THE OXFORD COMPANION TO SHIPS AND THE SEA

THE OXFORD COMPANION TO SHIPS AND THE SEA

Second Edition

Edited by I. C. B. Dear
and Peter Kemp

OXFORD
UNIVERSITY PRESS

OXFORD
UNIVERSITY PRESS

Great Clarendon Street, Oxford OX2 6DP

Oxford University Press is a department of the University of Oxford.
It furthers the University's objective of excellence in research, scholarship,
and education by publishing worldwide in

Oxford New York

Auckland Cape Town Dar es Salaam Hong Kong Karachi
Kuala Lumpur Madrid Melbourne Mexico City Nairobi
New Delhi Shanghai Taipei Toronto

With offices in

Argentina Austria Brazil Chile Czech Republic France Greece
Guatemala Hungary Italy Japan Poland Portugal
Singapore South Korea Switzerland Thailand Turkey Ukraine Vietnam

Published in the United States
by Oxford University Press Inc., New York

First edition 1976
Second edition 2005

British Library Cataloguing in Publication Data
Data available

Library of Congress Cataloging in Publication Data
Data available

ISBN 0–19–860616–8

ISBN 978–0–19–860616–1

1

Typeset by Alliance Interactive Technology, Pondicherry, India
Printed in Great Britain
on acid-free paper by
Clays Ltd, St Ives plc

INTRODUCTION

The design and employment of ships, and our attitude to the seas on which they sail, have altered radically since this ever-popular, and frequently reprinted, book was first published in 1976. It is a shift that is reflected in this new edition. Oceanography and marine archaeology are just two of the subjects which now take their place more fully alongside the original entries of biographies of famous seamen, the ships they sailed, the literature and paintings they inspired, the seamanship they practised, and the saltwater terms they used—'the rich language of the sea' in the words of the book's original editor, the late Peter Kemp. Altogether there are over 2,600 entries in this new edition, accompanied by 250 illustrations. All have now been cross-referenced to make the information they contain easily and immediately accessible to the reader, and there is also a select index of those subjects and individuals who do not have entries of their own.

Many of the original entries, written by Peter Kemp and his panel of distinguished experts, have been updated to take account of events and developments during the last three decades. Piracy, for example, which many may think a part of history, is still very much with us today, while the square-rigged sailing ship is definitely making a comeback. Recent scholarship on such personalities as Prince Henry the Navigator, the revolution in navigation created by satellite technology, and the development of different types of ship, like the Seacat and the SWATH, have also been incorporated into the text. The increased interest in, and awareness of, subjects like ship preservation and sail training has also been catered for and covered by the relevant experts; and there are, too, extensive new contributions on exploration by sea, warfare at sea, the development of steam propulsion, and the history of navigation. Where possible websites have been included with the longer entries as well as a short bibliography.

But I believe the most important additions to this new edition are those written by the oceanographer, Dr Martin Angel. These range from the oceans and seas and what lives in them, to the hazards they currently face and the new maritime laws and organizations that have been introduced to try to preserve them. His entries include vital global topics like climate change, environmental issues, tsunami, and marine pollution; they introduce the reader to such subjects as marine pharmaceuticals and the Economic Exclusion Zone; and they cover in detail the enormous diversity of marine wildlife that exists on and beneath the surface of the open waters of the world.

What I found most gratifying while updating this book was the unstinting help I was given by everyone I contacted about it, and the team at OUP—Pam Coote, Judith Wilson, and John Mackrell among them—were, as ever, both supportive and cogent in their advice.

April 2005 I.C.B.D.

ACKNOWLEDGMENTS

I would like to thank, and warmly acknowledge the help of, Dr Ian Dand, Janet Grosvenor, Royal Ocean Racing Club (RORC); International Maritime Pilots' Association; International Maritime Organization; Jubilee Sailing Trust; Professor Andrew Lambert; Maritime & Coastguard Agency; Roy Mullender MBE; Northshore; John Reed, Secretary, World Sailing Speed Record Council; Frank Scott; Kenneth Swan, Swan Hellenic; Trinity House; Mike Urwin, RORC rating office; and Dept. of Maritime Archaeology, Western Australian Maritime Museum, Fremantle.

My advisory board, nearly all of whom are also contributors, have been of invaluable help to me, and I owe them my gratitude. However, any errors in the text are mine and mine alone. They are: Dr Martin Angel, Maldwin Drummond OBE, Jeremy Lines, Commander Tyrone Martin US Navy (retd.), Colin Mudie, Mike Richey, John Rousmaniere, Fred M. Walker.

Contributors

Dr Martin Angel (Southampton Oceanography Centre)
Dr Mensun Bound (Triton Fellow in Marine Archaeology, St. Peter's College, Oxford)
Laurie Bradt (Mystic Aquarium & Institute for Exploration)
Peter Dick (former offshore underwater engineer and editor, *Historical Diving Times*, newsletter of the Historical Diving Society)
Dr Denis Griffiths (former sea-going engineer and lecturer)
Professor Eric Grove (Dept. of Politics & International Studies, University of Hull)
Warwick Jacobs (Trustee, Hovercraft Museum)
Captain Adam Kerr (President, International Hydrographic Management Consulting)
Professor Andrew Lambert (King's College London)
Captain Martin Lee (master mariner and researcher, maritime history)
Jeremy Lines (yacht designer and archivist, Camper & Nicholsons)
Commander Tyrone Martin (US Navy (retd.), author and naval historian)
Colin Mudie (naval architect and designer)
Rosemary Mudie (Partner, Colin Mudie Naval Architects, Editorial Director, 1990–8 'Tall Ships News')
Mike Richey (formerly Director, The Royal Institute of Navigation, single-handed yachtsman)
John Robinson (Adviser, World Ship Trust)
John Rousmaniere (American writer and sailor specializing in maritime topics)
Fred M. Walker (naval architect, formerly Consulting Naval Architect, National Maritime Museum, Greenwich)
Bryan Willis (member ISAF Racing Rules Committee)

There are also entries from the contributors to the original edition but it has not been possible to identify who wrote what. They are: Terence Armstrong, Captain Geoffrey Bennett, Miss Evelyn Berckman, Captain Charles H. Cotter, Captain John Creswell,

Vice Admiral Sir Archibald Day, Ernest S. Dodge, Major J. de C. Glover, Vice Admiral Sir Peter Gretton, Maurice Griffiths, Miss Vivienne Heath, Rear Admiral John B. Heffernan, USN, Richard Hough, H. G. R. King, Professor Christopher Lloyd, Captain Donald Macintyre, Professor Arthur J. Marder, Rear Admiral Samuel E. Morison USNR, Peter Padfield, Rear Admiral G. S. Ritchie, Commander W. B. Rowbotham, Vice Admiral Brian B. Schofield, R. A. Skelton, Commander Gilbert A. Titterton, Oliver Warner, David Woodward, and, of course, the original conceiver and editor of this well-loved and long-running compendium, the late Peter Kemp.

NOTE TO THE READER

Entries are arranged in alphabetical order up to the first punctuation in the headword. Cross-references are indicated by an asterisk—the exceptions are listed below—or by the use in brackets of 'See' followed by the relevant entry headword in small capitals. Sometimes 'See also' is used to inform the reader of related subjects which may be of interest. A cross-reference to a headword appears only once in an entry. For simplicity, verbs and nouns sharing the same headword are included in one entry. Where the headword has several different meanings, the sub-entries have been numbered. For example, the entry 'rake (1)' includes the meaning of '(2) to rake', as well. The cross-reference is not always identical to the headword but is close enough to it not to cause confusion. For example, crustacean is cross-referenced to Crustacea.

To avoid too many asterisks some of the most frequently used nautical words in the text have not been cross-referenced, though they do have entries or extended cross-references. These are: afloat, anchor, bay and bight (in their geographical senses), boat, boom, cannon, compass, deck, flag, fishing boat, fleet, gun, to haul, HMS, hull, keel, knot, mainsail, mast, navy, ocean, port (in the sense of a place where ships load and unload), oceans, to pull, rig, to rig, rope, sails, seas, to set, sheet, to sheet, to steer, ship, USS, wind, and all naval ranks in current use except Petty Officer.

Two other points: printed on a tea towel sold by the Royal National Lifeboat Institution is a ditty which encapsulates how most people have always regarded a ship's gender: 'A ship is called a "she" because there is always a great deal of bustle around her; there is usually a gang of men about; she has a waist and stays; it is not the initial expense that breaks you, it is the upkeep; it takes an experienced man to handle her correctly; and, without a man at the helm, she is uncontrollable. She shows her topsides, hides her bottom and, when coming into port, always heads for the buoys.'

However, in 2002, the principal British shipping magazine, *Lloyd's List*, decided to refer to all merchant ships as 'it', the editor commenting that he saw this 'as a reflection of the modern business of shipping', though the Ministry of Defence confirmed that warships would continue to be described as feminine. There was a flurry of correspondence in the press that showed nautically-minded people still took sides in this matter. I have therefore tried to steer a middle course and readers must forgive me if I have occasionally described a ship as 'it' when they consider a 'she' to be more appropriate, and vice versa of course. Yachts I have continued to call 'she'. Incidentally, in Japan a ship is always masculine.

Secondly, the tonnage of a ship is now almost always expressed in metric tonnes. This is very close to the old imperial ton, so close that when the change was made to metric ships did not have to be re-registered. However, as I found it odd to describe a Roman galley in metric tonnes, and pedantic to give both imperial and metric tonnage, I have tried to use one or the other depending on the era of the ship being described. But like the gender question I must ask the reader for a degree of latitude.

Aaron Manby**,** the first steamship to be built of iron. She was fitted with an engine designed by the Scottish engineer Henry Bell (1767–1830), and made her first voyage in 1822 when she carried passengers across the English Channel from London and up the River Seine to Paris, during which she averaged a speed of 8–9 knots. After a few regular passenger trips on this run she was purchased by a group of French shipowners who used her for several more years running pleasure trips on the Seine. Though the **Vulcan* had already been built, it was the first time that iron plates, and not wood, had been used to construct a seagoing ship, a landmark in the science of *shipbuilding. See also PADDLE STEAMER; STEAM PROPULSION.

AB, the abbreviated title for the *rating of able seaman, indicating someone able to perform all the duties of a seaman on board ship. In the days of sail it was someone who could *hand, *reef, and *steer, but today he or she must have many more maritime skills than that. The initials have been thought to refer to an 'able-bodied' seaman, but this is not so: they are merely the first two letters of 'able'.

aback, the situation of the sails of a *square-rigged ship when the *yards are trimmed to bring the wind to bear on their forward side. Sails are laid aback purposely to stop a ship's way through the water or to assist her in *tacking; they are taken aback inadvertently when the ship is brought to by an unexpected change of wind or by the helmsman's lack of attention.

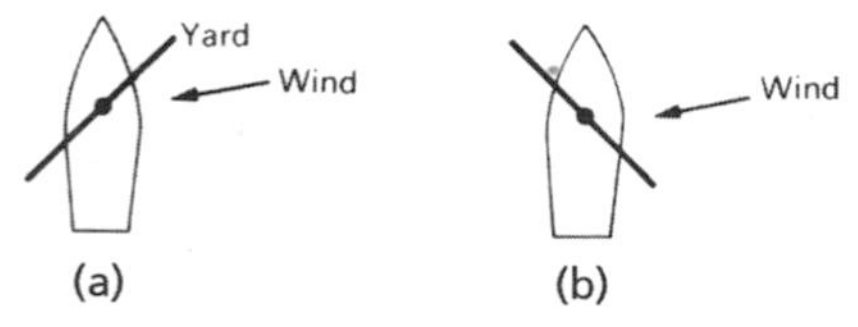

[a] Sails drawing [b] Sails aback

'Lay all flat aback' was the order in square-rigged ships to lay all sails aback in order to stop the ship and give her *sternway. When lying at a single anchor such ships normally spread a *mizzen *topsail laid aback to prevent the vessel *surging to the anchor and *fouling it with her *cable.

abaft, towards the stern of a ship, relative to some other object or position. Abaft the *beam is any *bearing or direction between the beam of a ship and its stern. See also AFT; but 'abaft' is always relative, e.g. abaft the mainmast (opposite to 'before'); 'aft' is general (opposite to 'forward').

abalone, a large limpet-like *shellfish, with a series of holes along the shell. It is prized commercially in the Far East and in New Zealand for its edible flesh and also for the shell, known by the Maoris as **paua**, which has a beautiful blue and green iridescence and is used to make decorative jewellery. M. V. Angel

abandonment, a term used in marine insurance indicating the surrender of a ship and its cargo to the insurers when the ship is a *constructive total loss. Once notice of such a loss has been promulgated it is irrevocable and the insurers can then take whatever measures are necessary to recover the ship and its cargo.

'abandon ship', the order given when a ship is sinking or on fire for the crew to take to the boats and liferafts. See also LIFESAVING.

abatement of false lights, a right, under the authority of the Merchant Shipping Acts, by which *Trinity House could order the extinction or screening of any light visible to seaward which could be mistaken for that emanating from a *lighthouse.

abeam, on a *bearing or direction at right angles to the fore-and-aft line of a ship. See also ABREAST.

able seaman, see AB.

aboard, in or on board a ship. The word is also widely used in other maritime meanings: for one ship **to fall aboard another** was for it to fall *foul of another; in the days of sailing navies **to lay an enemy aboard** was to sail alongside it with the intention of *carrying it with *boarders; in *square-rigged ships **to haul the tacks aboard** is to *brace the *yards round for sailing *close hauled.

about, a term used in sailing, meaning across the wind in relation to the bow of a sailing vessel. Thus, when a ship *tacks across the wind to bring the wind from one side of the ship to the other, the ship is said to be **going about**. **'Ready about'**, the order given in a sailing ship to tack across the wind, the actual moment of the *helm being put down being signified by the order **'about ship'**. In *yachts and smaller craft, this order is usually **'ready about—lee-oh'**, indicating that the helm is being put down to *leeward.

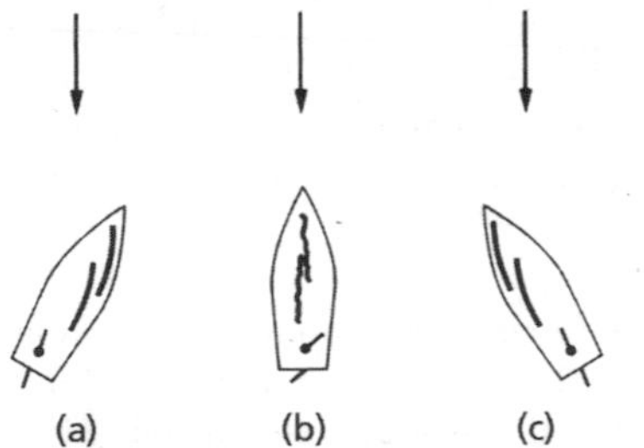

Three stages in going about [a] Port tack [b] Head to wind [c] Starboard tack

above board, above the deck and therefore open and visible, which gave rise to the term used to denote open and fair dealing.

abox, an old sailing ship expression used in the days of *square-riggers rigged with *yards. To lay the head-yards **abox** was to lay them square to the foremast in order to *heave to. This brought the ship more under command if it was subsequently required to *wear or to *stay the vessel. But to **brace abox** was to *brace the head-yards flat *aback to the wind, not square to the mast, in order to ensure that the wind acted on the sails so that the bows of the ship *cast the required way.

A-bracket, the triangular bracket that extends from the hull of a powered vessel to give support to the *propeller shafts. See also SHIPBUILDING.

abreast, a position of a ship in relation to another or to a recognizable mark or place, being directly opposite to the ship, mark, or place. Thus when a vessel is abreast, say, a *lightship, then the lightship is *abeam of it. **Line abreast**, a naval fleet formation in which ships steam in position abeam of the *flagship, forming a line at right angles to the *course they are steering.

a-burton, a term used in the old days of seafaring in the stowage of casks in the *hold of a ship when they are laid *athwartships, in line with the deck *beams. In those times all ships had to take a great number of casks on board, as they were the only means of carrying fresh water and provisions, such as beef and pork pickled in brine, for the crew. The method of their stowage in the hold was therefore a matter of great importance, both to accommodate the greatest number in the smallest possible space and to make sure that they were easily accessible when required.

accommodation, an old term for a *cabin when fitted for the use of passengers.

accommodation ladder, steps or a flight of steps leading from deck to deck in a ship for convenience of access and egress.

account, to go on the, a term used by *buccaneers to describe their somewhat irregular way of life at sea and to give it an apparently more respectable backing than in fact it had. The dividing line between buccaneering and *piracy was very shadowy indeed; 'to go on the account' perhaps sounded a little better to some ears than 'to turn pirate'. But it may well be that the origin of the term lay in the meaning of account as responsibility for conduct, that if caught and charged with illegal practices they would be able to account for their actions as being within the law.

a-cockbill, orig. **a-cockbell,** see COCKBILL.

acorn, the small ornamental piece of wood, usually in the shape of either an acorn or a cone, which was fixed on the top of the spindle on the masthead of a sailing vessel which carried the *vane. Its purpose was to prevent the vane, which had a very loose-fitting sleeve, from being blown off the spindle.

acrostolium, the symbolic ornament, usually in the form of a shield or helmet, which ancient Greek or Roman ships carried on their *prows either to seek favour with the *sea gods or to ward off evil. It was the forerunner of the *figurehead with which later ships were sometimes decorated.

acting, a prefix used in most navies and *merchant marine, and in similar services, to denote that a higher rank is being temporarily held. Payment is usually at the full rate for the acting rank or rating, though not in the US Navy. See also FROCKING.

active list, the list of officers of a navy or a *merchant marine who, as in all similar services, are actually serving or are liable to be called upon for active service at any time. Officers on the retired list may also be liable to recall to active service if below a certain age.

actuaire (French), 18th- and early 19th-century open *transport for troops, propelled by both *oars and sails.

actuairole (French), a small *galley propelled by *oars and used as a *transport for troops up and down the French coast in the 18th and early 19th centuries.

acumba, another term for *oakum.

Adams, William (1564–1620), English *navigator, who was apprenticed to a shipwright aged 12, and learned *shipbuilding and *navigation. He then served for a short time in the English Navy under Sir Francis *Drake before joining the Company of Barbary Merchants as a *pilot and navigator, during which time he sailed on an *exploration by sea in search of the North-East Passage. In 1598, attracted by the Dutch trade to India, he sailed with a small *squadron of five ships from the Texel, bound for India via the Straits of Magellan. During the voyage he changed ship and this vessel, the *Liefde*, was the sole survivor of the expedition which finally reached Kyushu, in Japan, with a crew of sick and dying men. Adams's knowledge of ships and *pilotage, as well as shipbuilding, made him a valuable man in the eyes of the shogun, Tokugawa Ieyasu. He used him in various capacities and ordered Adams to build two western-style sailing ships, one of 80 tons, the other of 120 tons, which he did.

Adams became known in Japan as *Miura Anjin* (Miura Pilot) after the estate he was granted on the Miura Peninsula, for though he had a wife and children in England he was forbidden to return to them. Instead, the shogun arranged for him to marry the daughter of a samurai warrior—by whom he had two children—but before doing so he declared that Adams was dead and that the samurai *Miura Anjin* was born. This was convenient for everyone as it freed Adams to serve the shogun and to marry, as only a samurai could marry the daughter of a samurai.

In 1612 Adams heard news of an English trading station which had been set up at Bantam (now Banten) on north-west Java, and after managing to communicate with it, was visited a year later by an English ship from there, the *Clove*. She was commanded by Captain John Saris, and Adams assisted him in obtaining trading concessions from the shogun in favour of the British *East India Company. He took a leading part in the company's organization in the Far East and, having now obtained permission to leave Japan, made many voyages to Siam and Cochin China on behalf of the company. However, he always returned to Japan, and died there.

His adventures have been the subject of several books including the novel *Shogun* (1976) by James Clavell.

admiral, in all maritime nations the title of the commander of a fleet or of a subdivision of it. The word comes from the Arabic word *amir*, prince or leader, and in the Mediterranean, as early as the 12th century, the leader of the Muslim fleets had the title *amir-al-bar*, commander of the sea. The substantive *amir* and the article *al* were combined by other developing maritime nations in the Mediterranean to form the title *amiral* (French) and *almirante* (Spanish). The title reached other north European nations probably as a result of the Crusades, but became confused with the Roman *admirabilis*. In England the title of admiral did not originally confer command at sea, but jurisdiction in maritime affairs and authority to establish courts of *Admiralty.

As well as signifying the chief commander of the fleet, the title was also applied to his ship, and in many of the Elizabethan descriptions of voyages published in England the word almost invariably applied to the ship; the commander himself frequently being described as 'general' or 'captain', or a combination of the two.

The senior admiral in the British Navy carried, from the earliest days, the title of **admiral of the fleet**. His presence at sea was originally signified by the Royal Standard flown from the mainmast head, replaced at the end of the 17th century by the Union flag. He held his post until death and even today an admiral of the fleet always remains on the active list. Equivalent ranks in other navies are fleet admiral (USA), *Grossadmiral* (Germany), and *grande ammiraglio* (Italy), though in the US Navy the rank of admiral of the navy was given to Rear Admiral George Dewey in 1899 after the Spanish-American War. This was considered senior in rank to **fleet admiral** when that rank was created during the Second World War (1939–45), but has long been abolished. Both the Royal Navy and the US Navy also have vice admirals and rear admirals, as do most other navies. However, in the US Navy the rank of rear admiral has two halves, the upper half wearing a broad stripe and a thin stripe on the sleeve, the lower half a broad stripe only. See also ADMIRALTY; COMMODORE; FLAG RANK; LORD HIGH ADMIRAL; NARROW SEAS.

Admiralty, originally the generic term for jurisdiction over maritime causes, with authority to establish courts, known as the High Court of Admiralty, presided over by a judge of Admiralty. This was a particularly British institution, dealing with maritime causes, such as *piracy and *prize, which provided the *Lord High Admiral, one of the great officers of state, with the majority of his income. According to the *Black Book of the Admiralty*, the English codification of the Laws of *Oleron, this court of jurisdiction was founded during the reign of Edward III (1327–77).

At about the same time, Admiralty came also to be applied to the office of the Lord High Admiral in its military and administrative aspects with regard to the Royal Navy. The officials executing this office were known as Lords Commissioners for executing the office of Lord High Admiral, and their committee as the Board of Admiralty. By the beginning of the Second World War (1939–45) this board comprised the First Lord, a political appointment who was also known as the First Lord of the Admiralty; the First Sea Lord and Chief of Naval Staff; the Second Sea Lord, who was responsible for manning and recruiting; the Third Sea Lord, also known as the Controller of the Navy, who dealt with *shipbuilding, ship repair, and naval dockyards; the Fourth Sea Lord, who was responsible for victualling, supplies, and naval hospitals; and the Fifth Sea Lord, who was in charge of the Fleet Air Arm. Unlike its air and army equivalents, the Admiralty was an operational centre with operations being under the direct control of the First Sea Lord in his capacity as Chief of the Naval Staff. He exercised this control through the Vice Chief of the Naval Staff, who also had responsibility for such matters as intelligence, *hydrography, and *navigation. In 1964 the board was absorbed, with its army and air force equivalents, into a Ministry of Defence. However, as a concession to long tradition, those within the Ministry of Defence charged with the overall direction of naval affairs were collectively called the Admiralty Board, but were no longer Lords Commissioners.

In other maritime nations the overall direction of their naval affairs is usually conducted by a Ministry of Marine or a Navy Department. See also ADMIRAL.

Admiralty midshipman, a term used in the British Navy during the 18th and 19th centuries to describe a midshipman who had served his time (six years) and passed his examination. He was appointed to a ship by *Admiralty order as compared to those rated by the captain and appointed by an admiral. The US Navy's equivalent was 'Passed Midshipman'.

adornings, a general name often used to describe the *gingerbread work on the stern and *quarters galleries of the old sailing ships, particularly naval, from about the 15th to the 19th centuries.

adrift, a term denoting floating at random, as of a boat or ship broken away from its *moorings and at the mercy of wind and *waves. To cast adrift a ship is to abandon it at sea; of persons, to place them in a ship's boat or *raft and leave them. The word is also used to describe a seaman absent from his *watch, or his work, or failing to return when his leave expires. It also can refer to an item that is not in its proper place, or is missing.

advantage, the term used to describe the method used to *reeve a *tackle in order to gain the maximum increase in power. The power increase in a tackle is equal, if friction is disregarded, to the number of parts of the *fall at the moving *block, and a tackle has been rove to advantage when the hauling part of the fall leads from the moving block. Where a tackle is rigged so that the hauling part leads from the *standing part, the power gained is less and the tackle is said to be rove to disadvantage. See also PURCHASE.

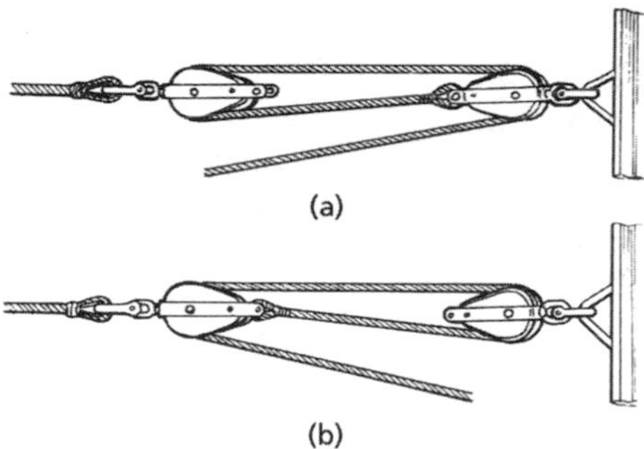

[a] Tackle rove to disadvantage
[b] Tackle rove to advantage

adventure, a commercial term, now defunct, which was recognized in international maritime law to denote consignments of cargo sent abroad in a ship to be sold or bartered by the *master to best advantage, hence cargo carried without fixed destination but to be sold when opportunity offered. A **bill of adventure**, one signed by a merchant in which he took the chances of the voyage. In French maritime law a bill of **gross adventure** was an instrument making a loan on a maritime security. Nowadays in marine insurance it is the period during which something is exposed to peril whether insured or not.

advice boat, a small vessel used during the period of sailing navies to carry orders or dispatches to and from fleets and single ships at sea. They were of no particular size or rig, the only criterion of their employment being speed.

adze, or sometimes spelt **addes** in old books on the art of *shipbuilding, the principal tool of the old-time shipbuilder in the days of wooden ships. It resembled a garden mattock but with a longer and sharper blade slightly curved inwards towards the handle. It was always considered a most difficult tool to use, but with it an experienced shipbuilder could smooth, or 'dub', an oak plank and leave it as smooth as if it had been planed.

aerodynamics, a branch of the science of pneumatics which deals with air and other gases in motion and with their mechanical effects. In its maritime connection it can be used to explain how a wind produces forward motion in a sailing vessel even when it blows from before the vessel's *beam.

When a wind strikes a surface at an angle, its force can be resolved into two components, one acting at right angles to the surface and the other along the surface. If this surface is the sail of a boat, the component blowing along the sail can be disregarded, as it is providing no force on the sail, but the component at right angles to the sail does exert a force. That component can now similarly be resolved into two more components, not in relation to the angle of the sail but to the fore-and-*aft line of the boat. The larger of these two components exerts a force which tries to blow the boat directly to *leeward, and the smaller of them, blowing along the fore-and-aft line, is all that is left of the wind to drive the boat forward. It is at this point that the boat's keel, or the *centreboard in the case of *dinghies, comes into play. It provides a lateral grip on the water which offers considerable resistance to the larger component and very little resistance to the smaller, so that the boat moves forward and makes only a small amount of *leeway.

The aerodynamic forces on the sail, described above, arise from the flow of air over the sail and the changes in the pressures acting on the sail which this produces. In plain view, a section of a sail is roughly parabolic in form, with the steepest part of the curve at its *luff. When an airstream strikes such a surface at an angle, it accelerates over the upper surface, thereby reducing pressure there. Accelerations are not so great over the lower surface so the overall effect is to create a force acting on the sail to leeward. Resolving this force into longitudinal and lateral components provides the driving and *heeling/sideslipping forces mentioned above.

The greater the speed of flow over the upper surface of the sail, the greater the aerodynamic force, and the faster the *yacht moves forward. With this in mind, modern sail plans increase the speed of the airflow by means of a *foresail (or sails) so aligned to produce a slot or 'funnel' along the luff of the mainsail. The slot increases the flow by acting as a form of venturi (duct). In designs where the *clew of the foresail overlaps the luff of the mainsail, the airflow is funneled with even greater speed over the steepest part of the mainsail's curve, thereby increasing the aerodynamic force.

Therefore, when a vessel is sailing *close-hauled, with the wind blowing forward of the beam, the aerodynamic forces resulting from pressure changes over the sails allow it to move against the wind. These also cause heel, which is resisted by the crew (of a sailing dinghy) or the ballast keel (of a displacement yacht), and *leeway which is resisted by hydrodynamic forces generated by the centreboard or keel.

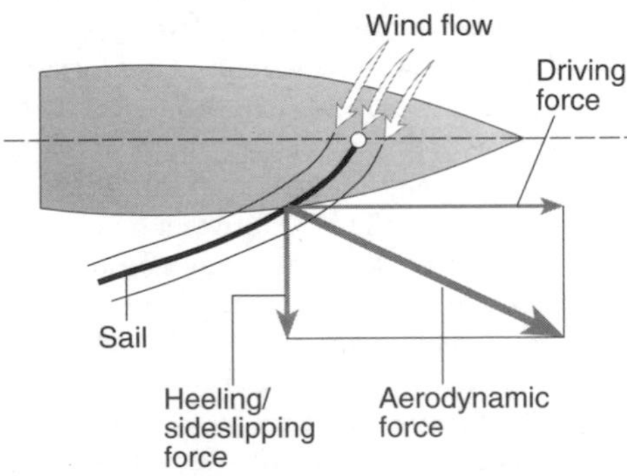

Components of the wind

affreightment, contract of. In chartering terms this refers to the shipowner's undertaking to carry goods by sea in return for a payment known as *freight. This contract may take the form of a *charter party or a *bill of lading. Martin Lee

afloat, the condition of a vessel when it is wholly supported by the water and clear of the ground. The word is also often used in a more general sense to mean at sea, or of life at sea.

aft, at or towards the stern or after part of a ship, as a word describing either position or motion. A gun may be **mounted aft** (an expression of position), and seamen **sent aft** to man it (an expression of motion), while **fore and aft** means from *stem to stern. Aft is a contraction of *abaft, though used in a general, not relative, sense. The adjective is **after**, e.g. the after part of a ship, as above.

afterbody, that part of a ship's hull which lies *aft of the midship section. It embraces the whole of the after half of the hull from upper deck to keel, and on the designed shape of the afterbody depends the *run of the ship. See also ENTRY; SHIPBUILDING.

afterguard, seamen whose station in the days of sail was on the *poop or *quarterdeck to work the after gear of the ship. Also a term often used in grander *yachts to denote the owner and his, or her, guests. In yacht racing it means the helmsman and his advisers. See also AFT.

afterturn, the twist given to rope, when the *strands are *laid up to form it in the opposite direction to the twist of the strands. See also FORETURN.

age of the moon, the number of days since the last new moon (also known as the change of the moon). A **lunation**, which is the average interval between the times of successive new moons, is 29½ days, so that the age of the moon at first quarter is seven days; at full moon fifteen days; and at third quarter 22 days.

aground, said of a ship when it is resting on the bottom. When put there purposely, it is said to **'take the ground'**; when by accident it **'runs aground'**, or is *stranded.

ahead, the opposite to *astern, is used in two senses at sea. Referring to direction, it means any distance directly in front of a ship on its current heading; referring to movement, it means the passage of a ship through the water in the direction in which its bows are pointing. It is a word much associated with the orders to work a ship's engines, as the engine room telegraph traditionally has the words 'ahead', 'astern', and 'stop' printed on the dial.

'ahoy!', the normal hail to a ship or boat to attract attention.

a-hull, or **lying a-hull,** the condition of a sailing vessel which is obliged, because of heavy weather, to *heave to under *bare poles with its helm *a-lee in order to ride out the *storm.

aircraft carriers are warships which operate aircraft from their decks. In January 1910 Commander Charles Samson RN flew off a Short biplane from a platform constructed on HMS *Africa*. In November that year the American aviator Eugene Ely, also using a specially built platform, performed the same feat from USS *Birmingham*. Then in January 1911 he landed on USS *Pennsylvania* after a landing platform and primitive arresting gear had been constructed over her aft guns. Though aircraft were regularly flown off numerous British warships during the First World War (1914–18)—and, in 1917, a Sopwith 'Pup' aircraft was landed on the flight deck superimposed on the forecastle of HMS *Furious*—it was not until *Furious* had a landing deck built *abaft her *bridge that regular attempts to land on her were made. These were in the main a failure and it was not until HMS *Argus* was built in 1918 with an unobstructed deck over her whole length that the problem of landing was satisfactorily solved. *Argus* dispensed with any *superstructure or funnel by incorporating a hydraulically raised and lowered bridge, and by discharging her boiler smoke and gases over the stern.

Argus was followed in 1920 by HMS *Eagle*, converted from an uncompleted battleship, which had a superstructure and funnels offset on the *starboard side of an otherwise unobstructed flight deck. This design was followed by HMS *Hermes*, completed three years later, the first ship to be built as a carrier from the keel up. These were known as 'island' carriers. The *Furious* emerged in her final form in 1925, a flush-deck carrier like the *Argus*.

The US and Japanese navies had meanwhile commissioned their first small carriers in 1922, the *Langley* and the *Hoshi* respectively. These were flush decked with funnels to one side which could be lowered horizontally during flying operations. No further carriers were built until after the conclusion of the Washington Treaty in 1922, when, by the treaty, the US and Japanese navies were each allowed to select for conversion to aircraft carriers two *capital ships due to be scrapped. These were the US *battlecruisers *Lexington* and *Saratoga* and the Japanese battlecruiser *Akagi* and battleship *Kaga*. These were all island carriers (i.e. carriers with the bridge structure offset to the side) of some 36,000 tons, though the superstructure in the Japanese ships was comparatively small as it did not incorporate the funnels. Instead, these projected horizontally over the side, a feature common to the majority of Japanese carriers.

The British selected two smaller ships, *Courageous* and *Glorious*, originally sister ships of the *Furious*, for conversion to island carriers. However, from 1937, when the British laid down the first of their post-Washington Treaty carriers, HMS *Illustrious*, their design differed from that of other navies in the incorporation of armoured flight decks and hangar sides which increased their resistance to bomb attack but reduced the number of aircraft they could operate. The Second World War (1939–45), in which aircraft carriers played a vital part, particularly in the Pacific, proved the necessity for such increased protection, and both the Americans and the Japanese adopted it for fleet carriers laid down after 1942. Three main types were used, 1939–45: large fleet carriers operating up to 100 aircraft; light fleet carriers, operating about 40; and escort carriers, converted from merchant ships, which operated up to 35 aircraft. None of the last type remained in service after the war, and most light fleet carriers were relegated to auxiliary roles. The US Navy was the only navy to continue operating large carriers in any number and it currently has nine Carrier Battle Groups, each having a nuclear-powered 80,000-tonne carrier of the *Nimitz* class which operate around 100 aircraft. It now (2004) has a new class under development and these carriers will have larger flight decks and very powerful nuclear power plants.

The British and other European navies opted for smaller carriers after the war. The British ones operated jump jets during the Falklands War (1982), and showed that carriers were still a vital asset for any navy in modern warfare. The British have two new ones on order as has the French Navy. See also WARFARE AT SEA.

Alabama, a *cruiser of the American *Confederate States Navy built by the Laird Company of Birkenhead in 1862 under a contract with Commander James Bulloch of the Confederate Navy. She was a three-masted *schooner with auxiliary *steam propulsion. The British government, which had declared its neutrality in the American Civil War (1861–5), issued an order of detention on her. However, before the officers enforcing this order could reach Birkenhead the ship steamed down the Mersey without clearance but with a party of ladies and musicians on board, ostensibly to carry out steaming trials. In the open sea she headed for Holyhead, landed her passengers, and, easily eluding the pursuing Federal *frigate *Tuscaloosa*, made for the Azores, where she picked up her armament which had been brought from Liverpool in two British ships. Under the command of Captain Raphael Semmes, she swept the seas of Federal shipping for two years until, on 19 June 1864, she was sunk in the English Channel off Cherbourg by the Federal warship USS **Kearsage*.

After a long period of arbitration, based on the lack of proper diligence in its duty as a neutral, Britain agreed to pay damages of $15.5 million to the USA in compensation for the direct losses attributed to the *Alabama* and two other Confederate cruisers built in Britain, the *Florida* and the *Shenandoah*.

In 1984 the remains of the *Alabama* were detected by the *sonar of a French warship and in the following years the site was excavated by French and American marine archaeologists who recovered many artefacts, the most significant one being a gun which was still loaded with a shell. Swift-flowing *currents made it difficult to work on, and the site is now being used to experiment with *marine archaeology techniques in a hostile environment.

'Albany beef', a slang name among British seamen during the US War of Independence (1775–83), for the sturgeon they caught in the Hudson River. The term became popular on among seafaring men and remained in general circulation for nearly a century. See also FISH.

albatross. There are 21 species of these large, long-winged, long-lived *seabirds that are superb gliders, certain smaller species being known as *mollymawks. The **wandering albatross** (*Diomedea exultans*) is continually on the wing from when it leaves the nest, and seven years later it first mates and nests itself. During that time, using its 4.6-metre (15-ft) wingspan, it glides hundreds of thousands of kilometres, encircling the Southern Ocean south of the *Roaring Forties many times. Albatrosses mate for life, and so are seriously threatened by *long-lining. During the past 30 years the wandering albatross's population in the Indian Ocean has halved and it is among the species threatened with extinction. The **black-browed albatross** (*Thalassarche melanophris*) is the most under threat, declining at 5% per annum. However, in 2004 the **short-tailed albatross** (*Phoebastria albatrus*), which was thought to be extinct, was discovered on a Japanese island. Australia and New Zealand have ratified an international agreement for the conservation of the albatross and petrel, and it is hoped other countries will soon follow suit.

About 100,000 albatrosses of all types are killed per annum, mostly by unregistered fishermen, fishing mainly for *tuna, who fail to take quite elementary precautions to avoid snagging the birds. Females are more vulnerable because they tend to feed at the Sub-Antarctic Convergence, where long-lining activity is most intense; males feed further south at the *Antarctic Convergence. Albatrosses are rarely seen in the North Atlantic, but several species occur in the North Pacific including the **Laysan albatross** (*D. immutabilis*), which only nests on Midway *Atoll, and the **waved albatross** (*D. irrorata*), which nests on the Galapagos Islands.

Early mariners believed albatrosses embodied the souls of drowned sailors and hence it was bad luck to kill one. This myth was immortalized in the 'Rime of the *Ancient Mariner', the poem written by Samuel Taylor Coleridge in 1798. M. V. Angel

Albemarle, CSS, an *ironclad ship built as a *ram in the Roanoke River at Edwards Ferry, North Carolina, in 1863–4. Her construction, far from any shipyard, reflected considerable credit on Commander J. W. Cooke of the *Confederate States Navy, formerly of the US Navy, who supervised it. He and his assistants scoured the surrounding country for iron, and built her from the miscellaneous materials gathered together. She was commissioned on 17 April 1864 and two days later, at Plymouth, New England, she rammed and sank the USS *Southfield* and forced three other Federal vessels to withdraw. The immediate effect was to yield the town of Plymouth to Confederate forces. On 5 May the *Albemarle*, accompanied by a converted vessel captured from the Federal Army, attacked Union vessels below Plymouth, suffering slight damage. She was taken back up the river and was torpedoed there and sunk with a *spar torpedo by an improvised torpedo boat in October 1864.

Aldis lamp, a hand-held electric lamp fitted with a finger-operated mirror used for sending *Morse code signals at sea.

a-lee, the position of the *helm of a vessel when it has been pushed down to *leeward. 'Helm's a-lee' is the response of the helmsman of a sailing vessel after putting the helm down on the order to *tack. When a sailing vessel *heaves to in rough weather, the helm is lashed a-lee so that the bows are continuously forced into the wind, in which position the vessel lies more easily.

Alfred the Great (848–*c.*900), English king of Wessex, is often said to be the founder of the English Navy. There is no real validity in this claim because naval actions against the Danes had been fought before Alfred began to build any ships to combat their raids, and later no navy existed for long periods but had to be recruited when the need arose from the *Cinque Ports and other sources. Early encounters with the Danes and their *longships, according to the *Anglo-Saxon Chronicle*, took place inshore, and not until 885 does it mention that Alfred 'went out to sea with ships and fought against four ships' companies of Danes'. In 897 Alfred started to build a new type of ship which was equipped with at least 60 *oars and was 'swifter, steadier, and with more freeboard' than those used by the marauding Danes.

Algerine pirates, *Barbary pirates who owed allegiance to the Dey of Algiers and operated from that port between the 14th and 19th centuries.

all-a-taunt-o, the condition of a *square-rigged sailing vessel where all the running *rigging is hauled *taut and *belayed, and all her *yards are crossed on the masts, i.e. have not been sent down. In general it refers more to ships with very tall masts than to more rugged ships with shorter masts.

alleyway, the name usually given in merchant vessels to a passageway along the decks below the upper deck, giving access to *cabins or other parts of the ship.

'all hands', an order on board ship for the seamen of every *watch to muster on deck immediately. It is an order usually given either in an emergency or for performing an evolution requiring the use of the entire crew. The full order is **'all hands on deck'**, but it is commonly shortened to 'all hands'.

all in the wind, an expression used to describe the situation when a sailing vessel, in the process of *tacking, is head to wind and all her sails are shivering.

all standing. A ship is said to be brought up 'all standing' when it lets go its anchor with too much *way on and so is brought suddenly to a stop when the anchor bites. In earlier sailing-ship days, 'all standing' was also an expression sometimes used to denote that a ship was fully equipped.

aloft, above, overhead, also anywhere about the upper *yards, masts, and *rigging of a *square-rigged ship and other sailing vessels. **'Away aloft'** was the command for *topmen in square-riggers to take up their stations on the masts and yards. In the days of sail **gone aloft** was a sailor's phrase for a seaman who had died.

aloof, an old expression meaning 'keep your *luff', or sail as close to the wind as possible. Sometimes, in old books of voyages, it was written as **aluffe**. It was most often used when a ship was sailing along a *lee shore, the order to 'keep aloof' being given to prevent it being driven closer to the shore.

alow, the opposite to *aloft, meaning on or near the deck of a ship. When a sailing vessel was said to be carrying all sail alow and aloft, it had all its sails, including *studding sails, set and all *reefs shaken out.

alternating light, see CHARACTERISTIC.

altitude, from the Latin *altitudo*, height, the angular distance of a celestial body above the horizon. The angle required in *celestial navigation is that between the centre of the earth and the centre of the body observed. Corrections thus have to be made to the *sextant altitude (the reading shown on the instrument) to obtain the observed altitude, which is that required to work up the *sight, to use the time-honoured phrase. The altitude corrections, as they are called, are given in *nautical almanacs and most nautical tables. They are, for index and any other instrumental error, *dip (for height of eye), *refraction, and, for the sun and moon only (because of their proximity to the earth), a correction for *semi-diameter. The term **computed altitude** as used in modern tables of computed altitude and azimuth may be defined as the theoretical altitude of a body at a particular place and time. Mike Richey

amain, an old maritime word meaning 'immediately', as **'let go amain'**, let go the anchor at once. Another naval expression of the 15th and 16th centuries was **'waving amain'**, which was a direction by a warship to a merchant vessel to give the time-honoured *salute at sea. The actual waving was done with swords or pikes to indicate the warlike nature of the ship demanding the salute. In the same context, the merchant ship would **'strike amain'**, i.e. let fall her *topsails immediately.

ambergris is a grey, light waxy, rather malodorous substance occasionally found floating in tropical seas in blackish lumps varying in weight from a few grams to a hundred kilograms. Each lump consists of concentric opaque waxy layers with colours ranging from grey to brownish yellow. Ambergris is probably regurgitated by sperm *whales (*Physeter macrocephalus*); in the days of *whaling it was found in the guts of slaughtered whales. It commands a high price, being used in perfumes and also dissolved in hot alcohol, in expensive cocktails. See also MARINE PHARMACEUTICALS.

www.netstrider.com/documents/ambergris/miscellany/ M. V. Angel

America, a *schooner yacht of 170 tons measurement built in New York in 1851 for a syndicate headed by John Cox Stevens, commodore and founder of the New York Yacht Club. Her dimensions were: length 28.5 metres (93 ft 6 in.), *beam 6.8 metres (22 ft 6 in.), *draught 3.3 metres (11 ft), mainmast 24.7 metres (81 ft), foremast 24.2 metres (79 ft 6 in.). Designed by George Steers, she was constructed under his supervision in the New York yard of William Brown (see Fig. 1 on p. 644 for her plans). She was then raced in English waters in the year of the Great Exhibition, 1851, as an example of American *shipbuilding. On 22 August 1851 she won with ease a race around the Isle of Wight organized by Britain's senior *yacht club, the Royal Yacht Squadron, and was awarded the 100-guinea silver Queen's Cup. Though without a bottom, and looking more akin to a claret jug, the trophy is now known as the *America's Cup. Of her performance the great Scottish *yacht designer G. L. Watson wrote that she was 'undoubtedly the great epoch-making vessel in yacht designing'.

She was bought by one Englishman and then another, was renamed *Camilla*, and after being laid up was bought 'at the price of old junk' (W. Thompson and T. Lawson, *The Lawson History of the America's Cup* (1911), 40), by the owner of a boatyard, who rebuilt her and sold her. In 1861 a former Royal Navy officer sold her to the *Confederate States Navy. She had a gun mounted on her, was renamed *Memphis*, and was used as a dispatch boat and *blockade runner during the American Civil War (1861–5). She was eventually scuttled in the St John's River, Florida, but was raised by the Federal Navy for use as a training vessel at the US Naval Academy at Newport, RI, and then Annapolis.

After taking part in the first defence of the America's Cup in 1870, she was rebuilt by General Butler, and used for cruising and racing until she was decommissioned in 1901 and put under covers in Boston. In 1921 she was presented to the Eastern Yacht Club at Marblehead which then sold her, for the sum of one dollar, to the US government. She was exhibited at the Naval Academy at Annapolis where, having been poorly maintained, she was placed in a shed in 1940. Two years later the shed's roof collapsed under a heavy snowfall and shattered many of her timbers. Despite protests by yachtsmen, who wanted her preserved, her remains were sold in 1945 for $990.90.

Rousmaniere, John, *The Big Black Hull* (1985).

America's Cup, sailing's most important competition as well as the oldest continuously held event in international sport. The name is that of the event's trophy, a silver ewer originally called 'the Squadron Cup', or (referring to its cost) 'the £100 Cup' or 'Hundred Guinea Cup'. It was first awarded in 1851 by the Royal Yacht Squadron to the winner of a race around England's Isle of Wight. It came to be called by the name of the American *schooner *yacht **America*, which first won it. Since then there have been 31 contests for it, held between 1870 and 2003.

When the surviving members of *America*'s syndicate donated the trophy to the New York Yacht Club (NYYC) they ruled in the deed of gift that it was to belong to the club which won it, and that it was to be 'perpetually a Challenge Cup for friendly competition between foreign countries'. Races occur when the *yacht club that holds the Cup is challenged by a yacht club from another country. Since 1871 it has been a match race, that is, between two competitors only.

Traditionally, the competition was always sailed in the largest boats of the time—some of them 27.5 metres (90 ft) on the waterline—and was held in waters of the defender's choice. A 'mutual consent' provision encourages the defender and challenger to negotiate many of the conditions, such as the type of boat, the number of races to be sailed, and the maximum wind strength so as not to damage the boats, many of which have been fragile. It is because of the simple, flexible structure of its rules that the America's Cup has thrived for so many years.

In the first challenge, in 1870, James Ashbury, an Englishman, had to face a fleet of yachts in a single race, just as *America* had done, though he had argued for a match race. He came tenth on corrected time and when he challenged again in 1871 the Americans relented and agreed to a match race—though in the best-of-seven series they claimed the right to have more than one defending yacht. Ashbury did win one race, but lost the other four against two different boats. From that time there was only one defending yacht.

After two Canadian challenges, Britain challenged thirteen times from 1885 to 1958. In the event's low point, in 1895, the challenger, the Earl of Dunraven, charged the NYYC with cheating. Bad feelings hung over the event until 1899, when Sir Thomas Lipton, a genial Scots-Irish food and tea merchant, issued the first of his five challenges. An exemplar of the rule that grand events attract grandiose personalities, Lipton came close to winning in 1901 and 1920 but none of his five **Shamrock* challengers managed to take home what he called 'the auld mug'.

Between 1930 and 1937 the matches were sailed in the high-tech *J-class yachts as large as 41.8 metres (137 ft) on deck. But they cost too much for a world impoverished by war and in 1956 the deed of gift was altered to permit the largest *international metre class boat then sailing, the 12-metre, to be used. About 20 metres (65 ft) long, they had crews of eleven, most of them amateur. The NYYC beat the Royal Yacht Squadron in 1958, then met an Australian challenge in 1962. In this, their first try, the Australians won one race and came close to taking a second. They subsequently challenged regularly, often with very fast boats. The Americans kept winning because their teams were better organized, their boats were better sailed, and their crews were more familiar with the waters off Newport, RI, where the races were moved in 1930.

From 1970 the NYYC permitted multiple challenges from two or more foreign yacht clubs. Because all the challenging clubs underwent lengthy elimination trials while racing for the Louis Vuitton Cup, even a losing team gained experience at Newport. In 1983 a challenger finally won, beating the NYYC's defending yacht. *Australia II*, owned by Alan Bond, was faster than Dennis Conner's *Liberty*, in part due to an ingenious winged keel. Conner had already won the Cup twice before this bitterly fought series came down to the final race for the second time in cup history—the first was in 1920—and the Australians came from behind to win. Four years later Conner, representing the San Diego Yacht Club (SDYC) of California, earned the right to challenge and won the first America's Cup match held outside the United States, at Fremantle, Western Australia.

Feelings have always run high in the America's Cup, but mutual consent about the conditions for a match did not collapse until 1988. This led to legal action and a bizarre mismatch between a 36.6-metre (120-ft) overall keel boat from New Zealand and Conner's much faster *catamaran, which won easily. After more legal action, *yacht designers developed the new International America's Cup Class of 24.4-metre (80-ft) *sloops, and in 1992 the new design was used when SDYC's defending yacht, sailed by Bill Koch and Buddy Melges, defeated the Italian challenger. Three years later New Zealand, the world's most successful sailing nation in the late 20th century, beat Conner in a dominating performance by Russell Coutts and his team. When racing resumed at Auckland in 2000, Coutts defended successfully against Italy.

Year	*Challenging yacht*	*Defending yacht*	*Result*
1870	*Cambria*, s. (England)	*Magic*, s. (USA)	defender 1-0
1871	*Livonia*, s. (England)	*Columbia*, s. (USA)	defender 3-0
		Sappho, s. (USA)	defender 2-0
1876	*Countess of Dufferin*, s. (Canada)	*Madeleine*, s. (USA)	defender 2-0
1881	*Atalanta*, sl. (Canada)	*Mischief*, cut. (USA)	defender 2-0
1885	*Genesta*, cut. (England)	*Puritan*, cut. (USA)	defender 2-0
1886	*Galatea*, cut. (England)	*Mayflower*, cut. (USA)	defender 2-0
1887	*Thistle*, cut. (Scotland)	*Volunteer*, cut. (USA)	defender 2-0
1893	*Valkyrie II*, cut. (England)	*Vigilant*, cut. (USA)	defender 3-0
1895	*Valkyrie III*, cut. (England)	*Defender*, cut. (USA)	challenger disqualified
1899	*Shamrock I*, cut. (N. Ireland)	*Columbia*, cut. (USA)	defender 3-0
1901	*Shamrock II*, cut. (N. Ireland)	*Columbia*, cut. (USA)	defender 3-0
1903	*Shamrock III*, cut. (N. Ireland)	*Reliance*, cut. (USA)	defender 3-0
1920	*Shamrock IV*, cut. (N. Ireland)	*Resolute*, cut. (USA)	defender 3-2
1930	*Shamrock V*, sl. (N. Ireland)	*Enterprise*, cut. (USA)	defender 4-0
1934	*Endeavour*, sl. (England)	*Rainbow*, cut. (USA)	defender 4-2
1937	*Endeavour II*, sl. (England)	*Ranger*, cut. (USA)	defender 4-0
1958	*Sceptre*, 12-m sl. (England)	*Columbia*, 12-m sl. (USA)	defender 4-0
1962	*Gretel*, 12-m sl. (Australia)	*Weatherly* 12-m sl. (USA)	defender 4-1
1964	*Sovereign*, 12-m sl. (England)	*Constellation*, 12-m sl. (USA)	defender 4-0
1967	*Dame Pattie*, 12-m sl. (Australia)	*Intrepid*, 12-m sl. (USA)	defender 4-0
1970	*Gretel II*, 12-m sl. (Australia)	*Intrepid*, 12-m sl. (USA)	defender 4-1
1974	*Southern Cross*, 12-m sl. (Australia)	*Courageous*, 12-m sl. (USA)	defender 4-0
1977	*Australia*, 12-m sl. (Australia)	*Courageous*, 12-m sl. (USA)	defender 4-0
1980	*Australia*, 12-m sl. (Australia)	*Freedom*, 12-m sl. (USA)	defender 4-1
1983	*Australia II*, 12-m sl. (Australia)	*Liberty*, 12-m sl. (USA)	challenger 4-3
1987	*Stars and Stripes*, 12-m sl. (USA)	*Kookaburra III*, 12-m sl. (Australia)	challenger 4-0
1988	*New Zealand*, sl. (New Zealand)	*Stars and Stripes*, cat. (USA)	defender 4-0
1992	*Il Moro di Venezia*, IACC (Italy)	*America 3*, IACC (USA)	defender 4-1
1995	*Black Magic*, IACC (New Zealand)	*Young America*, IACC (USA)	challenger 5-0
2000	*Luna Rossa*, IACC (Italy)	*Black Magic*, IACC (New Zealand)	defender 5-0
2003	*Alinghi*, IACC (Switzerland)	*Team New Zealand* IACC (New Zealand)	challenger 5-0

Despite costs as high as $US60 million a team, the Cup was more popular than ever, with international television coverage of months of elimination races between boats from half a dozen countries crewed in most cases by international teams of professional sailors supported by commercial sponsors. With the stakes rising, many top people on the superb 1995 and 2000 New Zealand boats were recruited by other teams. They included Coutts and his key people, who joined the *Alinghi* team from Switzerland that easily beat the New Zealand defender in 2003.

All previous Cup winners had represented yacht clubs and nations fronting on the sea, but Switzerland's Société Nautique de Genève (SNG) qualified because it held its annual regatta on salt water, on the Mediterranean. The Swiss defenders chose to hold the next series of Cup races at Valencia, Spain, in 2007. The first Cup regatta to be held off Continental Europe, the 32nd match is expected to be even more closely followed than the previous matches in the America's Cup's almost 160-year history.

John Rousmaniere

amidships, in the middle of the ship, whether longitudinally or laterally. It is more usually known as a *helm order, normally shortened to **'midships'**, to centre the helm in line with the keel.

amplitude, the angle between the point at which the sun rises and sets, and the true east and west points of the horizon. Amplitudes were used historically to find the error of the *magnetic compass in order to establish the *variation, the difference of either the morning or evening amplitude from the mean being the correction required. This was first suggested by Francisco Faleiro in his *Tratado del sphera y del arte del marear* (1535). In 1595 the mathematician Thomas Hariot produced the first table of amplitudes for use at sea which was published in the introduction to the *Instructions for Ralegh's Voyage to Guinea*.

Amundsen, Roald (1872–1928), Polar explorer, born at Borgo, southern Norway. Inspired as a boy by the exploits of Sir John *Franklin, he determined to explore the polar regions himself and abandoned a career in medicine in order to serve as a seaman in Arctic waters and to obtain his *mate's certificate. In 1897 he secured the position of first mate on an expedition to the Antarctic and was one of the first to spend an involuntary winter in these regions when the ship became trapped in the *ice. On his return in 1899 Amundsen obtained his *master's certificate. Thus equipped with a first-hand knowledge of ice *navigation and survival techniques he resolved to lead an expedition of his own to traverse the *North-West Passage, which, in 1905–6, he managed to do in a 50-ton fishing *smack, the first vessel to achieve this feat.

Two years later he planned to reach the North Pole by emulating *Nansen's drift in the **Fram*. The Norwegian government gave him the *Fram* for this expedition, but the news of *Peary's claim to have reached the Pole in the autumn of 1909 brought the scheme to a halt. Instead, Amundsen, emboldened by *Shackleton's recent expedition there, switched his ambitions to be the first to reach the South Pole. Carefully avoiding *Scott's planned route to the polar plateau up the Beardmore glacier, Amundsen and four companions achieved their goal by an untried route, reaching the pole on 14 December 1911. The return journey was equally successful.

After the First World War (1914–18), Amundsen used a considerable personal fortune to build a polar ship called the *Maud* with the idea of following a north-east passage to the *Bering Strait, but in this he failed. This experience convinced him that the Arctic Ocean was best explored from the air. In 1925 he achieved a *latitude of 87° 43' N. in a Dornier flying boat and in 1926 he was the first to fly across the North Pole when he flew in an airship from Spitsbergen to Telfer, Alaska, a distance of 5,424 kilometres (3,390 mls.). He disappeared in June 1928 while flying to Spitsbergen to rescue those aboard a crashed airship.

Amundsen, A., *The South Pole* (1912).
Huntford, R., *The Last Place on Earth: Scott and Amundsen's Race to the South Pole* (1999).
Mason, T. K., *Two Against the Ice: Amundsen and Ellsworth* (1982).

AMVER or **Automated Mutual Assistance Vessel Rescue System,** *lifesaving organization operated by the *US Coast Guard which reports to the AMVER headquarters in

New York the positions and movement of all vessels at sea off the US coastline. The system maximizes the efficiency of any lifesaving search and rescue operation which might have to be *launched to help a vessel in distress, and is part of the *Global Maritime Distress and Safety System. John Rousmaniere

anchor. The earliest forms, used by the ancient Greeks, were large stones, or baskets filled with stones, which were lowered to the seabed by ropes. As ships grew larger, more efficient anchors were required to hold them, and iron hooks, designed to dig themselves into the seabed as any strain came upon them, were introduced. Their invention has been credited variously to King Midas of Phrygia and to the seamen of Tuscany. A second arm to the hook, making them double headed, was added shortly afterwards, and the anchor thus took the general shape which we know today. An early improvement was the addition of a *stock, or horizontal arm, at the top of the *shank of the anchor and set at right angles to the hooks, or *flukes, which ensured the flukes lay vertically on the seabed and thus dug themselves in to provide maximum holding power. The shape of the **Chinese adze** anchor, where the arms are at an acute angle with the shaft, was also known in the West from Roman times, but the Chinese developed it differently, having the stock close to the crown.

The basic anchor, known as the **Admiralty** or **fisherman's** anchor, has two flukes and the stock at right angles at the ring end of the shaft. It remained the standard pattern of anchor for centuries. A variation of it was the **porter**, patented in 1838, which had swivelling flukes. In the early part of the 19th century a further improvement to this type was made by curving the arms, which provided added strength in a period when welding was still an imperfect art. A persistent drawback to this type of anchor was the difficulty of stowing it, and the likelihood of it *fouling the anchor *cable. These disadvantages were largely overcome by the invention of the **martin** close-stowing anchor. In this type the stock was in the same plane as the arms, which themselves canted about a pivot in the *crown of the anchor and thus forced the flukes downwards into the seabed to provide holding power. These anchors were stowed flat on an anchor bed when not in use.

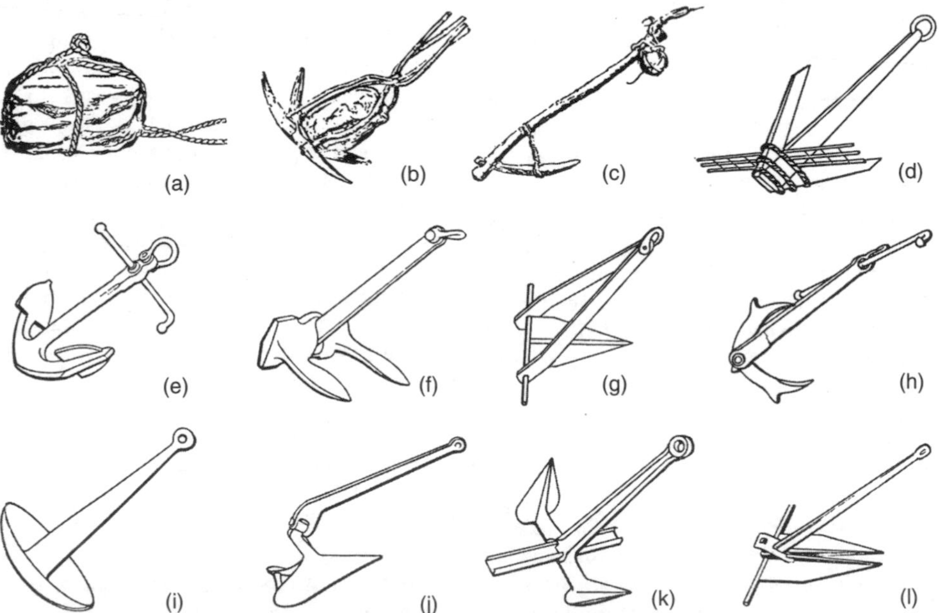

Types of anchor [a] Stone and rope [b] Primitive [c] East Indian [d] Chinese [e] Admiralty [f] Stockless [g] Wishbone [h] Porter [i] Mushroom [j] Plow [k] Northill [l] Danforth

It was a short step from the close-stowing to the **stockless**, or **'patent'**, anchor, the invention of an Englishman called Hawkins. Like the Martin this had two flukes pivoted at the crown, but had the advantages of making anchor beds unnecessary, as it could be stowed in the *hawsepipe, and of simplicity in working with a resulting saving of time and labour. Another early stockless anchor was the **wishbone**, patented in 1822, where the fluke pivoted between its forked shank.

A further development of the stockless anchor resulted in simpler and more efficient designs, such as the **CQR**, a type of anchor mostly used by small vessels and *yachts. The fluke is roughly in the form of two ploughshares set back to back and is held to the shank by a pin about which it can pivot to some extent. The CQR anchor has no stock, but when it reaches the bottom, any pull on it automatically turns it over so that the point of the fluke digs into the ground. It has considerably greater holding power than other anchors of a similar weight and, having no stock, cannot be fouled by the anchor cable. The CQR, which is not suitable for large vessels because of the difficulty of stowing it on board, was patented by Sir Geoffrey Taylor in 1933. He originally proposed to name it the 'Secure' anchor, but decided that the letters CQR, which give approximately the same sound, would be better remembered. In the USA it is usually known as a **plow** anchor.

An anchor that was originally specially developed for mooring *offshore oil and gas rigs is the **bruce** anchor, but it is awkwardly shaped for stowing on deck. However, if weight is a critical factor a lighter Bruce anchor has the same holding power as, say, the CQR. The **danforth** is an American-designed anchor which appeared in 1939, in which the two pivoting flukes are placed close together with the shank between them. The stock is across the crown of the anchor instead of in the more usual place at the top of the shank, and this makes it impossible for the anchor to be fouled by the cable. It has great holding power for its weight, similar to that of the CQR anchor, but has the advantage of stowing flatter on the deck. It is deservedly popular for small craft such as yachts. The two most recent developments for motor boats or yachts are the **delta** anchor, introduced in 1990 after intensive research and development by its manufacturers, and the **steadfast** anchor which first appeared in 1992. Both these have superior holding power for their weight.

Efficiency factors of the different types of anchor have been worked out but are apt to be misleading as so much depends on the type of ground into which the anchor beds itself.

To anchor, to let go the anchor.

See also ANCHORAGE; ANCHOR BUOY; ANCHOR WARP; ANCHOR WATCH; APEAK; A-TRIP; A-WEIGH; BACK, TO (4); BECUE, TO; BOWER ANCHORS; CATHEAD; COCKBILL; DRAG; FISH, TO; KEDGE; KILLICK; LUNCH HOOK; SEA ANCHOR; SHEET ANCHOR; SHOE; STREAM ANCHOR.

anchorage, an area off the coast where the ground is suitable for ships to lie to an anchor, giving a good and secure holding. These areas are marked on a *chart with the symbol of an anchor. In olden days it was also the name given to a royal duty levied on vessels coming to a port or roadstead for shelter.

anchor buoy, a *buoy used to mark the position of a ship's anchor when it is on the bottom.

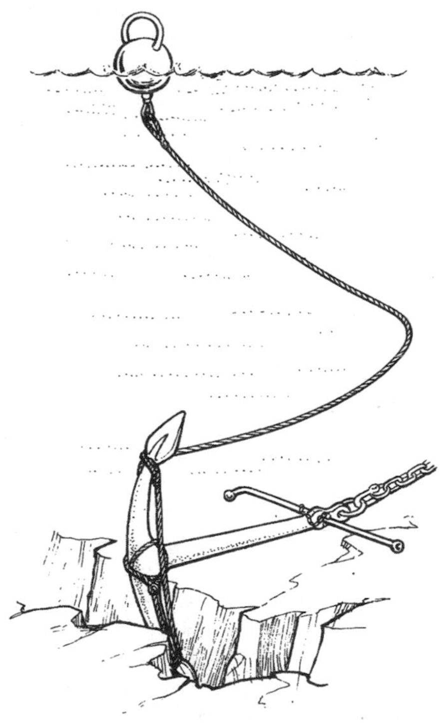

Anchor buoy

It is usually employed when anchoring on a rocky bottom. With small anchors, such as those used by *yachts, the buoy's rope is usually attached to the *crown of the anchor with a turn round one of the *flukes, or with a running *eye over one fluke and a *hitch taken over the other, so that it can be used to *weigh the anchor if its flukes are caught in rocks. In large anchors the rope is normally attached with a short length of *rigging chain to the gravity band or the crown to avoid damage by chafing on the bottom. An anchor buoy should always be *streamed before the anchor is let go. See also BECUE, TO.

anchor light, see RIDING LIGHT.

anchor warp, the name given to a *hawser or rope when it is attached to an anchor and used as a temporary *cable.

anchor watch, a precaution taken on board ship when lying to an anchor in bad weather with a danger of *dragging. The *watch normally consists of an officer who takes frequent compass *bearings of objects on shore to detect whether the ship is moving, and a small party on the *forecastle ready to watch and work the *cable. A dragging anchor can often also be detected by feeling vibration in the cable; another sign is when the cable slackens and tautens alternately in a marked manner.

ancient, an old name for an *ensign.

'Ancient Mariner, The Rime of the', written by Samuel Taylor Coleridge (1772–1834) and first published in *Lyrical Ballads* in 1798. The poem was almost certainly inspired by a remark made by William Wordsworth to Coleridge during a walk over the Quantock Hills in the summer of 1797. He told him that he had been reading *A Voyage round the World* (1726), written by the *privateer George *Shelvocke, and had been struck by the passage in the book describing the shooting of an *albatross by the second in command of Shelvocke's ship. Other suggestions of its origin were a dream said to have been told to Coleridge by his friend George Cruikshank after reading *Strange and Dangerous Voyage* (1633) by Thomas James (*c.*1593–1635), which described James's search for a *North-West Passage; and a letter of St Paulinus, Bishop of York (d. 644), to Macarius telling of the *shipwreck of an old man and how, with only one remaining member of the crew, the ship was *navigated by angels and steered by the 'pilot of the world'. However, the most likely source of the poem is unquestionably Shelvocke's account of his voyage. See also MARINE LITERATURE.

'Andrew', an obsolete slang name among sailors for the Royal Navy. It is said to have derived from an 18th-century *press-gang officer named Andrew Miller who impressed so many men into naval service during the Revolutionary and Napoleonic Wars (1793–1815) that he was said to own the Royal Navy.

anemometer, an instrument used to measure the velocity of the wind. It consists of a number of wind-driven cups connected to a vertical spindle which, as it rotates, moves a pointer on a scale marked in knots or miles an hour. In another type of anemometer, known as a **ventimeter**, the wind enters the bottom of a glass cylinder and pushes a disc up a vertical rod against the force of gravity, the wind strengths being marked up the side of the cylinder and indicated by the height reached by the disc.

angary, right of, the claim by a belligerent power to seize the ships of a neutral country for its own use when under stress of necessity. It is a right recognized in international maritime law but entails eventual restoration and the payment of indemnities for their use. A legitimate reason for the exercise of the right of angary is the prevention of the use of such ships by an enemy. See also WARFARE AT SEA.

angel-shot, another name used during the days of sailing navies for *chain shot.

angle of cut, in *navigation, the smaller angle at which two *position lines on a *chart intersect. The reliability of a *fix from intersecting position lines depends on the angle of cut. When fixing a ship's position by cross *bearings of two marks, the prudent *navigator will try to select marks whose bearings differ by not less than 50°. See also COCKED HAT.

Anson, Lord George (1697–1762), British admiral of the fleet, circumnavigator, strategist, and administrator, one of the founders of the naval profession as it became known to later generations. As a young man he had a variety of service including a spell in the Baltic, and he made extended cruises in American, West Indian, and African waters.

Anson's first great opportunity came as a *post-captain in 1740 at the beginning of the war with Spain and France. He was given charge of a small *squadron of six ships with the rank of commodore and ordered to the Pacific where he was to harry Spanish possessions and if possible to capture one of the *treasure ships which sailed yearly from Acapulco in Mexico across the Pacific to Manila.

Although he had some success, by June 1743 misadventure had reduced Anson's force to a single ship, the *Centurion*. However, she was by now well armed and manned with veterans trained to cope with every eventuality, so that when a treasure ship, the *Nuestra Señora de Covadonga*, was encountered off the Philippines on 20 June, the Spaniards *struck her flag after a 90-minute engagement. Her treasure was so enormous that it made Anson wealthy for life, and the voyage had proved to be the most successful of its kind since *Drake's circumnavigation in the *Golden Hinde*.

When Anson returned home the rest of his career was an uninterrupted success story. He became a *flag officer in 1745, and two years later, when cruising off Cape Finisterre, he defeated a French squadron which was protecting an outward-bound *convoy to Canada. He captured four *ships of the line and two *frigates, and took seven merchantmen, thus adding considerably to his wealth by his share of the *prize money. He was made a peer, and in 1748 married Lady Elizabeth Yorke, daughter of the Lord Chancellor. From then on, Anson moved freely in the corridors of power, enjoying two separate spells as First Lord of the *Admiralty.

At the Admiralty he proved a determined reformer, notably improving the *dockyards, which for generations had been a source of waste, inefficiency, and corruption; replacing the existing marine regiments with a corps of *marines; establishing the system of giving men-of-war a *rate; and drawing up a new code of the *Articles of War. The officers he trained were some of the most notable of their era, and it was in his time that a regular uniform was laid down for naval officers, though it was many years before the bulk of them readily conformed to it.

Le Fevre, P., and Harding, R. (eds.), *Precursors of Nelson: British Admirals of the 18th Century* (2000).

Williams, G., *The Prize of All the Oceans* (2000).

answering pennant, a red and white vertically striped *pennant hoisted when answering a flag signal at sea to indicate that it had been understood. Until the signal was fully understood, the answering pennant was hoisted at the dip, i.e. halfway up the signal *halyards. The same pennant was used both in the naval signal code and in the *International Code of Signals for merchant ships. In *yacht racing it is a postponement signal. See also SIGNALS AT SEA.

Antarctic Convergence, or Polar *Front, the northern circumpolar boundary of the Southern Ocean. It is one of the most important oceanographic features in the world's oceans, and its delineation was one of the achievements of the **Discovery* Investigations. At the convergence relatively cold and fresh surface sea water flowing northwards from the *ice sheets sinks beneath warmer, salty subantarctic water. Its position, between *latitudes 50° and 60° S., varies with both *longitude and season. Sea surface temperatures drop suddenly across the front from about 5 °C to 3 °C (41 °F to 37.4 °F) in summer and from 3 °C to 1 °C (37.4 °F to 33.8 °F) in winter. The convergence is often clearly visible both at *sea level and to satellites, as changes in the *waves and the colour of the water. The colour change indicates big shifts in the chemistry and biology of the surface water. Like all fronts, the convergence is a feature of high biological activity. Both plant and animal *plankton abound and attract in large numbers *seabirds like the male *albatross, and *marine mammals like seals and *whales. Islands like South Georgia that lie close to the convergence have climates that are strongly influenced by its presence, and offer breeding sites for seabirds and seals. See illustration overleaf and also BIOLOGICAL OCEANOGRAPHY; CHEMICAL OCEANOGRAPHY. M. V. Angel

antifouling, see COPPER SHEATHING; FOULING.

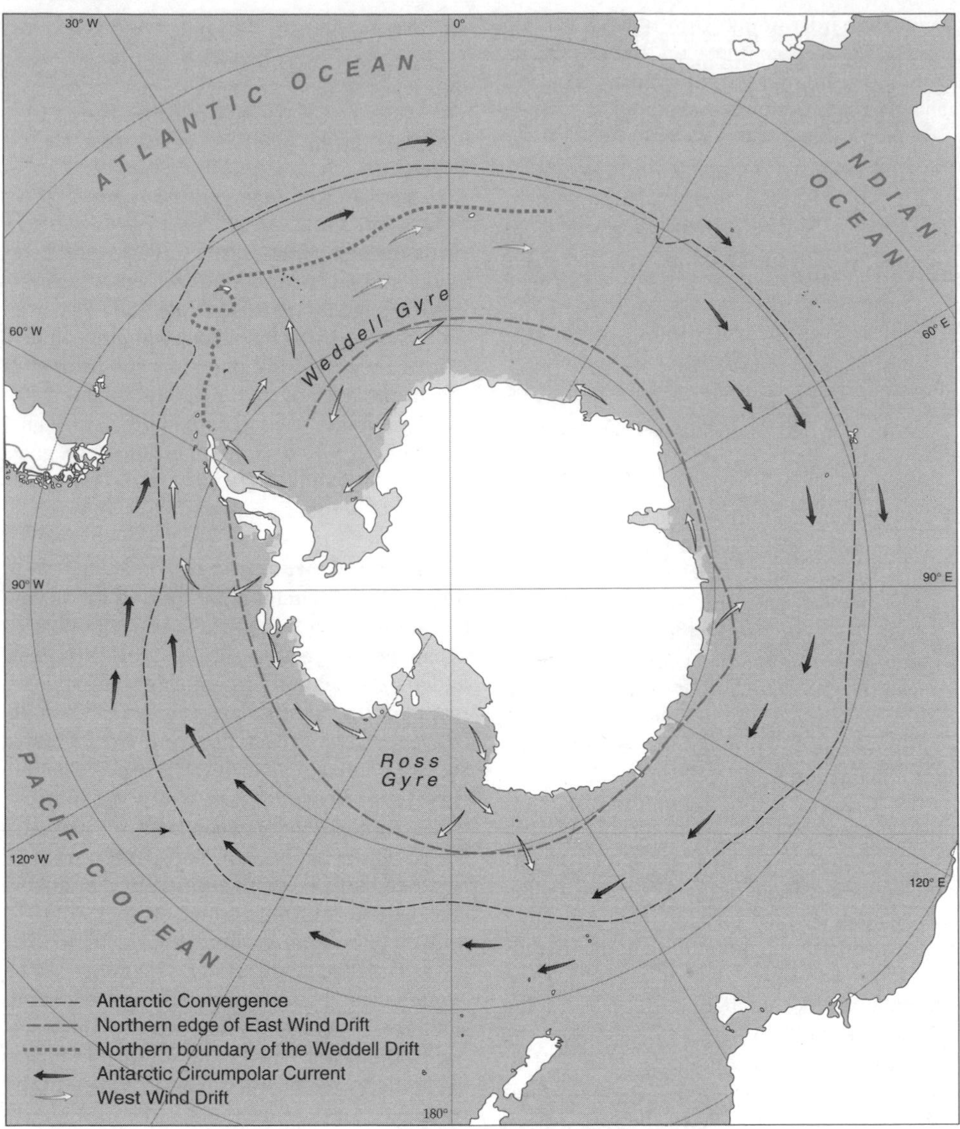

Antarctic Convergence

'anti-guggler', a straw or tube entered into a cask or bottle to steal the contents by sucking them out. It was a popular and relatively easy access to extra nourishment in hot climates during the 18th and 19th centuries when captains of ships often put their private stocks of wine and spirits in a hanging safe outside their quarters to keep them cool.

anti-rolling devices, see STABILIZERS.

apeak, orig. **apeek,** the position of the anchor when the bows of a ship have been drawn directly above it during *weighing, just before it is broken out of the ground.

apostles, the name given to the two large *bollards fixed to the main deck near the bows in larger *square-rigged ships, around which *hawsers or *cables were *belayed. In all the larger sailing vessels the anchor cables were brought inboard through the *hawseholes at main deck level since it was on that deck that the main *capstan was mounted. In some of the smaller merchant ships of the sailing era, where the anchor cables were brought in over the *forecastle deck, the *knightheads, which supported the heel of the *bowsprit, were used as apostles when belaying the anchor cables.

apparent wind, the direction of the wind as it appears to those on board a sailing vessel. It differs from the true wind in speed and direction by an amount which can be worked by a vector diagram: the vessel's speed through the water being represented by one leg of a triangle of which the true wind and the apparent wind form the other two sides. The difference between the true wind and the apparent wind is most pronounced when the true wind blows from directly *abeam, and is reduced as the vessel sails closer to, or further off, the true wind. It disappears completely with the wind from dead *astern. It is to the apparent wind, not the true, that a sailing vessel *trims her sails. In the diagram the strength of the wind has been taken as 12 knots and the speed of the vessel as 4 knots.

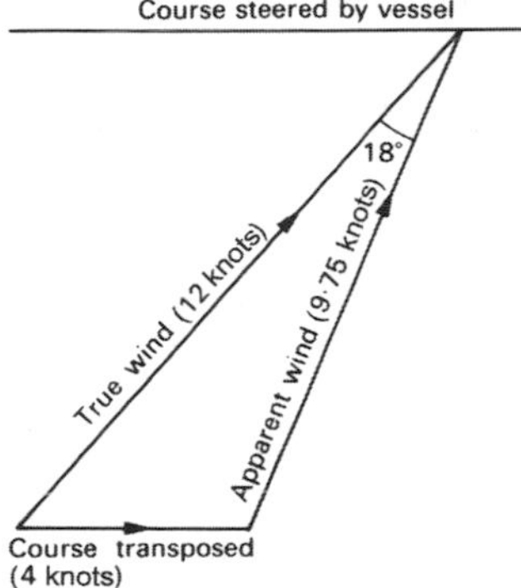

True and apparent wind

apron. **(1)** A strengthening timber used behind the lower part of the *stem and above the foremost end of the keel of a wooden boat or ship. It takes the fastenings of the fore-hoods or planking of the bow, and was also sometimes known as a stomach-piece. **(2) Apron of a gun**, a piece of lead sheet which, in the days of muzzle-loading guns, was laid over the touch-hole to protect the vent from damp. **(3) Apron of a *dock**, the platform rising where the gates are closed and on which the *sill is fastened.

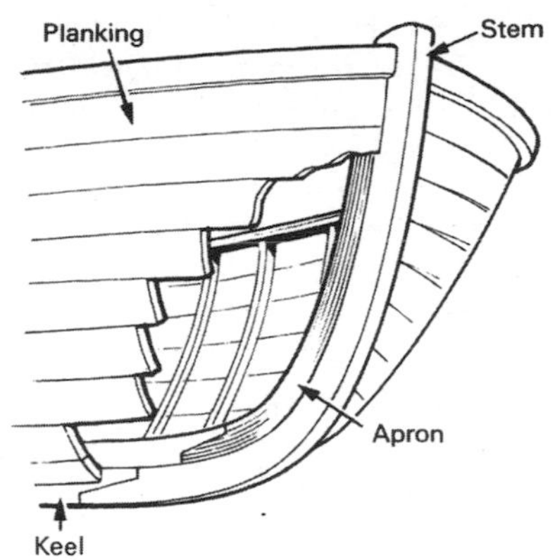

Apron (1)

Argonauts, in Greek legend a band of 50 heroes who undertook a sea expedition to bring back the Golden Fleece from Colchis on the farther shore of the Euxine (Black) Sea. It was led by Jason, who had the task imposed upon him by his uncle Pelias and sailed in the Greek equivalent of a *longship called the *Argo*, which in the legend was built by Argos, the son of Phrixus. She was constructed of pine cut from Mount Pelion which was supposed to have the property of never rotting, and was pierced for 50 *oars, one for each of the 50 heroes who manned her. It was recorded that her construction was supervised by the goddess *Athene, who inserted a piece of the holy oak from Dodona into the *prow so that she would never lose her way. Her bows were painted vermilion, and she was said to be the largest ship in the world.

The voyage of the Argonauts is one of the best known and oldest of mythological tales, but as a voyage to open up the Euxine Sea to Greek trade and colonization it may well have an element of truth about it. Certainly there were Greek settlements on the southern shores of the Euxine Sea as early as the 6th century BC. The legend of the Golden Fleece may also possibly have a basis in fact because of the practice of the inhabitants of Colchis of pegging down the skins of sheep in the rivers to catch in the wool the particles of gold washed down by the force of the streams.

Among the more notable of the Argonauts under Jason's command were Asclepius (Aesculapius), son of Apollo and doctor to the crew, Castor and Pollux, twin sons of Zeus (Jupiter), their brother Heracles (Hercules), Orpheus, to charm the crew with his lute, and Tiphys, the *pilot. Another member of the crew was Atalanta, daughter of Schoeneus, disguised in a man's dress.

argosy, the medieval name for a trading *carrack, principally in the Mediterranean. According to some sources, the name is derived from Ragusa, the original name of the modern Dubrovnik; others consider that the derivation is from the *Argonauts' famous ship, the *Argo*:

> Your mind is tossing on the ocean;
> There, where your argosies with portly sail,
> Like signiors and rich burghers of the flood,
> Do overpeer the petty traffickers.
> (Shakespeare, *The Merchant of Venice*)

In 1588, twelve of the best ships from Ragusa, with the generic name of argosies, were included in the *Spanish Armada. All were lost.

ark, a word commonly used to mean a box or chest, but see NOAH'S ARK.

arm, to, to place tallow in the cavity and over the base of the lead when taking a *sounding with a *lead line. It was done to discover the nature of the bottom by what adhered to the tallow.

Armada, see SPANISH ARMADA.

armillary sphere, a skeleton model of the celestial sphere, generally with the earth at the centre, showing the equator, poles, tropics, zodiac, etc. on the outer ring, with inner rings for the sun, moon, and planets. The instrument was used for *navigation during the late 14th or early 15th centuries to give the *navigator an understanding of the motions of the heavenly bodies. **Equatorial armillaries** were designed for determining the *declination of a celestial body, while **zodiacal armillaries** helped define a body's celestial *latitude and *longitude, without having to resort to computation. It is recorded that a brass armillary sphere, costing £4 7*s*. 6*d*., was supplied to Martin *Frobisher for his first expedition in search of the *North-West Passage in 1576.

'armstrong patent', a slang expression used in the big trading sailing ships, such as the *clipper, around the end of the 19th century and the beginning of the 20th century. It indicated that a ship was not fitted with any mechanical aids, and that all the work therefore had to be done by the crew's brawn alone.

artemon, the name of a small square sail set on a *yard. It was carried below a sharply *steeved *spar over the bows of Roman merchant vessels from about 200 BC to the decline of Roman shipping at the fall of the empire. The sail's function was largely as an aid to steering, while its spar, called an **artemon mast**, could be described as the forerunner of the *bowsprit. The artemon was virtually identical with the *spritsail of the 14th–17th centuries. The name was also used, somewhat loosely and erroneously, to describe the mainsail of ancient ships.

Oddly enough, the French word for *mizzen is *artimon*, and the mizzen-mast is *mât d'artimon*, which is of course at the stern of a ship not the bows. It is from the French word, and not the original, that the fourth mast of ships built with four or five masts during the 19th and early 20th centuries was sometimes known as the artemon mast. See also MAST.

articles of agreement, the condition of service signed by a seaman in the *merchant marine when joining a ship which formed a legal contract with his employers. Normally they embodied provisions governing rates of pay, scale of victuals, daily hours of work, etc., and specified the extremes of *latitude beyond which a seaman was not called upon to serve. Before the 1970s the *master had the authority to punish members of the crew who transgressed the articles, but nowadays discipline aboard UK ships is covered by the Code of Conduct for the Merchant Navy, though the master can still dismiss any crew member for a serious transgression. See also DEAD HORSE.

Articles of War, the disciplinary code for the Royal Navy. They were first issued in 1653 and were based on the ancient sea laws of *Oleron in which maritime crimes and punishments are specified. In Tudor times most captains of ships supplemented the Laws of Oleron with their own rules based on their own ingenuity in inventing punishments to fit the crime. In order to provide a code of punishment which would apply throughout the navy and not depend on the whims of individual captains, the Articles of War were introduced. They were incorporated into the first English Naval Discipline Act of 1661. It was under the 13th article of this harsh Act that Admiral John *Byng was executed.

Whereas the Articles of War were omitted from the Army Act of 1955, they were retained in the Naval Discipline Act of 1957. The US Navy's Articles of War were superseded in 1950 by the Uniform Code of Military Justice which applies to all American armed forces. It is likely that a British Tri-Services Act will follow the same route before 2010.

artificial horizon, see BUBBLE HORIZON.

ASDIC, the original name for the underwater sound-ranging apparatus for determining the range and bearing of a submerged submarine. The name was derived from the initial letters of the **Allied Submarine Detection Investigation Committee**, which was set up as an Anglo-French project immediately after the end of the First World War (1914–18). The invention was mainly French in conception. It is now known as *sonar.

ashore, on land as opposed to *aboard. A sailor **goes ashore** when he disembarks from a ship or boat and steps on land. A ship **runs ashore** when it strikes the land. **'A run ashore'** is the seaman's name for a short period of *liberty.

aspect ratio usually refers to the ratio between the length of the *luff and *foot of a *yacht's mainsail, but in some modern yachts may also refer to the ratio of the depth of a yacht's keel fin to its length. In the early days of *Bermudan mainsails the aspect ratio used to be as low as 2 : 1, but in modern racing yachts the luff-to-foot length ratio is generally between 3.5 : 1 and 4 : 1. Such a high aspect ratio means a tall and narrow sail which is like a glider's wing set up on end. It is highly efficient in sailing very close to the wind (as near as 3½ *points or about 39°) when set with suitable *headsails. See also AERODYNAMICS.

astern, backwards, behind. It is a word employed in two senses in maritime use. **(1)** In movement, that of a ship going backwards. **(2)** In direction, directly behind a ship. As an order given to the engine room of a ship for the movement of its engines, it indicates that they must be made to revolve in the reverse direction. See e.g. AHEAD, and for illus. see RELATIVE BEARINGS.

astrolabe, from the Greek *astron*, star, and *labin*, to take. The **planispheric astrolabe** was perhaps the earliest and certainly the most important of instruments to be used by astronomers. The earliest surviving description of its use dates to the 7th century. Chaucer, who seems to have possessed one, wrote an explanation of its use for his little son Lowys. The instrument is, in effect, a highly complex planisphere which rotates over a brass plate on which are engraved *azimuths and *altitudes as seen at the observer's latitude. The hours of the day, the days of the year, and the signs of the zodiac are set on the rim. Set to the right time and date the *bearings and altitudes of the fixed stars on the under plate will be correct. Data for the sun and planets had to be set at the time of observation.

On the back of the instrument is a sight rule, the alidade, which is the basis of the **seaman's astrolabe**, a simple instrument introduced during the 15th century, probably by the Portuguese, for measuring the altitude of celestial bodies at sea. It consisted essentially of a heavy graduated ring of brass fitted with the sighting device at its centre. The only engraving necessary was of two scales running from 0° to 90° so that both ends of the alidade could be read. Like the planispheric astrolabe the instrument was suspended by the thumb or possibly by a short line from a *shackle at the top of the ring so that it hung vertically. The alidade was then turned about its axis, so that the sun or star could be sighted along it, and the altitude read. The earliest recorded use of the mariner's astrolabe was by Diogo d'Azambuja in his *exploration by sea down the west coast of Africa in 1481.

After 1550 Portuguese mariners' astrolabes were graduated to read the *zenith distance of the body rather than the altitude. It would seem from contemporary accounts that English seamen at any rate found the astrolabe more convenient to use when the sun stood high in the sky, but preferred the *cross-staff when it was at lower altitudes.

Athene, also known as Pallas Athene and (in Latin) Minerva, the Greek goddess of wisdom, war, and all the liberal arts, was the mythological patroness of *shipbuilding and, according to legend, the first to build a ship. She is associated, also in legend, with the *Argonauts and their ship the *Argo*, and it was due to her care for them and her zeal for *navigation that they reached their destination safely.

athwartships, something which stretches from one side of the ship to the other. **Athwart**, something which is directly across the line of a ship's *course. **Athwart-hawse**, the position of a ship or other vessel driven by wind or tide across the *stem of another. **Athwart the tide**, the position of a ship held by the force of the wind lying across the direction of the *tide when at anchor. See also WIND-RODE.

Atlantis, a legendary island first mentioned by Plato in the *Timaeus*; a description of its supposed commonwealth is included in his *Critias*. It was supposed to have been engulfed by a tidal *wave after its armies had overrun most of western Europe, only Athens successfully defying its assault. Presumably it arose again from the sea, since it was later identified with other well-known mythical islands, particularly the Greek Isles of the Blest, the Portuguese Isle of Seven Cities, the Welsh *Avalon, and the legendary island of *Brasil. These islands were shown on the maps and *charts of the 14th and 15th centuries and formed the objectives of several early voyages of *exploration by sea, none of course successful. The actual position of Atlantis itself was marked on many charts of the Atlantic as a rock in 44° 48' N., 26° 10' W. at least as late as the mid-19th century, when it was proved by detailed surveys not to exist.

In 2004 a search for it began in the Mediterranean between Cyprus and Syria after Russian and Israeli scientists found an area there in 1989 which has features similar to those described by Plato. Claims have also been made to have found it off, among other places, the Azores, Crete, and Santorini. See also LYONESSE.

Atlas, in Greek mythology a brother of Prometheus who was originally a marine god before Perseus showed him the Gorgon's head and turned him into a rock mountain supporting the heavens. A mythical god, or Titan, he gave his name to the Atlas Mountains at the western end of the Mediterranean and also to the Atlantic Ocean. In the *Odyssey* (1. 52) Homer describes him as 'one who knows the depths of the whole sea, and keeps the tall pillars which hold heaven and earth asunder'. In his famous book of maps, the inventor of the *Mercator projection, Gerardus Mercator, used a picture of Atlas supporting the heavens as a frontispiece, and this use has led to the term 'atlas' being used to describe a volume of maps. See also CHARTMAKING.

atoll, a word derived from the Maldivian word *atollon* used to describe a ring of coral islets and *reefs enclosing a shallow *lagoon. They occur

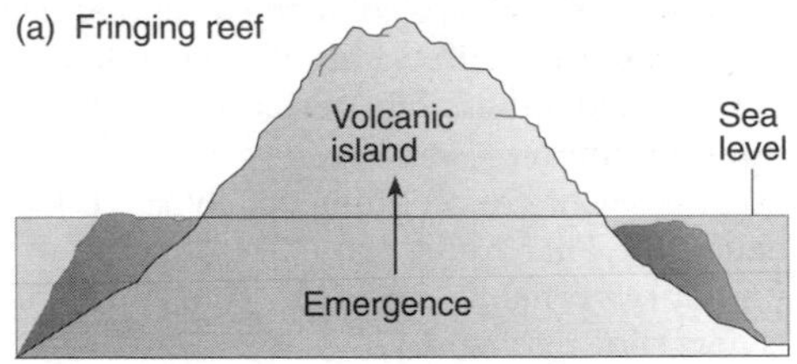

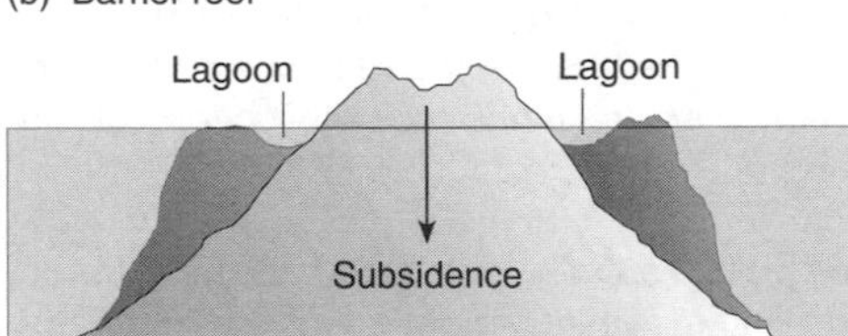

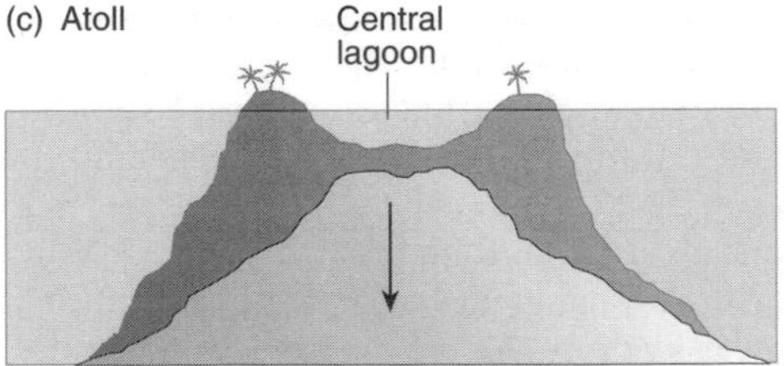

Formation of an atoll according to Darwin's theory of subsidence

exclusively in the tropical seas of the Pacific and Indian Oceans. Charles *Darwin first postulated that atolls form initially on the summits of volcanoes as fringing *coral reefs. The ocean crust then subsides under the weight of the new volcano and the *waves wash away the ash of the central cone leaving the ring of coral. As the volcano continues to subside the reefs keep above *sea level by continual growth. Islands form in the *lee of the reefs through the accumulation of coralline sand voided by *fish that graze on the coral. Deep boreholes drilled by the Americans into Eniwetak Atoll during preparations for nuclear weapon testing found hundreds of metres of coralline rocks sitting atop the remains of a volcano, thus demonstrating Darwin's theory was correct.

Most atolls are only a few metres above sea level, and are threatened by any rapid rise in sea level. Increases in the concentration of carbon dioxide in the atmosphere will inhibit the ability of the corals to lay down calcium carbonate, so the corals may no longer grow fast enough to keep pace with future rises in sea level. *Climate change may also result in an increased frequency and ferocity of *tropical storms. So, many atolls may be inundated within the next century.

Nunn, P., *Oceanic Islands* (1994).

M. V. Angel

a-trip. An anchor is said to be a-trip at the moment of *weighing when it is broken out of the ground by the pull of the *cable. In *square-rigged ships *topsails are a-trip when they are hoisted to their full extent and ready for *sheeting home and *yards are a-trip when they are *swayed up and their *stops cut ready for crossing. A *topmast or *topgallant mast is a-trip when the *fid is loosened ready for it to be struck, or lowered.

auks are diving *seabirds of the northern hemisphere which, like *penguins, have their legs at the back of their bodies and on land stand upright and are clumsy movers. They use their wings for both flying and swimming. The **great auk** (*Pinguinus impennis*), which lost the power of flight, was a northern version of a penguin. It was driven to extinction by over-exploitation; the last recorded specimen was collected in 1844. M. V. Angel

aurora, a display of lights high in the atmosphere, known as the **aurora borealis** in the northern hemisphere and the **aurora australis** in the southern hemisphere. In Scotland the former is also known as the Northern Lights. Both auroras are most frequently seen at *latitudes higher than 60°. A display consists of rapidly moving patches or columns of different coloured lights. They are most dramatic during disturbances in the earth's magnetic field and the sun is on the *equinoctial, when there are periods of extensive interference with radio and telephone transmissions. They are less intense when the sunspot cycle is at its peak, when the sun emits more ultraviolet light. The UV light alters the ionization of the upper atmosphere so that it absorbs the particles being emitted from the sunspots more efficiently. But once the sun's activity has peaked, the atomic particles are able to penetrate the Van Allen radiation belt, particularly within 20° of the magnetic poles. In the upper atmosphere the particles collide with the gas molecules, exciting them to emit light in the visible spectrum. Occasionally the sun emits huge pulses of particles known as solar winds, which result in particularly spectacular displays of auroras that are visible at lower latitudes than normal. M. V. Angel

auster, the old Latin name for the south wind, used in some of the accounts of very early voyages. It was this meaning of south or southerly which gave *Terra Australis Incognita its name.

automatic identification system, see SIGNALS AT SEA: MODERN RADIO COMMUNICATIONS.

automatic pilot, a device fitted to ships by which they are held on any desired *course without the need of anyone on the steering wheel. Any variation from the set course automatically supplies power to the steering engine so that the *helm is put over and the vessel brought back to its correct course. In most systems the automatic pilot is actuated by a *gyroscopic compass so that the course steered is a *true one. See also STEERING GEAR.

auxiliary. **(1)** The name by which an engine is known when fitted for occasional use in a sailing *yacht. **(2)** Machinery fitted in powered vessels which is not part of the main propelling machinery but used for ancillary purposes such as *pumps, *capstan engines, air compressors, etc. **(3)** A non-combatant vessel belonging to a *fleet train which refuels and resupplies warships.

Avalon, in Welsh mythology an earthly paradise in the western seas. The Welsh name is **Ynys Yr Afallon**, or Isle of Apples, after the largest fruit then known to the inhabitants of northern Europe, which symbolized the feasting which goes on in paradise. See also ATLANTIS; LYONESSE.

avast, the order in any *seamanship operation to stop or hold. It is generally thought to have been derived from the Italian *basta*, enough.

Avery, John (b. *c.*1653), pirate, alias Long Ben, born in Devon. In 1694, while a mate aboard the *Charles*, he incited a *mutiny and sailed the ship to the Indian Ocean. His most notable success at *piracy came in the Red Sea where he captured two pilgrim ships owned by the Mogul emperor. The loot accumulated from the pilgrims made them all rich men. Some of them elected to stay in the Indian Ocean, but the remainder went with Avery to the Bahamas where they bribed the governor to let them ashore. A number stayed in the area, others sailed to Carolina or, with Avery, to Ireland. The English government did its best to hunt them down and a few were captured and executed, but no one knows for certain what happened to Avery, though some sources say he died in poverty in England.

awash, the situation of an object almost submerged, as when seas wash over a *shipwreck or *shoal, or when a ship lies so low in the water that the seas wash over it. A falling *tide which exposes a rock or bank which is submerged at high water makes it awash.

a-weigh, or **aweigh,** the situation of the anchor at the moment it is broken out of the ground when being weighed. When the anchor is a-weigh the ship is no longer secured to the ground and will drift unless under sail or power. See also A-TRIP; UNDER WAY.

awning. **(1)** A *canvas canopy spread over a deck for protection from the sun. **(2)** In old sailing vessels that part of the *poop deck which used to project beyond the doors of the poop *cabins to form a shelter for the steering wheel and *binnacle was also called the awning.

axle-trees. **(1)** The name given to the two cross-pieces of a wooden gun carriage fixed under the fore and after parts of the cheeks and carrying the spindles of the wheels. **(2)** The iron spindle of the old-fashioned chain-*pump used for pumping out the *bilges of ships was also known as an axle-tree.

'aye aye, sir', the correct and seamanlike reply on *board ship on receipt of an order. In the days when officers were rowed ashore, or to their ships, 'Aye aye' was also a boat's reply in the Royal Navy when hailed from a ship if it had a commissioned officer below the rank of captain on board. If no commissioned officer was on board, the reply was 'No No'; if a captain was on board the reply was the name of his ship, and if an admiral, the reply was 'flag'. Boats were hailed in this fashion so that those on *watch would know the form of salute required when officers arrived on board.

azimuth, from the Arabic *as sumat*, way or direction, a term used in *navigation for the *bearing of a celestial body. Geometrically it is the measure of the arc of the *horizon that lies between the elevated pole (north in the northern hemisphere, south in the southern) and the point where the *great circle passing through the celestial body cuts the horizon. Separate azimuth tables were common in the days before modern altitude-azimuth tables came into use for sight reduction for *celestial navigation. Azimuth tables were also commonly used for checking *magnetic compass error at sea.

azimuth compass, a compass designed to observe the value of the local magnetic *variation. Early *navigators had no knowledge of the phenomenon, and it was not until the 15th century that it became clear that the compass needle did not point true north. It is sometimes claimed that it was *Columbus on his first voyage who discovered the existence of variation. However, the first recorded description of an azimuth compass occurs in John of Lisbon's *Livro de marinharia*, published in 1514, and for the next two centuries various types of compass were constructed to observe the variation. Most were completely separate from the steering compass. The function of the azimuth compass was simply to get a *bearing of the sun, moon, or a star that could be compared with the calculated bearing of the body, the difference between the two being the variation. A drawback of the azimuth compass was that it required two operators, one to take the bearing, the other to read the compass scale. Nowadays variation and its annual rate of change are recorded on every *chart. Azimuth rings are still used when *swinging a ship to find the *deviation, or to take bearings for *coastal navigation.

B

baboon watch, the unfortunate person detailed to remain on deck in harbour to watch over the ship's safety while the rest of the crew were below or ashore. The term is associated with the days of *square-rigged sailing ships, and the baboon was usually one of the apprentices carried on board.

babystay, or *jackstay, a short *stay attached on deck just forward of the mast and used to control the mast's lower part. A *storm jib may be set on it. John Rousmaniere

back, to. (1) The wind is said to back when it changes contrary to its normal pattern. In the northern hemisphere, north of the *trade wind belt, the wind usually changes clockwise—from north, through east, south, and west. When the change is anticlockwise, the wind is backing. In the southern *latitudes, the reverse is the general pattern of the winds. When the wind backs in either hemisphere it is generally taken as a sign that it will freshen. **(2) To back a square sail** in a *square-rigger is to *brace the *yards so that the wind presses on the forward side of the sail to take the *way off the ship. See also ABACK. **(3) To back water** is to push on the *oars when rowing a boat, instead of pulling on them, in order to bring the boat to a stop. **(4) To back an anchor**, to lay out a smaller anchor, usually a *kedge or *stream anchor, ahead of the *bower anchor in order to provide additional holding power and to prevent the bower from *coming home.

back a strand, to, when making a *long splice, to fill the *score vacated when unlaying a *strand with one of the opposite strands.

backboard, a board across the *sternsheets of a boat just *aft of the seats. It forms a support for passengers or for the helmsman if the boat is under sail.

back splice, a method of finishing off the end of a rope to prevent the *strands unravelling by forming a *crown knot with the strands and then tucking them back two or three times each.

Back splice

backstay, a part of the standing *rigging of a sailing vessel to support the upper part of a mast from *aft, while *forestays support it from forward. In *square-rigged sailing ships, backstays are taken from the heads of all the component mastheads of each mast, or the equivalent in pole-masted vessels, and are brought back to each side of the ship. In antiquity they were set up with *deadeyes and *lanyards to *chain-plates and in modern vessels with rigging screws that are made up to chain-plates. In *fore-and-aft-rigged vessels backstays are fitted to the mast(s) to balance the forestay(s). In old-fashioned vessels these are usually running, that is, made up at the deck with a *tackle or backstay lever. This allows the *lee backstay to be released so that the sail and its boom, and *gaff if fitted, are not constrained by it. Modern *Bermudan-rigged yachts have permanent backstays from the masthead to the *counter, called *preventer backstays, inside which the mainsail and boom can move without hindrance. For illus. see RIGGING: STANDING RIGGING.

badge, originally an ornamental stern in smaller sailing ships either framing a window of the *cabin or giving a representation of a window. It was usually heavily decorated with carvings of *sea gods or other marine figures. Today a ship's badge is normally a heraldic device based on the ship's name or on some other association she may have. It is often known as the ship's crest, and is usually displayed on board in some prominent place.

baggywrinkle, a home-made device designed to prevent chafe on sails from the *lifts, *stays, and *crosstrees during long periods of sailing. It is made by stretching two lengths of *marline at a convenient working height and cutting old *manila rope into lengths of about 10 centimetres (4 in.) which are then unlaid. The *strands are then laid across the two lengths of marline, the ends bent over and brought up between the two lengths, pulled tight, and pushed up against other pieces similarly worked, to provide a long length of bushy material. This is then cut into suitable lengths and *served round wire and *spars wherever there is a danger of these coming in contact with the sails.

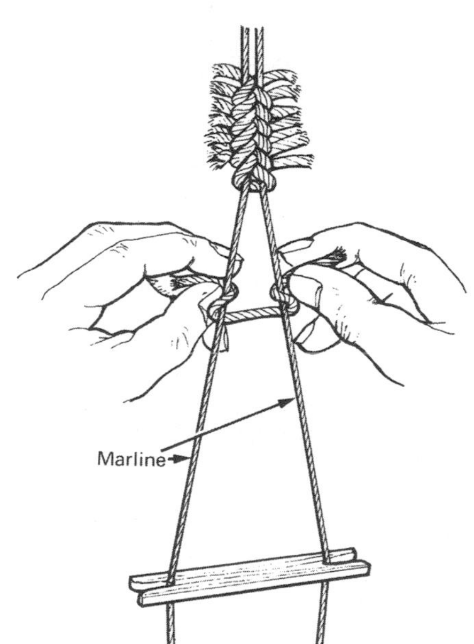

Baggywrinkle in the making

bagpipe the mizzen, to, an order given to lay *aback a sail set on the *mizzen-mast by hauling up the sheet to the mizzen *rigging, the purpose being to stop the way on a sailing vessel or slow it down. It was a quick and ready, if a little unseamanlike, means of bringing such a vessel to a halt.

bag reef, an additional fourth or lower row of *reef points on the sails of a *fore-and-aft rig. They were fitted in the smaller sailing ships of the British Navy. They took in only short reef to prevent large sails from bagging when *on the wind. In the US Navy it was the first reef of five in a *topsail, again to prevent bagging when on the wind.

bail, to, the process of emptying out water from the bottom of a boat or small vessel. The term implies that this is done by hand, not by mechanical means. Originally, a boat was bailed out with a **bail**, an old term for a bucket, but the modern word is a **bailer**. This is generally a plastic scoop with a handle which enables the water to be thrown out more rapidly than with a bucket.

balance, to, to reduce a *lateen sail by lowering the *yard and rolling part of the *peak of the sail onto the yard, securing it to the yard about one-fifth of the way down. When used as a noun it describes the part of the sail which lies forward of the mast.

balancelle, see SETTEE.

Balboa, Vasco Nuñez de (1475–1519), the first European to discover the Pacific Ocean. He first arrived in the New World in 1501 as a follower of Roderigo de Bastidas in his voyage of discovery along the coast of present-day Colombia. After an unsuccessful period as a plantation owner in *Hispaniola, Balboa was forced in 1510 to flee his creditors. He escaped as a *stowaway on an expedition to reinforce a colony on the Colombian coast of Urabá which included the future conqueror of Peru Francisco de Pizarro (*c.*1475–1541). On Balboa's advice, the colony moved to Darién on the Isthmus of Panama, and in 1511 Balboa was named the new colony's interim governor and captain general.

In the course of subjugating the hinterland Balboa heard of an ocean beyond the mountains and of a country full of gold. When this news reached Spain a large expedition was dispatched with great enthusiasm. However, Balboa was not given command of it, as his enemies had turned King Ferdinand of Spain against him. Instead, an elderly nobleman, Pedro Arias Dávila, was sent to replace him as governor. But Balboa did not await the arrival of the expedition or the new governor. On 1 September 1513 he gathered an expedition of 190 Spaniards, including Pizarro, and 1,000 of the local inhabitants, to try and find the ocean. Twenty-four days later he reached the summit of the mountain barrier where the distant ocean came in sight. Reaching the coast on 29 September, Balboa formally took possession of the 'Great South Sea', or the *South Seas as it came to be called, in the name of King Ferdinand of Spain. After visiting the Pearl Islands in the Gulf of Panama, he made a triumphant return to Darién loaded with treasure.

Balboa's discovery restored the king's confidence in him. He was appointed *adelantado*, or admiral, of the newly discovered 'Great South Sea' and governor of Panama and Coiba, but was still subject to Dávila's authority. The jealousy and rivalry between Balboa and Dávila intensified, but eventually Balboa was given grudging permission to explore the 'Great South Sea'. This he succeeded in doing by having two small ships built which were transported in pieces across the mountains to the ocean. In them Balboa explored the Gulf of San Miguel (1517–18), part of the Gulf of Panama, and took possession of the Pearl Islands; and only adverse weather prevented him from anticipating Pizarro's descent on Peru. He was then recalled by Dávila, ostensibly for a friendly meeting but in reality to face trumped up charges of treason. Dávila levelled these accusations at Balboa to protect himself from charges that he, Dávila, was facing and which he knew Balboa would support. Enticing him to Acla, near Darién, Dávila had Balboa seized, tried, and, largely on the evidence of Pizarro, condemned to death, and on 1 January 1519 he was executed in Acla's public square. See also EXPLORATION BY SEA.

bald headed, a sailing term used to indicate a *square-rigged ship without her *royals set, or permanently rigged without them. It is also used for *gaff-rigged vessels without their *topmasts.

bale, a curved metal strap usually attached to the *spar of a *yacht on which to hang a *block.

John Rousmaniere

balinger, a small seagoing vessel, without a *forecastle and carrying either a *square sail, or a sail extended by a *sprit on a single mast. It was used in the 15th and 16th centuries mainly for coastal trade, but sometimes as a transport carrying about 40 soldiers.

balk, an old term for naval timber, imported in roughly squared beams from Baltic countries. It is the origin of the present-day term 'baulk' used when describing timber.

Ballard, Robert D. (b. 1942), American oceanographer and deep-sea explorer, who has made important contributions to *marine archaeology and *oceanography, and is, perhaps, best known for his discovery in 1985 of the sunken *ocean liner **Titanic*. Before becoming president of the Institute for Exploration at Mystic Aquarium in Mystic, Conn., he worked for 30 years at the Woods Hole *Oceanographic Institution (WHOI), where he helped develop *underwater vehicles for marine research and founded the Deep Submergence Laboratory there.

In 1989, he created the JASON Project, an educational programe designed to inspire in students a lifelong passion to pursue learning in science, mathematics, and technology through exploration and discovery. He later developed telecommunications technology to create 'telepresence' for his JASON Project, which today allows hundreds of thousands of schoolchildren to accompany him from afar on undersea explorations around the globe.

During his career Ballard has conducted more than 100 deep-sea expeditions, using both manned and unmanned underwater vehicles. They include the first manned exploration of the Mid-Ocean Ridge which helped confirm the newly emerging theory of plate tectonics; the discovery of *hydrothermal vents and their exotic ecosystems during the 1977 Galapagos Rift expedition; and the 1979 exploration programme on the East Pacific Rise that discovered the first 'black smokers', a discovery that helped explain the chemistry of the world's oceans (see CHEMICAL OCEANOGRAPHY). He also mounted expeditions which found the sunken remains of the German *battleship *Bismarck*, the US *aircraft carrier *Yorktown*, 14 US warships lost in battle off Guadalcanal in 1942, and the torpedo boat PT-109, which was commanded by the future President John F. Kennedy during the Second World War (1939–45). More recent discoveries include the Mediterranean Sea finds of sunken remains of ships along ancient trade routes (1997), two ancient Phoenician ships off Israel, the oldest *shipwrecks ever found in deep water (1999), and four 1,500-year-old wooden ships—one almost perfectly preserved—in the Black Sea (2000). In 2003 he used satellite and Internet 2 technologies to bring thousands of students around the world into direct contact with his expedition team while in the Black Sea and Mediterranean Sea.

At the Institute for Exploration in Mystic, Ballard has developed a series of underwater vehicles, including the ROV Hercules, created specifically to conduct deep-water archaeological excavation to professional archaeological standards. Designed by a team of engineers, archaeologists, and marine geologists, Hercules, which was successfully field-tested in the Black Sea in 2003, uses sophisticated manipulation, optical, and acoustic sensors.

Ballard is a member of the *National Oceanic and Atmospheric Administration's Science Advisory Board, and is one of sixteen commissioners on the President's Commission on Ocean Policy. His publications include: *The Discovery of the Titanic* (1987), *The Discovery of the Bismarck* (1990), *The Lost Ships of Guadalcanal* (1993), *Exploring the Lusitania* (1995), *Return to Midway* (1999), *Adventures in Ocean Exploration* (2001), *Collision with History: The Search for John F. Kennedy's PT-109* (2002), *Mystery of the Ancient Seafarers* (2004), and *Return to Titanic* (2004).

www.ife.org
www.mysticaquarium.org
www.gso.uri.edu
www.jason.org

Laurie Bradt

ballast, additional weight carried in a ship to give it *stability and/or to provide a satisfactory *trim. Nowadays this is done by pumping water in or out of trimming tanks, but in the past ballast was usually in the form of pigs of soft iron, known as *kentledge, or stone or shingle was taken on board temporarily and stowed in the *holds. **Ballast tanks** are the external or internal tanks fitted in *submarines to control them when surfacing or diving. **In ballast**, the condition of a cargo vessel which has discharged its cargo and has taken ballast on board. *Yachts carry their ballast externally, as a keel. Sailing vessels insufficiently ballasted were said to be *crank.

banjo, the brass frame in which the *propeller fitted in early steamships. As a ship often had to rely on its sails, its propeller was fitted in a banjo which could be hoisted within the hull when not in use so the propeller did not cause drag. It worked in a well between slides fixed to the inner and outer *sternposts. See also 'UP FUNNEL, DOWN SCREW'.

banker, the old name for a fishing vessel employed exclusively in the great *cod fishing grounds on the *Grand Banks off Newfoundland. See also FISHERIES.

Banks, Sir Joseph (1743–1820), British landowner, botanist, explorer, and scientific leader. Banks inherited a landed fortune from his father, and devoted himself to the infant science of botany, using his wealth to fund a passage on Captain James *Cook's first Pacific voyage, on HMS *Endeavour*. Accompanied by a botanist, two artists, and servants Banks was the first European scientist to study the flora and fauna of the South Pacific, and the culture of the indigenous peoples. He also helped Cook develop an eye for natural evidence. On his return Banks acted as if he, and not Cook, had been the expedition leader. This attitude denied him the chance to sail on the second Cook expedition; instead he went to Iceland. In 1778 Banks became president of the Royal Society, a post he held until his death, and he did much to link the work of the society with the needs of government and the Royal Navy. In 1781 he was made a baronet. He recommended establishing a penal settlement in Australia, at Botany Bay. A giant of the Georgian state, Banks dominated British science for two generations. See also MARINE BIOLOGY; OCEANOGRAPHY.

Banks, Joseph, *The Endeavour Journals of Joseph Banks, 1768–1771*, ed. J. C. Beaglehole (1962).
Carter, H. B., *Sir Joseph Banks* (1988).

Andrew Lambert

banyan days were meatless days in the diet of seamen in the Royal Navy, so called from the name of Hindu merchants noted for their abstinence from eating flesh. The custom was introduced during the reign of Queen Elizabeth I to economize on the cost of meat, *fish or cheese being issued on banyan days in place of salt meat.

Barbarossa, the name by which the sons and grandson of Yakub of Mitylene, a coasting captain and trader, were generally known by Christians during the 16th century. Of his four sons, Arouj, Khizr, Elias, and Isaak, the first two took to *piracy and soon became feared throughout the Mediterranean for the ferocity of their attacks on both Christian shipping and the native African princes. Both were heavily bearded with red hair, which probably accounts for their name, but Khizr was also known as Khair-ed-Din. This was a name which struck even greater terror in many Christian hearts though earning for him a reputation as a great hero throughout Islam.

From 1510 to 1545–6, the two brothers engaged in almost continuous warfare, alternating their attacks on African states with descents on the Spanish or Italian coasts and the harrying of shipping in the Mediterranean. Arouj was eventually killed by Spanish troops, but Khair-ed-Din lived until 1547, his last exploit being a plundering expedition to the coast of Italy in 1544. With the vast riches he had gained, he built a large palace at Constantinople, and it was there that he died. His son Hassan, also known as Barbarossa, confined his operations mostly to the Levant and was not so terrifying a figure in Christian eyes, though his reputation as his father's son was often enough to suppress disorders along the North African coast as and when required. See also BARBARY PIRATES.

Barbarossa

Barbary pirates, generations of mainly Muslim *corsairs who operated from the coast of northern Africa and were notorious for their ferocity and the skill. The name Barbary comes from the Berber tribes who occupied most of the coast, and the Muslim corsairs' motives for attacking Christian shipping were fuelled as much by religious hatred as by pecuniary gain. Originally under Turkish suzerainty, the African coastal towns from which corsairs operated broke free of Turkish rule in the mid-17th century and became military republics, choosing their own governors and living by plunder. The principal ones were Tripoli, Tunis, Algiers, and Bône, and Salli, where they were commonly called *Sallee pirates. Although *piracy on this coast had existed more or less permanently from the time of the decline of Roman power, it found new recruits after Granada was captured by the Catholic forces of Spain in 1492. This drove many Moors into exile, who were thus ever ready to revenge themselves on Christianity in general and Spain in particular.

Originally conducted in oared *galleys, this Mediterranean piracy entered a new phase in the 17th century when a Flemish renegade, Simon Danzer, introduced the sailing ship to the corsairs, and so hugely increased the range of their operations. Using ships like the *xebec the Barbary pirates were able to reach into the Atlantic, and were seen as far away as Iceland. In 1631 they sacked the town of Baltimore in Ireland and carried off over 100 men, women, and children who were sold in the slave market in Algiers. Indeed, the *slave trade was very lucrative for them, and during the first half of the

17th century more than 20,000 Christian slaves were sold in the market of Algiers alone. Estimates vary as to the total numbers taken, but in his book *Christian Slaves, Muslim Masters* (2004) the American historian Professor Robert Davis has calculated that between the years 1500 and 1800 over a million European Christians were captured by Barbary pirates and sold into slavery. However, it was not entirely one-way traffic, as the Muslim corsairs 'had their exact Christian counterparts who attacked ships with Muslim passengers or goods aboard and raided the coasts of North Africa and the eastern Mediterranean in a search for Muslim captives to sell into captivity, and these attacks continued until Napoleon captured their base, Malta, in 1798' (P. Earle, *The Pirate Wars* (2003), 46).

The Muslim corsairs attracted many renegades from most European nations, dazzled by the ease with which fortunes could be made. One notorious turncoat was an Englishman named Verney, a member of the distinguished Buckinghamshire family of that name; another was a Fleming, who took the Arabic name of Murad Reis. It was he who led the raid on Baltimore and became famous as one of the most successful and savage of the corsairs. But perhaps the most notorious, and certainly the most feared, of the Mediterranean corsairs were known by the collective name of *Barbarossa.

Many naval expeditions against the pirate centres were carried out by various European nations from the 17th century onwards, and though piracy declined during the 18th century, none was completely successful in stamping it out for more than a year or two until the French finally eliminated it in 1830 when they captured Algiers and annexed Algeria. Before then one of the more notable of these expeditions was mounted by Admiral *Blake in 1655, whose fleet of 24 ships had been sent out to conduct reprisals for the injuries done to English shipping. When his demands for redress were refused by the Dey of Tunis, Blake attacked the forts and burnt the nine pirate vessels that were in Port Farina, situated about 40 kilometres (25 mls.) north of Tunis. Other expeditions included several sent by King Charles II (1660–85) in conjunction with the Dutch. The French also sent two, in 1682 and 1683; there were American operations in 1801–5, when the USS **Constitution* was in action, and again in 1815; and a combined British–Dutch expedition in 1816.

Earle, P., *The Pirate Wars* (2003).

barbette, the inside fixed trunk of a gun mounting in a warship on which the turret revolved. It contained the shell and cordite hoists from the shell-room and magazine. It was originally the name given to a raised platform on the deck of a warship protected by armour on the sides, on which heavy guns were mounted, and which fired over the armour. See also WARFARE AT SEA.

barca-longa, from the Italian *barca*, a *skiff or *barge, a large fishing boat particular to Spain in the 17th to 19th centuries, with two or three masts each carrying a single *lugsail. They were built up to an overall length of about 21 metres (70 ft) and had a *keel of about 15 centimetres (6 in.) extending the whole length of the hull. The word was also sometimes written as barqualonga or barcolongo.

barcarolle, or **barcarole,** originally the name given to songs sung by Venetian boatmen, or *barcaruoli*, while rowing their *gondolas. However, the meaning has been extended to cover any song reminiscent of the original Venetian barcarolle, which normally had a slow tempo and most often a sad or doleful air. The word dates back to the 17th century.

bare boat, or **demise, charter** is where the shipowner provides the vessel and puts her at the disposal of the charterer who provides the cargo and crew. This type of charter implies certain responsibilities to the charterer and its time can be measured in years. In the 1950s the Port Line chartered two vessels for seven and six years respectively. For a *yacht it means the vessel must be crewed by the charterer and his friends.

Martin Lee

Barents, Willem (*c.*1550–97), Dutch *navigator and explorer, born on the island of Terschelling. A Spanish decree forbidding the Netherlands to trade with Portugal turned the eyes of the Dutch towards the discovery of a North-East Arctic Passage to India and the Spice Islands (Moluccas), and in 1594 Barents, with two ships, sailed from Amsterdam to try and find it, though earlier English expeditions had failed to do so. He reached the coast of Novaya Zemlya, a Russian island in the Arctic Circle which divides what would become the Barents and the Kara Sea, and followed it northward until *ice prevented him from going further. The following year he repeated the attempt with seven ships but failed to reach the Kara Sea, being held up by ice off Vaygach Island, situated between the mainland and Novaya Zemlya. During a third voyage undertaken with two ships in 1596, he discovered Spitsbergen and Bear Island, before the two ships separated. It was these discoveries that sparked the *whaling industry in Arctic waters.

Barents made for the north point of Novaya Zemlya, which this time he succeeded in rounding into the Kara Sea before being beset by ice and compelled to winter there. The following spring, as the ship was still held fast, it was decided to abandon it. This was done in two open boats, but Barents, already suffering from the hardships of an Arctic winter, died seven days later, on 20 June. Part of his journal was found four years later, but it was not until 1871 that his headquarters on Novaya Zemlya were discovered and the contents removed to The Hague. His name was perpetuated when the Murmean Sea to the eastward of North Cape was renamed the Barents Sea in 1853. See also EXPLORATION BY SEA.

bare poles, the condition of a ship when, in a severe storm, all sail has had to be taken in because of the fierceness of the wind. A ship can attempt to lie a-try (see HEAVE TO, TO), or to *scud before the wind, very often a hazardous undertaking if there is a high sea running which can *poop it.

barge, probably from the Latin *barca*, which would make it the equivalent of *bark or barque. In its oldest use **(1)**, this is probably the case, as it was the name given to a small seagoing ship with sails, next in size above a *balinger. From about the 17th century onwards the names barge and bark diverged into separate meanings. **(2)** A ceremonial state vessel, richly decorated and propelled by rowers, used on state occasions and for river processions. Such was Cleopatra's barge described by Shakespeare in *Antony and Cleopatra* (Act II, sc. ii), which

> . . . like a burnished throne
> Burn'd on the water: the poop was beaten gold:
> Purple the sails, and so perfumed, that
> The winds were love-sick with them; the oars were silver;
> Which to the tune of flutes kept stroke, and made
> The water, which they beat, to follow faster,
> As amorous of their strokes . . .

Cleopatra's was probably carried a bit to extremes, but most state barges were immensely ornate even if their *oars were wooden not silver. Shakespeare must have seen such barges on the Thames in Elizabethan times, and they continued in use down to the 19th century. **(3)** A modern derivative of the barge as a ceremonial vessel is an admiral's barge, used by naval officers of *flag rank for harbour transport. When in *commission, the royal yacht, HMY **Britannia*, had a motor boat known as the Royal Barge, as does the Port of London Authority. **(4)** A large flat-bottomed coastal trading vessel having a large *spritsail and *jib-headed *topsail, a fore *staysail, and a very small *mizzen; occasionally a *jib was set on the *bowsprit. They were fitted with *leeboards in place of a keel so that they could operate without difficulty in *shoal water. This type of barge was normally only found in the River Thames and estuary, and on the south-eastern coast of England. Those still afloat have been turned into recreational sailing vessels or houseboats. **(5)** In the days of sail, the second boat of a warship, a double-banked *pulling boat with fourteen oars; later, the largest boat of a *battleship, with mast, sails, and a *centreboard but also fitted with fourteen oars. **(6)** In the USA, a double-decked vessel without sail or power, for carrying passengers and *freight, towed by steamboat. See also DUMB BARGE. **(7)** The name given on board ship to the wooden dish in which bread or *biscuit is placed on a mess table.

bargee, a man or boy who worked as a hand on trading *barges when they were employed commercially. Those who rowed the state barges were known as rowers, and never as bargees.

bark, from the Latin *barca*, and in England now synonymous with *barque, though the Americans always spell it this way. Originally, it was a term to describe any small merchant

Barque

sailing ship with a certain hull shape which could carry any rig. This is why Cook's *Endeavour*, an ex-*collier, was described as a 'cat built bark' by the *Admiralty but a 'square sterned bark' by her surveyors. See also BARGE.

bark's head, American term for a *cow-hitch.

barnacle, a small *crustacean that occurs in vast numbers attached to rocks, *jetties, *piers, etc., and on the hulls of ships and boats. The commonest on the shore are acorn barnacles (*Balanus* spp.), which live attached to rocks with their body enclosed within a shell formed of calcareous (limy) plates. During high *tide, they open their shells and use their hairy legs to comb food particles from the water. If barnacles settle on a ship's hull in large numbers they can cause serious problems. *Copper sheathing during the days of sail and now modern antifouling paints discourage *fouling, but such paints are an *environmental issue which has not been totally resolved. Goose barnacles (*Lepas anatifera*) are the worst offenders. They have long stalks, up to 10 centimetres (4 in.) long, and can grow to maturity in a matter of a couple of weeks. They normally settle on the floating debris that accumulates in *slicks and appear in European waters at about the time barnacle geese (*Branta leucopsis*) leave on migration. This coincidence, and the superficial resemblance between their comblike legs and birds' feathers, gave rise to the medieval myth that the geese hatched from the barnacles. In 1972, the *British Scientist*, a BP *tanker, came out of refit and sailed round the Cape to the Persian Gulf. On its return voyage the ship began to judder so violently that it had to be *dry-docked in Brest. The problem proved to be a covering of 70 tonnes of goose barnacles that had grown on the ship's hull in a matter of a few weeks. M. V. Angel

barograph, a self-recording *barometer which, by means of aneroid capsules, senses atmospheric pressure change and draws a trace on paper. It is above all useful as an indication of barometric tendency from which impending bad weather may be forecast. See also MARINE METEOROLOGY. Mike Richey

barometer, an instrument that measures atmospheric pressure either by a column of mercury or, in the case of the aneroid barometer, by a thin metal cylinder partially compressed by the atmosphere. Mike Richey

barque, or **bark** in the USA, a vessel with at least three masts all *square rigged except for the *mizzen which is *fore-and-aft rigged. Until the mid-19th century barques were relatively small commercial sailing ships of up to about 500 tons. Later they were built up to about 3,000 *GRT for the grain and nitrate trades. Finally four- and five-masted barques of over 5,000 GRT were built for this trade ranging up to the biggest sailing ship ever built, *France II*, of 5,806 gross register *tonnage. Although obsolete as trading vessels, several of the larger barques are still in commission as *sail training ships, and new barque-rigged vessels have been built for this purpose. Several decommissioned barques have also been preserved in many countries as museum ships. See also CLIPPER.

barquentine, or **barkenteen,** a vessel resembling a *barque but *square rigged on the

Barquentine

foremast only, main and *mizzen having a *fore-and-aft rig.

'barrack stanchion', a naval officer or rating who spent long periods of his service in barracks or a *stone frigate and seldom served at sea.

barratry, any fraudulent act on the part of the *master or crew of a ship committed to the prejudice of its owners or underwriters, such as deliberately casting it adrift, deserting it, selling it, or even diverting it from its proper course with evil intent.

barricade, a rail supported by posts across the forward end of the *quarterdeck of a sailing man-of-war. The spaces between the posts were filled before going into action with rope mats or spare *cable, and with *nettings above the rail. The purpose of the barricade was to provide protection from small arms fire from enemy ships for those whose action station was on the quarterdeck.

barricado, a 17th-century naval term for a *tender. It was usually a civilian oared or sailing boat which attended warships in harbour, and was used for odd jobs.

Bart, Jean (1650–1702), French naval officer. He was a native of Dunkirk, and, like many seamen from that port, distinguished himself chiefly as a *privateer. Going to sea as a boy, he first served under the legendary Dutch admiral Michiel Adrienszoon de Ruyter (1607–76), and had his first experience of battle during the Second Dutch War (1665–7). When war broke out between France and Holland (1672–78) he returned to Dunkirk and led a small fleet of privateers with great success, and was promoted to the rank of lieutenant. In the War of the Grand Alliance (1689–97) he was captured by English ships while escorting a *convoy off the Casquets and was briefly imprisoned at Plymouth. He managed to escape in a boat and rowed for over two days until he reached France. He was promoted to captain and defended Dunkirk from English attacks on the port, but his most outstanding success came in 1696. With France facing famine, he captured a Dutch convoy of 96 ships loaded with wheat, a feat for which he was ennobled by Louis XIV, and in 1697 he was promoted *chef d'escadre,* the equivalent rank of commodore in most other navies. His name has been commemorated by naming some of the French Navy's largest and most important warships after him. These included its last *battleship, of 35,000 tons, which took part in the Anglo-French operation in 1956 to seize the *Suez Canal. See also WARFARE AT SEA.

'Bartimeus', the pseudonym of Sir Lewis Ritchie (1886–1967), a British naval officer, the author of many fictional stories of naval life. See also MARINE LITERATURE.

basilisk, an old name for the long 48-pounder gun used in the Royal Navy in the 17th, 18th, and early 19th centuries, so-called from the snakes and dragons which were sculptured on it in place of the more usual *dolphins. It had a range of about 3,000 paces. See also WARFARE AT SEA.

Batavia, a Dutch *East Indiaman, widely known for its bloodthirsty *mutiny after it had hit a *reef in the Houtman Abrolhos off the Western Australian coast in 1629. About 250 of the 316 people aboard, including women and children, managed to reach some nearby, waterless, coral islands, and Francisco Pelsaert, the ship's commander, and 46 of the crew sailed two small boats to Batavia (now Djakarta) to get help. In his absence, an under-merchant, Jeronimus Cornelisz, took charge of the castaways and declared himself governor of the new community. Those who opposed Cornelisz were promptly murdered by his followers—a grave containing some of them was excavated in 2001—and many were also killed simply to give the mutineers more space and food. However, the ship's soldiers, who had been sent to another island (West Wallabi) to search for water, which they found, managed to warn Pelsaert about the mutiny when he eventually returned. They helped him round up the mutineers, who were put on trial, and many, including Cornelisz, were executed. Two were *marooned on the mainland, and were never heard of again. Pelsaert recovered nearly all the bullion that was aboard the *Batavia*, but on his return to Batavia he was criticized for leaving the survivors in the first place. The story stirred great interest in Holland and an account of the mutiny and murders was published in a highly illustrated book in 1648.

The site of the *shipwreck was not found until 1963, and between 1972 and 1976 experts in *marine archaeology at the Western Australian Maritime Museum carried out an extensive excavation of the site. Many artefacts and pieces of the ship were found, and parts of the hull were reconstructed and are now on view at the Western Australian Maritime Museum in Fremantle. Relics from the *Batavia*, including a large sandstone portico façade intended for the Castle of Batavia, may also be seen at the Western Australian Museum, Geraldton, and at the Australian National Maritime Museum, Sydney.

A 17th-century *replica ship based on the *Batavia*'s remains, and named after her, was *launched at Lelystad in Holland in 1995. In 2000 she was shipped to Australia to be exhibited, and to sail, during the Sydney Olympic Games, and was then shipped back to Lelystad.

Dash, M., *Batavia's Graveyard: The True Story of the Mad Heretic who Led History's Bloodiest Mutiny* (2002).
Drake-Brockman, H., *Voyage to Disaster* (1963).
Edwards, H., *Islands of Angry Ghosts* (1966).
www.mm.wa.gov.au

bateloe, a large wooden vessel with a crew of up to a dozen men, used on the river Madeira (widely known as the 'long cemetery') in Brazil to transport rubber from Bolivia to the Amazon, whence it was shipped abroad. They each carried about 10 tons of latex, and were strongly constructed to withstand the dangers of the nineteen cataracts of the 400-kilometre (250-m.) stretch of the river between Guajare-Merim and San Antonio. Mortality among the crews of the bateloes was heavy, mainly from fevers.

bathyscaphe, a small free-moving *underwater vehicle designed by the Swiss-born professor Auguste Piccard (1884–1962), for exploring the ocean depths. His first two were balloon shaped and in the second he reached a depth of 4,050 metres (13,284 ft) in February 1954. With Italian assistance, he constructed a third, *Trieste I*, in which the balloon shape was abandoned for that of a cylindrical tank beneath which was a spherical observation chamber. In 1958 this was acquired by the US Navy and, after extensive reconstruction, touched bottom at 10,915 metres (35,812 ft) in the Marianas *Trench on 25 January 1960.

bathysphere, an early observation chamber, a predecessor to the *bathyscaphe. It was spherical and made of steel and was fitted with Perspex windows. In 1934 its designer, the American zoologist Charles William Beebe (1872–1962), one of the pioneers of *oceanography, was lowered on a wire to a depth of 923 metres (3,028 ft), at that time a record for deep-sea *diving. See also UNDERWATER VEHICLE.

batten. **(1)** A thin iron bar used to secure the *tarpaulin cover over a cargo *hatch of a merchant ship. Several of them were used on each cover. When they were placed in position they were held securely in place by wedges under the batten-cleats—metal right-angled brackets welded on to the *coaming of cargo hatches—and the hatches were said to be **battened down** (see also next entry). **(2)** A thin wooden or plastic strip which fits into a long, narrow pocket in the *leech of a *Bermudan mainsail in *yachts to hold the leech out when sailing. The name is also given to the long, thin strips of bamboo which are inserted in *lateen sails to hold the form of the sail. These bamboo battens are also used in the sails of the *junk rig.

batten down, to, to secure the openings in the deck and sides of a vessel when heavy weather is forecast.

battlecruiser, a development of the Dreadnought *battleships pioneered in Britain. Battlecruisers were designed to function as advanced scouts of the battle fleet, powerful enough to push home their reconnaissance even up to the battle fleet of the enemy, but also fast enough to outstrip it. They carried guns of the same size as the Dreadnought battleships but had a speed of some 4 knots faster, which was attained by cutting down the thickness of their armour protection. They were the brainchild of Admiral Sir John Fisher when he became First Sea Lord in 1904. In fact, he called them fast armoured cruisers and it was not until 1912 that they were renamed generically as battlecruisers.

The first battlecruiser was HMS *Invincible*, a ship of 17,000 tons with a speed of 25.5 knots and carrying eight 12-in. (30-cm) guns. However, the first to be *commissioned was her sister ship, the *Indomitable*. Others included the *Lion*, Admiral Beatty's flagship at Jutland, *launched in 1910, and her sister ship the *Tiger*. They were followed by the 42,000-ton super battlecruiser HMS *Hood*, which carried eight 15-in. (37.5-cm) guns, the last battlecruiser to be built for the Royal Navy. She was completed in 1920 and was, at the time, the largest warship in the world, but was sunk by the German battleship *Bismarck* in 1941, a last bitter reminder that a thinly armoured ship was no match for one protected with adequate armour. See also WARFARE AT SEA.

battle honours, the names of battles or individual ship actions in which a warship has taken part. They are usually displayed on a board in a prominent place in the ship as a source of pride in her name. In the Royal Navy battle honours are hereditary, and a subsequent ship bearing the same name usually displays the honours gained by her predecessors. This is normal practice in most navies, though in the US Navy, where battle honours are known as **battle stars**, they are not hereditary. See also WARFARE AT SEA.

battleship, the modern equivalent of, and the name derived from, the older sailing *ship of the line.

From Ship of the Line to 'Ironclad'.The introduction into *warfare at sea during the 1840s and 1850s of the high-explosive shell, the rifled gun, armour plate, and *steam propulsion of acceptable reliability made obsolete the traditional three-decker wooden sailing ship of the line. However, the transition from ship of the line to battleship was a comparatively gradual process, many of the old sailing first *rates being converted to have iron protection on their hulls and lengthened to take steam propulsion, while the new iron ships retained the masts, sails, and gun batteries of the older wooden ships. It was only with the growth in reliability and radius of action of the steam engine, and the introduction of the breech-loading gun and a more efficient propellant than black powder, that the battleship at last broke clear from its wooden predecessor and evolved as a type of its own.

The first seagoing *'ironclad', the precursor to the 20th-century battleship, was the French **Gloire*, and she was followed in 1860 by the British iron-hulled HMS **Warrior*. Though classed as *frigates, these 13-knot men-of-war, powered by engines of over 3,000 horsepower but also carrying a full sailing rig, could overtake and overwhelm any contemporary three-decker ship of the line.

The first battleships to rely entirely on steam propulsion were known as mastless ships, though another feature, the *ram bow, lingered on longer than sails. The first such ship was the 9,300-ton British *Devastation*, designed in 1869. Having a very low *freeboard, and without *forecastle or *poop, she was virtually a seagoing *monitor. Here, again, the two types overlapped considerably in time, the masted iron battleships lasting until nearly 1890.

Guns, armour, and steam machinery improved so rapidly during the period 1870–1900 that the battleship began to settle down into a recognizable type, with the main guns mounted in *turrets, and most navies began to build them in classes instead of singly. *Tonnage increased with each new ship, in Britain rising to the 15,000 tons of the *Majestic*, completed in 1896.

By the last decade of the 19th century every permutation of large and small guns, high and moderate speed, thick and thin armour plate, had seemingly been exhausted, *naval architecture had settled on a basic specification for the battleship, and the term 'ironclad' had been dropped. This combined an armament of four big guns, about ten guns of various smaller *calibre, and a large number of quick-firers to deal with the new threat to the battleship, the torpedo boat.

The Dreadnought. In 1903 the naval annual *Fighting Ships* published an article by the distinguished Italian naval architect Vittorio Cuniberti, entitled 'An Ideal Battleship for the British Fleet', which called for a vessel combining an armament of twelve 12-in. (30-cm) guns, 12 inches of armour plate, and a speed of 24 knots—an unprecedented combination of qualities. HMS *Dreadnought* which was *launched in 1906 fell only marginally short of Cuniberti's ideal. She overturned all the long-established principles of compromise in *naval architecture, made every other battleship in the world obsolete, and created a furore in Britain as well as the world at large. She had many progenitors, but history justly gives the first credit to Admiral Sir John Fisher. With her armament of ten 12-in guns, displacement of 17,900 tons, and maximum speed of 21 knots, *Dreadnought*'s superiority to any other fighting ship was so manifest that no naval power could afford to build to any other pattern. Moreover, she was powered by turbine machinery (see STEAM PROPULSION), which offered greatly superior dependability, simplicity, and cleanliness. Such an advance in design was achieved that it was not imitated by foreign designers for several years and kept Britain ahead in what became known as the 'Dreadnought Race' for supremacy at sea.

The Decline of Battleship Supremacy. In 1936, when a new naval rearmament race was under way, the threat of aerial bombardment had been added to that of the *submarine, yet by the outbreak of the Second World War (1939–45) all the major powers had laid down new battleships. Germany, for example, laid down two, the 41,000-ton German *Bismarck*, and her sister ship, the 42,500-ton *Tirpitz*, both launched in 1941, but their so-called pocket battleships were in fact *cruisers. The Japanese built the biggest battleships ever constructed, ignoring the Washington Naval Limitation Treaty in doing so. These were the *Yamato* and *Musashi*, completed in 1941 and 1942. They displaced over 63,720 tons, carried nine 18-in. (45-cm) guns, and could steam at 27 knots.

However, early lessons in the Second World War, at Taranto in 1940, when the Italian fleet was crippled by a handful of obsolescent British Fleet Air Arm aircraft, and at Pearl Harbor in December 1941, when Japanese *aircraft carriers launched a devastating aircraft strike on the US Navy's Pacific Fleet, suggested that the battleship was an obsolete and expensive anachronism. This was underlined when in the same month, December 1941, the new British battleship HMS *Prince of Wales* and the older battlecruiser HMS *Repulse* were both sunk by Japanese aircraft off Malaya. And in spite of their size and speed, and elaborate protection against bombs and torpedoes, both the *Yamato* and *Musashi* were sunk at small cost after sustained attacks by US aircraft.

In the latter part of the war the battleship was used for shore bombardment, a role it continued to perform in the Korean (1950–3) and Vietnam Wars (1965–75). Four *Montana*-class battleships were laid down for the US Navy late in the Second World War but were never completed, and the Royal Navy's last battleship, the *Vanguard*, completed in 1946, was scrapped in 1960. The US Navy currently (2004) retains one battleship, *Iowa*, in reserve.

Hough, R., *Dreadnought: A History of the Modern Battleship* (1965).

Parkes, O., *British Battleships* (rev. edn. 1966).

bawley, a small coastal fishing vessel or oyster dredger, peculiar to Rochester and Whitstable in Kent, and to Leigh-on-Sea and Harwich in Essex, within the Thames estuary area. They were *cutter-rigged craft with a short mast and *topmast, and set a *loose-footed mainsail on a very long *gaff, a *topsail, and *staysail. The Leigh-on-Sea bawley was used chiefly for shrimping. They are now obsolete, though some may survive as recreational craft. See also FISHERIES.

bay. **(1)** The space between decks forward of the *bitts in sailing warships. They were often described as two separate spaces, the *starboard and *larboard bays; also, of course, **(2)** an indentation in the coastline between two headlands.

bayamo, a violent squall of wind off the land experienced on the southern coast of Cuba, especially in the Bight of Bayamo. The squall is accompanied by vivid flashes of lightning and usually ends in heavy rain.

beachcomber, originally a seaman who, not prepared to work, preferred to exist by hanging around ports and harbours and existing on the charity of others. It then became more generally accepted to describe any loafer around the waterfront, particularly in the Pacific Islands, who preferred a life of *dolce far niente* to work of any description. However, the continuing popularity of *Confessions of a Beachcomber*

(1908), E. J. Banfield's description of life on Dunk Island off Australia's Queensland coastline, has latterly given the word a far more respectable meaning.

beacon. **(1)** Normally a stake surmounted by a distinctive topmark erected over a *shoal or sandbank. In many coastal estuaries without important shipping the low water level is marked by local beacons, often withies. **(2)** A prominent erection on shore that indicates a safe line of approach to a harbour or a safe passage clear of an obstruction. With the widespread use of *GPS, sea traffic has tended to sail closer inshore by night so that there is an increasing demand for lit beacons. For *radar beacons see RACON; RAMARK. See also EPIRB; RADIO BEACON.

beak, the name sometimes given to the metal point or *ram fixed on the bows of war *galleys and used to pierce the hulls of enemy galleys, and thus sink or disable them.

beakhead, the space in a sailing man-of-war immediately forward of the *forecastle, and where originally a ship's *figurehead was erected. In those days the forecastle was built across the bows of the ship, from *cathead to cathead, and the beakhead was open to the sea. There were short ladders down to it from the forecastle deck, while the doors from the forecastle itself led directly onto the beakhead. This space was used in warships as the seamen's *heads. In some later warship designs the beakhead was decked with gratings so that the sea, breaking through them, helped to keep the space clean.

beam. **(1)** One of the transverse members of a ship's *frames on which the decks are laid. In vessels constructed of wood they are supported at their ends by being dovetailed into the beam shelf or *carlings. In steel ships they are bracketed to the frames. The depth of a beam is known as its *moulding, its width as its *siding. For illus. see SHIPBUILDING. **(2)** The transverse measurement of a ship at its widest part. It is also a term used in indicating direction in relation to a ship, thus **before the beam**, the arc of a semicircle extended to the horizon from the beam of the ship around the bows to the other beam; **abaft the beam**, the similar semicircle extending round the stern of the ship. For illus. see RELATIVE BEARINGS. **(3)** The wooden or metal bar which spreads the mouth of a *trawl when fishing. See also FISHERIES.

beam ends. A ship is said to be 'on its beam ends' when it has heeled over to such an extent that its deck *beams are nearly vertical.

bean-cod, the English name, probably given in jest, to a small Portuguese vessel used for inshore and estuary fishing. It had a sharp and very high curved bow, the curve being carried round inboard at the top. Single masted, they spread a very large *lateen sail which extended the whole length of the vessel, making it remarkably *weatherly. See also FISHERIES.

bear, to, verb describing the direction of an object from the observer's position, usually expressed in terms of a compass, e.g. the land bears NE by N., the enemy bears 047°, etc. In traditional seaman's language it was sometimes given with reference to the ship's head, e.g., the *wreck bore two *points on the *port bow. **To bear up**, in a sailing vessel, to sail closer to the wind; **to bear down**, to approach another ship from the windward side of it; **to bear in with** or **to bear off from**, to approach nearer or to stand further off, usually in connection with the land. See also BEARING.

bearing, the horizontal angle between the direction of north or south and the object of which the bearing is being taken.

beat, to. **(1)** To sail to *windward by a series of alternate *tacks across the wind. **(2) To beat to quarters**, the order given to the drummers on board a sailing man-of-war to summon the crew to their stations for action against an enemy. In the British Navy the drums were beaten to the rhythm of *'Heart of Oak'.

Beaufort Scale, the internationally recognized scale for wind and weather which was drawn up by Sir Francis Beaufort (1774–1857), a British rear admiral who served as Hydrographer of the Navy from 1829 to 1855. See also HYDROGRAPHY.

Courtney, N., *Gale Force 10: The Life and Legacy of Admiral Beaufort* (2002).

becalm, to, to blanket a ship by cutting off the wind, either by the proximity of the shore

Beaufort Scale

Used to indicate the force of the wind.

Force on Beaufort Scale	*Nautical miles per hr.*	*Description*	*Height of sea in ft*	*Deep sea criteria*
0	0–1	Calm	—	Flat calm, mirror smooth
1	1–3	Light Airs	¼	Small wavelets, no crests
2	4–6	Light Breeze	½	Small wavelets, crests glassy but do not break
3	7–10	Light Breeze	2	Large wavelets, crests begin to break
4	11–16	Moderate Breeze	3½	Small waves, becoming longer, crests break frequently
5	17–21	Fresh Breeze	6	Moderate waves, longer, breaking crests
6	22–27	Strong Breeze	9½	Large waves forming, crests break more frequently
7	28–33	Strong Wind	13½	Large waves, streaky foam
8	34–40	Near Gale	18	High waves of increasing length, crests form spindrift
9	41–47	Strong Gale	23	High waves, dense streaks of foam, crests roll over
10	48–55	Storm	29	Very high waves, long overhanging crests. Surface of sea white with foam
11	56–65	Violent Storm	37	Exceptionally high waves, sea completely covered with foam
12	above 65	Hurricane	—	The air filled with spray and visibility seriously affected

or by another ship. A ship motionless through the absence of wind is said to be becalmed.

becket. **(1)** A short length of rope whose ends have been *spliced together to form a circle. **(2)** A short length of rope with an *eye splice in one end and a *stopper knot in the other used in the days of the sailing navies to hold various articles (boarding pikes, cutlasses, etc.) together in their stowage. **(3)** A short rope with an eye splice in each end used to hold the *foot of a *sprit against the mast. **(4)** The eye at the base of a *block for making fast the *standing part of a *fall. **(5)** Rope loops spliced and *clove hitched to the *jackstays on *yards through which seamen put their arms to use both hands when *furling sails on a *square-rigged vessel.

becue, to, a method of making fast a rope to a boat's anchor for use on rocky ground. Before the anchor is lowered the rope is made fast to the *flukes of the anchor and then led to the ring of the anchor at the end of its *shank, where it is secured by a light *seizing. If the flukes are caught in the rocks, a sharp jerk will break the seizing and the anchor will then *come home easily, being hoisted from the flukes. See also ANCHOR BUOY.

bed. **(1)** A shaped piece of timber placed under the quarters of casks when stowed in a ship's *hold to keep the *bilge, the central part of a cask where it swells, clear of the ship's *floor. **(2)** **Anchor bed**, a flat space on either side of the bow of the ship on which, in the days before stockless anchors, the *bower and *sheet anchors were stowed after they had been *weighed and *catted. **(3)** **Engine bed**, the metal base on to which a ship's engines are bolted. **(4)** The stationary part of a carronade carriage upon which the gun slid.

bee, a ring or hoop of metal. **Bees of the *bowsprit**, pieces of hardwood bolted to the outer end of the bowsprit of an old-fashioned sailing vessel. The fore-*topmast *stays were *rove through these before they were brought in to the bow and secured.

bee blocks, wooden swells on each side of the after end of a boom of a small vessel such as an old-fashioned *smack or *yacht. It has *sheaves through which the *leech *reef *pendants, or reefing *tackle, were led.

beetle, a heavy mallet used by shipwrights to drive *reeming irons into the *seams of wooden-planked sides and decks of vessels in order to open them up. They could then be *caulked with *oakum and *pitch. See also HORSING IRON.

before the mast, literally, the position of men during the days of sail whose living quarters on board were in the *forecastle, but a term more generally used to describe seamen, as opposed to officers, in phrases such as 'he sailed before the mast'. The phrase is enshrined in Richard *Dana's classic of *marine literature *Two Years before the Mast.*

beitass, the old Norse name for a *luff *spar which was used in Viking ships, particularly the *knarr, to hold the luff of the sail taut, thus enabling the vessel to *claw off to *windward. A step was fitted in the vessel just forward of the mast with one or two socket holes each side, and the end of the *beitass* was *stepped in one of these when in use. See also FOREGIRT.

belay, to, to make fast a rope by taking turns with it round a *cleat or *belaying pin. In general terms it refers only to the smaller ropes in a ship, particularly the running *rigging in sailing vessels, as larger ropes and *cables are bitted, or brought to the *bitts, rather than belayed round them. It is also the general order to stop or cease.

belaying pins, short cylindrical lengths of wood, iron, or brass. They are held by *fife rails or *pinrails in convenient places in a sailing ship around which the running *rigging can be belayed.

***Belfast,* HMS,** a *cruiser of 11,500 tons with a main armament of twelve 6-in. (15-cm) guns in triple turrets. She has been preserved as a floating museum on the River Thames near Tower Bridge as an example of a type of ship used by the Royal Navy during the Second World War (1939–45). Built at Belfast and *launched in 1938, she was kept out of service until November 1942 after a magnetic mine broke her back. After playing an important role in the action off the North Cape of Norway in December 1943, in which the German *battlecruiser *Scharnhorst* was sunk, she was part of the bombardment force during the Normandy landings in June 1944, and then served in the Far East and in the Korean War (1950–3). She was paid off (see PAY OFF, TO) in 1971.

belfry, a small canopy or shelter supported on wooden brackets and often highly decorated with carvings and gold leaf, which used in older ships to be built over the *ship's bell.

bell buoy, a *buoy, normally unlighted, in which is mounted a bell. It is hung inside an iron cage, is rung by the motion of the sea, and serves as a warning to shipping of *shoal waters. In the USA, it is a buoy fitted with a single-toned bell which is used in the *IALA maritime buoyage system B.

***Bellerophon,* HMS,** the ship aboard which, on 15 July 1815, Napoleon surrendered to Captain Frederick Maitland in Basque Roads. Napoleon and his entourage remained in the *Bellerophon* until they were transferred to HMS *Northumberland* for passage to exile in St Helena.

Bellingshausen, Fabian Gottlieb von (1778–1852), Russian naval officer, born in Oesel, an island in the Gulf of Riga. He first saw service with the Imperial Russian Navy aged 25 when, as a junior officer, he was part of a Russian expedition commanded by Admiral Adam Krusenstern (1770–1846), undertaken to demonstrate to the Tsar the advantages of a direct sea route from Russia to China via Cape Horn. It took place between 1803 and 1806 and was the first voyage of circumnavigation ever undertaken by Russians.

Thirteen years later Bellingshausen was put in command of an expedition promoted by Tsar Alexander I to circumnavigate the world, which was to complement, rather than repeat, the discoveries of James *Cook in 1772–5. The expedition sailed in July 1819 with Bellingshausen aboard the *Mirny* and his second in command aboard the *Vostok.* In December they reached South Georgia and completed the coastal survey begun by Cook. From there the expedition proceeded to survey the South Sandwich Islands which showed they could not be part of any Antarctic land mass. Then followed a series of discoveries which brought the Russians within sight of the *ice cliffs of present-day Dronning Maud Land in Antarctica, though no claim to any sighting of an Antarctic continent was ever made by Bellingshausen.

Continuing clockwise round the continent Bellingshausen's ships penetrated further south than any previous expedition, reaching almost to Enderby Land, discovered over ten years later by the British seaman John Briscoe (1794–1843). After cruising in the South and central Pacific Bellingshausen continued his Antarctic circumnavigation in November 1820, approaching the continent through what is now the Bellingshausen Sea. On 22 January 1821 he sighted and named Peter I Island and, soon after, Alexander I Island. Bellingshausen's final mission was a survey of the South Shetland Islands, which he also proved could not be part of the Antarctic mainland.

Bellingshausen's Antarctic discoveries received little or no recognition from his contemporaries but were to prove the basis of Russia's interest in the region in the 20th century. See also EXPLORATION BY SEA.

bellum, the long *canoe-shaped boat of the Shatt-al-Arab and adjacent Iraq waters. They are paddled or poled, according to the depth of water, the larger ones being capable of carrying from fifteen to 25 men.

belly band, a strip of *canvas sometimes sewn midway between the lower *reef points and the *foot of a square sail to strengthen it. A more modern use is in the US Navy for the strap that prevents a ship's boat in the *davits from swinging as the ship rolls.

bend. **(1)** The generic maritime name for a knot which is used to join two ropes or *hawsers together or to attach a rope or *cable to an object. In strict maritime meaning, a knot is one which entails unravelling the *strands of a rope and tucking them over and under each other, such as in a *stopper knot, and is akin to a *splice in this respect. Bends, which are also known *hitches, have a variety of different forms designed to perform a particular function on board ship. When used as a verb, it is the operation aboard a ship of joining one rope to another or to some other object, originally with a

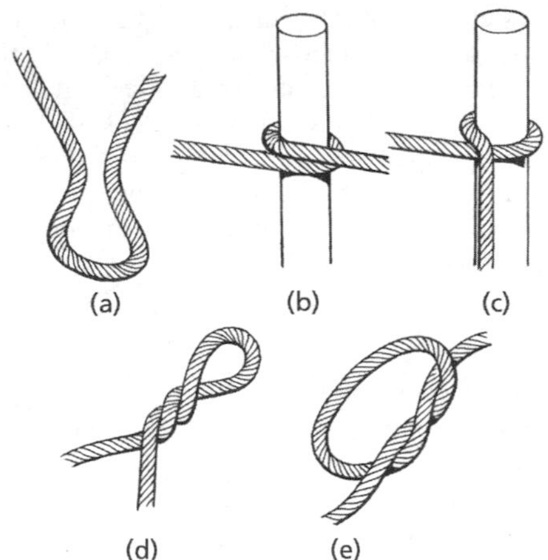

Some basic elements of bends [a] Bight [b] Round turn [c] Half hitch [d] Twist [e] Overhand knot

bend or hitch. It is also used still to describe the attachment of sails to the *spars or *forestays of sailing vessels and *yachts, though in fact more modern methods are employed for doing so. Also, a cable is still **bent to** an anchor even though it is in fact joined to it by an iron *shackle. **(2)** In sailing vessels, the chock of the *bowsprit.

bends. **(1)** A name sometimes applied to the thickest planks on the side of a wooden ship from the waterline or turn of the *bilge upwards. They are, however, more properly called *wales, and have the *beams and *knees of the hull structure bolted to them. **(2)** The colloquial name for *decompression sickness. See also DIVING.

beneaped, the situation of a vessel which has gone aground at the top of the *spring tides and has to wait for up to a fortnight (during which the *neap tides occur) for the next tide high enough to float it off. Vessels beneaped at around the time of the *equinoxes, when the highest spring tides occur, may have to wait up to six months to get off.

Bentinck. **(1)** The name given to a small triangular *course for use in *square-rigged ships. It was introduced by Captain Bentinck of the Royal Navy in the early years of the 19th century. The triangular form had a single *sheet to the deck on the centreline. This dispensed with the need to work the normally heavy sheeting loads of a square sail during *tacking and other manoeuvres. It also allowed the captain, *aft, to see signals from forward when manoeuvring. This was particularly useful for ships, such as *whalers, working amongst *ice. Sometimes a small *yard, called a Bentinck boom, was used to extend the *foot of the sail, while maintaining the single centreline sheet. **(2)** The name given to additional *shrouds rigged for heavy weather.

'bent on a splice', a traditional sailor's term for being about to get married. The allusion is obvious, a *splice being used to join two ropes together to make one. **About to be spliced** is the more common phrase nowadays.

bergantina, a small Mediterranean rowing and sailing vessel of the 14th–16th centuries, which could be considered as the Mediterranean counterpart of the English *pinnace of the same period. Bergantinas were built up to a maximum of about 12.2 metres (40 ft) in length and had from eight to sixteen rowing benches and a small *superstructure *aft for the captain and officers. They had one or two short masts, according to their length, to carry a single *lateen sail. They were essentially of light construction, relatively broad in the *beam, and drew a maximum of about 46 centimetres (18 in.). Their main function was as general purpose vessels for coastal and river work or for sailing to *windward against a contrary *current. They were in fact a member of the *galley family of vessels.

Like the English pinnace, bergantinas were carried 'knocked down' in the *holds of ships engaged in long voyages of *exploration by sea as they could be easily assembled on arrival at any coast for landing and surveying purposes. *Columbus carried bergantinas in the holds of his ships during his voyages to the New World, as did most other Spanish and Portuguese explorers of that period.

Bering or **Behring, Vitus** (1681–1741), Danish explorer, born at Horsem, Jutland. He entered the Russian Navy in 1704 and served in it during Russia's war with Sweden. In 1725 *Peter the Great, who was looking to expand his empire, sent him to discover whether Asia and North America were joined together. Bering crossed Siberia to Kamchatka, where he had several ships built, and in 1728 he sailed through the strait that now bears his name; and though he did not sight Alaska he rightly concluded the two continents were not connected. During this voyage he also discovered what are now known as the Big and Little Diomede Islands, St Lawrence Island, and the Bering Sea. However, he was not the first to discover what became the Bering Strait, as another Russian, Semyon Dezhnyov (1605–73), had sailed through it as early as 1648, but the description of his voyage lay unnoticed in an archive until 1736.

In 1730 Bering received a similar commission of exploration from the Empress Anna (reigned 1730–40). This became Russia's Great Northern Expedition which, between 1733 and 1743, surveyed much of the Arctic coast of Siberia. During this time Bering also founded the port of Petropavlovsk, and in 1741 he sailed from there with two ships, the *St Peter* and *St Paul*. They became separated, but Bering sailed on and this time discovered Alaska, later owned by Russia until purchased by the USA in 1867.

On the return voyage Bering suffered from *scurvy and was so debilitated that he could not command his ship properly. It was wrecked on the westernmost of the Aleutian Islands, now called after him and where he lies buried. See also EXPLORATION BY SEA.

Bermudan rig, or **Bermudian rig,** a sail plan, in which, unlike the *gaff rig, a triangular-shaped mainsail is attached to a track on a single pole mast. The Bermudan rig, or leg o' mutton rig as it was initially sometimes called, was commonly used by sailing craft in and

Bermudan sloop

around the West Indies from as early as the 17th century, and doubtless got its name from the island of Bermuda. It was first adopted for a racing boat by one of the contenders in the Seawanhaka Cup in 1896 and its popularity soon spread to small racing craft in Britain and elsewhere. Encouraged by the introduction of the *International Metre Class, the first of which appeared in 1907, it gradually replaced the gaff rig of racing yachts and most cruising yachts. It soon proved much easier to handle and was far more efficient, its high *aspect ratio allowing a boat to sail much closer to the wind, though its *aerodynamics was not properly understood for some time. See also MARCONI RIG.

Bermuda triangle, the area of the Sargasso Sea within the triangle formed by Bermuda, Miami, and Puerto Rico, which is subject to violent thunderstorms and *waterspouts. *Columbus reported unusual events in his *log when sailing through the region. In 1945 a training flight of five Avenger aircraft got lost, ran out of fuel, and crashed into the sea. A number of ships, like the USS *Cyclops* and the *Marine Sulphur Queen*, have either disappeared or been found, like the **Mary Celeste*, drifting and abandoned. In the region *magnetic compasses are subject to a 20° error. These losses have been attributed by more imaginative minds to paranormal happenings linked to UFOs or the lost world of *Atlantis, but statistically this region is probably no more dangerous and mysterious than any other.

www.fortunecity.com/roswell/warminster/167/index.html M. V. Angel

berth. **(1)** A place in which to sleep on board ship, either in a *bunk or, formerly in naval ships, a place in which to sling a *hammock. A **snug berth** is a situation a seaman finds himself in when he is given an easy job or post on board ship or ashore. **(2)** The place in harbour in which a ship rides to its anchors or is secured alongside with *berthing hawsers. In this sense it can also be used as a verb, i.e. to berth a ship. **(3)** A term used to indicate a clearance of danger, e.g. **to give a wide berth** to a rock, *shoal, or any other hazard, to steer a ship well clear of it.

berthing hawsers are used for *mooring a ship alongside a wall or *jetty. The two **breast ropes**, marked (2) and (5) in Fig. 1, are known respectively as the **fore** and **after breast ropes**, and are used to breast the ship bodily towards the jetty when coming alongside, and when *belayed they limit the ship's distance from the jetty. They can also be used to hold a small ship upright against a jetty when it is resting on the bottom. The *hawsers marked (3) and (4) are known respectively as the **fore spring** and the **after spring**. Any spring which leads forward is known as a **back spring** and any which leads *aft is known as a **head spring**. When a ship is secured alongside these prevent

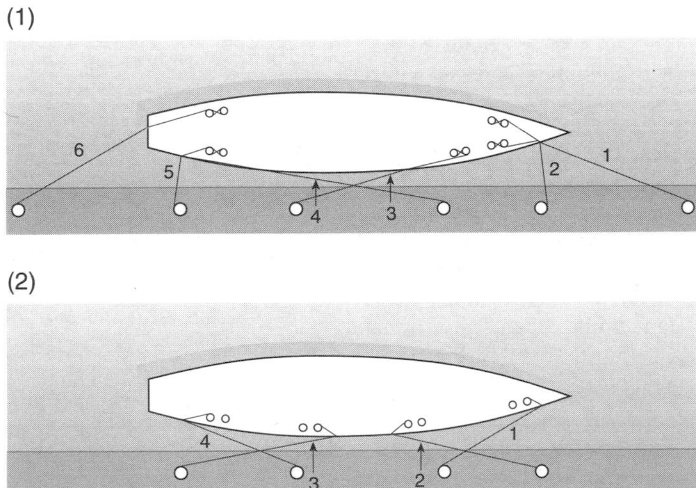

Berthing hawsers

it from surging ahead or astern at its *berth, and together they assist the breast ropes to keep it close alongside. They also enable the ship's bow or stern to be swung clear when leaving. By going ahead against a fore spring with the *helm over, the stern swings outwards while the ship is held from moving *ahead by the spring. Similarly, by going *astern against a back spring with the helm over, the bow can be swung clear. The **head-rope** (1) and **stern-rope** (6) help the springs in preventing the ship from surging and are also employed to move the ship into its correct berth when going alongside.

For a large ship, or one which is berthed near a busy *fairway where it is more likely to surge, or for any ship berthed in bad weather, the springs may be duplicated as shown in Fig. 2. These are then called the **fore head spring** (1), the **fore back spring** (2), the **after head spring** (3), and the **after back spring** (4).

Berthon boat, a folding or collapsible boat, of painted *canvas stretched on a wooden frame. It first appeared in 1849, and was the invention of Edward Berthon (1813–99). Its naval use was largely confined to *destroyers and *submarines as it could be folded away and stowed in a small space. However, some were supplied to General Gordon when he was besieged at Khartoum and a number were used in the Second World War (1939–45) to attack shipping in enemy-held harbours.

best bower, the *starboard of the two anchors carried at the bow of a ship in the days of sail. That on the *port side was known as the small bower, even though the two were identical in weight.

between decks, the space contained between any two whole decks of a ship. The term has become widely associated with the *steerage of a passenger vessel, the space below decks in which passengers, and particularly emigrants who could not afford *cabins, travelled, often enough in conditions of gross overcrowding and discomfort. The phrase is often shortened to **'tween decks**.

bezan, or **bizan,** from the Dutch *bezaan*, a small *yacht, usually *ketch rigged, of the 17th century. King Charles II named one of his many yachts *Bezan*; she was of 35 tons *burthen and was given to him by the Dutch in 1661. He had a second yacht, named *Isabella Bezan*, built for him in 1680.

bibbs, pieces of timber bolted to the *hounds of a mast of a *square-rigged ship to support the *trestle-trees.

'bible', see HOLYSTONE.

Big Class, the generic name given to the largest racing *yachts which raced together on handicap on the British regatta circuit between the two world wars. It included **Britannia*, which really brought the class into being when King George V announced he would race her in 1920, and later the *J-class yachts, but there were also others, some of which were built to the *International Metre Class Rule. In 1920 there were nine starters which took part in six races or more, but the public's interest only really took hold with the appearance of the J-class at the start of the next decade. In 1930 the 'Big Class' contained the products of three different classes: *Britannia*, *Lulworth*, *White Heather II*, and the *Herreshoff-designed schooner *Westward* were handicap yachts; *Astra*, *Cambria*, and *Candida* were *international metre class yachts; and, most significantly, **Shamrock V*, the 1930 challenger for the *America's Cup, was built to the American *Universal Rule. An earlier competitor had been Sir Thomas Lipton's 23-metre (75-ft) *Shamrock* (not to be confused with any of his five America's Cup challengers), but she was broken up in the mid-1920s.

Lulworth, *Cambria*, and *White Heather II* all dropped out after 1930 when it was decided that yachts over 14.5 metres (48 ft) should adopt the Universal Rule, though British yachts only had to comply with the rule's height of mast and draught. The class really reached its apogee in 1935 when the American J-class yacht *Yankee* crossed the Atlantic to join in the British regatta circuit to race against three British J-class yachts, *Shamrock* (as she was now called), *Endeavour*, and *Velsheda*, as well as *Astra*, *Britannia*, and *Candida*, all of which had adopted the Universal Rule; *Westward* occasionally joined in too. The stiff competition that year soon showed that *Britannia*, now in her 42nd season, was no longer competitive, and in August she was withdrawn from racing. The death of the King in January 1936, and the subsequent *scuttling of *Britannia*, proved the final death knell for the Big Class.

bight. (1) The name by which the loop of a rope is known when it is folded, or any part of a rope between its two ends when it lies or hangs in a curve or loop. For illus. see BEND. (2) The area of sea lying between two promontories, being in general wider than a gulf and larger than a bay, is also known as a bight.

bilander, or **billander,** from the Dutch *bijlander* and French *bilandre*, a small European two-masted merchant ship of the 17th and 18th centuries. It was occasionally used in the North Sea but was more frequently seen in the Mediterranean. The mainmast was *lateen rigged but its foremast carried the conventional square *course and square *topsail. They rarely reached a size of more than 100 tons.

bilboes, long bars or bolts, with a padlock on the end, on which iron shackles could slide. They were used on board ship to confine the legs of prisoners in a similar manner to putting someone in the stocks. It was a punishment usually known on board as putting a man in *irons and continued in use, particularly in American sailing ships, until the latter half of the 19th century. There are examples of bilboes in the Tower of London, taken out of ships of the *Spanish Armada. Thus Shakespeare's Hamlet, musing on a forthcoming fight:

> That would not let me sleep; methought I lay
> Worse than the mutines in the bilboes.

The name originates from the steel which was forged at Bilbao, in Spain, at that time reckoned to be the finest in Europe.

bilge. (1) That part of the *floors of a ship on either side of the keel which approaches nearer to a horizontal than a vertical direction. It is where the floors and the second *futtocks unite, and upon which the ship would rest when it took the ground. Hence, when a ship was holed in this part it was said to be **bilged**. Being the lowest part of the ship inside the hull, it is naturally where any internal water, known as **bilge water**, collects and where the suction of the bilge *pump is placed to clear it. These spaces on either side of the keel are collectively known as the **bilges**. (2) The largest circumference of a cask in the vicinity of its bung. (3) In naval parlance, the word used to describe an untrue, or nonsensical, statement.

bilge keel, see KEEL.

bill of health, a certificate properly authenticated by the consul or other recognized port authority certifying that a ship comes from a place where there is no contagious disease, and that none of its crew, at the time of its departure, was infected with such a disease. A certificate of this kind constitutes a clean bill of health; a foul bill of health indicates disease in the port of departure or among the crew. Nowadays, clearance is all done by e-mail, radio, or mobile phone.

bill of lading. An important document in the contract of carriage of goods by sea. It is not in itself a contract but a receipt acknowledging the shipment of goods in good order which are to be delivered in the same condition. Bills of lading can be signed by the *master of a merchant ship or by an export *wharfinger. Martin Lee

bill of sight, a bill Customs authorities, before releasing goods, require their importer to complete if the goods have arrived without documents or without the Customs knowing anything about them.

bill of store, a licence or custom-house permission for reimporting unsold goods from foreign ports free of duty within a specified limit of time.

billy-boy, or **billy-boat,** an east coast of England bluff-bowed trading vessel of river-barge build, originally single-masted with a *trysail, and usually with the sails tanned. Later it took on a *ketch rig, with *gaff mainsail and *mizzen, and square *topsails on the mainmast. Billy-boys remained in general trading use along the Yorkshire coast and rivers at least until the beginning of the 20th century.

Bimini top, US term for a *cockpit *awning for shading a *yacht's crew from the sun. The name derives from the Bimini Islands off Florida. John Rousmaniere

bingeing, the operation, long since obsolete, of 'bulling' or rinsing out a cask to prepare it for new contents. Before the invention of metal tanks, casks were the main means of carrying on board the necessary amount of victuals, fresh water, etc., for a voyage, and were thus an important part of any ship's equipment.

binnacle (formerly **bittacle**), the wooden housing of the mariner's *magnetic compass and its correctors and lighting arrangements. The change from bittacle to binnacle came in about 1750, although the former name did not entirely disappear until the mid-19th century. The origin of the term would appear to be the Italian *abitacola*, little house or habitation, and it was used by the early Portuguese *navigators to describe the compass housing. The French word for binnacle is still *habittacle*.

In addition to the compass and a light, the binnacle was the proper stowage for the *traverse board, the reel with the *log-lines and chip, and the 28-second *glass used for measuring a ship's speed. *Charts in actual use, if any, were also properly stowed in the binnacle. Later, when a ship's *deviation was established and had to be corrected, it was where the *Flinders bars and Kelvin spheres (see THOMSON, WILLIAM) were placed.

biological oceanography is the study of all aspects of the biology of the oceans particularly in the context of their physical and chemical environments, so that it overlaps with *marine biology in many respects. The range of living organisms extends from the smallest living things, like viruses and bacteria, to the largest animal ever to have lived on earth, the blue *whale (*Balaenoptera musculus*). This vast size range also reflects a wide range of life cycles—a bacterium's lifetime may be just a few hours during which it experiences the conditions in just a few millilitres of water, whereas a whale, which may live 50 years, will have repeatedly migrated halfway round the world. Techniques used to study bacteria and whales are totally different, yet the aim is to blend information for all organisms into an overall conceptual understanding of life in the oceans.

Life occurs at all depths, and there is 180 times more living space in the oceans than in terrestrial habitats. On land one can stand on a hilltop and survey the landscape, whereas oceans are remote, out of sight, and difficult to study. The classical questions investigated by biologists are: what species live where and when? How big are the populations? How are these species organized into communities? What are the dynamics of these populations and how do they cope with their environment's challenges? How are they responding to mankind's activities? Such questions cannot be studied in isolation from the other disciplines in *oceanography. Biological processes not only respond to physical and chemical processes but also play a central role in many biogeochemical cycles, especially the fate of pollutants and the dynamics of the carbon cycle (see ENVIRONMENTAL ISSUES). It is important to understand how marine communities are responding to fluctuations in ocean climate, how changes in the morphology of ocean basins have been reflected in the zoogeographical distribution of species today, and what the micro-fossils in ocean sediments can tell us about the *climate changes of past eras.

Whether a study focuses on a single species, like a whale or a species of *fish, or takes the broader approach of focusing on communities and how they change throughout the year, the organisms need to be sampled and quantified. Sampling the tiniest organisms (viruses, bacteria, and *marine plants like phytoplankton) involves collecting samples of water and filtering them. The extracts are either examined by microscopy or plated out to grow cultures. The volume of a water processed may be less than a litre, so studies of these micro-organisms are akin to studying the whole of the Sahara Desert by examining a few grains of sand. Living cells have to be distinguished from the abundant inanimate particles and aggregates if they are to be counted. The surfaces of bacteria suspended in the water are highly active chemically. The total surface area of bacteria, suspended in the water or attached to particles, greatly exceeds that of the inanimate particles, so bacteria play a major role in many aspects of water chemistry.

The tiniest animals, protozoans and their relatives, are equally hard to sample, identify, and quantify, and yet their activities are the key to understanding how the sun's energy fixed by the phytoplankton gets passed through to all parts of the oceanic ecosystem. *Plankton is sampled with various types of nets. Small fine-meshed nets are used to catch animals about a

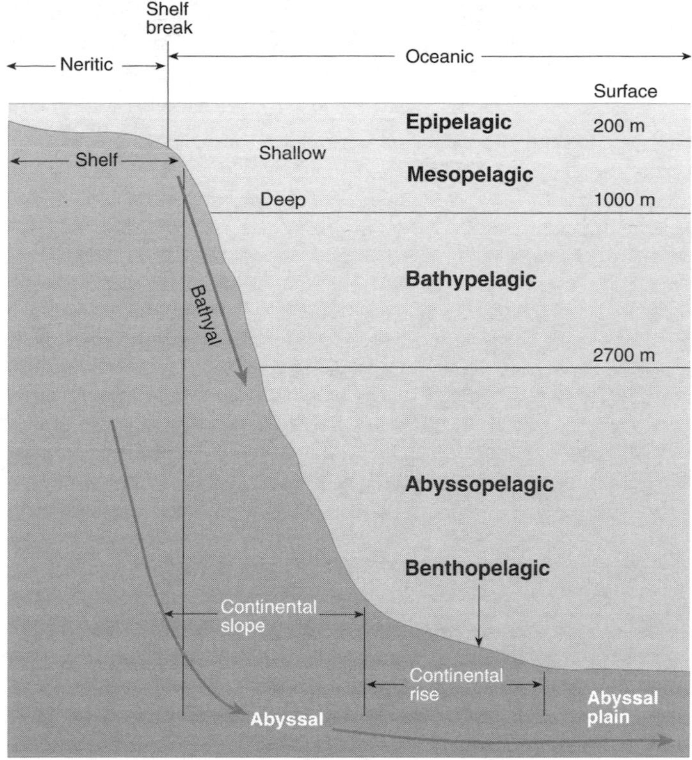

The main ecological zones of the oceans

millimetre in length, and much larger coarser-meshed nets to catch the faster-swimming *Crustacea like shrimps, and small fishes a few centimetres long. Larger animals can swim faster and so can dodge slowly towed nets. Even so, many of the abundant species are gelatinous and fragile, and when caught disintegrate and so are essentially 'invisible' to us. They have to be collected individually by *underwater vehicles or photographed *in situ*. In contrast, the larger animals, game fishes like *tuna and *marlin, *sharks and whales, are too large and too fast to be caught in conventional nets.

Studying the animals that live on the seabed (the benthos) is equally challenging. A few millilitres of surface sediment from the bed of the ocean at a depth of 4,000 metres (13,000 ft) may contain 100 species of both nematodes (round worms) and foraminifers (protozoans), but huge *trawls need to be towed many kilometres along the seabed to catch the bigger animals. But even the largest trawls cannot catch large sharks like the six-gilled shark (*Hexanthus*) and the mysterious megamouth (*Megachasma pelagios*). All these organisms occur irregularly in space and in time, so how representative is each sample? How can data from a few litres or even thousands of cubic metres of sea water be related to what is happening in the vast volumes of the oceans? It is clear that the oceanic communities in the water and on the seabed are zoned by depth, and they vary with *latitude and within different parts of ocean *currents. In addition, communities inhabiting coastal seas are very different from those living in and over very deep water.

Large-scale coverage of gross biological characteristics can be achieved by *remote sensing. At finer scales *sonars of different frequencies can discriminate variations in the concentrations of particles in the water, many of which are living organisms. Particle counters that continuously count abundances of animals and marine plants within prescribed size ranges can be towed or deployed on *moorings. These techniques neither identify the species nor

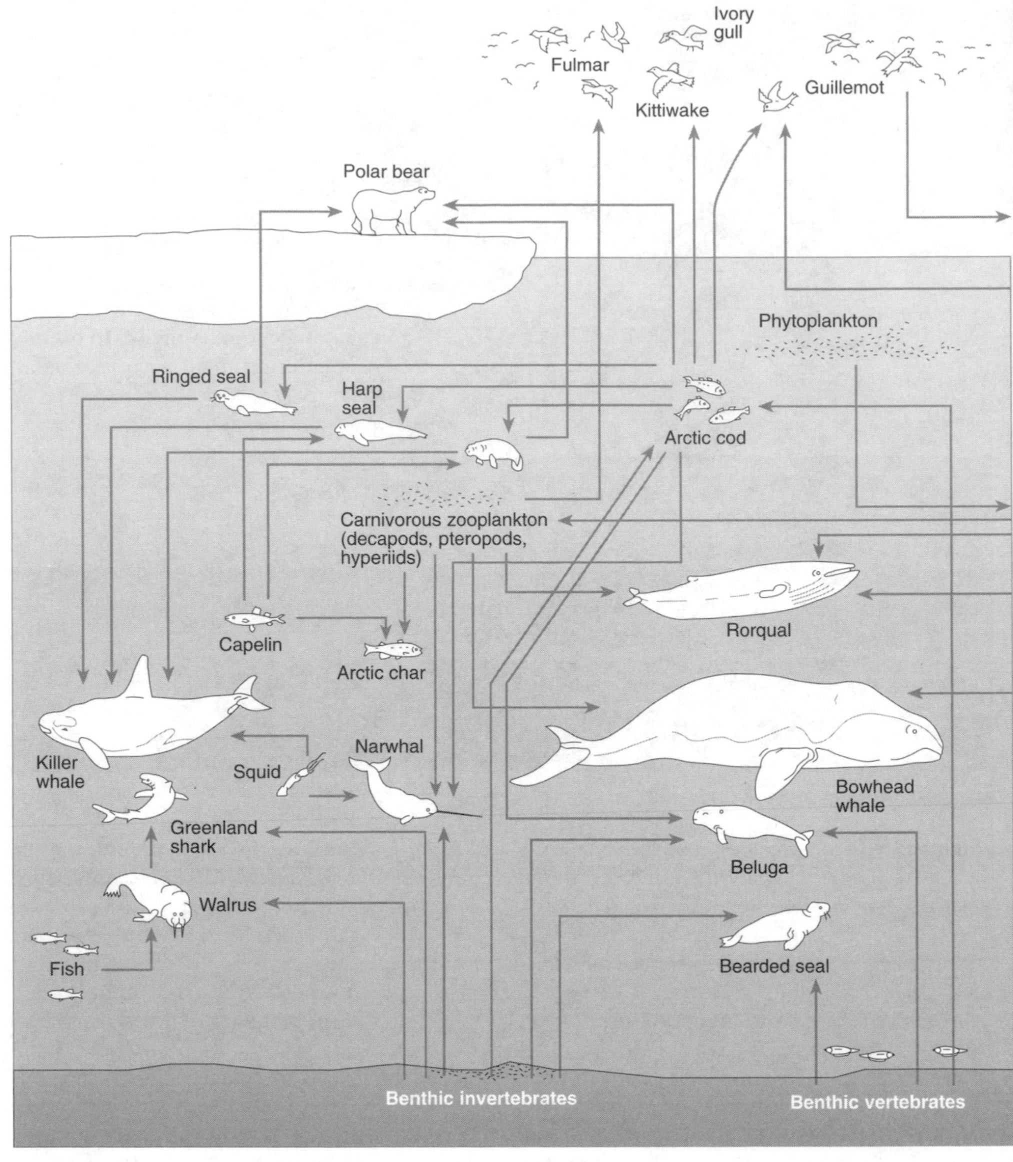

Schematic representation of the Arctic food web

discriminate between live and inanimate particles. However, they can be used to survey the variations in the gross distributions of the organisms and how they are influenced by currents and *eddies, and vertically by the *thermocline. They can be used to estimate the living mass of organisms in the water, how fast they are growing, and how energy is flowing through the ecosystem. But these techniques are akin to working out what a large painting looks like from a few dozen pinpoint samples of the colour and chemistry of paint. Computer models based on theories of how the ecosystems function are now being used to fill in the unavoidable gaps in the sampling to give some idea of what the big picture may look like. The strengths and weaknesses of the models are evaluated, so they can be tuned to

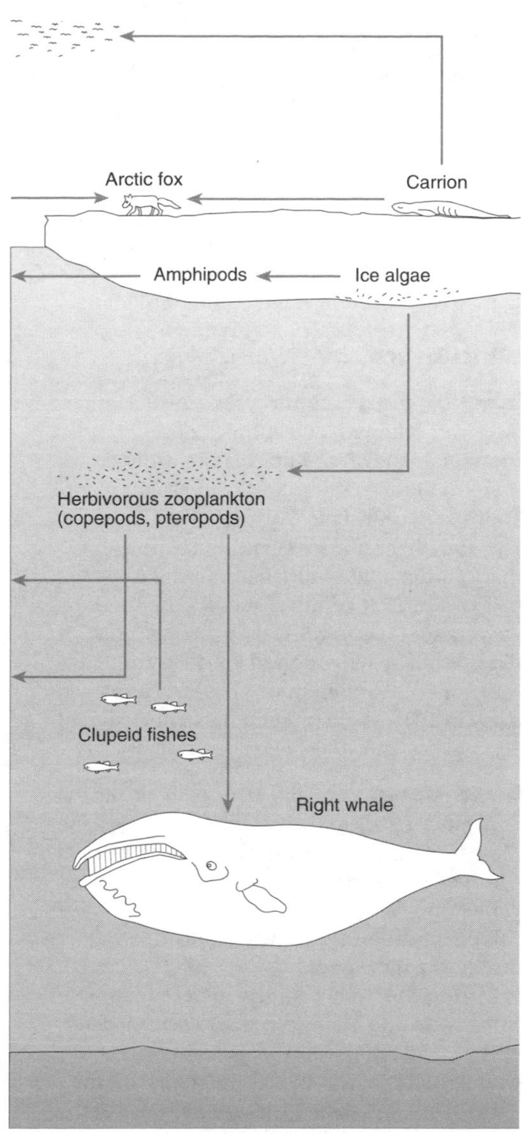

postdict known events and patterns. Ideally these tuned models will be effective in other scenarios, but this ideal is seldom if ever achieved. These approaches need the largest and fastest computers as well as some of the most sophisticated instrumentation to provide the real data needed to validate or to modify the theories.

Conducting biological surveys of the seabed is even more difficult, although enormous strides have been made with the development of sophisticated underwater vehicles, which can be used remotely to survey and conduct experiments on the seabed, or can even carry the scientist down to observe, sample, or set up experiments there. This task is made all the more demanding because there are twice as many of the basic types of animal (phyla) living on the seabed as in terrestrial environments, moreover the numbers of species found in tiny sediment samples is staggeringly large. Estimates of how many species may inhabit the seabed of the deep ocean range from a million to over a billion; if the latter estimate is correct then the deep ocean must be far richer in species than are all terrestrial habitats. A biologist may spend a lifetime naming a few hundred novel species and yet make almost no impression on the immense task of identifying the total inventory of fauna and flora. Yet the potential value to man of some of these organisms, particularly some of the bacteria, which are unique to the deep ocean, as sources of new *marine pharmaceuticals is enormous.

Perhaps the most unexpected discovery made using underwater vehicles has been the large communities of animals that inhabit *hydrothermal vents, which emit superheated, sulphide-laden waters. These communities are exceptional in that they are based on chemical synthesis to produce their organic material. Worms and *shellfish exploit internal gardens of bacteria to provide their energy, which is derived from oxidizing sulphide ions or methane contained in the vent waters. The bacteria involved are of very ancient lineages, and may have been linked to the origins of life on earth.

Another important discovery has come from using time-lapse cameras deployed on the seabed for several months. The sequences of pictures have revealed the rapidity with which plant material produced at the surface reaches the seabed. Phytoplankton cells are microscopic, and so they sink very slowly if at all. A cell that escapes being eaten will take many months to free-fall the 4–5 kilometres (2.5–3 mls.) to the seabed. However, sticky mucilage produced by various animals clumps them together into aggregates called marine snow, and the flakes of marine snow get progressively heavier and sink faster and faster and can reach the seabed within a very few days. Hence life on the seabed is dynamic and seasonal.

Herring, P., *The Biology of the Deep Ocean* (2002).
Lalli, C., and Parsons T., *Biological Oceanography: An Introduction* (1997). M. V. Angel

bird's nest. **(1)** A small round *top, smaller than a *crow's nest, which was placed right at the masthead to provide a greater range of vision from a ship at sea. **(2)** A tangle of rope.

bireme, a *galley having two banks of *oars. It was invariably fitted with a metal *ram and was used, particularly in battles at sea, in the Mediterranean until the mid-17th century. See also WARFARE AT SEA.

biscuit, the 'bread' which was supplied to ships, particularly naval ones, before bakeries were introduced on board. It was made with flour, mixed with the least possible quantity of water, and thoroughly kneaded into flat cakes and slowly baked.

bite, to, an anchor is said to bite when the *flukes bed themselves into the ground and hold firm without *dragging.

bitter, in the days of sail the name given to any turn of a ship's anchor *cable about its *bitts. Hence a ship is 'brought up to a bitter' when the cable is allowed to run out to that turn around the bitts or *cable stoppers, its modern equivalent. The **bitter end** was that part of the anchor cable *abaft the bitts which remained aboard when a ship was riding to its anchor. To *pay a rope or chain out **to the bitter end**, a phrase now more commonly used ashore to denote the extremity of a situation, meant that all was paid out and no more remained to be let go. **Bend to the bitter end** meant to reverse a cable, to *bend the inboard end of it to the anchor so that the strain on the cable came on a part of it that had been less used and was therefore more trustworthy.

bitts, in the days of sail, a frame composed of two strong pillars of straight oak timber, fixed upright in the fore part of the ship and bolted to the deck *beams. To them were secured the *cables when the ship rode to an anchor. Smaller bitts were fitted in *square-rigged sailing vessels for securing other parts of the running *rigging. They all served the same purpose, providing a convenient means of taking a securing turn with the *fall of whatever piece of rigging was involved.

bitt stopper, a length of rope, in the days of sail when ships had *hemp *cables for their anchors, used to bind the cable more securely to the *bitts to prevent it slipping. When a ship anchored with enough cable run out, the cable was brought to the bitts and secured by several turns round them. The bitt stopper was then passed round the turns to bind the cable in taut so that it could *render around the bitts.

'Blackbeard', see TEACH, EDWARD.

blackbirding was the practice of kidnapping, or otherwise ensnaring, South Pacific islanders—known as Kanakas—in order to sell them to those running cotton and sugar plantations in Queensland, Australia, and those on Fiji and the Samoan Islands. It was a trade that particularly flourished during the last half of the 19th century, and although efforts were made to control it they largely failed. It did not finally die out until 1904 after the new Australian Commonwealth government passed a law in 1901 which ordered the deportation of all Kanakas after 1906. See also SLAVE TRADE.

black-down, to, the operation of tarring and blacking a ship's *rigging, or of blacking its side. The best mixture was said to be coal *tar, vegetable tar, and salt water boiled together and laid on hot. In both cases the object was preservation against the action of salt water on *hemp and wood.

During the 18th century some captains of British warships, sent out to cruise independently against the enemy or his seaborne trade, would black-down the entire hulls of their ships. This was done as it was believed that a black ship appeared smaller at sea than it actually was and might therefore attract enemy ships, hopeful of an easy conquest, within range of its guns.

black jack. **(1)** Alternative name for the *Jolly Roger, said to be traditionally flown by those involved in *piracy. **(2)** The name popularly given by sailors to the bubonic plague, whose victims were said to turn black.

black ship, a description used by the British *shipbuilding industry during the days of sail of a ship built in India of Burmese teak. Wherever the term came from it was not from the type of wood the ship was built with, as teak is as light in colour as oak.

black squall, a sudden squall of wind, accompanied by lightning, encountered in the West Indies. It is usually caused by the heated state of the atmosphere near land where the warm expanded air is repelled by a colder medium to *leeward and driven back with great force, frequently engendering electrical storms of great intensity.

'black's the white of my eye', a sailor's term, now defunct, indicating an indignant rebuttal of a charge of misdemeanour and that all he has just said is the truth, the whole truth, and nothing but the truth.

black strake, a wide band of planking along a ship's side, just above the *wales, which was painted during the 17th and 18th centuries with *tar and lamp black as a preservative. It was also used to contrast the white *boottopping of the ship's bottom with the varnished wood of the sides. Oil paint was not used in ships, except very occasionally inboard, until the last quarter of the 18th century.

Blackwall frigates, the generic name given to a series of sail trading ships built between 1837 and 1869 for the Indian trade following the expiration of the *East India Company's exclusive charter in 1833, which threw the trade to the East open to all comers. They got their name because a number were built at Blackwall, on the River Thames, and because they were said to be 'frigate built'. This did not mean they bore any resemblance in design to the typical naval *frigate but that they were built with a finer *run, and were thus faster than the typical *East Indiaman. In this respect they could be compared in performance much in the same way as could a frigate with a *ship of the line.

Three firms were concerned with the building of the Blackwall frigates in Britain: Green and Wigram of Blackwall, T. and W. Smith of the Tyne, and Duncan Dunbar of Sunderland. The first Blackwall frigate was Green and Wigram's *Seringapatam*, a *packet ship of 818 tons, built in 1837, which set up a new record of 85 days from London to Bombay.

A large number of these Blackwall frigates were built, not all of them in Britain, as many were constructed of Burmese teak at Moulmein in Burma, and they dominated the trade to and from India until the opening of the *Suez Canal in 1869. Thereafter, though they continued to run successfully for a time in the wool trade from Australia, they were eclipsed by the *clipper ship.

Lubbock, B., *The Blackwall Frigates* (1922).

Blake, Sir Peter (1948–2001), yachtsman turned environmentalist. Blake, a New Zealander, was the only man to have won the Whitbread (now Volvo) Round-the-World Race (see YACHTING: ROUND-THE-WORLD COMPETITIONS) and the *America's Cup, and he also held the Jules Verne Trophy for the fastest non-stop crewed circumnavigation under sail. In 1995 he headed Team New Zealand's challenge for the America's Cup and its boat, *Black Magic*, won. For this feat he was knighted and he led the successful New Zealand cup defender team in 2000. He then decided to give up competitive sailing and founded Blake Expeditions to sail to those areas considered vital to the world's ecosystem. He was appointed special ambassador to the United Nations Environmental Programme and was visiting the Amazon River as part of a two-month expedition to monitor the effects of *pollution when he was shot aboard his *yacht, a victim of *piracy. See also ENVIRONMENTAL ISSUES.

Blake, Robert (1599–1657), British admiral and colonel, born at Bridgewater and educated at Wadham College, Oxford. Nothing is known about him until he distinguished himself as a soldier in the defence of Bristol and Lyme during the Civil War. In 1649 he was appointed as a 'general-at-sea' to chase Prince Rupert's *squadron which had declared for the royalist cause, and in 1651 he captured the Scilly Islands which were still holding out for the royalists.

In 1652, at the start of the First Dutch War (1652–4), he commanded in the Channel, from which he evicted the forces of two Dutch admirals, Marten Tromp (1597–1653) and Michiel de Ruyter (1607–76). However, he was later defeated off Dungeness in an action from which the legend originated that Tromp lashed a broom to his masthead to indicate that he would sweep the English from the seas. He was also defeated by Tromp the next year off Portland; but at the subsequent battle of the *Gabbard he forced Tromp to retreat to the Texel.

In 1655 he commanded a fleet of 24 ships in the Mediterranean to destroy the *Barbary pirates of Algiers. On the outbreak of war with Spain in 1656 he was sent to operate off Cadiz, where one of his captains captured a fleet of *treasure ships. In April 1657 Blake intercepted another treasure fleet at Santa Cruz, Tenerife, where, in spite of his wounds and the strong position of the enemy, he destroyed the escorting ships. Ill health compelled him to return home and he died entering Plymouth Sound on 7 August 1657. His body lay in state at Greenwich before being buried in Westminster Abbey, whence it was exhumed and thrown in the Thames after the restoration of King Charles II.

Blake laid the foundations of naval discipline and tactics in the British Navy by his introduction of the *Articles of War and the *Fighting Instructions. His short but brilliant career at sea fully entitled him to Lord Clarendon's tribute as 'the copy of naval courage'.

Baumber, M., *General at Sea: Robert Blake and the 17th-Century Revolution in Naval Warfare* (1989).
Powell, J., *Robert Blake* (1972).

blake slip, see CABLE STOPPERS.

bleed, to. **(1)** A British Navy term used in the days when *grog was issued to seamen to describe its surreptitious removal in transit between the point of issue from the grog-tub to the mess for which it was due. It was carried between these points in a tall *monkey and if a swig was taken en route, it was known as **bleeding** the monkey. **(2)** The operation of draining out of a *buoy any water which may have seeped inside after long use at sea.

Bligh, William (1754–1817), British vice admiral, who proved himself as a *navigator when he served as *master of the *Resolution* during Captain James *Cook's last voyage of exploration between 1776–9. In 1787 he was appointed to command the armed transport **Bounty* to take breadfruit seedlings from Tahiti to the West Indies. On 28 April 1789, when the ship was off Tofua in the Friendly Islands, a *mutiny broke out under the leadership of Fletcher *Christian, Bligh's protégé. Bligh with eighteen others was turned adrift in the ship's *launch, in which they made a remarkable open-boat voyage of 5,760 kilometres (3,600 mls.) to reach Timor.

Bligh's severity as a commanding officer has been cited as the cause of the mutiny, but this is disputed. In his subsequent career he showed courage on many occasions, but had a continuing difficulty in getting on with people. He played a distinguished part as a captain at the battles of Camperdown, in 1797, and Copenhagen, in 1801, during the Napoleonic Wars (1793–1815). However, when he was appointed governor of New South Wales he quarrelled with his deputy over the traffic of rum (see GROG), was arrested by the local militia, and was sent home in 1808. He was promoted rear admiral in 1811 and rose to vice admiral three years later.

Alexander, C., *The Bounty: The True Story of the Mutiny on the Bounty* (2004).

block, a wooden or metal case into which one or more *sheaves are fitted. They are used for various purposes in a ship or *yacht, either as part of a *purchase to increase the mechanical power applied to ropes, or to lead them to convenient positions for handling. Blocks are of various sizes and powers: a single block contains one sheave, a double block has two, and a threefold block has three, and so on. Modern blocks used on *yachts are generally made of aluminium or stainless steel and are fitted with roller, or ball, bearings and a *shackle or pin connection in the place of a *strop. See also FIDDLE BLOCK; TACKLE.

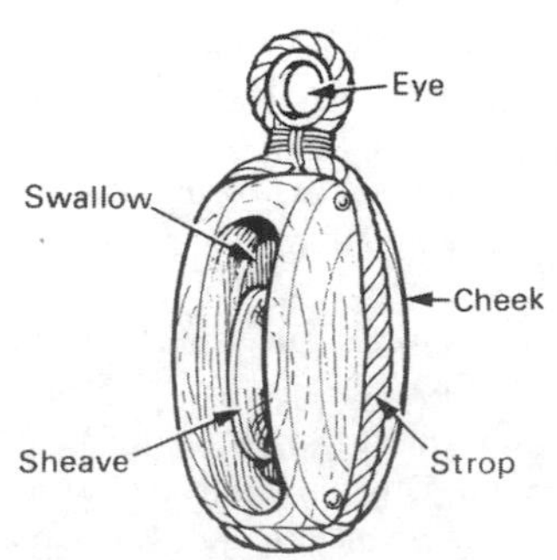

Single stropped block

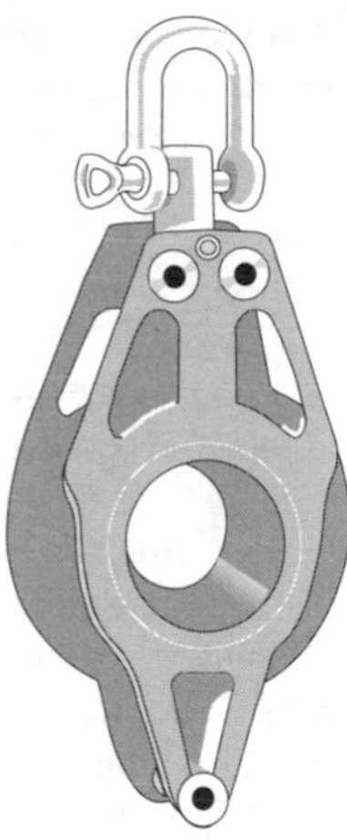

Modern blocks for racing yachts, like this 80 mm (3 in.) single one from Lewmar, have alloy cheeks and alloy sheaves which run on Torlon rollers with dual Delrin ball side thrust races

blockade, in *warfare at sea a declaration published by a belligerent power forbidding seaborne trade with an enemy. Originally, the days of the sailing warship and the short-range gun, blockade was virtually synonymous with investment, a *squadron patrolling off an enemy port to prevent all movement in and out. With the invention of the long-range gun, and mines and torpedoes, such close blockade became no longer a feasible operation of war. Instead, a distant blockade took its place, in which seaborne trade with a declared enemy was intercepted many kilometres out at sea from the blockaded coast. Blockade is universally admitted to be a belligerent right to which neutral countries are bound to submit.

block coefficient, in *naval architecture a measure of a hull's fineness. It compares the boat's actual displaced volume with that of a rectangular block of the same length, breadth, and mean depth as the immersed hull. A boat with a high block coefficient is full bodied and one with a low number is fine bodied.

Jeremy Lines

blockship, a *hulk, or obsolete vessel, which is stripped of its fittings and filled with cement or other suitable material, and *scuttled in position either to block the entrance to an enemy's port or anchorage; or occasionally to fill a gap in a *breakwater or to provide other shelter to an exposed anchorage.

'blood is thicker than water', a well-known saying attributed to Commodore Josiah Tattnall of the US Navy, when justifying his intervention in the British land attack on the Peiho forts in June 1859 during the Second Opium War (1856–60). With his ship, the *Toeywan*, he towed to safety from the shore British boats filled with the survivors of the attack, and is credited with using this expression in conversation with the British commander-in-chief, Sir James Hope, the following day.

'bloody flag', the colloquial description of the large square red flag which used to be hoisted at the mastheads of British men-of-war to indicate that they were about to go into battle. Other nations also hoisted distinctive flags at the mastheads of their ships during battle. The main purpose for these flags was to serve as an aid to distinguishing friend from foe in the smoke of action. More recently, warships of all nations going into battle hoisted their national *ensign, for this purpose known as a battle ensign, at the masthead or other prominent position.

'blowing great guns and small arms', an old maritime term for a heavy *gale or hurricane. It is still sometimes used, but is shortened to 'blowing great guns'.

'blowing the grampus', a term used in the days of sail for waking a sailor asleep on *watch by throwing a bucketful of cold water over him.

blue ensign. When the division of the British fleet by *squadronal colours was abolished in 1864, the blue ensign was reserved for naval auxiliary vessels. Owners of *yachts registered with certain *yacht clubs are granted permission by the British *Admiralty to fly the blue ensign. It is then sometimes defaced by an insignia or design in its *hoist, normally that of the club to which the yacht belongs. See also RED ENSIGN; WHITE ENSIGN.

bluejacket, a descriptive term used to describe the seaman of a British warship. It came into being in 1858 when rules for the uniform of seamen were promulgated, which included a jacket 'to be made of navy blue cloth double-breasted, with stand fall collar . . . to reach the hips . . . one inside breast-pocket and seven black horn crown and anchor buttons'. See also JACK TAR; SAILORS' DRESS.

blue light, a pyrotechnical preparation, also known as a Bengal light. Before the introduction of more modern methods of *signals at sea, it was used at night, in conjunction with gunfire, to transmit the orders of the admiral of a *squadron or fleet. By counting the number of gunshots fired, and observing the blue lights shown, the captain of a man-of-war could interpret through his night signal book what order the admiral was making.

blue peter, the signal that a ship is about to sail and that all persons concerned should report on board. It is a rectangular flag with a blue ground and a white rectangle in the centre. It also represents the letter 'P' in the *International Code of Signals.

'blue pigeon', the name sailors gave, during the days of sail, to the sounding *lead.

blue riband, or **ribband,** traditionally held by the *ocean liner making the fastest crossing of the Atlantic. It is said to have originated in the 1860s when shipping companies wanted to publicize the speed of their passenger ships, and the ship holding it flew a blue *pennant from one of its masts. It was formalized in 1933 when a 1.22-metre (4-ft) high trophy was donated by a British MP, Harold Hales, now known as the Hales Trophy. It was first awarded to the Italian liner *Rex*, but before it could be handed over a new record was established in 1935 by the French liner *Normandie*. So the trophy's trustees inserted a new clause into the deed of gift which allowed a holder to retain it for three months before passing it to the next winner. However, when the Cunarder *Queen Mary* established a new record in 1938, the company refused to accept it, implying it was more concerned with safety than speed. The trophy was therefore returned to the trustees who next awarded it to the *United States*, which in 1952 created a new transatlantic record of 3 days, 10 hours, 40 minutes. This remained unbroken until the end of the era of transatlantic liners, and when the *United States* retired from the North Atlantic route in 1969 the trophy was handed to the US Merchant Marine Academy, Long Island, USA.

In 1985 the 22-metre (72-ft) powerboat *Virgin Atlantic Challenger II* broke the record by 2 hours, 9 minutes. However, the Academy refused to hand over the trophy as it considered the powerboat ineligible to compete, since it was not a commercial passenger ship, a decision the trophy's new trustees later endorsed. In July 1990 a *Seacat, *Hoverspeed Great Britain*, a new breed of *catamaran *ferry, made the crossing in 3 days, 7 hours, 54 minutes, and after discussion the trophy was handed over to the Seacat's owners. Since 1998 the Hales Trophy has been held by a Danish catamaran ferry, the 91.3-metre (300-ft) *Cat-Link V*, which crossed in 2 days, 20 hours, 9 minutes at an average speed of just over 41 *knots. It also created another world record by covering 1,018.5 *nautical miles in 24 hours.

Mackenzie-Kennedy, C., *The Atlantic Blue Riband* (1993).

board. **(1)** The distance a sailing vessel runs between *tacks when working to *windward. Thus a ship tacking across the wind to reach a point to windward of its present position can make short or long boards according to the frequency of her tacks; the more she tacks the shorter the boards. **(2) To make a good board**, to sail in a straight line when *close hauled making only the minimum of *leeway. **(3) To make a stern board**, to come up head to wind so that the vessel stops and makes way *astern until she falls off on the opposite tack, often a very seamanlike operation when navigating in narrow channels. **(4) To board it up**, an old term used by seamen meaning to *beat up to windward. **(5) To go on board**, to go aboard a ship. **(6) To slip by the board**, to desert a ship by escaping down its side. **(7) By the board**, close to the deck as when a mast is broken off close to the deck, or goes by the board. **(8)** When used as a verb, it describes the action of going alongside an enemy vessel and overwhelming its crew with an armed **boarding party**. See also BOARDERS; ENTER, TO.

boarders, sailors appointed to *board an enemy ship, or to repel such attempts by an enemy. In the British Navy during the days of sail four men from each gun's crew were generally designated as boarders. Their duties, after capturing the enemy ship, were to man the pumps, repair the *rigging as much as possible to make the ship seaworthy, and *trim the sails so it could be sailed away as a *prize. See also ENTER, TO.

Board of Longitude, the general name by which the commissioners for the discovery of the *longitude at sea were known. The board was established by Act of Parliament in 1714 during the reign of Queen Anne. Its early history is closely associated with William Whiston, a dissenting clergyman, and Humphrey Ditton, mathematical master at Christ's Hospital School. On 14 July 1713, in a letter to a newspaper, they attributed the disaster that had overcome Admiral Sir Clowdisley *Shovel's fleet on September 1707 to its inability to determine its longitude. They appealed to Parliament to offer a substantial award to overcome this problem and in due course a committee was appointed to examine it. Eminent mathematicians and astronomers, including Sir Isaac Newton, president of the Royal Society, and Edmond Halley, who succeeded Flamsteed as Astronomer Royal, were consulted, and on their recommendation the Board of Longitude was established. This offered a prize of £20,000 for a solution to the problem, stipulating an accuracy to within 30 miles (48 km).

It had long been understood that since time measurement is a function of the earth's rotation on its axis, time and longitude must be interchangeable and, for example, if an event (such as an eclipse) could be seen simultaneously at two places on earth the difference in their local times at that instant would be (translated into angular measure) the difference in their longitudes. Local time was comparatively simple to establish—for instance, by taking equal altitudes of a body either side of the *meridian—but before the advent of radio there was no means of transmitting instantaneously the time of the event in question. However, as early as 1522, the Flemish astronomer Gemma Frisius had pointed out that if a voyager carried an accurate enough clock and kept it wound up he would only have to compare its reading with the local time to find the change in longitude.

An alternative solution, probably favoured by most astronomers, lay in the observation of *lunar distances using the moon's movements in the sky as a form of clock face. But the prize was ultimately awarded in 1765 to John Harrison, the designer of several remarkable timepieces, the most accurate of which, during its voyage from Britain to Barbados and back, lost only fifteen seconds in 156 days. Only half the prize money was awarded at first, as some commissioners expressed doubts as to the validity of Harrison's achievement, since the Act of Parliament called for a method to be generally applicable and a single *chronometer could scarcely be classed as a universal solution. However, in 1773 the balance of the prize money, to some extent due to the king's influence, was paid to Harrison.

The commissioners had also been empowered to grant sums of money up to £2,000 annually to assist bona fide investigators, and award prizes for minor discoveries and improvements in relation to the longitude problem. The first such grant was made in 1737 and the last in 1815. The board continued to operate until 1828, by which time the problem of longitude had ceased to attract attention. During its existence, it had disbursed more than £100,000.

This had been a remarkable period in the development of *celestial navigation that saw the invention of the double-reflection *sextant, an enormous increase in the knowledge of the theory of the motion of the moon that led to the practice of lunar distance observations, and finally the ultimate solution of the longitude problem by the development of the marine chronometer.

Andrewes, W. (ed.), *The Quest for Longitude* (1993).

Howse, D., *Greenwich Time and the Discovery of the Longitude* (1980).

Sobel, D., *Longitude* (1996).

Mike Richey

boat, the generic name for small open craft without any decking and usually propelled by *oars or outboard engine, and sometimes by a small *lugsail on a short mast. Some exceptions to this general definition are fishing vessels and *submarines, both of which are generally known as boats, irrespective of their size. Some coastal naval attack craft used during the two world wars were also called boats.

boathook. About the length of a broom handle, this has a two-pronged metal hook at the end, one prong larger than the other. A basic piece of equipment for all small vessels, such as *yachts, *launches, naval *pinnaces, it is used in a harbour, *marina, etc. to control a vessel coming alongside a *jetty, or another vessel, so as to avoid too heavy a contact. It can also be used to pick up *moorings or *fend off anything that might damage the vessel's hull. See also RICKERS.

boating, see YACHTING.

Boat People, refugees who escaped by sea from the Vietnamese communist regime after the fall of Saigon in 1975, a process that continued for about fifteen years. The exodus across the Gulf of Thailand and the South China Sea began slowly. About 5,240 escaped in 1976, but in 1977 there were 15,690, and in 1978, when ethnic Chinese joined the exodus, the numbers rose dramatically. In November 1978 alone the number of escapees exceeded 21,000, and January–July 1979 over 65,000, most of them ethnic Chinese, reached Hong Kong.

At first most Boat People attempted to reach the nearest landfall, southern Thailand, but acts of *piracy by Thai fishermen were so rampant that from 1977 most tried to reach Malaysia instead. However, they were often blown off *course or their rickety craft suffered engine failure, and they ended up as far away as Indonesia and Japan, and even Australia. The loss of life through bad weather, piracy, disease, and starvation amounted, according to a report by the United Nations High Commissioner for Refugees, to about one-third of those who attempted the voyage.

The brutality of the Thai fishermen who preyed on these vessels was quite shocking, and at first the Thai government, reluctant to receive large boatloads of refugees, did little to stop the killing, raping, and looting that was so often the fate of those trying to escape. In 1981, the year the United Nations launched its anti-piracy programme, 1,100 attacks were recorded. One of the most effective laws introduced by the $2.6 million programme, which was financed by the USA and ten other countries including the UK, was that all 15,000 Thai fishing boats were required to have numbers prominently displayed on their bows, and their crews were photographed on leaving harbour. The photographs were then circulated to refugee camps and other ports in an attempt to identify the pirates. The programme reduced the number of attacks as it deterred all but the most hardened criminals. However, it also resulted in even greater loss of life as the hardcore pirates attempted to kill every witness to their attacks.

Eventually, Vietnam agreed to take back any Boat People who wanted to return, and not punish them. As a result of this initiative, during the 1990s the exodus all but ceased, but not before it had created a refugee crisis of international proportions in places such as Hong Kong and Malaysia.

The term Boat People was also applied to asylum seekers from Iraq and Afghanistan, and elsewhere, who during the 1990s paid smugglers to take them by sea to Australia. Four thousand one hundred and seventy-five arrived in Australia between July 1999 and July 2000 and a further 4,141 arrived during the following twelve months. In one, well-publicized, incident in August 2001 the Norwegian *container ship *Tampa* picked up 433 mainly Afghan asylum seekers from their sinking vessel off the Indonesian coast, the captain citing his obligation to do so under the *International Convention for the Safety of Life at Sea. Both Australia and Indonesia refused them permission to land and eventually they were dispersed to other countries.

Cargill, M. (ed.), *Voices of the Vietnamese Boat People: Nineteen Narratives of Escape and Survival* (2001).

boatswain (pron. bo'sun), in the Royal Navy the officer, or warrant officer, in charge of all work on deck which is done under the general supervision of the officer of the deck or the executive officer. In spite of his title, the ship's boats do not normally come under his jurisdiction. In the US Navy he is also known as boats.

boatswain's chair, a short board, secured in a *bridle, used to *sway a man *aloft for scrapping and painting masts, and treating *yards and *rigging.

boatswain's pipe, a peculiarly shaped whistle of great antiquity, used by boatswain's mates of men-of-war to pipe—or wind as it was called before the 18th century—orders throughout the ship. A variety of cadences could be produced on it, and each order had its own particular, easily recognizable, cadence, or **call** as it was known in the Royal Navy. Up to Tudor times, the pipe, or whistle, often set with jewels, was the personal insignia of the *Lord High Admiral, and was worn around the neck on a long gold chain. Its only use today is for the ceremonial piping on board warships of visiting commanding officers and other dignitaries.

bobstay, a chain or heavy wire *rigging running from the end of the *bowsprit to the ship's *stem or *cutwater. Particularly heavy rigging was required in this position since the fore-topmast in sailing vessels was *stayed to the bowsprit, exerting a strong upward pull when the sails were full of wind. The bowsprit was also secured by *shrouds from either bow of the ship. Very few sailing vessels are fitted with bowsprits today and in consequence the bobstay is rarely seen as a piece of rigging; generally, the only sailing vessels still using it are the various *sail training ships and some classic *yachts.

body plan, a drawing made during the design stages of a ship giving a view at right angles to the *sheer draught and showing the *athwartships form of its sections. See also NAVAL ARCHITECTURE.

boeier, or **boier,** a craft used on the inland waterways of Holland, with apple-shaped bows and stern, rounded bottom, and broad fan-shaped *leeboards for sailing in very shallow waters. The boeier originated in the early part of the 16th century as a seagoing merchant vessel some 20 metres (65 ft) in length and 7–8 metres (23–6 ft) in breadth, *rigged with either a *spritsail or a *loose-footed mainsail having *brails and a standing *gaff, and often setting a square *topsail above. Some of the earliest and largest of the boeiers carried in addition a small *lateen *mizzen.

By the 19th century the boeier had changed to the present form of bluff-ended inland waterways type and been reduced in size, ranging generally from 12.3 metres (40 ft) to as little as 8 metres (26 ft) in length. The single mast, stepped in a *tabernacle for lowering at bridges, generally carried a boomed mainsail with the typical Dutch curved gaff, a *foresail set on the *forestay, and a *jib which could be set on a running *bowsprit. Later examples were built of steel. The boeier became the most common type of *pavilionenjacht*, or pleasure craft with *staterooms, until well into the 20th century.

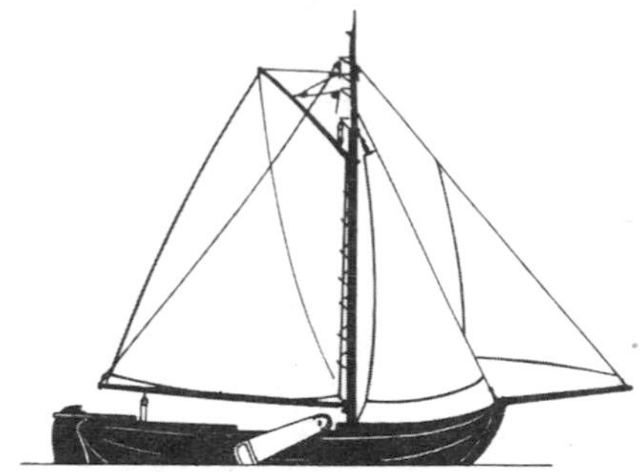

Boeier

bollard, a vertical piece of timber or iron, fixed to the ground, to which a ship's *mooring lines are made fast when alongside. When *whaling harpoons were launched by hand, the thick piece of wood fixed to the head of the *whaleboat, round which the harpooner took a turn of the line in order to *veer it steadily after the *whale had been struck, was also known as a bollard. The power of modern *tugs is measured by their **bollard pull** and is expressed in tonnes. See also NIGGER HEADS.

bolster, a piece of wood fitted in various places in a ship, mostly wooden sailing vessels, to act as a preventive to chafe or *nip. Powered ships sometimes have them fixed to the deck around the *hawseholes to prevent the *cable from rubbing against the hawsehole *cheeks. In old wooden sailing ships the pieces of soft wood, usually covered with *canvas, which rested on the *trestle-trees to prevent them getting nipped by the *rigging were also called bolsters.

bolt-rope, the name given to the rope which was sewn around the edges of a sail to keep it from fraying. While the whole rope was known as the bolt-rope, it was subdivided in name according to the side of the sail on which it was sewn, as *luff-rope, *footrope, etc. Bolt-ropes were always placed slightly to the left of centre of the edge on which they were sewn to enable seamen to orient the sail by feel in the dark.

Bombard, Alain (b. 1924), a French doctor of medicine and a pioneer of the art of survival at sea. He was born in Paris and qualified at the Faculty of Medicine there before taking a hospital post at Boulogne. There he began to study the problems connected with survival at sea and in 1952, to prove his theory that it was possible for shipwrecked mariners to survive and exist solely on the resources of the sea, he set out to cross the Atlantic on an inflatable raft called *L'Hérétique*. The voyage was successful and he published an account of it under the title *Histoire d'un naufragé volontaire* (*History of a Voluntary Castaway*). In 1959 he built a sea laboratory for the study of the physiopathology of sailors, and subsequently became Délégué Général to the Fondation Scientifique Ricard which sponsored research into *marine biology. He swam the Channel in 1951, became a Chevalier of the Legion of Honour, and in the 1980s was a member of the French government. See also HEYERDAHL, THOR.

bomb ketch, a ship of the old sailing navies, armed with one, or occasionally two, heavy howitzers or mortars and used for bombarding places ashore. Mostly the mortars were fitted in *ketches, either specially built or converted into such from a small three-masted vessel by the removal of its foremast to provide a good deck space forward for the mortars. When employed in bombardment, bomb vessels were *moored in position with *springs on their *cables so that the ships themselves were 'trained' for the mortars to fire on the desired bearing. Until 1804, in the British Navy, mortars in bomb vessels were manned and worked by the Royal Artillery; after that date by the newly formed Royal Marine Artillery. The development of naval guns which could be trained and elevated irrespective of the ship's *course made all bomb vessels obsolete.

During the latter part of the 18th century and the first half of the 19th century bomb ketches were also used extensively by the British *Admiralty to search for the *North-West Passage and for the *exploration by sea of the Arctic and Antarctic. They were always exceptionally strongly built and had had their decks stiffened with heavy beam bridges to support the shock of the recoil of the heavy mortars and thus were well suited to withstand the pressure of *ice when beset by it or frozen in.

bonaventure, an additional *mizzen-sail, *lateen in shape, which used to be carried on a fourth mast, known as a **bonaventure mizzen**, in the old sailing ships. It went out of use during the 17th century, when the standard three masts were adapted as the most efficient rig for ships.

bone. **(1)** The white feather of water under the bow of a ship when it is under way. A ship moving fast through the water and throwing up an appreciable feather is said to have a bone in its mouth, in its teeth. **(2)** As a verb, it is a naval term meaning to scrounge or pilfer. It derives from a *boatswain named Bone who served in the *flagship of Admiral Cornwallis during the French Revolutionary War (1793–1801), and who was adept at acquiring ship's stores from other ships to make good his deficits or build up a surplus. When the ship was decommissioned Cornwallis is said to have remarked, 'I trust, Mr Bone, that you will leave me my *bower anchors'.

bonnet. **(1)** An additional strip of *canvas laced originally to the *foot of sails on a *fore-and-aft rig and to *courses in *square-rigged ships to increase the area exposed to the wind. In the 19th century bonnets were also used to secure the foot of an upper *topsail to a lower topsail *yard. See also DRABLER. **(2)** The name given to a covering on the top of a *navel pipe to prevent water going down it. For illus. see CABLE-HOLDER.

booby, a *seabird of the gannet family which often perched on the *yards of *square-rigged ships in the days of sail. The name came from the ease with which it allowed itself to be caught after it had settled. 'One of the Saylers espying a Bird fitly called a Booby, he mounted to the top-mast and took her. The quality of which Bird is to sit still, not valuing danger' (Sir T. Herbert, *Travels* (1634)).

booby-hatch. **(1)** A small opening in the deck of a vessel used as an additional *companion to facilitate movement. **(2)** A name, in the past, that was sometimes given to the sliding hatch on the raised *cabin top of small cruising *yachts.

boom. **(1)** A *spar used to extend the *foot of a sail, or to which the foot is attached. In *square-rigged ships, *studding sails are set on studding-sail booms extended from the ends of the *yardarms. Such booms (including booms temporarily *rigged at deck level to extend the *clews of the lower sails) would normally be rigged only when it was required to make the most of a light wind. Thus a ship was said to come **booming forward** when carrying all the sail that it could make.

With a *fore-and-aft rig the boom is a permanent and important spar, to which the foot of the mainsail is attached by various means. The *foresail of some *schooner rigs also has a boom as does the *mizzen of a *ketch or *yawl. The boom is pivoted at the fore end to the mast by a *gooseneck, and controlled by a sheet at or near the *after end, by which the sail is *trimmed.

Until the mid-20th century a boom was normally a solid round wooden spar; nowadays in modern *yachts it is made of a metal which combines strength with lightness; as greater stiffness is required in the vertical than in the horizontal plane it is usually oblong or oval in section. Before the introduction of the *Bermudan rig, main booms were often extremely long, overhanging the *taffrail at the stern, just as the same rig often included a long *bowsprit and a *jackyard topsail, to obtain a very large total sail area. Modern sail plans have a Bermudan mainsail with a short boom, and a large fore-triangle without a bowsprit, which is obtained by *stepping the mast well aft from the bows. In the 1930s some *J-class yachts, and other large Bermudan *cutters, used the *Park Avenue boom.

The purpose of any boom is to enable the sail to which it is attached to set well, without undue 'belly' or sagging of the upper part of the sail to *leeward when sailing *close hauled. To increase flatness, the boom is sometimes prevented from rising when it swings outwards by a *kicking strap. Also in a fore-and-aft rig, the foot of the *spinnaker is normally extended by a spinnaker boom, one end of which is clipped onto the mast, the other end to the spinnaker. When the wind is dead *astern a *foresail may also be *goose winged, a manoeuvre also known as **booming out**. During the 1851 race for what was to become known as the *America's Cup, **America* was permitted to do this, though such a manoeuvre was not at that time allowed under the rules of the Royal Yacht Squadron which organized the race.

(2) A spar rigged outboard from a ship's side horizontally at deck level or between the deck and the waterline, to which boats are secured in harbour or when the ship is at anchor in calm weather; the boats thus lie clear of the ship's side and are ready for use.

(3) A barrier, usually floating, at water level across a harbour entrance or river to obstruct the entrance of an enemy or the passage of craft. Originally, perhaps, it was made of floating logs (German *Baum*, Dutch *boom*, a tree) secured together; it may also be of chain or *cable, buoyed to float. Its use in this connection has been extended to logging operations, and the size of log rafts floated down rivers is often controlled by booms of this type. Nowadays, floating plastic booms are used to prevent the spread of an oil spill.

(4) To boom off, to shove a boat or vessel away with a spar.

boom boats, the larger ship's boats which were hoisted inboard and stowed on the *skid booms, normally in the space between the ship's foremast and mainmast, known as the *booms. The smaller ship's boats were usually hoisted and secured at *davits.

boom-irons, metal rings fitted on the *yardarms of *square-rigged sailing ships through which the *studding-sail booms are traversed when setting the studding sails.

booms, the space in larger sailing vessels usually between the foremast and the mainmast. It was where the *skid booms, supported by *gallows, were stowed on board in the *waist of the ship, and which helped secure the ship's larger boats when the ship was at sea.

bootneck, nickname for a Royal *Marine.

boottop, a fine strip of paint around the hull of a *yacht which divides the antifouling (see FOULING) paint below the waterline from the paint on the topsides. The boottop is usually painted in a colour which contrasts with the colour of the antifouling and the topsides. In the merchant navy the term used is **boottopping**.

booty, a form of *prize which, when a ship was captured at sea, was permitted to be distributed among the captors at once. In an old definition it was everything that could be picked up by hand above the main deck, all else in the ship having to be legally condemned by a prize court before its value could be distributed among the captors. As may be imagined, it was a custom which allowed of much abuse. This form of prize 'pickings' was abolished at the end of the Napoleonic War (1803–15).

bora, a violent easterly squall experienced in the upper part of the Adriatic Sea, a weak one being known as a *borino* and a strong one as a *boraccia.* It is caused by heavy cold air from the Austrian Alps as it descends and flows out over the sea. The term is also applied to similar winds on the northern shore of the Black Sea and the island of Novaya Zemlya in the Russian Arctic.

bore, or **eagre,** a sudden and rapid flow of the *tide in certain rivers and estuaries which rolls up in the form of a *wave. Bores are caused either by the meeting of two tides, where the excess of water results in a rapid rise, or by a tide rushing up a narrowing estuary where the closeness of the banks or a shelving bottom encloses the tide so that it is forced to rise rapidly to accommodate the water coming in.

'born with a silver spoon', an old naval saying to indicate those young gentlemen who, through birth or connection, were able to enter the Royal Navy without examination and whose subsequent promotion was assured. They were said to enter the navy through *cabin windows in distinction from those others, said to have been born with a wooden ladle, who rose by merit and were said to enter the navy through the *hawseholes. See also CAPTAIN'S SERVANT.

boss, the swell of the ship's hull around the *propeller shaft and also the rounded hub of the propeller.

bo'sun, see BOATSWAIN.

botargo, a name sometimes used in the British Navy during the 16th and 17th centuries to describe the dried *fish issued to crews at sea in lieu of salt meat on *banyan days. It is really the name for the dried roes of fish, but was adopted in the navy to embrace the whole fish.

botter, originally a Dutch fishing boat normally based between Volendam and Harderwijk in what used to be the Zuider Zee. About 14 metres (45 ft) long and 4 metres (13 ft) in breadth, it was flat bottomed with curved sides and a high curved *stem and a low narrow stern. The *leeboards were long and narrow, sword shaped, for use in rough waters for offshore fishing. Fishing botters had a free flooding fishwell amidships for keeping the catch alive. Many botters were converted into *yachts, the large amount of space below decks providing comfortable and reasonably spacious accommodation, and many Dutch cruising yachts were also built on general botter lines.

'bottle', a term used in the Royal Navy for a reproof or criticism. It is said to have derived from an old naval saying, 'a dose from the foretopman's bottle', which was a purgative given in all cases of sickness; or, alternatively, from a 'bottle of acid', corrosive and painful.

bottlescrew, or **turnbuckle,** a type of screw, not perfected until the 1870s, which is used to adjust any rigging equipment for length or tension, the correct maritime term being to 'set up' the rigging. It consists of an internally threaded sleeve into which a right-handed screw takes at one end and a left-handed screw

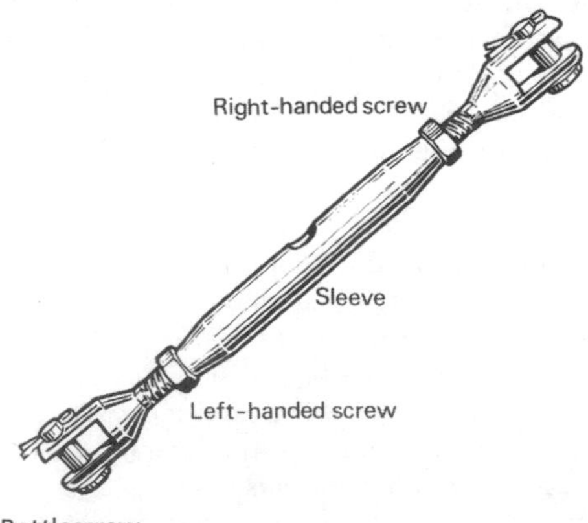

Bottlescrew

at the other. As the sleeve is revolved, the two contra-threaded screws are drawn together, thus increasing the tension of those parts of the rigging to which they are attached. Bottle-screws are largely used for setting up the *shrouds of sailing vessels and the *guardrails and *davit guys fitted in ships. A large bottle-screw is also used in a *cable stopper called a screw slip. This secures an anchor in a *hawse-pipe by screwing it home until the anchor *flukes are hard up against the rim of the hawse-pipe so that it cannot move when the ship *pitches in heavy seas.

bottomry, sometimes also known as **bummaree,** is a long defunct term for a mortgage on a ship executed by a *master who was out of touch with his owners and needed to raise money for repairs to complete a voyage. Money raised by bottomry had to be used only for the exact purpose stated and was always primarily for getting a ship back to its port of registry. A bottomry bond took priority over all other mortgages, but if the ship was lost at sea before the voyage was completed the lender lost his bond. Samuel *Pepys (*Diary*, 30 Nov. 1663) has the word as bottomaryne; another variant spelling is bottomarie. See also RESPONDENTIA.

Bougainville, Comte Louis Antoine de (1729–1811), best known as a French naval officer and *navigator although he was a professional soldier until he was 37. In the latter capacity he served with distinction under Montcalm in Canada during the Seven Years War (1756–63). However, after the peace his ambitions turned to the sea. At his own expense he established a colony on the Falkland Islands. This met with objections from Spain and, when Bougainville sailed in December 1766 in command of the *frigate *La Boudeuse*, accompanied by a storeship, his first task was the evacuation of the settlement.

The evacuation completed, the expedition passed through the Straits of *Magellan and crossed the Pacific in the *trade wind belt to Tahiti, which Bougainville formally annexed, though it had been discovered eight months previously by a British officer, Captain Samuel Wallis (1728–95). The Frenchman's eulogistic description of the island and its inhabitants gave support to the contemporary cult of 'the noble savage'. Sailing on westwards, he rediscovered the island of Espiritu Santo, first found by the Spanish explorer Pedro Quiros (1565–1615) in 1606. He then became the first European to sight Australia's eastern coastline when, in June 1768, he found his way barred by the *Great Barrier Reef in *latitude 15° S. To escape this area of perilous *lee shores, he *beat his way to *windward until he could *weather the eastern tip of New Guinea.

Passing through the Solomon Islands, one of which bears his name today, and visiting New Britain, the Moluccas, and Batavia, he completed his circumnavigation at Saint-Malo in March 1769, having lost only seven men out of 200, a remarkable achievement for the times.

In 1782 Bougainville commanded a division of the French Fleet at the battle of the Saints during the War of American Independence (1775–83), and in the French Revolution he narrowly escaped becoming a victim of the 'Terror'. He later gained the favour of Napoleon who made him a count of the empire, a senator, and a member of the Legion of Honour. The flamboyant climbing plant *Bougainvillaea* is named after him.

bounty, money that used to be paid at recruiting centres to encourage volunteers for service in the British Navy in time of war. At the beginning of the 18th century, state or royal bounties amounted to 30 shillings (£1.50) for an able seaman and 25 shillings for an ordinary seaman, rising later to four or five guineas. There were additional municipal bounties to encourage local recruitment, ranging from £2 to as much as £40. Thus in 1795 the City of London offered a supplementary bounty of ten guineas for able seamen, eight for ordinary seamen, six for *landsmen, and one or two for boys according to their height. The payment of recruitment bounties disappeared in Britain with the passage of the naval Continuous Service Act in 1857. In general, volunteers for naval service brought in by the bounties were objects of scorn to those in the navy who considered themselves real seamen.

Bounty, a ship's name made famous for the *mutiny which occurred on board. Originally a merchant ship called *Bethia*, the *Bounty* was built at Hull in 1784. She was bought, renamed, and fitted out as an armed transport for a voyage in 1788 to carry breadfruit seedlings from Tahiti to the West Indies, a scheme designed to acclimatize these plants there as a cheap source of food for those being transported in the *slave trade who were working on the sugar plantations. On 28 April 1789, under the leadership of Fletcher *Christian, part of the crew of 45 men mutinied. Opinions differ regarding the cause of the mutiny, the most common being that the commanding officer, William *Bligh, was an unduly stern disciplinarian who brutalized the *Bounty*'s crew by the severity of his punishments; but a more likely cause was the attractions to Christian and others like him of the women and way of life in the South Sea Islands.

At the time of the mutiny the ship was near Tofua, in the Tonga group of islands. Bligh and eighteen men who remained loyal to him were cast adrift in the ship's *launch and eventually reached safety at Timor after an epic open-boat voyage of 5,760 kilometres (3,600 mls.). The mutineers returned in the ship to Tahiti, then Christian and eight followers, accompanied by some islanders and several women, sailed to Pitcairn Island, where the *Bounty* was run ashore and burnt. The British *Admiralty, when they received news of the mutiny after the return of Bligh, sent HMS *Pandora* to Tahiti to bring back the mutineers for trial. Fourteen were secured at Tahiti, but Christian was not among them. Four of them were drowned when the *Pandora* was wrecked on the *Great Barrier Reef. The surviving ten were brought back to Portsmouth and court-martialled, three of them being hanged, some of them being identified by their *tattoos.

A copy of Captain James *Cook's three volumes describing his third voyage of 1776–9, which were completed by Captain King, belonged to Bligh; he took it with him in the *Bounty*, making many notes in the margins. It was taken after the mutiny by Christian to Pitcairn Island and was recovered about forty years later when a British *frigate visited the island. The last survivor of the mutineers, Seaman Adams, was still living there and exchanged the three volumes for a supply of pencils and paper. It says much for the new spirit of humanitarianism growing in the British Navy in the early 19th century that Adams was not brought home for trial on a charge of mutiny but allowed to remain to live out his life in peace. See also REPLICA SHIP; SHIPWRECKS.

bow, the foremost end of a ship, the opposite of stern. **From bow to stern**, the whole length of a ship. The word is frequently used in the plural, as 'the bows of a ship'. It was also used at one time to give an approximate *bearing of an object in relation to the fore-and-aft line of the ship, as e.g. 'the buoy bears 15° on the *port bow' or 'two *points on the *starboard bow', as the case may be. **On the bow**, within an arc of four points (45°) extending either side of the bow. It is the position in the ship where the *hawseholes for the anchors are situated and where the *jackstaff is stepped. See also BULBOUS BOW. For illus. see SHIPBUILDING.

bow-chaser, a long gun mounted forward in the bow-ports of sailing men-of-war and positioned to fire directly ahead. They were sometimes mounted in pairs and were always of small bore in relation to their length in order to carry their *shot for a greater distance. They were used particularly when chasing an enemy ship, to attempt to slow it down by shooting away its sails and *rigging. See also CHASE; CHASE GUNS.

bower anchors, the two largest anchors in a ship. They were usually, but by no means always, carried permanently attached to their *cables, one on either bow with the cables running through the *hawseholes so that the anchors were always ready for letting go in an emergency. They were originally known as *best bower and small bower, but are now just known as the *starboard and *port bower.

bow-grace, the name given to old *cable or chain hung over the bow of a wooden ship in very cold weather in a *tideway. This helped to protect the ship from the edges of thin drift *ice which can produce a cutting action serious enough to damage the bow.

bowline (pron. bolin as in no). **(1)** A knot tied in such a way as to produce an *eye, or loop, in the end of a rope. It is a knot with many uses at sea, whether to join two large *hawsers together, with one bowline tied with its eye

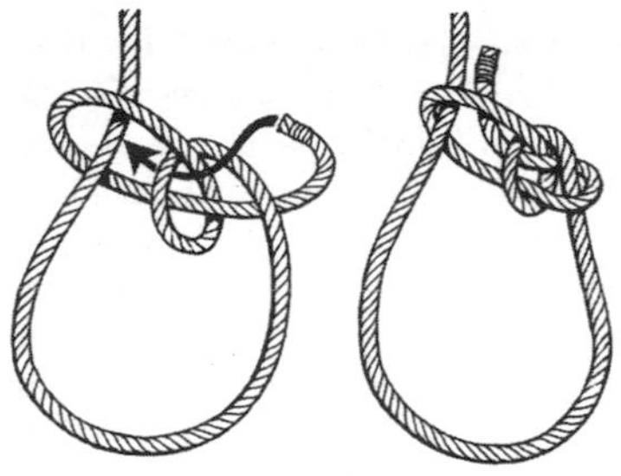

Running bowline

inside the eye of the other, or tied in the end of a hawser to provide a loop for dropping over a *bollard. It is a knot which will never slip and cannot jam. Variants of this knot are a **running bowline**, where the knot is tied around the *bight of the rope to form a noose, and a **bowline on the bight**, where the knot is made with the bight of the rope to produce two eyes. This variant is often used to form a temporary *boatswain's chair when a man is needed to work aloft. **(2)** The name of the rope attached with a bowline to, and leading forward from, a *bridle between *cringles on the *leeches of sails in a *square-rigged ship. Its purpose, when hauled hard in, is to keep the *weather edge of the sail *taut and steady when the ship is *close hauled to the wind. Thus a square-rigged ship is said to 'sail on a bowline', or 'stand on a taut bowline', when it is being sailed as close to the wind as possible.

bowse, to, to haul with a *tackle to make more *taut. Thus the *tack of a *lugsail is bowsed down with a tackle after the sail has been hoisted so that the *luff is drawn tauter than can be achieved merely by hauling on the *halyards. **'Bowse away'**, the order for all men on the hauling part of a tackle to haul away.

bowsprit (pron. bo- as in no), orig. **boltsprit,** a large *spar projecting from the *stem of sailing vessels to provide the means of staying a fore-topmast and from which the *jibs were set. When a fore-topgallant mast was set, the bowsprit was extended by a *jib-boom, to the end of which was led the fore-topgallant mast stay on which the *flying jibs were set. The bowsprit itself was held rigidly in place by *shrouds led to each bow of the vessel and by a *bobstay led from its outer end to the stem of the vessel just above the waterline. A **running bowsprit**, as opposed to a standing one, was where, in some smaller *cutter-rigged sailing vessels, the bowsprit was fitted so that it could be run in, or furled, by sliding inboard.

*Sail training ships and classic *yachts apart, the bowsprit has now virtually disappeared.

bow thruster, see PROPELLER: MODERN PROPELLER SYSTEMS.

box-hauling, a method of *wearing a *square-rigged ship in rough weather when

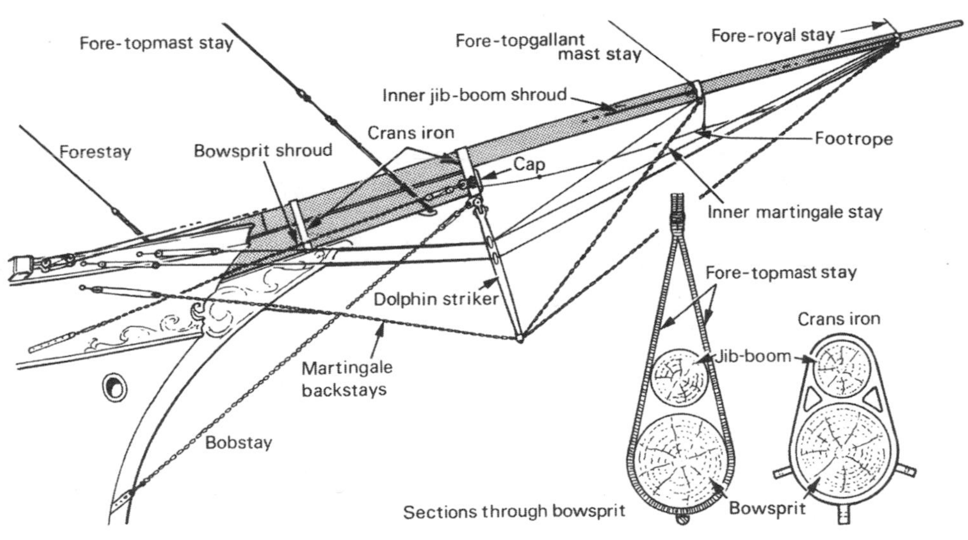

Bowsprit and jib-boom of a square-rigged ship

the force of the *waves makes it impractical for it to *tack. The procedure is to put the *helm *a-lee (1), as in *tacking, to bring the bows up into the wind, when the strength of the waves as they strike the *weather bow will force the bows down to *leeward (2). With the helm reversed, this movement is accelerated, and at the same time the aftermost sails are *brailed up to spill the wind out of them in order to give the foremost sails an added turning moment. As the stern of the ship crosses the wind the aftermost sails are *braced to catch the wind (3) and increase the rate of turn until the wind is forward of the *beam and the *yards can again be braced (4). Box-hauling, as well as being a rough weather tactic, was also used when ships were too near the shore to wear in the usual way.

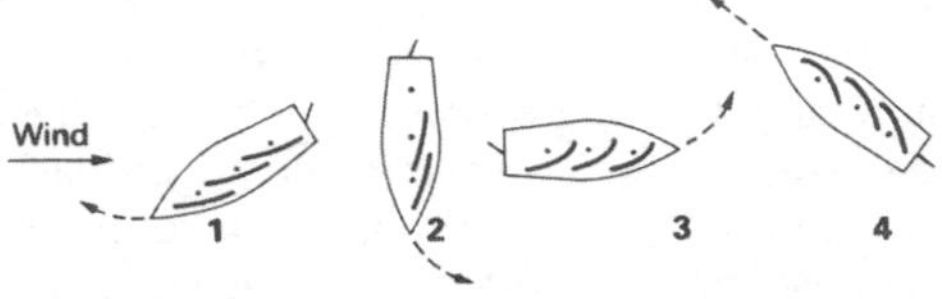

Box-hauling

box off, to, in a *square-rigged ship when *tacking, to haul the head-sheets to *windward and lay the head-yards flat *aback to *pay the ship's *head out of the wind, when the action of the *helm by itself is insufficient to produce that result. It is a means of ensuring that the ship does not miss *stays. In ships with a *fore-and-aft rig the same result can be achieved when the vessel hangs head to wind by hauling out the *clew of the *jib to windward.

box the compass, to, to know and to be able to recite the *points and quarter points of the *magnetic compass from north through south to north again, both clockwise and anti-clockwise. It is now a lost art, and was never a particularly easy thing to do because of the rule that quarter points were never read from a point beginning and ending with the same letter. Thus, for example, boxing the compass clockwise, the quarter point next to, say, ENE, would not be ENE ¼ E., but is taken from the next clockwise point, E. by N., with the quarter points read backwards, to become E. by N. ¾ N. Nowadays, a compass is read by what, when it was first introduced, was called the 'three-figure method' (see POINT).

brace, to, to swing round, by means of *braces, the *yards of a *square-rigged ship to present a more efficient sail surface to the direction of the wind. By bracing the yards at different angles to the fore-and-aft line of the ship, the best advantage can be taken of any wind which may be blowing. Thus, the yards are **braced *aback** to bring the wind on the forward side of the sails to take the way off the ship; are **braced *about** to bring the ship on the opposite tack when going about; are **braced *abox** to bring the head-yards flat aback to stop the ship; are **braced *by** to bring the yards in contrary directions on different masts to lie the ship to or *heave to; are **braced in** to lay the yards squarer to the fore-and-aft line for a *free wind; and are **braced sharp** to bring the yards round to make the smallest possible angle with the fore-and-aft line when sailing *close hauled.

'brace of shakes', originally a maritime term which has found its way into everyday language. It denoted a moment of time which could be measured by the shaking of a sail as a ship comes into the wind.

braces, ropes or wire ropes *rove to the ends of all *yards in a *square-rigged ship by which the yards are *braced, or swung, at different angles to the fore-and-aft line of the ship to make the most of the wind. For illus. see YARD.

brackets, small, shaped timbers or plates to connect two or more parts of a ship in *shipbuilding. They are known as *knees when joining a deck *beam to a *frame in a wooden vessel.

brails, ropes leading from the *leech on both sides of a *loose-footed sail on a *fore-and-aft rig and through leading *blocks secured on the mast *hoops of the sail to deck level. Their use was to gather in the sail close to the mast so that it was temporarily *furled when coming up to a *mooring or as required. The old-fashioned *whaler rig in which the mainsail was loose footed was always fitted with brails. **To brail in**, to haul on the brails and bring the leech of the sail up to the mast.

brake, the handle or lever by which the common ship's *pump was worked before the days of *auxiliary machinery. In ships of any size the pump was manned by up to six men working on the brake in short spells.

branch, the certificate or diploma which used to be given by *Trinity House to a *pilot qualified to *navigate a ship in British waters. A full branch from Trinity House qualified a pilot to navigate without any restrictions in British waters, which included the whole of the English Channel and all other waters around the British Isles even when they lay outside *territorial waters. A limited branch gave him a qualification to act as a pilot only in waters specifically named in the branch. Nowadays, a branch is the certificate awarded to Younger Brethren of Trinity House on election.

Brasil or **Brazil,** or **Hy Brazil,** a legendary island in the Atlantic Ocean. It was one of the *Insulae Purpuraricae* described by Pliny, and so convinced were the early geographers of its existence that they included it in their maps, sometimes attaching it to the Azores group but more often showing it in mid-ocean some hundreds of miles due west of Ireland. Its existence was shown on some *charts published as late as 1853. See also ATLANTIS; AVALON; LYONESSE.

brassbounder, a name used to describe an officer apprentice in a merchant shipping line, possibly because in most shipowning companies the apprentices wore caps with a thin gold *lace binding round them. The apprenticeship system was often much abused in some shipping companies, youths buying an apprenticeship and then frequently serving as unpaid deckhands under *masters and *mates who did little or nothing to teach them their trade. This was, perhaps, particularly the case in the big trading *barques in the late 19th and early 20th centuries, a period when these ships were struggling for their existence against the competition of the *tramp steamer and as a result were largely undermanned to save overhead costs.

breach, to. (1) When a *whale or *manta ray leaps clean out of the water, it is said to breach. (2) Of the sea, to break in, either in a ship or a coastal defence such as a sea wall. A sea which breaks completely across a ship is called **a clean breach**.

'bread-room jack', the name given in the British Navy during the days of sail to a *purser's assistant who issued the daily ration of *biscuit to the various messes on board. See also JACK OF THE DUST.

break, the sudden rise or fall of the deck when not flush, e.g. the break of the *forecastle, break of the *poop, etc.

break bulk, to, defunct term which meant to open up the *holds of a ship at the conclusion of its voyage and start unloading the cargo. For illus. of the break-bulk cargo ship see SHIPBUILDING.

breaker. (1) A small barrel or cask kept permanently in ships' boats for the stowage of drinking water for use in case of shipwreck. It is synonymous with barrico, which is the older word. It is thought possibly to be the Anglicized version of the Spanish *bareca*, a small keg, as barrico probably is, too. (2) In the plural, waves breaking over rocks or *shoals, and often a useful warning to ships off their *course that they are standing into danger.

breaking ground, the act of *weighing a ship's anchor when its *cable lifts it off the bottom and breaks it out of the ground.

break sheer, to. When a ship lying to its anchor is forced, perhaps by wind or *current, to swing across its anchor so as to risk fouling it with its own *cable, it is said to break sheer. When it swings clear the other way, it is said to **keep its sheer**.

breakwater. (1) An artificially placed construction in or around a harbour designed to break the force of the sea and to provide shelter for vessels lying within. (2) A low *bulkhead across the *forecastle deck of a ship which prevents seas which break over the bows or through the *hawseholes from running *aft. It diverts the water into the *scuppers where it is drained overboard.

breaming, in the early days of sail, the method of cleaning the *fouling off a ship's bottom by *careening, and then burning off the *seaweed, *barnacles, etc., which had grown there through long immersion. The clean bottom was then *payed with *tar, though applying a mixture of tallow, sulphur or lime, and rosin also did something to inhibit the growth of weed. The process was also called graving, which gave the *graving dock its name, and was an alternative to using a *hog.

Lighting fires under the hull was quite a dangerous operation, and many ships were set on fire and destroyed by breaming. Nevertheless, it was a necessary and frequent operation, and it was not until the introduction of *copper sheathing, as well as better docking facilities, that breaming became a thing of the past.

breast backstays, a pair of *stays which led from the *head of a *topmast or a *topgallant mast in a *square-rigged ship to *chain-plates forward of the standing *backstays to provide support for the upper masts from the *windward side of the ship. They formed part of the standing *rigging of the ship.

breeches buoy, a ring lifebuoy fitted with *canvas breeches used by the *Coastguard Service for *lifesaving when a ship ran aground on a coast and was in danger of breaking up or sinking. Contact with the wrecked ship was made from the shore by means of a line fired from a *Costain gun. A *jackstay was then *rigged between ship and shore, and the breeches buoy, supported in a sling attached to a *traveller, was hauled back and forth between ship and shore by an endless *whip along the jackstay. The seaman being rescued had his legs through the breeches to give him support as he was hauled ashore. The breeches buoy was then hauled back empty to the ship for the next man to be rescued. The advent of helicopters has made this method of rescue all but redundant.

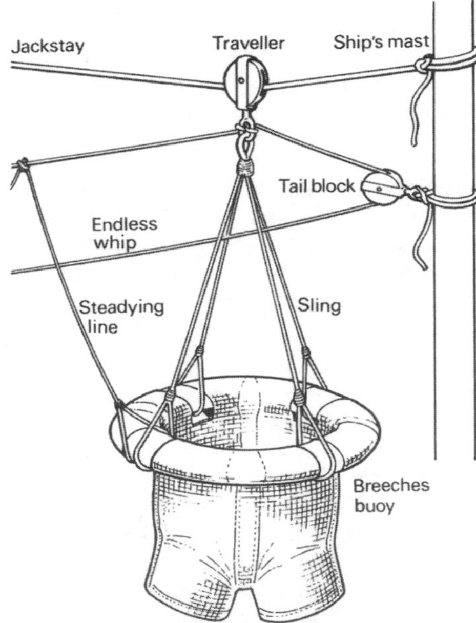

Breeches buoy

breeching, the name given to the thick rope used to secure the carriages of cannons in warships in the days of sail, and also to absorb the force of a gun's recoil. The centre of the breeching was passed through a *thimble stropped to the cascable (the knob on the breech end of the gun) and the ends led through ringbolts on the sides or *cheeks of the gun carriage and secured by *clench-knotting to other ringbolts in the ship's sides. It was of sufficient length to allow the muzzle of the gun to be brought back far enough inboard so that it could be loaded and the *shot rammed home, and also for housing and lashing the gun carriages inboard when the ship was on passage.

The strain on a gun breeching was tremendous, and one of the greatest dangers on board a wooden warship occurred when a breeching parted and the gun and its carriage took charge. This sometimes occurred during action through the force of the recoil or through damage caused by enemy shot, sometimes in very rough weather when the ship was rolling heavily. A 42-pounder gun and its carriage weighed several tons, and the scene on the gun-deck when one or more of these broke loose and took charge can be imagined. Hence the phrase **a loose cannon**, meaning someone who puts friends or colleagues, or a business, in jeopardy through his or her maverick behaviour.

breech of a block, the part of a *block opposite the *swallow, which is where the rope enters.

Brendan (*c.*484–578), Irish saint, the hero of a legendary voyage in the Atlantic. He is held by some to have been the first discoverer of America, on the basis of the text of *Navigatio Sancti Brendani Abbatis*, of which many manuscript copies exist, at least three dating from the 11th century. Between 519 and 527, he is supposed to have made several voyages, the early ones in a *currach, and on one of them was accompanied by seventeen monks. However, the many remarkable adventures recounted almost certainly place some of the voyages within the realm of legend, particularly as they also appear in the pagan Irish saga of *Maelduin and in Scandinavian mythology.

For many years St Brendan's Island was marked on *charts of the Atlantic. In his journal *Columbus records that the inhabitants of Madeira had seen it to the west, and on his Nuremberg globe the German *navigator Martin Behaim (*c.*1436–1507), shows it west of the Canaries. A great many voyages were undertaken to locate the island, so persistent was the belief in its existence, but it was never found. In 1859 it was accepted that, like *Atlantis, it did not exist.

It is virtually impossible that St Brendan could have reached America. If the voyage actually took place at all it is possible that it was to Iceland, and just possible that the monks then sailed southwards to the Canaries. See also EXPLORATION BY SEA.

O'Meara, J., *The Voyage of St. Brendan* (1976).

bridge, an elevated platform built above the upper deck of a powered vessel, from which a ship is normally *navigated and from where all activities on deck can be seen and controlled by the captain or officer of the *watch. Except in the case of some fishing and similar vessels, where it may be in the form of a *wheelhouse, it usually runs *athwartships. The bridge of a modern ship is normally totally enclosed by glass screens or windows to give protection from the weather, but in earlier vessels the bridge was usually open and protected from the weather only by a *canvas *dodger and, in very hot weather, from the sun by a canvas *awning. The main *magnetic compass and a repeater from the *gyroscopic compass are normally situated on the bridge together with the steering wheel, a *chart table for chart work, *GPS displays, and *radar scanners. In very large ships, such as *ocean liners etc., the bridge structure may contain two or even more bridges extending the full width of the ship.

A **flying bridge** in motor *yachts is a steering platform located a level above the deck. In the USA a **bridge deck** is the deck between the *cockpit and the *cabin in a monohull and between the hulls in a *catamaran.

In the days of sail, ships were controlled from the *quarterdeck, with the steering wheel in the after part of the *waist, but as *steam propulsion was developed, first in the *paddle steamer, it was discovered that the platform between the two paddle boxes, known at the time as a bridge, gave a much better all-round view of operations on deck. When the *propeller replaced the paddle wheel the elevated structure *amidships was retained as the navigational control position, and as further development took place, particularly in the number of boilers required to produce steam in sufficient quantity, this central bridge was moved forward and raised to keep it clear of the funnel smoke.

The modern tendency in larger ships, particularly *tankers and *bulk carriers, and some *cruise ships, is to construct the bridge well aft in the ship, mainly in order to keep the upper deck as clear as possible in order to give an uninterrupted view of it, and to provide easier and more economical working conditions at sea and in harbour. This is made possible because the propulsion machinery is placed as far aft as possible, with funnels or *diesel exhausts, which affect the position of the bridge in the ship, close to the stern. See also DODGER.

bridle. **(1)** A length of rope, wire, or chain secured at both ends to a *spar or other object, to the *bight of which a *purchase can be hooked. The purpose is to provide a better balance in an unhandy object for lifting purposes. **(2)** The upper end of fixed *moorings laid in harbours and anchorages. When a ship lies to moorings, it is secured to the bridle, or to the *buoy at the end of the bridle.

bridle-port, a square port cut in the bows on either side of the *stem of wooden ships on main deck level through which *mooring *bridles were led. The same ports were used in sailing warships for guns, moved up from the gunport next *abaft, when the ship was required to fire as nearly ahead as possible, as when chasing an enemy vessel. When used at sea for this purpose they were sometimes known as main deck *chase-ports instead of bridle-ports.

brig. **(1)** A two-masted vessel *square rigged on both masts. The word brig was originally an abbreviation of *brigantine before the latter became known as a different type of ship. Brigs were widely used for coastal and short trading voyages and the Scottish *clipper brigs were famous for trading to the Baltic. They were also used by several navies for training. Modern examples have been built for *sail training including *Royalist* owned by the British Sea Cadet Corps, and *Stavros S. Niarchos* and *Prince William* owned by the Tall Ships Youth Trust (formerly the Sail Training Association). The smallest brig in current sail training is the 9-metre (30-ft) *Bob Allen* owned by the Sea Cadets. See also HERMAPHRODITE BRIG; SNOW. **(2)** A largely American term for the jail cell of a ship or in a naval establishment ashore.

Brig

brigantine, a two-masted vessel *square rigged on the foremast and *fore-and-aft rigged on the mainmast. The name is thought to come from the sea brigands, particularly those operating in the Mediterranean, although the *Barbary pirates favoured oared galleys. Brigantines are currently built for *sail training and include the 35-metre (115-ft) *Young Endeavour*, in Australia, and the twin ships *Irving* and *Exy Johnson*, both 33.7 metres (110 ft) long, which were *launched in 2003 by the Los Angeles Maritime Institute.

brine, or **pickle,** the salted liquor in which beef or pork was preserved in casks for use in ships before the days of tinned or frozen meat.

bring to, to, to bring a sailing vessel to a stop with its sails still set. In the case of *square-rigged ships this was achieved by *bracing the *yards on the foremast *aback to counter the effect of those that were still drawing; in the case of a vessel with a *fore-and-aft rig it was achieved by bringing it head to wind. The term is also often used when forcing another vessel to stop by firing a *shot across its bows (see also HEAVE TO, TO). When anchoring, the correct term is to bring a ship to an anchor, because in the days of sail it was usual to bring to for anchoring by laying the *foresails aback to take *way off the ship.

bring up, to, to bring a ship to an anchor or a *mooring. The normal practice, particularly in small vessels under sail, is to bring up head to *tide, though at *slack water, a vessel normally brings up head to wind.

Britannia. **(1)** A ship's name associated with the Royal Navy since 1682, when the first of this name was built at Chatham. In 1859 the fifth ship named *Britannia* was allocated to the training of naval cadets and was eventually moored at Dartmouth in Devon for this purpose. Later a college was built there and this, too, was known as HMS *Britannia*, but changed its name to the Britannia Royal Naval College after the royal yacht *Britannia* was *launched (see (4) below).

(2) The first transatlantic *ocean liner to be built for what was later to become the Cunard Line. Constructed by Robert Napier, she was a 1,150-ton wooden *paddle steamer, 63 metres (207 ft) in length with a maximum speed of 9 knots.

(3) A 212-ton British racing yacht launched in 1893 for the Prince of Wales, later King Edward VII, and owned after his death by King George V. She was designed by the *yacht designer G. L. Watson, and was *composite built on the Clyde. During her first few seasons she was remarkably successful but a change in the *rating rule, introduced in 1896, did not favour her, and her supremacy was challenged by the German Kaiser's *Meteor*. In 1897 the Prince of Wales sold her but four years later he bought her back, but fitted her out for cruising only. After the First World War (1914–18), King George V fitted *Britannia* out for racing, which encouraged a resurgence in the sport. During much of the 1920s she competed with great success against other yachts in the *Big Class, but was eventually outclassed by the *J-class. In August 1935 she was withdrawn from racing having sailed a total of 635 races, winning 231 first prizes and 129 second and third prizes. During her lifetime she had seven different rigs, and could be justly called one of the most remarkable racing yachts ever built. After King George V died in January 1936 she was towed into the English Channel and sunk in deep water off the Isle of Wight, but a *replica of her is now being built.

(4) British royal yacht, launched in April 1953 by Queen Elizabeth II at the Clydebank shipyard of Messrs. John Brown & Co. Her dimensions were: length overall 125.7 metres (412 ft 3 in.), waterline length 116 metres (380 ft), *draught 5.2 metres (17 ft), gross *tonnage 5,862, seagoing speed 21 knots.

In July 1938 the British government decided to replace the ageing *Victoria and Albert* with a new royal yacht which would have a dual role in wartime as a hospital ship. Although preliminary plans were sent to leading shipbuilders in 1939, the Second World War (1939–45) intervened and it was not until October 1951 that the *Admiralty announced that a hospital ship, capable of carrying 200 patients and the necessary medical staff, would be added to the rearmament programme. In peacetime, the Admiralty announced, *Britannia* would be used as a royal yacht by King George VI, but the yacht was, at least theoretically, capable of being converted to her wartime role in 24 hours.

The contract with John Brown & Co. was signed in February 1952, shortly before the king died. The estimated cost was £1,615,090—though this had escalated to £2,098,000 by the time the vessel was launched. In addition, decorating the royal apartments cost £87,000. During her 44 years in *commission *Britannia* never acted as a hospital ship, but she undertook 85 state visits and many other worldwide tours, and was also used to sell British industry abroad. In the course of these duties she covered nearly 2 million kilometres (over a million *nautical miles) before being decommissioned in December 1997. She is now a static exhibit at Leith, Edinburgh, and is open to the public.

Britomart, more properly Britomartis, a Cretan goddess who is the patroness of hunters, fishermen, and sailors. She was a nymph, the daughter of Zeus and Carme. When pursued by Minos, King of Crete, who wanted to ravish her, she sprang into the sea but was saved from drowning by the nets of some fishermen.

'Britons, Strike Home', the title of a naval song much in favour in the 18th century and played on board British ships as they were sailing into battle. It was even more popular for this purpose than the equally well-known song 'Rule Britannia'. The song comes from Purcell's opera *Bonduca* of 1695. See also SEA SONGS; SHANTY.

broach to, to, the tendency of a sailing vessel to fly up into the wind when *running free or with the wind blowing strongly from the *quarter. In *square-rigged ships the chief danger of broaching to arose from the habit of many skippers of driving their ships too hard, keeping aloft too large a press of sail to make the most of strong winds. In extreme cases of broaching to, the sails could be caught flat *aback, in which situation the masts were likely to go by the *board, and the ship might even *founder. Ships with a *fore-and-aft rig are less likely to suffer from broaching to, though it does remain a major danger, particularly when sailing with a *spinnaker set. See also POOP.

Broaching to

broad pennant, a swallow-tailed pennant, flown from the masthead, and in most navies the distinguishing flag of a commodore. In Britain, until 1864, there were three qualities of broad pennants, red, white, and blue, indicating the commodores of the first, second, and third class and corresponding to the organization of the British Navy by *squadronal colours. After that date all commodores' broad pennants in the Royal Navy became white with a red St George's cross.

broadside, the full weight of metal which, before the days of missiles, could be fired simultaneously from all the guns on one side of a warship. **Broadside on**, sideways, the opposite of end on.

broke or **broken,** the sentence of a court martial which deprived an officer of his *commission. The full wording of the sentence in British courts martial was 'to be broke and rendered unfit to serve His Majesty at sea'. The modern equivalent is to be dismissed the service.

broom. **(1)** The old custom of indicating that a ship was for sale was to hoist a besom—a broom made of sticks—at the masthead. Some have held that the old, and unsubstantiated, story of the Dutch admiral Marten Tromp (1597–1653) hoisting a broom at his masthead during the First Anglo-Dutch War (1552–4), 'to sweep the English from the seas', really arose from an earlier derisory English statement that he had the broom at his masthead to denote that his fleet was for sale as it was so inefficient. There would however appear to be very little truth in either version of the story. **(2)** The shrub of that name was cut and used widely for the purpose of *breaming a ship. Brooming was often used as a synonym for breaming.

Brunel, Isambard Kingdom (1896–59), British-born engineer and ship designer. He began his engineering career in 1823 when he entered the office of his father, French-born Marc Isambard Brunel (1769–1849), who had fled to the USA to escape the French Revolution before settling in England in 1799 to work as an inventor and engineer. In 1825 Brunel was appointed his father's assistant engineer in the construction of the first tunnel under the River Thames, now used for the Rotherhithe–Wapping underground line, but in 1828 was injured in an inundation of the tunnel which delayed completion of its construction until 1843. He then worked on several projects constructing *docks and *piers in West Country ports before he was appointed engineer of the projected Great Western Railway in 1833, the design of which was mainly his work.

In addition to his railway and dock construction work, Brunel took a keen interest in the development of ocean steamships and *steam propulsion, and in 1835 suggested to the directors of the Great Western Railway that the line should be extended to 'have a steamboat to go from Bristol to New York and call it the **Great Western*'. His proposal was accepted and he designed and built the *Great Western* at Bristol, a wooden *paddle steamer larger than any steamer of the day. It was the first steamship built to make regular crossings of the Atlantic and proved a most successful vessel, its first voyage to New York and back being made in 1838.

Brunel next designed an even larger ship, the **Great Britain*, which was the first large iron steamship, the largest ship afloat at the time, and the first big one in which a screw *propeller was fitted. *Launched in 1843, the *Great Britain* made her first Atlantic crossing to New York in 1845, but the following year was carelessly run aground, and it was nearly a year before the ship was refloated. However, it was so little damaged that it was subsequently used for many years in the Australian trade, a great tribute to the strength of Brunel's design.

This connection with the Australian trade fired Brunel to envisage a 'great ship' large enough to carry in its *bunkers all the coal required for a voyage to Australia without the need of calling at a coaling station on the way and, if no coal was available at the ship's port of destination, enough coal as well for the return voyage. He took his designs for his 'great ship' to the directors of the Eastern Steam Navigation Company, who accepted them and appointed him as their engineer for the project. In collaboration with J. Scott Russell, Brunel's **Great Eastern* was laid down in December 1853, but many difficulties were experienced during construction and in the launching, and the ship did not get finally afloat until the end of January 1858. The *Great Eastern* was by far the largest ship ever built up to that time, and had both screw and paddle propulsion. Brunel did not see her leave on her maiden voyage; two days before she was due to sail he suffered a severe stroke and died ten days later.

Many of the elements of Brunel's designs, as for example the construction of *double bottoms in the *Great Britain*, remain standard practice in *shipbuilding today.

Rolt, L. T. C., *Isambard Kingdom Brunel* (1970).

bubble horizon, an attachment that screws onto the frame of a marine *sextant immediately in front of the horizon glass to provide an artificial *horizon in conditions when the real horizon is indistinct or invisible. When taking an *altitude of a celestial body, the *navigator's line of sight through the sextant's telescope passes through the clear part of the horizon glass and enters the attachment where, by means of mirrors and a lens, the rays of light from a bubble inside the attachment are projected in a true horizontal direction. This provides an artificial true horizon, and when the reflected image of the body, seen in the silvered part of the horizon glass, is brought down to the artificial horizon, its altitude can be read off on the scale.

buccaneers. Known among themselves by the romantic title of 'brethren of the coast', they were also called freebooters. They were seamen of several European nationalities who, from the 1620s onwards, cruised on their own *account on the *Spanish Main, raiding and plundering Spanish settlements, and sometimes ships, from their bases on some of the smaller West Indian islands and particularly from *Hispaniola. They adopted a code of laws, known as *Jamaica discipline, and styled themselves *privateers, but since they seldom carried *letters of marque, their actions differed from acts of *piracy only by virtue of the fact that they did not prey on ships belonging to their own nations. Called *zee-rovers* by the Dutch, *corsarios* by the Spanish, and *filibustiers* by the French, they were inspired by the tradition of the Elizabethan privateers. They became prominent for their marauding activities in the Caribbean after the capture of Jamaica in 1655, and later in the Pacific. One of the most bloodthirsty was a Frenchman, François l'Ollonois (d. 1668), so called because he was born at Les Sables d'Olonne. He joined the buccaneers at Hispaniola in about 1665 and was credited with tearing out and eating the hearts of his captives. He was eventually caught and lynched by local inhabitants on his way to the sack of Cartagena.

Early bands were composed of adventurers of all sorts. Perhaps one of the most successful was Sir Henry *Morgan, who led the first attack on Panama in 1671. Another band, led by Bartholomew *Sharp, included two English surgeons, Basil Ringrose (d. 1686), who was eventually killed in an attack on Santiago, Mexico, and Lionel Wafer (*c.*1660–1705). Wafer wrote a book based on his experiences of crossing the Isthmus of Panama, *Description of the Isthmus of America* (1699). Because of it he was made an adviser to the disastrous Darien Scheme in which 2,500 Scotsmen were induced to form a colony in the Isthmus before they were virtually exterminated by the Spaniards.

Some buccaneers, like Alexander *Selkirk, were remarkable characters; others, like *Dampier, were outstanding seamen. However, the outbreak of the European war in 1689 brought buccaneering to an end, and the buccaneers became legitimate privateers. Some of the last to operate were a band led by John Cook who, in 1683, captured a Danish ship of 40 guns off the coast of Guinea, and renamed it *Batchelor's Delight*. The ship was given this odd name presumably because the buccaneers had, near Freetown, exchanged their original

François l'Ollonois; engraving from Esquemeling's *The Bucaniers of America* (1684–5)

ship for sixty young females with whom they set sail for the Pacific, eventually discovering, so it is believed, Easter Island.

The word buccaneer is derived from the French *boucan*, or grill. On these the buccaneers cooked the dried strips of meat that came from the wild herds of cattle they hunted on Hispaniola. The word did not come into use until after the publication in 1678 of a book called *The Bucaniers of America* by a French surgeon, John Esquemeling (*c.*1660–1700), who apparently served with the buccaneers from 1666 to 1674. It was translated into English in 1684 and proved a useful, if not always accurate, source of information about buccaneers for later writers of *marine literature such as Daniel Defoe and John *Masefield.

Bucentaur, the traditional name of the state *galley of the doges of Venice, from the Italian *buzino d'or*, golden *bark. The name was also given to any great and sumptuous galley. The last and finest of the Venetian *Bucentaurs* was built in 1729 and, like all its predecessors, was used in the annual procession for the traditional symbolic ceremony of the wedding of the sea by the doge on Ascension Day, a ceremony which commemorates the victory of the Doge Pietro Orseolo II over the Dalmatian pirates (see PIRACY) in the year 1000. This *Bucentaur* was destroyed by the French for its golden decorations during their invasion of the Italian states in 1798. Its remains are in the Museo Civico Correr in Venice, and there is a fine model of it in the arsenal there.

The name, in the form of *Bucentaure*, was used as a warship name in the French Navy in the 17th and 18th centuries, and Admiral *Villeneuve flew his flag at the battle of Trafalgar in a man-of-war called *Bucentaure*. See also WARFARE AT SEA.

'bucko' mate, the term applied to the *mate of a sailing trading ship of the late 19th and early 20th centuries who drove his crew by the power of his fists, and his general brutality which made life a hell on board for the crew. 'Bucko' mates were notably prevalent in the American *square-rigged ships on the New York or Boston to California run after the discovery of the goldfields there and before the railway to California was built. The competition to make quick passage round Cape Horn was always very fierce among these ships, and many owners appointed *masters and mates on whom they could rely to drive their crews to the limit, and sometimes beyond, in their search for speed. These men did not spare their voices, fists, or rope-ends to keep their crews at work whatever the weather. Many seamen in these ships went to their deaths in the seas around Cape Horn, mainly because exhaustion from being driven too hard caused them to miss their footing on the *yards when working the sails in a *gale.

A typical ship of this type was the 800-ton American clipper ship *Challenge*. Built in 1850 by William H. Webb of New York, she was commanded by the murderous 'Bully' Waterman, with the equally notorious 'bucko' mate Douglas, and she held the record for many years for the fastest passages from New York to California around Cape Horn.

budge-barrel, the small barrel of gunpowder which, in the days before powder was made up into cartridges, was brought on deck to serve the guns. It held a hundredweight (about 50 kg) of powder and the top end was fitted with a leather flap or bag drawn tight by a string which, when the barrel was brought to the guns, covered the open end to lessen the danger of accidental firing. After the introduction of cartridges, which dates from about 1580, budge-barrels were generally only used in harbour for the purpose of firing salutes. In the US Navy in the early 19th century budge-barrels were used as ready service lockers for powder cartridges and *shot for the swivel guns in the fighting *tops. See also POWDER MONKEY.

bugeye, a later and larger development of the *skipjack, used for offshore fishing and general cargo-carrying in the Chesapeake Bay area of the USA. Built originally as work boats and later copies as shallow draught *yachts, bugeyes ranged from 12.3 metres (40 ft) to about 23 metres (75 ft) in length and were generally *ketch rigged with their sails set on masts *raking aft.

buggalow, or **bugalilo,** the name used by the warrior people native to the Indian state of Maharashtra, which has Bombay as its capital, for the trading *dhows which used to work on the Malabar coast of India and in the Persian Gulf.

Builders Old Measurement, a system of measuring a ship's *tonnage adopted in Britain by Act of Parliament passed in 1773. As a system of measurement it gradually replaced the *burthen method of calculating a ship's carrying capacity and was the method by which a ship's port and harbour dues etc. could be calculated. The formula was

$$\frac{(L - 3/5B) \times B \times \frac{1}{2}B}{94}$$

where L equals the length of the ship measured from the *aft end of the keel to the fore side of the stem at the deck and B equals its maximum *beam, the result giving its measurement in tons. This formula remained in force until the mid-19th century when the introduction of iron as the most efficient material for *shipbuilding, and *steam propulsion, meant a new method of calculation had to be devised. See also THAMES MEASUREMENT.

bulbous bow, a rounded underwater projection forward of the ship's *stem, which has been fitted on most seagoing ships, from *cruise liners to *tankers to fishing boats, since the 1960s. The object of the bulbous bow is to create a *wave pattern which in perfect conditions neutralizes the one generated by the ship's hull, enabling it to leave a smooth wake and consequently make significant fuel savings. This phenomenon was first investigated by Lord Kelvin (see THOMSON, WILLIAM) and William Froude in the 19th century after observing that in certain conditions, the *ram bow of a warship reduced fuel consumption. For illus. see TRAWLER. Fred M. Walker

bulge, often used in the same sense as *bilge. A ship which was bulged (or bilged) was one whose bottom had been holed. It was also an expression to indicate that additional width had been built into a ship below the waterline by the construction of outer compartments in order to provide greater stability or, in the case of warships, greater protection from attack by *submarine.

bulk carrier, a generic term for a vessel which carries large quantities of any material in bulk, but is now generally used to describe a large merchant vessel developed during the 1950s to transport large volumes of unpacked commodities such as oil, bauxite, coal, grains in bulk, phosphate, nitrate, and iron ore. Oil/ore carriers are designed to carry both commodities. OBO (oil/bulk/ore) carriers, more complicated to build and more expensive, but potentially more profitable, can switch between different cargoes. All are now constructed with *bulbous bows and nearly all have the *bridge, engines, and accommodation placed *aft. OBOs make up such a large proportion of the 5,500 bulk carriers operating worldwide that they are now considered as a separate category of the world's shipping. All such carriers face the problems of cargo movement and cargo self-ignition. They must allow for the carriage of high-density cargoes which will bring the ship down to its *load line while leaving much of the *hold space empty.

Building such large vessels with their huge holds brought with it serious problems, and by the 1980s the loss of bulk carriers had reached worrying proportions. No less than 151 OBOs were lost between September 1980 and August 1987, including the **Derbyshire*, 38 of them having foundered at sea, sometimes with heavy loss of life. Between 1990 and May 1997 99 bulk carriers sank at sea with the loss of 654 lives.

Structural failure has certainly been the cause of some of these incidents. Along with all merchant ships, bulk carriers are designed and built to standards laid down by various *classification societies. But because of the corrosive nature of some of their cargoes, OBOs are particularly vulnerable to rust and can deteriorate quickly if the hull is not rigorously maintained. This, combined with using some *flags of convenience to cut costs, the huge *tonnage of cargo carried, and the necessity for *masters sometimes to maintain a high speed in adverse weather conditions to keep to their schedule, all add up to an intolerable stress on a bulk carrier's hull if it is past its prime.

A study by the International Association of Classification Societies found that, if flooding occurred for any reason in the foremost hold, the *bulkhead between it and the adjacent hold was liable to collapse, leading to a domino effect which eventually sank the vessel. This led the Maritime Safety Committee of the *International Maritime Organization to bring in stricter regulations for both existing and new bulk carriers, and in December 2002 it adopted amendments to Chapter XII of the *International Convention for the Safety of Life at Sea (SOLAS) to include additional safety measures for them.

bulkhead, a vertical partition, either *fore and *aft or *athwartships, dividing the hull into separate compartments. Main bulkheads, running athwartships, are normally made watertight, with watertight doors fitted where access through the bulkhead is required. A **collision bulkhead** is a watertight bulkhead situated near the bows of a ship to prevent the flooding of the rest of the hull in the event of a collision at sea.

Chinese *junks were built with watertight bulkheads from the earliest days. However, the first wooden ships to be fitted with them in the western world were the *bomb ketches *Erebus* and *Terror* which in 1839 took part in Captain James Ross's Antarctic exploration. *Terror*, holed aft by the *ice, was saved by her after bulkhead, arriving home with her after section full of water. With the introduction of iron, and later steel, as the material employed for *shipbuilding, transverse bulkheads, and thus division into watertight compartments, became normal practice, *Brunel's **Great Eastern* being the first to be constructed in this manner. See also CUBBRIDGE HEADS.

'bullock', a name given by sailors in the Royal Navy to a member of the Royal Marine Artillery before their amalgamation with the Royal Marine Light Infantry in 1923 to form the Royal *Marines. They were also known as Grabbies, Jollies, or Turkeys.

bull rope. (1) A rope used for hoisting a *topmast or *topgallant mast in a *square-rigged ship. It was *rove from the *cap of the lower mast, through a *sheave in the *heel of the topmast, and then back through a *block on the lower masthead, with the hauling part led to the deck. When a topmast was hoisted, a pull on the hauling part of the bull rope sent the topmast up to the height where the *fid, which held it securely in place, could be inserted. The reverse operation lowered the topmast. But see also TRIPPING LINE. **(2)** A line rove temporarily through a *bullseye on the end of a *yacht's *bowsprit and secured to a *mooring *buoy. It was designed to hold the buoy well clear of the yacht's bows and prevent it striking or rubbing against the hull.

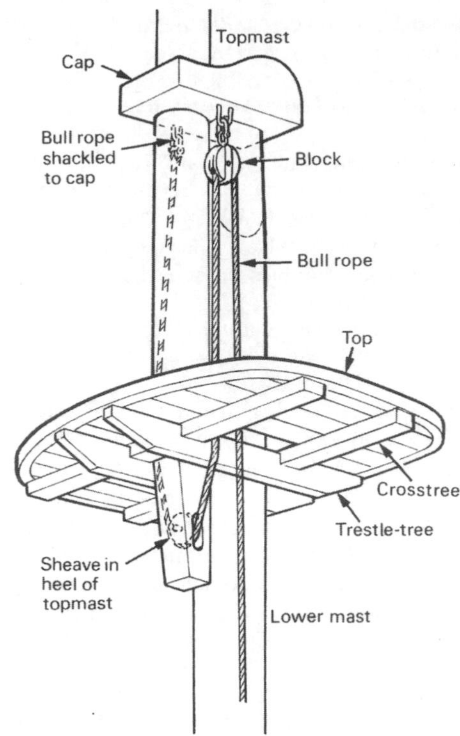

Bull rope

bullseye. (1) A circular piece of **lignum vitae*, hollowed in the centre to take a rope and grooved round the outside to accommodate a *strop which enables it to be fixed in position where required. Its main purpose is to change the lead, or direction, of a rope in cases where a *block for this purpose is not required. **(2)** It is also the name given to a piece of thick glass set flush in the deck of a ship to admit light to the deck below. **(3)** The small expanse of blue sky seen in the centre of a *tropical storm. **(4)** See PARREL.

bully beef, originally the seaman's name for the salt beef from which all the fat and substance has been boiled away by the cook to enrich his grease tub, which was one of his perquisites. The name comes from the French *bœuf bouilli*. See also FANNY ADAMS.

bulwark, the planking or woodwork, or steel plating in the case of steel ships, along the sides of a ship above its upper deck to prevent seas washing over the *gunwales. It also helped prevent any person on board who inadvertently fell from being washed overboard in rough weather. In sailing ships which used to round Cape Horn, nets were frequently rigged above the bulwarks to provide an added security against any of the crew being washed overboard.

bumboat, a small boat used for carrying vegetables, fruit, and provisions to ships lying in harbour. The term possibly derives from the Dutch *boomboat,* a broad-beamed fishing boat, but also possibly from *bumbay,* an old Suffolk word meaning quagmire. The word first appears in England in the by-laws of *Trinity House is 1685 under which scavenging boats attending ships in the Thames were regulated. These boats were employed to remove 'filth' from ships, and also to carry vegetables for sale on board. Apparently hygiene was not highly regarded by Trinity House in 1685.

bumpkin, or **bumkin,** originally a short boom projecting forward one either side of the bows of a *square-rigged sailing ship, used to extend the *clew of the *foresail to *windward. It had a *block fixed to the outer end through which the *tack was *rove and hauled aboard. Similarly, it was the name of a short boom which extended from each *quarter of a sailing vessel to carry the main *brace blocks. In its modern meaning it is a short *spar extending directly over the stern of a sailing vessel to which the *mizzen sheet is rove in cases where the mizzen-mast is stepped so far *aft that there is not enough room inboard to *trim the sheet. The name is also used to describe a short spar extending from the *stem of a *yacht in place of a *bowsprit.

'bundleman', a sailor's name, used in the Royal Navy during the days of sail, for another who is married. The term is derived from the days when men were allowed to purchase naval provisions at a cheap rate for their families, and a married man would be recognized by the bundle of provisions he carried when going ashore.

bunk, a built-in wooden bed on board ship. In the main *cabin of some sailing vessels engaged in trade during the 18th and 19th centuries the sides were lined with bunks fitted with sliding panels to provide privacy, since the captain, *mates, and any lady passengers, or the captain's wife, were all accommodated there. In the early *ocean liners, particularly on the Transatlantic route, passengers who could not afford a cabin went *steerage class instead, where bunks were erected in tiers one above the other, to obtain the maximum sleeping accommodation within the minimum space.

bunkers, compartments on board ship, most usually placed along the sides and bottom, for the stowage of fuel, whether coal or oil. The operation of filling or replenishing a ship's bunker with fuel is known as **bunkering**. See also STEAM PROPULSION.

bunt, the middle section of a square sail where it was cut full to form a belly. It applied more especially to *topsails than to lower sails which were generally cut square with only a small allowance for bunt. In a *square-rigged ship the bunt of the topsails was frequently so heavy and voluminous that a **bunt-jigger** was fitted to the sails to assist in *furling them. This was a small *tackle of two single *blocks by means of which the bunt of the sail was hauled up to the *yard so that the *gaskets could be secured. **Bunters**, the *topmen working in the centre of the yards who gathered in the bunt when furling the sails. When a square-rigged ship was sailing before the wind she was said to be **bunt-fair**.

bunting, a thin cloth of woven wool supplied in various colours from which are made flags of the *International Code of Signals, and other coloured flags such as *ensigns. Originally, the name for bunting was bewpars. It is the most satisfactory material for flags as it is light enough to spread well even in a gentle wind, and yet is more resistant to fraying in a hard wind than many heavier materials.

buntline hitch, used on *square-rigged ships to secure a line to rings on the *bunt of a sail. However much strain or movement it is subjected to it will not come undone.

buntlines, ropes fastened to *cringles on the bottom edges of square sails to draw the *bunt of the sail up to the *yards. They are *rove through *blocks attached to the yard and then inboard to centreline *blocks and down to the deck, usually to *belaying pins on *fife rails or *pinrails. A strip of *canvas called the **buntline band** is sometimes fitted on the forward side of a square sail to take the chafe of the buntlines. Crew often have to 'overhaul the buntlines' by slacking them from the yard to prevent them girding the *foot of the sail.

buoy, a floating mark used in the *IALA maritime buoyage system to mark a channel, bank, *spoil ground, or similar area which the *navigator needs to know about. The marking system in force in any particular area is given in the *sailing directions for those waters. However, buoys have other uses besides being aids to *navigation as they also mark the position of telegraph cables or mining grounds, sewer outfalls, etc. All these can have distinctive shapes and colours, the details of which are marked on navigational *charts. There are also strings of radio transmitting buoys worldwide which transmit weather conditions like wind strength and height of *waves.

Most buoys, particularly those marking main navigational channels, are lit for navigation at night, each type with its individual *characteristic. Cylinders of gas used to be the common method of lighting but most lighted buoys have now been converted to solar power. See also BEACONS; DAN BUOY; MOORING; WATCH BUOY.

buoyancy tank, or **airtank,** an airtight, watertight compartment that provides buoyancy to keep a small boat afloat in case it takes on water. John Rousmaniere

burgee, a broad, tapering pennant, normally with a swallow tail but occasionally without. Burgees of *yacht clubs are normally triangular, of a length twice that of the depth at the *hoist, and carry on them the particular insignia of the club concerned. Commodores of yacht clubs usually fly swallow-tailed burgees again carrying the insignia of the club. Burgees without a swallow tail are used as the substitute flags in the *International Code of Signals.

burgoo, an old seafaring dish from the days of sail, a sort of porridge or gruel made of boiled oatmeal seasoned with salt, sugar, and butter. It had the merit of being easily prepared in the *galley during rough weather and was sustaining enough for seamen to perform the heavy work of the ship.

burthen, the term used in Britain to express a ship's *tonnage, or carrying capacity. It was based on the number of *tuns of wine that a ship could carry in its *holds, the total number giving its burthen. The term remained as an expression of a ship's size until the end of the 18th century, but its use gradually declined after a new system of measurement, *Builders Old Measurement, was adopted by Act of Parliament in 1733.

Bushnell, David (*c.*1742–1824), American inventor, one of the fathers of the *submarine. Graduating from Yale in 1775, the year of the first skirmish between British troops in America and the colonists, he had bitter feelings against Britain and determined to put his engineering abilities to use in aid of the American colonies in revolt. He designed and built a small wooden 'submarine' named USS *Turtle*. It was shaped like an egg, floated upright in the water, and could be trimmed down until the *conning tower was *awash by admitting water to two small internal tanks. This curious vessel carried a detachable charge of 68 kilograms (150 lb) of gunpowder which could be fixed to the bottom of an enemy ship by means of a screw. In 1776, when the British fleet was lying off New York, Bushnell *launched his submarine with a sergeant in the American Army, Ezra Lee, operating it by turning a *propeller by hand. Lee managed to force it under the hull of HMS *Eagle*, flying the flag of Lord Howe (1726–99), but was unable to screw the charge home as Bushnell had not made allowance for the fact that the bottoms of British warships at that time had *copper sheathing. At the end of the war in 1782, Bushnell gave up his submarine experiments and, assuming another name, became a successful doctor.

busking, an old term, long obsolete, for a ship *beating to *windward along a coastline. It was also a term used when describing pirate vessels cruising in search of victims to attack. See PIRACY.

buss, a fishing vessel, mainly used in the *herring *fisheries, broad in the *beam with two, and sometimes three, masts with a single square sail on each and usually of from 50 to 70 tons, though it could be larger. The term, though known throughout Europe, was mainly used to signify Dutch and English fishing vessels in the North Sea, and by the 15th century the Dutch had a fleet of 300. By some the origin of the term is thought to be the old French *busse*, a cask. The development of the *ketch with its handier rig gradually superseded the older fishing busses.

'butcher's bill', old naval slang for the dead and wounded after battle.

butt. **(1)** The squared end of a plank used on the side or deck of a wooden vessel. It is also the name given to the space between the two squared ends of adjoining planks in a ship's side, which has to be *caulked. Similarly, the ends of plates used in the sides or decks of iron or steel ships are also known as butts. **To start a butt** is when the end of a plank springs clear of, or loosens from, its fastening to a ship's *timbers, usually as a result of heavy weather. See also SHIPBUILDING. **(2)** A cask containing 126 gallons (573 litres).

Butter-box, a derisory name used by British naval seamen during the First (1652–4) and Second (1665–7) Anglo-Dutch Wars to describe Dutch seamen. As a *sea song, written to commemorate the British victory at the St James's Day battle, 25 July 1666, has it:

> The cannons from the Tower did roar,
> When this good news did come to shore,
> The bells did ring and bone-fires shine,
> And healths carrous'd in beer and wine,
> God bless King Charles and all our fleet,
> And grant true friends may safely meet,
> *Then Butter-boxes brag no more,*
> *For now we have beaten you or'e and or'e.*

buttock lines, longitudinal sections of a ship's hull parallel to the centreline. See also NAVAL ARCHITECTURE.

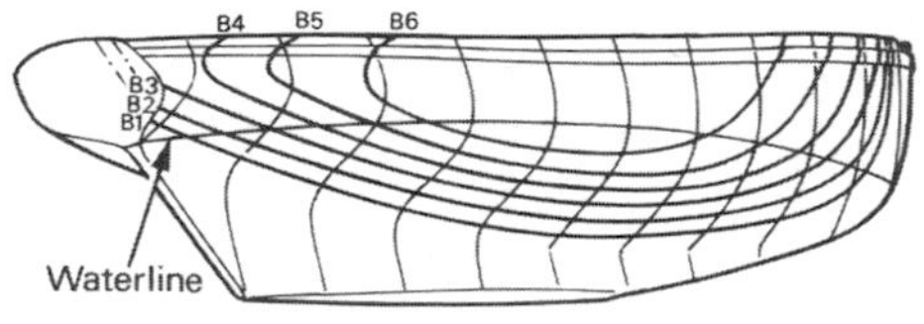

Buttock lines

Buys Ballot law, a rough and ready method of discovering the direction of the centre of a circular storm. If an observer faces the direction of the true wind, the centre of low pressure will be between eight and twelve *points (90°–135°) on his right hand in the northern hemisphere, and on his left hand in the southern. It takes its name from C. H. D. Buys Ballot, a Dutch meteorologist, who published it in his *Comptes rendus* (1857). See also MARINE METEOROLOGY.

by, in relation to the wind. To sail a vessel **by the wind** is to sail *square-riggers to *windward with the *yards fully braced, or, in *fore-and-aft-rigged vessels, with the sheets *hardened in. To sail a vessel **full and by** is to sail her to windward with the sails *eased and full of wind. When sailing **by the lee** the wind has been brought, when sailing downwind, to come across the stern and bear on the wrong side of the fore-and-aft sails. This may cause one or more sails to swing dangerously across the ship and may cause her to *broach.

by guess and by God, a phrase which in earlier days described a form of *navigation under which the ship's *master or *navigator relied more on his experience and memory to bring his vessel safely to her destination than on the formal processes of navigation.

Mike Richey

Byng, John (1704–57), British admiral, the fourth son of George Byng, Viscount Torrington and admiral of the fleet. With his father's influence to help him he quickly reached *flag rank though without any real experience of command. At the outbreak of the Seven Years War (1756–63), he was given command of a fleet to support British forces in the island of Minorca, then under siege by the French. He was delayed at Gibraltar by arguments with the governor, and on arrival off Minorca found the island held by the French but with the English garrison holding out in Port Mahon. He fought an indecisive action against the French fleet which was covering the French invasion, but four days later, after a council of war, returned to Gibraltar and left Port Mahon to its fate. He was arrested and brought back to England, where he was court-martialled on a charge of failing to do his utmost to save the island. He was found guilty and sentenced to death. A recommendation for mercy was refused, probably because the government needed a political scapegoat for the defeat. He was shot on the *quarterdeck of HMS *Monarch* on 14 March 1757 and his execution inspired Voltaire's remark in *Candide* that in England it was sometimes necessary to shoot an admiral 'pour encourager les autres'.

by the board, see BOARD (7).

by the head, a ship is said to be by the head when it draws more than its normal depth of water forward, with its bows lying deeper than its stern. Similarly, a ship is said to be **by the stern** when it is drawing more than its normal depth of water *aft. It is a result of the faulty trimming of the ship's internal *ballast or badly stowed cargo, or perhaps a leak.

by the lee, see BY.

C

cabin, (possibly from the Latin *capanna*, little house), a room or space in a ship partitioned off by *bulkheads to provide a private apartment for officers, passengers, and crew members for sleeping and/or eating. The 13th-century explorer *Marco Polo reported that Chinese *junks used by merchants had as many as 60 cabins for their passengers. In Europe the first cabin as such was probably the carosse, an open space under a *galley's *poop deck where the admiral or captain had his bed. In later ships, the same space was enclosed by bulkheads to provide the 'great cabin', which was the admiral's or captain's living quarters, often divided into sleeping cabin and day cabin, where he kept his 'table', served by his private cook and servants. Forward of the great cabin, in larger ships, was another cabin known as the *coach where in *flagships the flag-captain lived. As sailing ships, particularly warships, grew larger, with additional decks, there were two coaches, upper and lower, to provide additional cabins for officers. From about the early 17th century to mid-19th century, most officers of ships below the rank of captain were allowed temporary cabins, created by *canvas screens or removable wooden bulkheads, in which a *cot and a clothes chest took up most of the available room. These cabins could be quickly dismantled when necessary.

The use of iron, and later steel, as the main building material for ships, combined with the 19th-century expansion of travel and trade, brought about the construction in ships of permanent cabins for officers, and in *ocean liners for some of the higher-paying passengers, although during the period a majority of passengers still travelled in the *steerage. The continuing growth of travel led inevitably to the provision of cabins for all passengers, and ocean liners later had *staterooms as well as luxury cabins. See also HUDDOCK.

cabin sole, a *yachting term to describe the floorboards of the *cabin accommodation, or cabin deck space. The planks rest on sole bearers which are carried *athwartships beneath the sole.

cable. **(1)** Basically any very large *hemp or wire rope, but normally associated with the anchor of a ship, and thus the means by which the ship is attached to the anchor as it lies on the bottom or is stowed in the *hawsepipe or inboard. Originally, all such cables were of hemp, and an early definition of a cable, *c.*1740, was a hemp rope of 20 inches (50.8 cm) in circumference containing 1,943 yarns—a yarn being rope fibres twisted right handed—although the term was rapidly revised downwards to include any rope of 10 inches (25.4 cm) or more in circumference. By 1780 the general rule for the size of an anchor cable was half an inch (1.27 cm) for every foot (30.5 cm) in beam of the ship; thus a ship with a beam of 60 feet (18.3 m) had a cable 30 inches (76.2 cm) in circumference. Such a size of cable was that normally supplied to a first-*rate ship of war; it was tested to a breaking strain of 65 tons, and, in the days when *fathoms were used as a measurement of length (and depth), 100 fathoms (183 m/600 ft) weighed 12.5 tons. Chain cable first made an appearance in about 1800 (*Nelson's attack on the French invasion vessels anchored in Boulogne in 1801 was frustrated by the use of chain cables by the French ships), but was not introduced into the US Navy until after the War of 1812. In its larger sizes the links of chain cable are studded across the middle to prevent them kinking, and its size is measured by the diameter of the links. **(2)** A measure of length of cable. The length of a rope cable is 100–115 fathoms (600–90 ft/183–218 m), and a *hawser-laid cable 130 fathoms (780 ft/238 m). Studded chain anchor cable is made in lengths of 15 and 7.5 fathoms (90–45 ft/27.4–13.7 m), and is known as 'shackles of cable' and 'half-shackles of cable' respectively, though before 1949 a shackle of cable used in the Royal Navy was 12.5 fathoms (75 ft/22.8 m) long, eight shackles being considered as a cable length. **(3)** A measure of distance at sea. In Britain this equates to one-tenth of a *nautical mile (6,080 ft/ 1,854 m) or 608 feet (185 m), but sometimes 100 fathoms or 600 feet. In the USA a cable is 720 feet (220 m).

cable-holders, two *capstan-like fittings mounted on the *forecastle deck of larger ships by which the two *bower anchors are *weighed or *veered. They are set either side of the centreline of the ship in the line of the bower cables, and the chain links of the cables fit into cavities round the drum of the cable-holders so that they are held firmly. When a bower anchor is being weighed, its cable-holder is geared into the capstan engine so that the anchor is hove in mechanically; when the anchor is being let go or veered, the cable-holder is unclutched from the capstan engine and can run freely, its speed being controlled by a friction brake, which is also used to hold the cable when the ship lies to its anchor. In very large ships which carry a *sheet anchor in addition to two bower anchors, a third cable-holder is not fitted, the sheet anchor cable being brought to the capstan for weighing and veering.

In smaller vessels a *windlass takes the place of capstan and cable-holders, with *gypsies, fitted to take the links of the bower cables, mounted inboard of each warping drum.

cable-laid rope, a very thick and strong rope used only for the heaviest work on board ship and for the towing cable of a *tug. It is made by *laying up three ordinary ropes which have themselves been made by laying up three *strands. Whereas in ordinary rope, known as *hawser rope, the three strands are laid up from left to right, in cable-laid rope the three hawsers must be laid up from right to left; otherwise the strands in the hawser become untwisted and lose much of their strength and durability. If, in the days when *fathoms were used, three hawser-laid ropes of 120 fathoms (720 ft/220 m) each were laid up in this way, they made a cable-laid rope of 100 fathoms (600 ft/183 m).

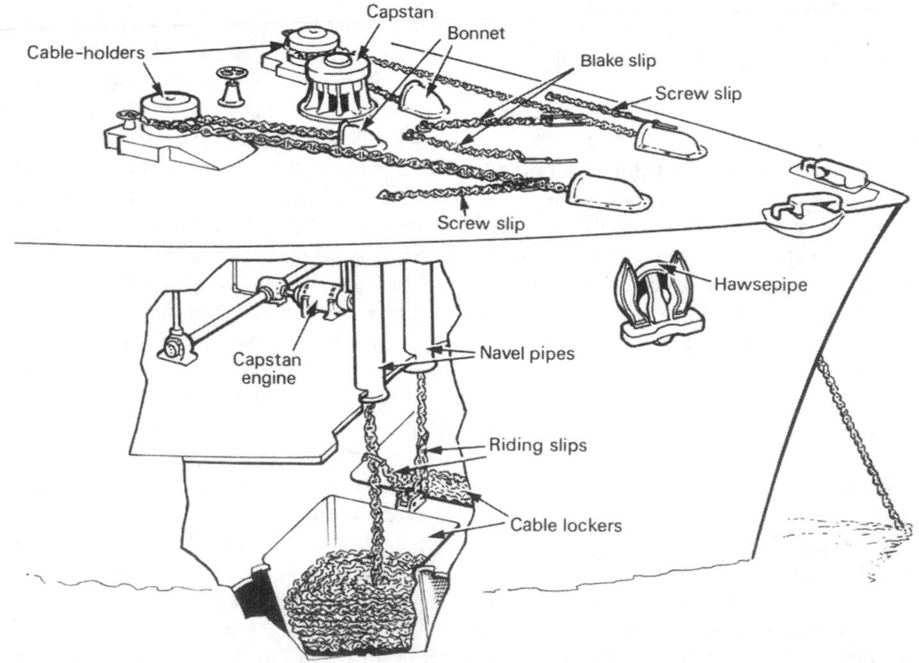

Cable-holders

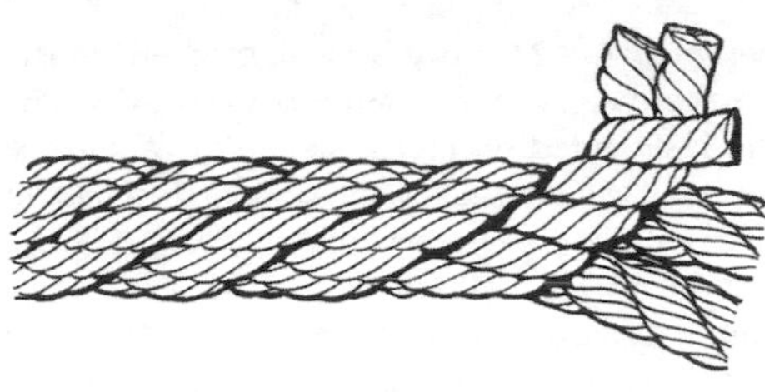

Cable-laid rope

Cable-laid rope is sometimes known as cablet, and also as water-laid rope, because it absorbs less water than hawser-laid rope.

cable ship, a vessel fitted for the laying and repairing of submarine telegraph and telephone cables. One of the earliest and best-known cable ships was the *Great Eastern*, so used after she had failed as an *ocean liner. A distinctive feature of modern cable ships is the large roller built out over the bows of the ship for paying out or underrunning cable.

cable stoppers, usually known as slips, are used to hold the *cable when a ship lies to an anchor, either as a preventer, or stand-by, when the cable is held by the brake of the *cable-holder, or to hold the cable temporarily so that the inboard part of it can be handled. There are four types of stopper normally used for cable work in larger ships, all tested to half the proof load of the cable.

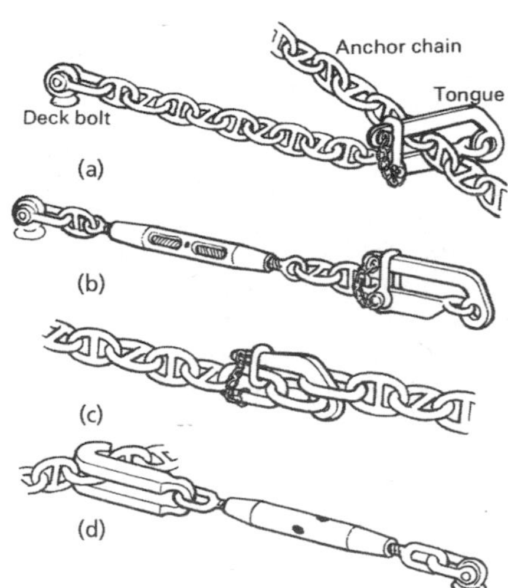

[a] Blake slip [b] Screw slip [c] Senhouse slip [d] Devil's claw

Blake slip, a general purpose slip, in which the tongue passes over a link of the cable. It consists of a short length of studded chain shackled to a deck bolt close to the line of the cable between the cable-holder and the *hawsehole, with the slip attached to the end of the chain. Its main use is as a preventer when the ship lies to its anchor but it is also used to hold the cable if work is necessary on its inboard end.

Screw slip, a Blake slip with a *bottlescrew incorporated in the length of chain. It is used when securing an anchor for sea, the bottlescrew being turned to bring the *flukes of the anchor hard home in the *hawsepipe.

Riding slip, again a Blake slip, usually shackled to a deck bolt immediately above each cable locker, though occasionally on the upper deck between the cable-holder and the *navel pipe. When a ship is lying to an anchor is riding to the brake on the cable-holder, the riding slip is put on as a preventer in case the brake *renders.

Senhouse slip, a slip designed to secure the end of a cable. In this slip the tongue passes through the end link of the cable, which is studless, and not across a link as in the other slips. Its normal place in a ship used to be in the cable lockers where the inboard end of the cable is secured, but in modern ships the end of the cable is shackled on to a deck bolt in the locker, no Senhouse slip being used. Smaller Senhouse slips are used in many smaller vessels and *yachts to hold the ends of the *guardrails to the *stanchions. In these cases the tongue passes through an eye in the end of the guardrail.

In many merchant vessels the cable is stoppered with a **devil's claw** in place of a slip. Here there is no tongue, its place being taken by a fitting in the shape of two claws, the gap between them being the diameter of a cable link. The claws are passed across a link that lies horizontally on the deck and hold the link next to it, which must lie vertically.

cable-tier, in the days of *hemp anchor *cables, the space left in the centre of a cable locker when the cable was coiled round the outside with the *flakes on top of each other.

caboose, also **camboose,** from the Dutch, a defunct term used to describe the *galley, or cookhouse, of a small vessel. It was normally built on deck, and in shape resembled a sentry box. It was originally a wooden box or covering of the galley chimney where it came through the deck, hence probably its association with cooking. The name applied only to smaller merchant ships, all larger ships having space for a galley between decks.

Cabot, John, the Anglicized form of **Caboto, Giovanni** (*c.*1450–98), Italian *navigator. Very little is known of his early life but it is believed that he was born in Genoa and as a boy went to Venice where he was naturalized as a Venetian citizen. He appears to have commanded a merchant ship which traded to the Levant and on one of these voyages is said to have visited Mecca where he was amazed by the market there in spices, silk, and jewels. Being told that they came overland by caravan from Asia, and knowing that the earth was a sphere, he was seized with the idea that it would be quicker to bring them to Europe by sea if he could reach Cathay and Cipangu, the names by China and Japan were known to Europeans in the 15th–17th centuries, by crossing the western ocean. Filled with this belief, but unable to convince the European courts to the extent of equipping an expedition, Cabot brought his family to London in 1484, and tried to persuade the more important merchants of Bristol that an attempt should be made to reach Cathay by sea. They agreed to take the risk of such a voyage but stipulated that he should first go by way of *Brasil and the Isle of the Seven Cities, those mythical islands which were shown on all the medieval maps of the western ocean.

Before the expedition could be organized and dispatched, news was received in England of Christopher *Columbus's voyage. The British merchants now decided that time should not be spent searching for either Brasil or the Isle of the Seven Cities, but that the expedition should go direct to Asia by sailing west. Letters patent were granted by King Henry VII in March 1496 to his 'well-beloved John Gabote, citizen of Venice . . . to seeke out, discover and finde whatsoever isles, countries, regions or provinces of the heathen and infidels which before this time have been unknown to all Christians'. He set sail from Bristol in May 1497 in a small ship called the *Matthew*, manned by eighteen men. On 24 June Cabot sighted one of the northern capes of Newfoundland, on which island he landed, and took possession of it in the name of the king. On its return the ship passed over what are now known as the *Grand Banks off the Newfoundland coast where the crew caught huge quantities of *cod merely by lowering baskets into the sea. It was this discovery which led directly to the development of the Newfoundland *fisheries.

On his return Cabot received £10 reward from the king for having discovered the 'new island' which he thought, and convinced the king, was off the coast of Cathay. He proposed to Henry VII that a new expedition could not only repeat the voyage but by sailing to the south after making the coast would surely reach Cipangu and thus make London the greatest trading centre in the world for the products of the East. Cabot, after the king's promise of a second expedition, made a visit to Seville and Lisbon in an effort to recruit men who had sailed with Columbus, but appears to have had little success. Henry VII issued new letters patent on 3 February 1498 giving Cabot the power to 'impress' six English ships for the voyage. However, only five were taken up; they were victualled for a year, and, in accord with the king's licence, Cabot, proceeding westwards from his last discovery until he reached the coast of Cipangu, was to set up a trading factory there for spices and silks.

This second expedition, of five ships and 300 men, sailed from Bristol in May 1498 and was never heard of again. For some 450 years it got somehow mixed up with a voyage made in 1500 by Jão Fernandez, known as Llavrador (farmer), to the east coast of Greenland, which was mistakenly named Labrador (after Fernandez) in the belief that it was a new discovery, and another in 1501 by Gaspar Corte Real, which seems to have visited Newfoundland or the mainland of America thereabouts. These two voyages appear to have become amalgamated and were held by some authorities to constitute Cabot's second voyage, from which they have him returning safely to Bristol and dying there shortly after. See also EXPLORATION BY SEA.

Harisse, H., *John Cabot* (1896).

Williamson, James A., *The Cabot Voyages and Bristol Discovery under Henry VII* (Hakluyt Society, 1962).

cabotage, the French name for the coasting trade. Many people believe that it is derived from *cabo*, Spanish for cape, as coasting ships generally sailed from cape to cape, but a more likely derivation is the French word *cabot*, a small vessel.

caique, from the Turkish *kaik*, a boat or *skiff. **(1)** In its strict meaning it refers to the light boats propelled by one or two *oars and used in Turkish waters, particularly the Bosporus, but it was also used as a term for the sultan's ceremonial barge when he went by water to a mosque or to his harem. The word has since been loosely applied to most small rowing boats and skiffs in the Levant. **(2)** A small Levantine sailing vessel, usually with a *lateen rig, but here again the name has been loosely expanded to include a variety of modern sailing and motorized vessels, used mainly for island trade.

caisson, from the French *caisson*, large chest, basically an enclosed space below water level with means of flooding with, or pumping out, water. **(1)** A fixed enclosure reaching to the bottom from which the water can be pumped out, or which can alternatively be filled with air under pressure, in order to give access to underwater areas for engineering works, such as the building of piers for bridges, breakwaters, etc. **(2)** The gate or movable structure which closes the entrance to a *dock or *dry-dock. **(3)** A floating platform or tank used by *salvage operators. It can be submerged by the admission of water and, when in position under a *wreck or other obstruction, pumped out in order to use the resulting buoyancy as a lifting force. See also CAMEL.

calashee, or **coolashi, watch,** a *watch on deck on a *square-rigged ship in which all hands, including the watch below, must stand by for a call. They were most frequently required when a sailing ship was *tacking in narrow waters or in a particularly heavy sea. The word came apparently from the Hindustani *khalasi*, sailor, as the system on board native ships was to work their watches in this fashion.

Cales, the name by which the Spanish port of Cadiz was known in Britain up to the beginning of the 17th century.

calf. (1) The name given to the young of *whales and *dolphins. **(2)** In polar regions calving occurs when a block of *ice breaks from a glacier to form an iceberg. An area of pack ice that has broken from the main area of pack by pressure generated by wind and *currents is also known as a calf. **(3)** The term used to describe the small islets which lie off larger islands, such the Calf of Mull, or the Calf of Man.

calibre, a term used for the measurement of guns. It is employed in two senses, but its strict meaning is the length of the gun expressed as a multiple of the bore or internal diameter measured at the muzzle; e.g. a 12-in. gun 30 feet (9 m) long would be a 12-in. (30-cm) gun of 30 calibres. In its second sense the word expresses the bore of the gun, again measured at the muzzle, such as 6-in. calibre, 12-in. calibre, etc.

call, see BOATSWAIN'S PIPE.

call sign, a particular group of letters or numbers in the *Morse code used for identification.

camber. (1) The *athwartships curve of a ship's deck, usually giving a fall towards the sides of a quarter of an inch (6.35 mm) to each foot (30.5 cm). **(2)** A small enclosed *dock in a *dockyard in which timber for masts and *yards was kept to weather and pickle in salt water, and used also to provide a shelter for small boats. In the USA such a dock was known as a **cob** or **cobb** dock.

camel. (1) Originally a wooden case made in two halves to fit on either side of a ship's keel. Both were filled with water and fitted to the keel by divers. The water was then pumped out to provide extra buoyancy if a ship had to pass over a *shoal. From this was evolved the *caisson. **(2)** A strong wooden stage sometimes used as a *fender when a ship lies alongside a *wharf.

camship, a merchant ship fitted in the Second World War (1939–45) with a catapult with which fighter aircraft could be launched to protect the ship, or the *convoy it was in, from air attacks. The fighter could not, of course, land back on board once it had been launched, and the pilot returned by ditching as close as possible to a merchant ship so he could be picked up, the aircraft being abandoned. The name came from the initial letters of **catapult aircraft merchant ship**.

can buoy, a *buoy in the form of a truncated cone used in the *IALA maritime buoyage system. See also LATERAL MARK.

cannon. Authorities differ regarding the date at which cannon were first mounted on board ships in the western world, confusion often arising from differences of interpretation of medieval Latin phrases used by scholars and historians with no personal knowledge of weapons. The first known record is that which states that guns made in Tournai were aboard the ships that Louis Mâle sent to attack Antwerp in 1336.

The early guns were either cast in bronze—a technique long known and used for making church bells—or made of wrought iron. The latter were built up from bars of iron welded into crude tubes and strengthened by hoops shrunk on to the outside. A bronze cylinder might be inserted at the breech end to serve as a powder chamber. However, cast iron replaced wrought iron for all but the largest pieces during the 16th century, bronze being too expensive when guns were manufactured in large quantities.

The cannon of the 15th and 16th centuries was of large calibre and medium length and range. Its two principal sub-types were the 'whole' cannon, of approximately 7-in. (18-cm) calibre, 11 feet (3.4 m) in length and firing a 50-lb (23-kg) ball; and the 'demi-cannon' of much the same length but of 6-in. (15.2-cm) calibre and firing a 32-lb (14.5-kg) shot. With improvement in the quality of gunpowder during the 17th century, guns were shortened, permitting greater calibres for the same weight. Even such large pieces as the 'cannon-royal', weighing some 8,000 lb (3,632 kg) and firing a 66-lb (30-kg) shot, were sometimes mounted. However, by the end of the period, by which time all ships' guns were identified by the weight of shot they fired, the usual sizes were the 42-pounder on the *lower decks and the 24-pounder on the upper gundecks. For other types mounted aboard ships, see GUN.

canoe, originally a small open boat which, by definition, was used by primitive nations. During the 17th–18th centuries the native craft seen by those involved in the *exploration by sea of the Pacific and other areas were also called canoes, though some found in the Pacific were, and are, remarkably large sailing vessels, usually either *catamarans or *outriggers; others were propelled by two banks of paddlers, up to 20 or 30 a side. Two of the most efficient ocean-going canoes were the twin-hulled *Pahi* of the Tahitian and Tuamotuan archipelago, and the Tongan *Tongiaki*, both of which were between 15 and 21 metres (50–70 ft) long. Some encountered by Captain *Cook were longer than his *Endeavour* and carried as many as 80–100 men. As David *Lewis noted in his book *We, the Navigators*, and as John *Voss proved, the seagoing canoe in all its varieties is extremely seaworthy and can cover great distances in safety. See also KAYAK; PROA; SEPULCHRAL SHIPS.

cant. (1) The name given to those *timbers in a ship towards the bow and the stern which are angled (or canted) from the *athwartships direction. **(2)** When used as a verb it is the operation of turning a ship's head one way or the other, according to the requirement at the time, when *weighing anchor or slipping from a *mooring. It may, for example, be necessary to cant the ship's head to *port, or *starboard, in order to avoid shipping or other hazards in the immediate vicinity. See also CAST, TO. **(3)** in *whaling, a cut made in a *whale between the neck and the fins to which the *purchase, known as a cant purchase, was secured in order to turn the animal round during the operation of *flensing.

cant rope, an old name for four-stranded rope *laid up without a central core. See also SHROUD-LAID ROPE; CABLE-LAID ROPE.

Canute, or **Cnut** (*c*.995–1035), the king of Denmark and England who sat on the bank of the Thames at Westminster and ordered the tide to go back. He did this, in fact, to demonstrate to his courtiers that there were forces in the world greater than war, and to prepare them for his submission to the Holy See in Rome. Among his many qualities he was a great leader and commanded fleets at sea, defeating the Swedish fleet at Stangeberg and the combined Norwegian–Swedish fleet at the mouth of the Helgeaa, both in 1028. See also WARFARE AT SEA.

canvas. (1) A cloth properly woven from *hemp, the word deriving from *kannabis*, the

Greek word for hemp. In the days of the *square-rigger it was used in *sailors' dress and is still occasionally used at sea, mainly for *awnings and coverings. Before the days of synthetic fibre, sails were also made from it and a ship's sail was generically known as its canvas. It is numbered according to the thickness and weave, the lowest number being the coarsest and strongest. **(2)** It is also a synonym for a ship being under sail, it being said to be **under canvas.** See also TARPAULIN.

cap, the wooden block on the top of a mast through which the mast above is drawn when being *stepped or being struck down (see STRIKE DOWN, TO). It has two holes, one of them square which is fixed firmly to the top of the lower mast, the other circular through which the topmast is hoisted, until its *heel is nearly level with the base of the cap. Once in position it is secured with a *fid and sometimes also with a *parrel lashing, and is held upright by *shrouds and *stays. In ships where *topgallant masts were stepped, there were similar caps on the tops of the topmasts. A *bowsprit cap serves a similar service for the *jib-boom. See also BULL ROPE.

Cape Horners. **(1)** Originally the American *square-rigged ships which during the 19th century ran regularly from the east to the west coast of America around Cape Horn. Comparatively few ships made this passage before 1847, but the discovery of gold in California in that year gave rise to the famous Californian *clipper ships which instituted a regular service. Commanded for the most part by hard-case captains and *'bucko' mates, they set many records and were driven unmercifully through the huge seas south of the Horn, frequently with loss of lives and *spars. This merciless driving quickly 'broke the heart' of these magnificent ships and few survived for more than five years at the most. The building of a railway across the Isthmus of Panama in 1857 was the signal for their decline and ultimate withdrawal from this trade.

By extension, the term Cape Horner has also been applied to all big sailing ships which regularly used the Cape Horn route, particularly those carrying cargo from Europe or Africa westwards to South American ports around the Horn and returning eastwards with grain, nitrates, guano, or hides. This was a regular trade until well into the first decades of the 20th century, but was virtually killed off by the opening of the *Panama Canal in 1914.

(2) Those who belonged to an association, Amicale Internationale des Captaines au Long Cours Cap Horniers (AICH), and who now belong to its latter-day equivalent, the International Association of Cape Horners (IACH). The AICH was founded at Saint-Malo, France, in 1937 for men who had sailed round Cape Horn in commercial square-riggers, as the founders wished to honour Professor Georges Delarney, who had held the Chair of Navigation at Saint-Malo, 1895–1910, under whom they had all studied. After the Second World War (1939–45) membership was extended to other countries and the association became an international one with affiliated national sections. The British one, which included Alan *Villiers, was formed in 1957, though the last commercial square-rigger to round the Horn had been the *Pamir* in July 1949. However, with the introduction of round-the-world *yacht races (see YACHTING: ROUND-THE-WORLD COMPETITIONS), the British section decided in 1973 to introduce a new category of membership, yacht members. In 1996 AICH decided not to accept this category and the British section therefore founded the IACH, which incorporated its original British AICH members. With the gradual passing of its original members, the AICH decided in May 2003 to lower its flag, but the IACH continues the traditions of the original association.

Cape Horn fever, an imaginary disease from which malingerers at sea were supposed to suffer. Its origin lay in the reluctance of many seamen to sign *articles in a ship making a passage of Cape Horn from east to west under sail, the contrary winds and heavy seas frequently entailing almost non-stop work on the *yards in numbing conditions.

caper, from the Frisian *kapen,* to steal, rob, plunder. It was a lightly armed ship of the 17th century used by the Dutch as a *privateer or *corsair. The word was, by extension, also used to designate the captain of a privateer.

capital ship, a term used in navies to denote the most important type of warship in the national fleet. For centuries throughout the era of sailing navies it was the *ship of the line, but after the introduction of iron, and later steel, construction, the *battleship was the capital ship of the world's navies. The development of ship-borne air power during and after the Second World War (1939–45), which rendered the battleship virtually obsolete, for a time made the *aircraft carrier into the capital ship of most navies. But this type of warship in its turn suffered from the development of its own original source of power into modern airborne, long-range weapons making it too vulnerable a target to be classed a capital ship any longer. When the missile-firing *submarine with nuclear weapons was introduced it was considered by some the true capital ship of the era, but nowadays the term is obsolete.

capping, a strip of wood, usually of Canadian elm, fitted to the top of the *gunwale or *washboard of wooden boats to strengthen it. In boats fitted to take *oars, it is pierced at intervals to take *crutches or *thole pins, or cut away to form *rowlocks.

capsize, to, to upset or overturn in connection with a vessel at sea or in harbour. In general the term is normally related to natural causes, such as high winds or heavy seas, but refers also to human error in such cases as faulty stowage of cargo which may cause a ship to become unstable and thus overturn. When a *tug is capsized by the vessel it is towing, it is known as **girding**.

capstan, a cylindrical barrel fitted in larger ships on the *forecastle deck and used for heavy lifting work, particularly when working anchors and *cables. It was normally placed on the centreline of the ship and was driven by *auxiliary machinery. The barrel was lined vertically with *whelps in order to provide a grip for *hawsers or cables when they were being hove in. Below the barrel a series of *pawls were attached which worked over a pawl-ring to prevent the capstan running back under a particularly heavy strain. In ships which were fitted with a capstan, two *cable-holders were normally geared into the capstan engine so that the *bower anchors could be *weighed direct without their cables having to be led to the capstan barrel.

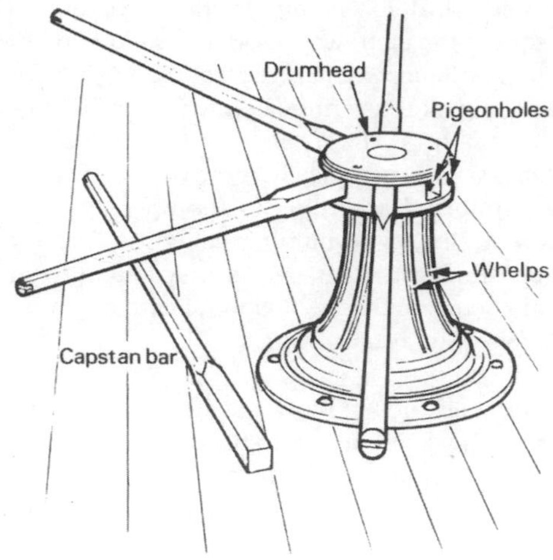

Capstan

Before the advent of auxiliary machinery, the capstan was always found on the main deck of the ship and used both for weighing an anchor and for *swaying up a *yard (but see also JEERS). There was a *drumhead above the barrel with square pigeonholes into which wooden capstan bars, made of ash or hickory, were inserted to work the capstan by hand. The bars could be connected at the ends with a *swifter to provide additional space for men to heave. In particularly heavy work a *messenger was rigged in addition to the swifter so that yet more men could be used on the capstan.

In most smaller ships the function of the capstan was taken by a *windlass. The difference between the two lies mainly in the fact that the spindle on which the barrel of a capstan is mounted is vertical, while that on which the drum and gypsies of a windlass are mounted is horizontal. For illus. see also CABLE-HOLDERS; NIPPER.

captain, in all navies the commissioned rank next below that of rear admiral (but see COMMODORE); also by custom the title of the commanding officer of any naval ship irrespective of his commissioned rank. In the *merchant marine, it is the *master of a merchant ship. By extension, captain is also the title of the senior rating in charge of a group of seamen engaged in particular duties, e.g. captain of the *hold, captain of the maintop, etc. French, *capitaine de* *vaisseau*; German, *Kapitän-zur-See*. See also POST-CAPTAIN.

captain's servant, the name that used to be given to boys entering the Royal Navy at about the age of 12, before they became *midshipmen. The custom of allowing *post-captains to take such 'servants' into their ships derived from the older apprenticeship system. Such servants or followers did no menial work since they were aspiring officers. They were accommodated in the *gunroom under the general supervision of the gunner before graduating to the midshipmen's mess in the *cockpit, and thence on promotion to the lieutenants' *wardroom. The name was changed in 1796 to volunteer, first class, boys of the second and third classes not aspiring to the rank of commissioned officers. Unlike *King's Letter boys, who were nominated by the *Admiralty, a captain's servant was a personal follower of a post-captain, taken on board to oblige relatives or friends. *Nelson and most officers of his day joined the navy in this way. See also 'BORN WITH A SILVER SPOON'.

caravel, originally a Portuguese fishing boat with *lateen sails for local trade; but by the start of the 14th century it became the name of a small merchantman with lateen sails on two masts, a larger version of which was developed by *Henry the Navigator for his *exploration by sea along the coast of West Africa. This type was *carvel-built, had no *beakhead or *stern castle, but a simple curved *stem and a plain *transom stern. Originally they carried lateen sails on all three masts (*caravela latina*), but they developed into three-masted, and occasionally four-masted, ships *square rigged on their two, or three, forward masts with a lateen-rigged *mizzen (*caravela redonda*). This provided a better balance of sail power and avoided to a great extent the main disability of the lateen sail, the immense length of the *yard on which the sail was set and the need when *tacking to lower the sail in order to bring the yard to the other side of the mast. It also enabled them to sail closer to the wind, and gave them greater manoeuvrability than would otherwise have been the case. The average overall length of a three-masted caravel was 23–5 metres (75–81 ft), although a few were built up to 30 metres (100 ft). Of the three ships in which *Columbus's expedition sailed in 1492, both the *Niña* and *Pinta* were caravels, as were those used by Vasco da *Gama.

carbon fibre is mainly produced by separating a chain of carbon atoms from polyacrynitrile through heating and oxidation. Combined with epoxy it is exceptionally strong and light for its weight. First used at sea in the masts of the International *America's Cup Class yachts in 1992, it is now employed in the construction of *yachts' hulls, *spars, and sails. In 2004 the largest vessel ever built of sandwich-constructed carbon fibre, the first of the Swedish Navy's Visby-class *corvettes, was launched. If the hull proves cost-effective, carbon fibre could become one of the *shipbuilding materials of the future.

carcass, an incendiary ship-to-ship weapon, used in the British Navy between the 17th and 19th centuries. It was an iron shell filled with a composition of saltpetre, sulphur, resin, turpentine, antimony, and tallow. It had three vents for the flame and was often also fitted with pistol barrels which discharged their bullets at random. Similar weapons were developed by most other navies during the days of sail, their main purpose being to set on fire the sails and *rigging of an opponent. They were never very successful. See also WARFARE AT SEA.

cardinal mark, a *buoy, normally a *pillar, or *spar, buoy. It is used in the *IALA maritime buoyage system to show that the deepest water in the area in which it is *moored is on the side of the *quadrant to which the mark belongs. It is also used to show the safe side on which to pass a danger, or to draw attention to a feature in a channel such as a bend, a junction, a bifurcation, or the end of a *shoal. Its name indicates which side it should be passed on, e.g., a north cardinal mark, covering between NW and NE, should be passed to the northward. It is coloured with black and yellow bands and the arrangement of these, and of the mark's black topmark consisting of two cones, identifies to which the four quadrants of the compass the mark belongs. The one covering the northern quadrant (NW and NE) has a top band of black and a bottom one of yellow with both topmark cones pointing upwards; the one covering the east quadrant (NE to SE) has its bands arranged black-yellow-black with both topmark cones pointing away from each other; the one covering the south quadrant (SE to SW) has a top band of yellow and a bottom one of black with both topmark cones pointing downwards; and the one covering the west quadrant (SW to NW) has its bands arranged yellow-black-yellow with its topmark cones pointing towards each other. Cardinal marks have a special *characteristic of quick flashing, or very quick flashing, white lights.

cardinal points, the four *points of north, south, east, and west on a *magnetic compass card. The points midway between these—north-east, south-east, south-west, and north-west—are known as the inter-cardinal points.

careen, to, the operation during the days of sail of heaving a ship down, by means of *tackles attached to its mastheads, so as to expose one side to *bream, or repair, it. The vessel was laid ashore on a steeply sloping beach, parallel to the shoreline. To control the angle of *heel, and to bring the vessel back onto an even keel after it had been cleaned or repaired, *relieving tackles were run under the keel and secured to convenient points on the exposed side. After one side had been cleaned, the ship was floated off on the *tide, turned round to face the other way, and the operation repeated so that the opposite side could be cleaned. Small craft are still occasionally careened for cleaning on suitable beaches, but the cleaning of larger vessels is always now done in a *dry-dock. A suitable beach where ships could be careened was known as a **careenage**. See also HOG; PARLIAMENT HEEL.

cargo jack, a large screw jack which was used in the stowage of cargo. Cotton and hides were always jacked into a *hold, in order to compress them into the smallest possible space so as to be able to stow the maximum quantity. Richard Dana describes the process well in that classic of *marine literature *Two Years before the Mast*. The modern equivalent of containing cargo in the most economic space is the *container ship.

cargo net, a large square net made of rope in which cased or packaged cargo is slung into and out of a ship's *hold. While modern methods of loading and unloading ships, such as the *container and *ro-ro ship, have made obsolete this method of handling cargo, there are still some smaller merchant ships which use it in the more remote corners of the world.

carley float, a raft used for *lifesaving. It was capable of supporting a large number of persons, up to 50 in the biggest type. It was a large oval ring of *canvas painted to make it watertight and stuffed with kapok or granulated cork, with a light wooden grid inside the oval and hand lines on the outer circumference. It was supplied mainly to warships but has long been superseded by inflatable rubber liferafts.

carlings, or **carlines,** pieces of squared timber fitted fore and aft between the deck *beams of a wooden ship. Their purpose is to provide support for the deck planking; in ships built of steel the usual practice is to lay a steel deck directly on the beams with planking, where necessary, laid on the steel. In *yachtbuilding and small wooden vessel construction, carlings carry the half beams in the way of *hatches and other deck openings, supporting the *coamings of the hatches or the *coach-roof above them. See also SHIPBUILDING.

carous, a sort of *gallery or *bridge, pivoted in the centre and fitted in ancient warships, such as *galleys, as a means of *boarding an enemy. On forcing a way alongside an enemy it was hoisted up by a *tackle and swung round until it projected over, or into, the enemy vessel, forming a means of access for boarders. The introduction of the gun mounted in ships and firing a solid *shot quickly put an end to this means of capturing ships as it was an unwieldy piece of equipment which even the most inexperienced of gunners could hardly miss.

carpenter's stopper, a metal stopper designed for holding a wire rope temporarily when it is under strain. It consists of a thick metal box with a hinged top and both ends open. One side of the box is grooved to take the *lay of the wire rope, the other, which is inclined to the lead of the wire, holds a wedge-shaped piece of metal similarly grooved. When using the stopper the wire is laid in the box against the grooved side and the top is closed. The wedge is then inserted and pushed home as far as it will go. As the pull comes on the wire the wedge is drawn down further into the box until it jams the wire. The box itself is fitted with a chain *bridle which is shackled to an eyeplate or deckbolt so that it is anchored to the deck while holding the wire.

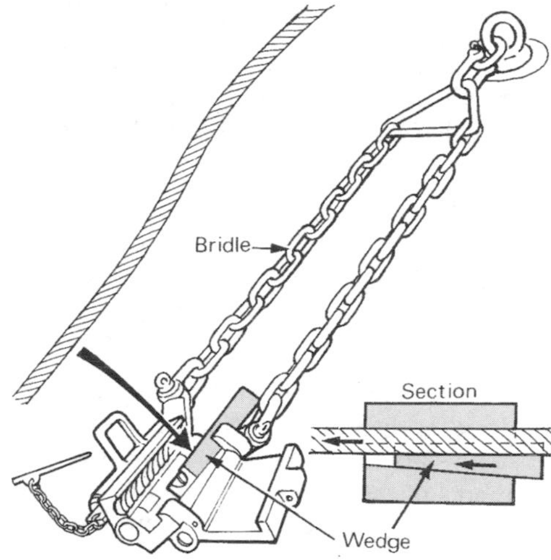

Carpenter's stopper

carrack, the larger type of trading vessel in use in northern and southern Europe during the 14th–17th centuries. It was developed as a compromise between the typical *square rig of the northern European nations and the *lateen rig of the Mediterranean. It was very similar in rig to the later three-masted development of the *caravel (*caravela rotunda*) though larger, beamier, and generally more robust, with very high fore and after castles. The carrack was the forerunner, and first example, of the larger three-masted ship which dominated *shipbuilding until the general introduction of *steam propulsion in the mid-19th century. It was square rigged on fore- and mainmasts, and lateen rigged on the *mizzen, the largest being about 1,200 tons. During the 16th and early 17th centuries, almost all the Spanish and Portuguese trading voyages to India, China, and America were performed in carracks. It was superseded during the 17th century by the more efficient *galleon.

carrick bend, a round knot created by two overhand loops which cross each other. It is a safe way of securing two rope *hawsers of different sizes. Because it assumes a round form when drawn tight it does not get jammed between the

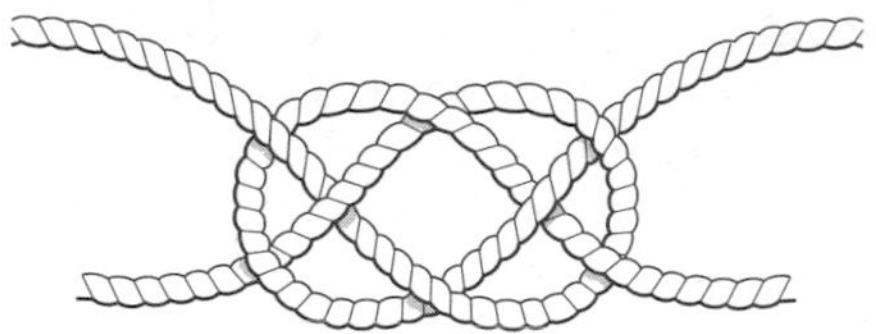
Carrick bend

*whelps of a *capstan barrel as might a flat knot like a *reef knot. To make it totally secure the two loose ends should be *stopped to the standing parts after the knot has been tightened.

carronade, so named after the Carron Iron Founding and Shipping Company where it was invented, a very short, light carriage gun which used a small propellant charge to fire a relatively heavy *shot for a limited range. Introduced in 1799 as an auxiliary to the main armament, it became known as a 'smasher', during the French Revolutionary and Napoleonic Wars (1793–1815). But until 1817 it was not included in the number of guns which decided the *rate of a British warship. See also GUN; WARFARE AT SEA.

carry, to, in its naval meaning, to capture a ship by coming alongside it in battle, and take possession of it by means of boarding parties.

carrying away, the breaking, or parting, of objects on board ship, particularly applicable in the case of masts and *yards. It is an expression used also in the case of ropes and *hawsers when they break as a result of sudden violence, such as a particularly heavy gust of wind or a ship with too much *way on it when attempting to secure alongside.

cartel. **(1)** A ship used in time of war, generally in the days of sailing navies but occasionally in the early days of *steam propulsion, when it was required to negotiate with an enemy. The sign of a ship used as a cartel was the flying of a white flag, a sign that was universally recognized and gave immunity from gunfire when approaching an enemy. Ships' boats, also flying a white flag, were sometimes used as cartels before and after battle in cases where the passing of some special message between belligerents was required. **(2)** An agreement between two belligerent nations for the exchange of prisoners of war while the war was being waged. See also WARFARE AT SEA.

carvel, a small *lateen-rigged Mediterranean vessel, normally with two masts. It was used for the carriage of small cargoes during the late Middle Ages, though it is thought by some to be a synonym for *caravel.

carvel built, a wooden vessel or boat in which the side planks are all flush, the edges laid close and *caulked to make a smooth finish, as compared with *clinker built. The word 'carvel' stems from the Portuguese *carvel or *caravel which was constructed by this method.

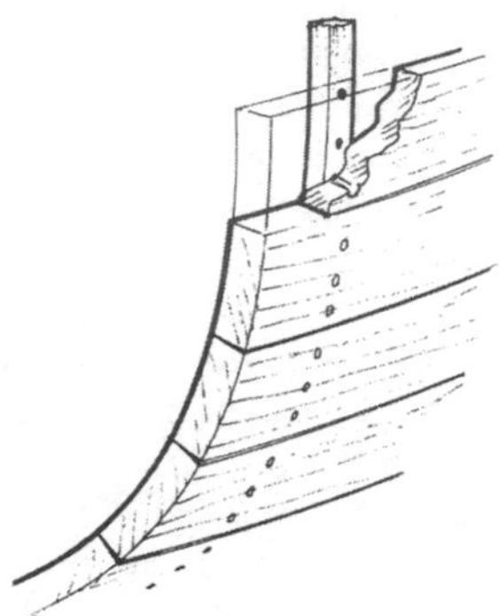

Carvel construction

casco, the local name given to a flat-bottomed, square-ended boat of the Philippine Islands, used as a *lighter for ferrying cargo from ship to shore and vice versa.

case-shot. Known in the US Navy as a **canister**, this was 'any kind of old iron, stones, musket-bullets or the like which we put into cases to shoot out of our great ordnance. These are of great use and do much execution amongst men . . . upon the upper deck when we come near or lie board by board.' Thus Sir Henry Mainwaring in *The Seaman's Dictionary* (1644). The cases in which the old iron etc. was stuffed were normally made of wood although occasionally *canvas bags were used if wooden cases were not readily available. But there was a danger that the bags might get caught and torn open by projections and irregularities inside the barrel of the gun, which could damage its bore, and wooden cases were always preferred.

cast, to, to bring the bows of a sailing ship onto the required *tack, just as the anchor is leaving the ground on being *weighed. This is done by hauling on the sheet of a *foresail so that the wind will force the bows off in the required direction. When there is insufficient wind to cast with a headsail but a *tide is running, it is often possible to cast onto the required tack by putting the *helm over and letting the force of the tide act on the *rudder to turn the bows.

castaway, a shipwrecked sailor, as opposed to one who has been *marooned, or deliberately put ashore from his ship.

cast off, to, to let go a *cable or rope securing a ship to a *buoy, *wharf, *mole, or alongside another ship, so that it may move away and proceed to sea or to another *berth in harbour.

cast of the lead, the act of heaving the *lead and line to ascertain the depth of water. At each cast, the leadsman called out the depth in *fathoms of the water alongside the ship according to the *marks or deeps of the line.

cat. (1) The name of the *purchase by which a ship's anchor, before the days of the stockless anchor, was hoisted to the *cathead before stowing it or letting it go. **(2)** Originally, one of the five principal types of merchant ship hulls in the days before sailing ships were identified by their rig. It was also the name given to Northumbrian vessels which moved coal around the east coast of England. **(3)** The short name by which the *cat-o'-nine-tails was known. **(4)** When used as a verb it was the process of hoisting an anchor by its ring so that it hung at the cathead, either in readiness for letting go or, after it has been *weighed, in preparation for securing it on the anchor bed. Catting an anchor was only necessary with anchors fitted with *stocks. See also CATBOAT.

catamaran, from the Tamil *katta,* to tie, *maram,* wood. **(1)** A sort of raft consisting of two or more logs or tree trunks lashed together and used as a *surf boat in the East and West Indies. The term was also used to describe the much larger rafts, made normally from the trunks of balsa trees, which used to be seen on the western coast of South America. **(2)** A raft used in the St Lawrence River, made by lashing two boats together. **(3)** A British naval explosive invention which was specially designed to attack the French invasion *flotilla as it lay in harbour at Boulogne in the autumn of 1804. **(4)** A small rectangular raft used in *dockyards to protect the hulls of large ships from damage when lying alongside a *mole or *jetty. **(5)** A twin-hulled vessel, present in the Pacific and Indian Oceans for hundreds of years, although its appearance in European and North American waters was much later. The first *steam propulsion warship, designed by Robert *Fulton in 1814, had two hulls and in 1874 the London, Chatham, and Dover Railway built a twin-hulled *ferry of 1,533 tons for their cross-Channel service. During the 1990s a cross-Channel ferry company started using twin-hulled *Seacats, wave-piercing designs where the hulls were designed to slice through the waves instead of over them, and they are now in use throughout the world. Similar designs are being used for military purposes by the Royal Australian and US Navies. The Royal Navy is also experimenting with a twin-hulled warship, and the UK's first purpose-built floating ambulance, *Star of Life*, is a catamaran. See also SURFACE EFFECT SHIP; SWATH SHIP.

The catamaran is very popular for recreational sailing, as it is both stable and fast, though a catamaran cannot sail as close to the wind as a monohull. One of the earliest, if not the earliest, sailing catamarans to be built for racing was designed by Nat *Herreshoff, the American *yacht designer, in 1876, and one was used successfully to defend the *America's Cup in 1988. Wave-piercing catamarans have also been developed for ocean racing. See also CANOE; TRIMARAN; YACHTING: TRANSOCEANIC RACING.

catboat, a type of sailing boat which originated in the middle of the 19th century in the Cape Cod region of the USA, used primarily in the local *fisheries but later adopted as a *sandbagger for racing, as well as for coastal cruising. The catboat was very shallow and of great *beam (some measured only two beams to the length) with a large weighted *centreboard of wood and a barndoor-like *rudder. The mast, supporting a mainsail on a *gaff and boom, was stepped right in the bows, close to the *stem. One, the 5-metre (16-ft 6-in.) *Una*, was shipped to Cowes in 1852 and gave her name in English waters to the *Una rig. Later, some of the racing catboats also set a *foresail on a long *bowsprit.

catenary, the curve of an anchor *cable between the anchor on the sea bottom and the vessel which lies to it: the deeper the curve, the more the catenary. A good catenary is essential for two reasons, the first being that the eventual pull on the anchor is horizontal, which tends to bury the anchor *flukes deeper into the ground; the second being that with the elasticity provided by a deep curve in the cable a vessel is prevented from *snubbing to her anchor as it rides to a sea. It is for this reason that most anchor cables, except in the very smallest of craft, are made of chain, where the weight of the chain tends to form a natural catenary.

catharpings, or **catharpins. (1)** Short ropes attached to the *futtock shrouds under the *tops in *square-rigged vessels. They are used to brace in the *shrouds more tightly and thus give space to brace the *yards at a sharper angle to the fore-and-aft line when a square-rigged ship sails *close hauled. For illus. see FUTTOCK SHROUDS. **(2)** The lashings used on *yachts to prevent *halyards frapping on the mast when moored up or at anchor, or in a *marina.

Cathay, the name by which China was known during the Mongol dynasty and by Europeans between the 15th and 17th centuries.

cathead, a heavy piece of curved timber projecting from each bow of a ship for the purpose

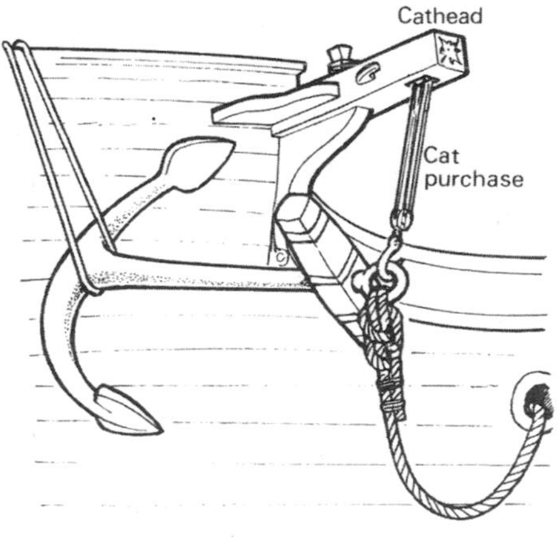

Cathead

of holding anchors which were fitted with a *stock in position for letting go or for securing them on their beds after *weighing. It holds the upper *sheaves of the cat *purchase which is used to *cat the anchor. Since the invention of the stockless anchor ships no longer have these large catheads, nor do they need to cat their anchors before letting them go.

catholes, two small circular holes cut in the stern of sailing men-of-war above the *gunroom *ports and on the same level as the *capstan. They were used for leading in a stern *hawser to the capstan when it was required to heave the ship *astern. The gunroom ports, being cut on a lower plane than the capstan, would have been subjected to great strain had the stern hawsers been led in through them.

cat-o'-nine-tails, an instrument of punishment with which, in the days of sail, seamen were flogged on their bare backs. It was made of nine lengths of *cord, each about 46 centimetres (18 in.) long and with three knots in each, fixed to the end of a larger rope which was used as a handle, and was used in almost every navy in the world. In both the US and the British Navies a captain was limited by regulations to ordering a maximum of twelve lashes for any crime. Any greater number could, in theory, only be awarded by a court martial, but few took any notice of this rule. In the US Navy also it was often avoided by finding an offender guilty of several crimes, and awarding the maximum number of lashes for each of them. The use of the cat-o'-nine-tails was ended in the US Navy in 1851. It was suspended in the Royal Navy in 1879 but had been falling into disuse long before that. See also COBBING; 'COMBING THE CAT'; FLOGGING ROUND THE FLEET; 'NO ROOM TO SWING A CAT'; 'ROGUE'S MARCH'; 'THREE SISTERS'.

catspaw. **(1)** A twisting *hitch made in the *bight of a rope to form two eyes, through which the hook of a *tackle is passed for hoisting purposes. **(2)** The name given to a ruffle on the water indicating a breath of wind during a calm. Old sailors, on seeing a catspaw on the surface while becalmed, would frequently rub the ship's *backstay (as though fondling a cat) and whistle to induce the wind to come to the ship.

catwalk, an elevated fore-and-aft passageway. It connected the midships *bridge structure, in the older design of merchant vessels and some warships, with the *forecastle and *poop decks so as to provide safe and relatively dry access forward and *aft from the bridge.

caulk, to, to drive, with a caulking iron, *oakum or rope fibre into the *seams of a ship's wooden deck or sides in order to render them impervious to water. After the oakum was driven in hard, the gap between the planks was filled with hot *pitch or some other composition to prevent the oakum from rotting through contact with water. On *yachts and small boats caulking cotton would be used.

The Chinese used quite different, but equally efficient, materials. The 13th-century explorer *Marco Polo noted that Chinese *junks were caulked inside and out with 'lime, and *hemp chopped small, and they pound it all together, mixed with an oil from a tree'. The result was sticky and when smeared onto the hulls held like birdlime. Other travellers reported that a putty-like composition of sifted lime and tung oil was used, and in some places the ashes of oyster shells replaced the lime. In Cambodia during the same era a mixture of fish oil and lime was used; in the Persian Gulf fish oil mixed with oakum; on the Somali coast whale oil and lime; while the ocean-going *canoes of the Pacific islanders were caulked with coconut fibre and adhesive breadfruit sap. See also CHINSE.

cavitation is the loss of effective *propeller thrust. It is caused by the impact of water against the propeller when vacuum pockets collapse. The vacuum pockets form when the propeller blade moves too quickly for the surrounding water to fill effectively the space left by the blade as it rotates. It can be caused by a propeller being too small, or too near the surface for the head of water pressure to supply a solid stream for the propeller to work in, by poor streamlining of the blades or of the after *run of the hull form, or by too thick a leading blade on the propeller itself. The head of water is the pressure which forces the water into the propeller blades, and amounts to normal atmospheric pressure plus 0.434 lb per sq. in. for every foot below the surface that the propeller is submerged. The effect of cavitation, besides loss of thrust, is heavy vibration of the ship and damage to the propeller blades.

ceiling, the inside planking or plating in the *holds of a merchant vessel, laid across the *floors and carried up the sides of the holds to the level of the *beams.

celestial navigation, or **astronomical navigation.** The *sextant, the *chronometer (nowadays possibly a quartz watch), the *nautical almanac, and navigation tables (now perhaps some form of calculator or computer) in one form or another remain the essential requirements for celestial navigation, by means of which, provided the heavenly bodies themselves are visible, the *navigator can find his position anywhere in the world. For long, navigation by sextant, or one of its predecessors, was the only position-fixing system in the deep ocean and all the great voyages of *exploration by sea have found their way by it. The practice has now largely been replaced by *satellite navigation, in its current (2004) form *GPS (Global Positioning System) or, less frequently, the Russian Glonass. The reason for the present supremacy of GPS is clear. For the first time in the long history of navigation a system exists that will give the navigator a position within a few metres, by day or by night, in any weather and in any part of the world. That astronomical navigation has not yet become obsolete is largely due to the fact that it remains self-contained, is wholly independent of any national or political authority, and is not subject to system failures.

For all the brilliance of its conception and performance satellite navigation as we know it remains for one reason or another vulnerable. As things stand, for example, GPS, which is provided free by the US Department of Defense, is still classed as a weapon-targeting system and could be withdrawn at any time. So a back-up still remains a requirement and celestial navigation remains at any rate one wholly viable alternative.

The practice of celestial navigation at sea remains in principle very much as it was in the days of Captain *Cook. But things have become easier. Time is universally available and the problem of *longitude has long been solved. The *ephemeris is now presented in the nautical almanac in such a manner that only the most elementary mathematics are required to solve the nautical triangle. Perhaps, above all, the concepts of the *position line and the *intercept have illuminated and simplified the whole business of astronomical position finding.

The predicted apparent positions of the heavenly bodies used in navigation, namely the sun, moon, planets, Aries, and the selected navigational stars, are tabulated for hourly intervals in the nautical almanac. The coordinates used are Greenwich *Hour Angle (GHA) and *declination which are adjusted by interpolation tables to the time of observation. The values extracted are used to enter the reduction tables (or calculator as the case may be). Each sextant observation or sight will produce a position line, somewhere along which the observer's position must lie. Two position lines taken at roughly the same time will indicate just where along the first position line the observer lies, and three sights in a series will normally produce a *cocked hat which gives a more reliable *fix. A single position line can be advanced along the ship's track and crossed with a later observation to give a position. Where the sun is used this is known as a sun-run-sun. The same principle of the transferred position line is of course frequently used in *coastal navigation.

To take a *sight the navigator measures the altitude of the heavenly body with his sextant, taking the time of observation (generally to within a second) since, due to the rotation of the earth, the body will be in constant motion. The *altitude corrections, given in the nautical almanac and elsewhere, are then applied; first

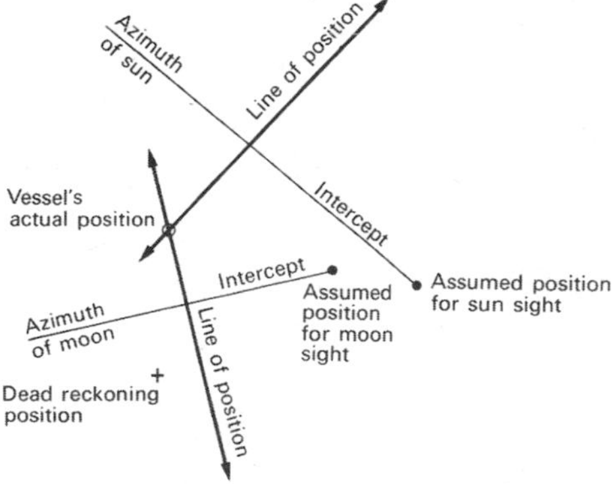

Celestial fix using simultaneous sights of sun and moon

*dip for the observer's height of eye, then atmospheric *refraction, then *semi-diameter for the sun or moon, and finally any index error of the instrument.

To work the sight up (to use the time-honoured phrase) the GHA is first of all converted to LHA (local hour angle) at the position from which the sight is being worked (generally the *dead reckoning position or a position that suits the tables) by adding or subtracting the longitude. Nowadays using modern direct entry altitude-azimuth tables, or a dedicated calculator, the declination and local hour angle are converted into *altitude and *azimuth. The altitude is compared with the observed (i.e. corrected) sextant altitude to obtain the *intercept or altitude difference. This whole process is known as sight reduction.

On the *chart or a *plotting sheet a distance on the chart scale equal to the intercept is measured along the azimuth line, towards the assumed or chosen position if the observed altitude is the greater and away from it if it is not. From that point the position line is drawn as a perpendicular, at right angles to the bearing.

There are many methods of sight reduction, tabular, instrumental, and mechanical. During and immediately following the Second World War (1939–45) logarithmic solutions such as the cosine-haversine method, or longitude by chronometer, held sway. These were later at least temporarily eclipsed by what were generally called the 'short' methods. These split the navigational triangle into two parts and lessened the work, but at the expense of introducing special rules for different situations. It was the introduction of large computers that made modern direct-entry tables possible. From these precomputed altitudes and azimuths could be extracted for any value of GMT (Universal Time). Bulky though the tables may be they still represent the most convenient form of tabular sight reduction. There are dedicated calculators, such as the Merlin II, that carry the ephemeris for the sun, moon, and navigational stars for a number of years and dispense altogether with the use of an almanac or reduction tables, or indeed the need to plot in order to establish the observed position. In some ways, given the altered status of celestial navigation, they perhaps represent the best way of reducing sights in the modern navigational environment.

The simplest form of sight is the *meridian altitude taken when the body observed, usually the sun, crosses the observer's meridian and reaches its maximum altitude. The altitude, adjusted by the altitude corrections and with the declination as appropriate taken into account, defines the latitude. The most accurate sight is a four-star fix with the stars in two opposed directions. The accuracy of celestial observations is a matter of some importance which affects not only the accuracy of position at sea but also the precision to which almanacs and nautical tables must be tabulated. The confidence level with which practising mariners are most concerned is the 95% level, which means that out of every 100 observations only five will be expected to exceed whatever the stated value is. In 1957 the Royal Institute of Navigation with the Royal Netherlands Navy and a number of shipping companies conducted an investigation into the accuracy of sextant observations actually achieved in different conditions at sea. The errors in question were position line errors, not errors in position. Some 4,000 observations were received and analysed by HM Nautical Almanac Office. The accuracy achieved by the average observer was 3 minutes of arc (or miles) and by the best observer 2 minutes. The figure, now generally accepted, was substantially greater than had been widely believed.

Blewitt, M., *Celestial Navigation for Yachtsmen* (1990).

Moody, A., *Navigation Afloat* (1980).

Mike Richey

celestial sphere, the imaginary sphere on to which the heavenly bodies appear to be projected. For astronomical work the radius of the celestial sphere is considered to be infinite. For some purposes the sun is regarded as occupying the central position, but for others the earth's centre or the observer's eye is considered to lie at the centre. Systems of *great circles on the celestial sphere, particularly the *horizon system, the *equinoctial system, and the *ecliptic system, have been devised to facilitate the solution of mathematical astronomical problems, especially those related to nautical astronomy. For illus. see ECLIPTIC.

centreboard, a device which is raised or lowered through the bottom of a sailing vessel, and is housed in a centreboard case. When lowered it increases the vessel's lateral area and its resistance to *leeway. Centreboards have been used in China since at least the 8th century, but they were slow to spread to Europe. The invention of the centreboard for small craft is generally attributed to the USA during colonial times. The need for centreboards arose from the great stretches of very shallow waters found in Chesapeake Bay and along the seaboard from Long Island Sound to Florida, where it was necessary to sail the flat-bottomed work boats of those areas to *windward.

In 1774 Lord Percy introduced the device to England when he had a small vessel built at Boston, Mass., on the lines of the local boats and fitted with one centreboard which was almost as long as the boat's keel, and had the boat shipped home for trials. Fifteen years later a larger boat was built at Deptford having three separate centreboards which were each narrow and deep, like a *dagger-board, and could be raised or lowered independently to aid steering and balance of the boat under varying sailing conditions.

In 1790 the British *Admiralty built a *revenue cutter, the *Trial*, 21 metres (68 ft) on deck, which was fitted with three centreboards working on the same principle. The success of this experiment led to the building of a 60-ton *brig, *Lady Nelson*, in 1798 with three similar centreboards expressly for a voyage of survey and *exploration by sea to New South Wales. The brig made a fast voyage out and was the first to sail round Tasmania and discover that it was an island. The favourable reports on the *Lady Nelson*'s voyage and the ease with which it *navigated in very shallow waters resulted in other vessels, including some merchantmen and work boats for the Teign and other shallow estuaries, being constructed on the same principle. About 1803 Commodore Taylor of the Cumberland Sailing Society, an early *yacht club, had a *yacht built on the Thames with five centreboards, a not uncommon number in Chinese craft. Named the *Cumberland*, he raced her with some success.

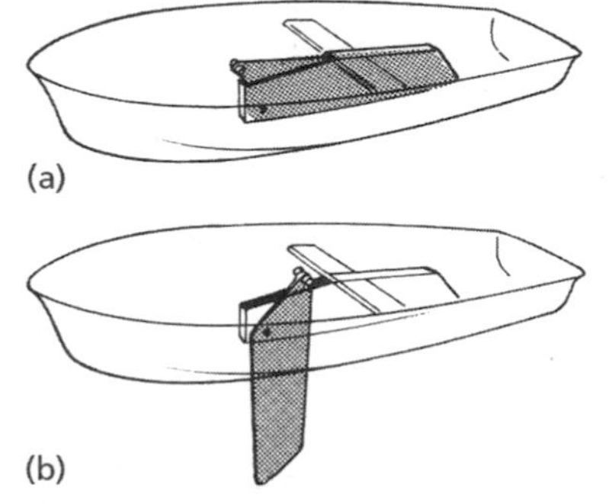

[a] Centreboard raised [b] Centreboard lowered

By altering the shape of the centreboard and hanging it on a pivot at the fore end, Captain Shuldham of the Royal Navy introduced a distinct improvement in 1809 which became the most common form of the centreboard today. In the USA a number of local types of work boat, such as *scows, *skipjacks, *bugeyes, *catboats, oyster *sloops, and trading *schooners up to 46 metres (150 ft) in length, as well as many yachts, were built with pivoted centreboards. In the larger vessels the centreboard was generally built up from wooden planks, weighted to make it sink; schooners over 24 metres (80 ft) in length sometimes had two such centreboards.

While centreboards and dagger plates are normally used in sailing and racing dinghies and yachts of shallow draught, metal centreplates, usually of bronze, are also fitted within the lead *ballast keels of racing yachts. With their use the yacht can gain a little over a similar fixed-keel competitor by increasing the lateral resistance to leeway when sailing close hauled. Then when the course brings the wind free the plate is raised and the amount of wetted surface friction is accordingly reduced, allowing the yacht a little extra speed down wind.

centre of buoyancy, a point through which the resultant of all buoyant forces on an immersed hull is assumed to act. It is about this point that a vessel afloat could be said so be poised.

centre of effort, a point of the sail plan of a sailing vessel through which the resultant of all wind forces is assumed to act. In a sail plan of a vessel each sail is assumed to have its centre of effort at its geometric centre, and on a drawing of a vessel's sail plan the resultant of these forces is assumed to be the centre of effort of the whole sail plan. In practice, however, the sails are never completely flat as shown on the plan, and the actual centre of effort moves at every fresh trimming of the sheets.

centre of lateral resistance, a point assumed to lie at the geometric centre of a sailing vessel's underwater profile. On a vessel's design plans this is indicated with the hull floating upright on its designed waterline. In practice, however, with sailing vessels heeled under a press of sail and lifting and *pitching over seas, the actual centre of lateral resistance is constantly shifting.

centring chains, chains stretched across the entrance to, and the head of, a *dry-dock with a red and white disc inserted in them which indicate the line of the keel blocks on which the vessel must rest when the dock is pumped out.

cesser clause, that clause in a *charter party under which the charterer's liability ceases when the ship is loaded and the *master has a lien on the cargo for *freight and *demurrage.

chain, see CABLE.

chain, or **cable, locker,** a compartment below decks in which a ship's *cable is stowed when the anchor has been *weighed and secured and the cable is all inboard. A ship has as many chain lockers as it has *bower and *sheet anchors.

chain-plates, strips of iron or bronze with their lower ends bolted to the ship's side under the chain-wales (see CHAINS (2)) of sailing vessels. They carry the *deadeyes or *rigging screws to which the standing *rigging is secured. In the older sailing ships these deadeyes were attached to short lengths of chain secured to the ship's side, and the name remained when chains were superseded by a plate.

chains. **(1)** A small platform on either side of a ship from which the *leadsman took *soundings to ascertain the depth of water. They were so called because originally, in the early days of sail, the leadsman cast his lead standing between the *shrouds, which were attached to the *chain-plates or, earlier still, to lengths of chain attached to the ship's side. The name was retained, and was still apposite while

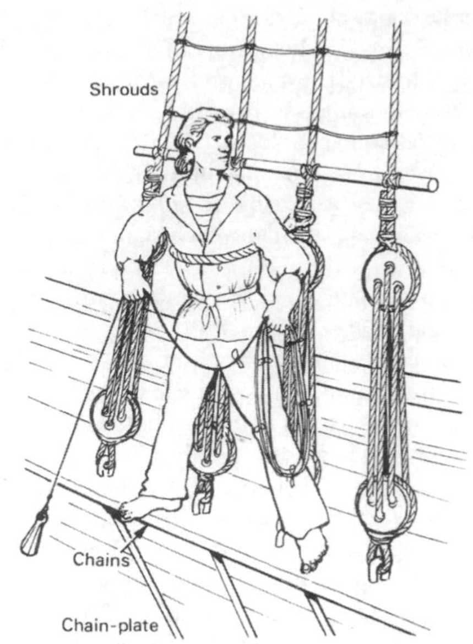

Old-fashioned chains

soundings were taken in this way, as a small chain was later threaded through *stanchions at waist height rigged round the platform to prevent the leadsman from falling overboard as he made a cast. See also LEAD LINE. **(2)** The wooden projections from the sides of *square-rigged ships, abreast each mast, which carry the chain-plates clear of the *gunwale capping to prevent chafe, and to give the shrouds a wider base and spread from which to support the masts. They are secured to the ship's side by *knees and bolts, each mast having its pair, one on each side of the ship. The name originated from the lengths of chain which preceded chain-plates as the fitting to which the *deadeyes of shrouds were secured. They are also known as **chain-wales** (spelt and pronounced **channels** in the US Navy).

chain shot, two cannon balls, connected together by either a chain or an iron bar, which when fired from a gun rotated at great speed through the air. It was designed to destroy the *spars and *rigging of an enemy ship and to clear the upper deck of men during an action.

***Challenger*, HMS,** a screw steam *corvette of 1,500 tons, which was lent to the Royal Society by the British *Admiralty in 1872 for what was to become the most important oceanographic expedition of the era. After being stripped of nearly all her armament, she was fitted out with laboratories and all the necessary equipment to plumb the ocean depths, and became, therefore, the earliest *research ship completely dedicated to *oceanography. She departed in December 1872 for a circumnavigation that lasted three and a half years during which time she steamed nearly 11,000 kilometres (70,000 mls.). The senior scientist aboard the *Challenger* was Wyville Thomson (1830–82), who had earlier completed two oceanographic expeditions to discover more about what lay on the ocean bed. His book, *The Depths of the Sea* (1873), was based on the findings of these expeditions and it is now generally regarded as the first book on the subject.

During the voyage the *Challenger* took hundreds of *soundings, including the first one of the Marianas *Trench, also making the discovery that there were mid-ocean ridges (see GEOLOGICAL OCEANOGRAPHY). She collected thousands of biological samples which showed that at all depths the oceans were teeming with life.

On his return Thomson was knighted by Queen Victoria. Such was the amount of information gained during the circumnavigation that it took the next twenty years to complete the 50-volume *Challenger Reports*. After Thomson's death, these were edited by his assistant, the geologist John Murray (1841–1914), who had accompanied him on the *Challenger*. The modern science of oceanography developed from these reports, and Murray is acknowledged to be the founder of geological oceanography. In 1951 scientists aboard a second research ship of the same name were able to sound the bottom of the Marianas Trench for the first time.

chambers. **(1)** An old legal term used to describe those areas of sea which lay between headlands but beyond *territorial waters. In 1634, for example, the Lords of the English *Admiralty instructed the judge of the Admiralty's High Court and the Attorney-General 'to compose a reglement whereby his Majesty's ancient right in the *Narrow Seas, and in his chambers and ports, might be preserved'. **(2)** Small pieces of ordnance during the 16th–17th centuries from which gun *salutes at sea were fired.

'channel fever', the seaman's name, during the days of sail, for the excitement on board ship as it approached its destination with the prospect for the crew of a spell of *liberty ashore.

chantey, or **chanty,** see SHANTY.

Chapelle, Howard Irving (1900–75), American naval architect and author, who studied *naval architecture in New York from 1920 onwards. In 1936 he started in business on his own, and produced in all some 120 different designs for fishing craft, *yachts, and sailing boats. During the Second World War (1939–45) he served in the US Army in charge of ship- and boat-building programmes, and in 1956 went to Turkey as adviser on the construction and equipping of their fishing fleets (see also FISHERIES). On his return to the USA he was appointed maritime historian at the Smithsonian Institution in Washington and was awarded the Smithsonian gold medal for distinguished service to the institution. Among the many books he wrote were: *The Baltimore Clipper, History of the American Sailing Ships, Yacht Design and Planning, History of the American Sailing Navy, Bark Canoes and Skin Boats of North America, American Small Sailing Craft, American Sailing Craft, Boatbuilding*, and *The American Fishing Schooners.*

chapelled, a ship is said to be chapelled, or to build a chapel, when, after losing *way through the water in a light or baffling wind (see also CATSPAW), it turns completely round or, when *close hauled, goes about without bracing its head-*yards and then comes back onto the same *tack as before. It can be caused either by the inattention of the helmsman or by a quick change in the wind's direction.

chapels, the name given to the grooves in a built-up, or 'made', wooden mast in which several pieces of timber were used to fashion it. In large sailing ships the lower masts were all 'made' *spars; the *topmasts and *topgallant masts were whole spars. The chapels occurred where the various pieces of the mast were joined together.

characteristic, the distinguishing qualities of a navigational light, whether from a *lighthouse, *lightship, light float, or lighted *buoy, by which the *navigator of a ship can easily identify it. In addition to their colours, white, red, yellow, or green, individual lights can be recognized by whether they are alternating, fixed, flashing, fixed and flashing, or occulting, and by the number, or group, of exposures in each cycle.

An **alternating light** is one in which two colours are used, exposed alternately in each cycle of the light and always in the same order. The colours are sometimes separated by periods of darkness, and sometimes alternate continuously. A **fixed light** shows a steady beam with no period of darkness, and thus has no cycle. A **fixed and flashing light** is one which shows a steady beam varied at regular intervals with a flash of brighter intensity. A **flashing light** is one in which the total duration of light in each cycle is less than the period of darkness. An **occulting light** is one in which the period of darkness is less than the period of light in each cycle.

These five main types are further varied for recognition purposes by what is known as grouping, in which a series of flashes or a series of eclipses (occulting) is separated by intervals of darkness or light. Thus in a **group flashing light** two or more flashes are visible at regular intervals in each cycle, while in a **group occulting light** there are two or more short intervals of darkness in each cycle. As an example, a light indicated on a *chart as a group flashing light with four flashes every 15 seconds (Fl. (4) 15 sec.) would show to the navigator four bright flashes with an interval of a second or so between them followed by a period of darkness occupying the rest of the 15 seconds. The 15 seconds is the period, or cycle, of the light, and is measured from the first flash in one group to the first flash in the next succeeding group. **Composite group flashing** is where the number of flashes alters and is used to identify modified *lateral marks in the *IALA maritime buoyage system. A light group flashing 2 + 1 every 15 seconds (Fl. (2 + 1) 15 sec.), for example, is where there are two flashes followed by the period of darkness, then one flash followed by the period of darkness, then two flashes again.

Other differentiations of characteristics are the **quick**, **very quick**, and **ultra quick**, **flashing lights** which are a modification of the flashing and group flashing systems. The quick flashing light is one which normally flashes at either 50 or 60 flashes per minute, the very quick flashing light normally flashes at a rate of either 100 or 120 flashes per minute, and the ultra quick flashing light normally flashes at between 240 to 300 flashes per minute.

Both very quick (VQ) and quick (Q) flashes are used to identify *cardinal marks in the IALA maritime buoyage system. A north cardinal mark has continuous very quick or quick flashes; east has three very quick or quick flashes, then darkness, in a period of five or ten seconds respectively; south has six very quick or quick flashes followed by a long flash, then darkness, in a period of ten or fifteen seconds respectively; and west has nine very quick or quick flashes then darkness, in a period of ten or fifteen seconds respectively. The long flash (not less than two seconds long) which is a characteristic of the south cardinal mark is merely a device for making certain the three or nine flashes cannot be mistaken for six.

Finally there is the **isophase light**, in which there are equal periods of light and darkness, and lights using *Morse rhythms. For instance a *safe water mark in the IALA maritime buoyage system uses the Morse code for 'A' (dot dash), followed by a period of darkness; while an offshore structure like an oil rig (see also OFFSHORE OIL AND GAS) is marked by the letter 'U' (dot dot dash) followed by a period of darkness.

The characteristic of every light, though not every lighted buoy, is clearly marked on all charts. Details of lighted buoys are listed in the *sailing directions appropriate to the waters in which they are situated and are also marked on the largest-scale chart of each area.

charley noble, originally the name of the chimney fitted when the *galley fires were lit to take the smoke above decks. The name was later extended to cover all portable chimneys fitted to the deck, i.e. for coal fires in admirals' and captains' cabins, wardrooms, etc.

Charlotte Dundas, the first vessel in the world to use *steam propulsion commercially. She was a small wooden *paddle steamer, with a steam engine designed by William Symington. Built on the River Clyde to the order of Lord Dundas, a governor of the Forth and Clyde

The *Charlotte Dundas*

Canal, she was named after his daughter. The engine drove a single paddle wheel fitted in the stern and made her first voyage in 1802 when she covered a distance of 32 kilometres (20 mls.) on the Forth and Clyde Canal in six hours with two 70-ton *lighters in tow, thus becoming the first steam *tugboat ever to operate. However, this experiment was not deemed a success—the canal's governors feared the wash would damage the canal—and she was withdrawn from service the following year. The first commercially successful steamboat is now acknowledged to be Roger *Fulton's 'North River Steamboat' otherwise known as the **Clermont*. See also VULCAN.

chart, a map primarily intended for *navigation, one of the earliest being the plane chart, hence *plain sailing. In very general terms, two types of nautical chart are used at sea, the straightforward *Mercator projection chart on which *rhumb lines appear as straight lines; and *gnomonic charts on which *great circles appear as straight lines. Normally ships sailing from one place to another steer rhumb line courses and use Mercator projection charts. Gnomonic charts are used to display great circles when that is necessary while special lattice charts are used for plotting fixes from *hyperbolic navigation fixing aids. The nautical chart is essentially a map of a sea area, showing coastlines and soundings with all hazards such as rocks as well as the position of *buoys, *lighthouses, and other visual aids to navigation. Charts are kept up to date by the regular issue of *notices to mariners by the charting authority. A *compass rose on the navigational chart enables the mariner to plot *courses and *bearings and to find the local *variation and its rate of change. See also CHARTMAKING; ISOBATH; ISOGONIC LINES; PORTULAN CHART.

chart datum, the datum to which the *soundings shown on a *chart are referred and above which heights of the *tide are expressed in tide tables. The level is essentially one below which the sea surface seldom falls. The default tidal datum of the International Hydrographic Organization is the Lowest Astronomical Tide (LAT). The water level will almost never be lower that LAT. Not all hydrographic offices have adopted this datum, but the one used is generally given on the chart. Mike Richey

charter, the contract for the employment of a merchant ship or *yacht. Charters are of two main types: a **time charter**, in which the owners of the ship provide the crew and all other requirements for operating it; and bare hull, bare pole, or *bare boat charter. Hence **charter party**, the written deed or contract for the hiring for *freight of the whole or part of a merchant vessel, for specific voyages or on a time basis.

chartmaking. The first man to draw charts for seamen was probably Marinus of Tyre (*c.*70–130), though the *periplus had been in use long before his time. He used an equidistant-cylindrical projection forming a grid of parallels and *meridians, the mid-parallel and *prime meridian passing through Rhodes, at that time the maritime centre of the known world. His proportion of the distances between parallels and meridians was four to five, giving an elongated appearance to the Mediterranean. Ptolemy (*c.*90–168), who laid the foundations of cartography, pays tribute to him in his *Geographia* and acknowledges his indebtedness to him in his own great work on the same subject.

Ptolemy was the first man to devise a projection whereby a portion of the surface of the spherical earth could be depicted on a plane surface. His first conical projection, covering the known world in 180° from west to east, had meridians every 10° converging on the pole, the point of contact of the cone providing a curved parallel through Rhodes centred on the pole, while two similar parallels passed through Meroe and Thule, the furthest known southerly and northerly places respectively. He also developed a projection giving a curvature to all meridians except the centre one while the parallels also remained curved. On this projection he drew a world map showing the Mediterranean with some accuracy, and England, Scotland, and Thule in the north. Africa appears as a vast continent stretching across the south of the Indian Ocean, making it an inland sea, and continuing northwards to join Asia. From this map it is clear that Ptolemy did not believe, as Herodotus had written, that Africa had been circumnavigated.

Though, in the middle of the 12th century, the cartographer of the Islamic world al-Idrisi made a similar but more detailed map, Ptolemy's projections and maps were forgotten for a thousand years until they were discovered in Constantinople in 1400, brought to Florence, and translated from classical Greek into Latin. Many learned men came to Italy during the ensuing century to make translations of his works for their own countries so that during the 16th century many cartographers in Europe were aware of the Ptolemy world map and were trying to fit into it the new discoveries. The development of printing and engraving made possible the wide publication of such maps.

Renaissance Chartmaking. The *wind-rose and the *magnetic compass were known to the 13th-century Mediterranean seaman, added to which he carried a *portolano which gave him seamanlike guidance along the coasts. At the end of the 13th century what is now called the *portulan chart appeared; sometimes they are known as 'compass charts' because magnetic compass roses, together with *rhumb lines of direction extended from them, were set down at frequent intervals of the parchment area. The rhumb lines were used by the cartographer to measure *bearings when laying down the coastline, and by the *navigator for setting his *course by pricking off from the rhumb line with dividers and a straight edge.

The prominence of Venice and Genoa during the Renaissance as two important maritime states provided the commercial demand which has motivated chartmakers throughout history. Later, the kingdom of Aragon, which included the ports of Palma, Barcelona, and Valencia, as well as those in Sicily, also became important cartographic centres. Then during the course of the 15th century Portugal, largely spurred on by *Henry the Navigator, became predominant. Among those who went there to pass on their skills as chartmakers was the Majorcan cartographer Abraham Cresques (d. 1387), who produced the Catalan atlas of 1375. Influenced by the voyages of *Marco Polo, this was a huge advance on earlier attempts to create a map of the world. For though Europe, North Africa, and Asia were still the only land masses to be depicted, Cresques had taken information from the early portulan charts so that the map is oriented to the north and the coastline of the Mediterranean is shown with great accuracy.

Early Portuguese *explorations by sea, and the greater understanding of navigation they had achieved because of them, led to many more maps being made, the Fra Mauro *c.*1450—its exact date is not known—and the Genoese map of 1457 being among the most important. The former included information from Mediterranean and Arab seafarers, and, like the Catalan atlas, it also drew heavily on the voyages of Marco Polo. The Genoese map, by an unknown cartographer, draws much information about India and south-east Asia from the Venetian traveller Niccolo Conti, and from the rediscovered Ptolemy material.

Another great advance in cartography was the Cantino map of 1502. Gathered from the voyages of Vasco da *Gama and another Portuguese navigator, Pedro Cabral (*c.*1467–1530), it included land masses never depicted before. The Indian peninsula, the entire African coastline, correctly oriented, and parts of the coasts of Brazil were all shown. Smuggled out of Portugal by an Italian, Alberto Cantino, it was available for study in Italy and was a huge influence on mapmakers for many years.

Around 1500 both Spain and Portugal established offices for controlling trade and exploration, the Casa da India in Lisbon and the Casa de Contrataçion in Seville, where up-to-date charts were kept and ocean *pilots examined. In 1530 the King of Portugal appointed Pedro Nuñes (1502–78), a skilled cosmographer, to head his department of *hydrography in the Casa da India, and it was to him that Portuguese navigators turned for a solution to the problem they found when trying to plot ocean courses on a plane portulan chart. Nuñes realized, and published the fact, that meridians converge towards the poles and that a course which crosses them at a constant angle is a spiral rhumb line leading to the pole.

North European Chartmakers. During the 16th century the focus of map- and chartmaking moved to the Netherlands where, in 1570, Abraham Ortelius (1527–98) published his atlas *Theatrum Orbis Terrarum* which, among others, contained a significant map of the world. Using the prime meridian through the Canary Islands, the world is drawn in a projection developed directly from that of Ptolemy, but showing the full 180° both to the west and to the east of the prime meridian. All the new discoveries are shown, giving a good picture of the land masses of the world in general. It also included a vast continent encircling the southern portion of the world named 'Australis Nondum Cognita'—called, on some later maps, *Terra Australis Incognita—a vestige of Ptolemy's concept. It was a mystery that eluded explorers for another 200 years until James *Cook disproved its existence.

The previous year, 1569, Gerardus Mercator (1512–94) had published a new world map in eighteen sheets. With this he abandoned Ptolemaic theories and introduced his own projection where parallels of *latitude and meridians of *longitude cut each other at right angles so that a rhumb line drawn on it appeared as a straight line, so solving the problem of steering ocean courses which Nuñes had described 40 years earlier. However, it was not until the end of the 16th century that an Englishman, Edward Wright (1558–1615), made clear to seamen the benefits of *Mercator's projection, describing it in his book *Certaine Errors of Navigation Detected and Corrected* (1599) with the aid of a diagram of great clarity.

But the problem of measuring longitude at sea simply was still a long way from being solved, so newly discovered lands were plotted on the charts with little east/west precision. The *Board of Longitude was formed to find a solution, one eventually brought about by the accurate timepieces produced by John Harrison (1693–1776). Cook carried an early copy of Harrison's No. 4 chronometer, Kendall's No. 1, on his second Pacific voyage in 1772, and testified to its excellence in keeping time accurately, and hence its precision in obtaining a correct longitude.

Waggoners. North European navigators had never felt the same need for charts as did the explorers from Spain and Portugal. Instead, they relied upon courses between one cape and another which had been handed down to them by their fathers, and on the use of the *lead line to warn them of shallow water. However, in 1582 a Dutch seaman, Lucas Janszoon Wagenaer (*c.*1534–1605), impressed by Ortelius' maps, and having seen the portulan charts carried by the Portuguese traders on their voyages to Flanders for wool, began to compile a pilot book for western Europe. This finally developed into *Spieghel der Zeevaerdt*, a manual of navigation, a pilot book, and a series of charts for navigation from the Zuider Zee to Cadiz along the coast of northern Europe. It was published in two parts in 1584–5 and the then *Lord High Admiral of England was so impressed with it that he commissioned a translation, and this was published in 1588 as *The Mariner's Mirrour*. These charts were widely used by British seamen for a century, calling them 'waggoners', a corruption of Wagenaer.

Over-reliance on the Dutch waggoners led Samuel *Pepys, then secretary of the *Admiralty, to commission a naval officer, Greenvile Collins (d. 1694), 'to make a survey of the sea coast of the Kingdom' in 1681. This was the first comprehensive survey of the British coast ever made and when it appeared as *Great Britain's Coasting Pilot* in 1693 it also was generally known as a waggoner. The name was even used for a sea atlas of the Pacific, *Wagoner of the Great South Sea*. This was redrawn by William Hack (*fl.* 1670–1700) from a Spanish *derroterro captured by the *buccaneer Bartholomew *Sharp in the South Pacific during Sharp's voyage there in 1681–2. Hack's atlas is in the King George III Maritime Collection at the British Library.

Wagenaer's charts still owed much to the portulan chart, as did Collins's. Nevertheless, they began to take on a more seamanlike look with *soundings reduced to a mean level datum shown in *anchorages and over harbour bars, and with sketches to assist recognition of the coast. Standard symbols were also introduced to show safe anchorages, *buoys, and submerged rocks, and these have survived on charts to the present day.

French Chartmaking. Neither Wagenaer's charts nor *Great Britain's Coasting Pilot* had used Mercator's projection but *Le Neptune françois*, also published in 1693 on the orders of Louis XIV, did. The newly established Observatoire de Paris had been founded to bring about a better understanding of the celestial sphere and it was here that a method of finding longitude by the observations of Jupiter's satellites was devised. Once the latitude and longitude of the observatory had been fixed, a triangulated survey of the whole of France was made, relating stations along the whole coastline to the prime meridian of Paris. The charts in *Le Neptune françois*, were based on this triangulated survey, employed Mercator projection for the smaller scales, and were beautifully engraved. They showed a distinct advance over both the Dutch and British charts, and gave France a clear lead in chartmaking. However, the first comprehensive collection of charts to use Mercator projection was the *Arcano del mare*, published in three volumes in 1645–6 by the Florence-based Englishman Sir Robert Dudley (1573–1649).

The Dépôt des Cartes et Plans de la Marine was established in 1720 and through this office during the 18th century further editions of *Le Neptune* were published, culminating in 1764 with the official publication of the cartographic masterpiece *Le Petit Atlas maritime*. Produced by Jacques Bellin (1703–72), who had published a chart of the Mediterranean in three sheets in 1737, these were beautiful, clear-cut charts covering the greater part of the navigable world. Both publications were of a standard of clarity and accuracy not previously achieved anywhere and mark Bellin out as an outstanding cartographer of his day.

Triangulation Adopted by the British. The use of a measured baseline from which a shore triangulation of fixed stations could be extended had reached Britain from France by the middle of the 18th century and was used to survey the Orkneys, and the west coasts of Scotland and Wales, and of Ireland, which was carried out for the Admiralty by Murdoch Mackenzie (b. 1712). In retirement, and when his nephew of the same name had taken over the coastal surveys, he devised an instrument, subsequently named a *station pointer, for plotting the position of a ship or boat with reference to three triangulated points onshore, the two angles between them having been observed simultaneously by two men on board. In those days these angles were taken with *Hadley's quadrant used horizontally; subsequently replaced by the *sextant, this method of station pointer fixing lasted well into the 20th century and accounts for the rapidly increasing number of soundings appearing on charts throughout the 19th century.

Early American Chartmaking. Contemporaneously with the work of the Murdoch Mackenzies, Joseph des Barres (1721–1824) and others working in support of the British Army in North America were making detailed coastal surveys of the east coast. Their work resulted in the publication by the Admiralty of the atlas *Atlantic Neptune* in 1777, the name of the Roman god *Neptune being often used in titles during the 18th century to describe collections of maps and charts, in much the same way as atlas. Beautifully engraved, using more symbols, and having extensive sounding coverage, this magnificent collection of charts recaptured from the French the ascendancy they had held since the beginning of the century, and served as the primary source for most North American charts for 50 years after the birth of the USA in 1783.

In 1807 the US Congress authorized President Jefferson 'to cause a survey to be taken of the coasts of the United States, in which shall be designated the islands and shoals, with the roads or places of anchorage, within 20 leagues of any part of the shore of the United States, and also the respective courses and distances between the principal capes, or head lands, together with such other matters as he may deem proper, completing an accurate chart of every port of the coasts within the extent aforesaid'.

It was not until 1816 that the Swiss-born Ferdinand Hassler was appointed superintendent of the survey of the coast but by 1836 the organization had become a flourishing agency called the US Coast Survey, the Federal government's oldest scientific agency. In 1871 a geodetic connection between the coastlines of the Pacific and Atlantic oceans was authorized which resulted in the agency being renamed the US Coast and Geodetic Survey in 1878, a name now retained by an office within the National Ocean Service, a part of the *National Oceanic and Atmospheric Administration.

Chartmaking in the 19th–20th Centuries. By 1800 virtually the whole of the inhabited world appeared on charts and world maps. Cook had finally disproved the supposed existence of the great southern continent, first drawn by Ptolemy 1,500 years earlier, and had put New Zealand on the map; *Flinders had laid down the coasts of Australia; and *Vancouver and others had delineated both shores of the North Pacific. Theirs were coastal running surveys, largely laid down from shipboard observations. The 19th century was devoted to detailed charting of bays and anchorages, passages, and approaches along every distant coastline. In this work the surveying service of the Royal Navy played a prominent part, and the first chart produced by the Admiralty from its own surveys was published in 1800.

An explanation of the construction of a *gnomonic chart, on which a *great circle sailing course appears as a straight line, first appeared as early as 1669, but it was not until Hugh Godfray published two polar gnomonic charts in 1858 that they became popular with mariners. Together these covered the greater part of the world, one for the northern, and the other for the southern hemisphere.

For a short period in the early 19th century when surveys were largely exploratory, surveyors were encouraged to send in drawings of their work fit for direct engraving, but soon it became necessary not to limit the surveyor in this way. Instead the Admiralty's hydrographic department, which had been established in 1795 under Alexander Dalrymple (1737–1808), was made responsible for converting his detailed work into what the navigator required, including the choice of scale for publication. Scale is subject to the dimensions of the projected chart and there has always been pressure for a standard size which would be practical in use, convenient for chart table and folio covers, and simplify the printing from, and the handling of, chart plates. A size of 965 × 635 millimetres (38 × 25 in.), known in the paper trade as double elephant, has been the most used, halved for smaller charts. The internationally accepted maximum size is 71 centimetres by one metre (28 in. × 40 in.).

In 1828 the Admiralty's Hydrographic Department published its first **Sailing Directions*, and in 1832 the promulgation of new information to keep charts up to date was begun in the *Nautical Magazine*. Two years later the issue of **Notices to Mariners* began for urgent items, and in 1907 paste-on reproductions of affected portions, known as 'block notices', were issued to facilitate corrections, a method the Japanese had begun in 1904. By the late 1960s there were some 3,000 notices every year which had to be entered on existing charts to take account of changes.

Traditionally there were three steps before the publication of a chart: a drawing based on a surveyor's work or a foreign chart; its engraving or inscription on copper or lithographic stone; and printing. A chart was originally judged for accuracy by the number and spacing of the soundings it showed; later it relied more on depth contours with fewer supporting depths and made more use of colours for depth differentiation. Depth lines, too, were simplified to speed reproduction stages. The representation of land features also changed, particularly in the hill-work. This went through stages of hachuring, perhaps accompanied by 'smoke shading', to the use of contours as on a land map. One reason for this was the introduction of *radar; another was simplicity in reproduction.

From 1939 the development of *hyperbolic navigation called for a new family of charts in which hyperbolic graticules were superimposed in colour on the navigational detail. Among other problems this involved was the adaptation of the reproduction process so as to ensure the accurate registration of the various printing plates. After the Second World War (1939–45) other developments in chartmaking included using chart plates made from plastic instead of copper or lithographic stone, and using metric measurement for depths instead of *fathoms, a change which started in the late 1960s. See also DEEP SCATTERING LAYERS.

Whitfield, P., *The Charting of the Oceans: Ten Centuries of Maritime Maps* (1996).

Modern Chartmaking by Adam Kerr

Chartmaking underwent a major change with the introduction of computer technology in the 1960s. Initially, the term 'computer-assisted cartography' was used—perhaps to stress that man had not been left out of the process entirely—with computers used to draft chart borders and grids, which had been previously a laborious undertaking. Another task that lent itself readily to early computer calculation was the lattices used for plotting hyperbolic navigation coordinates.

Nowadays most of the work is done by computers, although there are still important areas where the skills of the trained cartographer are essential. It is vital in the use of computers that all the data is in digital form. All modern surveys provide it, but historic data from graphic sources must be converted.

It is not always appreciated that the information appearing on a printed chart is a very small part of that obtained by the field surveys, which with modern systems collect huge quantities of data. It requires great skill to reduce this mass of information into something that the navigator can assimilate quickly and accurately. Efforts are currently being made to develop computer programs that will tackle this task.

Efforts, which have given rise to much debate, are also being directed towards finding suitable programs to calculate and draw depth contours, which are more numerous on modern charts than they were previously. More exotically, research is also in hand to show the configuration of the seafloor as a coloured three-dimensional image.

Chartmaking has traditionally tended to build a margin of safety for the navigator when interpreting the information received. For instance, all depths are shown as measured from the extreme low tide plane, so that the navigator has the height of the tide as a margin of additional depths. However scientists studying *oceanography and other aspects of the sea are more interested in the best interpretation of the actual depth.

Digital Charting. Traditionally printed paper charts have been used as the medium for plotting navigation. However, in the early 1980s interest developed in not only processing the hydrographic data digitally, but presenting it to the navigator in digital form that could be fed into an Electronic Chart System (ECS) that would display all the information on a computer monitor. Not only is the chart information displayed on screen but the ship itself is positioned continuously on the chart. This is a great help to the navigator, leaving him with his hands free while being able to monitor constantly the location of his ship. Such systems are being increasingly used, though paper charts are still common.

The capabilities of this technology have led to increased sophistication, not only in what basic chart information can be shown, but also in layers of other information, such as *ice or other *marine meteorological conditions. Specifications for the advanced systems that have these capabilities, called ECDIS (Electronic Chart Display and Information Systems), have now been approved by the *International Maritime

Organization (IMO). Unlike ECS, where paper charts still have to be carried, ships are legally permitted to use ECDIS without them, but it is a costly and complicated system, and tends only to be used on large vessels.

Oceanic Cartography. While the main focus of chartmaking has been to provide nautical charts for the purpose of navigation, there has always been a need by ocean scientists to plot and display numerous forms of data concerning the oceans. During the 18th and 19th centuries there had been a number of individual initiatives to develop ocean maps to show oceanographic phenomena. Perhaps the best known of these is Matthew *Maury's *Physical Geography of the Sea* which was published in 1855. However, towards the end of that century a group of eminent oceanographers met at the 7th International Geographic Congress at Berlin to discuss the need for a bathymetric map of all the world's oceans, bathymetric meaning the sounding of the seas. As a result, a major mapping project, called the General Bathymetric Map of the Oceans (GEBCO), was initiated to map the topography of the seafloor. This celebrated its 100th year in 2003.

Besides the topography of the seafloor, many other types of data are also mapped. This can include geophysical data such as gravity anomalies or magnetism or chemical or biological parameters. Frequently the maps are bound together as atlases so that comparisons of different parameters can be easily made.

Cartographers preparing oceanographic charts (or maps) will be generally less bound by navigation requirements, such as the general use of the Mercator projection that is used to show a ship's course as a straight line when plotted. Instead they may wish to use projections such as Equi-area, which shows all parts of the earth in strictly equal area, i.e. there is no distortion as in the Mercator projection. It has already been said that oceanic cartographers aim to show features in the most accurate form they are able, but as the data may sometimes be limited, very considerable interpretation is sometimes used. As the navigational chartmaker has moved to digital presentations, so also have the oceanic cartographers, who today make considerable use of mathematical models and digital displays on computer monitors.

Black, J., *Visions of the World: A History of Maps* (2003).

Scott, D., et al. (eds.), *The History of GEBCO, 1903–2003* (2003).

chase. **(1)** The name given to the guns mounted on the upper deck in the bows and on the *poop deck astern of a sailing man-of-war and fixed to fire directly ahead or astern. They were known as the bow chase, to fire at a vessel being chased, and the stern chase, to fire at a vessel chasing. But see also CHASE GUNS. Also the name given to a vessel being chased. **(2)** When used as a verb, it was pursuing a vessel in wartime with a view to its destruction or capture, or perhaps to acquire intelligence from those aboard.

chase guns, the name given to the guns which were temporarily moved from the normal *broadside gun tiers of a sailing man-of-war for use through chase ports cut on the gun-deck level in the bows of a ship, i.e. they were not permanently mounted to fire ahead, as was the bow *chase, and were fired from the gun-deck level and not from the upper deck.

chasse-marée, the French name for a coasting vessel, one which worked the tides. In the 16th century the typical French and other coasters were three masted, normally rigged with square main and *foresails, a *lateen *mizzen, a main *topsail, and a *spritsail carried below the *bowsprit. During the 18th century many coasters adopted the *lug rig, based on a design of fishing vessel, and during the Revolutionary and Napoleonic Wars (1793–1815) these *luggers, still known as *chasse-marées*, were used by the French largely for *smuggling and as *privateers, the rig being refined to the highest possible pitch to provide a good turn of speed. This was achieved by adopting a large sail plan on three masts, all three raked *aft, the mizzen being stepped hard up against the vessel's *transom. A long bowsprit and *bumpkin enabled a greater area of *canvas to be spread. All three masts carried a *standing lug rig, with a *jib to complete the rig, thus producing a very weatherly vessel. Some of the larger *chasse-marées* could also set a lug topsail on the mainmast. The need for the long bumpkin was to sheet the overhanging mizzen. One drawback of the *chasse-marée* in its role as a privateer was the comparatively large crew required to handle the considerable area of sail and also provide gun crews; another was that when *running free it could be overtaken relatively easily by a ship with normal *square rig.

Chatham Chest, a contributory benevolent fund for the English Navy established by Sir Francis *Drake, Sir John *Hawkins, and Lord Howard of Effingham (1536–1624) in 1590, to which seamen paid sixpence a month from their pay for the benefit of the wounded and the widows of those killed in action. To avoid peculation, the original Chatham Chest, which is preserved at Historic Dockyard, Chatham, was fitted with seven locks, the seven keys to which were held by different individuals so that all had to be present when the chest was opened. In spite of this precaution, large sums were regularly illegally abstracted from the chest. The funds of the Chatham Chest were amalgamated with those of Greenwich Royal Hospital in 1814.

chearly, an old sea expression meaning heartily or quickly. 'Row chearly in the boats', row heartily.

check, to. **(1)** To ease away slowly, particularly in connection with a *purchase such as the *falls of a lifeboat (see LIFESAVING) or the sheets or sails. **(2)** To bring a vessel to a stop, by letting go an anchor, by a *mooring wire made fast to a *wharf, or by going *astern on the engines.

cheeks. **(1)** Pieces of timber bolted to the mast of a sailing ship below the masthead to support the *trestle-trees. For illus. see RIGGING: STANDING RIGGING. **(2)** The two sidepieces of the wooden gun carriages in sailing warships. **(3)** The two sides of a *block. **(4)** The rounded portions of the bows of the old wooden men-of-war when they were extended by the erection of the *forecastle above the *beakhead, a feature of warship design introduced in the 15th century.

cheese down, to, a method of coiling down the tail of a rope on deck to present a neat appearance. The end of the tail is in the centre and the remainder coiled flat round it in a tight spiral, each *flake touching those on either side of it so that the finished *coil looks like a spiral rope mat lying on the deck. When a *fall has been cheesed down, the final result is itself called a cheese. The end of a rope should be never be cheesed down if it is required to *render quickly through a *block, as the tight coiling which forms a cheese is apt to make the rope kink when uncoiled quickly and it might therefore jam in the block. A rope so coiled is also known as a **Flemish coil**.

chemical oceanography is the study of the chemistry of the complex mixture of dilute chemicals in sea water. This is quite unlike classical chemistry in which pure unadulterated solutions are investigated.

Sea water contains every known naturally occurring element. Some like sodium and chlorine are in high concentrations but the majority occur only in trace concentrations. At the beginning of the 20th century the Germans believed they could extract enough gold from sea water to finance their war debt. They were led astray because the analyst's water samples were contaminated by his gold wedding ring, and he grossly overestimated the samples' gold content. Similar problems of contamination, caused by the wire on which the sample bottles were mounted, or even by cigarette smoke in the laboratory, have invalidated many subsequent analyses of the concentrations of more important trace metals in sea water, like iron, copper, and zinc. Sea water also contains a complex cocktail of organic compounds. Some of these are natural, but others are *pollution from industrial and agricultural activities. Man has even added novel elements such as minute traces of americium, an isotope synthesized by the nuclear industry and used in smoke detectors.

Water itself is a remarkable compound. As an oxide of hydrogen (H_2O) it might be expected to be a gas as is nitrous oxide (N_2O or laughing gas), which has a much heavier molecule. However, water molecules tend to stick together in fives, increasing its effective molecular weight, so pure water is liquid above 0 °C (32 °F). The freezing point of sea water is depressed to –1.9 °C (28.6 °F) by its salt content. *Ice is also exceptional, in that it floats. It is lighter than the liquid water because the molecules are arranged into an open lattice and are more spaced out. Quite of lot of heat is needed to melt a gram of ice (80 calories) and even more to evaporate it (532 calories). These 'latent heats' have far-reaching implications for understanding physical processes in the oceans.

The total amount of dissolved salts in sea water is known as its *salinity. Many chemical constituents of sea water are conservative, so their concentrations vary in direct proportion to the salinity. This is particularly true for those occurring at concentrations greater than one part per million, which together contribute 99.9% of the salinity. Most constituents are in 'steady state'—the rate at which they are being added to the oceans is exactly balanced by the rate that they are being lost. The total ocean is stirred about every 1,500 years (akin to taking over a millennium to stir a cup of tea). So any substance with a turnover rate of 10,000 years or more is uniformly distributed. However, the concentrations of many substances fluctuate widely, and most of these are involved in biological processes. For example, oxygen is used in the respiration of most organisms and is also produced during photosynthesis. Carbon compounds are involved in all biological processes, and many simple inorganic compounds, such as nitrates and phosphates, are essential for *marine plant growth. Recently, iron has been identified as being an important trace nutrient regulating biological production in certain areas of ocean. Many organisms regulate their internal chemical contents and thereby influence the concentrations of trace elements found in sea water. Some of the rarer elements are used in trace concentrations: iron is a constituent of haemoglobins in vertebrates including *whales and man, and vanadium and copper are constituents of the blood pigments of pelagic tunicates (sea squirts) and *crustaceans respectively.

Trace concentrations of some elements are essential to certain life forms, but at higher concentrations they become toxic, copper being an example. Some elements are not used directly by organisms but become attached to the outside of cell walls of marine plants and bacteria, and so their distributions in sea water resemble those of nutrients.

The vertical profiles of concentrations of these substances that are involved in biological interactions typically show much reduced concentrations near the surface, where they are stripped out by the heightened biological activity, and by the sinking of detrital material into deep water. However, in the deeper water below the *thermocline, detrital material is broken down, releasing these substances back into solution, so their concentrations increase. They are then returned back into the surface layers by vertical mixing during winter at high *latitudes when the thermocline is broken up by cooling. So the upper few hundred metres of water are mixed by winter storms, and by *upwelling.

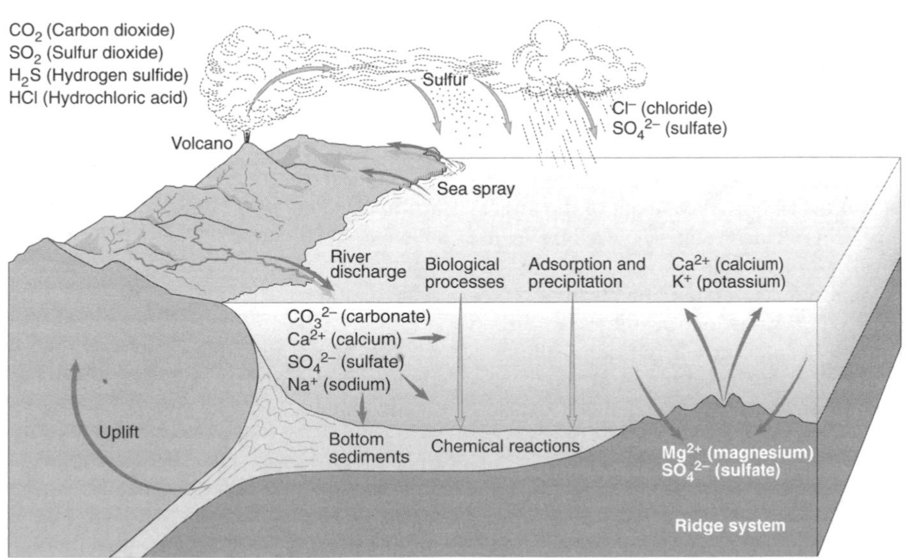

Processes that regulate the major constituents of sea water

Different behaviours of isotopes of the same element provide useful insights into differences in the dynamics of different parts of the cycles. For example, uranium-238 in continental rocks disintegrates into the radioactive gas radon, which is emitted to the atmosphere where it radioactively decays into lead-210, which is inert and insoluble. The lead isotope is washed into the ocean by rain where slowly it sinks to the bottom. However, lead-210 is also radioactive and decays into polonium-210, which readily gets absorbed onto biological surfaces and behaves like a nutrient. So measuring the ratio between the lead-210 and polonium-210 gives a measure of the differences in rates of sedimentation under gravity and the biological removal.

The exchange of gases across the surface of sea water is another important process, which is determined by the temperature of the water and the partial pressures of the gas. More gas can dissolve in cold water, because its partial pressure is lower, and if its partial pressure is lower than in the atmosphere, more gas will dissolve at the surface of the water. When the sea is rough, the breaking *waves carry bubbles several metres below the surface, so the equilibrium in the gas balance between the atmosphere and the water is achieved faster. In cold polar seas up to 9 millilitres of oxygen can dissolve in each litre of sea water, whereas in the tropics, where surface water temperatures are higher than 20 °C (68 °F), only 6 millilitres of oxygen can dissolve. The same effect is seen with carbon dioxide, but here the picture is complicated because when the marine plant phytoplankton is growing rapidly and using up the carbon dioxide in photosynthesis, the oceans draw carbon dioxide out of the atmosphere. Where cold water is upwelling in the tropics, carbon dioxide is vented back into the atmosphere. So understanding the importance of the oceans in ameliorating the rise of carbon dioxide concentrations in the atmosphere is highly complicated, and their effectiveness may be reduced by *climate change.

Other important processes that influence the chemistry of sea water and the sediments that accumulate on the seabed are associated first with *hydrothermal vents, which discharge fluids that are rich in the metal sulphides that precipitate to form manganese modules. Secondly, the organic matter that accumulates in profusion on the seabed underlying upwelling regions is, over geological time, converted into the *offshore oil and gas reserves that are now fuelling our industries.

Open University, *Ocean Chemistry and Deep-Sea Sediments* (1989). M. V. Angel

Chesapeake, USS, one of the six original *frigates authorized in 1794 to form the US Navy. Intended to be a 44-gun ship, its completion was delayed and it was actually built as a 36-gun frigate. On 1 June 1813, while under the command of James Lawrence, the *Chesapeake* left Boston Harbour to fight the British 38-gun frigate *Shannon*, lying offshore. It is a myth that Lawrence did so as a result of a challenge to come out and do battle from the British frigate: one was issued but arrived after Lawrence had sailed. However, in sailing as he did Lawrence not only disobeyed orders but departed from any kind of sensible strategy, and after two destructive *broadsides, the captain of the *Shannon*, Captain Sir Philip Broke (1776–1841), led a boarding party aboard the *Chesapeake*. Lawrence was killed and the *Chesapeake*, short of officers and with an untrained crew, surrendered after an action which lasted only fifteen minutes and which subsequently became one of the best-known frigate actions in naval history. The *Chesapeake* was taken to Halifax after its capture and later to Britain. Since Britain had recently suffered many humiliating defeats in such frigate actions, this success made Broke extremely popular in Britain and also had a salutary effect on naval gunnery and training which were largely remodelled on his methods.

In 1996 it was found that some of the timbers from the *Chesapeake*, auctioned in 1819, had been used to construct the Chesapeake Mill, which had been built in a Hampshire village in 1820 and which is still standing.

chesstrees, two pieces of oak secured to the *topsides of a *square-rigged sailing ship at the point where the curve of the bow began to straighten out for the *run *aft, one on each side of the ship. Normally they had a hole through them in the centre, but occasionally they were fitted with a *sheave. The *bowlines with which the main *tacks were hauled down were led through the hole or sheave in the chesstrees to give the crew a clear haul. See also VEER AND HAUL, TO.

Chiloé, a province of southern Chile (derived from *Chile* and *hué*, 'port'), a name which occurs frequently in English books of voyages of the 16th–18th centuries. It was the first sight of land—and therefore vastly welcome—to mariners as they entered the Pacific either round Cape Horn or through the Straits of *Magellan. Chiloé is also an island, part of the province of the same name.

chine, the angle where the bottom *strakes of a boat meet the sides. In a hard-chined boat this angle is pronounced; in a soft-chined one it is rounded off gradually.

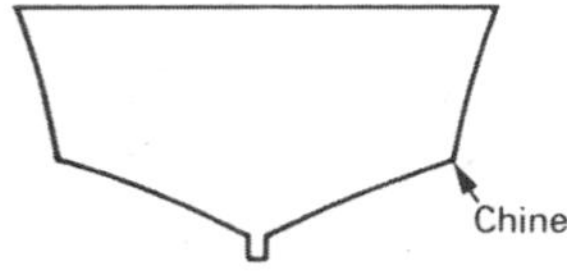

Chinese gybe, a type of wild and unpremeditated *gybe which occurs in a *gaff-rigged sailing vessel when the main boom gybes but the gaff does not follow.

chinse, orig. **chinch, to,** the operation of pressing *oakum into a *seam with a knife or chisel as a temporary measure until the seam can be properly *caulked. The full expression is that the oakum is chinched in. It is also used to denote the light caulking of a seam in places where the ship's structure cannot withstand the full force of caulking with a caulking iron and heavy hammer.

chip log, see LOG.

chips. (1) The pieces cut off timber in the *royal dockyards in Britain during the days of wooden ships when the dockyard carpenters shaped planks etc. for *shipbuilding and repairs. They were by tradition the perquisites of the carpenters and shipwrights, and could legally be carried out of the dockyard. It was a system which lent itself to considerable abuse, and whole planks and other timber were often carried out on the grounds that they were chips. There were many cases, particularly during the 17th century, when dockyard officials were found to have built whole houses and much of their furniture out the 'chips' they had taken out the dockyards. (2) In the US Navy, the ship's carpenter is nicknamed 'Chips'.

chock, to, an expression used by seamen meaning to secure articles stowed anywhere in a ship to prevent their breaking loose and taking charge in rough weather when the vessel rolled excessively. A wooden wedge used for this purpose is often called a chock.

chock-a-block, the position when two *blocks of a *tackle come together so that no further movement is possible. It is also known as 'two blocks'.

chocolate gale, the sailor's name for the brisk north-west wind which is the prevalent wind in the West Indies and off the *Spanish Main.

choking the luff, a quick and ready method of temporarily stopping all movement of a rope through a *block by placing the hauling part across the *sheave of the block, where it jams the sheave and holds it tight. A pull on the hauling part releases the sheave.

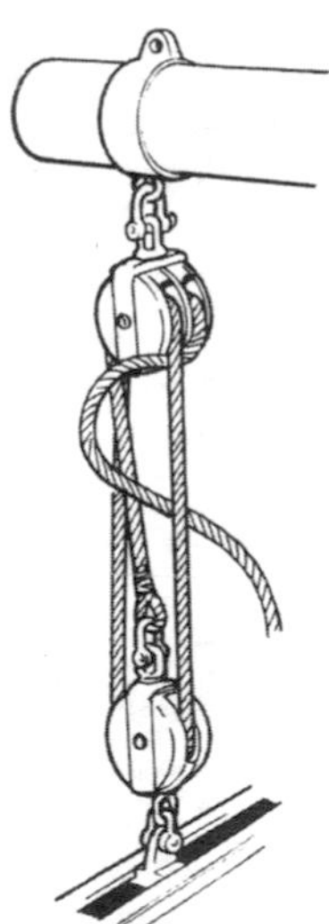

Choking the luff

chops, the area where *tides meet to cause an irregular sea, or where a channel meets the sea. 'Chops of the Channel', the western entrance of the English Channel when approaching from the Atlantic.

Christian, Fletcher (1764–93?), a Cumberland man of Manx origin, who was launched on a sea profession by William *Bligh and promoted by him from *master's mate to acting lieutenant in the *_Bounty_ for her voyage to Tahiti in 1788. Relations between the two deteriorated, however, and after a petty dispute Christian made preparations, using a makeshift raft, to desert the ship when passing the Tonga Islands. Discontented members of the crew discovered this and persuaded him to lead a general mutiny. His fate is uncertain. Though he probably died on Pitcairn Island, killed in a rising by the Tahitians, some slight evidence has been offered that he escaped from the island and returned clandestinely to England.

chronometer, a timepiece with a nearly constant *rate, intended primarily for the determination of *longitude by comparing local time, computed by *celestial or *satellite navigation, with time at the *prime meridian measured by a clock. In practice the chronometer would normally have been used to rate the error of the *hack watch which could be taken on deck so that the chronometer itself need not be shifted unnecessarily. The chronometer is normally set to *Greenwich Mean Time (Universal Time) and rated by radio time signals. Three chronometers used to be carried so as to detect the errant instrument if one of the three became unreliable. It was not until the 19th century that the mechanical construction of marine timepieces reached a sufficiently high standard, and improvements in manufacture resulted in a reduction of cost, that the chronometer became generally available at sea. See also BOARD OF LONGITUDE. Mike Richey

c.i.f., see FREIGHT.

Cinque Ports, an ancient association of towns on the Channel coast of England, mainly for juridical purposes. They originally comprised five ports: Dover, Hastings, Romney, Hythe, and Sandwich, to which were later added the 'ancient towns' of Rye and Winchelsea. They were charged with furnishing ships and men for the service of the crown in wartime, thus constituting the medieval equivalent of a navy, in return for charters guaranteeing them certain privileges in tolls and commercial *fisheries, and in maritime jurisdiction in the waters of the eastern English Channel, part of the *narrow seas. The oldest charter dates back to 1155–6, but the practice almost certainly went back much further. After 1444–5 there is no evidence that Cinque Port ships were employed by the crown and by that time, anyway, some of the ports had become so silted up that vessels could no longer use them. See also GROMET; WARFARE AT SEA.

Cipangu, the name by which Japan was known in the West in the 15th–17th centuries.

clamps. (1) Pieces of timber fixed longitudinally to the masts or *yards of *square-rigged ships to strengthen them if they showed signs of weakness or bursting under strain. See also FISH, TO. **(2)** Planks laid fore and *aft under the *beams of the *orlop and lower decks in wooden ships and *fayed to the timbers to add strength to the ship's structure. **(3)** *Strakes fastened to the inside of wooden ships' sides to form a support on which the ends of the deck beams can rest, the *knees being bolted or fastened with *treenails or bolts to the clamps.

clap on, to, the seaman's expression when something is added temporarily to an existing part. Thus, a *purchase is clapped onto a *guy or *fall when additional hauling power is required. Some *masters of sailing vessels used to order additional sails to be clapped on to take advantage of a fair wind. A *seizing is also clapped on.

class, see CLASSIFICATION. Also, a class of ships or *yachts are ones all built to the same design.

classification, the endorsement of a classification society which is awarded once the ships meets a minimum standard in design, quality of construction, etc. A vessel is classed in this way for a definite period of years, and on its expiry it must be resurveyed if its owners wish it to retain its original classification. In addition, after any accident such as a fire a ship has to be resurveyed to establish its classification. The advantages for a shipowner to have his vessels classified and to keep them 'in class' are numerous, as the construction and maintenance of a ship up to the standard required is mandatory for almost all insurance, *chartering, financing, and so on, and also for the issue of statutory certificates required by international conventions such as *SOLAS.

In 2003 there were nineteen classification societies that issued such classifications. Among the best known are the American Bureau of Shipping, Bureau Veritas, and *Lloyd's Register, the latter granting the well-known classification 100A1, where 100 = suitable for seagoing service, A = constructed or accepted into Lloyd's Register class and maintained in good and efficient condition, and 1 = good and efficient anchoring and mooring equipment. The mark indicating that a ship has been built to Lloyd's Register class is a Formée Cross, sometimes erroneously described as a Maltese Cross. It was adopted in 1853 as a distinguishing mark for all ships built under special Lloyd's survey anywhere in the world. Currently most classification societies encourage 'running surveys' whereby ships on constant voyages can have inspections on a regular basis, avoiding the need for a costly lay-up every fourth or fifth year. See also SHIPBUILDING.

claw off, to, to *beat to *windward in a sailing vessel to avoid being driven onto a *lee shore. The expression implies danger of being driven ashore because of a combination of a rough sea and a strong onshore wind.

claw ring, a fitting, long out of use, on the main boom of a *yacht to take the main sheet where roller *reefing was fitted.

clean, a word which refers to the lines of a vessel's hull when they give a fine and unobstructed *run from bow to stern so that the ship moves through the water smoothly without undue turbulence. It is normally used in terms such as **a clean entrance**, **a clean run aft**, and **a clean-lined hull**.

clean bill, the description of a ship when all the ship's company are in good health. A ship's *bill of health is a certificate signed by a consul or other port authority that no contagious disease existed in the ship's port of departure and that none of the crew was infected with a notifiable disease at the time of sailing. Such a bill of health, properly authenticated, is a clean bill; where it cannot be so authenticated because of infection in the port of departure, it is a foul bill.

clean slate, originally a log-slate, on which the *courses steered by a ship and the distances run as indicated on a *log were written in chalk during the course of a *watch. At the end of the watch, the information on the slate was entered in the deck-log and the slate wiped clean so that the officer keeping the next watch could enter on it the courses and distances made good during his watch. The term has entered the English language as an expression meaning that past action and occurrences are forgotten (wiped off the slate) and a new start can be made.

clear, to, a word that had, and has, many maritime meanings, such as to escape from, to unload, to empty, to prepare. **To clear for action**, to prepare for battle by securing everything on board, testing all communications in connection with the ship's armament, rigging fire hoses, *piping the ship's company to their

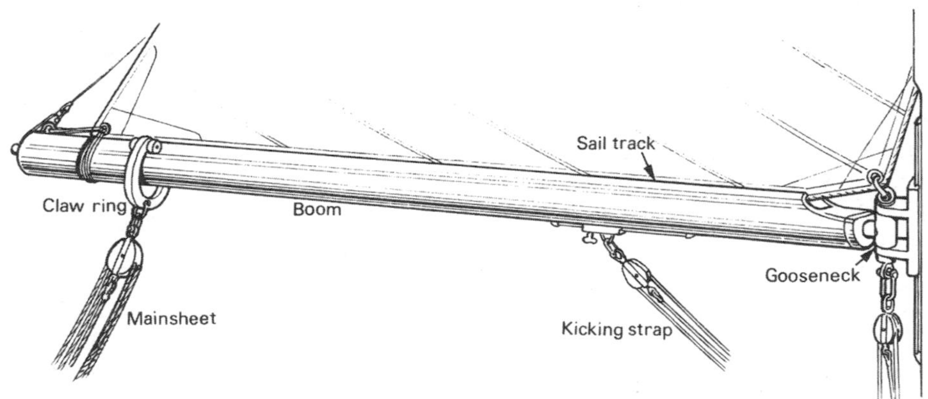

Claw ring

action stations, etc. In wooden sailing warships the order entailed also the rigging of additional chain *slings to the *yards as a precaution against their being shot away by gunfire, the dismantling of officers' *cabins, the *striking of all cabin furniture below decks, the hoisting out of all boats, which were towed astern during battle, and the rigging of protective nets above the upper deck to safeguard men working on deck against falling masts and *spars.

The term is also used in *navigation, as, for example, to *lay a ship's *course **to clear** a headland, a rock ledge, etc.

clearance, the document giving permission to sail by the custom house in a port to the *master of a vessel going foreign. It is given after inspection of the ship's registry, its crew list and *articles, receipts for port charges, the *bill of health, and the *manifest. The accuracy of all these papers has to be sworn by the master before clearance can be given. A ship is **cleared to sail** when all these formalities have been observed.

'clear lower deck', a naval order for all hands on board to muster on the upper deck. The only men exempt from such an order are those on *watch in the machinery spaces where the machinery is actually running.

clear-view screen, a circular disc of plate glass, which is revolved at high speed by an electric motor, incorporated in the glass screen of the navigating *bridge. The centrifugal motion throws off all rain, sleet, or snow and gives the *navigation officer a clear view ahead.

cleat. **(1)** A piece of wood or metal with two arms placed at convenient stations on board ship, or on a *yacht, to which ropes or *falls can be made fast by taking two or three turns under and over the arms. **(2)** Small wedges of elm or oak fastened to the *yards of *square-rigged sailing ships to prevent ropes or the *earings of the sails from slipping off the yard. See also THUMB CLEAT.

clench, to. **(1)** To make a permanent join. Thus a clenched *shackle, with which, for example, the end of a chain *cable is secured to the bottom of the *chain locker, has its bolt hammered over so that it cannot be removed, thus closing the shackle permanently. **(2)** To rivet with copper nails and roves (conical copper washers). A more simple method is to turn over the point of the nail without using roves. See also CLINCHING.

Clermont, or, more correctly, the 'North River Steamboat of Clermont', is generally acknowledged as the world's first commercially successful steamboat, though the one John Fitch (1743–98) built in 1788, which made regular scheduled trips on the Delaware River, was no failure. Built in 1807, the *Clermont* was a joint venture between two Americans, Robert Livingston (1746–1813), from whose home at Clermont, NY, this early *paddle steamer derived its name, and its designer, the engineer Robert *Fulton. In 1803, while Livingston, a politician of note, was in Paris negotiating the Louisiana Purchase, the two men demonstrated a small paddle steamer on the River Seine, and with Livingston having been granted a monopoly of steam *navigation on all waters with the state boundaries of New York, the two joined forces to exploit this as yet unproved method of transport.

Their paddle steamer was built on the East Hudson River, New York City, by Charles Brown, but the engine was made in Britain by Boulton and Watt of Birmingham, as no engineers in the USA had at that time sufficient experience to build an engine suitable for ship propulsion. The engine had a single vertical cylinder, 61 centimetres (24 in.) in diameter with a stroke of 122 centimetres (48 in.), which drove a pair of 4.6-metre (15-ft) paddle wheels, one on each side of its hull, through bell cranks and spur gearing. The North River Steamboat had an overall length of 40.5 metres (133 ft) and a displacement (see TONNAGE) of 100 tons. On its initial trip it steamed up the river to Albany and back, a distance of about 384 kilometres (240 mls.), in 62 hours. This gave it an average speed of just over 6 kph (3.8 mph), but in a run from Livingston's home to Albany against the flow of the river it made 8 kph (5 mph), rather higher than the terms of Livingston's monopoly required. After considerable alterations, which virtually made it a new boat, it was registered in 1808 as the 'North River Steamboat of Clermont'—quickly shortened by the press to *Clermont*—and it subsequently ran regularly between Albany and New York City.

clew. **(1)** In a *fore-and-aft rig, the lower aftermost corner of the sail; in a *square-rigged ship, the two lower corners of the square sail. In cases where sails on a fore-and-aft rig are not normally *laced to a boom, such as *jibs, *staysails, etc., it is the corner of the sail to which the *sheet is secured; with sails on a rig which normally are laced to a boom, the clew is usually fitted with an *outhaul so that the foot of the sail can be stretched tautly along the boom. For illus. see FORE-AND-AFT RIG. **(2)** The *lanyards and *nettles by which a naval *hammock was slung from hooks in a deck *beam. The hammock clews, one at each end of the hammock, consisted of a rope lanyard with a ring spliced into the end from which originally 22 nettles were secured into the same number of eyelet holes in each end of the hammock. Later the number of nettles was reduced to eight, though they were doubled through the ring, providing in effect sixteen nettles which were secured to sixteen eyelet holes in the two ends of the hammocks. See also DOUBLE CLEWS.

clew lines, the lines or *tackles used in *square-rigged ships to haul the *clews of the square sails up to their *yards. Those used for the *courses are often in the form of tackles and are called **clew garnets**. Colin Mudie

climate change. The earth's climate continually fluctuates as a result of the earth's elliptical orbit around the sun. When the earth is closer to the sun it receives more radiant energy. Long-term analyses of climate based on deep ocean deposits and *ice cores from the Antarctic and Greenland ice caps show there are climatic cycles lasting 25,000, 40,000, and 100,000 years, which have resulted in the oscillations between glacial and interglacial periods. There are also millennial scale oscillations: the Vikings were able to colonize Greenland in their *longboats during a mild climatic period about a thousand years ago, and from there visited *Vinland, whereas there was a mini-ice age in the early 18th century when goose fairs were regularly held on the frozen Thames. Recently, 70-year cycles have been identified in the *North Atlantic Oscillation. When pressure is high over the Azores, and low over Iceland, the flow of the *Gulf Stream increases, keeping north-western Europe's climate mild. In the opposite phase the flow reduces and the climate of Europe is cooler. Similar oscillations have been

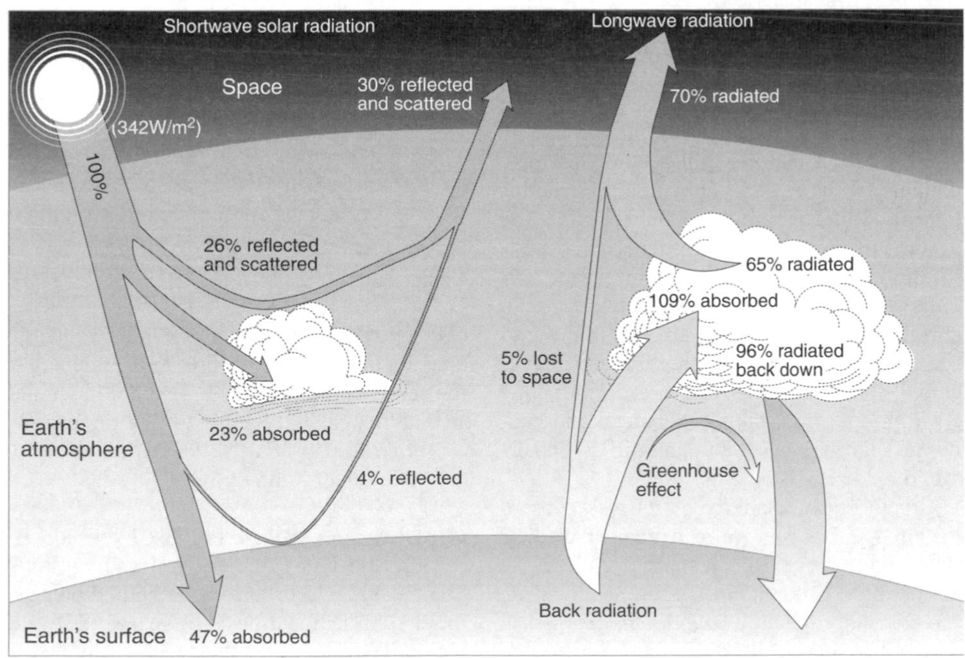

How part of the sun's radial energy is reflected back into space and part reaches the surface of the earth

identified in the North Pacific and both may be linked with *El Niño events.

The gases in past atmospheres can be measured in the gas bubbles trapped deep in the ice caps. These show that as climate has oscillated so have the amounts of carbon dioxide in the atmosphere. When CO_2 concentrations are high, more of the incoming radiant heat from the sun is trapped in the atmosphere—the so-called greenhouse effect. Other gases such as methane and CFCs (chlorofluorocarbons) are many more times more effective in trapping the heat, but their concentrations are rising more slowly. This link between carbon dioxide and climate is well established, but exactly what causes it is a matter of controversy. Since the start of the Industrial Revolution in the 18th century the burning of fossil fuels has increased the carbon dioxide content of the atmosphere from pre-industrial levels of 240 parts per million (ppm) to present levels of over 370 ppm. If we continue to burn oil and coal at the present rates it will rise to 500–600 ppm by the end of the century. As more and more of the sun's energy gets trapped in the atmosphere, the earth's climate will warm, but not uniformly across the planet; polar regions will warm more than the tropics. Although some countries will benefit from such shifts most will lose out. *Sea levels will rise as the polar ice caps melt and in 2003 Australian scientists produced fresh evidence showing that the area of sea ice surrounding Antarctica has shrunk by 20% in the last 50 years. Weather patterns will become less predictable with bigger and more destructive *storms. Shifts in rainfall will increase flooding in some places, but cause droughts and desertification in others. The pattern of ocean *currents will shift, and close links between ocean currents and local climate are contributing to the uncertainties of predicting the outcome of global climate change and are discouraging governments from taking the social and economic sacrifices needed to halt the rise in carbon dioxide emissions.

Already ocean *plankton off the west coast of Britain has become more typical of warmer seas, and there have been sharp decline in the abundances of keystone species, such as the *crustacean copepod (*Calanus finmarchicus*), which has been linked to the catastrophic decline in *cod stocks. Climate will continue to fluctuate because many of the causes are planetary, but the implications of the changes will become increasingly threatening as world population grows and industralization increases globally, one of the most serious *environmental issues facing us today. M. V. Angel

clinching, a method, used in the days of sail before the invention of *cable stoppers, of fastening or knotting large ropes to heavy objects by a *half hitch with the end stopped back on its own part by a *seizing. Thus a hemp *cable or *hawser would be clinched to the ring of a *kedge anchor when required for use, with the inboard end clinched to the mainmast as a stopper. Thus, **to run a cable out to clinch** means that there is no more to *veer.

clinker, or **clinch, built,** a method of boatbuilding in which the lower edge of each side plank overlaps the upper edge of the one below it. In the USA, this method of building is known as **lapstrake**. For a comparison, see CARVEL BUILT.

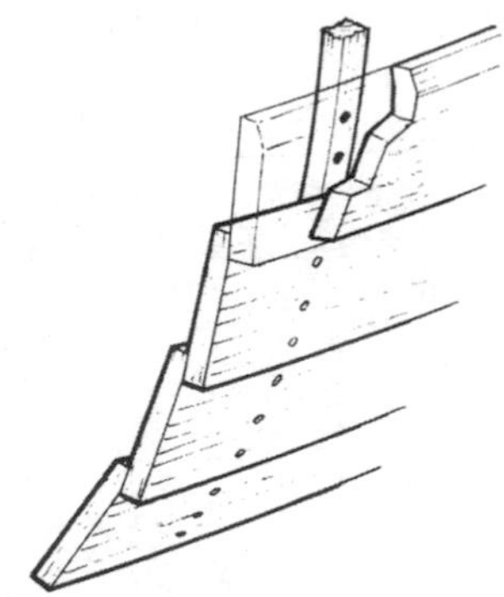

Clinker built

clip-hooks, two hooks of similar shape facing in opposite directions and attached to the same *thimble. They have a flat inner side so that they can lie together to form an *eye and are much used in small *tackles where an ordinary hook might jump out.

clipper, the generic name used very loosely to describe types of very fast sailing ships. The term is said to have been coined because they could clip the time taken on passage by the regular *packet ships, themselves very fast in their day.

The term was first applied to the speedy *fore-and-aft-rigged *schooners built in Virginia and Maryland, known as the Baltimore clippers, though they were not really clippers at all. These became famous during the War of 1812 as *blockade runners and *privateers, and subsequently notorious in the *slave trade carrying human cargoes from Africa to the USA. Their hulls were long and low with a *draught deeper *aft than *forward. They also had a very sharp-raked *stem (the true mark of the clipper), and an inclined, overhanging *counter stern, which reduced the area of hull in contact with the water. All these improvements in design were later combined with the three-masted *square rig to produce the beautiful clipper ships of the mid-19th century, the finest productions of the age of sail.

As early as 1833 an enlarged Baltimore clipper, the *Anne McKim*, had been given a square rig; and she is now generally acknowledged to be the first true clipper ship, though some hold it to have been the *Rainbow* built in 1845 at New York. The discovery of gold in California in 1848 and in Australia in 1850, raising a demand for the fastest passages to both places, and the repeal of the British Navigation Acts in 1849, opening the tea trade from China to London to foreign ships, gave a tremendous fillip to the production of American clippers. In this the outstanding shipbuilder Donald McKay (1810–80), of Boston took the lead, producing first the revolutionary *Stag Hound*, then *Flying Fish* and *Flying Cloud*. These were perhaps his most famous clippers, though his *Sovereign of the Seas* was a record-breaker, so much so that she was immortalized in a *shanty. Built in 1852 for the Swallow Tail Line, she made a name for herself through the speed of her voyages on the New York–California run.

As a result of this reputation *Sovereign of the Seas* was chartered to James Baines's Black Ball Line of Liverpool, and was used in the Australian wool trade, setting a new record of 65 days for the passage from London to Melbourne, a record which remained standing for 30 years until beaten by the famous clipper **Thermopylae*. She also established the all-time record of 13 days, 14 hours for a sailing passage from New York to Liverpool, being credited with a speed of 22 knots at times. Her performance impressed Baines so much that he ordered another four clippers from McKay, all of which were to become famous in the history of these great sailing ships: the *Lightning*, *Champion of the Seas*, *James Baines*, and *Donald McKay*, all built in 1854. Other American flyers were the New York-built *Challenge* (see 'BUCKO' MATE), and the Black Ball liner *Marco Polo*, built at St John's, New Brunswick, which broke all records for passages to and from Australia in 1852–3.

This competition now spurred British shipowners and *shipbuilding. Up to this time they had been mainly content with improving the sailing quality of the *Blackwall frigates, though schooner-rigged ships had been built since 1839 by Alexander Hall & Sons of Aberdeen for the England to Scotland passenger trade, and one of them, the *Scottish Maid*, *launched in 1847 and now regarded as the first British clipper ship, had reached London from Leith in 33 hours. The same firm now built the first small British clippers, the *Stornaway* and *Chrysolite*, for the tea trade, while R. & H. Green of Blackwall produced the *Challenger*.

The financial depression of 1857 and the American Civil War (1861–5) resulted in a decline in American commercial shipbuilding and in its place led to a revival in Britain which was to result in the golden age of the tea clipper. Tea from China was a very profitable cargo in those days and several clippers were specially built for the trade. The first arrivals in London of the new crop each year commanded the highest prices. The famous British clipper *Fiery Cross*, built by Chaloner of Liverpool in 1860, was the winner of the premium for the first ship home on no less than four occasions.

Robert Steele (*fl.* 1840–70), of Greenock, became one of the best known of the builders of tea clippers. Among them were the *Taeping*, *Aerial*, *Sir Lancelot*—said to be the most beautiful of all the clipper ships—and the *Serica*. All these ships were involved in the most famous of all the annual tea clipper races when the *Fiery Cross* left Foochow on 29 May 1866, the *Aerial*, *Taeping*, and *Serica* on the 30 May, and the *Taitsing* on the following day. The *Taeping* docked in London at 2145 on 6 September, the *Aerial* half an hour later, and the *Serica* at 2345 after having sailed the 25,600 km (16,000 mls.) from Foochow. The *Fiery Cross* and

Taitsing both reached London two days later. The *Thermopylae* and another tea clipper, **Cutty Sark*, which had been built to rival her, featured in another famous race, starting from Foochow in 1872, but off Cape Province, South Africa, the latter lost her *rudder in a *gale.

The opening of the *Suez Canal in 1869 struck at the *raison d'être* of the tea clippers, making the long trip round the Cape of Good Hope unprofitable for their specialized *freight. For a time these ships transferred to carrying wool from Australia, but were soon outmoded in a trade in which large cargoes, small crews, and less speed were more economical; these were better provided by the large, steel-hulled, four- and five-masted *barques with which the age of commercial sail finally came to an end.

The literature on clipper ships is extensive, but some of the most authoritative books on the subject were written by Basil Lubbock (1876–1944). His titles include *Round the Horn before the Mast: The China Clippers* (1919), *The Colonial Clippers* (1921), *The Log of the Cutty Sark* (1924), *The Down Easters* (1929), and *The Nitrate Clippers* (1933). More recent titles include: B. Bathe, *Seven Centuries of Sea Travel* (1972), J. Jobé (ed.), *The Great Age of Sail* (1967), F. Knight, *The Clipper Ship* (1973), O. Howe and F. Matthews, *American Clipper Ships, 1833–1858*, 2 vols. (1986), and R. McKay, *Donald McKay and his Famous Sailing Ships* (1995).

close hauled, the condition of sailing when a vessel sails as close to the wind as possible with her sails full and drawing. To achieve this a *square-rigger may brace her *yards to between about 30° to 40° off her centreline and achieve a heading of about 55°–70° off the *apparent wind. A *fore-and-aft-rigged vessel with her sails sheeted in close to her centreline can point considerably closer to the wind while modern *Bermudan-rigged racing *yachts can sail closer than 30° to the apparent wind.

close-quarters. **(1)** Strong barriers of wood erected across the decks of merchant ships in the days of sail, with loopholes through which muskets could be fired to resist boarding attacks from enemy *privateers. **(2)** A description of ships sailing in company very near one another.

close reefed. The description of a sailing vessel when her sails have been reduced by *furling and *reefing to a minimum for strong winds.

clothes, see GALLIGASKINS; LONG CLOTHES; SAILORS' DRESS; TARRY-BREEKS.

clothing, the name by which the various pieces of *rigging which hold a *bowsprit in position are known. The comparable name in the case of masts is **apparel**.

cloths, the strips of sailcloth which are *seamed together to form a sail. They are normally the width of the bolt from which they are cut in order that they may be seamed along the selvedges, which are considerably stronger than a cut edge.

cloud formations are a useful guide in weather prediction. There are four main types, **cirrus**, **cumulus**, **stratus**, and **nimbus**, but combinations of these main formations can also be indications at sea of the type of weather ahead. See MARINE METEOROLOGY.

clove hitch, a *bend formed by two half hitches, the second reversed so that the standing part is between the hitches. It is used at sea for making a line fast to a *spar and is also used when securing the *painter of a boat. It will not slip because the second half hitch rides over the standing part of the rope.

Clove hitch

club haul, to, to *tack a *square-rigged ship in a narrow space by letting go the *lee anchor from the bow—though with the *hawser led *aft and *stopped on the *quarter—as soon as the wind leaves the *foresails. As the ship gathers *sternway the pull of the anchor brings the ship's head round on the other tack and the anchor hawser is then cut. This method was only used in an emergency in heavy weather and when the ship was embayed.

clump block, a large single *block with a wide *swallow, which used to be used for a variety of daily purposes on board ships. They were made with a thicker case than usual so as to provide added strength to the *purchases in which they are used.

coach, a term used between the mid-17th and mid-19th centuries, probably derived from the word carosse, originally used to describe the forward part of the *cabin space under the *poop deck of a warship. Later, coach was also used to describe the fore-cabin under the *quarterdeck, just forward of the great cabin. About halfway through this period the term was used for both, the 'great coach or steerage' for the lower and the 'upper coach or *round house' for the upper.

'coach horses', the name given in the old Royal Navy to the men who rowed the admiral's *barge or captain's *galley. The name also spread from the navy to embrace the crews of state barges when they rowed with their livery.

coach-roof, the name by which the *cabin top of older *yachts is known.

coachwhipping, a form of decorative square *sinnet work worked with an even number of *strands to form a herringbone pattern. It was used occasionally in the decorative *pointing of a rope but more usually for covering *stanchions with a patterned sinnet to make a ship look smart and *'tiddley'. The making of sinnets, officially the duty of the *boatswain and his mates, was a favourite pastime of sailors during long voyages, but such fancy rope and knot work is very rarely seen at sea today.

coak. **(1)** Originally a wooden dowel, but the meaning has been extended to described the small brass bearing in the centre of the *sheave of a *block to keep it from splitting and to prevent wear by the pin on which it turns. Coaks, or dowels, used often to be fitted into the upper face of the wooden *knees to engage in corresponding holes in the *beams of ships to prevent them slipping. **(2)** As a verb, a *spar is **coaked** when it has been broken and the two pieces joined together by making a hollow in one of the broken ends and a projection in the other end which fits it exactly.

coaming, the name given to the raised lip, usually about 15–23 centimetres (6–9 in.) high, with which openings in the upper deck, such as *hatchways leading to the deck below, are framed to prevent any water on deck from running down the opening into the space below. They also serve as a framework for the cargo *hatches of old-fashioned merchant ships, though in this case somewhat higher, to which the strongbacks and hatch covers can be fitted and *battened down, and to which the *tarpaulin covers can be secured. In *yachts, coamings are the vertical sides of the *coach-roof or hatches above the deck.

coastal navigation. The difference between coastal navigation and *pilotage is narrow, but a general definition of the former would be the safe conduct of a ship where the *navigator has the land on one side of his *course and the open sea on the other, even though he is in fact navigating in what are known as pilotage waters. When a ship is proceeding in sight of a coastline, its navigator need not be in doubt as to his position, for the largest-scale *chart of the area will show all *landmarks, *lighthouses, *lightships, *buoys, etc., and by taking *bearings of objects on shore, and laying them off on the chart, he can *fix the ship's position. Where the chart shows only one conspicuous object in a long coastline, a position can be obtained by a **running fix**. A compass bearing of the object is transferred to the chart and later, when the bearing of the object has altered sufficiently to give an adequate *angle of cut, which should preferably not be less than 45°, a second bearing is taken and laid off on the chart. The first bearing is then transferred by parallel rulers by the distance the ship has run in the interval between the bearings along the course steered, making due allowance for the distance and direction the ship has been carried by the *tide. The point of intersection of the transferred bearing with the second bearing will be the ship's position.

Other methods of fixing the ship's position when in sight of land are by a *vertical sextant angle of, for instance, a lighthouse when its height above *sea level is known. Simple mathematics, a calculator, or distance-off tables, available in most *nautical almanacs, will give the distance off which can then be laid down on the chart on the correct bearing. A *horizontal sextant angle between two objects ashore will give a *position line which is the arc of a circle on which the ship and the two objects both lie. A second horizontal sextant angle between two other objects gives a similar position line, and again the ship's position is at the point of intersection of the two arcs.

*Satellite navigation systems such as *GPS, with its high accuracy and flexibility, will solve many of the navigator's problems. *Radar, too, will enable him to take bearings and ranges in poor visibility (keeping in mind that the bearings will be less accurate than the ranges).

The cautious navigator will not place complete reliance on buoys, which can occasionally drag their *moorings. For the history of navigation see NAVIGATION. Mike Richey

A fix

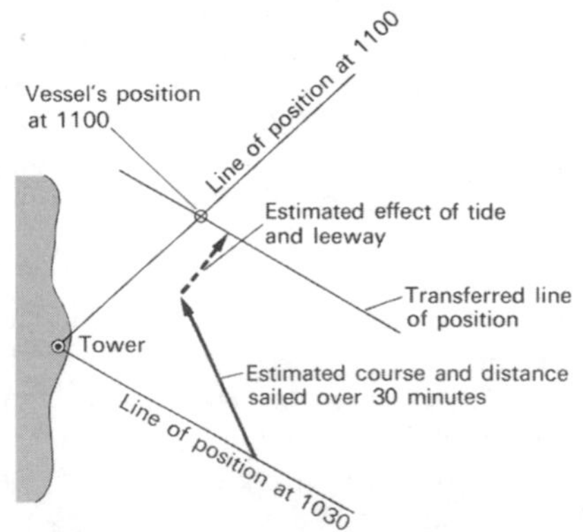

Running fix

coaster, generic term for small merchant ships, such as the *collier and the *tramp, which traded around the coasts of the British Isles during the late 19th–early 20th centuries. They still do so but in much reduced numbers.

coastguard, a service most maritime nations operate to patrol and guard their coastlines, to prevent *smuggling, and to supervise *traffic separation schemes and coastal shipping. In 1822 a British organization, known as the Coast Guard, was formed to prevent smuggling. After a period under the *Admiralty it became, in 1925, an independent service, as Her Majesty's (HM) Coastguard, and is now part of the *Maritime and Coastguard Agency. HM Coastguard's specific responsibility is coordinating and helping mount SAR (search and rescue) operations, both at sea and on the coastline, with the help of other *lifesaving organizations, Ministry of Defence helicopters, and any other of the emergency services they need to call on. See also NATIONAL COASTWATCH INSTITUTION; US COAST GUARD.

Webb, W., *Coastguard* (1975).

Coast Pilot, a US government publication which provides detailed descriptions of *yachting areas and harbours. John Rousmaniere

coat, *canvas painted with thick tar and secured around a mast or *bowsprit where it passed through a vessel's deck, or was bedded down over its *stem, to stop water penetrating into the vessel. Nowadays coats are made of rubber.

cobbing, an unofficial form of punishment in the British Navy during the days of sail, often inflicted as summary justice by the crew of a ship against a member who had transgressed the *lower-deck code of honour. It was also often used for the same purpose in the *midshipmen's mess. Originally it was administered with a flat piece of wood called a cobbingboard, the offender being tied down before the punishment was inflicted on his breeches. Later, in the 19th century it became a much more vicious punishment, the instrument used being a *hammock *clew which, with its 22 *nettles, became in effect not a *cat-o'-nine-tails but one with 22 tails. It was forbidden by the *Admiralty towards the end of the 19th century.

coble, a *clinker-built open boat, about 8.5 metres (28 ft) in length, used in coastal water *fisheries, particularly on the north-east coast of England, or for fishing and netting salmon in the mouths of rivers and in estuaries. The one used in coastal waters had a mast and *lugsail, and occasionally a *jib on a temporary *bowsprit, and was usually fitted for three pairs of *oars. A feature of the coastal coble was the *rudder which extended 1.2 metres (4 ft) or more below the keel. The *forefoot was also made slightly deeper than the keel, partly to balance the rudder and partly to give a better grip to *windward. The particular design allowed the boat to be *launched bows first from a beach, the deep forefoot helping to keep the coble straight and steady. The rudder was shipped when sufficient depth of water was reached. On landing on a beach the flared bows were always kept to seaward, and the boat was kept bows on to the *waves as it was backed in with the oars, or brought in with the waves. It was in a coble that Grace *Darling and her father rowed out to rescue the crew of the merchantman wrecked on the Farne Islands.

cockbill, or **a-cockbill.** **(1)** An anchor is said to be cockbilled or a-cockbill when hung vertically by its ring stopper from a timberhead or *cathead ready for use, or, temporarily, during the recovery process. **(2)** *Yards of a *square-rigger are said to be cockbilled, or a-cockbill, when they are canted to their maximum vertical angles as they are in the merchant navies as a sign of mourning. They were canted in opposite directions on each mast and the ends of the *spanker *gaff and boom were lowered. **(3)** The yards of a square-rigger are sometimes 'cockbilled' to reduce the overall width of the *rigging when the ship has to lie alongside a warehouse or transit the locks of a canal.

cocked hat, the small triangular space usually found at the intersection of *position lines on a *chart when a ship's position is determined by plotting three *bearings when employing *celestial, *coastal, or *hyperbolic navigation. With perfect observation and plotting, the three position lines should intersect at a common point. When they do not, a cocked hat is formed. This indicates minor errors when *fixing a ship's position, and, in general, the larger the cocked hat, the greater the error. *Navigators normally take the centre of the cocked hat, when it is not large, as the ship's position. In particular circumstances they may take the position nearest to danger. There are occasions when the true position may lie outside the cocked hat. See also ANGLE OF CUT.

cockpit. **(1)** The well of a *yacht or small sailing vessel where the steering wheel or *tiller is located. It normally gives access to the saloon, but in some yachts a separate central cockpit is incorporated where the steering wheel and navigational instruments are situated. **(2)** In the old sailing navies the space near the after *hatchway and below the lower gun-deck allotted originally to the senior midshipmen of the ship and later to the surgeon and his mates for their messes. In action it became the operating theatre to which men who had been wounded were carried for treatment. During the battle of Trafalgar it was to the cockpit of HMS **Victory* that *Nelson was carried after he had been wounded on deck, and where he died.

cockscomb, the name of a serrated *cleat often fitted to the ends of the *yards in *square-rigged ships to which the *reef earings were hauled out and lashed when a sail was being *reefed.

cod (*Gadus morhua*) is a commercial *fish species. The huge catches that could made off the *Grand Banks and other parts of the eastern seaboard of North America enticed large European fishing fleets, notably Basque fishermen from northern Spain and Biscay, to cross the Atlantic from the beginning of the 16th century onwards. It was claimed at the time that a man could walk across the sea on the backs of the cod. Annual catches peaked in the mid-1980s at over 2 million tonnes. The increase was partly a result of improvements in fishing technology and partly increases in the number

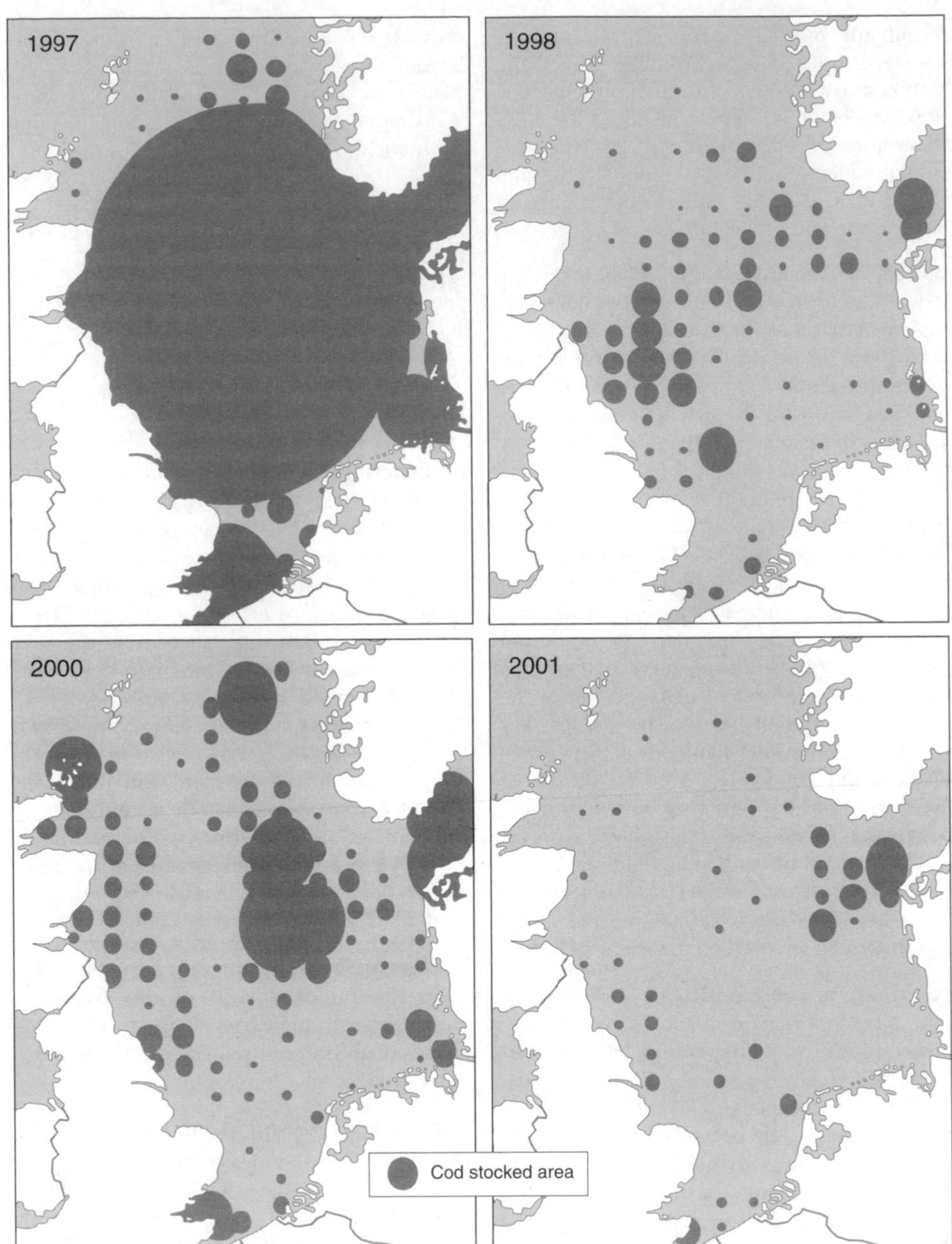

Distribution of one-year-old cod 1997–2001 in the North Sea

of boats working in the cod *fisheries as other stocks declined and fishing grounds were closed. Warning signs appeared: the average sizes diminished sharply and fewer old fish were caught. Suddenly the stocks crashed, probably because of the over-exploitation. But, at much the same time, big changes occurred in the ecology of the North Atlantic; the *currents changed, and the composition of the *plankton that the cod larvae feed on changed, too. The

Canadians closed their fishery causing economic disaster to local communities, but to no avail. The cod almost totally disappeared, and has failed to recover. Moderately large catches are still taken in Icelandic waters where, in the 1970s, Iceland closed its fishing grounds to the fleets of other nations, precipitating a feud with British fishermen that is remembered as the Cod Wars, but even round Iceland the stocks are in decline. This sudden and dramatic failure of this important fishery epitomizes the crisis being faced by the commercial fishing industry worldwide. Too many fishermen are chasing too few fish. The social and economic impacts on the local fishing communities have been devastating, yet to subsidize them to keep fishing is not a solution. The shifts in the ecology of the North Atlantic are thought to be linked to the *North Atlantic Oscillation.

Kurlanski, M., *Cod: A Biography of the Fish that Changed the World* (1997). M. V. Angel

cod-banger, a name in used during the mid-19th century to describe a vessel used in fishing for *cod. It applied particularly to those vessels which used lines, as opposed to *trawls, for catching this type of *fish. See also FISHERIES.

cod-end, the narrow pocket at the end of a *trawl in which the *fish caught up in the trawl are collected. See also FISHERIES.

codline, small line laid up with eighteen threads. It was originally the line used in fishing for *cod, but it also has a variety of uses on board ship where small rope would be too large and clumsy. It is also sometimes known as hambro line. See also MARLINE.

cofferdam. **(1)** A temporary structure in the form of an enclosed dam which can be erected on the seabed or the bed of a river and pumped dry to enable men to work within it below water level without having to wear *diving suits. They are used largely in harbour works and for the construction of the piers of bridges. See also CAISSON. **(2)** Heavy transverse *bulkheads in large merchant vessels, particularly *tankers, built as a safety measure between the *holds or oil tanks. They consist of a double bulkhead with a narrow space between them, the space frequently being used for the carriage of oil fuel or water *ballast.

cog. **(1)** An early coastal merchant ship. 'The consensus is that the cog, which began as a small flat-bottomed *coaster in the 10th century, or earlier, was developed by the Germans, perhaps out of the Rhine, and had become by 1400 a ship of 200 tons or more, 90 or more feet (27 metres) long and 30 or more feet (9 metres) in the beam . . . The cog was built either without a keel or with a simple keel-plank from which *stem and stern posts, straight but angled, rose sharply and in a straight line, the ship having a high *freeboard. The bottom-planking was laid flush or edge to edge, the steep sides being *clinker-built from the turn of the *bilge. A *bowsprit, or *spar, at the bow, appeared in the 13th century and a small square sail slung under it helped the vessel to move to *windward. *Superstructures or "castles" were added fore and *aft for purposes of defence, and a topcastle added to the mast. At the stern a *windlass was used to raise sail and haul the anchor. The cog of this ilk dominated the northern carrying trade, particularly from the Baltic, for about 150 years' (R. Hope, *A New History of British Shipping* (1988), 40). The *round ship of medieval times was virtually a cog. See also NEF. **(2)** A type of small sailing craft used for local commerce on the rivers Humber and Ouse in north-east England.

coil, the normal method for the stowage of rope on board ship, coiled in circular turns. The direction used to *lay up the coils depended on the lay of the rope; if it was laid up right handed the rope was coiled clockwise from left to right; if laid up left handed, it was coiled anticlockwise from right to left. The reason for this was that the correct direction of coiling kept the lay of the rope tight. *Hemp rope was always coiled clockwise since it was always laid up right handed. Wire rope is almost invariably coiled on a drum, as it will not hold its shape like rope made from fibres. See also CHEESE DOWN, TO; FLAKE; TIER.

coir, a very rough rope made from the fibre of the husks of the coconut, dark brown in colour. It had many uses aboard ship before natural fibre ropes were replaced by synthetic ones. In particular, it is lighter than other natural-fibre ropes, more resilient, and floats on water. This last property made it especially suitable for use as *warps and as a *grass-line.

collar. **(1)** A name given originally to the lower end of the principal *stays of a mast in a *square-rigged ship, but later to the rope, with a *deadeye in its end, to which the stay was secured at its lower end. Thus, the collar of the forestay was the short length of rope attached to the *stem of the ship to which the stay was set up and secured. See also MOUSE. **(2)** The *eye in the upper end of a stay, or in the *bight of the *shrouds, which was threaded over the masthead before being set up taut to hold the mast secure. **(3)** The neck of a ring-bolt.

collier, a vessel in the 17th and 18th centuries which carried coal in bulk. These collier *brigs, as they were called, carried 'sea coal' from the northern east coast ports of Britain to London, and from other ports to other destinations. Loading and discharging arrangements were both primitive and the amount of coal carried was very small, though it sufficed for domestic requirements during the sailing era. A typical collier brig could carry about 300–400 tons of coal, unloading it into *lighters moored alongside, by a system known as 'coal whipping'. Many of the Northumbrian collier brigs were known as *'cats' or 'cat-built', and it was these vessels which Captain James *Cook selected for his three great voyages of *exploration by sea 1768–80. He had first apprenticed to the sea in Northumbrian collier brigs and well knew their great strength of construction and hard-weather qualities.

The advent of *steam propulsion for ocean-going ships in the mid-19th century and the consequent necessity for establishing coal depots abroad for refuelling purposes, as well as growing industrial needs, gave rise to a requirement for vessels of much greater cargo-carrying capacity, and this was met by steam-driven ships with capacious *holds which could carry at least 6,000 tons. Many industries still use large quantities of coal and it is still carried by modern colliers built to carry it in bulk.

collision mat, a large square of very stout *canvas roped and fitted with ropes at each corner. Known as hogging lines, these ropes enabled crew members to manoeuvre the mat into position under the ship's bottom where the hull was damaged. The canvas was *thrummed with rope-yarn or *oakum to act as a sealing agent. When drawn over the damaged part of a hull, the pressure of the sea water forced the mat tight against the ship's side and limited the water inflow. The mat was invented in the mid-19th century by Rear Admiral Cochrane of the Royal Navy. See also FOTHERING.

Colossus, the bronze statue of the sun god Helios, one of the seven wonders of the world, which stood near the harbour at Rhodes. It was made by Chares of Lindus from the spoils of war left by Demetrius Poliorcetes when he raised the siege of Rhodes in 304 BC. The statue, reported to be 70 cubits (110 ft/33.5 m) high, took twelve years to complete. Legend has it that the statue held in its hand a light to act as a *beacon to shipping and that it stood across the entrance of the harbour, shipping passing between its legs, but this is unlikely. The statue was overthrown by an earthquake in, it is believed, 224 BC, the pieces lying where they fell for ten or eleven centuries, when they were purchased for conversion into weapons.

colours, the name by which the national flag flown by a ship at sea is known. 'What colours does it fly?' means what is its nationality? In British naval ships the colours are the *jack flown on the *jackstaff in the bows and the *white ensign flown at the *gaff when at sea or from an ensign staff at the stern in harbour. The colours of a British merchant ship are the *red ensign. Most other maritime nations use their national flag for the colours of their merchant marine, though in most such nations naval warships fly a special ensign in addition to the national flag.

The term also signifies the naval ceremony of the daily hoisting and lowering of national flags, both ashore and at sea. In the Royal Navy colours are hoisted at 0800 from 25 March to 20 September and at 0900 for the rest of the year. On foreign stations the time of hoisting is decided by the commander-in-chief. Colours are always lowered at sunset. See also FLAG ETIQUETTE.

Colregs, see INTERNATIONAL REGULATIONS FOR PREVENTING COLLISIONS AT SEA.

colt, in the old days of the Royal Navy a short piece of rope with a knot in the end used by *petty officers, with varying degrees of brutality, to urge men on to work. Its use was officially forbidden by the *Admiralty in 1809, though it persisted in some ships for a few years longer. See also START, TO.

Columbus, Christopher (1451–1506), born in Genoa between 25 August and 31 October 1451 to a family of wool weavers named Colombo, and christened Cristoforo. Later, in Spain, he was known as Cristobal Colón; the Latinized version was adopted by English writers. He grew up illiterate, helping his father Domenico at the loom, went to sea as a young lad, and made several voyages in the Mediterranean. In 1476, when serving as a seaman in a Genoese vessel which was sunk by a French fleet off Lagos, he swam ashore and made his way to Lisbon, joining his young brother Bartholomew in making *charts. The following year, in a Portuguese ship, he made a voyage to the north of Iceland and back, and in 1478, as *master or *supercargo, he engaged in a trading voyage from Madeira to Genoa.

In 1479, he married Felipa Perestrello, daughter of the hereditary captain of Port Santo in the Madeiras. The young couple settled at Funchal, whence Columbus made a voyage to the Gold Coast as master or *pilot of a Portuguese ship. Instead of following his promising beginnings as a professional mariner, Columbus moved to Lisbon to promote his 'Enterprise of the Indies', as he called it. This was to sail westwards to the Orient, as an easier and shorter route than around the Cape of Good Hope, which the Portuguese were pursuing and were shortly to attain. In preparation, he learned Portuguese, Castilian, and Latin, read widely, and annotated books in which he found support for his conviction that the Atlantic was relatively narrow and that the Eurasian continent lapped most of the way round the world. The vulgar notion that Columbus was trying to prove the world to be round is baseless; all educated Europeans then regarded the world as a sphere.

Columbus had immense difficulty finding someone to back him and had 'a terrible, continued, painful and prolonged battle' that lasted more than a decade to get his 'Enterprise' adopted. The main reasons for his ideas being rejected were, in the opinion of those he approached, his gross underestimate of the distance to be covered, and his unprecedented demands: three vessels and their crews to be provided, and, in the event of success, ennoblement, *admiralty jurisdiction, and viceroyalty over any new lands discovered, plus a 10% cut on all trade. Eventually, the joint sovereigns of Spain, Ferdinand and Isabella, who had already spurned him twice, agreed to give him all he demanded, not only for the voyage but for his future power, status, and profit.

By royal command two *caravels, *Pinta* and *Niña*, more properly called the *Santa Anna* and the *Santa Clara*, were fitted out, manned, and commanded by a family of merchant-ship owners; and a third caravel, the 100-ton *Santa Maria*, a Galician *nao* (ship). Manned by 40 northern Spaniards, she was chartered by Columbus and acted as his *flagship. On 3 August 1492 the three ships left for the Canary Islands, where the easterly *trade winds began and would help carry them westwards. After provisioning and carrying out some repairs at Las Palmas, they set sail on 6 September and followed the centuries-old technique of *latitude sailing, along latitude 28° N., which, according to existing geographical ideas, would hit either Japan or an island to the south of it. Once there Columbus proposed to set up a trading factory where products of the East and West could profitably be exchanged.

The voyage was plagued by light winds and a *mutiny, and as *variation was then unknown Columbus was disturbed by the fact that the further west they sailed the more his *magnetic compass differed from true north. However, on 12 October they made their first landfall, the Bahamian island of Guanahani which Columbus named San Salvador. Supposing it to be the East Indies Columbus landed there before sailing south-westwards in search of Japan. On 28 October he entered a harbour on the north coast of a big island that his native pilot called Cuba. It looked so unlike *Marco Polo's description of Japan that Columbus jumped to the conclusion that it must be an outlying promontory of China; he even sent an 'embassy' inland hoping to find the emperor.

After exploring the north coast of Cuba, Columbus crossed the Windward passage, and discovered and named *Hispaniola. The *Santa Maria* ran on to a *coral reef there, and as the natives appeared friendly Columbus decided to build a fort on the island from her timbers. He manned it with volunteers, whose task was to search for gold, while Columbus returned home in the *Niña*. Followed by the *Pinta* he set sail on 4 January 1493 and after a stormy passage dropped anchor near Lisbon on 4 March. The natives that he had brought back convinced the King of Portugal that he had indeed been to the Indies, and on Easter Sunday, shortly after returning to Palos, his port of departure, he received a letter from Ferdinand and Isabella confirming all his titles and privileges.

Between 1493 and 1502 Columbus made three other voyages of discovery in an effort to find a westerly route to Japan and to establish that Cuba was indeed a peninsula of China. During them he showed the excellence of his seamanship, but also the inability of himself and his two brothers to govern and administrate the lands he discovered. During his third voyage, which began in May 1498, he went ashore at Ensenada Yacua on the Paria Peninsula of what is now Venezuela. Assuming that John *Cabot did not sail beyond Newfoundland in 1497, that the site of *Vinland was also on that island, and that *Brendan never travelled that far, Columbus was probably the first European to land on the American mainland. However, the voyage ended in disaster and humiliation, for Hispaniola was in turmoil and the Spanish sovereign had felt obliged to dispatch a force to restore order on the island. The leader of it, Francisco de Bobadilla, took the side of the defeated rebels and clapped Columbus and his two brothers in jail, and then shipped them back to Spain in fetters. They reached Cadiz in October 1500.

After six weeks Ferdinand and Isabella ordered them to be released, and invited them to court; but instead of recalling Bobadilla in disgrace and restoring Columbus to his viceroyalty as he naturally expected, they appointed someone else as governor of the Indies, paying Columbus off by allowing him to fit out a fourth voyage at their expense.

His objective on this *alto viaje* (high voyage) as he called it, owing to the many adventures and difficulties he encountered during it, was to find a strait or passage through to what he thought would be the Indian Ocean, and after crossing the Caribbean to Honduras with four caravels, he landed where the city of Trujillo was later founded, before carrying on down the coast of Central America until he reached what is now the mouth of the *Panama Canal, never suspecting that the Pacific Ocean lay just over the horizon. After failing to establish a trading factory in the area, or to find the passage he was seeking, he sailed eastwards towards Hispaniola. By now two of his caravels, riddled with *teredo worm, had been abandoned and the remaining two had to be run aground in St Anne's Bay, Jamaica, where Columbus was forced to remain for a year before he was eventually rescued. On his return, in November 1504, he had less than eighteen months to live and he spent most of it in misery from arthritis, and outraged at the ingratitude of the Spanish monarchs. The queen, his benefactor, died, and Ferdinand, who had never cared for Columbus, would do nothing for him, and Columbus died full of sorrow and frustration.

Five centuries after Columbus's death there can be no reasonable doubt of his having been one of the greatest *navigators in modern history. Although his *celestial navigation was not remarkable, his *dead reckoning, always right when his *pilots called it wrong, was impeccable. *Magellan is the only navigator in history to have discovered more islands and a greater extent of coast than did Columbus. As a colonial administrator Columbus was a failure; but as an Italian attempting to govern Spaniards he was hindered from the start; and as someone wrote, any early governor of Hispaniola, to have been a success, must have been 'angelic indeed and superhuman'.

Bedini, S. (ed.), *The Christopher Columbus Encyclopedia*, 2 vols. (1992).

Fernández-Armesto, F., *Christopher Columbus* (1991).

Morison, S. E., *Admiral of the Ocean Sea*, 2 vols. (1942; reissued 1962), also available in 1 vol. (reissued 1991).

'combing the cat', the habit of a *boatswain's mate, during the flogging of a seaman, of running his fingers through the tails of a *cat-o'-nine-tails after each stroke in order to separate them in preparation for the next one. After several strokes, when the victim's back had begun to bleed, the tails of the cat were apt to become coated with blood and to stick together, and a stroke with the tails matted together could inflict serious and permanent damage. See also COBBING.

come, to, a verb with many maritime meanings. When a helmsman in a sailing vessel received an order to come no nearer, he had to hold the vessel as close as it already was to the wind and not attempt to sail it any closer. A ship **comes to an anchor** when it lets it go; **'come up the *capstan'**, an order to walk the *cable back to take off the strain or to *veer some of the cable; **'come up the *tackle'**, an order to let go the *fall.

come home, to. An anchor is said to come home, or be coming home, when its *flukes are not holding in the ground and it *drags.

commander. **(1)** The naval rank next below that of captain; in a large warship he is the executive officer and second in command. In the various branches of naval service (engineering, supply, medicine, etc.) the head of each branch on board a large ship would usually be of commander's rank. In smaller warships, such as *frigates, *submarines, etc., the commanding officer would normally be of commander's or lieutenant commander's rank.

Originally, in the British Navy, promotion to commander meant promotion to the command of a ship smaller than a 'post' ship, i.e. not a *rated ship, and after 1814 the *master aboard a warship was ranked **master and commander** as he was equivalent in rank to a commander. An officer promoted commander had the title of captain but not the actual full rank, only achieving this when he was posted to a rated ship as a *post-captain. In some European navies the nomenclature is still retained for the equivalent rank of commander, e.g. the French *capitaine de frégate*, the German *Fregatten-Kapitän*, etc. **(2)** The name given to a large wooden-headed mallet used for heavy work on board ship.

commission. **(1)** The documents by which naval officers hold their status as accredited officers in the navy in which they serve. It is normally issued when an officer reaches the rank of sub-lieutenant or its equivalent in other navies. In the case of 'royal' navies it is usually issued by the sovereign, and the cases of 'republican' navies by either the president or the national naval authority. **(2)** In the Royal Navy, the period in which a warship is allocated to particular duties which may be in any part of the world. She remains commissioned until she returns to her home, or occasionally another, port to *pay off and her company disperses. In the US Navy a ship is commissioned when she is formally turned over after her outfitting and trials and remains in commission until she is placed in reserve or is in a navy yard for a very long time. See also COMMISSIONING PENNANT; LETTER OF MARQUE.

commissioning pennant, the long, narrow *pennant flown at the masthead of warships commanded by commissioned officers. In the Royal Navy it is white with a red cross, in the US Navy white over red with thirteen white stars on a blue field at the hoist. In both cases it is flown permanently, by night as well as by day, so long as the ship remains in *commission. See also PAY OFF, TO.

commodore, in the Royal Navy an intermediate rank between captain and rear admiral, often held by a senior captain when appointed to certain commands or posts of extra responsibility. It is not a step in the ladder of promotion—a captain is normally promoted direct to rear admiral—but pertains only to the responsibility of the job. In the US Navy it is not a rank but a position held by an officer below *flag rank appointed to command two or more ships. A commodore in the Royal Navy flies a *broad pennant as the sign of his rank; a commodore in the US Navy flies a *burgee bearing the identification number of his command. In merchant navies the senior captain of a commercial shipping line is usually known as the commodore of the line. In a *yacht club the commodore is the senior officer of the club by election of its members.

common whipping, a whipping widely used to prevent the *strands at the end of a rope from unlaying or fraying. The end of the whipping twine is laid along the rope towards its end and a number of turns of the twine passed round the rope against its *lay, each turn being hauled taut. At about half the length of the required whipping, the other end of the twine is laid along the rope in the opposite direction and the whipping continued with the *bight of the twine, taking the bight over the end of the rope with each turn. When the bight becomes too small to pass over the end of the rope, the second end of the twine is hauled through the turns until the whole whipping is taut. The two ends are then cut off. See also SAILMAKER'S WHIPPING; WEST COUNTRY WHIPPING.

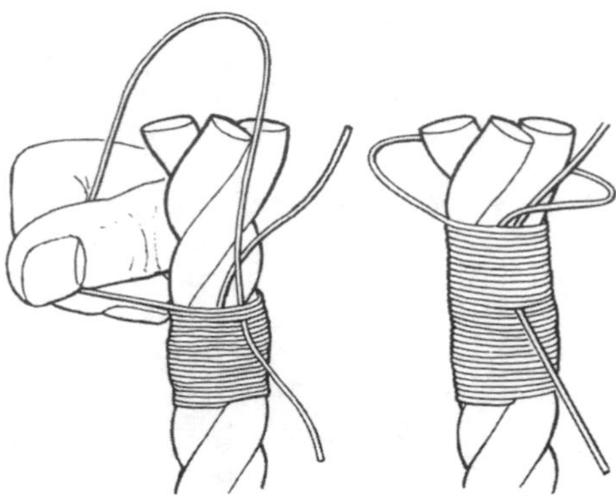

Common whipping

companion, in the days of sail the framing and sashlights on the *quarterdeck and of the *coach through which daylight entered to the *cabins below. Nowadays it is the covering over an upper-deck *hatchway which leads to the companionway and is generally understood to mean the *companion ladder.

companion ladder, the ladders leading down from the *quarterdeck to the upper deck, one on each side of the ship, in the sailing warships and merchant vessels which had a raised quarterdeck.

company, the whole crew of a ship, including all officers and men.

compartments. (1) The spaces between the transverse *bulkheads of a ship. **(2)** Another word for *chambers.

compass, in present parlance the instrument by means of which a ship may be steered on a course and by means of which *bearings may be taken to *fix the ship's position on the *chart. For the different types of maritime compasses see AZIMUTH COMPASS; GYROSCOPIC COMPASS; HAND-BEARING COMPASS; MAGNETIC COMPASS. See also VIKING COMPASS.

compass error, the amount by which the *magnetic compass direction differs from the true direction, the sum of *variation and *deviation. It is named east or west according to whether the compass points to the right or left of the true direction.

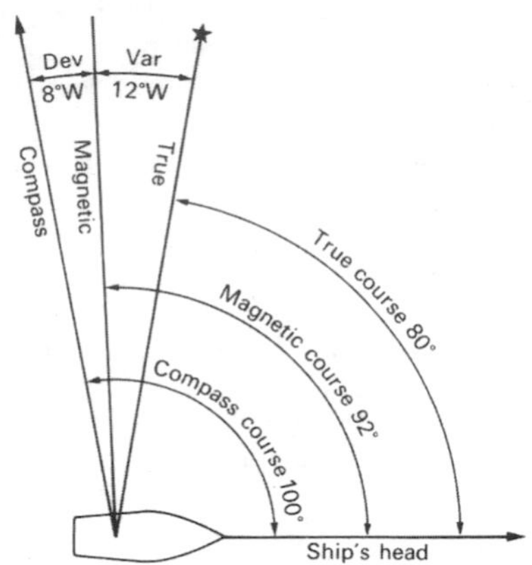

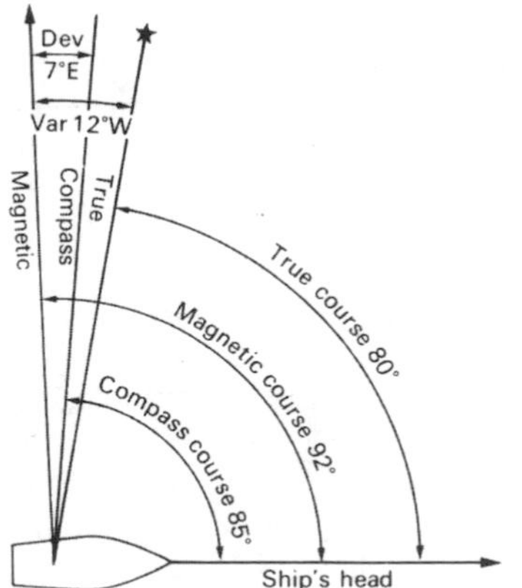

Compass error with westerly (above) and easterly (below) deviation

compass rose, a circular diagram displayed on the *chart to facilitate measurement of direction. It is graduated in degrees from 0 at the reference direction to 360 and sometimes includes compass points as well. On relatively large-scale charts the *magnetic compass rose is displayed, on British *Admiralty charts usually in magenta, inside the rose aligned with *true north. The date of the magnetic *variation is always given and the rate of change. Mike Richey

compass timber, the name given to *shipbuilding timber which has been steamed and curved to take up the desired shape when building the hull of a wooden ship.

composite built, a ship which is planked with wood on an iron or steel frame. A great many of the *clipper ships were composite built, and it was still a common method in *yacht-building before the introduction of *GRP. See also SHIPBUILDING.

composite great circle sailing, a method of sailing along the shortest route possible without crossing poleward of a specified *latitude. A feature of *great circle sailing is that a great circle route, unless it is along a *meridian, lies poleward of the corresponding *rhumb line route. In many ocean routes, especially in the South Pacific, a vessel following a great circle route could be carried into unnecessarily high latitudes, or indeed theoretically pass over land. In these cases, a composite route may be used. This comprises two great circle routes, the first starting at the place of departure with its *vertex on a limiting parallel of latitude. The second great circle route would have its vertex on the same limiting parallel but pass through the destination. When following a composite route the vessel is sailed due east or due west along the limiting parallel between the vertices of the two great circle arcs.

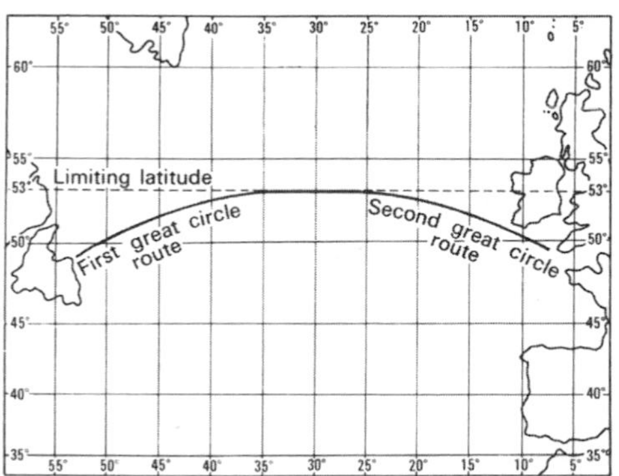

Composite great circle

compound engine, a development from the single cylinder *reciprocating marine engine in which the steam, after leaving the first cylinder, was passed through a second low-pressure cylinder of larger diameter before being drawn off to a *condenser to be changed back to boiler feed water. This second use of the steam added to the thrust produced by the engine results in a higher engine efficiency for the same amount of steam. Although the principle of compounding an engine was patented as early as 1781 by Jonathan Hornblower, a contemporary of James Watt, it was not until the 1850s, when higher boiler pressures were introduced in marine boilers, that the compound engine, designed by John Elder and Charles Randolph, became practicable at sea. As steam expands in a cylinder the temperature falls, and the greater the expansion the lower the temperature of the cylinder wall. When steam is admitted to the other side of the piston for the next stroke this steam encounters the cool cylinder wall and some of the steam condenses. This results in less steam being available to do useful work. To avoid this, steam was expanded in two states so that the temperature drop in each stage (cylinder) was less, resulting in reduced condensation and higher efficiency. See also STEAM PROPULSION; TRIPLE EXPANSION ENGINE.

comprador, the equivalent in the Far East of a ship chandler. The word entered the English language, and *marine literature, largely through the novels and stories of Joseph *Conrad and Somerset Maugham, who both wrote about the East. Originally it was a Portuguese word introduced in the East to denote a house steward and later adopted by business houses, and particularly those dealing with sea business, as the title of the chief native representative or manager.

compressor, or **compressor stopper,** a device for holding the chain *cable attached to an anchor against the side of the *navel pipe by choking it to prevent it running out. In some larger vessels separate compressors are mounted on the *forecastle in the line of the cables, which are then led directly through them. In such cases the cables are held on the compressors after anchoring until they can be permanently secured by the *slips. A more usual practice, however, is to hold them for this purpose by a brake on the *cable-holders. When *hemp cables were used in the days of the old *square-riggers, before the introduction of chain, the compressor was a curved iron bar, pivoted at one end, with a handle to give leverage which could be applied to the cable where it passed over a block of wood mounted on deck in the line of the run of the cable, either to check the speed at which it was running out or to bring it to a stop altogether and hold it until the cable could be *bitted and secured.

con, cond, or **cun, to,** from the Anglo-Saxon *connan*, to know, to be skilful, or possibly from the Latin *conducere*, to lead or conduct, the giving of the necessary orders to the helmsman to steer a ship in a required direction, usually in channels or in sight of land where it is not always necessary or desirable to steer by the *compass.

In the USA, where it is used as a noun and is spelt **conn**, it means the navigational direction of the ship; 'to take the conn', to take over the navigational duties on the *bridge of a ship. The naval *conning tower also derives from the verb, being in its original meaning the armoured tower from which a warship was controlled navigationally in battle.

concluding line, a small line *rove through the centre of the wooden steps of a *Jacob's ladder or a stern ladder. It is used for hauling up the ladder for stowage, when each step collapses on top of the step below it.

condemn, to, a legal term in *prize law by which the cargo of a ship, or a ship itself, may be declared in wartime, after the declaration by a belligerent of a *blockade, as contraband and confiscated by a Court of *Admiralty. See also CONTINUOUS VOYAGE.

condenser, a piece of equipment in the engine room of a steamship by which the steam, after use in the main engines, was reconverted into feed water for the boilers. The earliest form of condenser was the jet condenser introduced by James Watt for his steam engines. In this, the exhaust steam emitted from the cylinder entered an iron or brass chamber where it was condensed back into water by encountering a jet of cold sea water. The condensed steam, or condensate, was drawn off into the hot well for reuse in the ship's boiler.

An improvement on the jet condenser was the surface condenser, introduced around 1845, which is virtually the same type as that used in the few surviving steamships today. The principle was the same as the jet condenser, but the exhaust steam on entering the condenser chamber passed over a battery of small-bore pipes through which a continuous flow of cold sea water was led, and the condensate was then pumped as before to the supply tanks for reuse in the boilers. Twentieth-century steamships had an oil separator which was used to extract the cylinder lubricating oil which had become mixed with the exhaust steam and would have otherwise caused foaming or serious priming of the water in the boilers.

An additional effect of the condenser was to produce a partial vacuum which took the steam from the engines after use. This increased their efficiency by reducing the pressure on the exhaust side of the piston so that there was a lower force acting against the steam side of the piston. See also DIESEL ENGINE; STEAM PROPULSION.

Confederate States Navy (CSN), the navy of the southern states of the USA, when those states seceded from the Union and brought on the American Civil War (1861–5). With few resources and little industry, and only a few damaged units of the US Navy, acquired when southern bases fell, the Confederacy sought to create a naval force emphasizing the then cutting edge of technology: armoured ships, *'Davids', *submarines, mines, and modern guns to offset the extant Union Navy (see NAVY: UNITED STATES NAVY). In March 1862 the CSN employed an *ironclad, CSS *Virginia*, fashioned from a captured Union frigate, USS **Merrimac*, to destroy two Union sailing men-of-war, and then fought to a draw USS *Monitor*, the precursor of the *monitor warship, in the world's first battle between ironclads. In February 1864, the Confederate submarine *H. L. Hunley* used a *spar torpedo to sink USS *Housatonic* off Charleston, another 'first'. In October 1864 the Union Navy got its revenge when its improvised torpedo boat sank the CSS **Albemarle* with a spar torpedo.

Aside from the actions of the *Virginia* and the *Hunley*, the only successful Confederate operation was with its commerce raiders, when the CSS *Florida*, **Alabama*, and *Shenandoah* led the Union to divert many resources to bring them to bay. The last named never was stopped, and, after virtually destroying the American *whaling industry in the Pacific, finally returned to Great Britain and hauled down her flag in the summer of 1865, months after the Confederacy had ceased to exist. Tyrone G. Martin

conical buoy, a *buoy in the shape of a cone which is used in the *IALA maritime buoyage system. See also LATERAL MARK.

conning tower. **(1)** The armoured control centre of a major warship after the change from wood to iron and steel from which, originally, the ship was navigated in battle. Later, with the increasing sophistication of weapons and their control, it also became the centre of communications with the guns and *torpedoes, and all information, such as *radar plots and ranges, is fed into it. It was occupied only in battle; on all other occasions *navigation and weapon control was exercised from the *bridge. **(2)** The connecting structure between the bridge and the pressure hull of a *submarine. In the oldest submarines it was no more than a trunk with an internal ladder, sealed at both ends by watertight *hatches which were closed when the submarine submerged. In modern submarines the conning tower provides space for equipment and the captain's *cabin, and is usually known as the 'sail'.

Conrad, Joseph (1857–1924), the most outstanding contributor of fiction to *marine literature in the 20th century. He was born Josef Teodor Konrad Korzeniowski in Poland, when that country was part of the Russian empire, and his parents were Polish patriots who longed for national independence. His father Apollo Korzeniowski, a poet and translator by profession, was exiled to northern Russia in 1861 for subversive activities, and Conrad and his mother went with him. His mother died when he was 7 and his father when he was 11, and he was then put in the care of his uncle Thaddeus Bobrowski, who befriended and advised him. As a child he was a great reader in Polish and in French, having been first introduced to English literature when his father was working on a translation of Shakespeare. But at school, in Poland and then Switzerland, he was bored and expressed his desire to go to sea. Through family connections in Marseille he was allowed to migrate there in 1874 and began his experiences of the sea in French ships, visiting Mauritius once and the West Indies twice. On the second West Indian voyage he may have become involved in a gun-running episode, described later in *The Arrow of Gold* (1920), and a voyage down the Venezuelan coast was later vividly recalled when he wrote *Nostromo* (1904).

On his return Conrad ran heavily into debt and it is possible that he may have attempted suicide. He felt insecure in France and his uncle urged him to try and become a British citizen. With this aim in view he joined the crew of a British ship, which eventually landed him at Lowestoft, and it was then that he began to learn English. He subsequently worked on a *coaster between Lowestoft and Newcastle before joining a *square-rigger, the *Duke of Sutherland*, for a voyage from London to Sydney and back. On his return in 1879 he made one voyage to the Mediterranean and then sat, and passed, his examination for second *mate in London before sailing as a junior officer to Australia.

On his return in 1881 he began a series of voyages to eastern, especially Malayan, waters which deeply influenced his later thought and writing. In 1883 he was, for instance, second mate of the 425-ton *Palestine*, loaded with a cargo of coal for Bangkok, when her cargo caught fire and she was abandoned off Java Head, which became the basis for his story 'Youth' (1902). He also sailed from Bombay as second mate of the *Narcissus*, the name and some features of which he used in *The Nigger of the 'Narcissus'* (1898).

After obtaining his first mate's certificate in 1884 and his certificate as a *master in 1886, the year he became a naturalized British citizen, he then made more voyages to the Far East. Most notably in 1888 he took command of the *barque *Otago* at Bangkok whose master had died at sea—an experience described in *The Shadow Line* (1916), which is almost pure autobiography. Then in 1889 he sailed for the Congo to take up the command of a river boat he had been promised. He was disgusted by the oppression of Africans that he witnessed there, and when the command failed to materialize he returned home disillusioned, though with material that he afterwards used in the short story 'Heart of Darkness' (1899). By then he was writing his first novel, but still considered himself a seaman, and between 1891 and 1893 made two further voyages as the mate of the 1276-ton *clipper *Torrens*, from London to Australia.

On his return he still tried to obtain work at sea, but he settled in London with the ambition of finding a publisher for his novel. Throughout his career at sea he had been known by his Polish name, but when the novel (*Almayer's Folly*) was published in 1895, the year he married, he used the name Joseph Conrad, and continued to do so throughout his writing career. His second novel, *An Outcast of the Islands* (1896), had a similar theme and setting, and both show his remarkable command of English. However, his style in these books was not seamen's English but was based rather on his wide reading in English and French—he acknowledged his debt to Balzac and de Maupassant. With his next books, *The Nigger of the 'Narcissus'* and *Lord Jim* (1900), he developed a freer and more individual style.

He wrote later: 'In the *Nigger* I give the psychology of a group of men and render certain aspects of nature. But the problem that faces them is not a problem of the sea, it is merely a problem that has arisen on board a ship where the conditions of complete isolation from all land entanglements make it stand out with a particular force and colouring.'

This is typical of Conrad's attitude to the sea, which he regarded as the great testing and proving experience. In some men, and frequently among Conrad's characters, a fatal flaw or weakness leads to self-betrayal, as in *Lord Jim* when Jim, against his better instincts, joins the other white men in abandoning the *Patna*, leaving a shipload of Malayan pilgrims to their fate—though ironically she did not founder and Jim could have stayed on board.

Typhoon and Other Stories (1902) contains in the title story a classic of marine literature in which the unimaginative master ignores good *seamanship by taking his ship through the *eye of a typhoon (see TROPICAL STORMS). Next Conrad published his great novel *Nostromo*, followed by *The Mirror of the Sea* (1906), which contains some of his best work on subjects relating to the sea. Then came *The Secret Agent* (1907), *Under Western Eyes* (1911), *Chance* (1914), *Victory* (1915), and a collection of short stories called *Within the Tides* (1915). He also collaborated with his novelist friend Ford Madox Ford (F. M. Hueffer) in writing two novels, *The Inheritors* (1901) and *Romance* (1903), and his later works include *The Rescue* (1920) and *The Rover* (1923). He died in 1924 before he could finish his final work of fiction, *Suspense* (1925).

Conrad's early years as a writer were marked by poverty and lack of public recognition, and it was not until *Chance* was published in 1914 that he became established and sufficiently famous to be offered a knighthood, which he refused. His remarkable personal experiences of the sea and the Far East, and his unique ability to render it in works of literature in a language not his mother tongue, make him one of the outstanding novelists of the 20th century.

Najder, Z., *Joseph Conrad: A Chronicle* (1983).
Tennant, R., *Joseph Conrad* (1981).

Consol, originally the German wartime *Elektra Sonne*, a *hyperbolic navigation aid, now obsolete, described technically as a collapsed hyperbolic system. With a range of 1,600 kilometres (1,000 mls.) it required no special equipment beyond a beacon-band radio receiver with a BFO (beat frequency oscillator) facility. Each Consol station transmitted a sequence of 60 dots and dashes which the *navigator would count. The moment the dots or dashes changed from one to the other was known as the equisignal and the number of either dots or dashes before the equisignal represented a position line which would be either plotted on a Consol lattice *chart or taken from special tables. An observation from two stations would provide a *fix. The attraction of the system to many fishermen and yachtsmen on the Atlantic coasts of Europe in the 1950s was to some extent due to the fact that no special equipment was required. A similar system called Consolan, also defunct, was in operation in the USA. Mike Richey

***Constellation*, USS,** a 38-gun *frigate, one of the six original frigates authorized by the US Congress in 1794. When the stars and stripes became the national flag of the USA, the white stars on a blue field were called 'a new constellation', which is the origin of her name. She was built in Baltimore, and in June 1798 was the first of the frigates to go to sea, at the beginning of the undeclared naval war with France. Commanded by Thomas Truxton (1755–1822), she captured the French frigate *L'Insurgente* in February 1799 and the following year fought a night action against the 40-gun *La Vengeance*, but was unable to capture her when her mainmast went by the *board. She was broken up in 1853 and in 1855 a *corvette of the same name represented the United States in the Mediterranean during the American Civil War (1861–5). After further service in a training role, she was many decades in reserve until transferred in the 1950s to a private organization in Baltimore for preservation as a relic.

Constitution, USS, one of six original *frigates authorized by the US Congress in 1794, and generally regarded by Americans as the most famous ship in the history of the US Navy. *Rated at 44 guns, but generally carrying more than 50, her dimensions were: length, 62.2 metres (204 ft); beam, 13.3 metres (43 ft 6 in.); depth of hold, 4.3 metres (14 ft 3 in.); *displacement, 2,200 tons. She was *launched in 1797, served in the quasi-war with France, and fought against the *Barbary pirates in the Mediterranean, 1803–5. In the latter campaign she served as the flagship of Commodore Edward Preble (1761–1807) who conducted a *blockade of Tripoli, and then a bombardment (August 1804) of that city, and the peace treaty was signed aboard her. But it was in the War of 1812–15 against the British that she established her enduring reputation. Congress declared war on 18 June 1812 although no plans and no preparations had been made. The US Navy then consisted of eight frigates and eight smaller vessels. Morale in the USA was low after an initial setback in the war, when news came that the *Constitution*, then commanded by Captain Isaac Hull (1773–1843), had, on 19 August 1812, destroyed the British 38-gun frigate *Guerrière*. Tradition has it that much of the British *shot failed to penetrate the side of the American warship, and that as a result her own sailors gave her the name 'Old Ironsides'. She had other victories, too: on 29 December 1812 she destroyed the frigate *Java*; and on 20 February 1815 she captured two smaller British vessels in a battle lasting about four hours.

An inaccurate newspaper report that the *Constitution* was going to be broken up led the American poet Oliver Wendell Holmes to write a poem, 'Old Ironsides' (1830), which was intended to arouse public sentiment for the preservation of the old vessel. In fact, she stayed afloat for many more years. She made a circumnavigation in the mid-1840s and was not retired from front-line service until a decade later. She then served as a school ship, first at the Naval Academy, and then for apprentices, before being decommissioned in 1881. Public interest, aroused when her deteriorating condition was announced, led to her being restored between 1927 and 1931. Later, she made a tour of 90 US ports, and was visited by about 4.5 million people, before returning to Boston, where she had been built. She is now berthed, and is open to the public in the Charlestown Navy Yard section of the Boston National Historical Park. She is the oldest commissioned warship afloat anywhere in the world, and last put to sea in 1997.

Martin, Tyrone G., *A Most Fortunate Ship* (rev. edn. 1997).

constructive total loss, a marine insurance term indicating that the cost of repairing damage to a ship will exceed its total value. In such a case the insurance payment is the total sum for which it has been insured, and not the estimated cost of repairs. See also WRECK.

container ship, a cargo vessel, colloquially known as a 'boxboat'. It is specially designed and built to carry dry cargo prepacked in steel containers designed to be carried by trucks or freight trains. The system is called containerization and was invented in the 1930s in New Jersey by an American, Malcolm McLean. He later founded the Sea-Land Corporation, which *launched and operated the first container ship, the SS *Fairland*, in 1956.

Container ships have revolutionized the transport of dry cargo and carry 90% of it, with over 200 million containers being used between ports annually. There are two standard sizes of container, one 20 feet (6.1 m) long (20 ft × 8.5 ft × 8.5 ft) the other exactly twice the capacity. Although the 40-foot container is now the more common, the container capacity of a ship or port is still measured in 'twenty-foot equivalent units' or TEU, a 40-foot container being, of course, 2TEU.

In 2002 there were over 400 container ships worldwide with a capacity of over 3,000 TEUs. The largest currently (2004) operating is the *OOCL Shenzhen*, which holds 8,063 TEUs, but *Lloyd's Register has calculated that it is perfectly possible to build an Ultra Large Container Ship with a carrying capacity of 12,500 TEUs. As the world's container trade is increasing in the region of 8% annually, and economy of scale is essential in such a competitive industry, this will doubtlessly be achieved within the foreseeable future.

However, such huge ships do raise *environmental issues. Port authorities are obliged to widen and deepen shipping channels, and the dredging of these inevitably leads to the destruction of marine habitats. Cloudy water and sediments also adversely affect marine life.

Continental Navy, the sea service created by the American Continental Congress in October 1775 in furtherance of the American War of Independence (1775–83) against the British. A *squadron of eight converted merchantmen, none mounting more than 24 guns, became operational the following December. That same month, the Congress authorized an ambitious building programme of thirteen *frigates of from 24 to 32 guns. Most of these never reached service. During the winter of 1776, the entire squadron, under the command of Commodore Esek Hopkins, successfully raided Nassau in the Bahamas, carrying away more than 80 cannon and mortars and a quantity of powder, important gains for the struggling Continental Army fighting the British. Thereafter, the service largely pursued a **guerre de course*, individual units having varying successes in capturing British supply ships whose cargoes also went to the support of the army. While the exploits of the self-promoting John Paul *Jones have been widely published, captains like Gustavus Conyngham and Lambert Wickes were equally adept at wreaking havoc on British commerce in northern European waters.

During the course of the war, the Continental Navy acquired nearly 60 ships, but there were fewer than 40 owned in any one year and many fewer actually in service. The navy was in steady numerical decline after 1777 as the far superior British Navy gradually ran its ships down, and it went out of existence in August 1785 with the auction sale of its last unit into merchant service. Tyrone G. Martin

continental shelf, the shallow areas of sea fringing the continents underlain by rocks of continental origin. Across the shelf the seabed slopes gently offshore to a depth of about 200 metres (60 ft) to the shelf-break, where the seabed suddenly plunges into the deep ocean. Around Antarctica shelves are deeper, about 500 metres (1,640 ft), depressed by the vast weight of the *ice shelf. Continental shelves are important regions. They are criss-crossed by shipping lanes, and local *fisheries catch the vast majority of commercial *fish there. The definition of what a shelf is has become critical during recent years as the exploitation of *offshore oil and gas has extended. The wealth accruing from these resources within an *Exclusive Economic Zone is internationally accepted as being vested in the state that borders the shelf. Defining the exact positions of offshore national boundaries has at times been highly contentious, has excited several clashes of interests between neighbouring states, and has exercised conferences of the *United Nations Conference on the Law of the Sea for many sessions. For illus. see EXCLUSIVE ECONOMIC ZONE. M. V. Angel

continuous voyage, the legal doctrine in which the cargo of a ship may be *condemned in *prize even though it is consigned to a neutral port provided that it can be shown that the ultimate onward destination of the cargo is a belligerent. It is a doctrine which applies only after a declaration of *blockade by a belligerent in time of war.

contline, the modern name for the spiral grooves between the *strands of a rope after it has been laid up. It is, perhaps, a less suggestive and more refined name for these grooves than the original term, cunting.

contraband, goods which have been prohibited from entering a belligerent state by the declaration of a *blockade. Contraband is of two kinds, absolute contraband, which includes munitions, weapons, and other commodities which can be directly attributable to the prosecution of war; and conditional contraband, declared by the blockader, which is ancillary to the prosecution of war. Thus imports of food by a belligerent can be claimed by a blockader as conditional contraband since no army or navy can fight without it, irrespective of what effect the lack of such imports may have on a civilian population.

convoy, one or more merchant ships sailing in company to the same general destination under the protection of naval ships. Convoy has a very ancient history and specific cases of ships proceeding in groups under naval protection have been traced back to the 12th century. It is probable that the general principle existed even long before this, mainly as a protection against *piracy, and certainly later against *privateers. However, in such cases the reason for ships sailing in company was more likely to be mutual protection rather than naval protection, as most merchant vessels in those days carried their own armament.

*Warfare at sea has always resulted in an immense loss in merchant shipping. The only method of minimizing such loss is by the institution of convoy, in which adequate naval protection can usually deter enemy attacks on trade. During the Napoleonic Wars against France (1793–1815) losses of British merchant shipping were so immense that no merchant ship was allowed to sail out of convoy, and the owners and *masters of those which attempted to do so were liable to a fine of £100.

In the two world wars of the 20th century, immense losses of merchant shipping were again experienced, almost entirely at the hands of *submarines. In the First World War (1914–18) the principle of ocean convoy was not introduced until 1917, a failure in established and proved naval practice that very nearly lost the war for the Allied nations. In the Second World War (1939–45) convoy was instituted at the outbreak of war but a lack of sufficient escort vessels resulted in under-protection of convoys and once again tremendous merchant ship losses were experienced until an adequate strength in escort vessels was built up and the signalling code of the German submarines was broken.

Many of the great sea battles of naval history have been fought as a result of convoy protection, notably those of the *Spanish Armada in 1588, the Glorious First of June in 1794, and the great Mediterranean sea battles of the Second World War fought around the convoys taking supplies to the besieged island of Malta. See also FLOTA; WAFT, TO.

Cook, James (1728–79), captain in the British Navy, the son of a day labourer of Marton, in Yorkshire. He was taught reading, writing, and basic arithmetic at a 'dame' school there, but was otherwise self-educated. In 1746 John Walker, head of a Whitby, Yorkshire, shipping firm mainly engaged in the east coast coal trade, accepted him as a sea-apprentice. By a natural aptitude for mathematics, Cook quickly became skilled in *navigation as well as *seamanship, and became a mate of a Walker ship in 1752.

By 1755 Cook had decided that the merchant navy lacked scope for his ambitions and, though he had been offered his first command, he declined it and volunteered for the Royal Navy as an AB. Drafted to the 60-gun ship *Eagle*, his qualities quickly brought him advancement to the warrant rank of *boatswain. In July 1757 he was promoted *master of the *Solebay* and later of the *Pembroke*, in which he sailed in 1758 with the expedition for the capture of Louisburg and subsequently Quebec. It was at Quebec that he attracted notice for his efficiency during the survey of the St Lawrence River which played a decisive part in the capture of Quebec and the conquest of Canada. He was then appointed master of the *flagship of the *squadron remaining there, spent three summers engaged in further surveys, and then the next five years in Newfoundland where, given his first independent command, the schooner *Grenville*, he was engaged in surveying the coast. His observations of an eclipse of the sun visible in Newfoundland in 1766 and the accompanying calculations communicated to the Royal Society brought him to the favourable attention of that influential body. This made him acceptable as one of their official observers for an expedition to Tahiti to record the transit of the planet Venus across the face of the sun; a scientific expedition which he eventually led when the society's first choice of leader was vetoed by the *Admiralty which provided the ship and crew. This scientific expedition became part of a more extensive voyage of discovery, as the Admiralty decided that when the observations had been completed Cook was to sail south to search for the great southern continent, *Terra Australis Incognita, supposed to exist there. He was also to explore the coast of New Zealand, first discovered by Abel *Tasman, but still thought to be part of the southern unknown continent.

On Cook's advice, a *cat-built Whitby *collier, under 30 metres (98 ft) long, was chosen for the expedition and renamed *Endeavour*. She left Plymouth on 25 August 1768 and in a voyage that lasted until 12 July 1771 Cook completed the observations of the transit of Venus; proved New Zealand to be two islands and not the northerly promontory of the unknown continent; explored the eastern coast of Australia, where he anchored in Botany Bay, ran aground on the *Great Barrier Reef, and discovered Endeavour Strait; and then returned home via Batavia, bringing with him a new vogue, *tattooing, which has lasted to this day. Though a spectacular achievement, the voyage had not disproved the possible existence of Terra Australis Incognita and on 13 July 1772 Cook, now promoted to commander, set off again to try and find it. This time he was given two Whitby cats, the *Resolution* and the *Adventure*, the latter under the command of Tobias Furneaux.

This second voyage took Cook into the Antarctic Circle, the first *navigator to penetrate so far south, and by March 1773 he had conclusively proved that no southern continent existed in the one-third of the earth's circumference he had covered at an average *latitude of 60° S. He then spent the midwinter months making a similar negative proof by sailing eastwards from New Zealand between latitudes 41° and 46° S., never before covered, before swinging north and west for a period of rest at Tahiti which he reached on 16 July. From Tahiti he sailed west to locate the Friendly Islands (Tonga) before turning south for another penetration of Antarctica. On 30 January 1774 he reached a latitude of 71° 10' S. before being turned back by impenetrable *ice. In the mean time Furneaux, who had lost touch with the *Resolution*, left New Zealand in December 1773, and, sailing in latitudes between 56° and 61° S., became the first commander to complete a circumnavigation in an easterly direction.

That there could be no great habitable continent in the South Pacific had now been definitely proved, and Cook would have been justified in returning home in the wake of Furneaux. But his ship was still sound and his crew in good health and this persuaded him to undertake a third season of exploration of the still largely unknown Pacific. During the following months he charted Easter Island and the Marquesas, and then discovered and named New Caledonia and Norfolk Island, before setting sail for England from New Zealand on 11 November 1774.

After his return to Portsmouth on 29 July 1775 Cook was promoted *post-captain and elected a Fellow of the Royal Society, which awarded him the Copley Gold Medal. However, within a year he was off again with instructions to go via Cape Town, the French Indian Ocean islands, and on to Tahiti, whence he was to search for the Pacific end of the *North-West Passage after sailing up the North American coastline. For this third voyage he was again given the *Resolution* and a second Whitby cat called *Discovery*, commanded by Charles Clerke. The refit of both ships was shamefully skimped and there were continuous problems, particularly in the *rigging of the *Resolution*.

While sailing towards the North American coast, which he sighted at a latitude of 45° N. on 7 March 1778, Cook discovered the Polynesian-inhabited Hawaiian group, which he named the Sandwich Islands in honour of the then First Lord of the Admiralty, the Earl of Sandwich. After a brief stop he sailed on, followed the North American coastline as instructed, and eventually penetrated the Bering Strait. He reached 70° 30' N. but was then forced to turn back by a wall of ice.

The two ships now returned to the Sandwich Islands and anchored in Kealakekua Bay on 17 January 1779 for a refit. When Cook went ashore he was mystified to be greeted with prostrations and solemn ceremonies—he did not realize that he was being accepted as a Polynesian god whose return to the islands was prophesied in Polynesian legends. To welcome him adequately the priests and chiefs called upon their people to make gifts. However, these strained the islanders' resources to the limit and relations between them and Cook's men soon turned sour. There were a number of thefts, including the pilfering of one of the ship's boats, and on 13 February seamen sent ashore for water clashed with a group of hostile natives. The following day, Cook landed to take a chief hostage to force the return of the stolen boat, a tactic which had worked successfully in the past. But on this occasion the islanders resisted, and Cook was surrounded and stabbed to death before his guard of *marines were able to rescue him. Captain Clerke now took command and sailed again for the Bering Sea, but the ice was even worse than the previous year, and at the end of July the ships turned for home. A month later Clerke died of consumption and Lieutenant Gore of the *Resolution* took command, the two ships finally reaching the Thames in October 1780. See also CANOE; EXPLORATION BY SEA.

Beaglehole, J., *The Life of Captain Cook* (1974).
Cook, James, *The Journals of Captain Cook*, ed. J. Beaglehole, 4 vols. (The Hakluyt Society, 1955–67).
Thomas, N., *Discoveries: The Voyage of Captain Cook* (2003).

coordinates, the definition of the exact position of a point on the surface of the globe in relation to two lines, *latitude and *longitude, which intersect at right angles. Positions on the *celestial sphere are usually defined for navigational purposes using coordinates of the *ecliptic system, the *equinoctial system, or the *horizon system. Mike Richey

copper sheathing, the process of protecting the hull of a wooden ship with thin sheets of copper. It prevents the *teredo worm eating into the planks, and inhibits *seaweed and *barnacles from building up on the ship's bottom so as to improve the ship's performance at sea.

*Marine archaeology has unearthed evidence that copper and lead sheathing was used on some Roman and Greek vessels, and from the 15th century lead was used for sheathing by the Spanish and Portuguese navies. John *Cabot's son Sebastian, who in 1514 saw a Spanish ship sheathed in lead, may have brought back the idea of using lead to England, and certainly a number of English ships were clad underwater with lead in the 1670s. Other methods of protecting the hull were also tried in England and elsewhere, including an extra, sacrificial, layer of planks beyond which the teredo was unlikely to penetrate.

The Dutch admiral Piet Heyn may well have experimented with copper sheathing early in the 17th century, and the British dallied with the idea of using both copper and brass during the first half of the 18th century. However, the earliest evidence of it being used in the Royal Navy came when an examination of the wreck of the 74-gun *Invincible*, which sank in 1758, revealed that she was partly copper sheathed. The first documentary evidence that copper sheathing was ordered for the keels of two British naval ships is dated October 1759, and in December of that year the keels of two more ships were sheathed in this way.

Though experiments on other methods to prevent *fouling continued at the same time, the first trial of a ship with a fully coppered hull began in October 1761 when the 32-gun *frigate *Alarm* was sheathed in copper. This proved successful but few other ships were similarly treated. This was partly expense and partly because galvanic action had occurred between the copper sheets and the iron bolts by which the planks of the *Alarm*'s hull was secured to her *timbers. Though a *sloop called the *Swallow* was built in 1770 with copper bolts, thus becoming the first ship whose underwater hull was totally copper fastened, it was some years before the copper sheathing of smaller vessels began. Then in 1779 orders went out to copper the entire fleet, and in 1783 orders were issued that copper bolts should replace iron ones in naval *shipbuilding. Copper sheathing then became general, and other navies soon followed suit.

Copper-bottomed, a slang term for secure, to be trusted, cannot fail, was derived from the coppering of ships.

Cock, R., ' "The Finest Invention in the World": The Royal Navy's Early Trials of Copper Sheathing, 1708–1770', *Mariners' Mirror*, 87 (2001), 44.

coracle, from the Welsh *corwgl*, carcass, or Irish *curach*, meaning boat. It is a small boat, occasionally circular but more often rectangular with rounded corners, constructed of wicker work. It was originally made watertight with animal hides but in more recent times *pitch or some other watertight material was substituted. It was employed for river and coastal transport by the ancient Britons, and is still used today by fishermen, mainly for salmon, on the rivers and lakes of Wales and Ireland. It is light enough to be carried easily on a man's back.

This type of craft was far more widely distributed than might be thought. In China, where they were known as 'skin boats', they were widely used for many centuries, and they are present on Assyrian bas-reliefs. They were also extensively used in Iraq where they were called *quffah*—Arabic for basket—which has become Anglicized to *gufah.

coral reefs mostly develop in shallow tropical seas, though there are the cold-water *Darwin mounds. Typically, a coral reef consists of an inner *lagoon with a fringing reef at the edge of deeper water. They develop atop sea mounts forming *atolls and also along coasts as barrier reefs, with the *Great Barrier Reef being by far the largest.

Each reef has a complex structure built from the skeletons of species of hard (hermatypic) corals. Corals are coelenterates, relatives of anemones and *jellyfish, that lay down limestone skeletons (calcium carbonate). In their soft tissues live symbiotic microscopic plant cells called zooxanthellae, which provide their hosts with organic food in exchange for protection. Like all green plants these cells need sunlight to grow, so the reef-forming corals are restricted to the shallow sunlit waters and are very sensitive to any increases in turbidity of the water that may cut out the light.

The reefs are important not only for their rich diversity, but also because they protect the coastline from the ravages of *tropical storms. Many of the *fishes that live over the reefs graze on the coral, scraping off the soft tissues and the limy skeletons. The latter is voided and is the source of the white coralline sands that make tropical beaches so attractive. Traditionally they have been exploited by local *fisheries. One favoured, but highly destructive, method of fishing is to drop explosives, but this kills many more fish than are recovered. Another threat comes from the expansion of trade in colourful tropical fish for aquaria. Poisons are used to stun the fish, which also kill many of the other animals on which the ecology of the reefs depend. Yet another threat to coral reefs results from the sudden rises in sea temperatures generated by the *El Niños. Recently reefs in the Indian Ocean have been particularly badly affected, one scientist estimating that more than 90% of the corals were killed by the effects of the 1998 El Niño.

The expansion of *diving and ecotourism, while giving a measure of protection to some reefs, is exposing the fragile reefs to damage from boats' anchors, spearfishing and careless divers. On remote islands, coralline rocks from the reefs offer the only local source of building material, and their extraction can cause problems. Corals are now suffering from coral bleaching. When the water becomes too hot the zooanthellae are expelled and the coral dies back. This has been happening right across the tropics and may be a sign of global warming.

Some coral reefs are also under attack from population outbursts of the crown of thorns starfish, a species of *echinoderm that eats the corals' living tissue, and also from another of today's *environmental issues, eutrophication. Potentially an even more serious threat comes from the increasing concentrations of carbon dioxide in the atmosphere, which hampers the coral reefs' ability to lay down their skeletons of calcium carbonate, so they may no longer be able to grow fast enough to keep up with rising *sea levels. This is a major concern for people living along tropical coastlines and on coral islands, because the protection afforded to them from the impact of tropical storms by the reefs will be reduced. M. V. Angel

corbita, the merchant ship of imperial Rome, a large, full-bodied vessel massively built and capable of carrying as much as 400 tons of cargo. They set a single large square sail on a mast amidships, sometimes with two *raffee *topsails above the *yard, and a small square sail on an *artemon mast over the bows. It was steered with two deep *steering oars, one on each *quarter, which in strong winds and high seas required as many as four men on each oar to control the vessel. During the 1st century AD Roman corbitas made regular voyages between ports in the Red Sea and the west coast of India as well as normal Mediterranean passages.

cord, small laid-up rope of 2.5 centimetres (1 in.) or less in circumference, more often referred to in ships as 'line'. In size it is about

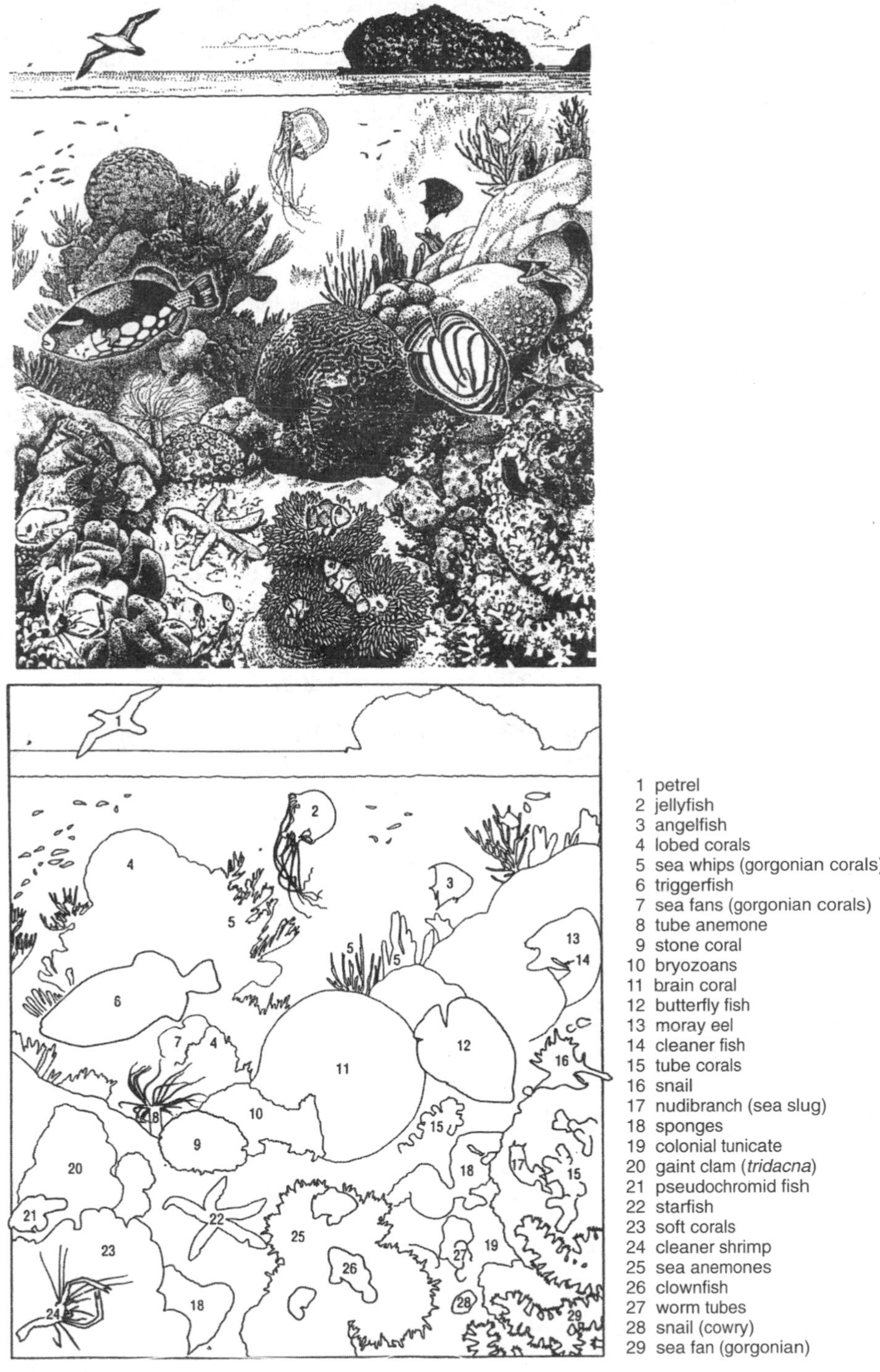

A coral reef habitat illustrating some of the many inhabitants of this diverse ecosystem

halfway between twine and rope, and is used on board for a variety of purposes where rope would be too large and clumsy. It is also widely described as *codline.

Corinthian, an amateur yachtsman who sailed his own *yacht without a professional skipper. It is a mid-19th-century American term for a rich amateur sportsman, and spread to Britain mainly in its yachting connotation. Some *yacht clubs used it when they were formed, i.e. Royal Corinthian Yacht Club.

Coriolis force is the name given to the inertial forces acting on a body moving across the surface of a rotating sphere. They result from accelerations generated through the conservation of angular momentum, a basic tenet of Newtonian laws of motion. So anywhere on the surface of the earth, apart from exactly on the equator or at the poles, anything that moves, including *currents and winds, will rotate. In the northern hemisphere the rotation is clockwise (cyclonic), and in the southern hemisphere it is anticlockwise (anticyclonic). It determines patterns of circulation in the atmosphere (prevailing winds and *tropical storms) and in the oceans (the major current gyres and *upwelling). The term commemorates the 19th-century French mathematician Gaspard-Gustave Coriolis. See also MARINE METEOROLOGY.

M. V. Angel

corsair, a private ship fitted out by an owner to operate under licence by the government against the merchant shipping of an enemy. The word is particularly applicable to Mediterranean waters and is most often associated with the privateering cruisers which operated off the Barbary (Saracen) coasts of North Africa as late as 1825 and preyed on the merchant ships of Christian states. Although many people regarded their actions as *piracy, corsairs were usually legitimate *privateers licensed by the Turkish government at Constantinople. The word is also used to describe the men who manned these ships. See also BARBARY PIRATES.

corvette, a warship of the 17th–18th centuries with a *flush deck and a single *tier of guns. It was smaller than a *frigate, and was *ship rigged. The design was originally French and was a development of the *lateen-rigged *galley, with virtually the same hull form being taken for the corvette. Proving fast and *weatherly, the design was adopted by the British Navy, the best British corvettes being those built of cedarwood in Bermuda.

The name corvette was also used in the Second World War (1939–45) to describe a small anti-submarine warship used for escorting *convoys, and some navies still have them (see table in NAVY). The Norwegian Navy has developed a 47-metre (154-ft) rigid-sidewall *surface effect ship, described as a coastal corvette. With a top speed of 55 knots, it can operate in only a metre of water, and is made of *GRP and *carbon fibre which gives it a low *radar signature. The Swedish Navy is building an equally radical corvette (see illus. opposite). Both types may be a glimpse of the future of smaller surface warships. See also WARFARE AT SEA.

Costain gun, a gun firing a small rocket projectile to which a thin line was attached. It was used mainly for *lifesaving in conjunction with a *breeches buoy, but it had other maritime uses such as when a line had to be passed between two vessels at sea.

cot, the wooden bed frame, enclosed in *canvas and slung from deck *beams, in which ships' officers slept before the permanent *bunks in *cabins were introduced.

counter, the overhanging stern of a vessel above the waterline, its top, or crown, being

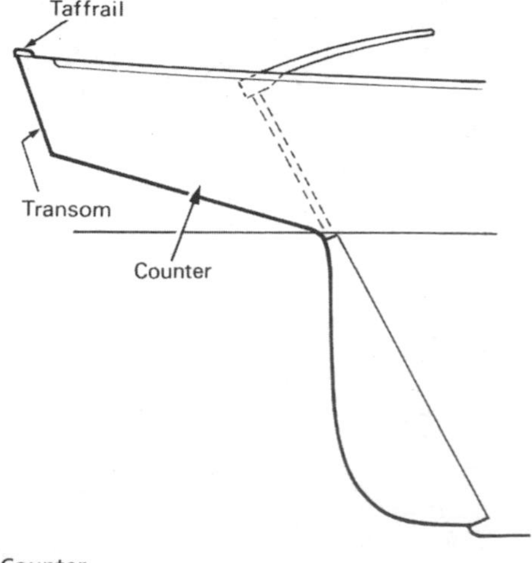

Counter

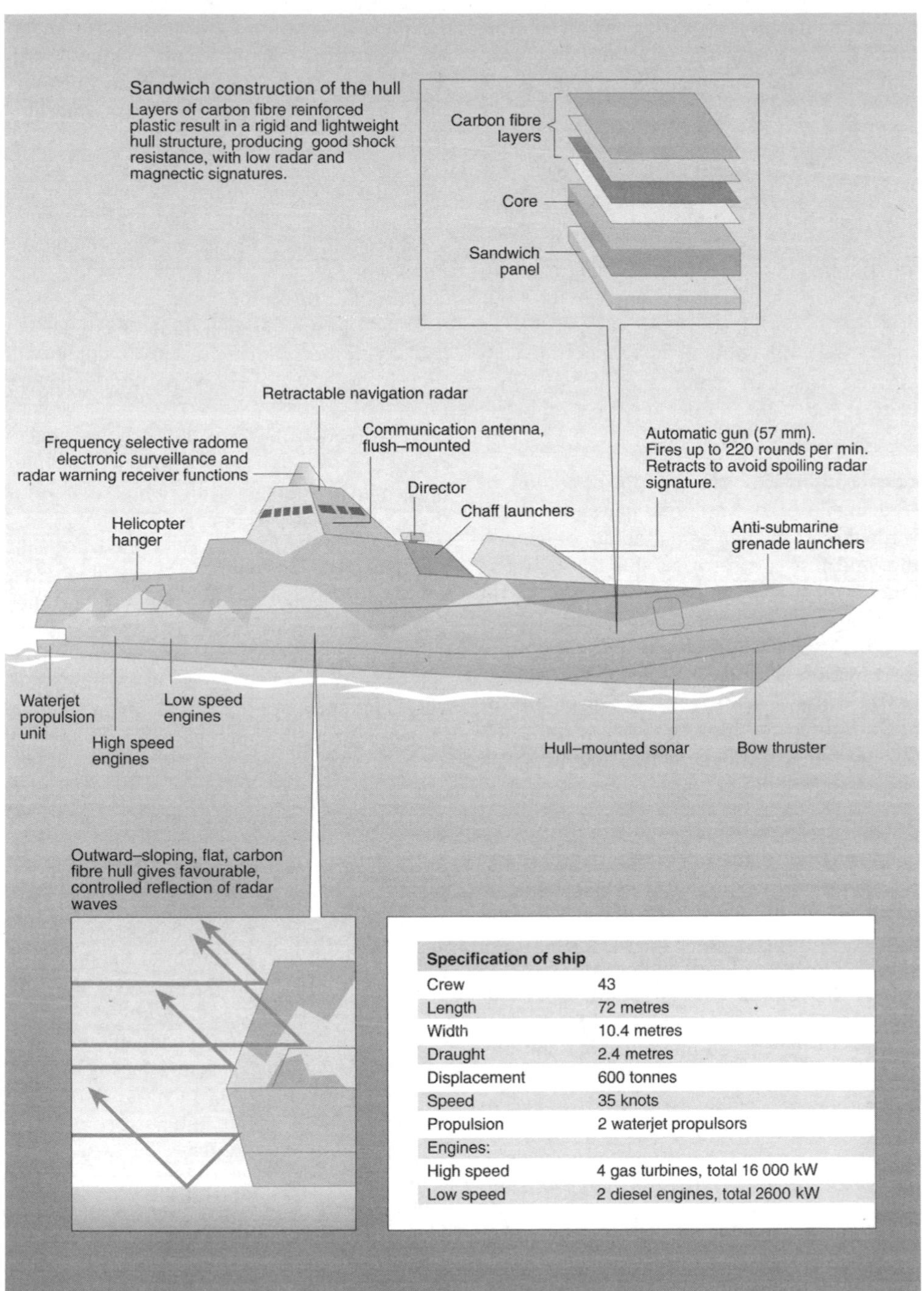

Specification of ship	
Crew	43
Length	72 metres
Width	10.4 metres
Draught	2.4 metres
Displacement	600 tonnes
Speed	35 knots
Propulsion	2 waterjet propulsors
Engines:	
High speed	4 gas turbines, total 16 000 kW
Low speed	2 diesel engines, total 2600 kW

The stealth ship. A Visby-class corvette built by the Swedish Navy which, besides its 57mm gun, is armed with anti-submarine torpedoes and uses underwater vehicles for mine-hunting and mine destruction. When it was launched in 2004 it was the largest vessel ever constructed of *carbon fibre. This makes it faster and lighter than conventional warships the same size, and also makes it much more difficult for *radar to detect it. This gives it a 'stealth advantage' over hostile aircraft as it can detect them before they detect it.

formed by the aftermost deck *beams and its bottom terminating in, or at, the *transom. The term is also loosely used to indicate the small area of deck *abaft the *sternpost. Most large ships today are built without a counter, the after end terminating in a transom, or a rounded or cruiser stern, but *tugs are always built with a pronounced counter, mainly to keep their towing *hawsers, when they fall into the water, clear of the *propellers. **Counter stern**, the overhang of the stern abaft the *rudder used in the sense of describing a type of stern. **Sawn-off counter**, as above, but with the aftermost part terminating abruptly in a vertical end instead of being carried on in the normal line of the hull form.

counter-brace, to. **(1)** The operation of *bracing the head-*yards one way and the after yards the other when going *about, or lying to the wind, in a *square-rigged ship. The counter-brace is the *lee brace of the fore *topsail yard at the time of going about. When the fore-topsail begins to shake as the ship is brought up into the wind, the lee brace is hauled in hard to flatten the sail against the *weather side of the topmast to force the ship's head across the wind. **(2)** The old term of the action required in a square-rigged ship to make it *heave to.

counter-currents are compensatory flows of water that balance the flows of the major *currents. Any flow in one direction has to be balanced by an equal volume of water flowing in the opposite direction. However, these counter-flows may lie either beneath or to one side of the main currents. For example beneath the north-eastern flow of the *Gulf Stream is a southward-flowing counter-current, and the counter-current of the Humboldt Current in the south-west Pacific is a mirror-image of the Gulf Stream flows. Similarly the strong currents that flow along the equator, especially in the Pacific, are flanked to north and south and underlain by counter-currents. The large-scale (or thermohaline) circulation of the oceans, which is such an important regulator of global climate, is the ultimate expression of the requirement for there to be compensatory flows. For illus. see CURRENTS. M. V. Angel

course. **(1)** The horizontal angle between the intended direction of travel of a vessel and a reference direction, generally north. The angles between *true, magnetic, and compass north and the path of the vessel are known respectively as true course, magnetic course, and compass course. The angular difference between the true and magnetic course is the *variation, and that between magnetic and compass course is the *deviation. The combination of variation and deviation is the *magnetic compass error.

Nowadays the compass course of a ship is denoted in three-figure notation from 000° to 359°. With the gyro compass the readings will be true. See also GREAT CIRCLE; LAY (3); RHUMB LINE.

(2) In theory, the sails set upon the lower *yards of a *square-rigged ship to which *bonnets could be attached. The original spelling for these sails was corps or corse. But the original definition of 'course' was extended to all sails set on the lower yards irrespective of whether they were adapted to carry bonnets, and they were designated by the name of the mast on which they were set, as fore course, main course, and *mizzen course. Gradually *staysails set on lower masts and the main staysails of *brigs and *schooners also became known as courses. A ship which set only *foresail, mainsail, and mizzen was said to be under its courses. For illus. see SQUARE RIG.

Cousteau, Jacques-Yves (1910–97), French naval officer, explorer, and one of the pioneers of *oceanography, best known for his invention with Emile Gagnan of the aqualung for *diving, and for his documentaries and books. He was born at Saint-André-de-Cubzac in the Gironde, and, after serving in the French Navy, worked in the Resistance during the Second World War (1939–45), and was awarded the Legion of Honour after it. In 1950 he converted a British minesweeper, *Calypso*, into a *research ship and made several expeditions aboard her. From these he made two full-length films, *Le Monde du silence* (The World of Silence), produced in 1956, and *Monde sans soleil* (World without Sun), produced in 1964, and the television series, 'The Undersea World of Jacques Cousteau'. In 1957 he was appointed director of the Oceanographic Museum at Monaco, and during the 1960s carried out several experiments in living underwater in undersea laboratories. In 1973 he formed the Cousteau Society, a non-profit-making organization devoted to marine conservation which has offices in France and the USA.

Besides the aqualung, he invented a number of useful tools for oceanographers including a highly manoeuvrable *underwater vehicle, underwater cameras, and a camera sled to facilitate photography of the seabed at great depths. His last book, *Man, the Octopus, and the Orchid,* was published posthumously. Among his other publications were: *The Silent World* (1953), *The Living Sea* (1963), *World without Sun* (1965), and a 20-volume encyclopedia, *The Ocean World of Jacques Cousteau,* published during the 1970s.

cove. **(1)** A small coastal inlet; its name implies that it is normally protected from the worst of the prevailing winds by high cliffs or promontories. **(2)** The wooden roof of the stern *gallery in the old sailing warships and *East Indiamen. **(3)** A thin, hollowed line cut along a *yacht's *sheer strake below deck level, and traditionally gilded. It is also known as a **caveta**.

covering board, the name given, particularly in *yacht construction, to the outmost plank of the main deck, which is usually wider then the other deck planks. In larger wooden ships it is usually called the *plank sheer.

cow-hitch, any *bend or *hitch which slips as a result of being improperly tied; or a 'home-made' knot which is not a recognized maritime knot as used at sea.

cowl. **(1)** A ship's ventilator with a bell-shaped top, which can be swivelled on deck to catch the wind and force it below. See also DORADE VENTILATOR. **(2)** The cover of a ship's funnel as used in harbour, and also the vertical projection at the forward end of a funnel to direct the smoke aft and away from the *bridge.

coxswain, orig. **cockswain** (pron. coxun). **(1)** The helmsman of a ship's boat and the senior member of its crew who has permanent charge of it. Originally all boats carried on board a ship were known as cockboats, or 'cocks', which gives the origin of the term. **(2)** The senior *petty officer on board small naval craft such as *destroyers, *submarines, etc. As these craft were originally known in navies as boats rather than ships (torpedo boat, submarine, etc.) the term was applied to the senior petty officer on board in the same way as it would be to the senior rating of a ship's boat.

crab, a *capstan but without a *drumhead, and in which the bars were inserted right through the top of the barrel instead of into pigeon-holes in the upper perimeter (drumhead) as in a capstan proper; the holes for the bars in a crab being in different planes. In the days of sail it was used for any heavy lifting work on board in exactly the same way as a capstan but sometimes extemporized for use in positions where the *fall of the purchase used for lifting a weight could not be led to an existing *winch or capstan. See also CRUSTACEA.

craft, in the 15th–17th centuries a term which denoted any kind of net, line, or hook used for catching *fish. Fishing vessels, such as *hoys and *busses, were in consequence usually described as small craft. The term has long since been expanded to include all small vessels whether they are fishing boats or not. See also FISHERIES.

cran, a unit of measurement for *herrings, being as many fresh or green unsalted herrings as will fill a barrel.

crance, crans, or **cranze.** **(1)** An iron band on the outer end of a *bowsprit fitted with *eyes to take the bowsprit *shrouds and the *bobstay. In larger sailing vessels where a *jib-boom is rigged the crance carries an additional opening through which the jib-boom is traversed, serving also to hold its *heel firmly in place on the bowsprit. It is sometimes known as crans-iron. For illus. see BOWSPRIT.

crane lines. **(1)** Small ropes which were set up to keep the *lee *backstays from chafing against the *yards of a *square-rigged ship when the wind is blowing from either *quarter. **(2)** The lines which were *rove from the *spritsail topmast to the centre of the *forestay to steady the former, acting somewhat in the manner of a backstay. With the spritsail topmast set up on the *bowsprit, there was no way of staying it except by such temporary means.

crank. A sailing ship which either by its construction, or by the stowage of its *ballast or cargo, heels too far to the wind, or one which through lack of ballast or cargo cannot carry sail without the danger of overturning, is said to be crank. Ships built excessively deep in relation to their breadth were notoriously crank. **Crank by the ground**, a ship whose *floor was so narrow that it could not be put ashore for *breaming or *careening without danger of overturning unless supported by *legs.

creeper, another name for a small four-hooked *grapnel used to recover articles dropped on the seabed by dragging for them. In clear water a white plate or dish dropped overboard immediately after the object falls gives a useful guide to where to use the creeper.

crib, the name widely used during the early 19th century to describe the small permanent sleeping berths in *packet ships. Its meaning was later expanded to cover any small sleeping berth in a small vessel.

crimp, one who, during the days of the *press gang, made it his business to persuade seamen to desert from a ship in order to sell them to another or to deliver them to the press gang on payment of head money. Most of them operated as keepers of seamen's lodging houses or taverns in ports with a busy turn-round of ships. The usual method of delivering seamen to a ship in need of hands was to make them drunk and deliver them on board, while still insensible, an hour or two before the ship's departure. One crimp, short of the number he had been required to collect, delivered a dead man aboard pretending he was drunk. The word is first noted in this sense in 1638. Although the practice was widespread around the world the most notorious port in which crimps flourished was San Francisco in the late 19th and early 20th centuries, when the rate for seamen delivered to a ship about to sail reached $30 a head plus expenses. Often crimps also claimed the first month's pay of the men they delivered. In Britain, crimping was an indictable offence leading to a prison sentence.

cringle, a short piece of rope worked *grommet fashion into the *bolt-rope of a sail and containing a metal thimble. In the days of sail they were used to hook in the *tack and sheet *tackles when they had to be moved up when a sail was *reefed. In the days of *square-rigged ships, cringles were used on the sails for extending the *leech of the sail by means of *bowline *bridles for extra driving power in a head wind. The word is derived from the Old English *crencled*, meaning circle, or circularly formed.

crossing the line, a ceremony performed on board ships when their passengers and crew are crossing the equator for the first time. Traditionally, it is performed by one of the ship's crew attired as King *Neptune, encrusted with *barnacles, wearing a golden crown and flowing beard, and clasping a *trident. He summons the novices one by one who, after receiving the attentions of both surgeon and barber, are tipped backwards into a bath of sea water, where King Neptune's assistants ensure they receive a good ducking. Nowadays, less onerous ceremonies are held for passengers aboard *cruise ships and other commercial vessels which cross the equator.

The ceremony undoubtedly owes its origin to ancient pagan rites connected with the propitiation of the Greek sea god *Poseidon, known to the Romans as Neptune. In classical times it was the custom to mark the successful rounding of prominent headlands by making a sacrifice to the appropriate deity, many of whom had temples erected in their honour on such points. With the spread of Christianity many of the vows and oblations paid to the heathen gods were transferred to the saints. In 1529 the French instituted an order of knighthood called *Les Chevaliers de la Mer* in which novices were given the accolade when rounding certain capes.

'crossing the T', a favourite manoeuvre in naval battle during the days of sail when opposing fleets sailed in the normal battle disposition of line ahead. If a fleet in this disposition, either by a superiority of speed or by approaching at an angle, could cross ahead of its enemy's line approximately at right angles, it had a considerable tactical advantage. This was because it could bring many more of its guns to bear, and fire them as a *broadside, while the enemy fleet could only reply with those guns which could be fired ahead. It was also a tactical situation which forced an enemy to turn away, and in the resulting loss of speed during the turn, and the difficulty of keeping guns bearing on an enemy while doing so, the fleet 'crossing the T' had a considerable advantage. See also WARFARE AT SEA.

cross-jack (pron. crojeck or crojick) **yard,** the lower *yard on the *mizzen or aftermost mast of a *ship-rigged sailing vessel to spread the sheets of the mizzen *topsail. It was so called because the term mizzen yard was in use for the *lateen sail which was later replaced by the trapezoidal *spanker sail set under a *gaff. From about 1800 some ships set a square sail called the cross-jack from the cross-jack yard but it had limited use because of the interference with the spanker.

cross lashing, a method of lashing with a rope in which the consecutive turns, instead of lying close up against each other in the same direction, are crossed diagonally. This type of lashing, by binding in upon itself with each turn, is less liable to give or *render.

cross sea, a sea running in a contrary direction to the wind. When the direction of the wind changes rapidly, such as during *tropical storms, the direction of the sea, whipped up by the wind, lasts for some hours after the wind has changed, throwing up a confused and irregular *wave pattern which can be dangerous for ships caught in it.

cross-staff, or **forestaff,** an early *navigation instrument for measuring the *meridian *altitude of the sun or a star to establish *latitude at sea. Its precise origins are obscure but the principle is clearly the same as that of the Jacob's staff (with which the cross-staff is often confused), a medieval instrument first referred to in 1342 in a treatise by the Catalan Jew Levi ben Gerson, and used principally by surveyors and for military purposes for distance measurement. The cross-staff measured with precision angles in degrees of arc and its use at sea seems to have been first proposed, somewhat earlier than contemporary technology warranted, by the astronomer Johannes Werner who had suggested the use of *lunar distances to find *longitude at sea. However, the earliest record of its employment in navigation, with proper instructions as to its use, seems to have been in John of Lisbon's *Livro de marinharia* written in about 1515. By the middle of that century the Portuguese in their southward *exploration by sea of the Atlantic Ocean were using the instrument, which was eventually to displace both the *seaman's quadrant and *astrolabe.

The cross-staff comprises a square-cut wooden staff about 76 centimetres (30 in.) in length with, at right angles to the shaft, a cross-piece known as the transversal that could slide up and down the staff. The instrument was aimed at the body being observed, much as a crossbow might be aimed, with one end on the observer's cheekbone. The staff was graduated to give the observer the angle of elevation, that is, the altitude of the body. To avoid altering the length of the staff to increase the range of angles, later instruments were fitted with three or four transversals. The back-staff or *Davis's quadrant supplemented it from the 1590s and among English seamen supplanted it almost entirely in the 17th century. Mike Richey

crosstrees, see SPREADERS.

crowd, to, to carry excessive sail particularly in *square-rigged ships, or to approach too closely another ship which has the right of way under the *International Regulations for Preventing Collisions at Sea.

crown. **(1)** A knot formed by tucking the *strands of a rope's end over and under each other to lock them and prevent them unravelling. A crown knot made on top of a *wall knot is the basis on which a manrope, or double wall and crown, knot is formed. **(2)** The lower part of an anchor where the arms are fixed to the *shank.

crow's foot, the name given to the method of attaching *reef-points to a sail. The points are cut to the required length and each end *whipped. A crow's foot is then formed in the middle by twisting against the *lay so that individual *strands are separated, pulling each one out and letting it twist up on itself. The crow's foot is then sewn to the *starboard side of the sail (if possible on a seam) after the reef point has been drawn through the sail.

crow's nest, a small shelter on the foremast for a ship's masthead lookout, early ones being made from a cask. It was used extensively in *whalers to watch for the blow of a *whale, and for *navigation in *ice-bound waters to distinguish the channels. See also BIRD'S NEST.

cruiser, orig. **cruizer,** in the days of sailing navies a ship, usually a fourth-*rate or large *frigate, detached from a fleet to cruise independently in search of the enemy. Frigates and smaller warships engaged in the protection of trade or in the **guerre de course* were also usually known as cruisers. The one essential characteristic of any ship detached for duty as a cruiser was a good sailing speed, superior to that of any enemy she might encounter.

With the introduction of *steam propulsion and iron armour in the mid-19th century, the cruiser gradually became a generic type of warship in its own right. It was built in three or four categories, ranging from armoured cruisers which were large ships of up to 15,000–16,000 tons *displacement, through belted cruisers (those protected only by a waterline belt of armour), second-class cruisers with only light armour, and light cruisers with virtually no armour but with a particularly high speed.

The Washington Naval Limitation Treaty of 1922 limited the cruiser to 10,000 tons and classified those with guns of 7.1 in. (17.7 cm) or larger as 'heavy' and those with 6 in. (15 cm) or smaller as 'light'. Virtually all subsequent cruisers carried either 6-in. (15-cm) or 8-in. (20-cm) guns, though the anti-aircraft cruisers built by the Royal Navy during the Second World War (1939–45) for *convoy protection were armed with 5.5-in. (13.7-cm) dual purpose guns. The three *diesel-engined German pocket battleships *Deutschland* (later renamed *Lützow*), *Admiral Graf Spee*, and *Admiral Scheer*, with their six 11-in. (27.5-cm) guns and eight 5.7-in. (14.2-cm) guns, were in fact heavily armoured cruisers of 10,000 tons displacement.

The US Navy *launched the last all-gun heavy cruiser, *Salem*, in 1947, but the advent of guided missiles rendered 'heavy' and 'light' designations for cruisers irrelevant; and, with larger and larger *destroyers being built, the difference between the two types of warship has virtually disappeared. No cruisers are built today though the US Navy continues to consider designs for them. See also BELFAST; WARFARE AT SEA.

cruise ship, a passenger ship which sails a prearranged itinerary to popular tourist destinations, though cruises can vary in length from a few days to a circumnavigation. Using a ship as a floating hotel, which is what a cruise ship is, is even older than the introduction of *ocean liners on regular scheduled routes as, in 1833, 80 passengers set off on a cruise in an Italian ship from Naples to Istanbul. It did not sound a great success as the diary of one passenger records there were constant disputes and that 'two duels are yet to be fought, when the voyage terminates'.

The British shipping line P & O (Peninsular & Orient) began running cruises in the 1840s and in 1844 employed the novelist William Makepeace Thackeray to publicize them. One of the first regular cruise schedules was by the North of Scotland, Orkney and Shetland Steam Navigation Company whose 1,500-ton steamer *St Sunniva*, with a capacity to take 132 passengers, made regular summer runs in the 1870s from Aberdeen to parts of Norway.

For many decades it was the scheduled ocean liners which garnered the publicity and the public's attention, and the smaller ones were employed for cruising during the winter months when the scheduled routes were not so busy. Between the two world wars cruising increased in popularity and shipping lines began to build passenger ships specifically for cruising. The main difference between the two types was that cruise liners were almost always one class. Also, because passengers lived aboard cruise ships longer than they did aboard scheduled ocean liners, the former were more luxurious and more space was allotted to the public rooms.

Shipping losses during the Second World War (1939–45), and the economic deprivation that followed it, meant little cruising took place in Europe until the early 1950s, though the Cunard Line's *Caronia*, *launched in 1949, was a dual purpose passenger ship which served as both an ocean liner and a cruise ship for nearly twenty years. The British firm of Swan Hellenic was founded in the early 1950s because a cruise ship was the only practical way to take those interested in antiquities to Greece, as stringent currency regulations were in force and Greece was just recovering from a civil war. The early Swan Hellenic cruises were somewhat spartan, with male and female passengers sleeping in separate dormitories, even if they were married. However, as soon as the world began to recover from the economic ravages of the war, more passenger ships started to be built in response to the demand for holidaying on a cruise ship. And once air travel began to supersede regularly scheduled ocean liners, particularly on the North Atlantic route, cruising became an even more important source of income to shipping companies, and new cruise ships of innovative design—*Southern Cross, Northern Star, Oriana, Canberra,* and *Rotterdam*—were launched. Each of these liners had unusual features, most of which are now standard. The most obvious one was placing the machinery *aft, saving space in the widest and therefore best part of the ship. Many of the *Canberra*'s first-class cabins had windows, not *scuttles, and some even had verandahs, and the toughened glass used aboard her was a forerunner of the immensely strong glass structures now seen in cruise ships everywhere. Noise suppression was another major feature, with steam turbines, *electric propulsion, and controllable pitch *propellers all helping to reduce vibration and increase passenger comfort. Great care was also taken, by air tunnel testing, to make sure the decks were as sheltered as possible in all wind conditions, *stabilizers were fitted to dampen the ship's movement at sea, and *evaporators ensured a constant supply of fresh water.

Perhaps the single most telling shift in emphasis towards cruise ships and away from ocean liners came in the early 1960s when, at the design stage of Cunard's *Queen Elizabeth II*, it was decided to build her for cruising as well as for maintaining a regular transatlantic schedule. It was just as well that this was done because, by the 1970s, scheduled all-the-year-round passenger routes by sea were a thing of the past, but the popularity of cruising continued to increase. New types of cruises which had been pioneered in the 1960s, where passengers flew to or from a destination before boarding their cruise ship, or stayed in a hotel ashore before or after doing so, now became routine. At the same time small specialist cruise ships began to be used specifically to cater for those who wanted to travel to unusual and exotic places, such as Antarctica, while others advertised cruises to a segment of the market, such as parents with children, or those devoted to gambling. Sailing cruise ships was another innovation which proved popular to those who could afford it.

The design of cruise ships, to accommodate the numbers wishing to use them, advanced enormously during the last four decades of the 20th century. When comparing the *Canberra* (1961), at that time the largest passenger carrier of her day, with the *Carnival Destiny* (1996), it can be seen that the latter, although very similar in displacement *tonnage, and being only 2% longer (between perpendiculars) and only 13% wider on the *beam (at the waterline), and with 20% less draught, can still accommodate nearly 40% more passengers (3,360) and crew (1,040) than the *Canberra* (2,200 + 960). The reason for this is that the gross tonnage of the *Carnival Destiny*, a measure of her capacity, is about two-thirds more than the *Canberra*'s, for the former has two more decks than the *Canberra* and all the passenger decks are much broader above the waterline. But because it was more economical to run one large ship rather than two smaller ones, cruise ships are also getting larger; and several exceeding 100,000 tonnes had been launched by 2004 which were nothing less than floating cities.

In the modern cruise ships safety is paramount. The *International Convention for the Safety of Life at Sea laid down the strictest regulations for *stability and for *lifesaving. Currently, cruise ships fit their lifeboats in recesses as close to the water as possible, and many have dedicated muster decks on the same level. Also important for those operating such large vessels, propeller systems, such as *bow thrusters and *propulsion pods, help manoeuvring in confined spaces. Combating *environmental issues is also essential and many cruise ships are now powered by *gas turbines to cut air *pollution. *MARPOL, which regulates this type of pollution, also prevents dumping at sea, so all water used aboard a cruise ship, and its sewage, is stored in its *double bottoms for later disposal ashore. The latest *Oriana* generates 8 tonnes of waste every day, of which only 3 tonnes can be burned in an environmentally friendly way, so it can be seen how essential it is that controls are in place.

In 2004 the most popular cruise destination was the Caribbean. However, Carnival, the world's largest cruise line conglomerate which owns Cunard, is building a new ocean shipping terminal close to the *Queen Mary*, now a hotel and conference centre at Long Beach, California. One of the reasons for this is to take full advantage of the untapped Asian cruise market, but the other is that *climate change is creating greater extremes of weather patterns in the Caribbean.

According to Cruise Lines International, 145 cruise ships carried 5.9 million passengers in 1999 and by 2004 the number of cruise ships in operation had risen to 180. This included the *Queen Mary 2* which sailed on her maiden voyage in January 2004. With a length of 345 metres (1,131 ft), a gross tonnage of 150,000, and a maximum speed of 30 knots, she was, at the time, the largest passenger ship ever built; but by then, other, even larger, cruise ships had been announced as being in the pipeline.

The Berlitz Complete Guide to Cruising Ships (2004).

'crusher', a Royal Navy slang term on the *lower deck for a member of the ship's police, or regulating *petty officer.

Crustacea, a group of invertebrate animals belonging to the phylum Arthropoda. It includes not only large *shellfish such as crabs, shrimps, and lobsters, but also smaller animals like copepods and *krill that are the most numerous and important animals of the *plankton. They have a hard outer skeleton or carapace, which in many species is hardened with calcium carbonate, and they have to shed this in order to grow. In crabs mating can only occur after the female has moulted and still has a soft carapace. In some species like the shore crab (*Carcinus maenas*) once a crab matures it no longer moults, and so can only mate once. In the spring the male common spider crabs (*Maia squinado*) assemble in huge piles in the centre of which are the moulting females. In contrast the edible crab (*Cancer pagurus*) and species of lobster (*Homarus*) continue to moult and grow, so mating is less of a crisis event and individual animals can attain much larger sizes. The heaviest on record is a 1.06-metre (3-ft 6-in.) long American lobster, which weighed 20.14 kilograms (44 lb 6 oz). The record for size is held by a giant spider crab (*Macrocheira kaempferi*) found off Japan, which had a leg span of over 3.7 metres (12 ft). Many of the larger crustaceans spend their larval stages in the plankton. The planktonic larvae of lobsters are highly transparent and leaflike, and are called phyllosoma; they spend nearly a year in the plankton during which time they may drift across an ocean.

Many types of crustacean live permanently in the plankton. One group, the copepods, make up 70% of the animals caught in nets and are probably the most numerous invertebrates on the planet. They are a key link in the food web between the phytoplankton and larger animals such as *fish and the smaller *seabirds. Another important planktonic group are the euphausiids. These shrimplike animals range in adult size from 1 to 3 centimetres (0.5–1.5 in.).

There are many important commercial species of crustaceans. Crabs and lobsters are trapped in baited pots and prawns are *trawled from the seabed. In tropical countries sea-water ponds are carved out of *mangrove swamps to make ponds in which prawns are cultured. The stocking of these ponds relies heavily on larvae from the wild populations that are introduced when the ponds are opened to the sea. Nearly 6.5 million tonnes of crustaceans are caught each year, and a nearly another million tonnes are produced by aquaculture. In all *crustaceans contribute 7% to global *fisheries.

M. V. Angel

crutch. **(1)** A *stanchion with two short, curved arms at the end shaped to take the main *boom of a *yacht, or other *fore-and-aft-rigged vessel, when the sails are stowed. It is fitted on the vessel's *counter and is used to secure the boom and prevent it swinging from side to side when the vessel rolls. See also GALLOWS. **(2)** Alternative name for a *rowlock.

CSS stands for Confederate States Ship. It was the prefix used for the warships of the states of the Confederacy (South) during the American Civil War between North and South (1861–5) to distinguish them from the warships of the Union or Federal states (North) which used the prefix *USS. See also NAVY: UNITED STATES NAVY.

cubbridge heads, the old name of the *bulkheads of the *forecastle and the half-decks in older sailing warships. They were fitted with sockets for mounting handguns, known as *murderers, to traverse the *waist of the ship in the event of being boarded by an enemy. See also PASSARADO.

cuddy, originally a *cabin in the after part of a sailing ship for the captain and his passengers, which was positioned under the *poop deck. The term is also sometimes used to denote a small cabin on board a boat, or *yacht, or very occasionally a small cookhouse on board, though *caboose was a more usual word for this. In larger ships the cuddy was the compartment where the officers had their meals.

culverin, a gun used aboard warships during the 15th and 16th centuries. It was of smaller *calibre relative to its length than a *cannon and therefore of greater range. It was preferred for arming ships during the 16th century rather than the heavy and comparatively unwieldy cannon and demi-cannon. The steady improvement in the quality and power of gunpowder and quicker combustion, together with increasing accuracy in the manufacture of the guns themselves, permitted smaller charges to be used and the length of the culverin to be reduced. This type of gun was subdivided into:

1. the **culverin**, a typical example of which would be of 5-in. calibre and firing a 7.7-kilogram (17-lb) shot; its length might vary greatly between 3.9 metres (13 ft) for a *bow-chaser and 2.4–2.7 metres (8–9 ft) for a *broadside gun;
2. the **demi-culverin**, a 9-pounder of 4-in. calibre and up to 3.3 metres (11 ft) in length;
3. the saker, a 5-pounder of 3-in. calibre and some 2.7 metres (9 ft) long;
4. the **minion**, a 4-pounder of 3-in. calibre and also some 2.7 metres (9 ft) in length;
5. the **falcon** and **falconet**, which were 2- to 3-pounders and 1- to 2-pounders respectively.

For other types of heavy weapons carried aboard ships see GUN.

Cunningham, a sail control line leading through a *cringle, in the lower part of the *luff of a sail. It is tightened as the wind increases so the sail retains its optimum shape. It is said to have been invented by the US yachtsman Briggs Cunningham.

John Rousmaniere

currach or **curragh,** a boat peculiar to Ireland, especially its western coast. It is of great antiquity, contemporary with, and very similar to, the *coracle, being originally constructed of animal skins attached to a wicker frame. Like the coracle it was often nearly circular in shape and was propelled by paddles. Possibly, the curraghs used by St *Brendan, 'who was born in Kerry, the home of the best curraghs, were capable of carrying twenty people and may have been constructed from as many as thirty hides' (R. Hope, *A New History of British Shipping* (1990), 21). A modern currach is constructed of two skins of calico or *canvas, tarred to make them watertight, stretched over an interlaced framework of elm laths, although other woods are used when elm is not easily available. Currachs are nowadays conventionally shaped for use with as many as eight *oars, though they are normally rather smaller. A small mast and a square sail are usually carried for use when the wind is favourable. Currachs are particularly associated with the Aran Islands, off the west coast of Ireland, where they are used for the transport not only of people and goods, but also cattle.

currents are driven by two main forces, wind and density differences. The friction of winds blowing over the surface of the ocean drives surface currents, whose direction is rotated by *Coriolis force. The rotational effects continue down into the water generating a phenomenon known as an Ekman spiral. The density of sea water is determined by hydrostatic pressure (i.e. depth) and the water's temperature and *salinity, and so changes markedly across any *thermocline. *Latitudinal variations in the sun's energy that reaches the surface, and rainfall, result in the surface waters tending to be buoyant in equatorial regions where there is high rainfall, heavier in the hot and arid *horse latitudes, and to vary seasonally, not only at temperate latitudes but also at polar latitudes where the sea *ice formation and melting directly effects salinity. These influences result in each ocean basin having a similar large-scale circulation pattern. Along the equator there is

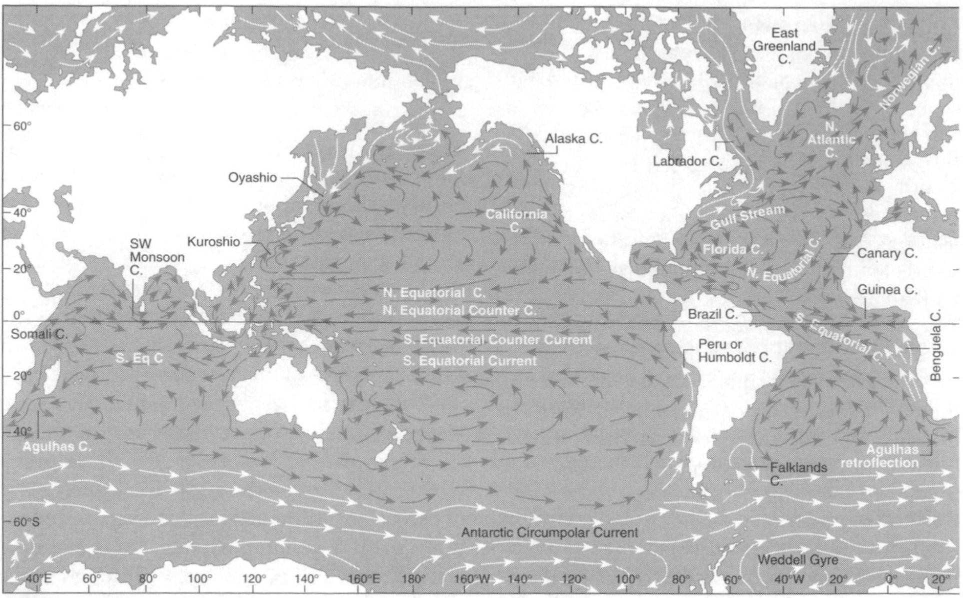

Highly generalized representation of the global surface current system. Cool currents are shown by white arrows; warm currents by black ones. The map shows average conditions for summer months in the northern hemisphere

a narrow band of current flowing from west to east. There is a subtropical clockwise current gyre with a narrow fast current flowing towards the poles along the western boundary, driven partly by the *trade winds and partly by the density differences. In the North Atlantic this boundary current is the ***Gulf Stream**, in the North Pacific it is the **Kuroshio**, and in the Southern Indian Ocean it is the **Agulhas**. These boundary currents feed transoceanic drifts, which are broader and slower. They, in turn, feed into flows towards the equator along the eastern boundaries, and on into return flows either side of the equator that flow counter to the fast equatorial current.

Similar gyres, or giant eddies, occur at northern sub-polar and polar latitudes, but in the Southern Ocean the circumpolar current, bounded by the *Antarctic Convergence, flows eastwards unimpeded around the globe. These currents have a major influence on climate by redistributing heat from equatorial regions towards the poles. For example, the mean annual temperature at Iqaluit in the North-West Territories of Canada is –9.1 °C (15.6 °F equivalent), whereas at Trondheim, at a similar latitude of the Atlantic margin, it is +4.8 °C (40.6 °F), because of the heat transported by the Gulf Stream and its extension, the **North Atlantic Drift**.

Knowledge of ocean currents has considerable value to navies as the book and film *The Hunt for Red October* illustrates, by showing how, during the Cold War, Russian nuclear *submarines escaped detection when entering the Atlantic. They did so by silently riding the fast flows of cold water that gush through the deep channels in the submarine ridge between the Norwegian Sea and the Atlantic.

M. V. Angel

cut and run, to, an expression often thought to imply the cutting of a *hemp *cable with an axe, thus abandoning an anchor, when a ship needed to get quickly *under way in an emergency. Another origin of the saying was the custom of *square-rigged ships, when at anchor in an exposed *anchorage, of *furling their sails with them *stopped to the *yards, so the sails could be quickly cut free and easily let fall when the need arose to get under way quickly.

cutch, a preservative dressing used to prolong the life of *canvas sails. It consisted of broken-up gum catechu boiled in fresh water in the proportion of 2.3 kilograms (5 lb) of gum to 36 litres (8 gals.). See also TAN, TO.

cutlass, originally a sabre with a curved blade, but generally recognized to mean the short swords issued to seamen in sailing warships for use when boarding an enemy or for fighting ashore. They were carried on board major warships of many navies up to the beginning of the 20th century.

cut of his (her) jib, the, a saying that has taken its place in the English language as meaning, originally, that a person was recognized by the shape of his (her) nose. It has now come to indicate what someone thinks of a person's appearance or demeanour: 'I like the cut of his jib', 'I like his attitude.' The term originated in the sailing navies of the mid-18th century, when the nationality of warships sighted at sea could be accurately determined by the shape of their *jib long before the national flag could be seen. For instance, French jibs were cut much shorter on the *luff than English ones, giving a distinctly more acute angle in the *clew.

cut splice, two ropes *spliced together to form an *eye. The splice is not made with the two ropes end to end, as in a *short splice, but overlapping to the extent required to form the eye, the end of each rope being spliced into the body of the other rope and splices then *whipped.

Cut splice

cutter, a term which embraces a variety of small vessels. **(1)** In its older meaning it referred to a small, decked ship with one mast and a *bowsprit, with a *gaff mainsail on a boom, a square *yard and *topsail, and two *jibs or a jib and a *staysail. The rig was introduced in about 1740. These vessels, armed with up to ten 4-pounder guns, were relatively fast on the wind and were employed mainly as *auxiliaries to the war fleets and in the preventive service against *smuggling. Later they were widely used by *Trinity House, which still class their light *tenders and *pilot vessels as cutters. **(2)** A *clinker-built ship's boat, 7.3–9.3 metres (24–32 ft) long, with 8–14 *oars. It was originally rigged with two masts with a *dipping lug *foresail and a *standing lug mainsail, giving way in the 20th century to a single mast with a *de Horsey rig. **(3)** A powered vessel of about 2,000 tonnes used by the *US Coast Guard for a variety of purposes.

cutter rig, a *fore-and-aft-rigged sailing *yacht with a *gaff or *Bermudan mainsail and two *foresails. In the USA such yachts are called *sloops, and the term cutter refers only to the old-fashioned rig with a very long *bowsprit.

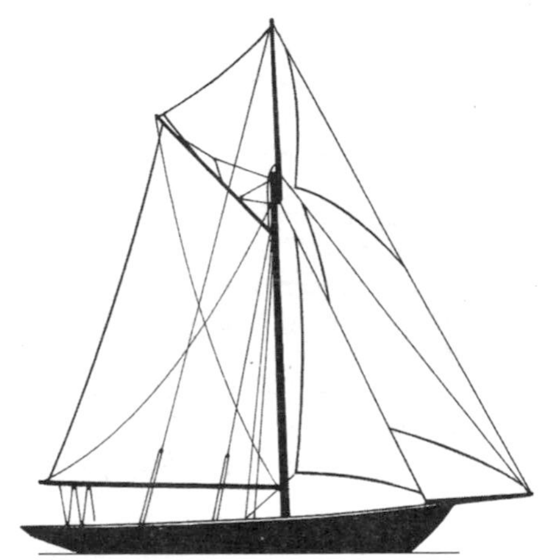

Gaff cutter with topsail

cutting his painter, an expression meaning, in terms of a ship in harbour, making a clandestine departure, but also, in seaman's language, and in terms of an individual, departing this life. Ships' boats are secured alongside by means of their *painters, and a silent or clandestine departure can only be made by cutting the painter and allowing the boat to drift silently away from the ship until it is out of earshot of those on board.

Cutty Sark, the only survivor of the British tea *clippers, is now preserved as a museum ship at Greenwich, London, as an example of the great days of sail. She was built to the order of Captain Jock Willis, son of the Captain Willis who was known as 'Old Stormy' and immortalized in the sea *shanty 'Stormalong'. She was built expressly as a challenge to the great British clipper **Thermopylae* and the two ships were almost identical in size, with a length of 64.6 metres (212 ft), a *beam of 10.9 metres (36 ft), and a *draught of 6.4 metres (21 ft). She was designed by Hercules Linton, and the firm of Linton and Scott was given the order to build her. However, the price it quoted was too low and the firm was forced into liquidation, and she was completed by William Denny and Brothers. *Launched at Dumbarton in November 1869 she took part the following year in the annual tea race from China to London.

Cutty Sark made eight voyages in the tea trade but never matched the times of the earlier clippers, her best being in 1871 when she sailed from Shanghai to the North Foreland in 107 days. Only once did she race home in company with the *Thermopylae*, but on that occasion lost her *rudder during heavy weather in the Indian Ocean when she had worked out a lead of 640 kilometres (400 mls.).

When the sailing clippers finally had to abandon the tea trade the *Cutty Sark* was forced to look for cargoes wherever they were to be had, but in 1883 she began regular voyages in the wool trade from Australia. Her last wool voyage from Australia was in 1894–5, and she was then sold to the Portuguese.

In 1922, a *gale forced her into Falmouth where she was seen by Captain Wilfred Dowman, who bought her and restored and re-rigged her to her original clipper rig. On his death in 1936 his widow presented her to the Thames Nautical Training College and she was towed to Greenhithe for use as a boys' training ship. In 1949, she was offered to the National Maritime Museum, Greenwich, which was unable to accept her. However, largely through the hard work and enthusiasm of Mr Frank Carr (director of the National Maritime Museum, 1947–66) the London County Council sponsored a scheme for her permanent preservation and she entered a specially constructed dock at Greenwich in 1954. Work on her hull and *rigging was completed in 1957, and she was then opened to the public. Funds are currently (2005) being raised for major restoration work to be undertaken.

The *Cutty Sark*'s name comes from Robert Burns's poem 'Tam O'Shanter', which tells the story of a Scottish farmer who was chased by the young witch Nannie, who wore only

> Her cutty sark, o'Paisley harn
> That while a lassie she had worn
> In longitude tho' sorely scanty
> It was her best, and she was vauntie.

The tea clipper's *figurehead is a representation of Nannie in her cutty sark (short shift), with her left arm outstretched to catch the tail of the farmer's grey mare on which he was trying to escape.

cutwater, the forward part of a ship's *stem around the waterline where the *bobstay is attached. Jeremy Lines

cyclone, see TROPICAL STORMS.

D

dagger, a steel bar which plays an essential part in the *launching mechanism of a ship. When the dog shores, the blocks of timber which support either side of a ship on the launching ways, are knocked out, the dagger acts as a trigger which releases the vessel and starts it down the launching *ways. Nowadays when a ship is launched the whole operation is performed by power, and men with sledge-hammers no longer knock out the dog shores, but the principle and mechanics remain unaltered. See also SHIPBUILDING.

dagger-board, a sliding *centreboard of wood or metal. It can be raised or lowered inside a case through a slot in the keel of a shallow-*draught boat, to increase the effective draught and so reduce *leeway when sailing *close hauled. It was one of the earliest types of sliding keel and originally used by the Chinese in some of their river *junks. It is so called because it is generally narrow in proportion to its length and, not being pivoted like a true centreboard, slides down from its case like a dagger from a sheath.

dahabeeyah, or **dahabiah,** from the Arabic *dahabiyah*, golden, a large river sailing vessel with high *lateen sails associated with the River Nile. Originally the term applied to the gilded state *barges of Egyptian rulers, hence its derivation.

damelopre, a Dutch sailing *barge or *coaster in which the mast is stepped in a *tabernacle so that it can be lowered for passing under a bridge. With the substitution of power in place of sail in such vessels, the name is now obsolete.

Dampier, William (1652–1715), British *navigator and surveyor who became first a *buccaneer and then a *privateer. He was born at East Coker, Somerset, and was orphaned while still a boy. He went to sea at 18 and after serving his apprenticeship joined an *East Indiaman as an able seaman and sailed in it to Java, a part of the world which delighted him and to which he was often to return. He returned to England in 1672 and, at the outbreak of the Third Dutch War (1672–4), enlisted in the Royal Navy. He was present at the two battles of Schooneveld but was invalided at the end of the war.

The offer of a job in Jamaica led him indirectly to joining a band of buccaneers, though he was probably attracted to this new life in the hope not so much of finding riches but of sailing to new places. In 1683 he joined a new band on a piratical voyage to the *South Seas which was eventually to take him round the world. His new companions were no more successful than his previous ones and he and some of the crew eventually left the ship and set off on their own *account, sailing to China and then to the Spice Islands (Moluccas) and New Holland (the Australian mainland). After a number of cruises in these waters, pillaging the few merchant ships they found, Dampier was *marooned with two others and half a dozen Malays on the Nicobar Islands. There they found a *canoe which Dampier managed to *navigate to Sumatra, and in 1691, after more dubious employment at sea, he found his way back to England.

During all these extraordinary adventures Dampier had been keeping a journal, not only recounting his voyages but, more notably, his observations on the winds and *tides, and the flora and fauna of the places he had visited. In 1697 he had it published under the title *A New Voyage round the World*. This brought him to the notice of the British *Admiralty and in 1699 he was sent out as captain of HMS *Roebuck* on a voyage of discovery around Australia. He made a careful survey of much of the west coast, but the lack of fresh water and provisions ashore, and of suitable harbours or inlets in which to refit his ship, forced him to abandon the voyage, and sail to Timor to refit his ship. From Timor he sailed to New Guinea where he resumed surveying, but this was cut short by a *mutiny, and he returned to Timor. He then set sail for England, but the *Roebuck* foundered off Ascension Island and Dampier and his men were lucky to attract the attention of a passing East Indiaman which took them to England. On his return in 1701 Dampier was court-martialled, declared unfit for any further employment in the Royal Navy, and fined the whole of his pay that he had accumulated during the voyage.

Despite this, in 1703 he managed to persuade the owners of two ships fitting out for a privateering voyage in the Pacific that he should take command of the venture and captain one of the ships, the *St George*. This voyage proved as disastrous as his previous one, his autocratic and erratic behaviour leading to another mutiny which left him with only 27 men. However, he managed to bring them back to England by way of the East Indies and the Cape of Good Hope, not in the *St George*, whose bottom fell out in the Gulf of Panama, but in a small Spanish ship which they had captured. It was during this voyage that one of the crew, Alexander *Selkirk, was marooned on Juan Fernandez Island at his own request. It was Selkirk's story of his time on the island that gave Daniel Defoe the basis for his famous novel **Robinson Crusoe*, one of the classics of *marine literature.

Dampier reached England in 1707, thus completing his second voyage round the world. Within a year he set out on another privateering adventure to the Pacific, this time as navigator of one of the ships, and during it Selkirk was rescued from Juan Fernandez Island after living alone there for over four years. The voyage proved financially successful, and when Dampier returned to England in 1711 he had not only circumnavigated the world for a third time but would have been a rich man if he had not died before receiving his full share of the profits.

A new edition of *A New Voyage round the World* with additional illustrations and a foreword was published in 1998.

Lloyd, C., *William Dampier* (1966).
Preston, D., and Preston, M., *A Pirate of Exquisite Mind: The Life of William Dampier* (2004).

Dana, Richard Henry (1815–82), born at Cambridge, Massachusetts. His family had been lawyers for generations, and Richard was sent to Harvard to study for the same profession, but an attack of measles during a period when he was rusticated from the university so affected his eyes that he was unable to continue his studies. He had the idea that a sea voyage and work on board a ship would cure his eye troubles, and he signed on as a paid hand in the Boston *brig *Pilgrim*, for a trading voyage round Cape Horn and up the Pacific seaboard. The brig sailed in August 1834, and Dana stepped ashore again in Boston in September 1836 with the eye weakness permanently cured. However, he returned in a larger ship, the *Alert*, which he joined halfway through the voyage to escape the brutalities of the brig's captain.

He kept a *log throughout the two years of his spell at sea, and during the intervals of his law studies prepared the log for publication under the title *Two Years before the Mast*. No New York publisher would look at it until eventually Harper's was persuaded to give it a trial. They bought all rights in the manuscript for $250, and the book was published in 1841. The simple, direct style of writing, the 'voice from the *forecastle' as Dana himself described the book, stamped it as one of the great masterpieces of *marine literature.

Dana became an authority on maritime law, and was also something of a politician, but public office in this field always just evaded him. Nor, in his writing, did he ever again reach the heights of his first book. He wrote a *Seaman's Manual* (1841) that went into four editions, and *A Voyage to Cuba and Back* (1859), which has none of the freshness and delightful simplicity of *Two Years before the Mast*.

dan buoy, a small, temporary *buoy used for marking a position at sea.

dandy-rig, another name, fallen into disuse, for the *ketch and *yawl rigs. It was also sometimes used to describe the rig when the *mizzen-sail was about one-third the size of the mainsail, the true ketch rig having a mizzen-sail about half the size of the mainsail and the true yawl rig having a mizzen-sail a quarter the size, or less. In some English West Country craft the mizzen-mast was stepped just forward of the *transom stern either to one side of the *tiller or with an iron tiller crooked around the mast. The sail, of triangular shape, sheeted to an *outrigger or *bumpkin, was called the dandy, and a boat so rigged, such as the Falmouth Quay punt, was called dandy rigged.

Darling, Grace Horsley (1815–42), the daughter of the keeper of the Longstone *lighthouse on the Farne Islands situated off the Northumberland coast of northern England. She achieved great fame for her part in the rescue she made, with her father, of some of the crew of the *Forfarshire* which was wrecked on the islands on 7 September 1838. On seeing the *shipwreck William Darling decided that he and his daughter must try and reach it, and rescue any survivors. In a tremendous sea, and knowing they would be unable to return unless helped by some of the survivors, they set out in a *coble and brought back four men and a woman. William Darling and two of the survivors then returned, and brought back four more men, but the remaining 43 members of the crew were drowned. Grace and her father each received the gold medal of the Royal Humane Society for their courage. Of a delicate constitution all her life, Grace Darling died of consumption at the age of 27.

Darwin, Charles (1809–82), best known for his theory of natural selection, which resulted in radical changes in religious and social attitudes in western societies. But he also made some direct contributions to *oceanography. While failing as a medical student in Edinburgh, he became friendly with Robert Grant, the professor of zoology, and they used to take walks and collect marine animals along the Firth of Forth. Darwin's first verbal contributions to marine science were presentations to the Plinian Society describing the larvae of the sea mat (*Flustra*), and identifying the black dots in old oyster shells as the eggs of marine leeches (*Pontobdella muricata*). While he was participating in the voyage of the *Beagle* (1831–6) under the captaincy of Robert *Fitzroy, he initially spent much of his time at sea observing arrow worms (chaetognaths) and other species of *plankton. However, visiting some of the volcanic islands in the Atlantic, and later going ashore in South America, he became more and more interested in geology and interpreting the significance of fossils that he collected. He was greatly influenced by the large earth movements that occurred when there was a major earthquake in Chile, and he began to realize that the earth is not as stable as fundamentalist interpretations of the creation story in the Bible require. His first writings on his return were narratives of the voyage and then a series of books on volcanic islands and *coral reefs, and his hypothesis on how *atolls formed eventually proved correct.

In 1851 and 1854 he produced two volumes on the systematics of recent and fossil *barnacles, which are have stood the test of time remarkably well. The fossils showed that large changes had occurred and that these changes were not consistent with a fundamental interpretation of the Genesis story. Subsequently Darwin's persistent poor health prevented him from developing his marine interests further, but some of his associates, notably Thomas Huxley (1825–95), continued to investigate *marine biology.

Bowler, P. J., *Charles Darwin: The Man and his Influence* (1996).

John van Wyhe, (ed.), *The Writings of Charles Darwin on the Web*,

http://pages.britishlibrary.net/charles.darwin/

www.aboutdarwin.com/index.html

M. V. Angel

Darwin mounds are features discovered in 1998 in deep water (1,000 m/3,280 ft) off Cape Wrath, Scotland. They extend over an area of about 100 square kilometres (38.6 sq. mls.); each mound being about 100 metres (300 ft) in diameter and 5 metres (15 ft) high. They are covered with a variety of cold-water corals, notably *Lophelia perusa*, and large numbers of xenophyophores, giant protozoans that can grow to be over 20 centimetres (8 in.) in size. The mounds attract a large variety of *fishes and invertebrates such as *sponges and *echinoderms like starfish, but even in the short time they have been known they have been heavily damaged by deep-sea *trawls of commercial *fisheries which target fish like orange roughy (*Hoplostethus atlanticus*). In 2004 their conservation was still the subject of active negotiations, and they may become one of the first deep-water no-take zones. The Norwegian government has already introduced emergency measure to protect similar reefs. See also CORAL REEFS.

www.wwf.org.uk/filelibrary/pdf/darwin_mounds.pdf M. V. Angel

'David', the name given to a series of small *submarines, built by the *Confederate States Navy during the American Civil War (1861–5). They were more submersibles than true submarines, were driven by *steam propulsion, and carried a *spar torpedo over their bows. The steam 'Davids' were not designed to dive fully, but were trimmed down so they proceeded *awash. One attacked a Federal ship during the American Civil War (1861–5). Its spar torpedo did not explode deeply enough to do any significant damage, and the *waves set up by the explosion swamped and sank it.

Davis's quadrant, or **back-staff,** named by the French the English quadrant. John Davis (*c.*1550–1605), the illustrious English *navigator and explorer of Elizabethan times who mounted three voyages in search of the *North-West Passage, invented this simple instrument for measuring the *altitude of the sun which obviated the need of sighting the sun direct. It consists of a graduated staff on which is fitted a half transom in the form of an arc of a circle which could be slid along the staff. At the fore end of the staff is a horizon vane with a slit through which the *horizon could be observed. In use the staff was held horizontally, the observer having his back to the sun. The half transom was then moved along the staff to a position at which the edge of its shadow struck the horizon vane and coincided with the horizon viewed through the slit in the vane. The staff was graduated to 45° and the instrument was useful for measuring altitudes of the sun of less than about 45°.

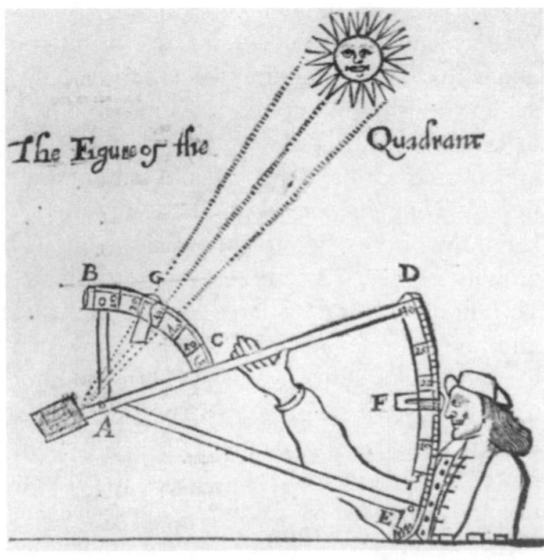

Back-staff also known as Davis's quadrant; from Sturmy's *Mariners Magazine*, 1669

For measuring greater altitudes Davis invented a 90° back-staff which used two half transoms, one straight, the other an arc. The straight half transom was fitted perpendicularly to, and stood vertically above, the staff when the instrument was in use. It was designed to slide along the staff. The arcuate half transom was fixed to the lower side of the staff and provided with a sighting vane. The fore end of the staff was fitted with a horizon vane through which the horizon could be sighted.

To take a *sight with the 90° back-staff the straight half transom was set at a graduation on the staff corresponding to a few degrees less than the sun's altitude. The instrument was then held in the vertical plane and the observer, with his back to the sun and his eye at the sighting vane, slid the latter to a position on the arc so that he was able to see the horizon through the slit in the horizon vane coincident with the shadow of a shadow vane fitted at the top of the straight half transom. The sun's altitude was the sum of the angles indicated on the staff and arc respectively.

Before the end of the 17th century the back-staff had all but replaced the *seaman's quadrant, the *astrolabe, and the *cross-staff; and it was not superseded for sea use until about 1731 when *Hadley's reflecting quadrant was introduced. The quadrant was not capable of adjustment and it was therefore necessary for the user to ascertain in advance its instrumental error. This was usually done by making *meridian altitude observations at places of known *latitude. Having thus discovered the error, the observer applied it to all altitudes measured with it. According to whether the error tended to increase or decrease the ship's northerly latitude the quadrant was said to be northerly or southerly.

Mike Richey

davits, small cranes from which a ship's boats are slung. The old-fashioned **radial davits** were manoeuvrable by twisting in their base sockets so that, when the boats were hoisted with *blocks and *tackles, they could be swung inboard so that they did not project beyond the side of the ship. **Luffing davits** have a geared quadrant fitted to their inboard end. This allows the boats to hang at the davits inboard of a ship's side though still suspended to seaward of the davits, a great saving of time and labour if the boats have to be used in an emergency. **Gravity-type davits** consist of two parts, the upper, which holds the lifeboat on its *falls, being mounted on rollers on the lower part. When the boat is stowed the upper part of the davit is hauled up by a wire so that the boat lies inboard. When it is being *launched, the wire is released and the upper part slides down the lower part. This brings the boat level with the deck and ready for lowering directly into the sea after its complement of passengers have climbed into it. See also LIFESAVING.

Davy Jones, in nautical slang the spirit of the sea, usually cast in the form of a sea devil. 'This same Davy Jones, according to the mythology of sailors, is the fiend that presides over all the evil spirits of the deep' (Tobias Smollett, *Peregrine Pickle* (1751), ch. XIII). **Davy Jones's locker**, the bottom of the sea, the final resting place of sunken ships, of articles lost or thrown overboard, of men buried at sea. The phrase also became a seaman's euphemism for death, saying 'He's gone to Davy Jones's locker', when someone has been buried at sea. The term is often shortened to Davy.

deadeye, orig. **dead-man's-eye,** a circular *block, usually of *lignum vitae*, though sometimes of elm, grooved around the circumference and pierced with three holes. In the days of the *square-rigger they were used in pairs to secure the end of a *shroud to the *chain-plate. A *lanyard was threaded through the holes in the deadeyes and by this means a *purchase was created to set up the shroud *taut.

The term 'dead' was used because, although deadeyes performed the function of triple blocks, they had no revolving *sheaves. No doubt the original name of dead-man's-eye arose from the remarkable resemblance of these blocks with their three holes to a human skull.

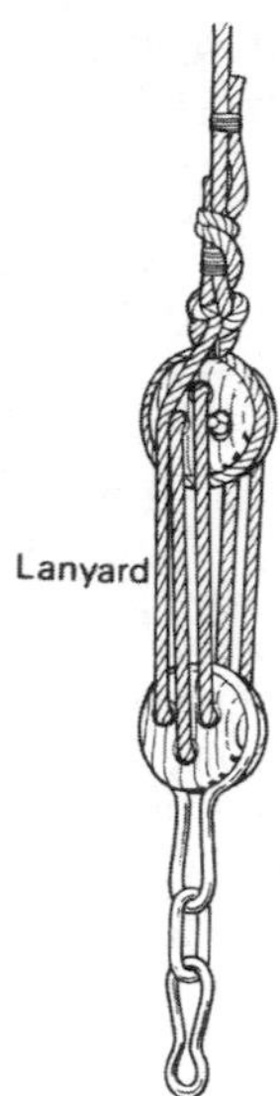

Deadeye

dead freight, the *freight charges for which a merchant is liable when he fails to ship cargo on board a merchant vessel for which he has reserved space in the *holds. But a shipowner cannot make more profit from dead freight than he would have by the carriage of the goods.

dead horse, obsolete term used by seamen to describe the period of work on board ship for which they had been paid in advance when signing their *articles. Having worked off the dead horse the crew celebrated by parading around the decks an effigy of a horse stuffed with straw. The parade was accompanied by the song 'Old man, your horse must die', before the effigy was *hoisted to the *yardarm and then cut *adrift to fall into the sea. In ships where passengers were carried, the stuffed horse was often put up to auction among them before being cut adrift, the money being divided among the crew. **To flog a dead horse**, to expect, vainly, to get extra work out of a ship's crew while they are working off the dead horse. See also HORSE LATITUDES.

deadlight, see SCUTTLE.

dead marine, an empty wine bottle after its contents have been drunk. The aphorism is supposed to have been first employed by the Duke of Clarence, the future King William IV, when, at a dinner on board one of his ships, he ordered the steward to remove the 'dead marine'. When a *marine officer present objected to this remark, the duke replied that he had used the expression in the sense that, like the marines, it had done its duty nobly and was ready to do it again.

dead men, *reef and *gasket ends left flapping instead of being tucked in out of sight when a sail has been *furled. See also IRISH PENNANTS.

dead reckoning, determining position at sea by advancing the last established position for *course and distance run. Before the advent of modern navigational systems dead reckoning was the basis of most offshore *navigation. The term 'estimated position' is sometimes used for the dead reckoning position corrected for the effects of *tides, *currents, *drift, *leeway, and so on. The origin of the term dead reckoning, which has been in use for at least four centuries, is obscure. It has been suggested that dead is a corruption of deduced, but there is no etymological, or other, evidence for this.

Mike Richey

dead shares, an additional allowance of pay enjoyed by the officers and warrant officers of the British Navy in the 16th and 17th centuries. It was achieved by the entry in the ship's *muster-book of fictitious names, for which sea pay and victuals were drawn and the proceeds divided among the ship's crew. The scale of payment ranged from 50 shares for an admiral to half a share for the cook's mate. It was introduced during the reign of King Henry VIII (1509–47) and remained in force until 1733. However, from 1695 the proceeds were diverted from the officers and given to Greenwich Royal Hospital to help provide pensions for widows of seamen killed in action. See also WIDOWS' MEN.

dead water, the eddy formed under the *counter of a ship.

deadweight tonnage, see TONNAGE.

deadwood, the solid timbering in the bow and stern of a sailing vessel just above the keel where the *lines narrow down to such an extent that the separate side timbers cannot each be accommodated. Generally the fore deadwood extends from the *stem to the foremost *frame, the after deadwood from the *sternpost to the after *balanced frame. Both deadwoods are firmly fixed to the keel to add strength to the ship's structure.

dead work, a defunct maritime expression meaning all that part of a ship above the waterline when it is fully laden. It is what we would today call the ship's *freeboard.

Decca, a continuous-wave *hyperbolic navigation system of high accuracy. It was first conceived in the USA in 1937 and further developed in the UK by the Decca Company with the *Admiralty's Signal Establishment. It was first used operationally for the navigation of minesweepers and landing craft in the Normandy landings in 1944, but is now defunct. The equipment was on hire, not for sale, from the Decca Navigator Company. Decca had a maximum range of something like 400 kilometres (250 mls.) by night and about 640 kilometres (400 mls.) by day. Its accuracy close to the base line was of the order of 90 metres (295 ft) and at 160 kilometres (100 mls.) between 1.6 kilometres (1 m.) and 0.8 kilometres (0.5 m.) A Decca chain consisted of a land-based master transmitter and three slave transmitters, designated red, green and purple, locked in a precise

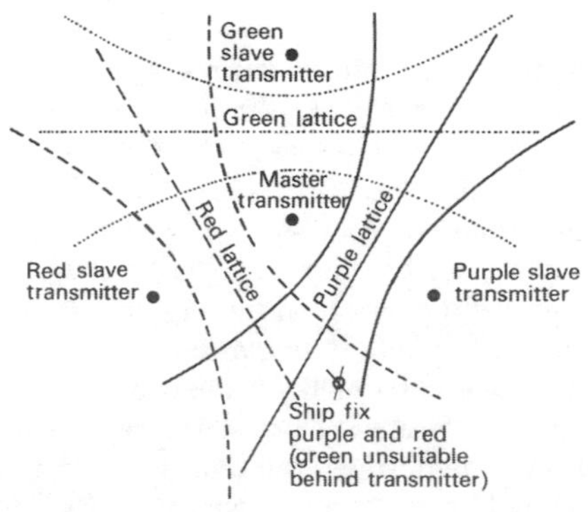

Decca chain

phase relationship with the master station and set up in a triangular pattern situated between 135 kilometres (85 mls.) and 385 kilometres (240 mls.) from the master.

A vessel fitted with Decca would carry the receiver and three decometers (red, green, and purple) and the appropriate nautical *charts overprinted with the Decca lattice displaying the hyperbolic position lines in the colours of the slave stations. The phase differences between waves emitted simultaneously from the master and one of the slave stations were displayed on decometers where a couple of clock-like pointers gave the lane number and the lane fraction. This enabled the *navigator to identify on the lattice chart the appropriate hyperbolic position lines, and their point of intersection would be the ship's position. Three slave stations were used, as the angle of intersection might not in all circumstances be suitable.

The coverage included the coastal waters of NW Europe and parts of Africa, the Persian Gulf, India, Australia, and Japan. In addition to merchant shipping it was widely used for fishing and for surveys. The system was the most accurate of the hyperbolic systems and enjoyed half a century of full operational life, longer than any other radio navigational aid except what is now known as *Loran-C. Its demise was at least in part due to the growing promise of *satellite navigation.

decker, a term used in the old sailing navies to describe the number of gun-decks, and therefore the size, of warships, such as a two-decker, three-decker, etc. It referred only to the decks on which batteries of guns were mounted and not to the total number of decks in the ship. The gun-decks of three-deckers, in ascending order, were the lower gun-deck, main gun-deck, and upper gun-deck, even though this upper gun-deck was next below the upper deck.

deckhouse, a square or oblong *cabin erected on the deck of a ship. In the sailing warships of the Royal Navy it was known, in a perverse sort of way, as the *round house because one could walk round it. Originally, in the 17th and 18th centuries, it was the name given to the upper *coach. However, by the end of the 18th century the term round house was used to describe the lavatory fitted in a warship's *sickbay for men who were unable, because of illness or wounds, to get forward to the *heads.

In many merchant vessels, particularly sailing ships in the days of the *clipper ships and, later, the big trading *barques, a large deckhouse was erected just *abaft the foremast to house the *galley and to provide quarters for the crew on *watch.

decks, the horizontal platforms in ships corresponding to floors in houses. Starting from the bottom, the decks in an average large ship are the *orlop, lower (though the two are now sometimes combined in a single deck known as the lower), main, upper, shelter, *bridge, and boat. These, however, may vary considerably from ship to ship according to its function. Smaller ships, of course, have fewer decks; larger ones have more. The *ocean liner *Queen Elizabeth II*, for instance, has thirteen. In some types of ships, these decks have other names: in large liners, for example, the shelter deck is frequently known as the promenade deck, and other names have been coined to denote different decks according to their main purpose, such as hurricane deck, cabin deck, etc. In the days of the sailing navies, the upper deck was often known as the spar deck, and the main deck as a gun-deck. But see also DECKER for warships with more than one gun-deck.

Properly speaking, a deck must extend the full length of the ship, but in cases where it does not extend the full length, the word is still used, if improperly, to describe the built-up portions *forward and *aft of a ship, the fore portion being known as the *forecastle deck and the after portion as the *poop deck. That portion of the upper deck which lies between forecastle and poop is often known in merchant ships as the **well deck**, and in many other types of ship as the *waist.

The origin of the term is obscure but it probably comes from the Old Dutch *dec*, a covering, cloak, or horse-cloth, although in its nautical meaning the word was in use in England at least a century and a half earlier than in Holland.

declination, in nautical astronomy the angular distance of a celestial body north or south of the equator, thus corresponding to the geographical *latitude of the body. The declination

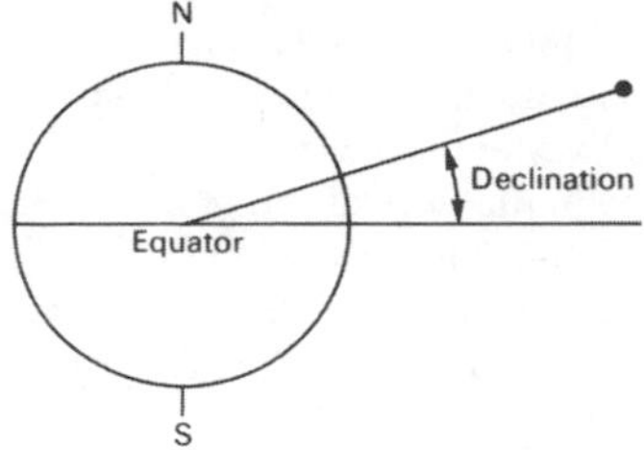

Declination

of bodies used in *celestial navigation are given in the *nautical almanac. Mike Richey

decompression sickness is what divers may be subject to if they rise too rapidly to the surface at the end of a dive, and is popularly known as 'the bends'. To avoid it all divers have to follow a procedure as they rise to the surface when they finish *diving, and even amateur divers breathing air need to be aware of what is involved.

Air is a mixture of oxygen and nitrogen, which pass from the lungs into the bloodstream and on to the body tissues. The oxygen is used in the body's metabolic processes, while the nitrogen remains dormant. However, as divers breathe air at ambient pressure—that is, the pressure of the depth of water surrounding them—nitrogen enters the body tissues and increases as they go deeper. The amount that has entered the tissues prior to the final ascent depends on the diver's blood supply—poorly supplied fatty tissue takes up nitrogen much more slowly than well-supplied major body organs—the maximum depth of the dive, and the time spent underwater.

The rate of ascent at the end of any dive must therefore be controlled, so that all the nitrogen in the various body tissues can move back into the bloodstream and be safely eliminated from the body. Should the ascent be too fast then nitrogen bubbles, much like those appearing in a bottle of soda water when the top is suddenly removed, may appear in any part of the body. These lead to a variety of symptoms, including rashes, itches, pain in the joints, and paralysis, which may take up to twelve hours or more to develop after the diver has surfaced. In extreme cases bubbles may form in the bloodstream, reach the heart, and cause death in a short time.

All decompression sickness symptoms should be treated as potentially dangerous and the victim removed to the nearest recompression facility as quickly as possible. Here, under medical supervision, they will be put into a recompression chamber where the pressure is increased to reduce the size of the nitrogen bubbles and relieve the symptoms. They will then be therapeutically decompressed which, hopefully, avoids any longer term effects.

At the beginning of the 20th century Professor Haldane developed stage decompression tables to avoid decompression sickness. These give a 'bottom time' for various depths: the deeper the dive, the shorter the bottom time. Dives made inside this time allow the diver to rise directly to the surface, but still following a maximum rate of ascent specified in the tables. If however, the diver exceeds the bottom time then, following the tables, he must rise to a specified safe depth where he makes a *stop* for a specified time. This allows the nitrogen level in his body to drop to a level where it is safe for him to ascend to a shallower depth where he again makes a stop, and so on in *stages* until he can safely surface. The stops become longer as the diver gets shallower, and even after surfacing he still has a residual nitrogen level in his body that takes around 24 hours to clear completely. Should he make a repeat dive during this period, this nitrogen must be taken into account. While repeat dive tables exist, it is now more common to use a wrist-mounted 'personal' decompression computer (DC). This remembers, and accounts for, nitrogen levels, and indicates the length of decompression that must be performed, and when a diver can move on to a shallower stop or to the surface. Like the original tables, they still specify a maximum rate of ascent which must be adhered to.

Decompression sickness is best avoided by learning to dive on a recognized diving course run by qualified instructors who will fully explain decompression procedures. Peter Dick

deep, see LEAD LINE; TRENCH.

Deep Scattering Layers (DSLs) appear on *echo sounders and other *sonar devices, and often resemble a false bottom. Immediately after the Second World War (1939–45) *shoals shallow enough to be a danger to shipping were shown on some *charts of the open ocean, because very dense DSLs were mistaken by *chartmakers for shallows. DSLs are the result of the sound transmissions of the echo sounder being reflected by dense concentrations of *fish or *plankton. Fishes with swim-bladders containing gas bubbles reflect the sounds efficiently, especially if the diameter of the gas bubble is more than half the wavelength of frequency of the transmitted sound. The higher the frequency of sound used, the smaller the organisms that reflect the sound. Some DSLs 'behave' in that they migrate up towards the surface at dusk and sink down again at dawn, indicating that the animals causing them are undertaking vertical migrations. M. V. Angel

degauss, to, or **degaussing,** a method used during the Second World War (1939–45) to prevent magnetic mines from exploding when a ship's steel hull passed over them. The magnetic field created by a steel hull was enough to activate such a mine, but it was a relatively simple matter, once the mine's polarity was known, to counteract or reverse the ship's magnetic field by passing a current through an electric cable encircling its hull.

degree, in circular measure $\frac{1}{360}$ of a circle.

de Horsey rig, a sail rig used in the larger pulling boats carried by British warships. It was introduced by Admiral de Horsey in the early 20th century and comprised a single mast stepped in a *tabernacle and carrying a *gaff rig *loose-footed mainsail and a single *foresail.

demurrage, the compensation payable to a shipowner when his ship is held up in port beyond the time specified in the *charter party in cases where it is the fault of the consignee through non-arrival of the cargo for which space in the ship has been reserved. It is also legally liable when, in time of war, a vessel has been detained in *prize but later is not *condemned by the prize court.

departure. (1) In the days before precise position fixing systems, the last position *fix on the *chart when a ship is outward bound. It is the correlative of landfall at the end of the voyage. **(2)** The distance in *nautical miles of one *meridian from another on the same *latitude. Mike Richey

depth charge, a weapon designed during the First World War (1914–18) for use against submerged *submarines. It comprised a canister filled with explosive and fitted with a hydrostatically controlled pistol which detonated the explosive at a pre-selected depth. Modern developments include a nuclear explosive to widen the lethal area of explosion, and the introduction of an active homing device which draws it close to the target before it explodes.

Derbyshire, a 169,000-tonne *bulk carrier, which sank off the coast of Okinawa in September 1980, the largest British ship ever to be lost at sea. Nearly 282 metres (925 ft) long and 44.2 metres (144 ft) wide, the *Derbyshire* was carrying a cargo of iron ore. Though of modern design, and constructed only four years previously, the bulk carrier failed to survive a *tropical storm it should easily have weathered, and sank so quickly that the crew had no time to radio a *mayday distress signal. Initially, the government resisted holding a formal inquiry. However, one was opened in October 1987 when it was claimed the loss might have been caused by structural failure—an identical fault had affected other bulk carriers of the same class. This came to no firm conclusion other than that the ship 'was probably overwhelmed by the forces of nature', possibly because it got *beam on to the wind and sea.

The families of the crew refused to accept the inquiry's conclusion and raised the money for an underwater survey in 1994, which found the ship's remains in two halves. Another survey in 1996 confirmed the whereabouts of the ship, and in March/April 1997 a special unit of the Woods Hole *Oceanographic Institution carried out a detailed survey. In what was declared by a British government minister to be 'one of the century's greatest feats of underwater detection work', the survey's conclusions were that though the *Derbyshire* undoubtedly did suffer from the structural weakness found in its sister ships, this did not appear to have been the cause of the disaster. Instead, the most likely, and principal, cause was the flooding of a tank in the bows through ventilators and an air pipe, the covers of which had been torn away. This flooding prevented the ship's bows riding the huge *waves whipped up by the typhoon; instead, these had come aboard with such force that the deck *hatches collapsed and this had led to the ship foundering. As a result of this survey, in November 2000 a High Court judge cleared the crew of any negligence.

derelict, any vessel or cargo abandoned at sea by those in charge of it, without any hope of recovery. In the UK, derelict now comes under the legal definition of *wreck, and any *salvage has to be reported to the Receiver of Wreck. However, boats lost from their *moorings are not classified as derelict as they have not been abandoned without any hope of recovery.

derrick, a large single *spar fixed on board ship, for hoisting boats, cargo, and other heavy weights, though it is now a relic of the past. It pivoted at the lower or inboard end and was fitted with *stays and *guy *pendants, and had a *topping lift and a *purchase attached to it. It was controlled laterally by the guy pendants, which allowed it to swing through a wide arc, and vertically by the topping lift, which positioned the hook of the purchase directly over the object to be lifted. The name comes from a 17th-century hangman named Derrick who was employed in his grisly trade at Tyburn, London, presumably because in both cases weights dangle from the ends of ropes.

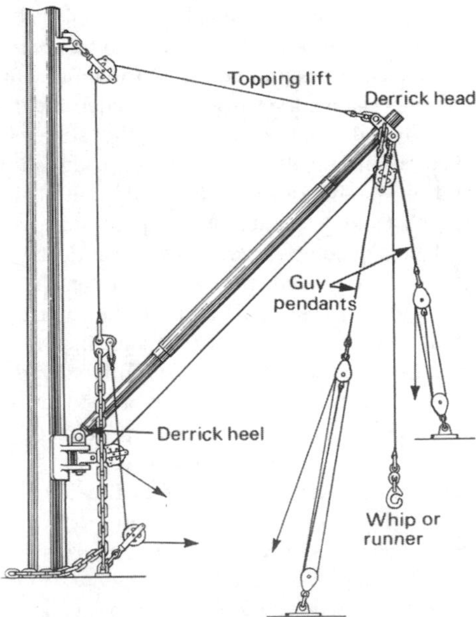

Mast derrick

derroterro, the Spanish version of a *rutter or *sailing directions, incorporating views of the coast from seaward. It forms, as the pages are turned, a complete picture of the coastline in the general area covered.

destroyer, a light, fast warship developed in the last decades of the 19th century. Originally called a torpedo boat catcher, it was introduced as a counter to the fast torpedo boats which had become a significant weapon in most fleets. The first two were *launched in Britain in 1886, but both they and their immediate successors proved too slow to fulfil their primary task efficiently. Then in 1893 the firm of the British marine engineer Alfred Yarrow (1842–1932), which had already established itself for its successful manufacture of torpedo boats, launched two ships of a radical new design. Called HMS *Havock* and HMS *Hornet*, they were the first true destroyers in the world. With a speed of 27 knots and a combined gun/torpedo armament, they were able successfully to demonstrate their superiority over the existing torpedo boats, and indeed quickly assumed the torpedo boats' role in modern naval warfare in addition to proving to be their antidote. By the time of the First World War (1914–18), the displacement *tonnage of destroyers had increased from around 250 tons to 2,000 or more,

The development of the *submarine during the first decades of the 20th century added appreciably to the traditional tasks of the destroyer in war. It already had the dual role in battle of attacking an enemy battle line with torpedoes from above-water tubes, and of beating back similar attacks on the fleet made by enemy destroyers. To this was now added the task of screening the fleet and *convoys against possible submarine attack, and during the First World War many destroyers were also fitted as minelayers.

Developments between the two world wars and during the Second World War (1939–45) brought yet further fleet responsibilities. The big expansion in naval air techniques meant some destroyers being fitted as air-direction ships to control the activities of carrier-borne and shore-based aircraft, and the development of *sonar gave them improved anti-submarine capability, and therefore increased responsibilities in combating this threat.

After the Second World War destroyers were largely relieved of their anti-submarine tasks by the development of the modern *frigate. However, the introduction of guided missiles brought destroyers new tasks in naval warfare and these, in general, were responsible for increasing their size from an average tonnage of 2,000 to 5,000 tonnes or more, so that they have virtually become light *cruisers. The Royal Navy's Type 42 destroyers which have been built since the 1970s are to be replaced by the Type 45.

deviation, an error of a *magnetic compass caused by the ship's own residual magnetism. If a ship had no residual magnetism, the needle of the magnetic compass would point directly along the earth's magnetic *meridian, but as every modern ship has metal fittings which affect the compass, there is always some error. Deviation varies according to the heading of the ship because, as a ship changes *course, the metal in it changes its position in relation to the compass as the ship swings round. Deviation is therefore read off for every quarter *point (about 4°) as the ship is swung through 360° and is tabulated on a deviation card so that it can be applied, together with *variation, to every compass course or *bearings. Deviation can rarely be completely eliminated, though it can be reduced by the use of soft iron balls, known as Kelvin spheres (see THOMSON, WILLIAM), mounted on each side of the compass, and by bar magnets, called *Flinders bars, placed in the *binnacle below the compass bowl.

devil, the caulker's name for the *seam in the upper deck planking next to a ship's waterways. No doubt they gave it that name as there was very little space to get at this seam to *caulk it with a caulking iron, making it a particularly difficult and awkward job. This is the origin of the saying **'between the devil and the deep blue sea'**, since there is only the thickness of the ship's hull planking between this seam and the sea.

Devil was also the name given by caulkers to the *garboard seam, which was always, when a ship was *careened, not only the most awkward to get at but usually the wettest and most difficult to keep above water and caulk. Hence the old seafaring term **'devil to pay'**, meaning something very difficult or awkward, as it was always difficult to *pay this particular seam.

dghaisa (pron. duyser as in buy), a rowing boat for ferrying passengers, used in Malta's harbours and around its coast. Dghaisas are propelled by one or two men with *oars to which they stand and push instead of sitting and pulling. They are characterized by a very high vertical bow and stern projections similar to Venetian *gondolas, but are straight up and down, not curved. Many of them, particularly those used in Grand Harbour, Valletta, are highly decorated with coloured paintwork and are a source of great pride to their owners.

dhow, in its strict meaning a trading vessel of 150 to 200 tonnes, *lateen rigged on a single mast, and indigenous to the Red Sea, Persian Gulf, and Indian Ocean. However, the name has been extended to embrace any trading vessel of similar size in those waters, irrespective of the number of masts rigged. Nowadays, many modern dhows are fitted with *diesel engines. They were formerly used extensively in the *slave trade from East Africa to the Arabian countries.

diagonal built, see DOUBLE DIAGONAL BUILD.

diamond knot, a stopper knot made in a length of rope. The *strands are unlaid, and the knot is formed by tucking the strands through the *bights of each other, and *laying up the rope again. A double diamond knot is made by tucking the strands twice. Its primary

Single diamond knot

purpose is to prevent a rope from running through an *eye.

diamond shrouds, masthead *stays in the *rigging of some old-fashioned *Bermudan-rigged *yachts. They were generally made of steel wire arranged on each side of the mast over spreaders, and secured to the mast above and below to form a diamond shape. Nowadays they are only used on *catamarans which have *rotating rigs. Jeremy Lines

diaphone, a type of sound signal emitted from *lighthouses and *lightships in fog. It is characterized by a powerful low note ending with a sharply descending tone known as the grunt.

Diaz de Novaes, Bartholomew (*c.*1455–1500), also spelt **Dias,** Portuguese explorer and discoverer of the Cape of Good Hope. He was first heard of in 1481 when he commanded a ship in an expedition to the Gold Coast. By 1487 he had achieved distinction as a *navigator and was placed in command of an expedition of three ships to extend Portuguese *exploration by sea along the African west coast. His mission was to sail beyond the 22° 10' S., which had been reached by Diogo Cam (*fl.* 1482–6).

Diaz sailed his ships as far south as the point in present-day Namibia which today bears his name (26° 38' S.) where he erected a commemorative pillar. He was then swept southward for thirteen days by strong gales. Steering east as soon as a moderation of the weather permitted, and finding no land after several days, he turned north and made a landfall in February 1488 at Mossel Bay on the south coast of Cape Colony. From there he sailed up the coast, reaching the mouth of the Great Fish River before his officers and men, alarmed by this venturing into the unknown, forced him to return. However, by this time the north-easterly trend of the coast made it clear that the southernmost point of Africa had been rounded.

On his return voyage, Diaz sighted a distinctive cape and named it the Cape of Storms (*Cabo Tormentoso*), but either he or King John of Portugal later renamed it the Cape of Good Hope. Diaz received little or no reward for his discovery and was only second in command to Pedro Cabral (1467–1530) during the latter's voyage to India in 1500. It was during this voyage that Diaz's ship sank in a storm off his own Cape of Storms.

dickies, the two small seats in large square-sterned rowing boats, such as old-fashioned naval *cutters. They were fitted in the angles between the *transom and the *gunwale, for the *coxswain to sit on when the boat was being rowed.

diesel engine, an internal combustion engine, which means that the fuel is burned inside the engine cylinders, as opposed to a steam engine where the fuel is burned externally in a boiler for *steam propulsion. A diesel engine may operate on a two-stroke cycle or a four-stroke cycle. A two-stroke engine gives one power stroke for every two strokes (up or down) of the piston or for every one revolution of the crankshaft. A four-stroke engine gives one power stroke for every four strokes of the piston or for every two revolutions of the crankshaft. This means that for the same size and rotational speed a two-stroke engine is likely to develop twice as much power as a four-stroke engine. The engine has a number of cylinders, each with a piston which attaches to the crankshaft by means of a connecting rod.

Marine diesel engines for ships are of the **crosshead type** or the **trunk piston type**. The crosshead type is similar to a *reciprocating steam engine, in that it is tall, and runs at relatively low speed. It is connected directly to the *propeller shaft, which means the engine speed is changed to change the ship's speed, and it is stopped and reversed to make the ship go *astern. It almost always operates on the two-stroke cycle, and is used to power *container ships, *tankers, and *bulk carriers because there is plenty of space to fit such an engine into them. The trunk piston type of engine is similar to an outsize car engine. Most of these are not connected directly to the propeller shaft but via a gearbox, though some are used to drive an electric generator for *electric propulsion. Unlike the crosshead-type engine, it is uncommon for them to be reversible and, as the engine's speed is constant, a controllable pitch propeller is used to change the ship's speed and direction. This type of engine is not as tall as a crosshead type which makes them ideal for *ferries and *cruise ships where low engine-room height means additional car or passenger decks can be fitted. Medium-speed trunk piston engines can also be used to drive electrical generators for purposes other than the ship's propulsion.

Diesel engines were introduced to ship propulsion in the early years of the 20th century. The first installations were for river and harbour craft, but as they became more reliable their use for marine propulsion gradually increased. The *Fram, which in 1911 took *Amundsen to the North Pole, had a diesel engine, and the first successful ocean-going ship powered by diesel machinery, the Danish *Selandia*, *launched in 1912, showed that the diesel was a practical and economic alternative to coal- and oil-fired ships. By the end of the First World War (1914–18) many ships had diesel engines, although these tended to be the smaller cargo ships; and its lower fuel consumption, greater range, and the availability worldwide of bunkering stations, led to a further increase in diesel's popularity during the 1920s. One of the earliest diesel-engined passenger ships was the 18,815 gross ton Swedish American liner *Gripsholm*. Built in 1925, she remained in service with her original engines until 1966.

The early diesel engines burned diesel oil, similar to the diesel fuels used in modern diesel-engined road vehicles. This is a distillate fuel and much more expensive than the boiler oil used for oil-fired steamships. However, during the 1950s diesel engines were developed which could burn the residual oil used by oil-burning steamships, which is also known as fuel oil, bunker C, and heavy fuel oil. Residual oil is what remains after crude oil has been processed and the lighter, higher-value commodities, such as kerosene, gasoline, gas oil, and diesel oil, have been extracted. With the development of residual fuel oil-burning marine diesel engines in the 1950s, the last economic advantage the steam plant had over the diesel engine, using cheaper fuel, was gone; and from that time diesels gradually replaced steam engines for all forms of conventional ship propulsion.

With few exceptions, all commercial ships built from the late 1980s onwards have been fitted with diesel engines and some ships have been re-engined with diesels. For example, the liner *Queen Elizabeth II* had its steam turbine plant replaced in 1986/7 with nine diesel engines, and the ship is now powered by diesel electric propulsion. Not only did this reduce the fuel consumption, it reduced the number of engineers running the plant. The efficiency of diesel-powered ships is further increased by using the engine's exhaust gas to generate steam. This can be used for various heating purposes within the ship, and waste heat in the engine cooling water can be employed in *evaporator plants to generate fresh water from sea water.

Apart from its economy, the diesel-engined cargo ship could also often travel twice as far as a similarly sized steamship on the fuel stored in its *double-bottom tanks, and the diesel's thermal efficiency, just over 50%, means that just over half of the chemical energy in the fuel is converted into work at the engine crankshaft. This compares very favourably with the best marine steam-turbine plant which only achieves a thermal efficiency of about 30%.

However, residual fuel oil does have its drawbacks. It has a very high viscosity which, at room temperature, has the consistency of treacle. For it to be pumped and burned it must be heated, so that its viscosity is the same as diesel oil. It also creates a major *pollution problem if it gets into the sea, particularly in large quantities from oil tankers that founder or run aground. It does not break down easily and if washed ashore it coats rocks and beaches with a tarlike substance which is very difficult to remove, destroying local *fisheries and tourism. Such accidents raise important *environmental issues as does the fact that residual oil emits chemical impurities when burnt. A large cruise or container ship may burn over of 200 tonnes per day and, if this contains 3% sulphur, over 12 tonnes of sulphuric acid can be directed into the atmosphere each day, a problem that *MARPOL is addressing.

Before the introduction of nuclear power, and with the exception of *K-boats, *submarines used diesel engines when surfaced, or when employing a *schnorkel. Denis Griffiths

differential global satellite navigation systems, see SATELLITE NAVIGATION.

digital selective calling (DSC) is part of the *Global Maritime Distress and Safety System. Each ship and relevant shore station has a nine-digit number, called a **Maritime**

Mobile Service Identity. This is used for identification purposes when DSC is employed to transmit radio distress calls from ships, to receive acknowledgements of distress calls from ships or shore stations which have heard them, for relaying other urgent or safety messages, and for transmitting messages on a one-to-one basis to another ship. When the distress button is pressed on a VHF radio using DSC a coded distress message, known as a **distress alert**, is transmitted on channel 70. The radio then automatically retunes itself to channel 16, and any ship receiving the call will reply by voice on this channel. However, before a coast radio station receiving the *distress signal acknowledges it on channel 16, it will send a 'Distress Acknowledge' on channel 70 which automatically turns off the distress transmission. If no 'Distress Acknowledge' is sent the distress signal is repeated every five minutes until it is acknowledged by a coast radio station.

dinghy, from the Hindi *dengi* or *dingi*, a small boat used on rivers, originally a small open rowing boat, with one pair of *oars. In the days of sail it was used as a general work boat by warships or merchant vessels and was often *clinker built. Nowadays the word is usually used to describe the *tender for a *yacht or a small open racing boat.

dip (1) of the *horizon, the first of the *altitude corrections applied to the *sextant altitude of a heavenly body. It is the vertical angle at the observer's eye between the horizontal and the line of sight to the visible horizon. Its value depends on the height of eye and the correction is always minus. The correction table given in *nautical tables and almanacs is frequently combined with the correction for terrestrial *refraction. For illus. see HORIZON. **(2)** When an *answering pennant was hoisted at sea, it was **hoisted at the dip**, that is, halfway up the signal *halyards, until the signal received was fully understood. See also SIGNALS AT SEA. Mike Richey

dipping lug, a rig in which the forward end of the *yard carrying a *lugsail project forward of the mast of a sailing boat. Unlike the *standing lug, this entails lowering the sail and dipping the yard round the mast whenever the vessel is required to go *about. Once the vessel *tacks the sail is rehoisted. For this purpose dipping lines are secured to the end of the yard, one on either side of the sail. See also GUNTER RIG.

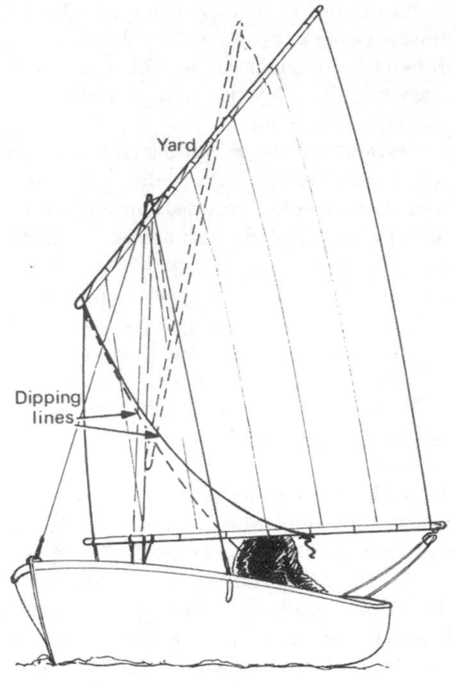

Dipping lug

director sight, a means of directing and controlling the gunfire aboard warships. It was introduced into the British Navy in 1912 by Admiral Sir Percy Scott (1853–1924). Previously, guns had been laid and fired individually by a gunlayer at each gun, but in the heat of firing it was always difficult to make sure that each gunlayer in a ship was firing at the same target. Funnel smoke, cordite smoke, and mist and haze were additional hazards militating against accurate gunnery. Scott's system involved a single telescopic sight mounted in the foretop of warships (see TOP), well above funnel and cordite smoke, and connected electrically to the sights of each gun, so that individual gunlayers had only to line up their gunsights with a pointer on a dial to ensure that all fired at the target selected by the director with the same elevation and allowance for deflection. The guns were all fired simultaneously by electric contact by the single gunlayer in the foretop so that their shells always fell together and were thus easier to spot.

dirk, the small naval sword worn by midshipmen or their equivalents in most navies, when in full dress uniform. In the British Navy it was originally a naval dagger worn, and used, by junior officers when boarding an enemy ship but it gradually developed as a ceremonial adjunct to the uniform worn on board. As a naval weapon it dates from the late 17th or early 18th century, the name probably coming from the Scottish dirk, or durk, a short sword worn by Highlanders.

disadvantage, see ADVANTAGE.

***Discovery* Investigations,** a programme of research into the oceanic resources of the Antarctic, with the particular object of providing a scientific foundation for the *whaling industry. In 1918 a British government committee was formed to consider how best to conserve the industry's future and its principal natural resource, the *whale. In 1920 a tax was imposed on whale oil and the revenues that accrued were devoted to finding out more about whales and their habitat in the Southern Ocean. The *Discovery*, in which *Scott sailed to the Antarctic, was refitted as a *research ship, and a base, Discovery House, was built on South Georgia for the team of scientists who were to undertake what became known as the *Discovery* Investigations. Their main tasks were to provide information on the life histories of whales and their food chain, in particular the *krill, and to discover as much as possible about the Antarctic environment in which whales live. During a series of commissions between 1925 and 1939, the crews of the *Discovery* (replaced by *Discovery II* in 1929) and the *William Scoresby* carried out thousands of routine oceanographic observations, undertook a number of whale-marking cruises, completed *charts of several island groups in the area, discovered the presence of the *Antarctic Convergence, and circumnavigated the Antarctic continent twice. The results of the Investigations were eventually published in 38 volumes. After the Second World War (1939–45), *Discovery* Investigations became part of the newly formed National Institute of Oceanography, which after further name changes brought about the formation of one of Britain's foremost *oceanographic institutes, the Southampton Oceanography Centre. A new *Discovery* was *launched in 1962 to participate in the International Indian Ocean Expedition, and is still operational. See also OCEANOGRAPHY.

dismast, to, to lose a mast. It is used most often in the past tense; a vessel is dismasted when its mast goes by the *board.

displacement, see TONNAGE.

distant signals, objects, such as balls, cones, etc., which, before the days of modern communications, were hoisted instead of flags, when the distance at which they were read was too great to distinguish the colours of the flags. Before the battle of Trafalgar in 1805, information of the sailing of the Franco-Spanish fleet from Cadiz was transmitted to Lord *Nelson some 65 kilometres (40 mls.) away below the horizon by distant signals which were relayed by three ships. The information reached him in less than ten minutes. See also STORM SIGNALS; SIGNALS AT SEA.

distress signals, a means of calling for help or assistance at sea. All ships over 300 tonnes are required to have equipment specified by *Global Maritime Distress and Safety System (GMDSS) regulations. The following list of distress signals includes some of the required equipment, but is primarily intended as a guide for the crews of those vessels who cannot use it because of malfunction, loss of power, etc. It must be understood that these signals must only be used if the vessel displaying or sending them is in imminent danger and that help is urgently required.

1. a gun or other explosive signal fired at intervals of about a minute
2. a continuous blast on any fog-signalling apparatus
3. *rockets or shells, throwing red stars fired singly at short intervals
4. signalling *SOS by sound or light (dot dot dot dash dash dash dot dot dot)
5. the flags 'N' over 'C' of the *International Code of Signals

6. a signal comprising a square flag with a ball, or anything resembling a ball, above or below it
7. the burning of a tar or oil barrel, or anything else which gives off flames
8. a rocket parachute flare or a hand *flare which shows a red light
9. a smoke signal emanating orange-coloured smoke
10. slowly and repeatedly raising and lowering outstretched arms
11. signals transmitted by *EPIRB
12. *digital selective calling distress signal
13. a piece of *canvas orange in colour with either a black square and circle or other appropriate symbol (for identification from the air)
14. a dye marker
15. SART (Search and Rescue Radar Transponders)

The earliest distress signals were probably made by smoke or flames by burning pitch or tar on board, but when gunpowder came into general use during the 15th century the firing of *cannon became the usual signal of distress. Although at that period there was no internationally agreed code, there are many instances of ships drifting ashore and summoning help by firing their guns.

In 1857 the International Code of Signals was established and a special flag was allocated for distress; other signals which came into use during the 19th century were a square flag with a ball above it, the *distant signal of a cone pointed upwards with a ball above or below it, continuous sounding on *foghorns, and, for night use, flames or shells or rockets throwing stars of any colour. It was not until 1954 that agreement was reached that distress rockets had to be red.

The most profound change in distress signalling was brought about by the invention of wireless telegraphy and the formation of the Marconi International Marine Communication Company in 1900. Several *ocean liners were fitted with Marconi equipment the same year, as also was the Borkum *lightship, whose crew were probably the first lives to be saved by a wireless call after their ship broke *adrift in a *gale. In January 1904 the Marconi Company issued a circular stating that the call 'to be given by ships in distress or in any way requiring assistance shall be "CQD" '. 'CQ' stood for all stations and 'D' stood for distress, although it became widely known as 'Come Quickly, Danger'.

Because of the **Titanic* disaster, a 1919 Act of Parliament required British ships with 200 or more persons on board to have sufficient radio operators to keep a 24-hour *watch. Experiments were also made with auto-alarms actuated by wireless distress calls, and in 1927 the British government approved such a device. It exempted any ship fitted with one from carrying the two additional wireless operators who were otherwise necessary to keep a continuous watch. In 1933 wirelesses became compulsory on all passenger ships, and on cargo ships of 1,600 tons upwards, and from 1954 it was internationally compulsory for all such ships to keep a continuous watch on the distress frequency, with either a radio officer or an auto-alarm. The distress call to actuate the auto-alarm was twelve dashes, each lasting four seconds, with one second between each. As from February 2005 ships and shore stations were no longer required to keep a listening watch for *'mayday' distress signals made manually. These now have to be transmitted automatically with GMDSS equipment. See also SIGNALS AT SEA.

ditty box, a small wooden box in which a sailor kept his personal belongings, such as letters from home.

diving. A simple definition of diving is that it is the art of going underwater and coming to the surface again. In antiquity it offered communities living at subsistence level a means of harvesting rivers and the shallower margins of the sea. A brief glimpse of what was involved in this was provided in 8th-century Japanese chronicles which detailed the activities of the *Ama*, sea folk, originally both male and female, who lived by making salt, catching *fish, gathering *seaweeds, *shellfish, and sea slugs. Sometimes they worked from the surface, but often they had to dive quite deep while holding their breath.

The epic of Gilgamesh (*c.*2800–2500 BC), a Sumerian king from the head of the Persian Gulf, relates how he made a voyage beyond the waters of death in search of a magical plant capable of granting immortality. Learning that it only grew on the seabed he attached stone weights to his feet so that he could descend and make his search, cutting them loose once he had reached the bottom. This is a technique that may have been associated with pearl fishing, as in the ancient world the island of Dilmun, modern day Bahrain in the Persian Gulf, traded in pearls with southern India.

Some divers in the distant past appear to have mastered the technique that modern divers call 'ear clearing'. This is the equalization of air and water pressures across the eardrums during a descent to avoid pain and possible physical damage, a mild form of which will be recognized by anyone who has been in a descending aircraft. Those who did master this technique could then dive relatively deep, repeatedly, and without problem. One of them must have been the ancient Greek sea god Glaucus, who was considered a good fisherman and diver before he drowned in a *storm, and became immortal in legend.

Early Diving Equipment. The main limitation of what is now called free-diving, or simply holding your breath, is that it allowed, and still allows, a maximum of around two minutes underwater. It was, however, the only way of diving available until the early first millennium AD when equipment began to be invented that allowed the diver to stay much longer beneath the surface. The earliest example of such equipment is attributed to Aristotle and appeared in a work called *Problems*. This described an upturned cauldron containing air being carefully lowered to the bottom, so that the diver could enter it if necessary and make use of the air it contained.

Other influences on the later development of diving equipment may well have come from stories which began to circulate early in the 12th century AD, for example Alexander the Great's supposed descent in a glass vessel, and a contemporary German poem describing how Salman and Morolff descended in a boat with an air pipe attached. Then in the 15th century diving helmets began to be mentioned in treatises written by German and Italian military engineers, which were intended to help recover goods and guns lost when merchants or armies crossed rivers. They probably worked, albeit for a limited time and in the shallows, though some danger would have been attached to their use. Some even had an air pipe attached, and all represented attempts to make the diver mobile and able to work more efficiently than free-diving divers.

The beginning of the 16th century saw the introduction of 'larger-volume diving bells', as they were called, which potentially offered more time underwater. The first such bell on record was 'mobile', as it could be carried around by the diver. Undoubtedly based on practical experience, it was designed by a Maestro Lorena and used by Franco di Marchi (1539) for a dive on the *shipwreck of one of the Emperor Caligula's pleasure craft in Lake Nemi, near Rome. It became noticeably heavier when the diver was on the bottom, which he found impeded his movement. We now know that this was due to the bell's air volume being progressively compressed by water pressure during the descent, though an explanation for this phenomenon had to wait until Robert Boyle (1627–91) finally explained the mathematical relationship between (water) pressure and gas volumes. His work not only left us what we now call Boyle's law, but a better understanding of buoyancy and how better to control it.

While there is some evidence of mobile bells being used successfully in the first half of the 17th century, Aristotelian ideas still held sway and consequently most bells followed the upturned cauldron design described in *Problems*. They had to be heavy enough to sink easily, but this caused problems for their support ships which often had difficulties lowering them onto a worksite, then lifting them again using an ordinary ship's *tackle. A further difficulty concerning mobility was that the bell divers could only work for as far as they could reach out under the bell rim, and this often meant lifting and moving the bell over short distances.

This is probably why, at the end of the 17th century and in the early 18th century, the first attempts were made to make more lightweight individual gear. Typically, this comprised a 'pressure-proof' body armour, from which the arms and/or legs protruded within a leather suit. There were a number of accidents with this equipment, but from 1720 John Lethbridge, then Jacob Rowe, both of them employed in *salvage, used pressure-proof wooden 'barrels' from which only their arms protruded. This not only worked successfully in depths up to 20 metres (66 ft) but gave them a degree of mobility while working on a site. Lethbridge and Rowe survived on the air they took down with them inside their 'barrel', but from the mid-17th century there were several attempts to supply air continuously with an air pipe and bellows. The civil engineer John Smeaton is the first on record to make this work successfully when in 1779 he used a pump on a very small diving bell to repair, in very shallow water, the foundations of a bridge at Hexham in Northumberland.

More Advanced Diving Bells and Diving Suits. As a result of the Industrial Revolution, the early 19th century saw an increased use of diving bells fabricated in cast iron, which were heavy enough to require dedicated handling systems. Some were even mounted on ships, with the bell being launched through a central 'moon pool', or *hatch. Air pump design and efficiency also began to improve, allowing bells to work at greater depth, stay down much longer, and so find an application in the building of a number of harbour *breakwaters. The civil engineer John Rennie first became involved in these construction projects early in the century and he soon improved work safety and efficiency. He first placed a one-way air inlet valve where the air pipe entered the bell, and then designed a gantry that allowed the bell and its pump to be moved around and located over any position on a work site.

The beginning of the 19th century also saw more reliable air pumps being used to supply 'flexible' diving dresses which, unlike the 18th-century armoured equipment and barrels, allowed divers to walk around freely, use their hands, and potentially become much more cost-effective and productive when tackling intricate jobs. In 1823 Charles Deane patented a 'smoke' helmet design, for use in firefighting. It failed to make an impact but in September 1830 his brother John adapted it to inspect a pier of Blackfriars Bridge over London's River Thames in what was to be the first recorded commercial use of a flexible diving dress. The helmet was attached to a short canvas jacket, pulled on over a full-length waterproof dress made of the newly invented Macintosh material. Later termed an 'open' dress design, because surplus air was free to escape under the canvas jacket's lower edge, experience soon showed that the helmet could easily displace and drown the diver. To remedy this, an American, John Norcross, introduced a completely 'closed' dress design in 1834 that in theory allowed a diver to turn a somersault underwater. To stop the 'closed' dress from ballooning, due to excess air being trapped, Norcross used an air-escape pipe hanging down from his helmet. In 1835 Mr Fraser proposed a reliable mechanical air-escape valve attached to the helmet, after which a German, Augustus Siebe (1788–1872), perfected the 'closed dress' design between 1839 and 1844, during successful salvage work on the warship **Royal George*. The resultant familiar copper helmet became standard equipment which remains in use today in many parts of the world.

Salvage worker wearing Augustus Siebe's diving suit: engraving c.1885

Early SCUBA Equipment. In 1664, Robert Boyle's one-time assistant Robert Hooke had both proposed and supervised the development and first practical use of what we now call self-contained equipment, known by the acronym SCUBA (self-contained underwater breathing apparatus), in which air was fed to the diver from inverted lead boxes. Intended for use by a diver walking out to work from a bell, as a way of getting around the problems of moving heavy bells around, it laid the foundations for lightweight equipment that allowed the diver to carry around his own air supply and so remain independent of the surface. In the early 19th century it was realized that the globes and cylinders designed to hold combustible gases under (relatively low) pressure for industrial and domestic lighting use could also be used to hold air for self-contained diving. Similarly, it was the valves required to control the pressure of coal gas supplies in towns that, in 1826, led the Frenchman Jean Jérémie Pouilliot to propose the first regulator, intended to provide air from a cylinder to the diver on his demand (i.e. only when he inhaled, which cut down air wastage) and at ambient pressure according to his depth. The best-known 19th-century self-contained equipment, based on a mechanical regulator, was later designed by Rouquayrol and Denayrouze (1864) and fictionally used by Captain Nemo in Jules *Verne's classic *Twenty Thousand Leagues under the Sea* (1868).

Advances in Knowledge and Equipment. All this self-contained equipment was 'open circuit', where the diver exhaled into the water. This was not very efficient, as the diver only ever used a small part of the 20% oxygen available in a breath of air. Around the middle of the 19th century a remedy for this was found with 'closed circuit' or 're-breather' equipment where the diver breathed pure oxygen and his exhalations then passed through a chemical (often caustic potash) which removed the dangerous carbon dioxide. The volume was then 'made up', as divers now say, by introducing a small amount of oxygen so that the gas could be safely re-breathed. The viability of this method was shown by Henry Fleuss's successful gear which was patented in 1879.

Improvements in steel manufacture led, from the beginning of the 20th century, to the introduction of cylinders which worked at higher pressures (typically, 100–120 bars) and held more gas, and these were to aid the further development of SCUBA diving. The same period also saw an increased use of *submarines by various navies, some of which were soon involved in accidents. This, along with a requirement for practice torpedo recovery, led to a greater demand for safe deep-diving practices, and in 1905 the British *Admiralty convened a committee to review the requirements for these. An important outcome was that its physiological member, Professor J. B. S. Haldane, developed tables to combat *decompression sickness. These were soon in use by the Royal Navy and other navies and, while there are more modern decompression theories, the procedures the tables laid out are still followed, although in amateur diving wrist-mounted decompression computers have come into widespread use.

Another important advance had by this time already occurred when, in 1878, the French physiologist Paul Bert recognized that oxygen became toxic to breathe above a certain pressure. This led, just prior to the First World War (1914–18), to the development of safer mixed-gas closed-circuit equipment (typically using oxygen-nitrogen mixtures) in both Britain and Germany. However, as the Royal Navy initially used pure oxygen submarine-escape equipment during the Second World War (1939–45), there were some deaths in training before mixed gases, along with much improved equipment, were adopted.

The Aqualung. In 1918, a Japanese inventor named Ogushi patented 'The Peerless Respirator'. Reportedly used in the Pacific pearling industry, the diver wore a full-face mask, which covered eyes, nose, and mouth, into which air flowed from a back-mounted cylinder when he compressed a spring-loaded valve held in his mouth. In 1924 Commandant Yves Le Prieur introduced a similar mask into which air free-flowed by way of a reduction valve from a cylinder mounted on the diver's chest. To save air, in 1933 he made the reduction valve diver-adjustable, though, being free flow, dive times still remained very short. Le Prieur is important to the history of recreational diving because, with Jean Painlevé, he started a club in Paris in 1935 which introduced any number of young and old alike to the pleasures of diving.

The mobility of the self-contained diver was assured when, in 1933, Commandant Corlieu introduced the modern foot-fin, and in 1938 the modern spectacle style of face mask started to be marketed by Alexandre Kramarenko of Nice. The same year Maxime Forjot patented the snorkel tube, though it is said that one had been in use for some time by Steve Butler, 'the English librarian of Juan-les-Pins'. Then in July 1943 an oft forgotten pioneer, Georges Commeinhes, used his own design of demand regulator to reach a depth of 53 metres (175 ft) off Marseille. The same year Frédéric Dumas descended to 64 metres (210 ft) to set a new depth record, using an early version of the 'twin hose' regulator.

This regulator, marketed from the mid-1940s under the name of 'Aqualung', was the invention of two more Frenchmen, Commandant Jacques-Yves *Cousteau and Émile Gagnan. On the diver's demand this delivered air from a back-mounted cylinder in two stages of pressure reduction. The modern 'single-hose' regulator first appeared in the 1950s, and it is still in use today. This combined in one unit, which was held in the diver's mouth, the diaphragm that sensed water pressure differentials and the exhaust valve. Over the years its design has seen further improvement, and today it is used in conjunction with cylinders capable of holding air or gas mixtures at pressures up to 300 bar. This gives divers much more control over the way they plan their diving, which for amateur sports is diving in depths up to 50 metres (165 ft).

The deeper diving carried out by Cousteau's team from the early 1940s also led to an appreciation of the dangers of nitrogen narcosis, the narcotic effect due to nitrogen in air that increases as a diver descends. Its study in the 1950s led to the use of the less narcotic helium gas in place of nitrogen in gas mixtures. This in turn paved the way for the development of modern deep-diving techniques and to deeper amateur 'technical diving', as it is called, which makes use of both 'open'-and 'closed'-circuit equipment.

Modern Commercial Diving. Commercial deep diving is often carried out using 'saturation' diving techniques, where the divers live for weeks in a chamber on the surface held at a pressure slightly less than the ambient pressure on the seabed. The chamber connects to a 'closed' diving bell, which can be disconnected so that two divers can descend to the seabed to work perhaps a twelve-hour shift, or even more. As the *offshore oil and gas industry has moved into much deeper water, underwater maintenance is nowadays often planned around using *underwater vehicles, some fitted with tools designed to carry out simple tasks. However, diver intervention with its 'hands-on' capability often remains as a back-up. Atmospheric Diving Suits (ADS), which resist pressure at great depths, allow a diver to apply his or her 'hands-on' skills.

The HARDSUIT 2000, an ADS developed for the US Navy, allows a diver to descend as deep as 610 metres (2,000 ft) while the suit in which he is enclosed maintains the same pressure regardless of depth. It is equipped with hydraulic rotary joints, which allow the diver to move his arms and legs, and manipulators which allow him to grasp and move objects underwater. The diver is also able to control four thruster modules, two vertical and two horizontal, with which he can manoeuvre the frame in which he stands. However, the limitation of ADS outside military use is that, even in commercial diving, international regulations stipulate that there must always be a 'stand-by' diver ready to assist in an emergency. For some applications, then, this requirement reduces the cost effectiveness of ADS units, as it implies that there must always be a second one immediately available.

Davis, R., *Deep Diving and Submarine Operations* (5th edn. 1951).

Harris, G., *IRONSUIT: The History of the Atmospheric Diving Suit* (1995).

Vallintine, R., *Divers and Diving* (1981).

Anyone wishing to dive should first receive training from qualified and experienced instructors working in a recognized diving school.
British Sub-Aqua Club **www.bsac.org**
PADI **www.padi.com/english**

Peter Dick

dock, in Britain the area of water in a port or harbour enclosed by *piers or *wharves. Some refer to the wharves themselves as the dock, but in the strict meaning of the word it is the area of water in between. However, in the USA the word is always used to mean only the wharf or pier. See also DRY-DOCK; FLOATING DOCK.

dockyard, in its naval sense an establishment in a strategic position ashore which not only serves as a base for warships but also provides all services they can require, such as repair, refit, replenishment, etc. Most naval dockyards of any size also have building slips for the construction of warships, and *dry-docks for their servicing. In Britain the naval dockyards are known as *royal dockyards; in the USA they are called naval shipyards or navy yards.

Civilian dockyards exist around the world to provide the same services for merchant ships, though often without the building facilities, being geared more to the repair and refit of ships than their construction. However, one of the best-known English dockyards was at Deptford on the River Thames where the English *East India Company had its *East Indiamen built. See also SHIPBUILDING.

dodger, before the days of the enclosed *bridge, a painted *canvas screen erected at chest height around the forward side and wing ends of a ship's bridge as a protection against the weather. Up to the 1920s, when strengthened glass was introduced, all small steamships, and even some large ones, used dodgers for protection. The totally protected bridge did not come into general use in small vessels such as fishing *trawlers and *drifters, *tugs, etc. until after the Second World War (1939–45).

dog, to, the operation of backing the tail of a *block with several turns around a *stay or *shroud, with the tail going with the *lay of the rope. This is one way of *clapping on a *purchase where additional hauling power is required.

dogger, originally a two-masted Dutch fishing vessel. In England, it was a development of the original *ketch, *square rigged on the main and carrying a *lugsail on the *mizzen, with two *jibs on a long *bowsprit. Short, wide beamed, and small, it was a fishing vessel which used *trawls or *long-lining on the *Dogger Bank. The name dates from the early 17th century, but was virtually synonymous with ketch until the latter began to increase in size—over about 50 tons—in the mid-17th century. See also FISHERIES.

Dogger Bank, an extensive *shoal in the North Sea about 96 kilometres (60 mls.) off the coast of Northumberland in north-east England. It has a minimum depth over it of about 11 metres (36 ft), but large portions of it lie at depths varying from 18 to 36 metres (60–120 ft). The origin of its name is obscure, though the word *dogger in Dutch originally meant a two-masted fishing vessel.

doghouse, an American term for the topside sleeping hutches provided for crewmen on ships involved in the *slave trade, so as to leave more space below for the living 'cargo'. The word evolved into a yachting term, to denote the short *deckhouse or main hatchway which is raised above the level of a *yacht's *cabin top.

dogs. (1) The metal hand clips fitted to *bulkheads and decks around watertight doors, small *hatch covers, etc., which when turned, force the rubber gasket lining the doors and hatches hard up against the sealing to ensure a watertight seal. **(2)** Metal bars, with their ends turned down and ending in a point, are also known as dogs. They were used for holding a baulk of timber steady while carpenters shaped it with an *adze, or for holding *frames on bending slabs while the frames are being bent to the shape of the hull. They are, of course, still in use for temporarily securing timber against unwanted movement, as much ashore as at sea.

dog-stopper, a heavy rope, secured round the mainmast of a sailing ship and used to back up the *stopper on the anchor *cable when the ship rode in a heavy sea in the days before chain cable and *cable-holders. It was not in any way a permanent fitting and was used only as an additional safety measure to secure the ship when anchored in very rough weather.

dog vane, a small temporary *vane, often of cork and feathers threaded on a thin line and attached to a short staff. It was fixed on the *weather *gunwale of sailing ships to enable the helmsman to judge the direction of the wind.

> The Dog-vane staff the Quartermaster moves,
> The wind upon the *larboard quarter proves.
> (H. B. Gascoigne, *The Navigator's Fame* (1825))

dog watches, the two half *watches of two hours each into which the period from 1600 to 2000 hours is divided. The purpose of this is to produce an uneven number of watches in the 24 hours, seven instead of six, thereby ensuring that watchkeepers, whether organized in two or three watches, do not keep the same watches every day. The two half watches are known as the First Dog and the Last Dog, and *never*, except by landlubbers, as First Dog and Second Dog. How they came by these names is not known: they were certainly in use by the 17th century. One suggestion, that they were called dog watches because they were curtailed, though ingenious, does not appear to have any foundation in fact.

doldrums, the belt of low pressure that extends 5° to 10° either side of the equator in a region known as the Intertropical Convergence Zone. The doldrums were notorious in the days of sail, because vessels could become becalmed there for many days and even weeks. This equatorial belt of windlessness and calm is often hot and sultry, so subject to violent thunderstorms and heavy rain. Being in the doldrums has now become synonymous with being listless, depressed, and generally stuck in a rut.

M. V. Angel

dolly. **(1)** A heavy iron anvil held against the head of a rivet while the other end is beaten. **(2)** A timber similar to a single *bollard which was set horizontally in the *bulwarks of a sailing ship. It was used as a convenient means for securing temporarily the *fall of a *purchase by taking a jamming turn round it when there was no *cleat nearby.

dolphin. **(1)** A large wooden pile, or collection of piles, serving as a *mooring post for ships, or occasionally as a *beacon. **(2)** Small brass guns carried in a ship and fitted with two lifting handles over the trunnions. They were used mainly as anti-personnel guns during the 15th, 16th, and early 17th centuries, much like a *murderer or *robinet. **(3)** The plaited rope strap (also known as dolphin of the mast) round the mast of a *square-rigged ship to prevent *nip between the lower *yard and the mast and at the same time to secure the *puddening round the mast which prevented the lower yard falling to the deck if the *jeers and *slings were both shot away. **(4)** A small light rowing boat of ancient times. It was from this name that arose the story recounted by Pliny of a boy going daily to school across the Lake of Lucerne on a dolphin. **(5)** Small toothed *whales. There are 34 known species, which include killer whales or orcas (*Orcinus orca*). Many of the smaller species of dolphin have the habit of riding the bow *waves of ships under way. They often associate with large schools of *tuna or whale *sharks, and this makes them vulnerable to being accidentally caught in *purse seine nets set around *fish *shoals. It was estimated that in 2003 as many as 8,000 dolphins were accidentally killed in this way in the North Sea, and the British government is currently (2004) experimenting with nets fitted with escape grids.

Dolphins usually associate in extended family units, some of which can be quite large, and occasionally large numbers of them become stranded. Sometimes the cause of their deaths is evident from clear signs of injuries from fishing nets but often there are no obvious reasons for their stranding. Being top predators dolphins tend to accumulate high concentrations of pollutants such as heavy metals and PCBs, one of today's *environmental issues, and these may disorient them, as may the powerful *sonars used by naval vessels. However, recently dolphins stranded off Southern California have tested positive for domoic acid, a natural toxin produced by a *red-tide diatom *Pseudonitschia*, so one cause may be the results of eutrophication, another environmental issue.

In orcas the *pods are led, and the hunts are organized, by the senior females, whereas the males, recognizable by their tall dorsal fins, tend to move between the family units. Like all dolphins they are highly vocal, using sounds both to communicate within the pod and as sonar to find and track their prey. Each killer whale group tends to have an identifiably different dialect for communication; even more interesting is that the dialects of groups of orcas that specialize in hunting other *marine mammals are distinct from those that specialize in hunting fish. Off southern Argentina a group of orcas has developed a unique hunting technique of beaching themselves to snatch cubs from a breeding colony of fur seals.

Dolphins, particularly the bottlenose or bluenose (*Tursopis truncatus*), are highly intelligent. For example, those kept by the Institute of Marine Mammals in Mississippi are trained to keep their pools clean by holding on to any litter until they see a trainer, and the litter is then traded for fish. They have a very sophisticated sonar system, which enables them to acquire detailed information about an object in the water, so some have been trained by the US Navy to detect mines, either floating in the water or lying on the bottom. They are taught not to touch the mines, but mark them with electronic floats, while cameras on their bodies transmit images to their handlers. See also PELORUS JACK. M. V. Angel

dolphin striker, a short perpendicular *spar under the *cap of the *bowsprit of a sailing vessel used for holding down or guying the *jib-boom by means of *martingales. It was a necessary spar to support the rigging needed to counteract the upward pull on the jib-boom of the *topgallant mast's fore-topgallant *stay. The name, of course, comes from the position of the spar, pointing vertically downwards towards the sea just beyond the bows of the vessel; that is, it would strike a *dolphin were one to leap out of the water just beneath it. For illus. see BOWSPRIT.

donkey engine, a small *auxiliary engine with its own small boiler employed during the early days of *steam propulsion aboard ship. It was used for furnishing power for a variety of smaller mechanical duties in harbour for which it would be uneconomic to produce steam from the main boilers. It was accommodated on deck in what was appropriately called a **donkey-house**.

donkey frigate, a class of small warships built for the Royal Navy at the end of the 18th century and the beginning of the 19th century. They carried 28 guns and were, more accurately, *ship-rigged *sloops built *frigate fashion, having guns protected by the upper deck, i.e. on a single gun-deck, with additional guns on the *forecastle and *quarterdeck.

donkey's breakfast, the merchant seaman's name for his mattress in the days when it was normally stuffed with straw. These mattresses were used by seamen right up into the 20th century in a majority of ships until the growth in the power of the trade unions and the passage of the Merchant Shipping Acts in Britain, or their equivalents in the various maritime countries, which led to their abolition.

Dorade ventilator, a deck vent that allows air to flow below decks without taking water with it. The ventilator cowl is mounted on a box screwed to the deck with its pipe extending into about half the box's depth. The top of the downtake spout is fitted more or less level with, and close to, the bottom end of the cowl piping, and extends through the deck into the vessel's accommodation. Any spray that enters the box through the cowl runs into the *scuppers from holes in the bottom of the box, while the dry air flows through the downtake spout. It first appeared in 1933 on the ocean-racing *yawl *Dorade*, and was invented by Roderick Stephens, Jr., the younger brother of Olin Stephens, *Dorade*'s designer.

dory. **(1)** A small flat-bottomed boat originating from the coast of New England, USA. It used to be used widely for line fishing on the *Grand Banks off the coast of Newfoundland. One of its great advantages for this purpose was that several could be stacked on board fishing boats one within the other, the collective noun being a nest of dories. Small boats, capable of landing commandos through surf for raids on the French coast and elsewhere during the Second World War (1939–45), were also called dories. After the war the name became associated with a type of hard-*chine *dinghy with flared sides, suitable for an outboard engine and widely used by yachtsmen and amateur fishermen. **(2)** A *fish, *Zeus faber*, known as a **John Dory**. The name comes from the French *jaune d'orée*, by which name it was known to the French fisherman of the Grand Banks on account of its golden-coloured scales. See also FISHERIES.

double bottoms are spaces in ships between the bottom of the hull and the lower part of the engine room or the cargo holds. Engine-room machinery cannot be fitted directly to the bottom of the hull, so it must be attached to plating located above the hull. Similarly, except in *tankers, cargo is not loaded directly onto the hull frames at the bottom of a hold but is loaded onto flat plates. The space between the bottom of the hull and these plates, known as the tank top, is made watertight and becomes a double-bottom tank for the ship. This provides a safeguard against the spillage of liquid cargoes, especially from oil tankers, and is also a precaution to prevent flooding in the event of an accident. The Chinese always built their *junks with double bottoms, but the first watertight double-bottomed ship to be *launched in the West was *Brunel's **Great Eastern*.

The double bottom can also be used to store a ship's fuel oil, a major advantage as it allows for increased cargo space. However, if the ship is *diesel powered, as most are nowadays, steam heating coils must be fitted in its double bottom tanks so that its residual fuel oil can be heated to enable it to be pumped. *Ballast water can be pumped into some of the double-bottom tanks in order to maintain the desired trim of the ship and keep the *propeller immersed when there is not much cargo on board. In *cruise ships the double bottoms may be used for holding grey water (washing and laundry water) until it can be discharged overboard when in open waters. Although ballast water tanks may be used for grey water, double-bottom fuel oil storage tanks must only be used for fuel oil. Denis Griffiths

double capstan, two *capstan barrels on the same central shaft designed to provide a capstan on two adjacent decks. In the old sailing *ships of the line double capstans were almost always fitted to provide lifting power on an upper and a lower deck with a single installation.

double-clewed jib, a *headsail which was also known as a quadrilateral jib. It was introduced aboard the *J-class *Endeavour* by her owner Mr (later Sir) Thomas Sopwith prior to the 1934 challenge for the *America's Cup. It was really an extra-large *jib with the clew cut off to form a four-sided sail *sheeted with two sheets, with the new fourth side corresponding to the *leech of a normal four-sided mainsail on a *gaff rig. It was almost certainly the invention of John Nicholson, the son of *yacht designer Charles E. Nicholson, who designed *Endeavour* and whose firm, Camper & Nicholsons, built her. It was believed by the British to be more efficient than the normal triangular jib. It was known to the Americans, who quickly adopted it, as a 'Greta Garbo', but it never caught on as a racing sail.

double clews, or **clues,** an old sea term used by seamen when one of them got married. *Clews, with their *nettles, were the cords which supported a seaman's *hammock. A double set of clews, in seamen's humour, were required to support a seaman's wife as well as himself. Double clews were also supposed to give a wider spread to a hammock, and the extra width thus obtained may also have had something to do with the origin of the term.

double diagonal build, a system of planking in which the *strakes are laid diagonally. Usually double skinned, the outer skin also being normally diagonal in the other direction but sometimes fore and *aft. The main purpose of double diagonal planking is to give the hull additional strength. Before the introduction of modern materials, such as *GRP, it was a system of construction used for small naval vessels, some *yachts, and also in sailing *dinghies.

double ender describes a vessel, usually a *yacht, with a *canoe stern.

doubling. **(1)** The name given to that portion of the mast of a large sailing vessel where an upper mast overlaps the lower, as a *topmast with a lower mast, or a *topgallant mast with a topmast. It is a word more often used in the plural than in the singular, as in normal *square-rigged sailing vessels each mast will have two doublings. **(2)** The operation of covering a ship with extra planking or plates when the original skin is weak or worn. In wooden ships the term was only used when the new planking was more than 5 centimetres (2 in.) thick. **(3)** Doubling a cape or other point of land means sailing a vessel round it so that on completion the land is between the ship and its original position. The verb, to double, can also be used for the last two definitions.

'Down Easter', the term given to *Cape Horners which, during the latter half of the 19th century and the early years of the 20th century, carried Californian grain around Cape Horn to the US east coast, and to Europe. 'Down Easter' comes from the phrase 'down east', at that time a US term for the coasts of Maine, Massachusetts, New Hampshire, and Connecticut where these medium-sized *clipper ships were built. Nowadays 'Down East' usually describes only the coast of Maine, especially north and east of Mt Desert Island.

Lubbock, B., *The Down Easters* (1929).

downhaul, in the days of sail a single rope fitted in large ships for hauling down a *jib or *staysail when shortening sail. It was led up along a *stay and through the *cringles of the sail and then made fast to the upper corner of the sail. Downhauls were also rigged for similar use with *studding sails, being led through *blocks on the outer *clews of the sails to the outer *yardarms of the studding sail. But in general, any rope fitted for the purpose of hauling down a sail used to be called a downhaul. Nowadays the word is used for the rope attached to a *yacht's *spinnaker pole to help control it. A yacht's *vang is also sometimes called a downhaul.

Downs, an *anchorage much used during the days of sail. It is situated on the east coast of England and lies inside the *Goodwin Sands, and between the North and South *Foreland. The Goodwins provide shelter from all easterly winds, the land shelter from the west.

drabler, or **drabbler,** an additional length of *canvas laced onto the *foot of the *bonnet of a sail in a *square-rigged ship to give it a greater area when *running free in light winds.

drag. **(1)** The amount by which a ship floats lower *aft than *forward. Almost all ships are designed, when in proper *trim, to *draw slightly more water aft than forward, to aid steering and to give the *rudder a slightly deeper immersion which helps to turn the ship more effectively. In the days of sail a ship with a tendency to *gripe and carry excessive *weather helm was eased by being trimmed down aft to give it more drag. Similarly, a ship with a tendency to *pay off, needing *lee helm to correct, could be improved by giving it less drag through being trimmed down forward. **(2)** When used as a verb, it is used to indicate that the *flukes of a ship's anchor are not holding in the ground. Though the phrase to describe this is 'the ship is dragging its anchor'—sometimes just abbreviated to the 'the ship is dragging'—it is, of course, the anchor which is dragging.

drag chains, lengths of chain shackled to weighted drags which act as a brake and bring a ship to a halt after it has been *launched into the water down the launching *ways. They are mostly used when the *slipway is in a narrow waterway where there is not sufficient room for the ship to be launched without stopping it, for fear of it running ashore on the opposite bank.

Drake, Sir Francis (*c*.1543–96), born at Crowndale, near Tavistock, Devon, though the date of his birth is uncertain. Nor is anything known about his early years beyond the assumption that, after his father became a preacher at Chatham, he served his apprenticeship in the Thames coastal trade. In 1567 Drake, who was a cousin of John *Hawkins, was given command of the 50-ton *Judith*, on Hawkins's third, financially unsuccessful, *slave-trade voyage. A clash with the Spaniards during it left Drake, who had strong Protestant convictions, with a passionate desire for revenge. He spent the next few years as a *privateer taking part in raids on the *Spanish Main, but his opportunity only really came in 1577 when he was engaged by a syndicate headed by Elizabeth I to make the first circumnavigation of the world by a captain commanding his own ship, through seas claimed exclusively by Spain.

It has long been assumed that the only objective for the voyage was plunder, and that his declared intention to find *Terra Australis Incognita before returning home via the elusive *North-West Passage was merely a cover story. However, recent research has intimated that Drake really did try and find the North-West Passage, though he certainly made no attempt to discover Terra Australis Incognita. Whatever his motives, the voyage became an exceedingly successful privateering expedition, which not only paid £47 for every £1 invested but also put England on the map as a rising sea power.

Drake sailed from Plymouth on 13 December 1577 in command of the 100-ton *Pelican* (later renamed *Golden Hinde*), together with four smaller ships and about 160 men. Since he had no *charts, a Portuguese *pilot was kidnapped and later put on shore when they reached the Pacific. The whole expedition had been planned in the greatest secrecy but one of Drake's closest friends, Thomas Doughty, whom Drake had taken into his confidence, informed Lord Burleigh, the Lord Treasurer of England, of its imminent departure. Burleigh, aghast at the effect of such a voyage on English relations with Spain, already made difficult by Drake's previous exploits, did all in his power to prevent the expedition taking place, and apparently persuaded Doughty to disrupt it should it succeed in sailing. This Doughty proceeded to do, making trouble and inciting the crews to *mutiny, and by the time the expedition reached Port St Julian, close to the entrance of the *Magellan Straits, Drake had to take drastic action. He had Doughty arrested, convened a 'court of law' complete with a jury of twelve men, and charged Doughty with treason and mutiny. Doughty was acquitted on the charge of treason but found guilty on that of mutiny, and was immediately executed.

After sailing through the Straits of Magellan Drake was driven south by a *storm to about *latitude 57° S., thus proving that Tierra del Fuego was an island, not a part of the great southern continent. By this time he had become separated from two of the ships and during the storm he lost touch with the only other one, the *Elizabeth*. When he could find no trace of the *Golden Hinde*, her captain turned for home. Drake, therefore, entered the *South Seas alone, but as the Spanish settlements along the western coast of South American were unguarded, he made several successful raids along the coastline, his richest prize being the *treasure ship *Cacafuego* which he took off Lima.

He then continued north to search for the strait that the Flemish cartographer Abraham Ortelius (1527–98) theorized would lead to the elusive North-West Passage, and there is some evidence to suppose that he reached a latitude of about 56° N. However, great secrecy and subterfuge surrounded the voyage on his return and there can be no great certainty about this. He may well have thought he had found the entrance to the Strait before being forced to turn back because of *ice. He then sailed south, and landed at a place he named New Albion, probably Vancouver Island, before sailing across the Pacific to the Moluccas, returning to Plymouth on 26 September 1580. His treasure, estimated at half a million pounds in Elizabethan currency, was taken by land to the Tower of London while he sailed the *Golden Hinde* round to Deptford. There, six months later, he was knighted by Elizabeth I aboard his ship, though for the actual accolade she handed the sword to the French ambassador.

Sir Francis Drake; the 'Jewel' portrait

Drake's next command, with Sir Martin *Frobisher as his vice admiral, was an amphibious expedition to the West Indies in 1585, the first act of open war with Spain. During it, Drake proved himself a master of combined operations, sacking San Domingo, Cartagena, St Augustine in Florida, and then taking off the first Virginian colonists. He returned to England to the news of the preparations for the *Spanish Armada, some ships of which he proceeded to destroy at Cadiz in April 1587, operations known as 'the singeing of the King of Spain's beard'. Soon afterwards he captured his greatest prize, the Portuguese *carrack *San Felipe* laden with goods from the East Indies valued at £114,000.

When the Spanish Armada sailed in 1588 Drake was appointed vice admiral of the English fleet at Plymouth under Lord Howard of Effingham. There, on Plymouth Hoe, the first news of the Armada's appearance off the Lizard was received on 19 July (29 July new style) when, it is said, a game of bowls was being played. Drake is reputed to have remarked, 'there is time to finish the game and beat the Spaniards, too', but as the English fleet was embayed, and as the remark is first recorded in 1736, it is doubtful whether he made it, though that he was playing bowls when he heard the news is quite possible.

Drake's part in defeating the Armada, while in command of the **Revenge*, was that of leader of the fleet during the first night of the week-long chase up the Channel, when he took the opportunity to capture the *Rosario* *galleon which he sent into Dartmouth. He may well have suggested the *fireship attack at Calais, and he certainly took the leading part in the gun battle off Gravelines.

The following year it was decided to destroy the remnants of the Armada on the north coast of Spain, and Drake commanded the ships which took the troops to Corunna and Lisbon. They failed to achieve anything and disease soon decimated their numbers. Drake was not employed again for five years, during which time he became mayor of Plymouth and represented the city in Parliament. His last expedition, to the Indies again in 1595, was also a failure and in January 1596, after sacking several places on the mainland in a fruitless search for treasure, he died of yellow fever off Porto Bello and was buried at sea.

Drake became a legend in his own lifetime. Though he spent comparatively few years in the service of the state, he was a founder of the British naval tradition because of the heroic quality of his exploits. He, not Magellan, was the first captain to take his ship around the world, and he was the greatest privateer of all time. In appearance he was short, stocky, and red haired. Essentially a man of action, he was a brilliant tactician both at sea and on land, but he was less successful as an administrator. He may have been ruthless, ambitious, and boastful, but he was also generous, cheerful, and an ideal leader of men. See also DRAKE'S DRUM; REPLICA SHIP; WARFARE AT SEA.

Bawlf, S., *The Secret Voyage of Sir Francis Drake* (2003).

Kelsey, H., *Sir Francis Drake, the Queen's Pirate* (1998).

Sugden, J., *Sir Francis Drake* (1990).

Drake's drum, a drum said to have been in the possession of Sir Francis *Drake and carried by him on board his ships to beat the crews to *quarters and now at Buckland Abbey, Devon, Drake's old home. According to legend, the drum gives a drumbeat whenever England is in danger of invasion from the sea. Doubts have been cast on its authenticity. It is the subject of a famous poem of the same name by Sir Henry Newbolt (1862–1938). First published in the *St James's Gazette* in 1897, this was later set to music by Ralph Vaughan Williams.

Take my drum to England, hang et by the shore,
Strike et when your powder's running low;
If the Dons sight Devon, I'll quit the port o' Heaven,
An' drum them up the Channel as we drummed them long ago.

draught. **(1)** Sometimes written as **draft,** the depth of water a ship draws, which of course varies according to how heavily it is loaded. The legal maximum draught for British ships used to be the *Plimsoll Line, but *load lines, with metric markings, are now governed by an international convention drawn up by the *International Maritime Organization. **(2)** In *naval architecture, a vessel's drawings or *lines from which the shipbuilder works. See also SHIPBUILDING.

draw, to. **(1)** When a sail is full of wind, it is said to be **drawing. To let draw**, to *trim the *jib of a small sailing vessel with the *lee sheet after it has been held to *windward by the *weather sheet in order to assist in forcing the vessel's bows across the wind when *tacking. In very light winds, where the vessel may not have sufficient *way to make tacking easy, the jib is held out to windward when the vessel is head to wind to assist its bows across. As soon as this is achieved, the order to let draw ensures the jib being sheeted normally on the new tack. When a ship *heaves to at sea, with the jib sheeted to windward, the order to let draw gets it sailing again. **(2)** Said of a ship to indicate its *draught, e.g. 'the ship draws, or is drawing, so much *forward and so much *aft'.

Dreadnought, see BATTLESHIP.

dredge, an iron, wedge-shaped contrivance with a small net attached, by which *shellfish are brought up from their beds. Towed along the bottom by a *smack, the iron wedge loosens the hold of the shellfish and guides them into the net. See also FISHERIES.

dredger, a vessel fitted with mechanical means for deepening harbours or clearing the entrances to rivers by removing part of the bottom. It is mostly self-propelled but some are *towed into position. The **'hopper' dredger** is fitted with an endless chain of buckets which scoops up the bottom and discharges the contents of the buckets into *hoppers or *dumb barges secured alongside it, though some have *holds in which to put the spoil. These have hinged doors on the bottom so that the dredger can dispose of the spoil out at sea. Another type is the **'bucket' dredger** where the endless chain of buckets operates through a central well so that the area of the bottom being dredged is immediately below the vessel. A **'dipper' dredger** has one bucket attached to an arm. These types are always stationary when operating.

With the modern **'suction' dredger** the bottom is removed by a vacuum pipe which sucks up the silt or mud before discharging it into the dredger's holds, a process which is done while the dredger is under *way. Some employ cutters to loosen the bottom which can then be sucked up. The *hovercraft principle has also been developed for small dredgers of up to 150 tonnes for use in very shallow waters and along the banks of rivers and estuaries.

dress ship, to, to deck out a vessel with flags for a ceremonial occasion. A ship can be either dressed overall or with flags at the masthead. A ship is only dressed overall in harbour while masthead flags are normally worn when under way in, or in the vicinity of, a harbour, though it is allowed as an alternative to dressing overall if the vessel does not have dressing lines.

A vessel is dressed overall only by flying the flags of the *International Code of Signals, and no others should be used. These are strung on dressing lines from the bow, or from below the bow in the USA, to the masthead, from masthead to masthead if the vessel has more than one mast, and from the masthead, or after masthead, to the *taffrail, or, in the USA, the water below it. There is a recommended order for doing this which spaces the code's triangular flags and *pennants between its rectangular flags, and this gives a pleasant contrast in colours.

The vessel's *ensign is worn at its usual position, and the same ensign is usually also flown at each masthead. In the UK the *burgee of a *yacht's *yacht club is flown side by side with the appropriate ensign at the principal masthead. Strictly speaking, if someone aboard the vessel is a flag officer of a yacht club, then his flag officer's burgee is flown on the main mast without the ensign, though ensigns are flown on any other masts. If a vessel displays more than one ensign it is important that they are of the same design. The correct *jack must also be flown on the *jackstaff.

Vessels dress ship on special days like Independence Day in the USA and the sovereign's official birthday in the UK. If dressing ship for a local occasion such as a regatta or a *launching ceremony a yacht's club burgee is flown at the main masthead without an ensign, though the ensign should be flown at any other masthead and the correct jack flown on the jackstaff.

The procedure for dressing with masthead flags is the same but without dressing lines.

Where dressing for foreign national festivals, in the UK or elsewhere, a vessel flies the ensign of the country whose festival is being celebrated. It is flown with a yacht's club burgee at the masthead if the yacht has only one mast, and at the *mizzen masthead in ketches and yawls, and on the foremast of a schooner. Despite this rule it is probably better to fly the ensign of the guest country at the masthead when there is only one mast, and the club burgee at the crosstrees or *spreader.

drift. **(1)** The distance a vessel makes to *leeward, by the action of either the *tide or the wind. **(2)** The term used to indicate the rate in knots of ocean *currents, as for example for the 'west wind drift' which circles the globe in southern *latitudes under the influence of the *Roaring Forties. **(3)** The distance a shell fired from a rifled barrel deviates from its aimed trajectory because of the rotation imparted to it by the rifling, a matter that used to be of considerable importance in the days when big naval guns were fired long distances at sea. **(4)** The accumulation of pieces of wood, trunks of trees, etc., or fragments of small *ice broken away from the edges of icefields, collected together by the action of wind or current and lying on the surface in a mass.

drifter, a type of fishing vessel, originally fitted with sails but today fitted with an engine or engines. It uses a *drift net which is shot by the drifter, which then lies at the *leeward end of the net, drifting with it, until is time to haul the net in.

Drifters are essentially fishing boats which operate in home waters, and are found mainly in the North Sea and around the coasts of Scotland and Ireland, but they are also common in other parts of the world. See also FISHERIES.

drift net or, more correctly, a **drift of nets,** a long shallow net or series of nets buoyed on the top edge with cork or with glass or plastic balls and weighted along the bottom edge with pieces of lead. Operated by a *drifter, it hangs vertically downwards in the sea from the surface to a depth of 12–15 metres (40–50 ft). It is employed mainly in relatively shallow waters and is the means of taking *fish which do not normally lie on the bottom, of which the more usual types are *herring, mackerel, and pilchard. See also FISHERIES.

drive, to. **(1)** A ship drives when its anchor fails to hold the ground it is at the mercy of wind and *tide. In the case of a sailing vessel, it drives to *leeward when the force of the wind is so great that it cannot be controlled by sails or *rudder. In a full *gale, too violent for the sails to be hoisted, the ship drives under *bare poles before the wind. Similarly, a powered vessel will drive before the wind if its engines are broken down or are not powerful enough to hold it against the wind.

> She drove in the dark to leeward,
> She struck, not a reef or a rock,
> But the combs of a smother of sand. Night drew her
> Dead to the Kentish Knock.
> (G. M. Hopkins, 'The Wreck of the Deutschland')

(2) In modern parlance to drive a ship or *yacht is to *steer her.

driver. **(1)** A sail in the form of a *studding sail set to augment, and sometimes replace, the *spanker. In its original form, about 1700, it was a narrow sail hoisted to the *peak of a *loose-footed *mizzen with a short *jackyard and sheeted independently to an *outrigger extended from the *poop. When used with a boomed spanker the driver used a lower *yard, and was sheeted directly to the *boom end. Development included the use of a large light sail set with the spanker *furled. **(2)** A term sometimes used for the spanker especially if the boom extends over the *transom.

drogue, usually an improvised contraption by which a sailing vessel is slowed down in a following sea to prevent it being *pooped by *waves coming up *astern. It can vary from a long *warp towed astern in small sailing craft to a *spar with a weighted sail in larger sailing ships. A drogue is very widely confused with a *sea anchor, but in fact the two serve different purposes. Sir Francis *Drake used a drogue

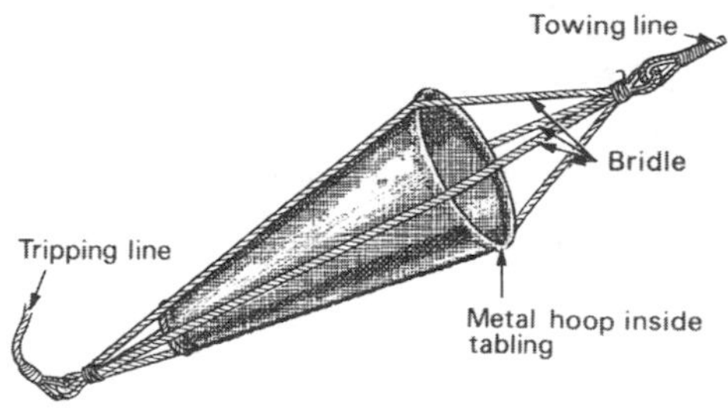

A drogue

comprised of wineskins in the *Golden Hinde* when chasing the *treasure ship *Cacafuego* in the Pacific as he did not wish to alarm its crew by coming up to it too fast. Also, when an open boat approaches the shore through breakers, a *grass-line over the stern acts as an efficient drogue, both slowing the boat down and holding it steady so that the waves do not turn it broadside to the beach so that it *capsizes.

dromon, or **dromond,** a large vessel of the Mediterranean which operated between the 9th and 15th centuries. Byzantine in origin, the name was at first used to denote a royal ship, but came into general use as describing any very large ship propelled by many *oars and with a single mast and a large square sail. They were used principally for trade or as transports in war.

drop keel. **(1)** A portion of the keel in early *submarines which could be detached in emergency to give additional buoyancy. By releasing this portion of the keel, usually weighing up to about 20 tons, a submerged submarine had a chance of returning to the surface if it could not regain positive buoyancy by any other means. It was released by a mechanism within the pressure hull. As the submarine developed into more reliable forms, the drop keel was omitted from the design. **(2)** A term often used to describe a *centreboard or *dagger plate.

drown the miller, to, an old expression much used by sailors in the Royal Navy during the days of sail to indicate that more than the statutory amount of water had been mixed with the rum in the daily ration of *grog. The statutory mixture was three parts of water to one part of rum, but some *pursers were tempted to 'drown the miller' to make the rum go further, pocketing the difference in value.

drumhead, the top part of the barrel of a *capstan, in which are the square pigeon-holes to take the ends of the capstan bars when an anchor, before the days of *auxiliary power, had to be *weighed, or a heavy weight lifted, by hand.

dry-dock, a watertight basin, with one end, which can be closed and sealed by a *caisson, open to the sea, in which ships can be docked for repair, examination, or cleaning of the underwater body. When a ship is to enter a dry-dock, the dock is flooded, the caisson withdrawn, and the ship floated in and held in position so that its keel is immediately above the lines of blocks prearranged on the floor of the dock. The caisson is replaced and the water in the dock pumped out, and the ship's keel settles on the blocks to support the weight of the hull as the water level falls. After the repair or cleaning of the ship, the dock is flooded, lifting the ship off the blocks, the caisson is withdrawn, and the ship is floated out. See also FLOATING DOCK; GRAVING DOCK.

dub, or **dubb, to,** the operation of smoothing away a plank with an *adze to make it suitable for use in planking the sides or deck of a wooden vessel under construction. The operation of taking a thin cut with an adze on the side planking of an existing ship in order to examine the condition of the wood was also known as dubbing. See also SHIPBUILDING.

ducking at the yardarm, an early form of naval punishment said to be first instituted by the French for blasphemy, sedition, or desertion. 'The ducking at the main *yard-arm is when a malefactor,' wrote Captain Nathaniel Boteler (*c.*1577–*c.*1643) in his manuscript *A Dialogicall Discourse Concerning Marine Affaires* (1634), 'by having a rope fastened under his arms and about his middle and under his breech, is thus hoisted up to the end of the yard and from thence is violently let fall into the sea, sometimes three several times one after another, and if the offence be very foul, he is also drawn under the keel of the ship, which is termed *keel-hauling. And while he is thus under water a great gun is fired right over his head, the which is done as well to astonish him so much the more with the thunder of the shot, as to give warning unto all others of the fleet to look out and be wary by his harms.'

These forms of punishment went out of fashion in most navies at about the end of the 17th century, being superseded by the less elaborate but more brutal form of punishment with the *cat-o'-nine-tails or by *cobbing.

'duck up', an order used in the sailing navies to haul on the *clew lines and clew garnets of the mainsail and *foresail so that the man at the wheel could see where the ship was going. The same term was used in the case of a *spritsail when a warship was chasing an enemy and wished to fire her forward *chase guns, as the spritsail would obscure the line of sight. 'Duck up the clew lines', hoist the clews (bottom corners) of the lower sails to provide a clear view forward.

dugout, the primitive form of a *canoe consisting of a tree trunk hollowed out by burning or other means. The two ends were sometimes roughly pointed. They were propelled in the earliest days presumably by the hands of the occupant, later by paddles when these were developed during the third millennium BC. Such primitive canoes are still in use in some South Pacific Islands and the West Indies, and by some riverine inhabitants of Central and South America.

DUKW, the code letters used for a military amphibious vehicle developed during the Second World War (1939–45) capable of being driven normally on land and across rivers and estuaries. Its official description was Amphibian Vehicle All-Wheel Drive Dual Rear Axle.

Dulcibella, the name of the small *yacht in the classic novel *The Riddle of the Sands*, by Erskine Childers (1870–1922), which was published in 1903. She was a converted lifeboat. See also MARINE LITERATURE.

dumb barge, a barge which has no power.

dunnage, loose wood or wooden blocks used in the *holds of the old-fashioned cargo ship. They were employed to secure the cargo above the *floors and away from the ship's sides to protect it from any sweating of the ship's plates, and also to wedge it firmly so that it did not get thrown about in a heavy sea. *Container ships and containerization have replaced the old methods of transporting cargo. See also FARDAGE.

dwt, see TONNAGE.

'dynaship', a project launched during the 1970s in Germany to examine the possibility of using wind as the main motive power for merchant vessels. The proposition was to reintroduce *square-rigged ships of up to 17,000 tonnes as *bulk carriers with an aerodynamically designed sail plan allied to a mechanical means of handling it. The main impetus behind this project was fear over the cost and scarcity of oil, but none was ever built. However, the technology was later purchased by a yachtsman who in 2005 launched a 87.2-metre (286-ft) three-masted square-rigger on the same principles. It has an *unstayed rig which should allow it to sail as *close hauled as a *Bermudan rig.

eagre, see BORE.

earing, a small rope used to fasten the upper corners of a square sail to its *yard. The outer turns of the earings, after being passed through the head *cringles on the sail, are then passed beyond the *lifts and rigging on the *yardarm and are designed to stretch the *head of the sail tight along the yard, while the remaining turns, known as inner turns, draw the sail close up to the yard and are passed within the lifts. Below the earings are the reef earings, by which the reef cringles are similarly made fast to the yard when the sail is *reefed.

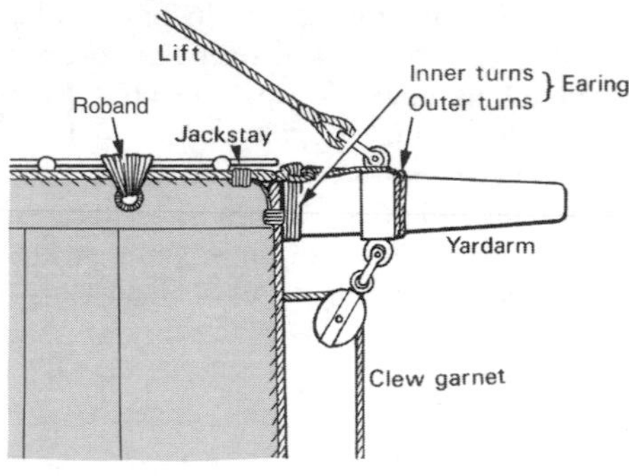

Earing

ease, to, or **easy,** a good maritime term meaning, in general, to take the pressure off. A sailing ship, on the order to 'ease her', is *luffed, to reduce the wind pressure on her sails in a heavy blow; the *helm in a powered vessel is eased by reducing the angle previously ordered, so as to reduce the rate of swing; and so on. Similarly, in sailing *yachts, the sheets are eased, sometimes to take the pressure off the sail to reduce the angle of heel, at others to produce a squarer aspect of the sail to the wind.

East India Company, the name of eight incorporated companies for the exploitation of trade in India, the East Indies, and the Far East. They were formed in England, Holland, France, Denmark, Scotland, Spain, Austria, and Sweden, but only the first three were of any importance. They built magnificent ships, called *East Indiamen, with which to trade and fight off competitors.

English East India Company. The English organization, known as the Honourable East India Company but also colloquially as 'John Company', was founded towards the end of the 15th century and was incorporated by Elizabeth I by royal charter on 31 December 1600. It was formed with a capital of £72,000 subscribed by 125 shareholders, and was founded to share in the East Indies spice trade. This had been a Spanish and Portuguese monopoly until the defeat of the *Spanish Armada in 1588 had weakened the hold of these countries on the lucrative commodities it produced. The first governor was Sir Thomas Smythe, and the early voyages, known as 'separate' voyages, were made by individual shareholders who bore the cost and took the profit from them, but from 1612 onwards all voyages were made by the company as a whole. During these years the company's ships reached as far as Japan, where friendly relations were established, and trading centres, or factories as they were called, were created on the coasts of India.

The company's early trading ventures were rigorously opposed by the Dutch East India Company, and a state of virtual war existed between the two. In 1619 an agreement was reached to stop these disputes, but it lasted for only one hour, recriminations and fighting breaking out as soon as the smoke from the saluting guns had cleared. This period of fighting reached its peak in 1623 with the massacre of Amboyna, where English merchants, though protected by a flag of truce, were tortured and killed by the Dutch governor. Despite this opposition the company was successful from the start, and it was given further impetus by

Charles II, who enlarged its charter by giving it the right to acquire territory, exercise civil and criminal jurisdiction, make treaties, wage war, command armies, and issue its own money.

With the company already established in India after the defeat of the Portuguese there, it became only a matter of time before the whole country was subdued and the various native rulers brought under the company's control; and when Robert Clive's victory at Plassey in 1757 resulted in the takeover of Bengal, the British government began to intervene. Over the next decades it ensured that the top company appointments became subject to its approval, and gradually through this means political, financial, and military control passed to it.

In 1813 the trade with India was thrown open to public competition, though the company was allowed to retain its monopoly of trade with China, a situation which only lasted until 1833. At the start of the 19th century it had financed the tea trade by illegally exporting opium to China, and this eventually caused the Opium Wars (1839–42 and 1856–60) which China lost, and which led to Britain acquiring several treaty ports and favourable trading rights.

The opening of the eastern trade routes for ships of other companies spelt the end of the East India Company as a trading monopoly, though it was still allowed to govern India. This it continued to do until the outbreak of the Indian Mutiny at Meerut in 1857. This forced the British government to step in and take over the civil administration, and in 1873 the company was wound up. See also ADAMS, WILLIAM.

Dutch East India Company. The Verenigde Oostindische Compagnie (VOG) was founded by charter from the States-General in 1602 to regulate and amalgamate all the various Dutch trading ventures to the East Indies already in existence. It was directed in Holland by local boards for each province of the States-General acting under a main directorate of seventeen members elected by the local boards. It was granted a monopoly of the East Indian trade, exempted from import taxes, and authorized to maintain armed forces, erect forts, make war or peace, and coin its own money.

Its early history is mainly a history of warfare, driving out of the East Indies first the Portuguese and then the English. It established its main capital in Batavia (now Djakarta), with subsidiary capitals in the Malay Archipelago, Ceylon, Malacca, Amboyna, and Ternate, with a fortified post at the Cape of Good Hope to ensure the safety of the route to and from Holland.

At the height of its success, which lasted for most of the 17th century, the company possessed 40 warships, 150 merchant ships, and 10,000 soldiers. But it held in its own success the seeds of its ultimate decline. Its policy in the East Indies was total monopoly of trade, maintained by force of arms when required, and this inevitably led to rivalry and hostility with the English and French interests in the area. By the early 18th century it had been driven from the mainland of Asia and from Ceylon, and vanishing profits, combined with a big increase in military costs, brought eventual bankruptcy, and in 1799 the company was officially wound up after Holland was invaded by the French revolutionary armies.

The Dutch also founded a West India Company, in 1621, but this was more interested in its *privateers, which attacked Spanish shipping, and the *slave trade than in ordinary commercial activities. For a time it successfully attacked Spanish and Portuguese colonies in the New World, and it also established colonies of its own there. One of these, New Netherland, was established in 1624 at what is now Albany after Henry *Hudson visited it in 1609 while employed by the Dutch East India Company. However, in 1664 it was captured by the British who renamed it New York State.

French East India Company. Formed in 1664, the French East India Company, Compagnie des Indes Orientales, was established by Louis XIV's finance minister, Jean-Baptiste Colbert. It traded under several different names during its existence and was in constant confrontation with the Dutch and English. It founded the French colony of Mauritius in 1721, and that of Mahé in Malabar (India) three years later. Its ablest leader was Joseph-François Dupleix who in 1742 was appointed governor-general of French India, the capital of which was Pondicherry. Dupleix waged open war with the British in India but Pondicherry was eventually captured by the British during the Seven Years War (1756–63). It never had the same support from its government or merchants as the English company and its monopoly of trade with India was ended in 1769. It ceased to exist in 1789.

East Indiamen, the name given to the ships of the various *East India companies. The great national importance of these companies, particularly those of England and Holland, coupled with the rich returns of their monopoly of trade in the East, resulted in the building of proud and magnificent ships, as much for national and company prestige as for the actual trade. Ships of these companies, as large as any built in the world, were highly gilded and decorated with carving, and were finished internally as much for comfort and luxury for the officers and passengers as for cargo capacity. They were always armed as warships for protection against *piracy and against the warships of other nations, and were very effective not only at protecting themselves but at taking the fight to the enemy as did the one commanded by John Paul *Jones.

In 1609 the English company built its own *dockyard at Deptford, on the River Thames, where its East Indiamen were built, and the Dutch company also had its own dockyard. It was only in the 19th century, when the monopoly of eastern trade began to be eroded by private competition, that the British company gave its *shipbuilding to outside interests, the greater part of it to the Blackwall yard of Green and Wigram.

Throughout the long histories of the individual companies, East Indiamen were regarded as the *ne plus ultra* of the shipping world. See also REPLICA SHIP.

ebb, the flow of the tidal stream as it recedes, from the ending of the period of *slack water at high *tide to the start of the period of slack water at low tide. Its period is about six hours, which is approximately divided into three parts: the first two hours being known as the first of the ebb, the middle two hours as the strength of the ebb, and the last two hours as the last of the ebb. It is also used as a verb. See also FLOOD.

echinoderms, a group of invertebrate animals including starfish (asteroids), sea urchins (echinoids), sea cucumbers (holothurians), brittle stars (ophuiroids), and sea lilies (crinoids). The basic design of the bodies is a radial symmetry with five arms as seen in starfish. They have internal skeletons constructed of plates of calcium carbonate elaborately slotted together. This skeleton provides support for their unique mode of movement based on tube feet. Each tube foot is a tiny, extensible, tubular structure that ends in a sucker and is powered by a hydraulic system. Individually, these are weak, but when acting in concert they are remarkably powerful.

Starfish are mostly predatory and can pull apart the shells of a clam far enough to evert their stomach into the victim and start to digest its flesh *in situ*. The most notorious starfish is the crown of thorns (*Acanthaster planci*) which eats the soft tissue of corals and causes considerable damage to *coral reefs. They are nocturnal, but if found should be handled with great care because their spines are poisonous.

Most other types of echinoderm either eat *seaweeds or feed on detritus by filtering water, or by swallowing mud. Many **sea urchins** graze on seaweeds using the teeth of the Aristotle's Lantern, the elaborate mouthparts on the underside of the body. Others burrow in sand and mud and have become asymmetric; the sand dollars (e.g. *Mellita* spp.) for example are very flattened and bury themselves just beneath the surface of clean sandy beaches. In the kelp forests fringing the coasts of California, sea urchins feed on the kelp and in turn are eaten by a *marine mammal, the sea otter. In some species of urchins the gonads, which hang around the insides of the shells like washing, are considered to be delicacies by gourmets. Urchins are also exploited for their shells, which are cleaned and sold to tourists as souvenirs. Many sea urchins need to be handled carefully, as the long spines of some readily break off and cause festering wounds, and others can inflict painful stings using special clawlike structures.

Sea cucumbers, which are almost devoid of any traces of radial symmetry, are more wormlike in their feeding behaviour. They either burrow in the sediment or crawl over the seabed, feeding by either swallowing mud or filtering particles from the water. A few deep-water species can swim. They are often abundant in the *lagoons on the landward side of coral *reefs. In Asia and Mediterranean countries they are collected, dried, and eaten as trepang or bêche-de-mer.

Brittle stars move by rowing themselves along using their arms, and feed on small food items. In areas where there is a rich supply of food they can form thick layers of animals several centimetres thick. **Basket stars** (*Astroboa* spp.) can be nearly a metre across and their writhing arms are repeatedly divided and used to trap particles suspended in the water.

Sea lilies either have their bodies on the end of long stalks or have clawlike appendages so that they sit with their mouths uppermost and use their long arms to entrap fine food particles from the water. Their limy skeletons preserve well and so there is a rich fossil record of echinoderms that stretches back 600 million years to the Cambrian era. M. V. Angel

echo sounder, an instrument based on the principle of *sonar by which the depth of water under a vessel's keel can be measured. By using a vertical sonar pulse and measuring the time taken between emission of the signal and the receipt of the echo off the bottom, the depth of water can be accurately calculated. For multi-beam echo sounders see HYDROGRAPHY: HYDROGRAPHY TODAY.

ecliptic, from the Greek *ekleipsis*, disappearance, the apparent path of the sun among the stars which is a *great circle inclined to the celestial equator at an angle of about 2° 27'. It is so named because, for an eclipse of the sun or moon to occur, the moon must lie on or near the ecliptic. It intersects the celestial equator, or *equinoctial, twice during the year at the equinoxes; on 21 March at the 'first point of Aries', which is 0° Right Ascension, and on 23 September at the 'first point of Libra', at 180° Right Ascension, and is furthest from the equator (23° 23' N., or S.) at the points marking the summer solstice (June) and winter solstice (December).

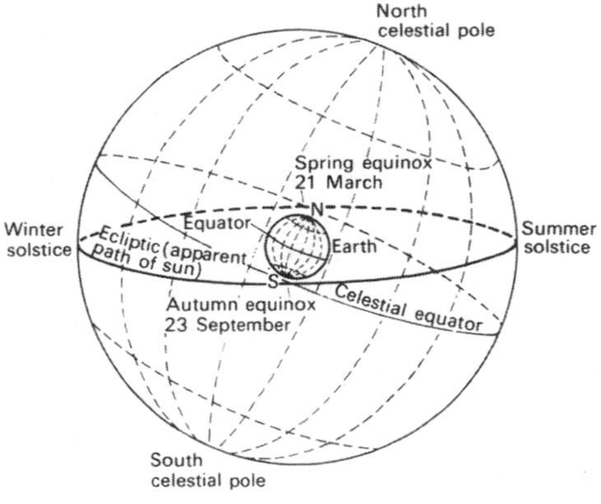

Ecliptic

eddy, a spiralling movement of water which occur at all spatial scales, from a few centimetres up to hundreds or even thousands of kilometres. Eddies play an important role in transferring heat and energy horizontally and vertically both in the ocean and in the atmosphere. In the ocean they contain far more dynamic energy than similar-sized features in the atmosphere, because water is so much denser than air. Mesoscale eddies in the oceans are tens to hundreds of kilometres across and can extend all the way to the bottom, where they generate disturbances known as 'benthic storms'. The tracks they follow are often 'steered' by the presence of seamounts and islands (see GEOLOGICAL OCEANOGRAPHY), and are equivalent to cyclones and anticyclones in the atmosphere. In the northern hemisphere those that spiral anticlockwise are analogous to depressions. They have lower *sea level and cooler water in their centres or cores. Conversely those that spiral clockwise are analogous to anticyclones and have higher sea levels and warm water in their cores. Changes in sea level associated with mesoscale eddies can be detected by *remote sensing. Meandering *fronts fringe the edges of these features.

Some of the most dramatic eddies are generated from the *Gulf Stream and the Kuroshio Current. Periodically, meanders in these currents pinch off to form ring structures. On the western landward side the rings are anticyclonic and introduce warm water into the cooler coastal seas. On the eastern side the rings are cyclonic, with a core of water from the main flow of the current wrapped around by a band of cold water from off the shelf water, which move out into the warm *Sargasso Sea. In the north-west Atlantic up to five cold core rings may be present at any one time. The fate of most of these eddies is to become reabsorbed back into the main flow of the Gulf Stream, but a few stay clear and persist for at least two years.

Other remarkable eddies are spawned from the deep outflow of relatively warm and salty Mediterranean water issuing from the Strait of Gibraltar. They consist of packets (boluses) of water that are confined to depths greater than about 500 metres (150 ft). They have no surface signatures, but have been tracked using neutrally buoyant floats drifting in their cores which are tracked acoustically from the sound signals they produce when they receive an appropriately coded sound signal. Most 'Meddies', as these boluses are called, move northwards, but a few move to the south-west and have been detected in the Sargasso Sea across the other side of the Atlantic. For illus. see CURRENTS; GULF STREAM. M. V. Angel

eels belong to the Anguilliformes, an order of *fishes with nineteen families that typically have snakelike bodies and a serpentine mode of moving. Most marine eels live on the seabed, but there are some extraordinary midwater species like gulper eels (e.g. *Eurypharynx* spp.). Cutthroat eels (*Synathobranchus* spp.) are attracted in large numbers to baited cameras deployed on the bottom at abyssal depths (>4,000 m/13,000 ft). Conger eels (*Conger conger*) are large predatory inhabitants of rocky areas that are frequently caught by anglers. The many species of moray eel (family Muraenidae) inhabit *coral reefs where they hunt fish and *Crustacea like crabs. The best-known eels are the *Anguilla* species (of which there are seventeen species). The European eel (*Anguilla anguilla*) lives most of its life in fresh water, but breeds in deep water somewhere in the *Sargasso Sea, no one is quite sure where. It evolved about 60 million years ago when the Atlantic was still quite narrow, but ever since has been steadily opening up 1–2 millimetres a year. So the larvae, which once had a journey of a few hundred kilometres to get to European rivers, now have to travel 4,800 kilometres (3000 mls.).

A newly hatched eel larva is known as a leptocephalus. It has an elongated flat leaflike body that is highly transparent. It is a weak swimmer, and takes about three years to drift across the Atlantic in the flow of the *Gulf Stream. Somehow the larvae find their way into estuaries, where they metamorphose into elvers. When they first enter the estuaries the elvers are still transparent and are known as glass eels, but soon become black. On high spring *tides elvers migrate, en masse, upstream keeping close to the banks. They even cross land during wet weather. They live in streams and rivers for about three years growing to over a metre in length. Then they migrate back to the sea, again metamorphosing to become silvery with enlarged eyes. It is not known how they find their way back to the Sargasso Sea to spawn, but it is likely they ride the return flow of the *current gyre. The numbers of elvers returning to European rivers are reported to be diminishing, which may reflect subtle changes in the currents of the North Atlantic.

Fort, T., *The Book of Eels* (2002). M. V. Angel

electric propulsion is basically the driving of a ship's *propeller shaft by an electric motor, with the electric power for it being produced in one or more generators driven by *steam propulsion, *diesel engines using residual fuel oil, or *gas turbines. Early electric propulsion systems used direct current but modern systems use alternating current. With early alternating current systems the electric motor speed was changed by changing the speed of the alternator, and the direction was changed by means of switchgear. This meant that the propulsion electrical generation system had to be separate from the system serving the rest of the ship. With a modern alternating current system the same electrical generation plant generates power for the propulsion motors and the rest of the ship. The propulsion motor generally runs at a constant speed and the speed and direction of the ship are changed by means of a controllable pitch *propeller.

The French *ocean liner *Normandie* was fitted with electric propulsion, the generators being driven by steam turbines, a type of installation known as **turbo-electric**. The advantage of this is that there is no need for long intermediate shafts from the turbine, or diesel engine, to the propeller shaft, thus increasing the space available for cargo or other machinery. Also, unlike the conventional system, only the propulsion motor, not the machinery driving it, has to be in line with the propeller shaft. This means that the machinery can be located where convenient and, particularly in the case of passenger ships, it allows for large open space areas in the middle of the ship. The P&O liner *Canberra* had a turbo-electric propulsion system located at the after end of the ship with boilers and turbines above the propulsion motors.

The USA has had considerably more experience with electrical systems than Europe and has used electric propulsion for many years in many types of ship. The *aircraft carriers *Lexington* and *Saratoga*, built in 1927, had electric propulsion as did many American-built merchant ships of the period, including the Second World War (1939–45) T2 *tankers. Today, electric propulsion is used extensively in cruise ships, the installations being the diesel electric type where a number of medium-speed diesel engines, each driving an alternator, supply electrical power. This electrical power is then used for the propulsion motors and the ship's hotel services, a transformer reducing the voltage of the electrical supply to serve the hotel needs. Large cruise ships need a lot of power for services such as lighting and air conditioning. So some of them, including *Queen Mary 2*, also have gas turbines which drive alternators to supplement their diesel-driven alternators.

Denis Griffiths

electronic charts, see CHARTMAKING: MODERN CHARTMAKING.

El Niño is a phenomenon that occurs every three to seven years in the Pacific Ocean. During a normal year sea temperatures warm up briefly during the Christmas season off the coasts of Peru and Ecuador (El Niño is Spanish for the infant Jesus). However, during an El Niño these warm temperatures persist for many months, coinciding with aberrant changes in air pressure and wind patterns throughout the southern Pacific, known as El Niño Southern Oscillations (ENSOs). Periodically, the Intertropical Convergence Zone (ITCZ) in the atmosphere, which normally sits over the Indonesian region, migrates eastwards over the central Pacific. The ITCZ is a zone of high atmospheric pressure where the rising air triggers heavy

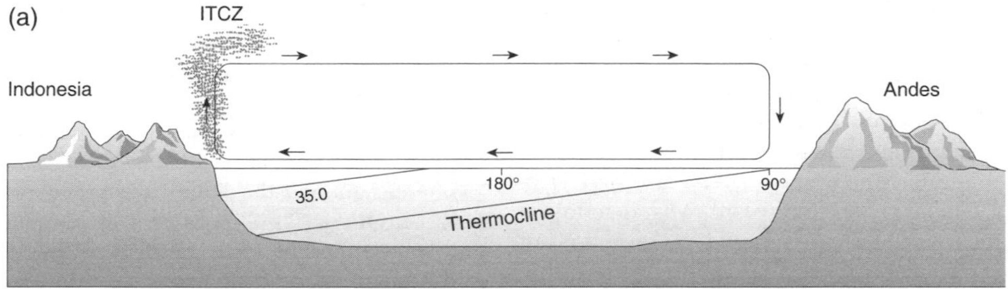

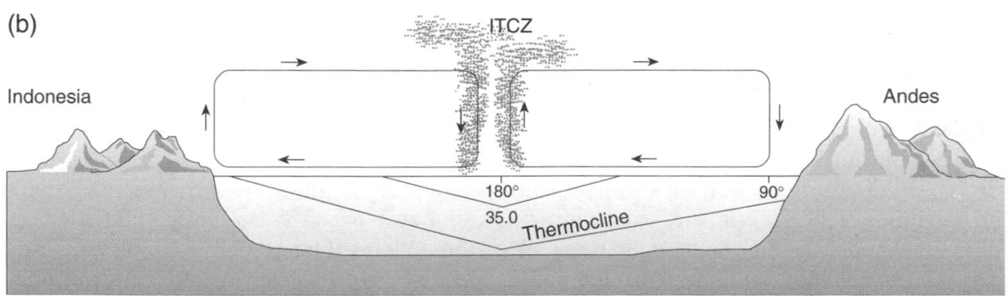

El Niño events are triggered by the Intertropical Convergence Zone (ITCZ) shifting eastwards from its usual position over Indonesia (a) into the central Pacific (b)

rainfall and high air temperatures. This warms the ocean surface and triggers a planetary *wave that travels eastwards. This wave is slow moving and takes about a year to cross the Pacific along the equator. Its effect is to deepen the *thermocline so that the *upwelling that occurs along the equator no longer brings cool nutrient-rich water from below the thermocline up to the surface. Normally the cool waters that occur off the coasts of Peru and Ecuador are not only highly productive, but they also keep the coastal climate arid.

During an El Niño event the major *fishery for anchovetta (*Centegraulis mysticetus*), normally one of the biggest in the world, collapses and there are mass mortalities of *seabirds, such as pelicans and guanay cormorants, whose droppings were the main source of nitrates used to manufacture the gunpowder used in 19th-century European wars. The warm seas also trigger heavy rainfall over the normally arid coastal regions, resulting in disastrous flooding. When the planetary wave encounters the continental margin of America it is diverted both north and south, resulting in similarly anomalous warm seas and heavy rainfall along the normally arid coasts of North and South America. The repercussions are felt in other regions such as South Africa, India, and South-East Asia, where seasonal rains fail resulting in disastrous droughts and human misery.

The El Niño events of 1982 and 1997 were the most extreme on record. What determines the irregular occurrences of ENSO events is not understood, but many scientists believe that the recent increase in their frequency and severity is one expression of global *climate change. If this is indeed so then these events may become the norm with severe implications for human societies. See also ENVIRONMENTAL ISSUES.

www.ogp.noaa.gov/enso/ M. V. Angel

embargo, a temporary arrest or injunction laid on ships or cargo to prevent their arrival or departure in time of war. An embargo can be general, affecting all ships of whatever nationality, or partial, in which only ships of certain nationalities are affected. Originally embargoes could be declared in anticipation of a declaration of war, a method used by many nations to detain ships belonging to the enemy that might be in port. However, in the Hague Convention of 1907, a clause laid down that it was desirable that ships in an enemy port on the outbreak of war should be allowed to depart freely but did not make it binding on the belligerent. A ship stopped by embargo may not be confiscated but only detained without compensation, and must be restored to its owners after the war. It was customary to give a respite to enemy merchant ships to leave port on the outbreak of war so that neither ship nor cargo is subject to embargo.

embark, to, has three meanings: **(1)** to put on board a vessel, **(2)** to go on board a vessel, and **(3)** of a ship, to receive on board. **Embarkation**, the process or action of embarking.

engines, See AUXILIARY; COMPOUND ENGINE; DIESEL ENGINE; DONKEY ENGINE; GAS-TURBINE ENGINE; MONKEY(S); RECIPROCATING ENGINE; SIDE LEVER ENGINE; STEAM PROPULSION; TRIPLE EXPANSION ENGINE; WALKING BEAM ENGINE. See also CONDENSER.

ensign. (1) The national flag as worn by the ships of a nation. Some countries use two ensigns, one for naval ships and one for merchant vessels. However, since the division of the British fleet by *squadronal colours was abolished in 1864, British ships have always flown three different types of ensign: the *red ensign, the *white ensign, and the *blue ensign. See also FLAG ETIQUETTE. **(2)** A naval rank in the US, and some other, navies equivalent to that of midshipman or sub-lieutenant.

enter, to. (1) To sign on voluntarily for service in the Royal Navy, in the days of *impressment. It has been fairly reliably estimated that from about one-third to one-half of the seamen enrolled during these years entered voluntarily, the remainder being supplied by the *press gangs and the Quota Acts. These were passed in the British Parliament in March 1795, under the stress of the Revolutionary War against France (1793–1801), to provide seamen for the Royal Navy. The number varied widely from ship to ship, according to the popularity or otherwise of her captain and the nature of the service to which she was ordered. It varied, too, according to current naval successes in battle, a notable victory being frequently followed by a surge in voluntary recruitment. **(2)** To board an enemy ship. A boarding party, or *boarders, enters the enemy, after his deck has been cleared as much as possible with fire or *stinkpots. 'It happens many times that there are more men lost in a minute by entering than in long fight board by board.' Mainwaring, *The Seaman's Dictionary* (1644). **(3) Entering ladder**, the wooden steps fixed up the side of a sailing warship level with the *waist. They led to the **entry port** (or entering port) which was cut down on the middle gun-deck of the old three-decker *ships of the line, by which seamen came on board from a boat lying alongside, or through which they boarded an enemy ship. **(4) Entering rope**, a rope which hung down the ship's side alongside the entering ladder to assist men coming on board. **(5) Entering** or **entered**, a term which indicates that the *master of a ship which has arrived from a foreign port has sworn the contents of his ship's papers before the customs authorities.

Enterprize, a 275-ton, 43-metre (141-ft) wooden *paddle steamer, launched at Deptford in 1825. She was noteworthy for making the first long passage where *steam propulsion was used to a significant extent. In 1823 the Indian government offered a prize of 20,000 rupees for whoever established a regular steamship route between England and Calcutta before the end of 1826, provided the voyage took no more than 70 days. *Enterprize* was built to challenge for this prize. Apart from the *lugger sails on her three masts, she was powered by *side lever engines of 120 nominal horsepower, and her owners had fitted her with a copper boiler, in the hope that it would stand the strain of the long voyage better than an iron one. She left Falmouth on 16 August 1825 with seventeen passengers aboard, but only managed to steam for 64 of the 113 days the voyage took via Cape Town. She was bought by the Indian government, and the owners were awarded half the prize, but she was never used for the mail service the Indian government required. She was broken up in 1838.

entrepôt, often used, but now fallen into disuse, to describe the particular type of trade of a port. The strict meaning of the word was a place to which goods were brought for distribution to other parts of the world. When used in connection with a port it was generally taken to mean the centre to which manufacturers or produce was brought for export. However, it was frequently used to indicate trade in the opposite direction; a port was said to be an entrepôt for the goods imported from overseas for distribution in its immediate neighbourhood.

entry, the form of the fore-body of a ship under the load line as it thrusts through the sea. A ship, or a *yacht, with a slim bow is said to have a **fine entry**. It is in many ways the complement of *run. See also SHIPBUILDING.

environmental issues. Mankind has continually abused the sea, regarding it as an inexhaustible source of food and minerals, and a dumping ground for rubbish. Now it is more widely accepted that the oceans are finite, and there is a need to use and manage them carefully, especially as globally environmental pressures are mounting because of the burgeoning human population. *Pollution is important enough to be discussed separately.

Carbon Dioxide. Regarded by some people as a pollutant, this is a key substance in natural cycles and so cannot be treated like man-made substances. As a greenhouse gas, increasing concentrations of carbon dioxide in the atmosphere threaten *climate change globally, modify ocean circulation, and so reduce the viability of many marine species. Sharp reductions in emissions per capita (>60%) are needed to avoid irreversible changes, bearing in mind the rate at which the human population is growing and future industrial expansion by the developing world, especially China. No one of the suite of solutions, which range from improving energy efficiency and switching to renewable energy sources, to capturing carbon dioxide and storing it somewhere—for instance, in deep geological deposits that formerly contained *offshore oil and gas—is likely to be sufficient.

Over-exploitation of Living Resources. This is now a growing and controversial problem. *Fish, *shellfish, and, in Asia, *seaweeds are important sources of food, particularly in developing countries. Improvements in technology for locating and catching fish, and the considerable post-war expansion of commercial *fisheries, resulted in fish catches peaking at over 100 million tonnes a year in 2000. But these catches are now declining, and the evidence is that the majority of fish stocks are either over-exploited, or close to being so. A seemingly logical solution is to develop farming techniques for fish and certain *Crustacea, such as shrimps. However, these place a high demand on coastal areas and lead to habitat destruction and degradation, notably of the *mangrove swamps in the Far East. Providing suitable feed for such farms is also a problem. A substantial proportion of the million tonnes of sand *eels (*Ammodytes* sp.) caught by commercial fisheries in the North Sea gets used to feed not humans but poultry and farmed fishes.

Habitat Destruction and Alteration. This is a major environmental issue in places. In the tropics the clearance of mangrove swamps not only destroys the nursery feeding grounds of many fishes, but also makes the coastline vulnerable to flooding and *tsunami. In developed countries coastal defences, sea walls and groynes, alter coastal habitats and can result in coastal erosion elsewhere. Dredging shipping channels for deep-draught vessels like *container ships and *ro-ro ships, the building of port facilities, and removal of hazards to *navigation, all lead to small pieces of habitat loss that globally lead to massive losses of coastal environments. The biggest problem is associated with the urbanization of the coastline. Most of the world's megalopolises (cities with more than 10 million people) are sited on coastlines and there is a general migration of people to coastal environments; over half of all people now live within 60 kilometres (37 mls.) of the sea, putting enormous environmental pressure on coastal habitats, with all the concomitant pollution problems.

Non-living Resources. These include hydrocarbons, aggregates, and minerals such as phosphates and placers. The exploitation of hydrocarbons for fossil fuels has direct implications for the marine environment. Enormous quantities are shipped around the world, about 1,500 million tonnes annually. Accidents inevitably happen, and the big spills caused by the foundering of large *tankers such as the *Torrey Canyon*, *Exxon Valdez*, and *Prestige* are amongst a number of notorious events that have resulted in major environmental catastrophes, often in highly sensitive marine habitats. The firing of the oil wells and terminals during the 1991 Gulf War had an immense impact on the Persian Gulf. But such spectacularly awful events only result in the discharge of relatively small quantities of oil compared to the minor spills during the day-to-day operations of ports and offshore oil and gas facilities. These have a negligible effect on deep ocean habitats but have a serious impact on coastal and inshore environments, and on charismatic animals such as *seabirds and *marine mammals like sea otters.

The exploitation of mineral and aggregate resources, both from the sea and on the neighbouring land, also has considerable impact on the coastal seas. Diamonds are dredged from marine sands off Namibia, and tin from Malaysia. These, and other developing countries, mining for gems, precious metals, and iron minerals, generate large quantities of spoils and their disposal is a real problem. Land is becoming more and more important to conserve; discharging into rivers is almost always unacceptable, which leaves marine disposal as the least damaging option.

Dredging marine aggregates for building can be very damaging to marine habitats, though its overall impact may be less than using land deposits, especially when the impact of transporting the material to the site is taken into consideration. Delivery of aggregates by ship to a building site in central London or New York can be achieved with less disruption and environmental damage than by road.

Introduction of Exotic Species. This is an environmental issue that emerged in the 1990s, though the reasons for it go back much further. For example, the building of the *Suez Canal has resulted in the movement of many species from the Red Sea into the eastern Mediterranean, some of which, like large *sharks, are not popular newcomers. Another route is the expansion of shellfish culture, especially of oysters, in which the local stocks have been 'improved' by the introduction of larger, faster-growing species from far afield, often bringing with them pests and diseases that have subsequently run rampant. The growing popularity of keeping marine species in aquaria has also resulted in the importation of undesirable new species,

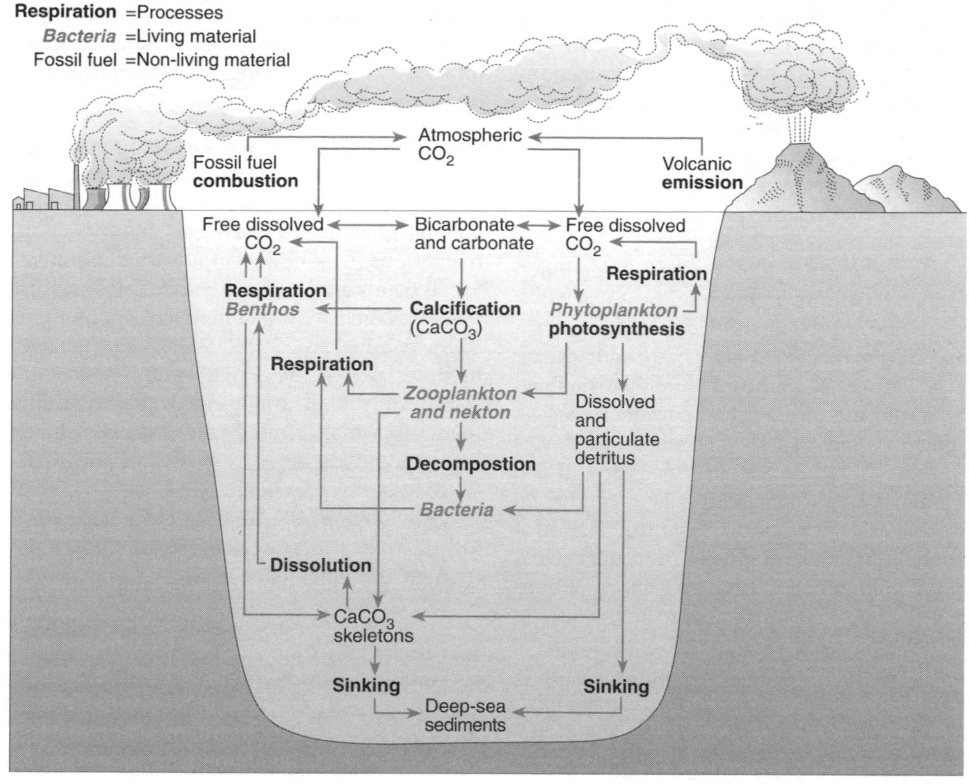

The basic scheme of the carbon cycle

the most notorious of these being the appearance of a vigorous sport of a highly invasive green seaweed, *Caulerpa*, beneath the windows of the marine aquarium in Monaco. This male sport can only reproduce by fragments of it being carried around by ships. However, once established it overgrows the local seaweed communities, drastically reducing the diversity, and destroying local fisheries. Not being able to breed sexually has been no bar to its dispersal; in two decades it has become established all round the western Mediterranean and is now in the eastern Mediterranean, most probably carried on the anchors of pleasure craft. Even more surprising has been its recent appearance in the seas off Japan, Australia, and California, in each case probably as a result of establishing marine aquaria.

However, the most serious introductions of exotic species have arrived in the *ballast water discharged from large *bulk carriers. Almost all the animals now inhabiting San Francisco Bay are species native to the seas off Japan rather than the Californian coast. Similarly, around many Australian ports returning large bulk carriers delivering iron ore to Japanese steel mills have brought back hundreds of unwanted and undesirable marine species in their ballast tanks. Most worrying are the large numbers of dinoflagellates that are implicated in *red tides. But many of the other species are able to out-compete and displace the native species because they arrive free of disease and the predators that normally keep them in check.

Eutrophication. The over-enrichment of environments with excessive amounts of organic matter and fertilizers coming from run-off from land and rivers. It results in excessive plant growth, and the plant and animal communities become dominated by just a few rampant species. These changes in ecology lead to reductions in the numbers of species present including many commercial fish species. They also lead to an increase in the frequency of red tides. *Coral reefs are particularly sensitive to the impacts of eutrophication, becoming overgrown with seaweeds and eventually dying. Eventually, under extreme conditions, overenrichment results in all the oxygen in the sediments being used up, and hydrogen sulphide and then methane is generated in the sediments, and creates dead zones, which are devoid of normal life. In 2004 the United Nations Environment Programme warned that 'dead zones' are being created in many waters—including parts of the Baltic, Irish, and Adriatic seas. The areas of these zones had doubled in the previous fifteen years and were becoming a greater threat to some fish stocks than overfishing.

Water. Water itself is the final environmental issue. In arid countries there is a proliferation of desalination plants to provide the water needed by the human population, agriculture, and industry. Locally, these increase the *salinity of the sea water and so alter the local pattern of *currents. On a global scale, however, the major impact is the interception of fresh water for irrigation schemes before it reaches the ocean. For this reason, some seas such as the Aral Sea have completely dried up. It is estimated that around 50% of all river discharges are now intercepted and used for irrigation. This is best illustrated by the building of the High Aswan Dam in Egypt. This single project decreased the freshwater inflow into the eastern Mediterranean by over half. In the short term, this resulted in the collapse of the delta fishery and substantial decline in the productivity of the offshore waters. In 2004, over 30 years after the completion of the dam, the currents in the eastern Mediterranean are changing and it is only a matter of time before the western Mediterranean will show signs of being affected as well. The environmental fallout cannot be predicted, but is likely to be deleterious to both marine communities and fisheries, and perhaps even to the tourists on the beaches. M. V. Angel

ephemeris, from the Greek word meaning a diary, a periodical astronomical almanac in which are tabulated the predicted celestial positions of the heavenly bodies on the *equinoctial system against a standard time. The *nautical almanac includes ephemerides for the sun, moon, planets, and 57 stars selected for their availability as well as other information of use to the *navigator.

EPIRB, or **Electronic Position Indicator Radio Beacon,** a small, floating, battery-operated, rescue device. Under the *Global Maritime Distress and Safety System regulations, it is now compulsory equipment for all commercial vessels, and for all seagoing *yachts. When activated manually, or automatically by a hydrostatic release switch triggered by water, it sends out a signal that is picked up by orbiting satellites or by search aircraft, which relay the signal to rescue services. The signal includes the identity, and owner, of the vessel so that authorities know what kind of ship they are looking for. Four hundred and six MHz EPIRBs transmit the device's geographical position to the emergency services using an internal *GPS instrument.

equinoctial, from the Latin *aequus*, equal, and *nox*, night, the *great circle on the *celestial sphere in the plane of the earth's equator, sometimes called the celestial equator. The sun is on the equinoctial on two occasions each year, these occurring on 21 March and 23 September, days known as the equinoxes. On these days the sun rises at 6 a.m. and sets at 6 p.m. (local time) at every place on earth. The two points of intersection of the equinoctial with the *ecliptic are called the spring and autumnal equinoctial points respectively, or more usually the first points of Aries and Libra for the spring and autumnal equinoxes.

The word is also used as an adjective to describe phenomena happening at or about the time of the equinox, e.g. equinoctial gales, equinoctial rains.

Erik the Red (*fl.* 985), Norse explorer, so called from the colour of his hair. He was forced to leave Norway, probably in the year 984, to escape trial for murder or manslaughter, and fled to Iceland. He was quickly in trouble again in Iceland and, hearing that another trader had sighted new land to the westward, decided to investigate. He verified its existence, gave it the name of Greenland, and returned to Iceland to persuade a group of people to join him in colonizing the new land which, at that time, was quite feasible because of *climate change. He returned to Greenland in the summer of 985 with a band of colonists, rounded Cape Farewell, and landed in Eriksfjord (near the present Julianehaab) where he founded the settlement of Brattahlid. It was from Greenland that his son Leif Eriksson (*fl.* 11th century) discovered *Vinland.

esnecca, or **snekkja,** a long *galley or *longship, propelled by *oar or sail, used by Scandinavian seamen as a warship probably between the 5th and 11th centuries. It is generally described as having twenty rowing benches, but occasionally up to 30 were fitted. The Scandinavian meaning of the word was snake, probably in reference to its extra length in comparison with the normal longship. No illustration of an esnecca is known to exist though it has been suggested that the ship incorporated in the seal of the city of Monmouth may be one.

Later, the word was used in England to describe a vessel belonging personally to the king in which he made voyages of state. Both Henry I and Henry II are recorded as having esneccas during the 12th century, the equivalent of a royal *yacht.

establishment of the port, the interval between the time of *meridian passage of the new or the full moon and the time of the following high *tide. This interval which is constant for a given port is also known as the High Water Full and Change constant (HWF & C). The average interval is known as the mean high water lunitidal interval. Because the tides are governed largely by the moon, and because the time of meridian passage of the moon is later each day by about 50 minutes, it follows that, if the *age of the moon and the establishment of the port are known, the approximate times of high and low water on any day may be found. If, for example, the HWF & C constant for a given port is 3 hours 45 minutes and the age of the moon is three days, the time of morning high water at the port will be approximately 0345 + (3 × 50) min. = 0615.

Eugenie, the name given to a woollen cap worn by seamen in the late 19th century in Arctic and Antarctic waters. The name originates from the caps presented by the ex-Empress Eugénie of France to every officer and man on board the *Alert* and *Discovery* during the Royal Navy's Arctic expedition of 1875.

evaporators are used at sea to produce distilled water from sea water. Though the **Sirius* was an exception, early steamships used sea water for boilers, but the salt scale caused loss of efficiency and the sea water was corrosive. Freshwater feed avoided these problems but there was a limit to how much fresh water a ship could conveniently carry. By the 1880s evaporators were fitted on ships to make distilled water from sea water, where the sea water was boiled and the vapour condensed to give distilled water. A modern ship, whether *tanker, *container ship, or *cruise ship, can meet all of its fresh water needs by making fresh water from sea water in an evaporator plant, though the water has to be treated in order to destroy all bacteria as this is not destroyed by the low temperature heating. Essential minerals must also be added as drinking distilled water is harmful.

Denis Griffiths

even keel. A vessel is said to be on an even keel when it floats exactly upright in the water without any *list on either side.

Exclusive Economic Zone (EEZ). The establishment of the EEZ under the *United Nations Conference on the Law of the Sea (UNCLOS) has had a profound effect on the exploitation of ocean resources. A coastal state has full sovereign rights over its *territorial waters, which extend 12 *nautical miles (22.2 km) offshore. It has jurisdictional rights to exploit and manage all resources in the water and on and beneath the seabed over an area extending 200 nautical miles (370 km) from its shore. About 87% of all known hydrocarbon reserves of *offshore oil and gas fields lie within EEZs, and the majority of the world's commercial *fish stocks are found within them. With these exclusive rights come responsibilities. Coastal states must manage the fish stocks in a sustainable way and are encouraged to share surpluses with landlocked states. They have to limit *pollution and other *environmental issues, and facilitate scientific research such as *oceanography. They are required to allow innocent right of passage through the EEZ to shipping, although they have the right to insist on ship-

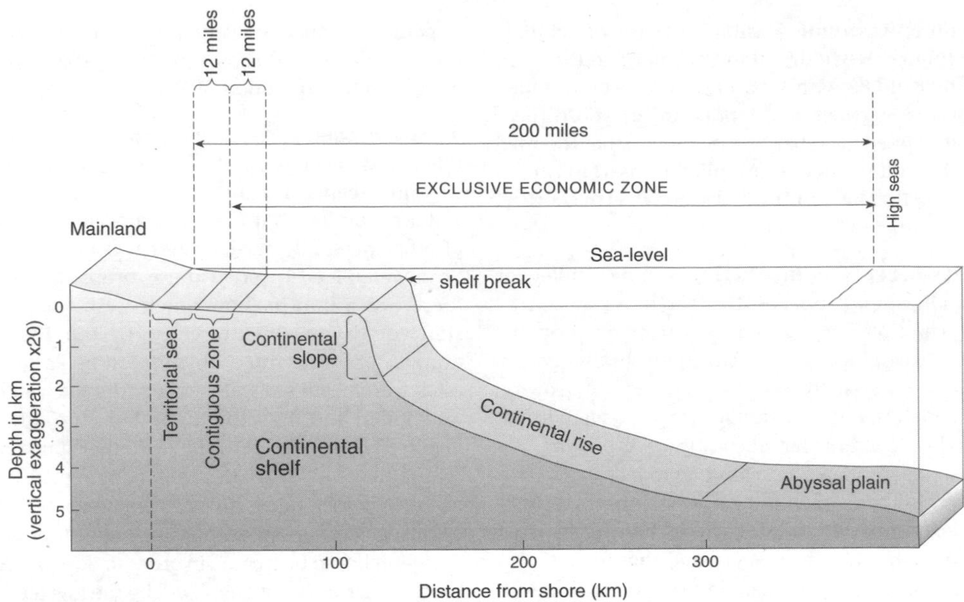

Diagrammatic cross-section (not to scale) to illustrate the maritime zones in the Exclusive Economic Zone

ping lanes and *traffic separation schemes being used to reduce the risks of collisions.

M. V. Angel

Execution Dock, the place on the bank of the River Thames, near Wapping in London, where, traditionally, men convicted of *piracy were executed. Originally the method of execution was to peg them down at low water below the high water mark on the river bank, so that the rising tide would drown them slowly. By the 16th century the method of execution had changed to being hanged in chains at a tall gallows. The body remained exposed on the gallows until it decomposed, or was eaten by seagulls, as a warning to others of the fate meted out to pirates such as Captain *Kidd.

exploration by sea for Europeans was, for many centuries, nearly always motivated by trade and profit. The desire for conquest and to spread Christianity were also important corollaries for exploration, and in more recent times science has been the motivator. The Arabs were commercially oriented, too, as were the Chinese, who, as they expanded southwards and eastwards, sent trading fleets to Japan and Korea, and into the Indian Ocean.

It should be remembered that many voyages of exploration were clouded in secrecy, so important was it to keep sea routes from trading rivals. That, and the loss of documentary evidence, both in Europe and the Orient, may have left undocumented the achievements of some of the earliest voyagers. It should also be remembered that what is called exploration by some is called invasion by others.

The Earliest Voyages. Exploration by sea began centuries before the time of Christ. The Greek historian Herodotus (*c*.480–*c*.425 BC) wrote how the Pharaoh Necho II, who lived in the late 7th and early 6th centuries BC, sent Phoenicians in ships from the Arabian Gulf with orders to return by way of the Pillars of Hercules (the Straits of Gibraltar) which, after three years, they duly did. In the 3rd century BC the Greek navigator Pytheas sailed to northern Europe and reached as far north as the Orkneys. Possibly he also reached Iceland, which may have been the Arctic land shrouded in mist to which he give the name Thule.

For centuries the south-west *monsoon wind in the Indian Ocean was known as Hippalus, after the Greek pilot who first sailed with it in about 100 BC from the Gulf of Aden to India. By then western traders had certainly sailed to several South-East Asian countries and may even have reached China, or Cathay as it was then called. By the time of the Roman Empire Greek ships, using the monsoon winds, traded regularly between the Red Sea ports and India. From the 3rd century, when the Roman Empire was in crisis, to the 15th century, when the European powers began to expand into the area, the Arabs dominated these sea routes. They founded trading posts down the east African coastline from the 8th century, and gradually explored southwards, reaching Madagascar in the following century. This is why, though fiction, the tales of *Sinbad the Sailor are based on centuries of the ways of the sea and the adventures of those who sailed them.

Later, the expansion of the Greek states into the western Mediterranean brought Greece into conflict with Rome, to whom control of that sea passed after the battle of Mylae in 260 BC. On the other hand, the Phoenicians, who founded Carthage, preferred trading to war. They sold their goods by sea from their ports in present-day Lebanon and before 1000 BC they had sailed beyond the Mediterranean to colonize the Spanish and North African coasts. *Gades, as Cadiz was at first known, was a typical Phoenician city. The Carthaginians also explored beyond the Mediterranean as early as 500 BC, with Hanno sailing forth around the African coastline with 60 ships and 30,000 colonists 'to found cities'; and Himilco, around the same time, sailing north to reach Brittany, and perhaps Britain.

The 9th–11th centuries were the time of the great Scandinavian exodus, when the Norsemen swarmed all over western Europe and the Mediterranean. They also headed westwards in their *longships, reaching Iceland in 875, Greenland in 984, and *Vinland in, or just after, 1000. Other early northern European explorers included Ohthere of Norway who, curious to know the northerly extent of his land, sailed round the North Cape in AD 890, and along the coast of Lapland to the White Sea, while the Irish saint *Brendan voyaged to western Scotland and, probably, Iceland, and maybe even further afield.

As the Greek and Roman civilizations spread westwards, the centre of sea power moved westwards too, with Spain and Portugal eventually becoming the dominant powers. However, it was two other great maritime galley-trading powers, Venice and Genoa, which first produced the *portulan charts that aided *navigation of the Mediterranean coastlines.

The Search for Trading Routes to Africa, India, and the Orient. By the end of the 14th century the Mogul Empire was disintegrating, making the overland routes to China insecure. Also, the power of the Ottoman Turks was increasing. They were hostile to Christians and blocked well-established trade from the East being shipped from eastern Mediterranean ports. Instead, *Henry the Navigator, Prince of Portugal, mounted many of the early voyages of discovery down the west coast of Africa in search of gold and slaves, and developed the *caravel for this purpose. By the time of Henry's death in 1460 the Portuguese had reached as far south as present-day Sierra Leone.

These early ventures were capped in 1488 by another Portuguese, Bartholomew *Diaz, who became the first European now known to have rounded what was later called the Cape of Good Hope. Four years later the Genoese-born Christopher *Columbus, funded by the Spanish throne, began his momentous voyage across the Atlantic in the vain hope of discovering the Orient by a western route. In doing so he inadvertently opened up the New World to Europeans, but it was a Florentine merchant-adventurer, Amerigo *Vespucci, who gave America its name; and another Florentine, Giovanni da *Verrazzano, who realized it was not part of Asia.

Early Chinese Voyages of Discovery. In the 3rd century BC it is possible that the Chinese emperors sent sailing *rafts to search for Pacific islands on which grew plants that would give them immortality, or at least longevity. From the 2nd century onwards diplomatic missions and *junk-rigged trading ships sailed westwards and had, by the 11th century, reached East Africa. In 1294 a fleet of fourteen ships escorted *Marco Polo to Ormuz (Hormuz) in the Persian Gulf; and in 1301 an even larger fleet returned there. Then, when China found its overland trade routes were barred by the Tartar warlord Tamerlane (1336–1405), it built a formidable fleet of warships, known as *treasure ships. Between 1405 and 1431 these ships mounted a series of trading expeditions which roamed far and wide. There is evidence to in-

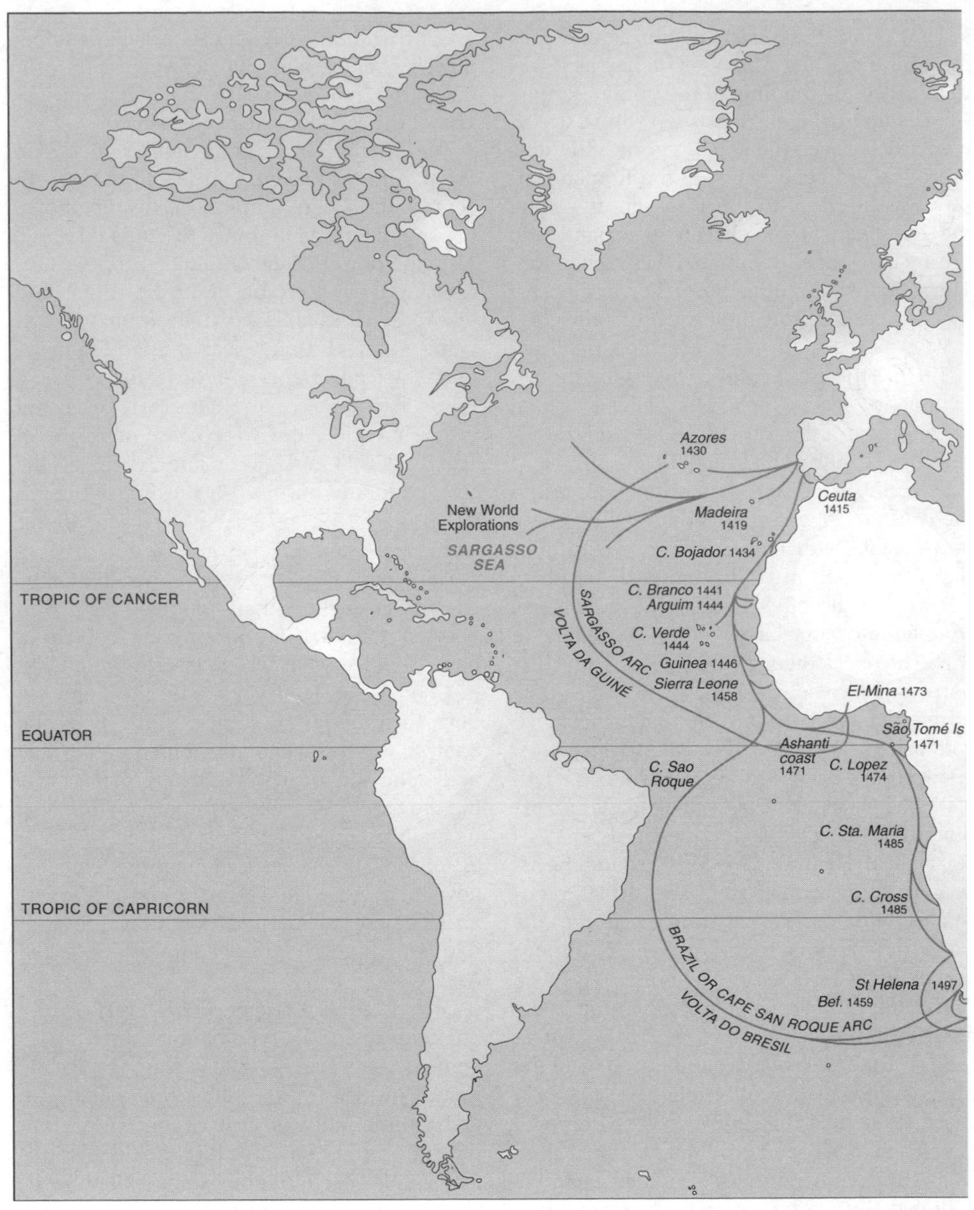

Comparative map of the voyages undertaken by the Chinese (dark lines) and the Portuguese (light lines) in the 15th century. The Portuguese knew all about the Atlantic currents and winds, and when returning from the Volta River (Ghana), where they had a fortified factory, they took a course known as the Volta da Guiné or the Sargasso Arc. To follow it they sailed far west into the Atlantic with the trade winds blowing from starboard, and then turned north for the westerlies

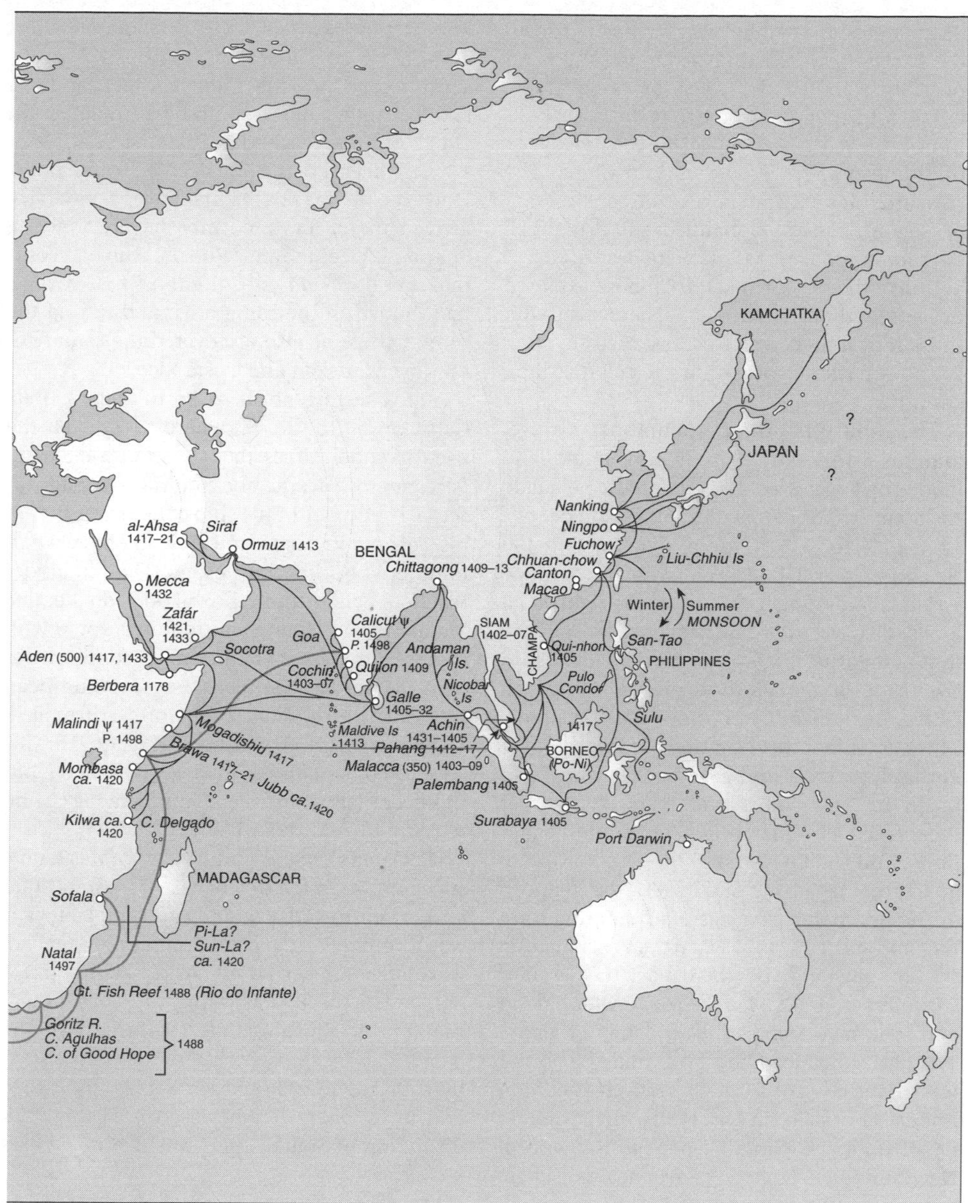

which they ran before to Lisbon. As they explored further southwards navigators like Vasco da Gama would leave the coast of Africa near Sierra Leone and sail across the Atlantic with the wind on their port beam. They would then, if necessary, make a landfall at Cape San Roque before sailing south until the Roaring Forties sped them into the Indian Ocean. This was known as the Volta do Bresil or Cape San Roque Arc.

dicate that some of them may have sailed down the East African coastline as far as 20° S., and possibly rounded the Cape of Good Hope, before returning. But by the time the last expedition returned new political forces, hostile to maritime power, were at work in China. The treasure ships fell from favour, the construction of seagoing vessels was banned, and virtually all documentation and charts were destroyed.

Unlike the Europeans, the Chinese explored peacefully, though in strength. They traded with those they visited, who were overawed by their sea power, without attempting to colonize their countries.

Treaty of Tordesillas. Columbus's voyage, and his conviction that he had found and landed on Cathay, led the Spaniards to persuade the Spanish-born Pope Alexander VI to decree, from pole to pole, a line of demarcation 100 *leagues (later 370 leagues) west of the Cape Verde Islands. Spain was given the right to all lands, discovered or undiscovered, west of the line, and Portugal was given the right to those to the east of it, though those already ruled by a Christian monarch were not to be occupied. This agreement was enshrined in the Treaty of Tordesillas (1494) and gave both Portugal and Spain the right to oust interlopers. It was never recognized by other European maritime nations, and the English and the Dutch were to go to great lengths to circumvent the treaty.

The first notable voyage of exploration from England started in 1497 when the Venetian John *Cabot sailed from Bristol to reach the East by a western sea route. He reached Newfoundland and took possession of it on behalf of Henry VII, and convinced the king that the island was off the coast of Cathay. A second expedition under Cabot sailed in May 1498 with the objective of finding Cipangu (Japan) to the west of Newfoundland, but it was never heard of again. Cabot's son Sebastian (1476–1557) was also an explorer. He led a Spanish expedition in 1525 to reach the Orient by way of the Magellan Strait but never got further than the mouth of the Paraguay River.

The Sea Route to India and Early Circumnavigations. In May 1498 the Portuguese Vasco da *Gama, with the help of Arab knowledge, reached India. To exploit his voyage a second expedition led by Pedro Cabral (*c.*1467–1530) was dispatched. He left Lisbon for India on 9 March 1500 with thirteen or fourteen ships and on the advice of da Gama steered south-south-west from the Cape Verde Islands to take advantage of the south-east *trade winds. On 22 April he reached Brazil, on a *latitude of 17° S., still east of the line decreed by the pope. However, he was not the first European to have arrived there, for three months previously a Spaniard, Vicente Yañez Pinzon, who had commanded the *Niña* on Columbus' first voyage, had landed in the same area; and during the same voyage he also discovered the estuary of the River Amazon and Costa Rica.

After coasting north to Porto Segura (Baia Cabralia) at 16° 20' S., where he erected the usual wooden cross that denoted a claim to Portuguese sovereignty, Cabral set sail for India. A number of his ships, including that of his second in command Bartholomew Diaz, foundered during this voyage. The remainder reached Calicut (now Kozhikode) on Kerala's Malabar coast, but when trouble erupted with the Arab traders there, he sailed south to Cochin. There he founded the first European settlement on Indian soil before returning to Lisbon in July 1501 with a rich cargo. He was appointed to command a second fleet, but this eventually went to da Gama, leaving Cabral to retire to enjoy his wealth.

Da Gama's second trading voyage was highly successful and the Portuguese began to build an empire in India. Among those taking part was a young Portuguese, Ferdinand *Magellan, who later transferred his loyalty to Spain. He persuaded the Spanish king to allow him to sail for the Spice Islands (Moluccas) in the East Indies by a western sea route—first visited by a Portuguese, Francisco Serrao, in 1512—and in October 1520 he discovered the strait off the tip of South America which now bears his name.

Magellan was possibly the first European to reach the Philippines and was killed there attempting to spread the Catholic faith. The survivors, in two ships, sailed on to the Moluccas, and so completed a momentous voyage of discovery. But only one ship, the *Vittoria*, commanded by a Spanish pilot, Juan Sebastian de Elcano (*c.*1486–1526), made it home, via the Cape of Good Hope, in July 1522. This made de Elcano and his surviving crew the first Europeans known to have sailed around the world, their voyage proving that Columbus had, indeed, discovered a New World. However, the first person known to make a circumnavigation was Magellan's Filipino manservant, whom Magellan had acquired during an earlier voyage to the East Indies.

Sailing into the Pacific from Peru, the Spanish navigator Alvaro de Mendaña (d. 1596) discovered the Solomon Islands in 1567 while trying to find *Terra Australis Incognita, the fabled great south land. In 1595 he and Pedro Fernandez de Quiros (1565–1615) came upon the Marquesas, and in 1606, during a later voyage, de Quiros discovered the New Hebrides group of islands before being forced to return. However, his second in command, the Portuguese navigator Luis Vaez de Torres (d. 1613), continued westwards. He sailed through the strait which now bears his name, before reaching the Moluccas and then the Philippines. It is not surprising, in the days when there was no accurate measurement of *longitude, that many of these discoveries were lost again, some for many years, but the explorations of both men were known to Captain *Cook, who made use of this knowledge on his first voyage.

The first captain to make a circumnavigation in his own ship was the Englishman Sir Francis *Drake, between 1577 and 1580. As much a *privateer as an explorer, he was, nevertheless, the first to discover that Tierra del Fuego was an island. He also sailed up the coast of North America to a high latitude in an attempt to find a strait that led to the *North-West Passage. Between 1586 and 1588 another Englishman, Thomas Cavendish (1555–92), also circumnavigated the world, discovering the island of St Helena on the way.

The Search for Arctic Routes to the East. Despite the successes of Drake and Cavendish, the Treaty of Tordesillas barred the way of the British and Dutch to the East's riches by the normal sea routes, just as the Ottoman Turks barred the land routes. During much of the 16th century they therefore tried to find other ways to reach China and Japan. Rumours had long circulated that a passage through Arctic waters to the Pacific existed, and in May 1553 an Englishman, Sir Hugh Willoughby (d. 1554), led an expedition of three ships in search of what was to become known as the North-East Passage. The crews of two perished in a Lapland harbour but the third, commanded by Hugh Chancellor (d. 1556), turned back and reached the White Sea. Chancellor landed, and visited Ivan the Terrible in Moscow, a meeting that led to the founding of the Muscovy Company designed to stimulate trade between England and Russia.

Spain annexed Portugal in 1580 and after the defeat of the *Spanish Armada eight years later, the British and the Dutch formed *East India Companies to exploit the spice trade via the sea routes which had so long been denied them. However, this did not prevent others from continuing to try and find a North-East Passage. They included the Dutchman Willem *Barents, who led three expeditions in the 16th century, and two Englishmen, Henry *Hudson and John *Franklin, who tried in the 17th and 19th centuries. But none managed to penetrate further east than the western part of the Kara Sea. This was still a long way from the Bering Strait, named after the Danish explorer Vitus *Bering. While sailing for the Russians, he built two ships at Kamchatka in eastern Siberia and passed through it in 1728.

In the 18th century the Russian Navy mapped the whole northern coast of Russia and established that a North-East Passage did exist, but it was not finally navigated until the Swedish Finn N. A. E. Nordensjkold (1832–1901) navigated it in two seasons. By then, science and national prestige vied with commerce as the principal motive for exploration. Several expeditions were mounted to the region for these reasons, those led by Fridtjof *Nansen and Roald *Amundsen, both from the new nation of Norway, being the most notable.

Frustrated at failing to find a North-East Passage, Hudson and Franklin, among others, searched for a North-West Passage instead. This search was primarily a British undertaking, though the French *navigator Jacques Cartier (1491–1557), with his exploration of the St Lawrence River between 1534 and 1541, was the first to claim he had found it. For well over three centuries huge amounts of British government money and resources, and a great deal of human effort and sacrifice, were poured into finding the passage before it was eventually navigated. It was never commercially reliable, but with *climate change it might still become so.

Southern Hemisphere Exploration. Even that great explorer James Cook was peripherally involved in attempting to find a North-West Passage. Though his main explorations were to find Terra Australis Incognita, which did not of course exist, his great achievement on his first voyage was to prove New Zealand was an island and to chart it and Australia's east coast. The Dutch navigator Jacob Le Maire (1585–1616) also sought the Great Unknown Land, by sailing south-east from the Magellan Straits until he came to the strait later named after him, and then became the first European to round South America's southernmost tip. This he named Cape Hoorn after the town in Holland where most of the backers of his expedition lived. It is an irony that when he eventually reached the East Indies his discovery was not believed and his ship's *log was branded a forgery.

By the mid-16th century French charts derived from Portuguese sources, known as the Dieppe maps, show an extensive coastline south of the Spice Islands. Some of these had Portuguese place names on the unknown land and this has led to speculation that the Portuguese were the first Europeans to discover Australia. However, there is no hard evidence to support this theory. What is incontrovertible—because he left an inscribed pewter plate nailed to a post on the West Australian island later named after him—was that the Dutchman Dirck Hartog, in 1616, became the first European known to have landed on Australian soil. However, the Dutch explorer Willem Jansz, who in 1605 sailed from the East Indies to search for New Guinea, was probably the first European to sight the continent. He reached the Torres Strait shortly before Luis Vaez de Torres himself and saw, and named, the western coastline of Cape York Peninsula; and another Dutchman, Pieter Nuyts, explored part of Australia's southern edge in 1627. Because of these early discoveries Australia was, for a time, known as New Holland, but the Dutch did nothing to exploit their knowledge of it.

In the following two centuries navigators such as *Tasman, George Bass (1771–*c.*1802), *Dampier, *Vancouver, *Flinders, and the Frenchman Nicolas Baudin mapped previously unknown parts of the coastline, and another Frenchmen, Louis Antoine de *Bougainville, added his discoveries to what was already known of the Pacific Islands.

The Final Phase. By the end of the first decade of the 19th century much of the exploration by sea, with the exception of the Arctic and Antarctic, had been completed. The Arctic had been known since the days of Pytheas' visit to the Orkneys, and in 1909 the North Pole was finally conquered, so it appeared, by Captain Robert *Peary USN. However, research undertaken in the 1980s and 1990s cast doubt on this achievement.

The Antarctic remained a mystery to Europeans for much longer, though it had long been postulated that a Great South Land existed, and that it was a rich and fertile region populated with natives anxious to trade. However, as voyagers penetrated further southwards the imaginary continent diminished. The discovery in 1739 by the French explorer Jean Baptiste-Charles Bouvet de Lozier (1705–86) of the ice-covered island that now bears his name; and the discovery of the equally frozen Kerguelen Islands in 1772 by the French navigator Yves-Joseph de Kerguélen-Trémarec (*fl.* 1771–4), convinced most people that the Great South Land, if it existed at all, would be a frozen, barren place. But it was Cook's second voyage which finally proved it did not exist.

Other explorers contributed to the discovery of Antarctica and its surrounding islands, one of the most outstanding being the Russian Fabian von *Bellingshausen, who circumnavigated the continent in 1819–21. Other voyages designed to open up new *sealing and *whaling grounds followed, and scientific expeditions were also mounted by several nations. Among them were those led by the Frenchman Jules-Sébastien-César Dumont d'Urville (1790–1842); the American Charles *Wilkes; the Belgian Adrien de Gerlache de Gomery (1866–1934); the Swede Otto Nordenskjöld (1870–1928); the Englishman Ernest *Shackleton; and the Australian Sir George *Wilkins. The Norwegian Roald *Amundsen, reached the South Pole first, in December 1911, beating the Englishman Captain Robert *Scott by a month.

In the 21st century *oceanography is opening up new areas of exploration by sea, not on the surface of the oceans but beneath them.

Seventy per cent of the earth is covered by water and 99% of it is still unexplored.

Whitfield, P., *New Found Lands* (1998).

explosion vessel, an ad hoc weapon at sea used for destroying or crippling objects with which it could be brought into contact. It was usually an old or obsolescent ship with its own means of propulsion, filled with explosive, and run alongside the object to be destroyed. The charge was exploded, either by slow match or by a time fuse, the crew making their escape by boat. See also WARFARE AT SEA.

eye. (1) Properly speaking, the circular loop in a *shroud or *stay where it passes over a mast at the *hounds. It is formed by *splicing the ends of two ropes or wires into each other to form a loop to fit over the mast. But by extension it has come to mean any loop spliced or *whipped at the end of a rope or wire, usually round a *thimble. A **Flemish eye** is a method of making the eye in a shroud or stay by dividing the *strands, knotting each part separately and then *parcelling and *serving. This method, though very neat, was frowned upon by all good seamen during the days of sail as it lacked strength where, for the safety of the ship, it was most needed. **(2)** The eye of the wind, or wind's eye, is a term used to describe the exact direction from which it blows, or when it is dead to *windward. **(3)** The eyes of the ship is a term used to describe its extreme forward end, the term being derived from the old eastern and Mediterranean custom of painting an eye on each bow so that the vessel could see where it was going. By some it is considered that the *hawseholes are equivalent to the eyes in a modern ship, but this is a somewhat doubtful attempt to fit the physical fact of modern ship construction to an older derivation. **(5)** The **eye of the storm** is the centre of a *tropical storm where there is an area of calm. **(6)** An **eye splice** is a loop or eye made in the end of a rope or wire by turning the end back and splicing it through the standing part, usually around a *thimble, with the length of the splice served to prevent fraying and to make a neater job.

Eye splice

eyebolts, metal bolts with an *eye in the end secured in various convenient places on board ship to which the *blocks of *purchases can be hooked or other lines secured.

fag-end, the end of any rope, but particularly applied to the end of a rope where the *strands have become unlayed and have *fagged out.

faggots, a name given in the British Navy during the days of sail to men who, for a small fee, could be persuaded to answer to the names of those absent from a ship when the crew were *mustered in a naval *dockyard. A man who failed to answer his name at a muster was liable to have R. for 'run' entered against his name. This automatically labelled him a deserter and subject to very heavy penalties if apprehended; and he was, moreover, unable to draw his pay when the ship eventually became due for payment. So there was always a temptation to find someone who would stand in and answer 'Aye' when an absentee's name was called. More efficient methods of naval bookkeeping introduced during the 19th century not only made the monthly muster of a ship's company unnecessary but also put an effective end to this fraudulent practice.

fag out, to, the tendency of the *strands of a rope to fray out at the ends. It is stopped either by holding them securely in place with a small *whipping, by a *back splice, or by *pointing the rope.

fair, a term applied to the direction of the wind when it is favourable to the *course being steered in a sailing vessel. It is more comprehensive than *large as it can blow from about four *points on the bow to right *astern. Any wind which will enable a sailing vessel to *fetch a desired point without *tacking or *pinching is a fair wind.

fairlead, a means of leading a rope in the most convenient direction for working, perhaps with a *leading block to alter its direction or with *eyes or *cringles to keep it clear of obstructions.

In the old sailing ships, a board with holes in it, through which various parts of the running *rigging were *rove, was used to provide fairleads. Similarly in these ships, the *chesstrees were fairleads for the *bowlines with which the main *tacks were hauled down.

fairway, the navigable channel of a harbour for ships entering or leaving. It is, in all harbours of any size, marked by *buoys, and usually in smaller harbours by withies or similar marks. Obstructions in a *fairway are also marked. See also IALA MARITIME BUOYAGE SYSTEM.

fall, the handling end of a *tackle, the end of the rope, *rove through *blocks, on which the pull is exerted in order to achieve power. When used in the plural the term refers to the complete *tackles by which a ship's boat is hoisted in or lowered from the *davits.

fall off, to, a sailing vessel falls off when it sags away to *leeward or further off the wind. It is the opposite to *griping, and similarly requires the movement of *ballast inside the vessel to correct the tendency. The shifting of ballast forward to *trim the vessel by the *head gives a greater grip of the water in the bows and thus less tendency to *sag away from the wind.

false fire, one of the *signals at sea used at night time during the days of sailing navies. A composition which burned with a blue flame was packed into a wooden tube and when ignited would burn for several minutes. As well as being used for night signals, false fires were sometimes employed to deceive an enemy, either by setting one alight in a drifting boat for the enemy to follow, or by burning one on board a fast *frigate to draw the enemy away on a false *course.

false keel, an additional keel secured outside the main keel of a wooden sailing ship, usually as a protection should the ship take the ground but sometimes also to increase its *draught in order to improve its sailing qualities.

fancy line. **(1)** A line *rove through a *block at the *jaws of a *gaff and used as a *downhaul when lowering the sail. It was only necessary in larger vessels setting a sail with a *gaff rig. **(2)** A line used for cross-hauling the lee *topping lift to hold it clear of the sail to *leeward. This was done to prevent it from beating or rubbing against the sail or to stop it reducing the sail's *aerodynamic properties by creating a ridge when the sail stood *taut.

Fanny Adams, an old Royal Navy *lower-deck slang term for tinned meat. Its origin lay in the murder in 1820 of a 7-year-old girl named Fanny Adams by a solicitor's clerk who disembowelled and cut up his victim. Tinned meat had recently been introduced in the British Navy and a sailor, finding a button in a tin, suggested to his messmates that it came from the murdered girl's clothing, which led to the use of the name to describe such tins. Its later meaning, absolutely nothing, has no maritime derivation.

fantail, the overhanging part of a ship's stern, a term used particularly in the case of large *yachts and *ocean liners. Although the correct word for the stern overhang of all ships, it is not often used in this connection except in the USA. It has not quite the same meaning as *counter, but comes very close to it.

fardage, loose wood or other substance used, before the introduction of *container ships, in the stowage of bulk cargoes to prevent them shifting in the *holds of a ship in a seaway.

farthell, to, a defunct nautical term meaning to *furl, using *gaskets at the *bunt of the sails but rope-yarns at the *yardarms as the weight of the sail there was not so great. The word referred only to the mainsail, *foresail, and *spritsail of *square-rigged ships. The *clew lines leading to the yardarms to furl the *topsails and *topgallant sails were sometimes called **farthelling lines**. It is an oddity of old-time maritime phraseology that topsails and topgallants were always described as furled, not farthelled, though they were fitted with farthelling lines.

fashion pieces, the aftermost *timbers in a vessel which form the shape of the *transom.

fast, in terms of a ship, secured, attached, fixed. Thus, to make a vessel fast is to secure it firmly to something.

fathom, a unit of measurement for the depths of the sea or the lengths of rope and *cables before the metric system was adopted. The word comes from the Old English *faedm*, to embrace, and is a measurement across the outstretched arms of a man, approximately 6 feet (1.83 m). The French *brasse* clearly has a similar derivation from arms.

fay, to, in *shipbuilding and boat-building, to fit together two pieces of timber so that they lie close to each other with no perceptible space between them.

feather, to. **(1)** To alter the angle of the blades of a *propeller so that they lie with the leading edge more or less in the line of advance of the vessel, normally a sailing vessel, to which they are fitted. The object of feathering a propeller is to reduce the drag when the vessel is under sail alone. **(2)** To turn the blade of an *oar from the vertical to the horizontal while it is being taken back for the next rowing stroke, performed by dropping the wrists at the end of the stroke. **(3)** To sail very close to the wind to prevent excess load on the sails.

feaze, to, an old word meaning to unlay old tarred rope and, by teasing it, convert it into *oakum for use in *caulking the sides and decks of wooden vessels.

felucca, a small sailing or rowing vessel of the Mediterranean, used for coastal transport or trading. The larger feluccas were narrow, decked, *galley-built vessels, with a *lateen rig carried on one or two masts, occasionally also with a small *mizzen. Smaller feluccas were propelled with six or eight *oars, though some of the smaller sailing feluccas used oars and sail simultaneously. The seagoing type has almost died out, but they are still in use on many eastern Mediterranean rivers, particularly the Nile.

fender, an appliance lowered over the side of a vessel to prevent chafing when lying alongside another vessel, or a *wharf or *pier, or to take the shock of a bump when going alongside. Fenders come in many shapes and sizes, and are nowadays generally air filled and made of rubber or synthetic moulding.

fend off, to, to bear a vessel off with a *boathook, or *fender, in order to prevent violent contact when coming alongside.

ferry, a vessel designed to carry passengers and/or vehicles, and which, like an *ocean liner, runs on a regular schedule. Ferries are of ancient origin—there was a guild of ferry ships at Dover in the early 14th century whose members took passengers and horses across the Channel—and can vary in size from small rowing boats up to ships with passenger accommodation that also transport cars, lorries, and *freight. Some are equipped with railway lines so that trains can be transported across stretches of water too wide for a bridge. The earliest of these was the *Leviathan* which carried loaded railway wagons across the Firth of Forth, Scotland, in 1850. Smaller ferries which connect the banks of sheltered waters, such as an estuary, are hauled over by chains. *Ro-ro (roll-on roll-off) ships are now the most popular form of ferry, but there are also a new generation of high-speed ones such as the *hovercraft, the *hydrofoil, and the *Seacat and Superseacat. For illus. of modern ferry, see SHIPBUILDING.

fetch, to, to reach, or arrive at, some place or point, particularly in conditions of an adverse wind or *tide. The word is used only in relation to sailing vessels when *close hauled or *on a wind, and implies being able to arrive at the desired point without having to *tack to windward. Fetch also signifies the distance of open water traversed by *waves before they reach a given point; the longer the fetch, the higher the waves generally are, and the more strongly the *swell will run after the wind has dropped. It is also used to indicate the distance a vessel must sail to reach open water, thus a *yacht can anchor in an inlet on a coast, and have a fetch of so many miles to reach the open sea.

fid. **(1)** A square bar of wood or iron, with a wider shoulder at one end, which in large sailing ships took the weight of a *topmast when attached to a lower mast. The topmast was hoisted up through a guide hole in the *cap of the lower mast until a square hole in its *heel was in line with a similar hole in the head of the lower mast. The fid was then driven through both and the hoisting *tackles slacked away until the fid was bearing the weight. The two masts were then generally secured firmly together with a *parrel lashing. Similarly a fid would support the weight of a *topgallant mast at the head of a topmast. **(2)** A tapered cylindrical pin, originally of hardwood such as **lignum vitae*, but now of stainless steel, used for opening the *strands of large cordage for splicing. It has a groove down one side used for feeding in the strand being tucked. **(3)** The piece of *oakum used to plug the vent of a muzzle-loading gun, to stop it getting blocked when the gun was not in use, was called a fid.

fiddle, a rack fixed to mess tables on board ships in rough weather to prevent crockery, glasses, knives and forks, etc. from sliding to the deck as the ship rolls and *pitches.

fiddle block, a double *block in which the two *sheaves lie in one plane one below the other instead of being mounted on the same central pin as in more normal double blocks. The upper sheave is larger than the lower so that it vaguely resembles a violin in shape. They were used chiefly for the lower-yard *tackles of *square-rigged ships as they lay flatter to the *yards.

fiddlehead bow, the stemhead of a vessel finished off with a scroll turning *aft or inwards, as at the top of a violin. This form of stemhead was originally adopted in small sailing warships which had no *figureheads as a piece of simple bow decoration; the term has remained to describe the termination of a *clipper bow which has this inward-turning decorative ending.

Fiddler's Green, a sailor's paradise, where public houses, dance halls, and other similar amusements are plentiful and the ladies are accommodating. It really had only a celestial and not a terrestrial connotation in the sailor's mind, a sort of permanent sensual Elysium or sailor's heaven but still vaguely related to the delights enjoyed by sailors ashore. A sailor who had died, and was known to have enjoyed such pleasures in his life, was often said to have gone aloft to Fiddler's Green.

fiddley, a raised deck grating fixed over the *hatches above the engine rooms of steam- or early *diesel-powered vessels to let the hot air and fumes escape. Fresh air would enter the engine room through the ventilators and force the hot air out through the fiddleys. In rough weather they were made watertight by *tarpaulins spread over them and secured by *battens.

fife rails. **(1)** The rails erected on the *bulwarks which bounded the *poop and *quarterdeck of old sailing warships, *East Indiamen, and the larger merchant vessels. As well as being decorative, they were useful in providing a convenient means of securing the *clew lines of the sail when under sail. **(2)** The circular or semicircular rails around the base of masts of sailing vessels which hold the *belaying pins to which the *halyards are belayed. They could also be positioned by the *chain-plates. See also PINRAILS.

fighting instructions, a code of tactical *signals at sea in the early days of the British Navy, first issued by Robert *Blake and others in 1653. The instructions, 21 in number, established the *line of battle and imposed some sort of tactical discipline on the *ships of the line that formed it. Later admirals such as *Anson issued additional instructions for use in the fleets they commanded, some of which were incorporated in the permanent or printed instructions, which first appeared in 1672 as the *Sailing and Fighting Instructions*. Similar French *Ordres et signaux généraux* date from 1690, but in France more theoretical treatises on the subject were written, including Père Hoste's *L'Art des armées navales* (1697).

Partly as a result of these French works, the old system of signalling in the British Navy, under which an instruction was conveyed to the fleet by the position of a particular flag, was improved during the last quarter of the 18th century, and made much more flexible. The *Signal Book for the Ships of War*, issued officially by the *Admiralty in 1799, distinguished between the old fighting instructions and the new methods of flag signalling which were further extended by Sir Home Popham's *Marine Vocabulary* (1800, 1803), with its 25 letter flags and a dictionary of 1,000 words, a precursor of the *International Code of Signals. *Nelson's famous Trafalgar signal was made by the three-flag hoists of this method, the word 'duty' having to be spelled out because it was not in the list of words.

From the mid-18th century onwards the introduction of the *general chase signal gave the commander on the spot a degree of flexibility when it came to forming the line of battle. See also WARFARE AT SEA.

'Fighting *Téméraire*', one of the best-known names in the Royal Navy on account of the poem 'The Fighting *Téméraire*', written by Sir Henry Newbolt (1862–1938) and first published in 1897.

> Now the sunset breezes shiver,
> And she's fading down the river,
> But in England's song for ever
> She's the fighting Téméraire.

There is also a famous *marine painting of her being towed away for breaking up by J. M. W. Turner, exhibited in the Royal Academy in 1839 and now in Tate Britain, London. A second warship of that name fought at the battle of Trafalgar in 1805.

fights, an old name for the waistcloths rigged above the *bulwarks along the *waists of sailing men-of-war before going into action to conceal the seamen working on deck from *sharpshooters in the *tops of enemy ships. The use of waistcloths lasted only a very few years beyond the 17th century because of the additional hazard presented by them of fire on board during battle. See also WARFARE AT SEA.

figurehead, an ornamental carved and painted figure, the successor of the *acrostolium. Figureheads were originally erected on the *beakhead of a vessel, but later on the continuation of the *stem below the *bowsprit as a decorative emblem generally expressed some aspect of the ship's name or function.

An Emblem for Protection. In the early days of seagoing it was probably a mixture of religious symbolism and a sign of treating a ship as a living entity. On the one hand, some propitiatory emblem was carried on board to claim the protection of a sea deity like *Poseidon or *Tethys while the vessel was at sea; on the other hand, there was a widely felt belief that a ship needed to find its own way across the waters, and could only do so if it had eyes. The ancient Egyptians drew on their extensive pantheon to provide both protection and eyes by mounting figures of the holy birds on the prows of their ships; Greek ships had a boar's head for both its quick sight and ferocious reaction; Roman ships often carried a carving of a centurion to indicate their prime fighting quality. William the Conqueror's ship pictured in the Bayeux Tapestry had a lion's head carved on the top of its stem; by the 13th century one of the favourite figureheads for ships was the head and neck of a swan, possibly in the hope that the ship would thereby possess the same mobility and *stability as that bird upon the water.

In northern Europe the favourite decoration for the high stem of the *longship was a serpent, though there were variations. Some Danish ships of the period had *dolphins or bulls as figureheads; one longship in AD 1004 was decorated in the form of a dragon, its head forming the figurehead and its tail the *sternpost. All these figureheads were carved onto, or mounted on, the beakhead.

Change of Design. The figurehead as we know it today was an effect of the change in the design of the ship which came about in the 14th–16th centuries. The examples mentioned above were mounted on, or carved directly onto, the beakhead or stem of the ship, but with the development of the *carrack, and its successor the *galleon, forecastles were built above and beyond the ship's stem, so that the position of the figurehead had to be moved. In the early stages of these designs there was no place for the figurehead, and although Henry VIII's ship *Holigost* of 1514 is recorded as being fitted with carvings of a swan and an antelope at a cost of £4 13*s.* 4*d.* (about £4.67), they were probably placed on the *quarterdeck or stern galley. In these early designs the beakhead was nearly horizontal, and figures of some sort could be placed on top of it; the earliest ships known to carry them, the *Salamander* and *Unicorn* of 1546, had carving representing their names.

In the century between about 1540 and 1640, the long beakhead developed into the rounded bow by the addition of *cheeks, and the position and stance of the figurehead consequently changed. At the beginning of the period the figurehead, nearly always an animal such as a lion or leopard, was virtually horizontal, but as the beakhead gradually disappeared into the bow it became more upright, finally reaching the perpendicular by about 1700 and then leaning further and further backwards, puffing out its chest, through most of the 18th century. In smaller ships, with little space available for a rounded figure, some form of heraldic carving frequently took its place. Of the larger ships which formed the navy of Elizabeth I, five had a figurehead of a lion (*Charles, Defiance, Repulse, Rainbow, Garland*), five had a dragon (*Bonaventure, Adventure, Dreadnought, Nonpareil, Hope*), the **Mary Rose* a unicorn, the *Swiftsure* a tiger, and the *White Bear* a figure of Jupiter sitting on an eagle. Most Dutch ships of the period also had a lion as their figurehead, as did many Spanish ships. Generally, French ships carried more elaborate figureheads, such as *Neptune driving a pair of seahorses or, a favourite, Jupiter sitting on his eagle.

Popular Figureheads. The lion remained the favourite figurehead for warships of most nations throughout the 17th century, though some of the larger and more important ships had more elaborate designs. The English *Prince Royal* of 1610 had a representation of St George slaying the dragon, and the *Sovereign of the Seas* of 1637 had as her figurehead King Edgar on horseback trampling upon seven kings. The *Naseby*, one of the great ships of Oliver Cromwell's Commonwealth Navy of 1649–60, had, according to the diarist John Evelyn, 'Oliver on horseback trampling six nations under foot: a Scot, Irishman, Dutchman, Frenchman, Spaniard, and English, as was easily made out by their several habits'.

The lion finally went out of fashion as a figurehead for warships in the second half of the 18th century, being replaced by carvings usually indicating the ship's name. For example, the *Edgar* of 1774 had a carving of King Edgar for her figurehead; the *Egmont* of 1768 and the *Bedford* of 1775 had figures of statesmen, presumably the First Lords of the *Admiralty after whom they were named. The *Brunswick*, which fought in the battle of the Glorious First of June in 1794, had a figure of the duke of that name wearing a cocked hat and a kilt. The cocked hat was shot away during the battle while the *Brunswick* was engaging the *Vengeur*, an accident which so concerned her crew that the captain gave them his own cocked hat and the carpenter nailed it onto the Duke of Brunswick's head.

Lord Sandwich, First Lord of the Admiralty 1771–82, introduced many classical names into the British Navy, a great opportunity for the carvers to let their imaginations loose. In the early 19th century a new system of training for shipwright apprentices was initiated at Portsmouth, and the well-known marine artist J. C. Schetky (1778–1874) was appointed as drawing master to train them in the carving of figureheads. He had a considerable talent for *marine painting and for a few years the carving of figureheads flourished under his tuition, although his designs were so elaborate that they were almost invariably vetoed by the Admiralty as being too costly, and its restriction on what could be spent resulted in British naval figureheads becoming generally uninteresting.

Figureheads in the 19th–20th Centuries. Up to about 1800 merchant ships followed naval practice fairly closely, and most vessels of the various *East India companies used lions as figureheads. With the advent of the *clipper ship, with its graceful lines, the figurehead blossomed, usually into a single figure, either full length or half-length. Women were, if anything, rather more popular than men, and very often reflected the *superstitions of sailors by having one or both breasts bared.

The 19th-century technological changes from sail to *steam propulsion spelled out the gradual end of the naval figurehead. The first two *ironclad warships built in Britain, the **Warrior* and *Black Prince*, did indeed have figureheads; later ships with their straight iron stem had no more than a medallion or shield, with supporters on either side. Figureheads for the larger warships were finally abolished in Britain in 1894 but some smaller ones kept them until the First World War (1914–18).

In merchant ships, too, the figurehead began to disappear when steam replaced sail, the loss of the bowsprit, under which the figurehead was traditionally placed, being the main reason for its disappearance. In some modern shipping lines a form of figurehead has been revived for decorative purposes.

Frere-Cook, G. (ed.), *The Decorative Arts of the Mariner* (1966).
Laughton, J. Carr, *Old Ship Figure-Heads & Sterns* (1925).

figure of eight knot, a knot made in the end of a rope by passing the end of the rope over and round the *standing part, over its own part, and through the *bight. Its purpose is to prevent a rope from unreeving (see REEVE, TO) when passed through a *block.

Figure of eight knot

filibuster, a name under which *buccaneers were originally known in Britain. It owes its derivation to the Dutch *vrybuiter* (freebooter), translated into French as *flibustier*, and from there into English as *filibuster*.

fill, to, to *trim the sails of a *fore-and-aft-rigged sailing vessel, or to *brace the *yards of a *square-rigged one, so that the wind could fill the sails. In square-rigged ships it was possible to move ahead, to stop, or to move *astern all on the same wind by bracing the yards so that the sails could fill, *shiver, or *back with the wind, i.e. with the wind blowing on the front of the sail.

'fire and lights', an old name on the *lower deck in the Royal Navy for the *master-at-arms. Its origin arose from the nightly duty of the master-at-arms, exercised through the ship's *marine corporals, to make frequent inspections below decks throughout the night to ensure that all fires were drawn and all lights extinguished, a very necessary precaution in the days of wooden ships.

fireships were a favourite weapon of the Chinese who used them from the earliest times, floating them downstream onto enemy ships. They liked to chain several together before setting them alight and letting them loose, so that they became entangled with the enemy's ships and it was very difficult, and dangerous, to clear them.

In Europe they were filled with combustibles and fitted with special ventilating ducts in order to ensure rapid combustion. The charge was ignited by a slow match and a train of powder, set to fire after a predetermined interval. An armament of around eight small guns was provided for defence when the vessel was not about to be used as a fireship. Its role in battle, or when attacking an enemy ship at anchor, was to secure itself to its victim with *grapnels, and its crew would then light the slow match before escaping in a boat.

In 1588 fireships were used with great success by the British to drive vessels belonging to the *Spanish Armada out of Calais into the English Channel where they were attacked by the English fleet. They were also used extensively in the battles of the three Anglo-Dutch wars of the 17th century. The last occasion they were employed by the Royal Navy was in 1811 when attacking French warships at anchor in the Basque Roads. The US Navy, which also called them 'infernals', used one, unsuccessfully, against the *Barbary pirates in Tripoli harbour in 1804, an attack which resulted in the deaths of all those on board. See also WARFARE AT SEA.

fireworks, an old naval term which embraced any means of setting fire to an enemy ship during battle. They included fire pots, fire-balls (cannon balls heated to red heat in a brazier before being fired), fire pikes (boarding pikes with burning tow attached which were thrown javelin fashion on board an enemy), arrows similarly tipped, etc. *Fireships were not included in this general description, although their contents were. See also WARFARE AT SEA.

First Fleet, the name given to the *squadron which, under the command of Captain Arthur Phillip, set sail on 13 May 1787 with the first 700 convicts destined for Botany Bay in Australia. It comprised the *frigate *Sirius*, the tender *Supply*, three storeships, and six *transports.

fish are vertebrate animals that live in almost every part of the ocean, from the surface to the bottom of the deepest *trenches, and even at the very edge of the sea. By 2004 over 20,000 species, including the 200 or so edible species, had been described, Since about 100 new species are being described each year, the total number of fishes may exceed 30,000 species.

About 60% of all vertebrate animals (animals with backbones) are fishes. About half the described species are marine, and approximately 75% of them live in shallow coastal waters. The types range from hagfish (*Myxine* spp.) to lungfish (Dipnoi), but here the discussion will centre on the bony fishes, or teleosts, which are by far the most diverse and species-rich group of fishes. They are distinct from the cartilaginous fishes, i.e. *sharks and their relatives, by having bony rather than cartilaginous skeletons, gills covered with a flap, and mouths that are usually on the front of the head. The mouths of some fishes are armed with teeth that are used to rasp soft tissue, grind up *molluscs, or scrape algae off rocks. Others, such as the *seahorses, have no teeth and have tubular-shaped mouths adapted to suck up individual *plankton.

The rich diversity of fishes is partly the result of their having adopted a great variety of ways of feeding. Their basic body form is spindle shaped, with dorsal fins on the back, two pairs of lateral fins, the pectorals and the pelvics, a ventral anal fin, and a large tail, or caudal, fin that is usually symmetrical. The fins are composed of fine bones, or fin rays that normally are webbed. These fin rays can be developed into long sensory structures or hard spiny structures that may be armed with poison glands. In **remoras** (family Echeneidae) the dorsal fin has been modified into a sucker. The spindle shape gives a good hydrodynamic shape that slides through the water with minimum resistance when the posterior region of the body, and the tail, beats from side to side. However, this basic body shape has been greatly modified in different families of fish, especially in those families that live around the seabed. ***Eels** have lost most of their fins and developed long sinuous bodies and a serpentine mode of movement, ideal for moving in and out of crannies in, *reefs, but less effective for swimming in midwater. **Flatfishes** (order Pleuronectiformes) have flattened bodies, with either the left side or the right side becoming the lower surface, and during development the head rotates 90°, whereas **scorpion fishes** (order Scorpaeniformes) have bodies that are flattened dorsoventrally. **Boxfishes** (family Ostraciidae) have inflexible armoured bodies, and so their mode of swimming is by sculling with their fins. **Mudskippers** (*Periophthalmus* spp.) that inhabit the fringes of *mangrove swamps use their pectoral fins to climb up out of the water.

The coloration of fishes is almost as diverse is their habits. Some, like flatfishes, can change their colour at will, either to blend in with

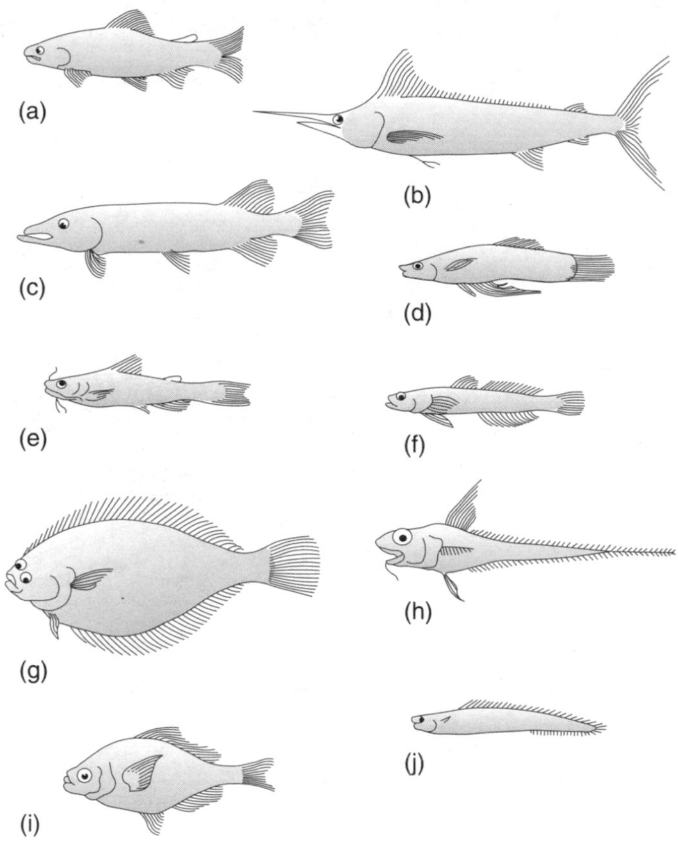

Typical fish body shapes [a] and [b] Rover-predator [c] Lie-in-wait predator [d] Surface-oriented fish [e] Bottom rover [f] Bottom clinger [g] Flatfish [h] Rattail [i] Deep-bodied fish [j] Eel-like fish

different backgrounds or to flash warnings to would-be predators. In many shallow *coral reef species, males display bright colours to guard their territories, but generally fishes use their coloration as camouflage. The commonest colour pattern in the fishes that swim in midwater is a counter-shading, with dark backs and pale bellies and flanks that may be banded with a disruptive pattern, often silvery or, in deep-sea species, lined with light organs. The brightness of light changes with depth, and its colour also changes—red light being absorbed very quickly—so the range of colours used by fish is restricted. Also, fish see only monochromatic blue-green light, which is the colour of light that penetrates furthest in water. In very deep water many fish species do not have functional eyes, since that there is almost nothing to see in the permanent darkness below about 1,000 metres (3,250 ft).

Another important sensory feature of fishes is their lateral line system. This is a chain of sense organs, similar to those in our ears, that can either be open to the water or semi-enclosed. With this system the fishes feel the water, sensing *currents and the low-frequency vibrations transmitted by the movements of other animals. Many deep-sea fishes have long filamentous tails that, by extending the length of the lateral line organ, enable them to feel the direction from which any movements are coming.

Fishes' blood is about half as salty as sea water—which is why thirsty shipwrecked mariners can safely drink it to slake their thirst—so fish continually have to get rid of salt from their bodies across their gills. Although this helps to make fishes less dense, many still have systems for adjusting the density of their bodies to be much the same as the sea water, so when they

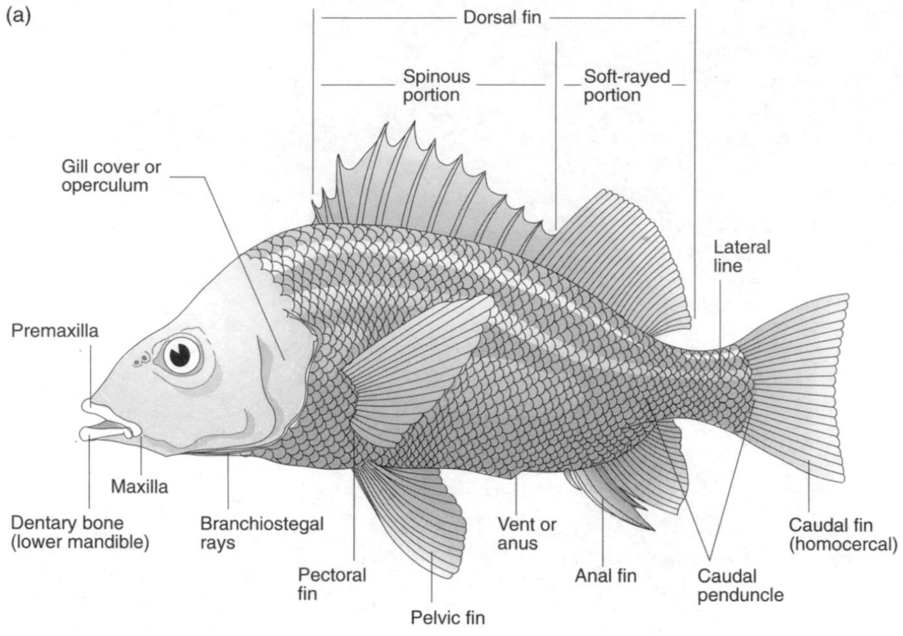

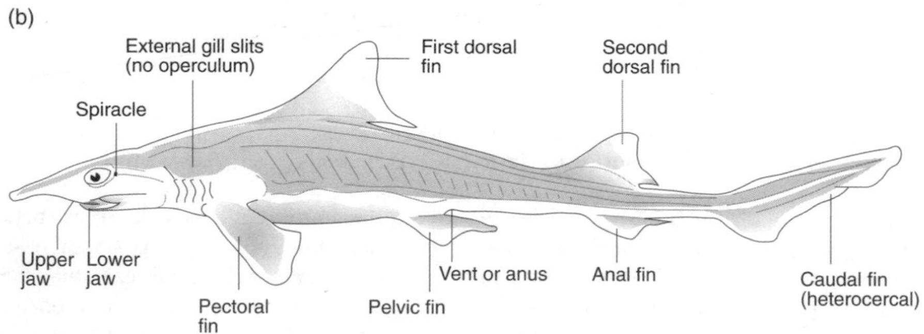

[a] External features of a bony fish (snapper)
[b] External features of a cartilaginous fish (smoothhound shark)

stop swimming they do not sink. Above the gut of many fishes is a swim-bladder that is filled with gas. In some fishes this is filled by gulping in air at the surface, but the vast majority never approach the sea surface, so the swim-bladder is filled by a special gland that extracts dissolved gases from the blood. Some fishes that swim continuously, like *tunas and *marlin, have no swim-bladder. Instead, they have rigid pectoral fins that act like hydroplanes to generate lift as they swim. Swim-bladders do not occur in many deep-sea fishes, because the greater the hydrostatic pressure (i.e. depth) the greater the energy required to fill them, so at depths below about 500 metres (1,625 ft) it becomes physiologically too expensive. In these fishes either the swim-bladder is filled with oily fats, or it disappears. Deep-sea fishes tend to have very watery tissues, and their bones contain very little calcium, which reduces their density. However, some still retain gas-filled swim-bladders in very deep water which are connected by bones to sensory organs, and function as hearing organs. They also often have drumming muscles attached to them for the fish to produce sounds for communication. During the Cold War when hydrophones were deployed in deep water to listen for the movements of *submarines, it was found that the deep ocean is quite noisy, especially during the breeding season for deep-sea fishes and when *whales migrate. See also FISHERIES.

Bone, Q., Marshal, N. B., and Blaxter, J. H. S., *The Biology of Fishes* (1995).

www.fishbase.org/home.htm M. V. Angel

fish, to. **(1)** To strengthen a *yard or a mast in a sailing vessel by using a fish, a long piece of wood, concave on one side and convex on the other. One of these is placed on each side of the weak point and secured either with metal bands or with a strong lashing known as a *woolding. **(2) To fish an anchor**, to draw up the *flukes of an *Admiralty pattern or fisherman's anchor to the *cat davit preparatory to its being stowed on an anchor bed. The modern stockless anchors have no need to be fished as their permanent stowage is in the *hawseholes and not on anchor beds.

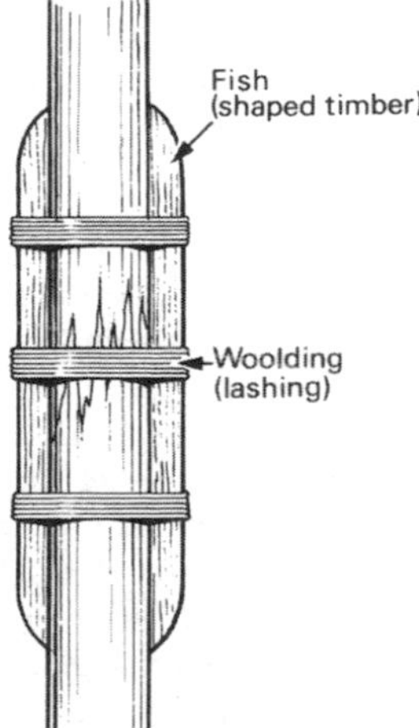

A fished spar

fisheries, a general term used to denote all the activities concerned with the catching of *fish commercially, whether by *long-lining, net, or other means. Until about 1900, commercial fishing was largely unregulated. However, the introduction of modern fishing boats fitted with refrigeration—which allows the boats to remain longer over fishing grounds—and electronic aids such as *sonar, meant that regulations on an international scale have had to be introduced. International efforts to try and curb overfishing, and to clamp down on those doing it illegally, are one of the *environmental issues facing mankind today.

The carbon dating of fish bones in kitchen middens has shown that humankind has been catching marine fish for tens of thousands of years. In the 19th century a committee of investigation chaired by T. H. Huxley (1825–95) concluded that the oceans offer an inexhaustible resource of fish, and this attitude prevailed for decades afterwards. According to the United Nations' Food and Agriculture Organization, in 2000 worldwide marine fisheries landed a little under 100 million tonnes of fish, providing 15% of animal protein, amounting to 13 kilograms (28 lb) per capita. However, this figure underestimates the fish that were killed, because at least 20% more were discarded as trash fish and by-catch.

*Trawls dragged along the seabed leave a trail of destruction. It is estimated that over half the area of the North Sea is trawled over each year, some parts as frequently as ten times. Globally, over 50% of fish stocks are either overfished or fished to their maximum sustainable capacity, so fishery scientists are desperately seeking to establish how the catches can be maintained while still enabling fishermen to make a living. Marine fishing and aquaculture gives employment to about 20 million people worldwide, and has an annual value of $55 billion. The scales of various fisheries range from individual artisanal fishermen using simple basic equipment catching fish for their own consumption, to large technically sophisticated fishing boats that are fishing to sell their catch for profit.

Commercial fisheries can be subdivided into **pelagic** (living in the water) and **demersal** (living on the seabed) fisheries, the former catching fish in the water using *purse seine nets and long-lines, whereas demersal fisheries target fish on the seabed using trawls, *dredges, and traps. Each population of fish that is targeted is called a stock. A stock may be the total population of a particular species, or populations of the same species that spawn in different areas and at different times of year. For example, in the North Sea there are several stocks of *herring. In theory a stock can be exploited to give the maximum sustainable yield (MSY) by catching fish at the same rate that they are being replaced. However, the number of new young fish (recruits) entering the stock fluctuates extensively year by year. This is because of variations in weather and climate, making accurate assessments of MSY impossible. So quotas of fish that can be harvested should, according to the Precautionary Principle, be set below the theoretical MSY. However, so strong are the economic and political pressures to set quotas at the maximum levels that what is set often exceeds the theoretical MSY, so stocks are constantly being over-exploited. Juvenile fish should not be caught until they have had a chance to spawn, which is achieved by regulating the minimum size of the mesh that can be used in the construction of trawls and purse seines. However, since in many fisheries several species of fish are caught, some undersized fish are taken and these have to be discarded.

The majority of commercial fish are caught in the shallow waters of the continental shelves, within the *Exclusive Economic Zones (EEZ) of coastal states. While these states have exclusive rights to the fish in their EEZ, they also have the obligation to exploit these stocks in a sustainable way, but many do not have sufficient resources to do so. Another major management problem arises with stocks that migrate between the EEZs of different countries: national boundaries have no environmental relevance as fish abundance is related to the productivity of the ocean waters, which is highest in regions where there are abundant nutrients in the surface waters. These areas are either in temperate regions where there is a seasonal cycle in the thermal stratification of the upper ocean, or where *upwelling brings nutrients up into the surface waters. The main upwelling regions mostly occur along the equator, particularly in the Pacific, along the eastern boundaries of the continents, off Peru, California, south-west Africa, and Mauritania, and the regions in the north-west Indian Ocean influenced by the *monsoon.

In 2000 the fishes contributing most to the global harvest were anchovetta off Peru (11.3 million tonnes) and the Alaskan species of pollock (3 million tonnes) and herring (2.4 million tonnes). See also DRIFTER; TRAWLER.

Merrett, N., and Haedrich, R., *Deep-Sea Demersal Fish and Fisheries* (1997).
www.defra.gov.uk/fish/fishindx.htm
www.fao.org/fi/default_all.asp M. V. Angel

fisherman's bend, a knot very similar to a *round turn and two half hitches, differing from it only in that the first of the two half hitches is made through the round turn and round the *standing part of the rope instead of round the standing part only. It is the recognized knot with which a *hawser is bent to the ring of an anchor. When used for this purpose the end of the rope, after the knot has been formed, is usually *seized as a safety measure to the standing part with two or three turns of *marline.

Fisherman's bend

fishing boat, see BANKER; BARCA-LONGA; BAWLEY; BEAN-COD; BOTTER; BUGEYE; BUSS; CAT-BOAT; COBLE; COD-BANGER; CRAFT; DOGGER; DRIFTER; FRIENDSHIP SLOOP; HENGST; HOOKER (1); HOY; JAEGT; LUGGER; PAREJA; PINK; PINKY; SCHOKKER; SHALLOP (1); SMACK; TRAWLER. See also BEAM (3); DORY; DREDGE; DRIFT NET; FISHERIES; GALLOWS (3); JYLSON BLOCK; PURSE SEINE NET; TRAWLS.

fishing fleet. **(1)** A collective term used to describe the fishing vessels owned by one individual or firm, or operating out of one port. It is also sometimes used, more loosely, to describe all the fishing vessels of one nation. Another use is to describe the fishing vessels of one type, e.g. the *trawler fleet. **(2)** A term used in the British Navy during the years when fleets and *squadrons were maintained on foreign stations, to describe the unmarried girls who, often with their families, stayed at these stations in the hope of finding an eligible young officer to marry.

fitting out, the general preparation of making a ship or *yacht fit for sea.

Fitzroy, Robert (1805–65), British naval officer who is, perhaps, best remembered for the voyage of the *Beagle*, 1831–6, in which he was accompanied by the naturalist Charles *Darwin. After working up the mass of data collected on the voyage, completing the *charts based on his surveys, and writing an account of the *Beagle*'s circumnavigation with Darwin, he was elected a Member of Parliament and introduced a Bill for the improvement of conditions in the *merchant marine. Although the Bill was defeated, it was the means of bringing about the introduction of voluntary certificates for *masters and *mates by the Board of Trade in 1845. Many other ideas embodied in Fitzroy's Bill were included in the Mercantile Act of 1850. In 1843 he was appointed governor of New Zealand but was recalled in 1845 after declaring that the land claims of the Maori population were as valid as those of the settlers. In 1850 he retired through ill health with the rank of rear admiral. Having always had an interest in *marine meteorology, in 1854 he was appointed by the Board of Trade to form its first meteorology department. He was the first man to draw a *synoptic chart for forecasting weather patterns based on observations at sea, and was also the first man in England to realize the usefulness of the newly invented electric telegraph to send warnings of imminent *gales to ports, a system that had already been introduced in the USA. He also arranged for the dissemination of this information from *coastguard stations by *semaphore to passing ships, and the hoisting of *storm signals at conspicuous places such as *lighthouses. He was always concerned with *lifesaving—he was for some time secretary of the Royal National Lifeboat Institution—and took the welfare of seamen very much to heart, so much so that he committed suicide when, so it was said, one of his forecasts proved incorrect. See also PORT (1).

Mellersh, H., *Fitzroy of the 'Beagle'* (1968).

fix, the process of determining the position of a ship without reference to a previous position, from observations of *landmarks or *seamarks, or by *celestial, *hyperbolic, or *satellite navigation. It has the same meaning when used as a verb.

fixed and flashing light, a navigational light in which a steady beam constantly visible is varied at fixed intervals by a flash of brighter intensity. See also CHARACTERISTIC.

fixed light, a navigational light displayed by a *lighthouse, *lightship, or lighted *buoy in which the light exposed is a steady beam with no intervals of darkness. See also CHARACTERISTIC.

flag, see BLUE ENSIGN; BLUE PETER; ENSIGN; INTERNATIONAL CODE OF SIGNALS; JACK; JOLLY ROGER; RED ENSIGN; WHITE ENSIGN. See also BUNTING; BURGEE; DIP (2); FLAG ETIQUETTE; FLAGS OF CONVENIENCE; FLY; HOIST; PENNANT; SQUADRONAL COLOURS; WEAR, TO.

flag etiquette, also called yacht routine in the USA, is concerned with what flags, *burgees, and *ensigns should be hoisted while afloat, and where they should be flown, or *worn, in order to obey national laws, or customs. Flags send important information about the vessels that fly them. Also, people have an emotional attachment to their national flags. If they are incorrectly displayed it can cause offence, and breaks the laws of some maritime nations. For example, it is illegal for a civilian vessel to fly the flag of St George; the European Union flag with a vessel's national flag at its *hoist has no status; and it is wrong for a powerboat to have the Union flag painted on its side, though the appropriate ensign is permitted.

All vessels, whether warships, commercial vessels, or pleasure craft, are entitled to fly the maritime ensign of the country to which the vessel belongs, though many merchant ships fly *flags of convenience. In the UK, the use of ensigns aboard merchant ships is regulated by various Merchant Shipping Acts. The USA is particularly strict about its national flag, the Stars and Stripes, which is derived from the British *East India Company flag, and the national flag is also the ensign of the US merchant fleet and the US Navy. Its use is controlled by Congress which also controls the flags and burgees for flag officers of American *yacht clubs, fleet captains, and *US Power Squadrons. All US pleasure craft, power or sail, fly the US yacht ensign, but only in US *territorial waters. Elsewhere, the US Stars and Stripes ensign must be flown. Unlike British and Commonwealth yacht clubs, US yacht clubs do not have individual ensigns. American yachtsmen are more punctilious about flag etiquette than their counterparts in Europe.

Any UK vessel of any type is entitled to fly the *red ensign, but a warrant has to be issued by the authorities before a defaced red or *blue ensign can be flown. A vessel's ensign must be hoisted: when requested by any British warship, on entering or leaving a foreign port, and on entering or leaving a British port if the vessel is over 50 tonnes gross. It is illegal for any ship, or *yacht, to fly an ensign to which it is not entitled.

The Union flag is only flown by British warships, and then only on their *jackstaffs in harbour or at anchor. It is then, and only then, properly called the Union *jack. However, other vessels may fly the pilot jack, the Union flag with a white boarder, at their jackstaffs when in harbour or anchored, and may also fly a house flag or something similar there, though this does not make it a jack. The Union jack flown by US warships is a blue flag with 50 white stars. It is only flown on certain occasions and only if the Stars and Stripes ensign is flown at the stern at the same time. Flying the Union flag upside down, particularly in Canada, UK, and USA, is traditionally a *distress signal, though not an official one.

An ensign is normally flown from an ensign staff on the stern, but a *gaff-rigged yacht can fly it from the *peak of its mainsail, or *mizzen sail if it is a *ketch or *yawl, and many *Bermudan-rigged yachts fly theirs from the *backstay or on the *leech of the mainsail. Wherever they are flown at sea, ensigns should only be flown from the stern when in harbour. The masthead is reserved for the club burgee or, in the case of merchant shipping, the house flag. Courtesy flags—the maritime ensign of the country a vessel is visiting—are flown from a *yard or *spreaders, as are signal flags and owners' flags. Occasionally, the club burgee is, too, though some clubs expressly forbid this. Some also forbid an owner to wear his flag at the same time as their burgee. If a powerboat has no mast, its club burgee can be worn from the jackstaff. Only one club burgee should be worn at any one time.

Burgees, house flags, owners' flags, and courtesy flags normally remain hoisted in harbour until it is no longer appropriate for them to be worn, though some yacht clubs require burgees to be hoisted and lowered with the ensign. Once at sea any courtesy flag is struck but the club burgee remains hoisted. It is quite usual to strike the ensign at sea, too, but it has to be raised if the crew wish to make their nationality known to another ship or to salute a warship. This is done by dipping the ensign about two-thirds of the way down the staff. It is raised again only after the ship being saluted dips its ensign in acknowledgement and then raises it. Only an ensign is used for *salutes at sea, and it is the only one flown at half-mast to mark a death.

Flags flown in harbour must be hoisted in order of seniority. For example, the courtesy flag of a country being visited takes precedence over a club burgee or owner's flag. The most senior, or most important, flag is hoisted close up on the *starboard spreader. The next senior is hoisted close up on the *port spreader; the third senior is hoisted below the top flag on the starboard spreader; and the fourth senior below the top flag on the port spreader. Where there is an inner *halyard, the outer one takes precedence.

In the USA, yachts fly special flags in harbour. For instance, in the port rigging, a dark blue rectangular one indicates the owner is temporarily absent; a dark blue rectangular one, intersected with a white stripe running diagonally upwards from the bottom corner of the *hoist, indicates that a guest is aboard; and a white rectangular one indicates that the owner is eating and visitors are therefore not welcome. Unofficial, light-hearted flags are also sometimes flown. A popular one has a white wine glass on a green background, known as the gin *pennant, which is often hoisted as an invitation for other yachtsmen to come aboard for a drink.

Some racing yachts have a battle flag to show their competitors they mean business, and all wear special racing flags when racing (see also RACING RULES). Flags belonging to the *International Code of Signals take on a different meaning when they are used by race organizers to communicate with competitors, and they are also used to *dress ship.

Johnson, P., *Reed's Maritime Flags: Usage and Recognition* (2002).

flag rank, a general term that embraces all officers of all navies of the rank of rear admiral, or its equivalent, and above, i.e. any officer who denotes his presence in command at sea by flying a flag. Commodores fly *broad pennants. **'He has got his flag'**, he has been promoted to flag rank. For **'flag'** as a boat's reply to a hail, see 'AYE, AYE, SIR'.

flagship, in navies, the ship that carries an admiral's flag or, in merchant shipping lines, the ship of the commodore or senior captain of the line.

flags of convenience, in some countries known as **flags of necessity,** a term applied to ships registered in countries by owners who are not nationals of those countries. This practice used to allow—and in a few cases still does—ships' owners to avoid the regulations, *classification, and restrictions governing ships' crews that other maritime countries have imposed for reasons of safety and to discourage the exploitation of seamen. The phrase retains such a pejorative meaning that the *International Maritime Organization prefers to use the term 'open register'.

Flying the flags of another country probably goes back to antiquity, but it is known that during the Napoleonic Wars (1793–1815) British ships flew the flags of minor German principalities into order to avoid French *blockades and *privateers; and in the 1812–15 War with Britain, US merchant ships flew Portuguese flags for the same reason.

However, the modern use, and meaning, of flags of convenience (FOC) probably started in the shipping slump of 1920–30 when a few owners sought to evade the inspections and regulations imposed by traditional maritime countries. Also, in the same era, American *cruise ships sailed under the flag of other countries during Prohibition so that there would be no restriction on carrying alcohol aboard. Whatever its origins, the real growth of the practice occurred after the Second World War (1939–45) when mainly Greek and Italian owners bought up war surplus *tonnage, often with US finance, and registered it in countries such as Panama, Liberia, Honduras, or Costa Rica, thus evading state inspections of ships and crews, currency restrictions, and all but nominal taxes.

Up to the 1960s these fleets were considered sub-standard, but freedom from taxes on profits soon allowed conditions at sea to improve and old vessels to be replaced by large, modern ships. At the same time Liberia particularly attracted what the USA called 'flag of necessity' ships; these were a product of the huge US stake in the international oil industry and her inability to compete in the oil-carrying trade because of the high wages and conditions of US seamen; at the time an American *tanker crew cost five times as much as a Greek or Spanish crew, though the Philippines is now the world's largest supplier of merchant seamen. Besides commercial necessity, the USA, as the world's greatest naval power, had a strategic necessity to maintain a *bulk carrier fleet and a cargo fleet on important supply routes, recognizing that the backbone of this power was the merchant ship.

Since the 1960s the number of FOC countries has increased to around twenty. A few of them, according to the International Transport Workers Federation, whose website (**www.itf.org.uk/seafarers/foc/report_2001**) carries much useful information on the subject, are unwilling, or are unable, to enforce minimal international standards on their vessels. Though many do now maintain the necessary standards, 699 merchant ships were detained in ports in 2001 for contravening regulations imposed by the country where they were detained, or those introduced by the *International Convention for the Safety of Life at Sea (SOLAS), or the *International Maritime Organization. Fifty-seven per cent of these were FOC ships, a disproportionately high percentage considering that though flags of convenience were flown by five of the world's six largest merchant fleets (see table in MERCHANT MARINE), only 23% of the world's fleet, in gross *tonnage, were FOC ships.

Flying flags of convenience also raises *environmental issues. Some fishing fleets pay FOC countries to allow them to fly their flag so that they can avoid the stricter controls imposed by some governments to conserve what remains of the world's commercial *fisheries, a practice that some *whaling fleets followed in the 1950s to evade the regulations laid down by the International Whaling Commission. Valuable species such as *tuna are particularly vulnerable to pirate fishing and in 1999 one regional fisheries organization, the International Commission for the Conservation of Atlantic Tunas (ICCAT), estimated that around 345 FOC fishing vessels from sixteen different

FOC countries were illegally fishing for tuna. In an effort to stop this type of pirate fishing some countries have taken action to ban the import of certain species from these sources. One, South Africa, where Cape Town was a favourite port for pirate tuna fleets, has said it will prohibit any fishing vessel from offloading in its ports if it is on the ICCAT's blacklist, or if it does not fly the flag of an ICCAT member. For more information on this subject go to **www.isanet.org/noarchive/desombre**.

flake, or **fake,** traditional term for a complete turn of a rope when it has been coiled either on deck or on a drum. It can also be used as a verb, so that when a rope has been properly flaked, or faked, down, it is clear for running, each flake running out without fouling those below it. As a verb, it is also the operation of laying out the chain anchor *cable of a ship on the *forecastle for examination.

flare. **(1)** The outward curve of the bows of a ship, which is designed to throw the water outwards when meeting a head sea, instead of letting it come straight up over the bows. **(2)** A signal, nowadays a *distress signal, fired from a *very pistol, but also hand held. They are part of the equipment of many *yachts for use in an emergency, and are also part of the equipment of a *lifesaving raft or inflatable.

flashing light, a navigational light displayed by a *lighthouse, *lightship, or lighted *buoy in which the period of light is shorter than the period of darkness separating the flashes. See also CHARACTERISTIC.

flatboat, a large flat-bottomed *pulling boat supplied during the 18th and early 19th centuries to warships which were to be engaged in amphibious operations and used for landing troops on open beaches.

fleet. **(1)** A company of vessels sailing together. This use of the word is also used to describe the whole of a national navy or all the ships owned by a shipping company. **(2)** A creek or ditch which is tidal. **(3)** As a verb, it is generally used to describe a means of obtaining a better haul on a rope, *purchases, or *cable. When a *tackle is approaching *'two blocks', so that no more movement is possible, the moving block is fleeted along to give a more advantageous haul. When *shrouds become stretched in sailing vessels, so that the *deadeyes come too close together, the upper set is fleeted further up the shroud so that there is room to haul it tauter. When an anchor was *weighed by hand, the *swifter was fleeted round the ends of the *capstan bars to provide space for additional men to be used on the capstan. **(4)** A colloquial expression of fishermen describing a vessel's first movement when it drags its keel along the ground as the rising *flood tide is just beginning to float it off.

fleet train, the generic term used during the Second World War (1939–45) to describe an assembly of *auxiliary vessels, such as oilers, repair ships, ammunition ships, provision and store ships, etc. This accompanied a fighting fleet to sea on operations and enabled it to remain operational for long periods without having to return to port. The term now usually employed for the function is **afloat support**.

Flemish horse, an additional short *footrope rigged at the end of those square sail *yards carrying reefing sails. It enabled seamen to reach the yard arms, particularly when passing the reef *earings. These are short ropes threaded through the *reef cringles of square sail and used to secure them to the yards. Colin Mudie

flense, to, to strip the blubber from a *whale when it has been caught and hauled up on to the deck of a whale factory ship. Flensing irons are used to cut the blubber loose, and *tackles then haul it away from the carcass. The deck on which the operation is performed is known as the flensing deck. See also WHALING.

Flinders, Matthew (1774–1814), British *navigator and explorer who entered the Royal Navy in 1789, served at the battle of the Glorious First of June in 1794, and in the following year sailed as a midshipman to Australia in the *Reliance* taking Captain John Hunter to govern New South Wales. He struck up a close friendship with the surgeon on board, George Bass (1771–*c.*1803?), with whom he shared an enthusiasm for *exploration by sea. After they reached Sydney in September 1795 the two, individually and in company, made several surveys, some of them in a small boat called *Tom Thumb* which Bass had brought with him from

England. At that time it was thought that Tasmania, then called Van Diemen's Land, was part of the Australian mainland, but Bass and Flinders came to the conclusion, independently, that this might not be the case. Governor Hunter was interested in their theory and gave them the chance of testing it, and on 7 October 1798 they sailed from Port Jackson in the *sloop *Norfolk*. After discovering the existence of what was later named Bass Strait, they accomplished the first circumnavigation of Tasmania. This was the last exploration the two made together and both returned to England. In 1803 Bass disappeared on a trading voyage to Peru.

In England, Flinders, who had been promoted to lieutenant while in Australia, was appointed to command the sloop *Investigator*. With his cousin John *Franklin aboard he sailed in July 1801 to Australia where, between December 1801 and May 1802, he surveyed much of the Great Bight, including St Vincent's Gulf (where Adelaide now stands), Bass Strait, and Port Phillip (site of Melbourne), before reaching Port Jackson (Sydney). In July 1802 he continued the circumnavigation of Australia in his ship, now worn out and leaky, surveying parts of the *Great Barrier Reef and the shores of the Gulf of Carpentaria, before sailing anticlockwise around the continent, returning to Port Jackson on 9 June 1803. It was a voyage of great privation for all aboard and resulted in the loss of many of Flinders's crew through *scurvy and other causes, and damaged his own health.

Besides his extensive surveys, Flinders made many scientific studies, particularly regarding the *deviation of the *magnetic compass caused by the iron components of his ship, which were to prove of the greatest importance; the compensating bars placed in the *binnacle of a magnetic compass are still named after him. With the massive collection of material and papers arising out of his voyages, he set off for England as a passenger, but was first of all wrecked on the Great Barrier Reef, and was then made a prisoner of war when the *schooner he was travelling in stopped at the French island of Mauritius in December 1803. This misfortune was caused because his French passport, which should have protected him, was made out specifically for the *Investigator* and not for the ship he was on. His captivity lasted until 1811 and his health deteriorated further during his detention, but on his return to England he nevertheless managed to compile his splendid account of his accomplishments, *A Voyage to Terra Australis*, dying on the day that it was published.

Estensen, M., *The Life of Matthew Flinders* (2003).

floating battery, originally a *razed sailing warship with guns on board for bombarding installations ashore, but in its better-known connotation, the first attempt to use armour in warships. They evolved from the abortive attack by British and French wooden *ships of the line against the Russian naval base of Sebastopol in 1854 during the Crimean War (1854–6), when the attack had to be hurriedly abandoned because of the damage the ships were receiving. Floating batteries, with their hulls protected by iron plates to the waterline and fitted with small steam engines, were constructed in Britain and France and reached the Crimea in 1855. Their first action was the bombardment of the Kinburn forts, where they created a great impression, inflicting great damage on the forts and receiving very little themselves. The ultimate development of the floating battery was the *monitor. See also WARFARE AT SEA.

floating dock, a dock constructed in the main of watertight tanks. When these are flooded, the dock is immersed in the sea to a depth where it can receive a ship's hull. As the tanks are pumped out, the dock rises, bringing the ship with it, until the hull is above water. The great value of a floating dock, as against a *graving dock which is a permanent structure, is that it can be towed to any place where its services are required.

float plan, US term for the written itinerary for a cruise. A copy of the plan is normally given to someone ashore before the start of the cruise so that the *US Coast Guard can be informed of its contents if the *yacht is overdue in returning to port, or in reaching its intended destination.

John Rousmaniere

flogging round the fleet, a form of punishment in the old days of the British Navy for the more serious crimes committed on board. It could be awarded only by sentence of a court martial. The man undergoing sentence was placed in a boat in which a ship's grating had been lashed upright across the *thwarts, and rowed alongside each ship lying in harbour. While bound to the grating he was given twelve strokes with a *cat-o'-nine-tails by a *boatswain's mate of the ship off which the boat was lying. After each infliction of a dozen strokes a blanket was thrown across his back while he was being rowed to the next ship, and it was usually necessary to *'comb the cat'. A naval doctor was always in attendance in the boat to make certain that the man undergoing punishment was fit to receive further instalments of his sentence as he came alongside each ship. In each ship visited the crew were mustered on deck and in the *rigging to witness the punishment, drums on board beating out the *'Rogue's March' as the boat approached. See also COBBING.

flog the glass, to, an expression used on board ship to indicate attempts to speed up the passage of a *watch in the days when it was timed by the half-hour *sand-glass. The run of the sand was supposed to be quickened by vibrating the glass, and when weary watch-keepers towards the end of their watches shook the glass to make the sand run out more quickly, they were said to flog the glass. See also WARM THE BELL, TO.

flood, the flow of the tidal stream as it rises from the ending of the period of *slack water at low *tide to the start of the period of slack water at high tide. Its period is about six hours which is divided into three parts of about two hours each, the first two hours being known as the young flood, the middle two hours as the main flood, and the last two as the last of the flood. An approximate rule for both the amount of the rise and speed of the flow of a flood tide for each of the six hours of the period of tide is $\frac{1}{12}$ for the first hours, $\frac{2}{12}$ for the second, $\frac{3}{12}$ for the third and fourth, $\frac{2}{12}$ for the fifth, and $\frac{1}{12}$ for the sixth.

floor, the lower part of a transverse *frame of a ship running each side of the *keelson to the *bilges. In the general run of *shipbuilding, this part of the frame is usually approximately horizontal, so that the floor of a vessel, i.e. the lower section of its transverse frames, is a virtually horizontal platform extending to the ship's sides at the point where they begin to turn towards the vertical.

flota, the name given to the annual *convoys of *treasure ships which brought treasure from Spanish colonies in Central and South America, and the Caribbean, to Spain during the 16th and 17th centuries. See also GALIZABRA.

flotilla, from the Spanish diminutive of *flota*, a fleet, *flotilla*, a little fleet, a name especially connected in navies with a group of *destroyers, *submarines, or other small warships below the size of a *cruiser. It was occasionally used in naval circles as a collective noun for all small surface craft. However, the more general meaning was restricted to the ships which made up one group under the command of a captain, the individual ships in a flotilla being commanded by lieutenant commanders or lieutenants.

In the Royal Navy the word has today almost completely died out, having been replaced by *squadron.

flotsam. **(1)** Cargo or goods lost from a ship which has sunk or otherwise perished which is found floating on the sea's surface. In Britain flotsam was originally a part of the perquisites of the *Lord High Admiral, but today comes under the legal definition of *wreck and, if recovered, must be reported to the Receiver of Wreck. To be flotsam, however, it must be floating and not on the bottom of the sea. **(2)** An archaic term for the spat, or spawn, of the oyster. See also SHELLFISH.

flowers of the wind, an old expression for the engraving of the *wind-rose on the earliest *charts and maps, and extended after the introduction of the *magnetic compass to include the compass rose on charts.

flowing. **(1)** The situation of the sheets of a sail in a *fore-and-aft-rigged sailing vessel when they are eased off as the wind comes from broad on or *abaft the *beam, and the *yards of a *square-rigged ship when they are *braced more squarely to the mast. A sailing vessel is said to have a flowing sheet when the wind crosses its beam and the sails are trimmed to take the greatest advantage of it. **(2)** A term used in connection with the *tide, a synonym of flooding. See FLOOD.

fluke. **(1)** The triangular shape at the end of each arm of an anchor which, by digging into the ground when any strain or pull comes on it, gives the anchor its holding power. They are also sometimes called *palms. Many seamen do not sound the 'k', pronouncing it as 'flue'. For illus. see ANCHOR. **(2)** The two triangular parts which make up the tail of a *whale. It was this which gave those involved in *whaling during the days of sailing *whalers the expression of 'fluking'. This meant the whalers were *running free with the *foresail *goose winged on the opposite side to the mainsail.

fluky, a description of a wind when it is light and variable in direction and has not settled down to blow steadily from any one *quarter.

flush deck, strictly speaking, a continuous deck of a ship laid from its bows to its stern, without any break. The term flush deck is also frequently used to denote a type of ship which has no *forecastle or *poop. In a *yacht it denotes a deck with no *coach-roof, *deckhouse, or other major obstructions.

fly. **(1)** The old maritime word for the *compass card from the time it was pivoted in the compass bowl and thus able to revolve freely. **(2)** The part of a flag, *ensign, or *pennant furthest from the *jackstaff or *halyard on which it is hoisted, i.e. the part which flutters in the wind. See also WEAR, TO.

fly-boat, a 16th–19th-century flat-bottomed trading Dutch vessel (*vlieboot*) with a very high and ornate stern, and with one or two masts either *square rigged on both or with a *spritsail on the mainmast. They were of about 100 tons, and used mainly for local coastal traffic. At the beginning of the 17th century they were replaced by the *fluyt* which in England was also known as a fly-boat. 'The major achievement of the Dutch ship designers, the fluyt was to have an enormous influence on shipbuilding, particularly in England. The herring *buss had a length to beam ratio of near 4 : 1. By 1610 the length to beam ratio of the fluyt had become 6 : 1 and the vessel—little more than a floating *hold with a flat bottom and near vertical stem and sternposts—was designed to carry a maximum amount of cargo' (R. Hope, *A New History of British Shipping* (1990), 169). It had one square sail on the foremast and two on the mainmast. It also had a *lateen *mizzen-mast and a spritsail under the *bowsprit. 'The early fluyts were about 150 tons, but the size increased rapidly to 200 tons and some were built to exceed 400 tons. It sailed well' (ibid.).

fly-by-night, the name given to an additional sail which acted as a sort of *studding sail. It was set by naval *sloops, which were not issued with studding sails, during the 18th and early 19th centuries. It was normally a square sail set on a temporary *yard when the wind came from directly *astern, but was occasionally a spare *jib set from the *topmast *head and sheeted by *tack and *clew to the upper *yardarms.

Flying Dutchman, the, perhaps the most famous of all legends of the sea. There are several variations of it. The most usual story is that of a Dutch skipper, Captain Vanderdecken, who, on a voyage home from Batavia and faced with a howling gale, swore by *Donner* and *Blitzen* that he would beat into Table Bay in spite of God's wrath. His ship foundered as he had this oath on his lips, and he was condemned to go on sailing until eternity in his attempt to reach Table Bay. The spectre of his ship is supposed to haunt the waters round the Cape of Good Hope and a strong *superstition among sailors is that anyone who sets eyes upon her will die by *shipwreck. A German legend concerns a Herr von Falkenberg condemned to sail for ever around the North Sea in a ship without *helm or helmsman and playing dice with the devil for his soul. A similar Dutch legend equates the Flying Dutchman with the ghost of the Dutch seaman van Straaten.

The theme of the Flying Dutchman has been used by novelists, poets, and dramatists in *marine literature, among the best known being Captain *Marryat in his book *The Phantam Ship*, Scott in his poem 'Rokeby', and Wagner in his opera *Der Fliegende Holländer*. In the opera the captain, Vanderdecken, is allowed ashore once every seven years to find a woman whose love alone can redeem him.

The origin of the legend is uncertain but it is possibly derived from a Norse saga which tells of the Viking Stöte who, having stolen a ring from the gods, was found later as a skeleton in a robe of fire seated on the mainmast of a black spectral ship.

flying jib, originally a triangular sail similar to a *staysail but set flying rather than *hanked to a *stay. The term is sometimes now used for *jibs hanked to a stay but set ahead of the other sails in the fore-triangle. Colin Mudie

f.o.b., see FREIGHT.

fo'c'sle, see FORECASTLE.

fog-buoy, a small *buoy that, before the days of *radar, was towed *astern at the end of a long *grass-line by naval vessels when steaming in line *ahead in thick fog. This gave an indication to the next ship astern of the distance away of the ship next ahead in the line, thus providing a means of retaining formation. When fog-buoys were in use, they were said to be *streamed.

foghorn, a sound appliance fitted in ships, or a portable horn carried on board small craft, used for giving warning of a vessel's presence in fog. *Fog signals are also made with foghorns by *lighthouses, and by *lightships but only when they are in their correct position.

fog signals. During the early days of sail *signals at sea in fog could only be made by ringing the *ship's bell or firing guns. Later, with the introduction of *steam propulsion, signals could be made on a siren, steam whistle, or *foghorn. These were used to indicate a ship's movements to other vessels in the immediate vicinity, indicating by the number of blasts whether it was turning to *port or *starboard, was stopped, or was going *astern. It was also possible for steamships to use their sirens to communicate with another ship by the *Morse code.

Fog signals are now laid down in the *International Regulations for Preventing Collisions at Sea. Vessels of less than 12 metres (39 ft) in length are not obliged to give any of the following signals, though they must make some other efficient sound signal at intervals of not more than two minutes.

1. A steamship under way sounds one prolonged blast on its steam whistle or foghorn not less than every two minutes.
2. A vessel under way but stopped sounds two prolonged blasts not less than every two minutes with two seconds between each blast.
3. A vessel not under command, a vessel restricted in its ability to manoeuvre or constrained by its draught, a sailing vessel, a vessel engaged in fishing, and a vessel engaged in *towing or pushing another vessel, shall sound, at intervals of not more than two minutes, one prolonged blast followed by two short ones.
4. A vessel at anchor shall, at intervals of not more than a minute, ring its bell rapidly for about five seconds. In a vessel exceeding 100 metres (328 ft) the bell must be sounded in the forepart of the vessel and immediately afterwards a gong must be sounded rapidly for about five seconds in the after part. In addition, a vessel at anchor may sound one short blast, then one prolonged one, then another short one, to warn an approaching vessel of possible collision.
5. Blasts, not just in fog, are also used by vessels to indicate a change of *course. One short blast indicates that the vessel is altering its course to starboard; two short blasts indicates that it is altering its course to port; and three short blasts indicates that it is going astern.

foot, the bottom side of a sail, whether triangular or four-sided. For illus. see FORE-AND-AFT RIG.

'foot it in', an order given to the men *furling the *bunt of a square sail when it was required to stow the sail especially snugly. It entailed the *topmen stamping this part of the sail in as hard as they could, supporting themselves by hanging on to a *topsail *tye. It was a process also known as **dancing it in**.

footropes, ropes extending from the middle of a *yard to its extremities on which the seamen stand when working on the yard. Footropes are supported at regular intervals by *stirrups which is perhaps why they were sometimes referred to as horses.

fore-and-aft rig. **(1)** The arrangement of sails in a sailing vessel so that the *luffs of the sails are attached to the masts or to *stays, as in the *Bermudan and *gaff rigs; or, as with the *lateen rig and *junk rig, by a fore-and-aft *yard hoisted on the mast, as is the *lugsail. With the exception of nearly all *foresails, but not a *staysail, the *foot of the sail is also usually attached to a boom, though they can be *loose footed.

The fore-and-aft rig dates back in Europe to the early 15th century, being introduced largely by the Dutch in or about 1420, though the Arabian lateen rig, a hermaphroditic development of a simple square sail, dates back to at least the 1st century AD. It is probable that, so far as Europe is concerned, the earliest form of fore-and-aft rig was a four-sided mainsail set on a *sprit, and that the staysail was introduced to provide a better sailing balance and prevent excessive *weather helm. In the Far East the fore-and-aft rig developed in the 3rd century. It probably came about when the Chinese developed the canted square sail used in Indonesia into the fore-and-aft *lugsail rig, this sail itself coming indirectly from the simple square sail of the ancient Egyptians. The earliest known illustration of the lugsail in the West was drawn by a Dutch artist, in 1584.

The invention of the gaff and boom came about a century later, the first known example being found in a *marine painting of Dutch ships dated 1525. Probably it developed naturally as vessels grew in size, for the larger the ship, the longer and heavier the sprit. A massive sprit would be well worth replacing on weight grounds alone by two smaller and handier *spars. This applied in even larger measure when experience showed that such substitution increased the overall efficiency of the rig, particularly when working to *windward. Indeed, for a great many years the gaff was known as a half-sprit.

Local development over the next two or three centuries produced a variety of fore-and-aft types of sailing vessel, the shoal waters of Holland and eastern England lending themselves particularly to types of barge rig, such as the *boeiers and *botters of Holland and the *wherries and Thames *barges of eastern England, where *leeboards are used in place of a fixed keel to avoid the danger of grounding when crossing sandbanks etc. In the Mediterranean, where deep water and steady winds are the governing factors, variations on the lateen rig provided the main types, while in American waters the *schooner, carrying more sail on the foremast than on the main, was widely used as a main type. In very general terms, the overall pattern of fore-and-aft rig, certainly in European waters, was a four-sided mainsail set on a gaff and boom, a triangular staysail, and a *jib set on a *bowsprit, and possibly a small four-sided sail set on a *mizzen-mast, as in *ketches and *yawls.

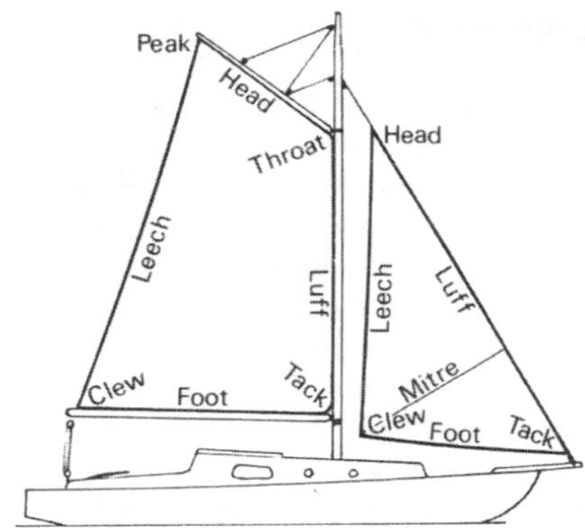

Parts of triangular and four-sided fore-and-aft sails

The next major development of the fore-and-aft rig came with the gradual abandonment of commercial sailing ships and the growth of *yachting as a sport. This period extended from about 1850 until the end of the century, by which time the fore-and-aft-rigged commercial sailing ship (with the exception of sailing barges) had been almost completely replaced by powered vessels, and yacht racing was growing fast in popularity. In the search for extra speed, the gaff mainsail was extended upwards by jib-headed or *jackyard topsails, the bowsprit was lengthened to enable additional jibs to be set, and the boom extended beyond the *counter so that a larger mainsail could be spread.

The next development was the introduction of the Bermudan rig, first used in a small racing yacht at the end of the 19th century. By the 1930s it was the norm for racing yachts though many cruising yachtsmen continued to prefer the gaff rig—and some still do.

(2) The expression **fore-and-aft** is also used to describe the seaman's uniform which consists of a jacket and peaked cap. See also SAILORS' DRESS.

forebitter, see SEA SONGS.

forecastle, (pron. fo'c'sle), the space beneath the short raised deck forward, known in sailing ships as the *topgallant forecastle, to be seen usually in smaller ships. The origin of the names lies in the castle built up over the bows of the old-time fighting ships in which archers were stationed to attack the crews of enemy vessels or to repulse *boarders *entering in the *waist of the ship. It used also to be the generic term to indicate the crew's living space in the forward end of the ship below the forecastle deck, but this meaning gradually died out as living conditions for crews improved. In this connection, it was also the name given to the *deckhouse on the upper deck of large sailing ships in which seamen had their living quarters.

forefoot, the point in a ship where the *stem is joined to the forward end of the keel.

fore-ganger. (1) Before the introduction of the metric system in the UK and elsewhere, it was a length of 15 *fathoms (90 ft/27.4 m) of chain, slightly heavier than the anchor *cable, which in some ships used to be inserted in the *cable between the anchor and first *shackle. This was done to take the additional wear on the cable as it lay in the *hawsepipe when the anchors were secured for sea. **(2)** In *whaling, a short piece of rope connecting the line with the shank of the harpoon.

foregirt, or **fargood,** a short wooden *spar lashed to the mast and used to *boom out the *luff of a *lugsail. It was chiefly used in small French and English fishing craft from about the middle of the 19th century, being probably an importation from a similar spar sometimes used in North American waters.

The foregirt may have been a late descendant of the early Norwegian **beitass*, a luff spar used in Viking ships, particularly the *knarr.

foreguy, a rope leading forward from the end of a mainsail *boom to the *bitts to prevent the boom from swinging inboard when the ship was *reaching or *running before a following wind which was patchy in force or direction. It applied mainly to *gaff-rigged vessels.

Foreland, North and **South,** two famous headlands on the eastern coast of Kent, the South Foreland being 4.8 kilometres (3 mls.) north-east of Dover and the North Foreland marking the southern end of the entry to the Thames estuary. Both appear widely in *marine literature and several battles during the 17th-century Anglo-Dutch wars were fought there. See also WARFARE AT SEA.

forelock, a flat wedge or pin driven through the hole in the *shackle of a large anchor to secure the shackle pin, much in the nature of a cotter pin. They were usually held in place by a pellet of lead which, when struck with a sledgehammer, expanded to fill the cavity behind the head. A later method was to insert a lead ring which fitted into a cavity and held the pin in position until removed with a shearing punch.

fore-reach, the distance a sailing vessel will shoot up to *windward when brought *head to wind in the act of *tacking. If a vessel has a good fore-reach, which is a function of its underbody design and its sailing speed at the time, it can sometimes be useful to make this distance to windward while remaining on the same tack, e.g. in those cases where it might mean rounding a mark or *fetching a point without having to go *about on the opposite tack, a tactic the *J-class yachts were particularly good at. The term can also be used as a verb to indicate that a sailing vessel can make progress to windward when going about or *heaving to. See also FETCH, TO; PINCH, TO.

foresail, generic name for the sails that are set on the forestays of a sailing vessel *forward of its foremost mast. However, a **big boy** or **blooper**, a light-weather foresail used by racing *yachts, is flown unattached to the forestay and is often hoisted with, and on the opposite side to, a *spinnaker. See also GENOA; GHOSTER; JIB; STAYSAIL; YANKEE.

fore-sheets, the *forward part of a boat, right in the bows, the opposite end to the *sternsheets. It has often been suggested that the origin of the term came from the fact that it was in that part of the boat that the sheets of the *foresails, when spread, are handled, but, while this is true of sternsheets, the sheets of foresails are almost invariably handled *amidships or *aft. It is more probable that because the *after part of a boat is called the sternsheets, someone decided that the forward part should be called by the opposite name.

forestay, part of the standing *rigging of a ship taken *forward to the hull from the mast. In small vessels there may be a single forestay but in sailing ships there is not only the forestay but other forward stays variously identified as to location and purpose.

Colin Mudie

Forester, Cecil Scott (1899–1966), novelist and creator of Horatio Hornblower. He was brought up in London and was originally destined for the medical profession. Failing his anatomy examinations, he took to writing in a way described in a fragment of autobiography, *Long before Forty,* which was published after his death. Among his best-known maritime stories are *Brown on Resolution* (1929), an imaginary episode during the First World War (1914–18); *The African Queen* (1935), later made into a hugely successful film; and *The Ship* (1943), in which the story centres on the second battle of Sirte in the Mediterranean during the Second World War (1939–45). However, he is, of course, best known for his series of twelve novels which traces the career, from midshipman to admiral, of a Royal Navy officer, Horatio Hornblower. Set during the Revolutionary and Napoleonic Wars (1793–1815), the series began in 1937 with *The Happy Return* (*Beat to Quarters* in the USA) and ended with the *Hornblower and the Crisis* published posthumously in 1967, their development being recorded in Forester's *The Hornblower Companion* (1964).

The Hornblower novels, based on detailed knowledge of *square-rig *seamanship and sound research, are meticulously accurate in their detail of 18th- and early 19th-century naval warfare, and are now part of *maritime literature. They brought Forester enormous popularity, and are as graphic as anything produced by his predecessor Frederick *Marryat. Forester, who was a keen yachtsman, was invalided from the *RNVR during the Second World War and spent his later years in California. Several other authors, among them Alexander Kent (Douglas Reeman), Patrick *O'Brian, and Richard Woodman, have followed in his footsteps.

fore-triangle, in *yachts, the area formed between the masthead, the base of the mast at deck level, and the lower end of the fore masthead *stay, whether it reaches the stemhead or the fore end of a *bowsprit if fitted. The size and area of the fore-triangle plays an important part in some *rating rules.

foreturn, the twist given to the *strands of which rope is made, before they are laid up into rope. See also AFTERTURN.

forge over, to. A sailing ship is said to forge over a *shoal or sandbank when it is forced over by the wind acting on a great press of sail. If the wind was *fair it was often possible to free a ship which had been caught on a shoal by setting additional sails and using the wind to push or forge it over.

former, a cylindrical piece of wood used for making the cartridges with which a naval gun was loaded in the days of sailing navies. It was slightly less than the diameter of the bore of the gun for which cartridges were to be made, and paper or linen was wrapped round it as a container for the gunpowder required to fire the ball. It was of a size to take exactly the amount of powder required for the charge.

Fortunus, originally a Roman god to whom sacrifices were made in Rome in honour of naval victories. However, in 31 BC Marcus Vipsanius Agrippa (63–12 BC) dedicated a temple to *Neptune in honour of the naval victory of Actium, thus confirming Neptune as the Roman god of the sea. See also WARFARE AT SEA.

forward (pron. forrard), towards the bows of a ship, or in its fore part. It has no particular boundary line, being used more in a relative or directional sense than as a definition of any area.

fothering, a method of stopping a leak at sea during the days of sail. The old practice was to fill a basket with ashes and chopped rope-yarns and cover it loosely with *canvas. The basket was then fixed to the end of a long pole and plunged repeatedly into the sea as near as possible to the leak. As the rope-yarns were gradually shaken through the side of the basket or over the top, they were drawn into the leak with the water entering it, and so choked it. A more efficient method, developed later, was to draw a sail, or a piece of canvas, closely *thrummed with yarns, under the bottom of the ship in the area of the leak, the pressure of water holding it close to the ship's side and thus stopping the leak. This is the same principle as that on which the *collision mat works, but was used in smaller vessels in which proper collision mats were not carried.

foul, an adjective and a verb with various nautical meanings, generally indicative of something wrong or difficult. When used as an adjective a **foul *hawse** is the expression used when a ship lying to two anchors gets its *cables crossed; a **foul wind** is one which, being too much ahead, prevents a sailing ship from laying its desired *course. When used as a verb it indicates much the same thing. One vessel can foul another when it drifts down on it, or can foul a ship's hawse by letting go an anchor and cable across that of the other. In a *yacht race, a yacht can foul another competitor by touching or hindering her. See also FOUL ANCHOR; FOULING.

foul, or **fouled, anchor.** **(1)** An anchor which has become hooked in some impediment on the seabed or, on *weighing, has its *cable wound round the *stock or the *flukes. **(2)** The foul anchor was also the official seal of the *Lord High Admiral of Britain. Its adoption as his official seal dates from the end of the 16th century when it was incorporated as part of the arms of Lord Howard of Effingham, then Lord High Admiral. A form of it, however, had been in use by the Lord High Admiral of Scotland about a century earlier.

The use of the foul, or fouled, anchor, an abomination to seamen when it occurs in practice, as the seal of the highest office of maritime administration is purely on the grounds of its decorative effect. The rope *cable around the *shank of the anchor gives a pleasing finish to the stark design of an anchor on its own.

Foul anchor

fouling. Any surface placed in the ocean soon gains a cover of bacteria, algae and *seaweeds, and animals such as *barnacles, and this is known as fouling. Fouling is a serious problem for vessels large and small because it causes loss of speed and costly increases in fuel. Static structures such as pilings, the legs of *offshore oil and gas platforms, and the cages of *fish farms are rendered dangerously susceptible to *wave damage by heavy fouling. Cleaning the hull of a modern merchant ship is an expensive and laborious task, and it is better to deter the organisms from settling in the first place. Anodic protection by attaching *copper sheathing to the hull is termed 'sacrificial' because the protection it gives results from its slowly dissolving and introducing toxic ions into the water flowing across the hull. This was particularly effective in protecting wooden-hulled ships against infestations of *teredo worm. Marine paints were then developed that also leached toxic substances, the most effective of which contained tributyltins (or TBTs). However, TBTs proved to be so persistent in the sea that they caused large and unacceptable changes in the faunas of ports and harbours, and began to spread further into the open sea. One of their effects (among many) was to cause 'imposex' in dog whelks (*Nucella* spp.), turning them all into sterile intermediates between male and female. The *International Maritime Organization's International Convention on the Control of Harmful Anti-fouling Systems on Ships was adopted in 2001, and using marine paints containing TBTs is now widely banned, but unfortunately not universally so. Traces of TBTs are still found contaminating marine organisms, even ones we eat.

So why are animals like fish and *whales rarely fouled? The answer seems to be because they are continually sloughing their skins so any fouling drops off; now new non-toxic paints are being developed that slough in much the same way.

M. V. Angel

founder, to, of a ship, to sink at sea, generally understood to be by the flooding of its hull either through springing a leak or through striking a rock. Other causes of a ship sinking, such as explosion etc., are not usually associated with the word.

fox, an old name for a *strand or fastening formed by twisting several rope-yarns together by hand for use as a *seizing or for weaving a *paunch mat.

Fram, a three-masted *schooner of 402 tons with *auxiliary steam power, was the first vessel designed to winter in the polar pack *ice, her hull being so shaped that no matter how strong the pressure of the ice she would lift free of it. The brainchild of the Norwegian polar explorer Fridtjof *Nansen, the *Fram* was first employed on his famous drift across the Arctic Ocean in 1893–6. In 1898–1902 Otto Sverdrup used her to explore the islands north-west of Greenland. In 1910 she was taken by Roald *Amundsen to the Antarctic where he and four companions successfully reached the South Pole.

Today the *Fram* is preserved as a national monument in a building specially constructed for her near Oslo. See also SHIP PRESERVATION.

frame, a *timber or rib of a ship, running from the keel to the side rail. A ship's frames form the shape of the hull and provide the skeleton on which the hull planking or plating is secured. In a wooden ship the frames are built up of sections called *futtocks; in steel ships they are normally of angle iron bent to the desired shape. A ship with its frames set up and ready for planning or plating is said to be 'in frame'. For illus. see SHIPBUILDING.

Franklin, Sir John (1786–1847), British naval officer and Arctic explorer, who was born at Spilsby, Lincolnshire. He experienced *warfare at sea at the battles of Copenhagen in 1801 and Trafalgar in 1805. In between he served under his cousin Matthew *Flinders in the *Investigator* where he showed his ability as a surveyor. In 1818 he was chosen to command the *Trent* in which Captain David Buchan tried to reach the North Pole. Between 1819 and 1827 he led two overland expeditions to the far north of the American continent which gained new knowledge of the coastline. During this time he was promoted *post-captain and was elected a Fellow of the Royal Society, and in 1829 he was knighted. He served as governor of Tasmania between 1836 and 1843 and on 19 May 1845, in command of the 372-ton *bomb ketch *Erebus*, he set out with another bomb ketch, *Terror*, to discover a *North-West Passage from the Atlantic to the Pacific. After being sighted on 26 July at the head of Baffin Bay, the two ships were never heard of again.

In 1850 the *Admiralty launched a search for the missing ships. The camp where the expedition overwintered in 1845–6 was found on a small island, as were the graves of three sailors. Modern autopsies on the bodies revealed a high level of lead in them which almost certainly came from the expedition's tinned food and would have had a disastrous effect on the entire crew. In 1859 the expedition sent in the steam yacht *Fox*, which had been purchased by Lady Franklin to discover the fate of her husband, found a cairn on the island. This contained the expedition's diaries, the *log book, and a letter which established the date of Franklin's death as June 1847. The cache also revealed that just as the ships were on the point of discovering a passage through Peel Sound in September 1846 they became fast in the *ice. In April 1848, the last entry in the expedition's diary, the ships were abandoned and their crews tried to march to safety, but none survived.

Later expeditions—and there were many of them—learnt from the local Inuit that Franklin and his men died on or near King William Island, probably from starvation. A number of articles were recovered from the Inuit who also mentioned cannibalism, and this was supported by a modern autopsy on some of the bodies found later. More bodies, some of them in the remains of the ships' boats, were recovered by further expeditions in the 19th century and by ones mounted by archaeologists during the last half of the 20th century. Scientific investigations into the tragedy were still ongoing in 2004.

Beattie, O., 'Franklin Expedition Graves', in James P. Delgado (ed.), *The British Museum Encyclopedia of Underwater and Marine Archaeology* (1997).
—— and Geiger, J., *Frozen in Time* (1993).
Lamb, G. F., *Franklin* (1956).
McClintock, F., *The Voyage of the Fox* (1859).

frap, to, to bind together to increase tension or to prevent from blowing loose, Thus *shrouds, if they have worked loose, are frapped together to increase their tension; a sail is frapped with turns of rope round it to prevent it from flapping in the wind. Frapping lines are passed across the tops of *awnings to hold them secure in a high wind. In the days of sail, ships' hulls were sometimes frapped by passing four or five turns of *cable-laid rope round them when it was thought that they might not otherwise be strong enough to resist rough weather.

free. A sailing ship is said to be **sailing free** when her sheets are eased, and **running free** when the wind is blowing from *astern. **To free the sheets**, to ease them off to present a squarer aspect of the sails to the wind. For illus. see POINTS OF SAILING.

freeboard, the distance, measured in the *waist, or centre, of a ship, from the waterline to the upper deck level.

freezing, the term sometimes used to describe the ornamental painting around the bows, stern, and *quarters of old sailing ships, most often in the form of arms and armour or maritime emblems. There can be little doubt that this was the contemporary shipwright's method of spelling friezing, from frieze, a band of ornament.

freight, goods transported in a ship, or the money paid for the transport of such goods. Freight, in its meaning of goods transported, is specified in the *bill of lading and when shipped c.i.f., which indicates that the quoted price for shipment includes cost, insurance, and freight, remains the property of the consignor until delivery is taken by the consignee at the port of unloading. Where freight is shipped f.o.b. (free on board) the goods become the property of the consignee immediately they arrive on board and he is responsible for the payment of insurance and freight charges.

In older forms of commerce the shipowner often owned the goods loaded in his ship and carried them to foreign ports to sell to the best advantage, replacing them when sold with goods purchased abroad and brought home for sale at a profit. In this case there were of course no actual freight charges as such, this element of the cost coming from the overall profit from the sales of outward-bound and inward-bound goods. An alternative to this general pattern was for a merchant to *charter a ship to carry his goods to foreign ports for the *master, or an agent known as a *supercargo or *husband, to sell to the best advantage. In this case the actual freight charges would not be specifically determined but would be a part of the sum paid in chartering the ship.

With the introduction of *steam propulsion and more rapid means of communications, the old pattern of freight changed. Instead of goods being taken aboard on the basis of *adventure, sales of specific goods were arranged directly between merchants, and the freight was arranged with a shipowner or a shipping line trading regularly to the port nearest to the consignee.

As the overall volume of world trade expanded from the late 19th century, the pattern of freight again changed, especially in the design of ships to carry one particular product, such as coal, grain, etc. The increasing volume of trade since then, in conjunction with the profits to be made in handling larger cargoes, has resulted in the building of ever larger *bulk carriers and *container ships.

Frenchman, the name given to a left-handed loop when coiling down wire rope right handed. Wire rope, especially in long lengths, does not absorb turns as easily as fibre rope, and if the wire being coiled is not free to revolve during coiling, it will become twisted. An occasional left-handed loop introduced into the coil will counteract the twists.

Frenchman

'freshening his hawse', an expression used by the old seamen, particularly in the days of *square-riggers, to describe the action of officers who took two or three nips of rum, known as *grog, or whisky, after a long spell on deck in stormy weather.

freshes, the name given to the fresh water which drains off the land after a period of heavy rain and increases the flow of the *ebb tide as it recedes from estuaries and the mouths of large tidal rivers, carrying the land silt to a considerable distance out to sea and discolouring the water. Thus, the freshes of the Nile are well known for carrying sand many kilometres to seaward, turning the water yellow. Other rivers whose freshes are notorious for the distance they discolour the water are the Amazon, Congo, Mississippi, Indus, Ganges, and Rhône. In the early days of *navigation, these freshes were often used as a useful indication of a ship's position.

Friendship sloop, originally a type of fishing boat working offshore out of the port of Friendship on the coast of Maine, USA. With fixed keel and deep *draught, a wide *beam and *fiddlehead bow, and a broad *counter, Friendship *sloops have been built in sizes from about 6 to 11 metres (20–35 ft) in length.

frigate, originally one of five principal types of merchant ship hulls in the days before sailing ships were identified by their rig. During the 18th century the word began to mean a three-masted vessel, *square rigged on each mast, then evolved into describing a class of warship which was part of all navies. They were normally armed with from 24 to 44 guns carried on a single gun-deck. In navies where ships had a *rate according to the number of guns they carried, they were fifth- or sixth-rate ships, and thus not expected to lie in the *line of battle. Possessing superior sailing qualities to the larger *ships of the line, they were used with the fleet as lookouts and, in battle, as repeating ships to fly the admiral's signals so that other ships in the line, which might be blanketed from the admiral by the smoke of gunfire, could read his signals. Alternatively, frigates worked independently of the fleet, cruising in search of *privateers or as escort ships for *convoys, in which case they were generally given the generic name of *cruisers.

There was a convention in the days of sailing navies that larger ships did not engage frigates during fleet battles unless the latter opened fire first, though it was not unknown for frigates occasionally to engage ships of the line. This convention only applied in fixed battle and did not hold good if a frigate were met at sea unaccompanied by a fleet.

During the Napoleonic Wars with France (1793–1815) a class of 44-gun frigates, rated as fourth rates, was introduced in Britain, carrying guns on two decks. In the Royal Navy they had little success as a class, being both too small to lie in the battle line and inferior in sailing qualities to the single-decked frigates. The Americans, on the other hand, had considerable success with theirs, USS **Constitution* gaining victories over HMS *Guerrière* and HMS *Java*, and the USS *United States* taking HMS *Macedonian*. The frigates built of fir for the British Navy towards the end of the Napoleonic Wars were known **square-tucked frigates** because of the shape of their *tuck.

During the Second World War (1939–45) the term frigate was revived for a class of medium-speed anti-*submarine vessels used on convoy escort work which, in size, were between *corvettes and *destroyer escorts (called 'patrol frigates' in the US Navy). Since then it has become the generic term for smaller warships in all navies with an anti-submarine, anti-aircraft, aircraft-direction, or general purpose capability. See also DONKEY FRIGATE; GALLEY FRIGATE; WARFARE AT SEA.

Frobisher, or **Forbisher, Sir Martin** (*c.*1535–94), English *navigator and explorer, one of the ablest of the great seamen of the Elizabethan age, endowed equally with courage, resource, and *seamanship. However, he made himself unpopular with his subordinates by the strict discipline he imposed and captains were not always willing to serve under him.

He first gained fame as leader of three expeditions in search of a *North-West Passage to *Cathay. The first of these, consisting of two little ships, *Gabriel* (25 tons) and *Michael* (20 tons), set out in 1576. In the course of it Frobisher, in the *Gabriel*, crossed what was later named the Davis Strait and discovered the bay—believed, until 1860, to be a strait—which has borne his own name ever since.

The glitter of mica in some stones he brought back encouraged a belief in the presence of gold. This brought him support for a second voyage the following year when Elizabeth I lent him the ship *Aid*, of 200 tons, to accompany the *Gabriel* and *Michael*. Though this voyage only achieved a more detailed survey of Frobisher Bay, the continuing lure of gold led to a third and larger expedition of fifteen vessels sailing under Frobisher's command in 1578. This voyage was of considerable navigational interest but brought no commercial profit and the discovery meanwhile that the glittering stones were valueless brought the expeditions to an end. In 1585 Frobisher commanded the *Primrose* as vice admiral in Sir Francis *Drake's expedition to the West Indies.

During the operations against the *Spanish Armada in 1588 Frobisher, in the *Triumph* of 1,110 tons, largest of the English men-of-war, distinguished himself in the fighting and, together with several others, was knighted. In 1590 and again in 1592, he commanded *squadrons stationed off the Spanish coast to intercept *treasure ships returning from the Spain's new colonies. In this he was not successful, though he dislocated the Spanish *convoy system.

Frobisher's last expedition was in 1594 when he was given command of a royal squadron to assist Henri IV of France to defeat a Spanish attempt to fortify the peninsula of Crozon and threaten the port of Brest. The assault from land and sea was successful but at the cost of heavy casualties of whom Frobisher was one. Though he survived his wound and brought his squadron back to Plymouth, he died of gangrene a few weeks later. See also EXPLORATION BY SEA.

McDermott, J., *Martin Frobisher, Elizabethan Privateer* (2001).

frocking, the term used in the US Navy where an individual has been selected for promotion and is authorized to assume the insignia, title, and seniority of his higher rank in advance of his official promotion date. However, as with an *acting rank, he does not receive any increase in pay until the official promotion date.

Tyrone G. Martin

front. (1) A surface feature of the sea caused by relatively sharp changes in either temperature or *salinity. Usually the temperature differences are small, a degree or so, but occasionally, along the boundaries of fast-flowing *currents, they can be as high as 5 or 6 °C (9–10 °F). Since the density of sea water is determined by both temperature and salinity, the denser water (cooler or saltier) tends to be sliding beneath the lighter water. So the surface water tends to be converging towards the front, but divergent fronts, where the water tends to be flowing outwards away from the front, can also be formed.

Fronts tend to be maintained dynamically along the edges of current flows, and can be generated by both local and large-scale mechanisms. One of the smaller-scale processes is the effect of a gentle wind blowing over the surface of a calm sea. This generates counter-rotating cylinders of water in the upper few metres that are called Langmuir cells. These cells lie parallel to the wind direction, with a convergent front along one side and a divergent front along the other. *Windrows and *slicks form along the convergent front, as any floating debris and *plankton tends to be accumulated. In coastal waters tidal fronts form which are generated by the *ebb and *flow of the *tide. At shallow depths the friction between the tidal currents and the seabed keeps the overlying water uniformly mixed, but there is a critical depth at which the mixing no longer extends all the way to the surface and here a tidal front develops. So on one side of such a tidal front the water is thermally stratified whereas on the other side the water temperature is uniform top to bottom. At still larger scales, mesoscale *eddies and rings that may be tens to hundreds of kilometres across are bounded by meandering fronts, along which there tend to be quite strong local surface currents. Following around the meanders the surface waters may tend to sink (where the water is turning clockwise around the meander in the northern hemisphere), or create an *upwelling. So not only does buoyant material tend to accumulate along fronts, but also, where nutrient-rich water is brought to the surface, *marine plant productivity is high. Since both phytoplankton and animal plankton tend to accumulate along fronts, they attract predators large and small, including turtles, *marlin and even *whales. Large currents like the *Gulf Stream, which are transporting warm (or cold) water from one region to another, are bounded by a complex of meandering fronts with quite large current shears across them. The breaking away of these meanders from the main flow of the current is the genesis of some of the eddies and rings. See also ANTARCTIC CONVERGENCE. **(2)** The forward edge of an advancing mass of cold or warm air. See MARINE METEOROLOGY.

M. V. Angel

full and by, the point of *sailing where a vessel keeps as close to the wind as it can without any shiver or lift in the *luffs of its sails, a condition also known as **rap full**. See also BY.

'full sea', an old term, used in the 15th–16th centuries, to describe the state of high water at the top of the *flood tide in a port or harbour.

fulmars are cliff-nesting *seabirds abundant in the North Atlantic and Pacific. They range further out into the open ocean than many other birds, feeding at the surface and gliding characteristically on stiff downward-curved wings. They eat almost anything and, because they do not regurgitate, scientists are able to assess the extent to which they are affected by marine *pollution from what they ingest. In 2003 it was found that the stomachs of 96% of dead fulmars that were picked up contained 0.6 gm of plastic fragments, almost double the amount found in the early 1980s. They are also known to ingest bits of rope and polystyrene cups, mattress foam, toys, tools, and cigarette ends. There are two forms of northern fulmar (*Fulmarus glacialis*), a pale, gull-like form and a dark, shearwater-like form. In the Southern Ocean there is the southern fulmar (*Fulmarus glacialoides*) which is a surface feeder and two species of giant fulmar (*Macronectes* spp.) that are aggressive scavengers.

Fulmars have no natural predators and can live to a great age. One female which frequently nests on the Orkney Isles has been monitored by scientists since 1951 and, at 50, became the world's oldest known wild bird. M. V. Angel

Fulton, Robert (1765–1815), American engineer. He was first apprenticed to a jeweller, then took up portrait and landscape painting as a profession, and finally, during a visit to England in 1794, decided that engineering was to be his career. His initial energies were devoted to canal engineering and he took out a British patent for superseding canal locks by inclined planes, an invention which failed to attract much attention. In 1797 he settled in Paris and in 1801, after a great many setbacks, managed to persuade Napoleon that the French answer to British sea power lay in the use of *submarines. He received a grant of 10,000 francs with which to construct a prototype and built the *Nautilus*. Ellipsoid in shape, with a length of 6.4 metres (21 ft) and a diameter of 2.1 metres (7 ft), she could submerge by flooding internal *ballast tanks. She was driven under water by a *propeller turned by hand and on the surface by a collapsible mast and sail. At a demonstration at Brest, Fulton succeeded in blowing up an old *schooner, moored in the centre of the harbour as a target, by diving the submarine beneath the vessel and attaching to her bottom an explosive charge carried externally on the submarine. Despite this success, the French Ministry of Marine was unimpressed, as were the British *Admiralty and the American authorities when he later demonstrated the submarine to them.

He was much more successful with his ventures into *steam propulsion and in 1803, with the help of the American politician Robert Livingston (1746–1813), who was in Paris to negotiate the Louisiana Purchase, demonstrated a 20-metre (65-ft) *paddle steamer, fitted with an 8-horsepower engine of French design, on the River Seine. Then in 1807, he designed a paddle steamer which he and Livingston, who had been granted the monopoly of steam navigation on all waters within the New York State boundaries, built. Later called the **Clermont*, she was commercially successful and in the following years Fulton designed several more. He also built the *turtle-boat; sat on the commission which recommended the construction of the Erie Canal; and in October 1814 *launched a 50-metre (167-ft), 6-knot, steam *catamaran, the world's first powered warship. Built for the US Navy Department she had her boiler in one hull and her engine in the other, and was armed with 26 32-pounder guns and fitted with a central paddle wheel. Fulton called her the *Demologos* ('the word of the people') but she was later renamed the *Fulton* in his honour. She was really a floating gun platform suited only for calm water. Designed to defend New York, the Anglo-American War (1812–14) ended before she saw any action.

Fulton spent much of his fortune on his submarine designs, and in litigation against those who pirated his steamboat patents and others who attempted to break the monopolies he and Livingston held. But he integrated the key inventions of other early ship designers, including David *Bushnell, and made them into successful prototype vessels.

furl, to, to take in the sails of a vessel and secure them with *gaskets. With *square-rigged ships this means hauling in on the *clew lines and *buntlines and rolling them up to the *yards. With the *fore-and-aft rig, the sails are lowered and secured to the booms with gaskets, or the *foresails are rolled up and secured to the *stays on which they are set. **To furl in a body**, a method of furling sail in square-rigged ships occasionally practised when the ship is expected to remain in harbour for some time. It entails gathering the sail into the *top of the heel of the *topmast by releasing the *earings at the *yardarms, so that the sail can be drawn in towards the centre of the yard.

furniture, the whole movable equipment of a ship—*rigging, sails, *spars, anchors, boats, and everything with which it is fitted out to operate it, but not including its consumable stores, such as fuel and victuals.

furring, an old term used by shipwrights meaning replanking a vessel to give it more *beam and *freeboard.

futtock, the separate pieces of timber which form a *frame or *rib in a wooden ship. There are normally four, or occasionally five, futtocks to a rib in a ship of moderate size. The one nearest the keel is known as a **ground** or **naval futtock**, the remainder being called **upper futtocks**.

futtock shrouds, or **puttock shrouds,** short *shrouds used to counteract the load of upper shrouds and connected to them at the *crosstrees at the *top, and down and into the mast. Alternatively, they are sometimes taken to a stave secured to the lower shrouds. In doing so they cross the shrouds coming up to that top. The exact placing of this crossing is planned at the height of the *yard to give it the maximum bracing angle. The futtock shrouds are fitted with *ratlines to provide a quick route for seamen to the upper shrouds or to the top. The name puttock is thought to be derived from the resemblance of the early metal bars used for this purpose to the pothooks in common use ashore. The name futtock is thought to be derived from puttock. Colin Mudie

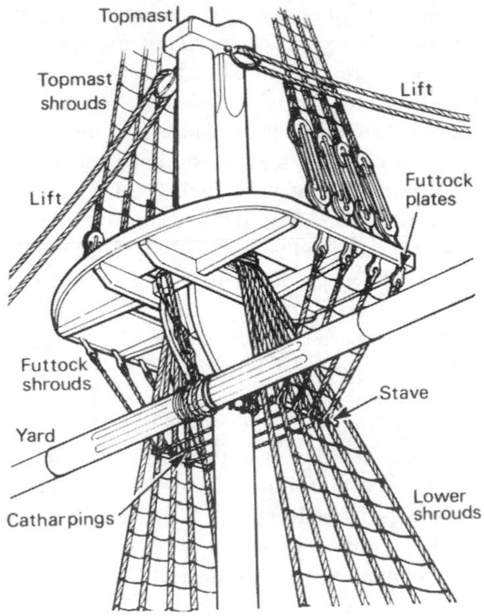

Futtock shrouds

G

Gabbard, the, a sandbank lying off the coast of Suffolk, England, to seaward of Orfordness, and the name given to a battle during the First Anglo-Dutch War (1652–4). See also WARFARE AT SEA.

Gades, now Cadiz, an independent state founded by the Phoenicians in 1100 BC and occupied by the Carthaginians around 500 BC. It allied itself with Rome during the Second Punic War (206 BC). The name occurs in the many histories and accounts of the port up to the 14th century.

gaff, see GAFF RIG.

gaff rig, a *fore-and-aft rig, development of the *spritsail rig. It was, according to the evidence from *marine paintings, in existence in Sweden as early as 1525, although it is generally believed to have originated some years earlier in Holland. For the first hundred years or so of its existence the gaff, a *spar to which the *head of the rig's mainsail is attached and from which the rig took its name, was known as a half-sprit. It was the logical development of the earlier sprit, serving the same purpose of spreading the sail, but with much greater efficiency and with considerably lighter and handier spars.

The forward end of the gaff is held against the mast by *jaws, or pivoted to a wrought-iron *saddle, to fit round the mast. To hold the gaff against the mast in all conditions, the gaff jaws were often joined by a *parrel. Two sets of *halyards are used to hoist a gaff sail, *throat halyards at the mast end and *peak halyards at the outer end, but on many traditional types of Dutch craft the gaff is a very short spar, usually cut into an arched curve, and only a single halyard, attached to a span on the gaff, is used to hoist it.

For some centuries, up to the introduction of mechanical power, the gaff rig was the sailing rig of the great majority of small craft, including *trawlers and *drifters, with the exception perhaps of those in eastern waters of the Mediterranean where the *lateen rig predominated. It remained as such until the gradual introduction, during the first two decades of the 20th century, of the *Bermudan rig. However, the gaff rig remains the preferred rig for some cruising yachtsmen.

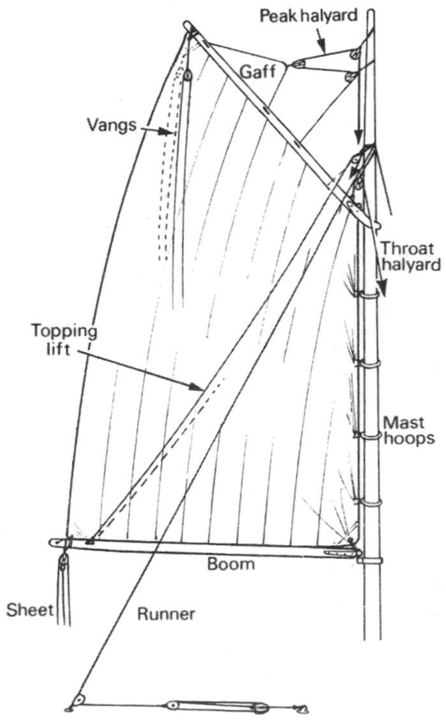

Gaff mainsail—an example of fore-and-aft rig

A gaff mainsail was commonly extended by setting a *jackyard topsail or a *jib-headed topsail above it to fill the area between the mast and the gaff.

gage, sometimes **gauge,** a term used at sea in relation to the direction of the wind. A ship which is to *windward of another has the ***weather gage** of it; one to *leeward has the ***lee gage**. It was a point of great significance in naval battle during the days of sail, either gage giving certain advantages to the fleet commander according to the way in which he wished to fight the battle. See also LINE OF BATTLE; WARFARE AT SEA.

gale, a wind blowing at a speed of between 34 and 47 knots, force 8 and 9 on the *Beaufort Scale. Winds of this strength are usually divided into two general descriptions, a gale when the wind speed is between 34 and 40 knots and a strong gale when it blows between 40 and 47 knots.

An indication of gale strength winds is also provided by the state of the sea. When the *waves are high and the crests begin to break into spindrift, a gale is blowing. Crests beginning to topple and roll over, with dense streaks of foam along the direction of the wind, are signs of a strong gale. See also MARINE METEOROLOGY; TROPICAL STORMS.

galizabra, a particular design of ship used by the Spanish in the 17th and 18th centuries. Galizabras were of similar size to a *frigate, fast, *weatherly, and very heavily armed. Their purpose was to bring the treasure over from the Spanish colonies in Central and South America, and the Caribbean, to Spain. Unlike the *treasure ships, which returned to Spain in the annual *flota, they sailed independently and relied on their speed and gun power to avoid capture.

galleass, or **galleasse,** a compromise between the oared *galley and the *galleon, in which *oars were retained to provide free movement irrespective of the direction of the wind, although masts and sails were also carried. In order to accommodate the masts and *rigging, galleasses had to be built with a great *beam and a deeper *draught than the galley. They were *lateen rigged on two or three masts, but suffered from the inevitable defects of compromise, being unable to carry the more effective *square rig of the sailing ship because of the modified galley hull form. For the same reason, they were unable to retain the speed and manoeuvrability of the true galley. Six galleasses were included in the *Spanish Armada but were unable to accomplish anything in the stormier waters of the English Channel and North Sea. The type died a fairly rapid death as warships.

The name was also used to describe the oared sailing vessels of the Mediterranean, widely used for the carriage of *freight during the 16th and 17th centuries. These were large vessels of up to 46 metres (150 ft) long with a beam of between 7 and 8 metres (25 ft), two or three masted with a lateen rig and a single bank of oars, and designed for the longer trading voyages. During the summer months they were frequently to be seen as far away from the Mediterranean as the ports of north Europe, laden with produce from India and China which had been taken on board at Genoa or Venice.

galleon, a development of the *carrack following the successful experiments of Sir John *Hawkins at the end of the 16th century. This new design, which made a ship much more *weatherly and manoeuvrable, reached Spain about seventeen years after its introduction in England. Its arrival resulted in the development of the galleon. It was originally a warship but during the next 30 to 40 years it also began to take the place of the carrack as the principal type of merchantman. Most 17th-century *treasure ships were galleons. Although the design was essentially English, the actual name was never adopted in England or among the north European nations.

gallery, the walk built out from the admiral's or captain's *cabin in larger sailing warships and extending beyond the stern. They were often highly decorated with carved work, gilded or painted, and were covered in with a wooden roof, known as a *cove, and protected from the weather with elaborate glassed windows. First- and second-*rate men-of-war normally had three galleries, a large stern gallery with smaller galleries on either *quarter. In these ships the galleries extended over two decks, thus giving six individual galleries. See also STERNWALK.

galley. (1) The oared fighting ship of the Mediterranean dating from about 3000 BC, and lasting into the 18th century. Originally propelled by *oars arranged on a single level, galleys were developed with oars arranged in banks, or different levels, known as biremes (two banks) and triremes (three banks). Galleys are mentioned in ancient writings with more banks of oars than three—quadreremes, quinqueremes, and in fact up to seventeen banks—but obviously this cannot refer to banks of oars, and some other method of classification must have been adopted, though no records exist of the methods today. In multibank galleys, up to the trireme, the length of oars differed according to the bank on which they were mounted, and it is generally thought that the length of oar in the upper bank was about 4.3 metres (14 ft), in the middle bank about 3.2 metres (10 ft 6 in.), and in the lower bank 2.3 metres (7 ft 6 in.). The number of rowers in each bank also varied, and in a typical Greek trireme with an overall length of about 39 metres (130 ft) and a beam of between 5 and 6 metres (18–19 ft), there would be 31 oars each side in the upper bank (known as thranites), and 27 oars each side in the middle (zygotes) and lower (thalamites) banks.

The weapon of the galley was the *ram, and from the 16th century guns were mounted on a platform in the bows, but they could not be trained and had to fire only directly ahead.

The galley was basically an unstable vessel, suitable only for use in calm waters. They were capable of sailing before the wind and had one or two masts, depending on their length, carrying in their early days one square sail on each mast but *lateen sails in later periods of their existence. Masts and sails were used only for passage-making and were always lowered and stowed away before action, to ensure that the great manoeuvrability given by the oars was always available in battle. A trireme, with all three banks of oars operating, was estimated to be capable of a speed of between 8 and 9 knots, but only for a short period depending on the stamina and strength of the rowers. The last naval action in which Mediterranean galleys took part was fought in 1717; in the Baltic, galleys were still employed as warships as late as the Russo-Swedish War of 1809. See also GALLIOT; WARFARE AT SEA.

(2) (*a*) An open rowing boat, with six or eight oars, used largely by customs officers in the 18th and 19th centuries, and in the British Navy by *press gangs visiting ships afloat in search of recruits. (*b*) A warship's boat, originally *clinker built but more recently of *carvel construction, rowing six oars and usually reserved for the use of the captain. Two masts, carrying lateen or *lug sails, could be stepped for sailing.

(3) The ship's kitchen, sometimes also called the *caboose in smaller merchant vessels.

galley frigate, a *frigate of a type built for the British Navy in the reign of King Charles II (1660–85) to take *oars or *sweeps as well as sails. Very few were built and, being generally inefficient, they were quickly discarded.

galley pepper, the sailor's name for the soot and ashes which used on occasions to fall accidentally into the victuals while they were being cooked.

galligaskins, the wide breeches worn by seamen in the old sailing warship days, also known as petticoat-trousers. They were most prevalent in the 16th and 17th centuries, but did not finally disappear in warships until the beginning of the 19th century. Being made of *canvas, the wide apron-like front was a protection for the men lying out on the *yards when the weather was wet. See SAILORS' DRESS; TARRY-BREEKS.

galliot, originally a small *galley, rowed by sixteen or twenty oarsmen, with a single mast and sail. It was used in the 17th and 18th centuries to chase and capture enemy ships by *boarding them, the entire crew being armed for this purpose. During the 18th century it became the accepted term for a small Dutch trading vessel, the hull built *barge fashion with a bluff, rounded bow, fitted with *leeboards, and *fore-and-aft rigged on a single mast, often with a *sprit.

gallows. **(1)** A raised wooden frame consisting of two uprights and a cross-piece on which the *skid booms of a *square-rigged ship rested. See also BOOMS. **(2)** A temporary wooden structure, also known as a boom crutch, erected on the *counter of small *fore-and-aft-rigged sailing craft on which the main boom is stowed and secured when the vessel is at anchor or lying on a *mooring. **(3)** Inverted U-shaped iron or steel frames fitted in pairs on one or both sides of a *trawler and carrying a large *sheave to take the trawl *warps. They were colloquially known as the 'the galluses'.

Gama, Vasco da (*c.*1460–1524), Portuguese *navigator, conquistador, and the first European known to have discovered the sea route to India. In 1497 he was selected by the King of Portugal to command a *squadron of four ships to follow up the discovery by Bartholomew *Diaz, nine years earlier, that there was a great ocean to the east of the Cape of Good Hope across which a route to the Orient might well exist.

Rounding the Cape of Good Hope successfully, Vasco da Gama followed the east coast of Africa to Malindi whence, under the direction of a Gujarati pilot, he crossed the Indian Ocean, reaching Calicut (now Kozhikode) on the Malabar Coast on 20 May 1498. There he set up the marble pillar by which Portuguese navigators marked any new discovery, and claimed possession of it for Portugal. The Arab traders already in the area prevented him from establishing a trading post, but he did load a full cargo of spices with which he returned home in September 1499. The voyage showed a profit of 600% and da Gama was given honours and awards by the Portuguese king.

A second expedition, commanded by Pedro Cabral (*c.*1467–1530), was dispatched in March 1500 to exploit da Gama's discoveries. Cabral established a trading post at Calicut, but, at the instigation of the Arab traders, this was later treacherously attacked and its occupants either killed or wounded. To avenge this attack a fleet of ten ships was dispatched under the command of da Gama, who was given the title of Admiral of India. He arrived off Calicut in 1502, bombarded it, and then treated the inhabitants with merciless cruelty before sailing on to Cochin where he obtained an immensely rich cargo for his ships.

On his return da Gama was created Count of Vidigueira and granted other honours and privileges, and retired to enjoy his great wealth. However, in 1524 he was appointed viceroy of the expanding Portuguese possessions in India and given the specific task of ensuring a thorough reform of the administration there. He arrived at Goa in September 1524 but had hardly begun work when he fell ill and died at Cochin. See also KAMAL.

Watkins, R., *Unknown Seas: How Vasco da Gama Opened the East* (2003).

gammon iron, a circular iron band used to hold a *bowsprit to the *stem of a sailing vessel. In the days when a bowsprit was fitted to a *yacht, the gammon iron had two metal *sheaves fixed on either side which acted as *fairleads for the anchor *cable.

gammon lashing, or **gammoning,** seven or eight turns of a rope lashing passed alternately over the *bowsprit and through a hole in the *stem of a sailing vessel to secure the bowsprit at the *knightheads. Good gammoning was a skilled operation, and when properly performed made a *cross lashing. Later a *gammon iron replaced the old gammon lashing.

gang, an old name used to describe the full set of standing *rigging used to stand up a mast in a *square-rigged sailing vessel.

gangway, originally the name given to the platforms on either side of the *skid-booms in the *waist of a *square-rigger, connecting the *quarterdeck to the *forecastle. It provided a convenient means of walking from one to the other without descending to the deck level of the waist. By extension it has today come to mean the movable passageway operated from the shore by which passengers and crews can enter or leave a ship when it is *moored alongside. See also PASSERELLE.

gantline, the modern corruption of **girtline.** It was a single *whip originally used to hoist to the masthead, or to the *hounds, the standing *rigging which was to be secured there while the ship was *fitting out, and also to hoist the *riggers, in *boatswain's chairs, to do the work. The gantline was also used for hoisting sails in *square-rigged ships from the deck to *bend them on to their *yards, as they were far too heavy to be carried up the rigging by the *topmen.

gantlope, or **gauntlope** (pron. gantlet), a form of punishment employed in the British Navy in the late 17th, 18th, and early 19th centuries which involved the whole crew of the ship. In the most serious cases the man under punishment was drawn in a sawn-down cask through a double line of the ship's company, each man armed with a *nettle, and lashed as he passed. For minor offences the man under punishment ran through a double line up to three times. Originally it was a punishment for stealing from messmates, but it was occasionally awarded for the more serious forms of naval crime. It was known as 'running the gantlope', and was abolished by order of the British *Admiralty in 1806. It has given its name to the expression 'running the gauntlet', usually used today in reference to sustained criticism. See also CAT-O'-NINE TAILS; COBBING.

garboard, or **garboard strake,** the first plank on the outer hull of a wooden vessel next to the keel, into which it is *rabbeted. It runs from the *stem to the *sternpost, and is similarly rabbeted into those timbers. The term was also used in wooden ships to describe the first *seam nearest the keel, the most difficult of all to *caulk. Similarly, in steel *shipbuilding the plates next to the keel are known as the garboard plates. It seems to have been a garbled version of 'gathering-board' and came into the English language from the Dutch *gaarboord*, itself derived from *gadaren*, to gather, and *boord*, board.

garland. **(1)** A collar of rope round a mast to support the standing *rigging and prevent it from chafing the mast. In the earliest days of sail, when ships only had single pole masts, the *tops were circular or semicircular platforms built round the masts, and that part of the pole mast above the top was known as the *topmast. The only mark on the mast above the top was the garland which supported the *stays, and that part of the pole mast above the garland was known as the 'top-garland' mast, which may have become *topgallant. **(2)** The wreath of carved wood, most often in the form of foliage, which for decorative purposes surrounded the circular *ports cut in the sides of the *forecastle and *quarterdeck of warships for the upper-deck guns. **(3)** The racks between the gun carriages and around the *hatches on the gun-decks of wooden warships, with holes cut for the stowage of *shot, were known as shot garlands. **(4)** A small circular net extended by a wooden hoop slung from the *beam above each mess in a warship in which seamen could stow their provisions to keep them beyond the reach of cats, cockroaches, rats, etc. It would also take a mug of beer or rum since, as it swung with the movement of the ship, there was no danger of spillage. See also WEDDING GARLAND.

garnet, a *tackle used in a *square-rigged ship for hoisting in casks and provisions. It was rigged from a *guy or *pendant made fast to the mainmast head with a block *seized to the mainstay over the *hatchway. In some merchant ships the tackle was large enough to be used for loading and unloading cargo as well as provisions.

'garters', seaman's slang for the *bilboes, or *irons, which were used to secure men under punishment by leg-irons shackled to a long bar.

gasket, a rope, plaited cord, or strip of *canvas used to secure a sail, when *furled, to a *yard or boom of a vessel. In large *square-rigged ships gaskets were passed with three or four turns round both sail and yard, with the turns spaced well out. The bunt gasket, which had to hold the *bunt, the heaviest part of a square sail when furled, was sometimes made of strong netting. In the old *seamanship manuals of the 17th and early 18th centuries the word is sometimes written as caskets. The modern term, used by yachtsmen, is 'tier'.

gas-turbine engines are derived from the aircraft engine and burn expensive high-quality fuel such as kerosene or gas oil, not the residual oil which the modern marine *diesel uses. A ship's main turbine unit generates high-temperature gas which drives a number of turbine wheels, and these act as its propulsion. The wheels are connected to a *propeller shaft by a gearbox which reduces the shaft speed, while the ship's speed and direction is changed by a controllable pitch propeller. This is the type of arrangement often used in gas-turbine-driven naval vessels, and most warships in the Royal Navy and US Navy which are not nuclear powered are driven by them because of the gas-turbine plant's high power to weight/size. The high cost of the fuel is not the prime concern with a naval vessel but the saving in space for the use of armaments is critical. The *aircraft carriers on order for the French and British navies will be powered by gas turbines.

For commercial ships expense does matter. The first one to be fitted with a gas-turbine propulsion plant was the American *Liberty ship *John Sergeant*, which was re-engined with one in 1956. This comprised a separate free piston gas generation unit and a gas turbine, connected via gearing to the propeller shaft. Although the gas turbine operated effectively, it could not compete with *steam propulsion or the diesel engine. An attempt was also made in the 1970s to use the gas turbine commercially when a series of fast transatlantic *container ships were constructed and fitted with aero-engine type gas turbines. But they also proved too expensive to operate and they were soon converted to diesel propulsion.

Nevertheless, gas-turbine plants are fitted in some modern *cruise ships where they are used as generators to supply power to the ship's *electrical propulsion system, as well as electricity for the ship's hotel services. The expense of the fuel is offset by the fact that the plant can be located at the funnel which frees up space elsewhere within the ship for use by passengers. They have other major advantages, too. Compared with the diesel engine, a gas-turbine plant has a low level of exhaust emissions such as oxides of nitrogen and sulphur—kerosene and gas oil contain no sulphur. This makes it an ideal power generator for cruise ships operating in environmentally sensitive areas such as Alaska, and its efficient insulation system means that it does not cause a noise problem. It is also well balanced so there is no vibration, and it can be started and put on load without any long preparation period. Denis Griffiths

gate vessel, a small ship, often a *trawler or similar vessel, which operated the central section of an anti-submarine *boom, comprising *submarine nets, across the entrance to a harbour or anchorage in time of war.

gaussin error, a *magnetic compass error temporarily induced through the soft iron in a ship when it has been steering one *course for a long time, or has been lying in one direction alongside a *pier or *wharf. It can be counteracted by the temporary adjustment of the compass correctors mounted in or on the *binnacle.

general-at-sea, the title given in England during the Protectorate of Oliver Cromwell, 1649–60, to those men appointed by Parliament to lead the English fleet in battle. Some of them, such as Robert *Blake, were appointed direct from the army. They were, of course, the equivalent of admirals.

general average, a term in marine insurance for the adjustment of a loss when cargo on board a ship belonging to one or more owners has been sacrificed for the safety of the whole, whereby the amount of the loss is shared by all who have shipped cargo in the vessel. A case for general average would occur, for example, if the deck cargo of a ship had to be jettisoned to safeguard the ship in rough weather. There are strict rules which bind a claim for general average; the loss must have been voluntary and not accidental, must not have been caused by any fault on the part of the owner claiming general average, must have been necessary and successful in saving the remainder of the cargo, and must have been made by order of the ship's *master. See also FLOTSAM; JETSAM.

general chase, a naval signal introduced into the British Navy in the mid-18th century in an attempt to circumvent the rigid *line of battle laid down for naval action by the current *fighting instructions. Few admirals were prepared to risk their reputations by departing from the tactical rules in these instructions, one of which was that battle could not be joined with an enemy fleet until the *ships of the line had been formed into line of battle and were directly opposite the enemy's line. As a result of this order, naval battles were somewhat formal affairs in which each ship fought its opposite number in the enemy's line while remaining rigidly on station in its own line. In order to break this sterility the general chase signal was introduced. This allowed each ship of war to make all sail towards the enemy and engage the nearest ship as she came up to it, even though it was not the ship she would have engaged in a line battle, succeeding ships coming up, passing her on her disengaged side, and engaging the next enemy ship within reach. It was a signal which restored initiative to the naval commander and flexibility to the line of battle and, when employed, produced some notable victories. The battles of Cape Finisterre (1747) and Quiberon Bay (1759) are fine examples of naval battles fought with the signal flying for a general chase. See also WARFARE AT SEA.

Gennaker, trademarked name for an asymmetrical or cruising *spinnaker. The word is a combination of *genoa and spinnaker.

John Rousmaniere

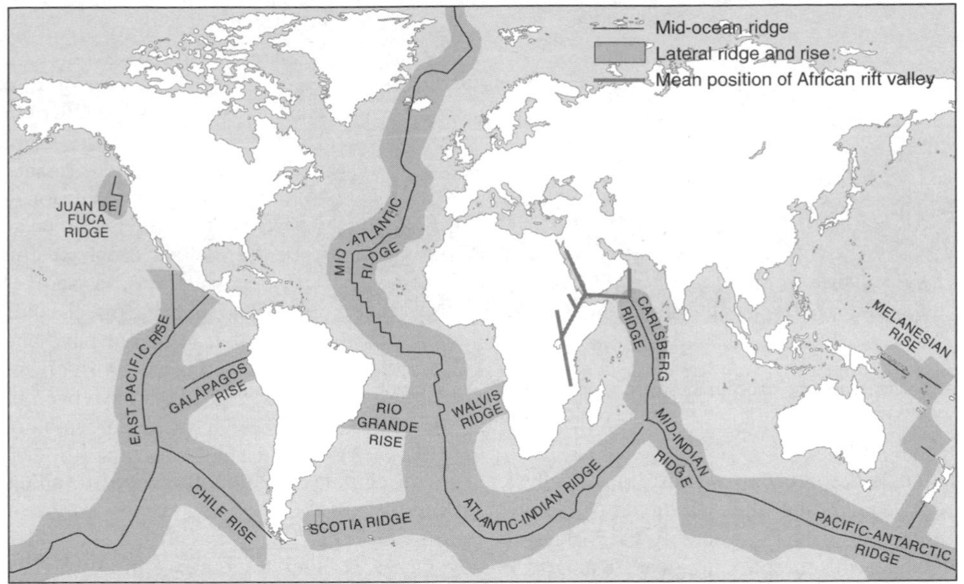

The global distribution of mid-ocean ridge systems with their central rift valleys

genoa, a large *foresail used in racing and cruising *yachts. Its features are (*a*) its size, considerably larger than a standard *jib and often larger than the *mainsail, and (*b*) its shape, with the *clew extended much farther aft than in an ordinary jib, overlapping the mainsail by an appreciable amount, its *foot often parallel with the deck *sheer. In effect, it combines jib and *staysail in a large single sail. As well as transferring the main driving power of a yacht's sails to the *fore-triangle, it also, by the sheeting of its *clew well *aft of the mast, increases the speed of the airflow over the *luff of the mainsail. This increases the partial vacuum there which helps to pull the yacht forward. See AERODYNAMICS for an analysis of this forward pull.

gentlemen captains, court favourites of the Tudor and Stuart kings and queens of England who were appointed to command ships in the British Navy without having had to work their way up by promotion from lower ranks. Very often they had no knowledge of the sea or the ways of a ship, but solicited these appointments for the opportunities of plunder and *prize money which they offered. Such captains were disliked by the crews of the ships they commanded and particularly by *tarpaulin captains. Equally disgusted by this backstairs method of appointment was Samuel *Pepys who, as secretary of the *Admiralty, 1673–9 and 1684–9, made the lives of gentlemen captains a misery by insisting that they remained on board their ships unless given official leave. He also required them to forward *log books for their ships punctually every month to the Navy Office. Under this strict regime few courtiers found it worthwhile to solicit appointments to command ships and the practice was effectively stamped out.

geological oceanography is the study of the rocks and sediments that compose the seabed. Two hundred million years ago there was a single great ocean surrounding one great continent, Pangea. The theory of plate tectonics describes the mechanism that led to the break-up of Pangea and the development of the ocean basins that we see today. The rocks underlying the ocean floor are totally different from those beneath the continents in both their origin and character. The rocks (or ocean crust) underlying the oceans are mostly less than 200 million years old, whereas on the continents the oldest rocks are 3 billion years old. Along the centre of each ocean lies a mountain ridge with a rift valley along its axis. Within the rift valley new ocean crust is continually being formed and

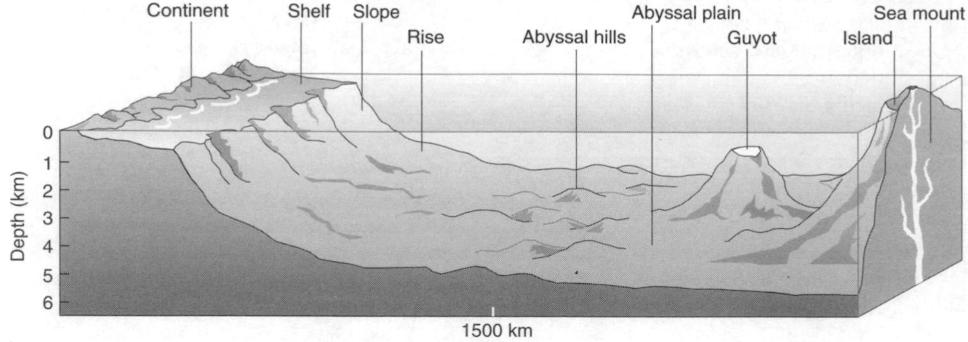

An idealized portion of ocean basin floor with abyssal hills, a guyot, and a sea mount on the abyssal plain. Sea mounts and guyots are known to be volcanic in origin

spreads sideways; also within the rift valleys are *hydrothermal vents. As the lavas that are erupted along the ridge solidify, the rock crystals align with the prevailing earth's magnetic field, which periodically reverses. This creates parallel lines of small, alternating, positive and negative anomalies in the magnetic field across the seabed, providing a sort of tape recording of the formation and subsequent spread of the ocean crust.

It is impossible to move a flat plate across the surface of a sphere without fracturing (try laying orange peel out flat without breaking it) so inevitably a pattern of faults develops. As the new crust moves away from the ridge, it cools and shrinks, so the ocean basins deepen towards their margins. Where the crust abuts against the continents, one of two processes occurs. At 'active' margins the ocean crust buckles down under the continent forming deep *trenches, and is destroyed in the molten interior of the earth. The 'passive' margins are stable and so continents are shunted sideways, constantly shifting their positions on the surface of the planet.

As the crust spreads away from the ridge it becomes covered by increasing thicknesses of sediments that include dust blown off the continents and myriads of skeletal remains of *planktonic species. The sediments eventually fill in the rough topography and create vast tracks of featureless seabed, known as **abyssal plains**, that underlie about half of the world's oceans. These accumulations of sediment become thicker with time, and contain chemical tracers and microfossils that, like tree rings, record the climate conditions that were prevailing at the time of their deposition. The extensive coring of ocean deposits carried out under the Ocean Drilling Programme, and its predecessor the Deep Sea Drilling Programme, has provided the main evidence for the way *climate change has occurred over geological time. In very deep water, particularly in the Pacific, the calcium carbonate and silicate constituents of the skeletal remains dissolve, leaving deposits of red clays that contain no climate record.

Another source of the material that infills the ocean basins are flows of debris derived from underwater landslides, which, triggered by earthquakes, slip off the continental slopes. Along active margins, the deep trenches trap these debris flows, but where the margins are passive, as they are around the Atlantic, massive flows of sediment-laden water flood out unchecked across the abyssal plains. When they reach the foothills of the mid-ocean ridge, they deposit thick layers of mud and debris, known as turbidites. Ash deposited after violent volcanic eruptions also contributes to the infill, and it can form thick local deposits, which can be dated from their content of radioactive isotopes.

Yet another source of infill identified in the North Atlantic are thick layers of stones and gravel, called **Heinrich layers**, dropped from vast numbers of melting icebergs that have periodically broken out from the Arctic.

The monotony of the abyssal plains is also broken in places by **sea mounts**, which are volcanic cones truncated by wave action that have developed over hot spots in the ocean floor. These hot spots are created by convection in the underlying magma, the liquid inner core of the earth. These hot spots are often stationary relative to the earth's surface so, as the ocean crust spreads across, a chain of sea mounts develops; thus the Hawaiian chain of islands lies at the end of the 6,000-kilometre (3,725-m.) Hawaiian-Emperor chain of sea mounts. This has a dog-leg in it that resulted from a change in the direction of ocean spreading 43 million years ago.

The geology of the seabed on the continental margins is an extension of the land geology. So surveying the structures underlying seas like the North Sea is based on the same techniques as those used on land, but with the added difficulty of coping with the covering of sea water. The rise in *sea level since the last ice age has submerged many oil- and gas-bearing strata, hence the development of the *offshore oil and gas industry. In the Mediterranean the constant jostling of the African continental land mass against the Eurasian land mass has resulted in the repeated opening and closing of the Strait of Gibraltar. Each time the strait closed the Mediterranean Sea evaporated to dryness leaving thick deposits of salt. The volume of these salt deposits implies that the sea emptied and refilled at least seven times during the Miocene era, causing fluctuations in sea level globally of around 70 metres (200 ft). The salt is porous, so oil has migrated through it and accumulated in domes, hence the rich oil deposits found in Libya. There are other mineral resources with commercial potential, placers of heavy metals (e.g. gold, tin, and diamonds) that get washed into the sea from rivers; phosphates that accumulate under productive regions of sea; manganese nodules that are precipitated at great ocean depths; and sands and gravels, many dropped in glacial moraines during the glaciations, which are now exploited as aggregates for construction projects.

Allaby, A., and Allaby, M., *The Concise Oxford Dictionary of Earth Sciences* (1991).

Crowley. T., and North, G., *Paleoclimatology* (1991).

http://pubs.usgs.gov/publications/text/dynamic.html

www.oceansonline.com/lib_geo_ocean.htm

M. V. Angel

German mile, a sea measurement used mainly by Dutch *navigators in the 17th and early 18th centuries. It was equal in length to 4 *nautical miles.

get spliced, to, see SPLICED, TO GET.

ghoster, a light-weather sail used in *yachts. It is attached to the topmast *stay by *hanks and is set when the winds are very light. It is very similar in shape to either a *genoa or a *yankee, according to choice, but with its *luff extending the whole length of the stay instead of short of the masthead as is often the case with a genoa or yankee. It is made of much lighter cloth than a genoa, usually very light Terylene, or even nylon, and is suitable for use in winds of upto force 2 on the *Beaufort scale.

ghosting, the art of making headway in a sailing ship without any *apparent wind to fill its sails. By taking advantage of such breaths of wind as may occur, a well-trimmed vessel can often make quite an appreciable way through the water, appearing to move, or ghost, even in a flat calm.

gig, a light, narrow ship's boat, built for speed, originally *clinker built but then more usually of *carvel construction, rowing four or six *oars. It had *steps or *tabernacles for two short masts which could be shipped when required, setting two *lug or *lateen sails. Powered boats have long since replaced them, but some are still used for recreational purposes. In the US Navy it is the name of the captain's personal boat.

gimbals, two concentric metal rings which form the mounting and suspension for the compasses and *chronometers on board ship. The rings are mounted on knife edges, the bearings of one being fixed fore and aft in the ship's line and the other *athwartships, thus allowing the compass or chronometer to remain level irrespective of the rolling or *pitching of the ship. Gimbals are also used to mount lamps, cooking stoves, etc. in small vessels. The earliest description of a gimbal mounting dates from the beginning of the 17th century.

gimblet, to, or **gimbleting,** the action of turning an anchor around on its *fluke in the days before stockless anchors and when they were stowed ready for sea on an anchor bed. It was a necessary operation in order to get the anchor into position so that it would lie flat on its bed before being secured. The origin of the term appears to be that the action of turning the anchor by rotating the *stock resembled that of turning a gimlet by hand.

gin block, a *sheave in a metal cruciform frame used as a *whip for general purposes, such as shifting cargo. They are usually used with a chain rather than with rope.

gingerbread, or **gingerbread work,** the gilded scroll work and carving with which the hulls of large ships, particularly men-of-war and *East Indiamen of the 15th to 18th centuries, were decorated. 'To take some of the gilt off the gingerbread', an act which diminishes the full enjoyment of the whole.

gin palace, derogatory name yachtsmen sometimes use to describe motor *yachts at the more expensive end of the market. See also YACHTING: POWER.

gird, to, to haul in or to bind something together with the object of securing more space. It is an expression used particularly in regard to *rigging and more especially to the rigging of a *square-rigged ship, where extra space was needed to *brace the lower *yards round when sailing *close hauled. The standing rigging of a mast when it reached the *hounds often formed a limit to the degree a lower yard could be braced round; if this rigging could be girded in to the mast, extra space for the yard was made and it could be braced sharper. See also CATHARPINGS.

girdle, an additional thickness of planking secured along the *wales, or bends, of a wooden ship about its waterline for the purpose of giving it more *stability in the water. It was a common practice in the 16th and 17th centuries, when the art of *shipbuilding was still largely experimental, to build ships too narrow in the *beam to carry their sail. This was particularly the case when *topmasts and *topgallant masts became a commonplace and the amount of sail carried increased accordingly. The word was used both as a noun and a verb; a ship was **girdled** when it was fitted with a girdle.

girt. A ship is girt when it is *moored with two anchors out with both cables hauled in so taut that they prevent the ship swinging to wind or *tide. The *cables as they *grow out tautly to the anchors catch the ship's *forefoot as it attempts to swing and prevent any such movement. It is a situation easily corrected by *veering one of the cables slightly.

glass, the seaman's name for a telescope, a *barometer, and—before clocks suitable for use on board ship were developed—a *sandglass. Although the word telescope is as old as the instrument itself, being used by Galileo in 1611 to describe his invention, the name did not become used in maritime circles until very much later. In 1619 there is a reference to it in England under the name 'trunke-spectacle', but the first naval use of the name appears to have been by Murdoch Mackenzie (b. 1712) in 1744 in his treatise on surveying (see also HYDROGRAPHY). In general maritime use the name glass was an abbreviation of long-glass or spyglass, and Captain *Marryat was using that name in his naval novels at least as late as 1844.

The barometer was, and is, almost invariably known as a glass, even when in the form of a *barograph, 'the glass is high, low, rising, falling' being the usual description of its movements.

Global Maritime Distress and Safety System (GMDSS), introduced by the *International maritime organization in 1992 this forms part of the regulations laid down by the *International Convention for the Safety of Life at Sea. It broadcasts Marine Safety Information (MSI), such as weather warnings, automatically through *Inmarsat and *NAVTEX when previously such information had to be obtained manually. Its regulations apply to all passenger and cargo ships over 300 tonnes though smaller vessels are obliged to be equipped with its automated *distress signals as it has now supplanted the system where a continuous radio watch on the three main international distress frequencies was kept by coast radio stations and certain ships.

GMDSS caters for three independent methods of relaying distress signals. (1) The *EPIRB, the signals of which when activated are picked up by the COSPAS-SARSAT satellite system. This was originally developed by Russia

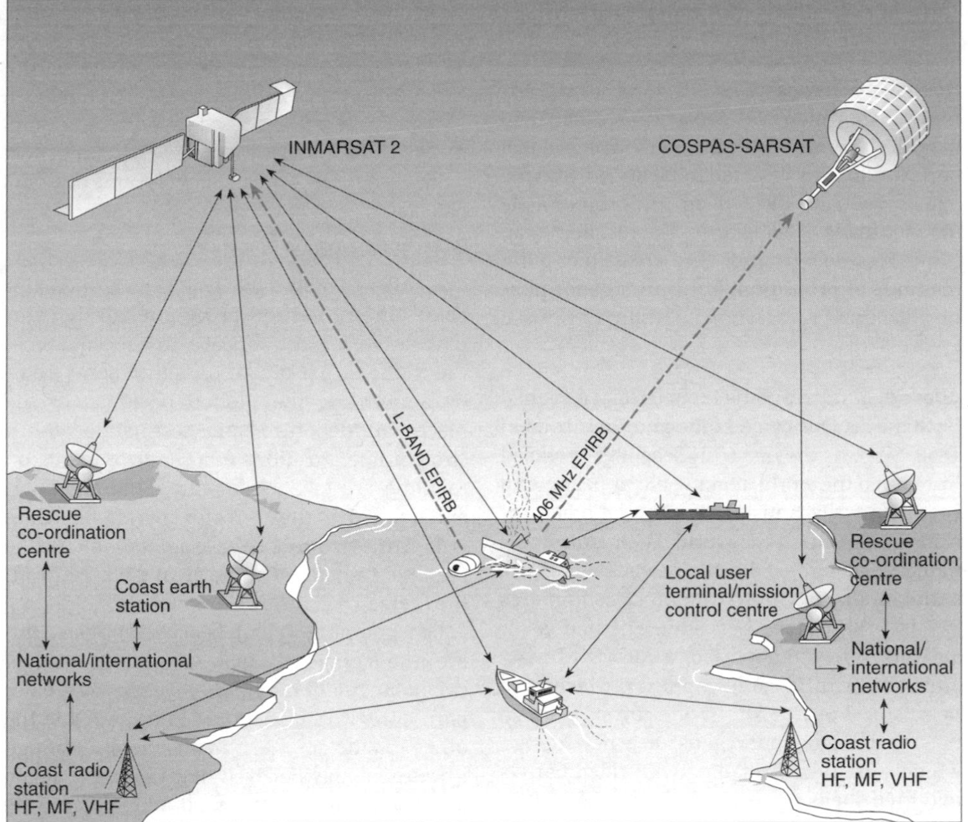

GMDSS communications systems as at 2004

(COSPAS) and the USA, Canada, and France (SARSAT). It currently (2004) has 45 ground stations and 23 mission control centres in over 30 countries. (2) *Digital selective calling (DSC). (3) Inmarsat. See also AMVER; LIFESAVING.

global positioning system, see GPS.

globe, a depiction, in the form of a revolving sphere mounted at the poles, of the earth or the constellations of the heavens. They are known as **terrestrial** (earth) and **celestial** (heavens) globes. Although often designed as furniture for libraries, there is some evidence that they were used, especially during the 16th century, as instruments of *navigation, although it seems very doubtful that they were put to practical use at sea. In the days before logarithms and the principle of the true *Mercator projection, the problems of nautical astronomy could be solved only by prolix mathematics which, in general, were foreign to *navigators. Globes, however, offered the means of demonstrating many of the problems instrumentally by inspection. Finding the *latitude from two *altitude observations of the sun or a pair of stars, finding the true *azimuth of a heavenly body, or finding the *rhumb line *course and distance from one position to another were problems easily solved with a celestial or terrestrial globe.

An important treatise on the use of globes, including navigation, was written by Robert Hues and published in Latin in 1592. It was 'made English for the benefit of the Unlearned' by Edmund Chilmead in 1638. In the eyes of the original author, the most important part of the treatise was that dealing with the practical uses to which globes could be put by the navigator.

With the advent of the Mercator chart and arithmetical navigation, facilitated by the use of logarithms, the fragile, cumbersome, and costly globes fell into disuse so far as ship navigation was concerned.

globular projection, a form of *chart-making in which the central *meridian and the periphery are arbitrarily marked off in equal parts for lines of *latitude to be drawn, and the equator equally divided up to accommodate the meridians of *longitude. The resultant map shows less distortion of land areas than other methods of projection, but is useless for plotting distances or directions. See also GNOMONIC CHART.

Gloire, a *frigate of the French Navy, designed by Stanislas Dupuy de Lôme and *launched in 1859. She was the first truly seagoing *ironclad warship in the world, making her appearance a year before the British **Warrior*, the first ironclad *battleship in the world. With a displacement of 5,000 tons, the *Gloire* was built of oak and had a belt of iron armour 12 centimetres (4.7 in.) thick along her sides. She had, as in all warships of this period, a full rig of mast and sails, with *steam propulsion which gave her a speed of 13.5 knots. She carried a single tier of 36 66-pounder guns of a new design which were breech-loading with rifled barrels and fired shells.

glut. **(1)** A term used for a *becket secured to the *aft side of the heavier *course sails on the centreline just above the *reef-bands. The bunt *jigger, or bunt *whip, was hooked into the glut when the sail was nearly *furled and used to roll it up into its stowed position. The sail is reinforced with a *canvas patch for the glut. **(2)** When used as a verb it denotes the prevention of slipping; e.g. a *messenger was said to be glutted when it was prevented by *nippers from slipping on the *cable to which it was bound.

GMDSS, see GLOBAL MARITIME DISTRESS AND SAFETY SYSTEM.

gnomonic chart, a chart which is very useful in *great circle sailing based on the gnomonic projection. This is a perspective projection in which part of a spherical surface is projected from the centre of the sphere onto a plane surface tangential to the sphere's surface. The principal property of this projection is that great circle arcs are projected as straight lines.

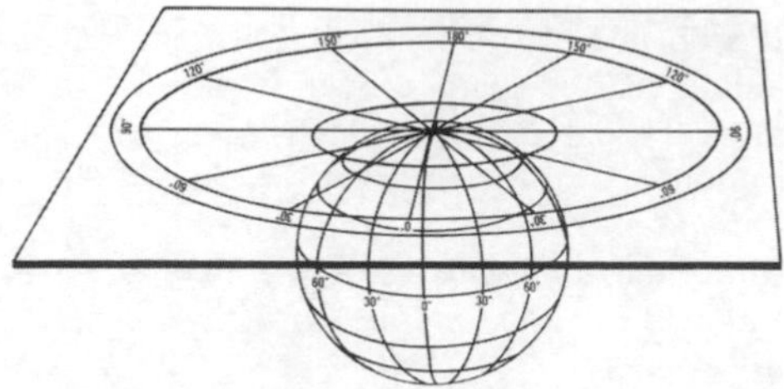

Projection of a gnomonic chart

In order to draw a great circle on a *Mercator chart—the projection being a relatively complex curve always concave to the equator—the route is first drawn on a gnomonic chart by connecting the plotted positions of the places of *departure and destination with a straight line. Positions of a series of points on this line are taken from the gnomonic chart and marked on the Mercator chart. A fair curve is then drawn through these points, which is the required projection of the great circle route on the Mercator chart.

The gnomonic chart became popular with the publication by Hugh Godfray in 1858 of two polar gnomonic charts covering the greater part of the world, one for the northern and the other for the southern hemisphere. Although it was generally believed that Godfray was the original inventor of this method of great circle sailing, it is interesting to note that a complete explanation of the construction of a polar gnomonic chart, with a detailed example of a great circle route from the Lizard to the Bermudas, appeared in Samuel Sturmey's *Mariners' Mirror*, of 1669.

'gobbie', in the days of sail the sailor's name for a *coastguard. Its origin is obscure, but until 1925 the British coastguard service was administered by the *Admiralty and manned by naval pensioners, and the term was probably a slang name for a pensioner. In the US Navy a coastguard was known as a 'gob'.

going about, see ABOUT.

goke, a 17th-century name for the heart, or core, around which a rope with four *strands was normally laid up.

gondola, a light open boat, much ornamented, with a high rising and curving *stem and *sternpost used on the canals of Venice and propelled by one man with a single *oar, standing near the stern, though until the 19th century there were two men. The high stem is surmounted by the *ferro*, a bright metal beak in the shape of the ancient *rostrum tridens*. The origin of the gondola is unknown though it is mentioned in contemporary writings as early as 1094.

gong buoy, a multi-toned sound *buoy used in the US *IALA maritime buoyage system B. It has four gongs and sounds four different notes as it sways in the *waves. John Rousmaniere

Goodwin Sands, the, a large bank of *shoal sands, which are partially exposed at low water. It lies nearly 10 kilometres (6 mls.) off the Kent coast near the entrance to the English Channel from the North Sea. The sands are shifting and attempts in the past to erect a *lighthouse on them to mark the danger always failed. Today they are marked by *lightships.

The shoal forms the eastern shelter of the anchorage known as the *Downs and is traditionally the site of an island known as Lomea, part of the lands of Earl Godwine. The island is said to have submerged during the 11th century when Godwine diverted the money earmarked for its protection to building the steeple of Tenterden church. The present name is derived from Godwine.

The sands, because of their shifting habit, are particularly dangerous to shipping, and many good ships have met their end on them. During the great *storm of 1703, thirteen British men-of-war anchored in the Downs, together with several merchant ships, were driven onto the Goodwin Sands and all were lost, perhaps the most terrible of the many disasters associated with the Sands.

gooseneck, a metal fitting on the inboard end of a boom of a sailing vessel by which it is connected to a metal ring round the base of the mast on which the sail is set. It has reference only to the *fore-and-aft rig or to the *spanker of a *square-rigged ship. The fitting allows for the swing of the boom sideways and is also hinged to allow the boom upward movement. It is a device of some antiquity, being mentioned in the 1771 edition of William Falconer's *An Universal Dictionary of the Marine*, an accurate record of 18th-century seamanship practices.

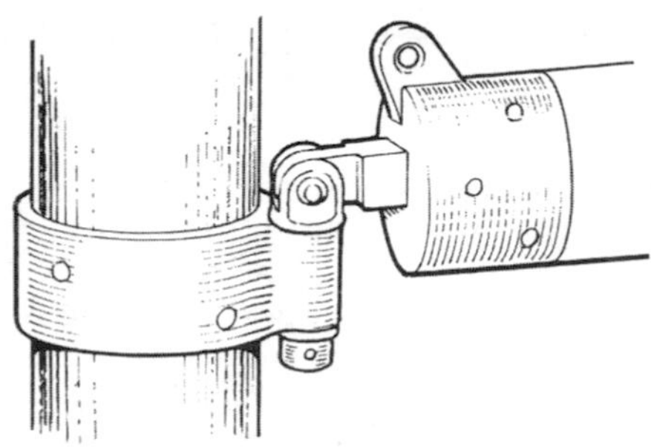

Gooseneck

goose-winged, a term applied in *fore-and-aft-rigged sailing craft to indicate the *jib or *staysail being boomed out on the opposite side to the mainsail in a following wind to present the largest possible area of sail to the wind. The assumption when this happens is that the vessel concerned does not carry, or does not wish to set, a *spinnaker, which is the most efficient means of getting the most out of a following wind in a fore-and-aft-rigged vessel.

goose-wings were the *clews of a *course or *topsail a *square-rigged ship used to *scud under when the wind was too strong for the whole sail, fully *reefed, to be used. With the *bunt of the sail hauled up to the *yard, only the clews would remain spread.

gores, sail *cloths with their ends cut at an angle to give the required outline shape of the sail. The seaming of the cloths gives it its aerofoil shape in section. Jeremy Lines

GPS, or **global positioning system,** is a US-government-owned *satellite navigation system. Receivers on board constantly calculate a vessel's position based on signals received from at least three of the 24 satellites orbiting at about 20,000 kilometres (12,500 mls.) above the earth. It was invented by two American scientists, Ivan A. Getting (1912–2003) and Bradford W. Parkinson (b. 1935). When the first GPS satellites were launched in 1978, it was initially a military system, but a degraded version was made available for civilian use in 1984 and during the 1990s GPS became widely available for many civilian purposes including *navigation at sea and *marine archaeology. The Russians have developed a similar system called Glonass. In 2004 the European Union came to an agreement with the USA whereby the 30 satellites of the EU's new Galileo system will be compatible with GPS. Galileo is due to come into operation in 2008.

grab, a coasting vessel used along the coasts of India during the 18th and 19th centuries. They ranged from about 150 to 300 tons and were normally *lateen rigged on two masts, though some of the smaller ones had only a single mast with a lateen sail. These smaller ones also had *sweeps for rowing when the wind failed.

grain, a five-pronged harpoon attached to a line and carried on board many ships in the days of sail for fishing, particularly for catching *dolphins. The fisherman usually climbed out on to the *jib-boom or the *bumpkin and drove the grain into the dolphin as it swam beneath him.

Grand Banks, the, also known as the Newfoundland Bank, an extensive shallow patch of the North Atlantic ocean lying south and east of Newfoundland, which used to be a prolific breeding ground of *cod. The Banks were first discovered by John *Cabot in 1497 and attracted fishing vessels from Britain and several other European countries, but, with the cod proving, so it seemed, virtually inexhaustible, there was only occasional friction between the fishing fleets of the various nations.

As North America grew, the Grand Banks proved an irresistible source of *fish and a number of ports were developed along the coast, chiefly of Massachusetts and Maine, to handle the trade, of which Gloucester, Mass., was probably the largest and most important. These ports each had fleets of *schooners with which they exploited the Grand Banks and which were named after them. However, the increasing popularity of cod, and the introduction of powered fishing boats with more efficient means of using *trawls, eventually led to overfishing, and in July 1992 the Canadian government closed the Grand Banks, along with Newfoundland waters and most of the Gulf of St Lawrence, to all commercial *fisheries.

Grand Fleet, the name given on two occasions in the naval history of Britain to the principal fleet gathered together for prosecuting the war. The first occasion was during the Revolutionary (1793–1801) and the Napoleonic (1803–15) Wars against France; the second was during the First World War (1914–18) when *K-class *submarines were designed to accompany its ships. See also HIGH SEAS FLEET.

The Japanese fleet commanded by Admiral Togo at the battle of Tsushima in 1905 was also known at that time as the 'grand fleet'. See also WARFARE AT SEA.

grapnel, sometimes **grapple,** a small four-pronged anchor often used as such in *dinghies and other small craft. Grapnels were also used in the sailing navy days to hold a ship alongside an enemy for the purpose of *boarding it by hooking them in the *rigging or over the *gunwale. They were also used by *fireships when attaching themselves to their victims, but when used for this purpose the four arms were barbed like fishhooks. A grapnel can also be used for dragging the bottom for articles lost overboard.

grass-line, a rope made of *coir, not particularly strong but which has the useful property of floating on the surface of the water. It had several uses at sea before synthetic rope superseded natural fibre, particularly in cases of rescue and *salvage, when a grass-line floated down across the bows of a disabled ship in rough weather could be easily picked up and used to haul across a towing *cable. It was also used by naval ships when streaming a *fog-buoy. It was also valuable as a *drogue to slow down and steady a small sailing boat in a following sea. Similarly, when a small boat approached a shore on which *waves were breaking, a grass-line towed *astern provided an extra grip on the water and helped prevent the boat being turned *broadside on to the breakers, rolled over, and *capsized.

graticule. **(1)** The network of projected parallels of *latitude and *longitude on a map or *chart. **(2)** The scale inserted into *submarine periscopes, rangefinders, and marine binoculars.

grave, to, to insert a new piece of timber, known as a graving piece, in place of timber which has rotted in the hull of a wooden vessel. See also GRAVING DOCK.

graving dock, a permanent dock with walls usually constructed of stone or concrete, and sealed in the normal way with a *caisson. The term originated from the old practice of graving, or *breaming, a ship's bottom. Today, a graving dock is synonymous with a *drydock.

Great Barrier Reef, the world's largest reef system, situated off Queensland, Australia, and one of the natural wonders of the world. It is a complex of 2,900 individual *coral reefs, islands, and *lagoons that stretches for over 1,900 kilometres (1,200 mls.). The full extent of the reef was first recognized in 1770 by Captain James *Cook when on his first voyage he found himself trapped inside the outer reef and was unable to reach the safety of the open sea. Currently managed as a national park, it is home for about 350 species of hard coral as well as vast numbers of *fish and invertebrates like worms, *shellfish, and *echinoderms. It also harbours species that are very dangerous to man, including the three species of cone shell (*Conus* spp.), two species of stone fish (*Synanceja* spp.), the blue-ringed octopus (*Hapalochlaena maculosa*), a relative of *squid, and the sea wasp (*Chironex fleckeri*), a box *jellyfish.

Like all reefs, the Great Barrier Reef is under pressure from *environmental issues. Nutrient runoff from the land has increased fourfold since Europeans colonized the area, pressures from commercial *fisheries are increasing inexorably, and the waxing of tourism is threatening the near pristine reefs the tourists flock to see. There have been population outbursts of the echinoderm, the crown of thorns starfish (*Acanthaster planci*) which eats the soft tissue of the coral, but more serious were two major coral bleaching events between 1999 and 2003 as a result of anomalously warm water temperatures possibly resulting from *climate change.

www.gbrmpa.gov.au/ M. V. Angel

Great Britain, The first large iron ship to be built as an *ocean liner, and the first to have a *propeller. She was designed by Isambard Kingdom *Brunel and *launched at Bristol in 1843. She was 98.2 metres (322 ft) in length, with a *displacement of 3,270 tons, and had engines that developed 1,500 horsepower which gave her a speed of 12 knots. As originally designed she had six masts and her hull, as a safety measure, was divided into six *compartments by watertight *bulkheads, the first western passenger ship to adopt a construction long used in Chinese *shipbuilding. She was also built with *bilge keels and had a chain drive for her propeller. On her maiden voyage to New York in 1845 she carried 60 first-class passengers in single *staterooms, as well as a full complement of *steerage passengers and 600 tons of cargo. After this crossing she ran ashore on rocks in Dundrum Bay where she lay *stranded for eleven months. Her still excellent condition when she was finally salvaged was a convincing tribute to her design and iron construction. Later, she was used as a cargo and passenger ship to Australia, on one voyage carrying more than 600 passengers. Finally, after nearly 40 years in service, she was damaged in a severe *gale off Cape Horn and was beached at Port Stanley, Falkland Islands, and used as a coal hulk.

In 1970 she was raised and placed on a pontoon which was towed first to Montevideo and then to Bristol, where she was put in the very dock in which she was built and from which she had been floated 127 years previously. After years of restoration she is now on view to the public.

great circle, the largest circle which can be inscribed on the surface of a sphere. In terms of the earth, the equator, and all the *meridians of *longitude, since they pass through both poles, are great circles, i.e. the centres of all these circles lie at the centre of the earth. It follows therefore that any circle inscribed around the earth which has its centre at the centre of the earth is a great circle.

The shortest distance between any two points on the earth's surface lies along the great circle which passes through them both. Radio signals follow the path of great circles. See also GNOMONIC CHART; MERCATOR PROJECTION.

great circle sailing, a method of navigating a ship along the shortest navigable distance between the point of *departure and the point of arrival. The shortest distance between any two points on a sphere is the circumference of the circle which joins them and whose centre is at the centre of the sphere. In terms of the earth, this is a *great circle, and if it were possible for a ship to sail along the great circle connecting its point of departure with its point of arrival, it would sail the shortest distance between the two. But unless both these points lie on the equator, which is of course a great circle, and along which it can steer a steady *course due east or west, the ship cannot do this unless it sails a continuing curve, permanently altering course to keep itself on the great circle.

The theory of great circle sailing has long been known and understood and is described in many early books on *navigation. But it was of little use to a ship dependent on the wind to get from one place to another since it was impossible for such a vessel to stick to a predetermined course. However, when *steam propulsion was introduced a ship could steer a course irrespective of the wind, so the economics of great circle sailing in terms of fuel consumption and voyage time were quickly appreciated.

One of the properties of a *gnomonic chart is that a great circle appears on it as a straight line. To plot a great circle track on a *Mercator chart the *navigator joins his point of departure and his point of arrival by a straight line drawn on a gnomonic chart, and then transfers a series of positions on this straight line—read off in *latitude and *longitude—to his Mercator chart. These positions will then lie on a curve, which he can sketch in although he will not be able to steer along it. He approximates to the curve by joining up successive points on the curve with straight courses which are in effect chords of the great circle and which appear as straight lines on the Mercator chart. He will thus keep his ship as close as possible to the great circle, altering course as each position on the curve is reached. In this way he will be sailing the shortest reasonable approximation to the great circle, thus saving fuel and time. For illus. see MERCATOR PROJECTION.

Great Eastern, The third of Isambard Kingdom *Brunel's great *shipbuilding masterpieces, the others being the **Great Western* and **Great Britain*, was a ship far in advance of its day. Laid down in 1854 and *launched in 1858, at a time when the largest ships afloat were under 5,000 tons, the *Great Eastern* had a designed *tonnage of 18,914.

The launch of the *Great Eastern*

Brunel designed her to carry 4,000 passengers (or 10,000 soldiers if used as a troopship) as well as 6,000 tons of cargo to India or Australia without recoaling. An oscillating engine drove a pair of paddle wheels and a horizontal direct-acting engine drove a *propeller. With a length of 211 metres (692 ft) and a *beam of 25 metres (82 ft), she had a top speed of 15 knots. She was the first ship to incorporate an engine for her *steering gear, and was also the first to be fitted with a cellular *double bottom. This, and her very strong construction, was demonstrated when she escaped with minor damage after running onto a rock.

Construction difficulties and launching delays ruined Brunel's collaborator John Scott Russell (1808–82), in whose yard the ship was built, and caused a breakdown in Brunel's own health from which he died before the *Great Eastern* was able to make her maiden trip. Although Brunel designed her for the Australia or India run, because of the large numbers of settlers or soldiers going to these countries, she was mistakenly used on the transatlantic run where she proved a failure. She was later converted to a cable carrier and employed in laying four cables across the Atlantic and one from Aden to Bombay, before she was finally beached at New Ferry, Cheshire, in 1888 for breaking up.

Great Harry, see HENRY GRÂCE À DIEU.

Great Western, with the **Sirius*, the first *paddle steamer to compete to establish a regular mail and passenger route across the North Atlantic. Unlike the *Sirius*, she was specially designed for the task by Isambard Kingdom *Brunel; and on her maiden voyage she arrived at New York on 23 April 1838, fifteen days out from Bristol, having made an average speed of 8 knots. Although she started three days before the *Sirius* she arrived at New York only four hours after her. Built of wood, she was 72 metres (236 ft) long and of 1,321 tons *burthen. Half her interior space was taken up by her four boilers and the two-cylinder Maudslay *side lever engine which drove her paddle wheels. On this trip 24 first-class passengers paid a fare of 35 guineas each, but she later carried up to 148 passengers. The most important aspect of her passage was that she still had 40 tons of coal remaining in her *bunkers when she reached New York, proving that the old problem of carrying sufficient fuel for long voyages was easily solved with proper ship design. She was broken up in 1856, one of her last tasks being to transport troops to the Crimean War (1854–6).

Greek fire, a liquid charge made largely from naphtha. It was thrown from mortars as an off-

A galley using Greek fire from a blow-tube; detail from a Byzantine MS

ensive weapon against ships, acting as a flaming torch against masts and sails. It was developed in the Byzantine Empire during the 7th century AD, and came into general use after it was employed with conspicuous success against the Arab fleet when the fleet attacked Constantinople in 678. Greek fire was then widely adopted as a naval weapon by most of the maritime countries of the Mediterranean, but fell into disuse after the introduction of guns as naval weapons and the consequent increase in range at which battles at sea were fought. This made it useless, since the charge always burned out before it was able to reach its target. See also WARFARE AT SEA.

green men, the five supernumerary hands which British *whalers fishing in Arctic waters had, by British regulations, to sign on to qualify for the government bounty on *tonnage. A condition of qualification for the bounty was that none of the five had previously been on a voyage to the Arctic. The regulation was in force between approximately 1820 and 1880, a period of fairly intense Arctic exploration, and its purpose was to create a pool of men who had experienced the rigours of an Arctic voyage from which the many expeditions could be manned. See also EXPLORATION BY SEA.

Greenwich Mean Time (GMT), or Universal Time (UT), mean solar time on the *prime meridian. Universal Time does not increase uniformly and is therefore unsatisfactory for theoretical astronomical and frequency control purposes. *Ephemeris Time, based on atomic clocks rather than solar time and coordinated from Paris, has taken the place of UT for purely scientific purposes but Greenwich, at *longitude zero, remains the prime meridian for all navigational purposes. By the middle of the 19th century some dozen prime meridians were in use for navigational charts and many more for the calculation of time.

In October 1884 an international intergovernmental conference met in Washington, DC, with the purpose of fixing a Prime Meridian and Universal Day. After many months of probably fairly leisurely deliberation the conference agreed to recommend to the governments represented that they should adopt the meridian passing through the transit instrument at the Observatory of Greenwich as the initial *meridian for *longitude; that the longitude should be counted in two directions from this meridian; and that the universal day should be a mean solar day to begin for all the world at mean midnight at the initial meridian. In due course the recommendations were universally adopted, as was the time zone convention based on Greenwich.

Astronomers by and large prefer the term Universal Time to Greenwich Mean Time but for most nautical and navigational work GMT still prevails.

Howse, D., *Greenwich Time and the Discovery of Longitude* (1980).

——'The Centenary of the Adoption of Greenwich as the Zero Meridian', *Journal of Navigation*, 38 (1985), 191.

Mike Richey

gregale, a Mediterranean wind blowing from the north-east, usually in sudden squalls. It is particularly associated with Malta and Sicily.

Grenville, Sir Richard (1542–91), English landowner whose name will always be associated with the last fight of the **Revenge*. He was born at Buckland Abbey, Devon, and was Sir Walter *Raleigh's cousin. Little is known of his early life except that he killed a man in a duel, was admitted a student of the Inner Temple in 1559, was elected a Member of Parliament in 1563, and took part in the Emperor Maximilian II's campaign against the Turks in 1567. In 1576 he was made sheriff of Cornwall and knighted, and in 1585 he made the first of two voyages to Virginia to further development of a colony there. By now a wealthy shipowner, he contributed three ships to the fleet being assembled at Plymouth in 1588 to resist the *Spanish Armada and, after the enemy had been routed in the North Sea, he commanded a small naval force in Irish waters to try and pick up some Spanish ships as *prizes.

These were the years when the lure of Spanish gold was an irresistible urge to Englishmen to take to the seas, and in 1591, Grenville got himself appointed as vice admiral and second in command of a naval force which was dispatched to the Azores to lie in wait for a homeward-bound Spanish *flota of *treasure ships. While awaiting its arrival, the ships' companies became seriously depleted through sickness, Grenville's flagship the *Revenge* being obliged to land over half her crew of 250.

Unknown to the English, a strong Spanish fleet had been sent out to escort the flota, and by the time it was reported in the *offing on 30 August the English ships were much too weak to give battle, and they only just managed to embark the sick and escape from the clutches of a greatly superior force. However, the *Revenge*, having most men ashore, was the last to leave and she was cut off and surrounded. For fifteen hours she fought the Spaniards, but Grenville's knowledge of *warfare at sea seems to have been limited for he fought in the old-fashioned manner, at close quarters. However, he did sink one ship and heavily damaged another, but the odds against the *Revenge* were too great and eventually she was forced to *strike her *colours to prevent further slaughter. Grenville, mortally wounded, was taken on board the Spanish flagship, *San Pablo*, and died three days later; the *Revenge*, shattered in the fight, sank in a *gale before she could be taken as a prize to Spain.

The action is immortalized in Tennyson's 'The Last Fight of the *Revenge*', first published in his *Ballads and Other Poems* (1880).

'Greta Garbo', the slang name which was given to a quadrilateral or *double-clewed jib used by some *J-class yachts.

grid, or **gridiron,** a stage, usually in a boatbuilders' yard on the water's edge, formed by cross beams, which is above water at low tide. Flat-bottomed vessels, particularly *barges and the like, are floated over it at high water and secured. As the *tide recedes the vessel rests on the grid where, at low water, its bottom is exposed for repairs or cleaning.

gripe, to, the tendency of a sailing vessel to come up into the wind when sailing *close hauled, and requiring too much *weather *helm to correct this. It is sometimes an effect of the overall *trim of the vessel and if so it can be reduced by lightening the vessel *forward or trimming down *aft to make its stern draw deeper into the water. More usually it is caused by an ill-balanced hull with too fat *quarters. An unbalanced rig can also cause a vessel to gripe, which can be corrected by increasing the amount of sail forward.

gripes, broad plaited bands of small rope, *canvas, or Terylene webbing used to secure boats on deck when at sea and to hold a ship's boats steady against the *davits. For boats normally stowed on deck the gripes are secured to ringbolts on the deck, passed over the boat, and set up on the other side by *lanyards.

grog, a dilution of rum with water, from which is derived the word 'groggy' meaning the result of having an excess of the spirit. In 1687, following the conquest of Jamaica, rum was introduced into the Royal Navy in place of brandy as a daily ration. In 1740 Admiral Edward Vernon (1684–1757) issued an order that the daily ration of rum, one pint (568 ml) of neat rum for men and half a pint (284 ml) for boys, was to be diluted by adding a quart of water (1,135 ml), an attempt to reduce the incidence of drunkenness in his fleet. This was issued in two halves, to the tune of *'Nancy Dawson', at a grog-tub at noon and 6 p.m. daily before being carried to the seamen's messes in a *monkey which it became common practice to *bleed, hence the phrase 'bleeding the monkey'. In the West Indies, to obtain extra rations, seamen also practised *sucking the monkey. The words 'God Save the King (or Queen)' were traditionally fixed to a grog-tub in large brass letters. Any grog left over in the grog-tub was known as *plush.

Dispensing the rum ration was always done in the presence of an officer to protect seamen from being given a short allowance by adding too much water, a practice by which some of the old-time *pursers used to enrich themselves. As Vernon was known throughout the navy as 'Old Grog' or 'Old Grogram'—on account of the material (grogram) from which his boat cloak was made—watered-down rum has always been known since that day as grog.

The evening issue of grog was abolished in the Royal Navy in 1824 and the daily ration reduced to one gill, or quarter of a pint (142 ml), in 1850. The issue to officers was stopped in 1881, the popularity of gin having replaced that of rum among them. The issue to warrant officers ceased in 1918. For all other ratings, except for chief and *petty officers who drew theirs undiluted, the grog ration was one and a half gills (213 ml) of water to half a gill (71 ml) of rum until 1970, when its issue was totally discontinued.

When the US Navy was reconstituted in 1798, many British practices were adopted, including the serving of grog. However, early in his tenure as secretary of the Navy (1801–9), Robert Smith ordered bourbon whiskey to be substituted for the rum, and US seamen commemorated his action by calling the altered mixture 'Bob Smith'. Spirits ceased to be issued in the US Navy in 1862. See also SPLICE THE MAIN BRACE, TO.

'grog-blossom', the sailor's name for a red nose or an inflamed pimple.

gromet, or **grummett,** from the medieval Latin *gromettus*, a youth or servant in the British Navy. Gromets ranked above ship's boys and below ordinary seamen. They formed a regular part of a ship's company until in the 18th century they were rated as volunteers, second class. In the days when the *Cinque Ports supplied fighting ships and men, gromets were the boys who tended the ships while in harbour.

grommet (pron. grummet), a ring formed by *laying up a single *strand of rope three times, and used originally to form *eyes on the *boltropes of sails. It has long been replaced by the spring-loaded *hank or clip-hook. Grommets have various other uses on board ship and, when the two sides of one are brought together by a *serving, it forms a couple of connected eyes, always a useful article to have available on deck. Grommets were also used to hold the *oars to *thole pins when rowing.

ground tackle, a general term embracing all the gear carried by a ship to enable it to anchor or to *moor. By some it is also held to include permanent *moorings for ships and smaller vessels, including *trots, but more usually the term refers only to a vessel's own means of anchoring or mooring alongside.

ground tier, the lowest tier of casks stowed in the *holds of a ship. In the US Navy they were always water casks with the largest sizes near the ship's centre of gravity. Before the days of refrigeration and freshwater tanks, most of the provisions carried for a voyage had to be carried in casks, and in view of the very long periods during which a sailing ship might remain at sea in those days, sufficient provisions for six months were usually carried. Several tiers of casks were necessary to carry this amount, and they were known as ground, second, third, etc., to the top tier.

group, a term used in *navigation to indicate the number of exposures of a fixed navigational light—whether from *lighthouse, *lightship, or lighted *buoy—in each cycle of operation. See CHARACTERISTIC.

grow, to, the term used with reference to the direction in which an anchor *cable lies in relation to the ship to which it is attached.

growler, a piece of low-lying *ice floating in the sea in high northern or southern *latitudes. It is difficult to see from a ship approaching it because of its dark colour. Growlers are formed of blocks of ice which have broken away from the ice pack or from icebergs, and have been blown or have drifted clear.

GRP, glass reinforced plastic, see YACHT-BUILDING.

GRT, gross register tonnage, see TONNAGE.

guarda-costa, the name for Spanish *coastguard vessels in the West Indies during the 17th century.

guardrail, the upper deck rail along both sides of a vessel to prevent anyone on board from falling overboard. In smaller ships they are usually of wire, supported at intervals by *stanchions and sometimes secured at each end to the foremost and aftermost stanchion by a small *cable stopper called a Senhouse slip. In larger vessels they are usually solid metal bars supported by the stanchions. Ships with *bulwarks do not need a guardrail as the bulwark takes its place.

guard-ship, a warship stationed at a port to act as a guard. In the days of sail it was the ship which received men brought in by the *press gangs and was usually the *flagship of the port admiral. Nowadays, the Royal Navy warship, usually a *frigate, which is present at some *yacht regattas for ceremonial duties is known as the guard-ship.

gudgeon, orig. **googing.** In its simple, original form this was an *eye fixed at the bottom of the *rudder which fitted over a *pintle fixed to the bottom of the *sternpost. Another gudgeon and pintle were fitted higher up so that the rudder was secure and free to swing. This allowed the rudder to be lifted off if required. The same basic principle and terminology is still used today in the largest ships. Jeremy Lines

guerre de course, a term originally accepted in international maritime law to indicate the practice of *privateering, or the right in wartime of individual owners of ships to arm them in order to attack the merchant ships of an enemy power when licensed to do so by a *letter of marque. In all maritime wars up to the mid-19th century, the merchant shipping of belligerent powers suffered severe losses under the *guerre de course*, and it was brought to an end by international agreement at the Declaration of Paris in 1856, only the USA refusing to sign the declaration. As a result, US merchant shipping suffered severe losses during the American Civil War (1861–5).

A form of *guerre de course* was reinstated at the Hague Convention of 1907 when it was agreed among the signatories that merchant ships of a belligerent power could be taken up for war service as armed merchant cruisers. However, this differed from the proper meaning of the term as such ships had to be manned by the navy of the belligerent power and fly its naval *ensign. It was not a return to privateering and the letter of marque, which enabled private owners of ships to operate their vessels as warships for private gain. Nevertheless, the result was much the same insofar as commerce-raiding was concerned.

guest-rope, a rope thrown to a boat from a ship, either to *tow it or to enable it to make fast alongside; it is also sometimes known as a guess-rope or gift-rope.

gufah, or **gopher,** a *coracle, shaped like a cauldron and constructed of dried reeds coated with *tar, indigenous to the River Tigris. They vary in size from just over one metre to over 3.5 metres (4–12 ft) in diameter. This type of craft was far more widely distributed than might be thought. In China, where they were known as 'skin boats', they were widely used for many centuries, and they are present on Assyrian bas-reliefs. Herodotus, who visited Babylon in the 5th century BC, describes them as being made of willow with a covering of skin outside and that they were 'round like a shield, without either stem or stern'. Describing them in the late 1930s one writer (see J. Hornell, 'The Coracles of the Tigris and the Euphrates', *Mariner's Mirror*, 24 (1938), 153) reported that, though on the decline, they were still being extensively used in Iraq where they were called *quffah*—Arabic for basket. This was very much how they were shaped and constructed, though the modern version was made watertight, not with animal skins, but with hot pitch covering the outside. They were used as water taxis and for transporting local produce, and varied considerably in size, some being large enough to carry two horses and several men. Even larger ones were used as *lighters to discharge the cargoes of grain brought downriver from Mosul to Baghdad and it has been suggested they may have been the basis for designing *Noah's Ark.

Gulf Stream, a narrow fast-flowing warm *current that originates in the Gulf of Mexico and flows up the eastern seaboard of North America. It carries warm water up towards Newfoundland. To the west of Cape Cod a chain of sea mounts (see also GEOLOGICAL OCEANOGRAPHY) diverts the flow of the current eastwards to feed the North Atlantic drift, and the flow broadens from 80 to several hundred kilometres wide, and its speed drops from nearly 3 knots to 1 knot. This extension is the North Atlantic Drift and it carries warm water to the seas off north-west Europe keeping the climate mild and keeping the seas around northern Norway free of *ice. Off the American coast it meanders extensively and these meanders pinch off to form mesoscale *eddies, which are typically 200 kilometres (125 mls.) in diameter.

The first person to describe the Gulf Stream was a Spanish *navigator, Juan Ponce de Leon, and Benjamin Franklin was the first to map it by collating temperature data and the time taken by sailing ships to cross the Atlantic. Vessels made a much faster passage from the Americas to Europe by sailing with the current than in the opposite direction. See illustration overleaf and also PHYSICAL OCEANOGRAPHY.

http://podaac.jpl.nasa.gov/kids/history.html
www.volvooceanadventure.org/article.php/rz_1_rom_06_rl_0005_00100.html

M. V. Angel

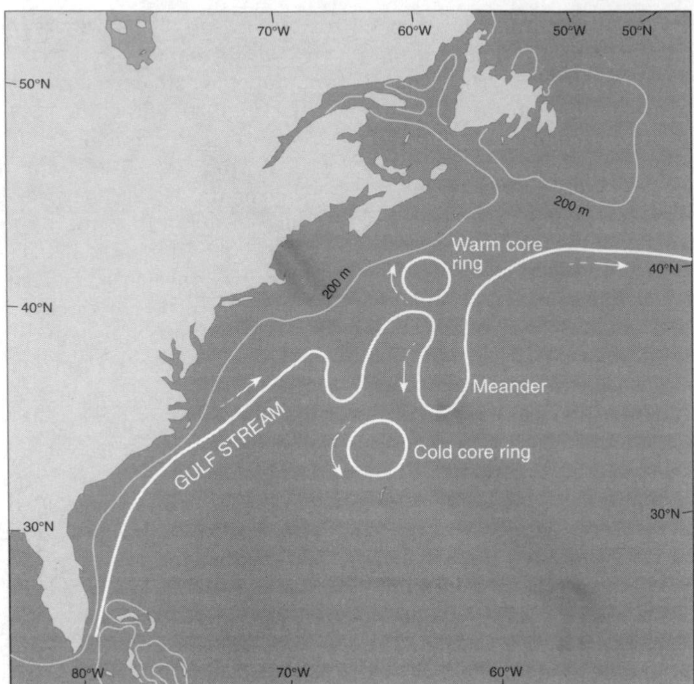

A schematic illustration of meanders in the Gulf Stream and the formation of eddies

gull, see SEABIRD.

gull, to, of the pin of a *block, to wear away the *sheave, round which the rope of a *tackle revolves. When the sheave begins to wobble in the block because of wear by the pin, it is called gulling. Similarly, when the *yards of a *square-rigged ship rub against the mast, they are said to gull the mast.

gun, see BASILISK; BOW-CHASER; CANNON; CARRONADE; CHASE (1); CHASE GUNS; CULVERIN; DOLPHIN (2); MURDERER; ROBINET; SERPENTINE. See also APRON (2); AXLE-TREES (1); BREECHING; BRIDLE-PORT; BROADSIDE; BUDGE-BARREL; CALIBRE; CASE-SHOT; CHAIN SHOT; 'CROSSING THE T'; DIRECTOR SIGHT; DRIFT (3); FID (3); FORMER; GUNPORT; GUN TACKLE; HALF-MUSKET SHOT; LANGREL; POWDER MONKEY; PRIME, TO; PRIMING IRON; QUARTER-GUNNER; QUOIN; RANDOM RANGE; SHOT; TRAIN; TRAIN-TACKLE; TRANSOM (3); WARFARE AT SEA.

gunboat, a small lightly armed vessel which used to be part of most navies for a variety of war or policing duties, particularly in rivers and on shallow coasts which precluded the use of larger warships. Many of the river gunboats during the 19th century, used for police duties in such places as the Yangtze River and the Persian Gulf, were stern-wheeled *paddle steamers so that they could operate in areas where the depth of water was very shallow.

gundalow, or **gundelo,** a form of river *barge, long obsolete, used in the USA. It had a high carved bow and a large *lateen sail set on a short, stumpy mast. The lateen *yard was very high in the *peak and the lower end was heavily weighed and balanced so that it could easily be lowered on deck. The small offshore fishing *schooners of Maine, USA, which had high sterns, were also known as gundalows. They, too, are obsolete.

gunner's daughter, the name of the gun to which the boys serving in a warship of the British Navy were 'married', or tied, when receiving punishment.

gunport, the square hole cut in the side of wooden men-of-war during the years of sail through which the broadside cannon were fired. Each had its own port, and they lined the gun-decks at the height of the gun's muzzle, being closed with a port-lid, hinged on the top, when not in use. Early gunports, being open to the sea, were a hazard and both the **Mary Rose* and the **Vasa* were swamped through them.

Until the Revolutionary War with France (1793–1801) the outside of the port-lid in the British Navy was painted the same colour as the outside of the ship; the inside was red, as also were the sides of the ship and, in a few cases, a strip of the gun-decks in the vicinity of the guns as well. The reason for this, it was said, was that any blood spilled in action would not show against the red paint and would therefore not have a depressing effect on the gun crews. Later the fashion changed, and port-lids were painted in contrasting colours on the outside, usually black against white or yellow *wales level with the gun-decks. This was known in the British Navy as 'Nelson fashion', and was introduced around 1805 when *Nelson fought the battle of Trafalgar. This gave the familiar chequer pattern of British *ships of the line. At about the same time, the inside colour was changed to yellow. See also WARFARE AT SEA.

gunroom, originally a compartment on the lower gundeck of a sailing man-of-war which was used as a mess by the junior midshipmen. Later, when the gunroom was also the mess of sub-lieutenants, it was moved up to the main deck. Today, there are no gunrooms in Royal Navy warships, all officers using the *wardroom as their mess.

gun tackle, a *tackle comprising a rope *rove through two single *blocks with the *standing part of the rope made fast to the *strop of one of the blocks. It multiplies the power exerted on the *fall of the tackle by three when rove to *advantage. Its original use was to run out a gun after it had been loaded so that the muzzle projected through the gunport ready for firing, but being a useful tackle for many purposes it is still used afloat. See also PURCHASE.

gunter rig, a rig in which the sail is cut with a very short *luff and very long *leech. The *head of the sail is laced to a *yard, which when fully hoisted, and with the *tack of the sail *bowsed hard down, lies virtually as an extension of the

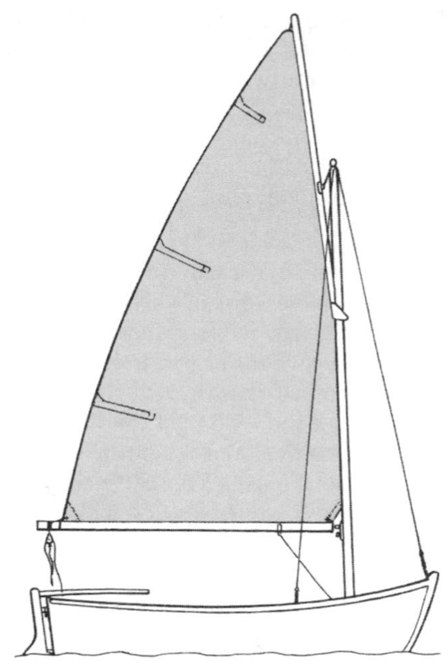

Typical gunter rig

mast, making the sail in effect very similar to a *Bermudan sail. It is also known as a 'sliding gunter'. For similar rigs see also DIPPING LUG; STANDING LUG.

gunwale (pron. gunnel). **(1)** A piece of timber going round the upper *sheer strake of a boat to bind in the top work. **(2)** The plank which covers the heads of the *timbers in a wooden ship. **(3)** In modern terms, the projection above the upper deck level of the two sides of a small vessel as a means of preventing the influx of sea water when the vessel heels over.

guy. **(1)** A rope or *tackle used to control the lateral movement of a *derrick. **(2)** A rope or wire led forward from a *boom as part of the running *rigging of a *fore-and-aft-rigged vessel. In sailing *yachts, a guy, called a **boom guy**, may be rigged between the end of the boom and a point well forward when *running free, particularly in light winds, or when the yacht is rolling in a swell. A *spinnaker boom nearly always needs a boom guy (or spinnaker guy) because the sheet of this sail has less control of it than the sheet of a mainsail.

gyassi, or **gaiassa,** the traditional sail trading vessel of the upper Nile. They were not unlike the *nugger of the lower Nile but mostly had only one mast and spread a very large *lateen sail on a *yard twice as long as the mast and as long as, or longer than, the vessel itself. Some of the larger gyassis carried two masts with normal lateen sails. They were all flat bottomed with broad, square sterns and large *rudders like barn doors.

gybe, or **jibe, to,** the action when *wearing a sailing vessel at the moment when the *boom of the mainsail swings across as the wind crosses the stern. The word can also be used as a noun, e.g. a ship can make a gybe.

The stronger the wind, and the greater the area of the mainsail and weight of the main boom, the more strain a gybe will put on gear and crew, but if properly sailed a *fore-and-aft-rigged vessel should be able to gybe in any strength of wind in which it can carry normal sail. The force of the gybe is broken by hauling in the main sheet before the boom is allowed to swing across, thus considerably reducing the strain as the gybe takes place. If the wind is so strong that a gybe would be dangerous, this may be a reason for setting a *trysail. An involuntary gybe, caused by running *by the lee through bad steering, or by a sudden squall from an unexpected quarter, is always dangerous.

If the vessel is not fitted with a permanent *backstay, the operation of gybing requires the setting up of the *weather *runner (when the vessel is on its new *tack) before the boom swings across the stern, and the *overhauling of the *lee runner to allow the boom to swing forward as the wind takes it. To gybe without attending the runners, or to do so involuntarily, is known as to **gybe all standing**, and is dangerous as it could dismast the vessel.

gyn, a form of temporary *derrick used on board ship which consists of three *spars with their *heels splayed out and their heads lashed together to form a tripod. A gyn can lift heavier weights than *sheer legs but can be used only for a straight lift and cannot be traversed as can *sheer legs.

gypsy, an attachment to a ship's *windlass shaped to take the links of a chain *cable for anchor work in a small ship where no *capstan or *cable-holders are fitted.

gyroscopic, or **gyro, compass,** an electrically driven compass that owes its directional properties to a perfectly balanced wheel, or rotor, that spins at high speed symmetrically about an axis. The operation of the gyro compass depends on four phenomena: (1) gyroscopic *inertia* which enables the rotor to maintain the direction of its plane of rotation unless an external force of sufficient amplitude alters its direction; (2) gyroscopic *precession* which causes movement at 90° to any applied force; (3) gravity; and (4) the rotation of the earth. Unless subjected to any external force the perfect gyroscope will continue to point in the same direction in space. Gravity and the rotation of the earth are used in the gyro compass, with gyroscopic inertia and precession, to give the gyroscope its north-seeking properties which have given the instrument its unique advantage.

The gyro compass has now replaced the *magnetic compass in virtually all commercial shipping. It is not affected by magnetism so that compass adjustment is no longer necessary, nor corrections from compass to *true *bearings. Repeaters are normally driven by the master gyro compass for use on the *bridge and to feed electronic equipment such as *radar and electronic dead reckoning instruments. A minor disadvantage of the gyro compass is that it takes, typically, 75 minutes to settle down after it has been switched on.

The first successful gyroscopic compass, which was introduced in 1908, was invented by the German engineer Dr Anschütz-Kaempfe for use in an *underwater vehicle. In 1911 the American Dr Elmer *Sperry patented his gyroscopic compass, and some five years later the British scientist and inventor S. G. Brown introduced a similar compass.

Mike Richey

hack watch, a *chronometer watch used on deck when taking a *sight for the purposes of *celestial navigation.

Hadley's reflecting quadrant, the replacement of the far less accurate *Davis's quadrant for taking a *sight for the purposes of *celestial navigation. It was invented by the English mathematician and scientist John Hadley (1682–1744) and was in fact an *octant. However, as the principle of double reflection made one degree of the octant's arc represent two degrees between the observed objects, it was called a *quadrant. After details of Hadley's new invention had been announced in the Royal Society in 1731 the British *Admiralty ordered a series of observations to be made to test the instrument, and as a result the quadrant was widely accepted at sea as a vastly improved aid to *navigation and *hydrography. The incorporation of a spirit level in 1734 made it possible to take a meridional *altitude at sea without the *horizon being visible.

Hakluyt, Richard (pron. Hacklit) (*c.*1552–1616), English collector and editor of sea narratives, born of a Herefordshire family and educated at Westminster School and Christ Church, Oxford. He found an early delight in reading books of travel and when at Oxford learned five or six languages to assist him in reading books of voyages written in other languages, and to enable him to talk to seamen of other nationalities. While there, he also studied *navigation and the art of *chartmaking, and by reading as many of the original journals kept by mariners as he could lay his hands on he compiled a collection of voyages to America and the West Indies which was published in 1582 as *Divers Voyages Touching upon the Discovery of America.*

On leaving Oxford he took holy orders and in 1583 went to Paris as chaplain to the English ambassador. During the next six years he compiled the great work for which he is famous, *The Principall Navigations, Voiages, Traffiques and Discoveries of the English Nation*, of which a first edition in one folio volume was published in 1589, and a second and enlarged edition in three folio volumes ten years later. It was one of the really great books of the English language, and one of the best loved in *marine literature.

Throughout his life Hakluyt was a strong advocate for exploring the American continent and discovering the *North-West Passage, and he continued to collect, read, copy, and make notes of every account of a voyage he could find, often travelling long distances to copy original sea journals or to talk with a seaman who had made a long or difficult voyage. He assembled a huge collection of manuscripts, many more than appear in his *Principall Navigations*, and he was working on these at the time of his death. They were acquired by a friend, a priest called Samuel Purchas (*c.*1575–1626), who in 1626 published some of them in five folio volumes under the title of *Hakluytus Posthumous, or Purchas his Pilgrimes*. Sadly Purchas was no editor and many of the accounts Hakluyt had gathered were garbled and truncated.

Among the publications of the Hakluyt Society, which was founded in Britain in 1847 to edit and publish the texts and accounts of voyages, was Hakluyt's *Principall Navigations* in twelve volumes and Purchas's *Pilgrimes* in twenty volumes.

Bridges, R., and Hair, P. (eds.), *Compassing the Globe: Studies in the History of the Hakluyt Society* (1996).

half beams, short *beams which extend from a ship's side to the *coamings of the *hatchways. Normally a beam extends the whole distance across the ship from side to side, but where a *hatchway leading to the cargo *holds intervenes, only half beams can be used.

half-deck, traditionally the apartment or structure on the upper deck of a merchant vessel in which the apprentices were berthed, usually in the *waist of the vessel.

half hitch, a single turn of a rope around a *spar or other object with the end of the rope being led back through the *bight. It is the basis on which many knots used at sea are constructed. For illus. see BEND.

half-musket shot, the traditional range at which British *ships of the line preferred to fight their battles during the days of sailing navies. The maximum killing range of a musket was around 180 metres (600 ft) and, in general, British fleets on engaging an enemy fleet would withhold their fire until they had approached to about half that distance, when every *shot fired would tell. It was for this reason that British naval gunners concentrated their fire on the hulls of enemy ships, while those of most other navies, who usually opened fire at a rather longer range, concentrated on the masts and *yards of British ships. They could then close in on the crippled vessels to what was virtually point-blank range. See also WARFARE AT SEA.

'half seas over', the condition of a ship *stranded on a *reef or rock when the seas break over its deck. In this condition the ship is usually unable to take any action to ease its situation. The expression has passed into the English language to describe the situation of a person incapacitated by drink and incapable of walking straight.

halyards, or **halliards,** the ropes, wires, or *tackles used to hoist or lower sails, either to their *yards in *square-rigged ships—with the exception of the fore, main, and *mizzen *course—or on their *gaffs, or by their *peaks, in *fore-and-aft-rigged vessels. The courses, which are very heavy sails, are hoisted by the *jeers or *gantlines. For illus. of peak and throat halyards see GAFF RIG.

hambro line, see CODLINE.

hammock, from the Carib *hamorca*, a type of native bed, and the bed of the naval seaman for hundreds of years, but not any longer, as the modern seaman sleeps in a *bunk. The hammock was invented, it is said, by Alcibiades, but its introduction in ships dates from the time of Christopher *Columbus who noted that the natives of the Carib islands used them slung between trees. The maritime version is made of *canvas with a row of small eyelet holes at each end through which are *rove *nettles which spread from a ring. When used on board, hammocks were slung from hooks in the deck *beams. When not in use they were lashed up, with the blankets inside them, by nine turns of a rope. In the days of sailing warships, hammock *nettings, protected by *quarter-cloths, were placed along the sides of the upper deck and along the break of the *poop so that the hammocks in them could act as a protection from musket fire from an enemy ship during battle. They were also stowed like this so that they would float free in the event of *shipwreck or disaster in battle, as a properly lashed hammock could support the weight of a man in the water for a considerable time.

hance, a step where the rail of a ship drops to a lower level in cases where a deck is not continuous, as from *poop to upper deck, etc. As such a step, if unfilled, is square and unsightly they were, in the days when most wooden ships were highly decorated with carved work, filled by **hancing pieces**, usually combined with long drop carvings often in the form of a human figure, to produce a curve instead of a square step. The elaborately carved hancing pieces of the Tudor and Stuart periods (1550–1690) gave way to a more restrained and simplified design in the 18th century as an economy measure.

hand, to, to *furl the sails of a *square-rigged ship. A typical sequence for the upper sails commences with an order to lower the *yard by means of its *halyard, followed by the pulling of it right down with the sheets held fast and hauling on the *clew lines. This is followed by slacking the sheets and bunching up the sail by means of the *buntlines. If required the crew then go aloft and secure the sail to the yard with *gaskets. Where the yards are not rigged to be lowered, the sail is first brought up to the yard by easing the sheets and pulling on the *leech lines.

hand-bearing compass, a small hand-held *magnetic compass for taking *bearings from the ship. Mostly used in *coastal navigation.

hand over hand, to haul rapidly on a rope or *tackle by passing one's hands alternately one before the other and thus keeping the hauling part in motion. A seaman was said to go 'hand over hand' when he went up the mast by means of a *stay or *shroud without using the *ratlines. The expression also means rapidly, as in 'We are coming up with the ship ahead hand over hand'.

handsomely, the order given when it is required to ease off a line or *tackle gradually and carefully. '**Lower away handsomely**', the order when lowering a boat from the *davits of a ship so that it may go evenly down the ship's side and be kept level during the process.

handy billy, the name of a small *jigger purchase or watch *tackle, used on board ship in the past for a variety of purposes, especially for handling cargo in the *holds. It was *rove with one double and one single *block and multiplied the power by four when rove to *advantage.

Today, the term in the US Navy refers to a portable pump, driven by a petrol engine, used by damage control parties to pump out flooded *compartments.

hank. **(1)** A small ring or hoop of metal used to *bend the *luff of a *headsail to the *forestay of a sailing vessel. Modern hanks are spring-loaded so that they can easily be slipped on or off the *stays as desired. It can also be used as a verb so that a sail can be **hanked** to a stay. **(2)** A length of small three-stranded rope used on board to *lace sails and for *lashings where strength is needed.

Hanseatic League, a trading federation of north German towns dating from about 1240. The league, mainly operating maritime trade, led to a huge expansion in merchant shipping especially during the 14th and early 15th centuries. When it was at the height of its powers, almost the whole of the trade of Germany and Flanders, both inwards and outwards, was channelled through its ports. The first two Hansa ports were Lübeck and Hamburg, later joined by Lüneberg, Wismar, Rostock, Stralsund, and Danzig. It eventually united the merchants of over 30 German towns, and set up 'hansas', or trading guildhalls, in foreign cities, including London, King's Lynn, Boston, York, Hull, Yarmouth, and Bristol, in England, and Bergen in Norway.

At the height of its power the league could claim and operate a monopoly in seaborne trade. However, industrial growth throughout Europe, particularly in Holland and England with the formation of companies of merchant adventurers, quickly produced a challenge to the monopoly which the league was unable to withstand, and in the late 15th century its power began to fail. Over a period of about twenty years, approximately 1480–1500, so many merchants challenged the trade monopoly that the league no longer existed in its former monopolistic shape and soon began to disintegrate under the growing liberalization of trade, with the Dutch dominating the former Hansa staple trade in the Baltic by 1600. By then the league was virtually dead, and although an attempt was made to revive it at a general assembly held in 1669, it was unsuccessful.

*Shipbuilding and ship design flourished under the Hanseatic League. It also claimed monopolies over North Sea and Baltic fishing. See also FISHERIES; HERRING.

Scammell, G., *The World Encompassed* (1981).

harbour dues, the amount of money the owner of a ship has to pay to a port authority for the use of the port and its facilities. Ships pay on their net *tonnage, that is, on their earning capacity; *yachts pay per metre of their overall length. As most ports are now recognized as competent *pilotage authorities pilotage charges are included in their disbursements.

harden in, to, the operation of hauling in the *sheets of a sailing vessel to present the sails at a more acute angle to the wind.

harmattan, an easterly wind which occasionally blows during the dry season (December, January, February) on the west coast of Africa, coming off the land, instead of the more normal wind which blows off the sea. It is a very dry wind, usually accompanied by dust storms the wind has picked up from the desert. It is sometimes also known as the 'doctor', as it is cooler than the normal temperatures of the coast.

harness cask, a large cask usually kept on deck in the days of sail which contained the salted provisions for immediate use. Salt pork and salt beef were usually known among sailors as salt horse because the meat was so hard and unsavoury, and the harness cask was where the horse without its harness was stabled. See also IRISH HORSE.

harpings, or **harpens.** **(1)** The forward parts of the *wales at the bows of a wooden ship where they are fixed into the *stem. They are normally thicker than the after part of the wales in order to provide additional strength at the bows, where most of the strain on a ship falls. **(2)** *Ribbands of timber used during the construction of a wooden ship to hold its *frames until it is planked.

hatch, an opening in the ship's deck for either persons or cargo to enter or leave. The cover that closes it is known as a hatch cover, though many seamen also call this a hatch. The term **hatchway** is generally taken to mean the vertical space through a series of hatches, one below the other, through the decks of a vessel. *Research ships have special hatches in the bottom of their hulls called **moon pools**.

haul, to, the seaman's word meaning to pull. Virtually every rope that needs a pull to perform its function is hauled at sea, never pulled. '**Mainsail-haul**', the order given in a *square-rigged ship to haul round the after *yards when it is nearly head to wind when *tacking. A ship also **hauls its wind** when it is brought nearer to the wind after *running free.

Hawkins, Sir John (1532–95), English admiral, and the architect of the Elizabethan navy. The son of William Hawkins, mayor of Plymouth, and the cousin of Sir Francis *Drake, Hawkins became the first English seaman to be involved in the *slave trade when, in 1562, he transported slaves from West Africa to *Hispaniola. This antagonized not only the Portuguese, whose practice he was adopting, but also the Spanish, who did not want their monopoly in the Caribbean infringed. His second voyage, 1564–5, was backed by a syndicate of merchants and by Queen Elizabeth I, who lent him a royal ship, and he sold slaves to the Spanish colonists at a great profit. However, his third voyage, 1567–8, ended in disaster when the queen's ship, *Jesus of Lubeck*, was captured, and only those commanded by Drake and himself returned home safely. This marked the beginning of the long quarrel with Spain which later led to open war.

Having married the daughter of Benjamin Gonson, treasurer of the navy, Hawkins became involved in naval administration. In 1577 he succeeded Gonson and added the post of comptroller in 1589. These two posts made him virtually responsible for the Elizabethan navy, and he built new and faster, and better-armed, ships. He also improved the pay and conditions of the seamen, and, with Drake and Lord Howard of Effingham, founded the *Chatham Chest fund for their relief.

In the campaign of 1588 against the *Spanish Armada he was knighted during the battle. In 1595 he and Drake were appointed to the joint command of an expedition to the West Indies, but by then, aged 63, he was undoubtedly too old for a sea command. He died off Puerto Rico on 12 November of that year.

Williamson, J. A., *Hawkins of Plymouth* (1949).

hawse, strictly, that part of a ship's bow where the *hawseholes and *hawsepipes are situated through which the anchor *cables pass. But it is by extension, and in its most generally accepted meaning, also the distance between the ship's *head and its anchor as it lies on the bottom. Thus another vessel which crosses this space is said to **cross the hawse**. When a ship lies to two anchors, it has **a clear hawse** when the two cables *grow from the ship without crossing; when they do cross, the ship has **a *foul hawse**. The normal practice in ships when they lie to two anchors is to insert a *mooring swivel between the two cables so that the ship swings in a restricted circle without the cables becoming crossed.

hawse bag, a *canvas bag stuffed with *oakum. It was used in heavy seas during the days of sail to stuff into the *hawseholes so that sea water was prevented from coming aboard through them. In the US Navy hawse bags were known as *jackasses.

hawsehole, the hole in the *forecastle deck, or upper deck in those vessels without a forecastle, in the bows of a ship, through which the anchor *cable passes. The hawseholes form the entries to the *hawsepipes which lead the cables from the deck to the outside of the ship's hull. Large ships are usually fitted with three hawseholes, one each side of the *stem, through which are led the cables for the *port and *starboard *bower anchors, and a third just *aft of the starboard bower through which is led the cable for the *sheet anchor.

hawse-pieces, in a wooden ship the timbers which form the bow, usually parallel to the *stem and through which the *hawseholes are cut; in a steel ship, the plates similarly placed. They are strengthened in the general construction of the ship by the *breast hooks.

hawsepipe, the inclined pipe or tube which leads from the *hawsehole of a ship to the outside of the vessel. A seaman who reached a position of *mate or *master, having begun his seagoing career as an ordinary member of the crew, was said to have **come up through the hawsepipe**.

hawser, a heavy rope used for a variety of purposes on board ship such as a *warp for a *kedge anchor, or as *berthing hawsers.

hawser-laid rope, the description given to rope in which three *strands are laid up (see LAY UP, TO) against the twist to form the rope. See also CABLE-LAID ROPE.

haze, to, to make life on board a ship as uncomfortable as possible for the crew by keeping them hard at work at all hours of the day and night, often unnecessarily so. It used to be the practice of some *masters and *'bucko' mates, particularly in the big sail trading ships and *barques of the 19th century, to try to assert their authority by hazing their crew unmercifully, even to the extent of inventing work to deprive the *watch below of the legitimate hours of rest. Richard Henry *Dana, in his *Two Years before the Mast*, describes how Captain Thompson used to haze the crew by turning out the watch below, rain or fine. He then made them stand round the deck far enough apart to be unable to speak to each other, and pick *oakum.

head, a much used maritime word meaning the top or forward part. The top edge of a four-sided sail is the head, the top of the mast is the masthead, the head of a ship is the bows (but the ship's head means the *compass direction in which it is pointing). **Headsails** are the *jibs and *staysails hoisted at the forward end of a sailing vessel.

The word is also used as a verb in very much the same sense; a sailing vessel is **headed** by the wind when it swings round towards the vessel's bows so that the original course can no longer be laid. **By the head**, a ship which is drawing more water *forward than *aft.

headboard, a small rigid section at the *head of a *Bermudan mainsail to spread the *halyard load and minimize the *luff length.

head-rope, that part of the *bolt-rope of a sail which lies along the *head of a four-sided sail. Triangular sails, of course, have no head and therefore no head-rope. See also BERTHING HAWSERS.

heads, the name given to that part of the older sailing ships forward of the *forecastle and around the *beak which was used by the crew as their lavatory. In the US Navy it was simply known as the head, but in the Royal Navy the word was always used in the plural to indicate the *weather and *lee sides, seamen being expected to use the lee side so that all effluent fell clear into the sea. They were floored with gratings so that the sea could assist in washing them clean. The name is still used today for the modern flush toilets fitted aboard every ship and *yacht.

headsail, see HEAD.

heart, a block of a wood such as **lignum vitae*, usually circular but sometimes triangular in early ships. It has a single D-shaped hole in the centre and is grooved around its circumference to take standing *rigging. The straight side of the D is usually scored for three *lanyards. Hearts are usually used in pairs and in the manner of *deadeyes for setting up the *stays of sailing ships. They are set up with a *tackle and the running end *seized. Modern sailing ships use *rigging screws for this purpose.

'Heart of Oak', a patriotic *sea song written by David Garrick and beginning:

> Come cheer up, my lads, 'tis to glory we steer,
> To add something more to this wonderful year.

It was set to music by William Boyce in 1759, and first performed in the pantomime *Harlequin's Invasion*. It commemorated the achievements of 1759, the year of victories, 'this wonderful year' as the song has it, during the Seven Years War (1756–63), when the army had triumphed at Minden, the navy at Lagos and Quiberon Bay, and both together at the capture of Quebec. The song was later traditionally played on board British *ships of the line when they sailed into battle, and when the drums on board beat to *quarters, they did so to the rhythm of 'Heart of Oak'. See also 'BRITONS STRIKE HOME'; SHANTY.

heave to, to. **(1)** To lay a sailing ship on the wind with its *helm *a-lee and its sails shortened and so trimmed that as it comes up to the wind it will fall off again on the same *tack and thus make no headway. Vessels normally heave to when the weather is too rough and the wind too strong to make normal sailing practicable. A powered vessel can similarly heave to by heading up into the sea and using its engines just enough to hold it in position. The whole idea in heaving to is to bring the wind on to the *weather bow and hold the ship in that position, where it rides most safely and easily. Heaving to is also known as **lying a-try** or **lying to**. **(2)** When a ship is ordered to heave to it is being told to stop, usually so that it can be *boarded.

heaving line, a light line with a small weighted bag at the end, or perhaps a *monkey's fist, used for throwing from a ship to shore when coming alongside; a heavier wire rope or *hawser is attached which can then be hauled over by the heaving line.

heel. **(1)** The after end of a ship's keel and the lower end of the *sternpost, to which it is connected. **(2)** The lower end of a mast, *boom, or *bowsprit in a sailing vessel. The heel of a mast is normally squared off and is lowered through a hole in the deck(s) until it fits in a square step cut in the *keelson of the vessel. Alternatively it can be held in a *tabernacle on deck so that it can be lowered, or raised, at will. **(3)** The amount, or angle, to which a vessel is heeled. **(4)** As a verb, in relation to a ship, it means to lean over to one side, though not permanently, as with a *list, or spasmodically, as when a vessel rolls in a sea, but somewhere between the two. Thus a sailing vessel will heel over when the wind catches its sails, unless it has the wind directly *astern, and it will retain that heel until it alters *course by coming nearer the wind, or bearing away, or the wind changes in strength or direction. A powered vessel will heel outwards, when turning at speed, through its centrifugal force, returning to the upright when the turn is over.

heeling error, an error in a *yacht's *magnetic compass which can be caused when she *heels. Most ships' compasses are stabilized and corrected with small magnets to prevent errors when the vessel is rolling or takes a slight *list, but a sailing yacht's compass is more liable to become affected when the yacht heels sharply. The cause is usually the shifting positions of adjacent ferrous metal objects in relation to the compass card, which remains level to the horizon by means of its *gimbals. See also SWING A SHIP, TO.

heeling moment, an expression of the power required to rotate or heel a vessel against its *stability. Colin Mudie

Hellespont, the ancient name for the Dardanelles, the strait which separates Turkey in Europe from Turkey in Asia and which connects the north-eastern corner of the Mediterranean with the Sea of Marmara.

helm, another name for the *tiller, by which the *rudder of small sailing vessels, such as *yachts, dinghies, etc., is moved. It also the general term associated with orders connected with the steering of a ship, so that the man who is steering is known as the **helmsman**.

After the replacement of the original *steering oar by the rudder, steering by tiller, aided in larger ships by the *whipstaff, was the general form of steering for all ships, and although the tiller gave way early in the 18th century to the steering wheel in ships of any size, the original helm orders (applicable to the tiller) remained in operation. The steering wheel is connected to the rudder so that the direction of turn is the same as the movement of the rudder, i.e. when the wheel is put over to *starboard, the rudder moves to starboard and the ship's head moves the same way. The reverse is the case with the tiller, which moves in the opposite way to the rudder: when the tiller is put to starboard the rudder moves to *port and the ship's head swings to port as well.

For some three centuries all helm orders given in ships remained applicable to the tiller, and an order from the *navigator of a ship to a helmsman of, for example, 'port 20' meant that the helmsman put the wheel over 20° to starboard, the equivalent direction of moving the tiller 20° to port, and the rudder and the ship's head moved to starboard. This practice was universal until after the First World War (1914–18), when some nations began to adopt the practice of relating helm orders to the rudder and not to the tiller, so that an order of 'starboard 20', for instance, meant turning the wheel, the rudder, and the ship's head all to starboard. By the mid-1930s all maritime nations had adopted this practice, which removed the anomaly of a navigator giving the order 'port' when he wanted to turn the ship to starboard, and vice versa. See also STEERING GEAR.

hemp, the fibres of *Cannabis sativa*, originally native to central Asia. Its cultivation, first recorded in China around 2800 BC, had spread to the Mediterranean by early Christian times. Also known as white rope when new, it makes a hard, smooth rope, pale straw in colour, which has a good ability to stretch. In the days of sail it was usually tarred to preserve it against deterioration when it got wet, and was originally used for *hawsers, running *rigging, etc., but has now been replaced by synthetic rope.

hengst, a typical Dutch fishing vessel of south Holland with a flat bottom, two *chines a side, a rounded low stern, narrow *leeboards, and straight *stem at about 45° *rake. They are small craft with an average overall length of 9–10.5 metres (30–35 ft) with the traditional Dutch rig of a *foresail set on the stemhead *forestay and a tall, narrow, *loose-footed mainsail with a short boom and curved *gaff. Later fishing hengsts, and those converted into *yachts, were fitted with *auxiliary engines. Like the somewhat larger **hoogaarts** they are decked forward of the mast.

Henry Grâce à Dieu, in her day the largest warship in the world, was *launched at Erith, in Kent, in June 1514 (see illstration overleaf). She was in her time, and still is, widely known under the name *Great Harry*. She was built by William Bond, master shipwright, directed by Robert Brygandine, clerk of the ships, at the command of Henry VIII, and was probably of 1,000 tons, although some contemporary accounts give the figure of 1,500. She had four pole masts, each, except the *bonaventure *mizzen, with two circular *tops, and set three square sails on fore- and main-masts and *lateen sails on mizzen and bonaventure mizzen. She had a complement of 700 men and was armed with 21 heavy guns of 'brass', which in those days meant bronze, and a light armament of 231 weapons of various types, mainly *murderers. She was accidentally destroyed by fire at Woolwich in August 1553.

Henry the Navigator (1394–1460), Prince of Portugal, was the third son of John I of Portugal and grandson of John of Gaunt. He gained military renown when the Portuguese captured Ceuta from the Moors in 1415 and, as a fervent Christian, was an ardent crusader against Islam. However, some of the military campaigns he was later involved in were less successful. The expedition he sent in 1424 to capture Gran Canaria from its indigenous inhabitants ended in humiliation; his ambitions to oust the Moors from Granada never came to anything; and his attempt to capture Tangiers in 1437 was a disaster, particularly as he reneged on his agreement to return Ceuta to the Moors, a volte-face which led directly to the death of his younger brother whom he had handed over as a hostage. But his determination to expand Portuguese trade and territory elsewhere, under the guise of spreading Christianity amongst the heathen, was more successful. It also brought him the fame, though not the fortune, he was almost certainly seeking.

Ceuta's garrison, for which Henry became responsible, had to be provisioned from Portugal. This led to the development of the *caravel, and it was not long before Henry began to send some of his out into the Atlantic to search for the places he had heard about and which were marked on the early *charts he studied. Some like *Brasil were fictitious, but Madeira was rediscovered by his ships during the 1420s, as almost certainly were the Azores, and Henry's financial support of the colonization of these

Henry Grâce à Dieu

islands paid him handsome dividends, though he spent lavishly and died in debt.

But Henry is best remembered for his patronage of a succession of seamen, Portuguese and others, who from 1434 onwards made voyages of discovery down the west coast of Africa (Guinea) in search of gold and slaves, and who in the 1450s found the first islands of the Cape Verde archipelago. His captains brought back little gold, but the number of slaves captured or traded made these ventures well worthwhile. At the time of Henry's death this *exploration by sea had reached present-day Gambia, and later led to the discovery of the Cape of Good Hope by Bartholomew *Diaz and the sea route to India.

Henry's sobriquet, 'the navigator', is something of a misnomer. He was no sailor and historians now dismiss the stories of his school of *navigation at Sagres. 'Far from teaching practical navigation to his pilots as the myth has it,' writes one (P. Russell, *Prince Henry 'The Navigator': A Life* (2001), 238), 'it is much more probable that at first it was they who taught the Prince about their craft, so enabling him to relate his book knowledge of astrology, astronomy and cartography to the needs of practical navigation, even though he had little direct experience of the latter . . . His own unshakeable self-confidence that it was his destiny to succeed as a sponsor of oceanic exploration communicated itself to mariners and sea-going knights and squires alike, even before the caravel started to trade profitably in Guinea. All these people trusted Henry because they believed, probably not always correctly, that he knew what he was about. It was also a touch of genius on his part to exploit the religious and chivalric sentiments of the squires of his overlarge household by offering them the chance to win in great waters, as crusaders for the Faith on remote African shores, the fame and glory they sought.'

hermaphrodite brig, the generic term for those sailing ships which incorporated facets of the *fore-and-aft rig into the *square rig, principally the *barque, *barquentine, *brigantine, and *brig. The brig-schooner was also sometimes known by this name. This had two masts, the foremast being rigged as a brig and the mainmast as a *schooner, with a square *topsail set above a *gaff mainsail. She differed from a brigantine by the square topsail set on the mainmast, brigantines being fore-and-aft-rigged on the main.

Herreshoff, Nathanael Greene (1848–1938), American naval architect and *yacht designer, nicknamed 'the wizard of Bristol', who was the progenitor of the *Universal Rule. He was born near Bristol, RI, on the shores of Narragansett Bay, and was one of a gifted family of six sons and three daughters. After a course at the Massachusetts Institute of Technology in mechanical engineering, the nearest subject to *naval architecture then available, Herreshoff spent the next nine years with the Corliss Steam Engine Company at Providence, largely on the design side. In 1876 he produced a 9-metre (30-ft) *catamaran, *Amaryllis*, an innovation to Narragansett waters, which soundly beat all the local *sandbaggers and gave a number of twin-hulled imitators of his design a brief triumph until catamarans were outlawed by changes in the *racing rules.

When the family business, the Herreshoff Manufacturing Company, was formed at Bristol, Herreshoff turned his talents to the design of steam *yachts and *launches, and their machinery, while designing a succession of beautiful racing yachts. Among them was the *cutter *Gloriana* (1891), a revolutionary design, and the schooner *Westward*, which raced with the British *Big Class between the wars. But today Herreshoff is best known for his string of successful defenders of the *America's Cup: *Vigilant* (1893), *Defender* (1895), *Columbia* (1899 and 1901), *Reliance* (1903), and *Resolute* (1920).

herring are one of the 216 species of the Clupeidae, a family of *fishes that includes some of the most important commercial species in the world. They are all pelagic fishes that form dense *shoals and feed on *plankton. They are caught commercially using *purse seine and *drift nets. In European waters the herring *Clupea harengus* is the most important of these fishes, together with sprats and pilchards and, in the Mediterranean, anchovies. A herring, given the chance, will live for over ten years and grow to nearly a kilogram (2 lb) in weight. They have quite specific demands for their spawning grounds, preferring shallow regions where the seabed is muddy and the *currents are weak. Their eggs are heavy and settle onto the seabed before hatching. One result of this preference is that the overall population of herring is divided into a number of different stocks, each with a specific spawning area and each tending to spawn at different seasons.

Historically, the herring played a significant political role because wealth from herring *fisheries and the salt trade underpinned the power of the *Hanseatic League. One of the factors that contributed to the waning in the power of the league was the collapse of the stocks of herring in northern European waters, probably because of *climate change with the onset of the mini-ice age in the 17th century.

Hardy, A., *The Open Sea: Its Natural History Pt II. Fish and Fisheries* (1959).

http://home.eznet.net/~dminor/O&E9706.html

http://192.171.163.165/history.htm

M. V. Angel

Heyerdahl, Thor (1914–2002), controversial Norwegian scientist and adventurer, who was born at Larvik. While at Oslo University he became fascinated by the study of early civilizations and movements of oceanic peoples. In 1937 he went to the Marquesas Islands in the Pacific to continue his research at first hand. While there, he first began to suspect that the Polynesian civilization might have had its roots in an earlier migration of South American Indians; though it seemed impossible to conceive how the long ocean voyage could have been made without ships, unknown in the Pacific at that time, and with no knowledge of *navigation and ocean *currents.

Heyerdahl decided that if his theories were correct, it could have happened by drifting across the ocean on *rafts, and in 1947 he set about testing his theory. Using only such fastenings as would have been available to the Indians at the time of their supposed migration, he built a raft from the trunks of the indigenous *Ochroma lagopus* tree (also known as 'balsa'), and with five companions set off to drift and sail across the Pacific from Callao, Peru. The raft, named *Kon-Tiki* after the legendary sun king of the South American Indians, was 13.7 metres (45 ft) long with a *beam of 5.5 metres (18 ft), and was rigged with a short mast and single square sail.

Aided by the Humboldt current, and using *plankton and *fish as part of their diet, the six men covered 6,880 kilometres (4300 mls.) in 101 days before beaching on Raroia Reef, in the Tuamoto Islands. This proved that his theory about the colonization of the Polynesian islands was a physical possibility, and that it could have come from the east, and not from the west as was the current academic thinking. It is now accepted that there was indeed early contact between South America and Polynesia. However, anthropologists, aided by modern genetics, have found no evidence that intermarriage occurred on a scale to support Heyerdahl's theory of colonization, and it seems more probable that early sailing rafts first sailed eastwards not westwards.

After mounting expeditions to the Galapagos and Easter Islands in pursuit of his theory, Heyerdahl turned his attention to very early Egyptian voyages. His interest in these had been sparked, not just by ancient accounts, but by the small reed boats he had found on Lake Titicaca, and the discovery on the Galapagos of what he believed to be the images of triple-masted boats made of reed. This led him to speculate on the possibility that ancient Egyptians may have crossed the Atlantic in boats made of papyrus reed, and he determined, with the aid of companions, to attempt an ocean passage in such a boat. He constructed the 15-metre (49-ft) *Ra*, and when this disintegrated in heavy seas close to the West Indies, he built the slightly shorter *Ra II*, on which, in 1970, he crossed the Atlantic from Safi, Morocco, to Bridgetown, Barbados. In covering 3,300 *nautical miles (6,578 km) in 57 days, he demonstrated that oceanic voyages by the ancient Egyptians were at least a possibility. Then in 1978 he built another 15-metre (49-ft) reed boat, called *Tigris*, and, with a crew of eleven, sailed it down the River Tigris to the Indian Ocean, again seeking to prove a possible communication between different early civilizations.

Heyerdahl wrote two best-selling books about his adventures: *The Kon-Tiki Expedition* (1948) and *Aku-Aku: The Secret of Easter Island* (1958), and published a number of others. He made several documentary films—his one on the *Kon-Tiki* won an Oscar in 1951—and lectured extensively. As one of his obituarists pointed out, he encouraged conservation and environmental awareness, and in the field of Polynesian studies contributed, among other enduring ideas, the notion that the sea was a connector, not a barrier.

Highfield lever, a form of hand-operated lever used aboard early *Bermudan-rigged *yachts as a rapid method of setting up or tautening running *backstays or *forestays. The end of the backstay wire was led to a *block which slid along a lever pivoted above deck so that the lever worked in a fore-and-aft direction. When the lever was turned *aft and its end pressed down onto the deck, the block holding the backstay wire came below the line of the pivot bolt, thus holding the *stay taught. To slacken the stay, the end of the lever merely had to be tripped up, and the stay was immediately released. Forestays could also be set up and released in the same manner.

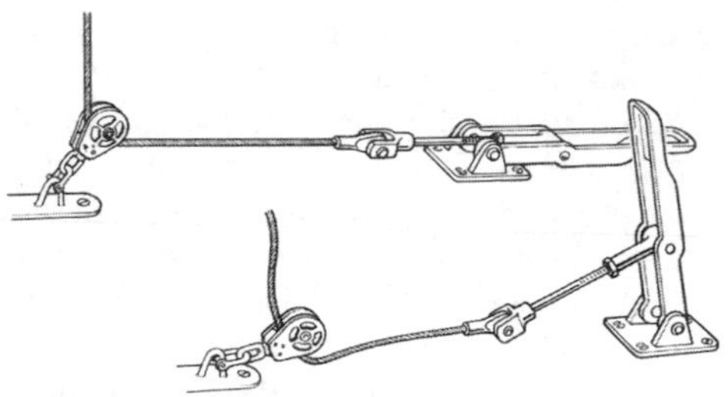

Highfield lever

high seas, all seas not under the sovereignty of states with a seaboard. See EXCLUSIVE ECONOMIC ZONE; TERRITORIAL WATERS; UNITED NATIONS CONFERENCE ON THE LAW OF THE SEA.

High Seas Fleet, the principal fleet of the German Navy, 1907–18. It was interned at *Scapa Flow after the Armistice of November 1918 which ended the First World War (1914–18). One of the greatest feats of *salvage was the raising of most of this fleet after its commander, Admiral Ludwig von Reuter (1869–1943), gave his crews orders to *scuttle their ships in June 1919. The fleet comprised eleven *battleships, five *battle cruisers and eight light *cruisers, and 50 *destroyers, and 51 of them were scuttled. Most of them were raised by the salvage firm of Cox and Danks with the aid of *caissons, and were towed away to be broken up. Of those sunk, all but one was salvaged. See also GRAND FLEET.

Hispaniola, the old Spanish name by which the West Indian island of Haiti and Dominica was known.

hitch, a series of knots by which one rope is joined to another or made fast to some object, such as a *spar. There are many types of hitches used for various purposes, such as a *half hitch, a *rolling hitch, a *clove hitch, etc. They come within the overall genus of *bends, which include all the more common knots in use at sea.

HMS, the prefix placed before the name of a Royal Navy warship to indicate that she is Her (His) Majesty's ship. The abbreviation came into use from about 1790, the custom before this date being to indicate a ship of the Royal Navy in the form 'His Maties Ship'. The earliest example of the use of HMS as an abbreviation is a reference to HMS *Phoenix* in 1789.

hog. (1) A device from the days of sail for cleaning the *fouling off a ship's bottom when it was not *copper sheathed. It was formed by enclosing a number of birch twigs between two planks, binding them together securely. The tops of the twigs were then cut off to form a stiff broom. The hog was guided under the ship's bottom by a long staff attached to the hog and drawn upwards by two ropes, one at each end of the hog, which was held hard against the ship's side by the staff. This operation was usually conducted from one of the ship's boats and was an alternative to *breaming. For **hogging lines** see COLLISION MAT. **(2)** When used as a verb, a ship is said to be **hogged** when its bow and stern have drooped. It is also used as an adjective: when a ship's bow and stern are poised over the trough either side of a wave, the ship is said to be subject to a **hogging stress**.

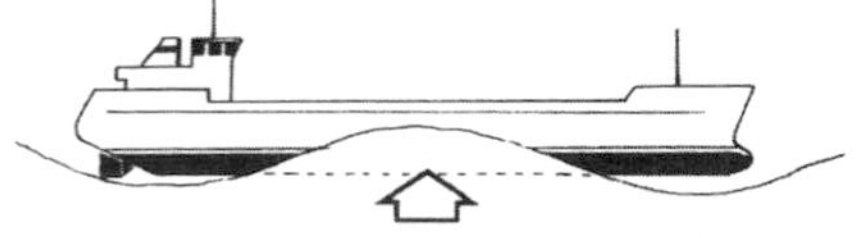

Hogging stress

hoist. (1) The name given to the *luff of a sail of a vessel with a *fore-and-aft rig; the distance which it must be hoisted to get a *taut luff. In a square sail it is the depth of the sail measured from its midpoint. **(2)** That part of a flag or ensign which lies along the flagstaff and to which the *halyards are bent. **(3)** The lift which carries a shell from a ship's magazine to the gun from which it is to be fired. **(4)** As a verb, the operation of hauling something up, particularly a sail or a flag, though the word is used in connection with most things which have to be lifted. An exception is a *yard of a *square-rigged ship which is *swayed up, never hoisted.

hold, a large compartment below decks in a ship mainly for the stowage of cargo but also, in the days of sail, for stowing provisions for a voyage, and often the ship's gear. Modern *dredgers discharge into their holds and vessels employed in the fresh food trade have special refrigerated holds to preserve the produce. Other specialized carriers have their holds designed for the particular cargo they carry. For example, *trawlers have refrigerated holds for the stowage and preservation of the *fish they catch. For safety reasons *bulk carriers can only have their huge holds partly filled.

holiday, a gap unintentionally left uncovered when painting or varnishing on board ship. It is also a gap left, equally unintentionally, in *paying a deck seam with *oakum and *pitch.

holystone, a piece of sandstone used for scrubbing wooden decks on board ship. Opinions differ as to how it received its name: because it was used originally for scrubbing the decks on Sundays, because the easiest method of supply was by robbing churchyards of their tombstones, or because seamen had to use it on their hands and knees to get a good result. Large holystones were known as 'bibles', smaller ones, for use in difficult corners, were 'prayer books', and these names certainly came into use because seamen had to get down on their knees when using them.

hood, the *canvas cover set up over a *companion hatch or a *skylight to give protection from sun and rain. In older sailing ships, it was the tarred canvas covering the *eyes of the standing *rigging to keep water out and thus prevent the rope from rotting. It was also the name given to the top of the *galley chimney, which was made to turn round so that the galley smoke might go down to *leeward.

hood-ends, the ends of those planks in the hull structure of a wooden vessel which fit into the *rabbets of the *stem and *sternpost.

hooker. **(1)** A fishing vessel which, as its name suggested, was probably used for line fishing. A development of the original *ketch, it was a short, tubby little vessel with main- and *mizzen-masts, originally *square rigged on the main and with a small *topsail above a *fore-and-aft-rigged sail hoisted on a *gaff on the mizzen. It usually set two *jibs on a high-*steeved *bowsprit, and early in the 18th century it became a distinct type of vessel in its own right, as opposed to the generic ketch. The rig was much favoured for Dutch fishing craft. **(2)** The name is also used, slightly contemptuously, for any vessel when it grows old and slow, or has perhaps come down a bit in the maritime world.

hoop. **(1)** In old-fashioned *gaff-rigged sailing craft the *luff of the mainsail was secured to the mast by wooden hoops which slid up and down the mast as the sail was hoisted and lowered. **(2)** Although square in form, the metal bands which held the *stock of the old-fashioned anchors to the *shank were called hoops. **(3)** The name given to an old form of naval punishment for two men accused of fighting each other below decks. They were stripped to the waist, their left hands bound to a wooden hoop, and with a knotted cord in their right hand had to lash each other until one of them gave in. The loser knew that he would usually also receive a few lashes with the *cat-o'-nine-tails, a means of ensuring that neither man was anxious to capitulate first.

hopper, a *dumb barge or *lighter used in conjunction with old-fashioned *dredgers for receiving the spoil brought up in the buckets, or for the carriage of sewage or similar material for disposal.

Horatio Hornblower, see FORESTER, CECIL SCOTT. See also MARINE LITERATURE.

horizon, from Greek *horos*, a boundary, *horizo*, form a boundary, limit. **(1)** The line which limits an observer's view of the surface of the earth and of the visible heavens. In *celestial navigation three meanings must be distinguished: (*a*) the visible horizon, that which is actually seen. This, however, is affected

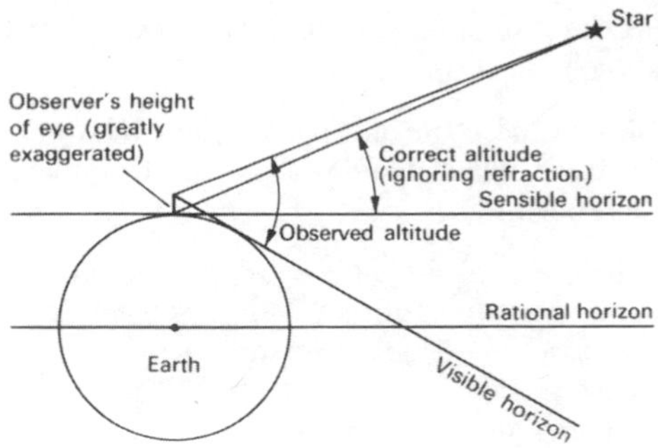

Horizon

by the *dip of the horizon which depends on the *refraction of light by the atmosphere and the observer's height above the sea; (*b*) the sensible horizon, the true horizon at sea level at the observer's position on the earth's surface, corrected for dip; it is the projection on the *celestial sphere of a plane tangential to the earth's surface at that point; (*c*) the rational horizon; this is the projection on the celestial sphere of a plane parallel to the sensible horizon but passing through the centre of the earth instead of tangential to its surface. In measuring the *altitude of a heavenly body considered as infinitely distant, the radius of the earth is insignificant, and normally the sensible and rational horizons coincide. For some purposes, however, they must be distinguished. **(2)** The broad ring in which a globe of the earth is fixed. The upper surface of the ring, level with the centre of the globe, represents the plane of the rational horizon. See also BUBBLE HORIZON.

horizontal sextant angle, the angle in the horizontal plane between two *landmarks

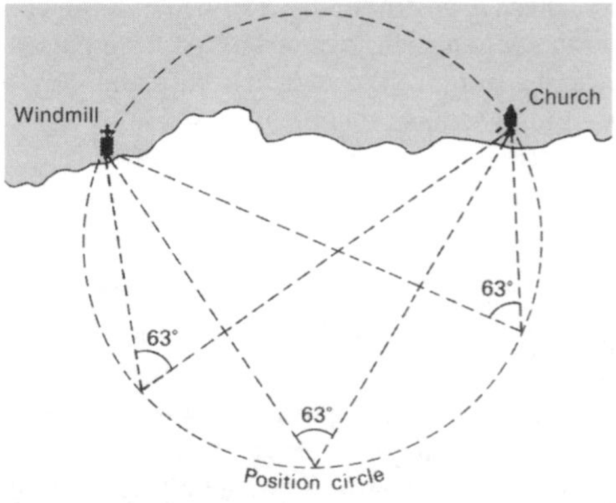

Horizontal sextant angle

British sailors dancing the hornpipe at Constantinople; engraving, 1878

or sea-marks. By measuring such an angle, the *navigator is able to plot a position circle on his *chart. Somewhere on this circle is his ship's position. By intersecting it with a second one obtained in the same way, or by intersecting it with a straight *position line, he then knows that the point of intersection is his ship's exact position. See also COASTAL NAVIGATION.

hornpipe, in its maritime sense a dance once popular with seamen. It was originally an old solo dance, danced three-in-a-measure to the Celtic instrument known as a hornpipe. However, by the beginning of the 18th century, when its maritime popularity began, it was changed to two-in-a-measure. Its adoption as a dance for sailors was purely fortuitous, as it previously had no maritime associations.

horns. **(1)** The points of the *jaws of a *boom or *gaff in a *gaff-rigged sailing vessel where they meet the mast. **(2)** The name of the outer ends of a mast's *crosstrees. **(3)** Two projecting bars sometimes bolted to the after part of a *rudder. From these chains could be led as an alternative method of working the rudder should the rudder head be damaged or broken off. See also STEERING GEAR.

horse. **(1)** An elevated rod, fixed at both ends and parallel with the deck of a sailing vessel, to which the sheets of sails can be led. Lateral movement of the sheet is made by means of a *traveller which can slide from side to side of the horse according to the *trim of the sail. Before *yachts were *Bermudan rigged with *foresails that overlapped the mainsail, a horse was fitted mainly for use with foresails. In old-fashioned sailing *dinghies, the mainsail sheet is sometimes led to a small horse fitted on the boat's *counter or *taffrail. See also FLEMISH HORSE. **(2)** See FOOTROPES.

horse latitudes, areas of the ocean between *latitudes 30° and 35° which lie between the generally westerly winds of the higher latitudes and the *trade winds, usually areas of prolonged calms. The name is said to come from the act of throwing the *'dead horse' overboard. This was because, in the days of *square-riggers, it took, from the start of the voyage to sailing clear of these areas of calm, about the same amount of time as it did for seamen to work off the advance of pay they had received on signing their *articles.

horsing iron, a *caulking iron attached to a wooden handle so that it could be held in position along a deck *seam while another man drove it in hard with a *beetle to consolidate the *oakum. **Horsing up**, to harden up the oakum in the deck seams by means of a horsing iron.

'hot chase', a so-called principle of *warfare at sea with no valid basis in law. It was sometimes quoted by admirals in their own defence after committing a breach of international law. The principle is that a fleeing enemy may be followed into neutral waters and destroyed there if the chase began in international waters. An example of this occurred at the battle of Lagos in 1759 when four French *ships of the line tried to escape from Admiral Boscawen's fleet by taking shelter in neutral Portuguese waters in Lagos Bay. Boscawen, who had been chasing them all night, followed them in, captured two of them, and burned a third. The fourth, the French *flagship, was burned by her crew after she ran ashore under full sail. On this occasion the Portuguese authorities accepted the principle of 'hot chase', possibly because the French were not popular in Portugal at that time. Boscawen, in his report to the *Admiralty, wrote that it was better to destroy the ships first and argue the principle later.

hounds, wooden shoulders bolted below the masthead to either side of a wooden mast of a sailing vessel which originally supported the *trestle-trees. In smaller vessels without trestle-trees hounds were used to support the *shrouds by which the mast was stayed laterally. In the days of large sailing ships the hounds of the lower masts were more properly known as *cheeks.

hour angle, the angular distance west of a celestial *meridian. It is normally specified as Local (LHA), Greenwich (GHA), or Sidereal (SHA), that is, measured westward from the observer's celestial meridian, or that of Greenwich, or that of the hour circle of the spring *equinoctial. In *sight reduction, LHA = GHA – W.Long. or GHA + E.Long. Mike Richey

house, to, in general terms a word meaning to secure or make secure. Thus a *topmast or *topgallant mast was housed by being lowered until its top was level with the top of the mast next below it. Topmasts and/or topgallant masts were normally housed when high winds were expected that might endanger them. In *gales of exceptional severity, topmasts and topgallant masts were *struck down to the deck. Guns of the old sailing men-of-war were housed when not in use by running them in from the gunports and securing them with *tackles, muzzle lashings, and *breechings to ensure they did not break free if the ship rolled in a seaway.

hovercraft, also known as a ground effect machine and air cushion vehicle. It supports its own weight by generating and containing an air cushion beneath its hull. The air cushion, usually generated by fans, is created by blowing air beneath the hull. This air hits the surface the vehicle is travelling over and, because it cannot escape, it turns back upwards which lifts the hull clear of the surface. More air coming in keeps the hull off the surface, and air escaping from under the hull ensures an equilibrium is maintained. Flexible skirts contain the cushion of air and raise the hull higher to allow it to clear obstacles.

Although there were experiments in the air cushion principle in Europe in the late 19th century, it was not until Dr Christopher (Sir Christopher from 1969) Cockerell (1910–99) patented his ideas in December 1955, and then approached the British Ministry of Supply for funding, that work on building the first hovercraft began. Called the SR-N1, it was built by Saunders-Roe on the Isle of Wight, weighed 4 tons, and had a maximum speed of 25 knots. In 1959 it crossed the English Channel with its inventor and a crew of two, proving the practicability of fast amphibious travel.

Improvements in the hovercraft's skirt resulted in bigger versions being possible and by 1966 a regular service across the English Channel had started. Various types were built, the largest and most commercially viable being the SR-N4 that came into service in 1968. It weighed 177 tonnes and was powered by four Proteus *gas-turbine, and two Rover turbine, engines. In 1978 it was stretched to double the capacity and was driven by the world's largest *propellers, 6.4 metres (21 ft) in diameter. These were mounted on swivelling pylons and were used to manoeuvre the 300-tonne craft. Its 30-tonne skirts lifted the hull between 3 and 4 metres (12 ft) clear of the water at the bow and nearly 3 metres (9 ft) at the stern, and it carried up to 61 cars and 426 passengers across the 34-kilometre (21-m.) wide channel at 112 kph (70 mph). In total the SR-N4s conveyed over 70 million passengers and 15 million cars, and continued in service until October 2000 when they were withdrawn in favour of the *Seacat. However, hovercraft still maintain services between the mainland and the Isle of Wight, and Oita Hoverferries still operate around the shallow coastal waters of Japan. Russia and the USA built large numbers of hovercraft and many have been built for export in Britain.

Sidewall hovercraft have also been developed. These have rigid sides which contain the air more efficiently. Though non-amphibious they have the advantage of using screw water propulsion, and remain popular passenger vessels in many parts of the world such as China and the Mediterranean.

Without the friction of a hull travelling through water, the hovercraft is one of the world's fastest *ferries and two SR-N4s amassed over 44,000 operational hours each. However, the real advantage of the hovercraft is its ability to operate where no other vessel can, in shallows, on mud flats and *ice, and across *shoals. This gives it a unique potential which can be exploited for survey work, for exploration, *lifesaving, and military purposes. Nowadays, they tend to be built more like boats than aircraft, often constructed with welded hulls and *diesel engines, rather than riveted airframes and gas turbines. This makes them cheaper to build and buy, and they are more robust and cheaper to operate. The US Navy has almost one hundred 100-tonne hovercraft some of which were used in the 2003 Iraq War. Britain's Royal *Marines also operated them there, and many *coastguards and other paramilitary organizations use them worldwide. The Greek Navy operates the world's largest hovercraft, the 350-tonne *Zubr* (buffalo class), employing them to guard the Adriatic coastline.

The future for hovercraft is secure, albeit in a niche market. Once regarded as overly sophisticated, they are now reliable workhorses that perform specific duties throughout the world. The word hovercraft is the same in the plural and the singular. See also SURFACE EFFECT SHIP.

www.hovercraft-museum.org Warwick Jacobs

hoy, a small coastal sailing vessel of Dutch origin of up to 60 tons. In England, where it began to be used in the 15th century and continued to be for the next three centuries, it usually had a single mast and a *fore-and-aft rig, sometimes with a boom and sometimes *loose footed. It was used largely for carrying passengers from port to port. Hoys in Holland mainly had two masts, usually with *lugsails on both.

huddock, the name by which, in the days of sail, the *cabin on board a *collier was known.

> 'Twas between Ebbron and Yarrow,
> There cam' on a bluidy strong *gale.
> The skipper luicked out o' th' huddock,
> Crying 'smash, man, lower the sail'. (anon.)

Hudson, Henry (b. *c.*1565, d. after June 1611), English *navigator and explorer, first heard of in 1607 when he made the first of two voyages for the English Muscovy Company seeking a route to China initially by way of the North Pole. When that proved impossible, he tried by way of a North-East Passage (see EXPLORATION BY SEA). Following the east coast of Greenland northwards, he was met by the *ice barrier, which he sailed along as far as Spitsbergen before turning for home. On his homeward passage he discovered the island later called Jan Mayen.

On his second voyage he followed the track of the Dutch navigator Willem *Barents, again seeking a North-East Passage, but failed to find any way through the ice in the Barents Sea. At the end of 1608 he was invited to undertake a similar search on behalf of the Dutch *East India Company for a passage to China either by the north-west or north-east; and in April 1609 he sailed from the Texel in the *Half Moon*, reaching the Barents Sea again by 5 May. Frustrated once more by impenetrable ice, Hudson persuaded his crew to follow an alternative proposal to cross the Atlantic to North

Virginia and seek a *North-West Passage, believed by some to exist in *latitude 40° N.

Reaching Virginia on 28 August, he coasted north, entered New York Bay, and sailed 240 kilometres (150 mls.) up the river that now bears his name and, from his observations, proved that it was not a strait as some had believed. Returning to Europe, the *Half Moon* put in at Dartmouth where Hudson was forbidden to give his services again to the Dutch.

Still confident in the existence of a North-West Passage, Hudson sailed again on 17 April 1610 in the 55-ton *Discovery*, reaching the strait since known by his name and sailing on entered Hudson Bay on 3 August. After three months spent examining the eastern shore of the Bay, the *Discovery* went into winter quarters in the south-west corner of James Bay, remaining frozen in until the spring. Hardship and privation led to discontent among the crew and finally to a *mutiny. It was led by Hudson's worthless protégé Henry Green, who had Hudson and others, some of them sick, set adrift in a boat before sailing for England on 22 June 1611.

On the way Green and several others were killed in a fight with the Inuit; others died before the ship reached England in September, and the survivors were imprisoned. No evidence of Hudson's fate has ever been discovered.

Asher, G. M., *Henry Hudson the Navigator* (1860).
Powys, L., *Henry Hudson* (1927).

hulk. **(1)** An early (8th–9th century), unwieldy ship of simple construction with a sail, a rounded bow and stern, and without a keel. The remains of one was found downriver from London Bridge and there is an image of one on a 9th-century Anglo-Saxon coin. By the 14th century it had become as large as a *cog, and thereafter the two types may have merged into one which became known as a cog. **(2)** Another name for the hull of a ship, but this use of the word had fallen into disuse by the end of the 18th century. **(3)** An old ship converted for some use which did not require it to move. Early hulks were used as floating storehouses, as the temporary abode of naval seamen, recruited by *impressment, who were awaiting draft to a seagoing ship, and particularly for *quarantine purposes. Some were also fitted out for use in *stepping or lifting out masts in seagoing ships. Later, particularly in the late 18th and early 19th centuries, they were used as prisons. 'It was as a means of devising a severe mode of punishment short of death that the Hulks on the Thames were introduced in 1776' (Robert Chambers's *Book of Days* (1864), ii, 67).

hull. **(1)** Probably from the German *hulla* or *hulle*, a cloak or covering, the main body of a ship apart from its masts, *rigging, and all internal fittings, including engines, etc. It consists virtually of the upper deck, sides, and bottom of a ship. **Hull-down**, a ship so far distant that only its masts and/or sails, funnels, etc. are visible above the *horizon.

Before the 18th century merchant sailing vessels were traditionally classified by their hulls, not their rigs. In 1768 Frederik af Chapman, a naval architect, published a book, *Architectura Navalis Mercatoria*. This divided the various hull shapes into five categories: *frigate, hagboat (or heck-boat), *pink, *cat, and *bark (barque), and each of these could have any of the rigs by which sailing ships were later identified, i.e. *schooner, *brig, *brigantine, etc.

The change to identifying a ship by its rig was gradual, though by 1769 William Falconer in *The Dictionary of the Marine* was writing that most of the different categories of hull form were becoming very similar and that the term 'bark' was 'a general name given to small ships; it is, however, peculiarly appropriated by seamen to those which carry three masts without a *mizzen *topsail'. **(2)** When used as a verb, to **hull a ship** is to penetrate its hull with *shot; to **strike hull**, in a sailing vessel, is to take in all sail in a *storm and to lie with the *helm lashed *alee so that it could *heave to; and a ship is said to be **hulling** when it drives to and fro without *rudder or sail or engine power.

hullock, an old maritime term for a small piece of a sail hoisted in heavy weather when it is impossible to spread more because of the strength of the wind. The term referred only to two sails, either the *mizzen *course, when a hullock was loosed at the mizzen *yardarm to keep the ship's bow to the sea, or the *foresail, to lay its head the other way. The correct nautical term used with hullock was to loose, as in 'let loose a hullock'.

husband, or **ship's husband,** before the days of modern communications, the title given to an agent appointed by deed, executed by all the owners of *freight carried on board. This gave him the power to advance and lend money, to make all necessary payments in regard to the freight carried, and to receive all money obtained from the sale of any freight, being accountable to the owners for all his transactions. See also SUPERCARGO.

Hy Brazil, see BRASIL.

hydrodynamics, a branch of physics concerned with pressures and behaviour of fluids, and is an important consideration in *naval architecture. Its origins may be traced to the middle of the 18th century when Euler formalized earlier work of Bernoulli, Newton and d'Alembert into the study of what Bernoulli referred to 'hyrodynamics'. Its, largely empirical, application to the design of ships was pioneered by the English engineer, naval architect, and mathematician, William Froude (1810–79). When he discovered that the wavemaking resistance (or 'residuary' resistance as it was then called) of scale models of ships towed at scale speeds through water along a towing tank varied in accordance with their full-size prototypes, he was able to propound his Law of Comparison, also known as the Law of Mechanical Similitude. He also showed that the behaviour of models in *waves represented their full scale behaviour, some of which he was able to measure on ships at sea. This demonstrated that scale models could be used to determine in advance the seagoing and performance characteristics of a design in various sea conditions. This was an important breakthrough in naval architecture as running model tests is less time-consuming and less costly than building the ship first and making the required modifications afterwards.

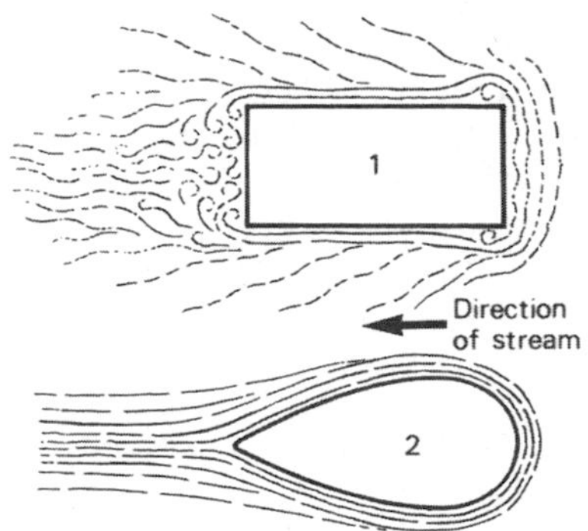

Streamlined flow: [1] Box in flowing stream [2] Sheet of ice in flowing stream

Study of the movements of liquids around bodies immersed in them also resulted in the discovery of what came to be termed the streamlined form, a body which presents the lowest resistance to a liquid moving through it. For example, if a floating rectangular box is towed through water, or is anchored and the water is allowed to flow past, a wave will build up against the front face of the box, forming an area of high pressure. The disturbed water then flows round both sides and underneath the box, producing friction drag over its surface. Behind the flat rear end the water flow endeavours to close in upon itself. It cannot do this because the change in body slope is too great for the flow to adhere. Pressure recovery therefore breaks down, as does the flow, forcing a series of eddies and 'dead' flow to occur which results in a disturbed wake for some distance downstream. This lack of pressure recovery creates a suction on the *aft face of the box which in turn acts as a significant source of resistance. This, when added to the high pressure resistance on the forward face and the friction over the wetted surface of the box, creates a considerable amount of drag as is shown in diagram 1.

If a streamlined form is adopted for the body, its resistance will be very much reduced. Developed in the first 30 years of the 20th century, streamlined forms were necessary in the quest for speed with aircraft of the time. These unstreamlined vehicles had very high so-called form and parasitic resistance (the former from the bluff shapes used for the fuselage, wheels and supports etc and the latter from the many struts, bracing wires and various protuberances) and this, coupled with the limited power-to-weight ratios of the engines of the time, limited speed. Streamlined forms and smooth structures were therefore adopted, resistance dropped dramatically and speeds increased as a result. The streamlined form is teardrop-shaped, as in diagram 2, whose main purpose is to prevent (or at least minimize) the eddying, separated and 'dead' flow seen *astern of the box in diagram 1. This it does by a nose designed to split the flow and allow it to accelerate smoothly to the thickest part of the body. At this point the pressures on the body are low and must carefully recover to their original undisturbed values by the time the end of the body is reached if separation is to be avoided. The aft body is therefore carefully shaped to give gentle slopes which the decelerating flow can follow without separating. By so doing form resistance is significantly reduced. By going further and smoothing the body, and minimizing all protuberances, parasite drag is reduced and the overall resistance, composed largely of frictional forces, is considerably reduced.

It might be thought that such a streamlined form would be eminently suitable for the design of a ship's hull, for like a *fish it seems ideal for offering the minimum resistance to the ship's progress. During the 18th and 19th centuries *shipbuilding did in fact copy a modified 'cod's head and mackerel tail' form of hull below the waterline in different types of sailing ships and in *yachts.

However, considerations other than the quest for speed in commercial ship design often make a fully streamlined hull impractical; but its principal features are still used in design. For maximum cargo capacity and stowage, the ideal shape for the hull of a cargo ship is a box, but, as has been shown, such a shape suffers from excessive drag. For large cargo carriers, running at comparatively low speeds, a bow can be added to a 'box' which, while not quite as rounded as that of a streamlined body, has similar features and may be quite bluff. Considerable care is taken in the design of the aft body to minimize or eliminate eddying or dead, separated, flow and this part of the hull will be elongated for the same reasons as its counterpart in the streamlined body. As a result, the *propeller(s) act efficiently in well-behaved flow. The bluff shape of the forebody may be enhanced by the addition of another streamlined body below the waterline: the *bulbous bow. This reduces drag at or near service speed by reducing bow waves and improving the flow (and hence pressures) over the forebody.

All vessels moving on the sea 'squat' or settle in the water. This comprises a bodily sinkage and trim by the bow at low speeds, changing to a bodily rise and trim by the stern at high speeds when the vessel, if it is able to move fast enough, is said to be *planing. This is aided by the fact that water is virtually incompressible so that the planing vessel behaves like a small flat stone being skimmed. As much of the hull is out of the water, drag is considerably reduced with the result that very high speeds can be obtained. When only early *steam propulsion was available, its weight in relation to the power it developed, that is the power/weight ratio, rendered it impracticable to drive a boat fast enough for it to do this, and it was only when the development of the internal combustion engine and lightweight boat construction produced a more advantageous power/weight ratio that boats could be made to *plane.

To make a vessel plane, the old concept of a fast hull with a fine entrance *forward, narrow *beam, and a fine *run to the stern, so as to make as few waves as possible, was discarded. Instead, a new type of hull was designed on the principle of a water sledge which would be able to rise onto the surface at high speed, with only its after part, *rudder, and propeller in the water. The design was found to need a broad flat stern to prevent squatting at speed, and sharply V'd bow sections. At velocities of 40 knots and over, water can be treated as though it were almost solid. To assist boats to start planing, many hydroplanes, as they were called, were built in the early days with one, two, or more steps on the underside of their hulls, on which they were designed to ride like a sledge.

The *hydrofoil is also based on the same principle, having a series of curved vanes or hydrofins which are fitted to a leg attached to each side of the hull forward, and similar vanes to another pair of legs fitted aft. As soon as the speed reaches a certain point the vessel rides up until its hull is completely clear of the water, and so runs on only the hydrofins.

Sailing vessels can plane too, though it is essential to have one of light construction with a V'd bow sections and a flat bottom at the stern together with a highly efficient rig to supply the necessary drive. Although some light-displacement yachts and some *multihulls can sail downwind with short bursts of speed in a state bordering on planing, true planing—riding along the surface at high speed for considerable periods—is normally achieved only by certain classes of high-performance dinghies.

Making use of this property of water the *hovercraft is able to lift itself just clear of the surface by maintaining a cushion of air at low pressure which is more or less imprisoned within the skirt surrounding the vessel's bottom. Here the water acts almost like a solid surface, and only a small amount of surface water is dissipated in spray while the vehicle is hovering. See also WAVE LINE THEORY.

hydrofoil, a type of craft beneath which planes or foils are fitted which lift the hull of the vessel clear of the water when travelling at high speed. Research in this field began in 1891 and trials took place on Lake Maggiore in 1906 with a craft designed by Enrico Forlanini, which was fitted with ladder-type foils, and reached a speed of 38 knots. Three years later the USA conducted successful experiments with submerged foils and in 1927 German engineers evolved what is known as a surface-piercing foil. In 1956 the first commercial hydrofoil went into operation between Sicily and Italy, and the following year the first passenger-carrying hydrofoil was *launched in the Soviet Union.

Today there are basically two types of hydrofoil craft, those fitted with the 'canard'-type foil in which 30% of the boat's weight is supported by the forward foil and 70% by the after foil, and the conventional type in which the weight distribution is reversed. With the former the boat rides clear of the water above the surface-piercing foils, whereas with the latter, though the hull is lifted clear of the water, the foils remain submerged, giving greater stability though not such high speed.

The naval use of hydrofoils has been pursued by a number of countries without any significant lasting results. However, their commercial use as *ferries is quite widespread, particularly in Russia.

hydrography, the science of marine surveying and of determining the position of points and objects on the globe's surface, depths of the sea, etc.

Most of the world's hydrographic knowledge and practice has come from the operations of the world's navies. A general requirement, before the birth of the various national hydrographic departments, was for the *masters, or *navigators, of the naval ships of all nations to observe, survey, and report to their respective admiralties on all possible occasions. Towards the end of the 18th century most maritime nations had thus collected large volumes of mainly uncollated hydrographic information, and most of them appointed official hydrographers during the course of the next half-century to organize the mass of knowledge and to publish it for the benefit of seamen of all nations.

The extent of a nation's overseas possessions or trade initially governed each maritime country's source of information and its ability as well as its need to produce *charts for its own naval and merchant shipping. France soon built up, and has since maintained, an extensive coverage and was the first to establish a hydrographer's department, in 1720. She was followed by Denmark (1784), Britain (1795), Spain (1800), the US Coast and Geodetic Survey (1816), Russia (1827), Germany (1861), Japan (1871), Italy and Sweden (1872), Norway, the Netherlands, and Chile (1874). Others followed and in 1921 the International Hydrographic Bureau at Monaco was formed by interested nations, the objective being to promote rapid and informed exchange of hydrographic information in standardized terms between member states. Information is exchanged by the United Nations-sponsored International Hydrographic Organization which was formed in 1970.

Maritime countries have commonly organized their surveying services within their navies, since the information obtained was often of national significance whether for military or commercial purposes. However, notable exceptions to this general rule include the French Corps of Hydrographic Engineers and the US Coast and Geodetic Survey, now an office within the National Ocean Service, a part of the *National Oceanic and Atmospheric Administration, which has responsibilities for US home waters. The development of the methods used in hydrography from the 18th century onwards can be found in Alexander Dalrymple's *Essay on Nautical Surveying* (1771), Murdoch Mackenzie's *Treatise on Maritime Surveying* (1774), Edward Belcher's *Treatise on Nautical Surveying* (1835), William Wharton's *Hydrographical Surveying* (1882), *U.S. Coast and Geodetic Survey* (Washington, 1963), *Admiralty Manual of Hydrographic Surveying* (1968), G. S. Ritchie, *The Admiralty Chart* (1967), and A. Day, *The Admiralty Hydrographic Service 1793–1919* (1967).

Hydrography Today by Adam Kerr

Originally, hydrography had a very broad remit of studying the sea and all that it contained, but it is now mainly concentrated on seafloor surveys and studies of tidal phenomena. Until the middle of the 20th century the results of this work were primarily used for *chartmaking. However, the development of interest in offshore petroleum deposits led to the need for hydrography on a broader commercial base for such tasks as positioning *offshore oil and gas rigs and laying pipelines on the seafloor. There is a rather indistinct line between *oceanography and hydrography because the former is involved in a very broad range of maritime studies, particularly the tidal phenomena.

For over 200 years the technology of hydrography changed very little, with survey ships being positioned by *celestial navigation and the depths measured by *lead line. However in the 1920s it was found possible to measure depths by sending out an acoustic impulse and measuring the time for it to travel to the seafloor, be reflected, and return to the instrument. Another major development was the result of the needs of the Second World War (1939–45) to position aircraft and ships by *hyperbolic navigation that allowed survey ships to be positioned at all times and in all weather conditions. The final step in providing precise positioning of survey vessels, and consequently the depths and other data that were collected, was the introduction of *satellite navigation. Initially this was based on the Doppler (changing frequency) of satellite signals, as the satellite passed along polar orbits. In the 1970s *GPS (global positioning system) and its Russian counterpart, Glonass, were introduced. These systems are very precise indeed, not only in the horizontal plane but also in the vertical height determination.

Depth measurement has also undergone great improvement. The early acoustic *echo sounders measured only a single profile of depth under the ship as it moved along. This was much better than the single-point lead-line measurements, but still left much to be interpreted between the sounding lines, which were normally arranged as a series of parallel tracks. To ensure that no obstructions extended from the seabed between the measured depth profiles **side-scan *sonar** was introduced. This device sent out acoustic signals perpendicular to the ship's track and, although it did not provide a precise measurement of the depths, the strength of the reflected signals from the seafloor gave an indication of changing depths or changing type of material on the bottom.

The most recent development in acoustic technology has been **multi-beam echo sounders**. This is similar to side-scan sonar except that it provides a fan of acoustic beams, again perpendicular to the ship's track, but now able to provide precise measurements of the depth along a swathe of the seafloor. When the survey plan is arranged with sufficiently close parallel swathes it is possible to obtain practically total measurement of the entire seafloor, leaving little to be interpolated or interpreted between measured points. The technology is particularly useful in deep water where the swathe can be very wide and large areas of the seafloor can be rapidly measured.

In very clear water a system using lasers from an aircraft, called LIDAR (Light Detection and Ranging), is now available that can be used to measure depths to approximately two to three times the visible depth, which in extremely clear water may be as much as 60 metres (197 ft). The system uses a red and a green laser that are fired at the water beneath the aircraft. Because of its higher frequency, the red laser is reflected from the water surface, but the green laser penetrates to the bottom, and the difference of return time of these two signals provides a measure of the water depth. The system has been used to a great extent in complex areas such as the *Great Barrier Reef.

These new depth-measuring systems collect vast amounts of data, and processing it has become a major challenge. All survey ships now carry computer systems that process it on line, and in some cases produce digital plots on board. Data visualization has become an important task both for the purpose of refining survey work while still in the field, and as a final product in forms such as the *electronic chart for *navigators and other users.

hydroplanes, see HYDRODYNAMICS.

hydrothermal vents are springs of superheated water that are found scattered along the rift valleys that occur at the crests of the

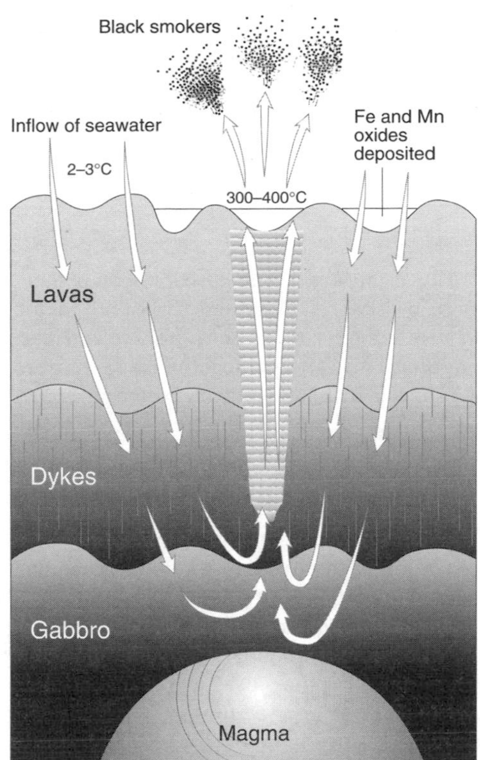

Illustration of circulation of water in the vicinity of hydrothermal vents, showing how water is superheated as it circulates down close to the molten magma

mid-ocean ridges. These valleys are the axes along which new ocean floor is being produced through eruptions of basalts. As the basalts erupt into the ocean water they tend to crack, creating channels through which water can percolate. The hot rocks generate convection currents in the fluids that penetrate deep within the ocean crust. The water is superheated, induces considerable changes in the mineralization of the rocks, and becomes saturated with metallic sulphides. The hottest water emitted from the vents is at a temperature of 350 °C (660 °F) and is kept from boiling by the high hydrostatic pressure. As it gushes out, it is rapidly cooled by mixing with the ambient sea water to temperatures of 2–5 °C (36–41 °F). The metal sulphides precipitate out of solution in black clouds, hence the colloquial name **'black smokers'**. In the immediate vicinity of the vents lives an extraordinary assemblage of clams, mussels, giant tube worms, and shrimps. These animals are characterized by having bacteria in their tissues that can synthesize organic molecules chemically using the energy derived from the oxidation of sulphide ions to sulphate. It is thought that these communities provide an analogue for the first living things that evolved on earth.

Because they occur where there are many earthquakes, many vents are destroyed by seismic events. Those that are destroyed gradually get furred up with metal deposits. The vent waters being emitted become cooler and no longer precipitate sulphides, and are then known as **'white smokers'**.

Fossil vents are found in a few places on land such as the Troodos mountains in Cyprus, and these were important sources of copper in the Bronze Age. The geochemistry of the vents is an important part of the long-term cycling of metals in both the oceans and continental rocks. It is estimated that all ocean water circulates through a vent system every 40,000 years. They are also remarkable in that their existence was predicted from theoretical considerations of seafloor spreading a decade before the first vent system was discovered near the Galapagos in 1977 by Dr *Ballard. See also CHEMICAL OCEANOGRAPHY.

http://seawifs.gsfc.nasa.gov/OCEAN_PLANET/HTML/oceanography_recently_revealed1.html

M. V. Angel

hyperbolic navigation system. If an observer measures the *difference* in distance from two identifiable points he will establish a *position line in the shape of a hyperbola. The speed of radio waves being constant, the difference in arrival time of synchronized signals from a pair of separate transmitters will locate the receiver on a hyperbolic line of position. This is the basis of those radio navigation systems known as hyperbolic. In practice the transmitters are so grouped as to provide a number of hyperbolic position lines that will intersect to provide a *fix. All hyperbolic systems require special receivers and lattice *charts on which to plot the signals received. All except *Loran-C are now operationally obsolete. See also CONSOL; DECCA; OMEGA.

Mike Richey

I

IALA maritime buoyage system, an international system of *buoys used globally for *navigation. Up to 1976 there were more than 30 different systems worldwide, many having rules which contradicted each other, and the history of attempting to find a universal system is a long one. In 1882 *Trinity House, the British authority then responsible for buoys, called a conference of all other national authorities concerned. This eventually took the form of an international marine conference at Washington, DC, in 1889 at which a uniform system was one of the subjects discussed. Most of the maritime nations attended, and the conference recommended the adoption of a lateral, or side-marking, system based partly on shape but primarily on colour. It was agreed that buoys marking the *starboard side of a channel, defined as that on the right hand of a ship entering from seaward or going with the main *flood tidal stream, should be coloured black and be conical in shape. Those marking the *port side should be red or chequered, and can, or truncated cone, in shape. No agreement was reached on the marking of the middle grounds, which in Britain was always done with spherical buoys.

Another international marine conference took place at St Petersburg in 1912 and an attempt was made to reverse the Washington decision, but the proposal was not accepted. But later some countries, particularly those bordering the Baltic Sea, found the lateral system not entirely suitable for their waters, and adopted a new system known as the cardinal, or directional, in which a combination of shape, colour, and topmark was used to indicate the compass quadrant in which the buoy was moored relative to the danger it marked. Countries exclusively using the cardinal system were Norway, Sweden, and Russia; Germany, Italy, and Turkey also used it either in addition to or in combination with the lateral system.

The catalyst for change came when there were a series of disastrous collisions in the Dover Strait in 1971. As a result the International Association of Lighthouse Authorities (IALA) began implementing two new systems, A and B. The rules of these were later combined into what is now known as the 'IALA maritime buoyage system' which operates in two regions, A and B. A, comprising Europe, South Africa, Australasia, and some Asian countries, uses red to mark the port-hand side of a channel when entering with the flood tide, and green for the starboard side. Region B, comprising North, Central and South America, Japan, Korea, and the Philippines, uses green to mark the port-hand side and red for the starboard. The system uses five types of marks: *lateral, *cardinal, *isolated danger, *safe water, and *special. Exact details of the buoyage system in use in any particular country are given in the *sailing directions appropriate to those waters.

ice, the solid phase of water, which, unusually, is lighter than liquid water. The molecules in ice crystals are arranged in a lattice and are more spaced out than in the liquid. The freezing point of sea water is about −1.9 °C (28.5 °F), depressed below 0 °C (32 °F) by the dissolved salts. It takes 80 calories to melt a gram of ice, enough heat to heat up the gram of liquid water to 80 °C (176 °F); this is termed the latent heat of ice formation. For the sea to freeze, it not only has to be extremely cold but also very windy to keep areas of water open and prevent a skin of ice from insulating the water surface from further cooling. Areas of open water are know as polynyas and are important for *marine mammals like beluga *whales and walruses, giving them access to air. When ice forms, the salts the water contained are left in solution, making the unfrozen water saltier. Because ice takes time to melt, it can drift well into warmer seas before finally melting. As it melts it dilutes the surface sea water, so the formation and melting of ice is one of the processes that modifies the *salinity of surface sea water.

Frozen sea water forms **pack ice**. In the Arctic, the pack ice tends to last for up to five years. This multi-year ice gets deformed into pressure ridges by the surface *currents and the wind. The pack ice moves with the drift of the surface current, whereas **icebergs**, with five-sixths of their volume below the surface, move with the deeper currents. A large tabular berg in the Southern Ocean can be as much as 200–300 metres (655–985 ft) deep. The deeper currents flow at an angle to the surface drift, because of the effects of *Coriolis force generating a spiral profile to the currents known as an Ekman spiral, so big bergs often plough across pack ice.

Icebergs have a different origin: they are spawned from glaciers in the Arctic, and from the ice shelf in the Southern Ocean, where at any one time there may be up to 300,000 icebergs. In 2000 a massive berg 290 × 37 kilometres (180 × 23 mls.), roughly the size of Jamaica, broke off the ice shelf in the Ross Sea, devastating the food chain for *penguins and cutting them off from their rookeries. Such a large berg will persist for several years. Fortunately, the currents of the Southern Ocean keep such *navigational hazards well to the south. However, 1–2% of the 40,000 icebergs spawned annually from the glaciers of Greenland are carried well south down the east coast of Canada to Newfoundland and beyond, presenting a potent threat to shipping; the **Titanic* was sunk by one. Nowadays, satellites are used to track these icebergs and alerts are issued by the Canadian *Coastguard as initiated by the *International Convention for the Safety of Life at Sea (SOLAS). It is estimated that the ice in most Atlantic icebergs was formed at least 15,000 years ago, so is uncontaminated by industrial pollutants, one of today's *environmental issues. Various uses have been suggested for icebergs: during the Second World War (1939–45) Admiral Mountbatten suggested one be converted into a floating airstrip; and it has been proposed to tow bergs to the arid coasts of Chile and south-west Africa where they can be used to supply fresh water.

www.weather-wise.com/polar/b15.htm
www.wordplay.com/tourism/icebergs/

M. V. Angel

ice-breaker, a vessel specially designed to force a way through pack *ice in extreme *latitudes. Modern ones have a massively reinforced hull that is designed to help the ship rise on top of the ice and then crush downwards through it. The Germans have a *research ship which is an ice-breaker, and several other nations with an interest in the Arctic and Antarctic regions have them, too, but the Russians have by far the largest fleet.

The first nuclear-powered ice-breaker was the 16,000-ton, 44,000 shaft horsepower *Lenin*, which was *launched by the USSR in 1960. In 1978 the first successful attempt was made to navigate the Northern Sea Route (NSR)—a 5,000-kilometre (3125-m.) stretch of Arctic water across northern Siberia from Murmansk to the port of Dudinka—on a year-round basis, but normally the route is only open to commercial traffic during the summer months. With the industrialization of Siberia the route is a vital one and in 1988 it was estimated that 6 million tonnes of cargo was carried on it.

During the 1970s and 1980s the Russians built up a fleet of more than 75 ships of different types of ice-breakers. The most important of these were those constructed to *convoy merchant ships along the NSR. Besides the *Lenin*, these include three other nuclear-powered vessels of 75,000 horsepower, and in August 1978 one of them, the *Arktika*, became the first surface ship to reach the North Pole. In cooperation with Finnish shipbuilders a fleet of specialized multi-purpose freighters were also built which are capable of transiting the NSR independently. Such ships must be capable of operating in ice that is up to five metres (3 ft) thick and in a temperature that can be as low as –50 °C.

Following the end of the Cold War in 1989, and then the collapse of the USSR, several Russian ice-breakers have been converted into *cruise ships. For example, the 134-metre (440-ft), 15,000-tonne *Kapitan Khlebnikov* carries 114 passengers as well as 60 crew, who can be taken to places in Arctic and Antarctic waters quite inaccessible to normal cruise ships.

http://members.shaw.ca/diesel-duck/library/articles/Russian.htm

idlers, the name used in the days of sail for those members of a ship's crew who, because of their job aboard, did not stand the normal *watches. Among these were the ship's carpenter, cook, and sailmaker.

impressment, the name given to the British government's requirements for an individual to serve in defence of his country; it was never employed in the US Navy. Although universally known as 'press' or 'impress', the origin of the word is 'prest', a sum of money advanced to a man in the form of conduct money to reach a naval recruiting centre, or *rendezvous as they were called. These were set up in the 18th and early 19th centuries, usually in some tavern near the waterfront of seaport towns. They had a strong lock-up room, known as a press room, where the recruits taken by the *press gangs could be held until a *tender took them to a receiving ship, or to a *hulk, before they were drafted to seagoing ships.

Impressment was a general and recognized method of recruitment in most countries, and applied equally to service ashore and afloat. In England, for example, the famous 'New Model' army of Oliver Cromwell was largely recruited by impressments. But because service in the navy was always unpopular, and the demand for seamen always so great, it is the naval element of impressments on which most attention has been focused.

Under early Acts of Parliament, the first of which was passed in 1556, some 'seamen' and 'mariners' were exempt from impressment, as were *landsmen. However, in practice, because of the chronic and persistent need for naval manpower, no authority questioned closely whether a man brought in by the press was exempt or not. The most prolific sources of recruitment came under the various Vagrancy Acts, which encouraged local justices to clear their jails and get rid of their worst characters by drafting them into the navy. During times of particular emergency, such as the Revolutionary War against France (1793–1801), each town and county had to provide a quota of men for service at sea, though the *Sea Fencibles and those with *protection were exempt.

The operations of the impressment service were widespread throughout Britain. They were also employed at sea, where homeward-bound merchant ships could be stopped and a proportion of the crew taken off, essential men

The Press Gang; watercolour by T. Rowlandson

being replaced by *men-in-lieu. Outward-bound vessels frequently suffered the same fate; by the time any complaint from an outward-bound ship reached the authorities in London, the incident would be too far in the past to command any action. This pressing at sea, which the men concerned could not evade as they could ashore, was the subject of much abuse.

The impressment service operated only in time of war. It was last employed in Britain during the Napoleonic War (1803–15), although the right to operate a press was still retained. Under an Act of 1835, men who had once been pressed for service and had served five years were exempted from further impressment. But with the introduction of continuous service in the navy in 1853, under which seamen could make service in the navy a career with a pension after a fixed number of years, the need for impressment faded. When, again, large numbers of men were required, as in the two world wars of the 20th century, Acts of compulsory national service were passed and men were drafted into the various fighting services in a more fair and orderly fashion than under the haphazard method of the press gangs. See also MACARONI MATE.

inertial navigation. The determination of (*a*) position relative to an established starting point, (*b*) velocity, and (*c*) heading, by the measurement of accelerations in known space-oriented directions, and processing the data by computer. Inertial navigation is founded on the work of Newton in 1687, Foucault in 1851, and Schuler in 1908.

The system of navigation known as SINS (Ship's Inertial Navigation System), was developed after the Second World War (1939–45) for use in nuclear *submarines which remain submerged for prolonged periods. The system must also be completely secure from outside detection. If a submarine's position is accurately plotted at the start of its voyage, and if all subsequent accelerations in their component directions can be measured, they can then be translated by calculation into speeds and distances which, when applied to the initial position, give the present position.

Inertial navigation is in fact an extremely sophisticated and precise method of *dead reckoning, using accelerometers. The system can measure every acceleration due to speed and *course changes, and can eliminate the effects of gravitational attraction, *pitching and rolling, etc. The first major public demonstration of the system accuracy was in 1958 when the US nuclear submarines **Nautilus* and *Skate* navigated under the polar ice cap. Since then nuclear submarines have made submerged circumnavigations navigated by SINS. So accurate is the system that a margin of error of not more than 100–200 metres (330–650 ft) is expected after a circumnavigation. Mike Richey

Inmarsat, abbreviation for the International Mobile Satellite Organization, which was formed by a convention of the *International Maritime Organization in 1975, and began operations in 1982. Inmarsat's obligations to provide maritime distress and safety services via satellite were part of the 1988 amendments to the *International Convention for the Safety of Life at Sea (SOLAS) which introduced the *Global Maritime Distress and Safety System. In 1999 Inmarsat was privatized and the new structure comprises Inmarsat Ltd., a public limited company, and the International Mobile Satellite Organization (IMSO), an intergovernmental body that ensures its commercial arm continues to meet its public service obligations.

Inmarsat's four satellites provide communications for the four ocean areas except the extreme polar regions. It has various mobile systems (Inmarsat-A, -B, etc.) which provide different facilities for mariners and other users. They include direct-dial telephone, fax, e-mail, and data communications, and provide for the transmission and reception of high-quality photographs and video film. Some can be connected to *satellite navigation devices such as *GPS, and meet the long-range communications requirements of the Global Maritime Distress and Safety System. Inmarsat-E is currently (2004) an alternative system for alerting *life-saving services through L-band *EPIRBs.

in soundings, or **on soundings.** A vessel was said to be in, or on, soundings when it was being *navigated in water sufficiently shallow to *sound the bottom to ascertain the approximate position of the ship. Traditionally, a ship was reckoned to be in soundings when it was within the 100-*fathom (183-m/600-ft) line, this *isobath being taken as marking the edge of the *continental shelf.

in stays, when a sailing vessel, during the operation of *tacking, is head to wind and hangs there instead of continuing to *pay off on the opposite tack. If the vessel's *head fails to pay off but falls back on the original tack, it is said to have **missed stays**.

intercept, *altitude difference; in *celestial navigation the difference between the corrected *sextant altitude and the altitude at the position from which the *sight has been worked. The observed (i.e. corrected) altitude is plotted on the *chart towards or away from the body observed according to whether the calculated or the observed position is the greater. See also MARCQ SAINT-HILAIRE METHOD.

Mike Richey

International Code of Signals, originally a specific method of communication between ships, or between ship and shore, by hoisting flags and *pennants, which in a group, or singly, conveyed a message. However, the phrase later included other means of communication at sea, such as *Morse code.

The original code was founded in 1817 on the one invented by Captain F. *Marryat, and at first comprised only fifteen flags and pennants. By 1855 it was being widely challenged by codes developed in France by Captain Reynold-Chauvaney, in Great Britain by Rohdė (1836) and Watson (1842), and in the USA by Rogers, and an international committee was set up in 1856 to try to reach agreement on a single code for universal use. The committee's final recommendation was based almost entirely on Marryat's original flags and it published a *Commercial Code of Signals* which received universal recognition. In 1887 the existing code ran into difficulties because the adoption of *signal letters for ship identification, and additional coloured flags and pennants, had to be incorporated into the code. This was universally agreed in 1900, and brought into use in 1902. The current code, which came into effect in 1969, provides for nine languages—English, French, German, Greek, Italian, Japanese, Norwegian, Russian, and Spanish.

The system provides for one flag for each letter of the alphabet and eleven pendants, numerals 0 and 9, and the answering pendant; and three triangular-shaped flags, the First, Second, and Third substitutes, which are used to repeat one or more letters in a group. Each letter flag has a meaning which, when hoisted by itself, indicates a very urgent message, or one which is important or common. For example, the letter 'O' indicates there is a man overboard, the letter 'B' that the ship flying it is taking in, or discharging, or carrying dangerous goods.

These single signals were well recognized by professional seamen, but when it came to decoding groups of two, three, and four flags (for ship identification) a code book was used. Each signal was normally a complete message in itself, but sometimes what was known as complements were used to alter a message, or to make it more specific. For example, the two-letter group KT meant 'you should send me a towing *hawser' but when the numeral 1 was added it meant 'I am sending towing hawser'; and the letter group CB meant 'I require immediate assistance' but when the numeral 4 was added it meant 'I require immediate assistance; I am aground'. There were many other complements as well as instructions for signalling such information as dates and times and *latitude and *longitude so that it was clear and unambiguous.

In today's world of instant satellite communications, signalling by flag is almost a thing of the past, though some of the single flags, such as the *blue peter, are still used. However, unlike *semaphore, the International Code of Signals has not yet been made redundant by the *International Maritime Organization which oversees international maritime communications. See also SIGNALS AT SEA; TACKLINE.

International Congress of Maritime Museums (ICMM), the international organization which represents maritime museums worldwide. It was established at its first meeting, at the National Maritime Museum, Greenwich, in 1972 and now provides standards and guidelines for *marine archaeology and *ship preservation, nurtures maritime museums and maritime preservation activities on an international scale, and is developing strategies to ensure long-term public awareness and appreciation of the significance of maritime preservation. There is no space in this book to cover the world's major maritime museums, but the ICMM website—**www.icmmonline.org**—lists all its members from 35 countries.

International Convention for the Safety of Life at Sea (SOLAS), possibly the most important of all international treaties affecting merchant shipping. The first SOLAS convention was adopted in 1914 as a result of the **Titanic* disaster, and was followed by the second in 1929, the third in 1948, and the fourth in 1960. The 1960 convention became effective in May 1965 and was the first major task for IMCO, now the *International Maritime Organization, after its foundation. It represented a significant advance in the modernization of regulations for the shipping industry.

The original idea had been to keep the convention up to date by periodical amendments, but this proved impracticable if the amendments were to be brought into force within a reasonable period of time. A new convention, which took in all the amendments up to that time, was adopted in 1974 and a new procedure, known as the tacit amendment procedure—which ensured that changes could be brought into force without undue delay—was adopted. This provided for the adoption of any amendment by a certain date unless objections were received from a set number of parties. The 1974 convention, known as SOLAS 1974, has been amended several times.

Among matters that come under the jurisdiction of the convention are *traffic separation schemes and revisions to the *International Regulations for Preventing Collisions at Sea, commonly known as the Colregs. Mike Richey

International Date Line, a line running mainly along the *longitude of 180° but with adjustments to avoid the division of certain Island groups which lie astride it, the Aleutian Islands in the north and the Fiji, Tonga, and Kermadoc groups, with New Zealand, in the south. It is on this international dateline that the *zone times of +12 hours and −12 hours meet and the date changes. If a traveller round the world sets out from Greenwich (see GREENWICH MEAN TIME), on 0° longitude, and travels eastwards, he puts his clock forward by one hour as he crosses each 15° of longitude, so that by the time he reaches Greenwich again, his clock has been put forward by 24 hours and he is one day ahead in date. To correct this anomaly, he subtracts a day when he crosses the international dateline eastwards and adds a day when he crosses it westwards. So in the former case the same calendar date is used for two successive periods of 24 hours; in the latter case one calendar date is omitted altogether.

International Lifeboat Federation (ILF), the independent charity for national search and rescue (SAR) operations, such as Australia's Royal Volunteer Coastal Patrol, Britain's RNLI (Royal National Lifeboat Institution), and the *US Coast Guard, whose common aim is *lifesaving on the world's waters. The first international lifeboat conference was held in London in 1924 and has been held every four years since then. Participation has grown significantly from the eight delegations which attended the first conference, to a current (2004) 89 organizations from 62 countries.

Over the years, the ILF has played a central role in the development of maritime rescue and it continues to be the primary vehicle for the exchange of technology and experience in maritime search and rescue. Members freely share experiences and research, and help one another to build better rescue craft, to provide better training for rescue crews, and to improve SAR techniques.

The *International Maritime Organization (IMO) recognizes the ILF as the global representative of the world's maritime search and rescue providers. It is regarded by IMO and by its sister organization, the International Civil Aviation Organization (ICOA), as a key partner in the achievement of their joint plan to deliver consistent aeronautical and maritime SAR coverage around the globe. To achieve this the ILF is promoting the establishment of new SAR organizations in parts of the world where adequate services are not yet available and is providing practical assistance where necessary.

The ILF has a fourteen-member council which advises the charity's trustees on matters of technical and developmental policy, and this is developing a new constitution for the federation which is expected to be formally ratified at the next conference, in Gothenburg, in 2007. See also GLOBAL MARITIME DISTRESS AND SAFETY SYSTEM.

international maritime law, see ADMIRALTY; CONTINUOUS VOYAGE; EXCLUSIVE ECONOMIC ZONE; HIGH SEAS; MARE CLAUSUM; MARPOL; NARROW SEAS; OLERON, THE LAWS OF; TERRITORIAL WATERS; UNITED NATIONS CONFERENCE ON THE LAW OF THE SEA.

International Maritime Organization (IMO), a special agency of the United Nations established in 1958 with responsibility for improving maritime safety and preventing *pollution from ships. It has its headquarters on the Albert Embankment in London. IMO deals with the administration and legal aspects of a number of important maritime conventions. One of the first treaties it was concerned with was SOLAS—the *International Convention for the Safety of Life at Sea—and it later addressed conventions on facilitating marine traffic, determining *load lines, measuring the *tonnage of ships, and regulating antifouling systems (see FOULING) and the transportation of dangerous cargoes. The grounding of the *tanker *Torrey Canyon* in 1967 resulted in the adoption of the Convention for the Prevention of Pollution from Ships, known as *MARPOL, and the establishment of treaties which provide rapid compensation to anyone who has suffered from the impact of marine pollution, one of today's most important *environmental issues. IMO also sets international standards for the training and certification of seafarers, and for *watchkeeping at sea, and it introduced the *Global Maritime Distress and Safety System (GMDSS), which became fully operational in 1999. Its activities touch everyone who has anything to do with the sea, making life at sea and along the coasts safer for everyone. See also INTERNATIONAL LIFEBOAT FEDERATION.

www.imo.org/index.htm M. V. Angel

International Metre Class, a class of racing *yacht designed under the International Rule of the International Yacht Racing Union (IYRU), now the *International Sailing Federation (ISAF), which was formulated in 1906 and came into force in 1908, though yachts built to it were racing in 1907. It was to be in force for ten years, but the First World War (1914–18) delayed revisions to it until 1920. They rated as 23, 19, 12, 10, 8, 6, and 5.5 metres, according to the rule restrictions of the class.

Yachts of the same metre class were not all identical, as in a *one-design class, but bore the characteristics of the individual *yacht designer and his interpretation of the rule. A yacht's *rating was calculated by a formula which took into account such measurements as its length overall, length on waterline, breadths at different points between bow and stern, depths inside the hull, *draught, displacement *tonnage, and the measurements of various sails including the overall height of the rig. These measurements could differ for each yacht in a class, but when applied to the rating formula the resultant figure had to produce the rating of 23 metres—Lipton's **Shamrock* being an example of this class—19 metres, 15 metres, 12 metres, 6 metres, and so on. Towards the end of the 1920s two new classes, the 22 square metre and the 30 square metre, were introduced into Scandinavia, and particularly Sweden, as lighter, faster, and less expensive than the traditional metre class of the same size. Other square metre classes included the 50 and 100 sq. metre, which were popular in Germany before the Second World War (1939–45).

Twelve metres were used in challenges for the *America's Cup, 1958–87, but mainstream racing in all the other metre class boats died out, though a form of the 5.5-metre class has survived as the Daring Class. However, many metre boats survive and are raced competitively, particularly in the 6-, 8-, and 12-metre classes, in classic yacht regattas.

International Regulations for Preventing Collisions at Sea, the official title, commonly shortened to Colregs, of the internationally agreed rules by which ships at sea keep clear of each other. The first international conference to consider such rules was held in Washington in 1889 and the regulations agreed were brought into force in several countries, including Britain and the USA, in 1897. A further international conference was held in Brussels in 1910 and the regulations then agreed remained in force until 1954 when revisions made at the *International Convention for the Safety of Life at Sea (SOLAS) conference in 1948 came into force. In 1960 the intergovernmental maritime consultative organization, now the *International Maritime Organization (IMO), an agency of the United Nations, convened a SOLAS conference which agreed certain alterations to the rules. Today the IMO has the responsibility, exercised through its maritime safety committee, for altering the regulations.

There are 38 rules which are divided into four parts, *a* to *d*, which cover application, responsibility, and general definitions; steering and sailing rules to keep vessels apart when they are approaching each other or are in restricted visibility; lights and shapes to be carried by vessels at night or by day by which they can be recognized; and sound and light signals. There are also four annexes covering the positioning and technical details of lights and shapes; additional signals for fishing vessels fishing in close proximity; technical details of sound signal appliances; and *distress signals. One of the most important new rules, which applies to yachtsmen and fishermen as well as to merchant shipping, is Rule 10 which deals with *traffic separation schemes.

Of the definitions laid down, the most important are those which define a power-driven and a sailing vessel. A vessel with any form of mechanical propulsion, including *oars, counts as a power-driven vessel; a sailing vessel is one propelled by sails only; a *yacht with her sails spread which is also using her *auxiliary engine is a power-driven vessel.

Under the regulations the lights a vessel is obliged to carry at night serve two purposes. Its *navigation lights, or steaming lights as they are also called, are so designed and placed that any other ship sighting them can tell reasonably accurately the *course of the vessel carrying them. The regulations also lay down other lights which must be carried by certain vessels to indicate their type and actual employment. For example, a fishing vessel engaged in *trawling must show an all-round green light above an all-round white light, in addition to its navigation lights.

During daylight signals are displayed by hoisting cones or black balls, and in restricted visibility, day or night, *fog signals are used to indicate a vessel's movements and sometimes its employment. Below are extracts from the regulations about the more commonplace sound and visual signals, including *distress signals, but if in doubt mariners should refer to the regulations themselves as there are exemptions and qualifications to some of the rules, and some do not apply to small craft.

1. Blasts from a ship's whistle or foghorn can be used by it to indicate a change of course. One short blast indicates that the vessel is altering its course to *starboard; two short blasts indicate that it is altering course to *port; and three short blasts indicate that it is going *astern.
2. When one vessel is in sight of another in a narrow channel or *fairway the overtaking vessel should indicate its intentions by two prolonged blasts and one short one, indicating that it is intending to overtake the other vessel on that vessel's starboard side, and by two prolonged blasts and two short blasts when it intends overtaking the other vessel on that vessel's port side. The vessel being overtaken should indicate its agreement by one prolonged and one short blast, repeated once immediately.
3. If one vessel, for any reason, does not understand the intentions or actions of another vessel which is approaching it, or is unsure that sufficient action is being taken to avoid a collision, then it shall immediately indicate such doubt by giving at least five short and rapid blasts.
4. When a vessel is approaching a bend or an area of a channel where other vessels may be obscured it should sound one prolonged blast. This signal should be answered by any vessel hearing it by a similar blast.
5. A vessel not under command during the day displays two balls or similar shapes in a vertical line where they can best be seen. At night it displays two all-round red lights in a vertical line where they can best be seen.
6. A vessel restricted in its ability to manoeuvre (except one engaged in clearing mines) shall display a ball shape, a diamond shape, and another ball shape in a vertical line where they can best be seen.
7. A vessel at anchor shall display in its fore part one ball.
8. A vessel *aground shall display three balls in a vertical line.
9. A vessel *towing another vessel, or vessels, in excess of 200 metres (656 ft) shall display a diamond shape where it can best be seen.

The most important group of rules are the steering and sailing ones, which lay down the procedures to be followed when ships approach each other and there is a danger of collision. Where this happens, the rules lay down which ship is to give way to the other. In a broad sense, vessels keep to the right when at sea. If, for example, two ships are approaching each other head on, both must alter course to starboard (to the right) so that they pass each other port side to port side. Where a vessel is on the starboard hand of another, and steering a course which may result in a collision, it has the right of way and should maintain its course and speed, the other vessel giving way to it. Where a vessel is on the port hand of another, and its course, if it maintains it, may result in a collision, it is the giving way vessel and must alter course to avoid the other. These basic tenets are enshrined in the well-known doggerel written by Thomas Gray, head of the British Board of Trade's marine department towards the end of the 19th century:

> When both side-lights you see ahead,
> Port your helm and show your red.
> Green to green, and red to red,
> Perfect safety go ahead.
> When on your starboard red appear,
> It is *your* duty to keep clear,
> To act as judgment says is proper,
> To port or starboard, back or stop her.
> But when upon your port is seen,
> A steamer's starboard light of green,
> There's not much for you to do,
> For green to port keeps clear of you.
> Both in safety and in doubt,
> Always keep a good look-out.
> In danger with no room to turn,
> Ease her, stop her, go astern.

However, any ship overtaking another, i.e. approaching at any angle from two *points *abaft the *beam on either side, must keep clear. Also, generally speaking, all power-driven vessels must keep clear of all vessels under sail, although there are always circumstances (e.g. a sailing vessel approaching a very large *bulk carrier in narrow waters) where the sailing vessel will keep clear. The only rule to which this does not apply is the overtaking rule; a sailing vessel overtaking a power-driven vessel must keep clear of it. When a vessel has the duty of giving way to another under the rules, it normally does so by altering course to pass astern of the other, and should make a clear and significant alteration of course in plenty of time to indicate to the other vessel that it is taking the appropriate action.

The rules which govern vessels under sail are clear and precise. They lay down that when two sailing vessels approach each other with the wind on a different side, the vessel with the wind on the port side must give way to the other. When both have the wind on the same side, the vessel to *windward keeps clear of the vessel to *leeward. When yachts are racing they have additional *racing rules which apply among themselves when competing, but the regulations always override these.

The sailing and steering rules lay down that if a collision between two vessels appears possible, both vessels must take avoiding action even if such action involves a departure from the regulations on the part of one of them.

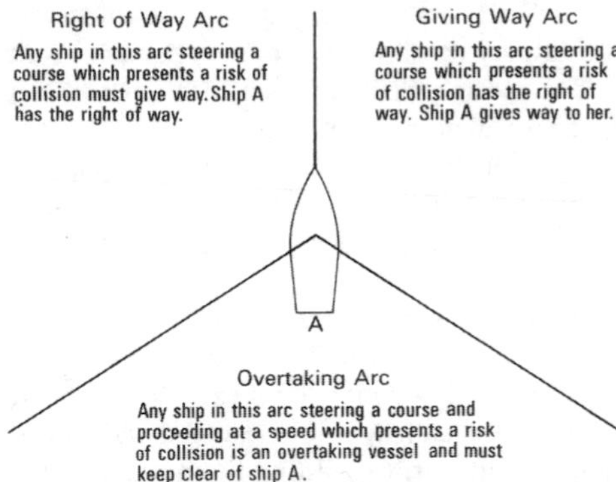

Colregs for powered vessels

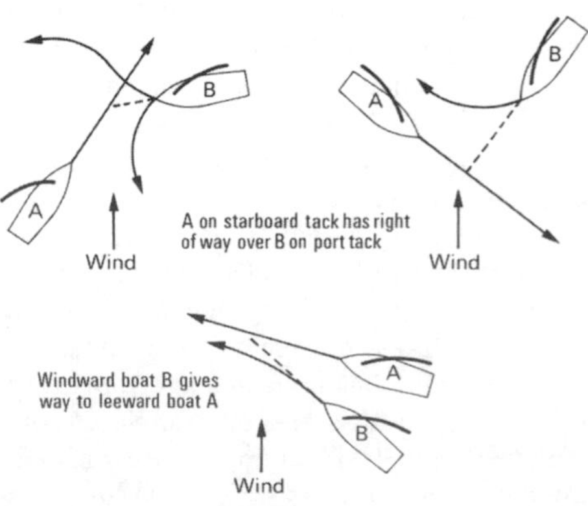

Colregs for sailing vessels

This requirement is perhaps best summed up by the little verse which most seamen learn early on in their careers:

here lies the body of Michael O'Day
who died maintaining the right of way;
he was right, dead right, as he sailed along,
but he's just as dead as if he'd been wrong.

International Rule, see INTERNATIONAL METRE CLASS.

International Sailing Federation (ISAF), the governing body for the sport of *yachting. Previously called the International Yacht Racing Union (IYRU), which introduced the *International Metre Class in 1907, it changed its name in August 1996. The ISAF, which currently (2004) consists of 114 member nations, is officially recognized by the International Olympic Committee as the governing authority for sailing worldwide. As such, it is responsible for the promotion and development of the sport internationally and has established several international events including the ISAF Team Racing and Match Racing World Championships. It also manages sailing at the Olympic Games, develops the *racing rules for all sailing competitions, trains judges, umpires, and other administrators, and represents sailors in all matters concerning the sport. There are currently 79 ISAF International and Recognized Classes, ranging from the smallest, the Optimist Dinghy, to the largest, the Maxi One-Design.

Irish horse, the sailor's name in the old days of sail for salt beef that was kept at sea in a *harness cask and that was tougher than usual. Its name was probably based on the belief in those days that the Irish, being so poor, worked their horses much harder and longer than the English. There was a sailor's *sea song of the 18th century in which he addressed his ration of salt beef:

Salt horse, salt horse, what brought you here?
You've carried turf for many a year.
From Dublin quay to Ballyack
You've carried turf upon your back.

Irish pennants, a seaman's name for loose ends of twine or ropes left hanging over a ship's side or from the *rigging, a sure sign of a slovenly crew. Similarly, the name given to the ends of *gaskets and *reefpoints left flapping on the *yard when the sail is furled in a *square-rigged ship. See also DEAD MEN.

ironclads, the early name for warships built of iron, or whose wooden hulls were protected by iron plates. The name was adopted as a generic description for such warships in *warfare at sea after the action at Sinope in 1853 in which a Turkish *squadron of wooden ships was set on fire and destroyed by Russian shellfire. It was this event which influenced all navies in the world to adopt iron as the main *shipbuilding material. The world's first true ironclad warship was the French *frigate **Gloire*, *launched in 1859, but the British soon outbuilt her with HMS **Warrior*. In the following decades many ironclads were built with a *ram. The first battle between ironclads took place during the American Civil War (1861–5) between the USS *Monitor*, which subsequently gave its name to the *monitor type of warship, and the Confederate warship CSS *Virginia* (previously the USS **Merrimac*). The name continued as a generic description of iron or steel warships until 1906 when it was replaced by the term Dreadnought, the precursor of the modern *battleship.

irons. **(1)** A sailing ship is in irons when, by carelessness or through a fickle wind, it has been allowed to come up into the wind and lose its *way through the water so that it will not *pay off again. It is in the process of *tacking, which entails a vessel coming up *head to wind and bringing the wind on the other side, that the most frequent cause of a ship being in irons occurs. **(2)** A man was **in irons** when he was shackled to *bilboes as a punishment. In the US Navy a man was in **double irons** when he was both shackled and manacled.

irradiation, an optical phenomenon whereby bright objects viewed against a darker background appear to be bigger than they are; and dark objects viewed against a lighter background appear to be smaller. The sun viewed against the darker background of the sky, and the sky viewed against the normally darker background of the sea, result in irradiation effects for which an allowance should be made when correcting the observed *altitude of the sun in *celestial navigation. The same conditions apply to moon altitude observations. An interesting effect of irradiation of the moon is often to be seen when it is crescent shaped and the remainder of its surface is faintly illuminated by reflected earth-shine. When the moon is young—not more than three or four days after it is new—this phenomenon is sometimes known, rather poetically, as 'the old moon in the new moon's arms'.

isobath, from the Greek *iso*, equal, and *bathos*, depth, a line on a *chart linking points of equal depth, sometimes called a depth contour.

isogonic lines, lines drawn on a *chart which connects points of equal *variation of the *magnetic compass. The first world chart to incorporate isogonic lines was published in 1701 by Edmund Halley (1656–1742). Called a *General Chart of the Variations of the Compass*, it was a notable landmark in the history and development of *chartmaking and *navigation.

isolated danger mark, a *buoy, normally a *pillar, or *spar, buoy, used in the *IALA maritime buoyage system. It is erected on, or *moored on or above, an isolated danger which has navigable water all around it. It is coloured black with one or more broad horizontal red bands, and has a distinctive topmark of two black spheres, one above the other. The *characteristic of its light, when fitted, is a white light group flashing (2) within a period of five or ten seconds.

J

jack. **(1)** The national flag which is flown from a *jackstaff on the *stem of naval ships when at anchor. **(2)** **Pilot jack**, originally the name given to the flag, which was a Union flag surrounded by a white border, flown by ships in need of a *pilot. Later, this requirement was met by 'G' flag in the *International Code of Signals, which has yellow and blue vertical stripes. **(3)** **Cargo jack**, sometimes also known as a **jack screw**, an appliance used in the *holds of merchant ships, before the introduction of *container ships, for moving cargo and for compressing cargo such as cotton, hides, etc. into as small a space as possible to increase the carrying capacity.

jackanapes coat, see MONKEY JACKET.

jackass. **(1)** A type of heavily built open boat used in Newfoundland. **(2)** See HAWSE BAGS.

jackass-barque, a four-masted sailing ship *square rigged on the two foremost masts and with a *fore-and-aft rig on the two after masts. A number of these jackass-barques were used in the late 19th- and early 20th-century nitrate trade around Cape Horn to Chilean ports, many owners and skippers considering them to be more efficient in the particularly stormy weather so frequently experienced around the Horn.

jack in the basket, before the days of the *IALA maritime buoyage sytem, the name given to a mark in coastal waters to show the edge of a sandbank or other obstruction. It was made of a wooden box or basket on the top of a pole.

Jack of the Dust, a colloquial term in the old days of the British and US navies for the *purser's assistant who was employed in the bread room, where the flour, issued as part of the daily victuals, was stored.

jackstaff, a short pole mast erected perpendicularly on the *stem of a modern ship, or at the end of the *bowsprit in the days of sail. It is where the national flag of a nation is hoisted in naval ships when at anchor.

jackstay, a wire or *hemp rope, or *pendant, secured firmly between two points and used as a support. When refuelling at sea, the oil hosepipe is suspended on a jackstay between the *tanker and the ship being refuelled. When an *awning is spread over a deck in hot weather as protection from the sun, it is supported centrally on a jackstay, though it is often called a ridge-rope. Also, when a *breeches buoy was employed in *lifesaving, a jackstay was rigged between ship and shore along which the *buoy was hauled to and from the ship. A jackstay, or **jackline**, is also the name for a line, wire, or length of webbing secured on the deck of a *yacht so that those working on deck in heavy weather can hook their safety harnesses onto it to prevent being swept overboard.

Jackstays are rigged with a minimum safety factor of four, i.e. the load supported by a jackstay including its own weight should not be more than one-quarter the breaking strain of the wire or rope used.

Jack tar, a familiar name for a British seaman. Tar is the shortened version of *tarpaulin, the tarred *canvas which seamen, and especially *topmen, used to wear as protection against the weather during the days of sail. Also, when pigtails were the fashionable hairstyle afloat, seamen always dressed theirs with tar. Originally, the name was applied only to ABs and men whose station in the ship was on the masts and *yards of *square-rigged warships, but it was later extended to cover all British naval seamen. See also SAILORS' DRESS.

jackyard, a light *spar used to extend a light-weather sail.

jackyard topsail, a triangular topsail set above the mainsail in a *gaff-rigged sailing vessel. It sets a larger area of sail than a *jib-headed topsail as both the *luff and the *foot of the *topsail are *laced to jackyards which extend beyond the top of the mast and the *peak of the gaff. But see also MARCONI RIG.

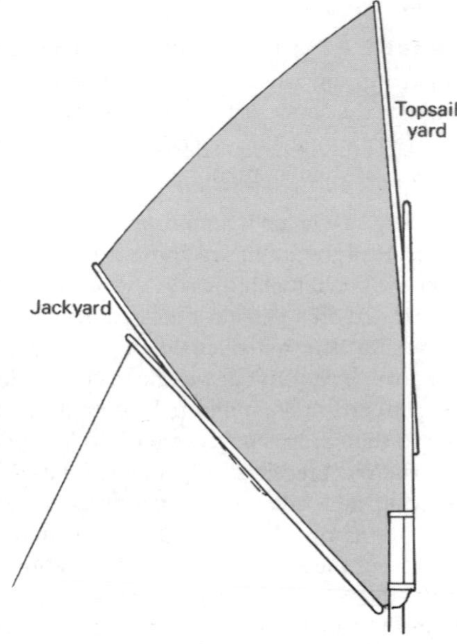

Jackyard topsail

Jacob's ladder. **(1)** Formerly a ladder, with rope sides and steps, fitted on the after side of a *topgallant mast where there were no *ratlines for ascending the *rigging. **(2)** A term also used to describe the shakes and short fractures, rising one above another, in a defective pole *spar. **(3)** The name of the rope ladder which hangs from the lower boom of a warship to which a ship's boats are made fast in harbour.

jaegt, the typical sailing boat of the Norwegian coast, now obsolete. The true jaegt was the direct descendant of the Viking *longship, with the same high stern and *stem and a large square sail carried on a single mast; they remained in use from about the 14th to the 19th centuries. Their main use was to take the *fish catch, from the Lofoten Islands, the centre of the Norwegian *cod *fisheries, to Bergen, returning up the coast with, it was said, mainly elm boards for coffins which were offloaded at the various ports of call.

Jamaica discipline, a code of laws, operative in the 17th and early 18th centuries, which was adopted by the *buccaneers of the West Indies, and later by *privateers of the same area, respecting the running of their ship and the division of *prize captured by them. Under these laws, the captain of a buccaneer ship received two shares of any booty, officers one and a half shares each, and seamen one share each. In some ships additional rules were adopted dealing with women on board and drinking hours. The ships were run very democratically with captains being voted into their positions and one, or sometimes two, men being appointed to speak on behalf of the crew; and any ship's crew, if they voted against it, or any individual, could freely decide not to take part in a raid if they did not wish to do so. One French buccaneer recorded that the regulations drawn up on his ship condemned anyone to forfeit his share of the loot 'if convicted of cowardliness, rape, drunkenness, disobedience, larceny, and failure to obey orders' (R. de Lussan, *Journal of a Voyage into the South Seas in 1684*, trans. Marguerite Eyer Wilbur (1930), from P. Earle, *The Pirate Wars* (2003), 121).

jaw. **(1)** The fitting at the end of a gaff or boom that permits it to ride smoothly against a mast. See also HORNS. **(2)** The distance between adjacent *strands on a rope. It gives a measure of the hardness or tightness of the *lay—the shorter the distance the harder the lay. See also LONG-JAWED.

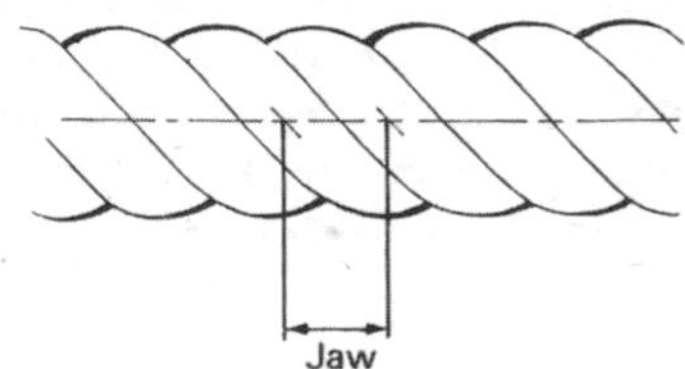

Jaw

J-class yachts, racing yachts built during the inter-war period to the American *Universal Rule. They were 23–6 metres (75–87 ft) on the waterline, and so conformed to the New York Yacht Club's J-class. As a generic term, the J-class also usually includes those yachts which were built to another rule, such as the *International Metre Class, but which were altered in 1931 to conform to the J-class rules for *Big

Class regatta racing in British waters (*Astra*, **Britannia*, and *Candida*).

When Sir Thomas Lipton challenged for the *America's Cup in 1929 the New York Yacht Club chose the J-class for the races. None of the six J-class built in the USA—*Weetamoe, Whirlwind, Enterprise, Yankee* (all built for the 1930 defence), *Rainbow* (1934), and *Ranger* (1937)—has survived, though a *replica of *Ranger* has been built. But of the four British ones—**Shamrock V* (built for the 1930 challenge), *Velsheda* (never a challenger), *Endeavour* (1934), and *Endeavour II* (1937)—only *Endeavour II* was scrapped, in 1963, though only *Shamrock V* continued to sail, with a cruising rig. There was a great revival of these elegant reminders of a bygone *yachting age during the 1980s and 1990s. The three remaining Js, plus two other yachts converted to the J-class to race with them (*Astra, Candida*), and one (*Cambria*) which raced in the Big Class but was never altered to conform to J-class rules, were all restored as closely as possible to their original rig. There is now a possibility of more new Js being built.

jeers, a heavy *tackle with double or treble *blocks with the upper blocks at the head of the lower masts of *square-rigged ships. Used for lifting or lowering the *course and its *yard. The *fall is usually taken to a *capstan between the masts or to a power *winch. Some modern ships do not fit jeers and rely on the *lifts, or on dockyard cranes, for this operation. The jeer capstan was often the scene for punishments in early sailing ships.

jellyfish are simple animals with a basic body structure of two layers, padded with a gelatinous infilling called mesoglea. They belong to the phylum Coelenterata along with sea anemones (actinians) and the ***Portuguese man-of-war** (*Physalia physalis*). The main body or bell is umbrella shaped and in the middle of its underside is a mouth that opens into a sacklike stomach. Muscles around the edge of the bell contract rhythmically and by jetting water propel the jellyfish through the water. Around the edge of the bell is a ring of tentacles, which can be extremely long and extensible in some of the species. Also around the mouth there is another ring of tentacles that manoeuvre food into the mouth. Both sets of tentacles carry stinging cells called nematocysts, which discharge when stimulated both by chemicals in the water and by touch. Many of the commoner species like the harmless **moon jellyfish** (*Aurelia aurita*) are filter feeders and have weak nematocysts. But the predatory

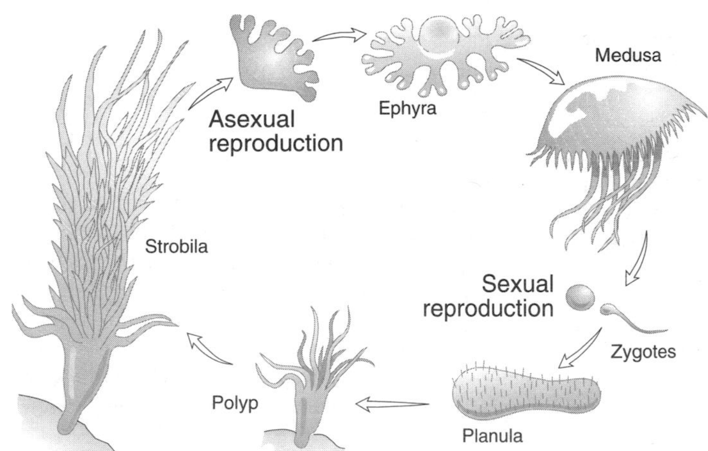

The life cycle of the jellyfish. It involves six stages: the adult form, or medusa, has male and female forms which sexually reproduce by releasing eggs and sperm into the water. The fertilized eggs, or zygotes, float away with the currents, for how far and for how long is not known. The zygotes then transform into the next stage, planulas, which can crawl across the seabed. The planula finds a suitable site and anchors itself to the sea bottom as a polyp, a plantlike form. As the polyp grows it forms a strobila, a stack of tiny jellyfish called ephyra, that gradually break off from the strobila, a form of asexual reproduction

species that feed on *fish have nematocysts that are powerful enough to pierce human skin and are the ones that can give painful nettle-like stings. Not only are they painful, but in some species they also inject neurotoxins that in extreme cases can cause paralysis in swimmers. The most extreme example is the **sea wasp** (*Chironex fleckeri*), a type of box jellyfish which occurs seasonally around some coasts of Australia above a *latitude of 26° S., mostly between May and October. Their stings can cause death within a few minutes, so take warnings about them seriously. If you are stung remember that nematocysts are triggered mechanically, so do not rub the area where you have been stung but wash it under a running tap. In Scotland, wives of trawlermen who repaired the nets used to suffer from a painful eye condition. When the nets were shaken, nematocysts from the dried tentacles of jellyfish, especially the **lion's mane jellyfish** (*Cyanea capillata*), would float around as dust in the air and get into their eyes. One rub and they would discharge, causing painful inflammation.

Other species that sting and may be found in British waters is the **compass jellyfish** (*Chrysaora hysoscella*), which has an umbrella-shaped bell with V-shaped markings and the **blue jellyfish** (*Cyanea lamarckii*), which is also umbrella shaped. The **barrel or root mouth jellyfish** (*Rhizostoma octopus*), which measures up to one metre in diameter and has a large solid bell fringed with purple, is harmless.

M. V. Angel

jetboats are propelled by water drawn in by a centrifugal water pump and then expelled again through a steerable nozzle above the waterline. The discharge of a high-velocity jet stream generates a reaction force in the opposite direction, which is transferred through the body of the jet unit to the craft's hull, propelling it forward. The first *Seacats were propelled in this manner.

The principle is an old one. It was first patented by two Englishmen in 1661 who proposed using a bellows to force out water as a means of propelling a vessel forward. With the coming of *steam propulsion the number of experiments increased, but none was particularly successful. However, in 1785 an American, James Rumsey of Virginia, built a boat with a steam pump which drew water in at the bows and forced it out at the stern, and took a voyage on the Potomac River in it.

In the modern jetboat, the jet unit is mounted inboard in the *aft section of the hull. Water enters the jet unit intake—via a vent flush in the bottom of the boat—at boat speed, and is accelerated through the jet propulsion unit and discharged through the *transom at a high velocity. Reverse is achieved by lowering an *astern deflector into the jetstream after it leaves the nozzle.

This method, which has proved highly successful, was the invention of a New Zealander, Sir William Hamilton (1899–1978), who began experimenting with marine jets in the early 1950s, following the lead of the American Hanley Hydrojet. Hamilton's breakthrough came when he modified the Hydrojet so that the jet stream was expelled above the waterline—as with some Seacats—instead of below it. This design eliminates all underwater appendages, which makes it ideal for travelling over very shallow, fast-running water.

Hamilton's first jetboat had a 3.6-metre (12-ft) plywood hull with a 100 E Ford engine which is now in the Auckland Maritime Museum. Improvements in the pumping system followed, and by the 1990s waterjets were being built for craft up to 60 metres (197 ft) and for ones with speeds of 60–65 knots.

Nowadays jetboats are widely used for flood relief, *hydrography, and recreation. They are also employed as patrol boats and fishing vessels, and the jet propulsion units have been sold to many navies.

jetsam, the legal term for goods or equipment thrown overboard from a ship at sea. It differs from *flotsam in that the goods are deliberately thrown overboard from a ship, for instance to lighten it if it is in danger. In the UK, jetsam now legally comes under the definition of *wreck, and any jetsam recovered, however insignificant, has to be reported to the Receiver of Wreck.

jettison, to, to throw goods or equipment overboard to lighten a ship in stress of weather or other danger. See also JETSAM.

jetty, normally considered to be a solid structure built out, usually into the sea but in some cases along the shore as part of a port or *dockyard alongside which ships could lie for loading or discharging cargo, repair work, etc. Nowadays, some jetties, as for example those alongside which *tankers lie to load or discharge oil, are built out on piles like a *pier.

jewel blocks, the *blocks attached to *eyebolts on those *yards (lower and *topsail yards) on which *studding sails were set in *square-rigged ships and through which the studding-sail *halyards were *rove. They were also used for reeving the rope by which men sentenced to death were hanged at the *yardarm in naval ships.

jew's harp, a name sometimes given to the *shackle with which a chain *cable is attached to an anchor. It is always secured with the bow of the shackle outboard so that, when the anchor is let go, the *lugs of the shackle do not catch up on the rim of the *hawsehole.

jib, a triangular sail set by sailing vessels on the *stays of the foremast. The largest *square-rigged sailing vessels of the late 19th century and early 20th century carried as many as six jibs, named from aft to forward: storm, inner, outer, flying, spindle, and *jib-of-jibs, the last being hoisted in only very light weather. Smaller sailing vessels, particularly those *fore-and-aft rigged, normally only set one jib, other triangular sails set before the foremast being known as *staysails. In the old-fashioned fore-and-aft rig, where a *bowsprit carried a fore-*topmast stay beyond the stem of the vessel to give additional support to the mast, it was on this stay that the jib was carried, with a staysail set on the forestay. The modern *Bermudan rig has no bowsprit and the single forestay is set up on, or even inboard of, the stem and this usually only carries one large jib, no staysail being set. These large jibs, of which the *clew extends well *abaft the mast, are known as *genoa or *yankee jibs, and for a period during the 1930s some of the *J-class racing yachts set a *double-clewed jib.

The jib and *jib-boom were introduced in 1705 for smaller ships as a replacement for the older *spritsail and spritsail topmast, and by 1719 had been also adopted by the largest ships then built. From its inception it proved a great step forward in the efficiency of a sailing vessel *on the wind and was, as the author of the *Marine Dictionary* (1771) wrote, 'a sail of great command on a side wind, and particularly when sailing *close-hauled'. See also CUT OF HIS (HER) JIB, THE.

jib-boom, a continuation of the *bowsprit in large ships by means of a *spar run out forward to extend the *foot of the outer *jib and the *stay of the fore *topgallant mast. It is supported laterally by stays and *whiskers and vertically by a *martingale stay. **Flying jib-boom**, a further extension with yet another spar to the end of which the *tack of the flying jib was hauled out and the fore *royal stay secured. The schooner **America* lost her flying jib-boom during the historic race in 1851 for the trophy which was later called the *America's Cup. For illus. see BOWSPRIT.

jibe, to, see GYBING.

jib-headed topsail, a triangular *topsail set above the mainsail in a *gaff-rigged vessel. The *peak of the topsail is hoisted to the masthead and the *foot is stretched along the top of the gaff, so that the sail just fills the triangle formed by the masthead, the peak of the gaff, and the *jaws of the gaff. See also JACKYARD TOPSAIL.

jib-of-jibs, a *jib sail set from the **jib-of-jib-boom** which was sometimes used in early sailing ships as an extension of the flying *jib-boom. Colin Mudie

jigger. (1) A light *tackle comprising a double and single *block, multiplying the power by four when *rove to *advantage and used for many small purposes on board ship. Originally it was designed to hold on to the *cable as it was being hove on board in the form of a temporary *stopper when anchors were *weighed by hand. In *fore-and-aft-rigged ships a jigger was also often used on the standing part of the *throat and *peak *halyards to give them the final *sweating up. A **boom jigger** was one used to rig the *studding-sail booms in and out from the lower and *topsail *yards of *square-rigged ships. It is in effect a *luff tackle used with a rope of smaller size. See also PURCHASE. **(2)** The name given to the small sail set on a *jigger-mast.

jigger-mast, a small mast set right aft in some smaller sailing craft, and a name sometimes given to the after mast of a small *yawl, though this is more properly called a *mizzen, and to the small mast set right aft in some *sprit-sail *barges. It is also the name given to the fourth mast of a five- or six-masted *schooner, and sometimes used for the fourth mast of a four-masted *square-rigger.

jockey pole, a *spar used on *yachts to bear out the *spinnaker *guy to relieve the load on the guy when the spinnaker pole is *forward. The inboard end is attached to the mast, the outer end with a *sheave for the guy.

joggle shackle, a long, slightly curved *shackle used in anchor work to haul the *cable of one anchor round the bows of a ship when *mooring to two anchors. It is used when a mooring swivel is inserted into the two cables to prevent a *foul hawse with two anchors on the ground.

'jollies', a nickname for the Royal *Marines in the British Navy. Originally all soldiers carried on board a British warship were known as jollies, a 'tame jolly' being a militiaman and a 'royal jolly' a marine, but later the name was only applied to marines.

> ''E was scrapin' the paint from off of 'er plates an'
> I sez to 'im, "Oo are you?"
> 'Sez 'e, "I'm a Jolly—'er Majesty's Jolly—soldier
> an' sailor too!"'
> (R. Kipling, *Barrack-Room Ballads*, 1896)

jolly-boat, possibly from the Dutch and German *Jolle*, Swedish *jol*, a small *bark or boat, though this may be the derivation of the English *yawl. It is more likely to be a perversion of gellywatte, a small ship's boat of the 18th and 19th centuries, which was used for a variety of purposes such as going round a ship to see that the *yards were square, taking the steward ashore to buy fresh provisions, etc. It was *clinker built, propelled by *oars, and was normally hoisted on a *davit at the ship's stern. When it was included as part of a warship's outfit of ship's boats, it pulled six oars on three *thwarts.

Jolly Roger, the name popularly given to a flag flown by pirate ships as seen through the eyes of writers of *piracy stories. It was supposed to be a white skull on a black ground, sometimes with crossed bones below the skull. There is, however, no evidence that such a flag was ever flown by a pirate ship at sea. If there ever were a general flag which might be recognized as a pirate flag, it would probably be the plain black flag which some pirate ships were occasionally reported as flying from their main masthead.

Another version of a pirate flag was said to be a black skeleton on a yellow field, but this may have been a mistaken impression of the imperial flag of Austria, which was a black double-headed eagle on a yellow field. During the 18th century a number of *privateers sailed under Austrian *letters of marque, which were much easier to obtain than those of other nations. As many privateers flying the imperial flag of Austria behaved little better than pirates, the impression may well have gained ground that this was in fact the pirate flag.

Jonah, one of the minor prophets of the Old Testament who, after being instructed by Jehovah to go to Nineveh to preach repentance of sins, attempted to avoid his task by running away by sea to Tarshish. During the voyage a great *storm arose and the sailors, suspecting Jonah to be the cause of it, threw him overboard. He was swallowed by a *whale, but was spewed up three days later, and, chastened by his experience, he proceeded to carry out his original orders. His name has survived in maritime circles as the description of a man who brings ill fortune to a ship, and has spread from its original maritime use to become a part of the English language as a person who brings ill fortune to all with whom he comes into contact.

The development of zoological science showed that whales have throats too small to swallow a man, and it is now regarded as legendary or allegorical, especially as a mythical sea monster like a *kraken, not a whale, is implied in the original Hebrew.

Jones, John Paul (1747–92), American naval officer, born at Kirkbean, Galloway, son of John Paul, gardener on the Arbigland estate. At the age of 12 he sailed as a *cabin boy to Virginia, where his elder brother had settled as a tailor, and in 1766 obtained work as chief *mate aboard a ship involved in the *slave trade. He returned home two years later and was appointed a *master, making voyages from the Solway Firth, London, and Africa to the West Indies and Virginia. In 1772 he bought a ship in the West Indies, but having killed a mutinous seaman in self-defence, he changed his name to John Jones, and fled to Virginia in 1773. When fighting broke out between England and the thirteen colonies, and Congress formed the *Continental Navy, John Paul Jones, as he now called himself, was commissioned as first lieutenant, and distinguished himself in action against the British, capturing several *prizes and sinking several others.

In 1777, after promotion to captain, he was appointed to command a *sloop. He sailed to Nantes and then visited Paris, where Benjamin Franklin, commissioner of the American colonies in France, judging him to be a brave fighting man, took him under his wing. On receiving orders to cruise about the British Isles to 'distress' the enemy, Jones launched a series of shore raids. On the night of 22/23 April 1778, he raided Whitehaven, hoping to destroy with incendiaries the large number of ships in the harbour. However, the landings were bungled and little damage was done, but the moral effect was immense.

Then, on the morning of 23 April Jones landed with a boat's crew on St Mary's Isle, intending to abduct the owner, the fourth Earl of Selkirk, so as to obtain the release of several hundred American sailors who had been captured in battle and were in English jails with indictments for treason hanging over them. The earl was not there and Jones's men, who disliked profitless raids, seized the family silver, but afterwards Jones apologized, bought back the silver from his men, and returned it. A more satisfactory exploit, on 24 April, was the sloop's battle off Belfast Lough with HMS *Drake* which, after an hour of close combat, surrendered. Jones eventually got his prize safely into Brest, together with 200 prisoners of war who were exchanged for the American sailors in English prisons.

Jones's next command was a *squadron comprising the new USS *Alliance*, three French vessels, a *frigate, *corvette, and *cutter, all flying the American *ensign, and Jones's *flagship, an *East Indiaman bought for him by the French government and renamed *Bon Homme Richard* as a compliment to Franklin. With infinite difficulty Jones got the *Bon Homme Richard* converted, gunned, equipped, and manned, and the squadron sailed from Lorient

John Paul Jones; 19th-century engraving

on 14 August 1779. It was soon weakened—the cutter got lost, the *Alliance* went off prize-taking on her own account—but on 23 September 1779 Jones bravely intercepted a Baltic convoy of 44 vessels escorted by two Royal Navy warships, HMS *Serapis* and HMS *Countess of Scarborough*. What ensued was one of the bitterest naval encounters of the century, known as the battle of Flamborough Head. The two naval escorts, after covering the escape of the convoy, closed with the squadron. The *Serapis* grappled the *Bon Homme Richard*, in an attempt to *board her, and a desperate fight ensued which caused heavy casualties on both sides, but eventually the *Serapis* caught fire and was forced to surrender. The losses in each ship were high, 128 killed and wounded in the *Serapis*, 150 in the *Bon Homme Richard*.

Jones's flagship was so badly damaged that she sank two days later, and Jones transferred with the remains of his crew to the captured *Serapis*. With the rest of his squadron, he then sought refuge in the Texel on 3 October; and after delays, caused by repairs, neutrality complications, and a British *blockade, he sailed for Corunna on 27 December, now flying his flag in the *Alliance* which had rejoined him. After sailing to Corunna, he reached Lorient on 17 February 1780 and proceeded to Paris where he found himself a hero. After some weeks he returned to America in the sloop *Ariel*, where

Congress gave him command of the *America*, the only 74-gun ship in the country, then being built at Portsmouth, NH. However, after working hard to get her completed and *launched, he lost her in 1782 because Congress, unwilling to support a peacetime navy, presented her to France.

Jones spent much of the rest of his life in France, going through the tiresome business of collecting prize money due to his squadron, and endeavouring without success to obtain a command in the French Navy. Eventually, he obtained the rank of rear admiral in the Imperial Russian Navy, and was given command of a squadron of nine frigates on the Liman of the Dnieper, where Russia was trying to capture Ochakov from the Turks.

The Russian Black Sea Fleet was a scratch collection of shoal draft vessels manned by impressed serfs, Cossacks, Volga boatmen, and Levantine pirates, officered in part by adventurers of six or seven nations. The Empress Catherine felt that only an outstanding naval officer from another country could weld this motley collection into a real fighting force. Possibly Jones could have done so had he not got into the ill graces of Prince Potemkin, the commander-in-chief after whom the *battleship **Potemkin* was later named. Potemkin resented having another foreign officer of *flag rank on his hands, but Jones got to fight the Turks and won the two battles of Liman, on 6 and 17 June 1788. But Prince Nassau-Siegen, commander of the light flotilla, received all the credit from Potemkin, and Jones was left out of the list of honours. He won the respect and loyalty of the Russian naval officers under him, but that did not help him with the commander-in-chief who relieved him of his post and sent him to St Petersburg to await orders.

Jones waited there through the winter of 1788–9. In the spring an important personage, probably Prince Nassau-Siegen, arranged to have him falsely charged with rape. Jones now had little alternative but to leave Russia and between 1790 and 1792 he lived in Paris and spent his time writing letters to anyone who might find him a post at sea or in the diplomatic service. Eventually, two commissions from President Washington, dated 1 and 2 June 1792, appointed him American consul in Algeria and plenipotentiary to negotiate with the Dey of Algiers for the release of American prisoners. It was too late, for on 18 July 1792, before the commissions reached France, Jones died from an attack of bronchial pneumonia, complicated by jaundice and nephritis.

The Legislative Assembly gave him a state funeral, and he was buried in an unmarked grave in the Protestant cemetery on rue Granges-aux-Belles. In 1905 the lead coffin was exhumed, and the body identified. It was then carried across the Atlantic in an American *cruiser escorted by three others, and was met off Nantucket by seven *battleships, and his remains were laid to rest in a marble sarcophagus in the crypt of the Naval Academy chapel at Annapolis.

The diminutive Jones was egotistical, extremely ambitious, and an aggressive self-promoter. He wanted most to be an admiral, and when that was not forthcoming in American service, he readily went elsewhere. Nevertheless, he proved himself to be a superb fighter, an impeccable seaman, and a thoughtful and forceful writer on naval education.

Morison, S. E., *John Paul Jones* (1959).

Jubilee Sailing Trust, British charitable organization formed in 1978 to promote the integration of able-bodied and physically disabled people through *sail training. After successfully experimenting with having disabled people crewing alongside the able-bodied, funds were raised to construct a 55-metre (180-ft) steel *barque of 490 tonnes *displacement which was specially designed and built to be sailed by physically disabled people. Called *Lord Nelson*, she was *launched in 1985 and by 2002 had taken over 17,800 people to sea, of whom 7,064 were physically disabled, including 2,860 who were wheelchair users. Such was her popularity that it was decided to build a second purpose-built ship and the funds were raised to launch the 65-metre (213-ft) *Tenacious* in 2000. Constructed of Siberian larch and sapele from renewable sources, this 680-tonne barque, the largest wooden sailing ship built for over 100 years, was completed with the help of a volunteer workforce, both able-bodied and disabled, who worked alongside a dedicated professional team of shipwrights. Both ships are based in and around the UK in summer and the Canary Islands in the winter, and they compete in the *Tall Ships Race every year.

jugle, or **joggle,** a notch cut in the edge of a plank to admit the narrow butt of another when planking up a wooden vessel. Its purpose is to make a more watertight joint and also to make it less likely for the butt of the plank to start or *spring. See also SHIPBUILDING.

'jumbo', the name often used for the fore *staysail in a *fore-and-aft-rigged ship. It is the largest of the *foresails, which perhaps explains the name, and in general terms corresponds to the *genoa jib used aboard *yachts.

jumper, a pair of *stays used to support the masthead of a *Bermudan-rigged vessel where the *forestay is attached below the masthead. Their lower ends are attached to the mast at a lower *spreader band where their forward pull is counteracted by *aft lower *shrouds. These stays are extended forward in way of the forestay by short **jumper struts** usually arranged at about 45° to the centreline. The term is also sometimes used on *square-riggers for *preventer braces used to augment the lead of the *braces of the *lee main *course when hard braced in bad weather. A single strut on the foreside of a *mizzen-mast, which takes a jumper stay to support the masthead, is known as a **parrot perch**.

jumping, or **jumper, wire,** a serrated wire leading from the stemhead of a *submarine to the forward edge of the *bridge casing above the *conning tower, and from the after edge of the bridge casing to the stern. It was used for cutting a way through defensive nets when submerged. Such nets were used extensively during the First World War (1914–18), but the modern submarine does not have a jumping wire.

junk. (1) A Chinese vessel. See JUNK RIG. **(2)** Old and condemned rope cut into short lengths and used for making swabs, mats, *fenders, *oakum, etc. **(3)** The word applied colloquially by seamen during the days of sail to the salt beef and pork used on board, presumably to imply that it was old and ripe to be condemned as in meaning (2) of the word.

junk rig. The word junk is derived from the Portuguese *junco*. The traditional Chinese *unstayed rig which is essentially a fully battened balanced *lugsail rig set traditionally on a completely unstayed mast, supported only at the *partners and *step. The sail lies permanently on one side of the mast and a proportion of it, known as the balance, lies ahead of the mast. The sail is hoisted by a *halyard from the masthead and is divided into a series of panels by full-length *battens which keep the sail stretched from *luff to *leech. Through a series of rope spans secured to the *aft end of each batten that spread the load, the single sheet controls the whole of the leech, so that the sail sets with little twist. Rope *parrels secure each batten to the mast. A system of *lazyjacks gathers the sail as it is dropped and supports the boom and sail when furled. The forward end of the boom is supported by a separate mast lift. Both lift and lazyjacks are adjustable. Only one sail is set on each mast but there seem to be no set limits on the number of masts, and as many as nine were reported by early travellers.

The Chinese rig is the earliest of the *fore-and-aft rigs in which the wind blows either side of the sail, and for many centuries it will have been the most efficient. The traditional sail was made of bamboo matting stiffened by

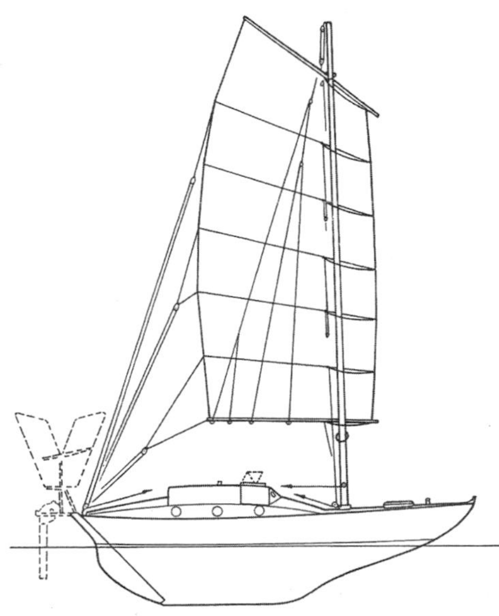

The fully enclosed junk-rigged Folkboat *Jester*, with self-steering gear. She is well known for her ocean passages and single-handed transatlantic races

bamboo battens. By western standards it could be extremely heavy, of the order of 5 tons for a large vessel, which required expert crews to handle it. On the other hand, because of the subdivision of the sail by the battens, each panel is controlled by its own system of battens and parrels, and the loading on the sailcloth and sheets is much less than with western rigs. The rig is not close winded in comparison with western fore-and-aft rigs such as the *Bermudan, but sheeted correctly, with the sheet slacker than it would be with the Bermudan sail, the junk will make up well to *windward with very little *leeway.

Since 1960, when the junk-rigged Folkboat *Jester* took part in the first Single-Handed Transatlantic Race (see YACHTING: TRANSOCEANIC RACING), there has been a revival of interest in the use of junk rig for cruising yachts. Larger junk-rigged vessels are also still being built. For example, in 2004, the 34.5-metre (113-ft) 200-tonne junk *Jockey Club Huan* was constructed in Guandong for the Adventure Trust of Hong Kong as a *sail training ship. Like those belonging to the *Jubilee Sailing Trust, she is specifically designed to be crewed by the disabled as well as the able-bodied.

According to Joseph Needham the origins of the junk rig in China go back to about AD 300. By 1430 ships of the Ming dynasty appear to have been considerably larger than anything in the western world. In large fleets these *treasure ships, as they were called, sailed at least as far as the Red Sea and East Africa.

Hasler, H. G., and McLeod, J. K., *Practical Junk Rig* (1988).

Ronan, C., *The Shorter Science and Civilisation in China*, abridged from Joseph Needham's text (1986).

Worcester, G., *The Junks and Sampans of the Yangtze* (1971).

Mike Richey

jury rig, a temporary makeshift rig to bring a disabled vessel into harbour. A **jury mast** is one erected in place of a mast which has been *carried away. A **jury rudder** is a makeshift arrangement to give a ship the ability to steer when it has lost its *rudder.

jylson, or **jillson, block,** a heavy *sheave fitted on the foremast of fishing vessels. It was used to hoist the *trawl off the deck before the *cod-end was opened. See also FISHERIES.

K

kamal, from the Arabic word meaning guide, a *navigation instrument of great antiquity. It was used by Arab seamen in the Red Sea and the Indian Ocean for at least six centuries for measuring the *altitude of a celestial body. The instrument became known to European *navigators through Vasco da *Gama after he had rounded the African continent from the Atlantic to the Indian Ocean in 1497. The principle of the kamal, which is the same as that of the *cross-staff, depends upon the geometrical properties of similar triangles. The simplest form comprised a rectangular board or tablet of wood, to the centre of which was secured a knotted cord. The tablet was held so that the upper and lower edges coincided respectively with the observed body and the *horizon vertically below it. In this position the cord was stretched taut to the observer's eye, and the ratio between the fixed length of the tablet and variable length of the cord between tablet and eye, being a function of the altitude of the observed body, gave the measurement. The positions of the knots on the cord were related to the *meridian altitudes of a given star appropriate to the *latitudes of headlands and harbours along the route. In a modified form, it can still be seen in use by the Arab navigators of *dhows in the Red Sea and off the East African coast.

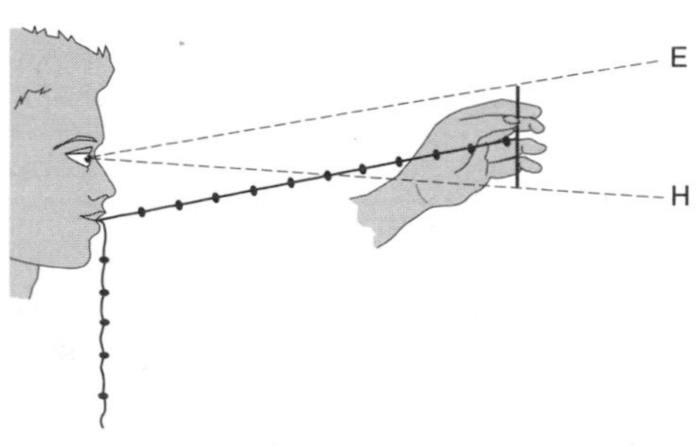

Observing the altitude with the kamal

kamikaze, the 'divine wind' which in 1281 sprang up in the Sea of Japan and destroyed the invasion fleet of Kublai Khan. It was also the name given by the Japanese during the Second World War (1939–45) to their 'special attack units' of suicide pilots which flew their aircraft into Allied warships.

kapal, a *square-rigged trading vessel, usually two masted but very occasionally with three. It was used in Far Eastern waters, particularly in Malaya, for inter-island trade before it was replaced by powered vessels.

kayak, an Inuit word for a light, covered-in, *canoe-type boat used for fishing, in common use in northern waters from Greenland to Alaska. It is made by covering a wooden framework with sealskin, with a hole in the centre of the top of the boat into which the kayaker, also dressed in sealskin, laces himself to prevent the entry of water. It is propelled by a double-bladed paddle. The word kayak, in its strict meaning, applies only to a boat when it is occupied by a man; if a woman uses one, it is called a **umiak**. It is thought by some people that the origin of the word is from the Arabic *caique, the name being given to these native boats when they were first seen by the early explorers and subsequently taken into the Inuit language. However, this seems unlikely as the name is the same in all Inuit and Greenland dialects.

Kayaks made of *GRP are also very popular for recreational purposes.

K-class submarine, a revolutionary *submarine design produced by the British Navy between 1916 and 1923. The basis of its design was the requirement in the British *Grand Fleet for a submarine fast enough on the surface to accompany the fleet in its searches for the German *High Seas Fleet and to dive and attack the enemy fleet with torpedoes when contact had been made. Since the normal *diesel engine could not produce the required surface speed, around 21 knots, a steam turbine (see STEAM PROPULSION) seemed the only answer, and steam, of course, requires a boiler to produce it.

Admiral Fisher, the First Sea Lord in October 1914, was fiercely opposed to the principle of steam-driven submarines, an opinion reinforced by the unfortunate experiences of the *Archimède*, a steam-driven French submarine temporarily attached to a British naval force. While in the Heligoland Bight, she was struck by such a heavy sea that it bent her funnel so that it could not be retracted. Unable to dive she was exposed to enemy surface ships, and matters were made worse when the heavy seas started to pour down the buckled funnel. Luckily, she managed to make port, but Fisher told his director of naval construction to concentrate on designing a diesel submarine which had the required surface speed. However, when 19 knots was the fastest the latest design could be expected to achieve, Fisher gave in and in 1916, after Fisher had resigned as First Sea Lord, two prototype steam-driven submarines were *launched. Neither was a success, but it was from these two boats that the K-class was produced. The class needed to be very large in order to accommodate boiler, fuel tanks, and turbine for surface propulsion, coupled with electric batteries and motors for submerged propulsion. They were, therefore, 103 metres (338 ft) in length overall with a submerged displacement of 2,500 tons. They had two collapsible funnels to carry away the boiler fumes, and these were shut down, and the boiler room completely sealed off, when the submarine dived. Their surface speed was 24 knots, their submerged speed 10 knots, and they were fitted with ten torpedo tubes.

Eighteen K-class submarines were completed during the First World War (1914–18), and they had a disastrous history. Their main failure was their initial high diving speed, but they were also difficult to steer on the surface and were liable to mechanical failures. Out of the eighteen, K1, K4, K17, and K18 sank in separate collisions, K5 disappeared during exercises, K13 sank on her acceptance trials, and K15 sank in Portsmouth harbour. Between November 1919 and May 1923 three more were commissioned (K19, K20, and K26). These, with K18, were renamed the M-class (Monitor Class). Their record was equally disastrous: M1 (K18) sank after a collision and M2 (K19) sank on exercises, and the other two were scrapped. Yet in their use of steam propulsion, the K-class were, in a way, the forerunners of today's nuclear-powered submarines.

Everett, D., *The K Boats* (1963).

***Kearsage*, USS,** one of the Federal *sloops of war built during the early years of the American Civil War (1861–5). A screw steamer of 1,031 tons, her armament included four 32-pounder guns. Her most notable action was when she sank the Confederate *cruiser **Alabama* off Cherbourg on 19 June 1864. She ran aground and was wrecked on 10 February 1894.

keckle, to, to cover a *hemp cable spirally with old rope to protect it from chafing in the *hawsehole, a necessary precaution in the days before chain anchor *cables.

kedge, a small ship's anchor formerly carried on board to *warp a ship from one *berth to another or to haul it off into deeper water after grounding; also the name by which the spare anchor normally carried in *yachts is known.

The original name was *cagger*, an early derivation from *catch* (i.e. to catch the ground), and certainly dates back to the 14th century, but it had developed into kedge at least by the end of the 16th century. It was also frequently used in harbour by sailing vessels as the main anchor to which the ship lay in order to save labour when the time came to *weigh it for departure. In the days of sail a kedge was also sometimes used to back up the *bower anchor when a ship was anchored in bad holding ground or when heavy weather was expected.

keel. **(1)** The lowest and principal *timber of a wooden ship, or the lowest continuous line of plates of a steel or iron ship, which extend the whole length of the vessel and to which the *stem, *sternpost, and *ribs or timbers of the vessel are attached. It could be called the backbone of the ship and is its strongest single member. In the sailing *barges of the Thames the keel is a continuous run of oak some 40 centimetres (16 in.) square, an indication of the great strength required in the keel of any ship,

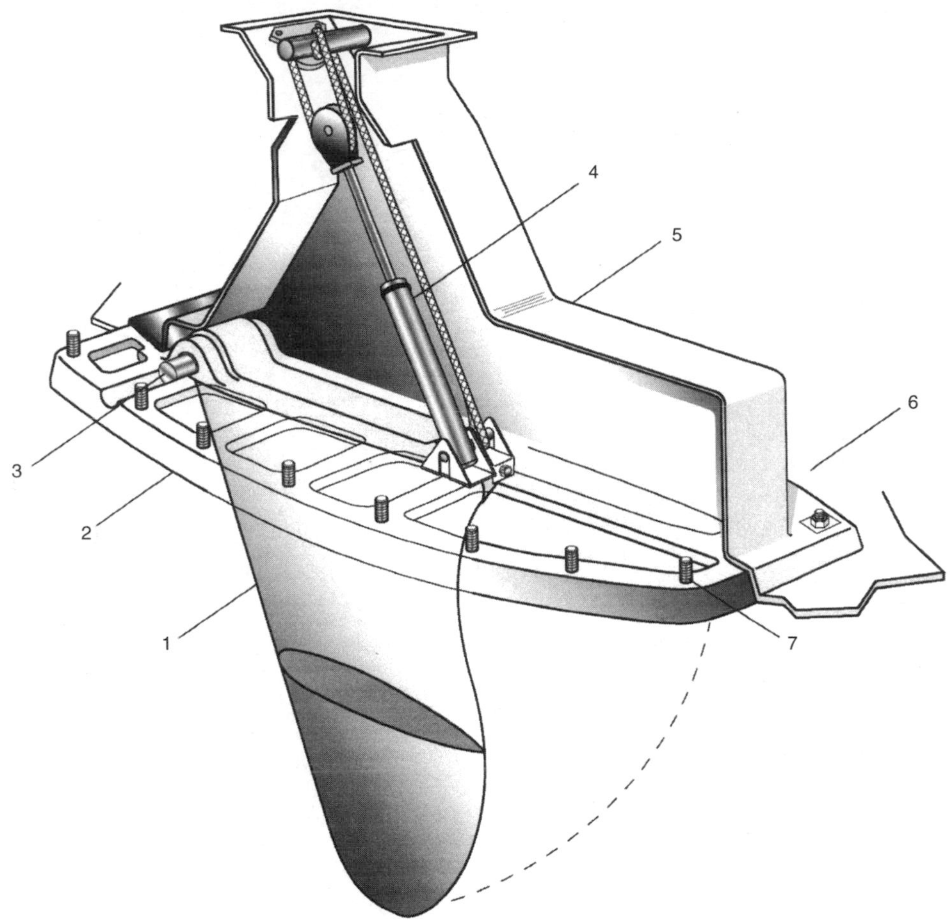

Southerly swing keel

though *junks were traditionally built without keels.

*Yachts have been built with a variety of keels:

(*a*) *Centreline Ballast Keel.* This is the traditional yacht keel developed early in the 20th century. It had the ballast bolted onto the wood keel above and being fairly long it allowed the yacht to take the ground safely, gave protection to the *rudder, and the hull shape allowed tanks to be installed beneath the *cabin sole.

(*b*) *Bilge Keel.* Although the first yacht to be recorded with this configuration was the 18.3-metre (60-ft) *Iris,* a *ketch built in Dublin Bay in 1894, it only became popular during the 1930s as it allowed cheaper, shallow tidal *moorings. With the added pressure on mooring in the last few decades it has become even more popular with its ability to stay upright on level ground and requiring no shoring up on *slipways or trailers.

(*c*) *Fin and Skeg Keel.* First used on small racing yachts during the 19th century, this configuration was only introduced for cruising yachts in the 1960s, particularly with the lighter *GRP yachts then being produced. It also proved the most successful configuration for racing yachts, but was not so well suited for cruising unless the fin was relatively large.

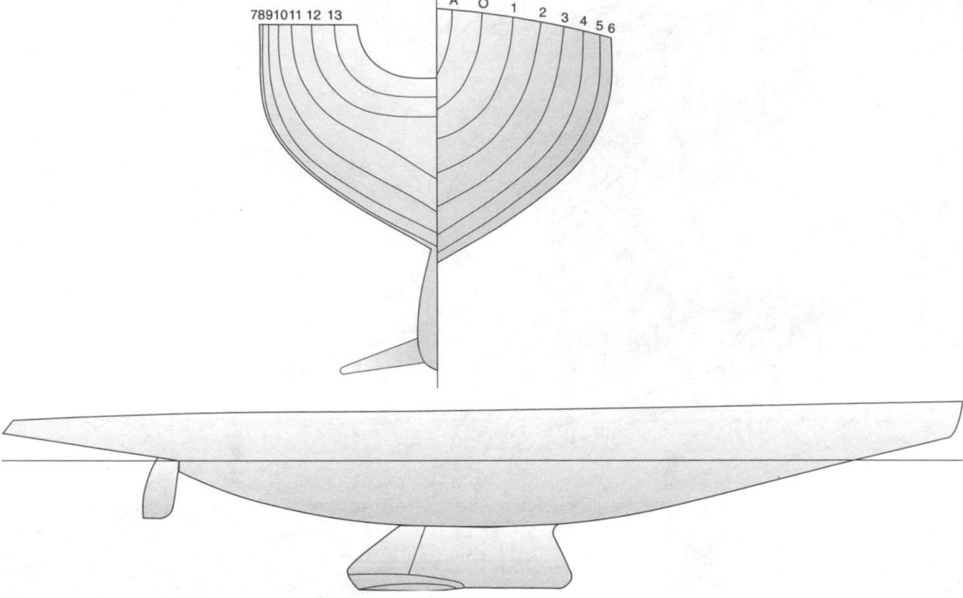

The profile and body plan of *Australia II*

(*d*) *Fin and Bulb Keel.* First developed in the 19th century by *yacht designers such as Sibbick with his small *skimming dish raters. Changes to the *rating rules stopped this type, but the recent introduction of the modern high-performance racing yacht, such as the *America's Cup class, the open 60, and many others, has led to an enormous development of this type of keel where the fin is machined from solid steel, maybe 6 metres (14.3 ft) deep and perhaps only a metre (3 ft 3 in.) long with a lead bulb at the bottom, weighing perhaps twice as much as the rest of the yacht.

(*e*) *Canting Keel.* This is a development of the fin and bulb keel where the whole fin and bulb can be swung mechanically out to *windward, the pivot being at the top of the keel, so that more righting moment is provided.

(*f*) *Swing Keel.* The large, cast-iron aerofoil (1) is pivoted in the grounding plate (2) by a pivot pin (3) with a hydraulic ram (4) which retracts the keel into the keel case (5) at the touch of a button. The whole assembly is attached to the hull (6) with keel attachment bolts (7). The substantial cast-iron grounding plate serves as fixed *ballast and protects the bottom of the boat when drying out. If the keel hits a submerged object, it will take the full impact of the blow and, by simply swinging from its pivot point and retracting into the hull, will absorb the impact.

(*g*) *Wing Keel.* Developed initially by Ben Lexcen and Peter van Oossanen for the Australian America's Cup challenger *Australia II*, it became perhaps unduly credited for her winning the Cup in 1983. Previous work on winglets on aircraft wing tips had improved the efficiency of the wing by reducing tip vertices and induced drag. These keel winglets were also well positioned to allow ballast weight to be lower and so provide a greater righting moment and less heel. The keel was also innovative in that it was smallest at the hull and largest at the bottom, so improving its efficiency and compensating for the added *wetted surface of the wings. The plan form and size of the wings depends greatly on the *aspect ratio of the keel itself, but in cruising yachts, where *draught or the practicability of taking the ground are important, the ballast weight may be in a single wing with a relatively small vertical fin.

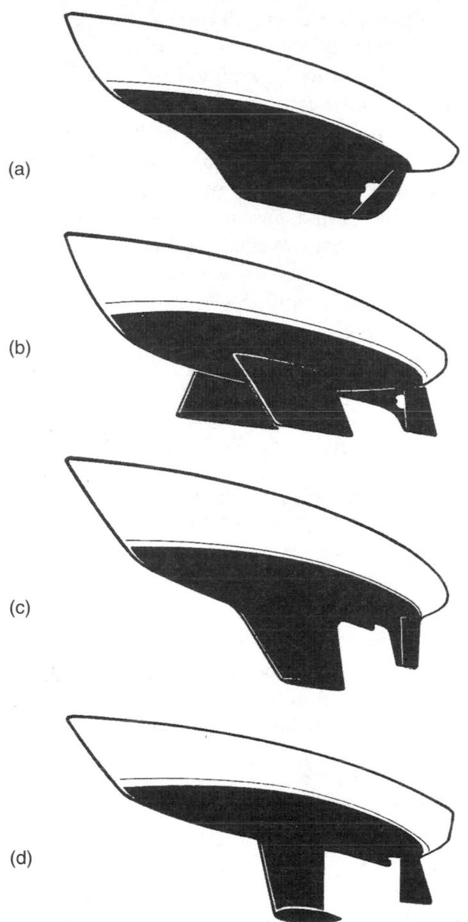

[a] Centreline ballast keel [b] Bilge keel [c] Fin and skeg keel [d] Fin and bulb keel

The Collins keel, with two related fins above a single delta-shaped wing, successfully combines efficiency with reduced draught.

Jeremy Lines

(2) An early English trading vessel. It was *clinker built and had a keel and therefore sailed better in open water than its contemporary, the *hulk. It was also the name given to a vessel employed extensively in north-eastern England up to the beginning of the 20th century for carrying goods. The Tyne keel was like a *lighter, but the Humber keel was decked in and driven by a square sail, and was therefore more suitable for the North Sea. They have been immortalized in the song 'We'el may the keel row that my laddie's in', first published in *Tyneside Songs* in 1863.

keel blocks, the line of blocks on the floor of a building slip on which the keel of the ship to be constructed is laid. Also the line of blocks in a *dry-dock on which the ship rests when the dock is pumped dry.

keel-hauling, also sometimes called keel-raking, was a naval punishment said to have been invented by the Dutch, but introduced into other navies around the 15th and 16th centuries. A rope was rigged from *yardarm to yardarm passing under the bottom of the ship, and the unfortunate individual to undergo the punishment was secured to it, sometimes with lead or iron weights attached to his legs. He was hoisted up to one yardarm and then dropped suddenly into the sea, hauled underneath the ship, and hoisted up to the opposite yardarm, the punishment being repeated after he had had time to recover his breath. As with a similar punishment, *ducking at the yardarm, a gun was apparently fired over the miscreant while he was undergoing his punishment, not only to give him a good fright but as a warning to anyone else in the fleet who might misbehave.

Keel-hauling went out of fashion as a punishment in most navies at the beginning of the 18th century, being replaced with the *cat-o'-nine-tails.

keelson, or **kelson,** an internal keel in the form of a *stringer bolted onto the keel, to provide additional strength and to support the *floors.

kelpie, a sea spirit said to haunt the northern British Isles. Local mythology attributed several shapes to it, but it is mostly depicted as a horse. It was a malignant spirit whose chief delight was drowning seamen and travellers.

Kentish Knock, a sandbank in the southern North Sea which gave its name to a naval battle fought near it during the First Anglo-Dutch War (1652–4). See also WARFARE AT SEA.

kentledge, the pigs of iron cast as *ballast and laid over the *keelson plates to provide additional *stability to a vessel. If they were laid in the *limbers, they were known as limber-kentledge. Following this reasoning, heavy items of cargo stowed low in the *holds of a ship as an addition to ballasting during a voyage were sometimes known as kentledge-goods.

ketch, a sailing vessel with two masts, the recognized description being that the *mizzen is stepped before the *rudder head, while in a *yawl it is stepped *abaft it. However, this is not an exact definition, the true difference between the two rigs depending more on the size of the mizzen-sail; if the difference depended on the position of the mizzen-mast, most of the yawl-rigged beach boats, including the well-known Norfolk yawls, would be ketches. From the ketch rig were also developed the *hooker and the *dogger.

The original name in England was 'catch', but although this suggests that they were used primarily for exploiting local *fisheries, their main use was in fact as small coastal trading vessels. Suggestions have also been made that the name indicated vessels used to chase or pursue others in time of war, but this appears to be negated by a description of them written in 1625 that 'catches, being short and round built, be very apt to turn up and down, and useful to go to and fro, and to carry messages between ship and shore almost with any wind'.

They were small vessels, originally of 50 tons or less, *square rigged on both masts, but they roughly doubled in size during the reign of Charles II (1660–85), who used the ketch design for his royal yachts. Large numbers were built by the English, French, and Dutch navies during the wars of the late 17th and early 18th centuries to act as *tenders to the fleets, and the design was also adopted by the English to serve as *bomb ketches, the large open space forward of the mainmast being an ideal place for the large mortar which fired the bombs. For this particular use the length of the average ketch was increased, and as a result they became fast and *weatherly, and a new use for them was developed as *packets.

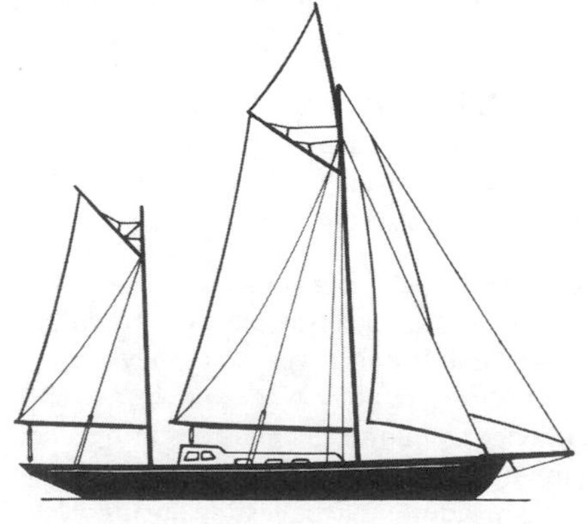

Gaff ketch

With the wide naval use of bomb vessels dying out in the mid-19th century, the naval value of the ketch diminished and it largely resumed its original use as a coastal trading vessel, though some specially strengthened bomb ketches for use in *ice were used during the many expeditions to the *North-West Passage and elsewhere. With the growing popularity of *yachting during the second half of the 19th century, and the weatherly qualities of a ketch as a *fore-and-aft rig, it became popular amongst yachtsmen. See also DANDY-RIG.

kevel, sometimes known as **kennet,** a large *cleat formed of two upright pieces of wood usually fitted on the *gunwale of a sailing vessel and used for *belaying ropes. **Kevel-heads**, used for the same purpose, are the ends of a vessel's top *timbers projected beyond the level of the gunwale. **Kevel posts** are the vertical posts holding the *pinrails or *fife rails. They pass through the deck and are bolted to a *beam or *bulkhead.

Kevlar, a brand name for the Aramid low-stretch nylon-related fibre that is used in sails, rope, and boat construction. It is also used for body armour, and combines great strength with great lightness, being five times stronger than the same weight in steel.

key, or **cay,** from the Spanish *cayos*, rocks, a small islet in the West Indies covered with scrub or sparse vegetation. The name was introduced into the English language by the *buccaneers who infested that area in the late 17th and early 18th centuries. They are sometimes coral formations, sometimes outcrops of sand and rock.

khamsin, or **kamsin,** a hot wind, usually from the south-west, which blows over Egypt and the eastern Mediterranean Sea, normally only in the months of March and April. It is a source of much discomfort, very similar to the *sirocco of the central Mediterranean. When blowing strongly it causes sandstorms, sometimes far out at sea. There is an ancient Arab saying, 'When the khamsin has blown for three days a man is justified in killing his wife.'

Khizr, the East Indian deity of the sea. Until modern times he was propitiated in many small coastal communities by burning small wooden boats known as *beera*, either annually as a festival or before the start of long voyages.

kicking strap, a fastening which prevents the mainsail boom on a *yacht from rising when it swings outwards. This helps the boom present a flatter sail to the wind and increases its driving power.

Kidd, or **Kid, Captain William** (*c.*1645–1701), an English merchant seaman who became noted for his *piracy. He was first heard of in 1696 when a syndicate of some of London's most powerful men backed his request to hunt down the pirates that were causing such trouble at the time in the Indian Ocean. He was placed in command of the *Adventure Galley* and received a commission as a *privateer from the Lord Keeper of the Great Seal, who just happened to be one of his backers. However, he and his crew soon turned to piracy themselves. In January 1698 they captured the *Quedah Merchant* which belonged to a rich and powerful merchant, Muklis Khan. They divided up their booty, disposed of the *Adventure Galley*, by now in a poor state of repair, and sailed in the *Quedah Merchant* to the pirates' stronghold off Mauritius where they drank with the very people they were supposed to be arresting.

Most of his crew were wise enough to stay there but Kidd decided to go to Boston in the hope that the governor, who had been one of the backers of his expedition, would overlook his lapse into piracy. This was a serious misjudgement on his part as, in his absence, the powerful men who had backed him had fallen from power and the government's attitude towards piracy had hardened. He was promptly arrested and sent to London, and in May 1701 he was tried for piracy and for the murder of his gunner William Moore whom he had killed with a blow from a bucket. He was found guilty and hanged immediately at *Execution Dock.

The money raised from his effects, valued at £6,472, was given to help fund Greenwich Royal Hospital and part of it was used to purchase what is now the National Maritime Museum. Kidd certainly buried other treasure when operating as a pirate in the West Indies and many later expeditions were mounted to search for it. Some of it, worth £14,000, was reputedly found on Gardiner's Island, off the eastern end of Long Island, USA, during the 19th century.

Ritchie, R., *Captain Kidd and the War against the Pirates* (1986).

Kiel Canal, German ship canal built across the isthmus of Schleswig-Holstein, 1887–95, to link the Baltic and North Seas. It extends for 98 kilometres (61 mls.) from Holtenau, at Kiel Harbour on the Baltic, to Brunsbüttelkoog at the mouth of the Elbe River. Known when it was built as the Kaiser Wilhelm Canal, its construction was a strategic move by the German emperor to link the principal German naval bases of Kiel and Wilhelmshaven, and it was designed to take the largest warships then in existence. The *launching in 1906 of the first British Dreadnought, a new type of *battleship, negated the strategic purpose of the canal, since all navies, including that of Germany, were forced to follow suit and build the new type, and the canal was not at first capable of taking them. However, it was enlarged between 1907 and 1914 and is currently 103 metres (338 ft) long and 11 metres (37 ft) deep. After the First World War (1914–18) it was, for all intents and purposes, internationalized by the Treaty of Versailles (1919), though its administration was left in German hands. In 1936 Hitler repudiated the terms under which it was run, but after the Second World War (1939–45) freedom of *navigation was again guaranteed.

killick, or **killock,** a small anchor, or more usually a large stone at the end of a rope used as an anchor, carried by small craft, a name which became defunct when proper anchors were developed. However, it remained as a slang term amongst seamen for an anchor of any size, and, in the British Navy, for the *rating of leading seaman whose badge is a *foul anchor sewn on his jumper.

kingpost, a short mast close to the cargo *hatches of old-fashioned cargo ships from which was worked the smaller cargo *derrick. In the days before *container ships, when cargo was loaded and unloaded into *lighters, kingposts were used where normal port cranes were not available or there was no room for the ship to lie alongside in port.

king spoke, the spoke of the hand steering wheel in a ship which is uppermost when the *helm is amidships. It is often marked with a ring carved on it or by a *turk's head knot fixed round the spoke.

King's Letter boy, the usual description in the British Navy given to the *rating of 'volunteer-per-order', which was an early method of entry into the Royal Navy of 'young gentlemen' destined to become officers. The rating was introduced by Samuel *Pepys in 1676 and the recipient received £24 a year and a letter from the crown which virtually guaranteed him promotion to commissioned rank after the specified training and passing the examination for lieutenant. The last entry by this system was in 1732 but a similar one, as *captain's servant, continued for some decades. See also GENTLEMEN CAPTAINS.

kite. (1) A fitting attached to a *hawser or wire which is being towed by a vessel, designed to hold it at a certain depth beneath the surface. It works on exactly the same principle as an *otter, though in the vertical plane it comprises an inclined surface attached to the hawser or wire, the pressure of the water upon it as it is being towed forcing it down. The required depth is arranged by varying the distance from the point of tow at which it is attached to the hawser. It is particularly used in certain minesweeping techniques such as the *Oropesa sweep. (2) A general name used to describe an additional light sail spread in a *square-rigged ship to make the most of light following winds. Originally kites meant all sails set above the *topsails but as the square rig was extended in the 18th and 19th centuries, and the *topgallant sail became standard, the term referred only to sails set above that sail, but included the *studding-sails and *jib-topsails.

klipper, a larger type of Dutch cargo carrier or *barge, about 20–24 metres (65–80 ft) in length, steel built with *leeboards. Before the introduction of the *diesel engine it was *ketch rigged when used under sail. They are recognizable by the upright *stem curved at the top into a form of *clipper bow and a round *counter stern.

knarr, the name of the old Norse merchant ship at the time of the Vikings. It was modelled on the traditional *longship, with one mast and a single square sail set on a *yard. When working to *windward a **beitass* was fitted to hold the *luff of the sail *taut. By the second half of the 9th century it could 'carry thirty people, together with their cattle, fodder, goods and furniture, west to Iceland or south Britain' and might have 'short half-decks at bow and stern and a fully-integrated keel, but was never, so far as we are aware, provided with *cabins' (R. Hope, *A New History of British Shipping* (1990), 28).

knee, a right-angled timber or metal bar used for strengthening and for support at the points of intersection of ship's *timbers in a wooden ship. They are of various kinds, such as a **hanging knee**, which fits vertically under a deck *beam and supports its ends; a **lodging knee**, which is fixed horizontally between the forward side of a beam and the ship's side; a **bosom knee** which performs the same purpose on the after side of a beam; and a **carling knee**, which strengthens the right angle between a *carling and a beam. Knees of ships' boats, which support the *thwarts, or in small sailing craft, which support the deck beams, are preferably fashioned from naturally grown timber in which the grain of the wood follows the right angle round. In the days of sail trees used to be artificially bent during growth to provide knee-timber for *shipbuilding.

knightheads, the name given to two large timbers, one on each side of the *stem of a wooden ship, that rose above the deck and supported the heel of the *bowsprit between them. In older wooden merchant ships, the name was also frequently given to the two timber *frames *abaft the foremast which supported the ends of the *windlasses. In some smaller vessels the knightheads of the bowsprit were also called *bitts, as with no space for separate bitts to be fixed to the deck, the anchor *cable was brought to the knightheads for securing.

knock down, to, to knock off the hoops of a cask when it is empty and gather up the *staves for stowage until they are required for remaking the cask. In the days of sail, casks were a very important part of a ship's equipment, as most food for the voyage and all drinking water were carried in them. In those days all sailing ships of any size carried a cooper on board whose duty it was to maintain the casks in good condition, making new ones to replace any that had been *staved accidentally, and retaining for future use those casks which had been knocked down.

knot. **(1)** The nautical measure of speed, one knot being one *nautical mile (1,852 m/6,076 ft) an hour. The term comes from the knots in the line of a common *log which were spaced at a distance of 14 metres (47 ft 3 in.). The number of knots which ran out while a 28-second *sandglass emptied itself gave the speed of the ship in nautical miles an hour. A knot is a speed not a distance so that it is incorrect to say 'knots an hour'. However, in the past nautical terminology may have been less rigid in the merchant service than the Royal Navy for even Joseph *Conrad occasionally wrote 'knots an hour'.

(2) It is also a generally used term to describe a *bend or *hitch in ropes, but in its strict maritime sense only refers to a tucking knot in which the *strands of a rope are tucked over and under each other to form a *stopper knot or a *splice. In more general terms, a knot is meant to be permanent, a bend or hitch temporary. The term is very rarely used in this strict definition today and is widely employed to embrace every form of knot, bend, or hitch.

Ashley, C., *The Ashley Book of Knots* (1972).

Fry, E., *The Complete Book of Knots and Ropework* (1996).

kraken, a mythical sea monster of enormous size said to inhabit the waters off the coasts of Norway and Sweden. According to one legend the kraken lies sleeping on the seabed battening on huge sea worms in its sleep; when the waters at the bottom of the sea grow warm from the fires of hell, the monster will rise to the surface and die. Another legend has the monster rising from the sea and lying on the surface like an island, only to sink again to the bottom. It is sometimes depicted in the form of a giant *squid.

Belief in the kraken's existence can be traced back at least to 1555 when Bishop Olaus Magnus of Sweden described it as having a skin which looked like gravel on the seashore so that men were tempted, when it appeared on the surface, to think it was in fact an island, and to land on it and light fires to cook their victuals. It was also reported that in 1700 a Danish priest celebrated mass on its back. Bishop Pontoppidan of Norway described the kraken as an enormous sea monster but poured scorn

An artist's impression of the kraken; late 18th-century engraving

on it rising to the surface in the shape of an island.

krill, a Norwegian word applied to the stomach contents of the baleen *whales killed in the Southern Ocean. The contents weighing several tonnes were almost entirely a single species of *plankton, a euphausiid. This shrimplike *crustacean (*Euphausia superba*) is the keystone species in the ecosystem, and is the main food of several whales, seals, *penguins, *fish, and *seabirds. Initially 'krill' referred just to *E. superba*, but is now used generally for any of the 86 species of euphausiid that occur in the plankton of the world's oceans. Many krill species are herbivores, filtering phytoplankton out of the water. In the Southern Ocean the presence of huge swarms of *E. superba* has led to a *fishery developing to catch and process the krill. Commercial exploitation of krill by Russians and Japanese in the Southern Ocean began in 1972, and catches rapidly rose to over half a million tonnes a year. But annual catches have now (2004) fallen for political and logistical reasons to less than a hundred tonnes a year. Any exploitation of living resources in the Southern Ocean is now carefully regulated under the terms of the Antarctic Treaty—an international agreement to maintain Antarctica for exclusively peaceful purposes—to prevent further large-scale damage to the Southern Ocean ecosystem.

Prior to the days of *whaling, baleen whales in the Southern Ocean were consuming hundreds of millions of tonnes of krill each year. However, the slowness with which the whale populations have been recovering since the virtual cessation of whaling in 1985 suggests that other species have moved in to exploit the krill resource, and other krill-eating species including penguins and fur seals have undergone population explosions. Krill tends to be most abundant along the *ice edge where algal productivity is enhanced by the ice melt. If future *climate change alters the seasonal pattern of pack-ice formation and melting, the whole Southern Ocean ecosystem could be at risk. M. V. Angel

'kye', slang name in the British Navy for hot cocoa.

L

L. The 'three Ls of *navigation', much favoured by seamen less versed in the intricacies of mathematical navigation, provided a rough and ready means of ensuring the safety of the ship by observation. They were usually regarded as *lead, *latitude, and lookout, although some seamen would substitute *log for latitude.

Mike Richey

labour, to, of a ship, to roll or *pitch excessively in a rough sea. The expression, though applied to all ships, is most apt in its application to wooden sailing ships since pronounced rolling produces a great strain on masts and *rigging and may lead to severe leaks caused by an opening of the *seams.

lace. **(1)** Also known as gold lace or distinctive lace, the rings denoting rank worn on the sleeves of an officer's coat or on the shoulder-straps of tropical uniform and greatcoats. **(2)** As a verb, the act of attaching, in a sailing vessel, a sail to a *gaff or boom by passing a rope or cord alternately through eyelet holes and round the *spar. The rope or cord is known as a **lacing**. In *square-rigged ships, a sail is laced to a *yard, a *bonnet to a *course, and a *drabler to a bonnet.

ladder. **(1)** The general nautical term for what on shore would be called a staircase. Ladders leading from deck to deck are known as **accommodation ladders**; **gangway ladders**, rigged over the side when a ship is anchored or at a *mooring, extend from a small platform level with the upper deck down to the level of the water, and are used when embarking or disembarking from small boats. **(2)** A term used in the control of naval gunnery when finding the range of an enemy vessel.

lade, to, the old equivalent of to load, in relation to a ship and its cargo or a warship and its guns. Guns were **laded** when the cartridge was rammed home, the wad and ball similarly rammed, and the cartridge pierced with a *priming iron to expose the powder ready for firing. The present participle, **lading**, was used as a noun to denote the whole of the cargo on board and **ladebord**, which later became *larboard, as being the side of the ship on which it was loaded. See also PORT; SUPERSTITIONS OF SAILORS.

lagan, a term in maritime law for goods which are cast overboard from a sinking ship with a *buoy attached so that they may be recovered later. It is a term that was also sometimes used to refer to articles still within a sunken ship as it lies on the bottom. The word comes from the Old French *lagand*, lying. In the UK, lagan now legally comes under the definition of *wreck, and any lagan found has to be reported to the Receiver of Wreck.

lagoon, a shallow area of water separated from the open sea by a *coral reef or sandbank. Lagoons are a regular inshore feature of fringing coral reefs and support a rich variety of *marine plants and animals, and are important nursery grounds for the young fry of many *fishes. The coastal lagoons of Baja California in Mexico are important calving areas for Gray *whales (*Eschrichtius robustus*). Along coastlines exposed to the open sea, the lagoons perform a key role in absorbing much of the *wave energy that hits the shore during *tropical storms. In tropical lagoons, where exchanges of water with the open sea are limited, the water heats up rapidly and the high evaporation results in the water becoming very salty, so lagoons are often exploited as a source of sea salt. Their productive waters, high in *salinity, attract large numbers of *seabirds, particularly flamingos (*Phoenicopterus* spp.), whose bills are especially adapted for filtering the abundant fine algae from the water. Around Britain, lagoons are uncommon coastal features, and almost without exception they are considered important conservation sites because of the rarity of the animals and plants that inhabit them; they are threatened by eutrophication, an important *environmental issue, and coastal developments. For illus. see ATOLL. M. V. Angel

laid, a term associated with rope-making, from *lay, meaning the twist of the rope. **Single-laid** rope is one *strand of rope, the strand consisting of fibres twisted up. *Hawser-laid rope consists of three strands twisted together into a rope against the lay of the strands; *cable-laid rope is three hawser-laid ropes twisted up together to form a cable. Cable-laid rope was also frequently known as **water-laid** rope.

laminated construction, a method of construction of many parts of small wooden vessels as an alternative to suitable planks and crooks, in which the grain of the wood follows the required curve. With this method such parts of the hull as the *stem, the *sternpost, the keel, fore-and-aft *stringers, *frames, *knees, deck *beams, etc. are formed of several thin layers of timber which are bound together with water-resistant glue into the various curves required. By means of prefabricated jigs or rigid patterns, various parts of the hull can thus be laminated in large numbers, enabling production of identical wooden hulls to be carried out with a reduction in time and labour costs. A familiar form of laminated construction is plywood which is formed of three or more thin layers or veneers of wood bonded together with glue. See also SHIPBUILDING; YACHTBUILDING.

Lanby buoy, a special *buoy with a diameter of 12 metres (40 ft), developed to replace *lightships. The name is derived from the initials large automatic navigational buoy. They are now largely obsolete.

land breeze, an evening offshore wind which blows from the land to seaward when the temperature of the land falls below that of the sea. As the sun sets, areas of land cool more quickly than the sea adjoining them. The air over the land thus becomes heavier and flows out to sea to establish an equilibrium with the lighter air over the sea. The opposite occurs when the land heats more quickly than the sea during the day and draws heavier air from the sea, creating an onshore sea breeze. See also MARINE METEOROLOGY.

landmark, any fixed object on land whose position is marked on the *chart. Some, such as *lighthouses, *beacons, *leading marks, are set up specifically as guides to *navigation or warnings to seamen; others, such as prominent buildings, can be used as navigational guides where the chart clearly shows their positions.

landsmen, or **landmen,** a *rate given in the British Navy during the days of sail to men without any naval training who served on board warships. In theory they were volunteers since, because they did not use the sea as a profession, they enjoyed immunity from *impressment. But during the 18th century the demand for men was so prodigious that virtually any man brought in by the *press gangs was accepted and rated on board as a landsman, being paid less than an ordinary seaman. The rating was replaced in 1862 by ordinary seaman second class. The spelling 'landsman' for 'landman' begins to appear about 1800. The term was also used in the US Navy, especially after the War of 1812 when it denoted unskilled men of legal age. See also LORD MAYOR'S MEN.

langrel, or **langrace,** or, in American usage, **langrage,** a type of cannon *shot much used at sea by *privateers during the 18th and early 19th centuries when attacking merchant vessels. It comprised various pieces of iron gathered together in a thin casing to fit the bore of the gun, which scattered widely when fired. Though meant to cut the sails and *rigging of a ship, many privateer captains used it against the crews of their victims with lethal effect.

lanyard, a short length of rope used for a variety of purposes on board. In sailing vessels, before the introduction of *bottlescrews and similar fittings, the *shrouds of all masts were set up taut by means of lanyards *rove through the *deadeyes. A sailor carries his knife on a lanyard; and when flintlocks were introduced into navies as the firing mechanism of a warship's guns, they were fired with a lanyard which released the hammer.

lapstrake, see CLINKER BUILT.

larboard, the old term for the left-hand side of a ship when facing *forward, now known as *port. During the early years of the 19th century the term larboard began to give way to port as a helm order as this avoided confusion with the similar sounding *starboard. The change was made official in 1844. See also LADE, TO.

'larbolins', or **'larbolians',** an old word to describe that part of a ship's company who formed the *port watch, which obviously derived from *larboard.

> Larbolins stout, you must turn out,
> And sleep no more within,
> For if you do, we'll cut your clue,
> And let *starbolins in.

The 'clues' in this context are the *nettles which support a slung *hammock.

large, a point of sailing where the sheets which control the sails in a sailing vessel can be eased well away to make the most of a *quartering wind. In *square-rigged ships it was the point where *studding sails would draw if set. The term does not refer to a wind from dead *astern but to one from *abaft the *beam. **To sail large**, to ease away the sheets and sail further *off the wind. **By and large**, to sail a vessel near the wind but not fully on it.

lash, to, to secure anything with a rope or cord. *Hammocks, with the bedclothes inside, were lashed up every morning before being stowed away. **Lash**, as a noun, is a stroke with the *cat-o'-nine-tails. A **lashing** is when a rope or cord is used to secure anything. See also CROSS LASHING.

lask, to, an old sailing term meaning to sail *large.

laskets, small cords sewn in loops to the *bonnets and *drablers of a *square-rigged ship by which, when they were set, they were *laced to the *courses and bonnets respectively by means of a line threaded through the loops. They were also sometimes known as **latchings**.

lateen rig, a narrow triangular sail, probably of Arab origin, set on a very long *yard of which the forward end is *bowsed well down so that it sets obliquely to the mast and produces a high *peak. The origin of the word is obscure, though it has been suggested that it comes from *latin*, meaning Mediterranean. The first known depiction of it is in a Byzantine manuscript, *c.*AD 880, and it seems certain that it was in general use by the 9th century, though it could have been in use in pre-Christian times. It was used very effectively by the Portuguese in their *caravels from the 15th century, and became common in the West Indies.

Lateen rig

There are two types: the triangular which is found only in the Mediterranean, and the more primitive **seltee-lateen**, with a short *luff, found throughout the Indian Ocean. The yard of the former was formed of two or more pieces bound together so that the outer ends would whip more easily than the middle. Because no *forestay could be fitted, the mast usually had a pronounced *rake forward, and the yard was held to the mast by a form of easily released *slip knot. Two bow *tackles were used to haul down the forward end of the yard. The seltee-lateen, having a short luff to the forward edge of the sail, is a four-sided sail. The yard on which the sail is set is often longer than the ship itself, on occasions by as much as one-third.

It is not a handy rig to *tack as the crew, which needs to be a large one to perform this task, must first turn their boat away from the wind and at the same time bring the yard, or yards, round the front of the mast(s), and the *stays supporting the mast must also be moved across to the new *windward side. In a strong wind the sail, or sails, have to be lowered to perform this manoeuvre, during which a lot of ground is always lost to *leeward. The rig can still be seen on the Nile River, and the northern waters of the Indian Ocean. It is the typical sail of the Mediterranean *felucca and the Arabian *dhow. The later *driver and *spanker evolved from it. See also SETTEE.

lateral mark, a *buoy used in the *IALA maritime buoyage system. The buoy can be *can, *conical, or *pillar in shape, and it sometimes has a topmark which is either can shaped or cone shaped. In IALA region A, lateral marks utilize red and green (in exceptional cases, black) colours by day and night to denote respectively the *port and *starboard side of a channel when entering it, while in region B these colours are reversed so that red is used to mark the starboard side and green the port. When a ship moving in the direction of the buoyage system (i.e. into a river) comes to a division in the channel, the preferred channel might be shown by a modified lateral mark. For example, if the preferred channel is to starboard the port, or red, lateral mark has one broad green horizontal band, while if it is to port the starboard, or green, lateral mark has one broad red horizontal band.

latitude, from the Latin *latitudo*, breadth, one of the two spherical *coordinates used to describe a terrestrial position, the other being *longitude. The latitude of a point on the earth's surface will be the angular measure between that point and the plane of the *equator along the *meridian on which the point is located. This is equivalent to the corresponding angle at the earth's centre. The earth's shape, however, is not an exact sphere so that these two angles do not coincide exactly except for points on the equator (latitude 0° or 90°). Geographical latitude is equivalent to the true *altitude of the elevated celestial pole. See also NAUTICAL MILE.

Mike Richey

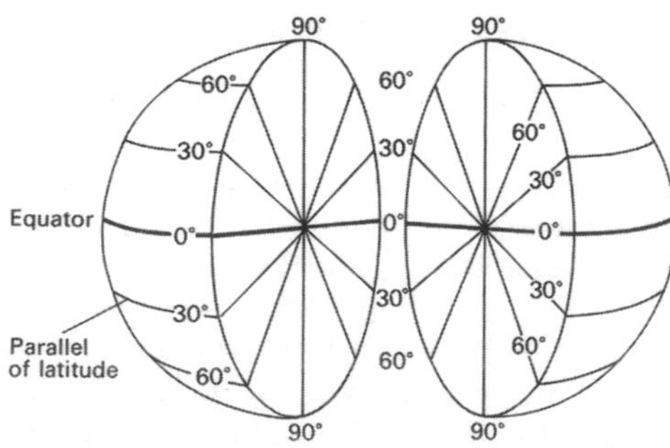

Parallels of latitude showing angular measurement

launch. **(1)** A type of flat-bottomed vessel with little *freeboard which was used as a *gunboat by some of the countries bordering the Mediterranean during the 18th and 19th centuries. **(2)** The largest ship's boat of a 19th- and early 20th-century *battleship and *battlecruiser, developed from the *longboat. They were 12 metres (39 ft) long, and pulled eighteen *oars, nine each side. They also had one mast with a *de Horsey rig, a *gaff-rigged *loose-footed mainsail, and a *staysail, but were later fitted with a paraffin engine and a *propeller. **(3)** Generic name for the small boat with an inboard engine carried as a *tender by large *yachts, or used for pleasure on rivers. **(4)** When used as a verb it is the act of putting a vessel into the water. See also LAUNCHING.

launching a ship is almost always preceded by a ceremony which often includes a blessing on the ship and its crew. Such a ceremony goes back hundreds of years. Thanks are expressed to the shipbuilders for their effort and skill, and to the owners for their faith and financial investment. This is followed by breaking a bottle of wine, or water, on the ship's hull. The bottle has been used for at least 150 years, and many traditions and customs have developed from its use, such as the Royal Navy's requirement that only Commonwealth wine be used.

The method of launching a ship in the traditional manner has been carried out for centuries. Even in today's changing world the shipwright would recognize the techniques of long ago, when it was a regular event to force ships bow-first down greased timbers, using *block and *tackle attached to the *sternpost, but nowadays most ships are built on a *slipway with their sterns pointed to the channel of deepest water. In narrow rivers ships are built at an acute angle to the riverbank.

Once the position of build has been selected, the standing *ways are laid on the ground and secured, and before the sliding ways are run in, the surfaces are covered with low-friction proprietary greases. As the ship nears completion, the space between the sliding ways and ship are packed with timber and long transverse wedges. Some hours before the launching these wedges are driven hard (a process known as 'ramming up'), ensuring the weight of the ship is transferred to the ways; at that stage all other supports are removed. To prevent the ship sliding into the water the standing ways and the sliding ways are kept together by *daggers. These are

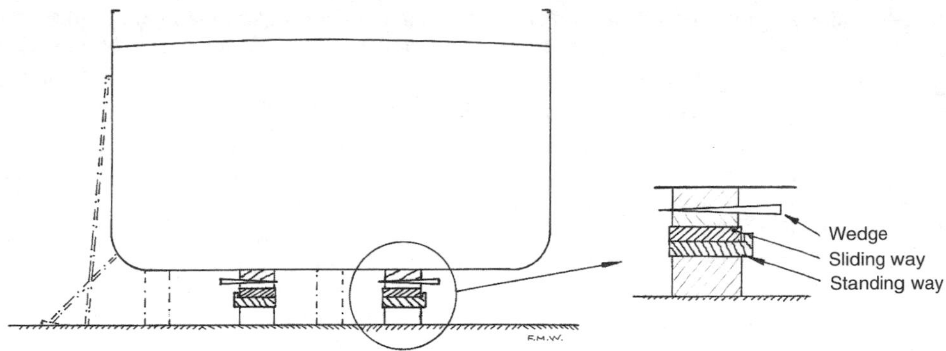

Section through ship about to be launched

released immediately after the naming ceremony, allowing the ship to slide backwards—probably travelling faster than ever again in her life!—though in some very restricted waterways ships are still launched sideways. The hull may have to be slowed quickly with *drag chains, or by temporary water brakes bolted to the hull. Every aspect of the launch must receive the closest attention of the naval architect (see NAVAL ARCHITECTURE) and the *shipbuilding manager.

Over time there have been many changes to launching practice and some yards have introduced stainless steel ways with, in one case, the sliding ways being coated with Teflon. Also, more and more ships are being built in *drydocks. This allows construction to be on the horizontal and the float out at a time conveni-

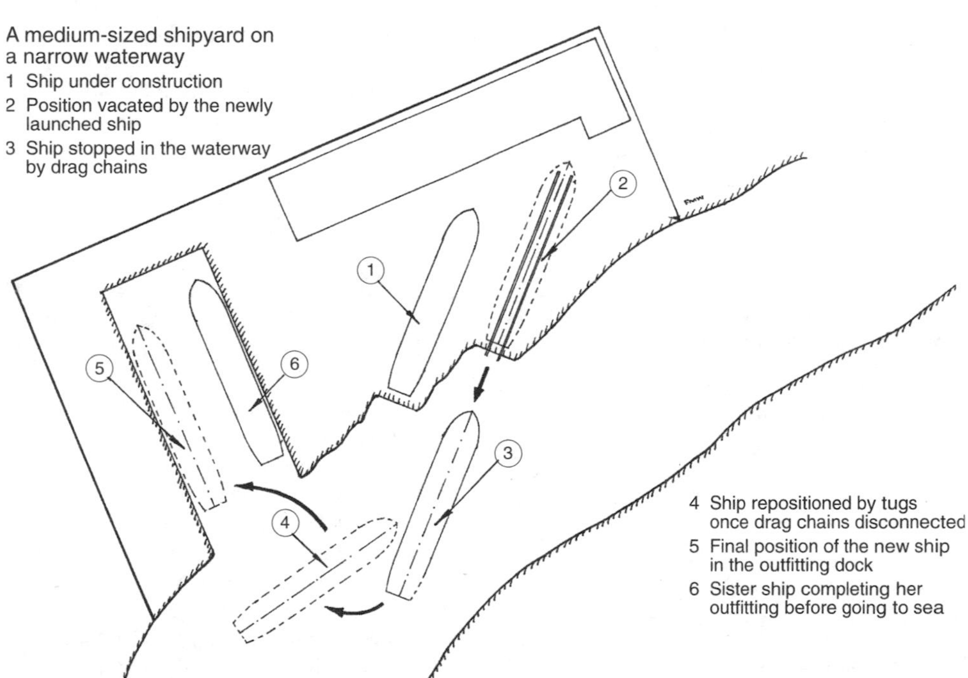

ent to the shipyard, and not dependent on tides.

Fred M. Walker

lay. **(1)** The twist given to the *strands of a rope. **(2)** A share in the profits of a *whaling voyage. **(3)** As a verb, it is much used by seamen and has a variety of meanings. A sailing vessel **lays its *course** when, if *close hauled, it can reach its objective without *tacking; a ship **lays to** when it *heaves to; *topmen **lay out** on the *yards in *square-rigged ships when handling the sails; **to lay *aft or *forward** is an order to seamen to move in the direction indicated.

lay days, the name given to the days which are allowed for the loading or discharging of the cargo of a merchant ship while it lies in port. On the expiration of the lay days, *demurrage becomes chargeable.

lay up, to. **(1)** To put a ship out of *commission or take a *yacht out of the water to overwinter in a boatyard. **(2)** To lay up a rope is to bring its different *strands together.

lazaretto, lazaret, lazarette. **(1)** A compartment in smaller ships, often in the stern, set for the stowage of provisions and stores. **(2)** An isolation hospital for men who may have infections or contagious diseases from ships which have been placed in *quarantine.

lazy guy, a small *tackle or rope used to prevent the boom of a sail swinging unduly when a sailing vessel is rolling heavily.

lazyjacks, light lines led from the *hounds or lower *spreaders to each side of the boom of a sailing vessel. They prevent the sail bellying out to *leeward when it is hoisted or lowered, a convenience for a short-handed crew.

lazy painter, a rope or wire with a *thimble in the end hanging vertically from a boat boom rigged out from a ship's side to which its boats are made fast when in harbour, the boat's own painter being *rove through the thimble and brought back inboard and secured. This form of lazy painter is necessary since the boom is rigged several metres above the level of the water and out of reach from a boat.

leading block, a single *block, frequently a *snatch block, used as a *fairlead to bring the hauling part of a rope or the *fall of a *tackle into a more convenient direction, or to lead it onto a *winch. In the case of a tackle, the fall is known, after it has been led through a leading block, as the **leading part**.

leading mark, a mark sometimes set up on shore or fixed on the bottom in shallow water. When brought into line with another mark or prominent object ashore, it will lead a ship clear of a local danger, such as a rock or *shoal, or guide it safely to a channel which leads to a harbour or the entrance to a port.

leading wind, the description given to a wind which is blowing *free in relation to the desired *course of a sailing vessel; i.e. any wind which enables the sheets of a sail to be eased off to present a square aspect of the sail to the wind.

lead line, a means, before the days of *echo sounders or *sonar, of finding the depth of water near coasts. It was probably the earliest device used by coastal *navigators to facilitate safe *navigation, especially in thick or hazy weather. It comprised a *hemp line to which was attached, by means of a leather *becket or a rope *strop, a lead weight, or plummet, of about 3 kilograms (7 lb). The lower end of the weight was cup shaped, into which a lump of tallow could be pressed, an action known as **arming the lead**. From the material that adhered to the tallow it was often possible for those aboard to identify what type of sea bottom the ship had beneath it. When the tallow came up clean, it indicated the bottom was rock.

A lead line of about 25 *fathoms (150 ft/45.7 m) was used in shallow water and an experienced and skilful leadsman could measure depths of as much as 20 fathoms (120 ft/36.5 m), with a ship making moderate headway of about 10 knots, by heaving the lead ahead of the ship so that when it reached the bottom it would be vertically beneath him. Traditionally, the line was marked with materials which could be easily distinguished by texture when taking a *sounding in the dark. There were pieces of leather at 2 (two strips), 3 (three strips), and 10 (a square piece with a hole in it) fathoms; white duck (strong cotton fabric) at 5 and 15 fathoms; red *bunting at 7 and 17; and blue serge (durable worsted) at 13 fathoms. The mark at 20 fathoms was a piece of cord with two knots in it, also easily distinguishable in the dark.

The fathoms on a longer lead line were marked with a piece of cord with one knot in it at each 5 fathoms and with three, four, five knots at 30, 40, and 50 fathoms (180, 240, 300 ft/55, 73.2, 91.5 m). When a seaman took a sounding with the lead line he called out the depth of water according to the mark on the line that was on or very near the surface of the sea when the lead reached the bottom beneath him. For example, if he saw that the first piece of red bunting was on the surface after his cast, he called out 'By the mark, seven'.

If, after heaving the lead, there was no distinguishing mark level with the sea, the leadsman had to estimate the depth of water by the nearest mark he could see above the sea. This was known as a **deep**, and the leadsman would call the depth of water with the words 'Deep —'. The navigator would then know that he had only got an approximate depth.

> For England when, with favouring *gale,
> Our gallant ship up Channel steered,
> And, *scudding under every sail,
> The high blue western land appeared
> To heave the lead the seaman sprung
> And to the *pilot cheerly sung,
> 'By the deep, nine'.
> (W. Pearce, *c.*1793)

For measuring depths greater than was possible with a hand lead line, the deep-sea lead line, which could measure depths of up to about 100 fathoms (600 ft/183 m), was used. In this case, the lead was about double the weight of a hand lead and the line was marked at each multiple of 10 fathoms with cord having a number of knots equal to the number of tens of fathoms. Each intermediate fifth fathom was marked with a piece of cord having a single knot. The lead was always cast from the *weather side of the ship, in the case of the hand lead from a platform called the *chains, with the depths being reported to the navigator or officer of the *watch by singing them out loudly in a traditional manner.

When using the deep-sea lead line, the vessel would *heave to and the lead be carried forward. The line was then passed *aft to the *poop clear of the weather *rigging and other obstructions. Seamen stationed at intervals along the weather side held a small *coil of the line in their hands, and at the order 'heave', the heavy lead was cast into the sea, the leadsman warning the seaman next *abaft that the weight was about to come on his hand, by the call 'watch there, watch'. This seaman, on letting go his coil, after first ensuring that the lead had not yet reached bottom, gave the same warning to the hand next abaft him; and so on until the lead was felt to reach the bottom.

league, a measurement of distance, long defunct. A league at sea measured 3.18 *nautical miles, or 5.8 kilometres, the equivalent of 4 Roman miles, though, for practical purposes, it was taken as 3 nautical miles. Leagues on land had different values according to the country, ranging from a minimum of 3.8 kilometres to a maximum of 7.4 kilometres (2.4–4.6 statute miles).

leatherneck, nickname for a member of the US *Marine Corps.

lee, probably from the Dutch *lij*, shelter, or the old English *hléo* with the same meaning, though some authorities quote the Scandinavian *loe* or *laa*, sea, as the derivation; the side of a ship, promontory, or other object away from the wind. The word can be used as both a noun and an adjective. Thus the lee side of a ship is that side which does not have the wind blowing on it. The lee of a rock or promontory, that side sheltered from the wind. **Lee helm**, the *helm of a vessel put down towards its lee side to bring the bows up into the wind. A sailing boat is also said to have lee helm when it tends to come up into the wind even despite the efforts of the helmsman to counter this with the *rudder. This is often caused by an imbalance in the sail plan.

In contradiction to the above, a **lee shore** is a coastline onto which the wind blows directly, i.e. it is downwind from any ship in the *offing, and thus can be dangerous as the wind tends to force a sailing vessel down on it.

leeboards. **(1)** An early type of keel or *centreboard, usually made of wood. Attached by a pivot at their upper end, they were positioned at approximately the midpoint on either side of the hull of a flat-bottomed or shallow-*draught sailing vessel. There is no evidence that leeboards existed in Europe before 1570, but when they were introduced—almost certainly from China where *rafts and ships had used them since at least the 8th century—they became particularly popular in the Low Countries where they are still in common use on the *boeier and other Dutch craft. They can also be seen on the few remaining examples of the Thames sailing *barge. The earliest representation of them in Europe is a *marine painting of Amsterdam harbour in 1600.

When the board on the *lee side is lowered it increases the effective draught, thereby reducing the *leeway made when sailing *close hauled. When the vessel has to turn through the wind to change from one *tack to the other, the board on the lee side is lowered as the sails fill on the new tack while the board on the *weather side is hauled up.

When constructed for use on inland waters and canals leeboards are generally very broad in relation to their length, in shape not unlike an opened fan, so as to present the greatest practicable area to resist leeway within the limits of the depth of water. In coastal waters, where rough seas can blow up with great rapidity, the leeboards are usually long and narrow, more like *dagger-boards. **(2)** A board or other preventive fitted to the side of a *bunk on board ship to keep the occupant from rolling out of it when the vessel is lively in a rough sea.

leech, the *after side, or *lee edge, of a sail in a *fore-and-aft rig and the outer edges of a square sail in *square-rigged vessels; in the latter they are known as *port and *starboard leeches according to which side of the ship they are nearest. The **leech-rope** is that part of the *bolt-rope which borders the leech of a sail. For illus. see FORE-AND-AFT RIG; SQUARE RIG.

lee-fang, obsolete name for a *vang.

'lee-oh', the warning given by the helmsman of a sailing vessel that he is starting to *tack. It is normally preceded by the warning 'ready about'.

leeskaertan, literally 'reading chart'. It was the Flemish name for a *rutter, the old-time equivalent of the modern *sailing directions and the forerunner of the *chart.

leeward (pron. loo'ard), a term meaning being situated, or having a direction, away from the wind, the opposite of *windward.

leeway, the distance a ship is set down to *leeward of its *course by the action of wind or *tide. A vessel can make a lot of leeway if a strong cross tide is running or if its keel is not long enough or deep enough to hold it up to the wind. The word also has a colloquial meaning as having fallen behind in something: **'he has a lot of leeway to catch up'** to reach the required position or standard.

leg, the seaman's term for the run or distance made on a single *tack by a sailing vessel. Thus, when making for a point directly to *windward, a sailing vessel will sail legs of equal length on each tack alternately; if the required *course is not directly to windward but still higher than the vessel can *fetch in a single tack, it will sail by means of long and short legs alternately.

legs, wooden supports lashed or bolted to each side of a deep-keeled vessel, such as a *yacht, to hold it upright when it takes the ground either for cleaning or repair. They extend to the depth of the keel.

lem, to, or **lemming,** the process of cutting the meat from the carcass of a *whale after the removal of the blubber by *flensing.

lemsteraak, a Dutch cargo-carrier originating in the Friesland town of Lemmer. They are built with a round bottom, and are generally similar in shape to the *boeier but can be up to 17 metres (55 ft) in length. Some lemsteraaks have been built as, or converted into, *yachts. The traditional rig was a *loose-footed mainsail having a curved *gaff and a large *foresail with the mast *stepped in the usual *tabernacle to facilitate lowering when required.

Lesseps, Ferdinand de (1805–94), French diplomat, best remembered in the maritime field as the creator of the *Suez Canal. A career diplomat, his interest in the possibility of building the canal was first raised in Alexandria in 1832 when he studied the proposals for the project by one of Napoleon's engineers. However, it was not until his diplomatic career had, through no fault of his own, been terminated that he turned once more to the possibility of constructing the canal, and in 1854 the new Khedive of Egypt, Sa'id Pasha, held discussions with him about it. At the end of that year an initial act of concession was signed and in 1856 de Lesseps formed a company with directors from fourteen countries to undertake the canal's construction. Such was his enthusiasm for the project that he persuaded the French people to subscribe most of the capital needed to form the company. Work was started in 25 April 1859, and it was formally opened on 17 November 1869, de Lesseps remaining the chief engineer throughout the project. When, in 1875, the British government decided to purchase the canal shares held by Sa'id Pasha, de Lesseps cooperated by helping in their transfer even though the British, suspicious of French intentions, had initially tried to prevent the canal's construction.

Following the success of the Suez Canal, in 1879 the International Congress of Geographical Sciences decided that a *Panama Canal should be built, and de Lesseps agreed to take on the project. However, he greatly underestimated the difficulties and in 1889 his company, Compagnie Universelle du Canal Interocéanique, was forced into liquidation. This caused not only a financial scandal but a political one too as it was found that government ministers had taken bribes. In 1892 the French government prosecuted the company's directors and both de Lesseps and his son were sentenced to a year in prison, though this sentence was later reversed. Despite this, de Lesseps's reputation remains high today and among his many awards he received the freedom of the City of London and was decorated with the Star of India.

let fly, to. to let go the sheets of a sailing vessel so that the sails flap directly down wind and lose all their forward driving force. It is a means, though possibly an unseamanlike one, of losing the *way quickly off a boat under sail when bringing it alongside or picking up a *mooring. In the Royal Navy it was also the form of salute in a boat under sail when passing a senior officer. See also SALUTES AT SEA.

'let go and haul', or **'afore haul',** one of the orders given during the process of *tacking a *square-rigged ship, being given when the bow of the ship has just passed across the wind and is about to *pay off. 'Let go' refers to the fore *bowline and what are now, after crossing the wind, the weather *braces, and 'haul' refers to the *lee braces.

letter of marque, a commission issued in Britain by the *Lord High Admiral, or by commissioners executing his office, and by the equivalent authorities in other countries, licensing the *master of a privately owned ship to cruise in search of enemy merchant vessels, either as reprisal for injuries suffered or as acts of war. Ships so licensed were themselves also sometimes referred to as letters of marque, though more usually called *privateers. The earliest mention of such a letter is in 1293 and they continued to be issued in time of war or of reprisal until privateering was abolished at the Convention of Paris in 1856.

The practice of licensing privateers by special commissions was very often a highly profitable affair and many owners were anxious to equip their ships with guns in wartime to prey on such merchant shipping as they could come across. In spite of the official commissions they carried, acts of *piracy were common. It was a form of *warfare at sea much criticized by all navies, as the rewards of a successful privateering voyage were often so great they attracted seamen away from service in regular warships.

levanter, a strong, raw wind from the east or north-east which blows in the Straits of Gibraltar and along the east coast of Spain. It is most frequent between October and December and again between February and May.

leviathan, in its scriptural meaning a gigantic sea animal, the maritime equivalent of the behemoth ashore. It has been described in the Bible as a crocodile (Job 41: 15) and as a sea dragon or serpent (Isaiah 27: 1). In modern usage it is mostly taken to mean a *whale and, by extension, a very large ship.

Lewis, David (1917–2003), New Zealand deep-sea yachtsman, anthropologist, doctor, and adventurer. He was awarded the New Zealand Order of Merit and also received many awards from nautical and scientific bodies. In 1960 he sailed his boat *Cardinal Vertue* in the first single-handed transatlantic race (see

YACHTING: TRANSOCEANIC RACING) and later, in *Rehu Moana*, completed the first circumnavigation of the globe by *catamaran accompanied by his wife and two small children. He wrote twelve books, at least two of which may well be numbered among the classics of contemporary *marine literature. *We, the Navigators* (and to some extent its sequel *The Voyaging Stars*) is a masterly account of a nine-month voyage in the auxiliary ketch *Isbjorn* to investigate the navigational concepts and methods used by indigenous Pacific islanders. These were essentially a system of *dead reckoning based on observation rather than measurement. No artefacts were used and myth and metaphor were the method of organizing navigational information.

We, the Navigators makes a profound and unique contribution to our understanding of the art of *navigation by means other than measurement. Lewis made his investigation just in time, before the indigenous methods of navigating used in the Micronesian, Polynesian, and Melanesian islands ceased to be practised by a *navigator caste, trained from boyhood and dedicated to their task.

Ice Bird, by contrast, is a hair-raising account of Lewis's attempt in 1972 to circumnavigate the Antarctic continent on his own. Quite apart from the atrocious conditions, the (finally abortive) voyage proved to be a remarkable feat of navigation. His later expeditions, always with some scientific purpose in mind, took him to the Australian desert and, in a wide variety of craft, three times to the Antarctic, to the Soviet Arctic tundra of Chukotea, and to Melanesia. From boyhood ('shy and solitary, a poor mixer and an indifferent student', as he relates) it seems to have been the beauty of the natural world that so challenged him. His contributions to navigation alone have, in many ways, been unique.

Dr Lewis's publications include: *Dreamers of the Day* (1964), *Daughters of the Wind* (1967), *Children of the Three Oceans* (1969), and *We, the Navigators* (1972), 2nd edn. ed. Sir Derek Oulton (1994). Mike Richey

liberty, the sailor's name for short leave from his ship. Sailors with permission to go ashore for the day or night are known as liberty men.

Liberty ships, mass-produced, prefabricated merchant vessels with all-welded hulls produced in quantity by American shipyards during the Second World War (1939–45). Their deadweight *tonnage was 10,500 and they were fitted with *triple expansion steam engines which gave them an overall speed of 11 knots. The original design was produced by the English Sunderland Company, Newcastle upon Tyne, as long ago as 1879. The British ships were given the prefix 'Sam', not as an indication of their origin but because it was the initials of their type of construction (Superstructure Aft of Midships). They were adopted by the Americans because they incorporated simplicity of design and operation, rapidity of construction, large cargo-carrying capacity, and were remarkably resistant to war damage. One even managed to sink a German armed merchantman with its 4-in. (10-cm) gun. Altogether 2,710 were built.

Elphick, P., *Liberty: The Ships that Won the War* (2002).

Sawyer, L., and Mitchell, W., *The Liberty Ships* (1970).

lie to, to, or **lying a-try,** see HEAVE TO, TO.

lieutenant, the rank in virtually every navy in the world next below that of lieutenant commander, or its equivalent. Originally there was no such rank as lieutenant commander, lieutenants being promoted direct to captain. In the days of sailing navies captain was the equivalent of the rank of commander today, while *post-captains were the equivalent of today's captain, though there was no such rank as post-captain in the US Navy. The origin of the term comes from the French *lieu*, place, and *tenant*, holder, one who holds his authority from a senior officer. The word, logically, is pronounced 'lootenant' in the USA, but in English it is pronounced 'leftenant', possibly derived from *luef*, the Old French for *lieu*.

lifeboat, see LIFESAVING.

lifelines, ropes or wires stretched fore and *aft along the decks of a ship in rough weather, so that the crew can hang on to them to prevent themselves being washed overboard. On *yachts, they are the lines permanently rigged *fore and aft on either side of the deck. They are supported by *stanchions and are connected at either end to the *pushpit and *pulpit.

lifesaving. Britain was the first nation in the world to adopt a comprehensive organization for saving life at sea. In 1824 a lifeboatman, William Hillary of the Isle of Man, founded the Royal National Institution for the Preservation of Life from Shipwreck, which then became the RNLI (Royal National Lifeboat Institution). The lifesaving service in Belgium was established in 1838, that of Denmark in 1848, Sweden in 1856, France in 1865, Germany in 1885, Turkey in 1868, Russia in 1872, Italy in 1879, and Spain in 1880.

In the USA the first local government lifesaving stations were set up in New Jersey in 1848, although one or two community-based organizations had been operating along the coasts since the pioneer Massachusetts Humane Society had been inaugurated in 1789. In 1871 Sumner Kimball (1834–1923) became head of the US Treasury's Revenue Marine Division and undertook a thorough reorganization of its various departments. In 1877 he established what is now the *US Coast Guard Academy, and in 1878 became General Superintendent of the new Life-Saving Service, previously part of the Revenue Marine Division. Nowadays, the responsibility for lifesaving in the USA rests with the US Coast Guard helped by *AMVER and the US Lifesaving Association.

The following is a brief rundown of the principal lifesaving equipment, but see also BREECHES BUOY; COSTAIN GUN.

1. *The Lifeboat.* A reasonable definition of a lifeboat would be a boat specifically designed for saving life at sea, although ordinary ships' boats are called lifeboats when engaged in saving life.

   In Britain Admiral Graves is credited with building a lifeboat in about 1760, but a better claim for being the real initiator in this field is usually given to Lionel Lukin, a coachbuilder. In 1785 he converted a Norwegian *yawl by giving it a projecting cork *gunwale, air chambers at bow and stern, and a false keel of iron, to provide buoyancy and *stability. This he called his 'insubmergible boat', but although he took out a patent for it, the invention had no success. However, he did also design an 'unimmergible' *coble for use at Bamborough, Yorkshire, which saved many lives. It was, incidentally, a coble which Grace *Darling and her father used for their famous rescue of several seamen in 1838.

   Despite Lukin's efforts, it took the *shipwreck of the *Adventure* in 1789 to dispel public apathy in saving life at sea. This ship was wrecked in rough seas off the mouth of the Tyne River, only 275 metres (900 ft) from the shore, and a large crowd watched helplessly as its crew, one by one, dropped to their death in the fierce seas. A public meeting was held and money raised for the best lifeboat design. Half the prize was won by William Wouldhave, and Henry Greathead, a South Shields boatbuilder, was asked to build a boat to part of Wouldhave's design. Called *Original,* she was *launched the following year, served for 40 years, and saved hundreds of lives. Another outstanding lifeboat designer was the Norwegian *yacht designer Colin Archer. Towards the end of the 19th century, he designed sailing rescue boats to work with the Norwegian fishing fleets which became famous for their seaworthiness and lifesaving abilities in the North Sea.

   From the time it was founded the RNLI has taken, as one of its prime objectives, the development of lifeboats that could survive in any kind of sea, and through the *International Lifeboat Federation, its lifeboat designs are used by many national search and rescue (SAR) organizations. It operates five all-weather lifeboat classes, all of which are constructed of fibre reinforced composite or *GRP. They are the 17-metre (55-ft 9-in.) 25-*knot 'Severn', the 16–16.5-metre (52–54-ft 4-in.) 18-knot 'Arun', the 14.3-metre (47-ft) 17.6-knot 'Tyne', the 14.3-metre (47-ft) 25-knot 'Trent', and the 11.8-metre (38-ft 6-in.) 16-knot 'Mersey', and they have operating ranges which vary from 140 *nautical miles ('Mersey') up to 250 nautical miles ('Severn' and 'Trent'). The last of the 'Arun' class, introduced in 1971, was built in 1990 and was then replaced by 'Trent' and 'Severn' class boats, though the 'Arun' remains the mainstay of other national SAR organizations. The RNLI currently (2004) operates three types of inshore lifeboats of *RIB construction and two small *hovercraft.

2. *The Lifebuoy*, or lifebelt, was traditionally a circular ring of cork covered in *canvas, for supporting the weight of a man who has fallen overboard, but nowadays it is more likely to be horseshoe shaped. In small craft, a lifebuoy is attached to the vessel by a line to make it easier to haul it back if it is supporting someone who has fallen overboard. It also has attached to it a *dan buoy and a lifebuoy light to mark its position, or sometimes a self-igniting smoke float. The best type of lifebuoy light is the one which is stored upside down, but which immediately starts to operate when it is thrown in the water with the lifebuoy and turns the right way up to float.
3. *The Life Jacket or PFD (personal flotation device)*. Designed to hold a body upright in the water, the old-fashioned type comprised sections of cork enclosed in canvas which was fashioned to slip over the head, before being secured by tapes round the waist. Nowadays the more modern inflatable type is generally used, which is inflated automatically by a carbon dioxide cylinder attached to the jacket. This is designed to turn an unconscious person so that his nose and mouth are clear of the water, and can support him in this position for at least 24 hours. A minimum of 8 kilograms (18 lb) of buoyancy is recommended by *SOLAS, but the British Department of Trade lays down 16 kilograms (35 lb) for adults and 9 (20 lb) for children. Regulations imposed by all maritime nations oblige their ships to carry one for every person on board, as do the various national yachting authorities.
4. *Liferafts* were, originally, any raft made on board ship from any available timber and used for saving life from a sinking ship. This was also one of the purposes of *hammocks being stored in *nettings during the days of sailing navies so that they could be used as liferafts. During the Second World War (1939–45) many warships and merchant ships carried *carley floats. Nowadays, all ships and *yachts are required to carry inflatable rubber rafts made of special waterproof material which have separate airtight chambers, survival packs, and emergency equipment such as an *EPIRB and distress *flares. Those carrying a large number of passengers, such as *cruise ships, also have inflatable chutes for the rapid evacuation of passengers into liferafts and lifeboats.
5. *Lifesling*, a rescue system for *yachts the main part of which is a horseshoe-shaped buoyancy device that is dragged *astern at the end of a long line to retrieve someone who has fallen into the water. Once the person is in the device the boat is stopped, a *halyard is attached to the Lifesling, and the person is lifted on deck.
6. *Helicopters* are, with national lifeboat organizations, an integral part of what are known as search and rescue (SAR) operations. For large commercial ships these operations are coordinated globally by the *Global Maritime Distress and Safety System. With smaller craft, the coordination is the responsibility of the *coastguard, or its equivalent. The helicopters are mostly supplied by a nation's air force, or air arm, which have air-sea rescue squadrons crewed by specially trained personnel, though the US Coast Guard has its own helicopters.

lifts, lines supporting the ends of the *yards of *square-riggers taken to the relevant masthead or the equivalent position in modern one-piece pole masts. Their principal purpose is to take the weight of the seamen working on the yard, but they are also used to keep the yard in equilibrium or to raise one end or the other (see COCKBILL).

lighter, a dumb vessel (i.e. one without its own means of propulsion), usually of *barge or similar build, used for the conveyance of cargo from ship to shore, or vice versa. They are towed by *tugs.

lighthouse, a building or other construction erected to display a *characteristic light as a warning of danger at sea and an aid to *navigation.

The lighthouse has a long history, and no doubt owes its origin to the *beacon fires which were maintained by priests in ancient Egypt. There is a description of a lighthouse at Sigeum (the present Cape Inchisari) in the writings of the poet Lesches in 660 BC. The most famous of the older lighthouses is the Pharos of Alexandria, which was built in the reign of Ptolemy II (283–247 BC) by Sostratus of Cnidus. This was well authenticated as one of the seven wonders of the world. Contemporary claims that the tower, which carried the light at the top, was 183 metres (600 ft) high are, however, open to some doubt and probably 45 metres (150 ft) is nearer the mark.

The oldest lighthouses in western Europe are said to be those erected by the Romans at Dover and Boulogne, in the 1st and 2nd centuries AD. There were famous lighthouses in Italy in the 1st century, those at Ostia, Ravenna, and Messina being the best known. The light exhibited at Cordouan, a rock in the sea in the Gironde estuary, is recognized as the first example of a lighthouse built out at sea. The earliest of the Cordouan towers dates from about AD 800.

One Chinese geographer, writing around the close of the 8th century, in describing the sea route from Canton to the Persian Gulf, mentions that the people living near the entrance to the Gulf 'set up ornamental pillars in the sea, on which at night they place torches so that people travelling on board ships shall not go astray'. By 1562 there were 711 beacons along the Chinese coast between western Kuangtun and northern Chiangsu.

For centuries lighthouses in the west were lit by wood or coal fires in braziers. Then, in 1763, the first catoptric system, which reflected oil light off parabolic mirrors, was designed and set up by Liverpool's dockmaster, William Hutchinson (1715–1891), a system later improved by the Scottish Lighthouse Board's engineer, Robert Stevenson (1772–1850). The next development, the dioptric system, where light rays were refracted through optic glass, was first described by the Scottish scientist Sir David Brewster (1781–1868) in 1812. But it was the French physicist Augustin Fresnel (1788–1827) who, independently, perfected it in 1822, while Stevenson promoted its installation, and invented a revolving dioptric apparatus which emitted intermittent and flashing light. A further refinement, Fresnel's catadioptric system, both refracted and reflected the light rays which intensified them so that they could be seen at a greater distance.

Until the 1990s most lighthouse using these systems were manned. However, because of the work of the Swedish scientist Gustaf Dalén (1869–1937), which won him the Nobel prize for physics in 1912, some had become automated by the 1930s, as all are nowadays.

light lists, periodical publications issued by most national hydrographic offices. They give the position and *characteristic of every navigational light, whether from *lighthouse, *lightship, or lighted *buoy, in the world. They supplement the information shown on *charts, which remain the primary source for such information.

lightship, normally a vessel without any means of self-propulsion, though in some countries they were, until recently, fitted with engines and *moored over navigational hazards such a *shoal or bank where, for whatever reason, it was impracticable to build a *lighthouse. The lightship, like a lighthouse, displays a *characteristic navigational light at night and a special mark by day, both easily identifiable and marked on *charts. They are also equipped with fog signalling equipment and *radar beacons, and come, like lighthouses, under the control of the national authorities like *Trinity House and the Northern Lighthouse Board. In British and many other waters, they are always painted red and used to carry a crew of three or four, but nowadays they are all automated.

'light to', an order, when *belaying a *hawser round a *bollard and the first turn has already been made, to fleet the hawser back along the deck to provide enough slack for additional turns to be made. When there is tension on the hawser, the first turn will hold it momentarily, but additional turns are then required to make it secure, and enough rope to do so quickly is provided by the order 'light to'.

lignum vitae, the hard smooth wood of the guaiacum tree, grown in the West Indies. It had many maritime uses, particularly for the *deadeyes and *chesstrees of sailing vessels and the *sheaves of wooden *blocks. It stood up well to the wear caused by ropes, and its smoothness allowed a rope to *render through it easily. One principal marine use during the 19th century was as a sea-water self-lubricating bush for the stern tubes of early screw steamships. It was first introduced for this purpose in 1854 by the marine engine builder John Penn, and until the introduction of more modern methods some 40 years later, it solved the problem of leaking stern bearings.

limbers, holes cut in the floor *timbers of wooden ships on either side of the *keelson to allow a free passage for the *bilge water to run down to the *pump well. In many ships a small chain or rope, known as a limber-rope, was threaded through the limbers extending the whole length of the bottom; by pulling it backwards and forwards any blockage could be cleared. As bilge water normally stank and was often a breeder of disease, it was most important to keep the limber-ways clear so that the bilges would drain properly.

'Limey', a name originally used by Americans when referring to a British seaman, though now frequently enlarged to embrace all British people. It originated from the British regulation that all ships registered in the UK were to carry a stock of lime juice on board for issue to the crew as a preventive against *scurvy. For the same reason, British ships were known in the USA as 'lime-juicers'.

line of battle, during the days of sailing navies, the line formed by *ships of the line before joining battle with an enemy fleet. The methods used to do this were rigidly enforced in the British Navy, and by other navies, by the *fighting instructions, and in the British Navy these remained inflexible until the introduction of the *general chase signal in the mid-18th century. Since most conventional sailing warships could only bring their maximum weight of gunfire to bear when they fired on the *beam or *quarter, the usual line of battle was either **line ahead**—that is, each ship following in the wake of the one ahead of it—or **quarter-line**. Wind direction, the position of the sun, visibility, and so on, were always factors which influenced a fleet commander in his choice of where and how he formed his line of battle. See also WARFARE AT SEA.

line of bearing, ships of a fleet disposed in a line on any particular bearing from their *flagship.

line officers in the US Navy are those who serve in various departments aboard ship who may one day be promoted to command. Restricted line officers, usually those with specialist skills such as intelligence and cryptanalysis, are those who will not be.

liner, see CRUISE SHIP; OCEAN LINERS.

lines, the drawing, known in the past as the sheer draught, which delineates the shape of a ship's hull. Normally it consists of three views: the sheer which shows the longitudinal elevation of the ship; the body plan which shows the vertical cross-sections; and the half-breadth plan which shows horizontal planes parallel to the waterline, including deck shapes. For illus. see NAVAL ARCHITECTURE.

linings, additional pieces of material sewn to a sail to prevent chafe, mainly in such places as the *reef-bands, *buntlines, etc. They are generally only seen in the sails of *square-rigged ships where the chances of chafing are much greater, due to the multiplicity of *rigging, than in *fore-and-aft-rigged sailing vessels.

list, the inclining of a ship to one side or the other due usually to a shift in the cargo or the flooding of some part of the hull. It is a more permanent situation than a *heel. See also LOLL.

lizard, a short length of rope with a *thimble spliced into the end, used for various purposes on board ship; in *square-rigged ships as a *fairlead for the *buntlines, for example. The length of wire rope, also with a thimble in the end, which hangs from the lower boom of a ship at anchor, and to which its boats can be made fast, is also known as a lizard.

Ljungstrom rig, a rig with a single sail shaped like a *jib, the *luff of which is attached, by a groove, to a round, revolving mast, though sometimes it is a double sail which can be set on either side of the mast when *running free. The sail is *reefed by spinning the mast with an endless rope, about ten turns rolling it up completely onto the mast. Ball bearings reduce the friction where the mast, which is *stepped on the keel, passes through the deck. The *halyard runs inside the mast and, for all practicable purposes, it is an *unstayed rig, as there is no standing *rigging apart from an adjustable *backstay.

Lloyd's, an association of *underwriters which traces its origin to daily meetings of London merchants in Edward Lloyd's Coffee House in the City of London. It has a continuous history of marine underwriting from 1601 and later formed the Register Society, now *Lloyd's Register. As well as its main business of marine and other insurance, it is also a centre of maritime intelligence of the daily movements of merchant ships, marine casualties, etc. See also LUTINE BELL.

Lloyd's Register, formerly Lloyd's Register of Shipping, was formed by *Lloyd's underwriters in 1760 to examine merchant ships and 'classify' them according to their condition. The first Register of Ships was printed in 1764 and is still produced annually as *Lloyd's Register of Ships*, which contains details of over 90,000 ships. *Lloyd's Register of Yachts* (1878–1980) was succeeded by *Lloyd's Register of Classed Yachts.* This ceased publication in 1996 but there have been three special editions since then. The Lloyd's Register Group, of which Lloyd's Register is a part, is an independent risk management organization whose business still principally involves the *classification of ships, which sets standards of quality and reliability during their design, construction, and operation. A ship's hull and machinery must conform to the standards required by its rules, and are inspected to help ensure they comply. It also carries out statutory inspections in line with international shipping conventions and codes. Much of its marine business concerns *tankers and *bulk carriers, but the group is also a world leader in some of the most technologically advanced vessels, including *cruise ships, *ro-ro ships, and naval vessels.

load line, the line on a merchant ship's hull which indicates the maximum depth to which it can be loaded, taking into account the potential hazards present in different zones at different seasons. The first International Convention on Load Lines, adopted in 1930, was based on the principle of reserve buoyancy. However, it was also recognized that a ship's *freeboard should also ensure adequate *stability and avoid excessive stress on the ship's hull as a result of overloading. In 1966 the Load Lines Convention was adopted by the *International Maritime Organization in which provisions were made to determine the freeboard of *tankers by subdivision and damage stability calculations. The latest (2004) amendments include regulations on such matters as the position, strength, and safety of openings in a ship including *hatches, doorways, and ventilators, etc. See also PLIMSOLL LINE.

loblolly boy, the name by which, during the days of sailing navies, a surgeon's assistant was known in a British warship. The origin of the name is the old country word *loblolly*, a kind of porridge or gruel, which was adopted in the navy to describe the surgeon's potions for the sick on board.

lobscouse, a well-known dish at sea during the days of sail. It was a mixture of salt meat cut small, broken biscuit, potatoes, onions, and such spices as were available, boiled up into a stew. See also SKILLYGALEE.

lodeman, from the Old English *lad*, a leader or guide, and thus occasionally used at sea to mean a *pilot. In the Laws of *Oleron it was laid down, 'If a ship is lost by default of the lodeman, the maryners may... bring the lodeman to the windlass or any other place and cut off his head'. Hence, **lodemanage** which meant pilotage or the hire of a pilot, a term which lasted into the 18th century. There was a Court of Lodemanage which sat at Dover during the days of the *Cinque Ports for the examination and appointment of pilots. Of his ship's captain Chaucer, in the prologue to the *Canterbury Tales*, wrote:

> His herborough, his moone, and his lodemanage,
> There was none such from Hull to Cartage.

lodestar, a sailor's name for *Polaris, or the Pole Star. The origin of the name presumably comes from the same old English source as *lodeman and *lodestone, to give a meaning as 'guiding star'.

lodestone, or **loadstone,** the seaman's name for magnetic oxide of iron. It is said that the ancient Chinese discovered that, when freely suspended, it would point to the north, and therefore used it to form the earliest crude *magnetic compass. Recent research suggests that this was not the case, although the Chinese were probably aware that a soft-iron bar, stroked with a lodestone, acquired a directional north–south property. There was, however, a long way to go before mariners were able to harness this directional property to a compass card. Presumably it was given its name from the old English *lad*, as did *lodeman and *lodestar.

Hitchens, H., and May, W., *From Lodestone to Gyro-Compass* (1954).

log. **(1)** The shortened name for a *log book. **(2)** The name given to any device for measuring the speed of a vessel through the water or the distance it has sailed in a given time. All the early types of devices for doing this were based on the same principle.

Common Log. This was first described in print in *A Regiment for the Sea* (1574) by William Bourne. In its earliest form it comprised a wooden board attached to a *log-line and hove from the stern of the vessel. The log-line was allowed to run out for a specified period of time. On the assumption that the board remained stationary in the water, the amount of line run out in a specified time indicated the distance sailed by the vessel through the water in that time. From this its speed could be easily calculated.

An early development of the first common log, introduced in about 1600, was the chip log, in which the original board was replaced by a wooden quadrant weighted with lead on the circular rim to make it float upright. This was designed to give it more resistance in the water to the drag of the log-line as it ran out, thus providing a more accurate reading.

Later, when the *nautical mile was introduced, the log-line was marked by knots, the derivation of the knot as a measurement of speed at sea.

Dutchman's Log. On much the same principle as the common log, the Dutchman's log was the method of estimating speed at sea favoured by Dutch mariners during the 17th and 18th centuries. The means of calculating the speed using this log involved measuring the time during which a chip of wood, dropped into the sea level with the bow, travelled between two marks cut on the vessel's *gunwale. Knowing the distance between the marks, it was a simple arithmetical matter to find the rate of sailing.

Patent or Self-recording Log. With the growth of the seaborne trade in the 17th and 18th centuries the need for a more accurate measurement of a ship's speed became widespread, and many inventors turned to a rotator towed by a ship as a means of measuring speed. The British engineer John Smeaton (1724–92), who improved Halley's *diving bell, was one of the earliest to develop a patent log, producing a lightweight rotator in 1754, and at about the same time similar inventions came from Britain, France, and Germany. But they all suffered from an unacceptable degree of friction which falsified the readings. A partial solution came in 1792 when Richard Gower fitted his rotator in a wooden cylinder which also contained the registering dials. Although this largely eliminated the friction, it entailed hauling in the log every time the ship changed *course as well as when the *watch changed. In 1802 Edward Massey produced a log which began to resemble a modern patent log. A streamlined rotator was attached to a case containing the dials by four lengths of cane jointed together, the whole being towed at the end of a log-line. It still involved hauling in the log to take a reading, but the results proved impressively accurate and it was the Massey log which was used extensively at sea throughout the 19th century.

Massey's nephew was Thomas Walker, a name widely associated with the modern development of the patent log. His 'Harpoon' log, similar to Massey's but with the dials incorporated in the outer casing of the rotator, was patented in 1861, and his famous 'Cherub' log was introduced in 1884. By this time, engineering development had reached the stage where revolutions of the rotator astern could be transmitted accurately to a register inboard without distortion by friction.

Bottom Logs. Other types of patent log are known as bottom logs, in that they are not towed *astern but protrude from the ship's bottom. There are three basic types, known as the pitometer, the Chernikeeff, and the electromagnetic.

The pitometer log was based on an invention by Henry Pitot who, in 1730, used an open L-shaped glass tube to measure current flow. By placing the foot of the L facing forward beneath a ship, water was forced up the tube as the ship proceeded, its speed being measured by how far up the tube the water was forced. A number of experiments were made with this device, and improvements introduced, but it was not until the 20th century that reliable logs on the Pitot principle were evolved.

The Chernikeeff principle relied on a small rotator in a retractable tub carried a metre or so below the hull of the ship. It was conceived by Captain B. Chernikeeff of the Russian Navy in 1917 and was later developed and widely used.

At sea, speed may be measured in relation to either the seabed or the water flowing past the hull. Modern logs measure both. The electromagnetic log, which is widely used, has two electrodes beneath the ship's hull. These measure the potential difference generated by the ship's movement relative to a magnetic field, which is produced by an electromagnet. Smaller vessels such as *yachts use an electronic log where an impeller fixed to the vessel's bottom is connected to the main instrument inboard which gives the readings of speed and distance run. Doppler *sonar systems, as well as measuring the depth below a ship's bottom, measure the ship's speed and distance run in relation to the ocean floor.

log book, usually referred to simply as a log, a compulsory document for all warships and commercial vessels in which is recorded information relating to the *navigation of the ship.

loggerhead. **(1)** The wooden *bitt in the stern of a *whaling boat around which the harpoon line was controlled as it ran out after striking a *whale in the days when harpoons were launched by hand. **(2)** A ball of iron attached to a long handle used for melting *tar or *pitch. The ball was heated in a fire to red heat and then plunged into the tar or pitch bucket.

log-line, classically, a specially woven line of contra-laid cotton used for towing a patent *log from the *taffrail of a ship. The reason for the special weaving was to prevent twist, so that it would faithfully repeat the number of revolutions made by the patent log as it is towed through the water. Such instruments are seldom used nowadays.

loll, a term used to describe the state of a ship which is unstable when upright and as a result floats at an angle of *heel on one side or the other. It is usually caused by a large area of free-surface water inside the hull, as for instance a ship with flooded compartments, but can also be caused by too much weight carried high up in the ship. It is not the same as *list, which is caused by quite different conditions. Loll in a ship can be reduced by removing top weight, adding to bottom weight, or by reducing the area, and particularly the width, of the free-surface water in the ship.

longboat, the largest boat carried on board ships in the 18th century. It was *carvel built with a full bow and high sides, and furnished with a mast and sails. A ship's gun could also be mounted in the bows. Its principal uses on board were to transport heavy stores to and from the ship and to take empty water casks ashore to be refilled whenever fresh water was required. It was also the principal lifeboat carried on board and was kept fully provisioned for use in any emergency. It was from the longboat that the *launch was developed as the major warship's boat during the 19th and early 20th centuries.

long clothes, the seaman's name, during the 18th and early 19th centuries, for the clothes worn by men ashore. It was a wise precaution for a British merchant seaman to have a suit of long clothes to wear when going ashore to avoid *impressment. 'When the [press] boat left the vessel we crept from our hiding hole,' wrote John Nicol in *The Life and Adventures of John Nicol, Mariner* (1822), 'and not long after, a custom-house officer came on board. When we cast anchor, as I had a suit of long clothes in my chest, I put them on immediately and gave the custom-house officer half a guinea for the loan of his cocked hat and powdered wig. I got a waterman to put me on shore. I am confident that my own father, had he been alive, could not have known me. All these precautions were necessary. Had the waterman suspected me to be a sailor, he would have informed the *press-gang in one minute.' See also SAILORS' DRESS.

longitude, from the Latin *longitudo*, length, one of the two spherical *coordinates used to describe a terrestrial position, the other being *latitude. It is the arc of the equator or the angle at either pole between the planes of the *prime meridian (0°) and the *meridian of the places measured eastwards or westwards. Before the *chronometer the longitude at sea would generally be calculated from *lunar distance observations which involved observations of the position of the moon relative to other astronomical bodies. The chronometer, which keeps accurate time, enabled the navigator to establish his longitude from the local time of noon compared to that at Greenwich. The longitude of a place is a function of the time it takes the earth to rotate through the angle between the planes of the prime meridian and the meridian of the place. Longitude and time are thus equivalent, the one expressed in arc, the other in hours, minutes, and seconds. See also BOARD OF LONGITUDE; GREENWICH MEAN TIME.

Mike Richey

long-jawed, the term used to describe rope which, through much use, had had the twist, or *lay, in its *strands straightened or pulled out and has no longer the resilience to resume its normal tightness of lay after use. See also JAW.

long-lining, a fishing method whereby baited hooks are attached to a headline, which is strung between a series of buoys. The length of a headline can be 40 kilometres (25 mls.) onto which are clipped up to 3,000 hooks on additional short lengths of line, or snoods. The snood lengths are adjusted so that the hooks fish in or around the *thermocline. Once a long-liner has shot the headline it returns to the start of the line and hauls in. Favoured regions for this type of *fishery are along ocean *fronts where the *fish being targeted, *tunas, swordfish (*Xiphias gladius*), and billfishes (family Istiophoridae), tend to congregate. When the fishing is good over 10% of the hooks take marketable fish, but now such good catches are rare. Large numbers of *shark are also taken. These are discarded after their fins have been cut off to be dried for making shark fin soup in Asia. Badly run long-line operations kill large numbers of *seabirds, especially *albatrosses, which snatch the baits as they are deployed, get snagged, and are drowned.

M. V. Angel

longship, a Norse or Viking *galley, used mainly for raiding and for war purposes approximately between the years AD 600 to AD 1000. The largest longships pulled up to 80 *oars, the smallest about 40 or 50. They also carried a mast, *housed in a *step, which was always lowered *aft when they were under oars. A single square sail was hoisted on a *yard, and by using *bowlines and a *beitass* to *brace the yard it was possible to use the sail for working to *windward as well as for *running free. As longships had neither deck nor keel, they gave no protection to their crews and also were poor seaboats, and normally did not operate in the winter when rough seas might be expected. The usual practice was to haul them up on shore during the autumn for *launching again the following spring. Yet they made many remarkable voyages, sailing as far west as *Vinland and as far south as the Mediterranean Sea.

Researches by J. Hornell during the 1930s revealed that the longship design was not confined to the northern hemisphere, for he found that similar vessels were used in the Pacific region. Not only did the two designs look alike, but they used identical methods of construction. So complex were these that it seems impossible they could have emerged independently, though no explanation could be found. See also SEPULCHRAL SHIPS.

Longship

long splice, a method of *splicing two ropes by unlaying the ends to a distance of eight times the circumference of the rope and then *laying up the *strands in the space left where the opposite strand has been unlayed. By this means the two ropes are joined without increasing the thickness over the area of the splice. A

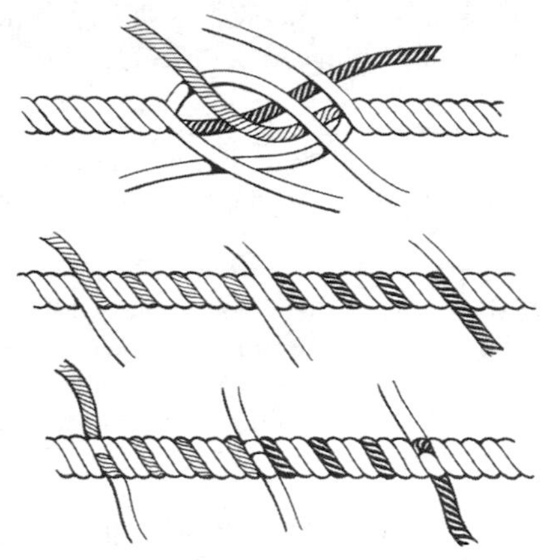

Long splice

long splice is used where the rope is required to *reeve through a *block after it has been spliced.

loof. **(1)** The after part of the bow of a *square-rigged ship just before the *chesstrees, at the point where the side planking—or plates when iron or steel was used for the hulls of large sailing ships—begins to curve in towards the stem of the ship. The term is now obsolete, and only ever applied to sailing ships. **(2)** The old word, sometimes also written as loofe, meaning *luff.

loom. **(1)** See OAR. **(2)** An effect of *refraction in a light fog at sea which makes objects look larger than they are. 'That ship looms large', the dim outline of a vessel through fog and appearing larger than it in fact is. The same effect is often observed when the land is seen through a fog from seawards, cliffs frequently appearing much higher than they really are. **(3)** Also an effect of reflection on low cloud in the case of the light from a *lighthouse or *lightship, when the light itself cannot be seen directly.

loose, to, of the sails of a *square-rigged ship, to cast loose the *gaskets, or stops, of a *furled sail so that the sail may be set.

The term refers only to sails set on *yards, and only when they are furled on the yards, implying the actual casting loose of the gaskets. Thus, if an additional sail, such as a *royal, is sent up in fair weather, it is set, not loosed, as it was not already in position furled on the yard with gaskets.

loose cannon, see BREECHING.

loose-footed, a sail in a *fore-and-aft rig set without a boom, as in the mainsail of a *barge, or in the *de Horsey rig. A sail which is set on a boom, but with only the *tack and *clew secured, is also said to be loose footed.

Loran-C. Loran is an acronym for long-range navigation, a *hyperbolic navigation system first proposed in the 1930s and implemented as the British Gee system in the early days of the Second World War (1939–45) to home bombers onto their targets. It was further developed by the radiation laboratory of the Massachusetts Institute of Technology, and by 1943 a chain of transmitters was in operation under the control of the *US Coast Guard. This became known as Loran-A, which was phased out in the USA in 1980. It is anticipated that in due course all Loran-A stations will be replaced by Loran-C ones. The system probably provides the best combination of accuracy and coverage area of any system yet devised for fixing a position by means of earth-based transmitting stations. It is favoured in some quarters as a possible earth-bound back-up for *GPS. There are some 30 Loran-C/Chakya chains, operated jointly by the Americans and Russians, each made up of three to five transmitter stations comprising one master and two secondary transmitters. Four Loran-C chains cover much of north-west Europe. As with all hyperbolic navigation systems the position is plotted by means of a lattice *chart and transferred to the nautical chart in use. See also CONSOL; DECCA; OMEGA.

Mike Richey

lorcha, a sailing vessel with a European-shaped hull and a Chinese *junk rig. They are believed to have originated at Macao when it was first settled by the Portuguese. Vessels with the typical *lateen rig of the Mediterranean, with its somewhat eastern look, led to many of them being wrongly called lorchas.

Lord High Admiral, an office first established in England in 1391 when Edward, Earl of Rutland, was appointed Admiral of England, uniting the offices of Admiral of the North and

Admiral of the South, instituted some 90 years earlier. Subsequently the titles 'High Admiral' and 'Lord Admiral' were indiscriminately used in the wording of the letters patent, crystallizing eventually as 'Lord High Admiral', ninth of the nine great officers of state of the crown. This title did not originally confer command at sea, but jurisdiction in maritime affairs and the authority to establish courts of *Admiralty. To give the Lord High Admiral military command, however, he was also appointed 'Captain General of Our Fleets and Seas'.

By the reign of Henry VIII (1509–47) the English Navy had grown too big to be administered by the Lord High Admiral alone, and its civil administration was delegated to a committee later known as the **Navy Board**. This board, which had Samuel *Pepys as one of its members during the reign of Charles II (1660–85), ran in parallel with the **Board of Admiralty** until it was merged with the Admiralty in 1832. However, the office of Lord High Admiral, which, except for brief periods during its long history, had remained extant, was not abolished until 1964. In that year the three separate service ministries were brought together into a single Ministry of Defence, and the title of Lord High Admiral was then resumed by the crown in the person of Elizabeth II.

Lord Mayor's Men, originally *landsmen who were induced to join the British Navy to avoid debts or disgrace, or were given the option by city magistrates to serve in the navy under the Quota Acts of 1795 in place of jail sentence for misdemeanours. The Quota Acts were passed in the British Parliament, under the stress of the Revolutionary War against France (1793–1801), to provide seamen for the Royal Navy. Later, in the Napoleonic War (1803–15), the phrase was unofficially applied to any landsman who joined the navy in order to qualify for a *bounty. They were held in great derision and contempt by professional seamen from whom they were easily distinguished by the clothes they wore on joining a ship.

low and aloft, a nautical expression describing a sailing ship with sail spread from deck to *truck; every stitch that it could carry. Many people are inclined to think that the phrase is an abbreviation of *alow and *aloft, but it is in fact the other way round, alow and aloft being an expansion of the correct term.

lower deck, the deck of a ship next above the *orlop deck. It is a term used to indicate the rating of naval ships, e.g. officers belong to the *quarterdeck, ratings to the lower deck. The expression possibly comes from the order *'clear lower deck', given when all seamen in the days of sailing navies were required on the upper deck, either to cope with an emergency or to hear some important announcement by their captain.

lubber's hole, an opening in the floor of the *tops on the fore-, main-, and *mizzen-mast of *square-rigged ships, to give access to the tops from below. It was so termed because timid climbers up the *rigging preferred to go through this hole to reach the top rather over the *futtock shrouds, the way experienced sailors went.

lubber's line, or **point,** the black vertical line or mark on the inside of a compass bowl which represents the bow of the ship. It enables a *course to be steered by bringing the lubber's line to the point on the compass card which shows the desired course.

luff, the leading edge of a sail in a *fore-and-aft rig. **'Hold your luff'**, an order to the helmsman of a sailing vessel to keep the vessel sailing as close to the wind as possible and not allow it to sag down to *leeward.

When used as a verb, 'luff' is an order to the helmsman to bring the ship's head up closer to the wind by putting the *helm down, or to leeward. In *yacht racing, to luff an opponent is to come up closer to the wind, or even head to wind if necessary, to prevent the opponent overtaking to *windward, a legitimate procedure under the *racing rules.

luff tackle, a *purchase which has a single and a double *block, the *standing part of the rope being secured to the *strop of the single block, and the hauling part coming from the double block. It increases the power by four times when *rove to *advantage. It was originally used for hauling down the *tack of a sail in a *fore-and-aft rig to make the *luff *taut, but the term is now used to describe any tackle rove through a single and a double block. **Luff**

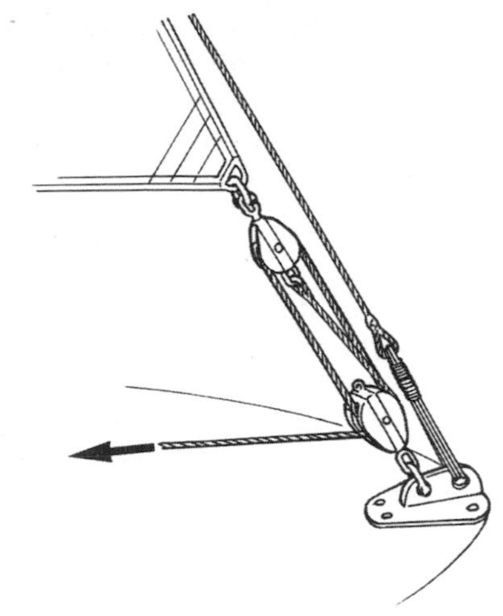

Luff tackle rove to disadvantage

upon luff, one luff tackle hooked onto the *fall of another in order to double the power.

lug. **(1)** The name, rarely used, of the *yard on which a *lugsail is set but more often employed to describe the sail of any small boat. **(2)** A projection on a mast or *bowsprit fitting with an *eye to take a *shackle of a *stay or *shroud.

lugger, a sailing vessel with a *lugsail rig, which appeared in western Europe at the end of the 16th century. It was normally fitted with a foremast and mainmast, except when it was used to *smuggle contraband or as a *privateer, when a *mizzen was stepped right *aft. It was used particularly for fishing and for the coastal trade. In these situations its increased weatherliness over the *square rig gave it considerable advantages when working the *tides.

As it appeared so quickly throughout Europe, it is open to question whether its development was indigenous. The possibility has been raised that it came from the *junk rig, losing its battens and multiple sheets in the process, particularly as it is said to have been disseminated from the Adriatic, *Marco Polo's home waters. Two types of lugger, the *trabaccolo* and the *braggozzi*, can still be found in Venetian ports and it may be no coincidence that they are flat bottomed and have exceptionally large *rudders which can be retracted, both features found in the junk. Multiple sheeting also appears in Turkish luggers, and certain Turkish boats possess similarities to the *sampan.

lugsail, a four-sided sail set on a *yard or *lug, used almost exclusively in small craft. The sail is very similar to the one used in a *gaff rig, but has a wider *throat, and depends on its *luff for *stability. The yard by which the sail is hoisted is normally two-thirds the length of the *foot of the sail and carries a *strop one-quarter of the way from throat to *peak. This strop is hooked to a *traveller on the mast and is hoisted in the normal way until the luff is as *taut as possible.

The earliest known drawing, by a Dutch artist, of what may have been a lugsail is dated 1584, but the name itself does not appear for another century. Suggestions that it is of much more ancient origin and first appeared in the Mediterranean in Egyptian and Phoenician craft around the 1st century BC are not borne out by any evidence and probably arose through confusing the *lateen rig with the true lug rig. The original lugsails were set on *dipping lugs and later on the *standing lug, of which the *gunter rig is the most modern and the most efficient type.

The **balanced lugsail**, which became popular in the west around the end of the 19th century, is laced to a boom which extends a short way forward of the mast, and set flat by a *tack *tackle. It is almost certainly a western adaptation of the short-boomed Chinese balanced lugsail, which itself developed during the 3rd century from the canted square sails of Indonesia.

lunar distance, an observation of the angle between the edge of the moon or sun, or a planet, in order to find *Greenwich Mean Time (GMT) at sea and so determine the *longitude. The moon has a relatively rapid motion across the heavens in relation to the fixed stars, so that the angular distance between the moon and any fixed star that lies in the moon's path changes comparatively rapidly. The earlier *nautical almanacs provided the *navigator with tables of predicted lunar distances (the angles between the moon and certain fixed stars, as well as the sun) against GMT. By observing a lunar distance it was possible to ascertain, by interpolation between tabulated values of lunar distances against GMT, the precise GMT of the observation. By comparing this with the local time of the observation, the longitude of the ship could be ascertained. The introduction of the *chronometer, bringing GMT permanently on board, made lunar observations no longer necessary for the accurate determination of longitude. See also BOARD OF LONGITUDE.

Mike Richey

lunar parallax, an *altitude correction applied to moon altitude observations because of the relative proximity of the moon to the earth. The true altitude of a heavenly body is a measure of an arc of a vertical circle between the celestial *horizon of an observer and the true direction of the body from the earth's centre. For all celestial bodies except the moon, the directions from the earth's centre are regarded as being the same as those from an observer on the earth's surface. For the moon, however, the angle subtended at the moon between lines which terminate respectively at the observer and at the earth's centre may be as much as nearly a degree of arc. The parallax correction for a moon *sight depends upon the distance between the earth and moon, the *latitude of the observer, and the altitude of the moon. Tables of parallax for moon observations are normally included in all compilations of *nautical tables and *almanacs. Mike Richey

lunch hook, US term for an unusually light anchor.

***Lusitania*,** an *ocean liner of just under 31,000 gross *tonnage which belonged to the Cunard Line. Built in 1906, she had quadruple screws, and the following year won the Atlantic *blue riband by crossing from Liverpool to New York at an average speed of 23.99 knots. She continued monthly sailings from Liverpool to New York and back after the outbreak of war in 1914.

Before she left New York on 1 May 1915 the German authorities in the USA published warnings that she would be attacked by *submarines, and advised passengers not to sail. The warnings were not regarded as serious, and it appears that warnings of German submarine activity in the area were not signalled to her by the British *Admiralty. On 6 May 1915 she approached southern Ireland. According to her sailing orders she should have been steering a zigzag *course and had been instructed to keep away from landfalls, but these instructions were ignored and she approached the Old Head of Kinsale on a steady course at a speed of 21 knots when at about 1415 on 7 May a torpedo struck her *starboard side, fired from the German submarine *U.20*, the explosion of the torpedo being shortly followed by a second. Great loss of life was caused by the rapidity with which she sank—she went under in twenty minutes—and because she was *listing so heavily, and was at so steep an angle bows-down when she sank, that it was difficult to get her lifeboats away. Out of the 1,959 passengers and crew aboard, 1,198 were drowned, including over 100 American citizens.

President Theodore Roosevelt called the sinking *piracy 'on a vaster scale than the worst pirates of history'. At the time the Germans claimed, quite wrongly, she was an armed merchant cruiser carrying troops from Canada. When the USA declared war on Germany in 1917 the latter's submarine warfare was given as one of the reasons for the declaration.

The ship was sunk in 90 metres (295 ft) of water and was first visited by a diver in 1935 after she had been located by *echo sounder, and in the 1960s an American diver bought her remains from the British government. Over a period of time he tried to establish what exactly had sunk her, but was unable to do so. Then with the advance in *diving technology, the ship's remains were explored properly in 1982 and a number of artefacts were brought to the surface as well as hundreds of military fuses. This appeared to verify suspicions that she had been illegally carrying military explosives, and that this had caused the second explosion. However, an expedition led by Dr Robert *Ballard in 1993 found no proof that this was what had sunk her. She is now protected by the Irish government.

Ballard, R., *Exploring the Lusitania* (1995).
Ramsay, D., *Lusitania: Saga and Myth* (2001).

lutchet, a mast fitting in the form of a *tabernacle used in *spritsail *barges and *wherries to enable the mast to be lowered to deck level when passing under bridges etc. The mast, stepped on deck, is held in place by the lutchet, the after side of which is left open to allow free passage of the mast when it is lowered. It differs from a tabernacle, whose forward side is left open, in that the mast is pivoted at the base and not at the top of the fitting.

Lutine bell, the bell of HMS *Lutine* which was recovered after she sank in a heavy gale off the mouth of what was the Zuider Zee in October 1799. She was carrying a large amount of coin and bullion, and since this was private and not government money the burden of the loss fell on the *underwriters who had insured it. The bell was brought to the surface during *salvage operations and, since the underwriters who had borne the loss were members of *Lloyd's of London, it was taken to Lloyd's where it still hangs. It is rung whenever there is an important announcement to be made to the underwriters.

Lyonesse, a legendary country supposed to lie off the southern coast of Cornwall, England, which is frequently mentioned in the various legends associated with King Arthur and his Knights of the Round Table. The country, including its sudden and unexplained disappearance beneath the sea, is described in great detail in several early English chronicles, such as that of Florence of Worcester, who died in 1118. See also ATLANTIS; AVALON; BRASIL.

macaroni lug, see STANDING LUG.

macaroni mate, a man signed on as *mate in a merchant vessel though without the required qualifications and without pay. The origin of the term, and the practice, is believed to have arisen at the time of the Napoleonic occupation of Genoa and Livorno in 1796. Many of the sons and favourite employees of the English merchants at these places were signed on in this way by American merchant ships to escape capture by the French, and possible *impressment at sea if the ship were stopped by British *cruisers.

Impressment at sea by the British Navy was permissible in the case of British nationals serving in foreign ships, but it was thought that British naval officers would be unlikely to question the nationality of a man serving as mate, or second-in-command, of an American ship. Such a rank automatically implied American nationality and it was not difficult for an Englishman to assume an American accent, if questioned, with a good chance of getting away with it.

Madoc, a Welsh sailor, probably legendary, who in the 12th century is said to have dreamed of a new continent beyond the western horizons and to have sailed in search of it, discovering America nearly 350 years before *Columbus reached it in 1492 and spending the remainder of his life with the indigenous people. The story was widely believed in Wales, and its acceptance grew with reports filtering back of hunters and traders in the new continent having met local inhabitants who spoke Welsh. It received a tremendous boost in 1669 when the Revd Morgan Jones returned from a missionary tour through North Carolina with a story of how he and some companions were captured by local inhabitants who threatened to kill them. When Jones turned to his companions and told them, in Welsh, to prepare themselves for death, their captors were said to have understood Jones's remark, welcomed them as cousins, and set them free. But when between 1792 and 1797 another Welsh preacher, John Evans, explored the valleys of the Mississippi, Missouri, and Ohio rivers in search of Welsh-speaking indigenous people he was unable to find one. There is general acceptance today that the story of Madoc's discovery is a complete myth and that Columbus can remain unchallenged in his claim to fame so far as Madoc is concerned.

Mae West, a large parachute *spinnaker used by large racing *yachts, particularly the *Big Class, during the 1930s. It acquired this nickname from the large swelling curve it took up when filled with wind, reminding the crew of the film actress Mae West, whose feminine curves delighted cinema audiences at that time.

***Maelduin,* The Voyage of,** a well-known Irish romance which dates back to the 8th century and records the travels of Maelduin, the foster-son of an Irish queen, who sailed with seventeen companions in search of his father's murderer. The account of their voyages is given in considerable detail in the manuscript *Imram Curaig Maildúin*, preserved in the Royal Irish Academy in Dublin. It has a distinct resemblance to the account of the voyage of St *Brendan, and is no doubt based to some extent on the older stories of the wanderings of Jason and *Odysseus.

maelstrom, a term commonly accepted as meaning a whirlpool, or a great *storm. In fact, it is a strong *current which rips past the southern end of Moskenaes Island in the Lofoten group off the west coast of Norway. Also known as the Maskenstrom, it is marked on a map of the area which appears in the 1594 edition of an *atlas by Gerhardus Mercator, who produced the *Mercator projection. The word would appear to come from the Dutch *malen*, to grind, and *strom*, stream or current.

Magellan, Ferdinand (*c.*1480–1521), Portuguese *navigator. He was born at Villa de Sabrosa in Trás-os-Montes and was the inspirer and commander of the first known circumnavigation of the globe. After passing his early years as a page and attendant at the Portuguese court of John II, he sailed to India in 1505 with Francisco d'Almeida, first Portuguese viceroy of the East. Four years later he joined Diogo Lopes de Sequeira for his voyage from Cochin to the Spice Islands (Moluccas), and was then employed on an expedition to explore them which produced apparently limitless amounts of spices.

In 1512 Magellan returned to Portugal where he was raised to the noble rank of *fidalgo escudeiro*. He was lamed for life in 1513 during the attack on a Moroccan town, was then accused of trading with the enemy, and fell into disfavour. Renouncing his nationality, he proceeded to Spain in October 1517 and was granted permission by the king, Charles I, to try and reach the Spice Islands by steering westwards, then sailing south of the New World into the *South Seas discovered four years earlier.

With his flag in the *Trinidad*, Magellan led his *squadron of five ships across the Atlantic in September 1519, making a landfall near Pernambuco. He then coasted south to the River Plate estuary, which he searched in the hope of finding a strait, before sailing on to reach Port St Julian on 31 March 1520. There, after crushing a dangerous *mutiny, he settled down to pass the winter. He named the natives of the place Patagonians (big feet) because of their great size.

Starting out again in August 1520, on 21 October 1520 he discovered the long and tortuous strait that today bears his name. Thirty-eight days later his squadron, with the exception of one ship which had deserted, emerged into the ocean which, from the gentle weather with which it received him, Magellan named the Pacific. Ninety-eight days of appalling hardship from starvation and *scurvy followed before an island, probably Guam, was reached. After three days of rest and refreshment there, the ships sailed on to reach Cebu in the Philippines on 9 March 1521.

Here Magellan made friends with the native ruler who, in order to endear himself to his Spanish visitors, embraced the Catholic faith. On the pretext of wishing to conquer the island of Mactan for Catholicism, he persuaded Magellan to lead an expedition against it. On 27 April 1521 Magellan was killed in the fight against the islanders and the ruler of Cebu then proceeded to murder many of the remaining leaders of the expedition. Two ships, the *Trinidad* and the *caravel, *Vittoria*, got away, but the *Trinidad*, being leaky and undermanned, was forced to remain in Borneo. However, the *Vittoria*, under Juan Sebastián del Cano (*c.*1476–1526), a *pilot whom Magellan

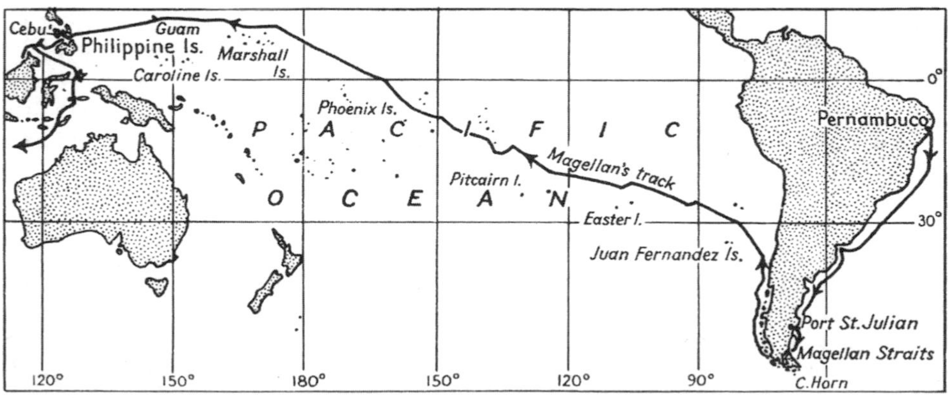

Magellan's track across the Pacific

had embarked for the circumnavigation, made her way home by way of the Cape of Good Hope. She eventually reached Seville in July 1522, with only 31 of the 270 men who had set out aboard her. Del Cano, especially, was lucky to be alive as he had only narrowly escaped execution for mutiny at Port St Julian.

Another of the survivors was Antonio Pigafetta, whom Magellan had taken with him to record the historic voyage, and he wrote an account of it. His original MS was widely copied, the best and most accurate versions being the Ambrosiana MS, which is the text followed in the *Hakluyt Society volume of 1874, and the Phillips MS, now in Yale University's library. A large number of anonymous narratives of the voyage appeared in due course, but only Pigafetta's is known to be genuinely contemporary.

magellanic clouds, a popular name for the two *nebiculae*, or cloudy-looking areas in the southern sky, which comprise a great number of small stars much resembling the Milky Way. They were named after Ferdinand *Magellan.

magnetic compass, a compass which depends for its directive property on the horizontal component of the earth's magnetic field. Its origins are obscure and although the earliest references to its use at sea are Chinese (before 1050), there is no direct evidence that it came to the West from China, nor that Arab ships were instrumental in bringing it. The earliest recorded mention of its use in the West was in 1180, although there are grounds for thinking it was in use well before that. No one person has been credited with the invention of the magnetic compass but it is clear that, in the West, it first appeared in the Mediterranean (by local legend in Amalfi).

The forerunner of the modern magnetic compass consisted of a magnetized needle thrust into a straw or piece of cork which floated freely in a basin of water. On settling, the marked end of the needle indicated the direction of magnetic north. In later times a primitive pivoted needle or needle system was used to serve the same purpose, and later still a compass card, on which the points of the compass were drawn, was attached to a needle magnetized by the oxide of iron *lodestone, and the whole was enclosed in a suitable bowl to afford protection, the bowl in turn being mounted in *gimbals in a *binnacle.

The magnetic compass was an imperfect instrument until after the time when the first iron ship appeared. The magnetism inherent in an iron ship's structure caused considerably difficulty in the early days, to such an extent that it was suggested seriously that such ships would never be successful for they would be quite unsafe in the absence of well-behaved compasses.

On wooden vessels the directive power of a magnetic compass is dependent, apart from relatively minor effects of ironwork fittings in its vicinity, on the earth's magnetism. Nevertheless, as far back as the beginning of the 19th century, Matthew *Flinders, the British *navigator and explorer, discovered that the compass needle might be deviated from the direction of magnetic north as a result of local attraction, as it was termed, of the ship's iron. He demonstrated that this *deviation was at a maximum with ships' *courses of east or west by compass and disappeared when a ship steered north or south. He also showed how the ship's magnetic effect could be neutralized by means of an unmagnetized rod of iron placed vertically near the compass. This form of corrector is still universally used and is named a **Flinders bar**.

With the advent of iron and steel ships, a great deal of study was directed to the nature of ship magnetism with the object of devising a method of neutralizing it at the compass position. Among those who engaged themselves in this important work was the Astronomer Royal, Sir G. B. Airy, who had the iron steamer *Rainbow* placed at his disposal in 1838. From his careful examination of the vessel's magnetic condition, he introduced a method of neutralizing a ship's magnetism by placing magnets and pieces of unmagnetized iron, or correctors, in the vicinity of the compass. To find what correctors are needed to neutralize a ship's magnetism it is necessary to *swing every vessel fitted with a magnetic compass, including *yachts. See also THOMSON, WILLIAM.

magnitude, as it applies to nautical astronomy, refers to the apparent brightness or luminosity of any of the navigational stars or planets.

First to classify stars according to their apparent brightness was Hipparchus (*c.*190–after 126 BC), the prince of ancient astronomers. His system comprised six magnitude classes, the small group of some fourteen of the brighter stars forming the group of first-magnitude stars, and the relatively large number of faint stars just visible to the naked eye forming the group of sixth-magnitude stars. This rough and ready classification was improved during the 19th century with the introduction of a decimal scale of magnitudes, and the extension of the magnitude scale to include telescopic stars whose magnitude numbers are more than 600, and fractional and negative magnitudes. Sir John Herschel, son of the astronomer Sir William Herschel, is credited with having suggested that a star of magnitude 1.0 should be regarded as being 100 times as bright as a star of magnitude 6.0.

*Nautical almanacs include tables providing for the navigational use of selected stars of the first and second magnitude, but those of lower magnitudes are never used for observation although they may form part of the constellation which enable the navigational stars to be identified. See also CELESTIAL NAVIGATION.

Mahan, Alfred Thayer (1840–1914), US naval officer and strategist, born at West Point. He graduated from the Naval Academy at Annapolis in 1859, and during the American Civil War (1861–5) served in blockading vessels and as a staff officer. Promoted captain in 1885, he served afloat before being appointed president of the Naval War College in 1886 where he had previously lectured. His first book, on the Civil War, *The Gulf and Inland Waters*, had appeared in 1883 and in 1890 *The Influence of Sea Power upon History, 1660–1783*, based on his lectures at the War College, was published in Boston. Two years later *The Influence of Sea Power upon the French Revolution and Empire, 1793–1812* was published in two volumes, and the same year he published a biography of Admiral Farragut.

In 1893 Mahan was appointed to command the *cruiser *Chicago*, flagship of the European station. In May and June 1894 the *Chicago* was at Gravesend, near London, and Mahan received honorary degrees from both Cambridge and Oxford universities, though at this time he had not received similar honours from any American university.

Mahon retired from the navy in 1896, but was recalled to active duty in 1898 for the Spanish–American War and made a member of the Naval War Board. Writing in 1901, he recorded that earlier in his career he had been an 'anti-imperialist' but declared that his studies had altered his views, and in 1893 had begun to advocate 'guardianship' of the Hawaiian Islands. As a member of the War Board he advocated the transfer of the Philippine Islands to the USA, a proposal which created a sharp conflict of political opinions.

Mahan was one of five American delegates to the first Hague Conference which took place in 1899. During the following years he wrote many articles on naval history, strategy, and foreign policy for various periodicals at home and abroad. Some of these, particularly those touching on questions in the political field, offended a number of Americans who held that political controversy was not the proper field for a historian.

In addition to the four works published before 1895, mentioned above, Mahan also wrote *The Life of Nelson: The Embodiment of the Sea Power of Great Britain* (2 vols., 1897), *Sea Power in its Relations to the War of 1812* (1905), and *The Major Operations of the Navies in the War of American Independence* (1913), and was a pioneer of geopolitics with *The Problems of Asia* (1900). His series of lectures between 1887 and 1911, published as *Naval Strategy Compared and Contrasted with the Principles and Practice of Military Operations on Land* (1911), summed up his views that command of the sea, gained in battle or by the possession of an all-powerful battle fleet, was the key to world power.

The influence of Mahan's works on the navies of most maritime nations was profound. His books were closely studied at most naval staff colleges and war colleges and his arguments were brought forward in many nations to divert a larger proportion of national income to the building of larger and more balanced navies.

Seager, R., *Alfred Thayer Mahan: The Man and his Letters* (1977).

mainsail, the principal sail of a sailing vessel. On a *square-rigged vessel this is the lowermost (and largest) sail carried on the mainmast, and is usually termed the main *course. The earliest known mainsails in European waters, as depicted on Roman pottery and mosaics of the 3rd century AD were set with a *sprit. This *rig held good in the Netherlands and North Sea ports until about the 15th century, when the sprit was superseded by the *gaff rig, while in the eastern Mediterranean it became the *lateen. Thames sailing barges, however, are still rigged with sprit mainsails for ease of handling with a crew of two.

In the past the mainsail on gaff-rigged *smacks was *loose footed while on other types of craft used for commercial *fisheries, such as the *bawley or Plymouth *hooker, it had an extra long gaff and no boom, the mainsheet being led from two or more points on the sail's *leech to *blocks on the *horse on the *counter. In Bermuda from the late 18th century a simple form of triangular or jib-headed mainsail was used on local *sloop-rigged boats, which was set on a sharply raked mast having a long boom but no gaff. In this early version the boom was almost as long as the *luff of the sail. A more sophisticated application of this type of sail is the *Bermudan rig, which was adapted by a few small racing yachts in the USA at the end of the 19th century. By the First World War (1914–18) it had become the normal rig for the smaller *International Metre Class yachts in Europe, and by the 1930s was almost universal amongst racing yachts of all sizes, including the *J-class. By then it had developed into a very tall and narrow sail with a luff-to-foot proportion—or *aspect ratio—of, in the case of the J-class, about 3 : 1. Nowadays many mainsails are fully *battened to provide an almost rigid aerofoil which does not flap or shiver, and which is just one step away from a solid aerofoil.

'mainsail haul', the order given when a *square-rigged ship was being *tacked in order to *brace round the after *yards. The timing of the order was vital during the operations if the ship was not to be caught in *stays. The moment was after the sails on the foremast had been *backed and the ship was almost head to wind.

make and mend, a half-day's holiday on board ship. The term originates from the custom of relieving men from ship's duties on one afternoon each week to give them a chance to make and mend their clothing. See also SAILORS' DRESS.

make her number, to, see SIGNAL LETTERS.

Mallows, the old English name for the French port of Saint-Malo, often to be found in English books of the sea of the 15th–17th centuries. Samuel *Pepys uses this version in his diary, as does Richard *Hakluyt in his *Principall Navigations.*

manger, a small space in the bows of a ship immediately abaft the *hawsepipes and bounded on the after side by a low *coaming called a manger-board. Its purpose was to prevent any water from running *aft along the deck should it enter through the hawsepipes. It applied principally to sailing ships and the early steamships when the hawsepipes were on the maindeck level. In modern ships, where the hawsepipes are on the *forecastle deck level, the same purpose is achieved by an *athwartships breakwater abaft the *cable-holders.

mangroves, tropical trees that grow with their roots in salt and brackish water. Worldwide there are 65 species belonging to twenty different plant families. Mangroves grow in dense thickets along sheltered muddy shorelines, often in estuaries where the sea water is diluted and temperatures stay above 24 °C (75.2 °F). Mangrove forests probably once lined 75% of tropical coastlines, but over half have now been destroyed. Currently throughout the world, mangrove forests cover 180,000 square kilometres (69,498 sq. mls.). Mangroves are used for timber and to make charcoal. They are being cleared because of urbanization, and to make way for prawn farms. A square metre of mangrove swamp annually produces a kilogram of leaf litter, which attracts large numbers of animals, including *seahorses. In northern Australia 75% of commercial *fish spend some of their lives in mangrove swamps. As the large quantities of leaf litter rot, the oxygen in the mud is used up, so it becomes black and smelly. Mangroves have various adaptations to cope with this, ranging from aerial roots (in *Avicennia*) to stilt roots (in *Rhizophora*). Conserving healthy mangrove forests is important not only because of the rich diversity they support, but also because they provide

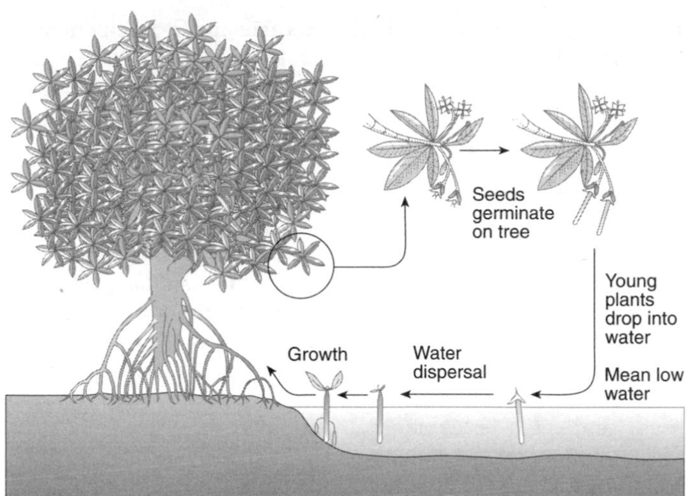

The life cycle of viviparous mangrove trees

protection against the destructive forces of *tropical storms and *tsunami. See also MARINE PLANTS.

http://www.env.qld.gov.au/environment/coast/habitats/m html
http://www.ncl.ac.uk/tcmweb/tcm/mglinks.htm

M. V. Angel

manifest, an official document for consular authorities and Customs, which is carried by all merchant ships. It differs from the *bill of lading in that it is drawn up when the cargo has been loaded, whereas the bill of lading details what has been delivered for loading. A ship cannot enter or clear a port unless its manifest has been passed at the custom house.

manila, the fibre of the wild banana plant, from which is manufactured a rope much used at sea before the introduction of synthetic rope, as it had good strength and spring. The plant is grown in the Philippines, and the rope takes its name from the capital of those islands. When made up into rope it is a golden brown in colour and was mainly used for such purposes as a boat's *falls, or in *tackles where considerable weights were liable to be lifted. It was the most dependable of the ropes made from natural fibres and did not need to be tarred, as did *hemp and *sisal rope.

manta ray (*Manta birostris*), a member of the family Mylobatidae that includes 42 species of rays that are relatives of *sharks with bodies that are flattened dorso-ventrally. Mantas swim using their pectoral fins like wings. The tail is rodlike and unarmed. On either side of the head are two lappets that protrude forward like horns, hence their popular name of devilfish—a misnomer because they are placid gentle giants. The lappets herd *plankton and small *fishes into the mouth. A fully-grown manta has a wingspan of 9 metres (29 ft) and it weighs 1,350 kilograms (3000 lb.). They occur everywhere in the tropics. A female manta gives birth to one or two large young, each having a wingspan of 1.2 metres (4 ft) and weighing 10 kilograms (22 lb). Mating mantas occasionally *breach, leaping 5 metres (16.5 ft) clear of the water.

M. V. Angel

man the yards, to, or **man ship, to,** a form of ceremonial salute in a warship with masts and *yards in the days of sail to honour the visit of a high official. The yards were lined by men standing upon them supported by *lifelines rigged between the *lifts and the masts and with one man, known as the button-man, standing on the *truck of each *topgallant mast. In the British Navy this form of salute continued until about 1885 when sail finally gave way to *steam propulsion. But the practice is still occasionally seen in *square-rigged ships used for *sail training, and in shore training establishments which have a mast crossed with yards.

marconi rig, sometimes confused with the *Bermudan rig, particularly in the USA where for a long time it was a synonymous term. It was introduced by the *yacht designer Charles E. Nicholson onto the 15-metre (49.5-ft) *Istria* in 1912. He did away with the traditional *gaff rig where the *topmast is fitted on to a *fid on the lower mast. Instead, he socketed a hollow topmast into the mainmast, so that it looked like a single *spar. This meant that the *luff of the triangular-shaped *jackyard topsail could be set on a track on the socketed topmast, which enabled it to be raised and lowered much more quickly during a race, a handy advantage. It also meant the topsail *yard could be discarded, which saved weight aloft, another advantage when racing. However, this type of mast had to have a complicated series of *stays to keep it upright as it was very much taller than that used in the gaff rig. The system of staying made it look like the new Marconi radio masts for transmitting *Morse code, hence its nickname.

The use of the Bermudan rig in the smaller racing classes had been encouraged by the introduction of the *International Metre Class in 1907, but the technical difficulties of staying the mast, and the conservatism of the owners, prevented its introduction into the larger classes. However, once the staying of the marconi mast had been mastered it was a logical step to introduce the Bermudan rig into the *Big Class which raced between the wars.

The marconi rig caused quite a stir when it was introduced, and when one old tar was asked during a regatta what he thought of it, he replied: 'If I was at the top o' one o' them, I should reckon I was a long way from home.'

Marco Polo (*c.*1254–1324), Venetian traveller who was famous for his overland journey to the court of Kublai Khan in Peking, his seventeen years in China in the Great Khan's service, and his sea voyage to Persia on his way home. Marco was his forename, but he is not normally referred to only by his surname. His father Nicolo had made an overland journey to Cambaluc (Peking) with Nicolo's brother Maffeo. The two brothers had returned to Venice in 1269, bringing letters from the Great Khan to the pope requesting the dispatch of a body of educated men to teach Christianity and the liberal arts.

After a delay of two years owing to an interregnum following the death of Pope Clement IV, the two brothers set out again with a reply from Pope Gregory X, though without teachers. With them they took the young Marco and arrived at the Khan's court in September 1275. The Great Khan was much taken with Marco, who decided to learn the many languages of the nationalities subject to the Mongol emperor. Kublai employed him in the public service in the course of which he travelled widely throughout the empire and, for three years, was governor of the city of Yangchow.

When the Polos had been in China more than ten years they became anxious to return home with the great wealth they had acquired. Kublai was unwilling to let them go, however, and it was not until their request was reinforced by the pleas of envoys from the Mongol king of Persia, the grandson of Kublai's brother Hulagu, that he relented. The envoys had arrived to escort back to Persia a Mongol bride for their master. Owing to the perils of the overland route, their journey was to be made by sea, and they begged that the Polos, particularly Marco, who had recently visited the Indies, might accompany them to give them the benefit of the Polos's experience. Reluctantly, the Khan consented and, at the beginning of 1292, the expedition, comprising some 600 sailors and courtiers in fourteen ships, sailed from Zaitun (Changchow). This fleet touched at what is now Vietnam before arriving at Sumatra, where the ships were delayed for some months waiting for the seasonal shift of the *monsoon winds. It then made its way past the Nicobar Islands before reaching Ceylon, and it then followed the west coast of India and southern Persia before arriving at Hormuz more than two years after its departure. These adventures did much to inspire later generations of *navigators, as did Marco Polo's written descriptions of what he had heard and seen during his time in China.

The Polos travelled on overland to Venice where they arrived towards the end of 1295. Three years later a maritime war between Genoa and Venice culminated in the great *galley battle of Curzola in which the former was completely victorious and more than 60 Venetian galleys were destroyed. One of these had been commanded by Marco Polo who became one of the 7,000 prisoners carried off to Genoa. There he was imprisoned for nearly a year during which he dictated the material for the book which described his experiences. Little is known of Marco Polo's history following his release. His will, now in St Mark's Library, Venice, was made on 9 January 1324 and it is almost certain that he died the same year.

The Travels of Marco Polo, trans. R. Latham (1958).
Olschki, L., *Marco Polo's Asia* (1960).

Marcq Saint-Hilaire method, a method of *sight reduction proposed by Captain (later Admiral) Marcq de Blond de Saint-Hilaire in an influential paper entitled 'Calcul du point observé' published in 1875 in the French *Revue maritime et coloniale*. The process described became known to the French as the *méthode du point rapproché* and, some years later, to the British *navigation establishment as the *intercept method, on which nearly all *sight reduction methods one way or another are still based. The concept of the astronomical *position line, a section of a circle of equal *altitude small enough to be treated as a straight line, was due to Captain Sumner and is now known as the *Sumner position line. Saint-Hilaire's contribution, some 70 years later, was not so much a new mathematical process as a fresh approach to the whole subject. This saw *zenith distance as the same thing as geographical distance, so that a *sextant observation of a celestial body in fact measures the distance from the body's geographical position in *nautical miles. The concepts are straightforward. For every heavenly body at a given instant there is a spot on the earth's surface, its geographical position, where it is at the *zenith. For anywhere else the body's observed altitude subtracted from 90° gives its zenith distance which determines a circle of equal altitude, with its centre at the geographical position of the body, somewhere along which the observer's position must lie.

The navigator is only interested in a small segment of this circle near his estimated position, which may without significant distortion be plotted as a straight line, the position line. The intercept is the difference between the calculated and the measured zenith distances and is plotted on the *chart towards or away from the position from which the sight has been worked according to whether the observed or calculated altitude is the greater. From that point the position line is drawn at right angles. See also CELESTIAL NAVIGATION. Mike Richey

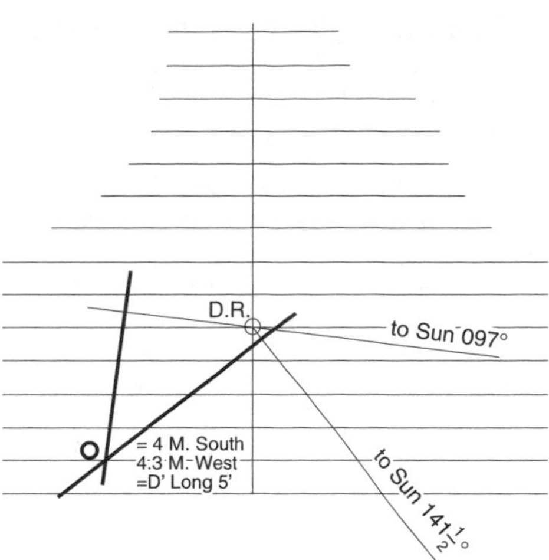

A Marcq Saint-Hilaire plot. The two position lines (in bold) are plotted at right angles to the azimuths at a distance from the D.R. corresponding to the length of the intercepts. The plot here is drawn in a notebook where one line space equals a mile. The only instrument required is a protractor

Marder, Arthur Jacob (1910–80), Harvard University-educated American historian who established his reputation as being the foremost proponent of British naval history of his day with his two earliest books, *The Anatomy of British Sea Power* (1940) and *Portrait of an Admiral* (1952), a biography of Admiral Sir Herbert Richmond. Both showed a remarkable degree of scholarship and insight into the period in which his main interest lay, from about 1896 to 1920. He followed these up with three volumes devoted to the correspondence of Admiral Sir John Fisher, under the title *Fear God and Dread Nought* (1952–9).

This interest in Fisher led naturally to an equal interest in his immediate naval successors, and thus to the activities of the British Navy in the First World War (1914–18). This was the theme of his next major work, in five volumes, published between 1961 and 1970, under the title *From the Dreadnought to Scapa Flow*. It is a work which is still widely regarded as a classic naval history of the years 1904–19.

Among his subsequent publications were *From the Dardenelles to Oran* (1974) and *Operation 'Menace'* (1976). Marder was awarded an honorary CBE in 1970.

mare clausum, or **'Closed Sea',** an old term used in connection with the claim by certain maritime nations to exclusive ownership of areas of open sea or ocean. Spain, in the 15th and 16th centuries, claimed dominion of whole oceans; Britain, in the 17th century, similarly claimed dominion of all the *Narrow Seas surrounding her. The obvious difficulties of such a doctrine, particularly for ships passing through these waters and for those involved in *fisheries etc., led to attempts to modify these outrageous claims among the nations concerned.

In 1609 Grotius wrote his *Mare Liberum*, or 'free sea', in which he advocated the unrestricted right of all ships to use all waters and particularly the right of Dutch fisherman to catch *fish in waters off the English coast. His argument was answered in 1631 by an English jurist, John Selden (1584–1654), who wrote *Mare Clausum*, which upheld the doctrine of that waters contiguous to the coastline of a country should be solely under the dominion of that country. Such arguments led eventually to the introduction of *territorial waters. See also EXCLUSIVE ECONOMIC ZONE; UNITED NATIONS CONFERENCE ON THE LAW OF THE SEA.

marina, a term said to have originated since the Second World War (1939–45) in the USA to describe a sheltered man-made harbour comprising a complex of floating *piers and *jetties which provides safe *berths for *yachts. Normally, marinas also have such facilities as food stores and a chandlery for yacht owners, and often a *yacht club, too.

marine and underwater archaeology. Humankind's artefacts litter the seabed, partly as a result of mercantile and naval activities, but also because landscapes have become submerged. This submergence is not only the result of the *sea level rising as the *ice caps melted at the end of last glaciation 20,000 years ago, but also a result of tectonic movements. For example, the southern half of the North Sea was only inundated by the sea about 7,000 years ago. Up until then it had been sparsely populated by bands of stone age hunter-gatherers and in 2003 two stone-age settlements dating back to the Mesolithic period, between 10,000 and 5,000 years ago, were found off the coast of Tyneside. The seashore always offered a rich abundance of resources for these early peoples. In historical times tribes of North American indigenous peoples such as the Haida of the Vancouver region had lifestyles intimately adapted to life on the coast. On islands in the Caribbean the refuse tips or middens left by the Caribs, when excavated, have shown how the diets of these coastal peoples changed, partly because of *climate change, but also because of their impact on the resources they were exploiting. *Sea levels also change locally because of tectonic movements. These can be slow, gradual shifts: for example in south-east Britain the land is sinking about 1 mm per year, fast enough to turn several coastal archaeological sites into marine sites over the centuries. However, in many places siltation has meant that harbours used in Roman and medieval times are now some distance from the sea. In the Mediterranean the impact of the African tectonic plate pushing up against the Eurasian plate has been rotating the island of Crete so that Graeco-Roman harbours are now high and dry above sea level on one side of the island but submerged on the other.

Some tectonic movements are sudden and violent. On Christmas Day 1968 a strong earthquake near Anchorage in Alaska resulted in vertical shifts of some parts of the coast by over a metre, and Charles *Darwin was greatly influenced by witnessing the impact of a metre shift in sea level near Santiago in Chile. But perhaps the most significant archaeological event was the explosive end of the island of Santorini in the Mediterranean that brought the Minoan civilization centred on Crete to an abrupt end. Such events add to the archaeological record not only by dropping local sea levels but also through the destructive power of the *tsunamis they generate, which wash immense numbers of artefacts into the sea.

Perhaps one of the most remarkable prehistorical underwater sites is the Cosquer Cave near Marseille, which is at the end of a 175-metre- (575-ft)-long tunnel 37 metres (120 ft) below sea level. The cave is not accessible to the general public, but it is now possible to make a virtual visit to see the remarkable paintings of horse, ibex, aurochs, *jellyfish, great *auks, and human hands, which were probably painted during the last glaciation when the sea was 70 metres (230 ft) lower than today.

However, in most people's minds marine archaeology is associated with *shipwrecks. The long history of seafaring stretches well back into prehistory and, inevitably, where there has been a high density of shipping accidents have occurred. Before the advent of effective *navigation instruments, seafarers tended to hug coastlines, where so many shipwrecks occurred. *Warfare at sea has also added to the profusion of shipwrecks on the seabed. Examples range from the great Mediterranean naval battles of early times, to sinkings of the **Mary Rose* off Portsmouth, the *Swan*, a Cromwellian warship, off Mull, the destruction of the *Spanish Armada by Atlantic storms in 1588, and the sinking of 20 million tonnes of shipping during the Second World War (1939–45). Some of the latter are now conserved as war graves, such as the *battleship HMS *Royal Oak* in *Scapa Flow and the USS *Arizona* in Pearl Harbor. Shipwrecks are a magnet to those whose techniques are destructive and aimed at maximizing financial profit, rather than maximizing the recovery of archaeological data. There is a fine dividing line between shipwrecks suitable for *salvage and those that should be treated as historical monuments.

Marine archaeology began in earnest once *diving technology had advanced sufficiently for the diving bell to be invented, although Roman 'urinators', or free divers, had salvaged cargoes from sunken ships in the Mediterranean. But the greatest advance, so far as marine archaeology was concerned, came with the aqualung, so long associated with Jacques *Cousteau, supplemented by the earlier invention of flippers. Since then technologies based on *satellite navigation, both above and under water, air-lifts, dynamic positioning of recovery vessels, use of gas mixtures, *sonars, and robotics have all added to the array of techniques used by marine archaeologists to solve the particular challenges presented by working in the hostile marine environment.

The first task is to locate a site. Recorded historical evidence and artefacts washed up or found in fishermen's *trawls can sometimes provide an approximate position. In shallow water or in the inter-tidal zone, shipwrecks may be discovered by chance by recreational divers or by walkers. In deeper water, beyond the safe limits for diving, side-scan sonars are now being used, supplemented by observations with *underwater vehicles.

Before any excavation is carried out, a fine-scale survey needs to be conducted, using traditional land-based techniques, of laying out grid lines with tapes, drawing, photographing, and mapping features on the seabed. Sediment is removed and sieved for tiny finds. The exact positions of artefacts as they are uncovered are plotted, and possibly removed for conservation. The lifting of whole sections of hull, such as occurred with the *Mary Rose* and the **Vasa*, requires the heavy lifting gear used in salvage operations, but the vast majority of wrecks are left *in situ*.

Artefacts are dated using various isotope techniques and dendrochronology—the use of tree rings, which yield a precise dating signature if the location where the original tree grew is known. Once in the air and light, deterioration is rapid unless immediate conservation action is taken. Metal objects are often X-rayed and treated by electrolysis, attaching them to anodes to reverse their degradation. Organic items, wood, fabric, and leather, need to be consolidated by infusing them with polyethylene glycol or freeze dried, a process that, in the case of the *timbers of the *Vasa* and the *Mary Rose*, is ongoing and requires decades of treatment. Such artefacts are rarely preserved in sites on land and provide direct evidence of trading practices, woodworking techniques, food storage, medicinal preparations, weaving techniques, and so on. Human remains are particularly interesting because they are the remains of people who died at the peak of their active lives. Their physical attributes are often very informative. For example, the archers drowned on the *Mary Rose* had physiques that made them able to draw weights greater than those of modern Olympic athletes; and the seamen on the *Swan* had suffered from rickets.

Delgado, J. (ed.), *Encylopaedia of Underwater and Maritime Archaeology* (1997).

Marx, R., *An Introduction to Marine Archaeology: The Underwater Dig* (1976).

www.indiana.edu/~classics/aegean/R17.html

www.decadevolcano.net/santorini/minoan-eruption.htm
www.adp.fsu.edu
www.maryrose.org
www.culture.fr/culture/archeosm/en

M. V. Angel

marine biology is the study of all aspects of ecology and life histories of marine organisms. The primary focus is on the organisms and their local interactions with their physical, chemical, and biological environments. Many marine biologists study the natural history of organisms that live in coastal and inshore environments, and so are more readily accessible and can be used in experimental studies. So the scope of marine biology as a scientific discipline overlaps that of *biological oceanography. Biological oceanographers tend to be more concerned about large-scale distribution patterns, how substances like carbon flow through the ocean system and how the living communities are responding to the motion of the ocean and different spatial scales. They often use 'proxies', for example using the volume of sound back-scattered echo-sounding to track and quantify *fish and *plankton, and estimating the quantities of the *marine plant called phytoplankton in a water sample by measuring the amount of chlorophyll it contains. Marine biologists are much more concerned with the organisms themselves and their responses to other species, and their chemical and physical environment.

Thus, on a rocky beach the *seaweeds and their grazers tend to be vertically zoned as a result of their differing abilities to withstand exposure to the air at low *tide. The species also vary in their abilities to withstand being battered by *waves, so different types of animal and plants are found on beaches that are either sheltered from, or exposed to, heavy surf. Predation and grazing pressures alter the structure of habitats. For example kelp, the straplike seaweeds that grow profusely in places at, and below, the low tide mark on rocky shores, form complex three-dimensional forests. These forests are full of local microhabitats each of which tends to be inhabited by different types of animals ranging from sea anemones to worms and *Crustacea. However, *echinoderms like sea urchins (*Echinus* spp.) can graze down these forests and reduce their diversity. Off California the populations of sea urchins are kept in check by one of the most charismatic of *marine mammals, the sea otter. When the sea otter populations crashed, because they were over-exploited for their fur, the sea urchins became so abundant they ate down the kelp forests along many shores.

Starfish (asteroids), another group of echinoderms, are active predators that consume many of the snails that graze down the seaweeds on the shore. They often feed selectively on the most abundant species and as a result the less common species are more successful, and the numbers of species able to live on the shore increases. In experimental areas on a rocky shore from which marine biologists removed all starfish, the populations of grazing snails became far less diverse.

Behaviour can be important to those studying marine biology. For example, the crustacean sandhoppers (*Talitrus* spp.) that are often found feeding in large numbers on the dead seaweed that piles up along the strandline on sandy beaches lay their eggs in the sand. The young hatchlings have to find their way down to the sea, but how do they know which way to hop? The answer seems to be that they navigate according to the patterns of polarized light in the sky, and the correct way down the beach is passed to the egg as chemical information by the female as she is laying. If a polarizing filter is placed over the eggs to that the sky pattern is reversed, the newly hatched youngsters hop inland.

Tait, R., and Dipper, F., *Elements of Marine Ecology* (1998).

M. V. Angel

marine literature. 'The history of the world', wrote Thomas Carlyle, 'is but the biography of great men', and the same can be said of the history of ships and the sea. It is through the biographies and literature of the men who have lived and fought on the sea, and who have undertaken great voyages of *exploration by sea, that we are able to chart the growth of the world as we know it today.

Early Literature. Although the Phoenicians and the Egyptians were among the earliest known users of the sea, the Greeks were the first to write about it. Homer's heroic epics provide some of the earliest examples of sea literature we possess. The Romans, less romantic and more practical mariners, wrote comparatively little about it. Virgil (70–19 BC), who studied Greek, appears to have borrowed some of Homer's nautical genius for expression when writing about ships and the sea, but the inspiration which led Catullus (*c*.84–54 BC) to write in such moving terms about the laying up of an old ship is exceptional.

Though doughty seamen, the Norsemen were men of action rather than of literature, and the eddas and sagas which they have left us are more in the nature of mythological stories of war and adventure than historical records, though the adventures of *Erik the Red and his son have been proved correct. The Welsh and the Irish had their sagas, too. The voyage of *Maelduin, and certainly that of *Madoc, are just fiction, but *Navigatio Brendani*, which describes the voyages of St *Brendan, is probably based on fact. That greatest of English writers, Geoffrey Chaucer (*c*.1342–1400), was familiar with the sea. He translated a treatise on the *astrolabe and 'knew all about English merchant shipping in the 14th century' (R. Hope, *A New History of British Shipping* (1990), 46), portraying the merchant in his Merchant's Tale as someone anxious to make sure the sea between East Anglia and the Low Countries was cleared of pirates.

Literature in the Age of Exploration. In 1516 Sir Thomas More (1478–1535) published *Utopia* which, for all its limited scope, managed to include the drama of seafaring. The early seamen knew little of the art of writing and their accounts of their voyages deal less with the hardships of their passages across the ocean than with the wonders they discovered at their journey's end. The first records of such discoveries come from Portuguese and Spanish sources and these accounts provoked the English seamen to emulate them. Such were *De Orbe Novo* (*c*.1511) by Peter Martyr d'Anghiera (1457–1526) and the collection of voyages by Giovanni Battista Ramusio (1485–1557) which began to appear in 1550. The doyen of English sea literature is Richard Eden (*c*.1512–76). In 1553 he translated Munster's *Cosmography* and in 1555 Peter Martyr's *Decades of the Newe Worlde or West India*, but he is chiefly remembered for his translation from the Spanish of Martin Cortes's *Breve compendio de la sphera y de la arte de navegar* (1551), which was published in English in 1561. As the practice of *navigation in England at that time was almost non-existent, this book gave a tremendous fillip to English explorers.

Eden has been described as a forerunner of the great Richard *Hakluyt to whom we owe an immense debt. Hakluyt rummaged through extant accounts of voyages, examining the papers of shipowners, merchants, and travellers, and was ably assisted in his work by Sir Walter *Raleigh. It was characteristic of him to include in his great anthology the first piece of naval propaganda of which we have knowledge, the anonymous 15th-century poem 'Libelle of Englysshe Policie'. Among the memorable pieces of narrative literature he preserved was the account of the last voyage of Sir Humphrey Gilbert (*c*.1539–83) in the *Squirrel* when, on his way home from founding the colony of Newfoundland, the little ship sank in a storm.

Hakluyt's successor, though not so gifted, was the English priest Samuel Purchas (*c*.1575–1626) who, as a friend of Hakluyt, inherited the vast collection of manuscripts Hakluyt was working on when he died. Some of this great collection was published by Purchas in five folio volumes in 1626 under the title *Hakluytus Posthumous, or Purchas his Pilgrimes*, but sadly they lack the perfection of editing which Hakluyt brought to his work. Purchas was an indifferent editor and he mutilated and garbled many of the accounts of voyages that Hakluyt had collected. Indeed, some were contracted to a degree which defies understanding, and some were accompanied with foolish editorial comment. Nevertheless, the *Pilgrimes* do contain the first accounts of voyages and travels that cannot be found elsewhere, and as such have an important place in English maritime literature. In the later part of the 17th century we find greater notice being taken of personnel problems and the manning and working of ships. Typical of these is Captain John Smith's *An Accidence or the Path-way to Experience Necessary for All Young Seamen, or Those that are Desirous to go to Sea* (1626), reprinted in 1627 as *A Sea Grammar* and reprinted many times.

The search for the *North-West Passage produced a literature of its own and during the reign of Charles I, when the British Navy was allowed to run down, attempts were made by writers like Sir Henry Mainwaring (1587–1653) and Captain Nathaniel Boteler (*c.*1577–*c.*1643) to remind their countrymen of its abiding importance. Mainwaring compiled the influential *The Seaman's Dictionary* (1644) and Boteler is best remembered for *A Dialogicall Discourse* (1634) in which an admiral and a captain discuss a large variety of subjects connected with ships and the sea. These six dialogues provide an interesting insight into the terms and customs of the British Navy at that time, and were reproduced by the Navy Records Society in 1929.

The last two centuries have produced some outstanding writing on life at sea, from war biographies and autobiographies to the adventures of modern cruising and racing circumnavigators. It is somewhat invidious to name names as there are so many but Richard *Dana's *Two Years before the Mast*, Joshua *Slocum's *Sailing Alone around the World*, Frederick William Wallace's *Under Sail in the Last of the Clippers*, Francis Chichester's *The Lonely Sea and the Sky*, and Eric Newby's *The Last Grain Race* must be essential reading for anyone interested in the sea.

Drama and Poetry. A wealth of folklore and *superstition connected with the sea had accumulated from time immemorial and this began to appear in literature, and in some of the plays of William Shakespeare (1564–1616) who seems to have been very well acquainted with them. His most nautical play is, of course, *The Tempest*, for which he is said to have derived the inspiration from the *shipwreck of Sir George Somers's ship *Sea Venture* on the Bermudas in 1609. However, generally speaking there are comparatively few theatrical works with a marine setting until Gilbert and Sullivan's light-hearted naval satire *HMS Pinafore*, first produced in 1878.

The influence of the sea is also revealed in the poetry of Edmund Spenser (1552–99), John Donne (1572–1631), and Samuel Taylor Coleridge (1772–1834) who wrote 'The Rime of the *Ancient Mariner'. Later, it is most apparent in the *sea songs and *shanties of the days of the *square-rigger and through the patriotic verse of Sir Henry Newbolt (1862–1938) and Rudyard Kipling (1865–1936). Newbolt is perhaps best known for his famous poems *'Drake's Drum' and *'Fighting *Téméraire*', while Kipling's prodigious output included a considerable amount of poetry as well as prose about the sea and seamen. Of a later generation, John *Masefield is perhaps the most outstanding.

Less famous poets were equally inspired by the sea. Just one example of their work are the evocative lines that appear in Frederick William Wallace's *Under Sail in the Last of the Clippers*, published in 1936:

> Aloft the ship they burn
> Down through the cloudless ether
> Through blue immensity to us;
> From nadir to zenith, a mighty dome.
> Of spangled worlds like diamond dust—
> Awesome, inspiring, tremendous!
>
> When day has fled
> And we stem the wide sea-paths,
> We note and mark them well.
> Observed, through countless miles of space,
> Our place upon the watery waste
> These stellar mile-posts tell.
>
> The seaman knows them,
> Vega, Sirius, Aldebaran,
> Capella, Rigel, Deneb, Mars,
> Friends of many a lonely watch
> At wheel, lookout, and pacing the deck,
> Under the stars.
>
> As in benediction hung,
> The Northern Cross above us swings
> Across the azure dark.
> Castor and Pollux by the tops'l leach shines bright,
> And Procyon beams
> 'Neath the fores'l's swelling arc.
>
> Betelgeuse and Bellatrix
> From Orion's lordly constellation
> To starboard scintillates.
> Dubhe and Merak point the way
> To where Polaris marks the magnet point
> Which compass indicates.
>
> The black sails swing
> Athwart the twinkling lights,
> Holding the seaman's soul in thrall.
> When winds are soft and South
> He meditates, and awed reflects
> On him who made them all.

The best-known couplet concerned with the sea was written by Mrs Felicia Hemans (1793–1835) and comes from her ballad 'Casabianca', first published in 1829. This immortalizes 10-year-old Jacques Casabianca who refused to leave the side of his father when the Frenchman's ship was set ablaze by the British during the battle of the Nile (1798). It begins:

> The boy stood on the burning deck
> Whence all but he had fled.

Novelists of the Sea. The earliest English novelist of the sea must surely be Daniel Defoe (*c*.1660–1731), a political pamphleteer and journalist, and it is as the author of **Robinson Crusoe* (1719) that he enters the maritime story. He also wrote several other novels connected with the sea: *Adventures of Captain Singleton* (1720), which relates, in the first person, how Singleton is kidnapped in his infancy, is sent to sea, takes part in a *mutiny, engages in *piracy, and finally acquires great wealth; *A New Voyage round the World* (1724), which appeared anonymously and though fiction was at first accepted as true; and *The Four Voyages of Capt. George Roberts* (1726).

Tobias George Smollett (1721–71) has been described as the first novelist of the British Navy and the literary father of the 'British tar'. He enlisted as a surgeon's mate and sailed for the West Indies during the War of the Austrian Succession (1739–48). After experiencing the abortive attack on Cartagena in 1741 he returned to London in 1744 where he practised as a surgeon, and began to write novels. His first was *The Adventures of Roderick Random* (1748) in which he drew upon his personal experiences at Cartagena and to which we owe today much of our knowledge about the British naval seaman at that time. It also introduced the well-known naval character of Lieutenant Tom Bowling.

However, it was not until the first half of the 19th century that the sea novelist proper appeared in the persons of Captain Frederick *Marryat and the Frenchman Eugène Sue (1804–57), the latter's novel *Kernok the Pirate* being considered by many to be the prototype for maritime fiction. It is necessary to distinguish between authors whose books deal with adventures of the sea and those who treat of the sea itself, as does Herman *Melville in his famous novel *Moby-Dick*. Joseph *Conrad followed along the course set by these pioneers in the realm of sea fiction, though he preferred to think of himself as a writer and not merely a novelist of the sea. His contemporary W. W. Jacobs (1863–1943), whose first book, a collection of short stories, *Many Cargoes*, was published in 1896, created for his readers a world peopled with sailors of a markedly humorous type.

Amongst 20th-century maritime novelists of note were C. S. *Forester and Patrick *O'Brian, who both wrote series of novels set during the Revolutionary and Napoleonic Wars (1793–1815); and Richard Hughes (1900–76), whose *In Hazard* (1938) rivals Conrad's *Typhoon* in portraying a ship's struggle to survive a *tropical storm. The Second World War (1939–45) produced some exceptional novels of *warfare at sea, *The Cruel Sea* (1951) by Nicholas Monsarrat (1910–79) and *The Caine Mutiny* (1952) by Herman Wouk (b. 1915) being two of the most popular. Nor must *The *Riddle of the Sands* be overlooked, for it is as widely read today as it was when it was first published over a century ago.

Naval History. The naval historian is of comparatively recent origin, though Herodotus (484–424 BC) includes in the wide sweep of his histories descriptions of warfare at sea such as the battle of Salamis. The great diarist Samuel *Pepys, whose record of naval administration during his period office is unique, does not quite fall into this category either. In fact, no attempt seems to have been made to separate naval history from the general chronicle of events until the French writers the Comte de Gueydon (1809–86) and Eugène Sue attempted to do so. De Gueydon, a student of naval warfare, wrote several penetrating analyses on the subject, including *The Truth about the Navy* (1849) and *Naval Tactics* (1868) while Sue wrote a history of the French Navy in five volumes.

It was the American naval officer Rear Admiral *Mahan and his English contemporary Sir John Laughton (1830–1915) who set the pattern for writing naval history which others were to follow, in not only chronicling it but expounding the lessons to be learned from a study of it. Their successors included such well-known historians as Arthur *Marder and Sir Herbert Richmond (1871–1946). Mention must also be made of the official historians Samuel Eliot Morison (1887–1976) and Stephen Roskill (1903–83). The former chronicled the operations of the US Navy during the Second World War (1939–45) in fifteen volumes; the latter those of the Royal Navy in three volumes.

Technical Literature. Ships have always attracted writers who liked to describe the way in which ships were built, and detail their *rigging and armament, and how they fought. The earliest of these date from the first half of the 17th century and they had numerous followers during later years. One of the most remarkable of them was the English-born Frederik Hendrik af Chapman (1721–1808), who emigrated to Sweden in 1715 and eventually became chief constructor of the Swedish Navy. His books, which include *Architectura Navalis Mercatoria* (1768), *A Treatise on Ship Building* (1775), *On Ships' Sails* (1793), *On Handling Ships* (1794), and *On War Ships* (1804), made a long-lasting impact on the future of *naval architecture and *dockyard practice. Also worthy of mention are John Charnock (1756–1807), whose beautifully illustrated three-volume *History of Marine Architecture* (1801) also had considerable influence on contemporary ship design, and the Frenchman Auguste Jal (1795–1875), whose great dictionary *Glossaire nautique* (1848) is still considered one of the main authorities on the seamanship of the period, as is the earlier *An Universal Dictionary of the Marine* (1768) by William Falconer (1732–69). Nor must be forgotten the internationally recognized German marine architect Henry Paasch (*c.*1840–*c.*1900), whose *Illustrated Marine Dictionary* (1885) and *From Keel to the Masthead* (1890) proved so popular that a facsimile edition in English of the former was published as late as 1977, while the latter went into four editions and was translated into five languages. The *Naval and Shipping Annual* founded by Earl Brassey (1836–1918) in 1889 carried technical information of this kind into the 20th century before being succeeded by a host of other technical books. The best known of these is probably the annual *All the World's Fighting Ships* by F. T. Jane (1865–1916). It is still published today and has its rivals in France, Germany, Italy, and the USA.

Obin, A., *The Bibliography of Nautical Books* (1996).

marine mammals comprise four groups: the Mustelidae (sea otter), the Phocidae (seals and sea lions), walruses, the cetaceans (*whales and porpoises), and the sirenians (dugongs and sea cows). All have been over-exploited in the past through *sealing or *whaling or hunting, either for their fur (sea otters and fur seals) or for their blubber and meat (seals, sea cows, whales). Within six years of the discovery of the South Shetland Islands in 1821, sealers had entirely exterminated the vast herds of elephant (*Miounga leonina*) and fur seals (*Arctocephalus gazellae*), killing over 300,000 a year. At least two species have been driven to extinction. Steller's sea cow (*Hydrodamalis gigas*) was discovered living around subarctic islands in the Bering Sea by a Russian expedition in 1741. These huge 7.5-metre- (24-ft)-long animals weighing about 4,000 kilograms (8,800 lb) were so easy to kill that by 1768 they had been exterminated. The last sighting of a Caribbean monk seal (*Monarchus tropicalis*) was in 1952 and in 1996 the species was declared extinct.

Apart from the sirenians that graze *marine plants, all marine mammals are carnivorous, feeding on *krill, *fish, *seabirds, or even other marine mammals. They show different degrees of adaptation to life in water. Cetaceans and sirenians are fully aquatic but still need to surface to breathe; sea otters, which have four well-developed legs and beat their tails from side to side to power their swimming underwater, are the least adapted and are fully mobile on land. Fur seals and sea lions have hind flippers that can hinge forwards and are used in their rather clumsy gait on land. The true seals and the walrus have hind flippers that point backwards. These are used for steering rather than to power swimming, and are useless on land. In sirenians and whales the hind flippers are fused into a tail fluke that beats vertically to power their swimming. Like walruses, sirenians have long bristly moustaches with which they sense out their food. Early sailors, presumably after many months of separation and deprivation at sea, thought they were *mermaids.

Recent results of attaching satellite tracking devices to seals have provided startling information about their behaviour. Elephant seals from South Georgia have been recorded foraging for *squid far down the Antarctic Peninsula, taking excursions of over 1,000 kilometres (625 mls.) and occasionally diving to depths of over 800 metres (2,625 ft). The most abundant seals in the world are crab-eater seals (*Lobodon carcinophagus*) in the Southern Ocean that specialize on eating krill that abound beneath

Examples of marine mammals: the elephant seal, harbour seal, and California sea lion are pinnipeds. The sea otter, related to river otters, feeds on clams and sea urchins while floating on its back. The tropic manatee of the Caribbean and the dugong of South-East Asia and Australia are herbivorous marine mammals. Walrus occur around the Arctic where they browse over the seabed detecting clams and worms with the long bristles of their moustaches

the pack *ice. The most predatory is the leopard seal (*Hydrurga leptonyx*) which supplements its diet of krill with Adelie *penguins and smaller seals. It grows to 7 metres (23 ft) and weighs half a tonne, and has also been known to attack humans, on at least one occasion with fatal results.

Perrin, W., Wirsig, B., and Thewissen, J., *Encyclopaedia of Marine Mammals* (2002).

www.press.jhu.edu/books/walkers_mammals_of_the_world/sirenia/sirenia.dugongidae.hydrodamalis.html

www.pinnipeds.org/contents.htm M. V. Angel

marine meteorology was founded by the American naval officer Lieutenant Matthew Fontaine *Maury, when he convened an international meeting in Brussels in 1853 to establish standards for the reporting of weather at sea and around coastlines. One result was the setting up of the International Meteorological Organization, which has now become the World Meteorological Organization. Thanks to Maury's efforts in standardization, and recent major advances in observational methods—especially through *remote sensing, the development of theoretical understanding, and increasingly powerful computers—today we benefit from high standards in weather forecasting. For example, 'sea winds' is an orbiting microwave *radar device that is used to predict big *storms. It measures wind, rain, and even *ice on the world's oceans, and data from it is supplemented by readings from ocean radio transmitting *buoys. It is particularly useful for surfers looking for outsize *waves.

Our weather is generated by the disparity in the amounts of radiant energy received from the sun at polar and tropical latitudes. In the tropics, as the warmed air rises, it is replaced by air coming from the poles. At the poles the cold air is continually sinking. This generates a basic pattern of convection, in which winds in the lower atmosphere blow towards the equator, while those in the upper atmosphere blow towards the poles. Once the air begins to move latitudinally, *Coriolis force comes into play and rotates its direction. So the basic pattern of airflow is broken up globally into a series of circulation cells.

Weather is latitudinally zoned. Near the equator are the *doldrums, the *trade winds blow between the *latitudes of 10° and 20°, and then around 30° are the *horse latitudes, which are high-pressure zones. At temperate latitudes cyclonic and anticyclonic pressure systems generate more variable weather patterns. At 60° is a zone of low-pressure systems, and finally over the poles high pressure dominates. The contrast in the high and low pressure

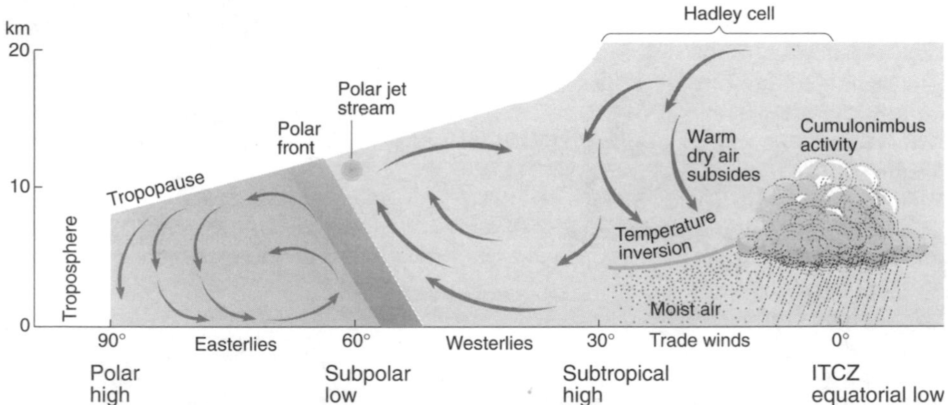

Section through the atmosphere, from polar regions to the equator, showing the general circulation, the relationship of the polar jet stream to the polar front (Antarctic Convergence), and the regions of tropical cloud formation. Note that much of the poleward return flow takes place in the upper part of the troposphere (the part of the atmosphere in which the temperature decreases with distance above the earth); the tropopause is the top of the troposphere and the base of the stratosphere. ITCZ = Intertropical Convergence Zone, the zone along which the wind systems of the northern and southern hemispheres meet

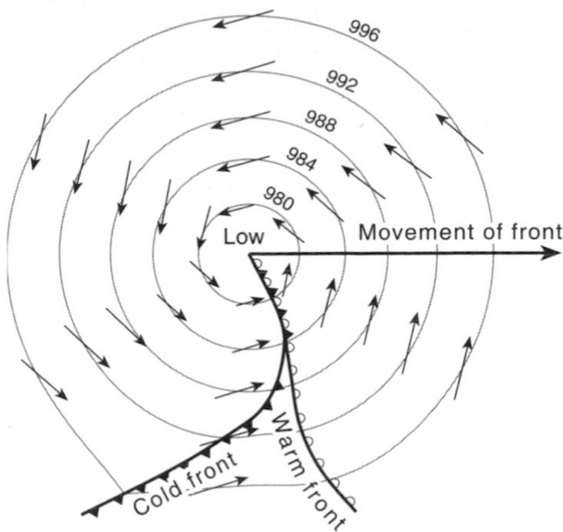

Pattern of isobars around a depression with associated cold and warm fronts

systems between these high latitude regions fluctuates, and leads to decadal cycles in climate. In the North Atlantic this cycle is known as the *North Atlantic Oscillation. In the tropics there are also significant variations in the geographical location of features like the Intertropical Convergence Zone (ITCZ), which irregularly generates *El Niño events.

The water cycle plays a central role in determining weather patterns. The evaporation of water vapour from the ocean's surface cools the sea surface temperature. In the atmosphere, water vapour is the third most abundant gas, although only about 0.001% of all the water on earth is in the atmosphere at any one time. The warmer the air the more water vapour it can contain. Conversely, if air is cooled some of the water condenses into cloud and mist. When the air rises, the atmospheric pressure it is subjected to falls, so it expands and cools, and clouds are formed. Where there are coastal hills and mountains, onshore winds are forced up by the topography so a line of clouds forms along the coast. In the days of sail, clouds on the horizon were a useful indication of the proximity of land. Clouds affect the heat balance of the ocean, as they insulate the surface of the ocean surface from much of the sun's radiant heat. Winds accelerate the rate at which heat is exchanged across the ocean's surface; the fiercer the wind the faster heat is exchanged. Convection resulting from rapid heat exchange in the tropics can generate *tropical storms.

In the atmosphere there are air masses, which are analogous to the water masses in the ocean. Boundaries between different air masses are also called *fronts. The main front between the cold polar air masses and the warm subtropical air masses is thrown into a series of long meandering waves that slowly travel around the globe. These meanders are regularly perturbed to form large-scale *eddies about 1,000 kilometres (625 mls.) across that are low-pressure or high-pressure systems; the former are depressions and the latter anticyclones, both familiar features of weather forecasts. Within a depression the boundaries between different air masses are either warm or cold fronts depending on which air mass is advancing. The cooler air mass pushes under a warmer one, so along the fronts air rises. The approach of a cold front is heralded by the cloud formations—changing from high-level cirrus, to lower cirro- and alto-cumulus clouds (mackerel sky), and then to lower-level stratocumulus clouds. These heavier, lower clouds along the fronts often bring rain. Clouds and rain tend to be heavier with the passage of a cold front because the gradient of the front between the air masses is steeper. Winds associated with depressions blow anticlockwise (veering) in the northern hemisphere and parallel to the isobars (lines of equal atmospheric pressure) rather than across them. So as a depression passes through the wind direction reverses.

Good forecasting is very much dependent on verification provided by the 10,000 mariners who participate in the **Voluntary Observing Ship Programme** by sending in regular weather reports while at sea. Their data help continually to update the theoretically derived forecasts. See also FITZROY, ROBERT.

Hamblyn, R., *The Invention of Clouds: How an Amateur Meteorologist Forged the Language of the Skies* (2001).

http://ww2010.atmos.uiuc.edu/(Gh)/guides/mtr/home.rxml

http://gmao.gsfc.nasa.gov/VLM/marine.html

www.aoml.noaa.gov/hrd/tcfaq/tcfaqE.html

www.wmo.ch/index-en.html

www.doc.mmu.ac.uk/aric/eae/index.html

www.atmosphere.mpg.de/enid/1442

M. V. Angel

marine painting. Historically, at least up to the late 19th century when the camera became generally available as an instrument of record, the overall volume of marine painting, of whatever country of origin, remains of great importance as a source of knowledge of *shipbuilding and design, of sails and *rigging, of ship decoration such as *figureheads, and of the transitional age when iron superseded wood as the material of construction, and *steam propulsion superseded sail as the means of propulsion. It is a record, too, of *warfare at sea throughout the great sea campaigns of the 16th–18th centuries. Of this historical value it is possible to speak with great certainty; of the aesthetic value of marine painting in the overall field of art, and of its inspirational value in focusing the endeavour and activity of man in his conquest of the sea, there can hardly be less doubt.

Early Marine Painting. The earliest known pictures of ships and boats are those which decorate Egyptian pottery of the period around 3200 BC. Wall paintings and reliefs of the two periods of Egyptian ascendancy, 2500–2300 BC and 1500–1085 BC, are often of such clarity and detail that contemporary methods of shipbuilding and rig are made clear. The methods and weapons employed in warfare at sea can be seen in a wall painting in the temple of Medinet Habu to the west of Thebes on the upper Nile. It depicts the victory of the Egyptian fleet of Rameses III (1198–1166 BC) over the combined fleets of sea-raiders from Crete, Cyprus, Philistia, and Libya.

Of the periods of Greek and Roman sea power, no true paintings exist beyond some pottery decoration. A Greek vase dating from 540 BC has a painting of a Greek merchant vessel being pursued by a pirate *galley, and a carving in relief from the temple of Fortune at Praesneste shows one of the Roman warships at the battle of Actium in 31 BC. There are also, of course, the coloured representations of French ships of 1066 in the Bayeux Tapestry, which provide details of contemporary building and rig.

Renaissance Painting. Representations of the sea and ships appear in many paintings of the early Renaissance. *The Birth of Venus* by Botticelli (1444/5–1510); Volpe's painting of Henry VIII leaving Dover on his way to the Field of the Cloth of Gold in 1520 in his great ship **Henry Grâce à Dieu*; and the equally well-known picture of Portuguese *carracks by the Dutch painter Cornelis Anthonisz (*c.*1499–*c.*1560), all show the features and build of ships with great skill and attention. However, they all lack any verisimilitude in representing the sea around them. These famous pictures are in no way seascapes, but merely portraits of ships.

Dutch Marine Painters. The true birth of marine painting, which can be taken as portraying the sea itself as well as the ships that sailed on it, occurred in Holland in the second half of the 16th century, coinciding with the rise to maritime power of the Dutch Republic, and the first Dutch painter to specialize in seascape as such was Hendrik Cornelisz Vroom (1566–1640), who painted a picture of Dutch ships running into the port of Flushing in the teeth of a *gale. It is his finest picture and shows a rare feeling for both ships battling against a high wind and the anger and force of a rough sea. It was the first true seascape in that it directly related the sea conditions with the behaviour of ships affected by them. Vroom, incidentally, is probably best known in Britain for his designs for the series of tapestries of the *Spanish Armada which the *Lord High Admiral, Lord Howard of Effingham (1536–1624), commissioned from him. Unfortunately, these tapestries were destroyed in a fire in the House of Lords in 1834, though they survive in the form of engravings made by John Pine (1699–1756).

Vroom began a school of painting which was carried on by such Dutch artists as Jan Porcellis (*c.*1585–1680), who has been described as the 'Raphael of sea painters', and Abraham Storck (*c.*1635–*c.*1710) who painted a magnificent picture, full of life, colour, and movement, of the Four Days Battle between the English and Dutch fleets in 1666 which now hangs in the National Maritime Museum at Greenwich. It was a school which reached its greatest heights with Willem van de Velde (1610–93) and his son, also called Willem (1633–1707). Another Dutch master of seascape of that era, Ludolf Bakhuyzen (1631–1708), made a speciality of *storm scenes at sea, and would gather his material by going to sea himself in bad weather.

British Marine Painters. The two van de Veldes came to England during the winter of 1672–3 to become marine painters to Charles II. They received pensions from the king, the father for 'taking and making draughts of seafights', the son for 'putting the said draughts into colour for our own particular use'. The son, in fact, settled in England and their paintings and drawings, particularly those of the father, are accepted as a historical archive of great value in portraying the *naval architecture and rig of the period, and the tactics and manoeuvres of naval battles. However, the son's paintings are considered superior to the father's because of his sensitive feeling for light, atmosphere, and the sea.

The period of the van de Veldes's later life in Britain corresponded with the rise of British sea power to a dominant position in the world, and the influence of their meticulous style can be seen in the early paintings of the British school of marine painting which grew up at about this time. The British marine artists Peter Monamy (1681–1749), the first eminent English marine artist, Charles Brooking (1723–59), and Samuel Scott (*c.*1702–72), if not exactly slavish copiers of the van de Veldes, owed much of their style and detail to these great masters. The van de Veldes were also an influence on a later marine painter of note, John Christian Schetky (1778–1874), though his work had a distinctive character all his own which revealed his great knowledge of, and affection for, his subject. A Hungarian by descent, Schetky became marine painter to no less than three British sovereigns, George IV, William IV, and Queen Victoria.

French Marine Painting. A French painter, Dominic Serres (*c.*1725–93), was also part of the British marine painting scene of this period. The *master of a French merchantman who was captured at sea and brought back to England, he decided to stay and study art, and he soon established himself as a painter of seascapes and naval battles. His practical experience of life at sea brought to his work an authenticity which, in conjunction with a brilliance of colouring and design, made his pictures outstanding examples of the painter's art in the mid-18th century. Ironically, he was to become probably the best of the marine painters of the English school of this period—ironically, because in France the genre received so little encouragement that marine artists never really prospered. A notable exception was Ambroise-Louis Garneray (1783–1857) who started to paint while a naval prisoner of war in a prison *hulk in Portsmouth harbour during the Napoleonic War (1803–15). On his return to France he studied art under his father, who was a professional painter, and in 1817 was appointed marine painter to the Duc d'Angoulême, Admiral of France. His best-known painting is perhaps his *Battle of Navarino*, now in the Musée de la Marine, Paris.

Marine Paintings of the 19th Century. J. M. W. Turner (1775–1851), the real father of Impressionism, was the outstanding landscape painter of his generation, and his seascapes, though not many in number, are of remarkable beauty in both atmosphere and colouring. He was not in any way an accurate portraitist of ships, as had been the van de Veldes, for instance, but he introduced a particular luminosity and drama in his studies which lifted them to new heights of pure artistry, most notably perhaps in *The *Fighting Téméraire*. Some of his sketches in oils of the River Thames and its shipping, though violently attacked by the art critics of the time for their lack of formal organization, brought a new dimension to the art of seascape.

This was the century when the sailing ship reached its perfection of design and the century which saw the introduction of the iron steamship. The many great English painters of the lovely *square-riggers which graced the 19th century are best represented by the Yorkshire artist George Chambers (1803–40), Clarkson Stanfield (1793–1876), who at one time served under Captain *Marryat, and Sir Oswald Brierly (1817–94), who studied naval architecture as well as art, and was appointed marine painter to Queen Victoria on the death of Schetky in 1874. Of this period, the pure seascape as such, not depending on the ship as its central theme, flourished under the brushes of Richard Parkes Bonington (1801–28) and John Sell Cotman (1782–1842), both of whom, though better known as landscape artists, produced seascapes of exquisite quality and atmosphere.

The transition from sail to steam propulsion is best represented in the work of W. L. Wyllie (1851–1931), a prolific artist whose watercolours of great delicacy and beauty are as much appreciated as many of his more stirring and dramatic oil paintings. His son Harold (1880–1973) was also a marine painter, and both of them were interested in *ship preservation, helping, in particular, with the restoration of HMS **Victory*. A contemporary of the senior

Wyllie was Charles Dixon (1872–1934), whose paintings covered the early days of steamships with loving detail, while another contemporary, known to everyone as *Marin-Marie, produced pictures and seascapes that showed his detailed knowledge of the sea and the craft which sailed on it.

In the USA, where Fritz Hugh Lane was the first painter to specialize in seascapes, Winslow Homer (1836–1910) became famous for his paintings of man against the elements. He travelled widely and in 1881 went to England, where he was drawn to the isolated fishing community of Tynemouth on the North Sea, and for two years he sketched and painted the life around him. It was a period in his life which proved crucial to his talent, for when he returned home he moved to a Maine fishing village where the rocky foreshore and the sea began to dominate his work. In the following years he produced such popular paintings as *The Life Line* (1884), which depicts the rescue of a woman from a *shipwreck; *Fog Warning* (1885); *Northeaster* (1895); and his best-known work, *The *Gulf Stream* (1899). In this a small sailing boat, wrecked by a storm and with its sole crewman unconscious on its deck, is menaced by *sharks and a *waterspout, and ignored by a passing ship.

Marine Paintings of the 20th Century. The two world wars produced a plethora of marine artists, in both Britain and the USA, as a result of naval appointments of painters as official artists to record scenes of naval activity. Sir Muirhead Bone (1876–1953) spanned both world wars as an official artist, and his drawings and etchings were powerful and evocative. Some others who made names in this particular field are Frank Mason, Norman Wilkinson (1878–1971), and Charles Pears (1873–1958), all of whom also produced some memorable paintings of *yacht racing between the wars. Other marine painters of note during the first half of the 20th century include Montague Dawson, a great portraitist of the vanishing *clipper.

Royal Society of Marine Artists, *A Celebration of Marine Art* (1996).

marine pharmaceuticals are chemical substances derived from marine organisms that are effective in various types of medical treatment and research. To date most pharmaceuticals have been derived from terrestrial organisms, but with twice as many animal phyla in the oceans as on land, as well as a plethora of different micro-organisms, the chances of finding novel natural compounds useful for biomedical purposes are high. In the sea, *seaweeds are an important source of iodine and are used for the treatment of patients with thyroid problems. Soft-bodied animals like *sponges, sea-squirts (Tunicata), and soft corals that inhabit *coral reefs both defend themselves from being eaten and wage territorial battles by producing noxious or distasteful chemicals, which are proving to be a treasure chest of useful chemicals. The dried remains of the seaweed *Desmarestia* is 18% sulphuric acid, strong enough to dissolve off the limy shells of *barnacles from rocks.

The chemicals produced by other organisms include terpenes, acetogenics, various alkaloids, and polyphenols. These have either proven or potential value that ranges from use as antibiotics, pain suppressors, and anti-inflammatory agents to sunscreens and anticancer agents. To give a few examples: neurotoxins (nerve poisons) like tetradotoxin —which renders pufferfish (Tetraodontidae) fatal to eat and is also the basis of the fatal bite of the *Great Barrier Reef's blue-ringed octopus *Hapalochlaena maculosa*—block sodium channels in nerve endings and have considerable value in biomedical research; and some sponges produce a substance, Halichondrin B, which shows promise in the treatment of ovarian cancer, melanomas, and leukaemia. The larvae of a type of shrimp are covered with bacteria which, if removed, result in over 90% of the larvae dying. It turns out that these bacteria secrete a toxic chemical, isatin (2,3-indoledione), that protects the larva from fungal infections, and may give us similar protection. A sea mat (*Bugula*) produces Bryostatin, which has immuno-stimulating properties and is used in the treatment of leukaemia. The blood of the horseshoe crab (*Limulus*) has a single, very sensitive, clotting agent that is used to detect any impurities and endotoxins contaminating surgical instruments.

Numerous laboratories around the world are actively screening marine organisms for biological active substances that may have a variety of potential uses. A British company dedicated to marine drug discovery announced in 2003 that it had discovered a marine microbe that in laboratory tests has produced a toxin that kills methicillin-resistant staphylococcus aureas (MRSA), currently (2004) such a threat to anyone undergoing surgery.

Antarctica is of particular interest to biotech companies and one firm has patented the molecule responsible for producing 'anti-freeze' in Antarctic *fish which could be used commercially to protect frozen food. However, 'bioprospecting' in Antarctica could prove a problem as it could infringe the international Antarctic Treaty, which protects the area from commercial exploitation. M. V. Angel

marine plants are the base of all food chains in the sea, except for the chemosynthetic communities associated with *hydrothermal vents. The few marine flowering plants that grow along the coastal fringes include *mangroves, eel and turtle grasses, and salt marsh plants. Most marine plants are varieties of algae. In coastal habitats large *seaweeds, the browns, reds, and greens, grow attached to the seabed, especially to submerged rocks. Only one species, *sargasso weed, is free floating.

In the open ocean marine plants are components of the *plankton, known as phytoplankton. The largest phytoplankton are 1–2 millimetres across, whereas the smallest are a thousand times smaller. Animals can sieve large cells out of the water but not those that are less than 0.005 mm across. So the grazers of these tiny cells either have to be extremely small themselves, or use sticky webs of mucus to entrap them. The phytoplankton includes several types of algae, including diatoms and dinoflagellates. Diatoms have cells enclosed within pill-box glassy walls, etched so finely that they are used to assess the quality of microscope lenses. Sinking diatoms are a major source of organic matter to the deep-living communities. Dinoflagellates can swim using long whiplike flagellae. Blooms of some form highly toxic *red tides; many produce the *phosphorescence seen in surf at night. The smallest cells are known as picoplankton. These are mostly tiny flagellates, and in tropical seas are often responsible for 80% of the photosynthesis. See also MARINE PHARMACEUTICALS. M. V. Angel

marine reptiles include some of the most charismatic marine vertebrates and some of the most deadly. There are not many of these relatives of the dinosaurs in the seas—seven species of turtles, 54 species of sea snake, the one salt-water crocodile, and the one marine iguana.

Turtles. The most charismatic of marine reptiles, these are gentle giants. They are under threat because they come ashore to lay their eggs on sandy tropical beaches that are ideal for tourist development. Their eggs, while they are incubating in the hot sand, are plundered by a variety of predators. Those hatchlings that survive have to run the gamut of *seabirds and *sea mammals as they scuttle across the beaches to the relative safety of the water, but even there they are gobbled up by hungry *fish and *sharks. Once safely at sea they roam the oceans feeding on gelatinous animals like *jellyfish drifting with the ocean *currents.

There are two families of sea turtles, the Dermochelyidae (leatherback) and the Cheloniidae (loggerhead, green turtle, ridley, and hawksbill). **Leatherbacks** (*Dermochelys coriacea*), the world's most endangered sea turtle, have been on earth 100 million years, 25 times longer than man, and can measure up to 2.1 metres (7 ft) in length and weigh well over 500 kilograms (1,000 lb). They are often the victims of *long-lining and fishermen's nets, and their numbers have declined disastrously during the last two decades. However, their extinction is not a foregone conclusion as international co-operation has reversed the decline of another species, **Kemp's ridleys** (*Lepidochelys kempii*), from 300 nesting females counted in the 1980s to the 6,200 counted in 2002. Leatherbacks regularly occur off the coasts of Britain, enticed there by the vast swarms of gelatinous animals called salps that appear there in early summer. **Hawksbill turtles** (*Caretta caretta*) will eat *Portuguese men-of-war. However, many are killed when their stomachs become clogged with discarded plastic bags (see also POLLUTION), which they mistake for gelatinous animals.

Sea Snakes occur mostly in tropical waters of the Indo-Pacific. Most species come ashore to lay eggs, but a few give birth to live young in the water. Being air-breathers, they have to keep close to the surface. Their tails are flattened laterally, making them more efficient at swimming. They feed on *fish, killing them by biting with highly venomous fangs. Their bites are lethal to humans, but being back-fanged they have difficulty biting us. Around Australia, the common **yellow-bellied sea snake** (*Pelamis platurus*) occasionally gets stranded in large numbers on beaches.

Crocodiles. Salt-water crocodiles are more dangerous than sea snakes, They inhabit the tropical estuaries of South-East Asia and northern Australia and can grow to huge sizes. Despite being protected they are heavily persecuted.

Iguanas. The marine iguana (*Amblyrhynchus cristatus*) is one of a range of reptiles unique to the Galapagos archipelago. They browse on the *seaweeds that grow on the larva rocks along the coasts. They are not great swimmers and, as noted by Charles *Darwin, the population on each island is subtly different, suggesting that each population is beginning to diverge and evolve into a separate species.

Salt-water crocodiles: **www.flmnh.ufl.edu/cnhc/csp_cpor.htm**
Marine turtles: **www.cccturtle.org/contents.htm**
Sea snakes: **www.reef.crc.org.au/aboutreef/wildlife/seasnake.html**

M. V. Angel

marines, soldiers specially trained and adapted for *warfare at sea, and latterly for amphibious operations. Several maritime nations have, or had, marine corps but only in Britain and the USA do they still serve at sea. The Royal Marines were formed in 1664, the US Marine Corps in 1798 (they were originally formed in 1775 but were disbanded at the same time as the *Continental Navy in 1783). Both have stirring regimental songs which reflect their past. The Royal Marines march to 'A Life on the Ocean Wave' while the hymn of the US Marine Corps, 'From the Halls of Montezuma to the Shore of Tripoli', recalls the first overseas expedition of the newly independent United States which defeated the *Barbary pirates of Tripoli in 1805.

Marine Society, founded in London in 1756 by Jonas Hanway (1712–86), a governor of the Foundling Hospital and a commissioner of the *Victualling Board. He started the society to save destitute boys from the streets of London and to help man the British Navy with them at the start of the Seven Years War (1756–63), and it is now the oldest public maritime charity in the world. Boys from this source were appreciated by naval captains of the time as they compared favourably with the men brought in by *impressment. In 1772 the society was incorporated by an Act of Parliament to clothe and equip all seafarers and from 1786 it provided pre-sea education and training in a succession of training ships moored on the Thames River. By 1940, when the last of these had been paid off, over 110,000 men had been recruited, equipped, and trained for both the Royal Navy and the Merchant Navy. After the Second World War (1939–45) the society concentrated on providing financial and material support for young people embarking on careers at sea, and on supporting other maritime youth organizations. Today, it continues to promote careers at sea with scholarships and loans, and through giving over 600 young people a year a taste of life at sea in its training ship, the 150-tonne *Earl of Romney*. It also provides seafarers with recreational and educational reading while at sea, and during 2002 over 375 ships and marine installations worldwide were supplied with libraries that are regularly updated.

Marin-Marie, the name by which the French yachtsman, painter, and author Couppel de Saint-Front Marin-Marie-Paul Durand (1901–87) was known. He made many notable single-handed cruises, and produced a number of outstanding *marine paintings. His best-known book was *Wind Aloft and Wind Below* (1939).

Maritime and Coastguard Agency (MCA), an executive agency of the UK's Department for Transport with overall responsibility for Britain's 16,800 kilometres (10,500 mls.) of coastline. It is the UK authority responsible for responding to *pollution from shipping and *offshore oil and gas installations, and its Counter Pollution & *Salvage Branch, with HM *Coastguard, responds to any emergency which may arise within the UK's search and rescue (SAR) area. SAR is coordinated through its network of six Maritime Rescue Coordination Centres, and its twelve Maritime Rescue sub-centres and sector bases, and civilian helicopters and fixed-wing aircraft are stationed around the UK for *lifesaving and anti-pollution measures.

It is also responsible for checking that ships entering UK waters meet UK and *International Convention for the Safety of Life at Sea (SOLAS) regulations; it monitors the policy on, and consistency of, port state control inspections and the inspections of UK vessels; and is the authority for the training and certification of UK seafarers. The Receiver of Wreck is also part of its organization.

maritime museums and museum ships, see INTERNATIONAL CONGRESS OF MARITIME MUSEUMS.

mark, see LEAD LINE.

marl, or **marle, to,** to *serve a rope, by which its *worming and *parcelling is secured. Ropes are frequently wormed and parcelled in place where heavy use may fray or gall (rub) them or where it is desired to make them impervious to water. An old rhyme instructs us to

> Worm and parcel with the lay,
> Turn and serve the other way.

The serving is secured on each turn by a *marling hitch, hence its name.

marlin, fast predatory warm-water *fish of the family Istiophoridae characterized by having a long bill on the upper jaw that they use to stun their prey. The largest is the blue marlin (*Maikaira nigricans*), which in 25 years grows to a length of 4.5 metres (14.7 ft), and weighs up to 1,300 kilograms (2866 lb). A relative, the sailfish (*Istiphorus platypterus*), holds the oceanic speed record, taking out 91 metres (300 ft) of line in 3 seconds—a speed of 109 kilometres per hour (68 mph).

Marlin generate such fast speeds by having red muscles, which are very rich in mitrochondria that generate the muscle's energy. Heat is conserved in the muscle by the blood supply flowing through a counter-flow system keeping the muscle 10 °C (50 °F) warmer than the surrounding sea water. When they sprint, their main bulk of white muscle comes into action providing the additional power, but as in all sprinters, an oxygen debt quickly builds up and the white muscles become exhausted.

Marlin are prime sporting fish. In the USA alone there are 200,000 deep-water anglers, whose ambition is to catch a record-sized marlin. When *long-lining was introduced in the 1960s, a quarter of a million marlin weighing 5,000 tonnes were caught annually in the Atlantic, but despite the conservation efforts of the International Commission for the Conservation of Atlantic Tunas (ICCAT), catches have fallen by 80%. ICCAT manages all the stocks of fishes that migrate transoceanically and are caught by long-lines and in *purse seine nets in the open ocean. So serious is the problem that sea-anglers now use unbarbed hooks so any marlin they bring alongside can be released.

M. V. Angel

marline, a small light line, supplied both tarred and untarred, used for a variety of purposes on board ship during the days of sail. It was two stranded, loosely twisted, and was originally used for bending light sails to their *yards or *stays. See also CODLINE.

marline spike, a steel spike pointed at one end and used for lifting the *strands of a rope to make room for another to be tucked in when *splicing.

marling hitch, a series of round turns in which the end is passed over the *standing part and under the *bight and pulled *taut on each turn. Unless there is an *eye in the end of the rope a marling hitch is usually started with a *timber hitch and is used for *lashing up sails, *awnings, *hammocks, etc.

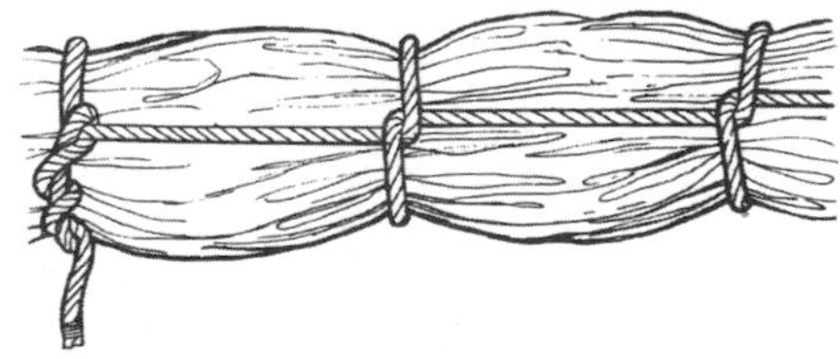

Marling hitch

maroon, to, to put ashore a sailor and leave him there. The action implies being left in some relatively inaccessible place. The best-known case of a marooned seaman was Alexander

*Selkirk, on whom Daniel Defoe based his character *Robinson Crusoe.

MARPOL, the International Convention for the Prevention of Pollution from Ships, one of several conventions that are the responsibility of the *International Maritime Organization (IMO). It incorporates the International Convention for the Prevention of Pollution of the Sea by Oil (OILPOL), which came into force in 1958 as an IMO convention, and the 1973 MARPOL Convention which was agreed after the *tanker the *Torrey Canyon* ran aground in 1967, causing the largest oil spillage ever recorded up to that time. The 1973 MARPOL Convention was more stringent than OILPOL, which was concerned with *pollution from routine tanker operations, as it included regulations against pollution from ships of oil, chemicals, harmful substances carried in packaged form, sewage, garbage, and air pollution. The 1973 MARPOL Convention had not been ratified when, in response to a spate of tanker accidents in 1976–7, the IMO held another conference in 1978 which agreed to a second convention. This absorbed the first convention as well as adopting measures affecting tanker design and operation, and was subsequently ratified. Its annexes dealing with oil and chemicals came into force in 1983, garbage in 1988, and sewage in 2003, and the one on air pollution from ships entered into force in May 2005. See also ENVIRONMENTAL ISSUES.

marry, to, to bring two ropes together, such as the *falls of a boat to be hoisted at the *davits of a ship, so that the haul on them can be combined so that the boat is hoisted level. The term is also used in other maritime contexts where two ropes, or other objects, are brought together and laid side by side.

Marryat, Frederick (1792–1848), British naval officer and novelist, born at Westminster, London. He was the son of Joseph Marryat, the agent for Grenada in the Windward Islands, and grandson of Thomas Marryat, a physician, author, and poet.

As a boy Marryat frequently ran away to sea and finally entered the Royal Navy in 1806. During his two-and-a-half years as a midshipman aboard his first ship, the *frigate *Imperieuse*, he took part in more than 50 engagements, an introduction to naval life which stood him in good stead for his later career as a writer. For example, his novel *Peter Simple* (1834) was based on the exploits of Lord Cochrane, who commanded the *Imperieuse* when Marryat was serving aboard her.

Marryat was promoted commander in 1815 and four years later took command of the *sloop *Beaver*, the guard-ship at St Helena until Napoleon's death there in 1821. Marryat was then given command of the *Larne* in the East Indies; was senior naval officer at Rangoon in 1824 during the Burmese War; and in 1825 commanded an expedition which ascended the Bassein River and captured the town of that name. He was, in fact, an officer with quite remarkable gifts. Apart from his distinguished naval career, he was awarded the medal of the Humane Society for 'a dozen or more' life-saving rescues and was responsible for the compilation of a code of signals which became the basis of the *International Code of Signals. For this latter achievement he was made a Fellow of the Royal Society in 1819, and appointed a Chevalier of the Legion of Honour in 1833.

He was promoted captain in 1830 but then resigned to devote himself to writing novels. His first, *Frank Mildmay*, had been published while he was still serving, and his second, *The King's Own*, came out the year he retired. *Frank Mildmay* had not been well received but it was in such contrast to the general run of historical romance that discerning readers prophesied a bright future for him as its mixture of adventure, high-spirited fun, distress and hardship, heroic action, friendship, and hatred was like a breath of fresh air to the contemporary novel. With the publication of *The King's Own*, any lingering doubts about his talent were set at rest. It was a great success and was followed in quick succession by *Newton Foster* (1832), *Peter Simple* (1834), *Jacob Faithful* (1834), *The Pacha of Many Tales* (1835), *Japhet in Search of a Father* (1836), *The Pirate of the Three Cutters* (1836), and *Mr Midshipman Easy* (1836), the best known of his stories.

Much of the naval adventure with which these books were packed was based on his experiences in the *Imperieuse*, and to all of them he brought the authentic smell of the briny and an intimate knowledge of the way of a ship at sea. He had a gift for characterization that suited his adventurous heroes admirably, and in 'Equality Jack' in *Mr Midshipman Easy* he possibly created the perfect hero in the realms of naval adventure.

Around this time Marryat began to write books for boys, of which *Masterman Ready* (1841) and *The Children of the New Forest* (1847) are the two best known. He also continued to produce many other books, the best of which were *The Phantom Ship*, a tale woven around the story of the *Flying Dutchman, and *Poor Jack*, set in Greenwich and around its great hospital for naval pensioners. In 1843 he bought an estate in Norfolk and took to farming, but he continued to write almost up to his demise, which was almost certainly hastened by the death of his son in a *shipwreck.

martingale. **(1)** The *stays, usually of chain, which hold down the ends of the *jib-boom and the flying jib-boom against the loading of the head stays just as the *bobstay does with the *bowsprit. They are taken from the end of each *spar down to the cap of the *dolphin striker which is supported by martingale stays taken to each side of the hull. In early usage before the term dolphin striker was in use the *bumpkin itself was called the martingale. **(2)** The *kicking strap of a sailing boat is also sometimes called a martingale.

martnets, a defunct term which was used in *square-rigged ships to describe the *leechlines of a square sail. When these martnets were used to haul the leeches of the sail up to the *yard, for *furling or shortening sail, they were said to be topped.

Mary Celeste, A *hermaphrodite brig of some 280 tons found abandoned in the Atlantic in November 1872. How she came to be in that condition remains one of the great mysteries of the sea.

She sailed from New York on 5 November with a cargo of 1,700 barrels of alcohol, bound for Genoa. Her *master was Benjamin Briggs, who had his wife and 2-year-old daughter on board, and his crew comprised a *mate, second mate, cook, and four seamen. On 24 November he made the Azores, but ran into a near *gale which forced him to shorten sail. On the morning of the 25th he sighted and sailed past the island of Santa Maria, leaving it to the southward and made a note to this effect on the deck slate so that it could be later entered into the ship's *log.

Nine days later the *Mary Celeste* was sighted some 560 kilometres (350 mls.) east of Santa Maria by the *brigantine *Dei Gratia*, also out of New York. The *Mary Celeste* was heading in an easterly direction on the *port *tack in a light breeze, with her reduced sail area set for the *starboard tack. To the crew of the *Dei Gratia* there was obviously something wrong and the brigantine's mate and one seaman boarded her. They found the vessel abandoned, her only boat gone, and the remains of the boat's *painter hanging over her stern. The side rails *abreast of the boat's stowage on board were lying on the deck, an evident sign of a hasty abandonment, and by the deck *pump was lying a sounding rod, with which the depth of water in the *bilges was measured. *Aloft, the running *rigging was snarled up, the *halyard to the main *gaff parted (the rest may have been used as the boat's painter), and the upper *topsail and *foresail blown out. The main *hatch and the cargo was secure but the small fore and after hatches were off, as was the *galley hatch, and the *skylight above the main *cabin was open. There was one metre of water in her, but this was not excessive for such a ship.

A *salvage crew from the *Dei Gratia* was put aboard the abandoned ship and she was sailed to Gibraltar, where she arrived on 13 December 1872. On the way she had made very little water. After her arrival an extensive survey was made but this revealed virtually no internal or external damage beyond very minor damage to the hull planking on either bow about a metre above the surface. A court of inquiry was then assembled to try to discover why she had been abandoned. A number of theories were put forward, some of them assisted by the evident desire of the assessor at Gibraltar to prove foul play. He tried to make much out of the discovery of an old sword on board covered with bloodstains, but on analysis these were found to be rust, and the theories of *mutiny and murder occasioned by its discovery had to be abandoned. A collision with a giant *squid was another theory, while the most popular suggestion for a long time was that there was collusion between Briggs and the master of the *Dei Gratia* so that salvage money could be claimed and later divided. The inquiry concentrated on this theory for many days but, somewhat regretfully, had to abandon it in the end.

A plausible explanation is that she was struck by a *waterspout and that the steep water pressure gradients associated with these forced water up the pump well, giving the impression to those sounding the well that she was filling rapidly. The presence of the sounding rod on the deck alongside the pump certainly indicates that the well was being sounded at the time, and the sight of water flowing out of the pump well onto the deck would certainly give the impression that the ship had such a large leak that the pump could never control it. As a precaution everyone took to the ship's boat but the captain would have been most reluctant to leave his ship if there was any chance of her staying afloat. However, the boat was veered well *astern to keep it clear of the ship in case she did sink, but the painter then parted—maybe the halyard was rotten—and the ship sailed on, and those in the boat could not row fast enough to catch her.

The subsequent career of the *Mary Celeste* was not a happy one. For thirteen years she went from owner to owner, seventeen in all, none being able to make her pay her way. Finally she was deliberately wrecked by her last owner on a reef off Haiti, in order to make a false insurance claim. Her remains were found by a Canadian expedition team in 2001.

Mary Rose, a 'great ship' of 600 tons, having an armament of about twenty heavy and 60 light guns and a complement of 400. She was built for Henry VIII and named in honour of his sister Mary Tudor. This ship, the first of her name in the British Navy, took part in the first (1512–14) and second (1522–5) French wars of Henry VIII, always as the flagship of the *Lord High Admiral, her good sailing qualities making her a favourite to perform this role. In 1536 she was rebuilt to some extent and given a complete lower deck of guns—probably the first of the British Navy's ships to be so fitted. In 1544–5 she was active in Henry VIII's third French war, but when going out to engage a French invasion fleet off Portsmouth on 19 July 1545 she was swamped through her lower-deck *gunports. She sank quickly with the loss of nearly all her company including her captain, Sir George Carew. In 1836 her remains were discovered by early pioneers in *diving and some guns and artefacts recovered, but she was then abandoned. Further efforts were made to find her in 1965, and in 1967 Professor Harold Edgerton of the Massachusetts Institute of Technology pinpointed the wreckage with side-scan *sonar. In 1979 the Mary Rose Trust was formed to undertake the necessary scientific programmes to examine the site and raise and preserve the remains, and to put them on display in the Mary Rose Museum situated in the Royal Naval base at Portsmouth. By the mid-1990s a three-stage conservation programme on the hull, which will take many years, was started. By then many thousands of finds, ranging from botanical specimens to the ship's guns and the remains of her crew, had been raised. See also MARINE AND UNDERWATER ARCHAEOLOGY; SHIPWRECKS.

Marsden, P., *Sealed by Time: The Loss and Recovery of the Mary Rose* (2003).

Masefield, John Edward (1878–1967), British poet. He was educated as a cadet on board the training ship HMS *Conway* and went to sea at the age of 15 as an apprentice in a *square-rigged ship in which he rounded Cape Horn. A few years later his health failed while his ship was in New York and he went ashore, supporting himself by taking any job, however humble, through which he could earn his keep. On his return to England he became a journalist and joined the staff of the *Manchester Guardian*.

He had already started to write poetry and was one of the pioneers in the revival of narrative poetry, of which his *Dauber*, published in 1913, was based in part on his early experience at sea. He settled in London during the early 1900s, and a volume of poems, *Salt Water Ballads*, came out in 1902, and was an instant success. Among the poems in it was 'Sea Fever', one of the best-loved ballads of the sea, which was later set to music by John Ireland.

I must go down to the sea again, to the lonely sea
and the sky,
And all I ask is a tall ship and a star to steer her by,
And the wheel's kick and the wind's song and the
white sail's shaking,
And a grey mist on the sea's face and a grey dawn
breaking.

Another book of poetry, *Ballads and Poems*, followed in 1910. At the same time he was writing short stories of the sea, published in *A Mainsail Haul* (1905) and *A Tarpaulin Muster* (1907), and he also wrote several plays.

His first novel was *Captain Margaret*, published in 1908, and among the dozen or so that he wrote, the two most connected with the sea were *The Bird of Dawning* (1933), a story of the tea *clippers, and *Victorious Troy* (1935) which tells the story of a sailing ship *dismasted and officerless, but brought back to safety by an apprentice on board.

However, it is by his poetry that he is best remembered, especially by such nostalgic and even sentimental poems as 'Sea Fever', and by his many verses in praise of the merchant navy in which he spent his early years, perhaps exemplified by his 'Cargoes' type of ballad. They were simple, direct, and held the true flavour of the sea.

Dirty British coaster with a salt-caked smoke stack,
Butting through the Channel in the mad March days,
With a cargo of Tyne coal,
Road-rails, pig lead,
Firewood, ironware, and cheap tin trays.

Masefield was appointed Poet Laureate in 1930 and was awarded the Order of Merit in 1935. See also MARINE LITERATURE.

mast, a vertical *spar which carries the sails of a sailing ship, though the *schooner **America* started a temporary vogue, when she appeared in English waters in 1851, for *yacht masts to have a pronounced *rake. Also, it is not necessarily a vertical spar in modern powered vessels when it usually serves to carry such essentials as radio aerials, *radar arrays, etc. The mast of a powered vessel also carries the compulsory *steaming lights which a powered vessel has to display when under way at night, and flag signals are hoisted on the mast's *halyards, or to a *yard across it.

In some sailing vessels, particularly *junks, the masts are stepped in *tabernacles so that they can be lowered if it is necessary to *navigate rivers and waterways with bridges. However, they are normally stepped through holes in the deck and their *heels, which are squared off, fitted into *steps in the ship's *keelson, hence the phrase 'to step a mast' means to set a mast up. In larger wooden sailing vessels they were held firm in the deck holes with wedges and the area around them strengthened by *partners. Except those vessels with an *unstayed rig, masts are secured in place by its standing *rigging. In *square-rigged ships the masts are crossed by the *yards, on which the sails are set. In *fore-and-aft-rigged vessels the sails are set on the masts themselves.

Bipod masts were a feature on the ships of some early civilizations and the Greeks used multiple masts, though this died out in the Mediterranean after the collapse of the Roman Empire and was not reintroduced until *Marco Polo reported their use in China in the 13th century. Two-masted vessels go back to this time in Europe, but the vessel of 1350, which could only run before the wind with its one or two square sails, quite quickly became the three-masted *caravel of the 15th century. This, with its use of the *lateen sail, first on all masts and then on the *mizzen alone, made possible the voyages organized by *Henry the Navigator and later the *exploration by sea by such *navigators as *Columbus, Vasco da *Gama, and *Cabot. However, something which did not spread beyond China was the system of staggering the masts of its 15th century *treasure ships in *port, *amidships, and *starboard positions, raking them at different angles, and stepping them in tabernacles, mostly without giving them standing rigging.

Before the growth in size of ships in the western world which occurred during the 17th century, ships' masts were single pole, or solid, spars, cut from the trunk of a fir tree. However, as the size of sailing ships increased, so did the number of sails and of upper masts. **Pole masts** were not strong enough or tall enough to carry the larger yards and extra sails, so masts had to be made of several pieces of timber to acquire the required strength, circumference, and height, and these were called **made masts**. In most ships of the 17th century and later, the lower masts were all made masts, *topmast and *topgallant masts being pole masts.

Very few, if any, sailing vessels in European and North American waters have solid wooden masts nowadays; and the lighter, hollow, wooden ones made up from spruce, and *scarfed and glued, that replaced them in *yachts must now be almost as rare. All modern sailing vessels have metal masts, and racing yachts have carbon composite ones laminated in moulds for a higher strength–weight ratio. See also MAST SHIP.

mast coat, a covering either of painted *canvas or of rubber, secured round the foot of a mast and to the deck around it, which prevents water running below through the opening in the deck where the masts goes down to its *step in the *keelson. It is mainly used in sailing vessels where the masts have to be allowed a certain amount of play as they go through the openings in the deck so as to absorb the pressure of wind on the sails.

master, originally a rank in the Royal Navy during the days of sail as well as a rank in the merchant service. The naval master was a specialist *navigator and ship handler whose function was to manoeuvre his ship into a position required by the captain. Appointed by the commissioners of the navy, he was required to be a good officer and seaman, and ranked as a subordinate to a lieutenant. After 1814 a master ranked with a commander and was known as **master and commander**, but this position was abolished towards the end of the 19th century when the navy established a professional hierarchy of navigators. He had assistants, classed as *master's mates, who kept *watch.

Nowadays a merchant service master is a qualified **master mariner**, though the term master mariner can apply to any merchant service officer who has the necessary qualifications but who has insufficient seagoing experience to hold the rank of master. A master is certified by the *Maritime and Coastguard Agency (MCA) in the United Kingdom, or its equivalent in other countries, his certificate being regulated by the *International Maritime Organization's Convention on Training, Certification and Watchkeeping for Seafarers (STCW), which now governs the certification of seafarers worldwide. The qualification has varying grades and endorsements for specialists in *tankers (chemical, gas, and oil), *bulk carriers, and *sail training vessels. One especially important feature of the Convention is that it applies to ships of non-party states when entering ports of states which are parties to the Convention. Currently, there are 144 signatories to it which together control over 98% of the world's shipping *tonnage.

Masters of ships carry heavy responsibilities to their owners, charterers, maritime organizations, safety executives, the environment, and their crew members, in addition to their seafaring functions of navigating and ship handling. The Indian master of the ultra-large crude oil carrier (ULCC) *Jahre Viking* was described as a 'hero' by a Royal Naval captain in appreciation of the skill and care required in navigating and handling this ship—the largest man-made moving object in the world. This vessel carries over 550,000 tonnes of crude oil at 14 knots with a draft of more than 23.7 metres (80 ft) and a turning circle of over 3 kilometres (2 mls.). The same epithet was also applied to the British master of *Brunel's **Great Eastern*, who carried an equally heavy burden in 1859. The master of a German ship negotiating, for instance, the Saimaa Canal locks in Finland, where the clearance is measured in centimetres, needs to exercise just as much skill and care. These different vessels point up the universal character of masters and their qualifications. The international status of STCW and its ongoing amendments reflect the many changes in seafaring since the days of master and commander.

Martin Lee

master-at-arms, the officer, appointed by warrant, who is responsible for police duties on board a naval ship. In the early days, when seamen knew him by the slang name of **Jaunty**, he was also responsible for exercising the crew in the use of small arms, which is the origin of his title. But this duty was later taken by the junior lieutenant on board who was known as the lieutenant-at-arms.

master's mate, an old naval rate in all navies during the days when the *master of a warship was the officer responsible for her *navigation. His mates were *petty officers entered in the ship's *muster-book to assist him in his duties.

mast ship, a vessel, during the days of sail, used for the transport of masts. They were ships which had extensive square *ports, sometimes known as raft-ports, cut in the stern, and occasionally also in the bows, so that the larger timbers intended for the manufacturer of lower masts and *topmasts could be loaded inboard through them. The traditional countries supplying suitable timbers for this purpose were those bordering the Baltic Sea, and the special mast ships carried on a flourishing trade from there through the centuries during which sail was the primary motive power of all shipping. However, with the great expansion of commerce during the 18th and early 19th centuries the Baltic countries were unable to meet the full demand for masts, and a second source of supply was discovered in North America, where the vast forests of firs proved an apparently inexhaustible reservoir of suitable timber. It was then that attempts were made to construct **temporary mast ships** made entirely of timber suitable for mast-making, by lashing them together in the rough shape of a ship's hull, setting up three masts, and trying to sail them across the Atlantic, the idea being they could be broken up into individual mast timbers on arrival. However, the lashings usually parted as the timbers worked in the sea, so that the 'ship' disintegrated en route; but properly constructed mast ships continued to operate until iron and steel replaced timber.

mate. In the navy during the days of sail the *master's mates were those professional *petty officers who assisted in the navigation and handling of the ship, keeping *watch with commissioned officers. The term mate developed, in merchant ships, to mean the officer next to the master who could deputize for him when necessary. Mates were part of the growing hierarchy of merchant service officers, chief mates, second mates, and so on down to junior fourth mates in *ocean liners. While mate is the recognized term for a watchkeeping officer, and is used as such by the *International Maritime Organization (IMO) to identify that position, most companies prefer to call the first mate the first officer, the second mate the second officer, etc. In legal terms the mate (that is the first mate) is an important signatory in *freight handling; the mate's receipt is a significant document. Mates, like *masters, have to satisfy the stringent requirements of the IMO's Convention on Training, Certification and Watchkeeping for Seafarers (STCW) and are required to meet equivalent international *radar, radio, specialized vessel knowledge, rule of the road (see INTERNATIONAL REGULATIONS FOR PREVENTING COLLISIONS AT SEA), and fitness parameters before certification by examination. Martin Lee

Matthew Walker knot, a *stopper knot near the end of a *lanyard to prevent it running through an *eye. It is made by forming a *half hitch with each *strand of the rope in the direction of the *lay and then tucking the strands over and under until the knot is formed. A finished Matthew Walker knot looks similar to other stopper knots. For illus. see DIAMOND KNOT.

Maury, Matthew Fontaine (1806–73), American naval officer, born in Fredericksburg, Virginia, who became a midshipman in 1825. He devoted his energies to the study of *navigation but is now best known for his work in *oceanography, which brought him a worldwide reputation. He was appointed to the USS *Vincennes* for her circumnavigation of the world and while on leave after this voyage published *A New Theoretical and Practical Treatise on Navigation*, which was highly successful.

In 1839 he was injured in an accident which ended his active service career, but in 1842 he was appointed superintendent of the Depot of Charts and Instruments of the Navy Department in Washington, and given additional duties as superintendent of the new Naval Observatory. His interest in *hydrography and *marine meteorology led him to issue special *logs to sea captains so that they could record the strength and direction of winds and *currents they encountered. With the information gathered from these sources he published his 'Wind and Current Chart of the North Atlantic' in 1847, and the following year issued *sailing directions for use with his chart, under the title, *Abstract Log for the Use of American Navigators*, bringing out new editions in 1850 and 1851.

Maury's publications made possible considerable savings in travel time and were enthusiastically received by mariners from many nations, with many masters cooperating with him by reporting their regular observations. Their success led to Maury organizing the first international maritime meteorology conference, convened in Brussels in 1853, and his uniform system of recording meteorological data was adopted for all naval and merchant vessels.

In 1855 Maury published *The Physical Geography of the Sea*, now acknowledged as being one of first text books of modern *oceanography, and prepared a chart representing the bottom profile of the Atlantic between Europe and America to demonstrate the practicability of a submarine cable across the ocean. In the same year a section of a third edition of his Sailing Directions suggested *traffic separation lanes in the North Atlantic, a recommendation that eventually bore fruit in 1898 when the five biggest transatlantic steamship companies of the day agreed to regular steamer lanes.

At the start of the American Civil War (1861–5) he joined the *Confederate States Navy. When it ended he went to Mexico and then returned to England where he had spent part of the Civil War trying to find suitable vessels for the Confederate Navy. In 1868, he was appointed professor of meteorology at Virginia Military Institute, Lexington, a post he held for the rest of his life.

'mayday', an international *distress signal said to originate from the French *m'aidez*, meaning 'help me'. It was made by radiotelephone from a vessel in distress on two internationally recognized frequencies, 2,182 kHz MF and Channel 16 (156.8 MHz) VHF, and many stations, both ashore and afloat, kept continuous watch on them. This manual system has now been superseded by the automated distress signals of the *Global Maritime Distress and Safety System, which are still known as 'may day' calls.

***Mayflower*,** the ship in which the Pilgrim Fathers sailed from Plymouth, England, in 1620, to establish the first permanent colony in New England. The original voyage, in company with the *Speedwell*, started from Southampton, England, but the *Speedwell* was found to be unseaworthy and the ships put into Plymouth, from which port the *Mayflower* sailed alone on 6 September. She was 32.5 metres (106 ft 6 in.) in length, with a *beam of 7.8 metres (25 ft 6 in.), and had a *displacement of 236 tons. Built before 1606, her home port was Harwich, and her *master was Christopher Jones who was hired to transport the 102 colonists to the 'northern parts of Virginia'. They reached Provincetown Harbor on 11 November 1620 and a small party, under the leadership of William Bradford, was sent ahead to choose a place for settlement. They landed at what is now Plymouth, Massachusetts, on 21 December.

The last record of the *Mayflower* was in May 1624 when an application was received by the High Court of *Admiralty from the ship's owners declaring the ship to be 'in ruins'. An appraisement was requested and she was valued at £128 8*s*. There have been several, unconvincing, claims that parts of the ship still exist. See also REPLICA SHIP.

Caffrey, K., *The Mayflower* (1975).

Melville, Herman (1819–91), American novelist of Scottish and Dutch descent, born in New York City. His father died in 1832 leaving the family in straitened circumstances and Melville was forced to leave school. He first went to sea aged 18 as a *cabin boy in a *packet ship plying between New York and Liverpool. In January 1841 he signed on in the *whaler *Acushnet* bound for the South Pacific. In June 1842 he deserted with another sailor at Nukahiva in the Marquesas Islands because of the living conditions on board and the harsh treatment meted out by the ship's *master and the *'bucko' mate. In August 1842 he was registered as a crew member of an Australian whaler, *Lucy Ann*, an unprofitable venture that provoked him to *mutiny. He was jailed in Tahiti but managed to escape without difficulty, and by November 1842 he was back in the USA where he signed on as a harpooner aboard the whaler *Charles & Henry*. Six months later he landed at Lahaina in the Hawaiian Islands, and three months after that signed on as an ordinary seaman in the US *frigate *United States* which discharged him at Boston in October 1844. He then returned home to write *Typee, a Peep at Polynesian Life* (1846), and followed it with a sequel,

Omoo, a Narrative of Adventures in the South Seas (1847). Both sold well and they soon made him one of America's most popular novelists. The same year as *Omoo* was published he married and in 1850 bought a farm near the novelist Nathaniel Hawthorne, who became a strong influence on his early career.

Melville's first two novels were, to some extent, autobiographical but were embellished with adventures and experiences which he had gleaned from other sources. Yet they are valuable for the vividness with which they describe the manners, conditions of life, and customs of the Polynesian tribes, at that time subject to the attempts of missionaries to convert them to Christianity. Melville's characters reveal the superficiality of these attempts and while there is little of the 'noble savage' belief in his writing, he does bring out the quick reversion to tribal customs and beliefs as the thin veneer of conversion wears off.

His next novel, a philosophical romance called *Mardi, and a Voyage Thither* (1849), was not well received and he followed it quickly with *Redburn: His First Voyage* (1849), for which he drew on his time as a cabin boy. Then in 1850 he published *White Jacket: Or the World in a Man-of-War*, a novel based on his experiences aboard the *United States*. It was highly critical of naval discipline and the issue of spirits aboard ship (see GROG), and it has been said the former criticism contributed to the end of flogging in the US Navy with the *cat-o'-nine-tails.

While writing these three books he began work on the novel by which he is best known today: *Moby-Dick or the White Whale* (1851), one of the true classics of *marine literature. For it he drew on his experience on whalers for the authentic flavour of *whaling in the days of sail. The book, made up of 135 chapters written in many different styles, is full of detail of *whales, their habits and anatomy, and tells the story of the undying love/hate relationship between Captain Ahab, of the whaler *Pequod*, and Moby-Dick, an immense and ferocious white whale which in an earlier encounter had been responsible for the loss of one of Ahab's legs. Ahab searches for the whale halfway round the world, having sworn to kill it to avenge his injury. The two meet in the end, Moby-Dick is harpooned by Ahab, but in the last *sound of the dying whale the harpoon line catches round Ahab and drags him down into the depths.

Moby-Dick did not sell well, and Melville's popularity as an author waned further when, in 1852, he published *Pièrre, or the Ambiguities*, a psychological novel of incestuous passion which alienated so many of his readers that the sales of his previous books dropped alarmingly. To add to his misfortune, a fire at his publishers in 1853 destroyed the plates of his books, and many unsold copies. Two years later he published a historical novel, *Israel Potter: His Fifty Years of Exile*, then came a collection of short stories *Piazza Tales* (1856), and a satire, *The Confidance-Man: His Masquerade* (1857). This was the last novel he was to publish in his lifetime for he then chose to abandon novels for poetry.

In 1863 he moved to New York. To earn a steady income, something he had always craved, he became a customs inspector in 1866, writing little more than occasional poems and articles. In 1888 he published a biography, *John Marr and Other Sailors*, and shortly before he died he finished *Billy Budd, Foretopman*, which was published posthumously in 1924. In this long short story, a great and deserved success, he wove his story around the activities of the *press gang in Britain and the bitter cruelties and injustices of life in the navy during the Napoleonic War (1803–15), a story that Benjamin Britten later turned into an opera. By the time he died Melville had been forgotten, and his death was marked by only one obituary.

Arvin, N., *Herman Melville* (1976).
Rosenberry, E., *Melville* (1979).

men-in-lieu, seamen put on board a merchant vessel by the British naval *impressment service after its prime seamen had been removed at sea, in order that the vessel could reach port in safety. It was legal in wartime for naval ships at sea to stop homeward-bound merchant ships and press seamen out of them, though there were regulations which made it unlawful to take so many men that the ship could not be sailed properly. But trained seamen were so valuable in the navy that many warships would wish to take more than they were allowed under the regulations; when this occurred they made up the merchant ship's crew by transferring some of their own men. It was a good way, from the naval point of view, of getting rid of some of their worst characters and untrained men. See also MACARONI MATE.

Mercator projection, the *chart projection in which parallels of *latitude and *longitude cut each other at right angles so that a *rhumb line appears as a straight line. The first work to embody these principles was published in 1569 by the Flemish mathematician Gerhard Kremer (1512–94), who used a Latinized form of his name, Gerardus Mercator. However, it was another 70 years before its use became widespread at sea.

This form of chart depends on the proposition that the convergence of the *meridians as they approach the poles will be proportional to the cosine of the latitude, and that if a proportional misplacement is introduced in the spacing between the parallels of latitude

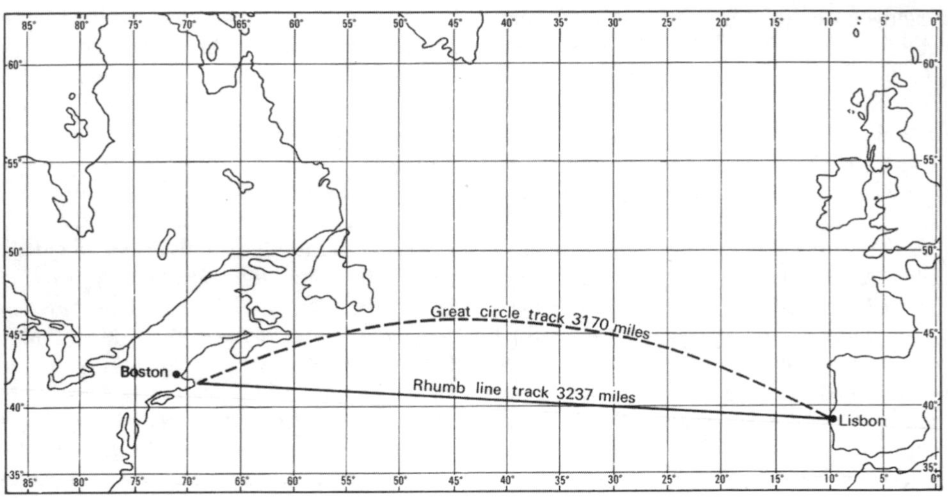

Mercator projection: rhumb lines appear straight

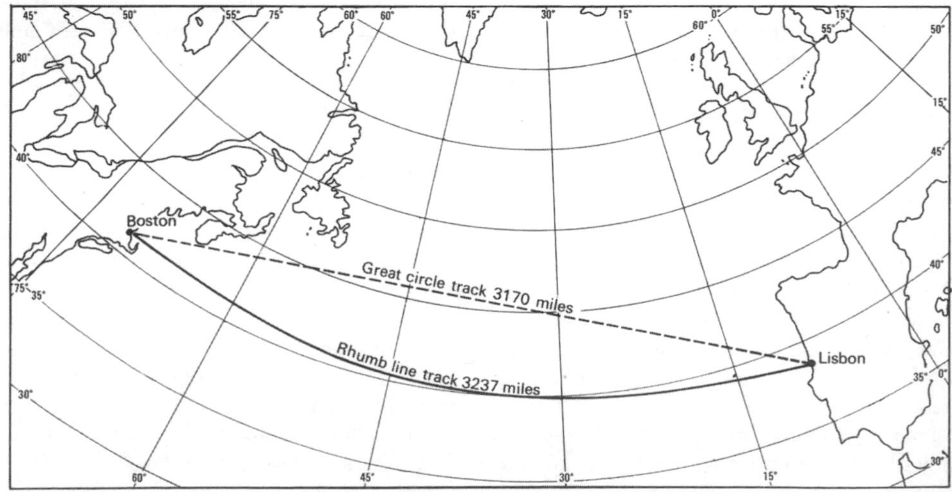

Gnomonic projection: great circles appear straight

on the chart as they move north and south from the equator, then a rhumb line, which cuts all meridians at the same angle, must become a straight line, although on a globe they are spirals. As ships normally steer rhumb line *courses such a projection would obviously be of great value for *navigation. Mercator's own description of his chart does not seem to have materialized, but towards the end of the century Edward Wright published an explanation of it in his *Certaine Errors in Navigation* (1599), and Mercator charts and Mercator sailing eventually replaced the old plain chart and *plain sailing.

In geometrical terms, Mercator's projection can be envisaged as a cylinder touching the globe at the equator, on to which the meridians and parallels are projected from the earth's centre, which is then developed (i.e. unwrapped) to form a flat chart. As the axis of the cylinder is the same as the polar axis of the globe, the projection of each pole will be at infinity and the polar regions therefore cannot be shown. The 'distortion' is least at the equator and increases progressively towards high latitudes. By distortion is meant that the linear scale for north–south distances becomes more and more divergent from that for east–west distances, increasing with the latitude, though not in the same proportion. This means that in a chart covering an area with a considerable north–south dimension, such as North or South America, the regions in high latitudes, e.g. Baffin Land or Tierra del Fuego, appear exaggerated in size compared with tropical areas such as the Isthmus of Panama; they also appear distorted in shape, e.g. Greenland appears to stretch out almost indefinitely to the north because, as the Arctic is approached, the projection become less and less convenient. Nevertheless, for nautical purposes the projection has the unique advantage that rhumb lines always appear as straight lines.

In measuring distances on a Mercator chart, therefore, it is essential to measure the span of degrees of latitude on the sides of the chart which lie on the same latitude as the distance being measured. These degrees will each represent 60 *nautical miles (112 km) for the measurement required. Degrees measured in other parts of the chart (i.e. not on the same latitude as the distance to be measured) will not, and of course the scale of degrees of longitude in the top and bottom margin is useless for measuring distances. For this reason no linear scale of miles can be included in any Mercator chart, except in the largest-scale ones showing a small area only. No linear scale could be drawn that would be accurate for different latitudes on a chart of any considerable area.

Mercator's projection can also be used with the axis of the cylinder not coinciding with the axis of the earth through the poles, and the resulting projections are known as **transverse Mercator** (if the axis is at right angles to the polar axis) or **oblique Mercator.** The former results in the projection being least distorted along a given meridian, instead of along the equator, and is useful for mapping regions extending in a north–south direction, e.g. the British Isles on the Ordnance Survey. Oblique Mercator gives a line of least distortion which can be arranged to suit the area being mapped, running at an angle to both meridians and parallels of latitude. Both these varieties, however, are useless for navigation.

Crane, N., *Mercator: The Man who Mapped the Planet* (2003).

merchant marine, a collective name to describe the merchant ships on the official registers of any one nation, though in Britain the merchant fleet is known as the **merchant navy** after King George V granted it this title in 1922. There are many different types of merchant ships (see Table 1) and in 2003 the world fleet of powered seagoing merchant ships of not less than 100 tonnes gross was 89,899 ships of 605.2 million gross *tonnage with an average age of 21 years. The world's cargo-carrying fleet was 46,918 ships of 846.6 million deadweight tonnage. Table 2 shows, in descending order of gross tonnage, the twenty largest merchant fleets in the world by registration. Those marked with an asterisk are *flags of convenience fleets. Table 3 shows the world's fleets by nationality of owner, 1,000 tonnes gross and above, which reveals that Greece and Japan have the two largest, with 16% and 13% respectively. See also INTERNATIONAL MARITIME ORGANIZATION; MASTER; MATE; SHIP; TICKET; TRAMP SHIP.

Hope, R., *A New History of British Shipping* (1990).
—— *Poor Jack: The Perilous History of the Merchant Seaman* (2003).

Table 1. Category of Cargo Ships over 100 GT

Shiptype Category	*No.*	*Dwt*	*GT*	*Age*
Bulk Dry	5,046	280,854,469	155,947,831	14
Crude Oil Tanker	1,810	247,805,236	134,497,497	11
Container	3,055	90,475,579	78,435,684	10
General Cargo	16,253	72,308,173	51,214,559	23
Oil Products Tanker	5,136	40,642,726	24,775,362	23
Chemical	2,828	36,400,153	22,490,309	14
Ro-ro Cargo	1,921	14,110,728	29,130,165	18
Bulk Dry/Oil	174	12,110,343	6,975,916	18
LPG Tanker	1,027	11,247,554	9,573,232	16
LNG Tanker	153	9,700,062	13,195,145	14
Other Bulk Dry	1,112	9,206,584	6,889,594	19
Refrigerated Cargo	1,272	6,849,261	6,375,829	19
Self-discharging Bulk Dry	168	5,507,994	3,257,346	28
Passenger/Ro-ro Cargo	2,737	4,152,782	15,133,063	22
Other Dry Cargo	250	2,054,561	1,913,920	26
Passenger (cruise)	432	1,399,001	10,650,564	22
Other Liquids	371	950,733	685,288	25
Passenger Ship	2,833	544,570	1,431,536	21
Passenger/General Cargo	340	328,096	628,316	33
Total cargo carrying	**46,918**	**846,648,605**	**573,201,156**	**20**

Table 2. Gross tonnage and average age of vessels by country of registration

Registration	*Totals*			*Cargo-carrying ships*				*Ships of miscellaneous activities*		
	No.	*GT*	*Age*	*No.*	*GT*	*Dwt*	*Age*	*No.*	*GT*	*Age*
*Panama	6,302	125,721,658	17	5,349	123,220,617	183,974,112	16	953	2,501,041	26
*Liberia	1,553	52,434,624	12	1,462	51,004,525	79,787,483	11	91	1,430,099	24
*Bahamas	1,297	34,751,748	15	1,127	33,226,958	45,473,151	15	170	1,524,790	20
Greece	1,558	32,203,117	22	1,325	32,130,644	54,519,431	21	233	72,473	32
*Malta	1,301	25,134,314	18	1,262	24,976,614	40,797,336	18	39	157,700	25
Singapore	1,761	23,240,945	11	1,056	22,807,969	35,998,380	12	705	432,976	9
*Cyprus	1,198	22,054,166	16	1,077	21,786,083	35,167,103	16	121	268,083	18
Hong Kong	901	20,507,453	12	846	20,483,481	34,456,489	12	55	23,972	10
China	3,376	18,427,955	22	2,374	17,554,128	26,257,775	22	1,002	873,827	21
*Marshall Is.	515	17,628,157	12	421	17,279,579	28,872,911	10	94	348,578	21
Norway (NIS)	705	16,996,583	16	608	16,660,889	23,979,689	16	97	335,694	13
Japan	7,151	13,561,521	13	4,137	12,457,304	15,993,791	12	3,014	1,104,217	15
UK	1,594	10,843,724	20	599	9,922,751	9,796,872	16	995	920,973	22
Russia	4,950	10,430,783	23	1,876	6,204,336	7,758,333	24	3,074	4,226,447	22
USA	6,185	10,408,896	24	467	8,358,332	11,052,013	26	5,718	2,050,564	24
Italy	1,504	10,245,809	22	871	9,955,275	10,403,001	19	633	290,534	25
Denmark (DIS)	425	7,246,602	17	330	7,078,157	8,840,014	16	95	168,445	21
India	1,028	6,960,567	18	429	6,537,456	10,999,548	17	599	423,111	19
Korea (South)	2,604	6,757,400	23	1,058	6,177,143	9,933,496	19	1,546	580,257	26
Isle of Man	302	6,416,425	10	243	6,017,856	9,883,089	10	59	398,569	12

Table 3. World's fleet by nationality of owner, 2003

Nationality	*Totals*			*Cargo-carrying ships*				*Ships of miscellaneous activities*		
	No.	*GT*	*Age*	*No.*	*GT*	*Dwt*	*Age*	*No.*	*GT*	*Age*
Greece	3,025	91,094,974	18	2,971	90,589,597	152,264,476	18	54	505,377	20
Japan	2,948	77,069,940	9	2,846	76,422,886	109,216,733	8	102	647,054	15
Norway	1,653	36,687,450	16	1,300	35,169,329	49,962,180	16	353	1,518,121	14
Germany	2,464	36,414,972	9	2,432	36,313,835	48,873,612	9	32	101,137	18
USA	1,549	34,505,581	18	890	31,395,892	42,620,674	19	659	3,109,689	17
China	2,416	30,611,974	20	2,175	29,883,768	46,734,721	20	241	728,206	20
Hong Kong, China	485	17,504,409	12	483	17,502,067	30,625,070	12	2	2,342	38
Korea (South)	865	16,823,726	15	793	16,665,331	25,062,978	14	72	158,395	24
China (Taiwan)	537	15,306,608	13	528	15,291,421	22,866,377	12	9	15,187	22
UK	793	15,247,093	14	603	14,522,121	18,921,620	13	190	724,972	15
Singapore	758	14,420,979	15	702	14,164,910	23,303,778	15	56	256,069	13
Russia	2,539	13,910,948	22	1,667	10,621,084	15,206,876	22	872	3,289,864	22
Denmark	686	12,815,017	12	574	12,347,043	15,868,511	12	112	467,974	14
Italy	656	10,690,165	15	590	10,302,046	12,082,959	15	66	388,119	23
India	394	7,363,160	17	291	7,079,110	12,021,659	16	103	284,050	18
Malaysia	335	7,290,745	14	306	7,210,512	9,668,090	14	29	80,233	17
Switzerland	278	6,706,956	17	271	6,526,805	8,209,505	16	7	180,151	25
Saudi Arabia	126	6,689,528	17	104	6,655,385	12,055,663	18	22	34,143	15
Turkey	576	5,574,578	18	575	5,573,414	8,687,038	18	1	1,164	24
Sweden	319	5,536,052	16	298	5,402,118	5,753,467	15	21	133,934	22

Source of these tables Lloyd's Register–Fairplay Ltd, *World Fleet Statistics* 2003.

mercy ships, global charity founded in 1978 by an American couple, Don and Deyon Stephens, when they raised funds to convert the 159-metre (522-ft) *Anastasis* into the world's largest non-governmental hospital ship. Equipped with three operating theatres, a dental clinic, a laboratory, and an X-ray unit, and manned by both permanent and temporary staff, she has been used to help the peoples of many Third World countries in need of medical and dental assistance. She is currently (2004) off Sierra Leone. In 1994 she was joined by the 78-metre (256-ft) *Caribbean Mercy* which covers the Caribbean basin and Central America, and a third ship, the 152-metre (499-ft), *Africa Mercy*, was converted in 2004 from a rail *ferry into a hospital ship with six operating theatres and an 80-bed ward.

meridian, from Latin *medius* meaning middle, and *dies* meaning day, a semi-*great circle joining the earth's poles. Meridians, better known as lines of *longitude, cross the equator and all parallels of *latitude at right angles. Owing to the rotation of the earth, all celestial bodies appear to revolve around the earth towards the west, making one revolution in a day. When the sun crosses an observer's meridian, the local time is midday. See also PRIME MERIDIAN.

mermaids, mythological denizens of the sea, half human and half *fish, have a history dating back into antiquity. It is generally believed there is a connection between the apsaras of Hindu mythology and the nymphs of the Greek legends. These last, together with Oceanids, *Nereids, naiads, and sirens, were believed to inhabit streams, lakes, and the sea. In the 3rd century BC the Greek historian Megasthenes, ambassador of Seleucus I to the Indian king Sandrocottus, reported that a

Sea-virgin, sea-monkey, and sea-Turk; engraving from *Cosmographia Universalis*, by S. Munster, 1555

creature like a woman inhabited the seas round Sri Lanka. Pliny the Elder (23 BC–AD 37) says in his *Historia Naturalis*, 'Nor are we to disbelieve the stories told of Nereids ... Several distinguished persons of Equestrian rank have assured me that they themselves have seen off the coast of Gades [Cadiz] a merman whose body was of human form.'

In 1187 a merman is said to have been taken off the coast of Suffolk, but he managed to escape. The Swiss physician Paracelsus (1493–1541) tells of mermaids 'who woo men to make them industrious and home-like', but he found mermen less friendly. This accords with the Norwegian belief that mermen were oldish with black beards and hair, whereas mermaids were young and attractive with golden hair. Icelandic mermaids were full of mischief and fond of playing tricks on fishermen.

Tales of mermaids come from all parts of the world. In 1825, one said to have been brought from Japan was exhibited at the Bartholomew's Fair, London, but on inspection she was found to be a woman with a fish's tail stitched to her skin. Although many of the legends concerning mermen and mermaids have their origin in mythology, the reported encounters with these supernatural beings are sometimes too circumstantial to be dismissed as mere hallucinations. The explanation doubtless lies in the existence of two *marine mammals, the manatee and the dugong, both of which bear a passable resemblance to the human face. The attitude of the female dugong when suckling her young takes on a particularly human appearance. Further, the plaintive cries of seals and sea lions have often been likened to those of human children. There is, in fact, ample natural evidence to support the mermaid mythology.

Merrimac, USS, a 40-gun warship, one of six naval vessels authorized by the US Congress in 1854 and named after rivers. She displaced 4,650 tons, was 84 metres (275 ft) long, with a 15.5-metre (51-ft) *beam, and a *draught of just over 7 metres (23 ft). Although often called a steam *frigate, she was really a sailing frigate with *auxiliary steam power. She was *scuttled during the American Civil War (1861–5) and fell into the hands of the Confederates who raised her and, as the *Virginia*, made her part of the *Confederate States Navy. In March 1862 the *Virginia* fought a duel with the USS *Monitor* (which gave her name to the *monitor type of warship). Although the action, which took place in Hampton Roads, was indecisive, it has gone down in naval history as the first encounter in war between *ironclads. In most accounts of this battle, the *Virginia* is referred to as the

Merrimac. She was destroyed by her own crew when the Confederates evacuated Norfolk.

merrow, the name by which a *mermaid is called in Ireland.

merry dancers, the name sometimes given to the streamers of coloured light associated with the *aurora borealis or northern lights.

Merry Men of May, a name given to the tide-rips formed during the *ebb in the Pentland Firth in the far north of Scotland.

messenger. **(1)** An endless rope which was used in *weighing the anchor in the days before the introduction of *auxiliary power aboard ships when the *capstan was worked by hand. As the *hemp anchor *cables of those days were generally too thick and heavy to be brought themselves round the capstan direct, a messenger was used instead. It was led through two single *blocks from the vicinity of the *hawseholes, along the main deck so that it ran close alongside and parallel with the cable, round the capstan, where three or four turns were taken round the barrel, and back along the main deck on the other side of the ship. As the capstan was turned, so the messenger moved with it, and the cable was bound fast to the messenger with *nippers so that it was hove in at the same rate as the messenger. **(2)** A small rope attached to the *eye of a *hawser and used to haul it out to the ring of a mooring *buoy is also called a messenger. **(3)** In the US Navy, the most junior member of a *watch.

metacentric height, see STABILITY.

meteorology, see MARINE METEOROLOGY.

middle ground, an obstruction in the form of a sand or mud bank, or an outcrop of rock, in a *fairway. Its extremities used to be marked by what were called middle ground *buoys so that vessels could pass either side of it in safety. Nowadays small areas of obstruction are marked by *isolated danger marks and larger ones by *cardinal marks belonging to the *IALA maritime buoyage system.

middle passage, see SLAVE TRADE.

midshipman, a non-commissioned rank in all navies (Fr. *aspirant*, Ger. *Führnich*, It. *guardiamarina*), immediately below that of sub-lieutenant in the Royal Navy and ensign in the US Navy. The name dates from the early 17th century when young gentlemen were sent to sea as *captain's servants or *King's Letter boys to obtain the necessary training to become midshipmen and then officers. The name comes, according to the *Shorter Oxford Dictionary*, from the fact that these young gentlemen were stationed *amidships where, doubtless, they could observe what was going on without getting in the way.

Nowadays, the service of midshipmen is essentially one of training for higher command. After graduating from naval college they are sent to sea where they are placed in charge of a ship's boats, keep *watch at sea and in harbour under the eye of a senior officer, and generally play a part, under supervision, in all the ship's activities, and at the end of their time at sea they take the necessary promotion exams. See also TALBOT, MARY ANNE.

millibar, a unit of measurement of atmospheric pressure, 1,000 millibars equalling the atmospheric pressure required to raise a column of mercury in a vacuum tube to a height of 750 mm (29.53 in.). Lines drawn on a *synoptic chart connecting points of equal atmospheric pressure in millibars are known as isobars. See also MARINE METEOROLOGY.

mirage, a natural optical illusion caused both at sea and on land by the refraction of light passing through layers of air of different densities. These are usually caused by temperature differences, but can be because the layers of air contain different amounts of water vapour. Particularly in tropical seas, heat hazes often result in the appearance, above the *horizon, of islands that normally would be below the horizon and too far away to be in line of sight.

M. V. Angel

mistral, a cold, and sometimes strong, wind from the north-west which blows down the Rhône Valley into the western Mediterranean Sea. It is sometimes spelt maestrale.

mitre, the seam in a sail where cloths which run in two directions are joined. Triangular sails, such as *staysails and *jibs (and occasionally *Bermudan mainsails), are normally made with the lines of the cloths running in two directions; for example, the upper cloths of a jib might run at right angles to the *leech, and the lower cloths at right angles to the *foot. The mitre seam usually forms a strengthened narrow cloth running diagonally from the *clew to some point on the *luff. Different sailmakers have their own ideas of the best method of setting the cloths and the mitre seam, but the latter is usually arranged to run more or less in line with the sheet so as to distribute the strain of the sheet evenly throughout the sail cloths.

mizzen, the name of the third, aftermost, mast of a *square-rigged sailing ship or of a three-masted *schooner, or the small after mast of a *ketch or a *yawl (but see also JIGGER-MAST). The word probably came into the English language either from the Italian *mezzana* or the French *misaine*, which are, in fact, the names in those languages for the foremast, but for some reason its position in the ship was changed round when the word was adopted in Britain. The word also possibly came from the Arabic *misn* meaning mast, and was associated with the *lateen sail, also of Arabic origin. See also ARTEMON.

Moby-Dick, the name of the great white *whale in Herman *Melville's famous classic novel of the same name.

moidore, a Portuguese gold coin much beloved by writers of stories of *piracy, struck between the years 1640 and 1732, and with a sterling value of approximately 67 pence ($US0.93). The double moidore, worth about £1.35 ($US3.25), was struck in 1688. It, too, figures in many pirate stories.

mole, a long pier or breakwater forming part of the sea defences of a port. It can be built either in the form of a detached mole constructed entirely in the sea or with one end of it connected to the shore. The ports of Dover and Gibraltar, for example, are protected by three moles, two of them attached to the shore with a detached mole to seaward, providing an entrance to the harbour at each end of it. In the distant past the word, sometimes written as **mole-head**, was also used, wrongly, to describe a harbour protected by a mole.

molluscs, the phylum of invertebrate animals that includes snails, bivalves, and *squid. Some are pelagic but most are bottom-living. Many have shells of calcium carbonate (lime). The edible ones, like oysters (*Ostraea* spp.) and scallops (*Pecten* spp.), are known generically as *shellfish.

Sea butterflies (Pteropoda) are members of the *plankton and have very light shells. Their foot (which corresponds to the flat process on which snails crawl) is developed into large swimming flaps that are covered in tiny hairs (cilia). These move across the foot a sheet of mucus that traps even the smallest phytoplankton cells. On the seabed the molluscs are either snail-like or have two shells (bivalves). The snails (Gastropoda) crawl over the bottom on a flattened foot. Many are grazers like the winkles (*Littorina* spp.), feeding by scraping algae off the rocks with a toothed tongue called a radula. Whelks (Buccinidae) are predatory snails that either bore holes in the shells of bivalves, or dissolve holes by secreting strong acids. Some cone shells (Conidae), which inhabit the *coral reefs including the *Great Barrier Reef, feed on *fish, killing them by shooting poisoned barbs into them; handle these at your peril! Bivalves are mostly sedentary bottom-dwellers either living burrowed in sand or mud like clams (Bivalvia), or anchored to rocks like mussels (e.g. *Mytilus* spp.) and oysters. They feed on particles they extract from the water by passing it through their large gills across which flow sheets of mucus. Scallops and queens (*Chlamys* spp.) are free living and can escape danger by swimming by rapidly opening and closing their shells. There are many commercially important species of mollusc, and oysters and mussels are farmed. Scallops are targeted by *dredgers and squid are caught in *purse seine nets for both food and bait.

Yonge, C., and Thompson T., *Living Marine Molluscs* (1976).

www.manandmollusc.net/ M. V. Angel

mollymawk is a seafarer's name for several species of small, black-backed *albatross including *Diomedia melanophrys*, but according to Webster's Dictionary it is also applied to *fulmars. The name is derived from a Dutch word *mallemowk*, meaning foolish gull, because seafarers found them so easy to catch when they landed on ships. See also SEABIRDS. M. V. Angel

monitor, a low-freeboard, shallow-draft ship mounting one or two large guns for coastal bombardment. The name comes from the original ship built for that purpose, an *ironclad designed during the American Civil War (1861–5) for the US Navy by a Swedish engineer, John Ericsson (1803–89). Ericsson, who had already designed the first warship with a *propeller, had the *Monitor* constructed to counter the *Confederate States Navy ironclad CSS *Virginia*, the former USS **Merrimac*, as well as Confederate shore batteries. She was significant in the history of warships for being the first vessel to be built with an armoured revolving turret. On 9 March 1862, soon after her *launch, she encountered the *Virginia* at Hampton Roads, but the battle proved inconclusive. By then she had already proved herself unseaworthy, and she foundered off Cape Hatteras on 31 December 1862. Her remains were found in 1973 by an American *research ship and in 1975 became the USA's first marine sanctuary. They are protected by the *National Oceanic and Atmospheric Administration (NOAA) which examined the hull but found it too fragile to be recoverable. However, the *turret was salvaged in 2003 and is now on display at the Mariners' Museum, Newport News, Virginia.

The name monitor was chosen from a phrase in a letter from Ericsson to the secretary of the navy about the design: 'The impregnable and aggressive character of the structure will admonish the leaders of the Southern Rebellion that the batteries on the banks of their rivers will no long present barriers to the entrance of the Union forces. The ironclad intruder will thus prove a severe monitor to those leaders ... Downing Street [a reference to the British Prime Minister and his government], in fact, will hardly view with indifference this last Yankee notion, this monitor.'

Britain, in fact, viewed the *Monitor* with complete indifference, having two years earlier launched the **Warrior*, which could have blown 50 *Monitors* out of the water. Nevertheless, Britain built monitors in large numbers during the First World War (1914–18) and also used them in the Second World War (1939–45).

monkey. **(1)** The name of a small coastal trading vessel of the 16th and 17th centuries, single masted with a square sail and, occasionally, a *topsail set above it. They ranged up to about 40–50 tons *burthen. **(2)** A name also given to a small wooden cask, wider at the bottom than at the top, in which *grog was carried to the seamen's messes in British Navy ships after issue from the grog-tub, and which it was common practice to *bleed en route. The name lingered on as a description of the metal mess kettles in which grog was later carried. **(3)** The name given to a form of marine steam reciprocating engine where two engines, either single cylinder or *compound, were used together in tandem on the same *propeller shaft. They were installed on opposite sides of the crankshaft so that when one engine pulled, the other pushed. See also STEAM PROPULSION.

monkey block, the name given to a small single *block stropped with a swivel, and used on board in places where it was awkward to get a straight haul. The name was also used in *square-rigged ships to describe the blocks fastened to the *yards through which the *buntlines were *rove.

monkey jacket, originally a thick, close-fitting, serge jacket worn by seamen while keeping *watch in ships at night or in stormy weather. It was also sometimes known as a **jackanapes coat**.

monkey's fist, a knot employed to weight the end of a *heaving line. Allow from 1.8 to 2.7 metres (6–9 ft) of the line to make it, and then (i) wind three turns round the palm of the hand before (ii) passing another lot of three turns across and round the first three, as indicated by the arrows in the diagram. Then (iii) pass a third lot of three turns round and across the second three, but inside the first three and in the direction indicated by the arrows. Note that if the knot has been made properly the end will come out alongside the *standing part of the rope. Finally, (iv) make all the turns *taut before *splicing the end into the standing part. Alternatively, before making the knot taut, tie an

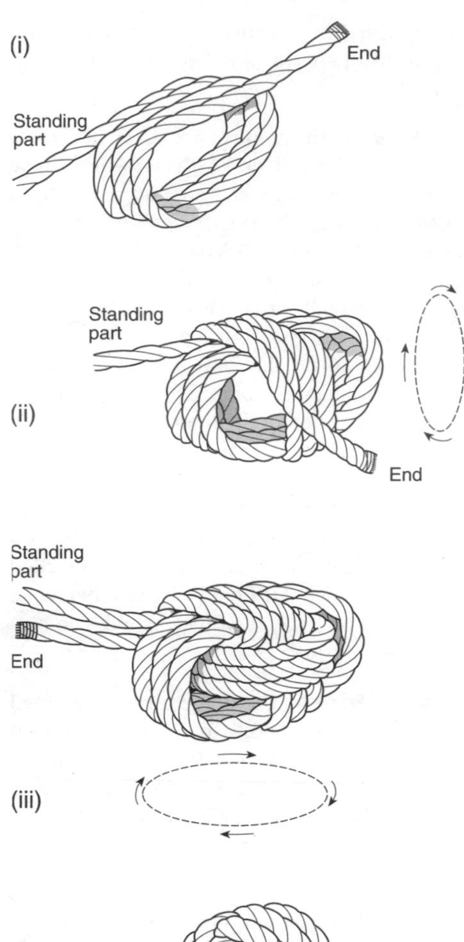

Monkey's fist

overhand knot in the end of the rope, and tuck it into the monkey's fist, which should then be made taut.

monk's seam, the seam made by a sailmaker after sewing the overlapping edges of *cloths together to make a sail. It is a line of stitches through the centre between the two rows of edging stitches. See also PRICK, TO.

monsoon, a seasonal wind in the Indian Ocean, generated by the large land mass to the north of the ocean, which heats up in summer and cools down in winter faster than the sea. The cycle of monsoon winds dominates the weather of the Indian subcontinent and South-East Asia, and strongly influences the ocean. When the land is hot, the air over the continent rises, and strong onshore winds develop carrying moisture-laden air that deposits torrential monsoon rains. The foothills of the Himalayas and the Ghats may receive as much as 10 metres (32.8 ft) of rain. When the continents cool down the winds reverse and blow offshore, and the climate becomes arid. Over the north-west Indian Ocean the wet south-west monsoon blows from May until September steadily at force 7–8 on the *Beaufort Scale. As these winds blow parallel to the Arabian coastline, the effects of *Coriolis force means they push surface water offshore and generate a strong seasonal *upwelling.

Off Somalia a huge *current gyre, the Great Whirl, develops creating surface currents as fast as 7 knots. Locally sea surface temperatures may fall to less than 15 °C (59 °F), and temperature *fronts develop across which the sea temperature may change by 7 °C. The cool upwelled water is rich in nutrients and stimulates intense blooms of algae. These algae become too abundant for the grazing *plankton to eat them all and as they die, they sink down, and their decomposition uses up all the oxygen in the water. In October, after a brief windless period, the winds start to blow from the north-east. The climate reverts to being hot and arid, the upwelling ceases, and the sea becomes unproductive.

On the equator, the reversing winds reverse the flows of the equatorial currents. These reversing winds were first described by Arab *navigators in AD 800 who were regularly sailing *dhows from the Persian Gulf and Oman to their trading posts along the east coast of Africa at Zanzibar, Mombasa, and Dar es Salaam during the north-east monsoon, and returning on the south-west monsoon with slaves and spices.

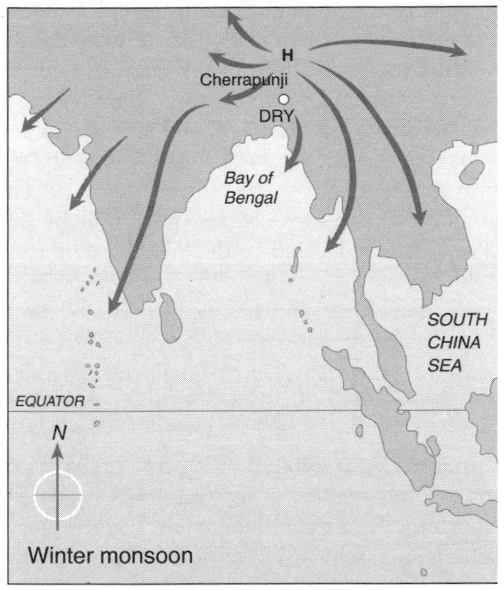

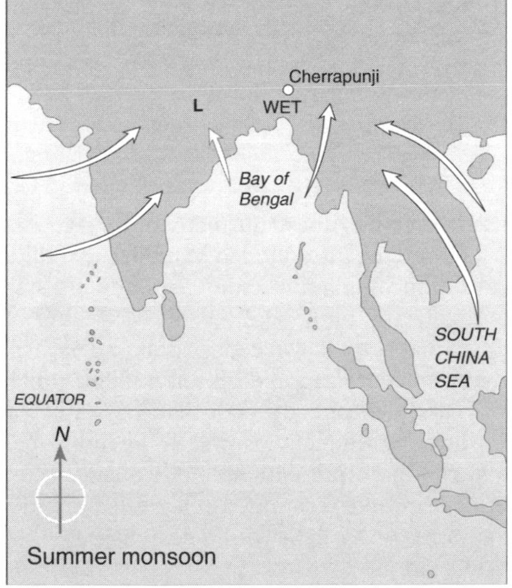

Changing annual wind-flow patterns associated with the winter and summer Asian monsoon

http://yang.gmu.edu/~yang/nasacd/www/indian_monsoon.html M. V. Angel

moon-lore. From the earliest times the phases of the moon have been important to seamen, and the regularity of its movements provided a means for recording the passage of time. The moon was credited with considerable influence on the weather and Virgil (70–19 BC) summarized some of the popular beliefs concerning it in one of the Georgics. According to Pliny (AD 23–79) the fourth and fifth days of new moon were to be watched with particular care. A new moon with horns erect on the fourth day was believed to forecast great *storms at sea. The Venerable Bede (673–735) in his *De Natura Rerum* says of the moon: 'If she looks like gold in her last quarter, there will be wind, if on top of the crescent black spots appear, it will be a rainy month, if in the middle, her full moon will be serene.' A star-dogged moon was regarded by sailors as a bad omen, and reference to this phenomenon is to be found in an old Scottish ballad of 1281, 'Sir Patrick Spens', and also in Samuel Taylor Coleridge's 'The Rime of the *Ancient Mariner'. In several of his plays, Shakespeare refers to the popular beliefs concerning the moon which, in *Hamlet,* he describes as 'The moist star upon whose influence Neptune's empire stands'.

While many of the *superstitions of sailors regarding the moon have no grounding in scientific fact, the lunar haloes to which Varro (116–27 BC) refers as foretelling wind from the bright quarter of the circle, with a double circle indicating a violent storm, are well authenticated as precursors of bad weather.

Although the Greek mathematician and astronomer Ptolemy (*c.*AD 90–168) appreciated the connection between the movements of the moon and the *tides, it was not until Sir Isaac Newton (1642–1727) discovered the law of gravity that this phenomenon was satisfactorily explained.

moonrakers, names given to the small light triangular-shaped sails set above the *skysails of *square-rigged ships in very fine weather. They were also often called moonsails or *raffees.

moor, to, in its strict meaning the condition of a ship when it lies in a harbour or anchorage with two anchors down and the ship middled between them. When a ship is moored in this fashion it is usual to bring both *cables to a mooring swivel just below the *hawsepipes so that the ship may swing to the *tide without getting a *foul hawse. The word is also loosely used to describe other ways of anchoring a ship, e.g. when a ship has a stern anchor laid out as well as a bow anchor, it is said to be moored

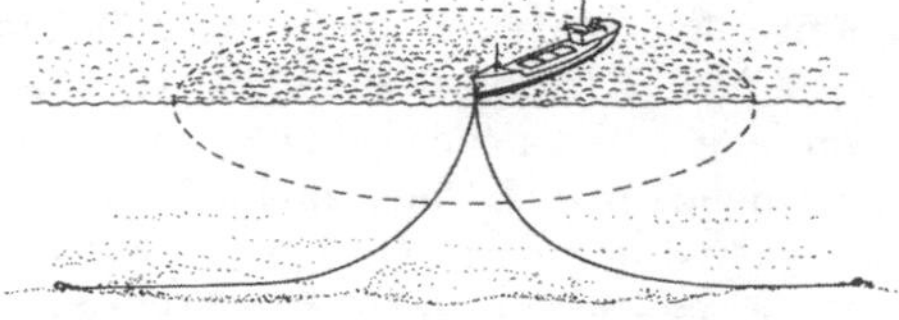

Ship moored

head and stern. It is also used to describe a vessel which is secured head and stern to a *quay; or alongside another vessel, with *berthing hawsers; or which lies with the bow or stern secured to a quay with an anchor laid out from the bow or stern, in which case a *passerelle is often used to gain access to the quay.

mooring, a permanent position in harbours and estuaries to which ships can be secured without using their own anchors. For large ships, a mooring comprises two or three large anchors laid out on the bottom and connected with a chain *bridle, from the centre of which a length of chain *cable leads upwards to a large mooring *buoy, usually cylindrical in shape, to the ring of which a ship can lie in safety by *shackling on its own cable. The vertical cable is short enough to ensure that the ship swings with the tide within its own length. Smaller moorings for smaller ships may require only one anchor or a block of concrete, with a chain rising to a small buoy. For *yachts, a very small buoy, light enough to be easily lifted on board, is attached by a length of rope to a light chain, itself attached to a concrete block. The buoy is brought aboard with a *boathook, and the rope is hauled up until the chain reaches the surface and the yacht is then secured with it. See also BERTHING HAWSERS; TROT.

Morgan, Sir Henry (*c.*1635–88), Welsh *privateer whose early life was obscure until he emerged as the leader of a band of *buccaneers at Jamaica in 1662. In 1671 he captured Porto Bello and Panama, after leading a band of buccaneers, which included Bartholomew *Sharp, in the first land crossing of the Isthmus of Panama in force. From Morgan's point of view he was acting legitimately, as he had been given a commission to act as a privateer by the governor of Jamaica. However, as the *commission antedated the 1670 peace treaty with Spain, the governor's action was illegal and, in an attempt to placate the Spaniards, both he and Morgan were arrested, and returned to England. But neither was punished and, with war against Spain threatening once more, Morgan was knighted by King Charles II and sent out to Jamaica as deputy governor. In this capacity he proved a scourge to the buccaneers and an embarrassment to successive governors of the island. He died a rich landowner at Lawrencefield, Jamaica.

Morgan's character has been traduced ever since the publication of *The Bucaniers of America*, though Morgan won a libel action against its printers. The book, first printed in Dutch in 1678, was written by a French surgeon, John Esquemeling (*c.*1660–1700), who served with the buccaneers from 1666 to 1674. It was then translated into many languages, but the English version, which first appeared in 1684, was taken from the Spanish version, which accounts for the libellous account of Morgan. He was, in fact, a fine leader of men, no more cruel or rapacious than others, and a good tactician.

Earle, P., *The Sack of Panama* (1981).

Morse code, one of the methods to *signal at sea before the introduction of modern satellite communications and radiotelephony. Its system gave the numerals 1–9 and each letter of the alphabet their own code of dots and dashes, e.g. A was dot dash, B dash dot dot dot. Quick and easy to master, the code made it simple for words and sentences, as well as the individual letters of the *International Code of Signals, to be transmitted by sound (wireless telegraphy or foghorn), or by light with a searchlight or an *Aldis lamp.

It was invented by an American portraitist, Samuel Finley Breese Morse (1791–1872), who eventually became professor of painting and sculpture at the University of the City of New York (later New York University). The idea came to him in 1832 while returning from Europe aboard a *packet ship, though he only turned his full attention to it in 1837. He endured great poverty while perfecting the code, only to discover that most of the nations to whom he offered it refused to give him a patent for it. However, eventually the US government gave him an appropriation to cover his costs, and the first Morse signals were passed between Washington and Baltimore on 24 May 1844.

However, when the code was introduced into Europe it soon became evident that it was inadequate for transmitting non-English messages, as it did not make allowances for letters with diacritic marks. A variant was therefore devised—among other alterations the length of a dash was made constant not variable—at a European Conference held in 1851, and this came to be known as the International Morse Code. In 1858 most nations in Europe contributed 400,000 francs as payment to Morse for the use they had made of the code.

Some minor alterations were made to the code in 1938 and more recently a new sign, A (dot dash) and C (dash dot dash dot) which stands for @, was added to it to help ham radio operators, its main users today, transmit email addresses in the code.

moses, a very broad flat-bottomed boat, propelled by *oars, which in the days of sailing ships was used in the Caribbean to bring hogsheads of sugar from the island beaches to shipping which had to lie off them because of the shallowness of the water.

Mother Carey's Chickens is a seafarer's name for *seabirds, the storm petrels (family Hydrobatidae). The name is a corruption of Mater Cara, darling mother. Sailors believed they came to warn them of approaching *storms, and since each bird contained the soul of a drowned seaman it was most unlucky to kill one. See also SUPERSTITIONS OF SAILORS.

M. V. Angel

motor yachts, see YACHTING: POWER.

moulding, the *shipbuilding term to describe the depth of any member of a ship's construction, such as its *frames, *keelson, keel, stern, *sternpost, *beams, etc. The width measurement is known as the *siding.

mould-loft, a long building with a considerable floor area on which the *lines produced by a naval architect or *yacht designer can be laid off in their full dimensions. These full-size drawings can then be copied with the aid of wooden moulds to which in turn the steel *frames or, in the case of wooden vessels, the hull moulds, are fashioned. See also SHIPBUILDING.

moulds, the name given to the thin flat wooden patterns made in the *mould-loft for all structural parts of the ship being built. They include not only the keel, *stem, and stern frame but all *frames, *bulkheads, and decks. Together with these moulds, bevel boards are produced to give the differing face angles of the frames and *beams. See also SHIPBUILDING.

mouse, a stop made of *spunyarn fixed to the *collar of the *stays in a *square-rigged ship to hold the running *eye of the *rigging from slipping down the stay. It is also a mark fixed on the *braces and other rigging of the *yards to indicate when they are square. In general, any small collar made with spunyarn round a wire or rope with the object of holding something in place, such as an eye threaded on the rope, would be called a mouse. A mouse can also be used to prevent a hook jumping out of a ringbolt or eye, or to prevent a rope running across the hook from jumping clear, and the operation of putting one in place is to **mouse a hook**.

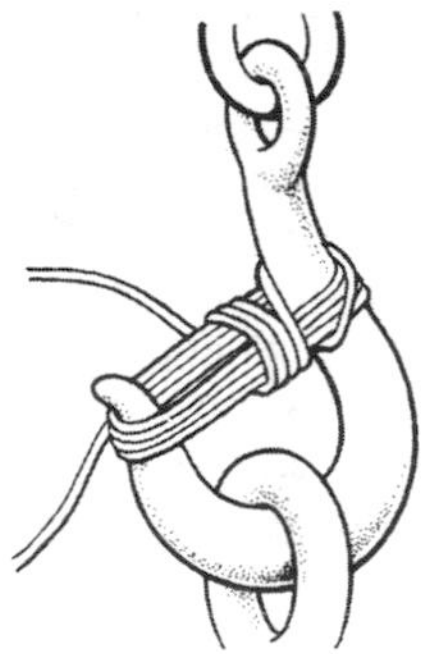

Hook half moused; to be finished with more turns and a reef knot

mudhook, the sailor's slang name for an anchor.

Mulberry Harbour, an artificial harbour constructed off the coast of Normandy during the Second World War (1939–45) to supply the Allied invasion forces which landed there on 6 June 1944.

multihull, see CATAMARAN; TRIMARAN.

murderer, a small iron or brass handgun employed during the days of sail. It was fitted with an iron pin on the stock which was inserted into a socket so that the gun could be traversed easily by hand. Sockets for these guns were fitted in several places in a ship so that they could quickly be taken where most needed. They were purely anti-personnel guns for use against *boarders. Their use in navies went out during the early 18th century, when *marines became a permanent part of a warship's complement, but they continued to be used by merchant ships as a protection against *privateers and *piracy up to the beginning of the 19th century.

muster, to, the operation of assembling the crew of a warship on deck and calling through a nominal list of the complement, to which men answered to their names. It was a necessary administrative action during the days of sailing navies before modern methods were introduced to check that fictitious names, for whom pay and victuals were being drawn, had not been entered on the **muster-book**. It was on the evidence of the monthly muster that naval seamen became entitled to their pay and rations, including their *grog. In the early days of the British Navy there was widespread abuse of the system of pay and victuals by drawing larger amounts than were required. These amounts were accounted for by retaining on the muster-book the names of men who had died or deserted, and also by entering in the book fictitious names to which other members of the crew answered when the names were called. See also DEAD SHARES; WIDOWS' MEN.

mutiny, a resistance by force to recognized authority, an insurrection, but applied particularly to any form of sedition in any naval or military force of a nation. In its strict legal sense the term implies the use of force, but by long custom a refusal to obey a legal order of a superior officer is considered to be mutiny. It is not necessarily restricted to naval and military forces: a crew which rises against its officers or a crew member who strikes a superior officer or refuses to obey a legal order is just as guilty of mutiny in a merchant vessel as in a naval ship. Mutiny in a naval or military force is always tried before a court martial, in a merchant ship before a civil court.

Those taking part in the early voyages of *exploration by sea frequently suffered mutinies among their crews, *Drake, *Magellan, and *Hudson being just three examples. Often blood was spilt, though the massacre of passengers and crew that followed the *shipwreck of the Dutch *East Indiaman **Batavia*, was exceptional. Those who mutinied and escaped often resorted to *piracy and any that were caught were hanged from the *yardarm without further ado. However, in the case of Magellan not only did one of the principal mutineers, Juan Sebastián del Cano (*c*.1476–1526), escape punishment—as a *pilot he was too valuable to be hanged—but, as the commander of the only ship to survive the expedition, he was honoured, *faute de mieux*, by the King of Spain with a coat of arms and a pension. A statue to him was also erected, a signal honour for a mutineer.

During the days of sailing navies, the penalty for mutiny in all navies was invariably hanging at the yardarm; when an entire ship's company mutinied, the ringleaders were hanged. However, in the naval mutiny at *Spithead in 1797, when all the ships of the Channel Fleet were in mutiny against the pay and conditions of naval service, there were no victims, and indeed no one was brought before a court martial as it was considered that the men were justified in their complaints. However, in the mutiny at the *Nore which immediately followed that at Spithead, a number of the ringleaders were hanged, since all the demands of the seamen had already been met at Spithead and there was, in the eyes of the *Admiralty, no justification for the mutiny.

One of the best known of all naval mutinies was that on board HMS **Bounty* in 1789; another was the mutiny aboard the Russian *battleship **Potemkin* in 1905; and a third was the mutiny in the German *High Seas Fleet in 1918, which led directly to the defeat of Germany in the First World War (1914–18). Another 20th-century naval mutiny occurred in the British Home Fleet at Invergordon in 1931 when the pay of naval seamen was reduced as a result of a crisis in Britain's economy. A proportion of crew members of several warships mutinied by refusing to obey orders and gathering on the foredeck of their ships, but quick action by the *Admiralty in rescinding the pay cuts brought the protests to a swift end.

MV, a prefix placed before the name of a ship to indicate that it is a motor (*diesel) vessel.

MY, a prefix used before the name of a *yacht to designate a motor yacht.

Mylar is a brand name for a strong polyester film. It was developed from Dacron, with which it is sometimes laminated to make sails.

N

'naked', the term used to describe the bottom of a sailing warship after the *copper sheathing had been removed, either by the action of rough seas or in *dock for examination or replacement.

'Nancy Dawson', the tune to which, by tradition, the daily issue of *grog was distributed in the 18th-century British Navy. It was a popular *sea song among seamen at that time and may perhaps have become associated with the daily grog issues because one of the effects of the spirit upon many men was to encourage them to burst into song. This pleasant little naval tradition died during the 19th century. *Nancy Dawson* was also the name of the first *yacht, probably, to sail round the world, making her circumnavigation in the late 1840s. See also SHANTY.

Nansen, Fridtjof (1861–1930), Norwegian explorer and zoologist, whose contribution to *oceanography included the Nansen bottle which he designed for collecting deep-water samples. Born near Oslo and educated at the university there, he was appointed assistant curator of the Natural History Museum at Bergen, and in 1888–9 he crossed the Greenland ice sheet from east to west, which he later described in his book *First Crossing of Greenland and Eskimo Life*. In order to test his theory of the existence of a polar *current flowing towards the east coast of Greenland, he set sail in June 1893 in the specially constructed wooden *topsail *schooner **Fram*, which spent the next 35 months drifting with the frozen *ice towards the North Pole. While the *Fram* was drifting north Nansen and her crew measured the depths of the Arctic Ocean through holes in the ice and discovered that it was not shallow, as had been thought, but a deep basin.

Other scientific investigations included recording air and water temperatures, and inspecting *plankton. Eventually, Nansen became impatient at the *Fram*'s progress and when she was still about 500 kilometres (300 mls.) from the North Pole he left the ship and, with a companion, sledged across the ice to try and reach it on foot. He reached *latitude 86° 13' N., further north than anyone had previously travelled, before having to turn back. He then turned south to Franz Josef Land where he wintered, and was picked up in 1896 by the British Jackson-Harmsworth polar expedition.

From 1905 to 1908 Nansen was the first Norwegian ambassador to Britain, but resigned in order to carry out oceanographic research round Iceland and Spitsbergen and also in the Kara Sea. In 1919 he was appointed Norwegian representative to the League of Nations and in 1920 director of an organization for the repatriation of prisoners of war. He was awarded the 1923 Nobel Peace Prize and in 1926 was made Lord Rector of St Andrews University, Scotland.

nao, the Spanish word for a ship during the 13th–16th centuries. It was not any particular type of vessel, only the general word meaning ship. The three ships with which Christopher *Columbus sailed across the Atlantic in 1492, though *caravels in type, were all described as *naos* in contemporary Spanish records.

Narrow Seas, those seas over which the King of England claimed sovereignty from the earliest days of England's emergence as a maritime power. They were the two seas which lay between England and France (the English Channel) and England and the Netherlands (the southern North Sea). Sovereignty of these seas implied the demanding of *salutes at sea from all foreign ships meeting an English warship in these waters, and also the right of regulating all fishing in them. One of the chief naval appointments of those days was that of admiral of the Narrow Seas, whose duties included patrolling the *fisheries and the enforcement of the salute. The claim of English sovereignty over these seas was maintained until the adoption of the three-mile limit in 1822 as *territorial waters by several European nations including Britain. See also VAIL, TO.

National Coastwatch Institution (NCI), a UK charity founded in 1994 to run Visual Watch Stations, often abandoned *coastguard stations, to help keep British coastal waters safe. Volunteer NCI watchkeepers keep a constant guard on large stretches of the UK coastline and are an important part of the UK network for search and rescue (SAR) operations. They log all small boat traffic to assist in tracing any missing craft and provide local weather conditions to yachtsmen, tourist offices, and local radio stations. In 2004 there were 24 NCI stations in operation, with more being planned.

National Oceanic and Atmospheric Administration (NOAA), a US government agency founded in 1970 to unify the piecemeal nationwide activities to combat *pollution and other *environmental issues into a rational and systematic approach to understanding, protecting, developing, and enhancing the total environment. In addition to a specific responsibility for the development and conservation of national *fisheries, NOAA led the development of a national oceanic and atmospheric search and development programme to provide a variety of scientific and technical services to other federal agencies and to the public. Today, its organization includes the Office of Fisheries, the Office of Coastal Zone Management, the Office of Oceanic and Atmospheric Services, the Office of Research and Development, the Office of Satellites, the Office of Minerals and Energy, and the Office of Policy and Planning which has within it the National Marine Pollution Program Office and the National Climate Program Office.

nautical almanac, a periodical publication of astronomical and other, primarily ephemeral, information intended for the *navigator and nautical astronomer. The earliest nautical almanac was the *Connoissance des temps ou des mouvements celestes* published in Paris under royal patent by the Bureau des Longitudes in 1679. The publication included full tables of the moon's motions and a long list of the *establishment of the port for French harbours.

Towards the middle of the 18th century the improvement in instruments and tables had made the determination of *longitude at sea by *lunar distance a practicable possibility. The Astronomer Royal, Nevil Maskelyne, was therefore authorized by the *Board of Longitude to compile a publication which would enable the mariner to compare the astronomical information and data contained in it with observations made at sea. *The Nautical Almanac and Astronomical Ephemeris for the Year 1767* was the first English nautical almanac and the earliest by far to give essential data for the practical determination of longitude at sea. It has, with periodic modifications of function and title, continued publication ever since.

Towards the end of the 19th century it was recognized that much of the matter contained in the almanac was of little interest to seamen and it was decided to issue the first part, consisting mainly of the *ephemeris and lunar distances, separately. In 1914 on the recommendation of the Royal Astronomical Society *The Nautical Almanac Abridged for the Use of Seamen*, as it then was, became an entirely separate publication. In 1948 the newly formed (and later Royal) Institute of Navigation, at the suggestion of the *Admiralty, was asked to advise on the complete redesign of the *Abridged Nautical Almanac*. As a result, from 1952 the revised almanac giving, as in the *Air Almanac*, Greenwich *Hour Angle (GHA) of the sun, moon, planets, and the first point of Aries tabulated against *Greenwich Mean Time was published. From 1958 the *Abridged Nautical Almanac* and the *American Nautical Almanac* were 'unified' and became identical in content, reproduced from identical material which has been made available to other national nautical almanacs. The title of the purely astronomical part of the Almanac was in 1960 changed to *The Astronomical Ephemeris*.

The Nautical Almanac tabulates the two coordinates *declination and GHA of the sun, moon, and planets at tabular intervals of 1 hour of GMT and, for the stars, GHA Aries, declination, and sidereal hour angle (SHA) at intervals of three days. In this way the almanac, in effect, determines the true direction, as it would be seen from the centre of the earth, of any object at the time of observation. By means of reduction tables, or a calculator or computer, this calculated *altitude is compared with the observed altitude to give an *intercept from which a *position line may be plotted.

There are in every maritime nation a number of commercially produced nautical almanacs containing a wide range of navigational information outside of that normally included in the official publications, such as tidal information, *light lists, navigation tables, *pilotage information, and so on. Some reproduce, with permission, matter from the official almanacs. For the most part such almanacs fulfil a very useful role for yachtsmen and other small craft navigators including fishermen who wish to cut down the number of publications carried. Mike Richey

nautical mile, the unit of distance used at sea, practically speaking a minute of *latitude. The publication in London in 1637 of *The Seaman's Practise* by the English surveyor Richard Norwood, who had measured an arc of the *meridian, effectively marked the distinction between the land mile and the sea mile. 'There are', he wrote in his preface, 'a greater number of feet contained in a degree than the common opinion that a thousand paces (of 5 feet) make a mile.' If the earth were a perfect sphere, a nautical mile would, of course, measure an arc length of one minute at all places and in all directions; but it is an oblate spheroid so that the nautical mile varies slightly with the latitude, and is shortest at the equator and longest at the poles. Norwood proposed a standard length of 6,120 feet (1,867 m) which he later changed to 6,000 feet (1,830 m) on the grounds that 'every man desires to have his reckoning something before the ship so that he fall not in with a place unexpected'. In other words the short mile was safer.

By 1730 the nautical mile as a minute of a great circle on the earth was well established. The question then arose as to which figure of the earth should be adopted. The difficulty was that although there may have been agreement about the figure of the earth there remained the problem that different countries and authorities adopted their own values for the land mile, the foot, and the metre. Finally in 1924 the International Hydrographic Bureau proposed a figure for an International Spheroid which was generally accepted and in 1929 the Bureau recommended a standard length of 1,852 metres (6,076 English ft) for the nautical mile which is now the accepted figure. Errors arising from the use of the standard nautical mile rather than its value at the latitude in which the ship lies are of no navigational significance. Thus for the seaman the nautical mile remains a minute of latitude.

Moody, A., 'Early Units of Measurement and the Nautical Mile', *Journ. Inst. Navigation*, 5 (1952), 262. Mike Richey

Nautilus, a species of cephalopod (*Nautilus pompilius*) of the warm waters of the tropical Pacific. It was also the name given to four *submarines of note: **(1)** the one built by Robert *Fulton in 1801; **(2)** a conventionally powered submarine of 1732 tons lent in 1931 to the Australian polar explorer Sir George Hubert *Wilkins for a voyage under the polar *ice cap. **(3)** The name of the world's first nuclear-powered submarine built by the General Dynamics (Electric Boat) Corporation for the US Navy. Her keel was laid on 14 June 1952 and on 17 January 1955 her captain sent the historic signal: 'under way on nuclear power.' Her length was 99 metres (324 ft) and she had a surface displacement of 3,539 tons, and a submerged top speed of 20 knots. In August 1958 she succeeded where the earlier submarine of the same name had failed, in making the passage from the Pacific to the Atlantic under the polar ice cap, reaching the pole itself on 3 August. An important factor in the success of this voyage was the system of *inertial navigation with which she was fitted. **(4)** The name of the submarine in which Captain Nemo sailed 20,000 *leagues under the sea in the well-known novel of that name by Jules *Verne (1828–1905), published in 1869.

nautophone, an electrically operated sound signal of high pitch used in fog, fitted on *buoys and *lightships.

naval architecture, the science of designing ships, *submarines, *floating docks, *yachts, oil rigs for the *offshore oil and gas industry, and any craft for use on water. Those qualified to work in this area are known as **naval architects**.

Until the late 16th century, when plans for constructing new ships began to be drawn

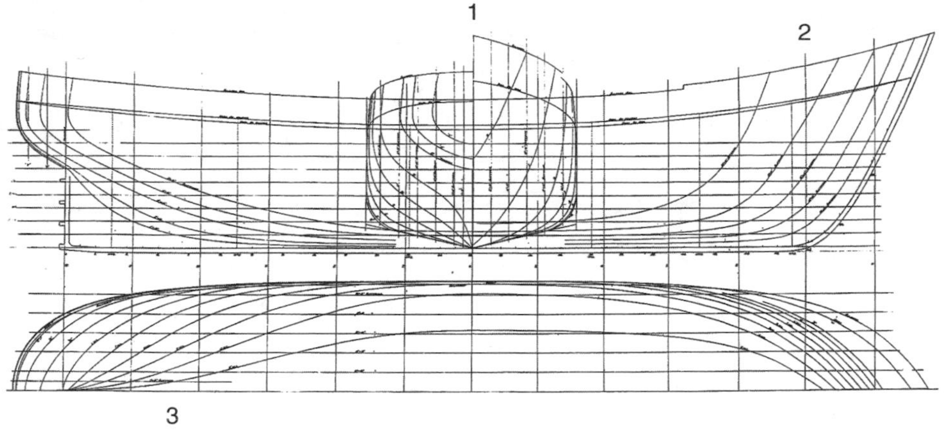

Ship's lines plan showing:

1The body plan 2 Elevation showing the bow and buttocks lines 3 The waterplanes in plan view

on paper, the shipwright's trade was a closely guarded mystique. The necessary expertise was handed down by word of mouth from father to son, as ships were built solely 'by eye' using traditional 'rule-of-thumb' methods. As a result, improvements in ship construction were introduced only slowly against deep-rooted suspicion and dogmatism.

The work of early naval architects was unscientific and generally followed specifications of shape and *scantlings which had been in use for generations. A more scientific approach was attempted by the Swedish naval architect Frederik af Chapman (1721–1808) and others. Chapman wrote a well-regarded treatise on the subject. But it was not until the British engineer William Froude (1810–79) began to study *hydrodynamics and ship behaviour in the late 1860s, by undertaking more sophisticated tank testing, that any advance of importance occurred.

Modern naval architecture by Fred M. Walker

Nowadays, naval architects must handle a wide variety of tasks including economic viability studies, conceptual design, strength and *stability calculations, as well as supplying the final working drawings for a ship. They may be asked to superintend ships under construction, to make the calculations for launching, and oversee the tests and trials required by a new vessel. The naval architect is also responsible for ensuring that the new ship meets *Classification Society regulations as well as the Statutes of International Law as defined by the *International Maritime Organization and other authorities. With the increase in complex technology there is now a much greater overlap with marine engineering, to the extent that most universities now offer combined degrees in Naval Architecture and Marine Engineering.

To design a ship, a series of calculations must take place, each defining one aspect of the ship, and in turn absorbing the results of previous calculations. The process has to be repeated several times—a process known as *iteration*—until the optimum ship design has been achieved. This is known as the **design spiral** (see illustration overleaf), and owing to the intense 'number crunching' required, is aided greatly by computers.

Basic Design. This incorporates the main dimensions of a ship, with estimates of displacement *tonnage and cargo-carrying capacity. In this part of the investigation, matters like depth of water in anticipated ports, air draft (maximum height allowable under bridges on the ship's anticipated route) and the owners' requirements for earning ability have to be incorporated into the calculations, and then a preliminary arrangement plan is drawn. The larger a ship, the more efficient is its capacity. For example, by doubling the dimensions of a ship, the cargo capacity increases eightfold,

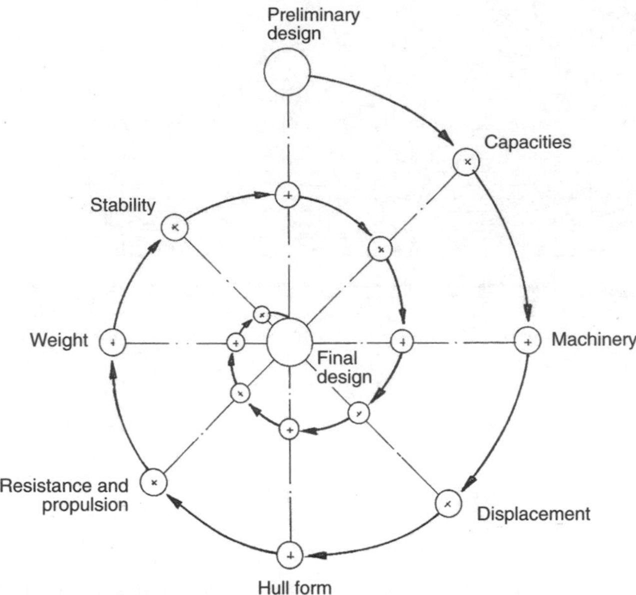

The design spiral

while the fuel consumption is unlikely to be more than double.

Amongst the plans of a ship, which may amount to hundreds, one should find:

- General arrangement (the internal layout)
- *Lines plan (showing the complex contouring of the hull)
- Midship section (showing the structural strength at midsection)
- Structural profile (showing *bulkheads and strength members)
- *Rigging plan (giving external fittings and profile)
- Machinery arrangement
- *Propellers (including bow and stern thrusters, propulsion pods)
- *Stabilizers
- Electrical layout
- Cargo capacity or passenger plan
- Paint lines

As a matter of principle, all plans are drawn with the ship 'steaming' to the right-hand side of the paper, so that a rigging plan shows its *starboard side. This international convention is vital, as information on the ship may be sent anywhere in the world, and all shipyards and ship repair establishments accept these conventions.

In the past few years the widespread introduction of computers has led to simplified ship plans, with in many cases the final drawings (where needed) being printed on paper as small as A3 size.

Selection of Machinery. To ensure decisions are made correctly, the naval architect must know the routes the ship will work, its range of operation, and the availability of fuel. The vast bulk of modern ships have two-stroke or medium-speed *diesel engines, and in these cases the weight, power, fuel consumption, and other matters can be predicted with great accuracy.

The availability of machinery spares must not be overlooked, although with modern air communications this seldom poses a problem. The options are immense, and the choice of machinery is endless.

In the final analysis an efficient design is one that uses material and local skills to produce a ship that is optimum for the trade envisaged. For example, the modern *cruise liner has a need for maximum passenger capacity and quick turnaround in port. The current answer is a ship with underslung or podded propulsors energized by *electric propulsion. The beauty of this configuration is that the alternators can be placed anywhere on the ship, whilst the main machinery is either within the propulsor or situated just above it, taking up little of the ship's vital earning capacity.

Once the ship has overall dimensions, machinery, and fuel capacity settled, the naval architect can compute capacity for passengers, crew, and cargo. Now the dimensions can be finalized and the final stages of the design spiral completed.

Tank Testing. To ensure that the ship has an efficient and sea-kindly hull form, an accurate scale model, usually about 3 metres (10 ft) long, is built and taken through a series of controlled experiments from which the ship's performance can be predicted with accuracy. This form of ship model experimentation has been carried out for nearly 130 years, following the 19th-century pioneering work of William Froude. Tank simulations allow for model testing of rudders, thrusters, and, for passenger ships, the ubiquitous stabilizer fins. Ships carrying passengers may have wind tunnel tests carried out on their funnels and *superstructures to ensure all soot and noxious exhaust fumes are blown clear of the decks.

With most decisions settled, the structure of the ship is designed to ensure the ship is strong enough for a long and arduous life. The key drawing is the Midship section which gives many technical particulars and the *scantlings of all steelwork parts at a point of significant stress. From this the weights and centres of gravity of the ship in various conditions including unladen, ballasted, fully laden, and so on can be analysed and stability checked out. Now the design spiral is complete, although it must be rechecked for every small change in the basic design before the final plans are drawn up and sent to the *shipbuilding yard responsible for the ship's construction.

For naval architecture terms not cross-referenced or mentioned in this entry see AFTERBODY; BLOCK COEFFICIENT; BODY PLAN; BUTTOCK LINES; CENTRE OF EFFORT; CENTRE OF LATERAL RESISTANCE; HEELING MOMENT; PRISMATIC COEFFICIENT; SECTIONS; SIMPSON'S RULES; WETTED SURFACE. See also YACHT-BUILDING.

naval hoods or **whoods,** large pieces of thick timber which were used in the days of sailing navies to encircle the *hawseholes in order to take the wear caused by the heavy *hemp *cables when a ship rode to its anchors.

navel pipe, the name of the pipe which led from the *forecastle deck—or from the main deck in the case of earlier warships when the *capstan was situated between decks—to the *chain, or *cable, lockers below, through which the anchor cable passed. The origin of the term was probably anatomical, coming from the similarity of feeding the cable into the chain locker to a mother feeding an unborn baby through the umbilical cord.

navicert, a certificate issued to a neutral merchant ship at its port of *departure during wartime. It was issued by a power enforcing a *blockade against an enemy country so that the ship could proceed through the blockaded zone without being brought in for examination. It was introduced by the British during the First World War (1914–18) and was used again during the Second World War (1939–45).

navigate, to, to steer or direct a vessel accurately and safely on the open ocean, along rivers, or in coastal waters. The noun, **navigation**, and the adjective, **navigable**, are derived from the verb when used in the sense of steering or directing a vessel, or describing waters through which a ship can be safely taken.

navigation, from the latin *navis* (a ship) and *agere* (to drive), the art and science of conducting a craft as it moves about its ways. See CELESTIAL NAVIGATION; COASTAL NAVIGATION; HYPERBOLIC NAVIGATION; INERTIAL NAVIGATION; SATELLITE NAVIGATION. What follows is a short history of navigation.

Navigation Without Artefacts. When James *Cook discovered Oceania in the 18th century the cultures were still at a Neolithic stage of development. But to Captain Cook, perhaps the most illustrious of all scientific *navigators, it was a matter of wonder the way the Polynesians navigated 'from Island to Island for several hundred *leagues, the sun serving them for a compass by day and the Moon and Stars by night'. Andia y Varela, leader of a Spanish expedition to Tahiti in 1744, was similarly impressed by the skill of the navigators. 'When the night is a clear one,' he wrote, 'they steer by the stars; and this is the easiest navigation for them because these being many [in number], not only do they note by them the *bearings on which the several islands with which they are in touch lie, but also the harbours in them, so that they make straight for the entrance by following the *rhumb of the particular star that rises or sets over it.'

The traditional navigation skills of the Pacific islanders will have encompassed the skills of all Neolithic navigators, and of navigators in the China Seas, the Indian Ocean, the Mediterranean, and the seas of northern Europe down to the Vikings of the 10th century and their Norman successors in the 11th. The methods, practised well into the 20th century by indigenous Pacific navigators, have been studied over the years by many scholars. Historically their interest is that they give us an idea of how other cultures in other seas and other centuries navigated before the introduction of the *magnetic compass enabled *sailing directions and *charts to be scientifically based, and navigation from then on founded on measurement. From the navigational point of view no work is more informative than *We, the Navigators* by David *Lewis, which describes his valuable and remarkable fieldwork.

In 1968–9 under a research fellowship of the Australian University Lewis spent nine months in *Isbjorn*, a 12-metre (39-ft) ketch, investigating native navigation in the western Pacific, learning from the surviving practising navigators and getting them to navigate *Isbjorn* by their methods. Hippour, as an example, an initiated Micronesian navigator from Puluwat, sailed *Isbjorn* on a voyage of some 1,840 kilometres (1,150 mls.) entirely without charts or instruments, relying only on his cyclopedic memory of *reefs and islands under the stars spanning some 2,400 kilometres (1,500 mls.). Hippour could neither read or write, nor understand the western concept of crossing *position lines to *fix position.

Basically, indigenous Pacific navigation is a system of *dead reckoning based on observation rather than measurement. There are, classically, no artefacts. *Waves, *winds, clouds, stars, sun, moon, *seabirds, *fish, the water itself are, to quote another authority, all there is to see, feel, smell, or hear. The navigational task is to integrate information from these sources into a system accurate and reliable enough to guide the mariner to his destination. The process is one of observation, judgement, and experience rather than measurement. The overall objective will be to bring the vessel into what Lewis terms the 'expanded target area', where signs of land such as birds, deflected swells, cloud formations, and so on will enable the navigator to home on to his destination.

The methods vary to some extent according to local conditions. In the Carolines, for example, wave direction is used to steer a steady *course, whereas in the Marshall Islands, where *atolls refract the waves, interference patterns themselves are used for orientation. In the tropics, equatorial stars near the *horizon change bearing very little as they rise and set, and the navigator chooses a guiding star for his destination and steers to keep it at a steady angle on the bow. Memory necessarily plays a vital part in the whole process and star courses for a large number of islands (about 60 in the Carolines) will be committed to memory by the navigator under training.

The ocean phase of the voyage may be divided, conceptually, into a number of segments (or *etak*) corresponding to the apparent passage of a notional reference island under successive navigational stars using a procedure analogous to the running fix. The island is conceived as moving backwards as the *canoe progresses and the segments so defined give the navigator his distance travelled and distance run. The first and last segments are identified with the dipping distance of the island of *departure and the expanded target area of the destination. The speed at which the reference island is taken to move backwards reflects, of course, simply the accuracy of the dead reckoning. The island is, if you like, a metaphor, a way of organizing navigation information. Like the chart it is an abstraction.

Birth of Navigation Based on Measurement. In the West at least, navigation based on meas-

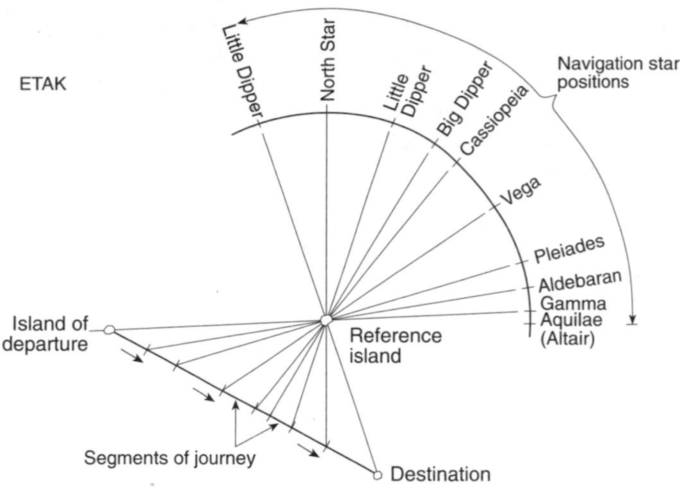

The concept of *etak*

urement was born in the Mediterranean and was developed rapidly by the Italian city states during the 13th century. By the end of it, Mediterranean seamen had the magnetic compass (the card already subdivided into 32 points), systematically compiled *sailing directions based on compass directions and estimated distances, and the nautical chart drawn from the same information.

It was, above all, the discovery and development of the magnetic compass that made mathematical navigation, the chart, and reliable *pilot books possible. It also altered the pattern of Mediterranean trade. Before its introduction the seas were normally closed in winter because of the weather and the difficulty of navigating with overcast skies. Once in use it enabled the number of voyages to be doubled so that the various trading fleets could make two round voyages each year without having to lay up overseas.

The word 'compass' originally meant the nautical division of the horizon into 32 'points' rather than an instrument or device of any kind, and compass directions were named after the familiar names of the winds that the seaman distinguished. Pliny, for instance, in his *Natural History* writes: 'From Carpathos is fifty miles with Africus to Rhodes', Africus being a wind; and the pilot bound for Rhodes might well wait for the wind to blow from that *quarter before setting sail.

Whether charts were used in antiquity is a matter of dispute, but none seems to have survived. In the late Middle Ages the *portulan chart appeared quite suddenly, the earliest surviving example in Italy, complete in all its parts and without apparent parentage. It was mathematically based and the first map of any kind to carry a scale. With the mariner's compass and the *sand-glass, which enabled the distance run to be calculated, it provided a self-contained system of navigation that seemed quite adequate for all normal purposes. Indeed, until the 17th century, there was no means of fixing a ship's position offshore in the Mediterranean. However, although voyages might now end anywhere from the Black Sea to Flanders, the Mediterranean seaman would seldom be out of sight of land for long. The fact that he would have followed magnetic, rather than *true, courses would have been of little consequence since both the sailing directions and the plain charts (hence the derivation of *plain sailing), were based on the same data. Nor did the inadequacy of the plain chart, where the *meridians were parallel to each other and did not converge towards the pole, matter much in a sea that stretches east–west over such a narrow belt of *latitude. The art of dead reckoning had been perfected, and to all intents and purposes seemed to suffice.

Early Navigation in Northern Europe. For those navigating the Atlantic coasts of Europe matters were quite different. Here a knowledge of the *tides was essential, both to determine the strong tidal streams on coastal passages and to predict the depths of water in ports and harbours. The emphasis in early English sailing directions, for instance, is on *soundings and the tides. 'Upon Portland is fair white sand and 24 *fathoms' runs one passage, showing the northern practice of establishing position on the *continental shelf by the depth of water and the nature of the bottom with an early form of *lead line.

A later entry reads 'A south moon maketh high water within Wight, and all the havens be full at west-south-west between Start and the Lizard', which refers to the practice of telling the time of high water by the bearing of the moon. For it had long been known that although high water does not occur simultaneously at all places on the same *longitude it does occur at any one place when the moon is at the same position in the sky. The daily retardation of the tides was well understood. However, for the unlettered seaman, accustomed to telling the time from a compass bearing of the sun—where each of the 32 points of the *compass rose represented 45 minutes—one point was, for him, close enough to the true retardation of 48 minutes. The mid-16th-century English pilot's skills in the *Narrow Seas, which he shared with the seamen of Normandy and Brittany, were considerable and the waters he navigated were as perilous as any, but they were not the navigational skills required in the ocean.

Early Ocean Navigation. From the 9th century onwards Norse traders and raiders in their *longships and *knarrs penetrated into the Mediterranean, and to Iceland, Greenland, and Norway in the north. Little is known of their precise navigational practices beyond what can be gleaned from the sagas, but they reached America some 500 years before *Columbus and for centuries conducted regular passages of some 1,400 *nautical miles to and from Greenland and Norway without the use of magnetic compass or chart. There is some archaeological evidence that they used a *Viking compass, but its use is unlikely to have been critical.

In the 1420s, when the *caravels of *Henry the Navigator began to sail down the West African coast, a better understanding of the wind and current systems of the Atlantic Ocean became necessary if regular trade routes were to be established. The practice adopted was to take a long *board out into the Atlantic, keeping the north-east *trade winds *abeam until the variables were met with further north and an easterly course could then be laid for home. To achieve this the pilot had to know when he had reached the parallel along which he was to run to his destination. At first this was done by comparing the *altitude of Polaris, as observed with the *seaman's quadrant, with what its altitude had been at the port of departure (say Lisbon). The difference was of course the difference in latitude but latitude meant nothing to the mariner at that time and was not marked on the charts. The difference in degrees and minutes was thus converted into linear distance by multiplying the readings by 16⅔ (the accepted degree of the meridian) to give the difference in leagues. Later the scale of the quadrant itself would often be marked with the names of ports and landfalls whose latitudes had been established. When the sun replaced the star as the equator was approached, first the mariner's *astrolabe and later the *cross-staff replaced the seaman's quadrant as the favoured instrument for observation.

Polaris is not, as sailors then believed, fixed in the sky, but circles the pole of the heavens so that its altitude will only correspond to that of the pole twice a day. Astronomers devised a simple rule for using the star to find latitude. Sailors had long used, as a form of clock, the rotation around Polaris of the two so-called Guards (or Pointers) in the Lesser Bear (Ursa Minor), a line from the front Guard (Kochab) to the star representing the hour hand. To help them memorize the midnight position of the Guards at different times of the year they imagined a giant figure in the sky, the pole at his stomach, whose head, feet, and outstretched arms, with cross lines between the limbs, defined an eightfold division of the circle. How this was used for timekeeping need not bother us but the new rules for observing Polaris made use of the familiar imagery to indicate the corrections to the star's altitude for different positions of the Guards. 'You are to know,' reads an English manual, 'that when the Guards are at the head of Polaris, the star is 3 degrees below the axis.'

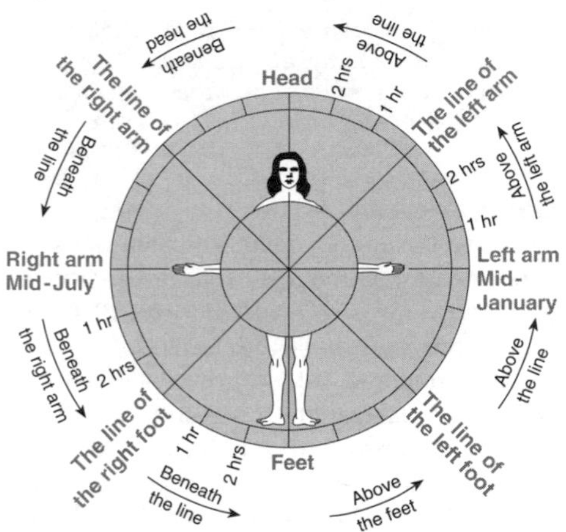

The 13th-century sky clock diagram in which the head, right arm, feet, and left arm marked the four seasonal positions of the clock hand at midnight in mid-April, mid-July, mid-October, and mid-January. The time by night was estimated from the position of the Guard stars. The diagram was later adapted to give the daily altitudes of the Pole Star at Lisbon and elsewhere

Developments of Charts and Manuals during the 15th–18th centuries. When the Portuguese explorers crossed the equator in 1471 Polaris was no longer visible and in 1484 King John II of Portugal appointed a mathematical commission to examine the problem of using the sun to determine latitude at sea, and its conclusions are described in the oldest surviving Portuguese navigation manual, *Regimento do astrolabio e do quadrante*. This gives seventeen examples of determining latitude from the sun's meridian altitude with different combinations of latitude and *declination, as well as rules for 'raising the pole' (finding how far the ship must run on a particular course to raise its latitude one degree).

In 1537 the great Portuguese mathematician Pedro Nuñes (1492–1577) published an important study on the errors of the plain chart. Navigation in the Atlantic had now become astronomical and the pilot required a meridian on his chart to identify the latitudes he was expected to attain and then 'run down'. The problem was that since the plain chart ignored the earth's curvature, an east–west compass course would eventually carry the ship off the east–west line of latitude marked on the chart. *Mercator's projection in his world map of 1569 solved this problem by introducing proportionally the same error into the spacing of the lines of latitude as there was in the lines of longitude.

While the Portuguese, and later the Spaniards, were transforming the practices of ocean navigation, the English, although they traded as far afield as Iceland and fished the *Grand Banks of Newfoundland, were still following earlier navigational methods. For England at that time lacked the Continent's common mathematical culture, which had led to English ships employing Spanish, Portuguese, or French pilots and having their instruments made in Flanders and their charts in Portugal.

The answer lay in scientific education which, during the latter half of the 16th century, English navigators had just started to acquire. The first English navigation manual was a translation of the leading Spanish one of the time and appeared in 1561 as *The Art of Navigation* by Martin Cortes. William Bourne, an instructor in mathematics described as an innkeeper, produced a popular version of the book, *A Regiment for the Sea* (1574), which was perhaps more suited to seamen. Then in 1599 Edward Wright published *Certaine Errors in Navigation*, perhaps the most important navigational work of the 16th century. It explained Mercator's projection (which Mercator had not) and included a table of meridional parts which gave the spacing of the minutes of latitude along the meridians so that anyone competent in *chartmaking could now draw a 'true' chart. Seventy years later, John Seller, an instrument maker, chartmaker, and instructor in navigation, published the first volume of his monumental *Practical Navigation*, a work that demonstrated how completely the navigational climate had changed under the influence of the talented astronomers, instrument makers, and mathematicians who so improved the practice of navigation and led ultimately to English supremacy at sea.

As navigation became increasingly based on mathematics, nautical publications assumed greater importance. For example, *amplitude tables enabled the pilot to establish the magnetic *variation at any place and so increase the accuracy of his compass readings. In 1686 the great scientist turned navigator Edmond Halley (1656–1742) published his study of ocean wind systems and, in the winter of 1669–1700, undertook a voyage to chart the world's *isogonic lines, lines connecting points of equal magnetic variation. The British *nautical almanac for 1767 became the first to publish data for the determination of longitude by *lunar distance. This method prevailed well after the *Board of Longitude had made its award to John Harrison (1693–1776).

Modern Navigational Aids. Until the 20th century, the only way of establishing a ship's position offshore was still *celestial navigation, although improved instruments, from the early *quadrants to the modern double-reflection *sextant, increased the accuracy and reliability of observation, whilst improvements in nautical tables and almanacs constantly evolved with the growth of nautical astronomy and, latterly, computers. Both the notion of the position line, stumbled across accidentally by the American Captain *Sumner in 1837 (it had been missed by the astronomers), and then the idea of the intercept propounded by the French naval officer *Marcq Saint-Hilaire, did much to make the principles of celestial navigation more widely understood and to ease the navigator's task.

Electronic aids to navigation, most of which were conceived either during or shortly after the Second World War (1939–45), revolutionized navigation at sea. *Radar could obtain the bearing of coastal echoes in poor visibility; electronic *echo sounders monitored the depth of water below a ship's keel; the electronic *log accurately recorded the distance it covered; and the various *hyperbolic navigation systems gave quick, simple, and accurate positions throughout much of the world, day or night. However, it is *satellite navigation, with its worldwide coverage, precision, and flexibility, that is the principal aid to navigation today.

Marcus, G., *The Conquest of the North Atlantic* (1980).

Ronan, C., *The Shorter Science & Civilisation in China, 3* (abridgment of Joseph Needham's text) (1986).

Seaver, K., 'Olaus Magnus and the "Compass" on Hvitsark', *Journal of Navigation*, 54 (May 2001), 235.

Taylor, E., *The Haven Finding Art: A History of Navigation from Odysseus to Captain Cook* (1954).

Williams, J., *From Sails to Satellites: The Origin and Development of Navigational Science* (1992).

Mike Richey

Navigation Acts, laws, long defunct, which restricted the employment of foreign ships in a nation's external trade. The first British Navigation Acts were passed in 1381 and 1390, and these expressly forbade the carriage of any merchandise out of British ports except in a British ship. Later Navigation Acts restricted the carriage of imports, as well as exports, either to British ships or to the ships of the exporting country. Much of the most profitable trade during the great period of expansion of the 17th–19th centuries came from India and China, countries which had only coastal shipping of their own, and this limitation on the carriage of imports was, of course, of tremendous value to the British *East India Company, an organization sufficiently powerful in its own right to demand the passing of such Acts. Almost all other nations engaged in the carriage of goods in ships passed similar Acts, and these were renewed from time to time as the individual nations strove to secure advantages for their own ships above those of other maritime powers.

It took the great increase in world trade during the Industrial Revolution to remove these limitations on the freedom of ships to trade irrespective of their nationality; in Britain this was achieved by the passage of the Customs Consolidation Act of 1853, under which foreign ships were put in the same position as British ships in relation to British trade. One provision of this Act, however, was that restrictions could be imposed on the ships of any nation in which British ships suffered similar restrictions. Until 1854 each nation, with few exceptions, restricted its coasting trade to the *masters of ships who were its own subjects; after that date this type of trade was opened to ships of any nationality, and they were protected from unfair discrimination by regulations that they were not to be charged higher rates (harbour dues, etc.).

navigational warnings, issued by Hydrographic Offices, are notices that are usually more urgent than *notices to mariners. They are normally concerned with changes of a temporary nature such as alterations to *charts and hydrographic publications as well as changes, or failures, to navigational aids and any other matter that affects the safety of *navigation. Such warnings are in text form and promulgated by coastal radio stations and on the *NAVTEX system. They are also sent directly to satellite communication centres for international delivery and are coordinated in the sixteen NAVAREAS as part of the World-Wide Navigational Warning Service (WWNWS). This was established jointly by the *International Maritime Organization and the International Hydrographic Organization in 1977 to promulgate by radio important information affecting the safety of navigation of ocean-going and coastal shipping. Adam Kerr

navigation lights, the lights laid down by the *International Regulations for Preventing Collisions at Sea which vessels must display when under way at sea at night. The most common are as follows:

(*a*) A power-driven vessel under way at night, less than 46 metres (150 ft) in length, carries one white *steaming light, *port (red) and *starboard (green) sidelights, also sometimes referred to as bow lights, and a white *overtaking light. If over 46 metres in length, it carries two white steaming lights, port and starboard sidelights, and a white overtaking light.

(*b*) A power-driven vessel towing another vessel carries its sidelights, overtaking light, and steaming light. If the length of the two is less than 183 metres (600 ft) an additional steaming light is carried; if the length of two is more than 183 metres a third steaming light is carried.

(*c*) Vessels engaged in *trawling show an all-round green light above an all-round white light, both visible 3.2 kilometres (2 mls.). They may carry in addition one steaming light, lower than and *abaft the all-round green and white lights. When making way through the water they show sidelights and overtaking light. Drift net vessels show an all-round red light above an all-round white light. When under way they show sidelights and an overtaking light. If outlying gear extends more than 152 metres (500 ft) an additional all-round white light shows the direction of the gear. See also FISHERIES.

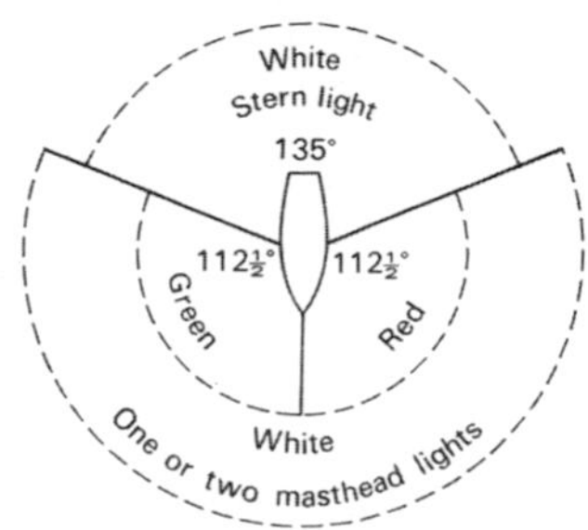

Navigation lights—arcs of visibility

(*d*) A vessel under way at night, but not under command and stopped, hoists two all-round red lights, one above the other, visible 3.2 kilometres (2 mls.), and switches off all other navigation lights. If the ship is making way through the water it also shows sidelights and overtaking light.

(*e*) A power-driven pilot vessel on duty and under way carries sidelights, overtaking light, and, at the masthead, a white all-round light above a red all-round light, both visible 4.8 kilometres (3 mls.). The vessel also shows one or more flare-ups at intervals not exceeding ten minutes or an intermittent all-round white light.

(*f*) A sailing vessel under way at night carries sidelights and an overtaking light. In addition she may carry on the top of the foremast a red light above a green light, visible 3.2 kilometres (2 mls.) and showing from ahead to two *points abaft the beam.

(*g*) A vessel of less than 46 metres (150 ft), when at anchor, carries in the forepart a white all-round light visible 3.2 kilometres (2 mls.). If 46 metres or more in length, the anchored ship carries two white all-round lights, visible 4.8 kilometres (3 mls.); one near the bow, the other at or near the stern and 4.5 metres (15 ft) lower.

navigator, in earlier centuries the term was applied to those in command of the great voyages of *exploration by sea. Nowadays, it is the description of the officer on board ship responsible for *navigation. The word is also responsible for the English term navvy, meaning a man who labours with his hands. This originated when the system of canals in England was being brought into existence during the 18th and 19th centuries. Canals were then generally called navigations, the men engaged to dig them being known as navigators, shortened to navvies. The term spread, and the workmen engaged in the railway construction were frequently known as railway navigators.

NAVTEX. Introduced during the 1980s, this allows ships' radio officers to receive Marine Safety Information (MSI) automatically and in printed form from a dedicated receiver. Under the *Global Maritime Distress and Safety System NAVTEX broadcasts MSI for coastal waters, up to about 480–640 kilometres (300–400 mls.) offshore. Mandatory for all commercial vessels, it is also suitable for larger *yachts.

navy, from the Latin, *naves*, ships, in its original meaning the entire shipping of a nation, but now only that part which is armed to defend the nation to which it belongs, its shipping routes, and its *merchant marine.

Navies have been described as instruments of national policy, and while this is an accurate enough definition from about the Middle Ages onwards, many of the world's earlier navies were no more than collections of vessels capable of warlike action and used for private gain in the raiding and harassing of weaker peoples. There were some, organized on a national basis, which were used to further national policies of conquest or defence, but it was more usual to find *squadrons of national ships in the hands of leaders licensed to use them for *piracy. Typical of these were the Danish and Viking *longships which harried western Europe in the 8th–10th centuries.

It was not until the early years of *exploration by sea, in the late 15th and early 16th centuries, that national navies began to grow and to assume a shape and function akin to the navies of today. As the known world opened up the growing volume of lucrative trade, and the national competition which it invoked, called for navies to control and defend these routes and the trade monopolies claimed as a result of the prior right of discovery. This was the start of the national struggle for sea power on which so much of the wealth of the trading nations depended. From the start of the 15th century to the early years of the 19th century, Spain, Holland, France, and Britain were more or less permanently engaged in *warfare at sea to win mastery of the oceans and control vital trade routes.

At the end of the 19th century three new navies, those of the USA, Japan, and Germany, emerged to challenge Britain's naval dominance, which had eventually triumphed at sea over all the other European powers. Following the Second World War (1939–45), the US Navy, though once challenged by the fleets of what was the Soviet Union, is now by far the largest in the world and is centred around its twelve Carrier Battle Groups, or Carrier Strike Groups as they are to be called. With the end of the Cold War, and the emergence of terrorism and rogue states, future US Navy strategy, known as 'Sea Power 21', provides the way forward for the next twenty years. The nuclear submarine fleet in particular is facing substantial changes.

Cuts in the Royal Navy surface fleet, announced in 2004, mean that for the first time since the 17th century it will be smaller than the French Navy, while the Russian government is making strenuous efforts to modernize and reorganize its sea forces. For a glimpse of how small surface warships may evolve, see illus. in CORVETTE. See also SURFACE EFFECT SHIP; SWATH SHIP.

Royal Navy. Two early English monarchs, *Alfred and *Canute, were both known for their abilities to conduct warfare at sea, but neither could be said to have founded the British Navy as none was permanently established until Tudor times. Before then ships and men were recruited as necessary, the *Cinque Ports being one of the mainstays of this system. The office of the *Lord High Admiral was established in 1391 but it was the Tudors, notably Henry VII (1457–1509) and his son Henry VIII (1491–1547), who laid the foundation for the modern navy, building such ships as the **Henry Grâce à Dieu* and the **Mary Rose*. During the latter's reign, in 1520, the beginnings of the *Admiralty took shape and later the navy prospered under the able administration of Sir John *Hawkins.

With the defeat of the *Spanish Armada in 1588, and the boldness of adventurers like *Drake and *Frobisher, the navy came of age under Elizabeth I. Neglect followed, but between 1642 and 1688, aided by that talented ad-

Major Warships of Selected Navies Built, Building, and Planned, 2003.

Country	*Carrier*	*Cruiser*	*Submarine*	*Destroyer*	*Frigate*	*Corvette*
Australia				4p		
Canada			4	4	12	
China	1p		2 ssbn 1 ssb 7 ssn + 3p 6 ssg + 2p 67 patrol	25 + 2p	45	
France	1 + 2p 1 helicopter		6 ssbn 6 ssn + 6p	14 + 2p	20 + 17p	
Germany			18	2	15	5
Italy	2	1	8 + 2p	6 + 2p	13 + 10p	8
NZ				c	3	
Russia	1	5 + 2(bc)	18 ssbn 25 ssgn/ ssn 12 ssk 6 ssa(n)	16	51	45
SA			2		4	
Spain	1		6 patrol + 4p		15	4
UK	3 + 2p		4 ssbn 15 attack + 2p	17 + 6p	20	
US*	10np + 1p 3	27gm + 27 gmp	16 ssbn 2 ssgn 59 ssn + 2p	49gm + 14gmp + 19	33gm	45

*excludes amphibious forces and military sealift command

p = planned, gm = guided missile,
np = nuclear powered
bc = battle-cruiser

Submarine Types
ssbn = ballistic missile, np
ssgn = surface-to-surface missile, np
ssn = attack, np
ssk = patrol, ASW capabilities
ssa(n) = auxiliary, np
ssg = guided missile, diesel engines

Source: compiled from *Jane's Fighting Ships*

ministrator Samuel *Pepys, its strength grew from 35 vessels to 151. Led by commanders such as *Blake, it fought three wars against the Dutch during this period, and fought the Spaniards and the *Barbary pirates as well. But it was during the next century and a quarter that the Royal Navy fought its most bitter battles, nearly all of them against France, which it mostly won, but against the new American nation as well, in which it lost the ones that mattered. These decades produced some of the country's outstanding leaders at sea, Hood, *Nelson, and many more, and the battles fought during the Napoleonic Wars (1793–1815), such as the Glorious First of June (June 1794) and Trafalgar (October 1805), are part of the nation's heritage. It was during this era that some of the great voyages of exploration by naval officers also took place, those led by James *Cook and those searching for the *North-West Passage being outstanding examples.

After 1815 the Royal Navy emerged bruised but triumphant, and led the 19th-century transition from sail to *steam propulsion, from *ships of the line to the early *ironclad warships such as HMS **Warrior*, to the Dreadnought *battleship. Its role during the First World War (1914–18) was to keep the world's sea lanes clear of German *submarines and commerce raiders, and few set battles were fought against the German Navy, the Falkland Islands (December 1914) and Jutland (May 1916) being the exceptions. After the First World War, when its decline as a maritime power was gathering pace, Britain remained in the forefront of developing a new type of warship, the *aircraft carrier, improving established ones, such as the submarine, and perfecting new seaborne weapons like *ASDIC and *radar.

The Royal Navy's role in the Second World War (1939–45) was a crucial one, for it not only had to keep open the sea lanes across the Atlantic and the Arctic Sea, escorting vital *convoys from the USA and to the beleaguered USSR, but had to counter a German Navy with powerful surface ships and U-boats which threatened to sever Britain's supply lines. For the Royal Navy the lowest points of the war came when the *battlecruiser HMS *Hood* was sunk by the German battleship *Bismarck* in May 1941, and when Japanese forces sank the battleship HMS *Prince of Wales* and the battlecruiser HMS *Repulse* off the Malayan coast in December 1941. The sinking of the *Hood* was soon revenged, when the Home Fleet tracked down and sank the *Bismarck* (see also BALLARD), but the Royal Navy's part in defeating the Japanese was relatively minor. Task Force 57, as the British Pacific Fleet was called, was the Royal Navy's largest fleet of the war, and worked as part of a numerically superior US Pacific Fleet. The Mediterranean Fleet defeated the Italian Navy at the battle of Cape Matapan (March 1941), played a vital role in supporting the British Army in North Africa, and ensured that its vital island base of Malta continued to be supplied. Further reductions in its size after the Second World War inevitably restricted its capabilities, but it was in the forefront of operating nuclear submarines and has been involved in numerous local conflicts, from the Korean War (1950–3) to the Gulf War of 2003.

United States Navy. The newly independent United States of America had no navy after 1785, when the last of its *Continental Navy's ships had been sold, although it then possessed the world's second largest *merchant marine. Depredations on this by the *Barbary pirates of North Africa led, in March 1794, to the construction of six *frigates, the *United States*, **Constellation*, **Constitution*, *President*, **Chesapeake*, and *Congress*. By the time the first three became operational in 1798, the dispute had been settled, but a 'quasi-war' with France began. In May 1801 trouble broke out again in the Mediterranean when the Pasha of Tripoli declared war, but after Commodore Edward Preble (1761–1807) had blockaded and then bombarded the Pasha's home port a peace treaty was signed in 1805, along with renewed treaties of friendship with Tunis, Algiers, and Morocco.

The War of 1812–15 pitted seventeen ships against the Royal Navy's thousand or more. The best-remembered actions are the three consecutive American victories scored by two of these original 44-gun frigates, which led to their becoming the world standard in this type of warship for the remaining age of fighting sail. However, the most important victories strategically, securing a lasting peace with Britain, were those on Lakes Erie (1813) and Champlain (1814), and at New Orleans (1815). During the following decades squadrons were deployed worldwide to protect US interests, naval forces saw action during a war with Mexico (1846–8), and Commodore *Perry opened Japan to American trade (1853).

In the American Civil War (1861–5) the US Navy, in its ultimately successful struggle with the *Confederate States Navy, became larger than ever before. In 1862 it promoted its first admirals and introduced the *monitor. It was also the first navy to lose a ship to a submarine, a weapon two Americans, David *Bushnell and Robert *Fulton, had earlier done so much to develop.

The post-war decline in naval strength was almost as rapid as its expansion, but fuelled by the writings of naval theorist Alfred Thayer *Mahan, the navy began a resurgence in the early 1880s. War with Spain in 1898 left the USA with overseas possessions in the Caribbean and the western Pacific which, in turn, led to the construction of the *Panama Canal. Involvement in the First World War (1914–18) came late and amounted to no more than convoy duties. Afterwards, the US Navy developed aircraft carriers and landing craft, and built battleships and *cruisers to the maximum size allowed. Further expansion, aimed at creating a 'two-ocean navy' capable of fighting simultaneously in the Pacific and the Atlantic, began before the USA entered the Second World War (1939–45).

When the Japanese attacked Pearl Harbor in December 1941 the American carriers were at sea. Their survival allowed a tactical victory over the Japanese in the Coral Sea (May 1942) and then a pivotal one at Midway (June 1942). Later others (Philippine Sea, Leyte Gulf, Okinawa) virtually destroyed Japanese naval power, and led to the Japanese surrendering aboard the battleship USS *Missouri* on 2 September 1945.

It was a different war in the Atlantic, where the US Navy's first task was to overcome Hitler's U-boats. This took time as it required the construction of anti-submarine forces, and their training, but by mid-1943 the Atlantic was secured. This underpinned the second task, the seaborne invasions of Nazi-occupied Europe—Sicily (July 1943), mainland Italy (September 1943), Normandy (June 1944), and southern France (August 1944). In each instance, the US Navy transported, landed, and provided supporting gunfire and logistic support that culminated in Germany's surrender on 8 May 1945.

At war's end, the US Navy had approximately 5,000 warships, auxiliaries, and large landing craft, and more than 30,000 aircraft. It was the mightiest navy the world had ever seen, but these numbers shrank rapidly as pre-war ships were scrapped and many war-built ones placed in reserve. During the second half of the 20th century the US Navy's biggest commitments were supporting United Nations forces in the Korean War (1950–3), providing air support, coastal interdiction, and special forces operations in the Vietnam War (1965–73), and, of course, ensuring an adequate submarine and surface screen, both nuclear and conventional, against the Soviet bloc.

After the Soviet Union collapsed in 1991, the US Navy was reduced to about 300 warships. However, individual units have, with the advent of long-range, extremely accurate missiles, extended range guns, and sophisticated detection and command and control systems, markedly increased their potency. On balance, it remains the most powerful navy in the world. See also LIBERTY SHIPS; MARINES; US COAST GUARD.

Miller, N., *The US Navy: A History* (3rd edn. 1997).

Sweetman, J., *American Naval History* (3rd edn. 2002).

www.history.navy.mil

Tyrone G. Martin

neal-to, an old expression meaning steep-to when describing a bank of sand underwater or the shoreline itself. A bank is neal-to when the water shoals suddenly from deep to shallow as the bank is reached; the shore is neal-to when deep water exists right up to the shoreline.

neap tides, those tides which occur during the first and third quarters of the moon when the pull of the sun is at right angles to that of the moon. The effect of this counteraction is to make the high water lower and the low water higher than when the sun and moon both exert their pull in the same direction, a condition which causes *spring tides. **To be neaped**, the expression used of a vessel which goes aground on the spring tides and has to wait for the next ones before there is enough depth of water to float it off.

nef, a French ship of the 15th and 16th centuries, a development and enlargement of the *cog up to 300–400 tons. They were three masted with square mainsail and *topsail on the mainmast and a single square sail on the fore and *mizzen, with a *spritsail under the *bowsprit. Some of the larger nefs carried a *bonaventure mizzen with a square sail in addition. They were of *carvel construction and were used for trade and war purposes alike. The word has come down to us today to describe the table ornaments, in the shape of a ship, which in those days decorated the dining tables of the nobility and in which was kept the salt, a costly commodity in medieval times. These ornaments were of very beautiful, intricate, and exquisite design, almost always of silver but very occasionally of crystal, and today are extremely rare and valuable.

Nelson, Horatio, first Viscount (1758–1805), British vice admiral and Sicilian duke, born at Burnham Thorpe in Norfolk, the third surviving son of the local vicar. After local schooling he joined the Royal Navy through the patronage of his maternal uncle Captain Maurice Suckling, who provided him with a first-class education, extensive practical experience, and a succession of personal contacts who pushed his career quickly to the rank of *post-captain in 1779. Not yet 21, Nelson was serving in the West Indies, but had also seen the Arctic and the Indian Ocean. With the War of American Independence (1776–83) raging his first mission was to escort troops attacking Spanish possessions in Nicaragua. Seeing the troops in difficulties he acted on his own initiative, with considerable success. However he nearly died of disease. After recuperating in England he took command of the frigate HMS *Albemarle* and by the end of war had joined the naval 'family' of the brilliant Admiral Lord Hood (1724–1816) a friend of his now deceased uncle. From Hood he learnt the art of an admiral.

Between 1784 and 1787 Nelson commanded the frigate HMS *Boreas* on the Leeward Islands station, where he demonstrated remarkable tenacity in suppressing illegal trade, and outmanoeuvring his naval and political superiors. He also married Frances Nisbet, a widow with a young son. He came close to ruining his career by backing Prince William (later King William IV, 1830–7), then a naval captain, in a petty dispute. He spent the next five years living quietly in Norfolk with his father, wife, and stepson. The French Revolutionary War (1793–1802) saw him recalled to service, commanding the battleship HMS *Agamemnon* (see also SHIPWRECKS) in Hood's Mediterranean Fleet. His active, intelligent service at sea and ashore on Corsica earned him the respect of his admiral, at the cost of the sight of his right eye, blinded at the siege of Calvi.

In 1795 Nelson demonstrated brilliant tactical judgement, and contempt for his pedestrian commander Admiral Hotham, in a battle near Toulon. He was then given an independent command on the Italian Riviera, blocking the French advance. When Admiral Sir John Jervis, later Earl St Vincent (1735–1823), took command of the fleet Nelson won his admiration, an emotion he reciprocated, finding in Jervis a role model for fleet command. Jervis appointed him commodore with an independent command. At the battle of Cape St Vincent on 14 February 1797 Nelson anticipated Jervis's orders, abandoning the rigid linear formation to break up a Spanish counter-attack, and then captured two Spanish ships of the line by *boarding, a unique, heroic achievement that, once he had written it up for the newspapers, made him a national celebrity. Six days later he reached the rank of rear admiral of the Blue (see SQUADRONAL COLOURS), and was made a Knight of the Bath for his conduct in battle.

On the night of 24–25 April Nelson led a daring attack on Tenerife in the Canary Islands, but was wounded in the right arm, which had to be amputated, and his force was defeated. Invalided home to recuperate he began to harvest the acclaim that he had earned since 1793. He was now a public figure, and once recovered was ordered back to the Mediterranean, for a detached mission to find and destroy General Bonaparte's expedition to Egypt. Jervis, ennobled as Earl St Vincent after his victory, sent a dozen of his best officers, all in 74-gun *ships of the line, to serve under Nelson, who referred to them with a Shakespearian flourish as his 'band of brothers'. On 1 August 1798 Nelson found the French fleet anchored in Aboukir Bay, the French Army having already landed in Egypt. Although night was falling, and the French were anchored in a strong position, Nelson immediately ordered his fleet to attack. In what came to be called the battle of the Nile all but two of the thirteen French battleships were taken or destroyed. Nelson's battle of annihilation had secured British domination of the Mediterranean, and transformed the art of *war at sea. At the height of the battle he was badly cut on the forehead by shrapnel, and concussed.

After securing the prizes Nelson split his fleet to exploit his victory, taking three ships to Naples where he helped the British minister, Sir William Hamilton, persuade the King of Naples to join the war against France. He was showered with honours by King George, the *East India Company, and foreign rulers. When the Neapolitan kingdom was overrun by the French, Nelson evacuated the royal family, before helping to restore the status quo, crushing the last remnants of the French-backed republic. His handling of the pro-French Neapolitan Jacobins gave rise to controversy, but Nelson was acting under the direct authority of the Neapolitan monarch, whose support was vital if the British fleet was to remain in the Mediterranean. He then oversaw the capture of Malta, and the two French ships that had escaped from the battle of the Nile. By 1800 the exhausted Nelson had begun a passionate affair with Emma, Lady Hamilton, the talented and beautiful wife of the minister. Nelson and Sir William were recalled to Britain, and went home through Europe in triumph.

Once in London Nelson abandoned his wife, with whom he had had no children, for his heavily pregnant mistress. Within weeks he was back at sea, second in command of the Baltic Fleet under Admiral Sir Hyde Parker (1739–1807). Sent to defeat a coalition of Baltic powers Nelson led part of the fleet in a decisive attack on Copenhagen on 2 April 1801. His judgement was, as ever, impeccable. At the height of the battle he ignored Hyde Parker's signal to retreat, before persuading the Danes to surrender. Once his *squadron was committed to battle in *shoal waters he had to win, or be destroyed. The ineffectual Hyde Parker was recalled, and Nelson was given the command. With the campaign over he came home, commanding the anti-invasion forces on the Channel coast. Here his presence gave the country peace of mind, and exposed Napoleon's invasion hoax, although his attack on invasion craft moored off Boulogne failed.

During the brief Peace of Amiens from March 1802 to May 1803 Nelson lived in a newly purchased house at Merton, south of London, with Emma and Sir William. They also undertook an astonishing public relations tour, which demonstrated that he was the most popular man in the country. By April 1803, when Sir William died, Nelson was already preparing for war. Sent to command the Mediterranean Fleet with his flag in HMS **Victory* he spent the next two years waiting for the French to leave Toulon. When they did, in April 1805, he pursued Admiral *Villeneuve's force all the way to the West Indies, saving the country millions in shipping and islands, and ruining Bonaparte's complex plans to open the Channel for an invasion.

In August 1805 Nelson went home, but was recalled to service by news that the Franco-Spanish combined fleet was moving. In late September he took command of the fleet off Cadiz, where Villeneuve and Admiral Gravina were blockaded. He allowed them to leave, and on 21 October engaged them off Cape Trafalgar. He had 27 ships of the line to face an enemy 33 strong, and he also knew the weather would break that night, so he had no time for fine manoeuvres. Sending the immortal signal 'England expects that every man will do his duty' with a new signal code, he demonstrated his mastery of leadership and morale. The fleet attacked the enemy line at right angles, in two loosely formed columns, one led by his *flagship *Victory*, the other by his second in command, Admiral Cuthbert Collingwood, in the *Royal Sovereign*. Although the leading ships were exposed to raking *broadsides, and suffered heavy casualties, Nelson's tactics worked. He passed under the stern of Villeneuve's *flagship, destroying her as a fighting ship and command centre, but then found the *Victory* hemmed in by enemy ships, amidst a cauldron of fire. He was calmly walking the quarterdeck with his long-serving flag captain Thomas Hardy, when at 1315 he was hit by a French musket ball, fired from the *mizzen top of *Redoutable*. The ball ripped through his left shoulder, cut a major artery in his left lung, and severed his spine. He was paralysed, slowly drowning in his own blood, and he died at 1630, just as the last shots of the battle were dying away. Most of the nineteen enemy ships that were taken were destroyed that night in the *storm Nelson had anticipated.

Trafalgar was the ultimate naval victory. The enemy had been out-thought and annihilated by the genius of one man, and the professional courage of many thousands more, inspired by his matchless example. Already an immortal, Nelson was, in death, transfigured into a national hero and war god. He was buried in St Paul's Cathedral, and in 1843 a majestic column was erected in Trafalgar Square, cementing his place in the national consciousness. A reflective and professional student of war, Nelson combined his mastery of ships and the sea, of winds and *currents, with irresistible leadership of officers and men alike, unequalled tactical insight, strategic vision, and the political courage to act at the highest levels of war. His tangled private life gave him a romantic fascination that has often attracted more interest than his professional qualities. He was, and remains, the ultimate naval commander.

Lambert, A., *Nelson: Britannia's God of War* (2004).
White, C., *The Nelson Encyclopedia* (2002).

Andrew Lambert

Neptune, a Roman god of unknown origin but thought have been associated with Salacia, the goddess of salt water. Later, in 399 BC, he was identified with the Greek god of the sea, *Poseidon. Up to that time sacrifices for naval victories had been made in Rome to *Fortunus. But the Emperor Augustus' right-hand man Marcus Vipsanius Agrippa changed that by dedicating a temple in the Campus Martius to Neptune in honour of the naval victory of Actium. See also CROSSING THE LINE.

Nereides, in Greek legend the 50 daughters of Doris and *Nereus, all nymphs of the sea, *Thetis being one of them.

Nereus, in Greek mythology the son of *Oceanus and Terra, and a deity of the sea. See also NEREIDES.

net register tonnage, see TONNAGE.

nettings. **(1)** Spaces around the upper deck, *forecastle, *poop, and the break of the *quarterdeck in sailing warships in which the crew's *hammocks, protected by *quarter-cloths, were stowed in the daytime. They had several uses. Exposure to fresh air limited the number of lice in the hammocks which also served as a defence in battle against enemy musket-fire. The hammocks also acted as liferafts as they could support a man for six hours before becoming waterlogged. **(2)** A net formed of small ropes seized together with yarns and spread across the *waist of a ship in hot weather. Sails were laid on them to form an *awning to provide protection from the sun. They were also used in some merchant ships as a defence against *boarders, since merchantmen usually lay lower in the water than warships and boarders would have to drop down on to the deck. However, it proved more dangerous than defensive, as boarders soon learnt the trick of cutting the netting down and enveloping the men beneath it. The purpose of **splinter-netting**, a stout rope netting rigged in battle in the days of sailing navies between the mainmast and *mizzen-mast at a height of about 3.6 metres (12 ft) above the quarterdeck, was to prevent those engaged there being injured if masts or *spars were shot away during the action. It also served to break the fall of men in the *tops or on the *yards if they fell as a result of the enemy's gunfire.

nettle, sometimes written as **knittle.** **(1)** A small line often used to *seize rope to form an *eye or to bind the tucks of an eye splice, or in other similar places where a *seizing may be required. **(2)** The small line used in the *clews of *hammocks, doubled round a ring and secured with a *half hitch in the eyelet holes at the head and foot of a hammock. See also GANTLOPE.

***New Ironsides*, USS,** an *ironclad, *launched in May 1862 at Philadelphia during the American Civil War (1861–5), whose name was intended to perpetuate the spirit of the sailing *frigate USS **Constitution*, long known as 'old ironsides'. With her heavy armament, which included fourteen 11-in. (28 cm) smoothbore guns, she was said by some to have been the most powerful ironclad of her day, but she had been planned and built hurriedly, and was an unhandy and uncomfortable ship. In April 1863 she took part in the attempt to persuade the Confederates to surrender the port of Charleston by a show of force, and was hit some 50 times but was not seriously damaged. She was destroyed by a fire in 1865.

nigger heads, a name sometimes given to the *bollards which line a *quay or *wharf and to which ships lying alongside secure their *berthing hawsers.

nip. **(1)** The name given by seamen to a short turn or twist in a rope or *hawser (see also FRENCHMAN). **(2)** That part of a rope bound by a *seizing around a *thimble or round the tucks of an *eye splice. **Nip in the hawse**, a twist in a ship's *cable when lying to an *anchor, which can usually be cured by *veering more cable to an order to **'freshen the nip'**, a phrase that can also mean to ease marginally or tighten a *sheet or halyard so that any point of chafe is moved. **(3)** As a verb, it is applied to a vessel when it is caught between two converging floes of *ice in Arctic or Antarctic waters.

nipper. **(1)** A short length of rope, usually braided or *marled from end to end, which was used to bind the anchor *cable temporarily to a *messenger when in the days of sail the anchor was *weighed by hand round the *capstan. **(2)** Boys or men who worked the nippers when the anchors were being weighed were called nippers. **(3)** When the *yards of *square-

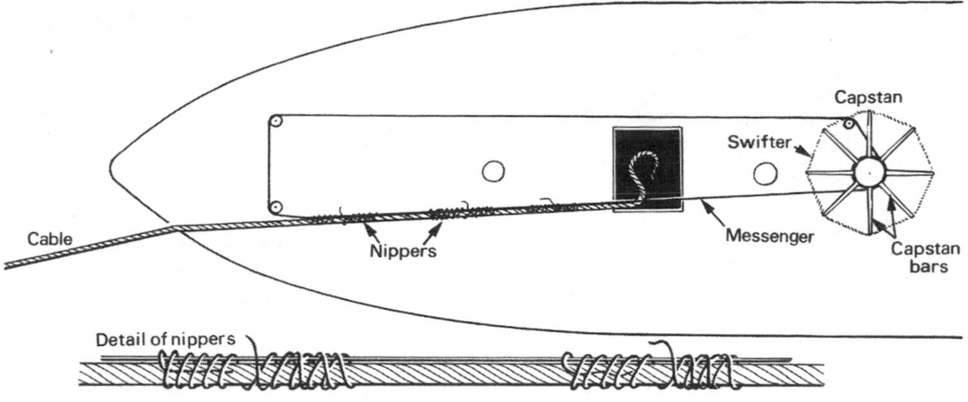

Use of nippers when weighing anchor

rigged ships were wet and slippery, nippers were often used to form slings for them when they were hoisted. **(4)** A *hammock lashed up with so little bedclothing in it that it would not stand on end in a hammock *netting was also known as a nipper.

Noah's Ark, said to have been constructed by Noah to accommodate his family, and representatives of each kind of animal, to save them from the great flood (Genesis 6–9). Its dimensions are given in the biblical account as 300 cubits long, 50 cubits broad, and 30 cubits high (1 cubit = 18–22 in./46–56 cm) and it was said to have been made of 'gopher' wood, which has been variously identified with cypress, cedar, and pine. It used to be an exercise of 'rationalist' theologians and others in the early 19th century to try to show that the ark was not big enough to house and feed all the species of animals aboard for the duration of the flood. As a consequence, some extraordinary theories were produced, one authority calculating that the ark would have needed to cover an area of half an acre, another estimating its *tonnage at 81,062.

More recent research suggests that the ark was a large raft made from bundles of papyrus reeds, with only the animals' stalls and the family's shelter constructed of timber. Smaller rafts of this type, such as the *gufah, or gopher, were at that time in normal use in the Euphrates–Tigris basin, where all timber suitable for *shipbuilding was scarce. In Genesis 6: 14, when Noah is told to make an ark of gopher wood in which to escape the coming flood, this may be a mistranslation from the original Hebrew and should possibly read 'an ark gopher of wood'. No wooden vessel, even an ark, is likely to be built of only one species of wood, and a gopher is a type of vessel which might well have been used as the basic design of the ark. The latest (2004) expedition to rediscover the remains of Noah's Ark is searching a part of Mount Ararat where high-resolution satellite photography has pinpointed what seems to be a large man-made object.

In the USA the term also used to be used to describe the large flat-bottomed vessels used for the carriage of produce down the major rivers.

nocturnal, an early instrument designed essentially for measuring the time of night by means of *Polaris and either the 'Pointers' of the Plough in the constellation Ursa Major, or the Guards of the constellation Ursa Minor. It was first described in print by Michel Coignet in 1581. The earliest nocturnals consisted of two concentric circular plates of brass or wood. The circumference of the larger was divided into twelve equal parts corresponding to the months of the year and that of the smaller into 24 equal parts corresponding to the hours of the day. The larger plate carried a handle and the inner plate was fitted with a long index, one end of which was pivoted to the centre of the plate. To ascertain the time by the nocturnal a projecting tooth at the position corresponding to 12 o'clock on the smaller plate was turned to coincide with the date on the larger plate. The instrument was then held at arm's length and Polaris viewed

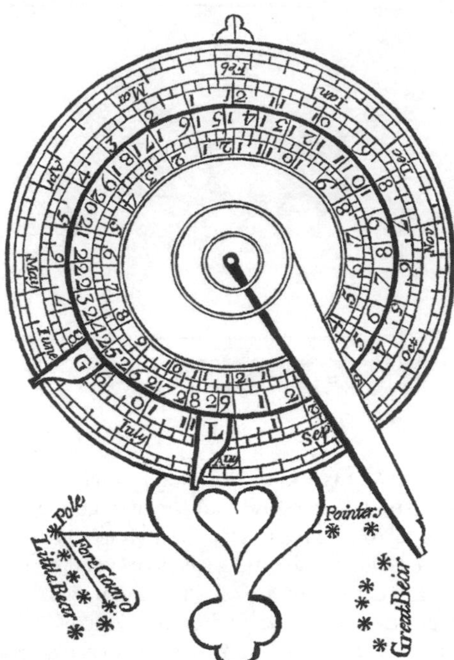

A nocturnal with scales to be used with Ursa Major and Minor

through a small hole at the centre of the instrument. The index arm was then turned until the bevelled edge coincided with the line joining the 'Pointers' of Ursa Major, or the Guards of Ursa Minor as the case might be, and the time of night was then read off the scale of hours on the smaller plate.

Nocturnals were also used for working out the time of high water for which the *establishment of the port was known. It was not too difficult a matter to relate the time of the moon's southing and the *age of the moon by means of circular scales attached to the nocturnal. By applying the establishment of the port to the time of the moon's southing, the approximate time of high water, or 'full sea' as it was called, could readily be found.

Nore, the, a sandbank at the mouth of the River Thames, England, lying off the entrance to the River Medway, and for many years a naval *anchorage which later gave its name to one of the chief commands of the British Navy. The first commander-in-chief appointed to the Nore Command was Admiral Isaac Townsend in 1752, and it included the naval *dockyard at Chatham. In 1797 it was the scene of a naval *mutiny which followed the one at *Spithead. During the late 19th century a smaller dockyard was constructed at Sheerness, at the mouth of River Medway, and this also became part of the Nore Command, the two forming, with Portsmouth and Plymouth, one of the three main home bases of the British fleet, with the commander-in-chief exercising naval operational control of the North Sea. After the Second World War (1939–45), Sheerness dockyard was turned over to civilian purposes, the Nore ceased to be an operational naval command in 1961, and Chatham Dockyard was closed in 1984.

Norman. **(1)** A short wooden bar which was thrust into one of the holes of a *windlass or *capstan and used to *veer a rope or to secure the anchor *cable if there was very little strain on it. **(2)** A preventer pin through the head of the *rudder to secure it against loss. **(3)** A metal pin placed in the *bitt cross-piece to prevent the cable falling off.

'no room to swing a cat', a term widely used to describe a small or confined space. It originates from the days of corporal punishment at sea with the *cat-o'-nine-tails, where ample space was needed to swing it properly to produce the maximum effect.

North Atlantic Oscillation (NAO), an index of climatic variation in the North Atlantic based on the ratio between the high atmospheric pressure centred over the Azores and the low pressure centred over Iceland. It undergoes long-term cycles of variation with periodicities of 2.1, 8, 24, and 70 years. For example, the index was particularly low during the 1880s and 1960s, and particularly high during the 1920s and 1990s.

When the index is high, winter *storms in the North Atlantic are more frequent and more violent, warmer and wetter winters are experienced in Europe and the north-eastern USA, but in Canada and Greenland the winters are colder and drier. When the index is low, winter storms in the North Atlantic are less frequent, Europe and North America experience colder and snowier winters, whereas the Mediterranean regions suffer from wetter conditions. Historically, these events are recorded in variations in the thickness of tree rings. The flow of the *Gulf

Stream appears to be reduced and no longer extends so far north, which provides a feedback mechanism between the ocean and climate.

The NAO also affects the growth and survival of marine *plankton, like the keystone copepod species *Calanus finmarchicus*, hence the success of many commercial *fish species, and may be one of the factors contributing for the spectacular decline and lack of recovery of *cod stocks in the North Sea and *Grand Banks *fisheries. There is a comparable climate index in the North Pacific, and both these indices appear to be linked to *El Niño events. See also CLIMATE CHANGE; MARINE METEOROLOGY.

www.ldeo.columbia.edu/NAO/

www.met.rdg.ac.uk/cag/NAO/

A plot of the index can be found on **www.met.rdg.ac.uk/cag/NAO/** M. V. Angel

north magnetic pole, the northerly point on the earth's surface where the magnetic *dip is 90° and towards which, along the magnetic *meridians, the needle of a *magnetic compass points. Although its approximate location had been known for many years, it was not until 1831 that James Clark Ross (1800–62) found, during his expedition to discover a *North-West Passage, that it was on the west side of the Boothia Peninsula. The angular difference between the magnetic and geographical meridians at any place is known as the *variation.

North-West Passage, a 1,450-kilometre (900-m.) sea route which lies off the northern coast of Canada, some 800 kilometres (500 mls.) north of the Arctic Circle, and links the Atlantic with the Pacific. From the earliest times it was sought to obtain a commercially practical passage to the Far East.

The First Voyages to Find the Passage. The search for the North-West Passage, which was always primarily an English undertaking, was concentrated in three periods, though there was also a rather drawn-out finale. In 1555 Sir Humphrey Gilbert (*c.*1539–83) petitioned Elizabeth I to allow him to undertake 'the discovering of a passage by the northe, to go to Cataia [Cathay, the name at that time given to China], & all other the east partes of the worlde' provided that he and his brothers were given a monopoly for trade through the passage. Nothing came of this but Gilbert followed his petition with a missive to his brother Sir John Gilbert in 1566, which he called 'A discourse of a discoverie for a new passage to Cataia'. This now famous document circulated in manuscript for ten years before it was published and quite possibly helped to inspire the expeditions which were launched to find the passage during the last quarter of the 16th century. Gilbert himself was eventually granted a charter in 1578, but his first voyage, started that year ended in disaster at the hands of the Spanish at the Cape Verde Islands. His second, in 1583, reached Newfoundland, which he took possession of in the queen's name and founded the first English colony in North America. On his way back across the Atlantic he went down with his ship during a *storm off the Azores.

Other expeditions that were mounted during this period were the three led by Martin *Frobisher in 1576–77, and 1578, and the three (1585, 1586, 1587) made by the English *navigator John Davis (*c.*1550–1605), the inventor of *Davis's quadrant, who penetrated as far north and west as Baffin Bay. Many of the names still on the map of the Arctic are memorials to Davis's endeavours, among them the great strait that bears his name. In 1579 Sir Francis *Drake was the first to try and find a way to the passage from the Pacific, with no more success than his contemporaries who were attempting to find it from the Atlantic.

The next expeditions of any consequence to seek the elusive passage were those of Henry *Hudson and William Baffin (1584–1622). Baffin, who usually sailed as a *pilot, made five voyages, and penetrated to the northern end of the bay which now bears his name. The last voyages of this first series were those of Luke Fox (1586–1636) and Thomas James (*c.*1593–1635) in 1631. Their expeditions proved conclusively what earlier *navigators had strongly suspected: there was no passage through the North American continent from the western shores of Hudson Bay. Foxe Channel and Basin to the north of the bay and James Bay on the south commemorate their endeavours.

Explorations by the Hudson Bay Company. The discoveries of these early adventurers led to the formation in 1670 of the Hudson Bay Company to exploit the trade in furs, and during the 18th century it began to be criticized for its lack of interest in attempts to find a North-West Passage, which by its charter it was bound to do.

Stung by this criticism it began a rather erratic search, consisting of minor sea voyages around Hudson Bay and various land journeys up into the north. The most important of these was the overland expedition of Samuel Hearne (1745–92) who, in 1771, discovered the long and winding Coppermine River and traced it to the Arctic Ocean; and the one led by the Canadian fur trader Sir Alexander Mackenzie (*c.*1755–1820), who in 1789 voyaged from the Great Slave Lake, down the river that was named after him, to the Arctic Ocean. Between these two dates Captain James *Cook, on his third voyage of circumnavigation, explored much of the coast of Alaska and penetrated through the Bering Strait to Icy Cape. Together, these expeditions revealed a more detailed understanding of the area, and in the third phase, which spanned much of the 19th century, the goal was more to fill in the remaining bits of the puzzle than to find a commercially viable route to the Far East.

The Admiralty Expeditions. This final phase was initially stimulated by amendments of an Act which had originally been passed by Parliament in 1745. This offered a reward of £20,000 to any British subject, excepting those on naval vessels, who discovered a North-West Passage through Hudson Strait, but there had been few takers. So twenty years later the naval restrictions were removed and the area of search was changed to north of *latitude 70° between the Atlantic and the Pacific. Then in 1817 the Act was further altered to provide a sliding scale of rewards for approaching the Pole and for reaching certain *meridians of *longitude.

It was this last amendment that inspired the first of the great 19th-century British *Admiralty expeditions. Commodore John Ross (1777–1856), with two ships, was dispatched in April 1818 and reached as far as Lancaster Sound. However, his progress was stopped by what he considered a high range of hills, which he named Croker's Mountains. He turned back and was in England again by November, and there followed a long and acrimonious argument over whether the mountains really existed.

Another expedition was sent to Lancaster Sound the following year, but this time Ross's former lieutenant William Edward Parry (1790–1855) was given command. His expedition sailed in May 1819 in the *Hecla*, a *bomb ketch, and the *Griper*, and did not return until October 1820. Not only was Parry the first to winter in those northern latitudes, his was also one of the most successful of the many expeditions. For Croker's Mountains proved to be a myth and Parry reached Melville Island, where he wintered before returning. However, hopes that Parry's success would make possible a transit of the North-West Passage were dashed when he, and then the Admiralty, mounted further expeditions.

Then, in 1829, John Ross returned to search for the passage in the *paddle steamer *Victory*, but after discovering and surveying the Boothia Peninsula and King William Island, his ship became ice bound. He endured four winters there before being rescued in 1833 by an expedition led by George Back (1796–1878). During these rescue operations, Back discovered both Artillery Lake and the Great Fish River. While Ross was marooned his nephew and second in command James Clark Ross (1800–62) located and discovered the *north magnetic pole while on a sledging expedition.

The Passage Discovered and Navigated. In 1845 Sir John *Franklin's expedition set out to find the North-West Passage. When he failed to return numerous searches were mounted to find him, and it was these that finally mapped the passage. One of them, commanded by Robert McClure (1807–73) in the *Investigator*, left Plymouth in January 1850 and entered the Arctic Sea through the Bering Strait. His two ships were separated off Cape Horn and though McClure successfully rounded Point Barrow, his other ship was prevented from doing so by *ice until the following year. When both failed to return yet another expedition, under the command of Captain Edward Belcher (1799–1877), was dispatched to try and find Franklin as well as McClure. He set sail in 1852 with five ships under his command, approaching the passage from the east.

Meanwhile, the *Investigator* had penetrated both the Prince of Wales and McClure Straits, and by doing so proved the existence of a North-West Passage, but McClure then had to abandon his ship in Mercy Bay and set off overland. It was the historic meeting between this overland party, and one sent from one of Belcher's ships, the *Resolute*, that put the final seal on the discovery that so many had sought for so long. However, in April 1854 Belcher was forced to abandon all his ships, and faced a court martial for doing so, but was acquitted. No more expeditions to the North-West Passage occurred for nearly 50 years. Then, on 16 June 1903, the Norwegian explorer Roald *Amundsen, set out to navigate the passage in a small fishing boat. This he managed to do over a period of three years, arriving in Alaska on 31 August 1906.

It was ironic that after all the huge expense of the British Admiralty expeditions, which lost many warships and hundreds of men, Amundsen, with a crew of six in a small fishing *smack, should be successful. However, it was not until 1940–2 that the passage was negotiated west to east. This was achieved by the *St Roch*, a *gaff-rigged, 323-ton *schooner. She was commanded by Staff Sergeant Henry A. Larsen, of the Royal Canadian Mounted Police, who then sailed her east to west as well. The *St Roch* is now on display in the Vancouver Maritime Museum.

The North-West Passage in the 20th and 21st Centuries. In 1969 the 150,000-ton *tanker *Manhattan*, protected by a special bow and a steel belt to protect her hull, transited the North-West Passage in both directions to test the practicability of shipping Alaskan oil via the passage. However, the difficulties proved so great, and the tanker suffered such damage, that it was decided to build an overland pipeline instead. But some authorities have estimated that at the present rate of *climate change, the North-West Passage will be clear of ice by the end of the 21st century. This will make it an important sea route for commercial traffic as it will cut over 11,000 kilometres (7,000 mls.) off the route from Europe to Asia for those vessels which can use the *Panama Canal, and over 19,000 kilometres (12,000 mls.) for those which have to go via Cape Horn.

notices to mariners, periodical or casual notices issued by the hydrographic offices of maritime nations, or other competent authorities, regarding changes in aids to *navigation, such as *buoys and *lighthouses, dangers to navigation, important new *soundings, and, in general, any information affecting *charts, *sailing directions, *light lists, and other nautical publications. Most major hydrographic offices issue such notices on a weekly basis but others issue them at two-weekly or monthly intervals. Traditionally issued as printed paper booklets, the *navigator adds the corrections to the publication. Larger corrections, known as 'patches', can be cut out and pasted on to the chart.

There is an increasing trend to post the notices on websites from which they can be downloaded by the navigator. For updating *electronic charts the information is frequently incorporated on a compact disk which is inserted into the system and automatically updates it. As there is a legal obligation for mariners to carry and use up-to-date charts and publications, the acquisition and application of the notices is essential for safe navigation.

Adam Kerr

nugger, or **nuggar,** the traditional sail trading vessel of the lower part of the River Nile. They were two masted with a very large *lateen sail on the mainmast and a much smaller one on the *mizzen. A distinctive feature of their construction was the very abrupt rise of the *stem as a precaution against the broken water which is very quickly knocked up by *squalls that come from the desert. They carried quite sizeable cargoes, mainly of grain coming downriver, and manufactured goods going upriver. See also GYASSI.

'number', the somewhat odd designation given to the *signal letters which used to be assigned to every merchant ship for identification purposes. Nowadays, all ships use a nine-digit Maritime Mobile Service Identity number when communicating by VHF radio.

nun buoy, US navigational aid in the *IALA maritime buoyage system B, where red is the starboard-hand mark. It is red, even numbered, and shaped like a truncated cone, though some are pointed on top, and is the US equivalent of the *conical green buoy used as the starboard-hand mark used in the IALA maritime buoyage system A.

John Rousmaniere

nut, the ball on the end of the *stock of an *Admiralty pattern anchor. Its purpose is to prevent the stock from penetrating the ground, thus forcing it to lie flat on the bottom so that the *flukes, at right angles to the stock, are driven into the ground to provide good holding.

O

oakum, tarred *hemp or *manila fibres made from old and condemned ropes which have been unpicked. It was used for *caulking the *seams of the decks and sides of a wooden ship in order to make them watertight. It was rammed down between the seams with a caulking iron and a heavy hammer, and then held in position with hot *pitch poured along the seams.

oar, a wooden instrument which, working as a lever, is used to pull a boat through the water. It has three parts: the **blade**, the part of the oar which enters the water; **the shaft**, the main body of the oar; and **the loom**, the inboard end on which the rower pulls, or pushes. The point of leverage is the *rowlock, *crutch, or *thole pin in the *gunwale of the boat.

Tomb reliefs show Egyptians standing to row as did the Chinese when propelling their *junks, but in western Europe rowers usually sat on *thwarts facing the stern as did the Phoenicians. In the Orient some oarsmen stand facing the vessel's bows and push on the loom, as does the Maltese oarsman in his *dghaisa.

The oar was a basic adjunct of the sea in classical times, when it was the only motive power for *galleys. According to legend, *Odysseus was told, on his retirement from a life at sea, that he should journey inland carrying an oar over his shoulder until he found a people who asked him what it was he was carrying. There, after making a sacrifice to *Neptune, he should build his house. See also SCULL, TO; YULOH.

O'Brian, Patrick (1914–2000), English-born novelist in the mould of C. S. *Forester who changed his name from Richard Patrick Russ and created the Aubrey–Maturin series of sea novels. His mother died when he was four and his father, a bacteriologist, was unsuccessful, and the boy's childhood was unhappy and dysfunctional. When he was 14 he started writing a novel about a fictional beast called *Caesar*. It was published as a children's book in 1930 and was well received. He then began writing for children's magazines, and published a book of stories, but he could not earn a living from his published work, and in 1934 he joined the Royal Air Force as an acting pilot officer. For whatever reason this was not a success and his commission was terminated at the end of the year. He continued to have his adventure stories for children published and in 1936 he married, but the marriage only lasted four years. He worked as a tourist guide and in 1938 another novel, *Hussain: An Entertainment*, was published to considerable acclaim in Britain and the USA. When war came poor health prevented him from enlisting; instead he joined the London Ambulance Service, but in 1942 he was recruited into the Political Warfare Executive. This was a secret intelligence organization whose task was to wage propaganda against the Germans and help sustain resistance in occupied countries, work that later encouraged him to cover his past in a veil of secrecy and subterfuge.

In July 1945 he married again and shortly afterwards changed his name to O'Brian. He moved to Wales, continued to write short stories, some of which were published in book form, and began encouraging the belief that he was Irish. In 1949 he and his wife Mary moved to France, and in 1952 he published a

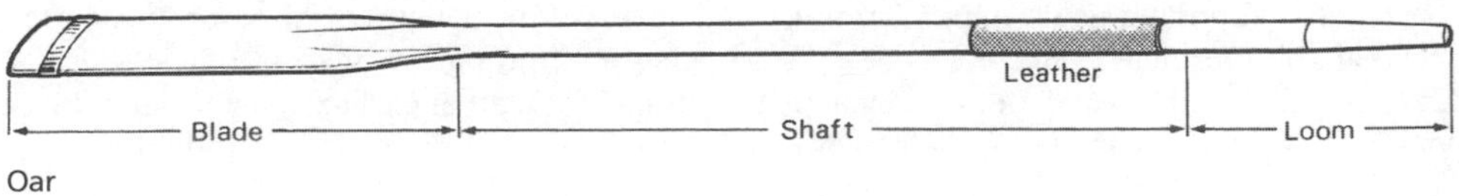

Oar

novel, *Three Bear Witness* (*Testimonies* in the USA). It established his reputation in America and between then and 1967 he wrote several others, two of them historical novels, *The Golden Ocean* (1956) and *The Unknown Shore* (1959), based on the voyages of *Anson. Both had been reviewed as children's books but when C. S. Forester died in 1966 an American publisher suggested O'Brian try and step into Forester's shoes. The idea appealed to O'Brian and in September 1967 he signed a contract for *Master and Commander* (1969/1970). It was the first of a series of twenty novels to follow the adventures at sea of Captain Jack Aubrey and the surgeon and philosopher Stephen Maturin during the Napoleonic Wars (1793–1815). Success and an international reputation came slowly but by the time O'Brian died, while working on the twenty-first novel in the series, the Aubrey–Maturin series had sold more than 3 million copies, and he had been awarded the CBE for services to literature and won the first Heywood Hill Literary Prize for 'a lifetime's contribution to the enjoyment of books'.

King, D., *Patrick O'Brian: A Life Revealed* (2000).
O'Neill, R. (ed.), *Patrick O'Brian's Navy: An Illustrated Companion to Jack Aubrey's World* (2002).

occulting light, a navigational light displayed by a *lighthouse, *lightship, or navigational *buoy in which the period of darkness is shorter than the period of light. See also CHARACTERISTIC.

Oceania, a term sometimes used to describe the *South Seas but more accurately those South Pacific islands included in the area bounded by Hawaii in the north, Easter Island in the east, New Zealand in the south, and New Guinea in the west. This area is subdivided into Polynesia in the east, Micronesia in the north-west, and Melanesia in the south-west.

Oceanides, or **Oceanitides,** the generic name given to the legendary sea nymphs, daughters of *Oceanus and *Tethys. Contemporary estimates of their number vary from 41 to 3,000. The Oceanides, like many of the rest of the inferior deities, were honoured with libations and sacrifices, in their case by seamen. Prayers were offered to them, and they were entreated to protect sailors from *storms and dangerous tempests. The *Argonauts, before they proceeded on their expedition, made an offering of flour, honey, and oil on the seashore to the deities of the sea, sacrificed bulls to them and entreated their protection throughout the voyage on which they were about to embark in the arduous quest for the Golden Fleece.

ocean liners may be defined as powered passenger-carrying vessels running a regular scheduled service across oceanic routes. Before the introduction of the jet passenger plane, it was the shipping lines, running passenger ships on a regular schedule, that were the primary means of connecting one continent with another. During the heyday of the passenger shipping companies the French had, and still have, the **Messageries Maritimes**, the Germans the **Hapag Lloyd** and the **Hamburg–South America Lines**, and the Italians the **Lloyd Triestino** and **Italia Lines**, and their ships linked their countries with every corner of the world. But it was the British, with their far-flung empire, that predominated in this form of transport: **P. & O.** (Peninsular & Orient) ships sailed to India and Australia, **Blue Funnel** ones went to China and Japan, **Union Castle** ships, each with the word 'castle' in its name, ran regularly to and from South Africa, while the **Royal Mail Line** went to South America. These were only a few of the best-known companies, and during a century or more (1840–1960) they, and many others, were founded and then grew, before merging with others, or with one another, until their names finally disappeared as the era of the ocean liner drew to a close. Nowadays, it is the transatlantic route that is best remembered for the biggest, fastest, and most luxurious, ocean liners.

The First Ocean Liners. The British *paddle steamer **Enterprize* was the first to attempt to establish a regular scheduled route—to India—in 1823. This came to nothing and it was an American, Junius Smith, who first started a regular ocean service after issuing the prospectus for the **British & American Steam Navigation Company** in 1835. His intention was to run a two-weekly service, with four paddle steamers, two built in the USA and two in Britain. The American steamers never materialized but in England the 1,850-ton *British Queen* and the 2,350-ton *President* were built for the company. Delays to the *British Queen* forced the company in April 1838 to charter another paddle steamer, the 700-ton **Sirius*. However, the *British Queen* made several crossings after that and was joined by the *President* in 1840. But the *President* was underpowered and when she foundered in 1841 she sank the company as well. A more successful early ocean liner was Isambard *Brunel's **Great Western*, which arrived in New York only hours behind the *Sirius*. The first passenger steamship built specifically for transatlantic crossings, she was followed by the two other Brunel creations, the **Great Britain* and the **Great Eastern*.

In 1840 the Peninsular and Oriental Steam Navigation Company, always known as P. & O., started a regular 'Steam conveyance from London and Falmouth to Vigo, Oporto, Lisbon, Cadiz, Gibraltar, Malta, Greece, the Ionian Islands, Egypt, and India', though those travelling to India had to travel overland between Alexandria and a Red Sea port to pick up a sea connection to their destination. With the aid of more *Admiralty contracts for delivering mail the service was extended to Singapore and Hong Kong in 1845, and to Australia in the early 1850s.

From this modest beginning P. & O. grew into a company which ran regular steamship services to the Far East and Australasia. Over the following decades it built many fine ocean liners to serve these routes, one of the best known being the 45,000-ton *Canberra*, *launched in 1961. With the Holland–America's *Rotterdam*, the *Canberra* produced a new look to ocean liners as her twin funnels and engine machinery were positioned well aft in the manner of *bulk carriers and *tankers. Affectionately christened the 'Great White Whale', she was, like *Queen Elizabeth II* (*QEII*), requisitioned as a troopship during the Falklands War of 1982.

Early Transatlantic Liners. The same year as P. & O. began its regular scheduled sailings, a Nova Scotian, Samuel Cunard (1787–1865), began a regular transatlantic passenger service after he had won a British government mail contract to replace the transatlantic mail *brigs with steamships (see also RMS). In the terms of his tender he guaranteed to build four ships that would operate two voyages to the USA and back every month, winter and summer. With Robert Napier, one of the best-known marine engineers of his day, Cunard formed the British & North American Royal Mail Steam Packet Company (known as the **Cunard Line** from 1878) with two *shipbuilding firms. They constructed for him four wooden-hulled paddle steamers, all of similar size—1,156 tons and 63 metres (207 ft) on the keel—and he began operating them from Liverpool to Boston with a voyage time of fifteen days. They each carried 115 passengers and 225 tons of cargo.

Cunard had the sensible but unexciting policy of letting others be the innovators, and he was averse to opulence, and it was left to shipowners like William Inman to break new ground. Inman's 1,600-ton, iron-hulled, *propeller-driven *City of Glasgow*, which he acquired in 1850, was the 'true prototype of the modern ocean steamship' (C. Gibbs, *Passenger Liners of the Western Ocean* (1952), 95). In 1850 paddle steamers could carry 500 tons of cargo; the *City of Glasgow* carried 1,200 tons and nearly as many passengers with far greater economy, and showed it was possible to make profits without being subsidized. More importantly, her fares were cheap enough to attract a new and profitable source of income, emigrants. Meals were provided, unheard of for *steerage passengers at that time, and a far cry from 1837 when seventeen steerage passengers died of starvation after a sailing *packet took 100 days to cross the Atlantic. Screw ships like the Inman line's record-breaking *City of Paris*, launched in 1865, soon proved they were also faster than the paddle steamer. Nevertheless, *City of Paris* was *ship-rigged on her three masts, a necessary precaution. The last Inman Line ship was launched in 1888. Called *City of Paris*, too, she was one of the first passenger ships with twin screws. But she still carried three masts rigged for sails, and it wasn't until the 1890s that passenger ships relied entirely on their engines.

The White Star and Cunard Lines. From 1871 a strong competitor to Cunard and Inman was the British Oceanic Steam Navigation Company, better known as the **White Star Line**. The line's fortunes lay in its partnership with the Belfast shipbuilding firm of Harland & Wolff that produced for it the 3,850-ton *Oceanic* class, which 'rendered all existing passenger tonnage obsolescent' (Gibbs, *Passenger Liners*). Their success was primarily due to their *compound engines which dramatically reduced fuel consumption, and therefore bunkerage space for coal, allowing more space for passengers or extra cargo. But Harland & Wolff also introduced a new hull form, raising the beam to length ratio from 8 : 1 to 10 : 1, that cut fuel costs further and increased speed. They also moved the saloon and best *cabins *amidships, away from their traditional place in the stern. This increased the level of comfort, as did the larger cabins which were fitted with electric bells and much larger *portholes. The White Star Line's best-known liners were the 45,300-ton *Olympic*, which became the largest ocean liner in the world when she was launched in 1911, the ill-fated 46,300-ton **Titanic* (1912), and the 48,150-ton *Britannic* (1915) which was sunk by a mine in the Aegean in 1916. The White Star Line continued in business into the 1920s before merging with the Cunard Line in 1934.

It is for its 20th-century ocean liners that Cunard is best known today and with them it set a new standard of luxury, speed, and size. 'The main consideration', one maritime historian has noted, 'is to convey the idea that one is not at sea, but on terra firma.' They include such famous names as the 31,950-ton *Mauretania* (1906)—a second larger one (35,750 tons) of the same name was launched in 1939—the 31,550-ton **Lusitania* (1906), and the 45,650-ton *Aquitania* (1913). The earlier *Mauretania* and the *Lusitania* were the first ocean liners to be fitted with quadruple screws driven by steam turbines. These vessels were followed in the 1930s by the 81,235-ton *Queen Mary* (1936), and the 83,673-ton *Queen Elizabeth* (1938). The latter did not enter service until after the Second World War (1939–45) and both were used as troopships. Out of the 865,000 US servicemen sent to the UK before the end of the war, these two liners transported 320,000 of them.

Twentieth-century Rivalry and Decline. The main rivals to the British for the coveted *blue riband during the first three decades of the 20th century were, at different times, the USA, Germany, and France, though Italy was also a contender. Immediately before the First World War (1914–18) the German Hamburg–America Line built three liners for the transatlantic route that were to remain the world's largest until 1935: the 51,950-ton *Imperator* (1912), the 54,300-ton *Vaterland* (1914), and the 56,550-ton *Bismarck* (1914), the fastest of the three. After the war they were all handed over as war reparations and became, respectively, the Cunard's *Berengaria*, the **United States Line**'s *Leviathan*, and the Cunard's *Majestic*, and all remained in service into the 1930s. By then a new generation of ocean liners had been launched and preeminent among them were the **French Line**'s 43,150-ton *Île de France* (1926) and the 79,300-ton *Normandie* (1932). The latter was the French answer to the *Queen Mary*, and was longer by almost three metres (9.5 ft).

But while the Cunarder was a natural development of earlier liners, the *Normandie* was full of innovations that included taking streamlining to the limit and a revolutionary turbo-electric propulsion system, and the luxury of her accommodation has probably never been equalled. On her maiden voyage in 1935 she broke all known speed records by a wide margin, crossing in a time of 4 days, 3 hours, 2 minutes, at an average speed of 29.98 knots. She was laid up in New York at the start of the Second World War, but was seized by the American authorities in December 1941. Renamed the *Lafayette*, work was started to convert her to a troopship but she caught fire in February 1942 and capsized at her berth.

The 1930s were undoubtedly the apogee of the age of the ocean liner and the glamour and the luxury could never quite be revived after the Second World War. However, Britain, France, and the USA all launched new liners which, for a while at least, earned their keep. In 1952 the 53,985-ton *United States* entered the North Atlantic service to compete with the *Queen Mary* and the *Queen Elizabeth*. Though ordered by the US Navy as a troopship, it was always the intention to sell the *United States* to the United States Line and the line acquired her, at a fraction of her original cost, immediately she was launched. She broke the record by a wide margin, crossing in 3 days, 10 hours, 40 minutes at an average speed of 35.59 knots, a speed that has never been equalled by a scheduled commercial passenger ship on the transatlantic route. The French Line also decided that a new luxury liner was still commercially viable on the North Atlantic route and in February 1962 the 66,348-ton *France* made her maiden voyage from Le Havre to New York. She added a late sparkle to the transatlantic route before being withdrawn in 1972 to become a *cruise ship. In

1974 she was laid up but in 1979 was acquired by a Florida-based cruise ship company and given a major refit. Renamed *Norway*, she was still operating in 2004.

Queen Mary made her last westbound voyage in 1967, and is now on display at Long Beach, California; *Queen Elizabeth* was withdrawn from service in 1968 and sold, first to the USA and then to a Hong Kong businessman, and in 1972 she was destroyed by fire in Hong Kong harbour. The *United States* was withdrawn in 1969, the year that Cunard's 65,863-ton *QEII* made her maiden voyage. But Cunard had already foreseen that the era was at an end and made a late decision—the liner's hull was nearly completed—to make *QEII* a suitable cruise ship, and she was changed from a three-class ship to a two-class one. See also DIESEL ENGINE; ELECTRIC PROPULSION; EVAPORATORS; STEERING GEAR.

Bathe, B., *Seven Centuries of Sea Travel* (1975).
Gibbs, G., *Passenger Liners of the Western Ocean* (1952).
Howarth, D. and S., *The Story of P. & O.* (1986).
Maxtone-Graham, J., *The North Atlantic Run* (1972).

oceanographic institutes. *Oceanography is a multidisciplinary science that requires large and expensive facilities such as *research ships, powerful computers, and the sophisticated instrumentation required for sampling and monitoring the ocean. So the world's oceanographic centres not only have a nucleus of full-time research staff but also technical support staff that service the equipment, computers, and ships. They also service a network of academic and industrial researchers and postgraduates who depend to a greater or lesser extent on the special facilities. Most of the major centres are on the coast, where the research ships can tie up alongside, and close to transport networks. Research ships on scientific missions to remote regions need to be serviced in ports, so close proximity to an international airport is an important asset.

Some centres are focused on the ocean near where they are situated. For example, the **Monterey Bay Aquarium Research Institute in California**, which is situated at the head of a deep canyon, is associated with an impressive public aquarium. This exhibits real-time images collected by *underwater vehicles that are used to investigate the inhabitants of the canyon. Another centre that is principally devoted to one specific facility is **Harbor Branch in Florida**. It runs the two Johnson Sea Link manned underwater vehicles which have plexiglass domes that are ideal for biologists since they give remarkably good all-round viewing. Some of the laboratories focus their researches on specific areas, like the **Institute of Antarctic and Southern Ocean Studies (IOASOS) in Hobart, Tasmania**, which, as its name suggests, focuses on studies of the Southern Ocean.

Some owe their existence to specific research projects, like the **Southampton Oceanography Centre (SOC) in Britain**, which originated from the **Discovery* Investigations. SOC was founded in 1994 through the amalgamation of the University of Southampton's Departments of Oceanography and Geology, and the Institute of Oceanographic Sciences that was then a government-funded laboratory run under the aegis of the Natural Environment Research Council. Although SOC no longer continues the work of the *Discovery* Investigations, which is now conducted by the British Antarctic Survey, it accommodates the independent unit that runs the UK's research ships. Other oceanographic centres include the laboratories at Plymouth where the emphasis is on *marine biology, at Liverpool where the emphasis is on *tides, and the Scottish Association for Marine Science laboratory at Oban, which focuses on the fascinating waters around Scotland where the *Darwin mounds were found.

One of the oldest of all oceanography centres is the **Scripps Institution at La Jolla near San Diego, California**, which was founded in 1903 as an independent research laboratory for marine biology, but is now concerned with all the oceanographic disciplines. It became part of the University of California in 1912, when it was given the Scripps name in recognition of its supporters Ellen Browning Scripps and E. W. Scripps. It has a staff of approximately 1,300, including about 90 faculty scientists, nearly 300 other scientists, and about 200 graduate students, and it runs four research vessels. The institution's annual expenditure totals more than $US140 million. On the opposite seaboard of the USA, on Cape Cod, Massachusetts, is another of the better-known oceanographic institutes, **Woods Hole (WHOI)**, which is close to the Georges Bank, still a major centre for commercial fisheries in the North Atlantic. WHOI has a mission that is typical of many oceanographic institutes which is to develop and effectively communicate a fundamental understanding of the processes and characteristics governing how the oceans function and how they interact with the earth as a whole.

To succeed in this basic mission WHOI seeks to recruit, retain, and support the highest-quality staff and students, and provide an organization that nurtures creativity and innovation. It takes a flexible, multidisciplinary, and collaborative approach to the research and education activities of its staff within an equitable working environment. In particular it promotes the development and use of advanced instrumentation and systems (including ships, underwater vehicles, and platforms) to make the required observations at sea and in the laboratory, and its Deep Submergence Laboratory, founded by Dr Robert *Ballard, has done much to develop underwater technology. It disseminates the results of its researches to the public and policy-makers, and fosters its applications to new technology and products in ways consistent with the wise use of the oceans. Like many oceanographic institutes, WHOI receives considerable support from its nation's navy, because so much of its research is relevant to successful naval operations, both offensive and defensive.

In Canada there are two major laboratories, one on the eastern seaboard, the **Bedford Institute at Halifax, Nova Scotia**, and the other on the western seaboard at Vancouver. The Bedford Institute is strategically placed close to the *Grand Banks, which have played such an important role in the development of both Nova Scotia and Newfoundland. Research there is now very much focused on Arctic studies and particularly on the potential effects of *climate change on the Arctic marine ecosystem. Similarly, at Vancouver the interest lies in the factors influencing the fluctuations in the stocks of Pacific salmon.

In Europe one of the largest oceanographic laboratories is the **Alfred Wegener Institute (AWI) at Bremerhaven** in Germany. Named after the palaeontologist who first proposed the idea of continental drift in 1912, AWI is the leading German research institute for marine and polar research and consists of a number of laboratories. Its main research ship is an *icebreaker, the *Polarstern*, which was specifically designed for work in polar seas and so can go where other more conventional research vessels cannot venture. Recently the *Polarstern* has been involved in iron fertilization experiments in the Southern Ocean. (See BIOLOGICAL OCEANOGRAPHY.)

The main French oceanographic organization is the **Institut Français de Recherche pour l'Exploitation de la Mer (IFREMER)**, which runs several laboratories, seven research ships, and two underwater vehicles. The largest laboratory is at Brest. In 2003 one of its underwater vehicles carried out a survey of the *tanker *Prestige*, which foundered off the Spanish coast that year, creating devastating oil *pollution of parts of the Spanish coastline. Thanks to the influence of Jacques *Cousteau and Auguste Piccard (1884–1962), the designer of the *bathyscaphe, IFREMER has always maintained an interest in underwater vehicles and it collaborated with WHOI in the successful search for the **Titanic* in 1985.

M. V. Angel

oceanography is the scientific study of the oceans. It is multidisciplinary, involving four major disciplines, *geological, *physical, *chemical, and *biological oceanography. Although each of these disciplines has its own technologies and addresses very different questions, results from one are often highly relevant to others. The overall intellectual challenge is how to integrate all aspects into an overarching (holistic) understanding of how the oceans work. Oceanography is also a component of global studies: what happens in the oceans is affected by and affects what happens in terrestrial and atmospheric systems, particularly through its influence on *climate change. See also MARINE BIOLOGY.

www.mth.uea.ac.uk/ocean/vl/by-subject.html#biological

M. V. Angel

ocean racing, see YACHTING: SAIL.

oceans. The waters of the oceans provide the most voluminous habitat on the planet; 71% of the earth's surface is covered by sea to an average depth of 3,800 metres (12,470 ft).

The volume of water in the oceans is estimated to be 1.368×10^9 cub. km (3.283×10^8 cub. mls.), which is 97% of all the water on the planet.

About 5% of the earth's surface is covered by the shallow waters of the *continental shelves that extend down to depths of up to 200 metres (650 ft). At the outer edge of the shelf seas is the shelf-break, where the slope of the seabed suddenly steepens. Across the continental slope ocean depths increase to 3,000 metres (10,000 ft) and the lower margin of the slope where the gradient slackens is known as the continental rise. Continental slopes and rises account for 13% of the earth's area. The slopes are underlain by continental rocks whereas beneath the rise is a talus (scree) slope of rock debris that has slipped from the slope. Beyond the rise stretch abyssal depths of 3,000–6,000 metres (10,000–20,000 ft), which cover about 51% of the earth's surface, and are underlain by oceanic crust (see GEOLOGICAL OCEANOGRAPHY) that is constantly being formed along the mid-ocean ridges. *Offshore oil and gas reserves are found in sedimentary rocks beneath the seabed of the continental shelves and slopes. They occur in regions which in the geological past have been highly productive, such as in the Persian Gulf, the Gulf of Mexico, the North Sea, and off Angola, Indonesia, and Brazil.

Along the margins of the Pacific Ocean and some island arcs the ocean crust is being subducted—buckled down beneath the continents. Here occur the deepest depths in *trenches of over 6,000 metres (20,000 ft). The continents are asymmetrically distributed across the surface of the earth, and so the intervening oceans are very disparate. For example 60.7% of the northern hemisphere is covered with ocean compared with 80.9% in the southern hemisphere. Consequently sea-surface temperatures range more widely at temperate *latitudes in the northern hemisphere than in the southern hemisphere. The boundaries of four of the major oceans are largely determined by the distribution of the continental land masses.

Pacific Ocean. This is the largest and oldest ocean. Its total area is around 165.38×10^6 sq. km (63.84×10^6 sq. mls.), with an average depth of 4,200 metres (13,750 ft), and its maximum depth of 11,015 metres (36,130 ft) in the Marianas Trench is the deepest anywhere. Its total volume is about 695×10^6 cub. km (167×10^6 cub. mls.) In the south it is fully open to the Southern Ocean, but to the north it has only a shallow connection with the Arctic Ocean via the Bering Strait. It connects with the Atlantic only though the Drake Passage to the south of the tip of South America, but as recently as 5 million years ago, there was a shallow water connection across the Panama Isthmus. The South Pacific is connected to the Indian Ocean near the equator via the shallow sills between the islands of the Indonesian archipelago and to the south of Australia at full ocean depths.

Atlantic Ocean. This is the second largest ocean, and has an area only half that of the Pacific, 82.22×10^6 sq. km (31.74×10^6 sq. mls.). It is a 'young' ocean; the North Atlantic began to open during the Jurassic era about 200 million years ago. Previous to that there was only one supercontinent, Pangea. The South Atlantic began to open up about 100 million years ago. The shapes and geology of Africa and South America are complementary and can be fitted together like pieces of a jig-saw. Because of its relative youth, the average depth of the Atlantic is only 3,600 metres (11,800 ft), and its volume is about 296×10^6 cub. km (71.04×10^6 cub. mls.). Its maximum depth of 9,560 metres (31,350 ft) is in the Puerto Rico Trench. It is the only ocean with a deep-water connection with the Arctic Ocean.

Warm Atlantic water flows north eastwards via the Norwegian Sea and feeds the Spitsbergen *Current. This flow not only keeps the climate of north-west Europe much milder than that of north-west America, but it has a major influence on the ecology of the Arctic and keeps the seas to the north of Norway free of *ice. These warm surface flows into the Arctic are balanced by cold outflows that spill over the ridges that stretch between Greenland, Iceland, the Faeroes, and Scotland, and also the flow of the East Greenland Current southwards along Greenland and Canada.

In the south, the Atlantic connects with the Indian Ocean around the southern tip of South Africa and large *eddies of water pass around the Cape from the Indian Ocean. Further south around Cape Horn there is a connection with the Pacific. To the south, the *Antarctic Convergence marks its boundary with the Southern Ocean.

Indian Ocean. This has an area of 73.48×10^6 sq. km (28.36×10^6 sq. mls.), and a volume of 282.9×10^6 cub. km (68.90×10^6 cub. mls.). It is connected to the Southern Ocean to the south, but to the north it is bounded by continental Asia. Its climate is modulated by the interaction between the atmosphere and the Asian land mass, resulting in seasonally reversing *monsoons. When the winds reverse, so do the surface currents particularly to the north of the equator. So in the Arabian Sea and to a lesser extent in the Bay of Bengal, the fertility of the ocean oscillates between being very rich during the south-west monsoon, and very unproductive during the north-east monsoon.

Arctic Ocean. This has an area of 14.1×10^6 sq. km (5.44×10^6 sq. mls.). It is a truly polar ocean, as it lies mostly within the Arctic Circle and is almost entirely encircled by land. Nearly half its area of consists of shallow seas, particularly north of Russia. Its greatest depth of 4,400 metres (14,400 ft) lies under the pack ice close to the North Pole. Its connection with the North Pacific via the Bering Strait is only a few kilometres wide and is very shallow, whereas its connection with the North Atlantic is broad and deep. The inflow of warm water from the Atlantic pushes the southern boundary of the winter pack ice far to the north. Even so, much of the Arctic Ocean remains covered throughout the year with pack ice that can be up to five years old, and 1.5–4 metres (5–13 ft) thick. Currently the Arctic pack ice is thinning so quickly that much of the Arctic may become ice free by the end of this century. While this may finally open up the *North-West Passage for commercial *fisheries, it will have a devastating effect on charismatic Arctic species like the polar bear and *marine mammals like the walrus, narwhal, and belugas. In the summer the area of the Arctic covered by pack ice normally shrinks by about 10%. The vast outflows of the great Siberian rivers keep the surface *salinity of the Arctic quite low, so that the sea freezes at slightly warmer temperatures.

Southern Ocean. Unlike the Arctic Ocean, which lies mostly in the Arctic Circle, only a relatively small part of this ocean lies south of the Antarctic Circle. This is why its former, popular name of Antarctic Ocean has been dropped. It is bounded in the south by the continent of Antarctica, but to the north it is open to the other major oceans, and is not separated from them by any geographical features. Its northern boundary is the Antarctic Convergence, whose position varies both seasonally and interannually. The major feature of its circulation is the Antarctic circumpolar current, which is driven by prevailing westerly winds of the *Roaring Forties (and the 'Filthy Fifties'). This current began to flow about 35 million years ago when the continent of Australia separated from the continent of Antarctica sufficiently to create an unimpeded circumpolar deep-water connection.

The Antarctic ice cap started to develop about 14 million years ago, becoming a major influence on the climate of the Southern Ocean and the evolution of characteristic Southern Ocean species such as the *penguin. The extreme conditions, with water temperatures that can fall as low as –2 °C (28.4 °F), have led to the evolution of some special adaptations. Some *fish have antifreeze in their blood and tissues, possibly one of the *marine pharmaceuticals of the future, as the blood of most species will freeze if water temperatures fall below –1.5 °C (29.3 °F).

The extent of pack ice in the Southern Ocean fluctuates enormously seasonally from about 20 million sq. km (7.7×10^6 sq. mls.) at the end of winter to 5 million sq. km (1.93×10^6 sq. mls.) in late summer. Most is renewed each year; only in the Weddell Sea, as in the Arctic, is there much multi-year ice. Immense tabular icebergs are spawned from the broad ice-shelves of the Ross and Weddell Seas where the depth of the continental shelf has been depressed to 400–500 metres (1,300–1,640 ft), by the massive weight of the ice sheet.

Along the margins of the pack ice the seas are highly productive, and attract large concentrations of marine mammals and *seabirds. During the 19th and 20th centuries *sealing and *whaling exploited the fur seals, penguins, and *whales. See also SEAS.

Cramer, D., *Great Waters: An Atlantic Passage* (2001).

Hardy, Sir Alister, *Great Waters* (1967).

M. V. Angel

Oceanus, an influential Greek deity of the sea, son of Coelus (the sky) and Terra (the earth). He married *Tethys, who gave birth to most of the principal rivers together with up to 3,000 daughters who are called *Oceanides after him. According to Homer, he was the father of all the gods, and on that account received frequent visits from the rest of the deities. Oceanus is generally represented as an old man with a long flowing beard sitting upon the *waves of the sea; he presided over every part of the sea, even the rivers being subject to his power. Mariners of the ancient world were deeply reverential in their worship of him, and served with great solemnity a deity to whose care they entrusted themselves when going on any voyage.

octant, a reflecting navigational instrument for measuring the *altitude of heavenly bodies, having an arc of one-eighth of a circle, but, because of its reflecting properties, capable of measuring altitudes of up to 90°. *Hadley's reflecting quadrant, which began replacing *Davis's quadrant in the 1730s, was in fact an octant, but was still called a quadrant because that was the name by which all seamen called the existing *seaman's quadrant. Octants remained in use by *navigators up to the 19th century. *Sextants, which were introduced during the second half of the 18th century, were generally used for *lunar distance in the calculation of *longitude. When the introduction of *chronometers made lunar calculations no longer necessary, the sextant replaced the octant as the standard navigational instrument for the measurement of altitudes.

Odysseus, according to Greek legend the son of Laertes and Anticleia and one of the most famous heroes of ancient Greece. After the capture of Troy, achieved by his stratagem of the wooden horse, he set sail for Ithaca but unfavourable winds carried him along the coast of North Africa and across the unknown seas to Italy, where he braved the dangers of *Scylla and Charybdis, a voyage recorded by Homer as the *Odyssey*. After many adventures he was, again according to legend, slain unknowingly in his old age by his son Telemachus.

Odysseus has been identified with *Poseidon, Hermes, and other legendary Greek gods by various subsequent writers and students of Greek mythology, but whoever he was he is generally accepted as the fount from which sprang the sailor race whose voyages and adventures so influenced and educated the Hellenic race. He was the archetype of the true Greek when their sea power was stretching out across the Mediterranean from the Black Sea to the western basin. The Latin equivalent of Odysseus is Ulixes, more often written Ulysses.

offing, the distance that a ship at sea keeps away from the land because of navigational dangers, fog, or other hazards. The term is generally, though not necessarily, understood to mean that the ship remains in waters too deep for anchoring. To keep, or to make, a **good offing** is to lay a *course which takes a ship well off the land and clear of all danger.

offshore oil and gas. Economically offshore oil and gas are the most important reserves in the *Exclusive Economic Zones (EEZ) of many countries. They were generated by chemical transformation from the remains of *marine plants and animals that sedimented to the bottom of stagnant anoxic shallow seas during past geological eras, and were then buried by movements of the earth. Initially deep within the rocks the high pressures and temperatures of 50–100 °C (122–212 °F) converted the organic remains into kerogen, a solid, waxy, organic substance, a forerunner of oil and gas. Further pressure cooking at temperatures of 100–160 °C (212–310 °F) converted the kerogen to oils and at still higher temperatures to natural gas (methane). The oil and gas then migrated laterally along porous rock strata, sandstones, or salt deposits, eventually becoming trapped where the strata domed or at faults where impermeable layers stopped further migration. In the North Sea the first gas was recovered in 1967, and the first oil in 1975. An example of a North Sea oil field is Forties. Discovered in 1970, it began production in 1975 and in 1982 produced its one billionth barrel of oil. It extends over a distance of 56 kilometres (35 mls.), covers an area larger than the city of Aberdeen, and each of its four main platforms, Alpha, Bravo, Charlie, and Delta, contains four times more steel than the Eiffel Tower.

To date about 132 million tonnes of oil and gas have been recovered in Britain's EEZ, annually contributing £4 billion a year in taxes since 1984, and in 2004 the industry was employing about 300,000 people. Even so UK oil and gas production is only about 4% of global production. The most important reserves are still in the Middle East, but many offshore regions have large untapped reserves, especially in deposits under the Caspian Sea, and under more than 1,000 metres (3,250 ft) of water off Brazil and Angola. Oil *pollution remains an unresolved issue, with serious spills from *tankers and other sources occurring with depressing regularity. The industry is concerned about what will happen when most reserves eventually run dry, maybe before, or during, the second half of the 21st century, but many environmentalists believe that the *climate change induced by burning all these hydrocarbons will by then have disrupted the world as we know it.

www.ukooa.co.uk/issues/storyofoil/index.htm

M. V. Angel

off soundings, a ship is off soundings when it is in waters which lie to seaward of the 100-*fathom line (600 ft/183 m). Before the days of *sounding machines and *echo sounders, the deep-sea *lead line could only measure depths up to about 100 fathoms, so that all greater depths were off, or beyond, soundings.

off the wind, said of a sailing ship when it is sailing with the sheets well eased off with the wind coming *free or from broad on the bow. See also ON THE WIND.

oldster, in the days of the sailing navies a *midshipman of more than four years' seniority who, with the *master's mates, also known as oldsters, occupied the *cockpit of the ship.

Oleron, the Laws of, a code of maritime law enacted by Eleanor of Aquitaine, who married Henry II of England in 1152. It was attributed by her to the Island of Oleron, which lies 32 kilometres (20 mls.) north of the mouth of the Gironde River in western France. The island was part of her duchy and was renowned for the skill and courage of its seafaring population. It is possible the laws were based on the older Rhodian Law of the Mediterranean. They dealt mainly with the rights and responsibilities of ships' captains in relation to discipline, *mutiny, pay, cargoes, sickness on board, *pilotage, accidents, and similar matters.

The Laws of Oleron were introduced into England in about 1190 by Richard I, son of Henry and Eleanor, and were codified in the *Black Book of the Admiralty* in 1336 which also contained a list of the ancient customs and usages of the sea. It is unfortunate that the original book disappeared from the registry of the High Court of *Admiralty at the beginning of the 19th century. Only a few manuscript copies of parts of it, some dating back to about 1420, are extant and are in the British Museum and Bodleian libraries. All known sources for it were collated in Sir Travers Twiss's *Black Book of the Admiralty* (4 vols., 1871).

Omega, a very low-frequency *hyperbolic navigation system introduced by the USA in 1982 with a 95% accuracy of about one and a half kilometres (1 m.) by day and just over 3 kilometres (2 mls.) by night. Obsolete. Mike Richey

one-design class, a class of *yacht or small racing boat all of which have been built to one accepted design. So as to give all yachts of a class an equal chance when racing against one another, and to eliminate the complications of handicapping, one-designs are built and rigged to be identical, or nearly so. Each yacht in a one-design class should have theoretically the same sailing performance, so that the results of a race should depend on the individual skills of the helmsmen and their crews. In practice, yachts reflect the amount of maintenance they receive and the care the owner gives to his boat's tuning-up and details of sails and gear, so, in fact, the relative performance of boats in a one-design class can vary widely. However, the principle of the one-design does limit the advantage the wealthy owner can have over the less affluent, and on the whole racing in any one-design class tends to be very fair.

'on the beach', said of seamen who have retired from sea service. See also 'SWALLOW THE ANCHOR, TO'.

on the wind, said of a sailing vessel when it is sailing with its sheets hauled as far in as possible, making the vessel sail as close to the wind as it will go. See also OFF THE WIND.

open hawse, the opposite of a *foul hawse, being the condition of a ship when it is lying to two anchors without the *cables being crossed.

order of sailing, the disposition of a fleet of sailing warships when sailing in company, or of a *convoy. It is from the order of sailing that the order of battle was formed when an enemy fleet was sighted.

ordinary, an old term from the days of sailing navies. It indicated that a ship had been laid up in a *dockyard or harbour, and its masts, *rigging, sails, and guns taken out and stored ashore, and the upper deck temporarily roofed over with timber to keep the ship dry. The term was also sometimes used to indicate the men who remained on board ships in this condition, usually the warrant officers and their servants.

ordinary seaman, the lowest rating on board British ships. Boys were rated ordinary seamen and began their man's time on board at the age of 18, normally being rated *Abs, or able seamen, at the age of 21. The abbreviation for this rank in the Royal Navy is 'OD', probably derived from OrDinary, while in the US Navy the most common abbreviations are 'OSea' or 'Ordy'.

orlop, orig. **over-lop,** the name given to the lowest deck in a sailing man-of-war. It was the platform laid over the *beams of a ship below the turn of the *bilge, and was the deck on which the *cables were coiled in their lockers when the anchors were *weighed and also the deck on which were found the powder magazines, the principal storerooms, and the *cabins of junior officers. In merchant ships, the orlop deck forms the floors of the cargo *holds.

Oropesa sweep, a method of sweeping moored mines by a wire *towed by a single minesweeper. It swept mines to the side of the minesweeper by means of a long wire fitted with wirecutters placed at intervals along the wire to cut the mines' *moorings. The wire was towed *astern of the minesweeper with a *kite fitted to the wire a short distance from the point of tow to keep the wire down to a fixed depth below water. Near the end of the wire was an *otter which forced it outwards as it was towed through the water, and at the end was a float to hold the wire at its fixed depth and prevent it sinking to the bottom. As the wire came into contact with the mines' mooring wires, they slid along it until meeting a cutter. This severed

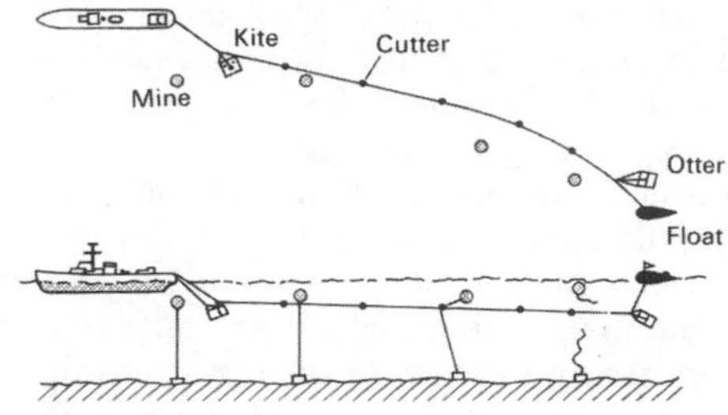

Oropesa sweep

the mooring wire so that the mine floated to the surface where it was destroyed by rifle fire.

This form of sweep was first developed in 1919 in the minesweeper *Oropesa* during the clearance of the northern mine barrage laid during the First World War (1914–18). This ran across the North Sea from the Orkney Islands to the Norwegian coast. It was improved between the two world wars by the substitution of multi-plane otters for the earlier single otter used for spreading the sweep, and by better designs of cutters.

otter, a board rigged with a line and bridle which, when towed underwater, stretches the line by reason of the outward angle at which the bridle holds it. It is used widely in fishing to spread out a net or to keep open the mouth of a *trawl—though when otter boards are used on a trawl they are normally called doors. The name comes from the otter board used by salmon fishermen to tauten their line or net as they *towed it along the shore, the otter being a great predator of salmon.

The principle of the otter board was also used in minesweeping devices. See OROPESA SWEEP; PARAVANE.

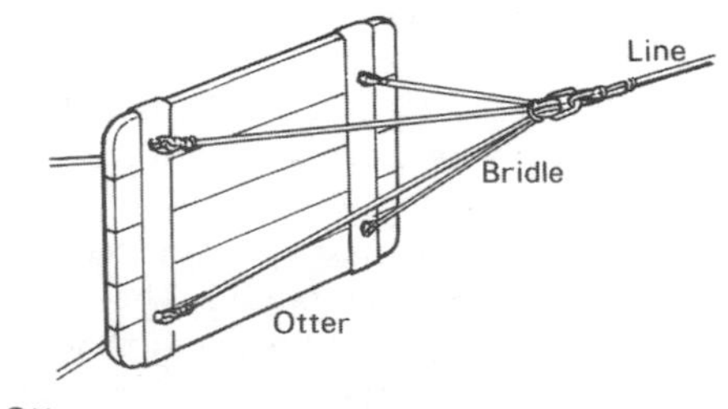

Otter

outhaul, a line or *purchase by which a sail is hauled outboard along a *spar. Aboard a *square-rigged ship the *studding sails and their booms were hauled out along the *yards by means of outhauls. On old-fashioned *yachts with long *bowsprits, the *tack of the *jib was hooked onto a *traveller, which was then hauled towards the outer, or *crance end, of the bowsprit by the outhaul.

outlicker, outligger, or **outleager,** a short boom which was extended *astern from the top of the *poop in the older *square-rigged ships. It was used to haul down (or 'lig-out' in the older phrase) the *mizzen sheet when the mizzen-mast was stepped so far *aft that there was no room to do so inboard. Most *carracks and four-masted *galleons were fitted with an outlicker. A later equivalent was the *bumpkin.

outrigger. **(1)** An extension to each side of the *crosstrees of a sailing vessel to spread the *backstays, in a *schooner the *topmast backstays, and in a *square-rigged ship the *topgallant and *royal backstays. **(2)** A type of Pacific or Indian Ocean *canoe or *proa where a counterpoising piece of wood, usually shorter than the vessel's hull, is rigged out from the vessel's side to provide *stability when sailing. **(3)** The projecting beams rigged on the sides of sailing men-of-war to which additional *shrouds were led for extra support of the masts when the ship was *careened. A great strain was exerted on the mast during careening as the ship was hauled down onto its side by *tackles secured to the mastheads, hence the need for extra support by additional, temporary, shrouds.

overfall, a condition of the sea when it falls into breaking *waves caused by wind or *current over an irregular bottom, or by currents meeting. *Tide-rips and *tide-races frequently cause overfalls.

overhaul, to. **(1)** To increase the distance apart of the *blocks of a *tackle by running the rope back through the *sheaves. **(2)** The expression used to describe the action of a ship when it overtakes, or is catching up with, another ship at sea. **(3)** An expression sometimes used in connection with the inspection, testing, and repair of a vessel's machinery, but the more correct nautical word in this respect is refit.

over-raked, a vessel is said to be over-raked when it is riding to its anchor(s) in bad weather and the seas break continuously over its bows. It is a condition which can often be ameliorated by increasing the *scope of the *cable through *veering an additional amount so that the vessel may lie more easily.

overtaking light, a white light displayed at the stern of a vessel under way at night, forming part of the compulsory *navigation lights which a ship must display under the regulations laid down by the *International Regulations for Preventing Collisions at Sea. The overtaking light, also known as a sternlight, must have a visibility of 3.2 kilometres (2 mls.) on a clear night and must show through an arc on either side of the vessel from right astern to two *points *abaft the *beam.

ox-eye, a name given to a small cloud which occasionally appears off the eastern coast of Africa and spreads quickly to cover the whole of the sky, presaging a severe *storm accompanied by a violent wind. It gets its name from its resemblance, when first seen, to the eye of an ox.

oxter plate, the name given to the hull shell plating which is riveted or welded to form the hull shape at the top of the sternpost where there is a rapid change of shape. Jeremy Lines

P

Pacific iron. **(1)** The cast-iron cappings at the *yardarms of a *square-rigged ship which support the *studding-sail *boom-irons and to which a *Flemish horse is made fast. **(2)** The *gooseneck at the deck end of a cargo *derrick which permits movement of the derrick in any required direction is also known as a Pacific iron.

packet, an abbreviation of packet boat, which was originally a vessel plying regularly between two ports for the carriage of mails, but available also for goods and passengers. The sailing packets of the early decades of the 19th century carried migrants to the USA and elsewhere for some years after the introduction of the early *ocean liners as they were much cheaper.

In the 16th century, state letters and dispatches were known as 'the Packet', and a Treasury account of 1598 gave details of 'Postes towards Ireland, Hollyheade, allowance as well for serving the packette by lande as for entertaining a bark to carie over and return the packet, x pounds the moneth'. They were essentially mail boats, and were also known as *post-barks.

By the 18th century they were built with a finer hull than average in order to give extra speed; still designed primarily for the carriage of mails, they were plying regularly as far from England as America, the West Indies, and India. They were armed with ten or twelve small guns, and also carried official passengers and special cargo for important persons such as ambassadors, commanders-in-chief, etc. They lost their role as mail carriers in the mid-19th century when, with the introduction of *steam propulsion, many governments gave contracts for the carriage of mails to private steamship owners. Soon after they lost their only other role, that of carrying migrants, when *steerage class was introduced aboard liners.

The name, however, in the form 'steam packet ship', remained for a few more years to describe those ships of a shipping line which made regular voyages between the same ports carrying passengers and cargo.

paddle steamer, a vessel with paddle wheels usually driven by the earliest forms of *steam propulsion. The type which has two, one on either side mounted amidships, was known as a side-wheeler; the other, where a single paddle wheel is mounted at the stern, was known as a stern-wheeler. They were powered by *reciprocating engines, though in the USA they often had a *walking beam engine.

Various forms of man-operated *paddle-wheel boats were in use long before the introduction of any kind of power, both in China and later in Europe. With the development of steam propulsion in the latter half of the 18th century various experiments were made in Europe to apply it to paddle wheels. The first to make a practical success of powering a boat in this way was a French engineer, the Marquis de Jouffroy d'Abbans (1751–1832). His 1776 experiment with a 13-metre (43-ft) boat on the Doubs River failed, but in 1783 his paddle steamer *Pyroscaphe*, with a displacement of 182 tons, was propelled against the current on the river Saône for fifteen minutes before it disintegrated. Another pioneer, the American John Fitch (1743–98), after a successful trial of a 14-metre (45-ft) paddle steamer in 1787, built a larger one the next year which ran regularly between Philadelphia and Burlington, NJ, though it was not large enough to be economically viable. The same year, in England, Patrick Miller also *launched a steamboat. This was powered by an engine made by William Symington which drove a paddle between two hulls, and in 1802 William Symington produced the **Charlotte Dundas*. The first paddle steamer in Europe to run a regular commercial service for passengers was the 13-metre (43-ft 6-in.) *Comet* which, from 1812, plied between Glasgow and Greenock. Other early paddle steamers such as the **Clermont*, **Savannah*, **Enterprize*, **Great Western*, and **Sirius*, all contributed to the slow transition from sail to steam.

The earliest powered paddle wheels carried six or more fixed floats, and some, like those fitted to the *Savannah*, could be dismantled and carried on deck when not in use. By about 1840 most paddle wheels were fitted with a feathering device in which radial rods mounted on an eccentric moved the floats in turn so that as they entered the water and left it they remained nearly upright, thereby gaining more propulsive power and causing less wash. In the early days of the 19th century there were also many experiments in the arrangement and shape of the floats, from single paddles to multiple shutters, all aimed at increasing the wheel's efficiency and reducing the shocks as the floats struck the water. Many variations of these ideas in model form can be seen in the Science Museum, South Kensington, London. Up to the end of the paddle steamer era, however, the traditional wheel with feathering floats was almost universal.

For the first fifty years of steam propulsion at sea the paddle steamer had few rivals. But shipowners were well aware of some of its disadvantages. One was the danger of broken paddle shafts and damaged engines when the ship rolled heavily in bad weather. Another was the varying effect in speed and coal consumption between a deeply laden cargo vessel, whose wheels would be well immersed, and one which was in *ballast, when the wheels would have little grip of the water. For warships, too, paddle wheels proved far too vulnerable to enemy gunfire or collision, which hastened the introduction of the *propeller.

However, passengers using the *ocean liners of the day were reluctant to trust themselves to the early screw-driven steamers. *Brunel, for one, recognized this reluctance and when his huge **Great Eastern* was launched in 1858, she had, in addition to a single 7.3-metre (24-ft) propeller, the largest pair of paddle wheels ever fitted to a steamship. The Cunard Line, too, was slow to abandon the paddle steamer, and continued to build them for its North Atlantic service until 1861. The last one, the 3,850-ton *Scotia*, was the most handsome—and powerful—ship on the Atlantic at that time and the ultimate in ocean-going paddle steamers. Her *side lever engines, built by Robert Napier, had cylinders 254 centimetres (100 in.) in diameter with a 3.6-metre (12-ft) stroke which developed 4,600 horsepower to give a service speed of 16 knots. As late as 1874 she was still able to make the year's second fastest crossing by a Cunard liner, in a time of 8 days, 16 hours.

With the introduction within the next ten years of high pressures in marine boilers, together with the introduction of the propeller and the *compound engine, with its greatly increased economy in coal and water consumption, the paddle wheel was gradually abandoned. But for passenger services on rivers and lakes, and in inshore waters, they held their own until well into the 20th century. Unlike the propeller, paddle wheels exert virtually as much power going *astern as *ahead, and a paddle steamer is far more manoeuvrable than a similar-sized screw steamer. This agility made the paddle steamers popular and well adapted for excursion services all over the world.

For the same reason paddle *tugs were built for all kinds of service except ocean work. As they carried no passengers, they were legally permitted to disconnect the shaft and to work each wheel independently of the other. By varying the speed of the wheels, or by going ahead on one wheel and astern on the other, a paddle tug could turn in almost its own length. The British *Admiralty thought so highly of them that even after the Second World War (1939–45) naval tugs were being built with paddle wheels operated with a *diesel-electric drive.

Even when propellers became the normal means of propulsion, stern-wheelers, flat-bottomed craft with a single paddle wheel at the stern, were retained to work in very shallow waters. The wheel, in this case usually of a simple type with fixed floats, was driven direct by two cylinders of long stroke placed on deck on a level with the paddle shaft and fed from a boiler, or boilers, mounted on the same deck right forward near the bows. Stern-wheelers were used extensively for police work in the Chinese rivers, in the form of river gunboats, and for *freight and passenger services on rivers in India, Iraq, and Australia.

However, in North America, although roughly half the river steamboats were stern wheelers, the larger and faster passenger riverboats were almost all side-wheelers. Some Mississippi and Ohio steamboats, powered by 12-metre (40-ft) paddle wheels turned by walking beam engines, were built as large as 5,000 tons gross with five or six decks rising above a flat hull shaped like a pointed tea tray. In the great steamboat races of the 1870s, speeds of 18 and 19 knots were claimed between Natchez and New Orleans. Larger numbers of stern-wheelers plied the rivers and lakes of British Columbia, Canada, than were employed on the Mississippi River. Modern versions of this type continue to be built, but only three of the original ones survive today and only one, the *Samson V*, is preserved afloat.

Spratt, H. Philip, *The Birth of the Steamboat* (1953).

paddle-wheel boat, like the pedalo off holiday beaches today, a vessel using a man-powered paddle wheel for propulsion.

In China, where they appeared in the 8th century, and perhaps even as early as the 5th, they were used as *tugs and as passenger river ships. They were also employed as warships, and enclosed ones—to protect the crews pedalling the wheels—were particularly effective, especially on lakes and rivers. One warship, built in the Sung dynasty (960–1279), had as many as 22 paddle wheels, 11 on each side, and was fitted with a stern wheel as well. Paddle-wheel

A Chinese paddle-wheel warship. The paddle wheels, two on each side, were worked by treadmills within the hull

warships were even employed against their modern counterpart, the *paddle steamer, during the Opium Wars (1839–42 and 1856–60) against Britain. Five of them fought a superior force of Royal Navy warships, leading many to suppose, quite incorrectly, that the Chinese had copied the paddle wheel from western ships. This mode of transport survived on Chinese rivers well into the 20th century.

In Europe the idea of constructing a paddle-wheel boat appears in several old manuscripts which date back to the 15th century, and such a mode of transport probably dates back much further. However, the first recorded use of them was in 1543 when, manned by a crew of 40 working on *capstans or treadmills, some were employed as tugs in Barcelona and Malaga harbours, and treadmill paddle boats were still in regular use on the River Loire at the start of the 19th century.

Needham, J., *Science and Civilisation in China*, iv/2 (1977).

painter, a length of small rope in a boat used for securing it when alongside a *pier or *jetty, or secured to a ship, at the *gangway, *astern, or on the lower boom. The inboard end is usually spliced with a *thimble to a ringbolt in the stern of the boat, the outboard end being prevented from unravelling by a *whipping or, more fancifully, by being *pointed.

pair of oars, the name by which a large river boat plying for hire on the River Thames in London was known during the 17th and 18th centuries. They were rowed by two men each pulling a pair of oars. In those days the Thames was one of the main highways of communication, and with only one bridge (London Bridge), a great number of boats plied for hire, both for crossing the river and for journeys up and down it. See also SCULLER.

palm. **(1)** The triangular face of the *fluke of an *Admiralty pattern anchor. **(2)** The sailmaker's thimble used in sewing *canvas, consisting of a flat thimble in a canvas or leather strip with a thumb hole. The whole is worn across the palm of the hand, which gives it its name.

pampero, a violent *squall, accompanied by heavy rain, thunder, and lightning. It blows up with great suddenness on the pampas of the Rio de la Plata plain and frequently drifts out to sea where it blows with the force of a hurricane, the wind usually coming from the south-west. The 5,900-ton five-masted *barque *France* was struck by a pampero in 1901 and had to be abandoned as a result of the damage she sustained.

Panama Canal, the canal cut through the Isthmus of Panama in order to connect the Atlantic and Pacific oceans. This shortened by many thousands of kilometres the previous route round Cape Horn or though the Magellan Straits, which, until then, was the only ice-free means of passing from one ocean to the other.

The length of the canal is 68 kilometres (42 mls.), and was a massive civil engineering problem to build. Since the mean levels of the two oceans lie at different heights, it was necessary to raise the canal to a height of 26 kilometres (85 ft) above sea level and at places, Lake Gatun in particular, this meant building a series of locks which had to be large enough to take the largest ocean-going vessels. This also entailed, since ships were unable to use their engines while in the locks, the provision of electric locomotives along the sides to *tow the ships within them.

Interest in building a canal dates back to the 16th century when the Isthmus of Panama became known to Spanish explorers. Ferdinand de *Lesseps, who had constructed the *Suez Canal, formed a company to build one but in 1889 it ran out of money. A fillip to the possibility of constructing one came in 1898 when, during the Spanish–American War, the *battleship *Oregon* was ordered from San Francisco to Cuba and took some weeks to negotiate the route round Cape Horn. This highlighted the strategic naval value of such a canal to the USA, then in the throes of building a navy large enough to control the two oceans that bounded her eastern and western shores. President Theodore Roosevelt, always a strong advocate of a Panama Canal, used the length of the *Oregon*'s voyage to great advantage in his political campaign to sanction the construction of the canal, and the acquisition of the necessary strip of land so that it would remain under the USA's political and operational control.

Preliminary work was begun in 1904, but it was not until 1908, when the construction was entrusted to the US Corps of Army Engineers, that real progress was made. The work proceeded under great difficulties because of the unhealthy conditions, mainly yellow fever and malarial diseases, in which it was carried out. However, eventually, all difficulties were overcome and the canal was opened to *navigation in 1914. The largest merchant ships able to transit the Panama Canal, that is, those with a maximum *beam of 32.5 metres (106 ft), are given the designation PANAMAX.

Panama plate, a metal plate bolted to the lugs of a *fairlead to close the gap between them when there is any risk of a *hawser or *warp jumping out. This could occur, for example, when a ship is secured alongside a high *quay and the hawser comes down through the fairlead at a steep angle. It originated in the *Panama Canal where ships have to secure to the sides of the many locks at constantly varying heights as the level of the water is raised or lowered.

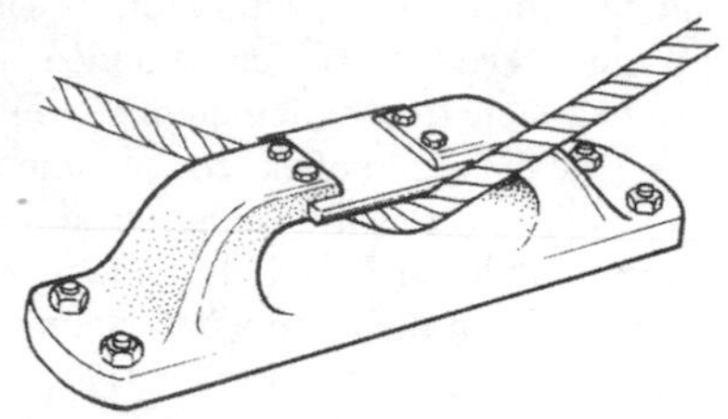

Panama plate on fairlead

papagayo, a *gale from the north-east which occasionally blows with great force off the coast of Central America, often without any warning signs of its approach. See also PAMPERO.

parallax. **(1)** The margin of error in reading a compass *course where the observer or helmsman stands to one side and there is an appreciable space between the graduated edge of the car and the *lubber's line. This of course can be eradicated by standing directly above the compass when reading off the course. **(2)** See LUNAR PARALLAX.

paraselene, sometimes known as a 'mock moon', a weakly coloured lunar halo, a result of refraction through *ice crystals, identical in form and optical origin to the solar *parhelion, which is frequently observed in high *latitudes. It is often taken as a sign of approaching wet weather. See also MARINE METEOROLOGY.

paravane, a device invented during the First World War (1914–18) as a defence against *moored mines for ships *under way. The paravane is essentially a glorified wirecutter which is towed, one on each bow of a ship, at the end of a length of toughened wire. The paravane itself works on the *otter principle to keep it at a fixed depth, to stretch its towing wire taut, and to hold it at an obtuse angle to the ship's course. If a moored mine lies in the path of a ship, the bow *wave pushes it aside and its mooring wire is deflected down the paravane's towing wire into the wirecutter where it is severed. The mine then floats to the surface where it can be sunk by rifle fire. Paravanes, introduced into the Royal Navy in 1916, were used by the larger warships when any danger from moored mines existed. It was invented by Commander Burney.

The paravane principle was also used in the *Oropesa method of sweeping mines.

parbuckle, a means of hauling up or lowering a cask or other cylindrical object where it is not possible to use a *purchase. The middle of a length of rope is passed round a *bitt, *bollard, or any convenient post and the two ends are led under the two quarters of the object to be hoisted or lowered and are brought back over it. The cask is hoisted by hauling away on the ends or lowered by lowering away on them.

Parbuckling

parcel, to, to wind strips of tarred *canvas round a rope after it had been *wormed and before it was *served or *marled. Parcelling, like worming, was always done with the *lay of the rope, and serving against the lay. As the old *seamanship rule suggested:

Worm and parcel with the lay,
Turn and serve the other way.

The object of worming, parcelling, and serving a rope was to make it resistant to water and chafe. Modern synthetic rope has made parcelling superfluous.

pareja, a Spanish or Portuguese fishing vessel, very similar to a *trawler, used off the Atlantic coasts of those countries.

parhelion, sometimes known as 'mock sun' or 'sun dog', either or both of two luminous spots having a reddish tinge on the inner edge that appear on both sides of the sun, usually in high *latitudes. The effect is caused by the *refraction of sunlight within hexagonal ice crystals whose axes are vertical. See also PARASELENE.

'parish-rigged', the seaman's term, in the days of *square-rigged ships, for a vessel which, through the parsimony of its owner, had worn or bad gear aloft and meagre victuals below.

Park Avenue boom, a main boom, first fitted to the American *J-class *yacht *Enterprise*, which successfully defended the *America's Cup in 1930. The conception of the *yacht designer Starling Burgess, it was triangular in section, 1.2 metres (4 ft) at its widest point with a wide flat top—so wide that two men could walk abreast along it, hence its name—and was fitted with a series of lateral rails about 46 centimetres (18 in.) apart along its length. Metal slides were sewn along the *foot of the mainsail which fitted these transverse rails, and stops, which limited the movement of the slides, were fitted into holes on the rails. These stops allowed the foot of the sail, or *roach, to take up a gentle curve to obtain a better *aerodynamic flow as the wind passed across the sail. To identify quickly the best positions for the stops in different sailing conditions, each line of holes was painted a different colour. These lines were called after the similarly coloured ones on the map of the New York subway system that marked the Seventh Avenue, Times Square shuttle, and Lexington Avenue subway lines.

The idea of such a boom was not entirely novel, as Dr Manfred Curry had written articles about its use in small boats, but it was the first time such a boom had been fitted to a large yacht. It was later used on other J-class yachts including *Endeavour*, the 1934 challenger for the America's Cup, and versions of it are still used in large yachts.

Parliament, or **parliamentary, heel,** a makeshift method of cleaning or repairing the sides of a British naval ship of the era of sail when there was neither time nor opportunity to *careen or dock her. She was heeled over by running the guns from one side of the ship over to the other side. Only the upper *strakes could be cleaned since the maximum angle of heel with the ship still afloat was limited by the level of the lower *gunports. According to an old belief, the name derived from the contempt in which parliamentary rule was held in the English Navy, implying that a half-done job was good enough to satisfy a parliamentarian. However, the more likely derivation is from the period of its introduction, the term coming into the British Navy during the First Anglo-Dutch War (1652–4) when England was governed by Cromwell's Parliament and when this process was much used. It did not spread into general use beyond the English Navy.

When, in 1782, HMS **Royal George* capsized and sank at *Spithead with a great loss of life, she was undergoing a Parliament heel to carry out underwater repairs.

parrel, or **parral,** used, before the introduction of the *truss, to attach a *yard to the masts of a *square-rigger, and it sometimes still is. The basic form uses a string of wooden parrel balls, sometime called **bullseyes** or **trucks**, to reduce chafe. With lighter yards a **parrel rope**, formed with an eye at each end and *seized to the *spar, is sometimes used. For heavier spars it was

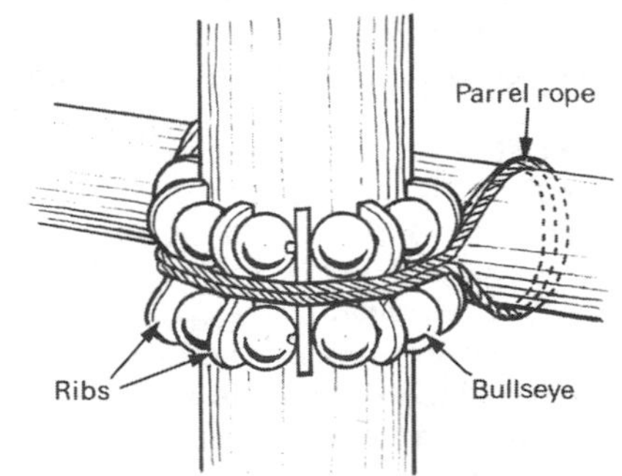

A parrel

common to have loose ribs interposed between each parrel ball, which were called **ribs of a parrel**. Metal collars called **parrel bands** are also used. A **parrel lashing** is sometimes used at the lower parts of upper masts for extra security.

partners, a framework, consisting of stout planks. It was secured to the decks of wooden ships round the holes though which passed the masts or the spindle of the *capstan. This strengthened the deck in these places and assisted in taking the strain when the masts carried a press of sail or the capstan was heaving in some considerable weight.

part of the ship, the division of a ship into areas as an administrative convenience in bringing a greater flexibility in the division of the crew for daily work purposes. In large ships, particularly large warships, the crew, in addition to their division into *watches, are further divided into parts of the ship, the normal number of divisions in the largest ships being four. In the British Navy, following the old navy pattern, these are the *forecastle, foretop, maintop, and *quarterdeck divisions. In smaller warships three parts of the ship (forecastle, topmen, quarterdeck) or two parts (forecastle, quarterdeck) are used. This method makes it simpler to detail men for the day-to-day work of the ship, as they can then be divided into large working parties by watches or small working parties by parts of the ship.

passarado, an old name for the rope used to haul down the *sheet blocks of the fore and main *courses of a *square-rigged ship when they were hauled *aft. This was done when it was required to sail the ship *large. The name may possibly have come from the Adriatic, where a 'passaro' was the lacing used to make fast the *foot of a sail to the *yard of a *trabacolo.

passaree, a rope used in *square-riggers to pull the *foot of a *course out to the side of the ship when running in light weather.

passat, the German name, dating from the mid-16th century, for the north-east *trade wind which blows in the North Atlantic. This was the wind which helped Christopher *Columbus in his first voyage to the West Indies in 1492. It was also the name given to one of the big four-masted German trading *barques of the early 20th century.

passenger ship, see CRUISE SHIP; FERRY; HOVERCRAFT; HYDROFOIL; OCEAN LINERS; PACKET; RO-RO SHIP; SEACAT.

passerelle, a *yacht's gangway, usually mounted on the stern to give access from a *quay. Nowadays it can be hydraulically operated, telescopic, and totally retractable.

paternoster, the framing of a chain *pump as fitted on board older sailing ships before the introduction of *auxiliary power. It was by the paternoster that the two copper tubes in which the chain with its washers worked were held firmly in place.

paunch, or **panch,** a thick mat made by weaving together twists of rope-yarns, known as *foxes, and forcing them home as close as possible. Paunch matting was used round *yards and *rigging to prevent rubbing and wear when the ship was rolling heavily. See also BAGGYWRINKLE.

pavesse, a wooden shield used on board English warships of the Tudor navy to line the fore and after castles. They were usually painted with the heraldic arms of the admiral, captain, or other noblemen on board, and in later Tudor times were extended to line the *waist of the ship as well as the fore and after castles. They were primarily intended as a protection for men on deck against small *shot from enemy ships, and were made of poplar, which did not splinter when pierced. Later they became much more of a form of ship decoration than of protection in days when warships were highly carved, gilded, and painted. They were copies from the shield protection which lined the *gunwales of the Viking *longships.

pawls, a series of metal dogs, hinged at one end, at the bottom of the barrel of a *capstan. They drop into scores in a pawl-ring round the capstan at deck level and prevent it from taking charge and overrunning when being used for *weighing an anchor or lifting a heavy load.

pay, to, a verb used during the days of sail, which had three meanings. **(1)** To pour hot *pitch into a deck or side *seam after it had been *caulked with *oakum, in order to prevent the oakum getting wet. **(2)** To dress a mast or *yard in a sailing vessel with *tar or varnish, or with tallow in the case of masts on which sails were frequently hoisted or lowered. **(3)** To cover the bottom of a vessel with a mixture of sulphur, rosin, and tallow. It is also still sometimes used in the sense of applying *antifouling paint. See also BREAMING.

pay off, to. **(1)** A sailing vessel's head pays off when it falls further away from the direction of the wind and therefore drops to *leeward. It is a term used particularly in relation to *tacking. **(2)** To close the accounts of a naval ship when she reached the end of a *commission—when the crew received any pay owing to them—or, in the case of a merchant ship, to close the accounts at the end of a voyage. In naval ships a **paying off *pennant** is flown.

pay out, to, to slacken a *cable or rope so that it can run out freely to a desired amount. It is not *cast off, but is secured in a new position when the desired amount has run out.

peak. **(1)** The upper, after corner of the four-sided *gaff-rigged sail. The *halyards used to hoist the outer end of a gaff sail are known as **peak halyards**. For illus. see GAFF RIG. **(2)** The end of the *palm of an anchor; the 'k' is not pronounced when used in connection with an anchor and the word is often written as 'pea'.

Peary, Robert Edwin (1856–1920), American naval officer and Arctic explorer who, for much of the 20th century, was generally acknowledged as being the first white man to reach the North Pole.

Peary was born at Cresson, Pa., and after studying engineering he joined the civil engineer corps of the US Navy in 1881 with the rank of lieutenant. He was always ambitious and in a letter to his mother wrote: 'remember, mother, I must have fame.' In 1886 he obtained leave of absence for a trip to Greenland and in 1891 organized an expedition there when he crossed the ice cap and proved for the first time that Greenland was an island. Over the next few years Peary continued his explorations, establishing that a polar ocean lay to the north of Greenland and reaching the highest *latitude yet achieved in the western hemisphere. In 1903 he supervised the construction of the *Roosevelt*, the first ship to be built specifically for Arctic exploration, and in April 1906 reached a latitude of 87° 6' N., beating his previous record by nearly 274 kilometres (170 mls.). In August 1908 the *Roosevelt* set sail again for Greenland, and in March 1909 Peary and his party set off on sledges to make another attempt to reach the North Pole. This time he apparently believed he succeeded when with his servant, Matthew Henson, and four Inuit, he had reached his goal on 6 April 1909.

A week before Peary returned to make public his success Dr Frederick A. Cook (1865–1940), who had accompanied Peary on his 1891 expedition before becoming a distinguished explorer in his own right, reappeared from the Arctic and claimed that he had reached the North Pole on 21 April 1908. He had accompanied an expedition to the Pole in 1907, but as nothing had been heard of him since his departure, it was thought that he had perished. A bitter controversy followed, but in December 1909 a committee of scientists decided Cook's evidence was not sufficient to prove he had reached the Pole, and ruled in favour of Peary. Cook's later life cast further doubts on his veracity; his claim to have climbed Mt McKinley was refuted, correctly as it turned out decades later, by his companion on that expedition; and he also served five years in prison for the fraudulent promotion of an oil company's stock, though he was granted a Presidential pardon for this a few months before he died. Peary, on the other hand, was lauded as a hero. He was thanked by the US Congress for his work and in 1911 was placed on the retired list with the rank of rear admiral.

Examination of Peary's papers when they were made available in 1984 and those of Cook, which were opened to scrutiny for the first time in 1990, probably show that neither reached the North Pole. If this is correct, then the first person to set foot there was Lt-Colonel Joseph Fletcher who climbed out of a US Air Force C-47 plane after it landed at the Pole in 1952. Both Peary and Cook still have their ardent supporters, and their detractors, but it seems likely that their rival claims will never be finally settled. See also EXPLORATION BY SEA; NORTH-WEST PASSAGE.

Bryce, R., *Cook & Peary: The Polar Controversy, Resolved* (1997).

peggy-mast, sometimes written as **pegy-, pygy-,** or **pege-mast,** occasionally a short mast or, more usually, a *yard, to which a *pennon was attached in very early warships. It was current during the 15th century but had fallen into disuse by the mid-16th century with the increased size of ships and consequently the increased number of places from which a pennon could be flown. In the accounts of the Lord High Treasurer for Scotland for 1496, there is an entry for 'one barel of pyk (pitch) and one pegy mast to the said schip'.

pelorus, a circular ring fitted to the rim of a *compass bowl and carrying two sighting vanes, used to take *azimuths of celestial objects. The ring can be easily revolved and the compass *bearing read off by sighting the vanes on the required object. Alternatively, the ring can be fitted to a 'dumb' compass (without a directive element) which can be set by hand to the *course of the ship before taking a bearing.

The word comes from the name of Hannibal's *pilot, probably a Greek, who sided with the Carthaginians, assisted Hannibal to get his troops across to Europe, and kept him in touch with Carthage by sea.

Pelorus Jack, the name given to a Risso's *dolphin (*Grampus griseus*) which, between 1888 and 1912, used regularly to accompany every ship which sailed through the French Pass, a narrow strait separating d'Urville Island from the mainland of South Island, New Zealand. The name came from Pelorus Sound, of which French Pass forms the westernmost part. A contemporary description gave Pelorus Jack a length of about 4.6 metres (15 ft) and a mainly white colour with brown stripes. He was so well known and so regular in his habit of accompanying every ship that used French Pass that in 1904 his life was protected by the New Zealand government. It was said that there was one ship which Pelorus Jack ignored whenever it appeared in those waters because, on its first passage through the pass, a member of the crew had fired a shot at him, which is why he was then protected. Risso's dolphins are rarely seen in New Zealand waters.

Another New Zealand dolphin that gained some notoriety was Opo who, in the summer of 1955/6, followed local boats at Hokianga in the North Island and frolicked with those swimming there.

pendant. **(1)** A *strop, or short length of rope or wire with a *thimble spliced into the end, fixed on each side of the main- and foremasts of a *square-rigged ship just below the *shrouds, and to which the main and fore *tackles were hooked. They received their name as they hung vertically downwards as low as the *catharpings. **(2)** Any length of rope or wire used in those places where it is required to transmit the power of a *purchase to a distant object. Generally they have a *thimble or a *block spliced into one end. They usually also have a qualifying name attached to indicate their use: e.g. a **cat pendant**, used to *cat an anchor; and a ***mooring pendant**, used to haul the end of a chain *cable round the bows of a ship when two anchors are down and it is necessary to insert a mooring swivel. See also PENNANT.

penguin. There are seventeen species of this flightless *seabird. They belong to the family Spheniscidae, which are almost exclusive to the southern hemisphere. Penguin wings are developed into powerful flippers for swimming. The legs are far back in the body so on land they walk upright. Since they no longer fly, there are no restrictions on their weight, so their bodies are invested with blubber. This insulates them in the water, but means they tend to overheat on land, so the warm tropics are a barrier to their spread into the northern hemisphere. The Galapagos penguin (*Spheniscus mendiculus*) lives on the equator, but where the sea temperatures are kept cool by *upwelling. The largest, the emperor penguin (*Aptenodytes forsteri*), stands over a metre high and weighs more than 40 kilograms (90 lb). Emperors have a unique life history. They breed in rookeries of up to 50,000 pairs on the Antarctic *ice shelf and the young are left in large crèches to overwinter hundreds of kilometres from the ice edge. They feed predominantly on *squid and can dive to depths of 265 metres (870 ft). Underwater they swim at speeds of 9–11 kilometres an hour (6–7 mph). Each species of penguin occupies a specific type of breeding ground, ranging from ice, to bare ground (chinstraps, Adelies, and gentoos), to cliffs (rockhoppers), to tussock grasses (mararonis), and in burrows (magellanic). Many of the penguins around the Antarctic feed on *krill. An individual Adelie penguin (*Pygoscelis adeliae*) catches about 2 kilograms (4.4 lb) a day during the breeding season. So the 5 million pairs that occupy just one rookery on Laurie Island in the South Orkney Islands take 9 tonnes of krill a day.

Peterson, R., *Penguins* (1998).

www.adelie.pwp.blueyonder.co.uk/

M. V. Angel

pennant, sometimes written as **pendant,** but always pronounced pennant. It is a narrow tapering flag used for signalling or, as with a *commissioning pennant, for some particular purpose. There are ten numbered pennants, an answering pennant, and three substitute pennants in the *International Code of Signals.

pennon, a long, coloured streamer flown from the mastheads or *yardarms of warships in the 15th and 16th centuries on occasions of state or national importance. Although it was not particularly a naval word, naval pennons were very much longer than those flown ashore, being on occasions as much as 18–24 metres (60–80 ft) in length.

Pepys, Samuel (1633–1703), naval administrator and noted diarist, born in London and educated at St Paul's School and Trinity Hall, Cambridge, from which he later transferred to Magdalene. Soon after obtaining his bachelor's degree Pepys entered the service of his first cousin once removed, Edward Montagu (1625–72), a *general-at-sea, who obtained for him a post as a clerk in the Exchequer. In December 1655 he married Elizabeth St Michel, an Anglo-French (Huguenot) girl of 14 with whom he lived in Montagu's lodgings.

In the republican administration set up by the army generals after Cromwell's death, Montagu's sympathies began to turn towards the royalist cause and he was driven from office. Pepys remained in charge of his cousin's affairs in London and set up his own household in Axe Yard, Westminster. The political turmoil of the times was one of the factors which encouraged him to begin his famous diary on 1 January 1660.

At the Restoration Montagu was again in office as general-at-sea and he took Pepys to sea with him as his secretary. On the return of the fleet with Charles II from Holland, Montagu was created Earl of Sandwich and showered with honours, and he promised Pepys that the two of them should rise together. As a first step he obtained for him the post of Clerk of the Acts to the Navy Board, the body responsible for the civil administration of the English Navy. Through hard work and long hours of labour Pepys soon became a leading member of the board, and his powers were soon tested to the full during the Second Dutch War (1665–7) when the board's work was crippled by lack of money. Only Pepys's efforts to drive his colleagues, clerks, and the contractors, and a campaign to root out the worst cases of corruption, prevented a complete breakdown of the system of supply of the fleet.

In June 1667, through the premature laying-up of the fleet while peace negotiations were still in progress, England suffered the humiliation of seeing the Dutch fleet in the Thames and Medway where for a time they set up a *blockade of London and destroyed a number of warships at Chatham. When attempts were later made to lay the blame on the Navy Board, Pepys addressed an elaborate and unanswerable memorandum to the Parliamentary Commission of Public Accounts justifying the conduct of the Navy Office throughout the war. He also made a memorable speech in Parliament proving that blame for the disaster lay elsewhere. Eyestrain and a belief that he was going blind led Pepys to end his diary, which was written in shorthand, in 1669.

In June 1673 Pepys left the Navy Board to become the first secretary to the *Admiralty or, more strictly, to the commission that exercised the office of the *Lord High Admiral. He now lodged at Derby House in Cannon Row, becoming one of the most important civil servants in the country. The Third Dutch War (1672–4) was drawing to a close and on its conclusion he launched a vigorous programme of recovery and reform. By 1678 he had developed the navy into a powerful, well-disciplined force and the previously unsystematic office of the Lord High Admiral into an efficient government department.

Pepys was Member of Parliament for Castle Rising, 1673–8, and for Harwich in 1679, being accepted in the Commons as spokesman for the service he had created and the administrative machine which managed it. Disaster now struck, however, when his old master and former Lord High Admiral, the Duke of York, was accused of conspiracy to betray the country to France and he himself was accused of being a secret papist and of selling naval secrets to France. After six weeks as a prisoner in the Tower of London, the charges against him were dropped; but for the next five years he was out of office.

Meanwhile Admiralty business suffered under an inept commission and in 1683—the year Pepys became president of the Royal Society—Charles II made him his Secretary for Admiralty Affairs, a post which he retained when the Duke of York came to the throne as James II. With the help of a special commission to perform most of the work of the Navy Board, set up in 1686, he set about a restoration of the good governance of the navy. Between 1685 and 1687 he was again Member of Parliament for Harwich and master of *Trinity House where he instituted many reforms.

However, after James II was dethroned in 1688, Pepys was once again falsely accused of treasonable relations with the French and of secret Jacobitism, and he was forced to resign. He now finally retired into private life. In 1700 his health began to break down and on 26 May 1703, after a long and painful illness, he died at the country home of his closest friend, William Hewer, at Clapham.

During his long service at the Navy Board and Admiralty, Pepys had an ambition to write an authoritative history of the English Navy. For this purpose he collected a great quantity of official and other papers, which passed on his death, together with his famous diary and library of 3,000 books, to Magdalene College, Cambridge. His great history was never written, but in 1690 he published his *Memoires Relating to the State of the Royal Navy*, a business-like account of the work of the commission of 1686 in restoring the administration of the navy to a sound footing.

An abbreviated version of his diary was published in 1825 and more complete versions appeared in the 1870s and 1890s. In 1970 the first three volumes of a new, complete, and annotated edition in eleven volumes was published.

Ollard, R., *Pepys* (1974).

Pepys, Samuel, *The Diary of Samuel Pepys*, ed. R. Latham and W. Matthews, 11 vols. (1970–83).

Tomalin, C., *Samuel Pepys: The Unequalled Self* (2003).

periagua, another name occasionally used for the type of *canoe known as a *pirogue.

periplus, or **periplous,** literally a sailing around or circumnavigation, was the word used to denote the earliest form of *sailing directions. One of the earliest examples is *The Periplous of Scylax of Caryanda*, a comprehensive pilot book for the Mediterranean which, starting at the mouth of the Nile, guides the mariner from port to port in a clockwise direction. Written about 500 BC, the book gave detailed directions for *coastal navigation including details of safe anchorages, adverse *currents, etc.

The Periplus of the Erythraean Sea, written about AD 60, is a combination of seaman's pilot book and merchant's handbook which describes the trades to be expected in the ports in the area, that of the Red Sea and Arabian Gulf. In addition, details of sailing routes to the western coasts of India are given according to the prevailing *monsoons. It was used by the distinguished Finnish polar explorer Otto Nordenskjöld (1870–1928), as the title of his great work on the history of *charts and sailing directions published in Stockholm in 1897. This has sometimes caused confusion in the minds of students new to the history of *chartmaking.

Perry, Matthew Calbraith (1794–1858), American naval officer and diplomat, born at Newport, RI. He joined the navy in 1809, seeing action in the war of 1812. However, his chief claim to fame rests on his success in 'opening' Japan to the rest of the world after he was selected to command the US Navy's East India *Squadron specially to make overtures to that isolated country. In 1852 he made his first visit there to persuade the Japanese to permit limited foreign trade and to repatriate shipwrecked seamen. With the steam *frigates *Mississippi* and *Susquehanna* he called first at Okinawa where, much against the will of the local authorities, he made a state visit to the regent. He reached Sagami Bay, Japan, in June 1853 bearing a letter from the American president to the emperor, and refused to leave until the letter had been properly received and acknowledged.

After five weeks of discussion, it was agreed that two high officials would receive the letter in a specially erected building near the village of Kurihama. On 14 July the two frigates anchored off the beach and trained their guns ashore, while Perry with some 250 *marines and sailors landed from the ships' boats. They were outnumbered on the spot by about forty to one, as the shogun had ordered mobilization, and the Americans were confronted by archers, pikemen, cavalry, musketeers, and earthworks armed with Dutch cannon. Excellent discipline on both sides prevented an outbreak of fighting which might have touched off a war instead of a treaty. In silence Perry presented the engrossed presidential letter in its gold casket and remarked that he would be back the following year.

On his return in February 1854, Perry anchored his squadron off Yokosuka. This time, satisfied that Perry's declarations of peaceable intentions were sincere, the shogunate did not mobilize. It persuaded Perry to negotiate at the village of Yokohama instead of at the capital and after a ceremonious landing the negotiations began through a Dutch interpreter. In the meantime the Americans set up and operated their presents for the emperor, of which a quarter-size steam railway and a telegraph instrument made the greatest impression.

On 31 March the Treaty of Kanagawa was signed. It opened Shimoda and Hakodate to the reciprocal return of shipwrecked seamen, and gave permission to set up an American consulate. Perry was careful to insist on nothing which might humiliate Japan, the commissioners felt that they had preserved national honour, and the proceedings concluded with banquets on board and ashore.

The rest of Perry's life was largely devoted to preparing the official narrative of the expedition in three volumes, edited by F. L. Hawks, which became a classic.

Schroder, J., *Mathew Calbraith Perry: Antebellum Sailor and Diplomat* (2001).

Peter the Great (1672–1725), or Peter Alekseyevich Romanov, was the first son of the second wife of Tsar Alexsis. His father died in 1676 and his half-brother Feodor ruled until his death in 1682. Peter then shared power with another half-brother, Ivan, and with his half-sister who acted as regent. During this time Peter obtained a broad education and developed his love of science, and his interest in *shipbuilding. In 1688 he found an old English-built 6-metre (20-ft) sailing boat at his estate in Ismailovo. This gave him his first experience of sailing, which led ultimately to an abiding love of the sea, and it remained one of his favourite boats. It is now on display in the Naval Museum of St Petersburg, and is known as 'The Grandfather of the Russian Navy'.

Peter instituted shipbuilding in Russia around 1695 with the construction of two 36-gun ships and a large number of galleys, all of them completed within one year. This new fleet won their first battle, at Azov in 1696, a date now regarded as the founding of the Russian navy. Shipyard complexes opened in Voronezh and continued there till the timber supplies from the surrounding country were exhausted in 1711. By then over 215 ships had been built for the Black Sea/Azov fleet, many with a direct input from Peter. One of them, armed with 58 guns, was designed by him with guidance from England.

On the death of Ivan in 1696, Peter became the sole ruler of Russia and commenced a quarter of a century of territorial expansion and reform to bring his country into the European arena. With this in mind he made a prolonged journey through Europe which became known as the Great Embassy. He stopped in what is now the Netherlands for nearly five months, first in Zaandam where there were 50 shipbuilding yards, and later in Amsterdam where he worked as a shipwright. Early in 1698, he sailed for Britain where he was welcomed by the new king, William of Orange, who presented him with a *yacht, the *Royal Transport*. Peter was delighted and during his five-month visit stayed in Deptford and was a regular visitor to the *Royal Dockyard there.

At that time Russia had no seagoing traditions. So, on his return, Peter took back with him about 60 specialists in shipbuilding, and he also started to recruit foreign naval and military officers, shipyard superintendents, academics, and others. By 1713, the Baltic Fleet (which he had begun building in 1703) had eleven senior commanders of whom only two were Russian. He opened a Naval Academy and a School of Mathematics and Navigational Science, and in 1720 edited the first edition of the Book of Maritime Regulations. By the end of his reign his Baltic Fleet, which had helped defeat Sweden in the Northern War (1700–21), totalled 49 warships, 800 smaller vessels, and 28,000 men.

As Russia had no outlet to the west, Peter ensured that the eastern end of the Gulf of Finland was in Russian hands, and on the unpromising marshlands where the River Neva meets the sea he built St Petersburg and moved the capital there in 1712. Strategically sited for both trade and defence it was protected by the fortress and naval base of Kronstadt. Shipbuilding commenced east of St Petersburg and ultimately the great Admiralty yards opened in the centre of the city around 1704, making Russia a significant shipbuilding nation in its own right. The Admiralty yards continued building the ships for the Baltic Fleet right up until1844.

Two years before he died, Peter held a fleet review of his ships, all constructed in his lifetime. He took the *tiller of the 'Grandfather of the Russian Navy' and four admirals pulled at the *oars.

Peter was very tall and in every sense of the word was 'larger than life'. He liked to take a hands-on approach, and regularly *piloted ships and more than once commanded part of a fleet during a naval action. Russia has great traditions of hospitality and kindness, and to this day there is enormous pride in the legacy of Peter the Great.

Massie, R., *Peter the Great: His Life and Work* (1980). Fred M. Walker

petty officer, the naval equivalent of the rank of sergeant in military forces. In the British Navy they are divided into two grades, chief petty officer and petty officer. The word petty comes from the French *petit*, small.

petty warrant, the scale of victualling allowed in the British Navy during the 16th–18th centuries to ships' companies when in port, generally at about two-thirds the scale allowed at sea. However, if victualling stores ran short at sea, the issue was reduced to the scale of petty warrant, it then being known as 'six upon four', that is, six men had to exist upon the victuals normally allowed for four. When this occurred, an addition to the rate of pay, known as short allowance money, was credited to the men for the period during which 'six upon four' applied. See also VICTUALLING BOARD.

PFD, or personal flotation device, US officialese for a life jacket, Lifesling, or other buoyancy aid. See LIFESAVING. John Rousmaniere

phosphorescence, a faint blue-green light emitted from the sea at night, either as a continuous glow or a series of tiny flashes. This light is produced by the bioluminescence of living organisms ranging from bacteria to the many species of *plankton, including phytoplankton, especially dinoflagellates. On moonless nights in late summer, flashes of light in the surf breaking on sandy beaches are often produced by the appropriately named dinoflagellate *Noctiluca*. Bioluminescence is produced by a chemical reaction and serves a wide range of functions. Deep in the ocean where there is little or no daylight, almost every species has some light-producing capability. The wavelength of the blue-green light emitted is the same as the residual daylight that penetrates to the greatest depths in the ocean. In a darkened environment signalling by light is an effective way of communicating with other animals of the same species, especially to confirm species identification during mating, or to indicate a readiness to mate. Lights are also used on lures to tempt prey within range. Bright flashes are used as a defence mechanism, startling the attacker. Glowing smoke screens or even phantom decoys are also used to avoid attack. In an environment where the brightest daylight comes from directly overhead, animals are particularly vulnerable to attack from below by predators that pick out their silhouettes. Lights arranged along the underside of *fish and some *Crustacea like prawns break up the silhouette, and act as a form of camouflage.

Some phosphorescent phenomena have a physical origin. During electrical storms structures like a ship's mast can become surrounded by a corona of electrical discharges giving an eerie bluish light called *St Elmo's Fire.

Herring, P., *The Biology of the Deep Ocean* (2002).
www.lifesci.ucsb.edu/~biolum/
www.islandnet.com/~see/weather/elements/stelmo.htm M. V. Angel

physical oceanography is the study of the physical processes taking place within the oceans and their interactions with the atmosphere. The high heat capacity of water relative to air means the oceans play a major role in the climate by redistributing heat around the globe. If the oceans did not exist, the poles would be much colder and the tropics much hotter. The mechanisms resulting in flows of water and the mixing of waters of different origins are of fundamental importance in understanding ocean processes. The rotation of the earth, and its influence on the atmosphere in generating winds, provide the basic processes whereby *currents develop in the oceans. In the absence of both continents and winds, a pattern of rotating cells (or gyres) of currents would develop. This basic pattern is strongly modified by the land barriers and the general shapes of the continental boundaries. The density of sea water is determined mainly by its temperature, *salinity, and the hydrostatic pressure. Sea-water temperatures are generally warmer at the surface and cooler at depth. The seasonal *thermocline, which at temperate latitudes forms in spring and disintegrates in autumn, is important biologically. Water below it is usually richer in the nutrients needed for the growth of the *marine plant phytoplankton than the water above it. The nutrient-rich waters from under the thermocline are only brought to the surface during *upwelling and in winter, when the surface waters are cooled and *storms mix the surface waters down to depths of several hundred metres.

At the surface, water temperatures fluctuate as a result of solar radiation, heat exchanges with atmosphere, and evaporation (the latent heat of evaporation means the surface skin of the ocean is cooled when water evaporates from the surface). When seawater is cooled it becomes denser. Its density also increases if its salinity is increased as a result of evaporation or the formation of *ice. Its density decreases (i.e. it becomes lighter) if it is warmed, or else diluted, with rain, the melting of ice, or the outflows from rivers. The outflow of the River Amazon can be traced several hundreds of kilometres from its delta, and the saltiness of the eastern Mediterranean has become higher since the building of the High Aswan Dam has reduced the outflow of the River Nile.

Thus, at *latitudes where rainfall is low and evaporation is high, the surface water becomes heavier and sinks into the ocean's interior. Once a mass of water has left the surface, its properties of temperature and salinity are conserved, and are only changed by mixing with other types of water. So the water column in the ocean tends to be stratified into layers, and these increase in density with depth.

Under exceptional circumstances, the water densities become uniform from the surface to the bottom, so that water at the surface can then sink freely all the way to the bottom. This occurs regularly in the Weddell Sea and until recently in the Greenland Sea, but *climate change has turned off this source of deep water, and it is now feared that this will lead to a change in the *Gulf Stream. This sinking of very cold—and hence oxygen-rich—water drives the so-called thermohaline circulation of the whole ocean. This results in the total turnover of the oceans every 1,500 years which supplies the oxygen to the bottom waters of all the oceans that is needed by most of the animals living there.

One possible effect of the cessation of bottom water formation in the Greenland Sea is to reduce the flow of the Gulf Stream, which would have a substantial effect in cooling the climate of northern Europe. In the Atlantic where the water at the bottom has most recently been formed—and is described as being young—the deep water is rich in oxygen. In the Pacific and Indian Oceans, the bottom waters are old and contain far less oxygen, but are richer in nutrients (nitrates, phosphates, and carbon dioxide), released by the decomposition (regeneration) of material that has sedimented from the surface.

Bottom water formation is one of the important processes whereby carbon dioxide is being removed from the atmosphere and stored in the deep ocean. If, as predicted, climate change slows the large-scale (thermohaline) circulation, then the rate of build-up of carbon dioxide in the atmosphere will increase.

The oceans are transferring energy absorbed from solar radiation in the tropics to the higher latitudes. This is well illustrated by the contrast in the climates on the two sides of the Atlantic. On the eastern side the Gulf Stream, and its extension the North Atlantic Drift, carries warm

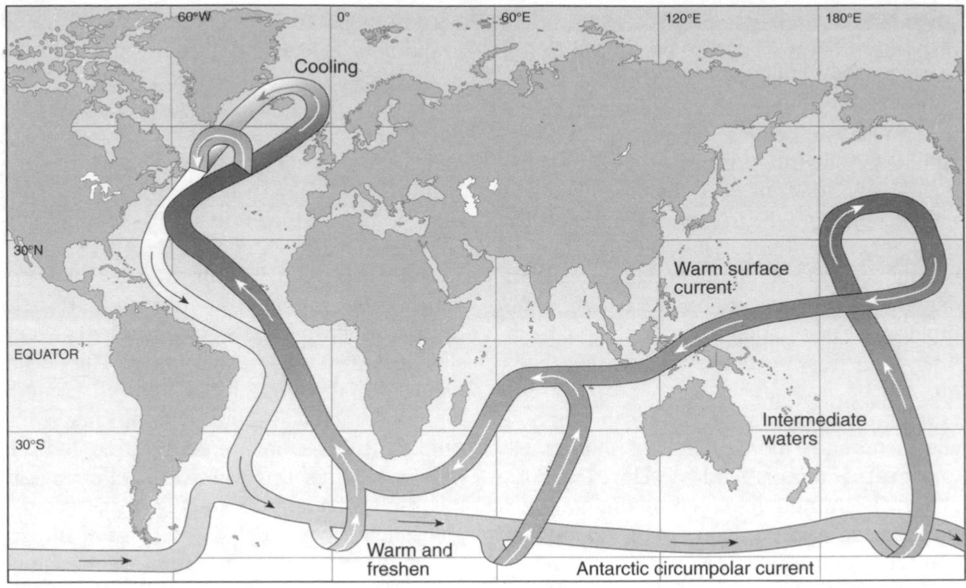

Schematic representation of the global thermohaline conveyor that drives the oceanic circulatory system. Surface water cools and sinks in the Norwegian Sea, flowing south and ultimately rising again from the southern hemisphere where it freshens and warms during its centuries-long circulation round the world's oceans

water far to the north into the Barents Sea. So the climate of western Europe is mild, whereas down the east coast of Canada the climate is kept cool by the Greenland Current, which carries cold water and icebergs southwards. Massive computer models are now being built to predict the responses of the oceans to climate change and how they may generate even greater climate changes.

Traditionally the method used by physical oceanographers was to collect water samples and measure their properties. However, with the development of technologies that allow these properties to be measured *in situ*, the approach has been, more and more, to use instruments to collect the data. Such instruments are either lowered on cables or attached to *moorings or to drifting *buoys, or most recently mounted either on *underwater vehicles or on towed bodies that undulate up and down as they are towed.

The use of satellites for *remote sensing and precision navigation has revolutionized physical oceanography. Even so, collecting enough data with sufficient precision to follow and quantify the influence of important small-scale features such as *eddies will require the total scientific budget for the whole world. As the power of computers has grown, so more and more effort is being devoted to constructing mathematical models to simulate the ocean. These can then be used to predict what is happening, and continually to check the model's output against real observations. Just as the accuracy of forecasts produced by *marine meteorology has improved dramatically since the 1980s, a remarkable improvement has taken place in the information being produced by physical oceanography.

Open University, *Ocean Circulation* (1989).

Open University, *Wave, Tide and Shallow Water Processes* (1989).

http://podaac-www.jpl.nasa.gov/

www.whoi.edu/science/PO/dept/

www.es.flinders.edu.au/~mattom/IntroOc/newstart.html

There is an excellent on-line textbook at **http://oceanworld.tamu.edu/home/course_book.htm**

M. V. Angel

picaroon, or **pickaroon,** an old 17th-century name for a *privateer or someone involved in *piracy. It comes from the Spanish *picarón*, pirate.

pickle. **(1)** The salt brine in which beef and pork was immersed in casks to preserve it for use as daily rations in the days of sail. **(2)** The salting of naval timber for masts and *yards in *dockyards by letting them float in sea water in mast docks or mast ponds in order to improve their durability and strength. Occasionally chloride of zinc was used for this purpose.

pieces of eight, Spanish coins much beloved by writers of stories about *piracy. They were the equivalent of a Spanish dollar of a value of eight reals. Such vast numbers of these coins were minted in Spain during the 17th and 18th centuries that they were accepted almost as a world currency during that time.

pier, a structure, usually of timber and supported on wooden piles, built out into the sea at seaside resorts as an attraction for holidaymakers and for excursion steamers to come alongside. However, some *jetties, which are basically solid structures, are, nevertheless, called piers, particularly where two of them may form the arms embracing a small harbour. Similarly, some piers, which are basically open structures, may be called jetties, such as those alongside which *tankers lie to load or discharge oil.

pierhead jump, an expression indicative of joining a ship at the last possible moment because of a sudden and unexpected appointment to it. Charles Powell, the central character in Joseph *Conrad's novel *Chance*, entered into a new world of experience with a totally unexpected pierhead jump into the ship *Ferndale*.

pig yoke, a name used in the 17th–18th centuries by many old seamen when describing *Davis's quadrant in the days before it was replaced by the reflecting quadrants, such as the *octant, and *sextants.

pillage, by an ancient law of the sea, the right of the captors of a ship taken in *prize to take everything found above the main deck except the *furniture and guns of the vessel. It was a right which, not unnaturally, could lead to great abuse as, in the heat and excitement of capture, there were few to swear what was, or was not, found above the main deck. In many cases the *holds of captured ships were broken open and the contents strewn on the upper deck, to be picked up a moment later and claimed as pillage.

pillar buoy, a *buoy with a relatively tall superstructure on a broad base. When used in the *IALA maritime buoyage system, only the colour of the buoy, and the colour and shape of the topmark, if fitted, is of navigational significance.

pillow, a block of timber fixed to the deck of a sailing vessel just inside the bow on which the inner end of the *bowsprit was supported. Its use was to take any wear on the deck caused by the working of the bowsprit.

pilot. **(1)** A qualified coastal *navigator, often a *master mariner, who is taken on board a ship at a particular place in order to conduct it into and from a port or through a channel, river, or approaches to a port. In the UK the jurisdiction over coastal pilots is invested in the relevant harbour authorities who specify the conditions under which pilots must be taken on board and the *pilotage fees to be charged. In many ports and navigable waterways, regulations make it compulsory for ships over a certain size to embark a pilot.

Before ships had radios, pilots would wait in pilot *cutters near the points of entry into pilotage waters so that they could be picked up by incoming ships; or a ship would anchor off a port and hoist flag 'G' of the *International Code of Signals to indicate that a pilot was required. Today any ship requiring a pilot makes arrangements by radio well in advance with the pilot being picked up at a predetermined rendezvous.

The International Maritime Pilots' Association, founded in 1970, is the voice of professional maritime pilots worldwide, and has its HQ on the *Wellington*, a converted *sloop moored on London's Victoria Embankment. Its consultative status at the *International Maritime Organization ensures that the practicalities of safe pilotage are taken into account before new regulations are implemented.

Masters of cross-Channel *ferries and other similar vessels which habitually navigate in pilotage waters normally hold pilotage exemption certificates from the relevant harbour/pilotage authority, and so do not require to embark a pilot for their passages. When a ship has a pilot on board, its master retains the responsibility for its safety, though the regulations require him to follow the pilot's instructions. **(2)** When used as a verb, the word embraces the acts of a pilot in taking a ship through pilotage waters. **(3)** A loose or affectionate term for the navigating officer of a ship. **(4)** The colloquial name for the volumes of *sailing directions. See also TRINITY HOUSE.

pilotage, from the Dutch *peillood,* *sounding lead, the act of navigating a vessel coastwise, especially when the land is nearby and the water shallow. See also PILOT.

pinch, to, to sail a vessel so close to the wind that the *luffs of its sails are continually lifting. This shows that the wind is not being used to best advantage. However, sometimes it is necessary to pinch a sailing vessel, when, for instance, it is desirable to *fetch a mark without having to make a *tack.

pink, a small, *square-rigged ship with a narrow and overhanging stern, often used for the carriage of masts. In the 15th and 16th centuries the name was loosely applied to all small ships with narrow sterns, a fairly common design in those days. It was later adopted by the Danish Navy to describe a small warship in which the stern was broadened out at upper-deck level to accommodate *quarter guns, though still remaining narrow below. Before the days of powered *drifters, the Dutch herring boats from Scheveningen were also called pinks. See also FISHERIES.

pinky, one of the oldest types of New England fishing and trading vessels. Built with a Baltic form of hull having a pointed stern similar to the bow, over which a false stern was carried out beyond the *rudder like a square *counter, it resembled the North Sea and Danish *pink of the early 18th century, from which it was named. These small craft, 15–21 metres (50–70 ft) in length, were generally *schooner rigged with or without a *staysail or *jib. See also FISHERIES.

pinnace. (1) A small vessel, usually square sterned, of about 20–30 tons which dates from the 16th century. It had two masts, normally *square rigged on both, but occasionally with a *lugsail on the main. Later, the square rig was abandoned for a *schooner rig. They carried *oars as well as sails and were used frequently as *advice boats. The first vessel to be built in America, the 30-ton *Virginia,* was described as a pinnace, though she had a *sprit rig on her single mast. About 50 metres (160 ft) long, she was built by English settlers on the mouth of the Kennebec River, Maine, in 1607–8 so that they could return to Britain. A *replica ship is planned for 2007 to celebrate the 400th anniversary of English settlement in America. **(2)** A ship's boat which, in the days of sailing ships, was rowed with eight oars but later was increased in length to accommodate sixteen oars. The larger variety were able to step a mast when required and set a *sloop rig.

pinrail, a rack of *belaying pins commonly set against the sides of a sailing ship abreast of each mast for the working and securing of items of running *rigging. See also FIFE RAIL.

pintle, a vertical metal pin attached to the leading edge of the *rudder of a small boat. Normally two pintles are fitted to such a rudder, and they drop into *gudgeons, or rings, fixed to the boat's stern, when the rudder is placed, or hung, in position. This method of hanging a rudder allows it to be swung as desired through the use of the *tiller. An advantage of this form of hanging a rudder is that it can be unshipped when not required. Also, in extremely shallow water the rudder will lift if it touches the seabed, thereby avoiding damage.

pipe, to, see BOATSWAIN'S PIPE.

pipe cot, a hinged cot fitted in many older small vessels where the space available did not permit the inclusion of a fixed *bunk. When not in use they are folded up and secured against the vessel's side.

pipe down, the *call on the *boatswain's pipe, made last thing at night in a naval vessel, for the hands to turn in. It is also a term used by sailors when they want to stop a man talking or making a nuisance of himself.

piping the side, the ceremonial call made on a *boatswain's pipe when distinguished visitors arrive on board a Royal Navy warship. With its long-drawn-out low, high, and low notes, the call dates from the days when visiting officers at sea were hoisted in and out of a ship in a *boatswain's chair at the end of a *yardarm *whip. The actual notes were the orders by which the men manning the whip knew when to hoist and lower.

piracy, the act of taking a ship on the *high seas from the possession or control of those lawfully entitled to it. This was sometimes done to acquire the ship itself, but more often just to plunder it, and to rob the crew and passengers. The operative word in that definition is 'lawfully', as international maritime law accepts the declaration, by a belligerent power, of a state of *blockade as a legitimate reason for the detention of any ship, whether neutral or belligerent, suspected of carrying *contraband. Without that legal right, every such act would by definition rank as piracy.

Pirates must be distinguished from *privateers and *buccaneers, though at different times in different places the distinguishing line was often perilously thin. Piracy was endemic among all seafaring nations until the birth of regular navies, but it was recognized very early on that the pirate was an enemy not of any particular state but of all mankind. Pirates could therefore be punished by the competent courts of any country. When captured, they were usually hanged in chains on prominent headlands, where they could be seen by passing ships as a warning. In England they were often staked to the ground at *Execution Dock, Wapping. The last pirate executed in England was in 1840, and in the USA in 1862.

Since the earliest times, no seas were free from piracy. Pirates were present everywhere, from the Indian Ocean to the *Barbary pirates of the Mediterranean, and the *Sallee pirates of Morocco, northwards to Ireland and south-west England. After the discovery of America, they flourished in the West Indies, the Gulf of Mexico, and along the western coast of South America. It was only when national navies began to develop as permanent institutions that a concerted stand against them became possible. Before that time they were often tolerated by the local populations, who benefited from their largesse, and by local officials who were often happy to accept bribes from them.

Pirates tended to operate from small ships—often captured ones—which were fast enough to *overhaul their prey at sea, out of reach of interference by other ships, and capture it by *boarding. As gunnery developed, pirates also equipped their vessels with guns, usually captured ones, so they resembled small warships.

Ann Bonny and Mary Read: women pirates; engraving c.1720

Often they were as powerful as, or more so than, the naval *frigates sent to sink them.

The classic age of piracy was the late 17th and early 18th centuries, when many of the privateers operating in the West Indies and the Indian Ocean became pirates. There is doubt that their flag, the *Jolly Roger, ever existed, but their exploits were real enough. They achieved wide notoriety with the publication of Charles Johnson's highly embroidered *A General History of the Robberies and Murders of the Most Notorious Pyrates* (1724–6), which some believe was written by Daniel Defoe, the author of **Robinson Crusoe*. It is from this source that many writers have taken their adventure stories, because of its lively accounts of such pirates as John *Avery, Edward *Teach, Bartholomew *Roberts, the female pirates Mary Read (*fl.* 1710–20) and Anne Bonny (*fl.* 1720), who were part of the crew of a *sloop commanded by the pirate Calico Jack Rackham; and, above all, William *Kidd, who committed his many acts of piracy in waters as far apart as the West Indies and the Indian Ocean.

Piracy is a modern scourge, too, and though robbery is the more common motive nowadays ships are still stolen. To conform to the modern definition of it the incident has to occur outside national *territorial waters as it is otherwise defined as armed robbery. Attacks covered by both definitions are frequent. In the period between 1980 and 1984 over 400 attacks worldwide on shipping were recorded, including numerous cruel assaults on Vietnamese *Boat People attempting to escape to Thailand. More recently the London-based International Maritime Bureau (IMB) reported 445 violent incidents in 2003 compared with 370 in 2002, and in February 2004 four crew members of an oil *tanker were shot dead by pirates in the Malacca Strait. Indonesia, the world's largest archipelago with over 17,500 islands, heads the list of countries where piracy is rampant. It accounted for 27% of the attacks, and Somalian waters have proved almost as dangerous.

Cordingly, D., *Life among the Pirates: The Romance and the Reality* (1995).
Earle, P., *The Pirate Wars* (2003).
Villar, Capt. R., *Piracy Today* (1985).

pirogue, or **piragua,** a seagoing *canoe formed out of the trunks of two trees, hollowed out and fastened together, usually of cedar or balsa wood. It was a common form of coastal transport in the Gulf of Mexico and on the west coast of South America during the 16th and 17th centuries and is frequently mentioned in the writings of European voyagers to those waters during that period.

pitch, **(1)** A mixture of *tar and coarse resin, fluid when heated and hard when cooled, used to cover the *oakum when *caulking the *seams of a vessel's deck or sides. **(2)** Pitch of a *propeller, the distance a propeller screws forward in one revolution assuming there is no slip. **(3)** As a verb, describes the motion of a ship when a *wave lifts its bows and then, after passing down its length, subsequently lifts its stern, giving it a rocking motion.

pitchpole, to, of a vessel, to be up-ended by heavy seas so that it turns over stern over bows.

plain sailing, in common parlance, means something simple and straightforward, but the origin of the term is purely maritime. When the *chart first appeared in Italy towards the end of the 13th century, it was drawn as plans are drawn, with no reference to the sphericity of the earth. The observed *bearings and measured distances were plotted irrespective of the principles of *celestial navigation and the convergence of the *meridians towards the poles. That the earth was a sphere was, of course, understood and taught in the universities. But the limited coverage of charts within the Mediterranean made any relationship to the spherical surface of the earth unnecessary. However, the expansion of *exploration by sea beyond the Mediterranean, and the practice of running down (i.e. along) an astronomically observed *latitude, made it impossible to ignore the shape of the earth. Nevertheless, seamen continued their practice of drawing the sketch maps in the sensible and uncomplicated way they were used to and let those involved in *chartmaking cope as best they could.

In 1599 Edward Wright published his *Certaine Errors in Navigation* which contained a table of meridional parts which gave the spacing of the minutes of latitude along the meridians. This enabled the ordinary chartmaker to produce a chart on *Mercator's projection with parallel meridians on which the mariner could still draw a *rhumb as a straight line. The chart became known as the true chart, as opposed to the ordinary, or simple, or plain chart, though one school of thought holds that the word 'plain' is simply a corruption of 'playne', meaning a flat surface. The references below give the arguments for either opinion. Whichever is right there can be no doubt that the introduction of the true chart was one of the most important advances in the practice of *navigation.

Taylor, E., 'All Plain Sailing', *Journal of Navigation*, 9 (1956), 230.

Waters, D., 'Plain Sailing or Horizontal Navigation', *Journal of Navigation*, 9 (1956), 454.

Mike Richey

plane, to, a term used to describe the action of a boat which attains sufficient speed to cause the forward part of the hull to rise and for the boat then to run along the surface of the water. In order to start planing the hull must have a suitable form and be very light in weight in relation to its sail area or power available. Power boats with a V-sectioned bow and a broad flat hull are noted for their ability to start to plane above a certain speed, and to skim along the surface with only the *after part of the hull and the *propeller and *rudder in the water.

Lightweight, high-performance racing *dinghies, given suitable wind and sea conditions, can get up and plane for shorter or longer periods depending on the continuing strength of the wind and the skill of the helmsman. While planing, a boat's speed can rise to twice or even two and a half times the theoretical maximum sailing speed of a displacement (normally heavy) boat of the same length obtained from the speed formula 1.4 times the square root of the waterline length in feet ($\sqrt[1.4]{\text{LWL}}$ = knots). Thus a dinghy with a waterline length of 4.9 metres (16 ft) has a theoretical maximum speed under sail of 5–6 knots if it cannot plane, but if it is of the planing type with a sufficiently high power–weight ratio, under the right wind and sea conditions its speed may rise to 8 or 9 knots, when it will surge along the surface with its speed rising in bursts to 12 or even 14 knots. While the boat is poised in this way on the surface, the *tiller feels almost rigid in the helmsman's hands, and great skill is needed to prevent a violent sheer to one side or the other, and a sudden *capsize. A powerboat, on the other hand, is usually quite stable as the thrust driving the boat is beneath the water surface, and the flat form of the underwater body enables the boat to be steered in sharp turns without much chance of a capsize. See also HYDRODYNAMICS.

plank sheer, the outermost deck plank covering the *gunwale of a wooden vessel or the plank covering the *timber heads of the *frames when they are brought up above the level of the gunwale. Another name for plank sheer, particularly in *yachtbuilding, is *covering board.

plankton are the tiny animals (zooplankton) and *marine plants (phytoplankton) that drift freely in the waters of the oceans. The herbivorous zooplankton graze on the phytoplankton, either sieving the cells from the water, or trapping them on sheets of mucus, or feeding on individual cells. Carnivorous zooplankton feed on the herbivores. Zooplankton range in size from microscopic single-celled protozoans (ciliates, foraminifers, and radiolarians) to large *crustaceans like copepods and *krill. They are all consumed by larger predators, some of which, like *fish larvae and arrow worms (Chaetognatha), are quite small, but others, like baleen *whales (*Balaenoptera* spp.) and basking *sharks (*Cetorhinus maximus*), are large. Many are permanently members of the plankton, but many are larvae that mature into larger adults and live in deeper water, or even on the seabed. Many of the larger planktonic species undertake extensive vertical migrations over 300 metres (1,000 ft) each day, commuting between the safety of deep water during the day and the food-rich upper layers at night. Larger planktonic species are sampled by towing fine-meshed nets, but the very small species are collected by filtering large volumes of water through fine membranes. There are very many fragile gelatinous species that are hard to sample and study, because they disintegrate either in the nets or when preserved.

The fossil remains of diatoms, microscopic marine plants, are used for keeping dynamite stable, for making luminous paint, and for filtering wine. See also PHOSPHORESCENCE.

Hardy, A., *The Open Sea. Its Natural History: The World of Plankton* (1956). M. V. Angel

plat, to. **(1)** To plait, or weave, braided rope which, before the days of chain cable, used to be made from *foxes and wound round the *cable where it lay in the *hawseholes to protect it from wear when the ship rode to its anchor in a rough sea. **(2)** To plot, in the sense of plotting a ship's *course or position on a *plotting sheet. **(3)** As a noun, an old name, *c.*17th century, for a *chart or map, usually, but not necessarily, engraved. 'Thence home, and took my Lord Sandwiches Draught of the Harbour of Portsmouth down to Ratcliffe to one Burston, to make a plat for the King and another for the Duke and another for himself—which will be very neat.' Samuel *Pepys, *Diary*, 18 February 1665.

plate. **(1)** The steel sheets used in *shipbuilding. They are riveted to the *frames and deck *beams to form the sides and decks. In most modern ship construction, the plates are welded together not riveted. **Armour plate**, the thick plates of case-hardened steel used for side, deck, and *turret armour to protect warships, such as *battleships and *cruisers, in the days when guns were the principle weapon of *warfare at sea. **(2)** The name sometimes given to the *dagger-board or *centreboard of a sailing boat. **(3)** Another name for *chainplates.

pledget, a string of *oakum rolled and ready for use in the *caulking of a deck or side *seam of a wooden vessel. It was inserted into the seam after it had been opened with a *reeming iron, rammed hard home, and then *payed with *pitch to make a watertight joint between the planks.

Plimsoll Line, a mark painted on the sides of British merchant ships which indicated the *load line to which a ship might be loaded with cargo for varying conditions of season and location. Load lines are now controlled by an International Convention adopted by the *International Maritime Organization.

The Plimsoll Mark was made compulsory in Britain under the conditions of the Merchant Shipping Act 1876, passed after a long and bitter parliamentary struggle conducted by Samuel Plimsoll MP (1824–98), a champion for better conditions for seamen. After an early life of hardship, which he later claimed introduced

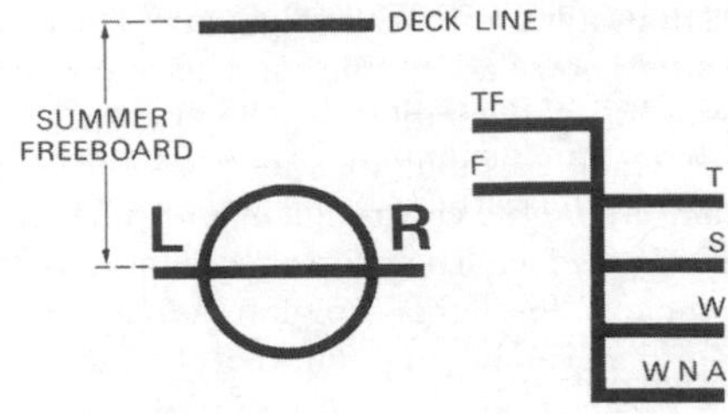

Plimsoll Mark and load line

him to the wretched conditions under which the poor lived, he became aware of what were known as 'coffin ships', those vessels which were unseaworthy and overloaded, heavily insured against loss, in which many shipowners, under the existing law, were permitted to risk their crews. After eventually succeeding in business, Plimsoll entered Parliament in 1868 and began his campaign to improve the lot of British seamen. He wrote a book called *Our Seamen* which aroused so much interest that in 1873 a royal commission was appointed which recommended changes. The government introduced a Bill in 1875 but this was abandoned due, so it was said, to the political pressure from shipowners. However, the depth of public feeling on the matter forced the government to reintroduce the Bill which became the 1876 Merchant Shipping Act.

plotting sheet, generally a sheet of squared paper on which the *navigator may plot *position lines to establish his position when, as is likely in the ocean, the scale of the *chart will be unsuitable. Plotting sheets for different *latitudes are published by the British Hydrographic Department and in the United States a Universal Plotting Chart, a partially constructed blank *Mercator projection chart, is often available and has many advantages for those wishing to use *celestial navigation to establish their position.

plug. **(1)** A tapering piece of wood or a screwed metal stopper, used to stop the drain hole in the bottom of a small boat. *Warfare at sea during the days of sail made it necessary to carry a number of wooden plugs of varying sizes to stop *shot holes after battle, particularly those below the waterline. It was one of the carpenter's duties after battle to inspect the hull for shot holes and hammer home the plugs. **(2)** The name given to the pattern, or male former, on which the moulds for hulls of small craft, such as *yachts and harbour boats, are moulded in *GRP.

plush, a naval term to describe the amount of *grog left over after the daily issue to the messes in a British warship. Official instructions were that any plush after the daily issue was to be poured into the *scuppers and allowed to run overboard to prevent anyone getting more than his ration, but seamen were adept at saving such waste. In its strictest connotation, plush was the amount of grog left over after its issue as a result of short measure given to the seamen; it was later surreptitiously divided between the cooks of the messes who came to the daily issue to collect the grog for their mess in their *monkeys. It involved a degree of conspiracy between the cooks, the *purser's assistant (later the regulating *petty officer) who measured out the allowances, and the officer who, by regulations, had to attend the issue to make sure that more grog was not issued to men than they were entitled to.

PLUTO, the code name given to the 'Pipe Line Under The Ocean' laid across the English Channel from Southampton to Cherbourg shortly after the Anglo-American invasion of northwest France on 6 June 1944 during the Second World War (1939–45). It was an entirely British achievement designed to provide a continuous supply of petrol to sustain the Allied armies as they drove the Germans eastwards. Further pipelines were laid as the Allied armies advanced. The pipe through which the petrol flowed was wound on huge floating drums, known as 'conundrums', which were then towed across the Channel unwinding the pipe as they progressed.

pocket battleship, see CRUISER.

pod, the collective name for a group of *whales and small groups of seals. M. V. Angel

point. **(1)** A division of the circumference of the conventional *compass rose on *charts and compass cards, divided and subdivided into 32 points, each of 11° 15'. It showed four *cardinal points (N., S., E., W.) and four intercardinal points (NE, SE, SW, NW), the remaining 24 divisions being full points. Each point on the card was subdivided into half and quarter points.

A point of the compass was, in the early days of the *square-rigged ship, about the smallest division to which an average helmsman could steer by wheel, but with the growing efficiency in the rig of these vessels it was later possible for a good helmsman to hold a *course between the points. This led to the introduction of half and quarter points, the half point measuring 5° 37.5' and the quarter point 2° 48.75'.

The requirements of more efficient *coastal navigation which came from the growing volume of shipping, and particularly with the realization of the effect of *variation and *deviation, on both the course steered by the ship and the accuracy of the compass *bearings in fixing its position on a chart, led to the abandonment of points as a means both of steering a vessel and of taking bearings. They were replaced by degrees, each *quadrant being divided into 90°, with the courses and bearing being read from the two cardinal points of north and south. Thus a ship with a *magnetic compass that might formerly have steered a course of, say, NE by E., would steer a course of N. 56° E.

For many decades now the compass has simply been divided into 360°, known as the three-figure method, and the helmsman steers by one of those degrees, but the term 'point' lingered on at sea for some time to express approximate bearings in relation to the ship's *head. A lookout, on sighting another vessel at sea, would

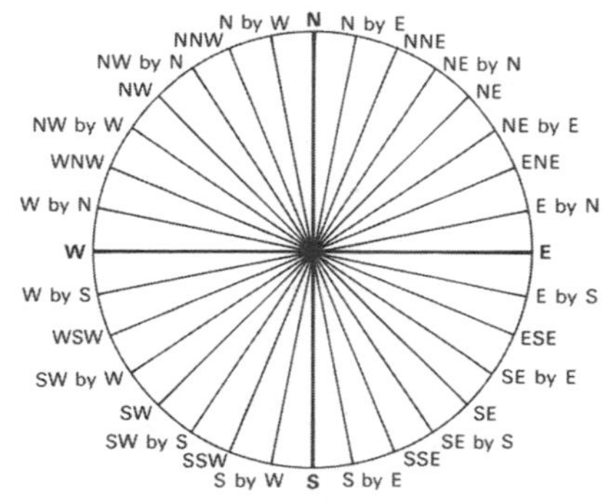

Points of the compass

report its position as being, for example, two points on the *starboard bow, or a point *abaft the *port *beam Nowadays such positions are reported in relation to red (port side) and green (starboard side). For example, another vessel sighted four points on the starboard side is reported as bearing Green 45. See also POINTS OF SAILING.

(2) As a verb it is the operation of tapering the end of a rope to prevent it becoming *fagged out and also to make it more handy to *reeve through a *block. The rope is unlayed for a short distance from the end and the *strands gradually thinned down until they finish in a point. The length of the pointing is then *whipped with a *West Country whipping to hold the strands together.

points of sailing, the headings of a sailing vessel in relation to the wind. When a vessel is sailing as near to the wind as it can, it is said to be *close hauled, i.e. with its sails sheeted (hardened) well in and just full of wind without any shivers in the sails. Modern racing *yachts can sail close hauled about 3½ points (39°) off the wind, a cruising yacht about 4 points (45°), a *gaff-rigged vessel about 4¾ points (50°–55°), and a *square-rigged one about 6 points (70°).

When a vessel's desired *course takes it further off the wind, it is said to be sailing *free, i.e. it can begin to free its sheets to present a squarer aspect of its sails to the wind. When the wind is within the angle of about two points (22°) before the *beam and four points (45°) *abaft the beam, a vessel is said to *reach across the wind, and in many cases this is its fastest point of sailing, particularly when the wind is blowing from *abaft the beam. On this point of sailing its sheets are eased well away so that that angle of the main boom is at a little less than a right angle to the direction of the wind.

When the wind is blowing within the angle of 4 points (45°) either side of the stern, a vessel is said to be running with the wind, and has its sheets eased right away to allow the boom to take up the broadest possible angle to the wind direction. See also BY.

polacre, a rig peculiar to the Mediterranean. The three-masted ones were usually *lateen rigged on the fore and *mizzen-masts, and *square rigged on the mainmast, but occasionally they were square rigged on all three. The two-masted version was usually square rigged on both masts. A feature of their design was that they had pole masts without either *tops or *crosstrees. This, and the arrangement for staying the masts, meant the *yards could be *braced much closer to the centreline than in the normal square-rigger. This made them extremely *weatherly—an English-built polacre constructed in 2004 could trim her yards 15° to the centreline—and as a result were much favoured by those involved in *piracy. There were no *footropes to the yards; the crew stood on the *topsail yards to loose, or *furl, the *topgallant sails and on the lower yards to loose,

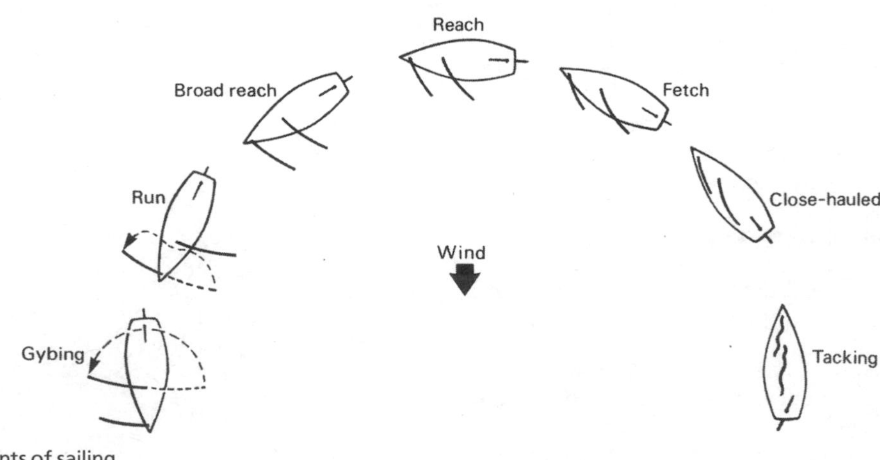

Points of sailing

Mediterranean polacre; engraving from *Recueil de veues etc.* by P. J. Gueroult de Pas, 1710

*reef, or furl the topsails, the yards themselves being lowered sufficiently for that purpose.

Polaris, the Pole Star, a second-magnitude star in the constellation Ursa Minor that describes a circle of about 2° 25' daily about the North Pole. It is thus of service to *navigators as it points within a degree or two of *true north. Corrected by Pole Star tables that are printed in most *nautical almanacs the *altitude of Polaris can be used to determine *latitude. During the 15th century, when *celestial navigation was in its infancy, a correction to the observed altitude of Polaris (known in the Mediterranean as *Stella Maris*, star of the sea) would be made according to the position of the two Guard stars as they encircle the pole of the sky. See also NAVIGATION.

poleaxe, a boarding weapon used by seamen in the days of sailing navies. It had a wooden handle about 38 centimetres (15 in.) long with an axe head which had a curved spike at the back. The blade of the axe was used to cut away the running *rigging of an enemy ship after it had been *boarded. The spike at the back was often used to assist men in clambering up the side of the ship in the act of boarding as several of these axes would be driven into the side of the enemy ship one above the other to form a sort of ladder. It was also, of course, a handy weapon to knock flat an adversary when boarding, which accounts for it becoming part of everyday language.

Pole Star, see POLARIS.

pollution is the introduction of substances and energy in concentrations that result in harm to the marine environment and its fauna and flora. But see also ENVIRONMENTAL ISSUES.

Dumping. Disposal of waste and raw sewage into the sea from ships and land became commonplace in the 19th and 20th centuries. At the time it provided a relatively cheap and very effective way of keeping the land clean and, following the construction of the sewage systems that discharged wastes either into rivers or the sea, the health of city-dwellers improved immensely. Sea water was thought to be effective in cleansing human waste and killing the pathogens, but after the Second World War (1939–45) it became clear that eating contaminated *fish and *shellfish from polluted water created a serious health risk, and even swimming in the sea could be hazardous and was linked to poliomyelitis.

At the end of the Second World War there was a major problem of what to do with large quantities of redundant munitions and toxic chemical agents. The solution, which seemed innocuous at the time, was to dispose of them in the sea. Similarly, when the newly emerging nuclear industries started to generate large quantities of dangerous radioactive waste, this too was dumped in the deep ocean. The first of the campaigns by Greenpeace led to banning of the disposal of radioactive waste in the sea and eventually to a complete reappraisal of marine dumping and a tightening of international regulations.

Once the relevant annexe of the 1978 International Convention for the Prevention of Pollution from Ships, known as *MARPOL, came into force, throwing and discharging most wastes from ships was also banned. All wastes now have to be off loaded in port, and the oceans are awarded greater protection from dumping of industrial waste than is afforded to the land or the atmosphere.

Toxic Chemicals. Marine ecosystems do have a limited capacity to cope with low levels of naturally occurring toxic chemicals. Organisms that take up some pollutants like heavy metals (e.g. mercury and lead), either directly from the water or via their food, can regulate their contents to some extent. Once the pollutant is absorbed into the body it may be excreted or converted into a non-toxic form and stored in the liver or in fatty tissues. However, if a predator eats prey containing such detoxified pollutants, it too absorbs and stores the pollutant and so it accumulates—a process known as biomagnification. Top predators tend to accumulate high concentrations of the pollutants in their tissues, and humans are, of course, the ultimate top predator. For example, in the Faeroe Islands the traditional hunt for pilot *whales has been abandoned because the whales are too heavily contaminated with heavy metals and PCBs (polychlorinated biphenyls) to be safe to eat.

Chemical industries continue to synthesize many thousands of novel substances each year. Many of these are specifically designed to be toxic and persistent. Ecosystems have no built-in ability to deal with novel substances, and so they have the potential to cause chronic long-term problems. Intensive agriculture, aquaculture, and industry all have high demands for chemicals that will boost production, control pests, and limit corrosion. The high cost of such chemicals favours the selection of persistent substances, which reduces the number of applications. The problems accruing from the synthesis and use of such novel substances were first recognized with DDT. Post-war, this was the most effective insecticide, particularly successful in controlling malaria-carrying mosquitoes and agricultural pests. However, DDT accumulated in body fat and interfered with the laying down of eggshells in birds, including *seabirds; populations of many charismatic species declined catastrophically. This was the first indication of a much greater environmental disaster as DDT residues were found to be accumulating not only in Antarctic species but also in human tissues, which persuaded governments to curb its manufacture and use.

Likewise the manufacture of PCBs (polychlorinated biphenyls), once widely used as lubricants and coolants, was halted in 1977, when they were found to be accumulating in both man and animals. By the time their manufacture was banned about 2 million tonnes had been synthesized, most of which still exist today as they are highly stable. About a third is in waste stores and the rest is out there contaminating the environment.

The use of TBTs (tributyltins) in antifouling paints was so effective at controlling *fouling organisms that they were rapidly and widely adopted. Soon their devastating impact as hormone disruptors was discovered; marine animals turned into sterile sexual intermediates, and some think reductions in human sperm counts have a similar cause. TBTs have largely been phased out, but they are so persistent that many harbours and *yacht basins still have substantial traces of TBTs in their sediments, which are inhabited by very aberrant faunas.

Atmospheric Disruption. Marine pollution is not all about direct impacts, it also involves the disruption of environmental processes. For example chorofluorocarbons (CFCs), once widely used as refrigerants, are inert in sea water and have no direct effect on the ocean life. But high in the earth's atmosphere, they lead to the breakdown of the ozone layer, which normally shields the surface of the earth from the damaging effects of the full intensity of the ultraviolet light coming from the sun. Once a hole appears in the ozone layer *marine plants and animals are exposed to the full intensity of UV radiation. The productivity of the Southern Ocean has probably been reduced by more than 10%. It may also have contributed to the increasing prevalence of coral bleaching in *coral reefs. It is estimated that it will take over 50 years for the ozone hole finally to return to normal. Also, the increase of greenhouse gases in the atmosphere, particularly carbon dioxide from the burning of fossil fuels, is threatening to cause *climate change that will disrupt the global ecosystem, including the oceans, in an unpredictable manner.

Garbage. Marine garbage, some thrown from or washed off ships, but most being carried in by rivers and blown into the sea from land, is not only unsightly but also causes real environmental problems. It accumulates in *slicks where it becomes a major cause of premature death in turtles (see MARINE REPTILES) through their mistaking plastic bags that block their guts for the *jellyfish they feed on. Three hundred *albatross chicks examined on the Pacific island of Midway, about as far as one can get from 'civilization', all had plastic items in their stomachs.

Inputs of some pollutants can be reduced by cleaning up our rivers and ground waters, and stopping direct discharges from land and ships. But controlling the inputs that arrive via the atmosphere will be much harder. The switch to unleaded fuel for vehicles has substantially reduced the lead entering the oceans from the atmosphere. Now anthropogenic radioactivity adds less than 1% to the natural background levels of radiation.

Oil Pollution. Another source of pollution is the foundering of large vessels carrying damaging cargoes. The effects of massive oil spills after notorious *tanker disasters, such as the *Torrey Canyon* and the *Exxon Valdez*, have been well publicized and have resulted in considerable improvements in *navigation, ship safety, and routeing that have curtailed the frequency of such accidents. However, human error ensures the risks can never be eliminated while we continue to transport materials around the oceans and exploit seabed minerals. The only sure way to stop marine pollution is to cease the manufacture, use, and transportation of the major pollutants, but so long as the human population continues to grow, marine pollution problems will continue.

Clark, R., *Marine Pollution* (1997).

Website on PCBs: **www.atsdr.cdc.gov/tfacts17.html**
www.epa.gov/owow/oceans/
www.pewoceans.org/inquiry/marine/

M. V. Angel

Polo, Marco, see MARCO POLO.

'Pompey', the British sailors' slang for Portsmouth, the English naval base. It is not known how or when the name came into being, though one theory is that it owes its origin to the fact that the local fire brigade, known by their French name *pompiers*, used to exercise on Southsea Common, adjacent to Portsmouth.

pontoon. **(1)** A flat-bottomed boat often used as a *lighter or *ferry. **(2)** A boat of special design to support a temporary road or footbridge across a river. **(3)** A hollow, watertight structure used in *salvage for its lifting power when the water it contains is pumped out. See also CAISSON. **(4)** A floating structure frequently used at the ends of fixed piers or alongside quays so that it rises and falls with the *tide to provide ease of access. **(5)** A low, flat vessel fitted with cranes, *tackles, and *capstans which was used in the days of sail to haul down, or *careen, ships for bottom cleaning or repair.

poop. **(1)** From the Latin *puppis*, stern, the name given to the short, aftermost deck raised above the *quarterdeck of a ship. In *square-rigged ships it formed the roof of the *coach, or *round house, where the *master normally had his *cabin. Only the larger sailing ships had poops, but the name has survived and is often used to describe any raised deck right *aft in the ship. It is also sometimes wrongly used to describe that part of the deck which lies at the *after end of a ship, regardless of whether raised or not. See also POOP ROYAL. **(2)** As a verb, a ship is pooped when a heavy sea breaks over its stern or *quarter when being driven before a high wind. It is a situation of considerable danger, particularly in a heavily laden ship, as it usually comes about when the speed of the ship is approximately the same as the speed of the following sea, so that the *rudder has little or no grip. In such cases, a sea which poops a ship is very apt to swing it off *course until it is broadside on to the sea, with the danger of being rolled over. It is even more dangerous in smaller craft, such as

A vessel pooped

a *yacht, as a pooping sea will bring a great weight of water aboard which might swamp it. The danger of being pooped can sometimes be reduced by slowing down the vessel's speed in relation to the speed of the sea by towing a *drogue or long *warp.

poop royal, a short deck above the after end of the *poop seen in many French and Spanish warships during the days of sailing navies, where the *master or *pilot had his *cabin. It was known in English *shipbuilding as a *topgallant poop, possibly because the gunports were usually decorated with *garlands, a typical English practice with regard to upper-deck gunports. Some of the largest British warships incorporated this deck to accommodate the upper *coach.

poor John, the name given by seamen to salted and dried *fish of the cheaper varieties, when supplied as part of the victualling allowance on board sailing warships of the British Navy. Issues of fish occasionally replaced issues of salt beef or pork and were never popular on the *lower deck.

port. **(1)** The name of the left-hand side of a vessel as viewed from *aft. The name probably owes its derivation to the fact that the old-fashioned merchant ships had a loading, or *lading, port on their left-hand side, and ladebord, later corrupted into *larboard, was the original term for the side of the vessel across which the cargo was always carried on board. The term larboard side was changed officially to port in 1844 to avoid any confusion with starboard. However, port had been used very much earlier than 1844, and Rear Admiral Robert *Fitzroy is usually credited with its introduction in the British Navy, in HMS *Beagle*, in 1828. Mainwaring, in his *Seaman's Dictionary* (1625), indicates the use of the word for *helm orders some 200 years earlier, and had: 'Port. Is a word used in conding [see CON] the Ship ... they will use the word steddy a-port, or steddy a-*starboard.'

The theory that the word port was chosen to replace larboard because a vessel burns a red light—the colour of port wine—at night on its left-hand side is demonstrably false, as the word port was used in this connection long before ships burned *navigation lights at night.

(2) A harbour with facilities for berthing ships, embarkation and disembarkation of passengers, and the loading and unloading of cargo.

porthole, see SCUTTLE (1).

port-last, or **portoise,** a word meaning level with the *gunwale, in connection with the *yards of a sailing vessel. An order to 'lower the yards, a-port-last', or 'a-portoise', was to lower them down to the gunwale. For a ship to ride in this manner was for it to ride out a *gale with its lower yards *struck down.

portolano, *sailing directions used in the Mediterranean between the 12th and 15th centuries, often backed up by an accompanying *portulan chart. Also known as a *compasso*. It described the coasts and ports, anchorages, rocks and shoals, *courses to steer, and the facilities available for trade at the various ports. The oldest surviving one is the *Compasso da navigare* that can be dated *c.*1250.

ports, square holes cut in the sides of the sailing men-of-war through which the guns were fired, or for other purposes such as *bridle-ports in the bows, entry ports in the *waist, and stern ports between the stern *timbers. When not in use they were closed by port-lids which were hinged along the top edge. See also SCUTTLE (1).

port sills, or **cills,** the name given to the lengths of timber used for lining the top and bottom edges of the *gunports in sailing men-of-war.

port tack, the situation of a sailing vessel with her sails trimmed for a wind which comes over her *port side. Although the verb to *tack postulates a vessel sailing *close hauled, a vessel on any point of sailing is on the port tack if the wind comes over her port side. However, if the wind is coming from *abaft the *beam on the port side of a *fore-and-aft-rigged sailing vessel it is sometimes said that she is on the **port gybe**.

Portuguese man-of-war (*Physalia physalis*), a relative of the *jellyfish that floats on the surface (neustonic) in warm oceans. They are blue in colour with a large gas-filled float beneath which hangs the main body, and are often found lined up in *windrows and *slicks. The body consists of polyps, modified as feeding tentacles, or for digesting prey, or for reproduction. The tentacles are enormously extensible and a 30-centimetre (12-in.) float may be trailing 30 metres (100 ft) of tentacles, which are armed with powerful stinging cells (nematocysts). These discharge in response to touch and chemical stimuli, killing their prey of small *fish and *plankton. They can also sting humans painfully and can cause anaphylactic shock that may temporarily paralyse a swimmer. The tentacles are blue and difficult to see in the water, and can still sting even after becoming detached from the colony. The float is set on the body so that some animals tack to the right and others to the left. In the sea individual Portuguese men-of-war are often accompanied by one or more man-of-war fish (*Nomeus gronovii*). This has blue and silver vertical stripes, swims with immunity amongst the animal's tentacles, and lives in symbiosis with it, gaining protection, and possibly some food, from its host. The Portuguese man-of-war is not without its predators; loggerhead turtles (*Caretta caretta*) eat them regularly.

www.aloha.com/~lifeguards/portugue.html

M. V. Angel

portulan, or **portolan, chart.** This derived its name from port books. It was not only the first sea *chart but the first true map of any kind for, based on measurement, it was intended for use rather than display or illustration. Unlike contemporary land maps where size might, for instance, be related to importance, it carried a scale. The earliest surviving example is the *Carta Pisana* housed in the Bibliothèque Nationale in Paris. Probably of Genoese origin, it is dated about 1275 and drawn on an outstretched sheepskin, the neck (untypically) to the right. The chart gives a remarkably accurate representation of the Mediterranean coastline, derived presumably from *sailing directions and the notes and sketches of *pilots. There is no graticule of *latitude and *longitude but a scale of miles is displayed at two places at right angles to each other, presumably to take into account shrinkage. With no projection, the chart is based on *bearing and distance, but within the latitude limits of the Mediterranean, convergence of the *meridians would be of little account. The bearings are of course magnetic not *true, but that again would have mattered little where both compass and sailing directions were also magnetic. The *wind-roses display sixteen 'rhumbs' corresponding to the *cardinal and inter-cardinal points of the compass which are then divided and subdivided by 'winds', as directions were then called, and half-winds to provide the network of *rhumb lines. By finding the rhumb most closely parallel to the bearing of his destination, and tracing it back to its parent rose, the *navigator could thus identify the rhumb, or *course, to sail on.

The mathematically precise construction diagrams by which the network of rhumbs was laid down on the chart appear for the first time on the Pisan Chart and continued to be used well into the 18th century. It is worth remembering that this was the period when, largely through the influence of Leonardo of Pisa, the Hindu ('Arabic') system of numerals was adopted in place of the clumsy Roman figures, which put arithmetic within the grasp of the ordinary man.

Campbell, T., 'Portolan Charts from the Late Thirteenth Century to 1500', in J. B. Harley and D. Woodward (eds.), *The History of Cartography* (1987).

Mike Richey

Poseidon. (1) The Greek god of the sea, known to the Romans as *Neptune. In Greek mythology he was lord and ruler of the sea. He was the son of Cronos and Rhea, and his palace was believed to lie at the bottom of the sea off Aegea in Euboea. His wife Amphitrite was a granddaughter of Titan (Ocean). He was credited with the power of gathering clouds, raising and calming the sea, letting loose *storms, and granting safe voyages. See also CROSSING THE LINE; FORTUNUS. **(2)** A nuclear weapons system fitted in *submarines. It is a later development of *Polaris. See also WARFARE AT SEA.

POSH, an acronym deriving from the phrase 'Port Out Starboard Home' which came to stand for the wealthy shipboard travellers who could afford to travel in this way. The letters were said to have been printed on the first-class tickets of passengers travelling on the P. & O. Line (see OCEAN LINERS) to the Far East, indicating that they had paid extra for *cabins on the *port side of the ship going out and the *starboard side coming home so as to avoid the heat and glare of the sun in the Indian Ocean. However, no ticket bearing these initials has ever been produced to confirm this.

position line, a line plotted on the *chart, whether from a terrestrial bearing, a *sextant *altitude, or a *hyperbolic system, somewhere along which the ship must lie. In *celestial navigation and in conventional chartwork the position line is usually indicated by a single arrowhead at each end, to distinguish it from other lines on the *chart or *plotting sheet. See also SUMNER'S POSITION LINE.

post-bark, a name often used in the 16th and 17th centuries for what was also known as a *packet boat, a vessel specially designated for the carriage of mails overseas.

post-captain, the rank in the British Navy in sailing warship days which corresponds with that of captain today, but it was never a rank in the US Navy. There were in those times two grades of captain, depending on the size and quality of the ship to which the appointments were made. On promotion, lieutenants were given the rank of captain and appointed to the command of a small warship, such as a *sloop, *cutter, etc. The equivalent rank today would be that of commander. After sufficient experience in command of such a ship they were 'posted', i.e. given command of a *rated ship, and took the rank of post-captain. See also MASTER.

Potemkin, more properly *Kniaz Potemkin Tavricheski*, a Russian *battleship of the Black Sea Fleet. She was named after Prince Potemkin, the commander-in-chief of the Black Sea Fleet under whom the naval officer John Paul *Jones served in 1788. The *Potemkin* was the scene, in June 1905, of a famous *mutiny, the ostensible reason for it being bad meat brought on board to be made into borscht, which the men refused to eat. The ship's commander, Giliarovsky, considering this refusal amounted to mutiny, and acting in accordance with an old Russian naval custom, ordered that a number of men should be selected at random, covered with a *tarpaulin, and shot. The men selected to do the shooting refused to fire. This account was later denied by officers of the ship who survived the mutiny, but one rating named Vakulinchuk was undoubtedly shot by Giliarovsky, whereupon Giliarovsky, the ship's captain, the chaplain, and four other officers were killed by the crew. When the *Potemkin* returned to Odessa, Vakulinchuk's body was exhibited to the crowd ashore and rioting followed, some 5,000–6,000 people losing their lives mainly during the famous charge of mounted Cossacks down the Richelieu Steps. After meandering round the Black Sea in search of support the battleship was *scuttled by her crew in shallow water off Constanza, but was later raised and refitted. She was broken up after the First World War (1914–18).

The mutiny is the subject of the Soviet film *Bronenosets Potemkin* (*The Battleship Potemkin*) which was made in 1925. It is now part of cinema history, although the ending, showing the Russian fleet rallying to the *Potemkin*'s leadership, is pure fiction.

pouches, an old name for the small *bulkheads, often temporary. They were erected in the *holds of a cargo ship when a shifting cargo, such as corn or coal, was loaded, their purpose being to prevent its movement when the ship rolled or *pitched. In the older sailing days, pouches were fitted in warships before they were *careened for bottom cleaning so that the shingle *ballast, which had been shifted by hand to *heel the ship, should not run back to the centreline.

powder monkey, a ship's boy during the days of sailing warships whose duty, when the crew was *piped to *quarters for battle, was to carry powder from the magazine to the gun-decks. They were helped in this task by any woman who might be on board, Mary Anne *Talbot being one example. Many of the larger ships carried three or four wives of trustworthy *petty officers or seamen when at sea, particularly for their value in nursing the wounded after battle. The powder they, and the powder monkeys, carried to the gun-decks was weighed out into silk bags in the form of cartridges for the guns. See also BUDGE-BARREL; WARFARE AT SEA.

powerboats, see YACHTING: POWER.

pram, praam, or **prame.** **(1)** A small two- or three-masted ship used by the French for coast defence purposes during the Revolutionary and Napoleonic Wars (1793–1815). They were flat bottomed, drew very little water, and carried from ten to twenty guns, being used as floating batteries or gunboats as a defence against coastal raids or assaults. The majority were *ketch rigged. **(2)** A *lighter used in Holland and in the Baltic for loading and unloading merchant vessels lying at anchor in the ports. They were first mentioned in this role as far back as the 14th century. **(3)** A small ship's boat of the 16th–18th centuries. **(4)** A *dinghy usually used as a small tender to a *yacht, frequently with a truncated or sawn-off bow.

pratique, a certificate given to a ship when it arrives from a foreign port when the port health officer at the port of arrival is satisfied that the health of all on board is good and that there are no cases of notifiable diseases in the ship. A ship remains in *quarantine on arrival in port until it has been granted its certificate of pratique.

press gang, the popular name for a group of seamen, under the command of an officer, who were employed in wartime to bring in men—and on at least one occasion a woman, Mary Anne *Talbot—for service in the navy. Although connected by most people with the British Navy other nations employed similar methods of recruitment for their navies and the *impressment of men for service in warships was widespread. In Britain these groups operated mainly in seaports, but occasionally visited inland towns to pick up seamen who may have been thought to reside or visit there, though during the Revolutionary (1793–1801) and Napoleonic (1803–1815) Wars against France the *Sea Fencibles were exempt. Men thus taken were, in the British Navy, entered in the ship's muster-book (see MUSTER, TO) as *landsmen, and were paid at a lower rate than those who had volunteered. **Hot press** was the name given to a condition of impressment when the need for men to man British warships was so acute that the press gangs were given instruction to take men regardless of any *protections they might carry. When news of a hot press in any district got around, all likely men usually went into hiding until the danger was past.

preventer, the name given to any additional rope or wire rigged temporarily to back up any standing *rigging in a ship in heavy wind and weather. It is most usually associated with sailing vessels, and particularly with the mast *stays of such ships.

prick, to. **(1)** To sew an additional central seam between the two seams which were normally employed to join the *cloths of a sail. This was normally only done when the sails were worn and the original stitching weakened by long wear. See SAILMAKER'S STITCHING. **(2)** To roll up leaf tobacco in *canvas and *serve it with tarred twine to compress it as solidly as possible; when matured and cut with a knife it was a favourite smoke or chew of old *tars. Those prepared to sacrifice a portion of their *grog ration in which to soak the tobacco before it was served always professed to enjoy it even more. A quantity of tobacco in its canvas and serving was known as a prick, qualified by the weight of leaf tobacco thus treated, as a half-pound prick, pound prick, etc.

prime, to, in general nautical terms, to make something ready for immediate use. A ***lead was primed before taking a *sounding** by inserting a piece of tallow or soft soap into the cavity at its end so that as it struck the bottom it would pick up sand, shells, or small stones to gave a *navigator information about the nature of the bottom. In the days of hand *pumps on board, **the pump was primed** by having water poured into the barrel so that the leather washers would take up firmly on the lining of the barrel. **Muzzle-loading guns in sailing warships were primed** by piercing the cartridge with a *priming iron to expose the powder, and a pinch of gunpowder, or later a quill firing-tube, was then inserted in the vent hole. When used as an adjective the term 'a prime seaman' meant someone who was fully trained and able to *hand, *reef, and *steer.

prime meridian, the terrestrial *meridian from which *longitudes are measured eastwards or westwards, the longitude of the prime meridian being 0°. Early Mediterranean *navigators used the meridian through the Fortunate Isles, or Canaries, as their first, or prime, meridian as they were then thought to be the westernmost part of the habitable globe. During the 15th and 16th centuries when the peoples of western Europe emerged as sea traders, almost every maritime nation used as a prime meridian a meridian passing through its own territory. The French, for example, used the meridian of Paris; the Dutch, that through Amsterdam; and the English the meridian through London. The inconvenience to navigators caused by the existence of a multitude of prime meridians, and so *charts with differing meridians east and west, was not resolved until the closing decade of the 19th century when it was decided by international agreement to adopt the meridian of Greenwich as the prime meridian. See also GREENWICH MEAN TIME.

priming iron, a thin piece of iron with a point at one end and a wooden handle at the other. This was thrust down the vent hole of a muzzle-loading cannon when loaded to pierce the cartridge and expose the powder. A quickmatch was then put to the powder train—or, later, the quill-tube inserted and fired—and the powder in the cartridge would ignite.

prismatic coefficient, in *naval architecture a measure of a hull's fineness. It compares the boat's actual displaced volume with that of a shape the length of the boat's waterline with a cross-section of the immersed midship section. A boat with a high prismatic is full ended and one with a low number is fine ended.

Jeremy Lines

privateer, a privately owned vessel armed with guns which operated in time of war against the trade of an enemy. The name came to embrace both the ships and the men who sailed in them, with the practice, known as **guerre de course*, becoming accepted in international maritime law. Such vessels were commissioned by *letters of marque, which licensed them to take *prizes in time of war, and which served as both official letters of *reprisal and bonds of good behaviour. The first letter of marque was issued in England in 1293, but only from 1589 did they provide for prizes to be condemned at an *Admiralty Court and a division of their value made between the crown and the owners. The division was usually on the basis of 10% to the crown and 90% to the owner.

In English history the reign of Elizabeth I (1558–1603) was the golden age of privateering, though it continued long after that to be a profitable business. Francis *Drake was essentially a privateer on his voyage round the world even though he did not have a letter of marque for the voyage, as also was John Paul *Jones two centuries later before he became a regular naval officer. By the time that national navies were established on a permanent basis, the authorities often disapproved of privateering because it drained off the best seamen. But it was such an efficient method of commerce destruction that the French, notably Jean *Bart and François *Thurot, and the Americans, made great use of it, to such an extent that all other nations were more or less forced to follow suit. In this way privateers may perhaps be considered as the strategic predecessors of *submarines, when used, as in the First and Second World Wars, in operations against the merchant shipping of an enemy state.

One of the most successful British privateers was Woodes Rogers (d. 1732). He was engaged by a syndicate of merchants during the War of the Spanish Succession (1702–13) to lead an expedition under a letter of marque to the *South Seas in the ships *Duke* and *Duchess*, described in his journal as *frigates of 20 and 26 guns respectively. With Rogers in the *Duke* was William *Dampier, who served as *navigator of the expedition. They sailed from Bristol in 1708, took a few prizes in the voyage south to Cape Horn, and eventually arrived at the island of Juan Fernandez where they chanced upon Alexander *Selkirk, who had been *marooned there four years earlier. The two ships then captured a Spanish *galleon off the coast of Mexico, and took aboard its precious cargo of bullion, silk, and precious stones. Rogers, who had been wounded in the battle, then sailed his ships across the Pacific to Guam before returning for England via the Cape of Good Hope. The prize goods taken during the voyage were sold for the considerable sum of £148,000 and Rogers wrote an entertaining account of his circumnavigation in *A Cruising Voyage round the World* (1712). From 1718 until his death he was governor of the Bahamas with a mandate to stamp out *piracy.

George *Shelvocke was another successful privateer in the South Seas, though some of his activities were closer to piracy. It was, incidentally, a passage from Shelvocke's book, *A Voyage round the World* (1726), which almost certainly inspired Coleridge to write 'The Rime of the *Ancient Mariner'. French privateers were most active in the century following the War of the Spanish Succession, and American privateers were far more numerous than naval ships in the War of American Independence (1775–82), and the War of 1812–14. Privateering was abolished by the Declaration of Paris in 1856. However, the USA refused to sign the declaration. As a result it suffered severely from this form of war against its trade throughout its Civil War of 1861–5 when both sides preferred to arm merchantmen as regular warships than to commission privateers.

The principles of the Declaration of Paris were reaffirmed at the Hague Convention of 1907. However, a form of *guerre de course* was approved there when a majority of the maritime nations endorsed the use of armed merchant cruisers, and in the two world wars waged during the 20th century, maritime attack on trade proved a major weapon. See also CORSAIR.

prize, the name normally used to describe an enemy vessel captured at sea by a ship of war of a *privateer. The word is also used to describe *contraband cargo taken from a merchant ship and *condemned in prize by a Court of *Admiralty. In its strict and original legal definition, prize in Britain is entirely a right of the crown, and no man may share in prize except through the gift of the crown. Most other maritime nations had similar definitions of prize, limiting it by right to the ruling body from whom it issued by gift. With the growth of maritime trade, and therefore the increase in value of prize, nations passed their prize laws under which the taking and condemnation of prize cargoes was controlled. At the Hague Convention in 1907, international rules were adopted to regularize the capture of prize. See also PRIZE MONEY.

prize money, the net proceeds from the sale of ships and goods captured in prize and condemned in an *Admiralty Court. In Britain, all prize captured at sea was forfeit to the crown, and was known as Droits of the Crown. Droits of Admiralty, that part of the *prize fund which accrued by right to the *Lord High Admiral, comprised ships improperly brought in for adjudication in a prize court before declaration of war or *reprisal; those brought in by those operating without a lawful commission or *letter of marque; and those forced into a British port by stress of weather, or shipwrecked. The High Court of Admiralty became the legal prize tribunal in 1589, with Vice-Admiralty Courts exercising local jurisdiction wherever they were set up. In 1692, with a view to making service in the British Navy more popular, the crown waived its right to part of the Droits of the Crown, granting it to the actual captors in a scale of shares laid down by royal proclamation. By an Act of Queen Anne (1665–1714) in 1708, known as the Cruisers Act, the whole of the Droits of the Crown were allocated to the captors, the value of the prize being divided into eighths, of which three went to the captain, one to the commander-in-chief, one to the officers, one to the warrant officers, and two to the crew. Any unclaimed prize money was allocated to Greenwich Hospital.

Prize Acts lapsed at the end of a war but were normally re-enacted at the start of the next. The last Prize Act in Great Britain came into force on the outbreak of the Second World War (1939–45). After the war it was announced that this was the last occasion on which prize money would be paid. This brought Britain into line with most other maritime countries which had, of course, their own prize law and decided their own method and scale of distribution.

Historically, prize in the British Navy was always a considerable incentive to recruitment and large numbers of men were tempted to join the navy for the chance of quick riches from this source. One of the most remarkable instances of prize distribution followed the capture in 1762 of the Spanish *treasure ship *Hermione* by the *frigates *Active* and *Favourite*. She was condemned in prize for £519,705, and each of the two captains received £65,000, every lieutenant £13,000, and every seaman £485. There were other captures as rich as this, but in most cases there were higher numbers entitled to a share in the distribution, making the payout proportionately smaller.

proa (Malayan *prau*), in the Malay language the term for all types of ship or vessel, from *sampan to *kapal. The South Pacific proa, which probably originates from Indonesia, has an *outrigger and is identical at both ends. It has a unique rig in that the crew, when *tacking, reverse the sail so that, on completing the manoeuvre, the bow becomes the stern with the outrigger remaining on the *windward side. The steering device, of course, then has to be moved from the old 'stern' to the new one. The proa's *lateen sail is, to western eyes, upside down, the wide base of the triangle being more or less level with the top of the mast, the apex of the triangle being secured to the bow. The hulls of some proas are just hollowed-out logs; more elaborate ones have their planks sewn edge to edge, a form of *carvel construction; the biggest are quite capable of sailing long distances between islands. See also CANOE; LEWIS, DAVID.

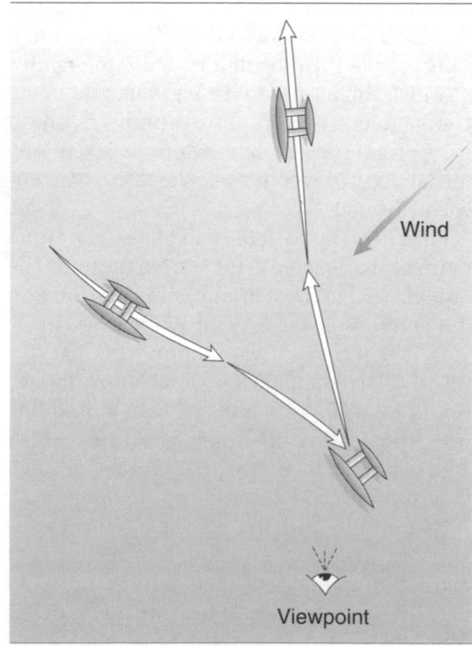

The course of a proa tacking

propeller, the rotating screw of a power-driven vessel by which it is forced through the water. The first mechanical propulsion of a ship had been a *paddle steamer's stern wheel or paddle wheels, but these had disadvantages which led to efforts to design a means of propulsion which would be permanently submerged and thus capable of being driven without straining the engine. The principle of the Archimedes screw was well enough known, and it was an adaptation of this principle which eventually produced the answer. Four engineers are usually credited with its invention, all at about the same period, between 1833 and 1836. They were the Englishman Robert Wilson, the Frenchman Frédéric Sauvage, the Swede John Ericsson (1803–89), and another Englishman, Francis Pettit *Smith, whose invention was finally awarded a patent. It was first tried out in 1838 in the 237-ton steamship *Archimedes*, but it was Ericsson who was responsible for the first propeller-driven warship when in 1843 he fitted a propeller to a ship for the US Navy which became the USS *Princeton*, a ten-gun *sloop.

Propeller design proceeded reasonably rapidly and with generally increasing horsepower. With the development of the original *reciprocating engine into the *compound and *triple expansion types, propellers increased in numbers from the single one driven by a shaft in the centreline of the ship, first to two, with one on each *quarter, and then, for the largest ships, to four, with two on each quarter. These arrangements were efficient but did not always increase steering control. The introduction of the turbine concentrated the attention of designers towards greater efficiency in the shape and *pitch of the propeller blades. Later, in order to absorb the ever-increasing power needed to propel single-screw *tankers, five-bladed and six-bladed propellers were introduced, their size closely approaching the 7.3-metre (24-ft) diameter of the **Great Eastern*'s four-bladed one.

For sailing *yachts with *auxiliary power, propellers are usually made to fold, to *feather, or to rotate freely when the vessel is under sail, in order to minimize drag as it goes through the water. Each type has its advantages, and it is usually a matter of personal choice as to which type is fitted.

Modern Propeller Systems by Denis Griffiths

Controllable Pitch Propeller. The conventional propeller has a fixed blade pitch which means that the blades are at a set angle to the axis of the shaft rotation. In order to change the speed of the ship the rotational speed of the propeller shaft must be changed, usually by changing the engine speed. In order for the ship to go *astern, the rotational direction of the propeller shaft must be changed. An alternative to changing the speed of the engine and to reversing the engine is to fit a controllable pitch propeller. In this case the individual propeller blades are mounted on the boss of the propeller in such a way that the pitch of each blade can be changed by means of an operating mechanism located within the propeller boss. The propeller shaft is rotating at all times when at sea or when the ship is manoeuvring. If the ship is to be stationary the blades are given zero pitch which means that they are at right angles to the axis of the propeller, and they exert no thrust. To move the ship forward, the blades are given a forward pitch and the larger the pitch the faster the ship will move. To move it astern, the blades are given a reverse pitch.

Thruster. This is a propeller unit located in a tunnel at the bow or stern of the ship. Called bow thrusters or stern thrusters, they are driven by an electric motor mounted above the thruster tunnel, the drive being through a bevel gearbox. They exert a sideways thrust on the ship to increase manoeuvrability, so that they can often do the work of *tugs when a ship is berthing or undocking. Their propellers, of the controllable pitch type, allow the magnitude and direction of the thrust to be varied, and using them in conjunction with the ship's propulsion propeller further increases manoeuvrability. Because they work by forcing water from one side of the ship to the other it is essential that they are placed well below the waterline to avoid air being drawn into the tunnels. They only function when the ship is at rest or moving very slowly. For illus. see TRAWLER.

Propulsion Pod. This has a controllable pitch propeller, which allows for variation in propulsive thrust, and is driven by an electric motor in the pod. The pod is positioned for maximum efficiency, usually at the stern for larger ships but may be at other locations. Because there is no direct drive from an engine within the ship the pod is able to be located anywhere on the hull, and it may be fixed or it may rotate. If a pod is steerable (can be rotated) it will provide a thrust in any direction and can therefore also act as a side thruster and as the *rudder, and it is rotated by a hydraulic motor unit located where the pod connects with the ship's hull. The hull at this point must be strengthened because of the thrust from the pod's propeller; this area effectively acts as what is technically called the thrust bearing. The power cables driving a fixed pod's electric propulsion motor go directly to the pod, but a rotating pod's electrical connection is with slip rings, similar to the system used in electric motors.

Apart from the advantage of acting as thrusters and rudders, pods provide for better propulsion efficiency. This is because the hull form can be designed to suit the needs of the water flow into the propeller, there being no conventional propeller shafts to consider in designing the hull form. Propulsion pods are fitted to many ships including, supply vessels for *offshore oil and gas rigs, *ferries, and *cruise ships. The *Queen Mary 2* has four propulsion pods, two fixed and two steerable, which act as thrusters and rudders. For illus. see TUG.

propulsion pod, see PROPELLER: MODERN PROPELLER SYSTEMS.

protection, the name given to the certificate carried by certain classes of men which rendered them immune from *impressment for the navy in Britain. They included *masters and *mates of merchant ships, seamen in outward-bound but not homeward-bound merchant ships (but see MEN-IN-LIEU), a proportion of the crews of *colliers, men employed by the Customs Office, Salt Office, and *Trinity House if laying *buoys, men employed in the royal *dockyards, and the crews of *privateers. Protections were also given to apprentices under 18 and men over 55, if they could prove their age. Harpooners employed in the Greenland *fisheries and fishermen on the east coast during the *herring season were also exempt from the *press gangs and normally carried protections. In general, a man had to prove his trade, and show that it fell into an exempt category, before he could be issued with an official protection. During the Napoleonic (1793–1801) and Revolutionary (1803–1815) Wars against France *Sea Fencibles were also exempt.

protest. **(1)** A formal document drawn up by the *master, first *mate, and a proportion of the crew of a merchant ship at the time of its arrival at a port, and sworn before a notary public, or a consul in a foreign port, that the weather conditions during the voyage were such that if the ship or cargo sustained damage it did not happen through neglect or misconduct on their part. It was a safeguard against the owners of the ship being held accountable for the damage, if any, if the cause of it was stress of wind and weather. One of the conditions of a protest was that the cargo *hatches were not to be removed until a survey had been carried out. It is not a legal requirement in the UK but is necessary in Europe within 24 hours of a ship's arrival. **(2)** See RACING RULES.

proviso. When a ship lay to a single anchor in the stream with its stern held fast to the shore by a *warp, it was said to be *moored a-proviso.

prow, a word used, though rarely by sailors, to describe the *forward end of a vessel. It was also a term used in the 16th and 17th centuries to denote the fore gun-deck of a naval vessel where the *bow-chasers were mounted, and later, in the 17th and 18th centuries, as specifically indicating the *beak of a *felucca or a *xebec.

puddening, a thick matting made of yarns, *oakum, etc., which, like *baggywrinkle, was used during the days of sail in places where there was a danger of chafing. Another form of puddening was fastened round the main and foremasts of *square-rigged sailing warships directly below the *trusses of the *yards, both to guard against undue chafe and to prevent the yards from falling if the *lifts were shot away in battle. It was made by taking a length of rope twice the circumference of the mast and splicing the two ends together to form a *strop, thus doubling it in thickness. A *thimble was then *seized into each end and the doubled rope was *parcelled and *served to an extent where it was thickest in the middle, tapering to each end. It was then *laced to the mast by lacing a *lanyard between the two thimbles. As an extra precaution to prevent it slipping under the weight of the yard if the lifts or sling were shot away, a *garland was passed over it to bind it even more securely to the mast.

In general, puddening was used in all places where undue chafe was likely. In the old days of sail, when anchor *cables were made of *hemp, the rings of anchors were protected with it to stop chafe in the cables. See also PAUNCH.

puffer, a bluff-bowed, Clyde-built, Scottish cargo boat, the heroine of Neil Munro's Para Handy tales, originally designed to fit the locks on the Forth and Clyde Canal. The first, the 20-metre (66-ft) iron-built *Thomas* launched in 1856, acquired the name because of the way her steam engine, which used fresh water from the canal instead of having a *condenser, 'puffed' with every stroke. Later ones had condensers, so they did not 'puff', but they were still called puffers. Simple to operate, by the 1870s three types were in use: those working the Forth and Clyde Canal; the 'shorehead' ones that operated above Bute in the Firth of Clyde and on Loch Fyne; and the longer, 27-metre (88-ft) ones that were employed for trading with outlying Scottish islands. Later ones had *diesel engines though the ones used as *tenders to service the British fleet at *Scapa Flow during both world wars were often steam powered. Puffers were still being built in the 1950s.

pull, to, in most navies, to row a boat with *oars. For some naval reason, boats are not rowed, they are pulled. Perhaps this came about because most naval seamen during the days of sail were not concerned with the finer points of rowing, such as *feathering the oar at the end of a stroke, but concentrated on getting the blade square into the water and pulling it through with maximum force.

pulpit. **(1)** A raised platform in the bows of the old-fashioned *oared *whaleboat from which the harpoon was launched by hand. **(2)** A metal tubular frame, U shaped in plan, at the bow of a *yacht. To it are fixed the *forward ends of the *lifelines or *guardrails rigged for the safety of hands working on deck. See also PUSHPIT.

pump, an essential piece of mechanism on board ship, used for emptying the *bilges of any water which may have collected in them. Three types of pumps were fitted in the old sailing vessels to clear the bilges. A small **hand-pump**, similar to those used ashore, was placed near the mainmast, used when there was only very little water in the bilge and a short spell of pumping would clear it. It was a slow and laborious method. Some ships, particularly Dutch and German ones, used a **burr-pump**, also known as a bilge pump, in which a spar of wood about 1.8 metres (6 ft) long had a burred end to which a leather was fixed. Two men standing over the pump thrust this down into the box in which the bilge water collected, and six men then hauled it up by a rope fixed to it, thus lifting the water which lay on top of the leather. The third type was the **chain-pump**, which worked on a similar system to the burr-pump but with an endless motion so that there was no need for men to thrust it down in the bilge-box on each stroke. This was a most efficient pump, and two men working on it could lift a ton of water in 55 seconds. According to Sir Walter *Raleigh, it was one of the improvements—*bonnets, *studsails, anchor *capstans, and the ability to *strike down a ship's topmast being the others—introduced into the British Navy during his time.

Modern pumps in ships are power driven and are capable of lifting some hundreds of tons of water an hour. Most smaller *yachts have hand-operated diaphragm pumps which are more efficient than the plunger type. In steamships and their modern equivalents there are many other types of pump, used in connection with their internal machinery, such as fuel pumps to feed the boilers, circulating pumps to draw in seawater for the *condensers, feed pumps to return condensed steam to the boilers, trimming pumps to transfer water *ballast from one tank to another, and so on. See also ROSE BOX.

punt. **(1)** A small flat-bottomed craft, built in the form of a floating platform or stage, for men working to *caulk a vessel's waterline seam, to *bream its side, or to repair its bottom. **(2)** A small wooden boat, with sharp pointed bows and stern, and a very low *freeboard, used by wildfowlers in estuaries and local waters. **(3)** A flat-bottomed pleasure boat with square ends and drawing very little water used on rivers and propelled with a pole.

purchase, a mechanical device to increase force, whether by means of levers, gears, or *blocks, or pulleys *rove with a rope or chain. In its maritime meaning it is only the last of these which is known as a purchase: a rope rove through one or more blocks by which the pull exerted on the hauling part of the rope is increased according to the number of *sheaves in the blocks over which it passes.

Where two or more blocks are involved in the purchase, it is generally known as a *tackle, though there are exceptions to this general rule when two double or two treble blocks are used, these being known as twofold and threefold purchases respectively. The blocks of a tackle are known as the standing block and moving block, the rope rove through them is known as the *fall and is divided into three parts known as the *standing, running, and hauling parts. The amount by which the pull on the hauling part is multiplied by the sheaves in the blocks is known as the mechanical *advantage.

Twofold and threefold purchases are used only for heavy lifting, such as hoisting boats

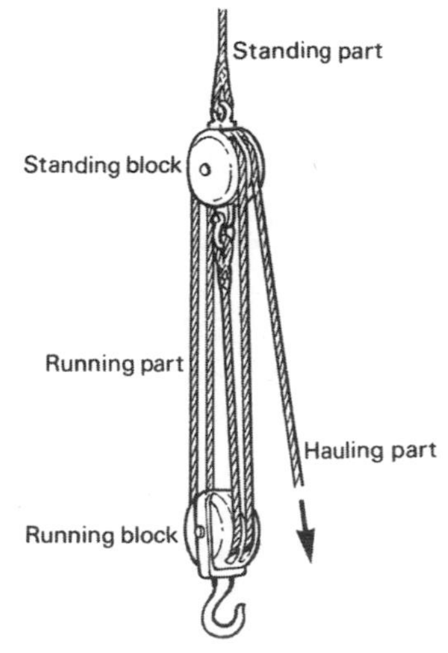

Twofold purchase rove to disadvantage, mechanical gain 2.26

inboard. When rove to advantage, their theoretical mechanical gains are 5 and 7 respectively, when rove to disadvantage, the gains are 4 and 6, though in each case the loss due to friction of the sheaves is considerable since more sheaves are used. Allowing for average friction these gains are reduced to 3.57 and 4.37 when rove to advantage, and 2.26 and 3.75 when rove to disadvantage. See also GUN TACKLE.

purser. **(1)** In the *merchant marine the officer in charge of the financial side of administering a ship's crew, and particularly the passengers of *cruise ships and *ferries. **(2)** The old name by which the paymaster, and officer responsible for provisions and clothing, was known in both the British and US navies during the days of sail. In the British Navy he was placed on board a ship by the *Victualling Board and was paid partly by a small direct salary and partly by a commission on the issue of the daily victualling allowance, a method of payment which led to some abuse of his responsibilities.

purse seine net, used in commercial *fisheries where the bottom can be drawn together after shooting to form a purse so that the *fish enclosed in it cannot escape. It is a means of catching surface fish at sea in cases where a *shoal of fish is visible or where they can be attracted into a small area by the use of powerful lights. The net is paid out around the shoal, from a fishing boat or sometimes from the *sternsheets of a rowing boat, the *warps from each end of the net being brought on board the fishing vessel. The bottom warps are then hauled in to close the purse seine underneath the shoal and, with the fish firmly enclosed, the whole net is hauled alongside and brought aboard, and the catch is deposited in the *hold.

pushpit, term for the curved tubular frame at the stern of a *yacht which carries the after ends of the *guardrails. It is a comparatively modern word which was perhaps introduced as an antonym for a yacht's *pulpit.

Q

Q-ship, a small merchant ship fitted with a concealed armament used by the British Navy during both world wars as a lure for German *submarines.

quadrant, from Latin *quadrans*, the fourth part. **(1)** The name given to a variety of nautical astronomical instruments. See CROSS-STAFF; DAVIS'S QUADRANT; HADLEY'S REFLECTING QUADRANT; QUINTANT; SEAMAN'S QUADRANT. **(2)** The quarter of a circle, used particularly in relation to the *magnetic compass card graduated in degrees instead of *points. **(3)** A fitting on a ship's *rudder which received the steering wires.

quadrilateral jib, see DOUBLE-CLEWED JIB.

quadruple expansion engine, see TRIPLE EXPANSION ENGINE.

quarantine, a harbour restriction placed on a ship which has an infectious disease on board or has arrived from a port or country which is notoriously unhealthy. While under quarantine the vessel must fly 'Q' flag in the *International Code of Signals, a square yellow flag usually known as the yellow *jack. Its crew may not land until either the infectious period has elapsed or it is granted *pratique as free from disease. These quarantine laws originated in the Council of Health held in Venice in the 14th century.

quarter, one of the two *after parts of the ship, one on each side of the centreline. Strictly, a ship's *port or *starboard quarter is on a bearing 45° from the stern, but the term is more often rather loosely applied to any point approximately on that bearing. Hence a **quartering wind**. The term is also applied to the direction from which the wind is blowing if it looks like remaining there for some time, e.g. the wind is in the south-west quarter. For illus. see RELATIVE BEARINGS.

quarter bands, the bands with which the arms of the centreline *truss are secured to the *yards of *square-riggers. They are also called **truss bands**. Colin Mudie

quarter-bill, a nominal list of officers and men in a warship which gave the **action station** of every man on board when the ship went into battle. It was the origin of the naval order to **'beat to quarters'** where the drummers aboard a sailing man-of-war beat to a particular rhythm, *'Heart of Oak', to indicate that men must go to their battle stations. See also WATCH-BILL.

quarter blocks. (1) Blocks attached to the *quarter bands of the *yards of *square-rigged ships. They are used to turn down to the deck running *rigging, such as the sheets of an upper sail and *clew lines of the lower sail, that runs along the yard. **(2)** Blocks on the deck on each side of the stern to take the mainsail or *spanker sheets, or to take the sheets of light headsails such as *spinnakers. For illus. see YARD.

quarter-cloths, strips of *canvas, normally painted red, which were fixed on the outboard side of the *nettings, extending from the *quarter galleries to the *gangways, in the sailing warships of most navies. Their purpose was to protect the *hammocks, stowed by day in the nettings, from any seas breaking aboard. See also TOP-ARMOURS.

quarterdeck, that part of the upper deck of a ship which is *abaft the mainmast or, with powered ships, approximately abaft of where the mainmast would be. In medieval British warships, the religious shrine was set up at the break of the quarterdeck and was saluted by every man as he passed it by taking off his hat or cap. This led to the habit in British warships of saluting whenever the quarterdeck was entered, a tradition still observed in the Royal Navy.

In sailing ships it is the part of the ship from which it was commanded by the captain or *master, or by the officer of the *watch, as there was no *bridge in sailing ships. It was also traditionally the part of the ship where the captain used to walk, usually on the *starboard side, when he came on deck to take the air or oversee the conduct of the ship, and also from which the *navigator took his *sights when *fixing the vessel's position. It was the custom in most ships that only officers might use the quarterdeck, ratings being allowed there only when detailed for specific duties.

quarter gallery, a small *gallery on each *quarter of a ship, with balustrades in the larger ships, which communicated with the stern gallery. Like the large gallery in the stern, they were used to provide a private walking space for the occupant of the *cabin with which they communicated. Also like the stern gallery, they were, in vessels such as warships and *East Indiamen, highly decorated with carvings. Galleries and quarter galleries first made an appearance in the late 14th or early 15th centuries and were still in use in the larger warships in the form of a sternwalk until the second decade of the 20th century.

quarter-gunner, a *petty officer in the days of sailing navies whose duty it was to assist the gunner of the ship in keeping the guns and their carriages in proper order, scaling the barrels when necessary, filling the cartridges with powder, etc. Quarter-gunners were appointed in each ship at the rate of one for every four guns.

quartermaster, originally a *petty officer appointed to assist the *master of a ship and his *mates in such duties as stowing the *hold, coiling the *cables, etc. It is now a term more generally applied to the senior helmsman who takes over when a ship is entering or leaving harbour. In the past he was also concerned with the upkeep and use of much of the navigational equipment, such as *sounding machines, patent *log, *lead and lines, etc.

quatuor maria, an old term, dating from the reign of Queen Mary I (1553–8), for the four British seas surrounding Great Britain. The term arose when there was trouble with France over the *salutes at sea demanded by English ships in these waters, now known as the North Sea, English Channel, Irish Sea, and the Atlantic Ocean bordering the Scottish west coast. Quatuor was the Tudor way of spelling quattuor, which is the better Latin.

quay, a projection, usually constructed of stone, along the boundaries of a harbour to provide accommodation for ships to lie alongside for the loading or unloading of cargo, embarkation and disembarkation of passengers, etc. When a quay is built out from the harbour boundary into the water, it is usually called a *mole. See also WHARF.

quick flashing light, a navigational light displayed by a navigational aid such as a *lightship in which quick flashes of less than one second duration are shown. See CHARACTERISTIC.

quickwork, the planking of a ship's *bulwarks between the *ports in a sailing man-of-war. Also that part of the inner upperworks above the *covering board in a wooden ship. See also SPIRKETTING, with which quickwork is largely synonymous.

quilting, the name given to *paunch matting secured to the outer planking of a wooden-hulled vessel to protect it against *drift ice.

quintant, a reflecting navigational instrument on the same general lines as a *quadrant or *sextant, and used specifically for calculating *lunar distance. Its arc subtended a fifth of a circle, or 72°, hence its name. Because of its reflecting property, it was able to measure angles of up to 144°. See also CELESTIAL NAVIGATION.

quoin, a wedge used to elevate a ship's cannon in the days of the sailing navies in order to obtain a greater range. They were also used to separate casks of wine, spirits, or oil when stowed on board so that their *bilges should not rub against each other or get stove in during rough weather.

rabbet, from the word rebate, an incision in a piece of timber to receive the ends or sides of planks which are to be secured to it. It is also used as a verb, so that the keel of a wooden ship is **rabbeted** to receive the sides of the *garboard *strakes, and the *stem and *sternpost are similarly rabbeted to take the ends of the side strakes. See also SHIPBUILDING.

rabelo, Portuguese working boat employed from at least the 9th century to transport wine downriver to Oporto. It was about 20 metres (65 ft) in length, had a large square sail, and was guided by a very long steering *oar, hence the vessel's name *barco rabelo*, meaning 'boat with a tail'. The oar, which made the rabelo very manoeuvrable, was operated by a crew member from a high platform and its *loom was counterweighted so that its blade remained immersed at the vessel's approximate *draught. Rabelos are no longer in use but some have been retained by the wine companies for local regattas.

race. (1) The name generally used to describe strong and confused *currents produced by the narrowness of channels, an uneven bottom producing *overfalls, or the crossing of two *tides. **(2)** As a verb, it describes the action of a ship's *propeller when the ship *pitches to the extent that the propeller is occasionally lifted out of the water. The lack of water resistance will cause the engine, and thus the propeller, to race, with a consequent strain on the engine.

racing rules. When taking part in a boat race, the participants agree to be subject to the racing rules which take the place of the *International Regulations for Preventing Collisions at Sea. The racing rules are produced by the *International Sailing Federation (ISAF), in which each country is represented by its national authority, and are revised every four years. No changes are envisaged until 2009. They are largely based on the Collision Regulations but differ from them in several important respects, particularly when boats are rounding marks or obstructions. When a boat that is racing meets a boat that is not, the Collision Regulations apply to both of them.

There are 89 racing rules divided into seven parts: (1) Fundamental Rules; (2) When Boats Meet; (3) Conduct of a Race; (4) Other Requirements When Racing; (5) Protests, Hearings, Misconduct, and Appeals; (6) Entry and Qualification; and (7) Race Organization. These are accompanied by sixteen appendices which cover such matters as the racing rules for sailboards, and match and team racing; Appeals Procedures; Identification on Sails; Banned Substances and Banned Methods; and Recommendations for Protest Committees. When the rules of an appendix apply, they take precedence over any conflicting rules in parts 1–7.

A *yacht engaged in a race is bound by the racing rules from the time she intends to race until she has left the vicinity of the course. However, she can normally be penalized for breaking a rule only when the incident occurs after the preparatory signal (which is almost invariably four minutes before the start of the race) and before clearing the finishing line having finished the race. To be eligible to race in any event under the racing rules a yacht must have on board, as the owner or his representative, a member of a *yacht club recognized by the appropriate national authority.

The basic 'when yachts meet' rules are similar to those that apply to sailing vessels in the Collision Regulations. Thus, when on opposite *tacks, a yacht on the *starboard tack has the right of way over the yacht on *port tack. When yachts are on the same tack, an overlapped yacht to *windward keeps clear of the yacht to *leeward, and a yacht clear *astern must keep clear of the yacht ahead.

Yachts racing have to manoeuvre in close proximity to each other, so the racing rules are designed to place clear obligations and rights to enable them to do so in safety. If during a race one yacht is being overtaken on her windward side by another, the leeward yacht has the right to *luff right up until she is head to wind if she likes. However, she must do so in such a way as to allow the windward yacht an opportunity to keep clear. The windward yacht must keep clear. When a yacht establishes an overlap to leeward of another yacht she becomes the right-of-way yacht but she must initially give room to the windward yacht to fulfil her new obligation to keep clear. However, the leeward yacht must sail no higher than her proper *course while the overlap exists and they remain within two lengths of each other. (This situation would be different under the Collision Regulations, where the overtaking boat would be required to keep clear.)

There are special rules that apply to yachts that are rounding or passing a mark or an obstruction. A yacht that has an inside overlap when the leading yacht comes within two lengths of a mark or obstruction has the right to room to round it, even if the overlap is broken inside the 'two lengths' zone. However, the outside yacht must be able to give the required room when the overlap was first established. If there is doubt about whether or not there was an overlap at two lengths, the doubt is resolved against a yacht claiming she was clear ahead having broken an earlier overlap, and against a yacht claiming a late inside overlap.

Another rule governs the situation when two yachts on the same tack are approaching an obstruction (which may be shallows or other dangers). When on a *close-hauled course and needing to tack, a yacht that cannot tack without risk of collision with another yacht behind or to windward may hail for room to tack. The hailed yacht must immediately tack, or reply 'you tack' and take on the responsibility to keep clear.

Another racing rule governs the rights of yachts at the start of a race. If any part of a yacht is on the course side of the starting line at the moment of her starting signal, she must return wholly behind the line and restart, while keeping clear of other yachts that have started correctly.

A yacht which touches a mark of the course during a race may exonerate herself by sailing well clear of other participants and making a turn including a tack and a *gybe. A yacht involved in an incident with another competitor which accepts that she is to blame may sail clear and make a 'two-turn penalty' which must include two tacks and two gybes. When neither accepts the blame for an incident, one or both may protest by shouting 'protest' and, if her overall length is 6 metres (19.7 ft) or more, by prominently displaying a red flag, and leaving it displayed until the end of the race. The protesting boat must then submit a written protest with the race committee, explaining her grounds for doing so.

As soon as possible after the race, a protest committee is appointed to hear the protest. Evidence is taken from the representatives and their witnesses. After assessing the evidence, the committee makes a decision and the parties are informed. The penalty for having been found to have broken a rule is usually disqualification from the race.

For most match racing (just two competing boats) events, such as the *America's Cup, umpires in an umpire boat accompany the competitors. One competing boat is identified by a blue flag on her backstay, the other by a yellow flag. In response to a protest flag, the umpires display a green and white flag when they decide no penalty is appropriate, or a blue or yellow flag to indicate which boat must take a penalty turn. The penalty may be taken any time after starting and before finishing. Umpiring is also sometimes used for small fleet races.

Bryan Willis

rack, to, to hold two ropes together temporarily with *marline or other small line in order to bind them firmly and prevent *rendering or slipping. This is done by taking the marline under and over each rope alternately and crossing it between them two or three times, much in the fashion of a series of figures of eight. This type of *seizing is often used to prevent a *tackle slipping when the hauling part is being secured if the strain on it is so great that the tackle cannot be held with the hands without overrunning. If a more permanent junction of two ropes is required, this is done by passing a **racking seizing** round them, as above but with more turns of

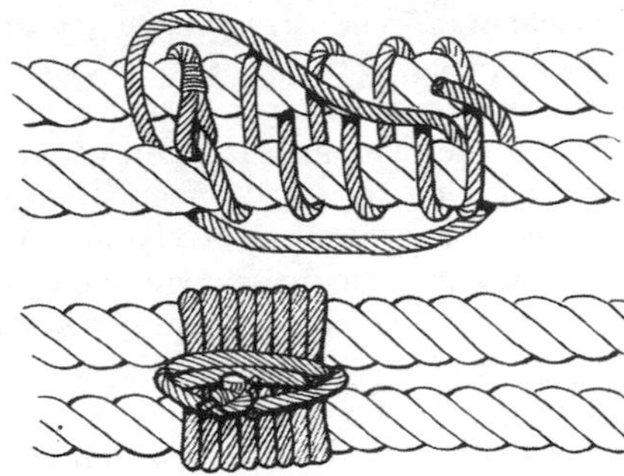

Racking seizing

the marline and the ends of it secured by tucking back under the turns.

racon, a transponder radar beacon fitted to many *lighthouses, *lightships, and *buoys which transmits a powerful signal when triggered by a transmission from a vessel's *radar. With racon buoys this facilitates detection and identification and overcomes the problem of sea-clutter which can obscure their presence.

radar, an acronym for Radio Detection and Ranging, a system for determining the range and bearing of an object by transmitting bursts of electromagnetic energy and timing the intervals between the transmission and return of the echoes. The main purposes of radar at sea are for collision avoidance and *navigation in poor visibility. The wavelength of seaborne radar is for the most part 3 cm or 10 cm; some ships carry both. There are several types of display for marine radar, the most common of which is the plan position indicator (PPI) which is either 'head-up' where the top of the display corresponds with the ship's heading, or stabilized where true *bearings are indicated. On true-motion radar, which is largely used for anti-collision, the origin on the display moves with the vessel. See also RACON; RAMARK; REMOTE SENSING.

Mike Richey

radar reflector, a device, generally a metallic corner reflector, that enhances the echo returned from a vessel or *buoy or sea-mark. Most small vessels that can be expected to give weak echoes mount them.

raddle, the name given to describe small lines such as *codline when they are interwoven to make flat *gaskets, or *gripes, for securing boats when hoisted on the *davits of a ship.

radio beacon, a land-based radio station which transmits characteristic medium-frequency radio signals the bearing of which can be measured from a ship fitted with a *radio direction finder and so provide the navigator with a *position line. For this purpose the system is now largely obsolete, but radio beacon stations are now used in over 30 countries, including most European maritime countries, for monitoring DGPS (Differential Global Navigation Satellite System) services for *satellite navigation. When the network is complete some 126 stations will be operational.

Mike Richey

radio direction finder, a navigational instrument, no longer in general use, by which the *bearing of a *radio beacon may be obtained and plotted on the *chart. Initial experiments in radio direction finding took place early in the 20th century and the first ship to be fitted with a radio receiver designed to take bearings was the *ocean liner *Mauretania*, in 1911. By the 1950s they were common aboard fishing vessels and even the smallest offshore *yacht.

raffee, a triangular topsail set between a standing *yard and the masthead of topsail *schooners. It is usually *furled to the yard and hoisted by a *halyard.

Colin Mudie

raft. **(1)** With the *dugout, perhaps man's earliest form of marine transport. The seagoing bamboo sailing raft of Taiwan, used for raids on the Chinese coast as far back as the 8th century, is a likely progenitor of the Chinese *junk, and rafts for transporting goods can still be seen on some Chinese rivers. Similar craft were used in Indo-China. Balsawood sailing rafts, which were manoeuvred by *centreboards only, were also widely employed off the coasts of Peru and Ecuador, and the northern coast of Brazil, in the days of the Inca. Thor *Heyerdahl constructed both a balsawood raft, and Egyptian ones made of papyrus, for his epic voyages across the Pacific and the Atlantic. **(2)** A flat, floating framework of *spars, planks, or other timber formerly used to carry goods or cargo from the shore to a ship lying off for loading on board. Similarly a temporary platform made on board for *lifesaving as a substitute for a boat. **(3)** Lumber, cut inland, lashed together, and floated down a river to the sea, is also known as a raft.

rake. **(1)** The angle, in relation to the perpendicular, of a ship's masts and funnels, which can be raked *forward or *aft. It is a word also sometimes used to describe the degree of overhang of its bow and stern. **(2)** As a verb, it describes the operation of manoeuvring a warship so that it could fire its guns down the length of an adversary. The manoeuvre was particularly used during the days of sailing navies when a ship's main cannons could fire broadsides only. This was why wooden *ships of the line were built immensely strong on their sides, with oak or teak planking 38–46 centimetres (15–18 in.) thick. Their weakest point was at the stern with its wide *galleries and windows. If a warship could manoeuvre to cross the stern of an enemy at right angles, it could fire its guns through the stern, creating immense damage and slaughter, without its adversary being able to reply. Almost equally advantageous was to cross its bows at right angles, as this part of the ship was also a weak point defensively. See also CROSSING THE T.

Raleigh, or **Ralegh, Sir Walter** *c.*1552–1618), English adventurer and explorer, born near Budleigh Salterton, Devon. As a young man he fought with the French Huguenots and attended Oriel College, Oxford.

Raleigh, whose name was almost certainly pronounced Rawley by his contemporaries, had a half-brother, Sir Humphrey Gilbert (*c.*1539–83), who, in 1578, obtained a patent from Elizabeth I to 'discover and take possession of any remote, barbarous and heathen lands not possessed by any Christian prince or people'. This was the type of adventure which had long attracted the gentlemen of Devon, and Raleigh accompanied Gilbert. However, the expedition was driven back after an engagement in the Atlantic, and a second expedition the following year was equally disastrous. Raleigh was forced to look elsewhere for his livelihood and attached himself to the court in London, obtaining employment as captain of a company of soldiers sent to Ireland to suppress the rebellion of the Desmonds in Ireland. He played a significant, if somewhat unsavoury, part in the ruthless defeat of the rebels, resorting to massacre and assassination.

He returned to England at the end of 1581, and immediately became a favourite of Queen Elizabeth I, who showered honours and rewards upon him—he was knighted in 1585—and he grew exceedingly rich with the grants and monopolies he received from her. Among them was nearly 65,000 acres of the land forfeited by the Desmonds after the rebellion; here he introduced the potato as a suitable crop, and attempted the cultivation of tobacco. He probably did lay his cloak over a puddle that the queen might walk dry-shod over it, and it is equally possible that he did scribble a verse with a diamond on a pane of glass where he was sure the queen would see it.

When Gilbert's patent ran out the year after his death, Raleigh had it renewed in his own favour, and used it to start a series of expeditions. In theory, these were designed to settle colonists in the new land of Virginia, but in practice they were an attempt to discover gold and silver mines. These expeditions were all unsuccessful and Raleigh claimed to have lost as much as £40,000 through them.

During 1588, the year of the *Spanish Armada, Raleigh was appointed vice admiral of Devon, a legal and administrative post, and he took no part in the defeat of the Spaniards. The following year he took part in an expedition to the coast of Portugal to foster a revolt against Philip II of Spain. This failed miserably, and, with the rise of the Earl of Essex as the queen's prime favourite, Raleigh's popularity with his sovereign now declined. He finally fell from favour in 1592 when the queen discovered his marriage to her maid of honour Elizabeth Throckmorton. Both Raleigh and his wife were imprisoned in the Tower of London and though Raleigh managed to buy their release he never regained his importance at the royal court. Raleigh then retired with his wife to an estate in Dorset, but in an effort to find favour with his queen he left for South America in 1595 to sail up the Orinoco River in search of the mythical golden city Eldorado. He found no gold, but wrote an account of his voyage in *The Discoverie of Guiana* which was more romantic than truthful; and though his attack on Cadiz in 1596 was largely successful the queen remained unimpressed.

Sir Walter Raleigh; miniature by N. Hilliard, *c.*1585

The death of Queen Elizabeth spelled Raleigh's ruin. One by one his estates and privileges, granted by the queen, were stripped from him. He was accused, perhaps with reason, of taking part in conspiracies against the life of James I, who succeeded Elizabeth in 1603. He was condemned to death, but instead of execution was confined in the Tower. However, James was chronically short of money, and in 1616 Raleigh was released on condition he discovered a gold mine in Guiana for the king without infringing any Spanish possession. This was impossible, as Spain had many settlements there. When the Spanish ambassador in London pointed this out, the king promised the ambassador that if a clash with the Spaniards did occur he would execute Raleigh on his return.

The ships reached the mouth of the Orinoco at the end of 1617. Raleigh, who was sick with fever and remained at Trinidad, sent five small vessels up the river under the command of his most trusted captain. Inevitably, they found a Spanish settlement in the way and fighting broke out in which Raleigh's son was killed, as well as some Spaniards. After a fruitless search for a gold mine, the vessels returned. Their commander committed suicide, and when the expedition returned home Raleigh was arrested and executed on 29 October 1618. He died, a brave man, with dignity and serenity.

During much of his life Raleigh was unpopular in England, particularly during his time as a favourite of Queen Elizabeth, mainly because of the grasping and extortionist means by which he built up his fortune. But with the death of the queen the mood changed. His hatred of Spain endeared him to a public that was suspicious of King James's close relations with that country, and the patent falsity of Raleigh's trial in 1603, and his long years in captivity in the Tower, made him a popular hero. His execution, at the Spanish ambassador's instigation and insistence, enhanced his popularity; and he has remained one of the heroes of Elizabethan England, whose name is linked with such men as Sir Francis *Drake, Sir Martin *Frobisher, and Sir John *Hawkins. He also had a persuasive pen, and his literary and historical works rank him among the first strategic writers on sea power.

Greenblatt, S. J., *Sir Walter Raleigh* (1973).
Hyland, P., *Ralegh's Last Journey* (2003).
Irwin, M., *That Great Lucifer* (1960).

ram. **(1)** A strengthened or armoured projection from a warship's bow used to disable or sink an enemy ship by ramming it. The rowed war *galleys of the Mediterranean were fitted with a sharp spike in their bows for this purpose. The ram as a naval weapon disappeared during the age of sail but made its reappearance when *steam propulsion was adopted by the world's navies. The best-known case of the ram being used successfully was when the Austrian *ironclad *Ferdinand Maximilian* rammed and sank the Italian *battleship *Re d'Italia* at the battle of Lissa in 1866. This success, allied to certain disasters in peacetime manoeuvres when ships were sunk after being accidentally rammed—for example, the *Vanguard* and *Iron Duke* in 1875 and the *Victoria* and *Camperdown* in 1893—prolonged the life of the ram far beyond its use as a practicable weapon in *warfare at sea, and most ironclads built up to the beginning of the 20th century were fitted with ram bows. The word was also used to describe a warship whose offensive power was centred mainly on its ram, a type extensively built by both sides in the American Civil War of 1861–5. During the 1860s both the French and British navies built warships specifically for ramming, and the British continued to build such ships until 1884. See also BULBOUS BOW.

(2) As a verb, an operation of war by which an attempt to sink an opponent by ramming it is made. During both world wars a number of warships, particularly *submarines, were sunk by being rammed. The word generally indicates a conscious act to sink an enemy, and although occasionally used for the purpose, does not properly cover the sinking of a vessel through an accidental collision.

ramark, a transponder radar beacon fitted to some *lighthouses, *lightships, and *buoys which transmits a powerful signal. Unlike a *racon, it does not have to be triggered by a vessel's radar.

ram schooner, the description of a *schooner which does not set *topmasts but is rigged with pole masts only. It is also sometimes known as a bald-headed schooner.

randan, a method of balancing three rowers in a boat so that equal thrust is generated on either side. Stroke and bow row one *oar each while the man in the centre rows a pair of oars.

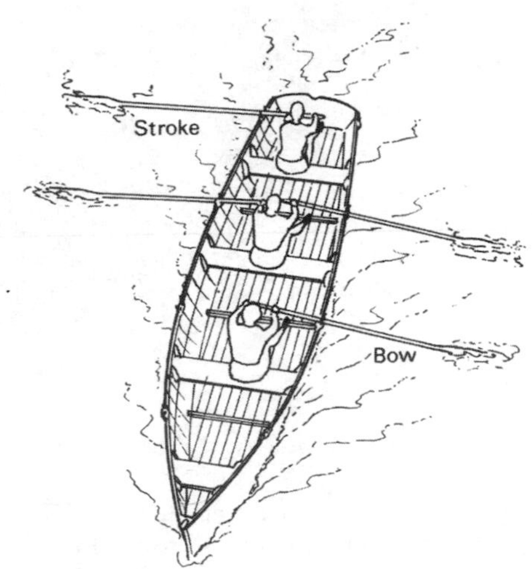

Randan

random range, the usual description of the maximum range of a warship's muzzle-loading guns during the days of sailing navies. It was anything up to 1,600 metres (2 mls.), according to the bore of the gun, the length of the barrel, and the weight of the charge of powder used. It was called random, as a gunner was not expected to hit an enemy ship at the maximum range of his gun, but might possibly do so with a lucky shot. Random range was rarely used in battle, ships usually preferring to get within *half-musket shot before firing their *broadsides. However, it was employed when in a *chase, or when being chased, in the hope that a lucky shot would damage a mast or *rigging.

range, to, the operation of heaving the anchor *cable of ships up from the *chain lockers and laying it out on deck. It was then examined to discover the presence of weak links, if any.

Ransome, Arthur (1884–1967), British journalist and author, a man of wide attainments, both in the literary field and as a fisherman and yachtsman. As a youth, books, fishing, and sailing absorbed his interests, and his first job after leaving school was in a small publishing firm. From that he turned to journalism, contributed notes and articles on fishing to many journals, and between 1909 and 1912 wrote three books, *A History of Story-Telling*, *The Hoofmarks of the Fawn*, and a book on Oscar Wilde which landed him in a libel action brought by Lord Alfred Douglas. In 1913 he went to Russia to learn the language, working as a newspaper correspondent in Moscow, and in 1916 he published *Old Peter's Russian Tales*, which sold well. While in the Baltic, he had a 13-ton *ketch, *Racundra*, built at Riga, and later wrote *Racundra's First Cruise* (1923) about his voyages in her.

In 1924 he married Evgenia Shelepin, who had been Trotsky's secretary. A serious illness cut short his career as a correspondent and he was forced to live carefully and quietly in the Lake District. It was during this period of convalescence that his mind turned towards writing the books which were to win the hearts and imaginations of a host of young readers worldwide, for he knew at first hand the ways of a boat in the water and he was able to impart that knowledge and lore in a way that was real to children. The first two, *Swallows and Amazons* (1930) and *Swallowdale* (1931), were only moderately successful, but the third, *Peter Duck* (1932), established his reputation. The last *Great Northern?*, was published in 1947. Papers released in 2005 revealed that he was recruited into the British Secret Intelligence service, or MI6, in 1919 while he was living in Russia.

Brogan, H., *The Life of Arthur Ransome* (1984).

rate. (1) The six divisions into which warships of almost all sailing navies were grouped according to the number of guns carried. The system was introduced in Britain by *Anson during his first term as First Lord of the *Admiralty between 1751 and 1756, but some naval writers have antedated it for the sake of convenience in describing earlier warships. For example, HMS *Resolution*, *launched in 1610, is frequently described as a first rate of 80 guns, meaning that she was one of the largest ships of her time in the British Navy and could therefore be considered a first rate. Later, first-rate ships were those that carried from 100 or 110 guns upwards, the change from 100 to 110 coming in 1810. Second rates carried from 84 (later 90) to 100 (110); third rates 70 (80); fourth rates 50 (60) to 79 (80); fifth rates 32 to 50 (60); and sixth rates, any number of guns up to 32 if commanded by a *post-captain. Such ships when commanded by a commander were rated as *sloops. Only ships of the first three rates were considered to be sufficiently powerful to be in the *line of battle in actions between main fleets. Ships of the fifth and sixth rates were generally known as *frigates; fourth-rate ships, of which very few were built, did not lie in the line of battle, except occasionally in the smaller fleets. It was not until 1817 that *carronades, first introduced into the Royal Navy in 1779, were included in the number of guns which decided the rating of a ship. **(2)** The rate, or rating, used to describe a seaman in a warship, but more accurately the status of seamen, corresponding to rank with officers. Men hold rates according to their abilities, the normal chain of *lower-deck promotion in the British Navy being ordinary seaman, able seaman, leading seaman, *petty officer, chief petty officer, with similar steps in most other navies.

rate of change, a correction applied to the reading of a *chronometer. This was done when a ship's *navigator worked out the *Greenwich Mean Time (GMT) of an observation of a heavenly body by *sextant to *fix his ship's position. Until well into the 20th century no man-made ship's chronometer was free of error, usually gaining or losing a second or two every day. If this rate of gain, or loss, known as the chronometer's rate of change, was calculated, it could then be applied to each reading to produce the exact time of the observation, and thus GMT. See also CELESTIAL NAVIGATION.

rating. For a seaman's rank see RATE (2). Otherwise, it is a calculation of a *yacht's expected performance relative to another yacht during a race, based on the physical measurements, and other definable characteristics, of the yacht. Two early methods in Britain of physical measuring were the *Builders Old Measurement and *Thames Measurement, but a common variant nowadays is performance handicap where observed performance, rather than physical measurement, is the determining factor. These rules are best suited to local racing because of the difficulty of assessing comparative performance across wide areas. In North America by far the most popular rule of this type is the well-established **Performance Handicap Racing Fleet (PHRF)**. This has been in use for many years and a version of it is used in other countries around the world. The **Portsmouth Yardstick** is the British equivalent. With this, the results of handicap racing are sent by clubs to the *Royal Yachting Association, which calculates a national figure for each class of boat. The result is a Portsmouth number and the corrected time (CT) is obtained with the formula CT = (Elapsed Time × 1000)/Portsmouth number.

However, the most widely used rating rules are still based on measurement, the principle underlying them being that a yacht's ultimate speed is related to her length. This speed is only reached in stronger winds, and the amount of sail area that a yacht carries, and also her *displacement, will affect her performance. Most rules therefore specify a measurement of length, which is usually some combination of the waterline length and the bow and stern overhangs, if any.

There are also rules for the measurement of sail areas in the different parts of the rig. The displacement of the yacht will be included in some form, either by weighing or by full measurement of the hull shape and then flotation depth. Corrections are also included for items such as *beam, *draught, *freeboard, engines and *propellers, *centreboards, and keels, all of which have some effect on a yacht's performance. Some measurement of *stability or *ballast ratio is also necessary.

The most common methods for combining these individual measurements to produce rating are either formula rules, where a series of linked formulae combine to produce the rating, or velocity prediction programme (VPP) rules. In the latter the performance of the yacht is mathematically predicted under a range of conditions using a computer program, and the rating derived from the outcome. Historically, ratings were expressed in linear units of feet or metres with race organizers then applying time allowances to them. More recently, ratings have been directly expressed as time allowances.

There have been many rating rules since *yachting became a popular sport and *yacht designers have always been ingenious in evading them. The earliest rating rules were intended to restrict the variations of proportions of yachts within classes that were to race without handicap. Examples of these rules were the rater classes of the late 19th century and the *International Metre Classes where the actual rules differed in their values and limits in determining the various metre class yachts which raced from 1907. More properly, these variants on rating rules are known as 'box' rules because they simply impose dimensional restrictions and do not generally incorporate any form of time allowance. Some of these classes are, as classic yachts, still competing today, perhaps the best known being the 12-metre which was used in the *America's Cup races from 1958 to 1987. In the USA the *Universal Rule was used the same way to rate the various classes, including the *J-class, until the International Rule which governed the metre classes was gradually adopted.

Between the two world wars the advent of ocean racing (see YACHTING: SAIL) required the use of rating rules under which cruising yachts of different types and sizes could race together with time allowances. The best known and most widely used were those devised by two *yacht clubs, the **Cruising Club of America** and the **Royal Ocean Racing Club (RORC)**. Both required a yacht to be measured manually by a measurer so its rating could be calculated. The two rules were brought together in 1970 to become the **International Offshore Rating Rule (IOR)**, Mk. II. Mk. III was introduced in 1973, and in November 1975 Mk. IIIA was introduced to cover existing yachts that were not out-and-out racing machines. The IOR rule governed ocean racing internationally until it was gradually replaced in the 1980s. The last large regatta to use it exclusively was the One Ton Cup held at Marseille in 1994, by which time the **Channel Handicap System (CHS)** and the **Measurement Handicap System (MHS)**, which became the **International Measurement System (IMS)** in 1985, were in the ascendancy.

Unlike IOR, which had become expensive and complicated, CHS was cheap and simple—boats did not need to be measured for it. Devised by the RORC and UNCL (Union Nationale de la Course au Large), the RORC's French equivalent, both clubs developed it and agreed to keep the formula secret to thwart designers trying to optimize it.

IMS, originally an American system, was introduced around the same time as CHS for high-level racing. IMS evolved from a system of measurement and computer prediction of speed developed in the 1970s by the Massachusetts Institute of Technology (MIT). In the past, yachts had always had to be measured manually to produce the measurements required to rate them. The MIT system employs a VPP to assess the potential speed of a boat. The data is obtained by measuring the hull with an electronic wand which transmits it to a computer, defining the entire geometrical shape of the hull, keel, and rudder. From the *hydrodynamics of this, and the *aerodynamics of the rig, the VPP calculates the boat's potential speed in a variety of wind speeds and directions. Unlike other rating rules, IMS provides a yacht with different time allowances for the actual course sailed during a race and the strength of wind encountered.

IMS has never been adopted to the same extent worldwide as IOR. In 1999, the RORC and UNCL introduced **IR2000**, a two-level rating system. At the lower level **IRC** is a development of CHS and was recognized by the *International Sailing Federation as an international rating system in 2003. It is now used extensively all around the world. IRM was intended as a high-level international rating rule but to date has only been adopted in British waters. In 2004, IRC and IRM were separated into two separate rules with the overall IR2000 name being dropped.

Johnson, P., *Yacht Rating* (1997).

ratline, one of a series of rope steps up the *shrouds of a mast, 38–40 centimetres (15–16 in.) apart, by which men working aloft in *square-rigged ships reach the *yards via the *tops and *crosstrees. In the days of sail, ratlines normally were made of 18-thread tarred rope with an *eye in each end and *seized to the outermost shrouds, being secured to each intermediate shroud by a *clove hitch.

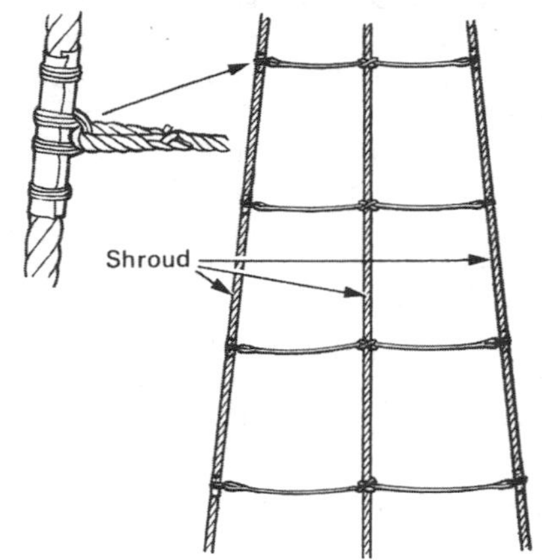

Ratline

rattle down, to, to secure the *ratlines to the *shrouds with a series of *clove hitches round each shroud except the foremost and aftermost, where the ratline is *seized to the shroud through an *eye.

razee, or **rasee,** a *ship of the line which had its upper works taken off so that the vessel was reduced by one deck; thus a razed two-decker would become a heavy *frigate. The word was used both as a noun and a verb, and was taken from the French *raser,* to cut.

reach. **(1)** The *point of sailing of a vessel which can point its *course with the wind reasonably *free and its sails full. A **broad reach** is the same but with the wind *abeam or from slightly *abaft the *beam. For illus. see POINTS OF SAILING. It can also be used as a verb. **(2)** A straight, or nearly straight, stretch of a navigable river or estuary. Thus a vessel coming up the River Thames will, after passing Tilbury, navigate through Long Reach, Erith Reach, Halfway Reach, Barking Reach, Gallion's Reach, Woolwich Reach, and Limehouse Reach. **(3)** As a verb, the act of sailing a vessel with the sails full and the wind free. A sailing vessel which overtakes another is sometimes said to reach ahead of her. It was also a word used to describe a sailing vessel when she was standing off and on, waiting perhaps to pick up a *pilot or for some other purposes. See also FORE-REACH.

'ready about', the order in a sailing vessel to be prepared to *tack. See also ABOUT; 'LEE-OH'.

reciprocating engine, a form of steam engine in which a piston moves back and forth inside a cylinder, transmitting its motion by connecting rod and crank to a driving shaft. Reciprocating engines used at sea to drive a *propeller shaft were usually installed so that the pistons moved vertically up and down the cylinders, but in some cases were installed to give a horizontal movement. After the introduction of the steam turbine at the end of the 19th century, the commonest form of ship's reciprocating engines, which had their cylinders in line above the crankshaft, were called by their crews the 'up and downers'.

Reciprocating engines were 'double-acting' which means that steam would be admitted on the top of the piston to force it downwards while the space below the piston would be open to exhaust so that the exhaust steam would go to the *condenser. When the piston reached the bottom of the stroke, steam would be admitted to the space below the piston to force it upwards, and the space above the piston would be open to exhaust. See also COMPOUND ENGINE; SIDE LEVER ENGINE; STEAM PROPULSION; TRIPLE EXPANSION ENGINE.

reckoning, the record of *courses steered and distances made good through the water from the time the ship's position was last reliably fixed. In the days of sail this record would be kept on a log-slate on which the times of altering course, and the distances made on each course as indicated by the *log, were chalked up on the slate. At the end of each *watch the record was transferred to the *log book and the relieving officer of the *watch began his watch with a clean slate. Hence the expression **'to start with a clean slate'**.

red ensign. After the division of the British fleet by *squadronal colours was abolished in 1864, the red ensign, or **red duster** as it is colloquially called, became the *ensign of the British merchant fleet. Today it is flown by all British merchant vessels and most *yachts. Some yachts are entitled to fly it defaced on the *hoist, normally by the insignia of the *yacht club they belong to, provided their owners have the requisite warrant from the *Admiralty. See also BLUE ENSIGN; WHITE ENSIGN.

red tides are caused by blooms of planktonic *marine plants (phytoplankton) that discolour the water. They occur especially in regions where *upwelling stimulates rapid growth in the algae, but their geographical range has been expanding and the frequency of their occurrence has been increasing, probably because of eutrophication, an important *environmental issue. Some red tides are merely nuisances, producing unsightly foams or bad smells. In some the algal species are very abrasive and mechanically damage the gills of *fish. Others are seriously toxic. Blooms of one type of phytoplankton, dinoflagellates, not only kill fish but also make *shellfish exceedingly poisonous. One species that has appeared off the eastern seaboard of the USA aggressively attacks fish and has caused the death of a researcher.

Ballast waters discharged from *bulk carriers have spread many toxic species from Japanese waters to Australia and the USA. The exotic species are introduced as dormant cysts. Since they arrive without their normal suite of predators and diseases, if they become established they tend to out-compete the native species. Around Australia shell *fisheries have been destroyed, and local people have experienced health problems. So if you see dense blooms of algae discolouring the sea, be careful about swimming and refrain from eating the local seafood.

M. V. Angel

reef. (1) The means of shortening a sail to the amount appropriate to the strength of the wind, and the same word is also used as a verb to describe this action. There are various ways of reefing a sailing vessel, depending on its rig and modernity. In *square-rigged ships, sails up to the *topsails normally carry two rows of *reef-points, enabling two reefs to be taken in. The first reef is at the *head of the sail and is reefed up to its *yard. The sails set above them usually have no reef-points as they are *furled or sent down in a wind strong enough to require the sails to be reefed. *Gaff-rigged vessels usually have three sets of reef-points in their mainsails. The mainsail is reefed by lowering it sufficiently for the reef-points to be tied under the boom, thus securing the reefed part of the sail to it. In a *Bermudan rig the mainsail is reduced in size by **roller reefing** or **slab reefing**. Roller reefing is achieved either by a patent reefing gear which winds the *foot of the mainsail onto the boom or the *luff into the mast. See also SPANISH REEF. **(2)** A group, or continuous line, of rocks lying low in, or just beneath, the sea. In 2004 Britain followed Canada, New Zealand, and Australia to create its first artificial reef with a ship when HMS *Scylla* was sunk at Whitsand Bay, Cornwall, a known nursery for flatfish. The new reef is being supervised by the National Marine Aquarium, Plymouth, which runs the UK Marine Fish Reporting Scheme. It is expected to attract many forms of sea life for conservationists and recreational divers to view. See also CORAL REEFS.

reef-band, a strip of extra *canvas *tabled onto a sail of a *square-rigged sailing vessel along the line of the *reef-points. It supports the strain on the reef-points when the sail is *reefed. A **balance-reef** is a reef-band which crosses a sail diagonally.

reef-cringles, *thimbles *spliced into the *bolt-rope on the *leeches of a *square-rigged sail at the end of the *reef-bands. When the sail is to be *reefed the *cringles are hauled up the *yard and lashed to it. In *fore-and-aft-rigged sails, the reef-cringles, similarly set in the lines of the *reef-points, become the new *tack and *clew of the sail when a reef is tied down.

reef knot, a square knot formed of two *half hitches in which the ends always fall in line with the outer parts. It is used when it is required to join two pieces of rope, particularly if they are of an equal thickness, and, of course, when tying *reef-points. It is one of the commonest and most useful knots used at sea.

Reef knot

reef-points, short lengths of rope, sometimes braided, set into the *reef-bands of square sails and used to tie down a *reef. In *fore-and-aft-rigged sails the reef-points are usually set into individual reef patches in the sail. The reef-points of heavier sails are usually secured to the sail by *crow's feet but smaller craft may use *stopper knots.

reef-tackle, a *tackle which is hooked into the *reef-cringle of a square sail to hoist it up to the *yard for *reefing. They are also used to pull *fore-and-aft-rigged sails down to the boom for reefing.

reeming iron, an iron wedge used by shipwrights to open up the *seams of wooden-planked vessels so that they could be *caulked with *oakum and *pitch. They were driven into the seams with a *beetle or caulking mallet.

reeve, to, to pass the end of a rope through the *throat and thus on to the *sheave of a *block when forming a *tackle, or through an *eye or *thimble. Generally, when the end of a rope is passed through anything, it is said to be **rove** through it.

reformado, or **reformade,** a 16th- and 17th-century name for a naval officer serving on board a ship without having obtained a commission from the *Admiralty or his country's equivalent. This was frequently necessary, as in those days disease or battle casualties often carried off officers, a state of affairs on board which required the temporary upgrading of midshipmen or a *rating so that the work and discipline of the ship might be maintained.

refraction, the bending of light rays as they pass from one medium to another of different optical density, an important consideration in *celestial navigation. Light from an observed celestial body or from the observer's visible *horizon suffers atmospheric refraction, the former being called **celestial refraction**, the latter **terrestrial refraction**. The effect of atmospheric refraction is to elevate celestial objects and the horizon, so that it is necessary to make allowance for this effect when converting observed *altitudes to true ones. The altitude correction, known as **mean refraction**, is defined as the angular measure along an arc of a vertical circle between the true and apparent directions of a celestial body, when atmospheric temperature, pressure, and humidity are normal. Abnormal refraction gives rise to effects such as *loom and *mirage. Mean refraction varies from about 33 minutes of arc for objects on the horizon to nothing for objects as the *zenith.

regime, a term used in *hydrography to describe the channels and the characteristics of *tides of a port or estuary. Building *moles, *jetties, and other port installations can alter the tidal flow, and thus the regime, of a port.

register ship, an old naval term to describe a Spanish treasure *galleon or plate ship. It originated from the requirement of the Spanish government that every Spanish ship trading to her American colonies required a licence to do so, those owners to whom licences were granted having their name entered on a register. It was a fairly widespread belief in England that every ship returning to Spain from America must be a *treasure ship. As these were always desirable ships to capture in time of war, they became widely known as register ships to distinguish them from Spanish ships trading in other parts of the world. See also FLOTA.

register tonnage, see TONNAGE.

regulating captain, a captain in the British Navy during the 18th–19th centuries who was appointed to a port during a war to administer a *rendezvous for the *impressment service. It was his duty to examine the men brought in by the *press gangs and to pay the official *bounty to volunteers. He was usually elderly and with no prospects of a sea appointment.

relative bearings, the *bearings of objects in relation to the ship's *head. They can be expressed in two ways, as bearings on the *port or *starboard bow, *beam, *quarters, etc., with the words 'fine' or 'broad' to add further definition. These can be expressed more accurately in degrees from ahead on each side of the vessel, with the prefix 'red' if on the port side and 'green' if on the starboard. When relative bearings are given in this way, the word 'degrees' is omitted.

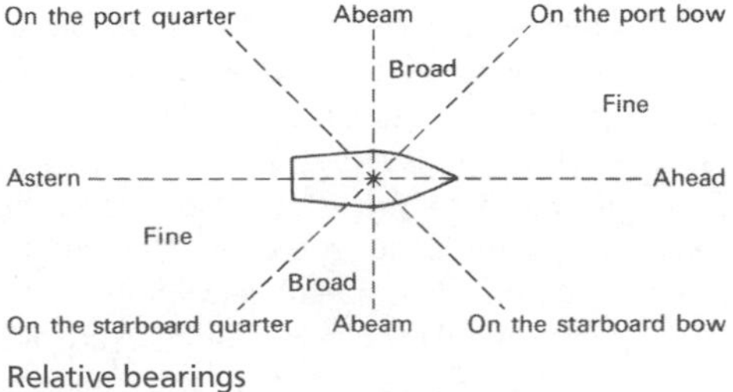

Relative bearings

relieving tackles. **(1)** Two strong *tackles used in sailing men-of-war to provide a safeguard against a ship overturning when it was being *careened on a beach with little slope down to the water. **(2)** Purchases rigged on either side of a vessel's *tiller, to ease the strain in heavy seas when the pressure on the *rudder was too great for the helmsman.

remote sensing is the use of earth-observing satellites to study the oceans and their weather. The sensors either passively detect radiations coming from the earth's surface, or atmosphere, or they actively use *radars to produce pulses of energy and then detect the energy reflected back. By using combinations of data from detectors of both visible and invisible light—that is, infra-red detectors—surface parameters like sea-surface temperatures and the concentrations of chlorophyll in the water can be estimated. However, corrections have to be applied to allow for the water vapour content of the air and the amount of suspended sediment in the water. Active radars of different frequency are used to measure surface wind speeds or as precision altimeters, which measure variations in the height of the sea surface caused by *eddies or the *waves (for illus. see GULF STREAM). The frequency of the radar and the altitude of the satellite influence the size of the footprint, the area of the surface observed. Observations may be averages of patches of ocean ranging from 25 metres (82 ft) to many kilometres across. The higher-frequency, short-wavelength radiations can 'see' through cloud, and can be used to detect some surprising features. For example, radars, which only detect the finest of ripples on the surface, can map underwater *shoals in coastal waters. This is because, as tidal *currents flow over these underwater features, they change the fine ripples on the surface.

The orbits of satellites are determined according to the phenomena being observed.

Those used for *satellite navigation, like *GPS, are geo-stationary, orbiting synchronously with the earth; others have tracks that are constantly repeated or follow tracks which shift, so the whole surface is observed every few days. Remote sensing has given those studying *oceanography and *marine meteorology the ability to observe the global oceans, but unfortunately it does not detect ocean conditions at depth.

M. V. Angel

render, to. **(1)** To ease away gently, such as by taking one or two turns with a rope or *hawser round a *bollard or *winch, and easing it slowly to absorb a heavy pull upon it. **(2)** The action of a rope as it passes over the *sheave of a *block. A seaman talks of a rope **rendering** through a block, not passing through it.

rendezvous, a British naval recruiting centre of the 18th and early 19th centuries, usually set up in times of war in some tavern near the waterfront of seaport towns with a strong lock-up room, known as a press room. It was the centre of the local *impressment service administered by a *regulating captain and was known colloquially as a 'rondy'. Recruits, both volunteers and pressed men, were held in the press room until they could be dispatched to a receiving ship, or *hulk, in a home port.

replica ship, a full-scale reproduction of a vessel, usually a ship from the past. Some have been used in *marine archaeology to assess the construction materials, handling ability, etc. of the original archaeological find. For example, the Kyrenia ship, a 4th-century BC Greek trading vessel found off Cyprus in the 1960s, was able to be accurately reconstructed as an unusually high percentage of the hull, 75%, was recovered. Called the *Kyrenia II*, this replica was *launched in 1985, and proved an invaluable source of information about the original find.

Replica ships have also been built to commemorate famous voyages undertaken by many of the men who have biographies in this volume—John *Cabot's *Matthew* is one example, William *Bligh's *Bounty* another—and they have proved a valuable source of information on how these ships behaved in a seaway, and how their crews lived. They also help to preserve man's seafaring heritage, as do the ocean-going Polynesian *canoes constructed for the Polynesian Voyaging Society. These have not only contributed to the knowledge of how the Pacific was explored, and settled, long before any European reached it, but have also helped to preserve a form of the ancient art of *navigation without artefacts so lucidly described in Dr David *Lewis's book *We, the Navigators*.

Some replicas are constructed, as was Thor *Heyerdahl's balsa raft *Kon Tiki*, to discover more about the movement of populations and the transference of early technology, language, and methods of cultivation from one culture to another. For instance, in 2003–4 an expedition took place to show that Indonesian seamen, who had reached Madagascar around the 5th century, could conceivably have reached West Africa as well. To prove it was possible for them to have done so, a ship was reconstructed from one illustrated in the reliefs of an 8th-century Javanese Buddhist temple, and sailed to Ghana from Indonesia.

One of the earliest replica ships was the *Mayflower II*, a faithful copy of the original ship which took the founding fathers from Plymouth to New England in 1620. Launched in September 1956 she was sailed across the Atlantic in 1957 by Alan *Villiers to commemorate this momentous voyage, and is now exhibited in the USA at the Plimoth Plantation, the Living History Museum of 17th-century Plymouth, Massachusetts. A second replica is due to be launched from the Devonport dockyard in 2005. Another ship which took emigrants to the USA was the 34-metre (111-ft) *barque *Jeanie Johnston*. The original was built at Quebec in 1847, and in 2000 a replica was launched near Tralee, Ireland. Effectively, she is 19th century in the *between-deck accommodation and on the weather decks, but 21st century below with twin *propellers, *bow thrusters, five *diesels, freshwater generator, and an eco-friendly sewage system, all of which are hidden from sight.

James *Cook's *Endeavour* is another well-known replica ship. Built in Fremantle, Australia, in 1993, she has undertaken extensive voyages and is currently based in the UK. Run and funded by the HM Bark Endeavour Foundation as a sailing museum replica ship, she is used for educational purposes and is manned by a professional crew. Another replica ship being used for educational purposes is the *Golden Hinde*,

The three-masted barque *Jeanie Johnston*, designed by Fred M. Walker. She was launched in May 2000 and is a replica of one of the 19th century's most successful Irish emigrant ships

the original being the ship in which Sir Francis *Drake circumnavigated the world, 1577–80. She was built and launched in Devon in 1973, sailed to San Francisco to commemorate Drake's claiming of California for Queen Elizabeth I in 1579, was used in several feature films, undertook voyages to the United States and round Britain in the 1980s, and is now berthed in London. Another Australian-inspired replica ship, launched in 1991, is the 27-metre (88-ft) topsail *schooner *Enterprize*, which is an exact copy of the vessel which brought the first European settlers to Melbourne in 1835.

On 13 October 1991 replicas of *La Pinta*, *La Santa Maria*, and *La Niña* sailed from the southern Spanish port of Huelva to re-enact the first historic voyage of *Columbus to the New World in 1492, and successfully followed his route across the Atlantic. In 2003 the replica of the *East Indiaman Götheborg* was launched 250 years after the original vessel had sunk in Göteborg harbour. With a length of 58.5 metres (192 ft), a beam of 11 metres (36 ft), and a *displacement of 1,250 tonnes, it has the same lines, hull, and rigging as the 18th-century *East Indiaman.

Mudie, C., *Sailing Ships: Designs and Reconstructions of Great Sailing Ships from Ancient Greece to the Present Day* (2004).

www.plimoth.org/Museum/Mayflower/mayflowe.htm

www.tallshipbounty.org/home_body.html

www.barkendeavour.com.au

www.goldenhinde.co.uk

www.enterprize.com.au

reprisal, originally a period of belligerency which preceded a declaration of war. Where a grievance existed against another country for acts committed, which might not rate a full declaration of war, the aggrieved nation could declare a state of reprisal, and undertake operations short of war until its grievances were settled. It was usually the signal to issue *letters of marque. Needless to say, a declaration of reprisal almost invariably drifted into full-scale war.

research ships are the most expensive research facility, both to build and run, required by *oceanographic institutes. They take the scientists and technicians to the study areas, to enable them to collect samples, deploy instruments, and carry out analyses and measurements at sea. Some oceanographic disciplines such as *geological oceanography have specific requirements that require dedicated vessels. For example, the Ocean Drilling Programme (ODP), which is collecting long cores from deep ocean sediments, operates a dedicated ship called the *JOIDES Resolution*; and some of the *underwater vehicles like *Alvin* require dedicated tenders. One of the most unusual research ships was aptly named *Flip*, which steamed out to its operating position like a normal ship, but then upended to drift with the currents for several months. It had to be specially designed so that its *aft *bulkheads became decks.

Most research vessels are used for multidisciplinary operations and often remain at sea for several weeks, especially when operating in remote regions. They carry parties of up to 25, or in the case of Russian ships 50, scientists, and are fitted out with a range of laboratories. They need to be able to keep station, i.e. stay on a fixed position in all but the most extreme weathers and *wave conditions, so instruments and samplers can be lowered on vertical wires. They also to have to be capable of maintaining low speeds of between 1 and 5 knots consistently and accurately. They are fitted out with a range of *winches for towing devices, such as *trawls, *dredges, and undulating devices. The latter are towed on *cables that are faired to reduce the drag so the device reaches greater depths and can be towed at speeds of up to 8 knots.

At least 10,000 metres (32,500 ft) of towing *cable is needed to tow a trawl at a depth of 5,000 metres (16,250 ft). Trace element chemistry requires special cables and clean laboratories to prevent contamination of the samples. Many types of gear are now towed or lowered on conducting cables that both deliver power to the device and transmit the data it collects back to the ship. The ships usually have large A-frames or cranes to handle heavy equipment over the side. Others have moon pools, *hatches in the ship's hull through which instruments can be lowered. Lowering instruments this way in the centre of a ship greatly reduces the effects of *pitching and rolling on wire tensions.

As it is impossible for research ships to stay at sea all the time, many types of instruments are deployed on moorings which are usually anchored to the seabed with subsurface buoyancy, and are left in the ocean for months and even years. Some of these devices are now programmed to come to the surface and transmit their data via satellite links to the laboratories on shore.

Research vessels have to have the most up-to-date *navigation equipment, powerful computers that constantly archive data that are collected continuously while *under way, and satellite communications like *Inmarsat for real-time processing of the data and receiving satellite imagery in real time. Because sound is used so much for probing the interior of the ocean and controlling instrumentation, research vessels have to be acoustically quiet. A noisy *propeller can completely drown the signal from an instrument on the seabed at a depth of 5 kilometres (3 mls.) at a slant range of 10–15 kilometres (6.2–9.3 mls.).

Many research ships have lent their names to the programmes they have operated under. Britain had the first one dedicated to *oceanography, HMS **Challenger*, and another gave its name to the **Discovery* Investigations. But the first ship built specifically for oceanographic research was the US Fish Commission's *Albatross* *launched in 1882. Such were the advances in the technology of her deep-sea equipment that on her earlier expeditions it proved possible to collect more deep-sea specimens in a single haul than the *Challenger* had collected during her entire voyage. Other famous research ships include *Atlantis* (USA), *Dana* (Denmark), *Meteor* (Germany), and *Vityaz* (Russia).

Rice, A., *British Oceanographic Vessels 1800–1959* (1986).

www-odp.tamu.edu/

www.whoi.edu/marops/research_vessels/index.html

www.marine.gov.uk/ships.htm M. V. Angel

respondentia, a loan made upon the goods laden in a ship for which the borrower was personally responsible. This is very similar to *bottomry, the difference being that in bottomry the ship and its equipment were security for the loan, in respondentia it was the goods alone. Like bottomry it plays no part in modern shipping business.

***Revenge*, HMS,** one of the best-known ship's names of the British Navy. The first of several ships called *Revenge* was made famous by Lord Tennyson's poem which tells of her last fight in 1591. She was a 34-gun ship of 441 tons, *launched at Deptford in 1577, and was Sir Francis *Drake's *flagship in the battle against the *Spanish Armada in 1588. In the following year, again commanded by Drake, she was part of the expedition which sailed from Plymouth to attack the Spaniards in Portugal. In 1590, under Sir Martin *Frobisher, she was engaged in an expedition to the coast of Spain, undertaken in the hope of intercepting the Spanish *treasure ships returning from the Indies. It was in August 1591, 'at Flores, in the Azores', that the *Revenge*, now the flagship of Sir Richard *Grenville, fought her last fight, which lasted for fifteen hours, against overwhelming odds. When there was no further hope of fighting her, Grenville ordered her to be sunk. However, his surviving officers would not agree to this and terms of surrender were made with the Spaniards on the understanding that the lives and liberties of the ship's company should be spared. Grenville, who had been wounded three times during the action, was carefully conveyed on board the ship of the Spanish admiral but died two days later. Five days after the battle the *Revenge* foundered in a *storm, taking with her 200 Spaniards who had been put on board.

revenue cutter, a single-masted *cutter with fine lines built expressly for the prevention of *smuggling. Their greatest period of activity was during the late 18th and early 19th centuries when high import duties made the running of certain dutiable goods a highly profitable business and the lack of adequate *coastguard stations presented smugglers with plenty of unguarded coastline to which to run their cargoes. This made it desirable to catch the smugglers at sea and led to the special design of these cutters to provide a margin of speed over the smugglers. They carried up to ten guns, usually 'long 9s', nine-pounders with extra-long barrels to provide a greater range.

rhumb line, from the Old French *rumb*, a line on the *chart which intersects all *meridians at the same oblique angle. Meridians and parallels of *latitude are special cases of the rhumb line, the angles of intersection being respectively 0° and 90°. Rhumb lines which cut meridians at oblique angles are loxodromic curves spiralling towards the poles. A rhumb line is a straight line on a *Mercator projection.

The radial lines on a compass card are also called rhumbs, and the term 'sailing on a rhumb' was often used in the 16th–19th centuries to indicate a particular compass heading. A line of constant *course is a rhumb line. On a plane surface (see PLAIN SAILING) this would be the shortest distance between two points. Over relatively short distances, where the curvature of the earth is negligible, it can also be considered so, so a rhumb can be used for plotting a ship's course.

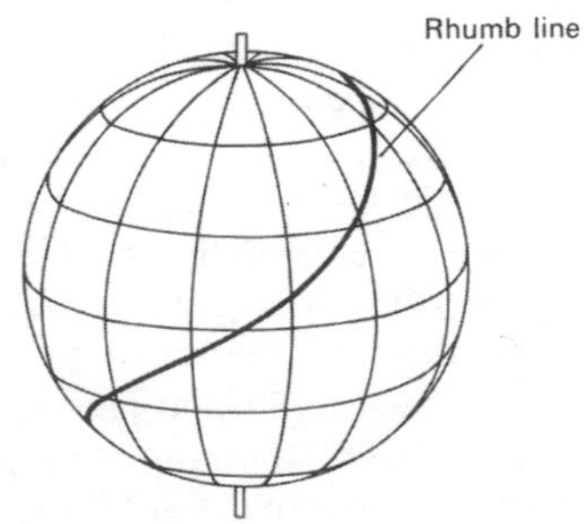

Rhumb line

Over longer distances at sea, and especially ocean passages, *great circle sailing provides a shorter course. But the inconvenience of having to change course continually when following the great circle course makes rhumb line sailing the general method of *navigation.

RIB, an acronym standing for Rigid Inflatable Boat. The origins of these fast, seaworthy craft, constructed of inflated rubber and powered by outboard engines, go back to the rubber inflatable craft of the Second World War (1939–45). During the 1950s improved rubber technology allowed for a more traditional boat shape to be constructed and for more powerful engines to be mounted. Around the same time a department of Atlantic College in west Wales, which used inflatables as safety boats for dinghy racing, started bonding sheets of plywood to the outside bottom of the inflatables to prevent excessive wear and tear. Experiments soon showed that altering an inflatable by adding plywood gave a more comfortable, and much faster, ride; and by the 1970s further development had incorporated the skills of *yacht designers Don Shead and Ray Hunt, whose powerboat designs were well known for their seaworthiness at high speeds. Nowadays, a RIB's V-shaped keel is usually made from *GRP. They are used by the armed forces of several nations, by the *offshore oil and gas industries, by *lifesaving organizations like the Royal National Lifeboat Institution, for *diving, and for many other recreational purposes. In 2003 an 8.8-metre (29-ft) RIB won the Round Britain race in a world-record time of 33 hours, 11 minutes.

Jones, C., *Rigid Inflatable Boats* (1992).

ribband, in *shipbuilding the long flexible lengths of fir fixed temporarily to the outsides of the *ribs of a wooden vessel and to the *stem and *sternpost to hold the *timbers together in *frame, until the deck *beams and *stringers are fitted. The term **ribband carvel** is used for a form of construction of lightweight wooden vessels, such as *yachts used for racing on lakes or rivers.

ribs, another name for the *frames or *timbers of a ship as they rise from the keel to form the shape of the hull. See also FUTTOCK.

rickers, the name used to describe the short, light *spars supplied for the masts of small ships' boats, *boathook staves, bearing-off spars, etc.

Riddle of the Sands, The, the famous spy novel of the North Sea and German islands written by the Irish author and politician Erskine Childers (1870–1922), and published in 1903. Its theme was the German preparation for an invasion of England and it was based on his own cruises in those waters in the 7-ton *Vixen*. See also MARINE LITERATURE.

ride, to, a verb with many maritime uses. A rope round a *winch or *capstan **rides** when the turn with the strain overlies and jams the following turn. A ship **rides to its anchor** when it is on the bottom and is holding it, and also **rides to the *tide or the wind** when anchored, or it can **ride out** a *gale. In a *square-rigged ship a seaman on the *yards who stamps down on the *bunt of a sail is said to be **riding it down.**

riders. **(1)** The name given to *timbers secured between the *keelson of a wooden ship and the *orlop *beams to give it additional strength if it was weakened by *stranding or other causes. They were normally only used when the *floors or *timbers had been broken or damaged in order to give the vessel enough strength to enable it to reach a port for repairs. They were also sometimes known as ground or upper *futtock riders according to the position in which they were required. **(2)** The name given to the upper tiers of casks stowed in the *hold of a ship.

ridge rope, the name given to the *jackstay on which an *awning over the deck of a ship is spread.

riding light, a navigational light displayed by a ship at night when it is lying to its anchor.

riding slip, see CABLE STOPPERS.

rig. **(1)** See BERMUDAN RIG; DE HORSEY RIG; FORE-AND-AFT RIG; GAFF RIG; JUNK RIG; LATEEN RIG; LJUNGSTROM RIG; LUGSAIL RIG; MARCONI RIG; ROTATING RIG; SHIP RIGGED; SQUARE RIG; UNA RIG; UNSTAYED RIG. See also OFFSHORE OIL AND GAS. **(2)** A term used in most navies and many shipping lines to describe the various sets of uniform worn by officers and men, such as No. 1 rig, working rig, etc. See also SAILORS' DRESS. **(3)** As a verb, it describes the operation in a sailing vessel to set up the standing *rigging and the *yards, and to *reeve the running rigging. The word is also used to describe many other operations on board ship, such as to rig an *awning, to rig a boom, to rig the *falls of a boat, etc.

rigger, a man employed on board ships or in shipyards during the days of sail to fit or dismantle the standing and running *rigging of ships. His duties included all the stretching, *splicing, *serving, and *seizing required before setting up a ship's rigging.

rigging, a term covering all the rope, chain, metalwork, and associated fittings used to support and operate the masts, *spars, flags, sails, booms, and *derricks of sailing vessels, and the masts, booms, and derricks of power vessels. The rigging used principally to support the masts and spars and which is fixed in nature is known as the **standing rigging**. That used to operate the sails and other equipment, which is adjustable, is known as **running rigging**.

Standing Rigging. Used where a mast is supported *athwartships by *shrouds and fore and aft by *forestays and *backstays. Historically, these were made of rope, sometimes specially built four-strand *hawser-laid rope which had less stretch than three strand. This has been generally superseded by steel wire and, occasionally, solid stainless steel bar is used for performance sailing *yachts where the smaller section can reduce wind drag. In early and small *square-rigged ships the rope shrouds were set up by *tackles which could be slacked or detached to allow the *yard to swing closer to the centreline. Later and bigger vessels used *deadeyes and *lanyards, and these could also be slacked away to allow the yards to be swung closer.

Wire rope was originally used with deadeyes but these were superseded by *bottlescrews.

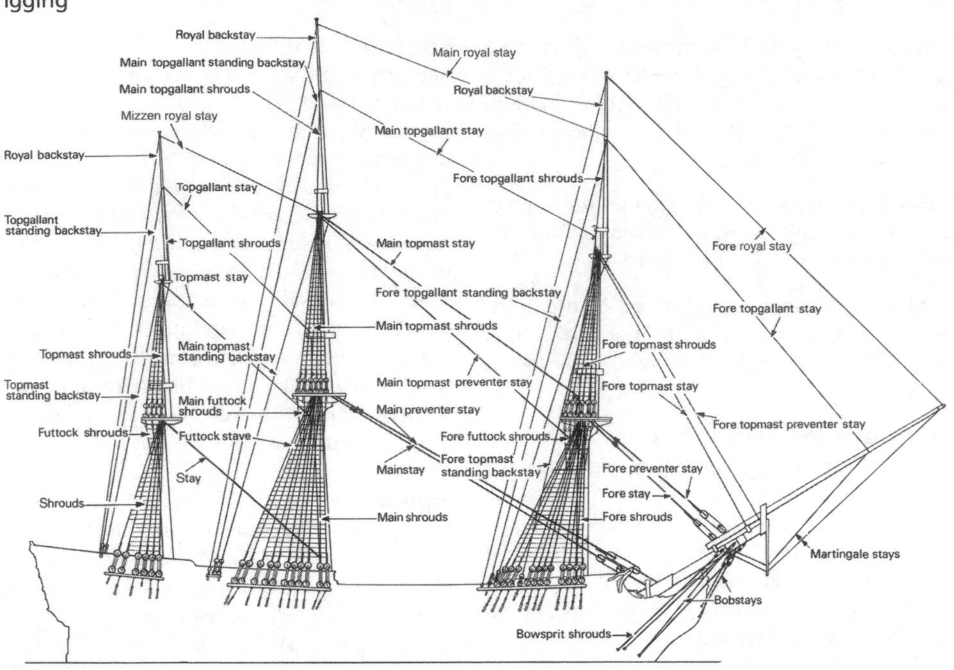

The principal elements of a ship's standing rigging

These are more efficient at stretching the longer and stronger wires, and can be retightened as required to counteract the stretching of the wire, but are not slacked away for any aspect of sailing. Stays followed a similar evolution except that they generally used *hearts instead of deadeyes. Forestays and the backstays of square-riggers were not commonly slacked away, but the **running backstays** of *fore-and-aft-rigged vessels have to be eased to allow the boom to swing clear over the ship's side when running before the wind. The running backstays of yachts are often operated by a lever system such as the *Highfield lever.

The degree of use of standing rigging varies heavily with the type and rig of the vessel. The *junk rig may not use any, and relies solely on the strength of its pole masts to support its sail; and vessels such as *dhows use the *falls of *halyards and *parrel *tackles (both classed as running rigging) for mast support. Power vessels usually rely on a minimum of standing rigging to support masts which may carry only *steaming lights, flags, aerials, and *radar. Fore-and-aft-rigged sailing yachts support their masts with only the most basic standing rigging, often as little as a single forestay and a single backstay together with twin lower shrouds, and a single upper shroud, each side.

Big square-riggers have a more extensive system of standing rigging due to their size, the complexity of their masting, and the specific need to swing their yards around the masts. Each stack of sails of a classic square-rigged ship was likely to have three or even four component masts. To the one stepped into the hull would be added a *topsail mast and a *topgallant mast, and sometimes a *royal mast. To these a *clipper might add a *skysail mast.

Traditionally each upper mast was separate and set forward of its lower mast so that it could be lowered past it. The lower masts were supported by shrouds taken from the masthead to the side of the ship. The shrouds of upper masts were taken from the masthead down to the *crosstrees and then to the lower mast or lower shrouds by means of the *futtock shrouds. The intersection between the futtock shrouds and the lower shrouds was arranged at yard height to maximize the scope for the rotation of the yard. Each masthead was usually supported in the forward direction by stays taken to the *bowsprit assembly, or to the mast immediately forward. Backstays from each masthead were

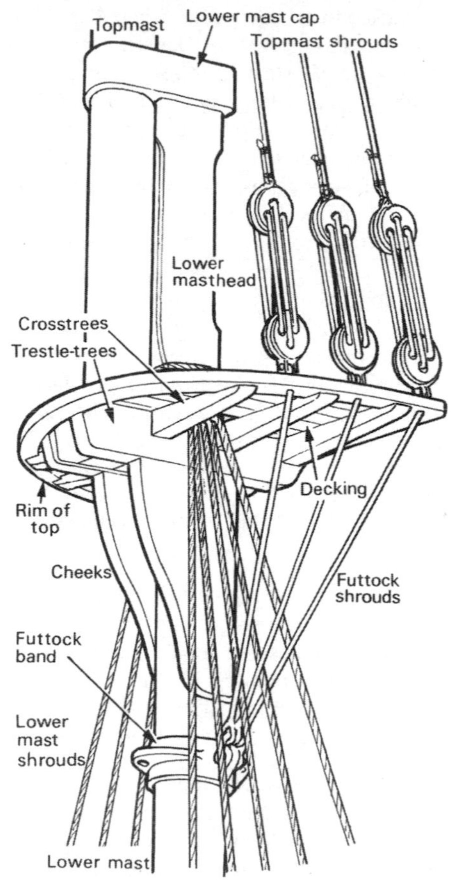

Mast top and standing rigging

taken to the side of the mast. Modern square-riggers with one-piece pole masts follow the same rigging pattern.

Bowsprits and their extensions, the *jib-boom and flying jib-boom, are supported *athwartships by shrouds led back to the hull. The loads from the various forestays are taken by *bobstays and *martingales back to the stem, generally making use of a *dolphin striker to improve the angle.

In square-rigged vessels those yards which are not arranged for hoisting or lowering may be fitted with fixed-length *lifts which would be classed as standing rigging, as are the *stirrups and *footropes used on yards and such items as *cran lines and *ratlines. Generally speaking all items of standing rigging are identified by their association with a particular mast.

Running Rigging. Sails are generally hoisted by *halyards and *trimmed by sheets; booms and *yards are held up by *lifts and adjusted by *braces or *guys. In bigger sailing ships the normal rope rigging often contains flexible steel wire components, and chain is sometimes used for square sail sheets. Modern yachts of any size often use wire halyards operated by *winches.

The sails of square-riggers are pulled up to their yards for *furling by *clew lines and *buntlines, and big sails of fore-and-aft-rigged vessels such as *spankers often use *brails to bundle

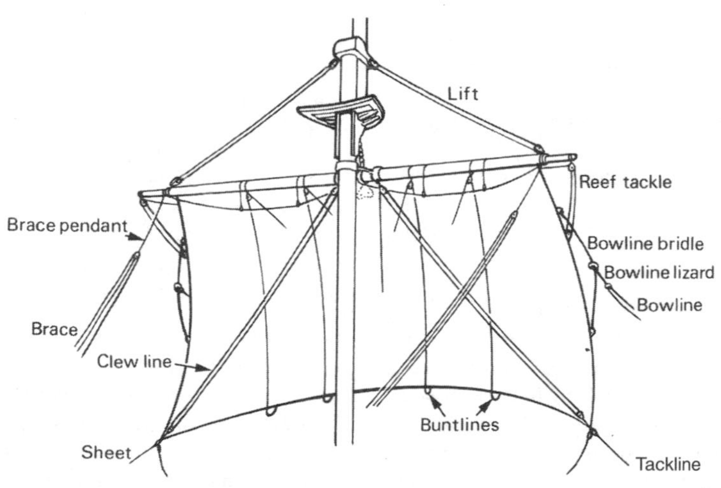

Elements of square sail running rigging

them up to their mast and yard. Brails have also been used on some headsails. The *course sheets of a square-rigger are normally taken *aft to the deck. But they also have a matching pair of forward sheets, called *tacklines, to allow the sail to be sheeted forward when sailing to *windward as this adds lift and reduces the *heeling moment. *Bowlines attached to *cringles in the weather *leeches were also used to pull the *luff of the sail forward.

The yards of square sails are controlled by braces attached to the *yardarms. Course braces are usually led aft and down to the deck, often to brace poles extending from the ship's side to give a better lead. Upper yard braces commonly lead aft to a convenient point on the next mast, but in vessels such as *brigs the braces from the *mizzen yards are often led forward to the foremast. In the later stages of commercial sail groups of braces were handled together by brace winches. Colin Mudie

rigging screw, see BOTTLESCREW.

rigol, a curved, semicircular steel strip riveted to a ship's side over a *scuttle. This deflects any water that runs down the side of the ship and prevents it from entering the scuttle when it is open.

ringtail, an extension fitted to the *leech of a *fore-and-aft *gaff-rigged mainsail to provide a greater area of sail to spread before a following wind. In the days of sail it was rectangular and was attached to the leech of the *spanker and extended by a ringtail boom attached to the main boom. Later it became triangular, with the *peak secured to the end of the *gaff and the *foot forming an extension of the mainsail.

rising, a narrow *strake secured to the inside of the *frames of a small rowing boat to support the *thwarts. Risings are often used for this purpose in place of *knees.

RMS, the prefix, short for Royal Mail Ship, placed before the name of a British merchant ship with a licence to carry the Royal Mails. It was the granting of mail licences to commercial shipowners during the 19th century which gave so great a fillip to British *shipbuilding and made possible the formation of the big steamship lines. Before then, the overseas mails had been carried in sailing *packets owned and operated by the Post Office. However, with the introduction of *steam propulsion it proved too great a financial burden on the Post Office to build new steamships, so carrying the mails was farmed out to commercial shipowners. Only the fastest ships, which were normally *ocean liners, received the licence and so had the right to use the prefix RMS. Synonymous with this type of trade was the appropriately named Royal Mail Steam Packet Company, later the Royal Mail Line. Founded in 1839, by the 1870s this offered a passenger service to many parts of the world. By 1919 it was one of the five largest shipping companies in the UK, but it went out of business in the 1960s.

RNLI, the Royal National Lifeboat Institution. See also INTERNATIONAL LIFEBOAT FEDERATION; LIFESAVING.

RNR, Royal Naval Reserve, originally a volunteer force of officers and men of the merchant service prepared to serve in the Royal Navy during times of war or emergency. It was reorganized in 1956 to include all naval reserves, not only those raised from the merchant service.

RNVR, Royal Naval Volunteer Reserve, a volunteer force of officers and men raised for service in the Royal Navy in time of war or emergency, colloquially known as the 'wavy navy' after the wavy gold braid worn on the sleeves of reserve officers to differentiate them from officers of the regular navy. The RNVR differed from the *RNR in that its members were not recruited from the merchant service. In 1956 the RNVR was absorbed into the RNR to form a single reserve force.

roach, the curve in the *leech or *foot of a sail. The square sails of a *square-rigger have a hollow roach in their foot to keep them clear of the mast *stays when the *yards on which they are set are *braced up, and this is known as a foot roach. See also PARK AVENUE BOOM.

Roaring Forties, the area in the southern hemisphere between the *latitudes of 40° and 50° S. where the prevailing wind blows strongly from the west unimpeded by continental land masses. Sailing ships in the Australian trade used to make for this area after rounding the Cape of Good Hope, as they could then rely on the westerly *gales to lift them along their way. The expression is also frequently used to describe the very rough parts of the oceans in the northern hemisphere between the same latitudes, particularly in the North Atlantic. See also RUN THE EASTING DOWN, TO.

robands (pron. robbins), the attachments or *lacings of square sails to the *yards of a *square-rigger. Originally they were small, sometimes plaited, ropes *rove through eyelet holes in the *head of the sail and taken around the yard. In modern ships the robands are lashings to a jackstay which runs along the top of the yard. The name is probably from the word *ra* which was used as the term for the yard in old English and the Germanic languages. For illus. see EARING.

Roberts, Bartholomew (1682–1722), English pirate who was probably the most successful of his profession in the history of *piracy. He never drank anything stronger than tea, went to bed early, was a strict Sabbatarian, and never gambled. He operated off the coast of Guinea and in the West Indies, where he is said to have captured as many as 400 vessels. He was killed in an action after a British warship had been sent out by the *Admiralty in 1722 to clear the west coast of Africa of pirates, having lived what he himself called 'a merry life and a short one'.

robinet, a small ship's handgun of the 15th and 16th centuries. It had a calibre of 2.5 centimetres (1 in.) and fired a 227-gram (8 oz) ball with a charge of the same weight. The *random range was a thousand paces. When the powder used was the same quality as that used in muskets, the charge was reduced by one-quarter. Robinets were upper-deck or 'castle' guns and were used purely in an anti-personnel role.

Robinson Crusoe, the castaway hero of Daniel Defoe's novel of the same name published in 1719. The story is based on the experiences of Alexander *Selkirk, who was marooned on Juan Fernandez Island in 1704 for over four years. See also MARINE LITERATURE.

rocket, a pyrotechnic device, one of the *distress signals used at sea. In the past it also had other uses aboard warships, such as indicating the executive order to start a particular manoeuvre. In the early days of *steam propulsion, rockets were also used as recognition signals between vessels of the same shipping company. See also COSTAIN GUN; FLARE; VERY LIGHTS.

roding, the old name for the anchor *warp or *cable of a coasting *schooner. The term is said to be derived from roadstead, the place where such craft usually anchored.

rogue knot, the seaman's name for a *reef knot tied 'upside down', the two short ends appearing on opposite sides of the knot after tying instead of on the same side. It is the knot which ashore would be called a **'granny knot'** and is very apt to slip when it takes any strain.

'Rogue's March', a particular cadence beaten on the drum when a man of bad character was dismissed the naval service in Britain for an offence committed on board ship. It was also used when a man was sentenced to be flogged around the fleet with a *cat-o'-nine-tails. It appears to have been introduced into the British Navy during the latter half of the 18th century and was in use for almost a century.

rogue's yarn, a coloured yarn of jute *laid up in a *strand of rope to identify the materials from which it was made. Commercially made *manila rope was marked with a black rogue's yarn, naval manila rope with red in each of two strands. Commercial *sisal rope had a red rogue's yarn, naval sisal had yellow in each of two strands. Commercial *hemp had no rogue's yarn, naval hemp had red in all three strands. *Coir rope was marked with a yellow rogue's yarn in one strand only. Originally, rogue's yarns were used only in naval rope and indicated from their colour the ropeyard in which they were made. They were introduced to stop thieving by making the rope easily recognizable, as in the days of sailing navies naval rope was considered far superior to any other, and there was a great temptation to smuggle it out of the *dockyards and sell it to owners or captains of merchant vessels.

roller furler, a device that *furls a sail by rolling it up around itself, usually on a *luff wire, so that the crew need not lower it. A roller furler may also be used to *reef a sail by rolling up only some of the sail. See also REEF.

John Rousmaniere

rolling hitch, a hitch used on board ship for *bending a rope to a *spar. The end of the rope is passed around the spar and then passed a second time round so that it rides over the *standing part; it is then carried across and up through the *bight. A rolling hitch properly tied will never slip.

Rolling hitch

rope, the name given in the maritime world to all cordage of over 2.5 centimetres (1 in.) in diameter, whether made from natural, or man-made, fibres, or wire. Prior to decimalization in the UK, rope sizes were expressed in inches of circumference, but since then, and in the USA and most other countries, the size is denoted by its diameter.

Natural Fibre Rope. The natural fibres used in rope-making are *hemp, *manila, *sisal, and *coir, each of which has its own particular characteristics and uses. Cotton was also occasionally used for rope in *yachts, but it was hard and difficult to handle when wet and was liable to mildew. The different ropes were often identified by *rogue's yarn.

The process of rope-making is the same for all natural fibres. Each fibre is generally about 1.5 metres (5 ft) in length and, in right-handed rope, known as Z-twist, is spun right handed to form yarns, sufficient overlapping fibres being used to form a continuous yarn. The spinning binds the fibres firmly together, the individual fibres being held in place by friction. The yarns are then gathered together and twisted left handed into *strands; three strands (or four in the case of four-stranded, or *shroud-laid, rope) being *laid up right handed, or anti-clockwise, to form a *hawser-laid rope. The contrary twists of the strands and the rope ensures that it remains compact with no tendency to spread. The twist of the strand is known as the *foreturn, that of the rope, the *afterturn. In left-handed rope, known as the S-twist, each component of the rope is twisted in the opposite direction, while Z-twist is laid up right handed.

Rope-making in the past was done in a building, some 275–365 metres (900–1,200 ft) long, called a ropewalk or ropehouse. The first process was to hackle the fibre by drawing it through hackleboards studded with steel prongs, to separate the fibres and get them all lying straight. These fibres were then spun into yarns and then into strands with a spinning machine, the rope-maker making fast a sufficient number of fibres to three rotating hooks in the spinning machine and walking backwards with the fibres to keep the proper tension on them while an assistant worked the spinning machine. When the necessary number and length of strands had been spun they were then laid up into rope, the strands being attached to the spinning machine and fed through grooves in

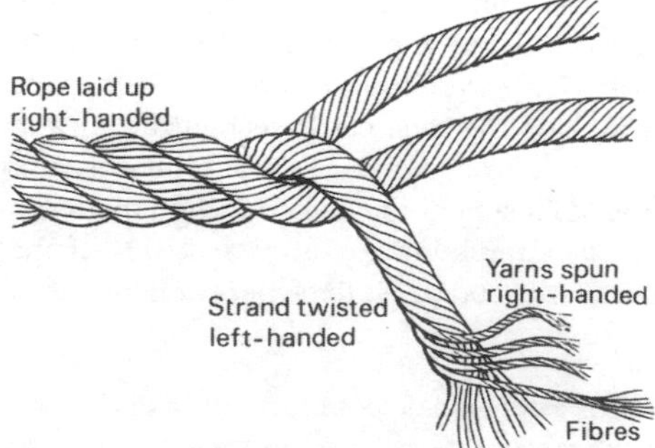

Right-handed hawser-laid rope

S-twist and Z-twist

a 'top', a conical piece of wood with the grooves merging at the thin end. Again the ropemaker walked backwards down the ropewalk holding the top, and the strands emerged from its thin end laid up into rope.

A rough and ready rule for finding the breaking strain of rope was to divide the square of its circumference in inches by three, the answer being in tons. Thus, the breaking strain in tons of 4-in rope would be $^{16}/_{3}$ or 5⅓ tons. A general rule with all rope was to divide the breaking strain by six in order to find the working load, a factor of safety of six to one.

Synthetic Rope. Manufactured from man-made fibres, this has almost entirely replaced rope made from natural fibres such as coir, hemp, and manila. The main fibres used are nylon, polyester, and polypropylene, and with the introduction of *Kevlar and other high-strength, low-stretch materials, synthetic rope can be made to suit every purpose. Nylon and polyester ropes have similar breaking strengths but nylon is much more elastic. Polypropylene may only have two-thirds the strength of nylon and polyester, but it is lighter and it floats.

The majority of yacht ropes have a braid sheath to protect and hold the load-bearing core in position, and the composition varies depending on what it is being used for, *halyards, sheets, *warps, etc. Apart from the great increase in strength the advantages of synthetic rope over natural fibre rope are that it does not absorb moisture, does not swell or rot, and does not lose much strength when frozen. The approximate breaking strain in tonnes can be calculated from the square of the diameter in millimetres. For nylon and polyester it is 2% of the square of the diameter and for polypropylene 1.5% of the square of the diameter.

Wire Rope. This is made with a number of small wires which extend continuously throughout the length of the rope and give it its great strength. The small wires are twisted left handed round a jute or wire core to form strands, and six strands are laid up right handed round a hemp or jute heart to form the rope. The heart has two functions, acting as a cushion in which the strands bed themselves and can take up their natural position as the wire rope is bent; and also as a lubricant by absorbing the oil with which wire rope is periodically dressed,

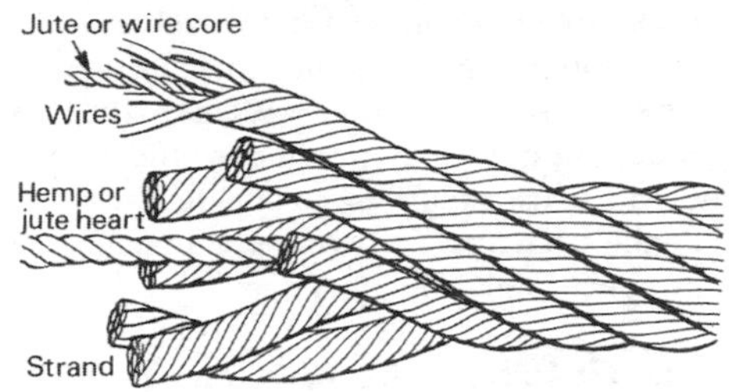

Wire rope

and forcing it between the individual wires when the rope is bent.

Wire rope is supplied in three grades. Where flexibility is not important, as with standing *rigging, **steel wire rope** (SWR) is the normal type used. Lack of flexibility in SWR is compensated for by its added strength. The individual wires are of larger gauge than in other wire ropes and are wound round a steel wire core, seven wires per strand being used in the least flexible and nineteen wires where a certain amount of flexibility is needed. In cases where considerable flexibility is required, as in wire *hawsers, a certain loss of strength is unavoidable. **Flexible steel wire rope** (FSWR) is supplied for this purpose, the individual wires being of medium gauge and wound round a large jute core. The number of wires used in each strand are 30 in very flexible wire, 24 in flexible wire, and 12 in less flexible. The third grade of wire rope is **extra special flexible steel wire rope** (ESFSWR), and this is supplied in cases where flexibility and strength are both necessities. The wire used is of small gauge wound round a hemp core, 61 wires per strand in EFWR and 37, 24, and 19 wires in the less flexible grades. The term 'extra special' refers to the quality of steel used, which is of a higher grade than in FSWR and SWR, thus producing the extra strength. All these are also available galvanized in which case they are prefixed with a G.

Since the Second World War (1939–45), there has been a big increase in the use of stainless steel wire rope. It is made in a similar manner to the old wire ropes but with a wire core in place of hemp, with 7×7 construction for stay wires and 7×19 where flexibility is required. A 1×19 construction giving more strength and less stretch is popular for standing rigging. With developments of this the individual wires are not round but shaped to fit snugly together to give even greater performance. Due to the large number of different types of construction it is not safe to use simple approximations to calculate the strengths of wire rope, so manufacturers' figures should be obtained.

rope clutch, a device for securing a *halyard or other line which is under strain. The line is led through the device, which allows it to run freely until a handle is pulled down and the line is engaged. John Rousmaniere

ro-ro (roll-on roll-off) ship, a vessel, both military and civilian, where vehicles are loaded on by means of a bow ramp and are offloaded by a similar ramp at the stern or by side ports. Commercial ships are connected to land by Linkspans, a ramp designed to alter in height and slope depending on the state of the *tide or loading of the ships. Many ro-ros have mezzanine, or portable, decks which can be taken to deck head height when handling large commercial vehicles, but lowered to half height allowing twice the deck area to be made available for cars. Unlike the old-fashioned cargo ship, the cargo space is open from bow to stern without any transverse *bulkheads.

Ro-ro ships are nothing new as they were being built in the 19th century to transport trains across rivers too wide for bridges, and Linkspans were first produced by the Glasgow shipbuilder Robert Napier around 1850. An early example of a ro-ro is the Firth of Forth ferry which started operations in 1851. The ships were equipped with rails which could be connected to the ones on land, and a train simply rolled onto the ship and then off it again at the other end. In its heyday the overnight Golden Arrow service from London to Paris was transported in exactly the same way.

During the Second World War (1939–45) the same principle was used to transport tanks and other equipment in landing craft for amphibious assaults. However, after the war anyone wanting to take his car across any stretch of water had to have it loaded and unloaded by crane, an expensive and time-consuming business. Statistics issued by the port of Dover showed that it handled about 10,000 cars annually in this way before the introduction in 1953 of ro-ro passenger ferries with terminals to service them. Within a year the numbers of cars handled by the port rose to 100,000 and by 1994 it was handling 4.5 million. By 1994 the world's ro-ro fleet of 4,600 vessels could be divided into several types, two-thirds of them dedicated to carrying cargo.

The US Navy's Military Sealift Command also runs a type of ro-ro ship with a slewing stern ramp which services two side ports. Designated a Large, Medium-speed, Roll-on Roll-off ship, or LMSR, these ships, of 55,000 displacement tonnes, have a carrying capacity of 35,000 square metres (380,000 sq. ft.), and are used to sealift the equipment of large combat forces.

However, the most widely known type of ro-ro is the car/passenger *ferry where vehicles, both private and commercial, drive on at one end and drive off at the other. They are extremely popular with holidaymakers and hauliers because of the speed with which they can be loaded and offloaded. Nevertheless, ro-ro ferries do have problems. Constructed with cargo doors at both ends, especially vulnerable to wear and tear when used as vehicle ramps, and without internal transverse bulkheads, they are vulnerable if an accident occurs. When flooding happens, either through the cargo doors or through the hull being pierced, there is nothing to stop water flowing rapidly onto the car deck. This can cause the ro-ro to list, the cargo shifts, and the ro-ro quickly capsizes. As a safeguard against this, modern ro-ros have bows which hinge upwards and a secondary door inside. This acts as both a collision bulkhead and a ramp which is attached to a Linkspan.

A conventional ship has watertight bulkheads which prevent it from sinking too fast, so that its passengers and crew usually have time to escape. Though statistics show the ro-ro ship's accident rate is no higher than any other type—between 1965 and 1982 it was considerably lower—other statistics are more disturbing. Between 1989 and 1994, when the two worst ro-ro accidents occurred, Lloyd's Register's figures reveal that 4,583 lives were lost in accidents at sea. Of these, 1,544 were lost in accidents involving passenger/ro-ro cargo ships, or one-third of the total, though ro-ro ships comprise a tiny percentage of the world's *merchant marine *tonnage. In other words, the accident rate for ro-ro ships is average, or below average, but when an accident does occur, a large loss of life can result.

The first civilian ro-ro ship to be lost was the rail ferry *Princess Victoria*, which was sunk in the Irish Sea in 1953 after huge seas stove in her stern cargo door: 133 lives were lost. In the following decades there were several other accidents with ro-ros, but it was not until *The Herald of Free Enterprise* capsized off Zeebrugge in March 1987, after her bow cargo door was left open, that the public's attention was drawn to the inherent dangers of the ro-ro. The ship capsized in a few minutes leaving passengers little time to escape, and 193 lives were lost. But at least *The Herald of Free Enterprise* capsized in shallow water so that some of the passengers, who might otherwise have perished, were rescued. With the *Estonia*, after its bow cargo door was ripped off in a Baltic storm in September 1994, the passengers had no chance at all, and over 900 people died when it sank in deep water.

These incidents focused the attention of the maritime authorities, and in 1996 eight European countries (Denmark, Finland, Germany, Ireland, the Netherlands, Norway, Sweden, UK) concluded the 1996 Stockholm agreement. Requirements were agreed that were additional to those implemented between 1994–2005 after the loss of *The Herald of Free Enterprise*. They will have to be implemented by all European Union countries by 2010.

rose box, the name given to the strainer at the end of the suction pipe of a bilge *pump. This prevents any solid material in the *bilges being sucked up into the pump and choking it. It is also widely known, particularly in *yachts, as a **strum box**.

rose lashing, a *'tiddley' piece of *seizing with which the *eye of a rope is secured to a *spar. The seizing is *rove in the form of a cross lashing by being passed over and under the parts of the eye, the end being brought round the whole to finish it off.

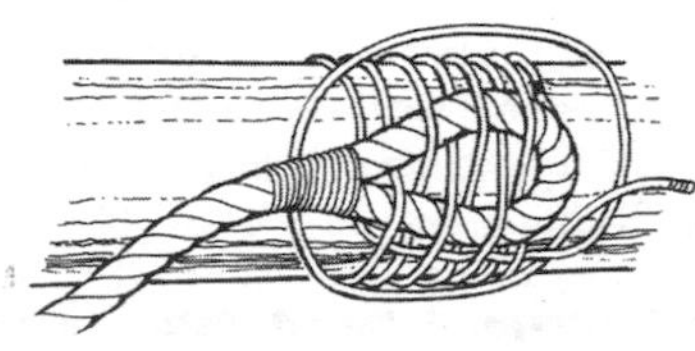

Rose lashing

rotating rig, where a *yacht's mast or sails pivot to present the best *aerodynamic shape to the *apparent wind to improve the airflow and minimize turbulence. Rotating rigs were developed from the experiments of Dr Manfred Curry in Germany in the 1930s. The French racing *catamaran *Elf Aquitaine II* used a rotating rig in the 1980s where the mast pivoted on a bearing under its *heel. Another version is the **Stollery Swing Rig** which, instead of a boom, has a *yard which pivots on the mast and extends both forward and aft of it. The *loose-footed mainsail is set on the after part and the foresail, on its own boom, is set on the fore part.

round, to. Used in conjunction with an adverb, this has a variety of maritime meanings. To **round down** a *tackle is to *overhaul it; to **round up** a tackle is to haul in on it before taking the strain. To **round in** is to haul in quickly, as on a *weather *brace in a *square-rigger; to **round to** is to bring a sailing vessel up into the wind.

round house, a name given to square or rectangular *cabins built on the *quarterdeck of passenger ships and *East Indiamen in the 18th–19th centuries, the *poop deck often forming the roof. They were called round because one could walk round them; they corresponded to what was called the *coach in a sailing warship.

round of a rope, the length of a single *strand when it makes one complete turn round the circumference of the rope.

round seizing, a *seizing used to lash two ropes together with a series of turns of small line with the end passing round the turns to finish it off. Two parts of the same rope can be secured by a round seizing to form an *eye.

round ship, the generic name for the medieval ship, at least up to the 15th century, with the exception of the *galley and the *longship. The average proportion of length to *beam was two, or two and a half, to one and they were normally single masted with a single square sail hoisted on a *yard. Within the generic term were subdivisions, such as *cog, *dromon, etc., all of them basically of the typical round ship design. They were the standard ship for almost all sea purposes, being used as warships, transports, and as cargo carriers.

round turn and two half hitches, a knot widely used when making a boat or small vessel fast to a post or *bollard. It is made by taking a full turn round the post or bollard and finishing the knot off with two half hitches round the standing part of the rope. If there is likely to be much strain on the knot, a better one for the purpose is a *fisherman's bend, as a round turn and two half hitches is liable to jam when there is a heavy pull on it.

Round turn and two half hitches

rouse in, to, to haul in any slack *cable, or *slatch, which may lie on the bottom when a vessel lies to a single anchor. The reason for rousing in the slack cable is that otherwise it might foul the anchor.

rouse out, to, the maritime term meaning to turn out all the hands on board ship in the morning, or call the *watch for duty on deck.

rov, remotely operated *underwater vehicle.

rove, see REEVE, TO.

rover, another name used to describe a freebooter (see FILIBUSTER), or anyone involved in *piracy. It comes from the Dutch word for pirate, *zee-rover*, literally sea-robber.

rowlock, a U-shaped space cut in a boat's *gunwale or *transom to take an *oar. In the past, when the boat was under sail, or secured alongside, the rowlocks were closed with shutters, or **poppets** as they were sometimes called. The word rowlock is now used, though wrongly, to describe the metal *crutches used for oars in rowing boats. See also THOLE PIN.

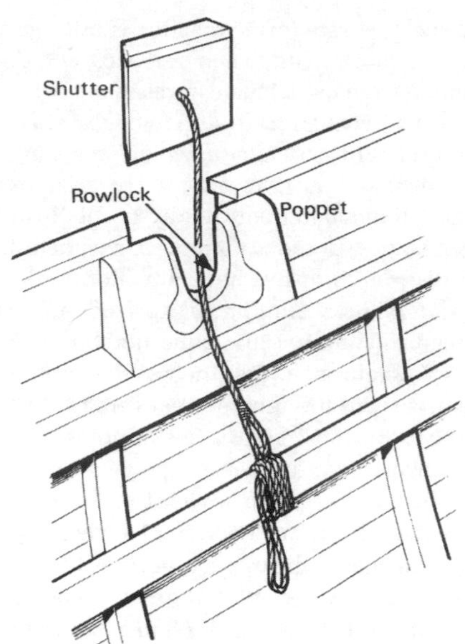

Rowlock

royal, the square sail set immediately above the *topgallant sail in square-rigged ships. It is usually set on an extended topgallant mast although sometimes on a separate *fidded *royal mast. This *spar was usually fidded on the forward side of the topgallant mast but was occasionally fidded on the aft side. It was originally known as the **topgallant royal**.

royal dockyards, the generic name given to the naval dockyards of the Royal Navy, probably an abbreviation of Royal Naval Dockyard. In the early days of the British Navy there were five royal dockyards in Britain: Deptford, Woolwich, Chatham, Portsmouth, and Plymouth. As the navy grew in size and complexity, the dockyards at Deptford and Woolwich were closed down, though Deptford remained as the principal victualling yard, and further naval dockyards in Britain were established at Sheerness, Haulbowline in south-west Ireland, and Rosyth in Scotland. In the colonial era of British expansion, a number of naval (royal) dockyards were constructed in other parts of the world, the principal ones being at Gibraltar, Malta, Halifax, Bermuda, Simonstown, Trincomalee, Singapore, and Hong Kong.

***Royal George*, loss of the,** one of the best-known examples of the *capsizing of a ship. She was a first-*rate warship with 100 guns and on 29 August 1782 she was lying at *Spithead with almost her entire crew and a large number of wives and other women and children on board. She was being given a *Parliament heel to expose part of her side for repairs. While she was heeled, she filled with water through her *gunports, and sank very quickly, with the loss of about 900 lives, including that of Rear Admiral Richard Kempenfelt (1718–82). The capsizing of so notable a ship was commemorated in the poem by William Cowper with its well-known opening line 'Toll for the brave, the brave that are no more'. Cowper, however, was no seaman and when he attributed the disaster to 'a land breeze [which] shook the *shrouds', he was very far off beam.

Several attempts were made to raise the hull but all were unsuccessful. Finally, in 1848, it was removed by the engineer Sir George Pasley, partly by being blown up with explosives and partly by being lifted. It was on this occasion that Augustus Siebe was able to demonstrate the efficiency of his newly invented *diving dress, receiving as a result a contract from the British *Admiralty to supply this equipment to the navy.

Royal Yachting Association, the controlling body in Britain for all matters concerning *yachting, both power and sail. It was founded in 1875 as the Yacht Racing Association by a representative body of yachtsmen to control yacht racing and the design of racing *yachts, with the authority to hold courts of appeal. One of the first *rating rules under which yachts could race was initiated by the *yacht designer Dixon Kemp, who was the association's first secretary. The Prince of Wales (later Edward VII) became its president in 1881 and as the popularity of competitive sailing increased so did its influence in Europe and elsewhere. Its name was changed to the Royal Yachting Association in 1952 and it is affiliated to the *International Sailing Federation and to the Union Internationale Motonautique (UIM).

The RYA's main objectives are:

- to increase participation in boating by promoting it as an accessible, safe, enjoyable, and healthy sport for people of all ages and abilities;
- to represent all who enjoy recreational boating, and protect their rights to enjoy their activity in a responsible way, in harmony with other water users;
- to provide information and advice on all aspects of boating;
- to promote proficiency and safety on the water, mainly through a range of voluntary training schemes. These take place at RYA-recognized training centres and are run by RYA-qualified instructors;
- to train coaches and officials and raise standards of event management;
- to identify and nurture talent and achieve success for Great Britain in international competition.

Fairley, G., *Minute by Minute: The Story of the Royal Yachting Association (1875–1982)* (1983).

rubber, a tool used by sailmakers, in the days when *canvas was used to make sails, to flatten a sail's *seams after the canvas had been sewn.

rubbing strake, a piece of half-rounded timber or rubber which runs the length of a small vessel or *dinghy. It runs on either side just below the *gunwale to act as a permanent *fender and protect the side of the boat when coming, or lying, alongside.

rudder, a logical development of the older *steering oar which the rudder began to replace in the West early in the 13th century, but see also WHIPSTAFF.

The earliest known representation of a *sternpost rudder in Europe appears on a font in a Belgian church (Zedelghem), dated around 1180, and, though this is disputed by some, another appears in an English church (Winchester). It is also represented on the seal of Ipswich, which is dated at about 1200, and some of the seals of the *Hanseatic League ports of this period show local *cogs with them.

In China the rudder was a much earlier invention. A model ship in pottery, with a rudder in place, was found in a tomb dating from the Later Han period (1st century). However, the rudder never totally replaced the steering oar as it did in the West and often coexisted with it. Oriental rudders were hung much deeper in the water than in the West and, as *junks lacked keels, the rudder helped, in conjunction

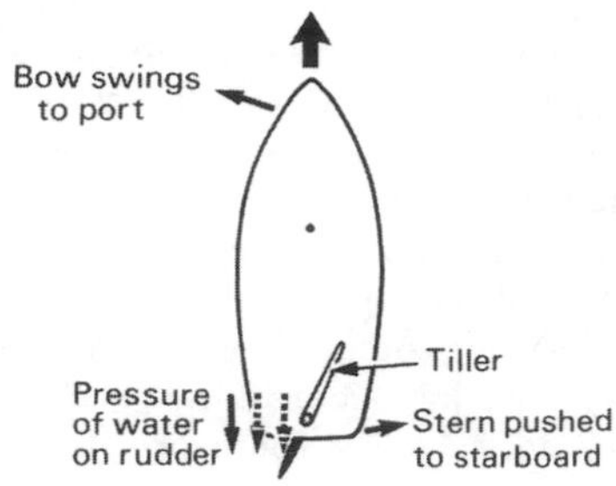

Rudder

with *centreboards or *leeboards, to prevent too much *leeward movement. Unlike in the West, therefore, rudders were hung so that they could be retracted. They were also often bored with holes as this decreased the force of the water on the rudder—easing the task of the helmsman—without affecting its efficiency. As with the *magnetic compass, it is thought that the rudder was transmitted from the Orient to the West.

Rudders in *dinghies and many other small boats are usually hung from the sternpost or *transom by means of *pintles, which engage in *gudgeons and allow lateral movement from side to side as required. In many *yachts they are hung on a rudder stock which is led through the *counter, movement being imparted to the rudder by either a steering wheel or a *tiller. Larger ships also have their rudders hung on a rudder stock, the rudder being turned by the *steering gear attached to it. In order to reduce the steering gear force required to turn the rudder, the rudder on larger ships is balanced or semi-balanced. A fully balanced rudder has the same surface area forward of the rudder stock as *aft, so the force of the water on the rudder, which tends to turn it in a clockwise direction, is balanced by the force of the water tending to turn it in a counter-clockwise direction. For technical reasons of design, most modern rudders are of the semi-balanced type. This means that a higher steering gear force is needed compared with a fully balanced rudder but that force is considerably less than that used to turn an unbalanced rudder.

Rudders on modern ships are of an aerofoil section in order to allow for smooth passage of the water and they are hollow in order to provide for a buoyancy effect. That buoyancy reduces the weight that the rudder carrier bearing, which supports the rudder, has to take. A carrier bearing is necessary, otherwise the weight of the rudder would act upon the steering gear.

Podded propulsors and ducted water jet systems do not have conventional rudders as the direction of the ship is controlled by the steering of the pod or water jet outlet. For a description of these see JET BOATS; PROPELLER: MODERN PROPELLER SYSTEMS; TUGS.

Rule of the Road, see INTERNATIONAL REGULATIONS FOR PREVENTING COLLISIONS AT SEA.

run, the shape of the *afterbody of a ship in relation to the resistance its underbody engenders as it goes through the water. A **clean run**, the shape at the after end of a ship's underbody that slips easily through the water without creating excessive turbulence. Run could be said to be the complement of *entry, which describes the shape of the *forward end of a ship's underbody.

runners, the two preventer *backstays, led from the mast to each *quarter of a sailing *yacht to support the mast and maintain tension in the *forestay. Whenever *tacking or *gybing the *lee runner is eased or cast off to allow the boom to swing over without restriction, the new *weather runner being set up *taut. See also RIGGING.

running free, the situation of a sailing vessel when the wind is either well *abaft the *beam and within a *point or two of blowing from directly *astern or blows directly from that direction. The term comes from the fact that with the wind from this direction, the sheets of the sails are freed right away in order to present the maximum possible sail area as square as possible to the wind. See also BROACH TO, TO; GYBE, TO; and for illus. POINTS OF SAILING.

running rigging, see RIGGING.

run the easting down, to, an expression which refers to the long easterly passage from the Cape of Good Hope to Australia between the *latitudes of 40° and 50° S., in the area known as the *Roaring Forties. It originally referred to the big *square-riggers on the Australian run which used the prevailing westerly *gales which blew in this area to help them on their way, but *yachts engaged in round-the-world races (see YACHTING: ROUND-THE-WORLD COMPETITIONS) also run their easting down in this area of the Indian Ocean.

rutter, from the French *routier*, itself from the Portuguese *roteiro*, a route or road, an early name for a book of *sailing directions—though the *periplus was even older. It was usually illustrated with views of ports and coastline seen from seaward. In 1483 a French sailor named Pierre Garcie wrote *Le Grand Routier et pilotage*, a *pilot book for the west coast of France, and a translation appeared in English, possibly the first of a long series of rutters which appeared over the next two centuries. A printed version appeared in 1521 with woodcut views to facilitate identification of the coast from seaward. There was also much information on *tides, and general advice on *navigation. In 1541 Richard Proude printed *The New Rutter of the Sea for the North Partes*, being sailing directions for the circumnavigation of the British Isles.

Rutter also referred to the English seaman's personal notebook in which he kept a record of *courses, anchorages, etc.; such notebooks were usually handed down from father to son, being valuable for the local information they held. See also DERROTERRO.

S

saddle, a block of wood, or a wooden bracket, fixed to a mast or *yard to support another *spar attached to it. Thus, the *bowsprit of a sailing vessel has a saddle attached to it to support the *heel of the *jib-boom, and a saddle on each lower *yardarm supports the *studding-sail boom in *square-riggers. It is also the name of the wrought-iron fixture which in some *gaff-rigged vessels holds, with the aid of a *parrel, the inner end of the gaff against the mast.

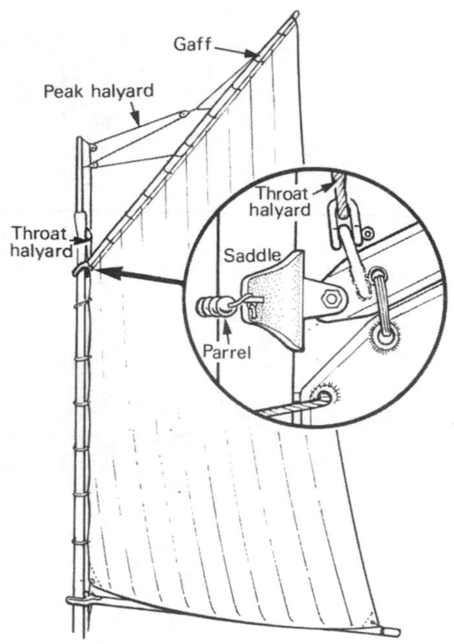

Saddle used on a gaff-rigged mainsail

safe water mark, part of the *IALA maritime buoyage system which indicates there is navigable water all round it. It may also be used as an alternative to a *cardinal or *lateral mark to indicate a landfall. It is either a spherical or *pillar buoy, or a *spar buoy with a spherical topmark, and is the only type of mark to be coloured with red and white vertical stripes. If it is lighted it is white using isophase, *occulting, one long flash (a single flashing light in which the light appears for not less than two seconds duration and is regularly repeated), or *Morse code 'A' rhythms. See CHARACTERISTIC.

sag, to. **(1)** The tendency of the hull of a ship to settle *amidships when in a seaway its weight is supported only at its bow or stern by *waves. It is the opposite of *hogging. **(2)** A word also used by seamen to describe a *leeward drift. A sailing ship is said to sag away to leeward when it makes excessive *leeway.

saic, a small Greek trading *ketch of about 200–300 tons, of the 18th–19th centuries, without a *mizzen *topsail. It was possibly an earlier form of the word *caique.

sail burton, the *purchase which extends from the heads of the *topmast to the deck in *square-rigged ships and is used for hoisting sails *aloft when it is required to *bend them onto the *yards.

sailing, see YACHTING.

sailing directions, or pilot books, are, as has been observed, as old as sailing. They provide a written description of the navigational information that *master and *pilot require and pre-date the *chart by many centuries. They are an original written source of worldwide information, relating almost entirely to *coastal navigation, to supplement the information presented on the chart. The earliest Mediterranean pilot to survive, entitled *Lo compasso da navigare,* dates from about 1250. The first printed French pilot book was Pierre Garcie's *Routier,* published in 1483, which accounts for the later English term *rutter.

During the reign of Charles II (1660–85) English mariners became acutely aware of the inadequacy of the *chartmaking of their coastline and in 1681 Samuel *Pepys appointed Captain Greenvile Collins (d. 1694) 'to make a survey of the sea coast of the Kingdom'. Collins took ten years over the work and prepared 120 plans of harbours and stretches of open coast, 48 of which were engraved and issued in his *Great Britain's Coasting Pilot* (1693). *Sailing Directions* as such were first published by the British Hydrographic Department in 1828, and updated versions continue in print to this day. Each volume covers a particular area of coast, such as the Channel Pilot (southern England and northern France), China Sea Pilot, Mediterranean Pilot, etc. The series is completed by the volume *Ocean Passages for the World*, the only non-coastal pilot. Mike Richey

sailing thwart, a fore-and-aft *thwart running down the centre of some *gigs and *galleys which were used as ships' boats. This was to give the extra strengthening needed to support the two masts such boats required.

sailmaker's stitching, the types of stitching used with sails, awnings, etc. when it is not possible to use a machine. There are three types: **flat sewing** is used to join two pieces of sailcloth or *canvas where strength is not of paramount importance. The selvedge of one piece of material is placed along the seam line of the other, both are hooked onto a sailmaker's hook to keep them taut, and the needles passed down through the single cloth close to the selvedge and then up through both cloths, and so on until the whole seam is completed, with a back stitch to terminate the line of sewing. The normal spacing is three stitches to 2.5 centimetres (1 in.). When the first seam is completed, the work is reversed and the selvedge of the piece of cloth sewn to the seam line in the same way. The direction of sewing in flat sewing is always away from the hook.

Round sewing is used where greater strength is required, the stitches passing through four thicknesses of the cloth instead of two. There are two forms, known as **single last** and **double last**. In single last, each cloth to be joined has its edge turned in about 1.8 centimetres, the two are then placed together, held taut with a sailmaker's hook, and joined at the edge by passing the needle through all four parts about 3 centimetres from the edge and back over the top, making four stitches every 2.5 centimetres. In double last, the selvedge of one piece of cloth is placed level with the doubled edge of the other and the seam sewn as in the single last. The work is then reversed and the selvedge of the other piece is similarly stitched to the other, which is doubled at the seam line. In round sewing, the direction of sewing is always towards the hook.

Darning is used to repair small tears. The first stitch is made by bringing the needle up through the sail about 2.5 centimeters (1 in.) from the side of the tear, down through it a similar distance on the other side, then up through the tear and through the *bight formed by the twine. Subsequent stitches are made by passing the needle through the tear, up through the sail on one side, down on the other side leaving a small bight, and then up through the tear and

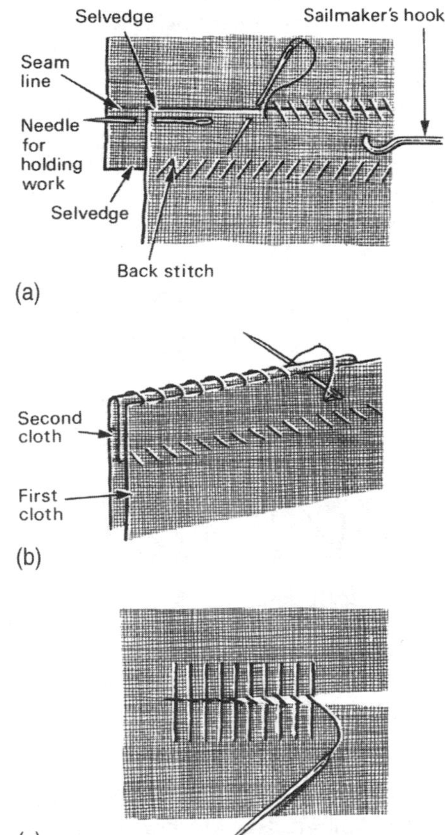

[a] Flat sewing [b] Round sewing [c] Sailmaker's darn

the bight. This forms a locked stitch, each one being drawn *taut as it is finished. The stitches are made close together to give greater strength. See also PRICK, TO; TABLE, TO; MONK'S SEAM.

sailmaker's whipping, used in cases where it is essential that whipping (see WHIP) will not slip or come adrift. It is made by unlaying the rope between 5 and 7 centimetres (2–3 in.) and passing a *bight of the whipping twine over the middle *strand, leaving the two ends of the twine, one short and one long, and the bight hanging downwards. The rope is then laid up again and the turns of the whipping passed round the rope using the long end of the twine and working against the lay of the rope and towards the end.

When the whipping is long enough to take the bight, it is passed up outside the whipping, following the *lay of the strand over which it was originally placed, and finally over the top of the same strand. The short end of the twine is now hauled *taut, so that the bight is tightened, and is itself then brought up outside the whipping, again following the lay of the rope. The whipping is completed by joining the two ends of the twine with a *reef knot concealed in the middle of the rope. See also COMMON WHIPPING; WEST COUNTRY WHIPPING.

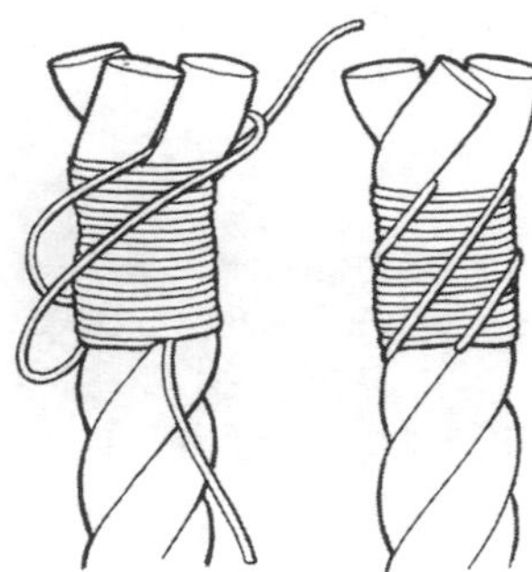

Sailmaker's whipping

sailor-by-the-wind (*Vellela vellela*), a subtropical cnidarian—a relative of *jellyfish—that is neustonic (floats at the sea surface). Its body is oval, grows to a length of 8 centimetres (3 in.) long, contains a gas-filled float, and has a sail on top that sticks up into the air. The sail is set so that some individuals tack to the right and other to the left, so they tend to accumulate along *slicks and *windrows. On the underside there are numerous delicate tentacles armed with stinging cells that stun its prey of small *plankton. Its blue coloration, typical of most neustonic animals, may either be camouflage, making the animals difficult to pick out against the blue of the ocean, or provide protection against the damaging effects of ultraviolet light. *Vellela* has its own predator, the purple sea snail (*Ianthina*). Seen from a boat, *Ianthina* looks like a cigarette end floating in the water because it secretes itself in a bubble float. Both are occasionally washed up on beaches in large numbers in Britain, usually in late summer after a period of south-westerly winds. M. V. Angel

sailors' dress. The earliest reference to any sort of uniform dress for seamen appears to date from a few years after the Roman invasion of Britain (55 BC) with an order that the sails of *longboats in the Roman fleet were to be dyed blue to match the colour of the sea and that their crew were to wear clothing of the same colour to lessen the chances of the boats being seen by an enemy. Over 2,000 years later, the prevailing colour of all sea uniforms is still blue.

Of the general cut of the clothing worn, one of the earliest descriptions is that given by Geoffrey Chaucer of his 'shipman' in the *Canterbury Tales*, who was dressed 'all in a gowne of falding to the knee'. This gives a date of about 1380 for this knee-length gown, possibly the forerunner of the English seaman's petticoat-trousers, which remained an article of his standard dress until the beginning of the 19th century. There was a good functional reason for the longevity of this odd piece of maritime clothing in the protection it offered to the trousers of men working *aloft on the *yards of *square-rigged ships, and also when rowing in the boats of the fleet, where the petticoat protected against rain and spray. As time passed the 'shipman's' gown became a *canvas frock tucked into breeches or trousers to form a blouse.

In general, the tendency to provide seamen with some sort of uniform clothing started in the fighting navies many years later. Thus, when men were hurriedly raised in England in 1587–8 to man the ships that fought against the *Spanish Armada, they were all given a blue coat by Elizabeth I, but the blue coat did not appear in merchant ships, and then only in a few ships, until nearly a century later. James I, who followed Elizabeth on the throne, was less generous to his seamen, writing to the *Lord High Admiral that 'it is not intended to clothe the men to make them handsome to run away'.

The elaborately illustrated title pages and cartouches with which the early chartmakers decorated sea *atlases provide much evidence about the contemporary dress of seamen. Those of the late 16th and early 17th centuries are virtually unanimous in showing seamen wearing very baggy breeches with woollen stockings, a thigh-length blouse or coat, and a tall, hairy hat, though one or two of the Dutch sea atlases show some of their seamen wearing long baggy trousers under an ankle-length coat. The *salvage of the **Mary Rose* has also added to our knowledge of clothing and habits of seamen of that time, so that we know now that English seamen also wore leather or canvas and probably a sleeveless leather jerkin. A 17th-century journal kept by one of the English *buccaneers cruising in the Pacific Ocean records sighting another ship, and 'we knew her to be English because the seamen wore breeches'. The only other ships in the Pacific at that time would be those of Spain, which argues that the fashion for breeches as a rig for seamen had not yet spread to that country.

These clothes did not differ very greatly from those worn on land, except for the coat or jerkin in place of the doublet. Certainly there was nothing that could be described as any sort of general uniform which differentiated the seaman from the *landsman. However, from the 16th century onwards, *exploration by sea increased the length of voyages, so there was a tendency for the dress of ships' crews to be similar in cut and colour. This was because they were dressed from the slop chest. Slops—the name comes from an Old English word *sloppe*, meaning breeches—originally referred only to the baggy trousers worn by seamen. Later it developed into a sort of unofficial uniform when the original clothing, in which men joined their ships, wore out. If only for economic reasons, the clothes tended to be all of the same pattern and colour. Slops were first officially issued in the Royal Navy in 1623 and were sold by *pursers, who were allowed one shilling in the pound commission, and who opened their slop chests *before the mast on certain days. Samuel *Pepys refers to the business as one 'wherein the seaman is much abused by the purser', as he continued to be until an official naval uniform for seamen was introduced in the navy in the mid-19th century. However, they were not a uniform, but replacement clothing for any articles worn out, and seamen were not forced to buy them if they could cobble together anything else which was serviceable.

In fact most seamen did make their own clothes on board, for few could afford the slop chest, and *make and mend was set aside for this. Worn-out canvas sails provided the basic cloth for home-made clothing, and a liberal application of *tar made the canvas weather resistant. Almost all seamen of all nations made themselves canvas hats with a brim and coated them with tar to make a waterproof headgear known as a *tarpaulin, later shortened to 'tar' which became a synonym for a sailor. Canvas blouses and trousers were also treated with tar to become the more or less standard heavy-weather clothing, from which came the other synonym of *'tarry-breeks' for a sailor. The tarpaulin hat and the tarred canvas blouse and trousers were the forerunners of the oilskin coat and sou'wester hat. Introduced in the 19th century, these were made of a very fine canvas impregnated with an oil-based preparation to give it a glossy surface which made it completely waterproof. This type of oilskin suffered from the defect that exposure to salt water eventually made it sticky and destroyed the waterproofing, and it has long since been replaced by more suitable material.

Until uniforms were officially introduced in the mid-19th century most sailors only owned the suit they were wearing when they first came on board, and they slept in the same clothes. This shortage of clothing was frequently responsible for the diseases which ravaged so many crews during the 16th–18th centuries. However, during the 18th century and the early part of the 19th they wore *long clothes when going ashore. Following the earlier fashion of baggy breeches and trousers, and spanning the last years of the petticoat-trousers, there was a period when striped waistcoats, shirts, and trousers, either red and white or blue and white, became a feature of the seaman's dress, as did straw hats. They originated in the main European navies and to some extent were copied by seamen in the *merchant marine. Introduced in the last decade of the 18th century, this type of clothing lasted until about 1820, when solid colours came back into favour. However, the straw hat lasted a great deal longer and was worn by many seamen until the beginning of the 20th century, particularly in warmer climates.

Full uniforms were not introduced into navies until about the mid-18th century for officers and in 1857 for ratings. From around that time, particularly in the large shipping lines, up to the First World War (1914–18) officers and sometimes ratings in the British merchant service were dressed in the liveries of their shipping companies. However, during the war the *master of a railway steamer rammed and sank a German *submarine. Unfortunately for him he was later captured, and recognized, by the Germans, who shot him because at the time he had sunk the submarine he was not in uniform but a civilian wearing his company's livery. To prevent this happening again in wartime, by ensuring that the merchant service became one of the armed services, 'an Order in Council was promulgated in 1918 to prescribe a standard merchant service uniform' (R. Hope, *A New History of British Shipping* (1990), 355), and in 1922 the British merchant marine became known as the merchant navy.

Jarrett, D., *British Naval Dress* (1960).

sails, generally, can be divided into two distinct types, those used in *square-riggers which are set on horizontal *yards crossing the masts, and those used in *fore-and-aft-rigged vessels which are set from their *luffs on masts or *stays. These two types are sometimes used together, as with the *jibs, *staysails, and *spanker set aboard a square-rigged ship or, in the past, the occasional square sail set from a yard aboard a fore-and-aft-rigged vessel when it was *running free. There are exceptions to this general rule: *lateen sails and *lugsails, though set on a yard, are generally accepted as fore-and-aft sails.

Before the days of synthetic materials and machine stitching, sails were made by hand using the techniques described in *sailmaker's stitching. Then, during the 1950s, synthetic materials such as Terylene replaced natural fibres and sails were stitched by machine. Now there is a whole range of new, lighter, and more stable sail materials such as *Kevlar and *Mylar. There

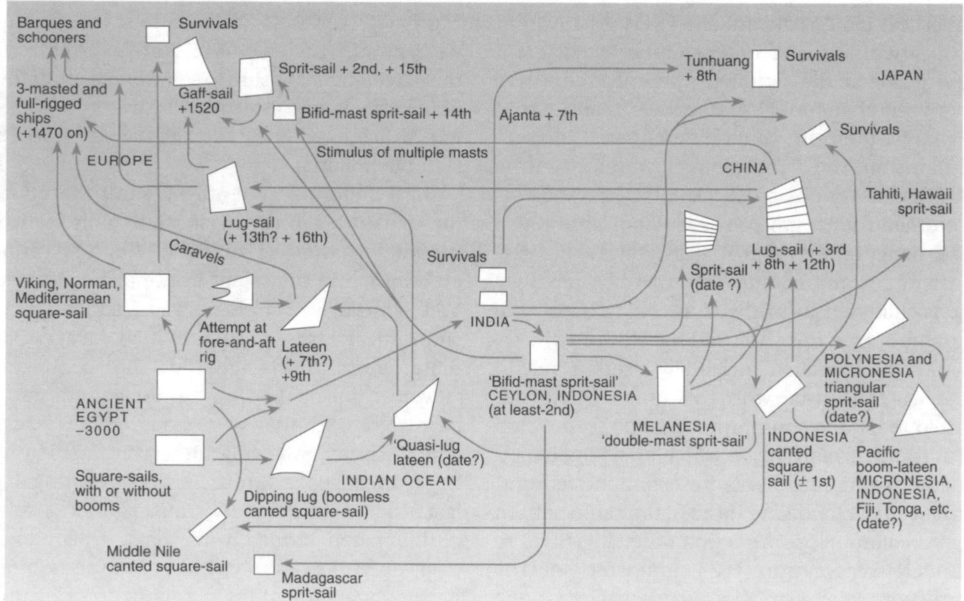

Chart, which follows the outlines of a map of the Old World, showing the distribution and possible genetic derivation of sails. Not to scale

are also new methods of sailmaking which use moulds and glues with computers controlling the cutting of the shape of a sail. Indeed, the shapes of the sails can be so closely controlled that they can be modified for different wind speeds. With the introduction in the 1960s of roller-*reefing headsails which were permanently *bent on, ultraviolet (uv) light degraded both the Terylene cloth and its stitching. At first a cover of uv-resistant cloth protected the *leech of the foresail which remained exposed when *furled, but better uv-resistant cloth now allows the whole sail to be made of this.

sail training, the modern term for crewing a sailing ship as a naval or *merchant marine cadet or as an adventure experience for those not following a seagoing career. The vessels sailed are known as tall ships, meaning that they have high masts, often *square rigged.

The advent of power-only vessels cancelled the necessity for career training in sail. However, the British Navy kept a sail training squadron and their *brigs were in *commission until the early years of the 20th century. Some commercial sailing shipowners also continued to take apprentices, believing in training in sail even for crews who would later serve in power-only ships. Up to the First World War (1914–18) some American states ran sea schools in vessels lent by the US Navy for boys intent on merchant service careers. Between the wars many navies continued to train cadets under sail, valuing the sail training ship environment where individual effort matters and the need for teamwork is apparent. Sailing school ships and cargo vessels also offered some adventure training and seagoing experience.

After the Second World War (1939–45) reparations changed ownership of several large sailing cargo and cadet ships but Britain took no part in the redistribution. In 1954 the Sail Training International Race Committee was started to organize an International Tall Ships' Race from Torbay to Lisbon, which took place in 1956, attracting twenty ships representing eleven nations. After the race the **Sail Training Association (STA)** was formed and ran races, at first every other year and then annually from 1964. The largest British crew in the 1956 Lisbon race competed in *Creole*, the 58-metre (190-ft) staysail schooner lent by Greek shipowner Stavros S. Niarchos. It was not until the STA had the 41-metre (136-ft) LOA three-masted topsail *schooner *Sir Winston Churchill* built in 1966, followed two years later by her sister ship *Malcolm Miller*, that the UK once again had sizeable sail training ships in regular use. The **American Sail Training Association (ASTA)** was established in 1973 on similar lines to the STA, and many other countries have followed suit with their own sail training organizations.

Many navies and merchant marine academies still train cadets in sailing ships; some also take civilian trainees. Dedicated school ships run courses in maritime and general studies and many other vessels offer adventure sailing. Passenger sailing ships take trainees for international races or port festivals. The modern sail training fleet includes ships of many different rigs (see table), either newly built or remaining from the later days of commercial sail, as well as reconstructions and *replicas. A significant number, many since 1990, were built specifically for sail training. Most tall ships are at sea throughout the year. Many regularly take part in the international races.

In 1972 the STA races became the Cutty Sark Tall Ships' Races and were run by the **International Sail Training Association (ISTA)**, a subsidiary of the STA. Then in 2002 **Sail Training International** was formed by organizations from Australia, Belgium, Bermuda, Canada, Denmark, Finland, France, Germany, Ireland, Italy, Latvia, the Netherlands, Norway, Poland, Portugal, Russia, Spain, Sweden, UK, and USA, and this now runs the European Tall Ships' Races. The races attract an average of 70–100 vessels representing twenty nations; they range from the largest sail training ship, the Russian barque *Sedov*, with a sparred length of 122 metres (400 ft), to yachts 9 metres (30 ft) on the waterline owned by clubs, scout groups, and similar organizations. There are usually two races and a cruise-in-company, and the ships visit four European ports where crew contests are held on shore. Transatlantic races are held at regular intervals. The STA no longer organizes the races and is now incorporated in the **Tall Ships Youth Trust** which runs the 60-metre (195-ft) brigs *Stavnos S. Nianchos* and *Prince William*.

Each year hundreds of thousands (often millions) of visitors come to see the tall ships,

Table of Sail Training Ships over 40 metres (131 ft) sparred length (that is, overall including *bowsprit, *bumpkin, etc.). Ships in Class A category in Sail Training International races are from 40 metres on deck (stempost to sternpost)

Ship	*Country*	*Built*	*Rig*	*Sparred length (metres)*	*Sparred length (feet)*
Sedov	Russia	1920	Barque	122.3	401.3
Kruzenshtern	Russia	1926	Barque	114.5	375.7
Esmeralda	Chile	1952	Barquentine	113.0	370.7
Nippon Maru II	Japan	1984	Barque	110.1	361.2
Kaiwo Maru II	Japan	1984	Barque	110.1	361.2
Mir	Russia	1987	Ship rigged	109.6	359.6
Khersones	Ukraine	1988	Ship rigged	109.6	359.6
Pallada	Russia	1988	Ship rigged	109.4	358.9
Nadezhda	Russia	1991	Ship rigged	109.4	358.9
Druzhba	Russia	1987	Ship rigged	109.4	358.9
Dar Mlodziezy	Poland	1982	Ship rigged	109.2	358.3
Juan Sebastian de Elcano	Spain	1927	Schooner	106.8	350.4
Amerigo Vespucci	Italy	1931	Ship rigged	104.2	341.9
Libertad	Argentina	1956	Ship rigged	102.6	336.6
Statsraad Lehmkuhl	Norway	1914	Barque	98.7	323.8
Cuauhtemoc	Mexico	1982	Barque	90.8	297.9
Eagle	USA	1936	Barque	89.9	295.0
Gorch Fock II	Germany	1958	Barque	89.2	292.7
Sagres II	Portugal	1937	Barque	88.9	291.7
Simon Bolivar	Venezuela	1979	Barque	86.2	282.8
Mircea	Romania	1938	Barque	82.1	269.4
Kajama	Canada	1930	Schooner	80.2	263.0
Guayas	Ecuador	1976	Barque	79.5	260.8
Mercator	Belgium	1932	Barquentine	78.5	257.6
Cisne Branco	Brazil	1999	Ship rigged	78.0	255.9
Stad Amsterdam	The Netherlands	1999	Ship rigged	78.0	255.9
Gloria	Colombia	1968	Barque	76.0	249.3
Danmark	Denmark	1932	Ship rigged	75.9	249.0
Caledonia	Canada	1962	Barquentine	74.7	245.0
Christian Radich	Norway	1937	Ship rigged	72.2	236.9
Palinuro	Italy	1934	Barquentine	69.6	228.4
Creoula	Portugal	1937	Schooner	67.4	221.1
Grossherzogin Elisabeth	Germany	1909	Schooner	65.8	216.0
Tenacious	UK	2000	Barque	65.0	213.3
Sorlandet	Norway	1927	Ship rigged	65.0	213.3
Alexander von Humboldt	Germany	1906	Barque	62.6	205.4
Elissa	USA	1877	Barque	62.5	205.0
Swan fan Makkum	The Netherlands	1993	Brigantine	62.0	203.4
Capitan Miranda	Uruguay	1930	Schooner	61.9	203.1
Niagara	USA	1998	Brig	60.4	198.0
Europa	The Netherlands	1911	Barque	60.0	196.9
Artemis	The Netherlands	1926	Barque	60.0	196.9
Gunilla	Sweden	1940	Barque	59.5	195.2
Stavros S. Niarchos	UK	2000	Brig	59.4	194.7
Prince William	UK	2001	Brig	59.4	194.7
Eendracht	The Netherlands	1989	Schooner	59.1	193.9
Dewarutji	Indonesia	1952	Barquentine	58.2	191.0
Belem	France	1896	Barque	58.0	190.3

Concordia	Bahamas	1992	Barquentine	57.5	188.7
Bluenose II	Canada	1963	Schooner	55.2	181.0
Lord Nelson	UK	1985	Barque	54.9	180.0
Picton Castle	Canada	1928	Barque	54.6	179.0
Gazela Philadelphia	USA	1883	Barquentine	54.3	178.0
Fryderyk Chopin	Poland	1990	Brig	54.1	177.5
Tarangini	India	1997	Barque	54.0	177.2
Georg Stage	Denmark	1934	Ship rigged	54.0	177.2
Akogare	Japan	1992	Schooner	52.2	171.2
Leeuwin	Australia	1986	Barquentine	52.1	170.9
Mare Frisium	The Netherlands	1916	Schooner	52.0	170.6
Victory Chimes	USA	1900	Schooner	51.8	170.0
Pride of Baltimore II	USA	1988	Schooner	51.8	170.0
Bounty	USA	1960	Ship rigged	51.5	169.0
Shabab Oman	Oman	1971	Barquentine	51.5	169.0
Jeanie Johnston	Ireland	2000	Barque	51.0	167.3
Fridtjof Nansen	Germany	1919	Schooner	51.0	167.3
Roald Amundsen	Germany	1952	Brig	50.0	164.1
Thor Heyerdahl	Germany	1930	Schooner	49.8	163.5
Pogoria	Poland	1980	Barquentine	49.6	162.7
Den Store Bjorn	Denmark	1902	Schooner	49.4	162.0
Iskra	Poland	1982	Barquentine	48.8	160.1
Zodiac	USA	1924	Schooner	48.8	160.0
Kaliakra	Bulgaria	1984	Barquentine	48.5	159.1
Linden	Finland	1992	Schooner	48.0	157.5
Oosterschelde	The Netherlands	1918	Schooner	47.8	156.8
Tole Mour	USA	1988	Schooner	47.6	156.0
Highlander Sea	USA	1924	Schooner	47.0	154.2
Kaskelot	UK	1948	Barque	46.6	153.0
Margaret Todd	USA	1998	Schooner	46.0	151.0
Kaisei	Japan	1990	Brigantine	46.0	150.9
Ernestina	USA	1984	Schooner	45.6	149.4
Alma Doepel	Australia	1903	Schooner	45.5	149.3
Spirit of New Zealand	New Zealand	1986	Barquentine	45.2	148.3
Windy II	USA	2001	Barquentine	45.1	148.0
Windy	USA	1996	Schooner	45.1	148.0
Endeavour	Australia	1993	Ship rigged	44.4	145.6
Earl of Pembroke	UK	1945	Barque	44.2	145.0
Young Endeavour	Australia	1997	Brigantine	44.0	144.4
Tunas Samudera	Malaysia	1989	Brigantine	44.0	144.4
One and All	Australia	1985	Brigantine	43.0	141.1
Zawisza Czarny	Poland	1952	Schooner	42.7	140.1
Kalmar Nyckel	USA	1997	Ship rigged	43.0	141.0
Soren Larsen	UK	1949	Brigantine	42.7	140.0
Pacific Grace	Canada	1999	Schooner	42.3	138.6
Denis Sullivan	USA	2000	Schooner	42.1	138.0
Bill of Rights	USA	1971	Schooner	41.5	136.0
Wilhelm Pieck	Germany	1951	Brigantine	41.0	134.5
Robert C. Seamans	USA	2000	Brigantine	41.0	134.5
La Recouvrance	France	1992	Schooner	41.0	134.5
Corwith Cramer	USA	1987	Brigantine	41.0	134.5
Ji Fung	Hong Kong	1980	Schooner	40.2	132.0
Svanen	Australia	1922	Barquentine	40.0	131.2

their crews and the parades of sail, and 3,000–4,000 trainees aged 15–25 take part. Some are regular cadets while others pay for their berths. Ships and their crews are viewed as ambassadors for their nations. See also JUBILEE SAILING TRUST. Rosemary Mudie

St Elmo's Fire, the brushlike electric discharge which, under certain atmospheric conditions, takes place at the mastheads and *yardarms of a ship. It is known by over 50 different names, including St Ermyn, St Telme, St Helm, St Ermo, St Anselmo, etc., and was sometimes described by British seamen as 'Jack with a lantern'. The name is believed by some to be a corruption of St Erasmus, a patron saint of Mediterranean sailors. But it has also been equated with St Peter Gonzales (*c*.1190–1246), a Dominican friar who, after crusading with Ferdinand III of Spain against the Moors, devoted much of his life to improving the conditions of seafaring people along the Spanish coasts. One of the earliest recorded uses of it appears in a vow invoking the aid of Pope Urban V (1362–70) which caused 'the light of St Elemi' to appear. In the Middle Ages the appearance of the phenomenon was greeted sometimes with joy, sometimes with dread, and it was the origin of a number of *superstitions held by seamen, some benevolent, some not. Italian mariners of the 15th and 16th centuries believed that the lights emanated from the body of Christ and gave them the name of Corposanto, of which again there are many derivatives. It is also occasionally seen on aircraft flying among thunderclouds and sometimes on shore on prominent points such as church spires.

salinity, a measure of the saltiness of sea water. On average each litre (0.22 gals.) of seawater contains 35.5 grams (1.25 oz) of salt dissolved in it (i.e. has a salinity of 35.5). In the open ocean, salinity ranges from about 32 to 40. The highest values occur in the Red Sea where evaporation is very high. Salinity is important because together with the water temperature, it determines the density of the sea water. In tropical regions where rainfall is heavy, the rain dilutes the sea water and makes it more buoyant, but at the more arid *latitudes around 30°, the low rainfall combined with strong solar radiation makes the surface water denser so that it tends to sink. As the sea freezes in winter in the polar oceans, the water left unfrozen is saltier and very much colder, so it tends to sink. Conversely, during summer when the *ice is melting, the surface water is diluted and becomes more buoyant.

Once a body of water leaves the ocean's surface, its characteristics of temperature and salinity are conserved, and are only changed by turbulent mixing between the water body and its surrounding waters. The waters sinking into the ocean's interior in different regions have predictable characteristic temperature and salinity properties, and are known as water masses. The distribution of these water masses is used to follow the flow of deep *currents and map the features of their large-scale circulation. M. V. Angel

Sallee pirates, *Barbary pirates, mostly Muslims expelled from Spain, but also European renegades. They operated from the Moroccan port of Salli (now part of Rabat) from the early decades of the 17th century. They harassed Christian trade, and raided the coast of Spain, a particular focus of their hatred, to acquire victims for the *slave trade. Salli was nominally under the control of the Emperor of Morocco but in 1627 it broke away and established a self-governing *corsair republic. So successful were they that they later extended their activities into the English Channel and the Atlantic, and even as far as Newfoundland, and they could put as many as 60 ships—vessels developed from the Mediterranean *tartan and *xebec—to sea. These 'were all very fast sailers and nearly always equipped with *oars as well as sails, so fast indeed that the French Admiral Tourville believed that a Sallee rover could only be caught at sea by a former Sallee rover taken as a *prize into French service' (P. Earle, *The Pirate Wars* (2003), 44–5). Uncoordinated expeditions were mounted against them by the British, Dutch, French, and Spanish. These sometimes achieved temporary success, but *piracy always broke out again when the expeditions withdrew, and lack of a concerted effort to crush them allowed their depredations to continue well into the 18th century.

sally port. (1) A large *port cut on each *quarter of a *fireship out of which officers and men made their escape into the boats towing alongside as soon as the fireship had *grappled an enemy ship and the powder train was fired. **(2)** The *entering port of a three-*decker warship during the days of sail. **(3)** A landing place in Portsmouth Harbour which was reserved for the use of boats from men-of-war in the harbour. It was from this landing place that Lord *Nelson was rowed out to HMS **Victory* before sailing in September 1805 to join the British fleet off Cadiz before the battle of Trafalgar. See also WARFARE AT SEA.

salt horse, the seaman's slang name during the days of sail for the salted beef issued as victuals at sea. The origin of the expression was of course the toughness of the beef as it came out of the cask. It was also known as salt junk, indicating the seaman's belief that any old meat was thrown into the casks for pickling in brine irrespective of the animal from it was supposed to have come.

salutes at sea, the recognized courtesies paid by ships at sea to the warships of all nations. They originally took two forms: a ship would fire its guns or would *vail its *topsails, the latter when within the *territorial waters or *narrow seas of the warship being saluted. Gun salutes were fired on every possible occasion and were often unlimited in extent, largely due to a predilection of naval officers of all nations for loud and prolonged noise, and it was not until 1675 that regulations were introduced in Britain, quickly followed by all other maritime nations, limiting the number of guns to be fired. The immediate cause of the limitation was the need to stop the severe wastage of gunpowder, and Samuel *Pepys, secretary of the British *Admiralty, worked out a scale based on a minimum salute of three guns up to nineteen guns for the admiral of the fleet. Two more guns were added for a salute to the monarch, and a royal or presidential salute still remains at 21 guns. The odd numbers were chosen for salutes because even numbers were always fired at naval funerals as a sign of mourning for the dead officer.

Gun salutes were always fired with the saluting ship's bows pointed towards the ship being saluted to avoid any possibility that a salute might be construed as a hostile act, since muzzle-loading guns had to have *shot in them to make a satisfactory bang and they could only be fired broadside on. A ship firing a salute bows-on to the ship saluted could not possibly hit her.

As the armed merchant ship went out of fashion and sail was gradually displaced by *steam propulsion, a new means of saluting had to be devised to take the place of the guns or the struck topsails. This was done by dipping the *ensign, lowering it halfway down the ensign staff and not rehoisting it until the warship had answered the salute by dipping her own ensign. As soon as the warship rehoisted her ensign the merchant ship followed suit and the salute was complete. This remains the current practice. See also FLAG ETIQUETTE.

Navies have a variety of salutes for officers of rank and ships of foreign nations, varying between gun salutes, guards and bands, guards without bands, bugle calls, and *piping the side, according to rank and circumstances. See also QUARTERDECK.

salvage. From around the 14th century many Italian and other coastal cities already had sea laws in place that defined a split between the finder and the original owner in the value of salvaged goods brought into their harbours. In most cases this was dependent on whether the goods were recovered floating on the surface (see FLOTSAM), or from the sea bottom (see LAGAN), and how close the *shipwrecks were to the harbour. In the late 19th century salvage became the compensation paid by the owner of a ship or a cargo in respect of services rendered by persons, other than the ship's company, in preserving a ship or cargo from shipwreck or fire, a process in which *tugs often played an important role. *Lloyd's Form of Salvage Agreement (Lloyd's Open Form) was first adopted in 1892 on the basis of 'no cure, no pay', and it has been evolving ever since. In the UK salvage by an individual or a company is governed by the legal definition of *wreck.

But the word salvage has other meanings, too, from the skilled techniques of firms employed to raise, or move, dangerous wrecks, to the activities of individuals who undertake *diving expeditions to recover sunken treasure. Nowadays, sites are protected from the activities of the latter and *marine archae-

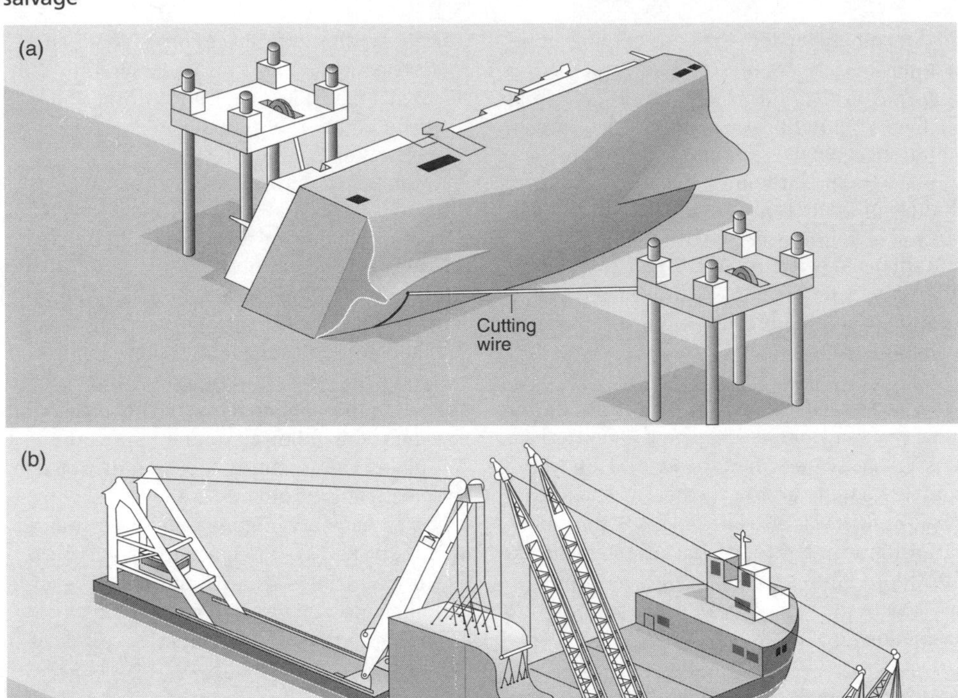

In December 2002 the 50,000 tonne Norwegian container ship *Tricolour* sank in a busy part of the English Channel after a collision. [a] After the ship's fuel had been drained out, divers drilled holes in the hull for the hoisting cables and a special cutting wire was strung under it from the platforms which had been erected either side of it. This moved to and fro between the two platforms to cut the hull into several segments [b] The hull segments were then removed by two floating cranes. The one on the left clamped onto the top of a segment and the hoisting cables of the other were attached to its side. The segments were then lifted onto a 'Giant' barge which is semi-submersible

ology plays a major role in preserving and interpreting what has been found. For example, the **Mary Rose* was a salvage operation but was undertaken by experts with conservation as the primary objective. However, marine archaeologists and salvage operators often use the same equipment, though their objectives are often different. Side-scan *sonars are used to locate wrecks accurately and divers' salvage reports have been replaced by television surveys carried out by *underwater vehicles.

From the second half of the 15th century onwards *exploration by sea saw many European ships being lost around the world. Among the Caribbean islands in particular, seasonal hurricanes sank any number of Spanish *treasure ships before they even reached the Atlantic Ocean for the voyage home. Salvage from such wrecks soon became a thriving business. Locals using free-diving techniques were pressed into service, not only by the Spanish themselves, but by many other nationalities who wanted to recover a fortune from under the sea.

In the late 17th century an American born Englishman, William Phips, found sponsors for an expedition to investigate the wreck of the *La Nuestra Señora de la Concepción* off the island of *Hispaniola. Sailing in a ship supplied by the king, he located her, against the odds, and his divers recovered a staggering 37 tons of treasure, worth at that time £207,600. Arriving back in England in June 1687, Phips received his one-sixteenth share and was knighted, while his main sponsor, the Duke of Albemarle, became a very rich man. In the years following Phips's success much of the coastline around Britain and the Americas, then owned by the British crown, was to be divided up and sold off to potential wreck hunters, with the crown taking a share of the profits. However, many investors went bankrupt, including the author of **Robinson Crusoe*, Daniel Defoe.

Early salvage methods usually involved the recovery of both goods and guns. *Grapnels, attached by divers, ripped off the decks of sunken wrecks to allow the divers vertical access. The alternative, described in 16th-century editions of Vitruvius, a Roman architect from the 4th century AD, was to lift and move an entire sunken vessel. In a method used successfully in a Venetian lagoon, two sailing ships positioned themselves either side of the wreck linked together with wooden beams. Lifting ropes were run under its hull and the wreck gradually moved into shallower water, helped by successive incoming tides. From then on this was the general method used in raising a wreck, though each one presented, and presents, a different set of problems. Certainly, salvage work became much more efficient with the introduction in the 19th century of steam winches. Using well-developed rigging techniques, and the wire rope which was introduced towards the end of the century, these provided enough power for wrecks even to be rolled over.

Many ships posed a danger to shipping by sinking very close to port or, as the **Vasa* did, in the harbour itself. Stockholm already had wreck removal measures under way in the early 17th century, as did Sheerness *dockyard in England. At Sheerness, gunpowder was employed to clear a channel of a shipwreck. It was sealed in barrels, lowered to the bottom and then ignited from the surface by means of a gunpowder fuse inside a long leather pipe. The same method was used later in the century, for clearing the River Tiber between the sea port of Ostia and Rome, and again for the removal of the wreck of the **Royal George*. As diving techniques improved, there began a golden age of stories of treasure recovered from wrecks. Typically, after the *Alphonse XII* sank off Grand Canary in 1885, divers descended 51 metres (160 ft) to smash their way through a number of decks and reach the strong room, recovering £90,000 of the £100,000 of gold being carried. In 1917 the liner *Laurentic*, a casualty of war, went down with £5,000,000 of bullion of which 99% was later recovered by salvage operators. When the *ocean liner *Egypt* sank in much deeper water in 1922, an observation chamber directed surface-operated grabs which recovered three-quarters of the £1,045,000 in gold aboard.

Improvements in water pump and air compressor efficiency opened up many more possibilities for innovative methods by professional salvage companies. After the German *High Seas Fleet scuttled itself in *Scapa Flow in 1919, all but one of the wrecks was removed using access tubes with airlocks so that workers could enter the hulls below water level and work under pressure. Divers could also install patches over holes in a sunken hull, then attach air hoses which pumped air into the hull to restore enough buoyancy for it to be moved. Lifting *caissons were often employed, as with the wreck of the US *submarine *Squalus*, which sank off the east coast of the USA in 1939. Caissons were rigid structures that offered a fixed volume and a known lifting capability, but small wrecks or objects are sometimes raised using flexible lifting bags. However, great care is needed, as once enough air is added for them to lift the weight from the bottom, water pressure lessens and the air begins to expand. This creates more buoyancy, and the lift can get increasingly out of control.

Where a wreck cannot be moved or hoisted it is cut up instead. In the past, a chain was used to cut through parts of a hull which was worked back and forth using winches or cranes. However, there is now a more efficient flexible wire saw available, and this was used to remove a dangerous wreck in the English Channel in 2003. With the sunken 14,000-tonne Russian submarine *Kursk*, whose salvage began in 2001 from 100 metres (330 ft) of water, the damaged bow was first cut away. Divers then cut holes in the hull, wire ropes were attached, and the two parts lifted separately. Peter Dick

sampan, the typical small and light boats of oriental waters and rivers. There are two types, the harbour sampan which usually has an *awning over the centre and after part and is normally propelled by a single *scull over the stern, and the coastal sampan fitted with a single mast and *junk rig. The origin of the name, first recorded in the 8th century, is generally said to come from the Chinese *san-pan*, meaning 'three boards', but some believe it has a Malayan origin.

samson post. In the old days when it was normal to *cat anchors before they were let go or on *weighing, a samson post was a post erected temporarily on deck to take a *tackle with a sufficiently long lead for the whole crew to man the *fall. When all anchors had to be handled entirely by manpower, a large number of men were required on the tackles used in lifting and stowing. Later, a small *derrick mast in a merchant ship to support the cargo booms came to be known as a samson post. They were usually fitted in pairs and were known colloquially as **goalposts**. It is also the name of a post fitted on the foredeck of *yachts and small craft. It is not a deck fitting but extends down to the keel, so is the strongest point on which to make fast *mooring chains or a *tow rope.

sandbagger, a type of broad, shallow, open or partly decked sailing boat which originated in America about 1850, in which movable *ballast in the form of sandbags was used while racing, and wagers were often made on the results. The boats, generally of the *catboat type, were divided into four classes: 8–9 metres (26–30 ft), 7–8 metres (23–26 ft), and under 6 metres (20 ft). They carried an immense area of sail, with a mainsail and *jib, and had agile crews of eight or more who shifted the sandbags onto the *weather deck every time the boat *tacked. The vogue lasted, mainly in New York harbour and at New Orleans, until the 1880s with the advent of finer designs of *yachts for racing, but it also became a popular sport in Australia's Sydney harbour.

sand-glass, an instrument for measuring the passage of time on board ship before suitable *chronometers had been developed. Basically the sand-glass comprises two vacuum glass globes connected by a narrow neck, like an egg-timer. The sand ran from the top globe into the bottom one through the neck, emptying itself in a given interval of time. When it had all run through the sand-glass was reversed and the process repeated. Four sizes of sand-glasses were manufactured for maritime use: half-minute, half-hour, hour, and four-hour glasses, but the two most in use were the half-minute and half-hour. The former, later changed to a 28-second glass, was used to estimate the speed of the ship with the aid of the ship's *log. The latter was the main means of measuring the passage of time on board ship, the *ship's bell being rung every time a half-hour glass emptied itself. A *watch on board amounted to eight half-hour glasses, or four hours.

SAR, search and rescue. See GLOBAL MARITIME DISTRESS AND SAFETY SYSTEM; LIFESAVING.

Sargasso Sea, see SARGASSO WEED.

sargasso weed is a brown *seaweed (*Sargassum natans*) which is a member of a genus with 150 species, nearly all of which live attached to the seabed in shallow water. Sargasso weed is the exception in that it is found floating freely in the tropical oceans, particularly in the Sargasso Sea where it gathers in large accumulations in the centre of a great *eddy lined up along *slicks and *windrows. The Sargasso Sea, the area of the North Atlantic east of the Bahamas Islands bounded by 25° and 30° N. and 40° and 60° W., derived its name from the Portuguese word for grapes *sargaco*, because of the grapelike floats on the brown fronds of the weed. Clumps of sargasso provide a unique pelagic habitat for an assortment of animals that have become specifically adapted for life within this floating forest. *Fishes like the sargassum anglerfish (*Histrio histrio*) have the same coloration as the weed and bodies covered with protuberances that mimic the fronds of the seaweed. *Sargassum muticum*, a relative of sargassum weed, is a notoriously aggressive invader. Originating in Japanese waters, it has been accidentally introduced to temperate coastal waters worldwide; such introduction of alien species is an *environmental issue. Once introduced it grows so rapidly that it tends to displace the native species of seaweeds and greatly reduces the diversity of inshore habitats.

The Sargasso Sea was mentioned by Christopher *Columbus in his accounts of his voyages to the New World, and has given rise to many stories of ships trapped in the weed and unable to make their way out. This was a belief prevalent among many seamen during the days of sail, but it was finally disproved by Sir John Murray's expedition in 1910 that discovered the surface was covered only in patches of weed. It is also the main breeding place of *eels, the elvers swimming to Europe in the *Gulf Stream.

M. V. Angel

satellite navigation, position finding by means of a space-based system of orbiting satellites. Now the most general way of navigating at sea, it has virtually displaced every other method of fixing the ship's position, whether *hyperbolic, *radio direction finding, or *celestial navigation, one reason for this being the low cost of the equipment, others being its accuracy and ease of use. However, as the whole system is owned by the military, and can be withdrawn at any time, it is inherently unlikely that more traditional methods of navigation will be abandoned, and celestial navigation, and at least one ground-based radio aid such as *Loran-C, will probably remain for the foreseeable future.

The Doppler shift is a well-documented phenomenon but its potential as a method of global positioning was only realized in the 1950s when radio signals picked up from the USSR's orbiting satellite Sputnik revealed a marked Doppler shift when received at fixed points on earth. From these transmissions American scientists were able to calculate Sputnik's orbit in no time. The corollary was that the Doppler shift of a satellite of known orbit could also be used to determine the position of the receiver.

The first satellite navigation system to become commercially available was the US Navy Navigation Satellite System known as Transit. Using the Doppler shift principle, it provided accurate position information to ships at sea up until the end of 1996 when the more advanced American military *GPS, known as Navstar, took its place. The other satellite navigation system in operation is the Russian Glonass which has much in common with GPS. Plans for a European system entitled Galileo are in hand and the system is expected to be operational by 2008. GPS III is expected to replace the present GPS system by 2010.

The GPS system consists of a master ground control, ground monitoring stations, and a constellation of satellites the positions and orbits of which will be precisely known through monitoring and regular correction. In the current system 24 operational satellites, four in each of six orbital planes inclined at 55° to the equator, orbit the earth at an altitude of 20,200 kilometres (12,625 m.) with an approximately twelve-hour orbit period. (Because of the difference between solar and sidereal time each of the satellites will appear above any fixed point on the earth four minutes earlier each day.) The accuracy of GPS depends critically on precise timekeeping and each satellite carries four atomic clocks. The GPS receiver stores and continuously updates time information from the satellite and can calculate the delay in the transmission of signals of each satellite, which provides a measure of the distance between the satellite and receiver.

The current (2004) satellites radiate two codes, a Precision Code (P) and a Coarse Acquisition Code (C/A), both of which are now available for civil use. In general the accuracy of GPS *fixes is taken to be of the order of 10–20 metres (33–65 ft), although in many cases it may well be considerably less. An important factor to remember is that the geodetic chart datum to which the receiver will normally be referenced is that known as WGS84, the World Geodetic System 1984, an ellipsoidal figure of the earth based on a centre equivalent to its centre of gravity. By no means the majority of nautical *charts are yet based on this datum and most receivers have a facility for altering the datum to that of the chart in use. Significant errors in position may arise from failing to adjust the datum in this way. Most GPS receivers offer a bewildering range of navigational facilities such as speed over the ground, speed through the water, distance to go, time to go, course to steer, estimated time of arrival, cross-track error, and so on. Most of them are related to *waypoints which form an essential feature of computerized navigation.

Differential GPS (DGNSS) is a system for improving the accuracy of GPS fixes. The main sources of error in satellite navigation are consistent over large geographical areas and the errors may be corrected by using reference stations, whose position is precisely known, to measure the errors of the signals from the satellites. Any corrections are transmitted to users' receivers which adjust their position measurements accordingly. Marine *radio beacon stations with a range of 160–240 kilometres (100–150 mls.) are commonly used to transmit these corrections to maritime users. Application of the corrections typically will give an accuracy of 1–2 metres. The requirements for such high accuracy could include improved voyage planning, freedom of manoeuvre in restricted waters, etc.

Sandford, W. H., *A Simple Guide to GPS for Marine Use* (2001). Mike Richey

Savannah, a US *paddle steamer of 380 tons, was the first vessel powered by *steam propulsion to cross the North Atlantic when in May 1819 she made a passage from Savannah to Liverpool in 27 days. She was originally a sailing vessel but was later fitted with a small auxiliary engine with detachable paddle wheels that were unshipped and laid on deck when she was under sail. During her passage she was, in fact, under power for only 85 hours. The rest of the voyage was made under sail, as her *master found that using wind and steam power together did not work—when she heeled while under sail one paddle dug deep into the water and the other beat on nothing but air. It was not until 1838 that one of the earliest *ocean liners, the **Sirius*, crossed the North Atlantic entirely under her own power.

save-all, the name given to a temporary sail set to catch the wind which might escape beneath the foot of any other sail.

scampavia, a type of small warship of the kingdom of the two Sicilies (Naples and Sicily) during the Napoleonic War (1803–15). It was basically a large rowing boat or *galley of up to 46 metres (150 ft) in length, pulled by twenty *oars or *sweeps a side, with each rower having his *bunk or sleeping place under his rowing bench. They were very fast in the water, whether sailing or being pulled. See also WARFARE AT SEA.

scandalize, to, to reduce sail in *gaff-rigged craft by hauling up the *tack and lowering the *peak of a sail. It was a method used by the old sailing *trawlers to reduce speed through the water when operating a *trawl. Also the *yards in a *square-rigged ship are said to be scandalized when they are not set square to the masts after the ship has anchored. Scandalizing the yards of a ship was a sign of mourning for a death on board.

scant, a defunct term which applied to the wind when it headed a *square-rigged ship so that she could just lay her *course with the *yards *braced.

scantlings, originally the dimensions of a *timber after it has been reduced to its standard size. Its modern meaning covers the dimensions of all parts which go into the construction of a ship's hull, including its *frames, *stringers, girders, plates, etc. Rules governing these sizes, based on long experience and study, are published by various *classification authorities, and most ships of any size built throughout the world are constructed to them.

When *yacht racing increased in popularity during the last quarter of the 19th century the introduction of proper scantlings prevented the construction of unseaworthy boats such as *skimming dishes.

Scapa Flow, a huge expanse of water in the Orkney Islands sheltered by the off-lying islands of Hoy, Flotta, South Ronaldsay, and Burray. It was used as the base for the British *Grand Fleet during the First World War (1914–18) and for the Royal Navy's Home Fleet during the Second (1939–45). At the end of the First World War the German *High Seas Fleet was interned there, where most of it was *scuttled by its crews in June 1919.

'Scarborough warning', a nautical expression meaning to let anything on board go with a run without giving due warning. The term comes from an incident in English history, the surprise attack on Scarborough Castle in 1557, when men encountered on the approach march were hanged without trial on suspicion of robbery. The poet and dramatist Thomas Heywood wrote of this:

This term *Scarborow warning* grew, some say,
By hasty hanging for rank robbery theare,
Who that was met, but suspected in that way,
Straight he was truss'd, whatever he were.

scarf, or **scarph,** the joining of two *timbers by bevelling off the edges so that the same thickness is maintained throughout the length of the joint. In the construction of a wooden ship, the *stem and *sternposts are scarfed to the keel. A scarf which embodies a step in the middle of the joint, so preventing the two parts from drawing apart, is called a lock scarf. It is a joint of great antiquity, having been used in early Egyptian and Phoenician *shipbuilding.

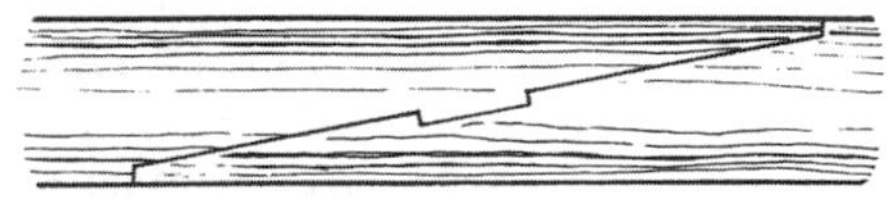
A scarfed spar

scend (pron. send), the quick upward motion when a ship *pitches in a heavy sea. In its old meaning it was the opposite of pitching, the quick roll when a sea knocks a vessel off its *course, but this meaning has now died out. **Scend of the sea**, the surge of the sea as it runs into a harbour.

schnorkel, or **snorkel. (1)** The German name given to a tube attachment providing an air supply to a *submarine at periscope depth. It was abbreviated in the British Navy as a 'snort' and was called a snorkel in the US Navy. A conventional submarine has to use its electric engines after it has dived as its *diesel engines depend on a constant supply of oxygen. When the Germans overran the Netherlands in 1940 during the Second World War (1939–45) they captured a half-completed Dutch submarine fitted with a tube which enabled the diesel engines to obtain air so long as the vessel did not go below periscope depth. **(2)** The name of the breathing tube recreational swimmers use. It allows them to keep their faces under water so that they can view what is below them. See DIVING.

schokker, a Dutch fishing vessel of the middle part of what used to be the Zuider Zee, usually from Enkhuizen, with a flat bottom, curved sides, a straight *stem raking at about 45°, and narrow *leeboards. They were similar to a *hengst but were generally larger. Dating from the early part of the 18th century, the schokker was normally built of oak in sizes varying between 13 and 16 metres (45–52 ft) in length and 5 and 6 metres (16–19 ft) in *beam. They were originally rigged with a *sprit mainsail and a *gaff-rigged *mizzen in addition to a *staysail and a *jib set flying on a *bowsprit. Later, schokkers were built of steel and some were converted, or were built, as *yachts.

schooner (Dutch *schooner*, German *schouer*, Danish *skonnert*, Spanish and Portuguese *escaña*), all possibly deriving from the Scottish verb to 'scon' or 'scoon', to skip over the water like a flat stone. The name is said to have come from a chance remark 'there she scoons' from a spectator at the *launch of the first vessel of the type at Gloucester, Mass., in 1713. There is some evidence that the schooner did originate in North America and probably at Gloucester.

A typical schooner has a *fore-and-aft rig on two or more masts. The type originally carried square *topsails on the foremast, though later, with the advance in rig designs, these were changed to *jib-headed or *jackyard topsails. *Yachts rigged as schooners generally set *Bermudan sails and so have no topsails. Properly speaking, a schooner has two masts only, with the mainmast taller than the foremast, but three-masted, four-masted, and five-masted schooners have been built, and one, the **Thomas W. Lawson*, the largest schooner ever built, had seven. These were commercial schooners, largely used in the coasting trade and also in local *fisheries on the *Grand Banks, their attraction to their owners being that they

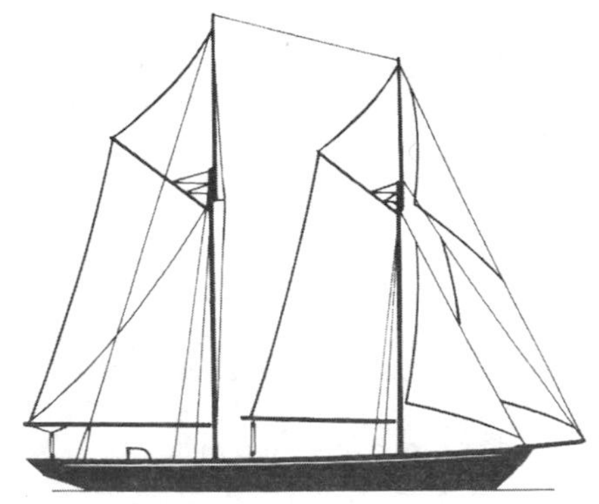
Gaff schooner rig

required a smaller crew than a *square-rigged vessel of comparable size.

The last remaining wooden-hulled topsail schooner in Britain is the three-masted 30-metre (100-ft) *Kathleen & May*, based at Bideford, north Devon. Built in 1900 she worked as a trading schooner until the 1960s and is still sailing. See also FRAM.

scope. (1) The amount of *cable run out when a ship lies to a single anchor. Its scope is approximately the radius of the circle through which the ships swings under the influence of the tide. **(2)** The display screen of a *radar or *sonar.

score. (1) The name given to the groove cut in the shell of a wooden *block in which the *strop is passed. Blocks are stropped with an *eye or hook at the top so that they can be used wherever necessary, and the score prevents the strop from slipping off the shell of the block. Similarly it is the groove cut round the body of a *deadeye for the same reason. **(2)** The space vacated in a rope when unlaying a *strand in the course of making a *long splice is also known as a score.

scotsman, a sacrificial strip of chafe protection aboard a ship. They are usually strips of metal or wood fitted on the deck to take chafe from the anchor chain or from slack running *rigging. Jeremy Lines

Scott, Robert Falcon (1868–1912), British naval officer and Antarctic explorer, a native of Devonport and the descendant of three generations of sailors. In 1899 he met the secretary of the Royal Geographical Society who recommended he lead the National Antarctic Expedition. The chief objective of this was the scientific exploration of Victoria Land, in the New Zealand sector of Antarctica, first discovered by Sir James Clark Ross (1800–62), and the 484-ton polar vessel *Discovery*, later used for the **Discovery* Investigations, was equipped for this task. Scott was promoted commander and the expedition sailed in August 1901, and after discovering King Edward VII Land, wintered at Hut point on Ross Island. During the two summer seasons of 1902–3 and 1903–4, several valuable sledging journeys were made. On one of these Scott, accompanied by Dr E. A. Wilson and Ernest *Shackleton, reached a southern *latitude of 82° 16' 33" on 30 December 1902, the most southerly point ever reached up to that time.

On his return to naval duties in England Scott was promoted *captain and in September 1908 married the sculptress Kathleen Bruce. He then served as naval assistant to the Second Sea Lord before he led a second expedition to continue the scientific work of the earlier one, with the added objective of reaching the South Pole. In June 1910 he sailed in the wooden 749-ton three-masted *barque *Terra Nova* which had been built in 1884 as the biggest *whaling ship afloat. On his arrival in New Zealand he heard that the Norwegian Roald *Amundsen was also planning to reach the South Pole, and while establishing his winter quarters at Cape Evan and laying supply depots he sent a northern party to Cape Adare in the *Terra Nova*. Then on 1 November 1911 he set out for the South Pole, and though his motorized transport failed him he reached the foot of the Beardmore Glacier using dogs and ponies. From then on he relied entirely on manhauling.

On 4 January 1912 the last supporting party set up 'One Ton Depot' and left for base and Scott, accompanied by Dr E. A. Wilson, Captain L. E. G. Oates, Lieutenant H. R. Bowers, and *Petty Officer Edgar Evans, pressed on across the Antarctic plateau to the pole which they reached on 18 January 1912, only to find that Amundsen had already been there. The return journey of over 1,280 kilometres (800 mls.) was marked by a series of disasters, a combination of deteriorating weather, inadequate diet, and shortage of fuel. On 17 February Evans died after a severe fall. On 17 March Oates, badly frost-bitten in the feet, and reluctant to be a hindrance to the others, walked out of the tent to his death in a blizzard. A week later another blizzard caught the remainder of the party only 7.6 kilometres (11 mls.) from 'One Ton Depot' and safety. Scott's body, with those of Wilson and Bowers, was found in their tent by a search party eight months later. Alongside them were their diaries, personal papers, and unique geological specimens.

Scott has been portrayed as incompetent, and he certainly did make mistakes, errors he freely admitted to in his diaries. However, in the 1980s a network of automated weather stations was installed, for aircraft safety, in an area which covered Scott's path from the pole. An American Antarctic scientist working for the *National Oceanic and Atmospheric Administration has analysed the meteorological data accumulated by the network and has concluded (see S. Solomon, *The Coldest March* (2001)) that it was exceptional weather, some 20 °F colder than normal, which was largely responsible for the tragedy. One of the contributing factors was that the extreme cold would have turned the snow to a consistency that made it incredibly hard for the sledges, on which Scott and his party carried their supplies, to run properly.

Huntford, R., *The Last Place on Earth: Scott and Amundsen's Race to the South Pole* (1999).
Huxley, E., *Scott of the Antarctic* (1990).
Savours, A., *The Voyages of Discovery* (2001).

scow, in the US a small flat-bottomed racing *yacht. In Britain it was a large boat, very full in the *bilges and with a flat bottom, used as a *lighter or as a *ferry to transport men a short distance at sea.

screw slip, see CABLE STOPPERS.

scrimshaw, the name given to the carving done by sailors of *whaling ships on the jawbone or teeth of *whales or the tusks of walrus. The origin of the word is not certain but the art was developed by the American whalemen of the early 19th century, but there is no evidence that the word derived from an Admiral Scrimshaw as some have suggested. Herman *Melville remarks of the whaler's crew in his novel *Moby-Dick*: 'Some of them have little boxes of dentistical-looking implements specially intended for the shrimshandering business. But in general they toil with the jack-knives alone.'

SCUBA, acronym for self-contained underwater breathing apparatus. See DIVING.

scud, to, a 19th-century term to describe a sailing vessel running before a *gale with reduced sails, or under *bare poles. It is a dangerous practice, especially if no *drogue is used to slow the vessel down, as the vessel risks being *pooped.

scull, to, to give a small boat headway by working a single *oar to and fro in its stern *rowlock. As a noun, it describes a very light oar used by racing oarsmen who are said to scull when in action. See also YULOH.

sculler, the name given to a small river boat which plied for hire on London's River Thames during the 17th and 18th centuries, when it was used as a main thoroughfare. It was rowed by a single man pulling a pair of *oars. See also PAIR OF OARS.

scupper, to, see SCUTTLE.

scuppers, draining holes, also known as freeing ports, cut through the *bulwarks of a sailing ship on the *waterways to allow any water on deck to drain away down the ship's side. **Scupper shutters** were flaps fitted over the outboard side of the scuppers and hinged on the top so that the pressure of water inboard will swing them open while water pressure outside the ship will keep them firmly closed. Pipes led internally to drain water off the deck are known as **scupper pipes**.

scurvy, a disease caused by vitamin C deficiency and the difficulty, during the days of sail, of preserving fresh fruit and vegetables. It usually became apparent after about six weeks on salt provisions, and was a common ailment when long voyages of *exploration by sea began in the 16th century. The first symptoms were usually swellings on the gums and the falling out of teeth, followed by blotches on the skin and a dull lethargy from which a man could be roused only when his life was threatened. In the 18th century more British Navy seamen died of the disease than were ever lost in battle.

To combat the disease the Chinese, as early as the 5th century, grew ginger plants aboard their ships and by the 14th century had, by purely empirical means, 'arrived at an understanding of the role some kinds of food could play in preventing or curing diseases like beri-beri. The Dutch, in contact with Chinese-influenced south-east Asia, probably learned there that greenstuffs and citrus fruits could be important in a sea diet and passed the message on to Europe' (R. Tannahill, *Food in History* (rev. edn. 1988), 227). After the appalling casualties caused by scurvy on *Anson's voyage round the world in 1740–4, Dr James Lind (1716–94), a British naval surgeon, published his *Treatise of the Scurvy* in 1753 in which he recommended the navy follow the Dutch practice of taking citrus fruits on long voyages. However, it was not until the naval physician Sir Gilbert Blane (1749–1834) became a commissioner of the Sick and Wounded Board in 1795 that Lind's recommendations were followed. Lemon juice was made a compulsory issue—usually in the *grog ration—and this virtually eradicated the disease in the Royal Navy.

In the mid-19th century lime juice replaced lemon as it was cheaper, and the Parliamentary Act of 1844, later reinforced by another Act in 1867, laid down its issue to the crews of merchant ships. But it was not then known that limes have only half the anti-scorbutic value of lemons, and scurvy recurred if insufficient doses of lime juice were used; and in merchant ships scurvy even increased in the decade 1873–83. The disease was not finally conquered until vitamins were discovered during the early decades of the 20th century. See also 'LIMEY'.

Carpenter, K., *History of Scurvy and Vitamin C* (rev. edn. 1988).

scuttle. **(1)** A circular window cut in the side of a ship to admit light and air, also known in the Royal Navy as a sidelight and in the merchant service as a porthole or portlight. It consists of a circular metal frame with a thick disc of glass which is hinged on one side and which can be tightly secured to the ship's side from inside by butterfly nuts. A **deadlight** is the part of the scuttle which is let down and secured with a butterfly nut to protect the glass in heavy weather. **(2)** As a verb, it means the deliberate sinking of a ship by opening its *seacocks or by blowing holes in its bottom. The origin of the word, as in the synonymous verb to scupper, presumably is to make the ship sink to the level of its scuttles at which point the sea will pour in through them and finish the job of sinking it. **(3)** A cask is said to be **scuttled** when its *staves are stove in or broken.

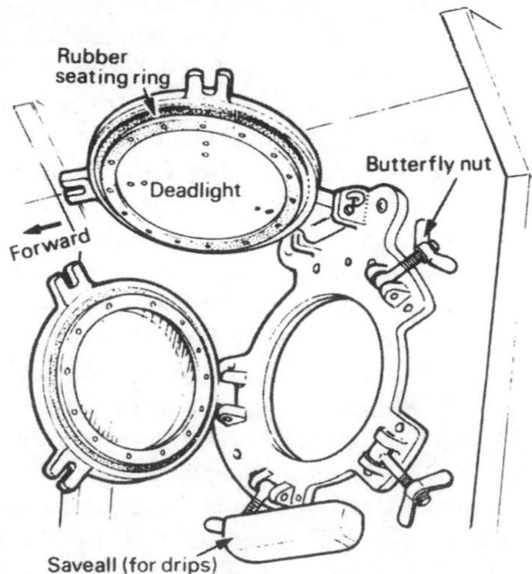

Scuttle

scuttle, or **scuttled, butt,** a cask lashed in a convenient part of the ship to hold water for daily use before the days when ships were fitted with fresh water tanks. All water in those days had to be carried on board in large casks and, on a long voyage, had to be used very sparingly to make it last until the next opportunity to land and refill the casks. To prevent more than half a butt full of water being available daily, the butt was, in effect, 'scuttled' by having a square piece sawn out of the widest part of its side, or *bilge. The grog-butt from which *grog was dispensed was a scuttle butt.

Scylla and **Charybdis,** the names of two mythical navigational hazards in the Straits of Messina between which, according to the Greek legend, the fleet of *Odysseus, or in the Latin legend that of Ulysses, passed after the capture of Troy. In the legend Scylla was a nymph seen bathing in the nude by the sea god Glaucus who fell in love with her but whose advances she repelled. Glaucus appealed to Circe for a love potion but she, jealous of his affection for Scylla, gave him instead a poisonous mixture which, when poured into the sea when she bathed, turned Scylla into a frightful monster, rooted to a rock on the Italian sides of the straits. Nevertheless, she retained her lovely voice and whenever a ship passed she sang songs enticing the mariners on board to their destruction.

Charybdis was a dangerous whirlpool on the Sicilian side of the straits opposite Scylla. She was said by legend originally to have been an avaricious woman who stole the oxen of Hercules and for this misdeed was punished by Zeus by being turned into a whirlpool. She was also said to swallow the sea three times a day and throw it up again, thus causing the whirlpool. Between Scylla on one side and Charybdis on the other, the unfortunate seamen of the time seemed to have little chance of survival.

sea anchor, anything that will hold a vessel's bow to the sea in heavy weather. *Oars, barricoes (see BREAKER), or loose sails *lashed together and *veered from the bow on as long a line as possible will act as a satisfactory sea anchor to which a vessel can ride out a *storm. Various forms of *drogue are often offered as sea anchors, but usually the vessel's own gear will prove as efficient a sea anchor as any. In very severe weather, such as *typhoons, a ship's anchor lowered to some depth on its *cable has often been used to hold the ship's *head to the sea.

Sea Beggars, the name given during the second half of the 16th and early part of the 17th centuries to the independent Protestants who lived in what was later to be known as the Dutch Republic.

The Low Countries were at that time occupied by Spain with great severity and cruelty, and it was against the Spaniards that the Sea Beggars led a popular revolt. Their initial success was an amphibious operation at Brill in 1572, and in the following year they defeated a Spanish *squadron off the port of Hoorn in what used to be the Zuider Zee. Two of the great Dutch naval heroes, Admirals Jacob van Heemskerk (1567–1607) and Piet Heyn (1578–1629), began their naval careers as Sea Beggars, and it was from these beginnings the Dutch Navy was established in the 17th century. See also WARFARE AT SEA.

seabirds. There are over 300 species of birds belonging to around sixteen families that rely on the sea for their food and only return to land to nest. Many, including most gulls (44 species), are restricted to coastal waters, but several are truly oceanic, and even when nesting, fly hundreds of kilometres to collect food. There are four main modes of feeding: diving, plunging, surface feeding, and stealing from other seabirds.

Diving is best developed in the seventeen species of *penguins. Penguins are restricted to the southern hemisphere and in the northern hemisphere their feeding niche is filled by the eighteen species of *auks and three species of puffins (*Fratercula* spp.), which can still fly, but also use their wings to swim underwater, which restricts their size. The 26 species of cormorant (*Phalacrocorax* spp.) also dive for fish using both their feet and their wings to swim underwater. One cormorant, the Galapagos cormorant (*Phalacrocorax harrisi*), has become flightless, a characteristic of island birds. The nine species of gannets and *boobies (*Sula* spp.) are plunge divers and eight species of pelican (*Pelecanus* spp.) mix plunge diving with surface fishing. The sight of a large flock of gannets over a *shoal of fish hurtling into the water at high speed is one of the more dramatic sights in inshore waters. The 40 species of terns (*Sterna* spp.) and noddies (e.g. *Anous* spp.), also known as sea swallows, also plunge dive. Terns are remarkable strong fliers: the Arctic tern (*Sterna paradisaea*) undertakes the longest migration of any bird, commuting from its nesting grounds in Arctic to overwinter in the Antarctic, a round trip of about 35,000 kilometres (22,000 mls.), and so enjoys almost continuous summer and almost continuous daylight.

Surface feeding, often along *slicks, is the mode used by the greatest number of seabirds. They tend to be more nocturnal, because at night many species of *plankton and small *fish migrate up to the surface. Some of these surface feeders are strong fliers, using gliding flight to cover vast distances with minimum expenditure of energy. The most efficient of these gliders are the thirteen species of *albatrosses and *mollymawks.

There are three species of sea eagle (*Haliaetus* spp.), which, together with the bald eagle (*Haliaetus leucocephalus*) and the osprey (*Pandion haliaetus*), can snatch fish out of the water with their talons. They are also scavengers, eating the bodies of spent salmon and following fishing boats to pick up their discards. The Steller's sea eagle (*Haliaeetus pelagicus*) is the largest of all eagles and occurs along the north-west Pacific coast.

Many of the 61 species of shearwaters (*Puffinus* spp.), *fulmars, prions, and petrels (Procellariidae) are also efficient gliders, effortlessly quartering the seas exploiting the updrafts of the waves and rarely having to resort to flapping flight, whereas the sixteen species of storm petrels (Hydrobatiidae), or *Mother Carey's Chickens, flutter almost ceaselessly over the troughs and crests of the *waves,

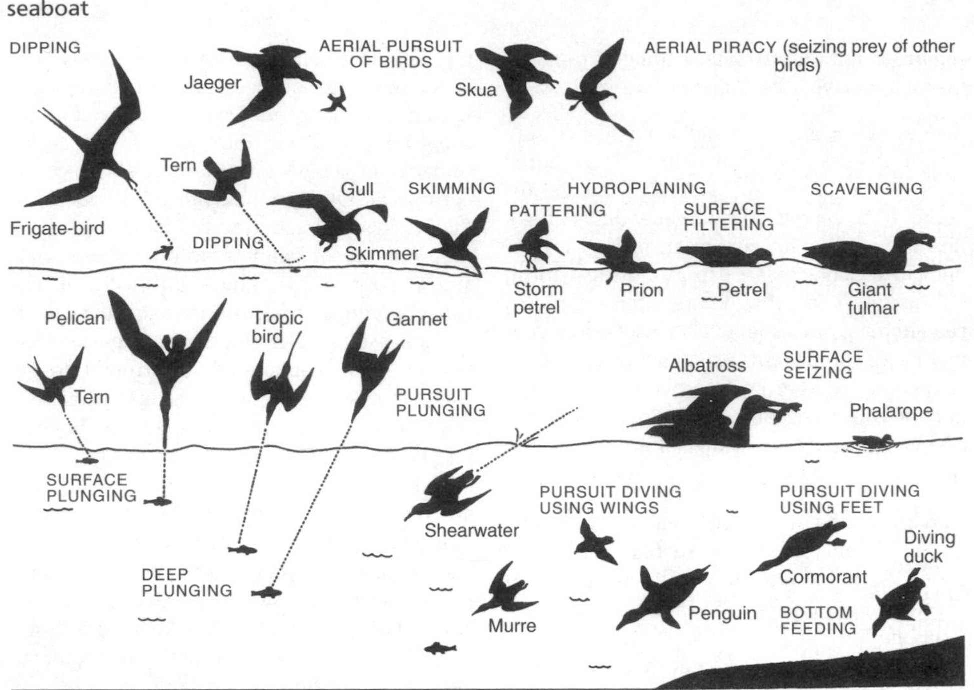

Seabird feeding methods. In most cases, the examples given represent only one of several types of bird that feed in the depicted manner

picking up the tiniest of plankton from the surface.

The 42 species of gulls (Lariidae) tend to be surface feeders and scavengers, often following fishing boats in large numbers waiting for the offal to be discarded. Recently many gull species have become more terrestrial, particularly during winter exploiting our rubbish tips and following the plough. Some gulls are highwaymen, harassing other birds to disgorge the food they have collected, and also indulging in egg predation and eating nestlings. The most efficient of these piratical birds are the seven species of skuas and jaegers (Stercorariidae) who have been given a variety of other names by mariners, such as bonxies and aulin. Every nesting colony of seabirds is attended by parties of these piratical raiders, and they are frequent visitors to seal and sea–lion colonies where they scavenge on corpses, and eat afterbirths, regurgitated food, and even faeces. The two species of giant petrel (*Macronectes* sp.) are also scavengers, and the three species of frigate, or man-of-war, birds (*Fregatta* spp.) are acrobatic aerial highwaymen harrying boobies to disgorge the contents of their crops. Perhaps the weirdest feeding mode is that of the two sheathbills (*Chionus* spp.) that walk around penguin colonies feeding almost exclusively on penguin faeces.

Seabirds are vulnerable to predation when nesting, so they often nest on remote islands or sea cliffs, where they can find a degree of safety from predators, such as rats, cats, foxes, and even man. Many shearwaters have also become nocturnal visitors to their nests, so avoiding being harried by the aerial pirates. The three tropic birds (*Phaethon* spp.) nest far inland on mountainous islands, but the most extreme precaution is taken by the snow petrel (*Pagodroma nivea*), which nests deep in the icy interior of Antarctica.

Harrison, P., *Seabirds: An Identification Guide* (1983).

Nelson, B., *Seabirds: Their Biology and Ecology* (1981).

M. V. Angel

seaboat, the name given in the Royal Navy in the days of sail to the ship's boats, such as *cutters and *whalers, which were suspended from *davits when at sea and not stowed inboard. They were used mainly for ship-to-ship communication at sea before the use of the *jackstay was introduced to pass gear between ships while at sea. When a seaboat was used for *lifesaving, it was invariably called a lifeboat and at the call of the *boatswain's pipe 'Away lifeboat's crew', the nearest men on deck would man it whether detailed as its crew or not.

Seacat, a high-speed (40–5 knot) *catamaran *ferry capable of carrying vehicles as well as passengers. It is manufactured by Incat of Hobart, Tasmania, and was introduced into Europe during the 1990s as a fast alternative to *ro-ro ferries. Instead of *propellers, the first two were powered by quadruple *diesel engines connected to a water-turbine system that, like *jetboats, sucks in water but, unlike jetboats, expels it beneath the surface. A Danish Seacat currently (2004) holds the *blue riband (Hales Trophy), but they are normally employed on shorter routes such as the English Channel. The 75-metre (246-ft) Seacat has now been replaced on some routes by the 100-metre (328-ft) **Superseacat**, a V-shaped steel monohull design built and designed by Fincantieri of Genoa, Italy. Superseacats have a service speed of not less than 38 knots with a full load of 340 tonnes and have a capacity of 774 passengers and 175 cars, rather more than the Seacat's 600 passengers and 80 vehicles.

seacock, the maritime term for what is called a tap on shore. Many of the essential pipes used in a ship or *yacht have their outlet to the sea, and it is necessary to fit a seacock at the outboard end to prevent sea water flooding in through the pipe.

Sea Fencibles, a maritime militia raised in Britain for limited service, and for a definite period, as a defence against invasion during the Revolutionary (1793–1801) and Napoleonic (1803–15) Wars against France. They were made up mainly of fishermen and local residents in coastal areas, and service in the Sea Fencibles protected a man from *impressment into the navy. They were ranked junior to *marines and soldiers of the line regiments, but senior to yeomanry and volunteers. The force was first raised in 1798 and reached its peak in 1810 with a strength of 23,000 men.

sea gods and goddesses, see ATHENE; ATLAS; BRITOMART; FORTUNUS; KHIZR; NEPTUNE; NEREIDES; NEREUS; OCEANIDES; OCEANUS; POSEIDON; TETHYS; THETIS; TRITON. See also KELPIE.

seahorses, are highly specialized *fishes of the family Syngnathidae (pipefishes and sea dragons). There are about 35 known species; the exact number is uncertain because, like chameleons, they are adept at changing colour to match their surroundings, which has misled some biologists into thinking they have caught a new species. They range in size from about 2 to 30 centimetres (1–12 in.) in length, and are most common in shallow tropical and temperate seas. They have tubular mouths, adapted to suck up individual small *plankton. Seahorses swim upright with their heads at right angles to their bony-plated bodies, sculling with their fins. The tail is prehensile and used to anchor the fish in its habitat on *coral reefs, and in beds of sea grass or *seaweeds, and *mangroves. Male and female seahorses form stable long-term partnerships. The female lays her eggs into the brood pouch on the male's chest. He then cares for the young until they have grown too large to fit in his pouch and are able to fend for themselves. In most species the average brood is 100–200. They are highly territorial and occupy quite small home ranges. They are easily disturbed and even if they were not in high demand, they would be under threat because of habitat degradation. However, seahorses are over-exploited because they are used in potions for folk medicine, to stock home aquaria, and dried as curios for tourists.

http://seahorse.fisheries.ubc.ca/ M. V. Angel

sea level. Variations in sea level over short time scales are familiar effects of *tides, winds and *waves, but globally mean sea levels are affected by fluctuations in the amount of water in the oceans, the shape of the oceanic basins and the warmth of the interior of the oceans. Ocean basins are constantly, albeit slowly, changing shape as a result of tectonic movements. Over geological time scales sea levels have fluctuated by several hundred metres.

During the Miocene Era the Strait of Gibraltar opened and closed several times. Each time the strait closed, the water that evaporated from the

Mediterranean basin fell as rain and filled up the rest of the oceans, raising sea level by about 70 metres (230 ft). Then when the strait reopened there was a rapid fall as sea water cascaded back into the Mediterranean. *Climate change has also played a major role in sea level fluctuations. Following the end of the last ice age sea level has risen by nearly 100 metres (325 ft) as the *ice sheets melted, and the interior of the ocean is still continuing to warm up; the thermal expansion of water is resulting in a small annual rise of one millimetre, a tiny but significant rise for those designing coastal protection and flood control for the next century.

Currently the polar ice caps contain enough water to raise global sea levels by 60 metres (195 ft). A modest amount of global warming that leads to some melting of polar ice will result in catastrophic rises in sea level. The precise amount of rise is difficult to estimate because as ice is removed from Antarctica and Greenland there will be local adjustments in the earth's crust. However, increased sea levels in the Bengal basin are threatening the Indian Sundarbans, the world's largest delta, and its *mangrove forests. Levels have risen by an average of 3.14 centimetres (1.2 in.) annually since the 1980s, submerging four islands, leaving many families homeless, and threatening local *fisheries and the food chain. If this continues, thousands of square kilometres of the Sundarbans will be submerged, destroying whole communities. In 2003 the government of the Pacific state of Tuvalu, where the sea level has risen nearly three times as fast as the world average, was considering the possibility of having to evacuate its 9,300 residents.

In the north-west of Britain, the land is still rising as a result of isostatic adjustments of the earth's crust after the last glaciation. In the south-east the land is sinking by more than a millimetre a year, adding to local sea-level rises. Hence how long will the Thames Barrier remain effective in protecting London from flooding? Globally, sea level is being observed by *remote sensing.

Levels oscillate about the surface of equal gravity, the so-called geoid. Sea levels over deep *trenches, where gravity is anomalously high, can be depressed by 40 metres (130 ft). Variations around the geoid result from the influences of *currents and *eddies as well as the underlying geological structure of the seabed. See also CHART DATUM; GEOLOGICAL OCEANOGRAPHY.

M. V. Angel

sealing has a history, like *whaling, that stretches back into prehistory; images of seals (see MARINE MAMMALS) appear in Palaeolithic rock art. It is still practised by Inuits today for whom seals are a key resource for pelts, food, and oil. Walrus (*Odobenus rosmarus*) are also hunted for their ivory, although trade in the ivory is banned under CITES (Convention on International Trade in Endangered Species). More bizarre seal products are their penile bones, which have a market as aphrodisiacs in Asia. Breeding harp seals (*Phoca groenlandica*) and hooded seals (*Cystophora cristata*) are hunted on the pack *ice in the North Atlantic particularly in the Gulf of St Lawrence. These seals breed on ice and have white-coated pups whose pelts were in high demand by the fur trade. The scenes of brutal clubbing of cubs and blood-stained ice floes excited strong protests from animal rights activists and the killing of cubs was banned in the St Lawrence in 1987. However, in 2004 the Canadian government announced a cull of 350,000 harp seals; the rationalization of this extreme measure is to protect the local *fish stocks.

Fur seals (*Arctocephalus* and *Callorhinus* species) were heavily exploited during the 17th and 18th centuries, when many of the populations around the North Pacific, South Africa, and Antarctica were almost driven to extinction. In 1911 the North Pacific Fur Seal Convention banned the killing of northern fur seals at sea and restricted killing on land to immature males. Fur seal pelts became very valuable commodities, but wearing fur went out of fashion, so even though the convention lapsed in 1984, no further sealing has taken place on the Pribilof Islands in the north-east Pacific, home to the largest breeding colonies of northern fur seals. In the southern hemisphere the exploitation was so intense that for much of the late 19th and early 20th centuries there were few if any sightings of fur seals around South Georgia and the South Sandwich Islands in the South Atlantic. They began to be seen regularly again in the post-war years, and now the population on South Georgia alone is estimated to be about 4 million.

Elephant seals (*Mirounga* sp.) were very heavily exploited, mostly for their blubber. At the beginning of the 20th century the population of northern elephant seals in the North Pacific had been reduced to under a thousand and restricted to the Mexican Isla de Guadalupe. Again, once given protection the population has recovered to about 100,000 and has spread up the coast of California. However, it is possible that a genetic bottleneck created by the reduction of the population will have left the animal with insufficient genetic diversity to cope with future environmental changes or infectious epidemics. The southern elephant seal was still being exploited as late as 1964 on South Georgia, but in common with all Southern Ocean seals south of 60° S. is now protected under the Convention for the Conservation of Antarctic Seals.

www.pinnipeds.org/contents.htm M. V. Angel

Sea Lord, see ADMIRALTY.

seam. **(1)** The narrow gap between the planks forming the sides and decks of vessels constructed of wood which is *caulked with *oakum and *pitch to keep out the water. As wood swells when it is in contact with water, a narrow seam between the planks must be left to accommodate the expansion, and as the planks 'take up' when immersed, they compress the oakum and add to the watertightness. **(2)** As a verb, the work of the sailmaker when he joins together the *cloths from which a sail is made with a double seam. See also MONK'S SEAM; SAILMAKER'S STITCHING; PRICK, TO; TABLE, TO.

seamanship, in its widest sense, is the whole art of taking a ship from one place to another at sea. It is an amalgam of all the arts of designing a ship and its motive power, whether sail, *steam propulsion, or other means, of working it when at sea, and in harbour, and the science of *navigation. It thus embraces every aspect of a ship's life in port and its progress at sea.

Seamanship, however, has also a narrower meaning. It is that area which is concerned with the rest of a ship's daily management and safe handling: its gear, boats, anchors and *cables, *rigging; its sails if it is a sailing vessel, and the organization of a *watch kept at sea and in harbour. The old definition of a prime seaman was a man who could *hand, *reef, and *steer—had, in fact, an intimate knowledge and understanding of the way of the sea and ships—and although the handing and reefing of sails in commercial vessels and warships is a thing of the past, the same general definition holds good if the modern equivalents are related to the powered ship of today, or to those who go *yachting for pleasure. It embodies a knowledge of *knots and how to *splice, of handling ropes and *hawsers, *blocks and *tackles; it embraces a knowledge of *marine meteorology and of winds and *tides, the means of riding out *storms, the skill to apply the *International Regulations for Preventing Collisions at Sea, and the necessary experience and judgement to interpret *navigation lights and distances at night, in fact the day-to-day work of running a ship at sea in a *shipshape and Bristol fashion.

seaman's quadrant, often called the simple *quadrant, the earliest instrument used by *navigators for measuring the *altitude of a heavenly body. It was in the form of a quarter circle of brass or wood with a plumb line suspended, when the instrument was in use, from the centre of the circle of which the quadrant formed part. One radial edge of the instrument was fitted with two pins or sights by means of which a *sight of the heavenly body was acquired. This quadrant required two observers, one to bring the observed body into the line of the two pins and the other to note the position where the plumb line crossed the arc of the instrument.

This type of quadrant was in use by the early Portuguese navigators during their *exploration by sea along the West African coast during the second half of the 15th century. Its first use appears to have been for measuring the altitude of *Polaris, the Pole Star, to find the distance made good south of Lisbon or any other port of departure. At that time the scale on the quadrants was often marked with the names of places where the *latitude had been established rather than in degrees. Once tables of the sun's *declination had been published—they appeared around 1480 in copies of *Regimento do astrolabio e do quadrante*, the first navigation manual ever published—the arc of the quadrant was graduated in degrees and minutes so that altitudes could be read in angles.

This simple quadrant could not be used on board ship unless the sea was smooth and the air calm, and even in the most suitable conditions its degree of accuracy was coarse. But it was an instrument which could be easily manufactured by the navigator himself if the need arose and, because the vertical was defined by a plumb line, the quadrant could be used for measuring altitudes when the *horizon was obscured by darkness or fog.

sea-mark, the seaman's name for any floating navigational mark, such as a *buoy or *lightship, as opposed to a *landmark. Because sea-marks are moored to the seabed and can drag their *mooring, *navigators tend to treat their position with some caution when using them to *fix their ship's position. Centuries ago, marks set up ashore in Britain were known as sea-marks, not landmarks, and in its original charter *Trinity House was empowered to place sea-marks ashore whenever necessary as an aid to *navigation. Any person found destroying them was fined or, if unable to pay, outlawed.

sea-pie, a favourite dish for the crew on board a ship in the days of sail. Almost anything could go into a sea-pie, but the proper dish consisted of layers of meat, vegetables, and *fish separated by crusts of bread or broken biscuit. By the number of layers it was known as a two- or three-decker.

seas. In the ancient world traditionally there were seven seas—the Red Sea, the Mediterranean, the Persian Gulf, the Black Sea, the Adriatic Sea, the Caspian Sea, and the Indian Ocean. Seven is a mystical number. The world was created in seven days, there are seven deadly sins, seven graces, seven divisions to the Lord's Prayer, and seven ages in the life of man. The Romans named the seven salt-water lagoons off Venice 'Septem Mare'. Rudyard Kipling further popularized the use of the term through the title of one of his books of poems.

Nowadays it tends to embrace all the oceans (two of the five oceans, the Pacific and the Atlantic, are divided into North and South). A sea usually describes an area of water that is geographically distinct, so the North Sea, the Baltic Sea, the Caribbean Sea, the Bering Sea, and the Sea of Okhotsk are bodies of water that are semi-enclosed by land or island arcs. However, others, like the *Sargasso and the Arabian Seas, are areas of the open ocean with special characteristics that set them apart. The Baltic and the North Seas are quite shallow, whereas the Mediterranean, Black, and Red Seas have areas of water that are over 2,000 metres (6,500 ft) deep and offer exceptional deep-sea environments.

The straits that give entry into the Mediterranean and Red Seas, Gibraltar and Bab-el-Mandeb respectively, are narrow and shallow and inhibit deep-water interchange with the neighbouring oceans. Both are situated at arid *latitudes, so the volumes of freshwater inputs by rainfall and by rivers are very much smaller than the volumes of water lost by evaporation. In the eastern Mediterranean this imbalance has been accentuated by the reductions in outflows from the Nile following the building of the High Aswan Dam. The imbalance both lowers *sea level and increases the *salinity at the far ends of the two seas. As a result strong surface *currents constantly flow in through the two straits. This was of great help to *Nelson when he was blockading the French fleet during the Napoleonic Wars (1793–1815). It also results in the deep water in these seas being unusually warm and salty.

In the western Mediterranean the water below 300 metres (985 ft) is 12.6 °C (54.6 °F) all the way to the bottom at over 2,000 metres (6,500 ft), whereas outside in the Atlantic the temperature at 2,000 metres is about 3–4 °C (37.4–39.2 °F). Deep-water temperatures in the Red Sea are even more extreme at 21.6 °C (71 °F). In contrast, the deep water of the Japan Sea is sub-zero year-round.

The Black Sea is even more extraordinary, being a Mediterranean-type sea within the Mediterranean. It opens into the main sea via two straits, the Dardanelles and the Bosporus, through which there is very limited exchange. It is quite deep, over 2,000 metres (6,500 ft), but for its size it receives substantial freshwater inputs from major European rivers, the Danube, the Dniester, and the Dnieper. These rivers drain the fertile steppes and introduce high concentrations of nutrients. So below a depth of 150 metres (490 ft) the water of the Black Sea is anoxic, that is, totally devoid of oxygen, and rich in hydrogen sulphide. Indeed, it gained its name from the way an iron implement, if lowered deep into the sea, comes up blackened with sulphide. The Arabian Sea is the region of the north-west Indian Ocean along the coast of Oman, and is one of the most variable seas as a result of the *monsoons. See also HIGH SEAS; NARROW SEAS; OCEANS; UNITED NATIONS CONFERENCE ON THE LAW OF THE SEA.

M. V. Angel

sea songs, the generic name given either to songs sung at sea by sailors in their leisure time, or to songs sung ashore about the sea, which more often than not were never sung by seamen. They differ entirely from the *shanty, which was always a working song, and never sung on board except when required for an actual job of work.

The songs sung on board ship were known as forebitter or forecastle songs. It is almost certain that these names arose because the sailors gathered around the fore *bitts on the forecastle to sing them. They were home-made songs which usually adopted the tune of an already existing song which was known by most men on board. The words could describe anything from a famous naval battle (see BUTTER-BOX) to a sailor's grouse about conditions on board his ship, could tell a story of an adventure ashore, usually amatory, or be rankly sentimental to start the seamen thinking of home and family life. One of the best known of the British forebitters was 'The Limejuice Ship', a song which recalls both the Merchant Shipping Acts of 1844 and 1867, which made a daily issue of lime juice (see LIMEY) compulsory to all merchant seamen to prevent *scurvy, and the Merchant Shipping Act of 1894, which laid down minimum scales of victuals in merchant ships and brought seamen other rights in the way of hours of employment, rates of pay, etc. The words of the song ran:

Now if you want a merchant ship to sail the seas at large,
You'll not have any trouble if you have a good discharge,
Signed by the Board of Trade, and everything exact,
For there's nothin' done on a limejuice ship contrary to the Act.
So haul, boys, your *weather main *brace and ease away your *lee,
Hoist *jib and *topsails, lads, an' let the ship go free,
Hurrah, boys, hurrah; we'll sing this jubilee,
'You can keep the navy, boys, a merchant ship for me.'

The other type of sea song, written, composed, and sung ashore, almost invariably tried to tell of the glories and delights of a life at sea, which the average sailor of the days of sail knew, only too well, painted a picture so false that he would have none of it. This was probably the reason why they were never adopted as part of the pattern of life on board. An early sea song was the aria 'Come away, fellow sailors, come away', which opens the second act of Henry Purcell's opera *Dido and Aeneas*, written in 1689, but the best known of them all was *'Heart of Oak'. This song was an exception in that it was played on board British warships, but not usually sung, when they were sailing into battle, as was *'Britons Strike Home'. 'Rule Britannia' was, too, though it was sung as well. It was, and is, so popular that it is generally recognized today as the official march of the Royal Navy.

The greatest writer of sea songs of this type was the British actor, dramatist, and song writer Charles Dibdin (1745–1814). In 1789 he produced a variety show *Oddities*, in which he introduced some nautical songs, the best known being *'Tom Bowling', 'Saturday Night at Sea', and 'The Good Ship *Rover*'. The *'Rogue's March', which was beaten on drums during the course of the naval punishment *flogging round the fleet, was based on Dibdin's 'Right Little, Tight Little Island'. He wrote some hundreds of such songs which he made popular by singing himself. As he lived during the period of the great naval wars at the end of the 18th century, many of his songs had a considerable recruiting value at a time when the British Navy was desperate for men to sail the greatly increasing number of ships. Such a song was:

A sailor's life's the life for me,
He takes his duty merrily;
If winds can whistle, he can sing;
Still faithful to his friend and King;
He gets beloved by all his ship,
And toasts his girl and drinks his flip.

One of the oldest, and probably best-known, and best-loved, songs of the sea is 'Spanish Ladies'. It was probably written and first sung in 1694–5, when the British fleet wintered at Cadiz.

Captain *Marryat, in his novel *Poor Jack*, gives the earliest complete version known but the song was an old one long before Marryat joined the British Navy. It has five verses and a chorus, and though there are many small differences in wording in the various versions, perhaps the best known runs as follows:

Fare ye well and adieu to you, fair Spanish ladies;
Fare ye well and adieu to you, ladies of Spain,
For we have got orders for to sail back to old England,
But we hope in a short time for to see you again.

Chorus: Then we'll rant and we'll roar like true British seamen,
We'll rant and we'll roar all across the salt seas,
Until we strike *soundings in the Channel of old England;
From Ushant to Scilly is thirty-five *leagues.

We *hove the ship to with the wind at sou'-west, my boys;
We *hove the ship to for to strike soundings clear.
We had forty-five *fathom and a fine sandy bottom,
So we filled the main *topsail and up Channel we *steer.

(*Chorus*, as before)

The first land we made, 'twas the head called the Dodman,
Next Rame Head near Plymouth, Start, Portland, and Wight;
So we sailed by Beachy, by Fairlee, and Dungeness,
Where we bore right away for the South Foreland Light.

(Chorus)

Then let every man toss off a full bumper,
And let every man swig off a full bowl;
For we'll drink and be jolly and drown melancholy,
With a 'Here's a good health to each true-hearted soul.'

(Chorus)

The 19th century brought Gilbert and Sullivan's HMS *Pinafore* with its quota of sea songs, immensely popular ashore but not sung on board, while perhaps the best-known 20th-century sea song is John Ireland's setting of John Masefield's haunting 'Sea Fever':

I must down to the seas again, to the lonely sea and the sky,
And all I ask is a tall ship and a star to steer her by,
And the wheel's kick and the wind's song and the white sail's shaking
And a grey mist on the sea's face, and a grey dawn breaking.

But here again, this was never a song sung by sailors at sea.

The most complete collection of sea songs is *Naval Songs and Ballads*, edited for the Navy Records Society by C. H. Firth in 1908. Also see:

Fox Smith, C., *Sea Songs and Ballads* (1923).
Palmer, R., *The Valiant Sailor* (1973).
Whall, W. H., *Sea Songs and Shanties* (1920).

seaweeds are the most familiar of all *marine plants. They are large algae, non-flowering plants. With the exception of *sargasso weed, seaweeds are restricted to shallow inshore waters where they can anchor themselves to the seabed. They are limited to depths that are shallow enough for sufficient sunlight to penetrate to support their photosynthesis. They are classified according to their pigmentation into reds, browns, greens, and blue-greens. On rocky shores around Europe ebbing low *spring tides reveal a zonation of the brown algae, mostly wracks. The species most tolerant of desiccation flourish at the top of the shore but are replaced down the shore by a succession of more vigorously growing species that are less and less tolerant of being exposed at low tide. Lowest down the shore are the kelps or oarweeds (e.g. *Laminaria*) that are anchored to rocks by their rootlike holdfasts from which grow their stipes (stalks) and leaflike blades. They form dense forests in the sublittoral (the zone just below the lowest tide mark), which are home to a rich fauna of invertebrate animals and fishes. Off California and Chile giant kelps can grow to lengths of 100 metres (325 ft), each year renewing their blades, whereas the stipes are perennial, They are grazed by sea urchins, types of *echinoderms, which in turn are eaten by sea otters (see MARINE MAMMALS). When the sea otters have gone into decline because of over-exploitation or *pollution, the urchins are unchecked and graze down the kelp forest so the numbers of other species inhabiting the region decline markedly. Molecular techniques have shown that clumps of seaweeds can be surprisingly old. Off the coast of Brittany quite modest clumps of bladder wrack (*Ascophyllum nodosum*) have been shown to be as much as 70 years old.

On *coral reefs eutrophication, one of today's *environmental issues, can lead to seaweeds overgrowing and destroying the coral by shading it. So what can be good for a rich diversity of species in one habitat can be bad for it in others.

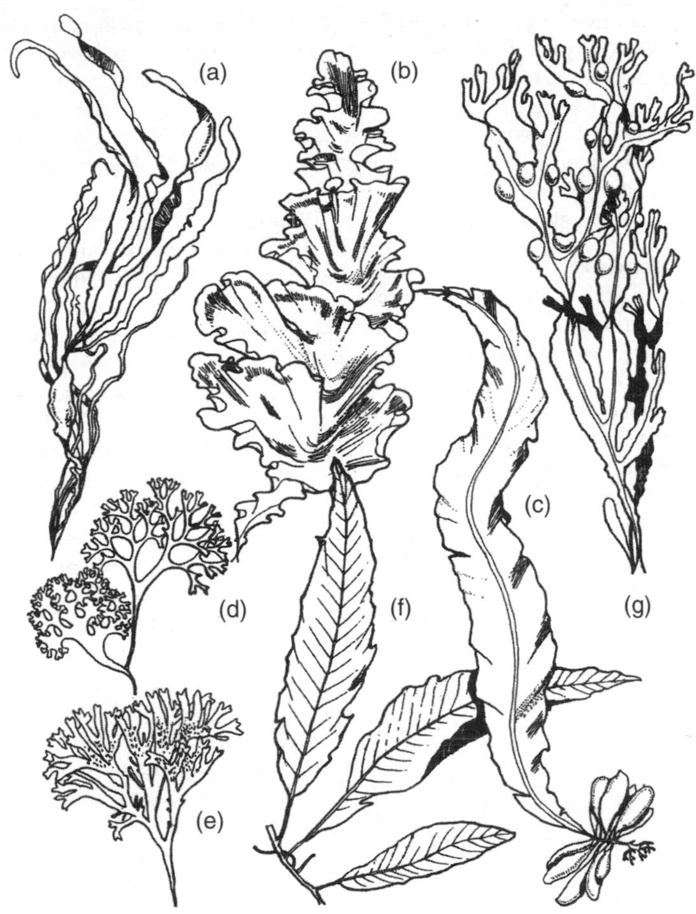

Examples of seaweeds: (a) *Enteromorpha* (up to 500 mm); (b) *Ulva* (up to 250 mm); (c) *Alaria* (up to 2 m); (d) *Chondrus* (up to 150 mm); (e) *Gigartina* (up to 200 mm); (f) *Delesseria* (up to 250 mm); (g) *Fucus vesiculosus* (up to 1 m). (a) and (b) are green algae; (c) and (g) are brown algae; and (e) and (f) are red algae

Some seaweeds are used for food and they are extensively cultured in China. In Britain the red alga (*Chrondrus crispus*), known as carragheen or Irish moss, is traditionally used to make blancmanges and jellies. In south Wales another species, *Porpyra umbilicalis*, is eaten fried with bacon or rolled in oatmeal as laverbread. Alginin, extracted from kelp, is used as an emulsifier in the manufacture of ice cream. See also MARINE BIOLOGY; MARINE PHARMACEUTICALS.

M. V. Angel

sections, drawings made during the design stages of a ship showing the transverse shape of the hull at different longitudinal positions. See also SHIPBUILDING.

seel, to, an old seafaring term meaning to lurch over in a roll, in connection with the motion of a sailing vessel at sea. Thus Sir Henry Mainwaring, in his *Seaman's Dictionary* (1644): 'so that seeling is but a suddaine heeling, forced by the motion and force of the sea or wind.' The word is also used as a noun to describe a sudden or unexpected roll. Glanville, in his *Voyage to Cadiz* (1625), wrote: 'Our ship did rolle more and fetch deeper and more dangerous Seeles than in the greatest storme.'

seize, to, to bind with cord or twine as, for instance, one rope to another, or the end of a rope to its own part to form an *eye.

seizing, the cord or twine by which ropes are seized to one another. It is also the name given to the finished product when the two parts have been seized together. There are many varieties of seizing according to the method of binding and the function to be served. There is a **flat** or *round seizing, a **racking seizing** (see RACK, TO), a *throat seizing, etc. See also CLAP ON, TO.

Selkirk, Alexander (1676–1721), British seaman and the model of *Robinson Crusoe in the story by the same name written by Daniel Defoe (*c.*1660–1731). He was born in Lower Largo, Fife, Scotland. In 1703 he volunteered to become a member of the crew of a *privateer, *Cinque Ports*, for a voyage to the *South Seas. In 1705, after a violent disagreement with with his captain, Thomas Stradling, Selkirk asked to be *marooned on the island of Juan Fernandez. He survived on the vegetables and fruit which grew there in abundance, and on the goats left there by the original Spanish discoverers of the island. He remained there until 1709 when he was rescued by Woodes Rogers (d. 1732) during the latter's circumnavigation. He was so good a seaman that Rogers put him in charge of one of the *prize ships captured by the expedition.

After his return to England in 1711, Selkirk told his story to Richard Steele, who wrote an account of Selkirk's adventures which was seen by Daniel Defoe. Shortly after his return, Selkirk volunteered for the Royal Navy and at the time of his death was *master's mate in HMS *Weymouth*. There is a statue of him on the wall of the house in Lower Largo in which he is thought to have been born.

selvagee, an untwisted skein of rope-yarn *marled together to form a *strop. Selvagee strops are used for a variety of purposes on board ship, such as slings for heavy weights required to be hoisted by a *purchase, or for securing masts and *oars in ships' boats to prevent them rolling about in a seaway, etc.

semaphore, from the Greek *sema*, a sign, and *pherein*, to bear, a means of communicating by a machine with movable arms, which was later also adapted for use with hand-held flags. It was the invention of two French brothers, Claude (1763–1805) and Ignace (1760–1829) Chappe, in the mid-1790s and the word itself was first introduced into Britain in 1816 by a British naval officer, Admiral Sir Home Popham (1762–1820). Popham had already made a major contribution to *signals at sea when his flag code, adopted by the *Admiralty in 1803, vastly extended the range of orders and instructions at the disposal of an admiral directing his fleet.

Popham's semaphore system replaced an earlier, more complicated, one invented by the Revd Lord George Murray. After a chain of fifteen stations had been built, the first message by Murray's system, which involved the use of six shutters working in a frame operated by men hauling on ropes, was passed by the Admiralty to Deal, on the Kent coast, in January 1796. After practice, it took only two minutes for such a message to be sent and acknowledged, and the system was extended to Portsmouth and Plymouth. However, one of the system's drawbacks was that it was entirely one-directional as the shutter frames had to be permanently fixed on the roof of buildings. Popham's semaphore had no such disadvantage, and was also more easily operated than Murray's shutters, the arms being worked by winches.

Once a vocabulary had been worked out, semaphore gave much more flexibility in the wording of messages and also considerably greater speed in transmission. Popham did not use the stations set up for Murray's telegraph but selected his own. On the Admiralty–Chatham line, opened on 3 July 1816, eight stations, including the Admiralty and Chatham Yard, were sufficient to complete the chain, though the one to Portsmouth, which opened in 1823, needed fifteen. An extension to Plymouth was started in 1825 but after reaching the borders of Hampshire and Dorset the Admiralty's money ran out, and there it stopped.

The days of Popham's semaphore as a long-distance signalling system began to be numbered in 1838 when Wheatstone's experiments in electric signalling had their first major success, with signals made in London being read in Birmingham. From then on the spread of the electric telegraph was rapid, and the last of Popham's naval signal stations, that at Portsmouth Dockyard, was closed in April 1849.

Popham's semaphore, however, did not die out for it was quickly recognized as an admirable method of short-distance direct communication for shore station-to-ship, and ship-to-ship messages. It became a universal code, widely used at sea by ships of all nations, either by means of a miniature Popham machine in which the arms were worked by chain and sprocket gear, or by hand flags used as an extension of a signalman's arms. Despite the advent of radio communication and signal lamps, it remained in use until well into the 20th century.

semi-diameter, one of the *altitude corrections to the *sextant reading of the sun or moon. It compensates for the fact that the *navigator will observe the altitude of either the lower or upper limb of either body, whereas the altitude required is that of their centre. This is necessary because these two bodies are close to the earth whereas the stars, which require no such correction, are at an infinite distance. The values of semi-diameter are given in *nautical almanacs and most nautical tables.

Mike Richey

sepulchral ships, the names commonly given to ships used in connection with burial rites. The use of such ships is of very ancient origin. The Egyptian sun god Osiris was said to have journeyed to the underworld in a golden *bark attended by the Hours, and in emulation, after embalming, Egyptian dead were often carried westward across the lakes and canals towards the setting sun where, it was thought, lay the earthly paradise. Many of the pharaohs of Egypt had a decorated and fully stocked boat burned alongside them for their later journey to the underworld. Others had ships buried alongside them. The oldest vessel known to exist anywhere is the one buried in a trench cut in the rock alongside the tomb of the Pharaoh Cheops (*fl.* 25th century BC) who built the Great Pyramid at Giza. When the trench was opened in 1954 the dismantled ship was found to be 40.5 metres (133 ft) long with a maximum *beam of 8 metres (26 ft), and was constructed from over 600 individual pieces of wood, some up to 23 metres (75 ft) in length. A second boat pit found at the same time was left undisturbed until 1987 when an investigation using special cameras discovered it contained a sister ship. Another important find, which has added enormously to the knowledge of this type of ship, was the discovery of a fleet of at least twelve boats at Abydos, some 11 kilometres (7 mls.) from the River Nile, in 1991. Buried in boat-shaped graves made of mud bricks, and ranging from 19 to 29 metres (62–95 ft) in length, they were discovered by a University of Pennsylvania–Yale University team of archaeologists.

In the Norse legend of Baldur, he was set afloat in his ship *Hringhorn* on a funeral pyre and, of course, there is ample evidence of the burial of Vikings in *longships, many of them having been excavated in recent years. The Arthurian legends also tell of death ships, King Arthur being borne to Avalon in such a vessel. In Brittany, near the Pointe du Raz, there is the Baie de Trépassés where, according to a local legend, boats were summoned to convey the souls of drowned men to the Île au Sein, while in the Aleutian Islands boat-shaped coffins were used, and many of the North American Indian tribes buried their dead in *canoes raised up on poles, although the Cherokees and Chinooks sometimes buried them so at sea.

There are similar legends among the Solomon Islanders, the Fijians, and the Maoris, and the Dyaks of Borneo used to place their dead in a canoe, together with some of the deceased's property, and set it adrift. In 1847, on the death of Thieu-tru, Emperor of Cochin China, the boats used in his funeral procession were burned on his pyre.

In England, burial ships are rare. The best-known example is the one found at Sutton Hoo, near Woodbridge, Suffolk, in 1939. It was a *clinker-built rowing boat 26 metres (85 ft) long, fully equipped for the afterlife. Artefacts found on the site have led to the supposition that it belonged to the East Anglian king Raedwald (d. 624–5), and among them were objects that came from the Mediterranean and the Near East, proof that trading between the two areas existed. However, in 2004 Yorkshire archaeologists announced that they had almost certainly found a Viking burial ship, the first ever found in England. Artefacts unearthed at the site date it to the 9th century, a time when it was a ritual to bury important personages in their longships.

serang, the Anglo-Indian name, from the Persian *sarhang*, commander, for a native *boatswain or the leader of a Lascar crew.

serpentine, a small ship's handgun of the 15th and 16th centuries. It had a calibre of 3.8 centimetres (1.5 in.) and fired a 156 gram (5.5 oz) *shot with a charge of the same weight of 'cannon corn' powder. The maximum, or *random, range was 1,300 paces. When the powder used was 'fine corn', the same quality as used in muskets, the charge was reduced by one-quarter. Serpentines were upper-deck or 'castle' guns, i.e. fired into the *waist of an enemy ship from a ship's *forecastle or after castle, and were used purely in an anti-personnel role. See also ROBINET.

serve, orig. **sarve, to,** winding *spunyarn close round a rope after the operation to *worm and *parcel it. This serving was wound on with a serving board or *serving mallet to obtain maximum tension, with the turns made against the *lay of the rope. The purpose of doing all this was, before the days of synthetic materials, to make the rope impervious to water and so preserve it against rot. The expression was also used in the case of sailing ships which, through age or weakness, had their hulls served round with *cables to hold them together. See also MARL, TO; POINT.

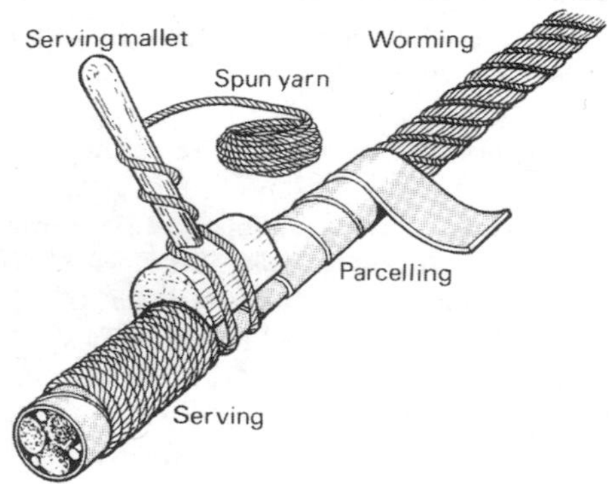

Worming, parcelling, and serving

serving mallet, a wooden hand mallet used on board ships, in the days of sail, for passing a *serving round a rope. The bottom of the mallet had a semicircular groove which fitted round the rope, and the *spunyarn with which a serving was made was led from the rope and a turn with it taken round the handle of the mallet. As the mallet was turned round the rope, the spunyarn rendered round the mallet handle, by which means it could be kept taut and the serving applied with the maximum tightness. A board, with a similar groove at the bottom, was sometimes used instead of a mallet.

set. (1) The word used to denote the direction in which a *current or *tide flows, e.g. 'the tide is setting to the southward'. It is also the distance and direction in which a vessel is moved by the tide in relation to its desired *course and distance run. **(2)** It is a word also applied to sails in relation to their angle with the wind as, for example, in the 'set of a *jib'. **(3)** As a verb, it has many maritime meanings. For example, a **current or tide sets** in the direction in which it flows; a **ship sets a course** when it is steadied down on it; **a sail is set** when it is hoisted and *sheeted home to the wind; a **ship sets sail**, regardless of whether it uses sails or not; and an ***anchor watch is set**.

settee, a two-masted ship of the Mediterranean. They were *lateen rigged on both masts, and were often used as a transport for spare *galley crews. They were single decked with a long, sharp bow, and belonged more to the eastern Mediterranean than to the western. Their dates are from the 16th to about the mid-19th century. Occasionally they were called balancelles, from the double lateen rig. It was a settee, or balancelle, that was used by gunrunners in Joseph *Conrad's novel *The Arrow of Gold*.

settle, to, a defunct maritime term used in connection with a *halyard after a sail had been hoisted. The term referred usually to a *peak halyard after a *gaff-rigged sail had been hoisted too high, creating wrinkles between the peak and the *tack. Where these occurred, the halyard was settled or eased until the wrinkles disappeared.

sewed, (pron. sued), an old maritime word used to describe a ship which had run ashore and had to await the next *tide before refloating. A vessel was said to be sewed by the difference between the level of the water and the flotation mark on its hull, e.g. it was sewed 60 centimetres (2 ft) if the level of the water was that amount below its normal flotation mark.

sextant, a double-reflecting instrument for measuring angles at sea, primarily the *altitude of astronomical bodies in *celestial navigation.

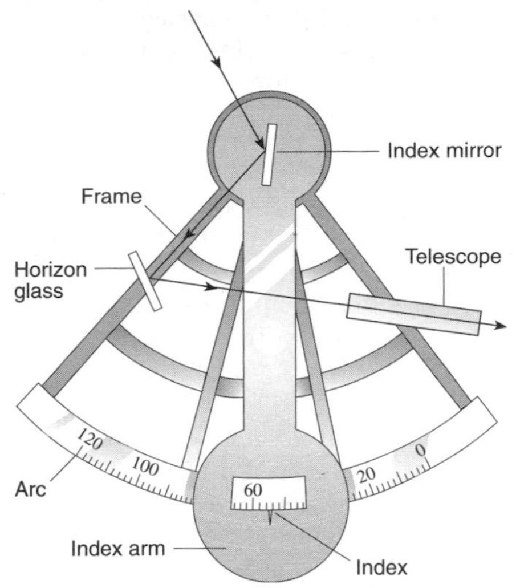

Simplified diagram of a marine sextant

The instrument may also be used for measuring other angles at sea such as for distance-off and horizontal angles for *coastal navigation. Although its arc subtends an angle of only 60°, by double reflection the sextant measure angles up to 120°. The instrument was designed by Captain (later Admiral) John Campbell of the British Navy in 1757 and based on *Hadley's reflecting quadrant (or octant), a double-reflection instrument proposed in principle by Newton and in 1731 demonstrated to the Royal Society by Robert Hooke. The principal requirement to measure more than 90° arose largely from the need to make *lunar distance observations to determine *longitude at sea. However, the overwhelming advantage of the double-reflecting principle was that, in a seaway, once the body observed has been brought down to the *horizon it will not leave it no matter what the weather. Observations could now be made to within a few minutes of arc. A vernier, which enabled single minutes of arc to be read off the scale, became normal, but was replaced much later by the micrometer drum.

At the same time as the development of Hadley's quadrant a young American optician, Thomas Godfrey, who was engaged with the problem of taking lunar distance observations at sea, had submitted an instrument of his own design based on the same principle as Hadley's, and he is now widely regarded as the joint inventor of the sextant.

The modern sextant employs the same optical principles as Hadley's reflecting quadrant. There are two mirrors: a fixed mirror, the horizon glass, is mounted on the frame of the sextant in line with the observer's telescope. Then there is the index mirror at the top of the arm which, when the index arm is set to zero on the scale, will lie precisely parallel to the horizon glass. The horizon glass is half silvered, so that the horizon can be seen through the plain half and the reflected object seen in the silvered half. To take a *sight the navigator, with the index arm set to zero, faces the body to be observed and, with the sextant held vertically, looks through the telescope and moves or rotates the sextant as necessary to get the horizon in view. He then moves the index arm along the scale until the body observed appears in the silvered half of the horizon glass and then adjusts the image so that the limb of the body coincides with the horizon. See CELESTIAL NAVIGATION.

Mike Richey

shackle. **(1)** A U-shaped iron closed with a pin across the jaws and used for securing such things as *halyards to sails, other parts of standing or running *rigging where required, anchors to their *cables, and joining lengths of chain cable, etc. Shackles used in the rigging normally have a threaded pin which is screwed into one of the jaws; those used to join lengths of cable are of two kinds. The old-fashioned type of joining shackle was closed by a bolt flush with the lugs of the jaws which was kept in place by a tapered pin. This was driven into place with a hammer and punch and secured by means of a leaden pellet or ring which, when hammered in, expanded into a socket cut round the inside of the hole. The modern joining shackle is made in two parts with a fitted stud, the stud being kept in place by a steel pin which runs diagonally through the stud and both parts of the shackle. The advantage of this type of shackle is that it is the same size and shape as an ordinary link of the cable and so fits better into the snugs of the *cable-holder when *veering or *weighing anchor. A universal form of shackle in *yachting is the **snap shackle**. This is shaped like a hook with the gap closed by a spring-loaded pin. The pin opens under pressure and closes when the pressure is taken off. **(2)** Before 1949 a shackle of cable supplied to the Royal Navy was 12.5

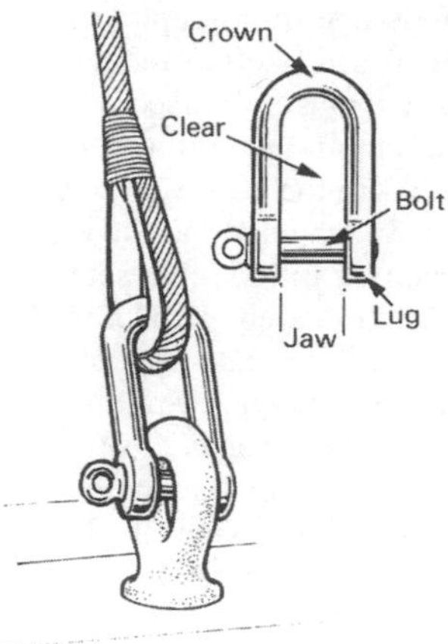

Shackle

*fathoms (75 ft/22.8 m) long, but was later made in lengths of 15 (90 ft/27.4 m) and 7.5 fathoms (45 ft/13.7 m), called 'shackles of cable' and 'half-shackles of cable'. **(3)** When used in the plural it is a term for *bilboes. It can also be used as a verb: two chains can be shackled together and a person is said to be shackled when put in irons.

Shackleton, Sir Ernest Henry (1874–1922), British explorer, born in Kilkee, Southern Ireland. He left Dulwich College at 16 to join the *merchant marine and served before the mast in various *square-riggers, before becoming an officer in the Union Castle shipping line. He then served in the 1901 National Antarctic Expedition under Captain *Scott as its third lieutenant, but was invalided home after an attack of *scurvy. In January 1908 he led the British National Expedition which accomplished some useful scientific work and reached to within 160 kilometres (100 mls.) of the pole. For these achievements Shackleton received a knighthood.

In 1914 he again sailed for the Antarctic in command of the Imperial Trans-Antarctic expedition on board the 350-ton Norwegian sealer *Endurance*, with the intention of crossing the continent of Antarctica from the Weddell to the Ross Seas. However, after a combination of adverse circumstances, the *Endurance* was beset by *ice in the Weddell Sea, and was eventually crushed after drifting for nine months. Only Shackleton's superb natural gifts of leadership and organization enabled the expedition's members to survive. After drifting on ice floes, they eventually took to the ship's boats and reached Elephant Island in the South Shetland group, in April 1916. Leaving his second in command, Frank Wild, in charge, Shackleton sailed one of the boats, a 7-metre (23-ft) *whaler which he named *James Caird*, to South Georgia, 480 kilometres (300 mls.) away, to seek help. After three unsuccessful attempts to rescue the Elephant Island party, they were taken off with the help of the Chilean *tug *Yelcho*.

In 1920 Shackleton, now in charge of the Shackleton–Rowett Antarctic expedition, sailed to the Antarctic on board the *Quest*, but off South Georgia he died of a heart attack. The *James Caird* is preserved at his old school.

Dunnett, H., *Shackleton's Boat* (1994).
Huntford, R., *Shackleton* (1985).

shake. **(1)** The name given to a longitudinal crack in a mast or *spar. **(2)** The staves of a cask after the cask has been taken to pieces; thus **'no great shakes'** means something of little value. **(3)** The shivers of a sail when a sailing vessel is steered too close to the wind. It is a meaning which has given rise to the expression **'a brace of shakes'** as very quickly or immediately, literally the time in which a sail shivers twice when too close to the wind.

'shake a cloth in the wind, to', a seaman's expression meaning to be slightly intoxicated but not helplessly drunk.

'shake a leg', see 'SHOW A LEG'.

shake out a reef, to, to enlarge a sail by casting off the *reef points and rehoisting it to spread a larger area to the wind. It is still a current expression though few sailing vessels have reef points nowadays.

shakings, the seaman's term to describe the ends of old rope and pieces of old *canvas sails which were unpicked for making *oakum.

shallop. **(1)** A light, small sailing vessel of about 25 tons, either *schooner rigged or with a *lugsail rig, employed in commercial *fisheries during the days of sail. Being fast and *weatherly, particularly with the lugsail rig, they were also frequently employed as *tenders during the days of sailing navies. **(2)** A large, heavy, undecked boat with a single mast, *fore-and-aft rigged. In many cases in the 17th and 18th centuries when ships were driven ashore in *storms, contemporary accounts mention the ship's carpenters building a shallop from the timber of a *shipwreck. This enabled some of the crew to sail to the nearest port to summon assistance. **(3)** A small French coastal gunboat of the 18th and early 19th centuries, single masted and armed with one gun. They were known as *chaloupes* and carried a crew of about 40 men. **(4)** Alternative name for a *skiff rowed by one or two men.

shamal, the name given to the prevailing wind from the north-west in the Persian Gulf. It sets in without warning, and in June and July blows more or less continuously. At other times it can last between one and five days, and is so dusty, as well as hot, that it can obscure visibility quite badly. Its speed rarely exceeds 48 kph (30 mph).

Shamrock, the name of six racing yachts owned by Sir Thomas Lipton (1850–1931). Lipton, who was born in Glasgow of Irish parentage, began his working life as an errand boy. He made a fortune in the grocery business, particularly tea. He was knighted in 1898 and created a baronet three years later. He conceived the idea of challenging for the *America's Cup after Lord Dunraven's second challenge, in 1895, had created a lot of ill feeling in America, ill feeling which Lipton successfully dissipated while at the same time gaining publicity for his business. In 1899 *Shamrock I,* a *cutter of 103 tons displacement with a sail area of 1,245 square metres (13,400 sq. ft), was beaten by the American defender, and *Shamrock II, III, IV,* and *V* suffered the same fate in 1901, 1903, 1919, and 1930. In 1908, during a hiatus in racing for the America's Cup, Lipton built an unnumbered *Shamrock,* a 23-metre *International Metre Class yacht which raced in the British regatta circuit until she was broken up in the 1920s. Lipton's final challenger, *Shamrock V,* is still afloat as a classic yacht and has been restored to her original rig.

shan, a word that has now disappeared from the nautical vocabulary; it was used to describe defects in wooden *spars, usually caused by knots in the wood that contracted and fell out; or to describe a naval plank that had been sawn obliquely to the central axis of the tree. It was used mainly as an adjective, as in 'a length of shan timber' or 'the timber is shan'.

shanghai, to. To be shanghaied, said of a sailor in the days of sail when he was shipped against his will, usually under the influence of drink or drugs, as one of the crew of a ship. The practice was especially prevalent in the USA during the 19th century at a time when the reputations of many *masters and their *'bucko' mates made normal recruitment unlikely. The sailors were delivered to the ships by *crimps.

The term comes from the USA, but its origin is obscure. It might possibly have arisen from the Australian word 'shanghai', meaning catapult, in that the unfortunate seamen were catapulted off to sea as soon as they were made insensible.

shank, that part of an anchor which connects the arms to the anchor ring.

shanty, or **chantey,** pronounced 'scanty' by the seamen who sang them, a song sung on board during the days of sail to lighten the labour of working a merchant ship. However, they were not actually called by this name until after 1834, as Richard *Dana does not give them this name in his book *Two Years before the Mast* which was published in that year. The earliest known example of this type of song, to coordinate the efforts of men working on the *capstan bars, occurs in the *Complaynt of Scotland*, published about 1450, and 'Haul the Bowline' must be very nearly as old, as in the earliest days of sail the *bowline rope was the most important one in a sailing ship.

The words of many shanties often varied from ship to ship, sometimes to incorporate local personalities or to lengthen the words of a song; if the words ran out before a task was completed, a good shantyman, who led the singing, could improvise new words to keep the song going without a break. But though the words might differ, the tunes never varied.

They were broadly divided into two classes: the capstan shanties, designed to produce a continuous effort such as would be required from men heaving on the capstan bars; and *halyard shanties, where the accent was placed on occasional words or notes to encourage the men to pull together, as when *swaying up a *spar. They all follow the same pattern, with short solo verses and rollicking choruses, with a shantyman to lead the singing. Many shanties became famous as much for their tunes as for their words, such as 'Shenandoah', 'Rolling Home', 'Billy Boy', 'Bound for the Rio Grande', and 'Blow the Man Down'. Perhaps the best known today is the one Robert Louis Stevenson (1850–94) put in his novel *Treasure Island* (1883):

> Fifteen Men on the Dead Man's Chest,
> Yo ho ho! And a bottle of rum,
> Drink and the Devil had done for the rest,
> Yo ho ho! And a bottle of rum.

Shanties were essentially *merchant marine songs, and were rarely heard in warships, where work was traditionally carried out in silence. Also, merchant ships were frequently undermanned so that the owners might make more profit, and to make up for the lack in numbers a shanty was necessary to coordinate the efforts of each man. Warships, on the other hand, were, by comparison, overmanned. The large number of men required to work the guns in battle were almost always available for duties which required a heavy effort, such as *weighing an anchor or swaying up a main *yard. See also SEA SONGS.

Carr Laughton, L. G., *The Mariner's Mirror*, 9 (1923), 48, 66.

shape, to, a verb frequently used in relation to the *course selected by the *navigator for a ship to sail; e.g. 'a course was shaped to avoid some danger' or 'we will shape a course to reach such-and-such a destination'.

sharks are elasmobranch *fishes with cartilaginous skeletons. Elasmobranchs include about 368 species of selachians (true sharks) belonging to 30 families, and a further 470 species of batioids (skates and rays, including *manta rays). They range in size from the pygmy lantern shark (*Etmopterus perryi*), which is 15 centimetres (6 in.) long, to the whale shark (*Rhinchodon typus*), which can grow to lengths of 12 metres (39 ft) and is the world's largest fish.

Sharks have gill slits rather than covered gills as in bony fishes. Instead of having swimbladders they keep their buoyancy close to that of sea water by having oily livers, blood rich in urea, and fins that act as hydrofoils. The larger species, such as the whale shark, the basking shark (*Cetorhinus maximus*), and the megamouth (*Megachasma pelagias*), are *plankton feeders, but the other species feed on fish, *marine mammals, or even young *seabirds leaving a nesting colony for the first time. They have poorly developed eyesight, but have an acute sense of smell, being able to detect a drop of blood in an area the size of a full-size swimming pool. They can also detect vibrations over long distances, by means of a lateral system that runs down each side of their bodies and onto their heads. Their skin comprises toothlike structures, known as denticles, which are shed as the shark grows, and are replaced by larger ones. They have triangular-shaped teeth that are frequently shed and replaced; a shark typically replaces many thousands of teeth during its lifetime.

The most curiously shaped is the hammerhead shark (*Sphyrna lewini*), which has a wing-shaped head (cephalafoil) with eyes at its extremities. This shape helps the hammerhead manoeuvre, but it also acts as a large sensor which can detect the electromagnetic fields of its prey, such as *herring, *squid, and other sharks. The giant hammerhead can grow to 6 metres (20 ft) in length.

The great white shark (*Carcharodon carcharias*) tends to frequent waters close to seal colonies or fish spawning grounds. This species, and others that are most dangerous to man, forage in shallow coastal waters where the waters are murky. Because they hunt using their senses of smell and vibration to detect their prey they sometimes mistakenly attack humans that are swimming or wading. Worldwide, in 2002 there were 86 incidents attributed to shark attacks of which only 60 were unprovoked and only three resulted in the death of the victim. So the dangers of shark attack are often exaggerated.

Sharks have internal fertilization, and male are easily distinguished from females by their pelvic fins being modified into claspers with which they impregnate the females. Female sharks either lay a small number of eggs in mermaid's purses or the development of the eggs is internal and the young are born live. There is also evidence that the young sometimes feed cannibalistically on their siblings within

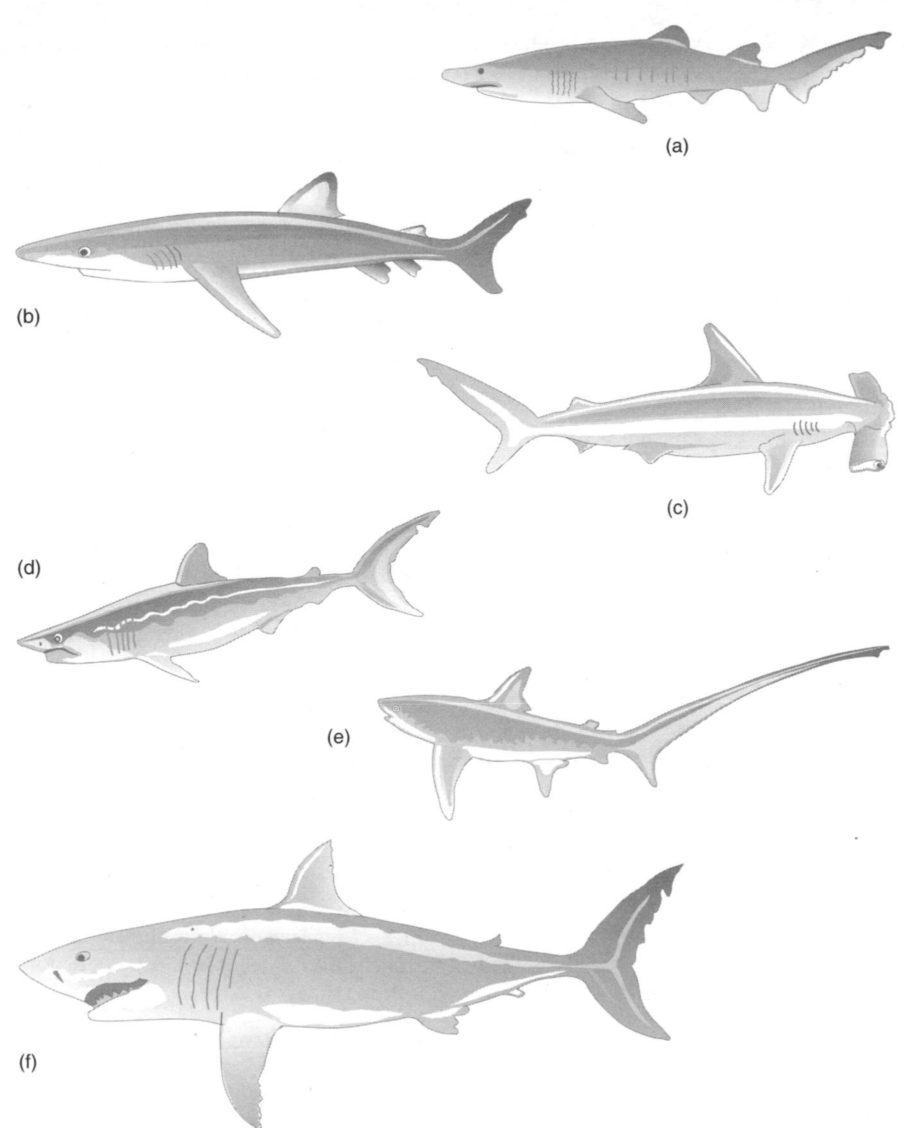

Endangered species of sharks [a] **Tiger** (*Galeocerdo cuvien*) grows up to 3.2 metres (10 ft 6 in.), solitary except when mating. They are found in tropical waters worldwide and in some more temperate seas. They are capable of swimming down to a depth of 340 metres (1,100 ft) and eat anything they can catch alive [b] **Blue** (*Prionace glauca*), which grows up to 3.2 metres (12 ft 6 in.), is one of the fastest swimming sharks. They eat mainly squid, but can prey upon almost anything. They are found in open water in all the world's oceans, and often form large all-male or all-female groups [c] **Hammerhead** (*Sphyrna lewini*) grows up to 3.4 metres (11 ft). It is found in tropical and warm temperate waters from the surface down to 300 metres (985 ft). It forms large schools during the daytime, and at night feeds on fish and squid in deep water [d] **Mako** (*Isurus oxyrinchus*), which grows up to 2.4 metres (8 ft), is also known as the mackerel shark. It is a fast swimmer and sometimes leaps out of the water. It can be found worldwide both on the surface and deep below it, up to 400 metres (1,310 ft) [e] **Thresher** (*Alopias superciliosus*) grows up to 3.4 metres (11 ft) and is found in coastal waters and far offshore in the great ocean basins. It hunts in packs, rounding up a school of fish and then using its long tail to stun or kill them [f] **Great White** (*Carcharodon carcharias*) grows up to 6.4 metres (21 ft). It has been seen off the coasts of most continents. No one knows how long it lives. It is a protected species along some parts of the Australian, South African, and US coastlines

the female's body. Their low reproduction rate makes them very susceptible to over-exploitation, and many sharks are killed as by-catch in *trawls or on *long-lines, and some species are now under such threat that they are protected in some parts of the world. Many taken on long-lines are finned—their fins are cut off and dried for shark-fin soup and the rest of the carcass is discarded. Such removal of top predators from any food web totally alters its structure and dynamics, and reduces its diversity.

Allen, T., *The Shark Almanac: A Fully Illustrated Natural History of Sharks, Skates and Rays* (1999).
Carwardine, M., and Watteron, K., *The Shark-Watchers Handbook: A Guide to Sharks and Where to See them* (2002). M. V. Angel

Sharp, or **Sharpe, Bartholomew** (*c*.1650–88), a *buccaneer who served under Henry *Morgan in the first piratical attack on Panama in 1671 and was a leader in the second in 1679. Having marched with his followers across the Isthmus of Panama, he seized a Spanish ship to cruise to the southward off the coasts of Peru and Chile. Later, while still in the Pacific, his buccaneering band broke up, some like William *Dampier returning to the Atlantic across the Panama Isthmus, the rest remaining with Sharp. In 1681 one of the Spanish *treasure ships he was chasing ran onto a reef off the coast of Ecuador and the captain burnt her to prevent Sharp plundering her. In retaliation Sharp killed all the survivors. He had better luck when he captured the Spanish ship *Rosario*, finding on board 'a Spanish manuscript of a prodigious value'. This was a *derroterro of the *South Seas, an outstanding example with the coastline painted in its natural colours, which is now in the British Library.

'Also I took in this prize another jewell, viz., a young lady about 18 years of age, a very comely creature.' History does not relate the fate of this second 'jewell', but the derroterro undoubtedly saved Sharp's life. After a remarkable voyage to the West Indies round Cape Horn—he was the first Englishman to round it—Sharp made his way back to London where the derroterro was redrawn and coloured by William Hack (*fl.* 1680–1700), who also had it translated. Called *Waggoner of the Great South Sea*, it was a superb piece of *chartmaking and in 1682 Sharp presented it to King Charles II. Charles made him a captain in the navy and he was appointed to command the *sloop *Bonetta*. But the call of a buccaneering life was too strong for him to resist. He deserted his ship, captured a small Dutch vessel off Ramsgate, and sailed back to the West Indies. He was last heard of as commander of a nest of pirates in the island of Anguilla. See also PIRACY.

sharpie. **(1)** A type of oyster *dredge which originated among the oystermen of New Haven, Connecticut, USA, about 1830. Having a flat bottom with single *chines and a large wooden *centreboard, sharpies were built in sizes from 9 to 18 metres (30–60 ft) in length as oyster dredgers in Chesapeake Bay. They were developed later as flat-bottomed cruising *yachts and were, traditionally, *Bermudan-rigged *ketches with no *headsails. **(2)** During the 1930s the name was adopted to describe a class of small, hard-chine racing boat with a Bermudan *sloop rig.

sharpshooter. **(1)** A type of small work boat with a straight *stem, a *transom stern, and fixed keel. It was native to the Bahamas and ranged in length from 7.6 to 8.5 metres (25–28 ft), and was often known as a Bahama sharpshooter to distinguish it from the small racing class of the same name. The sharply *raked mast carried a *Bermudan mainsail with sometimes a *headsail on a long *bowsprit. **(2)** In the US Navy, the name for a marksman in the fighting *top.

sharp up, the description of a *square-rigged ship with her sails *trimmed up as near as possible to the wind and with her *yards *braced up as far fore and aft as the *lee *rigging would allow.

shear. A ship is subject to shear whenever it is bending. It is an imbalance between weight and buoyancy along the ship.

sheave, the revolving wheel in a *block. In the days of sail they were mostly made of **lignum vitae* or brass, sometimes a combination of the two, in which case the brass formed the bush of the sheave. The older name for a sheave is *shiver, and many seamen used to spell sheave as shiv, using the same pronunciation. Modern sheaves are mostly made of aluminium or of composite construction with roller or ball bearings.

sheepshank, a temporary *hitch in a rope to shorten it. It consists of two long *bights in the rope and a half hitch over the end of each bight made in the standing part of the rope. A **knotted sheepshank** is formed by passing the two ends of the rope through the *eyes of the bights.

Sheepshank

sheer. (1) The upward curve of the deck of a ship towards the bows and stern, with the lowest point in the *waist. **Reverse sheer**, a downward curve of the deck level towards the bows and stern, the highest deck level being *amidships. Some *yachts have been built to this principle to provide more headroom below deck. **(2)** The angle which a ship takes to its *cable when lying to an anchor, caused by the effects of wind and/or *tide.

sheer draught, what is nowadays known as a *lines plan. See also NAVAL ARCHITECTURE.

sheer legs, or **sheers,** a temporary structure of two or three *spars raised at an angle and lashed together at the point of intersection, with their *heels placed on a plank or *shoe. With the aid of a *tackle secured to this point, the sheers could be used for lifting heavy weights on board ship where *derricks were not available. Their main original use was for lifting in and out the lower masts of *square-rigged ships.

sheer pole, a horizontal steel rod fitted at the base of the *shrouds supporting a mast. It was *seized to each shroud just above its *bottle-screw and served to keep any turns out of the shrouds when they were being set up.

sheer strake, the top *strake, or plank, of a wooden vessel immediately below the *gunwale. It runs from *stem to stern, level with the upper deck of the vessel. See also GARBOARD.

sheet. (1) A *purchase or single line used for *trimming sails to the wind. A square sail set on a *yard has two sheets, one to each *clew. Sails on a *fore-and-aft rig normally only have a single sheet to the clew, the *double-clewed jib being an exception to the rule. The *junk rig is notable for having multiple sheets that lead from the bamboo *batten ends on the *luff of the sail. **(2)** As a verb, such as to **sheet in** a sail, it indicates the action of hardening in a sail, usually when it is desired to sail closer to the wind.

sheet anchor, an additional anchor carried in the largest ships for security should the *bower anchors fail to hold the ship. Originally two additional anchors were carried, one at either *chesstree *abaft the fore *rigging, one anchor being termed the sheet, the other the spare.

The term sheet anchor is also used as a synonym for security generally. 'I never knew an appeal made to them for honour, courage or loyalty,' said Admiral of the Fleet Lord St Vincent (1735–1823) of the Royal *Marines during the Napoleonic War (1803–15), 'that they did not more than realise my highest expectations. If ever the hour of real danger should come to England, they will be found the country's sheet anchor.'

sheet bend, also sometimes known as a swab *hitch. It is used to secure a rope's end through a small *eye, as, for example, in securing a boat's *lazy painter to the eye at the end of a *Jacob's ladder hanging from a lower boom. It

Sheet bend

is a simple knot in which the end of the rope is threaded through the eye and the end led round the eye and underneath its own *standing part so that it is nipped in the eye. The greater the pull on the rope, the tighter the *nip. A **double sheet bend** is a similar knot but with the end of the rope led twice underneath the eye instead of once. A sheet bend is also useful to temporarily join two ropes of different sizes, the smaller rope being given two turns around the larger one, as in the double sheet bend.

The origin of the name presumably came from its original use as the means of bending a sheet to the *clew of a small sail.

shell. (1) The outer part or body of a *block inside which the *sheave revolves. The shells of wooden blocks are *scored to hold the *strop with which they are bound and which embraces the *eye or hook, at the top or bottom of the block. (2) The calcareous protective structure which encloses the bodies of *molluscs, namely snails and clams. Snails have a single shell, which is often twisted into a spiral and may be decorated with ribs and spines. In bivalve clams there is a pair of hinged shells which entirely encloses the body. The hard outer skeleton of *crustaceans like crabs is also colloquially referred to as a shell.

shellback, a slang name given to an old sailor during the days of sail; in theory one who has been at sea for so long there has been time for *barnacles to grow on his back. It was originally employed in a slightly derogatory sense to indicate an old seaman who was old-fashioned and had failed to move with the times. But it later became almost a term of affection as indicating an old seaman whose knowledge of *seamanship was vast and who had much to teach the youngster in his profession.

shellfish is a term used generally to describe most of the invertebrate animals that are exploited by commercial *fisheries. Hence it includes *molluscs such as oysters, mussels, clams, and *squid, and also *crustaceans such as crabs, shrimp, and lobsters.

M. V. Angel

Shelvocke, George (1675–1742), British *privateer. He was born at Deptford (see ROYAL DOCKYARDS) and entered the Royal Navy in about 1690, serving through the remainder of the War of the League of Augsburg (1689–97). He became a lieutenant in 1704, and in 1707 was made *purser of the *Monck*, a less honourable though more lucrative position than that of a lieutenant. He came out of the navy in 1713 and fell into great poverty. In 1718 he approached a syndicate which was about to fit out two privateers to operate against Spain and was offered command of the expedition with John Clipperton as his second in command. While the two vessels, the *Success* and the *Speedwell*, were fitting out, Shelvocke took matters so much into his own hands that the syndicate of owners reversed the command structure, making Shelvocke second in command to Clipperton.

In February 1719 the two ships sailed with British *letters of marque. Shelvocke, in command of the *Speedwell*, was determined to give Clipperton the slip and succeeded in doing so at the Cape Verde Islands. He then proceeded into the *South Seas, and engaged more in *piracy than in privateering. It was while the *Speedwell* was sailing through the Straits of Le Maire that there occurred the well-known incident when Simon Hatley, Shelvocke's second in command, shot a black *albatross which had been following the ship for several days, the action which gave Coleridge the theme for his 'Rime of the *Ancient Mariner'.

The *Speedwell* made her way to Juan Fernandez Island, capturing a number of *prizes on the way, and here she was lost, probably through Shelvocke's carelessness. On his return to England in August 1722 Shelvocke was imprisoned, at the instance of the owners, but he escaped and fled to France. He subsequently returned to England, dying at the home of his son in Lombard Street, London. In 1726 he published an entertaining but doubtful account of his expedition with the title *A Voyage round the World*.

Poolman, K., *The Speedwell Voyage* (1999).

shift, a term used at sea to denote a change in the direction of the wind. It is less positive than the terms *veer and *back, which indicate which way the wind is shifting. In a purely naval sense, and used as a verb, it indicates a change of clothing. 'Hands to shift into working rig', an order to change into working clothes.

shifter, an old naval term for the cook's mate, one of whose chief duties was shifting, washing, and steeping the salted provisions stowed in casks in the ship's *hold. The steeping was done to reduce the amount of salt acquired by the provisions during their long stowage in brine.

shifting boards, longitudinal wooden *bulkheads temporarily erected in the *holds of ships. They were used in the days before the modern *bulk carrier to prevent bulk cargo, such as coal, grain, etc., from shifting in heavy seas.

ship, from the Old English *scip*, the generic name for seagoing vessels, as opposed to *boats, though *submarines are known as boats as are the different types of fishing vessels. Ships were originally personified as masculine, but by the 16th century they had become feminine. In 2002 *Lloyd's of London decided that all merchant ships should be described as 'it', though the British Ministry of Defence has confirmed that warships shall still be defined as feminine. Up to the 1950s, *yachts were often described as 'ships', but it is rare to hear them called this nowadays. For different types of ships see: AIRCRAFT CARRIER; BALINGER; BARQUE; BARQUENTINE; BATTLECRUISER; BATTLESHIP; BILANDER; BIREME; BLACKWALL FRIGATES; BOMB KETCH; BRIG; BRIGANTINE; BULK CARRIER; CARAVEL; CARRACK; CLIPPER; COASTER; COG; COLLIER; CONTAINER SHIP; CORBITA; CORVETTE; CRUISER; CRUISE SHIP; DESTROYER; DROMON; EAST INDIAMAN; FERRY; FRIGATE; GALIZABRA; GALLEASS; GALLEON; GALLEY; GALLIOT; HERMAPHRODITE BRIG; HOVERCRAFT; HYDROFOIL; IRONCLADS; JACKASS BARQUE; KNARR; LIBERTY SHIPS; LONGSHIP; LORCHA; MERCY SHIPS; MONITOR; NAO; OCEAN LINERS; PACKET; PADDLE STEAMER; PINK; POLACRE; Q-SHIP; REPLICA SHIP; RESEARCH SHIPS; RO-RO SHIP; ROUND SHIP; SAIL TRAINING; SEPULCHRAL SHIPS; SLOOP; SNOW; SURFACE EFFECT SHIP; SWATH SHIP; TANKER; TARTAN; TRABACOLO; TRAMP SHIP; TREASURE SHIP; TRIREME; TUG; VICTORY SHIPS; WEATHER SHIP; WING-IN-SURFACE EFFECT SHIP; XEBEC.

ship broker, an agent who acts for the owners or charterers of a ship in securing cargoes, clearances, and any other business, including insurance, connected with merchant shipping. He also negotiates the sale and purchase of merchant ships.

shipbuilding. Transport over water is a necessity in most parts of the world. Since time immemorial ships have been constructed in any place with a suitable shoreline, easily procured supplies of timber, and an available workforce. The improvement in ship design and construction has been a process of evolution, slow at first, but gathering speed over the centuries, leading ultimately to the sophisticated ships of the 21st century. It is interesting to compare the simplest *dugouts still to be found in less developed parts of the world and to appreciate that the design of even these humble craft has variations brought about by experience in operation. Following on from carved logs, dugouts, and similar craft, early shipbuilders in many Middle Eastern lands produced vessels constructed with papyrus, and elsewhere craft, like the *coracle and the *kayak, were formed of animal skins stretched over timber framework.

Wooden Shipbuilding. Well over 1,500 years ago, the skill of building ships with wooden planks was developed, a method that continued until the middle of the 19th century for commercial ships and which is still in use today for smaller vessels. Methods of construction have altered little over a thousand years: The shape of the ship is constrained by *frames (or ribs) covered with a shell of thinner planks, the plank edges being secured and *caulked to prevent leakage. The ship has a spine, or keel, on which the frames are set up and which in turn support the *beams, longitudinals, and other parts. Timber is a flexible material, able to yield and adapt to complex shapes, and with centuries of experience, methods of construction have become fairly standard throughout the world.

The western tradition of shipbuilding evolved over a period of about 500 years. During it the sailing ship became a fairly efficient vehicle, but also one in which the layout and *rigging have a form which is constrained by conventions understandable to multilingual, international crews. Hence, over the years, improvements and developments were accepted on a worldwide scale.

For several reasons, wooden vessels cannot be constructed in the traditional way with a

Hull configurations: some basic definitions

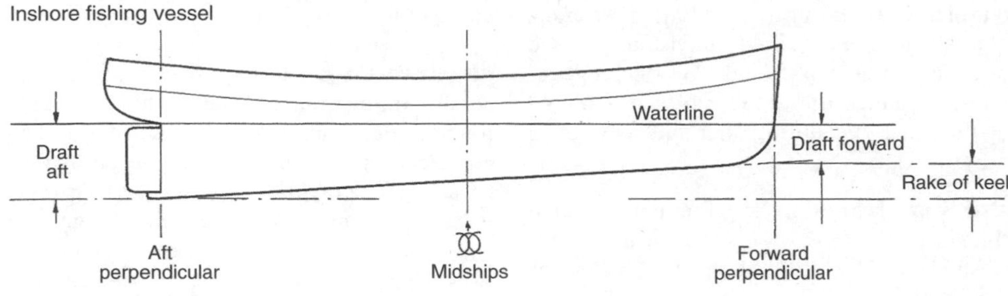

Definition of Ship Drafts—fore and aft

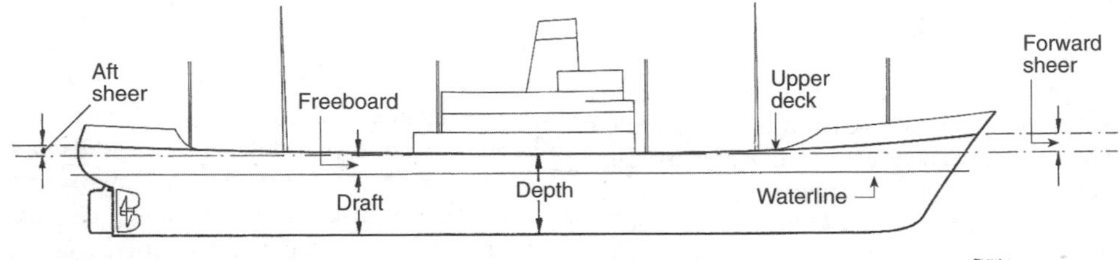

Sheer and Freeboard

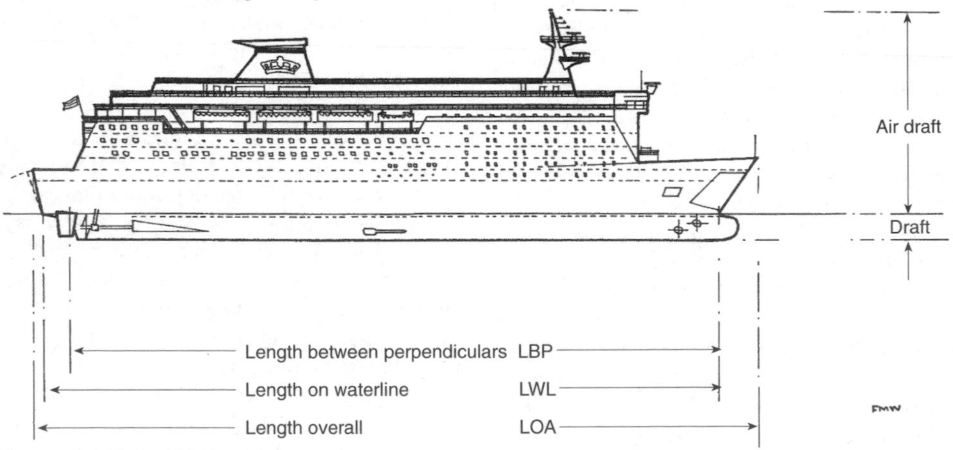

Means of defining ship lengths

waterline length much in excess of 80 metres (260 ft). As the ratios of the various dimensions, such as length to breadth, are fairly constant, this length limitation made it difficult to improve cargo-carrying capacity, and a plateau in efficiency was reached. Any small improvements came about by manipulation of the key proportions of ships. This often made them unseaworthy, a situation exacerbated by the elementary knowledge of *naval architecture at that time. Also wooden ships often had a fairly short lifespan if maintenance was lacking, or if they were *laid up for lengthy periods. A further problem came through demand for timber outstripping supply in many countries during the 18th century. At this time, industrial shipyards were being created in Europe, and for the first time there came an appreciation that shipbuilding was an assembly business requiring detailed planning, material control, ample manpower, and safe access to water. The stage was set for iron.

Iron and Steel Shipbuilding. The introduction of iron into shipbuilding was the industry's most dramatic change ever. In Britain the **Vulcan* was the first vessel to be built in it and *Brunel's **Great Britain* was the first large iron-built *ocean liner. The form of a ship's construction altered little, but the methods changed overnight. From a technical point of view there was practically no limit to the length, speed, and carrying capacity of a ship, its size being limited only by its ports of call. In addition, the basic principle that doubling a ship's length increased its carrying capacity eightfold made iron ships highly profitable, while improved hull strength enabled the fitting of heavy steam machinery, with adequately sized coal bunkers. As iron is a tough and unyielding material, the shipyards had to retool to enable them to produce component parts to the highest precision standards. New engineering techniques had to be introduced and shipyards were equipped with rollers, shears, punches, and frame-bending furnaces, while lofting departments became dedicated to the making of accurate full-scale templates for construction. Design and drawing offices were introduced as were specialist ordering departments for the procurement of all necessary materials. The tasks within a shipyard also had to be redefined and new trades, like plater, riveter, and driller, introduced and integrated into the labour force—not always an easy task.

For a short time in the mid-19th century, some owners ordered vessels of *composite construction. This led to slightly longer hulls and to ones which did not 'sweat' in the tropics. This method was used to build many *clipper ships during the 1850s and 1860s, and remained in use to a limited extent in *yachtbuilding into the early 20th century.

In the 1860s there was another change in material that was as significant as had been the one from wood to iron. This was the introduction of steel, an alloy of iron, which, though much more vulnerable to corrosion than iron, was stronger and lighter and it increased a ship's cargo capacity by as much as 10%. Such an improvement in earning power more than outweighed any increase in production costs, with the further benefit that the machine tools and systems for iron could be adapted to it. The *Rotomahana*, built at Dumbarton by William Denny in 1879, is credited with being the first large merchant ship to be built in mild steel and was the first steel ocean-going ship. Initially, steel was extremely expensive but by the 1880s a number of ships had been built in it, and by 1890 it was being used in every British shipyard. Europe and North America made the changeover somewhat later, completing it by 1900.

Ship Manufacture. Despite the introduction of new processes, new materials, and advanced ship designs, the traditional processes of a shipyard have altered little over the years.

First, the design settles the dimensions and overall appearance of the ship, and from this the detailed plans are generated. After careful investigation of the suppliers, and their ability to meet stipulated dates and costs, materials have to be ordered. Some, like steel, are ordered in bulk; others, like machinery, as individual items. The plans have to be submitted to a *Classification Society, like *Lloyd's Register, for acceptance, and also to statutory bodies like the UK's *Maritime and Coastguard Agency or the *US Coast Guard. Their approval of a design is mandatory and there must also be a plan for an ongoing inspection during construction, and then for the lifetime of the ship. Most countries of the world have accepted a new concept, known as State Port Control, where their maritime authorities can carry out random inspections of any ship and detain it if it fails to meet international standards laid down by the *International Maritime Organization.

The steelwork plans have to be transferred to some form of templates, or, as is now current practice, to computer-controlled machine tools. All parts are sub-assembled and then placed in assembly units, which can be as large as 500 tonnes, with most of the piping, wiring, and other small parts included. When these are moved to the erection berth or building dock they should require little work apart from assembly and the testing of the systems, and final paintwork. The Classification Society inspections continue throughout and all watertight

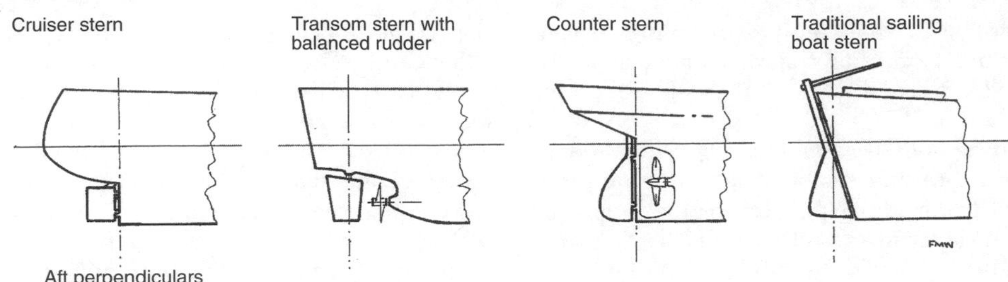

Means of ascertaining the aft perpendicular on different ships

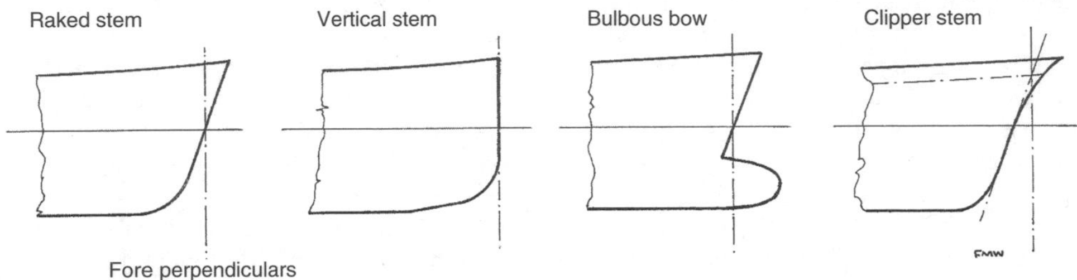

Means of ascertaining the fore perpendiculars

compartments must be tested under a head of water.

The task of final outfitting includes placing main machinery aboard and then testing in dock conditions. Following float out or the traditional *launching, the ship is prepared for exhaustive full-scale trials, often lasting several days. Indeed in many large ships a small team of test engineers will remain aboard for the first voyage to ensure all contractual obligations are fulfilled.

Modern Systems of Production. The number of people employed in a shipyard has fallen significantly and large portions of the traditional shipbuilding tasks are subcontracted out. A current example, from a north German shipyard, is that steel is sourced from another country and brought to the yard for primary cutting. It is then sent to another European country for machining and preparation, before being returned to the yard for painting and assembly. Almost every other task in the establishment is by subcontracted labour, and all parts, including the main engines, are brought to the shipyard by sea or land.

The computer has entered every field in shipbuilding and a very small group of people can plan and control the complex tasks of a ship's construction, from design and materials ordered, through to construction and delivery. The time scales required for construction have been greatly reduced, although the 'gestation period', when the design concepts are evaluated, has risen. This is because lengthy periods of planning and analysis are required for a ship that may be constructed in just a few months, something which adds weight to the commercial advantage of repeat orders and standardized ships.

Geographical Disposition of Shipyards. In the years up to the introduction of iron, shipyards were found in all places blessed with readily available timber supplies and adequate water for launching. Labour requirements were less problematical as from time immemorial shipyards could depend on groups of itinerant shipwrights, something that continues to this day in the *replica ship market. Shipbuilding sites were to be found on every part of the European coast and later in North America and Russia, all countries with an abundance of timber. With the demise of wooden shipbuilding, such sites became few and far between, although some are found still in Indonesia and other parts of South-East Asia.

The introduction of iron made it economical to set up of shipyards near iron suppliers, and therefore in areas adjacent to coalfields.

Examples include the River Clyde—which saw the founding of nearly 400 shipyards in a mere 200 years—and those based in the north-east of England on the Tyne, Wear, and Tees rivers. Despite the reduction in the use of coal, and the gradual centralization of iron and then steel smelting, European shipyards remained viable until the end of the Second World War (1939–45). Since then rationalization in Europe and North America has led to a vast reduction in shipbuilding sites in these areas, while, at the same time, they increased elsewhere, particularly in the Far East.

With modern methods of production and good transport infrastructures, the need to be near raw material supplies has vanished and shipyards now survive on their technical and commercial competence.

Worldwide Production. During the 19th century timber ships continued to be built but on an ever-decreasing scale, and by 1900 even the large North American yards were in decline. Britain enjoyed a head start in iron shipbuilding, and then with the changeover to steel, so that by 1913 British shipyards were the dominant force in the world. In that year, when British shipbuilding was at its peak, the industry produced 61% of the world's ships, with the River Clyde alone producing an amazing 23%. In that year the Clyde delivered more than one new ship every day of the year. The First World War (1914–18) ensured that the shipyards of both the United States and the United Kingdom were working at full stretch. During this period many of Britain's former customers, unable to obtain tonnage quickly in the profitable wartime market place, set up new shipyards themselves and even started to compete for Britain's former customers. Despite the Depression years, when shipyards throughout the world were struggling to survive, some wonderful ocean liners, including the *Empress of Britain*, *Normandie*, *Queen Mary*, and *Queen Elizabeth*, were produced for the passenger trades. However, closures—mostly of small and undercapitalized yards—were commonplace and when hostilities began again in 1939 the shipbuilding industry was poorly placed to produce what was required. As in the First World War, both the British and the American shipbuilding industries contributed in a superb manner to the Allied cause with the Americans, as they had during the First World War, concentrating on mass-produced war-standard cargo ships such as the *Liberty and *Victory ships, as well as on standard *tankers, known as T2s, producing them in astonishing numbers. Untrammelled by tradition, they capitalized on the known but under-utilized processes of welding and prefabrication-processes which are now accepted in every shipyard in the world.

In 2001, the number of merchant vessels completed was around 1,700 worldwide: totally 31 million gross tonnes. The largest shipbuilders are now in the Far East, with the People's Republic of China growing fast, the Republic of Korea producing 37% of the world's production, and Japan 38%.

New Techniques, New Types of Ship. Construction techniques, ship design, and construction materials developed dramatically in the final decades of the 20th century, allowing for a great increase in the size of existing vessels and the introduction of new types of ship. The greatest increase in size has been in the tanker trade, with ships now being built which can carry over 500,000 tonnes of crude oil. *Container ships are also increasing in size, but the most interesting statistics come from *cruise liners. Here, not only have passenger numbers increased, but the amount of space for each passenger has increased more than twofold.

In the area of new designs, two in particular stand out. The first, the *underwater vehicle, has given access to the deepest parts of the ocean. Whether manned or unmanned, it has opened up new avenues of research for scientists in *oceanography, *marine archaeology, and the *offshore oil and gas industry. The second is the continuing development of the *surface effect ship. See also MOULDING; MOULD-LOFT; MOULDS. Fred M. Walker

ship-money fleets, the annual fleets sent out by King Charles I between 1635 and 1641 to assert the sovereignty of the *Narrow Seas which at that time were plagued by *piracy and with the local *fisheries being plundered by Dutch fishing *busses. These fleets got their name from the fact that they were financed by the levy of a tax known as ship-money. No English parliament was sitting at that period and the king levied the tax by his own decrees. Such a tax had been levied previously, frequently during the

15th and 16th centuries and again in 1626 when a fleet had been fitted out during the war with Spain. The form of the tax was to assess each port and maritime town with a sum of money which the mayor had to raise however he thought best. Later, as the cost of succeeding fleets grew greater, the levy was made on all towns and parishes throughout the country.

These ship-money fleets achieved the object for which they were designed, clearing the English waters of the many pirates who were operating in them and policing the east coast *herring fisheries so efficiently that almost all illegal fishing by the Dutch was stopped. But as the annual levy of ship-money grew, it became more and more difficult to collect as resistance to paying it spread. Parliament was recalled in November 1641 and in January of the following year the House of Lords declared ship-money illegal. This brought Charles I into a head-on collision with Parliament, and in the fleet fitted out in 1642 all captains with royalist sympathies were removed from their commands. It was a signal for the start of the English Civil War.

ship of the line, a warship of the days of sailing navies which carried a sufficiently large gun armament to lie in the *line of battle. Until the time of the First Dutch War (1652–4), fleets of warships did not fight in formation, each ship sailing into battle with the purpose of finding an enemy vessel she could engage in single combat. The first attempt to make a fleet fight in formation was made by Robert *Blake at the battle of Portland in 1653, but the line of battle as such did not emerge until the Second Dutch War (1665–7), when fleets were more rigidly controlled by their admirals. And because a ship's guns of those days had no means of being trained, but could only fire through their *gunports at right angles to the fore-and-aft line of the ship, the line of battle had obviously to be in the line ahead formation, with each ship following in the track of the next warship ahead. This formation was rigidly laid down in the *fighting instructions issued to all admirals and captains of ships, and governed the conduct of all British ships in action until the introduction of the *general chase signal in the mid-18th century gave the admiral in command a degree of flexibility. See also RATE; WARFARE AT SEA.

ship preservation, the practice of deliberately extending a vessel's life beyond its normal economic span. Motives may be religious, as with the Egyptian Cheops *sepulchral ship; historical or patriotic, as with HMS **Victory* or USS **Constitution*; or utilitarian as with the 1897 river steamer *Melik*, now the headquarters for the Khartoum Sailing Club.

Without human intervention, ships decay steadily because of the hostile environment in which they usually operate. Sun, rain, and humidity are all hostile to a ship's structure, as is electrolytic action afloat. The Cheops ship has survived for more than 4,000 years thanks to the dry atmosphere of the tomb in which it was enclosed; and the almost original condition of the 1824 *frigate *Unicorn*, now displayed at Dundee, can be put down to the roof which covered her weather deck for most of her life. However, *Drake's *Golden Hinde*, perhaps the earliest example of ship preservation for patriotic reasons, soon decayed when displayed in the open air at Deptford following his circumnavigation of 1577–80. The fact is that a wooden ship open to the weather will require progressive replacement of its various timbers as they age and decay, so that, arguably, all that remains after many years is a *replica ship of what was originally preserved. To avoid this fate, *Amundsen's exploration vessel **Fram* has been totally enclosed in an exhibition building near Oslo, and other large museum ships may have to be similarly protected from the weather if they are to survive for posterity.

As a natural biocide, salt may actually extend the life of a wooden ship. During construction, merchant ships sometimes had rock-salt packed between their *frames to deter rot. An old wooden ship will often survive longer if it can be kept working gently, so that its decks are sluiced regularly by salt water—in which rot-causing organisms cannot live—and fresh air is able to circulate below decks to deter dry-rot. Regular use also reveals any leaks or structural defects more quickly than when a vessel remains tied up for months or even years.

Vessels displayed alongside a *quay for extended periods should be turned annually to equalize the exposure of each side to sun and wind. Rainwater encourages wet-rot in wooden decks, particularly where the vessels being exhibited are stationary, and there is no natural rolling to throw off the water. At Mystic Seaport Museum in Connecticut, vessels exhibited afloat benefit from a daily sluicing with salt water across their upper works to deter rot and shrinkage of timbers.

Steel corrodes steadily in a salty environment. Even with regular painting, the service life of a steel ship is about twenty years because of structural corrosion. Sacrificial anodes fitted to the external hull may inhibit electrolytic degradation if they are replaced regularly, but the waterlines of metal ships, where chlorides can combine with oxygen, are particularly affected by destructive corrosion. Wrought-iron ships fared better, and before the Bessemer process made steel widely available from the 1870s, wrought iron was frequently used in *shipbuilding. Among the largest iron ships was *Brunel's **Great Eastern*, still so strong when scrapped in 1888–90 that the labour of dismantling almost bankrupted her Merseyside shipbreakers. HMS **Warrior*, whose massive wrought-iron armour has contributed to her longevity, is another remarkable testament to the resistance of wrought iron to salt-water corrosion, and Brunel's earlier iron ship **Great Britain* survived nearly 50 years beached on the Falkland Islands, thanks to the durability of her riveted wrought-iron plates. But the ambient humidity within the dry-dock where she is now displayed in Bristol must be controlled if it is not to accelerate corrosion deep within her hull plates, where chlorides have penetrated over more than 150 years. A glass 'roof' is therefore being erected over her which will exclude rainwater from the dry-dock and help to inhibit further damage.

Several other nations besides Britain and the USA have preserved their most notable warships for historic or patriotic reasons, the 1865 turret ship *Huascar*, preserved at Talcahuano Naval Base in Chile, and the 1899 battleship *Mikasa*, dry-docked at Yokosuka, being just two examples. A number of merchant sailing ships like the **Cutty Sark* in Greenwich, and the iron barques *James Craig* and *Polly Woodside* in Sydney and Melbourne, have also been preserved to show future generations how cargoes were transported in the days of sail. The preservation of larger ships like these is usually the responsibility of governments, municipalities, or charitable organizations. Many of them struggle to maintain a historic vessel as a public amenity, as the costs far exceed what can be earned from admission revenues and corporate hire. Nobody ever got rich from ship preservation.

Since 1970, the explosion of interest in conserving fragile old ships has expanded faster than our technical knowledge of how best to achieve it. However, the US National Parks Service's *Standards for Historic Vessel Preservation Projects* (1990) is an important contribution to the methodology of ship preservation, and there are numerous organizations worldwide working actively in this area. Two of the most important are the World Ship Trust and European Maritime Heritage, both of them charities. The former was established in London in 1979 to encourage all nations to preserve ships important for their own history. Working with the National Maritime Historical Society in New York State, it has made more than twenty prestigious awards to preserved ships throughout the world, and individual achievement awards to some of the most eminent practitioners. The latter, believing that some traditional vessels survive best if they can find a new working role, perhaps in *sail training or for other educational purposes, has campaigned since 1994 for a regulatory regime which encourages such vessels to continue working in compliance with today's safety regulations. It acts equally on behalf of maritime museums and shipowners, and also works to harmonize national safety regulations, so that traditional vessels can more easily visit neighbouring countries and help to keep alive historic sealinks between nations.

The World Ship Trust's *International Register of Historic Ships*, compiled by Norman Brouwer (3rd edn. 1999), lists more than 1,800 ships preserved in 72 countries. With a 12.2-metre (40-ft) length threshold, the *Register* has to exclude the thousands of smaller vessels preserved worldwide, many by private owners who enjoy sailing them and attending festivals of traditional boats. Without the enthusiasm of such owners, most of these historic old vessels would already have disintegrated.

Bray, M. (ed.), *Taking Care of Wooden Ships* (1978).

Fuller, G. (ed.), *A Curatorial Handbook for Historic Naval Vessels* (1993).

John Robinson

ship rigged, a sailing ship which is *square rigged on all three masts.

ship's bell. This is traditionally made of brass with the ship's name engraved on it and with a short length of rope—known as the **bell rope**—spliced into the eye of the clapper. It is used for striking the **bells** which mark the passage of time on board ship, when the 24-hour day is divided into six *watches. The passage of time in each watch is marked by the bell every half-hour, one bell marking the end of the first half-hour, and eight bells the end of each watch. However, with the two *dog watches four bells is struck to indicate the end of the first one, then one is struck to mark the end of the first half-hour of the last dog watch. However, eight bells, not four, are struck to mark the end of the last dog watch. Seamen, when reporting the time, traditionally refer to it as bells. Thus, for example, half-past three is seven bells while five minutes to one is reported as five minutes to two bells and so on. In the US Navy sixteen bells is sometimes struck at midnight on 31 December to ring out the old and ring in the new year.

The ship's bell was also used, when no other audible signal was carried aboard, as a *fog signal by ringing the bell for five seconds every minute. When a ship is broken up its bell often becomes a highly prized memento of service in the ship and they frequently command very high prices when offered for sale. See also SOUTHERN CROSS; WARM THE BELL, TO.

shipshape and Bristol fashion, a phrase meaning in good and seamanlike order with reference to the condition of a ship. The expression had its origin when Bristol was the major west coast port of Britain at a time when all its shipping was maintained in good order.

ship's number, see SIGNAL LETTERS.

shipwrecks is a word with several connotations but here it means vessels that are of particular interest to those working in *marine archaeology. Many shipwrecks within the *Exclusive Economic Zone of coastal states are now protected sites, particularly those within their *territorial waters, and efforts are being made to give a measure of protection to those sunk outside those zones. In the USA such sites are protected by the Abandoned Shipwreck Act (1987); in the UK all *diving on shipwrecks is governed by the legal definition of *wreck. Most governments issue permits which impose restrictions and obligations on those wishing to *salvage artefacts from a shipwreck or to excavate a site. Marine parks and reserves have also been created for the management and preservation of shipwrecks. Unfortunately, in the past, the law was slow to catch up with treasure hunters who, helped by the advances in diving equipment and salvage techniques, have plundered many shipwrecks with little regard to recording their structures.

However, marine archaeologists are not just interested in a vessel's construction and fittings; whenever possible they also want information on its performance and seaworthiness, as well as the cargo it contained, the society on board, the socio-economic and historical framework within which it operated, and the environmental context within which it came to rest.

Shipwreck Environments. The most accessible sites are usually those found on dry land but, whether interred or abandoned, vessels in this environment rarely survive well. The timbers of the *sepulchral ship at Sutton Hoo, for instance, survived only as a buried print in the soil, and exposed hulls rarely last beyond 250 years. Those that end up in wet or submerged environments generally survive better, their state of preservation depending largely upon the botanical, biological, and chemical content of the water, as well as the dynamics and geomorphology of their resting place. Fresh water is an excellent preserver of wood and other organic remains, particularly if the remains are sealed, as was the case with the wetland boats of northern Europe, of which the 3rd-century BC Hjortspring boat from Denmark is an outstanding example. Some of these, to all appearances, were almost as fresh as the day they were abandoned.

Ships that sink in deep freshwater lakes also survive well. The armed *schooners *Hamilton* and *Scourge* that went down in Lake Ontario during the Anglo-American War of 1812–14 surprised the world in 1973 when they were found sitting upright on the bottom. Their guns were still in their carriages and their anti-boarding cutlasses were still in their racks; indeed one still had its boat hanging from the *davits. Cold also helps preserve structures: the

Breadalbane, lost in 1853 while searching for the *Franklin expedition, was found in 1980, upright and largely intact beneath the Arctic *ice.

Salt-water environments are less conducive to survival, though some are quite benign. The Baltic for instance, which has a relatively low level of salinity and oxygen, is free of the *teredo shipworm (*teredo navalis*) and most other wood-devouring organisms, which is why the great, four-deck fighting ship **Vasa* survived in such an excellent state of preservation.

But, generally speaking, shoreline, intertidal, and shallow-water shipwrecks tend to be badly eroded, much decayed, and, to varying extents, dispersed by the *waves and *currents that characterize shallow, open-coastal zones. Areas with particularly strong currents can produce surging waters and an unstable seabed. An Elizabethan wreck off Alderney in the Channel Islands, though over 30 metres (98 ft) down, has suffered much from this.

Ships that end up on a hard bottom generally fare worse than those that come to rest in soft sediments and work their way down into the seabed. Once within the silt and mud their environment is largely anaerobic, or oxygen free. This protects them from shipworm or other organisms of microbiological decay which destroy timbers and other organic materials. An example of a shipwreck being preserved in this manner is the **Mary Rose*.

Legendary Shipwrecks. As ancient writings attest repeatedly, shipwrecks have always been objects of fear and fascination, particularly if they are associated with tragedy or great events, famous people, battles, *mutiny, or *explorations by sea, and the discovery and investigation of them always attract public interest. The loss of the **Titanic*, which touched everybody for its drama and the heroism and self-sacrifice of those on board, is one outstanding example; the **Batavia*, an *East Indiaman wrecked off Western Australia in 1629, is another. The tragic events that followed the latter disaster, involving desertion, mutiny, massacres, and executions, have ensured that this became one of the most notorious shipwrecks of all time.

Shipwrecks associated with important historical figures also arouse the public's imagination. The excavation of *Nelson's first major command, the 64-gun *Agamemnon*, which sank in the River Plate in 1809, caused considerable interest in the mid-1990s. The one cannon not *salvaged when she sank was raised and examined, and a commemorative seal bearing Nelson's name in reverse was recovered. There was public interest, too, when items from Captain *Bligh's **Bounty*, which was burned at Pitcairn, were recovered in 1957; and when the *Pandora*, the vessel that went after the *Bounty* mutineers before being wrecked on the *Great Barrier Reef, was found in 1977. Surveys carried out on the latter suggest that much of the hull has survived in good condition as have some important artefacts. Excavation of the site is ongoing.

Shipwrecks of Warships. These are always interesting as they can sometimes add to our knowledge of *warfare at sea in earlier centuries. Those that have caused widespread interest include the early American *ironclad **Monitor* which sank off Cape Hatteras, North Carolina, in 1862. Her remains were found in 1973, but proved too fragile to move, though her *turret was recovered in 2003. Another Civil War shipwreck of great interest is the CSS **Alabama*, sunk by the USS *Kearsage* off Cherbourg, France, in June 1864. Of the many items recovered from her, the artillery and how it operated was of particular significance. Important work has also been done on *L'Orient*, the flagship of the French fleet that Nelson defeated at the battle of the Nile in 1797 from which 400 artefacts have been raised since the first excavations of the site in the 1980s.

In recent years the public gaze has shifted to the great battles and fighting ships of the 20th century. Examples include the German *battleship *Bismarck*, which was found and filmed by Dr *Ballard in 1989, and the remains of the German *pocket battleship *Admiral Graf Spee*, scuttled in the River Plate in 1939. A gun was raised from her in 1997 and the rangefinder and the remains of her *radar in 2004.

Cargoes of Shipwrecks. Many shipwrecks have become well known because of the artistic and historical importance of their cargoes. The first of these was found in 1900 by sponge divers off Antikythera, Greece, which contained a series of spectacular bronze and marble statues from the late classical period as well as later Roman copies of Greek originals. Another sensational cargo of similar art works, dated to the 1st–2nd centuries BC, was found in 1907 in a shipwreck off Mahdia, Tunisia.

If the importance of a wreck is measured by the extent to which it advances learning, then there can be few more important wrecks than the Hoi An *junk which sank in over 80 metres (260 ft) of water, 22 kilometres (14 mls.) from the Da Nang peninsula in Vietnam. The wreck appears to be of Thai origin and its spectacular cargo of blue and white and monochrome ceramics, painted with human figures, landscapes, fish, birds, and mythological animals, dates to Vietnam's Golden Age of the mid-15th century when Vietnamese potters filled the vacuum that China created by distmantling its fleets and forbidding exports. Over a third of a million pieces were raised during the late 1990s and they not only provide a new chapter in South-East Asian arts but also illuminate what happened when, for a few decades, China closed its doors on the world. Another cargo of great importance came from what is reported to be an Arab *dhow that went down at Batu Hitam in Indonesia's Karimata Straits. In 1998 over 65,000 9th-century AD Tang dynasty ceramics were recovered from it which were intended for the Malay, Indian, or Persian markets. They demonstrate that, even at this early date, there was a maritime alternative to the overland silk roads.

Sometimes the cargoes of shipwrecks are not only of historical, and artistic, importance but are also immensely valuable. The Dutch East Indiaman *Geldermalsen* (aka the *Nanking* wreck), lost in 1752 on a reef in the South China Sea, was located in 1985. Part of her cargo, some 160,000 pieces of Chinese porcelain and 126 gold ingots, was auctioned the following year in Amsterdam and created a buying frenzy the like of which Europe has not seen since similar cargoes were sold in the Low Countries in the 16th century. Another sensational find, made in 1987, was that of the *Central America*, a side-wheel *paddle steamer that went down in deep water during a storm off South Carolina in 1852. Four hundred and twenty-three lives were lost. On board was over US $2 million in California gold, a large part of which was recovered using *underwater vehicles.

Some of these last wrecks were not recovered in an archaeological manner, resulting in a great loss of information, particularly with regard to structure.

Construction Methods Learned from Early Shipwrecks. Shipwrecks also reveal to us how our ancestors built their ships. Bronze Age examples found off the Turkish coast had their cargoes contained within a shell-first hull where the planks had been edge joined with mortise and tenons before the installation of the frames. This method of assembly, which continued, with some variation and development, throughout the Graeco-Roman period, is best exemplified by the 4th-century BC Kyrenia ship. An amphora carrier that was found in 30 metres (100 ft) of water off northern Cyprus in the late 1960s, its remains and remnants of its cargo are now on display at Kyrenia Castle.

A wreck found at Yassi Ada, Turkey, dating from the 7th century, seems to mark the transition from shell-first to frame-first construction, but a different method of Mediterranean ship construction was found on several 6th-century BC shipwrecks where stitching was the principal method used to bond together the planking and much of the primary structure. The earliest example of this is the *Giglio* wreck from the Archaic period (*c.*600). It was found at 50 metres (165 ft) off Tuscany in 1961, and was excavated in the 1980s. Quite apart from its construction the *Giglio* had an astonishing cargo which included Etruscan storage jars, painted wares from Corinth, Lakonia, and Etruria, a range of weaponry, and a spectacular Greek helmet that had been engraved with boars and snakes.

Shipwrecks found outside the Mediterranean revealed a very different method of construction which, for want of a better term, has been called the Romano-Celtic tradition. Examples have come from various points across north-west Europe including the Thames, the Severn Estuary, the Channel Islands, and some German rivers and estuaries. Within this group there is much variety in hull forms and the fastening, design and installation of the individual components, but, in general, they feature dense, heavy framing with (usually) flush-laid, *caulked planking that is gripped to the *frames with clenched iron nails.

Other shipwrecks that contrast markedly with the mortise and tenon ships of the Mediterranean are the mainly *clinker-planked vessels of northern Europe and Scandinavia, whose best-known examples include the Nydam boats which were excavated from a former lake in

Jutland in 1859–63, and the Oseberg (*c.*815–20), Gokstad (late 9th century), and Tune (*c.*910) Viking Age ships from Norway. These vessels found their full expression in the *cogs, *hulks, and other Nordic ship types of the Middle Ages.

Types of 15th–18th-century Ships. Shipwrecks of later vessels include the *caravel, of which several examples have been found. One, the so-called Molasses Reef Wreck found on a Turks and Caicos Islands reef, appears to be dated to around 1510–30 and was about 19 metres (62 ft) long. Though very little of it survives, it stands out as one of a very few wrecks in the world that has been fully excavated, preserved, and published after the site was excavated by American marine archaeologists in the 1980s. Over 10 tonnes of artefacts were removed, much of which are now on display in the Turks and Caicos National Museum.

Far more discoveries have been made of 16th-century ships, including late examples of the *carrack. One of the best preserved is the Portuguese-built Fort San Sebastian wreck that went down off the island of Mozambique in the 1550s with a cargo of pepper, nutmeg, mace, porcelain, and gold, and which was excavated between 2001 and 2003. Several examples of the other vessel that helped shape the 16th-century world, the Iberian *galleon, have also been found and excavated, one off Saipan, another off Luzon in the Philippines, and a third, the *San Agustin*, California's first recorded shipwreck, which was lost in 1595 in Drake's Bay, California. The wreck itself has not yet been confirmed, but its presence is well attested by large numbers of late Ming porcelain fragments that have come from Indian graves. All these were involved in the so-called Manila Trade.

The evolutionary high point of 17th-century ship development was the fully-fledged East Indiaman of which many examples have been found and excavated. Of the Dutch examples the earliest are the *Nassau* (sunk in battle, Straits of Malacca, 1604) and the *Mauritius* (lost off Gabon, West Africa, 1609).

Numerous instances of East Indiamen shipwrecks belonging to other *East India Companies, and those of ships from later times, could be given, but they do not tell us much that we do not already know. Of the vessels that represent the peak of sailing ship development, and the advent of *steam propulsion, mention must be made of an important group of 19th- and early 20th-century hulks from the Falkland Islands, South Georgia, and Tierra del Fuego. They were mostly victims of Cape Horn but have survived mainly because of their isolation and climate. The most important of these is the **Great Britain*, which was returned in 1970 to Bristol where it had been built and is now on display to the public, a shining, if rare, example of how shipwrecks can be saved and restored as museum ships. See also WRECKERS.

Bound, M., *Lost Ships* (1998).
Monaghan, J., and Bound, M., *A Ship Cast away about Alderney: Investigations of an Elizabethan Shipwreck* (2001).
Sheaf, C., and Kilburn, R., *The Hatcher Porcelain Cargoes* (1988).

Mensun Bound

shiver. **(1)** See SHEAVE. **(2)** As a verb, it describes the condition of a vessel's sails when the vessel is brought so close to the wind that it lifts the *luffs of the sails and makes them shiver.

'shiver my timbers', an expression of surprise or unbelief, as when a ship strikes a rock or *shoal so hard that its timbers shiver. Although the saying has an obviously nautical origin, and is widely attributed to seamen by many writers of sea stories, it is unlikely that it was used much, if at all, by seamen afloat or ashore.

shoal. **(1)** A derivative of the word 'shallow', indicating a patch of water in the sea with a depth less than that of the surrounding water. They are the results of banks of sand, mud, or rock on the seabed, and are usually marked, in coastal waters, by *navigation marks such as *buoys. **(2)** A large number of *fish which swim together.

shoe. **(1)** A pair of triangular wooden boards which were occasionally fixed to the *palm of an anchor to increase its holding power on the bottom. An anchor treated in this way was said to be shod. **(2)** A block of wood with a hole in it which fitted the sharp bill of the anchor *flukes to protect the ship's side when the anchor was being *fished. **(3)** A term occasionally used to describe a *false keel. **(4)** The projection of the keel *abaft the stern *frame on which the spindle of the *rudder rests. **(5)** A plank on which the *heels of *sheer legs are placed.

shoot, to, a verb with more than one nautical meaning. A navigator is said **to shoot the sun**, or any heavenly body, when he takes its *altitude with a *sextant. A sailing vessel is said **to shoot**, or *fore-reach, when she *luffs into the wind and makes distance to *windward. A fisherman, when using a *drift net or *purse seine net, **shoots his nets** when he lays them, but the word does not apply when fishing with a *trawl. When a naval gunlayer's *shots were very wide of his target, he was said **to be shooting** the *compass.

shore, a stout wooden timber used to back up a *bulkhead in a ship when excessive pressure is applied to it from the other side, as with a flooded compartment. It is also the name of timber props used to hold vessels upright in *dry-dock and to hold small ones upright on shore.

short, an adjective with many uses at sea. An anchor *cable hove in short is when a vessel's anchor is nearly *up and down in preparation for getting *under way. A short sea is one in which the distance between *wave crests is less than normal. For short allowance, see PETTY WARRANT. See also SHORT SPLICE.

shorten in, to, to heave the anchor *cable in *short.

short splice, a method of *splicing two ropes together where the joined rope is not required to be *rove through a *block. The ends of the two ropes are unlayed and then married together with the *strands of one rope alternating with the strands of the other. Each strand is then tucked over its adjacent strand and under the next, and the splice is completed when each strand has been tucked twice. If the joined rope is intended for heavy use a third tuck is often made to provide an extra strong join. A short splice increases the diameter of the rope along the length of the splice, which is the reason why it is never employed when the joined rope is required to be used through a block. See also LONG SPLICE.

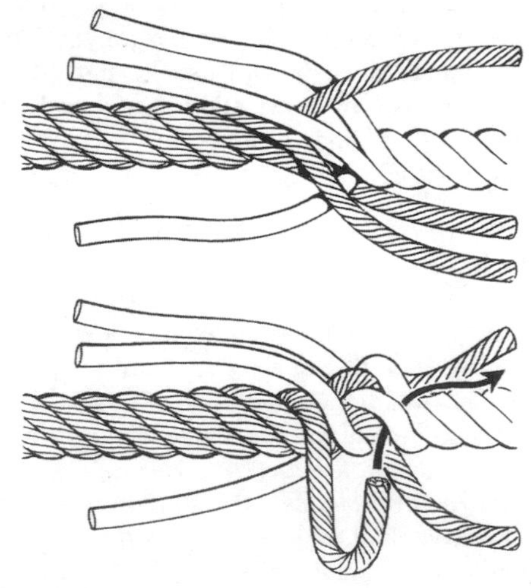

Short splice

shot, the name which applied to everything that was fired out of a naval gun except missiles filled with explosive. As Sir Henry Mainwaring remarks in his *Seaman's Dictionary* (1644): 'There are many kinds of shot. That which flies farthest and pierces most is round shot; the next is crossbar, which is good for ropes and sails and masts, the other *langrel, which will not fly so far but is very good for the rigging and the like, and for men; so is *chain shot and *case-shot, which is good to ply among men which stand naked [unprotected] on deck plying of their small shot.'

Shovel, or **Shovell, Sir Clowdisley** (1659–1707), talented English admiral, who was involved in one of the most famous *shipwrecks in English history. He first went to sea in 1664 as a cabin boy and probably took part in the Third Dutch War (1672–4). He served in the Mediterranean from 1673, and in 1676 commanded the boats of the fleet which burnt the ships belonging to the *Barbary pirates in their stronghold of Tripoli. Promoted *post-captain in 1677 he spent the next nine years serving in various ships in continuous operations against the Barbary pirates with notable success. He returned to England in November 1686, was knighted and promoted, and took part in several encounters against the French before commanding a *squadron which played a prominent part in capturing Gibraltar in 1704 during the War of the Spanish Succession (1702–13). Other victories followed when he commanded the fleet in the Mediterranean, and it was October 1707 before he sailed for home with the fleet, and it was then that disaster struck.

Nearing the English Channel, Shovel's flagship, the *Association*, a 2nd-*rate *ship of the line with 90 guns, and three other ships, were swept in heavy weather onto the Bishop and Clerk rocks off the Scilly Isles by an unsuspected northerly current. All four were wrecked and almost everyone aboard them perished. Shovel, who was very fat, was washed overboard and reached the shore alive, but was murdered by a local woman for his emerald ring. He is buried in Westminster Abbey, and the emerald ring was subsequently recovered and returned to his heirs.

In 1967 the *wreck of the *Association* was discovered and a considerable quantity of bullion, guns, and silver plate was recovered by amateur and professional divers who came from all over the world. So thoroughly did they plunder the wreck, and damage it, that when the 1973 Protection of Wrecks Act came into being it was decided the site was no longer worth protecting. See also WRECKERS.

'show a leg', or **'shake a leg',** the traditional call of the *boatswain's *mates in a British warship when the hands are called to turn out in the morning. It arose from the days of sail when seamen, who were signed on for the duration of a ship's *commission, were always refused shore leave when in harbour for fear that they would desert. Instead of going ashore, women, ostensibly wives, were allowed to live on board while the ship remained in harbour, and of course joined the men in their *hammocks at night. When hands were called in the morning, the women were allowed to lie in, and the boatswain's mates, when they saw a hammock still occupied, would check the occupant's sex by requiring a leg to be shown over the edge of the hammock. If it was hairy, it was probably male, if hairless, probably female. The call remained in use for many years after the custom of women living on board in harbour was finally abolished in the British Navy around 1840.

shroud-laid rope, the name given to rope *laid up with four *strands instead of the more usual three. The strands are laid up round a *heart, or central, strand, as the four strands would not bind close enough together, and without a heart would leave a central hollow. Size for size, shroud-laid rope is not as strong as *hawser-laid rope. However, it is less liable to stretch, and therefore proved more suitable to be used in sailing vessels as standing *rigging.

shrouds, the standing *rigging of a sailing vessel which gives a mast its lateral support, in the same way as *stays give it fore-and-aft support. In larger ships they were usually

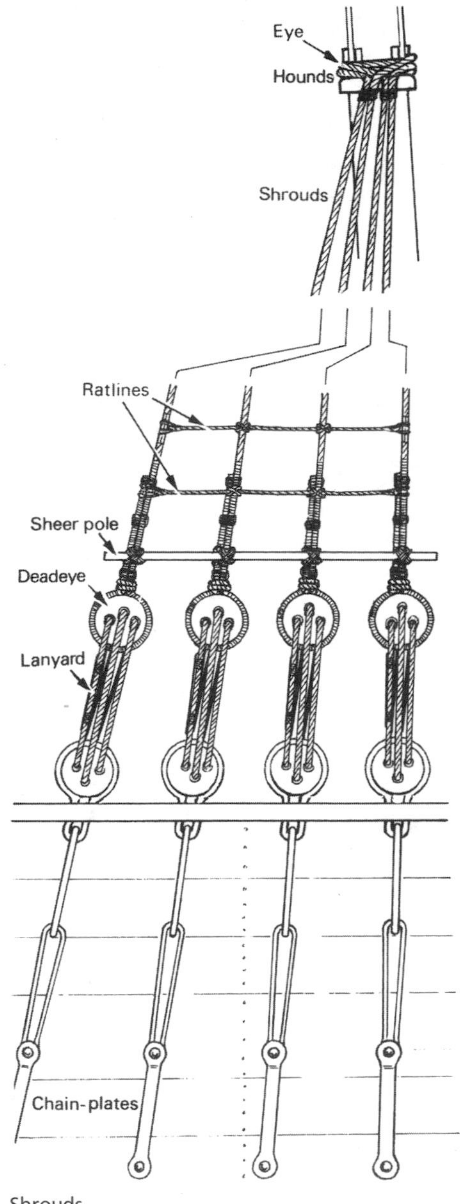

Shrouds

divided into pairs, or doubles, with an *eye *spliced at the halfway point that slipped over the masthead and was supported by the *hounds. The ends were brought down to deck level and secured to the *chain-plates on each side of the vessel abreast the mast, either through pairs of *deadeyes or with a *bottle-screw, enabling them to be set up taut. Each mast had its shrouds, and in the larger sailing ships many pairs were used for each mast. *Topmasts and *topgallant masts had their shrouds running to the edges of the *tops.

Originally *shroud-laid rope was used for shrouds, but it was later replaced by *wire rope, and in some *yachts by solid stainless steel wire in rods, the greater strength of which allows for a thinner shroud and consequently less windage when sailing. See also BENTINCK.

sickbay, a compartment *between decks in a large ship which is used for the treatment of sick or wounded men.

side lever engine, a development of the Watt beam engine and used for driving the paddle wheels of early *paddle steamers. Unlike the American *walking beam engine, the beam, which was driven by the steam cylinder at one end and connected with the paddle wheel at the other, was entirely within the ship. There were actually two beams, or levers, and these were placed low down at the sides of the engine. This low positioning was essential in order to allow the use of a long connecting rod attached to the paddle-wheel crankshaft. A long connecting rod was essential in order to minimize the side thrust which would act on the crankshaft if a short connecting rod was used. The steam cylinder was located at one end of the engine and the connection with the paddle shaft at the other end. The piston rod connected with the two side levers by means of a crosshead and two connecting rods. The opposite ends of the side levers were joined by a pin and this drove the paddle shaft with a connecting rod. The *condenser was located at the base of the engine; this was normally of the jet type although some engines were fitted with early tubular condensers. The side levers operated the air pump which removed water and air from the

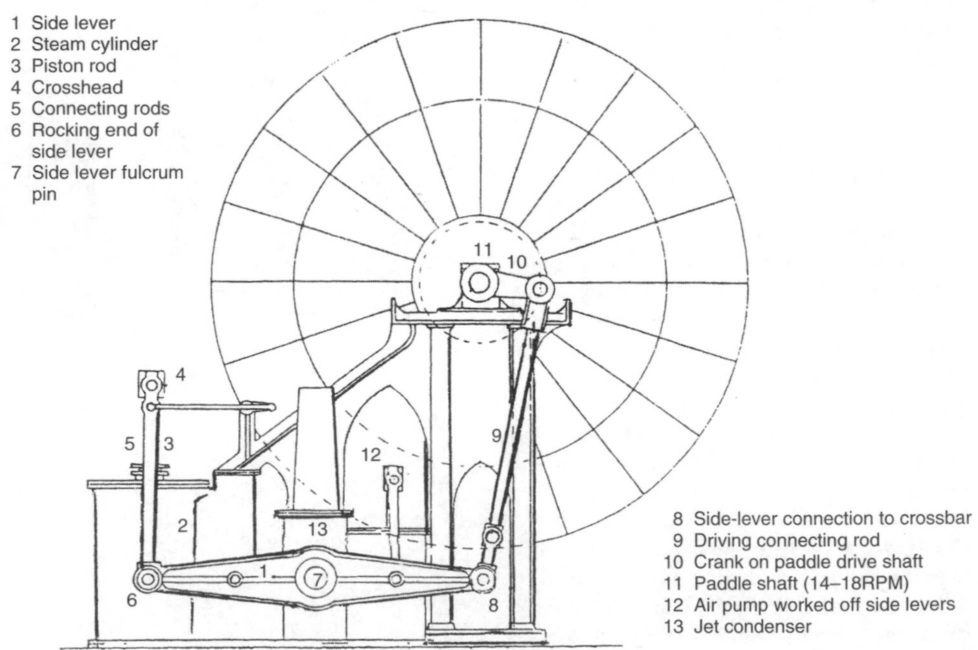

Diagram of typical side lever steam engine driving a paddle wheel

condenser, and discharged them into the hot well, the water from the hot well then being pumped back into the boiler. See also STEAM PROPULSION.

Denis Griffiths

siding, the width of *frames and *beams and other structural members of a vessel as opposed to the *moulding or depth of them. The width of the siding is usually constant while that of the moulding varies. See also SHIPBUILDING.

sight, an *altitude observation of sun, moon, planet, or star by which the ship's position can be calculated by *celestial navigation instead of *satellite navigation. It entails the simultaneous measurement of altitude, obtained with a *sextant, and of *Greenwich Mean Time. Most *navigators try to minimize random errors of observation by taking several observations of each body. Each observation in this case is referred to as a shot.

signal letters, the four letters that used to be assigned to every merchant ship as a means of identification. They were hoisted using the alphabetical flags of the *International Code of Signals so that the ship could be easily identified by another ship or by *coastguards. Nowadays all ships and shore stations have a nine-digit Maritime Mobile Service Identity number which is used when communicating by VHF radio.

signals at sea can be broadly divided historically into day signals, night signals, wireless telegraphy, and modern radio communications, and a brief history of the development of each can be found below.

Day Signals. The first record of a system of communication between ships with flags was the *fighting instructions of the 16th century. Only five flags were used at first and though their significance depended on where and how they were hoisted communication was very restricted. However, by the end of the 17th century five more flags, and the Union flag, had been added. When these were supplemented by firing a particular number of guns, it was possible to make 22 manoeuvring signals for the purposes of battle tactics. In the 18th century the number of flags, and flag signals, steadily increased. A code of signals for the *general chase was also introduced for warships, and these were the first signals to include *compass directions. By the 1790s there were 57 signals in the fighting instructions alone and these were increased further by a numbered code with 28 designs of flags (numbered 1 to 28) that could be used singly or in combination and could be hoisted anywhere without affecting their meaning. After modifications, the *Admiralty issued the *Signal Book for the Ships of War* in 1799 which remained in force with minor alterations for nearly 30 years. The numerical signals of the 1799 signal book were supplemented in 1803 by a vocabulary signal book, *Telegraphic Signals or Marine Vocabulary*. For this a different set of numeral flags was introduced, three or four flags denoting a word or phrase. Its use continued throughout the 19th century until the advent of the *International Code of Signals which was also used by merchant ships to hoist their *signal letters. By then there had been two important additions to signalling by day, *semaphore and the *Morse code.

Night Signals. In addition to signalling by flags during the day, various night signals were developed. From the 18th century to the middle of the 19th, they were based on arrangements of four lanterns or fewer, disposed in horizontal or vertical lines or in squares or triangles, sometimes supplemented by a masthead light, either alone or with *rockets, *blue lights, or *false fires. Then, in 1867 a British naval officer, Captain Philip Colomb (1831–99), invented a form of Morse code using short and long flashes from a lantern. Later the Morse code itself was adopted which, with the advent of electricity aboard ships, was transmitted by *Aldis lamp.

Wireless Telegraphy. A development of the electric telegraph, a 19th-century invention which used Morse code to send and receive messages. The first transmission took place in 1892, and by 1901 the Italian Guglielmo Marconi (1874–1937) was regularly transmitting Morse code signals to ships at sea. At first strong electrical power and a long wavelength were needed to send signals long distances. Initially, it was thought that short-wave sets on low power would be valuable in *warfare at sea because, it was assumed, they could not be detected more than a few kilometres away. However, it was later found that the transmissions included some waves that inclined upwards which bounced off a layer of the atmosphere so that after about 160 kilometres (100 mls.) the signal could again be received. An apparatus to signal to *submarines underwater was also invented early in the 20th century by the Canadian–American radio pioneer Reginald Fessenden (1866–1932), who was also one of the pioneers of radiotelephony. This directed sound waves over a distance of up to about 1.6 kilometres (1 m.). After the Second World War (1939–45) *sonar was used, in which a supersonic beam was transmitted underwater a considerably greater distance.

Modern Radio Communications. Radiotelephony, voice radio, was developed for use at sea during the first decades of the 20th century. Nowadays VHF (very high frequency) radio, with the help of various satellite systems such as *Inmarsat, is universally used for ship-to-ship and ship-to-shore communications. A more recent addition is the **Automatic Identification System (AIS)**, a Swedish invention, which transmits high-speed information about the movements of ships in an area. This broadcasts data, in digital format, on a dedicated VHF channel at very high speeds lasting only seconds. Because it transmits in very small bursts at least 2,000 ships in any one area can use the system simultaneously without causing radio interference with each other. The information is received aboard a ship via its AIS transponder which has three main components: a *GPS receiver, a VHF transceiver, and in between them a compturized data processor.

The minimum data a ship must broadcast using AIS is its nine-digit Maritime Mobile Service Identity number, what type of ship it is, and its position, *course, speed, and rate of turn. AIS collects this information from all ships within VHF range and then either sends it to the recipients as text or marks it alongside the blips on the recipient's *radar screen or *electronic chart. Such information is extremely useful if a ship's *master considers himself on a possible collision course with another ship, particularly as it is also possible to ask for additional information about the ship causing concern. AIS was developed for ships to inform VTS (vessel traffic systems) authorities of their hazardous cargoes. This is because, in certain congested shipping lanes such as the Straits of Dover, VHF voice traffic has just about reached saturation point. *Lighthouse authorities, and some port authorities, have also started to use it to broadcast instant data about their aids to *navigation. In the USA, the system, for security reasons, is now compulsory for vessels as small as 20 metres (65 ft) LOA. The European Union (EU) requires all its coastal states to have established the AIS infrastructure by 1 July 2007. See also DIGITAL SELECTIVE CALLING; NAVTEX.

sill, sometimes written as **cill.** **(1)** The upper and lower framing, or lining, of a square *port cut in a ship's side. **(2)** The step at the bottom of the entrance of a *dry-dock and, by extension, a ship's *draught if it is able to enter the dock over the sill.

simoon, the name given to the hot wind coming in off the desert, frequently laden with dust, which blows in the Red Sea. It is the Arabian name for the *sirocco.

Simpson's Rules were devised by the mathematician Thomas Simpson (1710–61) and revolutionized ship design. They are the means of calculating the areas bounded by smooth or 'fair' curves and, in turn, the volume of part of a non-regular shape. They formed the basis of hydrostatic ship design, and in the late 19th and early 20th centuries naval architects were assisted in applying them by the development of elegant drawing office instruments known as planimeters and integrators. Using the same principles, computers now carry out these tasks speedily and effectively. See also NAVAL ARCHITECTURE

'Sinbad the Sailor', the hero of the 291st tale of the great Persian–Arabian classic *A Thousand Nights and One Night*. The story concerns the adventures of a wealthy citizen of Baghdad, known as 'the sailor', during seven voyages which he undertook. Although parts of the tale are imaginative, such as the discovery of the Roc's egg, the valley of diamonds, and the Old Man of the Sea who had to be killed because he would not get off the 'sailor's' back, much of it is based on the voyages and experiences of Persian and Indian *navigators. Its telling occupied 25 of the 1001 nights.

'singeing the King of Spain's beard', the contemporary English description of an operation against Cadiz in April 1587 by Sir Francis

*Drake. He commanded a naval *squadron, which destroyed several Spanish ships and a vast quantity of stores being assembled for the invasion of England. The actual words were reported to have been said by Drake in jest after the exploit. See also SPANISH ARMADA.

sinnet, synet, sennet, sennit, or **sinnit,** a flat woven cordage formed by plaiting an odd number, usually five or seven, of rope-yarns together to form a decorative pattern. Its original maritime uses were for anti-chafing gear such as *baggywrinkle, *reef-points, *gaskets, *earings, etc., but as such fancy work fell out of fashion at sea, its later uses were purely decorative. Various forms of sinnet were developed, of which the major ones were **square plat**, **chain**, and **crown**. The straw hats worn in hot weather by many sailors during the 19th and early 20th centuries were made of the fibres of palm leaves worked up in plat sinnet.

SINS, the initial letters used to describe a ship's *inertial navigation system.

Sirens, or **Sirenes,** the sea nymphs who charmed seamen so much with their melodious voices that the men stopped working their ships to listen. Because they were unable to sail their vessels, they ultimately died of hunger. The names of these charmers were Parthenope, Ligeia, and Leucosia, daughters of the muse Calliope, and they lived on a small island near Cape Pelorus in Sicily. The Sirens had been told by the oracle that as soon as any persons passed them by without being charmed by their songs, they themselves would perish. They prevailed in calling the attention of all sailors until *Odysseus, who had been warned of the power of their voices by Circe, prepared for his encounter with them by stopping the ears of his companions with wax. He also ordered that he himself should be tied to the mast of his ship, and that no attention should be paid to his commands, should he wish to stay and listen to the Sirens' song. His plan succeeded and the fatal coast was passed in safety. The Sirens were so disappointed by their failure that they threw themselves into the sea and perished. The place on the coast of Sicily where they destroyed themselves was afterwards called Sirenis.

Sirius, the first steamship, with the **Great Western*, to compete in establishing a regular mail and passenger route across the North Atlantic. She is also generally acknowledged to be the first steamship to cross the North Atlantic entirely under *steam propulsion, though the Canadian steamship *Royal William*, which crossed in 1833, also has a claim to this distinction. But whereas the *Sirius*, unusually for her time, used fresh water in her boilers, and so could steam non-stop, the *Royal William* used salt water. This meant that every fourth day the salt water had to be drained and the boilers cleaned before the salt water was replaced. This took at least 24 hours, during which time the *Royal William* proceeded under sail.

The *Sirius* was a cross-Channel *paddle steamer of 700 tons, 54 metres (178 ft) long, with an engine developing 320 horsepower. She was chartered by the British and American Steam Navigation Company in 1838 when it became apparent that their own ship, the *British Queen*, would not be delivered in time from the builder to make the first Atlantic crossing. She left Cork, in Ireland, on 4 April 1838 with 40 passengers aboard, and reached New York on 22 April with only 22 tons of fuel remaining and having burned some of her *spars. Her passage took 18 days, 10 hours, and her average speed was 6–7 knots. The *Great Western* arrived in New York a few hours later, having left Bristol four days after the *Sirius* had departed from Cork. See also CONDENSER; EVAPORATORS; OCEAN LINERS; SAVANNAH.

sirocco, or **scirocco,** the name of a hot southerly wind which blows across the Mediterranean after crossing the Sahara Desert. On occasions it can blow for days or weeks on end, usually during the summer months, bringing sand and acute discomfort with it. When it crosses the Mediterranean it gathers a lot of moisture because of its high temperature and by the time it reaches Malta, Sicily, and southern Italy it is very humid and enervating. It is also often a precursor of a cyclonic *storm. See also KHAMSIN; SIMOON.

sisal, a fibre used in making rope obtained from the leaves of the *Agave sisalana*. It is a hard fibre native to Central America, with cultivation of it later spreading to South America, Africa, Indonesia, the Philippines, and elsewhere. A hairy rope, it is, like *hemp, a pale straw colour. In the days when it was used aboard ship it was frequently tarred to preserve it, though it resists deterioration in salt water well. It has a good ability to stretch, but is unreliable. Like all ropes made from natural fibres, it has now been replaced by synthetic ropes.

The *Henequin* plant, native to Mexico, produces a fibre sometimes known as Yucatán, or Cuban, sisal.

sister blocks, a set of two or more *blocks set in a frame in single plane. These are commonly used on *square-rigged ships to receive the *falls of the upper *braces at the ship's side before they reach the *pinrail.

six water grog, a punishment in the British Navy during the days of sail, inflicted on seamen found guilty of neglect or drunkenness. It consisted of their daily tot of *grog being diluted with six parts of water instead of the normal three. It was a punishment that fell into disuse around the start of the 20th century.

skeet, or **skeat,** a dipper with a long handle which was used to wet the sides and deck of a wooden ship in very hot weather to prevent the planking splitting or opening up in the heat of the sun. In small sailing vessels the skeet was also used to wet the sails in very light weather so that they might hold whatever breeze there might be.

skeg, the short length of keel, normally tapered or cut to a step, which in the days of sail used to project *aft beyond a ship's *sternpost. Its purpose was to protect the *rudder if a ship went aground and attempts were made to get it off stern first. The skeg did not last long as a *shipbuilding practice as it was soon found that it was liable to snap off, and by 1630 it had gone out of fashion. However, with the introduction of *steam propulsion, the skeg came back as an extension of the *deadwood to prevent a ship's *propellers digging into the ground if it went ashore. The rudders of many modern *yachts are fitted to an *after skeg. *Tugs often also have one fitted aft to give them extra directional *stability.

skid-booms, skids, or **skid beams,** the name given to the spare *spars, supported by *gallows, carried in the part of the *waist of a large sailing ship known as the *booms. They helped to secure the ship's larger boats when at sea.

skiff, in maritime terms a ship's working boat during the days of sail. It was usually a small *clinker-built boat pulling one or two pairs of *oars, used for small errands around a ship when it was in harbour. They should not be confused with the light pleasure craft used on rivers and inland waters.

skilly, a poor broth, often served as an evening meal at sea in the days of sail. It was made with oatmeal mixed with the water in which the salt meat had been boiled. It was often the basic food of prisoners of war and other prisoners kept in prison *hulks during the 17th–19th centuries.

skillygalee, or **skillygolee,** an oatmeal drink sweetened with sugar, which was often issued to seamen in British warships in place of cocoa up to the end of the Napoleonic War (1803–15). It was also a drink issued to stokers working in great heat in the stokeholds of British steam warships in the later 19th century as it was thought to protect them from stomach cramp.

skimming dish, originally a mid-19th century derogatory description used by anyone who disliked the look of a racing *yacht. However, it later came to describe the extreme designs constructed to exploit the *rating rules in force in both the USA and Britain towards the end of the Victorian era. *Yacht designers used lighter and lighter *scantlings as well as a low *freeboard, while longer and longer overhangs were employed at bow and stern to increase the waterline length when *heeled (the longer a boat's waterline, the faster it goes). These distortions grew gradually more extreme as each season passed, so that by the early 1890s owners of the smaller ½-rater, 1-rater, and 2½-rater classes in Britain were more or less obliged to have a new boat built every season. Also, larger racing yachts began to be constructed which exploited the existing rule in the same way, and this eventually threatened their seaworthiness. New rating rules were introduced to encourage a more wholesome type of sailing yacht, but were not really effective until the

*Universal Rule was adopted by the New York Yacht Club in 1903 and the International Rule which governed the *International Metre Class was officially adopted in Europe in 1908, though yachts built to this rule first raced in 1907. However, the old rule used by the New York Yacht Club still governed the *America's Cup challenge held in 1903, and this produced the *Reliance* as the defending yacht, the largest and one of the most extreme examples of a skimming dish ever built.

skipjack, a work boat of the east coast of the USA, *sloop rigged with a *Bermudan mainsail and a *foresail *set on a *bowsprit. They were hard-*chined boats with a large wooden *centreboard. A feature of the skipjack was the mast which was rigged to *rake some 25° *aft to enable cargo to be hoisted on board by means of the main *halyard. Skipjacks were introduced in Chesapeake Bay in about 1860 and largely superseded the *sharpie.

skipper, the person in charge of a ship, particularly applicable to smaller vessels, such as *yachts or fishing boats. The word was introduced in Britain in the late 14th century, probably from the Dutch *schipper*, captain, itself based on *schip*, ship. See also MASTER.

'skipper's daughters', a colloquial name for high *waves when they break at sea with a white crest.

skylight, a glazed window frame, usually in pairs, set at an angle in the deck of a ship to maximize light and ventilation to a compartment below, and protected with brass rods. They were only seen on smaller vessels. Once very common in *yachts, they were difficult to keep watertight and were superseded by *hatches with transparent plastic tops or by transparent panels, though they are still to be seen in classic yachts.

skysail, the square sail set immediately above the *royal in *square-rigged ships and usually set on an extended *topgallant mast or royal mast. They were only used on the extreme *clippers. Colin Mudie

slab-lines, light lines often attached to the *foot of a *course and taken up to a *block on the *yards, and then into the mast and down to the *fife rail. They are often used to lift the foot of the course sufficiently to allow the officer of the *watch or the helmsman to have a better view forward.

slack water, the periods at the change of the *tide when little or no stream runs. On a *flood tide, its maximum rate of flow occurs during the middle two hours; as it approaches high water the rate of flow slackens until there is virtually no appreciable movement. The same pattern occurs on the *ebb. The period of slack water is perhaps some twenty minutes or so each side of high and low water. During this period, the wind frequently drops or changes direction, and it is noticeable that bird life in and around estuaries becomes quiet.

slatch, the slack parts of any rope or *cable lying outside a ship, such as an anchor cable lying on the bottom in a loose *bight, or the *lee running *rigging slacked away too much, so that it hangs loose. Slatch of the cable is *roused in; slatch of the rigging is hauled up.

slave trade. In its maritime context, the shipping of slaves by sea. Slave trading by this method was practised in the Mediterranean from the late Middle Ages, particularly by the Genoese who bought, or captured, inhabitants of the Balkans and Black Sea and shipped them to Mediterranean slave markets, though long before then the Arabs had been shipping slaves to India, and elsewhere, from East Africa. The indigenous inhabitants of the Canaries were sometimes enslaved by raiding Europeans in the 14th century, and *Henry the Navigator established the first Atlantic long-distance slave trade in the mid-15th century when he traded slaves in Guinea. The *Barbary pirates thrived on the slave trade. They took their victims from captured ships, or during raids on the coasts of Christian countries, and sold them in the slave markets of Tunis and Algiers, or put them to row in their *galleys. Christian *corsairs, mainly based on Malta, were equally keen to acquire Muslim slaves for their galleys.

In 1501 Ferdinand and Isabella of Spain gave Spanish colonists permission to import black slaves into *Hispaniola from West Africa—mostly sold by the victors in local wars there—and the practice quickly spread to other parts of the Caribbean, and to Central and South

America. But although they were the first to purchase slaves, and to have them transported by sea, the Spaniards did not themselves start trading slaves in West Africa until the late 1700s.

From 1520 onwards slaves were shipped regularly to the New World by several European countries, but by the 18th century the British dominated the trade. Sir John *Hawkins was the first Englishman to have the dubious distinction of being involved in it and by the 1770s nearly 200 ships, with a capacity to cram aboard 45,000 slaves, were based at Bristol, London, and Liverpool. They undertook a triangular voyage. On the first leg they were loaded with goods that were exchanged for slaves along the coast of West Africa. These were loaded on board in appalling conditions and the slavers then sailed on the next leg, known as the **middle passage**, to North and South America and the West Indies. There, the survivors of these voyages were sold to the owners of tobacco, cotton, and sugar plantations. These goods, and rum (see GROG) and logwood as well, were then loaded aboard for the final leg across the Atlantic.

It was a very lucrative business as a profit was made on each stage of the voyage, but the slaves suffered a very high mortality rate and the cruelties inflicted on them were horrendous. Crew members, who often turned to *piracy when they had the chance of escaping, were equally at risk, and were described by one clergyman as being 'a third sort of persons, to be numbered neither with the living nor the dead; their lives hanging continually in suspense before them' (P. Earle, *Sailors: English Merchant Seamen, 1650–1775* (1998), 133–4).

It has been calculated that between 1795 and 1804 about 400,000 slaves were shipped from Africa by ships operating from British ports, and the total for the 18th century may have reached 6 or 7 million. The British abolished the trade in 1807 and the USA in the following year, though of course slavery continued there until after the Civil War (1861–5). Other European countries soon outlawed it, too, but it remained legal in Brazil until the 1850s.

The British made slave trading a felony in 1811, but it was not at all easy to stamp out the practice. Warships of both the Royal and US navies were deployed along the African coastline to intercept those flouting the law. It has been estimated that during the first 40 years of trying to suppress the trade only about one in eight slaves were freed, and the methods used were often questioned. It was even suggested that the British Navy were causing even greater suffering, as slaves were often dumped overboard when a British warship was sighted. However, by 1850 it had been stamped out on the west coast. It continued on the east coast until Zanzibar became a British Protectorate in 1890, though the advent of *steam propulsion made it progressively more difficult for the slaving *dhows to evade British naval patrols. Even then, the unsavoury business of *blackbirding continued in the Pacific, a practice that was not halted until the start of the 20th century. See also DOGHOUSE.

slicks are lines of smooth unrippled water at the surface of the sea. They mark where the surface tension has been lowered by floating oil or fats. Many slicks are natural phenomena, which develop where the surface water is converging and sinking. When the sea is calm, lines of smooth water appear which are the result of accumulations of natural oils from *plankton. *Seabirds, turtles (see MARINE REPTILES), and *marine mammals are attracted to these slicks because food like plankton and *seaweed is often more abundant along them. However, as well as natural products, floating *flotsam and *jetsam like plastics and polythene also accumulate along them, creating a dangerous form of *pollution to marine life. When there is a serious oil spill from a *tanker, slicks of oil spreading away from the accident are also a fatal attraction to marine life. See also FRONT.

M. V. Angel

slings, in general, the ropes or chains attached to any heavy article to hoist it. **Boat slings** are made of strong rope or wire with hooks and *thimbles in the ends to hook into the *stem, keel, and stern bolts so that boats may be hoisted into or out of a ship. **Butt slings** are used for hoisting casks, formed by passing a *strop round the two ends of a cask and bringing the *bight through the end of the strop. **Yard slings** are the ropes or chains which support a *yard on the mast. For illus. see YARD.

slip hook, a hinged hook of which the tongue is held in place by a link which, when knocked off, allows the hook to open. Small slip hooks are used to secure the *gripes of lifeboats when hoisted at a ship's *davits so that they can be quickly released when required. Large slip hooks, *cable stoppers, known as Blake slips or Blake stoppers, are used to hold the chain *cables before anchoring and to secure them when the anchors are *weighed.

slippery hitch, a *bend or *hitch used on board ship to attach a rope to a ring or *spar so that, by a pull on the rope, the hitch comes free. This is achieved by passing a *bight of the rope under the other part so that when the strain is taken the bight is jammed. A pull on the end of the bight will clear it, and the bend is then dissolved. Hitches most often used in slippery form are *sheet bends, *clove hitches, and *bowlines.

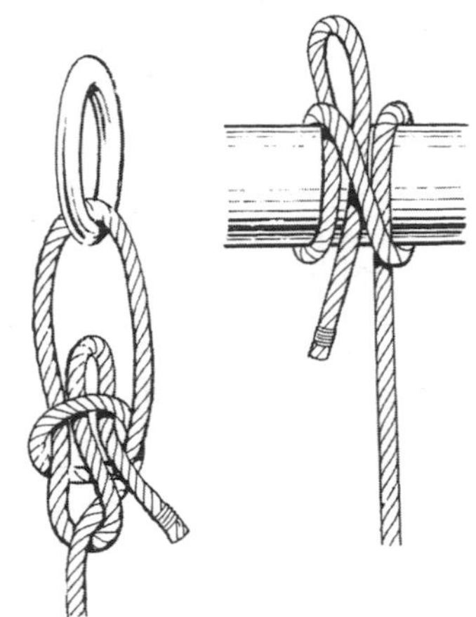

Slippery bowline and slippery clove hitch

slipway, a sloping foreshore in front of a shipyard on which ships are built on *ways in preparation for *launching. **A patent slipway** is an inclined plane on the shore extending into the water, usually gravelled or made of concrete, and fitted with rails up which a *yacht or other small vessel, secured in a cradle, can be hauled for cleaning or repair.

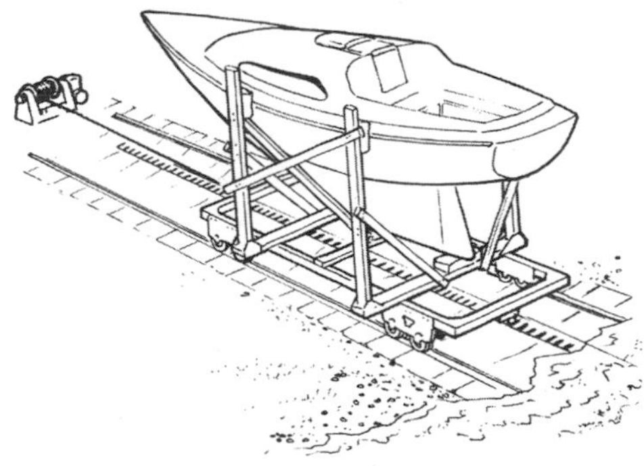

Patent slipway

Slocum, Joshua (1844–*c.*1910), American seaman. He was born at Wilmot Township, Nova Scotia, and went to sea as a ship's cook at the age of 12 after running away from home. In 1869 he was *master of a trading *schooner on the coast of California and a year later commanded the *barque *Washington* in which, after a voyage to Australia, he sailed to set up a salmon *fishery in Alaska. After an adventurous career, which included building a steamer of 150 tons on the jungle coast of Manila, Slocum became master and part-owner of the *square-rigged *Northern Light,* 'the finest American sailing vessel afloat', and then purchased the small barque *Aquidneck* in which he made several voyages before she was lost in 1886 on a sandbank off the coast of Brazil. His second wife and two sons by his first, one of whom was still a small boy, were on board at the time of the *shipwreck. From the remains of his ship Slocum completed a 10.6-metre (35-ft) sailing boat with a *canoe hull which he had been building on board. He named her *Liberdade* and brought his family safely back to New York in her after a voyage of over 8,000 kilometres (5,000 mls.). Slocum knew all about Chinese *shipbuilding, for he built her with bamboo-batten *lugsails, multiple *sheets, and a fenestrated *rudder. He wrote later that he thought the Chinese *sampan style 'the most convenient boat rig in the whole world'.

His book about this adventure, *Voyage of the Liberdade,* was published in 1894 and the *Liberdade* is now preserved in the Smithsonian Institution in Washington. In 1892, while he was writing it, he was offered what remained of a 11-metre (36-ft) *sloop called *Spray* which was lying under a *tarpaulin in a field at Fairhaven where she had been for the previous seven years. Slocum bought her, largely rebuilt her with oak which he felled, shaped, and treated himself, and in 1895 left Boston in her. His subsequent circumnavigation, by way of Gibraltar, the Magellan Straits, Australia, and South Africa, is believed to be first single-handed voyage round the world.

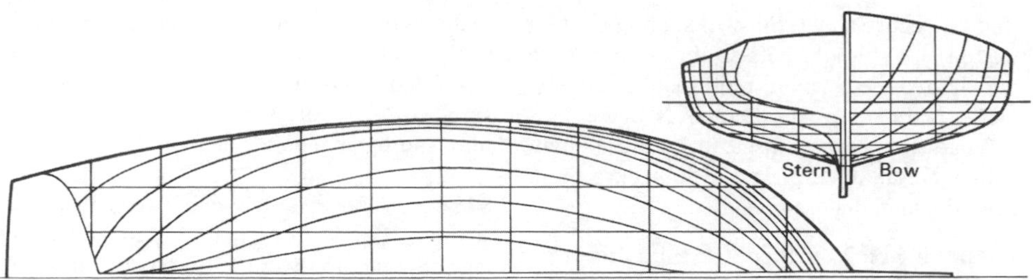

Spray, 11 m (36 ft), 1894

Having hardly any money, he supported himself by lectures at his various ports of call, earning enough to keep his family and cover his expenses. He arrived back at Newport, Rhode Island, in 1898 and wrote a book about his experiences. Called *Sailing Alone around the World* (1900), it has become a classic of its kind through its simple, direct style, wit, and dry humour. In November 1909, at the age of 65, he set out from Bristol, Rhode Island, on another lone voyage, but was never heard of again. It is thought that the *Spray* was either run down by a steamer in mid-ocean, or struck a *whale and sank, as she was too soundly built, and Slocum too experienced a sailor, to have been lost from any other cause.

sloop. **(1)** A sailing vessel with a single mast, *fore-and-aft rigged, setting, in western Europe, a single *headsail. Its development, in respect of dates etc., was parallel with that of the *cutter. In the USA, the term also embraces vessels setting two headsails, which in other parts of the world would be termed cutters. In 2003 *Mirabella V*, at 75.3 metres (247 ft) LOA (length overall) and with a rig 91.5 metres (300 ft) high, became the largest sloop ever built up to that time when she was *launched at Woolston, Southampton. **(2)** A designation used during the Second World War (1939–45) to describe a small class of anti-*submarine *convoy escort vessels used during the battle of the Atlantic. It was a resuscitation of the name of **(3)**, an older navy class of ships, 17th–19th century, used mainly for auxiliary naval duties. Until the late 18th century the term was used somewhat indiscriminately to embrace any of the smaller naval vessels that did not fit specifically into a recognized class of minor warship. However, by the beginning of the 19th century there were two accepted classes of sloop depending on the number of masts: the **ship sloop** (three masts) and ***brig sloop** (two masts), both of them *square rigged on all masts. As a distinctive type of warship, the sloop finally disappeared in the late 1880s although some navies, including the British, retained a few for *sail training. Those in Britain were attached to the boys' training ships and continued in use until 1904.

slush, originally the fat of the meat boiled on board in the coppers of naval ships which was the perquisite of the ship's cook. Usually he sold it to the *purser who made it into candles. It was later the name used for the grease with which masts and *spars of sailing vessels were rubbed down after they had been scraped.

smack, originally a *cutter or *ketch-rigged sailing vessel, normally from about 15 to 20 tons, used for inshore *fisheries. In older days it was often known as, and rigged as, a *hoy, and during the 18th and 19th centuries in Britain they were sometimes used as *tenders in the king's service, particularly in the service of Customs and Excise. Today, the word is frequently used as a generic term for all small fishing craft.

Smith, Sir Francis Pettit (1808–74), British inventor. He started life as a Kentish farmer, but became engrossed in the construction of model boats and in methods of propelling them. In 1835 he constructed one which was driven by a *propeller actuated by a spring. This was so successful that he became convinced of its superiority over the paddle wheel which was universally used at that time with *steam propulsion.

Smith was unaware that three others, including the Swedish engineer John Ericsson

(1803–89), were separately working to develop a propeller, and, in fact, his patent for his type of screw propulsion, taken out on 31 May 1836, pre-dated Ericsson's different type by only six weeks. Thus Smith's improved model exhibited in that year can claim to have been the first of its kind, though Ericsson was awarded part of the £20,000 offered by the British *Admiralty for the successful development of this method of propulsion.

With financial backing and some technical assistance, Smith now built a 10-ton vessel propelled by a 6-horsepower engine which successfully drove a wooden screw. To satisfy Admiralty demands for experiments in a larger ship, a company was formed to build the 237-ton propeller-driven *Archimedes*, which in October 1839 achieved a speed of 10 knots and later made a successful cruise to the major ports of Britain, to Amsterdam, and to Oporto. This convinced the Admiralty to build its first screw-driven warship, which was *launched in 1841, but Smith received only a meagre financial reward for his invention. He was also poorly paid as adviser to the Admiralty, a post he held until 1850. However, in recognition of his services he was knighted in 1871.

smiting line, a small rope made fast to the underside of the *mizzen *yardarm at its lower end during the period when the normal rig of sailing ships was a *lateen mizzen. When the mizzen-sail was *furled this rope was led along the *yard to the mizzen *peak with the sail and then down to the *poop. *Spunyarns are used to *stop the sail to the yard with the smiting lines inside them, so the sail could be set, or loosed, without having to *strike down the yard, simply by pulling on the smiting line and thus breaking the spunyarns. **'Smite the mizzen'**, the order to haul down on the smiting line.

SMS, the prefix used before the name of a ship of the German Imperial Navy during the period which ended with the abdication of Kaiser Wilhelm II in 1918. The initials stood for *Seiner Majestät Schiff*, the equivalent of the British HMS.

smuggle, to, to bring goods into a country clandestinely to avoid the payment of duty. Smuggling has a very old history, largely connected with the sea as one of the main highways of trade between countries. During the Revolutionary (1793–1801) and Napoleonic (1803–15) Wars, when Britain was largely cut off from trade with much of Europe, smuggling, particularly in French brandies and lace, became almost an industry, and the British government was forced to maintain a large fleet of fast sailing *cutters, known as the preventive service, to attempt to cut off the smugglers before they could reach the shore to land their cargoes.

snatch block, a *block with a single *sheave which has a hinged opening above the sheave to allow the *bight of a rope to be dropped in, thus saving the necessity of having to *reeve the whole length of the rope through the block. It is also sometimes known as a **notch-block**.

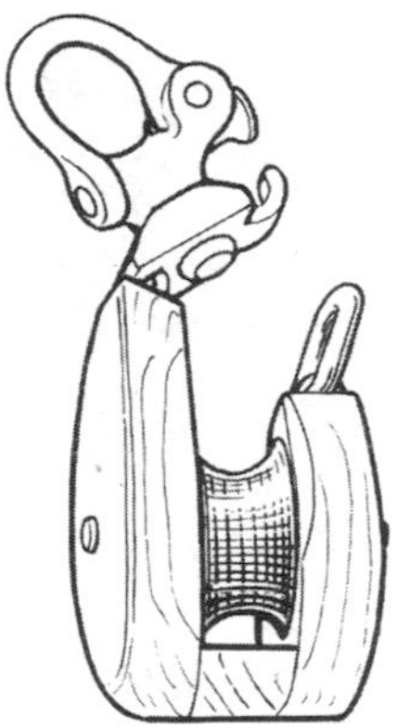

Snatch block

snotter, the name given to the fitting which holds the *heel of a *sprit close to the mast in a *spritsail-rigged sailing vessel. For illus. see SPRIT.

snotty, slang name for a midshipman.

snow, a two-masted merchant vessel of the 16th–19th centuries, the largest two-masted ship of its period with a *tonnage of up to 1,000 tons or so. It was rigged as a *brig, with square sails on both masts. It also had a small *trysail mast stepped immediately *abaft the mainmast from which a *trysail with a boom was set, the *luff of the trysail being attached to the mast with *hoops. In some cases this trysail mast was replaced by a *horse on the mainmast, the luff of the trysail being attached to it in

A Prussian snow; etching by E. W. Cooke, 1829

the same way. Snows were entirely European ships, not found in other parts of the world.

snub, to. **(1)** The action of bringing a ship to a sudden stop by letting go an anchor while having too much *way on. **(2)** The action of a ship when it is inclined to *pitch while at anchor making the anchor *cable tauten to such an extent that it holds the bows down at the top of the pitch. It is apt to occur when there is insufficient *scope to the cable, and is easily corrected by *veering some more. **(3)** A *hawser is also said to be snubbed when it is *checked suddenly while running out by taking a quick turn round a pair of *bollards.

Society for Nautical Research, a learned society founded in Britain in 1910 to foster research into matters relating to seafaring and *shipbuilding on a worldwide basis, and also into the language and customs of the sea, and other topics of maritime interest. Its principal work was carried out with the help of the naval historian Sir Geoffrey Callender (1875–1946), who, as the Society's honorary secretary and treasurer, founded the National Maritime Museum, Greenwich, and instigated the drive to raise sufficient funds to preserve HMS **Victory*. The Society also supported *sail training in the *frigate *Foudroyant* and the return of the **Great Britain* from the Falkland Islands to Bristol. It publishes the *Mariner's Mirror*, a quarterly journal devoted to matters of ships and the sea.

SOLAS, see INTERNATIONAL CONVENTION FOR THE SAFETY OF LIFE AT SEA.

'soldier's wind', a name given to a steady wind, around force 4 in strength on the *Beaufort Scale, when it blows on the *beam of a sailing vessel. This is sailing at its simplest and needs no great nautical skill to get the vessel to its destination and back.

sole, in some ships, and especially in *yachts, the name given to the decks of the *cabin(s).

sonar, or sound navigational ranging, is the use of sound to explore the oceans, and for military and *salvage purposes. And as the swim-bladders of *fish that are gas filled are good reflectors, sonar (fish-finders) is used by commercial *fisheries to detect fish *shoals.

Sound, particularly low-frequency sound, travels well through water—the singing of humpback *whales allows them to communicate over hundreds of kilometres underwater. *Dolphins have their own sonar systems, which they use to locate their prey. The sound pulses they produce are reflected back by any objects in the water that have a different acoustic density from the water. They may be either hard objects or gas bubbles that will reflect the sound so long as they are larger than the wavelength of the sound signal. High-frequency sounds have short wavelengths and so 'see' smaller objects, but do not travel through water as well as low-frequency sounds with long wavelengths.

Pulses of sound are used by *echo sounders; a series of pings of sound is transmitted from the vessel on the surface and the shortest time for the echo to return gives a measure of the depth. Sound travels at about 1,500 metres per second, so if the echo returns in two seconds, the depth is 1,500 metres (5,000 ft), that is, one second for the signal to reach the bottom and another second for it to return. But the speed of sound through water varies with the temperature of the water, so over very deep water an accurate sounding can only be gained if the temperature profile of the water column is known.

But sonar does not just work vertically downwards. **Upward-looking sonars** are mounted on autonomous *underwater vehicles that have been programmed to go far under pack *ice and ice shelves in polar regions. These sonars not only enable the vehicle to stay below the ice but have also provided direct measurements of the rate at which the ice is thinning as a result of *climate change. **Side-scan sonar** is the transmission of sound beams at an angle to insonify a swath of the seabed. The returning echoes generate a *radar-like record of the seabed, picking out variations in its topography and make-up. Strong echoes are returned from gravels and rocks, especially if the rock face is facing the transmitter, whereas muddy bottoms reflect weak echoes. GLORIA was a long-range oblique sonar system developed to survey large swaths of the deep ocean bed 12 kilometres (7.5 mls.) to either side of the ship's track. It was mounted in a large body that was towed on a faired cable below the *thermocline, so the reception of the faint acoustic echoes would be optimized. It revealed many new seabed features, such as immense debris flows fanning out from the volcanic islands of the Canary Islands and Hawaii. **Sea Beams** are hull-mounted devices that are simpler to operate, but achieve similar, if less extensive, seabed surveys.

Side-scan sonar not only reveals the characteristics of the bottom topography but in shallow water can be used to locate pipelines or, in *marine archaeology, to detect *shipwrecks on the seabed. The full technological development of side-scan is swath bathymetry in which multiple frequencies are used; the lower frequencies penetrating the sediments to provide data on the internal structure of the seabed. Sound signals can also be coded to switch devices such as acoustic releases to recover *current meter moorings in the deep ocean, or even transmit *in situ* data from devices being towed.

Marine archaeologists use **forward-sector scanning sonar**, targeting a site where there may be a shipwreck by making several runs from different directions so that a sonar 'shadow' picture can be built up of the feature on the seabed.

Other scientific sonars include **acoustic doppler current profilers** (ADCPs) in which an array of high-frequency sound (70–100 kHz) is transmitted into the water, and the frequencies of the return echoes are analysed by computer. At such high frequencies the echoes come from particles, including *plankton, suspended in the water. If these are moving relative to the device, the tones (frequencies) of the echoes are shifted (just as the sound of a train changes as it passes; the so-called Doppler shift). If the particles are drifting passively in the currents, this gives a direct measure of variations in the *currents with depth.

For military purposes, passive listening systems are used initially to detect the approach of enemy devices. Once something is heard, active sonars transmitting sounds are turned on to locate the potentially offensive devices (*submarines, torpedoes, or mines). However, the active sonar will not only locate any offensive devices, but also reveal the presence and position of the vessel transmitting it, so it is only used in the final stages of an engagement.

Recently (2004) the use of high-powered military sonars has been blamed for mass strandings of whales, the strong sound signals allegedly fatally damaging the whales' sonar systems. See also DEEP SCATTERING LAYERS; SALVAGE.

www.arl.psu.edu/capabilities/uss_acou_sonars.html

news.bbc.co.uk/1/hi/world/americas/2131524-.stm

M. V. Angel

songs, see SEA SONGS; SHANTY.

son of a gun, a description given by the lower deck to children born on board ships of the British Navy during the period when the wives of seamen were allowed to live on board in harbour and, occasionally, at sea. As the *gangways had to be kept clear, the only place on board where women in labour could give birth was in the spaces between the guns on the gundecks, so that, inevitably, any male child born on board was known as a 'son of a gun'. Such a birth gave rise to the saying: 'Begotten in the *galley and born under a gun. Every hair a ropeyarn, every tooth a *marline spike, every finger a fishhook, and his blood right good Stockholm *tar.'

'SOS', at one time the internationally agreed wireless distress call made by a ship requiring help at sea. It came into force on 1 July 1908 and is still one of the *distress signals which can be used by a vessel requiring urgent assistance. The three letters were chosen because they were easy to read and make in *Morse code—three dots, three dashes, three dots—but they did not stand for 'Save Our Souls', as is often thought. The first 'SOS' to be broadcast was in August 1909 when the American steamer *Azaoahoe* was disabled with a broken *propeller shaft. See also GLOBAL MARITIME DISTRESS AND SAFETY SYSTEM; MAYDAY; SIGNALS AT SEA.

sound, to. (1) From the Anglo-Saxon *sond*, a messenger, to ascertain the depth of the sea under a ship. See ECHO SOUNDER; LEAD LINE; SOUNDING MACHINE. **(2)** Of a *whale, to dive deep.

sounding. (1) The name given to a depth of water obtained by a *lead line, *sounding machine, *sonar, *echo sounder, or *sounding rod. The depth was traditionally measured in *fathoms, but is now standardized to metres everywhere except in the USA where it is expressed in feet. **(2)** The figures on a *chart which indicate the depth of water. See also IN SOUNDINGS; OFF SOUNDINGS.

sounding machine, a 19th-century mechanical device, long obsolete, invented by Lord Kelvin (see THOMSON, WILLIAM) by which the depth of the sea could be measured. He first demonstrated it in the 1870s in the Bay of Biscay, successfully measuring depths of over 2,000 *fathoms (12,000 ft/3,660 m).

sounding rod, one of the earliest aids to *coastal navigation. It was a graduated rod which could *sound the depth of shallow water while the vessel was under way merely by feeling the bottom with the rod.

Southern Cross, a constellation in the form of a cross visible in the southern hemisphere. It is of no particular significance for *navigation, as is, for example, the northern constellation of Ursa Minor which contains the Pole Star or *Polaris. However, the last sight of it was a sign for the crews of the *square-riggers which used South American ports during the late 19th and early 20th centuries to load nitrate, guano, or saltpetre that they were homeward bound. When a ship was loaded and ready to sail, the ship's carpenter made a large wooden cross to which were fixed red and white lights in the shape of the constellation. This was hoisted to the mainmast head and was greeted by the well-known *shanty 'Hurrah, my boys, we're homeward bound'. When the shanty was finished, the *ship's bell in the next ship alongside was rung, and her crew cheered the departing vessel, and so in turn until all ships in harbour had cheered her.

South Sea Bubble, a series of financial hoaxes, or speculations, in stocks of the South Sea Company which in 1720 produced ruin for many investors. The company, founded by Robert Harley in 1711, was formed on the supposed possibility of a vast increase in the *slave trade, particularly in the Pacific, once peace returned after the War of the Spanish Succession (1702–13). However, the Treaty of Utrecht, signed in

1713, provided only very limited possibilities for trade, an annual tax being imposed on imported slaves and the company being restricted to no more than one ship per year. Nevertheless, with the king becoming governor of the company in 1718, popular confidence was enhanced and a wild boom was engendered in which the value of the stock, issued at £100, rose to over £1,000 in the summer of 1719, and the directors even offered to take over part of the National Debt. However, by the end of the year the stock had dropped to £124, and six months later was virtually valueless. While a few holders of the stock had made vast fortunes, the great majority lost very heavily. Some holders fled the country because of their debts, many others committed suicide. A committee of inquiry found that three ministers of the crown had accepted bribes and speculated heavily in South Sea stock. The Chancellor of the Exchequer was sent to prison, the other two had their estates confiscated. The South Sea Company itself remained in existence until 1853, being mainly concerned, after selling its supposed trading right to Spain in 1750, with the Greenland *whaling industry.

South Seas, the old term for the Pacific Ocean. It was given this name by Vasco Nuñez de *Balboa in 1513 when, after sighting the ocean from the top of a mountain range, he reached the coast near Panama and took possession of the 'Great South Sea' in the name of King Ferdinand of Spain. The expression occurs in most of the books of voyages at least up to the middle of the 18th century. It embraced the whole of the Pacific Ocean, purely from the fact that the only means of reaching it from the east was round Cape Horn or through the Magellan Straits. See also EXPLORATION BY SEA.

spall, to, to fix ship *frames at the proper breadth by means of cross-spalls. They are, of course, finally replaced by the permanent deck *beams. See also SHIPBUILDING.

span. **(1)** A rope or wire with each end secured between fixed points, which is used for hooking on the standing *block of a *tackle where no other convenient point is available. **(2)** The distance between the *port and *starboard *bottle-screws, or the *deadeyes of the *chain-plates, measured over the masthead of a sailing vessel, is also known as the span of the *rigging.

Spanish Armada, called by the Spaniards before it sailed the *felicissima*, most fortunate, and *invencible*, invincible. It was a great fleet assembled by King Philip II of Spain to force the English Channel, pick up the army of the Prince of Parma then operating in the Low Countries, and invade England. The fleet, consisting of 130 ships, both large and small, was commanded by the Duke of Medina Sidonia (1550–1619). It left Lisbon in May 1588 but made such poor headway because of heavy weather that it had to put in to Corunna for repairs, water, and provisions, and it was another month before it again set sail.

The English fleet, initially larger in number but much smaller in *tonnage, was divided between Lord Howard of Effingham's *squadron at Plymouth, and Lord Henry Seymour's ships at Dover, which was watching Calais for the arrival of Parma's army. The western squadron sailed from Plymouth as soon as the Armada was sighted off the Lizard on 19 July, an event which gave rise to the well-known legend of Sir Francis *Drake and his game of bowls on Plymouth Hoe. The first shots of the battle were fired off the Eddystone on 21 July.

The Spanish fleet was sailing in a crescent-shaped formation, too strong for the English ships to attack in formation, but, being generally more *weatherly, they attacked singly at long range, exploiting superior naval gunnery techniques and equipment to keep the Spanish ships on the move. During the next four days the Armada was continually harassed, losing two ships, and by the evening of the 25 July the two fleets were abreast the Isle of Wight. By this time the English ships were running short of ammunition and Howard, when reporting this, stated his intention not to attack again until he had obtained a further supply.

Meanwhile the Armada continued its slow progress up Channel, losing an occasional straggler to the English ships, but in general keeping its crescent-shaped formation intact. It anchored off Calais on the evening of 27 July to await Parma's troops for the planned invasion. As it dropped its anchors, so also did Howard's squadron, which was promptly reinforced by Seymour's ships.

With the wind blowing from the south-west, the English fleet now anchored about 800 metres (2,640 ft) to *windward of the Spaniards, very well placed for an attack with *fireships. Six of these were sent down on the following night, causing much consternation and confusion among the tightly packed Spaniards. There was nothing they could do but cut their *cables and make sail before the wind to escape the threatened holocaust. They were followed by the whole English fleet and a major action developed off Gravelines, in which Medina Sidonia lost three of his best ships and found himself being driven by the wind and the English towards the Dutch *shoals. At the last moment the wind *backed into the south-east and enabled the Spanish ships to *claw off the dangerous shallows.

Without Parma's troops on board, and with the invasion now impossible, Medina Sidonia had no option but to make his way back to Spain as best he could. Short of ammunition and provisions, he could not fight his way back down Channel through the English fleet, and the only way left for him was around the north of Scotland and west of Ireland. Leaving Seymour and his squadron to guard the Channel and maintain a watch for any movement by Parma and his troops, Howard pursued the retreating Armada up the North Sea as far as the latitude of the Firth of Forth. There, running short of supplies himself, he decided to abandon the chase, though a few English *pinnaces continued to follow the Spaniards until they were past the Orkney Islands, and committed to returning to Spain by the west of Ireland. The weather, which had been rough in the North Sea, deteriorated further as the Armada ploughed its long way homewards, and many of its vessels were wrecked on the rocky coasts of Scotland and Ireland, where they were pillaged and their crews slaughtered. Of the 130 Spanish ships which had left Lisbon, almost half were lost.

Laughton, J., *State Papers Relating to the Defeat of the Spanish Armada* (Navy Records Society, 1895).
Martin, C., and Parker, G., *The Spanish Armada* (1988).

Spanish burton, a *purchase in which two single *blocks are used, the upper block being fitted with a hook, *eye, or tail and its standing

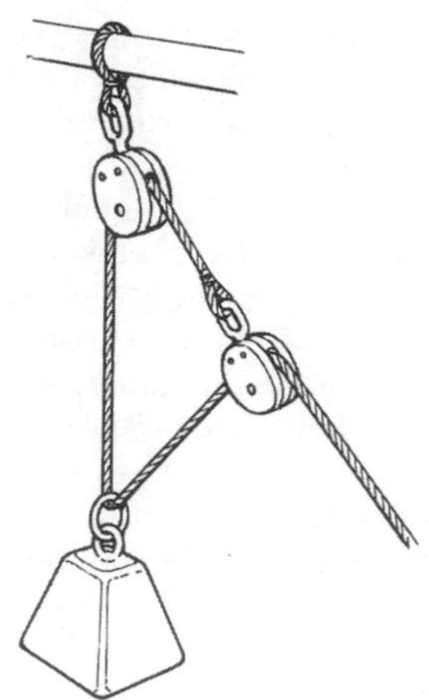

Single Spanish burton

part forming the *strop of the lower block. The power gained is four times, but the lift is very limited in comparison with a normal purchase. A double Spanish burton has the same arrangement but employs a double block in addition to the two singles, increasing the power gained to six times.

Spanish Main, a term much used by writers of romantic stories of the sea to describe the Spanish possessions in America during the 16th–18th centuries. In the strict and early meaning of the word it embraced that part of the mainland of the north-east coast of South America stretching from the Orinoco to the Isthmus of Panama, and the former Spanish mainland possessions bordering the Caribbean Sea and Gulf of Mexico. But by extension, particularly from the sense in which it was used by the *buccaneers of the late 17th and early 18th centuries, the term came to mean the Caribbean Sea itself. Thus the meaning changed completely; where originally it referred to the main land, it later came to mean the main sea.

Spanish reef, a method of *reefing the *topsails or *topgallant sails of a *square-rigged ship by lowering the *yard on to the *cap of the mast. It was, in British eyes in the days of the sailing navies, thought to be a slovenly method of shortening sail. Another form of Spanish reef, considered equally slovenly, was to shorten sail by tying a knot in the *head of the *jibs.

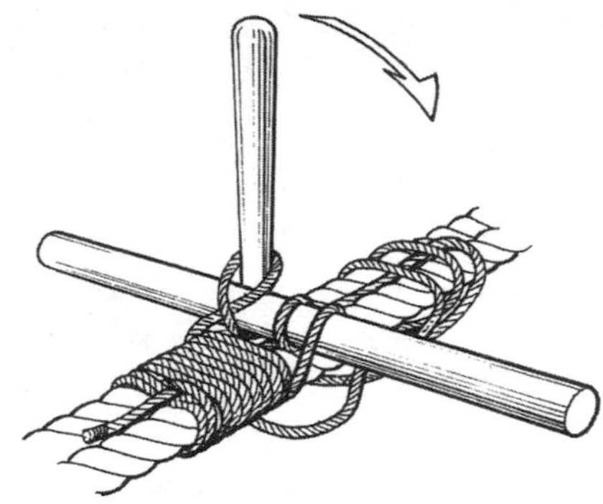

Spanish windlass

Spanish windlass, a means of increasing the tautness of a *seizing by taking a couple of turns with the seizing round a short bar and then turning the bar with a *marline spike, held to it by a *bight of the seizing and used as a lever. A Spanish windlass is used where maximum tautness is required, as in seizing together a couple of *hawsers or binding a *strop tightly round a large *block and holding it *taut while the neck is seized.

spanker, the fore-and-aft sail set from the *mizzen of *square-rigged ships, usually with a *gaff and a boom. Although used for propulsion, the principal function of the spanker is to aid the ship in manoeuvre and to be set to assist in the balance of the *helm. It grew so large in the big grain carriers that the Germans split it in two with double gaffs so that the two halves could be *furled independently. Many square-rigged ships also carry a spanker *topsail reaching to the mizzen masthead. In early ships a *driver was often used to augment the sail area in light conditions and the term driver is occasionally used in place of spanker.

Colin Mudie

spar, a general term for any wooden or metal support used in the *rigging of a ship; it embraces all *yards, *booms, etc.

spar buoy, a *spar-shaped *buoy *moored from its bottom so that it floats more or less upright. It is part of the *IALA maritime buoyage system.

spar deck, in its strict maritime meaning a temporary deck laid in any part of a ship, the *beams across which it is laid being known as skid beams. But the term was often used to describe the *quarterdeck or *forecastle deck of a deep-waisted ship, possibly because in the days of sail spare *spars could be lashed to these decks as replacements for those damaged in use, rather than in the ship's *waist. In the US Navy the term applied to the weather deck of its *frigates, where the flimsy gangways formerly used to connect the forecastle and quarterdeck had been so expanded and strengthened as to create a continuous deck capable of supporting guns. The ships themselves were sometimes referred to as 'spar deck frigates'. In modern usage, the term is sometimes employed to describe the upper deck of a flush-decked ship.

spar torpedo, an explosive charge, exploded by a contact pistol, fixed to the end of a long pole and carried over the bows of a small vessel for use against an enemy ship. They were developed during the American Civil War (1861–5) and the most notable example of their use was the sinking of the Confederate *ram *Albemarle* on 27 October 1864. They were rendered obsolete by the development of the modern torpedo which is still employed by *submarines today.

speak, to, or **speak to a ship, to,** to communicate with a ship at sea. The term includes all methods of communication and does not necessarily mean that the ships are in sight of each other, much less within hailing distance.

special mark, a yellow *buoy or *spar buoy, sometimes with an X-shaped topmark, which is used in the *IALA maritime buoyage system. It is not primarily intended to assist *navigation but to indicate a special area or feature like *spoil ground or a military exercise zone. It is also sometimes used as a mark for a *traffic separation scheme where use of conventional channel marking may cause confusion, and in this case its topmark, if fitted, is the same as a *lateral mark. A special mark can be any shape so long as it does not conflict with navigational marks. To avoid confusion, the yellow lights of these marks do not have any *characteristic used for white lights.

spectacle iron, or **plate,** fitted at the outer ends of *yards of a *square-rigger to hold the *studding-sail *booms.

spencer, similar to a *spanker but set, usually *loose footed, on the other masts of *square-riggers. Their principal function was to reduce rolling and to aid in the balance of the *helm.

spend, to. A mast or *yard, broken during bad weather, was said to be spent. But if broken in battle, it was 'shot by the board', or 'carried away by the board' if it was broken by the weight of other masts or yards bringing it down.

Sperry, Elmer Ambrose (1860–1930), American inventor, best known for his application of the gyroscopic principle in producing a *gyroscopic compass which, unlike a *magnetic compass, is unaffected by iron or steel and always points to the *true North Pole. First developed by a German engineer for use in a submersible, the gyroscopic compass underwent its first sea trials in 1908 and later proved to be an immense boon to *navigators. Sperry developed it initially for aircraft, forming the Sperry Gyroscope Company of Brooklyn in 1910, and the first surface vessel to be fitted with such a compass was the American *battleship *Delaware* in 1911.

Sperry is less well known for his invention of the high-intensity carbon arc searchlight which he brought out in 1915. These were used aboard warships of all navies during the 20th century for *signals at sea and for illuminating an enemy. He also adapted the gyroscopic principle to the control of naval gunnery and, especially, to the guidance of torpedoes. Following these successes he produced in 1921 a gyroscopically controlled *automatic pilot for ships and, later, gyroscopic *stabilizers. Sperry founded no less than eight companies to manufacture his inventions and took out over 400 patents.

spider. **(1)** The name given to a metal *outrigger to hold a *block clear of a mast or off the side of a ship. **(2)** In the USA it was the name given to a *pinrail attached around the *mizzen-mast in lieu of *fife rails, so as to provide more room to the ship's wheel when located just forward of that mast. It was also known as a **spider rail**.

spider band, a metal band with many *eyes, usually welded, fitted around the masts and *spars of *square-riggers and other ships, and used for many purposes.

spile, to, in *shipbuilding, to mark a curved line from the vessel onto a new part, usually planking, so that the new edge fits precisely with the previous edge. This is commonly first marked on a batten or template before being transferred to the new part.

spill, to, to take the wind out of a sail by bringing the vessel head to wind or by easing away the sheet to an extent where the sail can hold no wind.

spilling lines, a variation of *buntlines which are taken under the sail and back up to the *yard. They are principally used for ships commonly sailing in hard conditions where a quick method of spilling the wind from a sail is especially valuable. Colin Mudie

spinnaker. **(1)** A three-cornered lightweight sail which is normally set forward of a *yacht's mast, with or without a boom, to increase sail area with the wind *aft of the *beam.

The name of the sail seems to have come from the time it was first hoisted in a race in June 1865 aboard the yacht *Niobe*, whose owner, William Gordon, had a sailmaking business in Southampton (see *Mariner's Mirror*, 51 (1965) 355). It was called a 'niobe' by the crew, but the racing skipper Tom Diaper, whose grandfather was the professional skipper aboard *Niobe* that day, wrote in his memoirs in 1950 that one of the crew remarked, 'that's the sail to make 'er spin', and that Gordon reversed this comment to give the sail the name 'spinmaker'. The following year the owner of the yacht *Spinx* hoisted a similar sail which her crew dubbed a 'spinker' much as it had been called a 'niobe' the year before. The two words appear to have become combined so that when the word first appeared in print later that year it was spelled 'spiniker', and was not spelled as it is now until 1869.

However, the sail may have been invented well before this. In his well-known book *Down Channel*, the single-handed yachtsman Richard McMullen (1830–91) wrote: 'In 1852, contemplating longer passages, I gave *Leo* a topmast; and in 1855, wanting more sail for running before a light wind, I invented a sail which for want of a better name I called [a] studding-sail, but which was known about twelve years later as a spinnaker, when it came into use among larger yachts for match-sailing. It is made of very light material in the form of a jib, and sets from the topmast head to the deck where it is boomed out like a squaresail. As it is a sail that endangers the topmast, except in the lightest winds, I discarded it in 1864.'

Since its first appearance many variations of the spinnaker have been tried out. At first the sail was shaped like a *foresail, with only a moderate amount of flow or bulge in the belly, but with the introduction of synthetic fibres, such as Terylene, nylon, Dacron, etc., spinnakers began to be cut with a deep curve or *roach in the *foot, and a great deal of flow in the belly. So full was this amount of flow in some of these sails that they quickly earned the name of **parachute spinnakers**. During the 1930s sailmakers also experimented with the effect of having a large hole, or multiple holes, in the sail, sometimes known by British yachtsmen during the inter-war period as **'Tom Ratsey's peepholes'** after the English sailmaker of that name who produced them. These holes were incorporated to create a steady flow of air and prevent the wild gyrations that some spinnakers were prone to when running before a freshening breeze. In the early 1970s the **star-cut spinnaker**, also called a **reacher**, was introduced which could be used as close as 45° to the wind and was better than an ordinary spinnaker when running in heavy weather. Another innovation was the **all-round** or **radial spinnaker**. Radial refers to the layout of the panels making up the sail. These make it more stable in a strong wind and especially good when *reaching. A more recent development is the **asymmetrical spinnaker**, also known as an **A-sail**, or the trademarked **Gennaker**. This is a reaching or cruising spinnaker where the sail is longer on one *leech than on the other. It is made of very lightweight cloth, and is set when reaching, often without a spinnaker pole.

(2) Spinnaker was also the term bargees used to describe the *jib *topsail which Thames *spritsail *barges set on their topmast forestays.

spirketting, the name given to the extra thick *strake which used to be incorporated in the hull of a wooden ship to provide additional strength. It was fitted either at the outboard ends of the deck *beams or next above the *waterways.

spitfire jib, a small storm *jib made of very heavy sailcloth, used when the strength of the wind is such that the normal *foresails in a small sailing vessel cannot be carried. It is almost entirely applicable to *yachts, larger sailing ships carrying several jibs being able to reduce sail by lowering one or more of them.

Spithead, a well-known and historical stretch of water in the east Solent off the British naval base of Portsmouth. It is bounded on the north by the Spit Sand, on the east by the Horse and Dean Sand, on the south by the Sturbridge Shoal and the Motherbank, and on the west by the Ryde Middle Sand. It was the scene of the famous naval *mutiny of 1797 and of an indecisive action between the English fleet and a French invasion fleet in 1545, when the **Mary Rose* capsized and sank. It is the traditional anchorage where the British fleet is most frequently reviewed by the sovereign on great occasions. See also WARFARE AT SEA.

splice, to, a method of joining two ropes or wires together by unlaying the *strands at the two ends and tucking or relaying them. The end result is known as a **splice**. Ropes and wires are spliced together to join them permanently, but knots are knotted when the join is temporary. Ropes can be joined by a *long splice so as to *reeve them through a *block; a *short splice, or a *cut splice, is required if an *eye is to be incorporated at the point of junction. An eye required at the end of a rope or wire is produced by an *eye splice.

spliced, to get, the sailor's term for getting married. Just as two ropes or wires are joined together by being *spliced, so also are a man and woman when they get married.

splice the main brace, to, a traditional term in the British Navy meaning to serve out an additional tot of *grog to a ship's crew. The main *brace itself was a *purchase attached to the main lower *yard of a *square-rigged ship to brace the yard round to the wind. However, it probably has little to do with the saying beyond the fact that hauling on the main brace called for a maximum effort by the crew. In the days of sail the main brace was spliced (in terms of drink) in very bad weather or after a period of severe exertion by the crew, more as a pick-me-up than for any other purpose. But with the introduction of *steam propulsion, with machines to take most of the harder labour out of seagoing, the main brace was spliced only on occasions of celebration or, occasionally, after battle. Now that rum is no longer issued aboard ship, splicing the main brace is a thing of the past.

spoil ground, an area of the seabed, marked by *buoys, on which sewage, spoil from dredging, and other rubbish may be deposited by *lighters or *hoppers specially equipped for the task.

spoke, in any wheel a rod or bar extending outwards from the hub to support the rim. However, in a ship's steering wheel a spoke is the extension beyond the rim which forms a handle by which the wheel is turned to angle the *rudder. See also KING SPOKE.

sponges, the simplest of all multi-celled organisms. Their cells are not organized into tissues, so that some sponges can reconstitute themselves if they are strained through sieves. Most of the 5,000 species are marine and live attached to the seabed, although some bore into and infest the shells of *molluscs or the fabric of *coral reefs. They are filter-feeders, drawing water into their bodies through tiny pores in the body wall, and expelling it through a central exhalent siphon. Microscopic whiplike flagella power the flow of water. Each day a sponge can process a volume of water that is up to 20,000 times its own body volume and extract from it 90% of the bacteria suspended in it.

There are three major groups of sponges: **glass sponges** (500 species), which have skeletons of siliceous spicules and mostly live in the deep ocean; **calcareous sponges** (about 500 species), which have spicules of calcium carbonate and most live in shallow seas; and **demosponges** (about 4,000 species), whose skeletons are either siliceous or fibrous and which occur in both shallow and deep water. They include the bath sponge (*Spongia*), one of the few commercially important sponges that are collected by free divers *diving to astonishing depths. M. V. Angel

sponson, a platform formed on a ship's side either by an outboard bulge of the hull or by an indentation of the ship's side to form a flat surface on the deck level below. Sponsons were mainly associated with larger warships and were most often used to provide mountings for the secondary armament. Without a sponson the barrels of guns ranged along the ship's side would project beyond the line of the vessel's hull; when mounted in a ship with sponsons the barrels, when trained fore and aft, remained within the line of the hull. Modern warships, with the exception of *aircraft carriers, are no longer built with sponsons.

spoon, to, an old maritime term meaning to *scud, or to run before a *gale with reduced sail or under *bare poles. It passed out of use as a sea expression during the first half of the 18th century, but is sometimes to be seen in the *marine literature of the 16th and 17th centuries. For example, Samuel *Pepys, commenting on the St James's Day battle against the Dutch, wrote in his diary for 3 August 1666: 'And more, that we might have spooned before the wind as well as they, and have overtaken their ships in the pursuite in all that while.'

spreaders. (1) Metal or wooden struts placed in pairs *athwartships on a *yacht's mast to

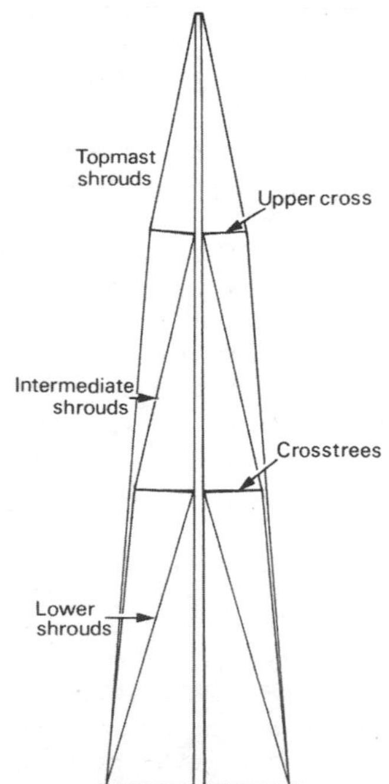

Spreaders (1)

spread the angle of the upper or masthead *shrouds. In the old-fashioned *gaff rig, they were commonly known as crosstrees. **(2)** Metal bars fitted to the bow of a *square-rigged ship to give more spread to the *tacks of the fore *course.

spring. **(1)** See BERTHING HAWSERS. **(2)** As a verb, it describes the action when one of the ends, or *butts, of a plank of a wooden hull breaks loose from the copper nails, or *tree-nails, that secure it to a ship's *timbers. Because the plank's shape is bent to the curve of the hull, it springs outwards and projects beyond the curve of the hull. When this happens it is said to be **sprung**. Similarly, the verb is used to describe the wooden mast or *spar of a vessel when a crack develops and needs to be *fished, or, if very badly sprung, replaced.

spring a leak, to, for a vessel to develop a crack or fracture in its hull which allows sea water to enter. The term originated from the occasional tendency of the hull planking of a wooden vessel to *spring, but the expression now applies to any hole or break in a ship's hull, however made, by which the sea can enter the hull.

spring stays, the name given to additional mast *stays carried on board sailing warships to replace those shot away in battle. *Chain and bar *shot were frequently used in action during those days specifically to sever the *rigging of enemy ships, making it advisable to carry on board spare rigging of all descriptions.

spring tides, those *tides, as opposed to *neap tides, which rise highest and fall lowest from the mean tide level. They occur when the pull of the moon and of the sun act in conjunction whether 0° or 180° apart. These conditions occur twice in each lunar month, so that there are two spring tides and two neap tides every 29 days.

sprit, a long *spar which stretches diagonally across a four-sided fore-and-aft sail, called a *spritsail, to support the sail's *peak. In the typical *barge rig, its heel or inboard end is held in a *snotter near the base of the mast.

Reliefs dating from the 2nd century BC show that the sprit was known to the Greeks and Romans for small boats. The first representa-

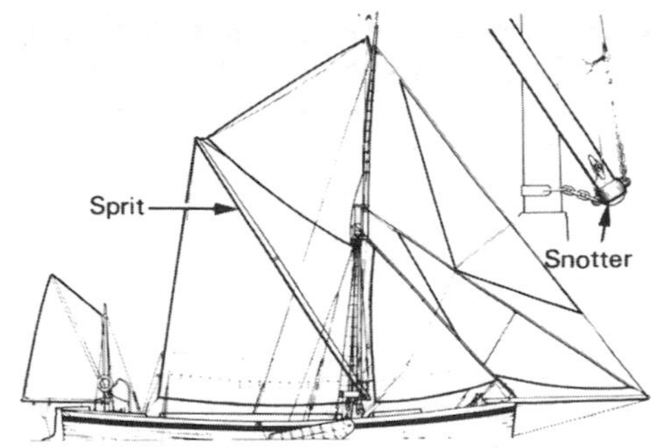

Thames barge with sprit

tion of it in western Europe is on the seal of the city of Kiel, dated 1365, though not all experts agree that this is what it is. The seal shows two sprits, shaped as a V, supporting a square sail, a type of sprit rig long associated with boats in the Indian Ocean and the Pacific. This kind of sprit may well have been transmitted from the Indian Ocean to the Mediterranean in classical times as some of the reliefs mentioned above show V-shaped sprits.

The single sprit was not used in western Europe for seagoing ships until the early 15th century. It was almost certainly introduced by the Dutch at that time as a rig for smaller, coastal craft, proving much more *weatherly than *square-rigged vessels in the *shoal and tidal waters off the Dutch coast.

spritsail. **(1)** A fore-and-aft quadrilateral sail extended from the mast by means of a *sprit set diagonally across the sail. This extends from the foot of the mast with the upper end attached to the *peak of the sail. It is particularly well known for its use on the Thames *barge. **(2)** A small square sail set beneath a highly *steeved *bowsprit on early square-rigged ships. An

16th-century rig with spritsail

additional sail, called the **spritsail topsail**, was sometimes set ahead of the spritsail, or on a short mast, called the **spritsail topmast**, stepped upright at the end of the bowsprit. These sails were superseded by the current system of *jibs and *staysails early in the 18th century.

spunyarn, a small line made of two, three, or four yarns, not laid but loosely twisted. It has a variety of uses, on board ship, particularly to *seize or *serve rope. It is also used aboard sailing vessels to *stop sails with.

spurling line, a line made fast to the *rudder head of a ship and brought up on either side to the position of the steering wheel. It operated the *telltale by which the angle of the rudder was indicated to the *quartermaster at the wheel.

squadron, from the Italian *squadrone*, a small number of warships which could comfortably be directed by a single flag officer. The term, in the British Navy, dates from 1588. Later, in the age of *steam propulsion, it became the collective name for a small number of warships, usually eight, of the same type. See also SQUADRONAL COLOURS.

squadronal colours, an early method of subdividing the English fleet into *squadrons. It is said to have been inaugurated in the reign of Elizabeth I; the earliest surviving instructions laying down the wearing of coloured flags to denote the three squadrons into which the fleet was divided are dated 1617. The admiral's squadron wore a red flag, the vice admiral's a white, and the rear admiral's a blue.

As fleets grew in size, and the three squadrons into which they were divided became correspondingly larger, it became impossible for one admiral to control the movements of his squadron efficiently from his position in the centre of it. In consequence, three admirals were, in theory, allocated to each squadron, a full admiral in command, a vice admiral as his second, and a rear admiral as his third in command. So the white squadron was commanded by an admiral of the White, with a vice admiral of the White and a rear admiral of the White as his second and third in command. The squadrons ranked in the order red, white, blue, and admirals took rank according to the colour of their squadron. Promotion of admirals also took place in this order, a rear admiral of the Blue on promotion becoming a rear admiral of the White as his first step in *flag rank, and a rear admiral of the Red becoming a vice admiral of the Blue when he received promotion. Only in the Red, or senior, squadron was this hierarchy not followed. There was no admiral of the Red since he was in overall command of the whole fleet and was therefore, in theory, admiral of the fleet.

The rank of admiral of the Red was introduced after the battle of Trafalgar in 1805 as a compliment to the British Navy for its successes in the Napoleonic War (1803–15), and as a means of rewarding the most successful admirals. It was not possible then to make promotions to the rank of admiral of the fleet since there was only one holder of this rank and he retained it for life.

In 1864 the organization of the British fleet into coloured squadrons was discarded, mainly because it had no further relevance in the age of steam warships. The *red, or senior, *ensign was allocated to the British merchant navy, the Royal Navy adopted the *white ensign, and the *blue ensign was used by naval auxiliary vessels. See also YELLOW ADMIRAL.

squall, a sudden gust of wind of considerable strength. Squalls usually follow the passage of a low-pressure system, when the *barometer begins to rise from its lowest point. This is because the barometer gradient is almost always steeper in the wake of such a system than ahead of its centre. **A line squall** is heralded by a dark cloud stretched across the *horizon, sometimes arched in form. It is caused by a narrow area of low pressure passing across the sea with an arc of high pressure following close behind it. Where the differences of pressure are considerable, a heavy squall blows up accompanied by a distinct drop in temperature See also MARINE METEOROLOGY.

square, the position of the *yards when a *square-rigged ship is at anchor and set up in harbour trim. The yards are square by the *braces when they are at right angles to the fore-and-aft line of the ship. They are square by the *lifts when they are horizontal.

square rig, a term that refers essentially to the use of square-cornered sails, usually approximately rectangular, set from horizontal *spars, or *yards, balanced across the mast. This arrangement is used from simple single sails to the complex and sophisticated multiple sail rigs developed over 2,000 years for the major ships of war, commerce, and exploration.

Vessels setting square sails are known from the earliest depictions of ships up to the present. The earliest sails may have been animal skins or woven fabrics, both essentially rectangular, which may explain the origins and early dominance of the form. A square sail hung from a spar balanced across a mast has the characteristics of maximizing the sail area for the height of mast while minimizing the operational loads to be handled by the crew. This favoured its use for light open craft where the mast might have had to be set up by those on board when sail was required and also for heavy vessels which needed sail area for power to drive them.

An early use of the square sail is evidenced by the contemporary depictions of Greek *galleys some 3,000 years ago. For such craft the limitations of the light hull meant that the square sail was essentially used for *running free and *reaching, a pattern of use that persisted up to perhaps the 10th century AD. The single square sail was generally set from the deck by hoisting it on a yard and it was removed by lowering the yard to the deck. To meet stronger wind conditions the sail could be replaced by a smaller version. A later practice was to add area to a small and strong sail by lacing one or more lighter additions, called *bonnets, along the *foot of the sail. These had the value of being able to be added or removed without slowing or stopping.

On early and small vessels the sail was set on a mast with simple supporting *rigging and the sail loads taken largely by *braces running *aft

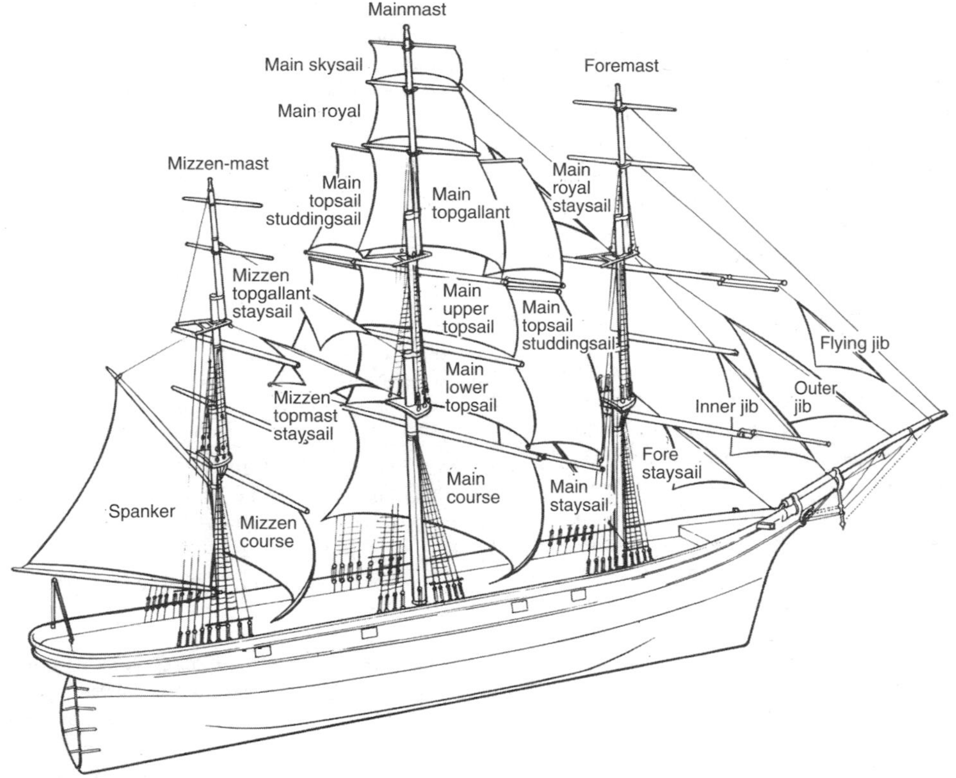

Sails of a typical 19th-century square-rigger

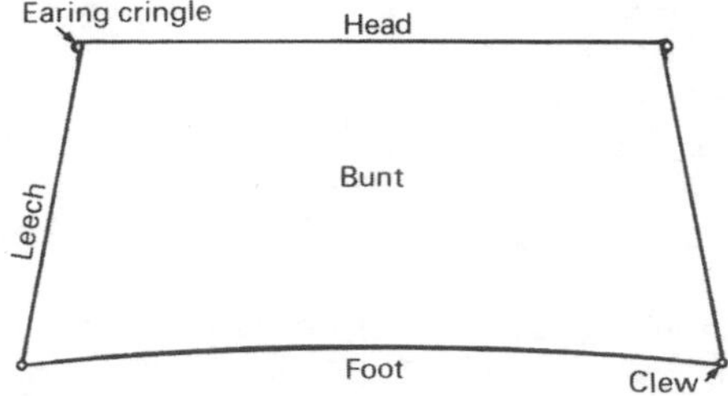

Parts of a square sail

from the ends of the yard and by sheets attached to the lower corners. The yard could be swivelled around the mast under the control of, and limited by, the braces. The *leeward-side rigging of the mast itself could be disengaged to allow closer bracing. The *windward working value of this manoeuvre was mostly limited by the hydrofoil abilities of the shallow hulls.

As ships grew bigger and heavier to meet more ambitious voyages, two factors controlled their planning. First was the need to increase sail area and this was done by multiplying the number of masts and adding further masts above these masts, each carrying its own sail. The other factor was to keep the length of the ship short, first because of the practicalities of the use of one-piece wooden keels, and second to maximize the relative water flow around the hull which had come to be recognized as an essential component in windward ability.

A typical ship of the 15th–16th centuries might, for instance, carry three masts, square rigged on the forward two and with a *bowsprit carrying a square *spritsail. The third mast would probably carry a *lateen steering sail. Some would carry a second tier of square sails called *topsails and in a few years these would extend to a third tier of *topgallant square sails.

Each stack of square sails acts as an engine for the ship. The lowest sail and biggest sail in a standard stack is called the *course and above that is set the topsail which may be subdivided into upper and lower topsails. The next sail upwards is the topgallant which may also be subdivided into upper and lower topgallants. Above these some ships set a single royal sail and only the most extreme set a single *skysail. Moonsails have been set above the skysail but to little effect.

The addition of further square sails into a vertical stack probably came from the use of light topsails initially set *athwartships to reduce rolling. The improved efficiency of sails set close together with wind slots between them led to the multiple stacking of square sails. The ultimate example of the China race *clippers saw as many as eight square sails on their mainmasts with their seven slots.

Generally speaking, square rig has an unmerited reputation for poor windward ability, but this is mostly due to its use in large and heavy vessels with relatively slow hull speeds. This brings a preference for the development of speed over pointing to minimize the resultant heavy angle of attack, or *leeway. However, it is noteworthy that no better rig was ever developed where windward working in such ships was regarded as essential. A further and valuable characteristic of square rig is the ability to stop, start, adjust speed, turn quickly, and even sail backwards. All these were unique and valuable to many aspects of seafaring before the development of *steam propulsion.

Ships rigged in this manner became one of mankind's most significant inventions, preserved today by the *sail training ships of many nations as square rig is especially valued for modern sail training. This refers to a relatively short period of sea experience for young people rather than any vocational education. The large numbers of crew required and the need for everyone to be completely involved for the success of sailing evolutions requires all on board to act as a team. Even ordinary housekeeping becomes a feat in a rolling ship, and climbing aloft at sea, very popular, can be an experience to remember.

Seafaring for exploration, commerce, and conflict has been one of the greatest spurs for the development of the human condition, and it has been dominated by square-rigged ships. In their full glory they became a system of sophisticated worldwide transport using little more than wind and timber. See also SHIP RIGGED.

Anderson, R., *The Rigging of Ships in the Days of the Spritsail Topmast 1600–1720* (1994).

Harland, J., and Myers, M., *Seamanship in the Age of Sail* (1984).

Underhill, H., *Masting and Rigging the Clipper Ship and Ocean Carrier* (1964). Colin Mudie

squid, predatory cephalopod *molluscs of the order Teuthoidea. The 298 species of squid range in size from 2 centimetres (1 in.) to 20 metres (65 ft) in the **giant squid** (*Architeuthis dux*). The fast-swimming species have some of the highest metabolic rates of all animals. The body is usually cigar shaped with two lateral fins. The head has well-developed eyes and around the mouth with its parrot-beak-like jaws is a ring of eight arms lined with suckers, and two others that are highly extensible tentacles with suckers only on their ends. These extensible arms are shot out to seize the prey. Most squid swim backwards, using jets of water squirted from the siphon just beneath the head. The powerhouse for the jets is the mantle cavity on the underside of the body, which is lined with powerful muscles. The body fins are used for steering, but in some species they undulate to provide the power for normal swimming.

Squid are a favoured food of sperm *whales, and titanic struggles have been witnessed between them and giant squid. The giant squid may have given rise to the Norwegian myth of a many-armed sea monster, the *kraken. Recently in 2003 a '**colossal squid**' (*Mesonychoteuthis hamiltoni*) was picked up by fishermen near the surface in Antarctic waters. It was about two-thirds of its potential full size but even so its mantle measured 2.5 metres (8 ft), and when stretched out its arms and tentacles measured 5–6 metres (16–19 ft), so potentially this species could be even larger than the giant squid. It has the largest eyes of any animal and is reported to be extremely aggressive, chasing large prey such as the Patagonian toothfish (*Dissostichus eleginoides*), which it grasps with the swivelling hooks on the insides of its tentacles, and rips apart with its parrot-like beak. Previously only six specimens had been found, five of which came from the stomachs of sperm whales. It has been estimated that this species makes up nearly 80% by weight of a bull sperm whale's diet in the Southern Ocean.

There are some remarkable deep-sea species. The **cock-eyed squid** (*Histioteuthis*) has one big eye and one small eye, and its underside is studded with light organs. **Cranchid squid** (*Cranchia* spp.) are jelly-like and concentrate ammonia in their blood making them neutrally buoyant, so they do not have to swim constantly.

There are some large *fisheries for squid, some of which are sold for human consumption, but many are used as bait for *long-lining. In Monterey Bay off California there is an annual event when millions of **market squid** (*Loligo opalescens*) gather in huge *shoals to spawn and then die. This species, like many squid, live for only a year.

Hunt, J., *Octopus and Squid* (1997).

www.cephbase.utmb.edu/ M. V. Angel

SS, the prefix placed before the name of a ship to indicate that it is a merchant ship. Originally the two letters stood for screw steamer—a steamer driven by a *propeller or propellers—to distinguish it from a *paddle steamer. But with the disappearance of the latter the designation came to be accepted as meaning steamship, and continued to be used even after the introduction of the marine *diesel engine.

stability is the ability of a ship to return to an upright position after being heeled by an external force, such as a weight being placed aboard or by rough sea conditions. If a ship is inclined at an angle and then naturally returns to the upright, it is known as being stable. Should the ship wish to continue moving from the upright and is heading for capsize, then it is described as unstable.

It is normal for ships to have their centre of gravity higher than the *centre of buoyancy (see Fig. 1) creating what appears on first sight to be an unstable situation. However, as can be seen (Fig. 2), the centre of buoyancy travels away from the centre line as the ship is heeled, producing a restoring force.

In Fig. 2 the distance G–M is known as the metacentric height and is a measure of the stiffness, or stability, of a ship. The larger the metacentric height of a ship, the greater the stability. On the down side, very large metacentric heights produce violent rolling motions. So passenger ship operators, in particular, must find a suitable compromise which keeps their ships safe yet creates a slow rolling movement which neither upsets fare-paying passengers, nor damages fragile cargo. To assist in keeping the ship from excessive rolling, fin *stabilizers are often fitted.

Naval architects (see NAVAL ARCHITECTURE) calculate the metacentric height of every ship in all conditions, from being in *ballast through

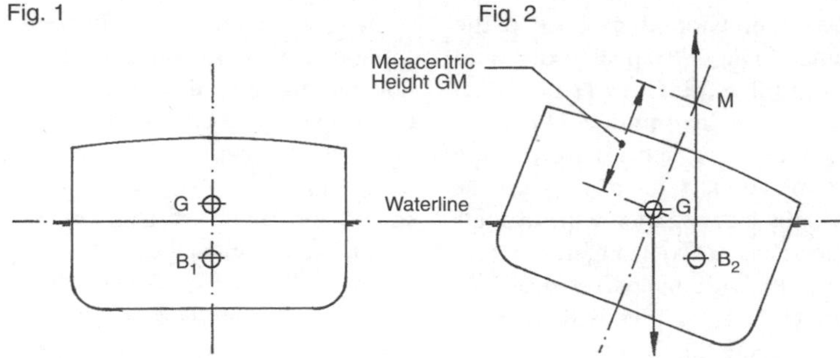

Stability

to part and fully laden. As the safety of the ship is a statutory obligation it is important that the metacentric height be confirmed at full scale. For this reason an inclining experiment is carried out when the ship is afloat in still conditions. The stability can be calculated from the angle of heel adopted by the ship when a known weight is moved across the deck an exact amount.

During a ship's lifetime, it acquires additional topside weight through coats of paint, loose stores, etc. The ship's managers and officers must keep aware of this, and it is recommended that further inclining experiments be carried out every few years. Fred M. Walker

stabilizers are used to minimize the rolling of a ship. They are normally fitted to *cruise ships and *ferries, where passenger comfort is essential, and to large *container ships, where it is necessary to minimize the rolling forces on the containers stacked on deck. They should not be confused with anti-heeling systems (see last paragraph of this entry) which are used to correct small angles of heel.

Anti-rolling tanks were introduced by a German inventor, Dr H. Frahm, and one of his first systems was fitted in the *ocean liner *Laconia* of 1912, his Frahm tanks being a development of an earlier system first used in the liner *City of New York* in 1889. The Frahm arrangement consists of two large tanks at the sides of the ship, joined by a connecting tank at the bottom, forming a large U-shaped tank; an air venting line joins the tanks at the top. As the ship rolls, water in the tanks moves from one side of the ship to the other and the effect of the moving water is to minimize the roll. As no operating system was used, the Frahm tanks are classed as passive tanks. The active tank stabilizing system, which is generally used on smaller ships, operates in the same way except that a pump is used to move water from one side of the ship to the other.

A disadvantage of a tank system is that it takes up valuable space inside the hull and so other stabilizing systems have been developed. A **gyroscopic stabilizer** unit was installed in the Italian liner *Conte di Savoia* during the late 1920s. Although it was effective in certain *wave conditions, it was not successful and the experiment was not repeated. However, the gyroscope was later used at sea in Elmer *Sperry's *gyroscopic compass. The **fin stabilizer** was first patented in 1898, and the Japanese introduced a fin stabilizer system in 1925. But it was the one introduced by Denny-Brown in the 1930s, which used gearing to operated the fins, that became the most successful for all types of ship.

A fin stabilizer system has two fins, one on each side of the ship; larger ships may have two sets of fins. If a fin is turned to the nose-up attitude as the ship moves through the water, there is a resulting upward force on the fin just like the effect on an aircraft wing. If the fin on the opposite side of the ship is given a nose-down attitude there is a downward force on the fin. The total effect of the forces on the two fins is to exert a turning moment on the ship which opposes the rolling effect on the ship caused by a wave.

An essential feature of this system is the monitoring and control arrangements. These have to react to the angle of roll and the rate at which that angle is changing, and must react quickly enough to move the fins to the correct position before the angle of roll becomes too large. Nowadays, electronic control systems are used and the fin actuators are similar to the hydraulic systems used for steering gear, generally of the rotary vane type as this is compact. When the ship is not rolling, and when it enters port, the fins must be drawn into the hull. Early systems had retractable fins but modern ones use hinged fins.

Anti-heeling systems are fitted in cruise ships and container ships in order to keep the vessel upright when it is at anchor or alongside a *berth. For cruise ships a level ship is essential for safety and for disembarking passengers, particularly into *tenders. It is also essential that a container ship, when loading or discharging, is as close to the upright position as possible to ensure that its containers are moved correctly in their cell guides without jamming. The anti-heeling system has two tanks, one on each side of the ship, joined by a connection pipe at the bottom and an air vent pipe at the top. In the connection pipe at the bottom there is a pump that can pump water in either direction, i.e. from *port to *starboard, or vice versa. This corrects small angles of list and maintains the ship in an upright position.

Denis Griffiths

staghorn, a metal bollard with horizontal arms forming the shape of a cross, fitted in big ships as a means of belaying larger *hawsers.

stanchions, the upright supports set along the side of the upper deck of a ship that carry the *guardrail or, in the case of smaller vessels, the wires acting as a guardrail. Longer stanchions are also used in large ships as the means of spreading an *awning over the deck in hot weather, and are also occasionally fitted to support a light deck above.

standing lug, a sailing rig, where, unlike the *dipping lug, the lower end of the *yard which carries the *lugsail hardly protrudes forward of the mast. This means the boat can go *about without having to lower the yard. An obsolete name for the standing lug was **macaroni lug**. See also GUNTER RIG.

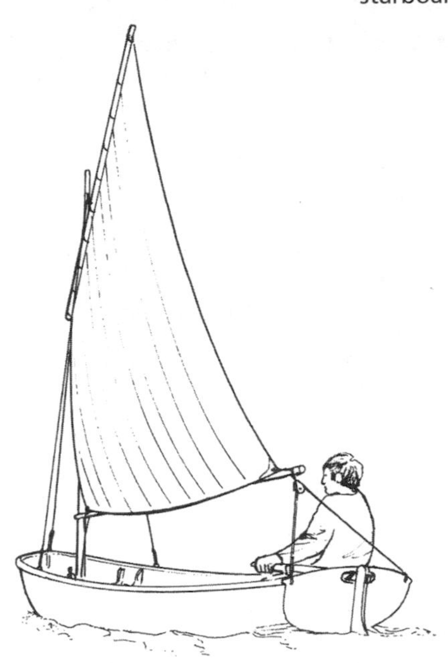

Typical standing lug

standing part, that part of the rope used in a *purchase, the end of which is secured to the *eye of the standing *block. The part of the rope between the standing and the moving blocks is the running part, and the remainder, as it comes out of the purchase, is the hauling part. The whole of the rope is known as the *fall.

standing rigging, see RIGGING.

starboard, the right-hand side of a vessel when looking forward. It is generally accepted to be a corruption of steer-board, the board or *oar which projected into the sea from the starboard quarter of ancient ships and by which they were steered before the invention of the hanging *rudder. See also LARBOARD; PORT; STEERING OAR.

In the days of sail the starboard side of a ship used to be the side usually reserved for the captain. He used the starboard ladder when going ashore or returning to the ship, everyone else would use the port ladder; the starboard side of the *poop deck or *quarterdeck was usually reserved for him when he came on deck for exercise; and his *cabin was normally on the starboard side of the ship.

starboard tack, the situation of a sailing vessel with her sails trimmed for a wind which comes over her *starboard side. Although the verb 'to *tack' postulates a vessel sailing *close hauled, a vessel on any *point of sailing is on the starboard tack if the wind comes over her starboard side. However, if the wind is coming from *abaft the *beam on the starboard side of a *fore-and-aft-rigged sailing vessel it is sometimes said that she is on the starboard *gybe.

'starbolins', a name given to the men of the *starboard *watch in a ship during the days of sail. See also LARBOLINS.

starshell, a shell containing a pyrotechnic flare suspended on a small parachute and fired to illuminate an enemy warship or fleet at night. See also WARFARE AT SEA.

start, to. (1) To ease away, as with the sheet of a sail, or with a *hawser, by *rendering it round a *bollard. A cask is started when it is topped or opened; a plank in the side of a wooden ship has started when it works loose. **(2)** An irregular punishment, widespread on board ships of the British Navy during the days of sail, where the *master-at-arms and *boatswain's mates were allowed to hit, or start, seamen with canes or rope-ends to get them moving at their work. It was made illegal by *Admiralty order in 1809, but it took some years for it to be completely eradicated. See also 'THREE SISTERS'.

stateroom, the name often given in *ocean liners to the *cabins occupied by first-class passengers.

station pointer, a navigational instrument, rarely seen nowadays, used in coastal waters by which a ship's position can be plotted on the *chart from *horizontal sextant angles. In its simplest form it consists of a circular perspex protractor about 15 centimetres (6 in.) in diameter fitted with three radial arms, each with a bevelled edge. The central arm is fixed at 0°, the other two pivoted at the axis so that each can be set to any angle relative to the fixed central arm. The horizontal sextant angles between three fixed points marked on the chart are set on the instrument's movable arms and the pointer laid on the chart so that the bevelled edges of the three arms correspond with the three fixed points on the chart, the ship's position being at the pointer's axis. It was of most use in hydrographic surveying. A similar procedure can be achieved by using tracing paper.

stationaire, a steam *yacht, manned by the Royal Navy. It used to be permanently stationed at some foreign ports for the exclusive use of the British ambassador accredited to the country, but the practice was discontinued early in the 20th century.

stave, to, to break in the planking of a boat or vessel in order to sink it, or to drive in the head of a cask to deliberately spill the contents. With boats, the past tense is **stove**, with casks it is **staved**.

staves, the curved wooden parts of a cask after it has been *knocked down.

stay. (1) A part of the standing *rigging of a sailing vessel which supports a mast in the fore-and-aft line, *forestays supporting it from forward and *backstays from aft. In vessels with more than one mast, they take their names from the one they support. **(2)** A term used in connection with a ship's anchor *cable in relation to the ship. A cable is said to be at **short stay** when it is taut and leads down to the anchor at a steep angle; it is at **long stay** when it is taut and leads out to the anchor well away from the ship's bows, entering the water at a less acute angle. See CATENARY. **(3)** As a verb, it is the operation of bringing the head of a sailing vessel up to the wind in order to *tack. See also IN STAYS. A mast is also **stayed forward** when it is inclined forward from the perpendicular.

stayband, a metal ring fitted near the top of a mast, with projecting lugs to which are secured the *shrouds and *stays supporting the mast. It is the modern equivalent of the *hounds. See also RIGGING.

staysail, a triangular fore-and-aft sail which is set by being *bent to a *stay. They are set both in *square-rigged and *fore-and-aft-rigged ships, and take their names from the stay on which they are set, such as fore staysail, fore *topmast staysail, etc.

steaming lights, the compulsory white *navigation lights carried on the masts of all vessels under way at sea by night by which the presence, and an indication of their *course, is made known to other vessels in the vicinity.

steam propulsion. The aphorism 'steam gives way to sail' came out of the marine steam revolution of the 19th century, for steam-powered vessels had a range of speeds and manoeuvrability denied to sailing ships. The *International Regulations for Preventing Collisions at Sea, ratified in the 1890s, recognized this new technology and steamships were nearly always required to keep clear of sailing ships. But in all other respects sail gave way to steam, in terms of economies of scale, reliability, speed, and profitability. Coastal and riverine traffic adapted to steam propulsion, but on the *high seas the transition was an extended one, with, ironically, sailing ships hastening their demise by carrying coal, and later fuel oil, to bunkering stations throughout the world.

Coal Burners. Early steamships fuelled by coal were all *paddle steamers and they had to carry large amounts of coal, which meant less space for cargo or passengers. The engines were unreliable and had a short steaming range, and this, combined with the innate conservatism of shipowners and navy boards, resulted in ocean-going ships being also rigged for sailing for many decades after they became powered by steam. It was an unsatisfactory combination, and even when steam engines became reliable, ships continued to be built with masts, though, eventually, not the *rigging and sails that went with them.

Steam is vaporized water. Its production requires high temperatures and pressures in efficient boilers using fossil or nuclear fuel. Before the last quarter of the 18th century steam machinery had no practical uses afloat, but in the 1780s James Watt did make it more efficient by means of the separate *condenser and other improvements. However, it was in France in 1776 that the practical application of steam technology on water was initiated by the French engineer the Marquis de Jouffroy d'Abbans (1751–1832). The American John Fitch (1743–98) was another pioneer and their experiments were followed in the early 1800s with the **Clermont* and the **Charlotte Dundas*.

The first transatlantic voyage by a steamship, the **Savannah*, took place in 1819, but she had to sail most of the way with her collapsible paddle wheels stowed on deck. The voyage was not commercially successful, nor was the one undertaken to India by the **Enterprize* in 1825, and it was not until 1838 that the **Sirius* proved a steamship could cross the Atlantic under power. Even so, the inefficiency of the double-acting single cylinder engine was not overcome, by John Elder on the Clyde, until the 1850s. He patented a system of compounding where high-pressure steam at high temperature was expanded in two stages—this was the *compound engine. Initially a two-stage expansion, it developed into the ubiquitous *triple and quadruple expansion *reciprocating engines which dominated the world's fleets for the rest of the 19th century. Compounding, combined with better, higher-pressure boilers, such as the cylindrical Scotch and Yarrow water tube boilers, reduced fuel consumption by at least 60%, allowing profitable passages to be made as far afield as the Far East and Australasia.

With the introduction of the screw *propeller, and iron and steel into *shipbuilding—large wooden ships were too flexible in a seaway and had difficulty coping with the increased stresses in power transmission—steam propulsion slowly gained the upper hand over sail. However, despite the success of *Brunel's **Great Britain*, both iron construction and propellers were initially treated with some scepticism. To see if the propeller was superior to the paddle wheel, the British *Admiralty even arranged a tug-of-war between two same-sized *frigates, HMS *Rattler* (screw) and HMS *Alecto* (paddle). It took place in 1845 and the former won. Although the relative power of their engines is debatable, it did show the inherent caution with which shipbuilders treated anything new. It was not until the late 1880s, when *ocean liners adapted the twin screw, that they 'at last dared to rely on their engines alone' (C. Gibbs, *Passenger Liners of the Western World* (1952), 101), and began to discard the heavy masts and *spars that were needed to raise sails in an emergency.

Steam-turbine Engine. Coal was the main fuel for steamships for many years. It was easily available but, besides taking up valuable space, the disposal of the residue of ashes was a perennial problem, and coal stocks had to be maintained at bunkering stations throughout the world. Nevertheless, by the last decade of the

19th century sail had finally given way to coal-burning ships, but it was the appearance of the steam-turbine engine that really heralded a revolution in marine steam propulsion. This is a marine rotary propulsion engine in which a jet of steam is directed onto blades set at an angle in a drum connected either direct or through gearing to the propeller shaft. The action of the steam on the blades revolves the drum and by this means the drive is transmitted to the propellers. In the late 1880s turbine-driven electric generators were fitted in some ocean liners, and a number of designers, such as Curtis in the USA and De Laval in Sweden, were active in this field. However, it is generally acknowledged that the marine turbine engine as we know it today was developed by the British marine engineer the Hon. Charles Parsons (1854–1931). The youngest son of the third Earl of Rosse, he founded the firm of C. A. Parsons at Heaton which produced the first turbo-dynamo machinery for a power station. In 1897 he designed the *Turbinia*, the first vessel in the world to be powered by steam turbines. She was built specifically to demonstrate this new invention and made her first appearance at the British Naval Review held at *Spithead in that year to celebrate the diamond jubilee of Queen Victoria, an international gathering of ships where she was bound to attract the maximum attention and publicity. She had three shafts, each carrying three propellers, and each driven by a turbine, which produced a speed of 31 knots, quite unheard of those days.

The high power to weight–size ratio of the steam turbine compared with the steam reciprocating engine made it popular with the owners of fast ocean liners and *ferries, but for cargo ships the tried and trusted steam reciprocating engine remained popular and some triple expansion engined merchant ships were still being built in the 1950s. For warships, the steam turbine was ideal as its low height allowed the machinery to be placed very low in the ship. The major disadvantage of the early steam turbine was its high rotational speed, and not until the development of the geared turbine about fifteen years after *Turbinia*'s run did the turbine find greater popularity. An efficient propeller operates at a speed between about 100 r.p.m. and 150 r.p.m., and only with gearing was the steam-turbine plant able to achieve such low speeds. Although the geared steam turbine was adopted by cargo ship operators as well as passenger ship owners, development of the marine *diesel engine at about the same time reduced the impact it might otherwise have had on the marine propulsion field.

Oil Burning. At about the same time as early steam-turbine engines appeared oil was just beginning to replace coal in steam propulsion. In 1866, Spakowski, in Russia, where the Baku oilfields promised a reliable oil supply, had developed a commercial oil burner for marine use, but the ready availability of coal supplies and the relative lack of oil stifled its adoption. However, as oil production increased, Britain and America began to use it instead of coal. In 1905 Royal Navy trials showed a distinct advantage in oil-fired warship boilers and in 1913 the Royal Navy started to convert all its warships to oil firing. After the First World War (1914–18) oil fuel was available at many bunker stations worldwide and the conversion of merchant ships, particularly the large ocean liners, became an economic proposition. Not only was oil cleaner than coal, it could be stored in *double bottoms, and so save space within the ship. It also required fewer people. The liner *Mauretania* was converted to oil burning in 1922. This reduced the engine-room staff from 366 men to 79 and the fuel consumption fell from 1,000 tons of coal per day to 620 tons of oil. In 1914 coal burners comprised 89% of steamships, but by the 1920s oil-fired boilers had taken over as the main method of steam propulsion and of the new *tonnage being built approximately 75% was oil fired and 25% coal burning.

Like modern diesel engines, oil-fired boilers burn residual fuel oil which must be heated before it can be pumped. But the fact that it can be pumped makes transportation between the storage tanks and the boilers much simpler than the movement of coal. At a boiler burner the heated fuel oil is sprayed into the furnace in fine droplets which will burn easily; the air supply is regulated by dampers in order to obtain good combustion of the oil. It is possible to vary the amount of oil sprayed into the furnace at any time in order to control the rate of steam generation; this is referred to as the 'turn down ratio' of the burner. An oil burner has a minimum flow below which it will not spray effectively and if a lower firing rate is required the burner has to be shut down. When firing is again required the fireman needs to ignite the burner manually. Automatically controlled boiler systems appeared in the 1960s and these allowed for the firing and ignition systems to be operated automatically, thus resulting in fewer firemen having to operate the boiler.

Nuclear Power. The most modern form of ship propulsion by steam is that produced by a nuclear reactor. The first reactor-powered submarine, the USS *Nautilus*, was *launched in 1955, and nuclear-powered surface vessels such as *cruisers, *ice-breakers, and *aircraft carriers are now also in service. However, the commercial use of nuclear fuel in merchant ships has not been successful. The American *Savannah*, the German *Otto Hahn*, the Japanese *Mutsu*, and the Russian *Sevmorput* were all dogged by technical, political, and economic problems and have either been withdrawn or converted to diesel propulsion.

Steam machinery was behind the Industrial Revolution; marine applications over the past 200 years have powered a revolution in efficient transportation. Today, the largest man-made moving object, the *tanker *Jahre Viking*, 564,650 deadweight *tonnage, is powered by four Stal-Laval geared steam turbines producing 265,000 shaft horsepower. See also GAS TURBINE ENGINE; 'UP FUNNEL, DOWN SCREW'.

Craig, R., *The Ship: Steam Tramps and Cargo Liners 1850–1950* (1986).
Gardiner, R. (ed.), *The Advent of Steam* (1995).
Jane's Fighting Ships (2002).
Padfield, P., *The Battleship Era* (1975).

Martin Lee/Denis Griffiths

steam-turbine engine, see STEAM PROPULSION.

steer, to, to direct a vessel by means of a *steering oar, or by a *tiller or steering wheel connected to a *rudder, so that it proceeds in the desired direction. Up to about the end of the first millennium AD, all steering was achieved by means of the steering oar, usually projecting from the *starboard quarter of the vessel. It was a short step, taken in about the late 12th or early 13th century, to replace the steering oar with a rudder hung on the *sternpost of the ship and worked by a tiller attached to the rudder head. This was very efficient until ships grew in size to the extent where the tiller had to be relatively long in order to provide sufficient leverage to counteract the pressure of the water on the rudder. In a high wind it could require several men to control the tiller of a large ship, even with the aid of *relieving tackles. The introduction of the steering wheel in the late 17th century replaced the long tiller in larger ships and made easier the manual task of controlling the rudder. **To steer small**, to keep a ship on its desired course with only small movements of the tiller or wheel. **To steer large**, the opposite of to steer small or, in the case of a sailing vessel, to steer it so that it has the wind *free. See also DRIVE, TO; HELM; STEERING GEAR.

steerage. (1) A large space below deck, usually above the *propellers, which in some merchant ships was used for crew accommodation and in the *ocean liners of the 19th and early 20th centuries was reserved for those passengers who could not afford a private *cabin. The sides were lined with wooden *bunks, often one or more tiers of them running longitudinally in the space between the sides. In those days passengers were expected to bring their own bedclothes, and also their own food, a large stove being erected on deck at which they could cook it. In the days when sailing ships carried passengers the steerage was that part of the ship next below the *quarterdeck and immediately before the *bulkhead of the great cabin. **(2)** In the US Navy it used to be the name for a midshipman's *berth.

steerage way, a vessel has steerage way when it has sufficient headway for its *rudder to grip the water so that the vessel will answer its *helm.

steering gear. In order to turn a *rudder a force is applied to a *tiller. As ships became larger the rudders also increased in size and the manpower necessary to turn the rudder increased. *Brunel's large steamship *Great Eastern* was the first ship fitted with a powered steering gear; this was a steam engine-driven system developed by John McFarlane Gray and it was fitted in 1867. Steering gear powered by steam engines continued to be used in ships until the 1930s by which time the **ram-type**

hydraulic steering gear proved more efficient and more reliable. This consisted of hydraulically driven rams connected with the tiller attached to the rudder stock. The hydraulic rams are supplied with oil from pumps which are driven by electric motors. Control instructions are relayed to the steering gear control system from the bridge by electronic means or by means of a hydraulic telemotor system.

The most modern system is the **rotary vane steering gear** which is very compact compared with the more traditional hydraulic ram type. A cylindrical actuator unit sits on top of the rudder stock with the vaned rotor connected to the rudder stock. The actuator cylinder has fixed vanes or stoppers which divide the actuator into a number of sections, usually two or three, and each section houses one of the rotor's vanes. The steering gear pump forces oil to one side of each rotor vane and takes oil from the other side of the rotor vane, thus causing the rotor to turn. As the rotor is connected to the rudder this causes the rudder to turn to the desired angle. As with the ram-type hydraulic steering gear, the rotary vane steering gear for large ships, particularly oil *tankers, has two separate hydraulic pump systems so that if one fails the other is available to steer the ship.

All steering gear in large ships can be controlled automatically by gyroscopic pilots. The ship's *course is set on a *gyro compass, and if it strays from this setting the rudder is automatically moved to bring the ship back on course. See also VANE SELF-STEERING GEAR.

Denis Griffiths

steering oar, the forerunner of the vertical *rudder hung on the *sternpost. Originally a single *oar projecting over the quarter of the boat, usually on the *starboard side, it was multiplied in larger vessels to two or three oars. A *quarter gallery pierced for such steering oars gave the necessary pivotal support, examples of this technique being seen in Egyptian bas-reliefs of 3000 BC. A somewhat later example from Egypt (2500 BC) shows a steering oar projecting over the stern of a vessel, lashed to the *counter and secured to a vertical post in the *sternsheets, and operated by a vertical *tiller dowelled into the *loom of the steering oar. By 1200 BC steering oars projecting from both quarters were common in Egypt, an obvious improvement in obtaining directional control of a vessel. In some pictures of the Phoenician trading ships, steering oars are shown projecting on both quarters through the hull of the ship itself, and they were also sometimes connected by a bar. In a Viking *longship dating back to the 9th century it was attached to a pivot and this development led to the oar becoming rudder shaped and hinged onto the side of the longship. However, as representations of them in the 11th century Bayeux Tapestry and elsewhere show, they remained the only means of directing the *course of a ship up to about the beginning of the 13th century, when they were gradually replaced by the vertical rudder. However, their use still continues in *surf boats and in some Chinese river *junks.

steeve, the angle of the *bowsprit in relation to the horizontal. A **high-steeved** bowsprit is one well cocked up towards the vertical. In ancient single-masted sailing ships the bowsprit was always very high steeved, and in fact became the forerunner of the foremast when the two- and three-masted rig was adopted.

stem. **(1)** The foremost *timber or steel member forming the bow of a vessel joined at the bottom to the keel either by *scarfing, in the case of wood, or riveting or welding in the case of steel. In wooden vessels all the timber *strakes are *rabbeted to the stem; in steel ships the fore plates are welded or riveted to it. See also CUTWATER. **(2)** As a verb, it is a seafaring term indicating that a vessel is holding its own, or making only slight headway, against a contrary *tide or *current.

step, a square framework of timber or steel built up and fixed to the *keelson of a ship to take the *heel of a mast. So to **step a mast** is to fit its *heel into the mast step. Masts are normally squared off at the heel, to fit securely into the square step to prevent them twisting or revolving. When a mast is stepped on the deck the deck is strengthened to provide extra support. But see also TABERNACLE.

stern, the after end of a vessel, generally accepted as that part of the vessel built around the *sternpost, from the *counter up to the *taffrail. For illus. see SHIPBUILDING.

sternboard, the manoeuvre of a ship when it wants to turn in narrow waters where there is insufficient room for it to turn normally while going *ahead. If it goes *astern with reversed *helm, its bows will continue to swing in the required direction of its original turn. It is the equivalent of backing and filling until the vessel is heading on its new *course. It was also a manoeuvre, though usually involuntary, in sailing ships when they were taken *aback while *tacking. But see also CLUB HAUL, TO.

sternpost, originally the timber member rising from the *aft end of the keel. It formed the centreline structure for the aft end of the vessel from which the *rudder was hung. In the early days of *steam propulsion the sternpost became part of the stern frame as modifications were made to accept shaft bearings and *propeller apertures. With the introduction of multiple propellers, and rudders supported by separate *skegs, the term is now seldom used in *shipbuilding or *naval architecture.

stern rope, see BERTHING HAWSERS.

sternsheets, that part of an open boat between the stern and the after *thwart, usually fitted with seats for passengers. It is occasionally written as stern-sheets but the single word is the more correct usage. No doubt it was so named because the main sheet was handled from this position when the boat was under sail.

sternwalk, a roofed platform built around the stern of some large ships, particularly warships, up to about 1914, when they were largely discarded. They connected with the main *cabin and were fitted so that the admiral or captain could take the air without having to come on deck. They were the more modern version of the *gallery of ancient sailing ships.

sternway, the movement of a ship when it is going backwards in relation to the ground. In its most usual form the term is used to mean motion backwards through the water, either by the use of engines running *astern or, in the case of a sailing vessel, by laying a sail *aback. But a ship lying stopped in the water and carried backwards by an adverse *tide is also said to be **carrying sternway** even though it may not be making any movement through the water.

stevedore, a docker who is employed loading or unloading a merchant ship in port.

stiff. **(1)** An adjective which, when applied to a ship, indicates that it returns quickly to the vertical when rolling in a heavy seaway and, when applied to a vessel under sail, that it is one that stands up well in a wind. This is a function in *naval architecture of the metacentric height which has been built into the ship. See also TENDER. **(2)** It is also an adjective which is applied to the strength of the wind, a stiff breeze being one in which a *square-rigger is able to carry all her sails.

stinkpot, a favourite weapon of the Chinese. It was an earthenware pot, part filled with sulphur, black powder, nails, and *shot, while the other part was filled with noxious materials designed to emit a highly unpleasant and suffocating smell when ignited. Several of these bombs were wrapped in calico bags and were then hoisted in a basket to the *truck of the mast. When an enemy ship was alongside, one of the crew climbed the mast and primed the stinkpots with lighted joss sticks. The stinkpots were then launched onto the deck of the enemy by cutting the rope by which the basket had been hoisted. The ensuing noise, flying debris, and smell would create, it was hoped, sufficient confusion for the enemy crew to be overcome.

More or less the same device, but fitted with a touch-hole and fuse, was employed by *privateers during the 18th and early 19th centuries when attempting to board and capture a ship. 'The fuses of the stinkpot being lighted, they are immediately thrown upon the deck of the enemy, where they burst and catch fire, producing an intolerable stench and smoke, and filling the deck with tumult and distraction. Amidst the confusion occasioned by this infernal apparatus the [boarding] detachment rush aboard sword in hand, under cover of the smoke' (Falconer, *Marine Dictionary* (1771)). Alternatively, the stinkpots were suspended from the *yardarms (as done by the Chinese), and cut adrift when the two ships came together. As the yardarms projected over the vessel being attacked, they fell on the enemy's deck.

stirrups, the name given to the short ropes which hang from the *yards of *square-rigged sailing ships and support at intervals the *footropes on which the *topmen stand when working on the sails aloft. For illus. see YARD.

stock, the horizontal crosspiece of an *Admiralty pattern, or fisherman's, anchor, set right angles to the arms of the anchor so that when hitting the sea bottom it will turn the anchor to bring the arms vertical, enabling the anchor *flukes to bite into the ground. For illus. see ANCHOR.

stocks, another name for *keel blocks, the line of blocks in a building berth on which the keel of a ship is laid when being constructed. So a vessel **on the stocks** is one being built. See also SHIPBUILDING.

stone frigate, Royal Navy slang for a shore establishment.

stop, to, to roll up, or bunch, with a few turns of *spunyarn, a sail which has been hoisted on its *halyards, but which is not required to operate as a sail immediately. When it is required, a sharp pull on its sheets will break it out of its **stops** and it will then set properly.

stopper, the name given to a short length of rope. While secured at one end it is used to hold temporarily, with a stopper *hitch, parts of the running *rigging of sailing ships while the *fall is being belayed. A **stopper hitch** is a *rolling hitch in which the second turn rides over the first. A **chain stopper** is a metal grab designed to hold a ship's anchor *cable. See also CABLE STOPPERS; COMPRESSOR; ROPE CLUTCH.

stopper knot, a name generally used for any knot in which the *strands are tucked back to form a knob at the end of the rope as a stop where, for example, the rope is threaded through an *eye or a ringbolt, perhaps for use as a handrope. Examples of this type of knot are a *turk's head or *Matthew Walker knot. However, strictly speaking, a stopper knot is another name for a single or double *wall knot.

storm, a wind whose average speed lies between 48 and 63 knots, i.e. force 10 and 11 on the *Beaufort Scale. The two types of storm recognized depend on the wind speed, from 48 to 53 knots being known as a storm, and from 56 to 63 knots being known as a violent storm. Winds blowing above 63 knots are classed as hurricanes, or *tropical storms. As with a *gale, the state of the sea gives an indication of the strength of the storm. When the *waves are very high with long, overhanging crests, and the sea takes on a white appearance from the foam blown from them, a storm is in progress. In a violent storm the waves are so high that small and medium-sized ships are for a long time lost to view behind the waves, the sea is covered with long white patches of foam, the wave crests are blown into froth, and visibility is seriously affected by blown spray. For a **storm surge** see WAVES.

storm signals, signals where black *canvas cones were hoisted at *coastguard stations and other prominent places along the coast when a *gale was forecast. The number of cones, and the way they were hoisted, indicated from which direction the gale was expected. Storm cones were introduced in 1861 by Robert *Fitzroy, and until recently were still used in some countries.

stowaway, a person who hides himself on board a ship just before it sails in order to obtain a free passage to the ship's destination, or to escape from a country unobserved.

strake, the name given to each line of planking in a wooden vessel, or plating in a vessel built of steel, which runs the length of the ship's hull. The hull form therefore consists of rows of strakes from the keel up to the top edge of the vessel's hull.

strand. (1) A number of rope-yarns twisted together, ready to be laid up into a rope with other strands. A rope is said to be **stranded** when one of its strands is broken by too great a strain or worn too thin by chafing. **(2)** As a verb, it describes the state of a ship when it is driven ashore, or onto a *shoal, usually by bad weather.

stray line, the name given to the length of line between the *log and the zero mark on the *log-line before the days of modern means of measuring a ship's speed. This allowed the log to drift well *astern, beyond the reach of any *eddies caused by the motion of the ship, before the *sand-glass was turned and the measurement of the vessel's speed begun.

stream, to, to let an *anchor buoy fall into the sea from the *after part of the ship before an anchor is let go to prevent the buoy-rope being fouled by the anchor or *cable as it ran out. Patent *logs, *fog-buoys, and *sea anchors are, like anchor buoys, said to be streamed when they are run out.

stream anchor, an anchor carried as a spare in some of the larger ships, normally about one-third the weight of the *bower anchors and *sheet anchor, but larger than the *kedge. In many of the larger ships the stream anchor became a stern anchor with its own *hawsepipe in the ship's stern. It had no permanent *cable but, if it was necessary to use it, one of the ship's wire *hawsers was *shackled onto it. It was *weighed by bringing the wire hawser to the *after *capstan.

stretcher. **(1)** A piece of wood fixed *athwartships in the bottom of a pulling boat against which the rowers can brace their feet. **(2)** A short length of wood, notched at both ends, for spreading the *clews of a *hammock when sleeping in it.

strike, to, to lower the *colours of a warship in battle as an indication of surrender. In the days of sail a vessel was also said to strike *soundings when it could reach the bottom with a deep-sea *lead when approaching land.

strike down, to, to lower a mast or *yard to the deck in a *square-rigged ship, or lower heavy articles into the *hold of a ship. Thus *topgallant masts, *topmasts, and yards were struck down when they were lowered to the deck (but see also HOUSE, TO, in the case of masts where they were lowered only sufficiently to lie alongside the mast next below them). Casks were also struck down into the hold of a ship. When, in the days of sailing navies, guns were lowered to the lower gun-deck in very rough weather, to get their weight carried as low as possible, they, too, were said to be struck down.

stringer, the name for what was called, in the early days of *shipbuilding, shelf-pieces, the fore-and-aft members of the structure of a ship's hull. There are **deck stringers** to give added strength to each deck in a ship, **bilge stringers**, and **hold stringers**, each designed to strengthen the frames in these particular localities by holding them firm in the fore-and-aft line.

stripped to the girt-line, the condition of a sailing vessel when all the standing *rigging, *yards, *topmasts, etc., have been stripped off the masts, so that the lower masts are mere poles standing upright without support.

strop, a rope *spliced into a circle for use around the *shell of a *block so as to form an *eye at the bottom; or to form a sling for heavy articles which need to be hoisted with the aid of a *purchase or a *parbuckle to lift them up a slope. Strops are also frequently used to double round a rope or *hawser to form an eye into which a *tackle can be hooked in order to give a greater purchase.

studding sails (pron. stuns'ls), additional sails set outside the main stacks of *square-riggers to increase sail area in suitable conditions. First introduced in the 16th century, they are set from light *spars called studding-sail booms which slide out from the *yards through hoops on the yard and at the *yardarm. The sail is hoisted by a *halyard from the end of the boom attached to a light yard to which it is *laced. The sheet is taken to a similar boom extending from a lower yard or from the deck. They are usually set between the *topgallant yards and the *topsail yards, and the topsail yards and the *course yards. **Lower studding sails** also used to be set below the course yards but this is rarely seen these days. A common practice was to use a topmast studding sail on the *weather side to help balance the *helm. For illus. see SQUARE RIG.

submarine, a vessel designed to operate below the surface of the sea. Its hull must be circular in transverse section to withstand the pressure of water to which it is subject when submerged. It must be fitted with *ballast tanks to which water can be admitted to destroy its positive buoyancy when it wants to dive and from which the water can be expelled by compressed air when it wants to surface. To control the depth when the submarine is under way submerged, it needs horizontal *rudders, and when dived it must have a propulsion system capable of operating without a supply of air.

Until the advent of nuclear power, this could only be provided by electric motors powered by batteries. The endurance of the batteries was comparatively limited. To recharge them submarine had to use its *diesel engines—on *steam propulsion in the case of the *K-class—which meant coming to the surface or employing its *schnorkel.

Lengthways, the hull of the earlier submarines was cigar shaped, but it has now been found that optimum results are attained with a teardrop design of hull. Until the advent of nuclear-powered submarines, all others were really submersibles, that is they could not remain underwater permanently, but see also UNDERWATER VEHICLES.

Early Submarines. Between 1578 and 1763 some seventeen designs of submarines have been recorded, and among the early pioneers of submarine design were the Americans David *Bushnell and Robert *Fulton. Further impetus was given to the design of submarines by the introduction of metal to *shipbuilding, and in the latter half of the 19th century American and French engineers produced a number of models. During the American Civil War (1861–5) the *'David' submersibles were not a success, but the *H. L. Hunley* of the *Confederate States Navy was the first submarine ever to sink a ship when she sank the USS *Housatonic* with a *spar torpedo, though all her crew were killed in doing so.

At the turn of the century the invention of the *diesel engine, coupled with that of the electric motor and the Whitehead torpedo, enabled real progress to be made with an effective design for a submarine. Credit for the design of the first really workable one belongs to the Irish-born American J. P. Holland (1840–1914), whose designs were accepted by the US Navy. The first five submarines built in Britain were also based on his design. They displaced 105 tons on the surface and had surface and submerged speeds of 8.5 and 7 knots respectively. Their surface endurance was 800 kilometres (500 mls.) at 7 knots using petrol-driven engines. In Germany it was decided to await the perfection of the much safer diesel engine before embarking on the construction of the first of a long line of U-boats (short for *Unterseeboot*) which were to play such an important part in the First (1914–18) and Second (1939–45) World Wars.

The Submarine in Two World Wars. In 1914 there were some 400 submarines distributed among sixteen navies, of which Britain and France accounted for about half the total. Britain entered the war with 74 submarines and 31 building, Germany with 33 built and 28 building, but whereas most of the British boats were of a small, coastal type, the majority of those in the German Navy were overseas types ranging between 550 and 850 tons *displacement. During the war both sides built a number of submarines of varying types which included minelayers, a role for which the submarine is specially suitable. German construction was far and away the largest and ranged from the coastal UB types of 125–250 tons to the cruiser types of 1,700–3,200 tons capable of crossing the Atlantic.

Though there was little change in the basic design of submarines between the two world wars, they did play a much larger part in the war than in 1914–18, and the battle of the Atlantic, in which wolfpacks of U-boats attacked Allied *convoys to sever the transatlantic supply route, was a crucial one. What were new were the midget-type submarines, developed initially by the Italians, who had pioneered them during the First World War, the Japanese, and later the British and Germans, to attack warships in defended harbours which conventional submarines had little chance of penetrating. Two of the most spectacular operations were the Japanese raid on Sydney harbour in May 1942, and the crippling of the German *battleship *Tirpitz* in September 1943 in Trondheim, Norway. Another important development in submarine warfare came in 1944 when Germany began to fit its U-boats with schnorkels which gave them a definite advantage, but by then the battle of the Atlantic had been won.

Nuclear-Powered Submarines. In 1948 the US Atomic Energy Commission awarded a contract to the Westinghouse Electrical Company to develop a nuclear propulsion plant suitable for installation in a submarine, and on 14 June 1952 the keel of the first nuclear-powered submarine, USS **Nautilus*, was laid. Its completion meant that at long last the true submarine was a reality and in 1960 another nuclear-powered submarine, the USS *Triton*, made a circumnavigation of just over 40,000 kilometres (30,708 mls.) in 61 days without surfacing. The nuclear reactor fitted in vessels of this type is used to generate steam in much the same way as the ordinary boiler, but with certain modifications to prevent radiation injury to the crew. Since the reactor functions without the use of oxygen, the only factor limiting the time the submarine can remain submerged is the revitalization of the air to enable the crew to breathe. This is overcome by air-purifying machinery which enables the vessel to remain submerged almost indefinitely, and the modern nuclear-powered submarine, which is armed with nuclear warheads which can be fired from below the surface, can operate submerged at or near its maximum speed of about 30 knots for as long as is operationally necessary.

With the end of the Cold War the US Navy's force of nuclear-powered submarines is having to face change to meet the requirements of the navy's future strategy which was made public in 2002. For a start, four 'Ohio'-class submarines have been armed with cruise missiles for attacking land targets and for handling Special Forces.

The problem of the only instance of a nuclear-powered submarine firing in anger was when HMS *Conqueror* torpedoed the Argentine cruiser *General Belgrano* during the Falklands conflict in 1982. She tracked her for two days before attacking, which would have been beyond the capability of any conventional submarine.

The problem of the disposal of Britain's redundant nuclear-powered submarines has yet to be solved. Currently (2004) there are eleven tied up in two British naval dockyards. The oldest, the *Dreadnought*, first brought into service in 1960, has been tied up since 1983. See also WARFARE AT SEA.

sucking the monkey, the illicit act by British naval seamen of using a straw to siphon off rum from its container, a 'monkey' being the sailors' description of the vessel in which they collected their *grog. During the American War of Independence (1775–82) British sailors persuaded the local West Indian women, who came aboard to sell fresh coconuts, to empty them of their milk beforehand and fill the coconuts with rum instead. When the contents were extracted with a straw this, too, was known as sucking the monkey. The drunkenness that resulted on board remained an unexplained phenomenon for years.

Suez Canal. The canal, still one of the world's most heavily used shipping lanes, is 163 kilometres (101 mls.) long, and connects the Mediterranean at Port Said with the Red Sea at Port Suez. Proposals for such a waterway date back over 4,000 years, and during the Roman occupation of Egypt work was started in cutting a canal. This linked the River Nile with the Red Sea along the course of a previous small canal which had been in existence 700 years earlier. However, this venture never reached fruition, nor did the plans drawn up by one of Napoleon's engineers when France occupied Egypt at the beginning of the 19th century. It was eventually begun in 1859 after its progenitor, the French diplomat Ferdinand de *Lesseps, won from the Egyptian Khedive the right to build the canal and to lease it until 1969. It took ten years to build instead of the expected six and was not constructed across the shortest part of the isthmus, which is 120 kilometres (75 mls.), but deviated in order to use several lakes. It has no locks.

The Canal was officially inaugurated by Empress Eugénie in November 1869. During its first full year only some 486 vessels used it, but by the end of the Second World War (1939–45) both passenger and commercial traffic had reached a high volume. However, in July 1956, after Britain and the USA had decided not to finance Egypt's Aswan Dam, the Egyptian President, Gamal Abdel Nasser, nationalized the Canal to pay for the dam, precipitating what became known as the Suez Crisis. After diplomacy failed, Britain, France, and Israel invaded Egypt, the first two on the pretext of restoring order between Egypt and Israel, but in reality to seize control of the Canal and overthrow Nasser. Pressure from the USA and the world community soon brought the invasion to an end, and the Canal, after being blocked by Egypt, was soon back in commercial use. By 1966 traffic had grown to 21,250 transits annually, but the following year, during the six-day Arab–Israeli War, the Egyptians blocked the Canal again and it remained closed until 1975. By the time it reopened the *tonnage of *tankers had necessarily increased to enable them to carry sufficient oil round the longer Cape of Good Hope route, which made many of them too large for the Canal. This, and a changing pattern in world trade, lost the Canal much of its strategic importance as a waterway. Nevertheless, employing a long-established *convoy system, and with the help of some enlargement along the route, the waterway, which takes around fourteen hours to negotiate, is currently (2004) used by *container ships and *ro-ro vessels, and by empty supertankers as big as 200,000 deadweight tonnes.

Sumner position line, effectively the concept on which nearly all modern *celestial navigation is based. The voyage which gave birth to the idea of the astronomical position line was made in December 1837 when an American, Captain Thomas H. Sumner, was approaching the south coast of Ireland on passage from Charleston, SC, to Greenock in Scotland. The weather had been overcast and foggy for some days, and Sumner, unable to get a *sight for days, was navigating by *dead reckoning. Of 17 December, Sumner wrote: 'the ship was kept on ENE under short sail with gales. At about 10 a.m. an *altitude of the sun was observed and the *chronometer time noted; but ... it was plain that the *latitude by DR could not be relied upon. Using this latitude in finding the *longitude by chronometer it was found to put the ship 15° of longitude east ... which is 9° *nautical miles. This seemed to agree ... with the DR ... but the observation was tried with a latitude 10 further north. This placed the ship ENE 27 miles of the former position and was tried again with a latitude 20° north of the DR. This also placed the ship still further ENE and still 27 miles. These three positions were then seen to lie in the direction of the Smalls Light. It appeared that the observed altitudes must have happened at all three points and at the Smalls Light and at the ship at the same time, and it followed that the Smalls Light must bear ENE,' which indeed proved to be the case. Although he (rightly) described the concept in terms of position circles the first astronomical position line was nevertheless undoubtedly that through the Smalls Light. Sumner described his method in a pamphlet published in Boston in 1843. See also MARCQ SAINT-HILAIRE METHOD.

Mike Richey

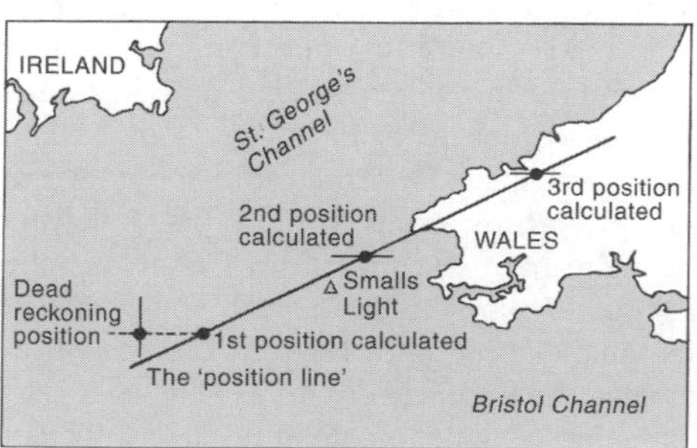

Sumner position line, 17 December 1837

'sundowner', a slang name for a bullying officer in a ship. The origin of the name comes from those captains who would only give shore leave to their crews up to the time of sunset.

'sun is over the yardarm, the', a traditional nautical saying to indicate that it is time for a morning drink. It was generally assumed in northern *latitudes the sun would show above the foreyard of a ship by 1100, which was about the time in many ships of the forenoon 'stand-easy', when many officers would slip below for their first drink of the day.

supercargo, an abbreviation of cargo superintendent, a representative of the ship's owner on board a merchant ship who looked after all commercial business in connection with the ship and its cargo during a voyage. Now obsolete. See also HUSBAND.

superstitions of sailors. Although a great many of the old superstitions of seamen, which initially owed their origin to the desire of mariners of ancient times to guard themselves against the unknown dangers of the sea, have been forgotten or are now ignored by the sophisticated sailor of today, some still linger on. For example, in classical times it was the custom when *launching a ship, or before sailing on a long voyage, to offer a libation to the gods of the sea, such as *Fortunus and *Neptune.

Another superstition dating from classical times was that to be successful a warship's keel must taste the blood of a live person during its launching, and the same ceremony was also practised when Norse *longships were launched. In the Mediterranean, when a *galley was launched, a slave was tied down on the *keel blocks so that as the galley gathered speed on its way into the sea, his body was crushed and his blood splashed the vessel's keel and hull, and his head was then mounted on the vessel's stemhead. This custom survived almost into the 20th century when Solomon Islanders were still fixing the head of a killed enemy onto the stemheads of their newly built *canoes. The natives of the Celebes used to do the same but by the mid-20th century they simply smeared the blood from a cock onto the bow and *sternpost. The ritual of mounting a head on the bows of a vessel has continued almost to the present day with *figureheads.

It used to be an ill omen to start a voyage on certain days of the week. Friday was one, the origin for this being that the Crucifixion took place on a Friday. Other days are the first Monday in April, believed to be the birthday of Cain and the day on which Abel was killed; the second Monday in August, thought to be the day on which Sodom and Gomorrah were destroyed; and 31 December, the anniversary of the day on which Judas Iscariot hanged himself. Another omen was that if the cargo being brought on board heeled the ship to steerboard, or *starboard, *storms would blow; but if it heeled to ladeboard (see LADE, TO) then the voyage would be successful.

Flowers carried on board ship were thought by some seamen to be destined to form a wreath, either for a death on board or for the loss of the ship with all its company. This belief used to be very strongly held among the crews of *submarines. Priests, because of their black dress and their office of burying the dead, were unlucky to have as passengers on board, as were women, it being held that the sea grew angry at the sight of a woman. This superstition was also strongly held by fishermen, and up to the end of the 19th century, in the Firth of Forth, a fisherman would refuse to go to sea if a bare-footed woman crossed his path while on his way to his boat. Yet many seamen used to believe that *gales and high winds would subside if a naked woman appeared before them. It was for this reason that so many ships' figureheads showed a woman with a naked breast.

In Kuwait, Alan *Villiers reported (*Geographical Magazine*, 20 (1948), 350, see R. Bowen, 'Maritime Superstitions of the Arabs', *American Neptune*, 15 (1955), 5), it was believed that if a barren woman leapt over the keel of a new boat before the planking was high enough to stop her, she would conceive a male child. However, if she did succeed in jumping over it, one of the carpenters working on the boat would die, or the captain would die during the vessel's maiden voyage. Guards were therefore posted to prevent any woman approaching the vessel. A similar superstition was prevalent among fishermen in western Europe where a woman was not allowed to step over their nets or gear.

When the art of *tattooing became popular a pig and a rooster tattooed onto a sailor's feet were said to prevent him from drowning by showing him the way ashore.

Phantom ships, such as the **Flying Dutchman*, were the source of many sailors' superstitions, one of them being that anyone sighting such a ship would be struck blind, or die, or his ship would be wrecked. *St Elmo's Fire was also the source of a similar superstition: if the light of the fire fell upon a man's face, he would die within 24 hours, and few of the older seamen would dare to look directly at the phenomenon when it appeared. Possibly the two superstitions were connected in some way. However, St Elmo's Fire was also held to be a heaven-sent warning either of an approaching storm, so that a ship's crew could prepare themselves, or that the worst of a storm had passed.

Some superstitions defy analysis. To some seamen the loss overboard of a bucket or a mop is an omen of misfortune, to others it is unlucky to repair a flag on a ship's *quarterdeck or to hand a flag to a sailor between the rungs of a ladder. Black travelling bags bring misfortune, and to hear bells at sea is a sign of forthcoming death. It is also considered unlucky to wear a *sailor's dress who has died at sea while the voyage is in progress; though once it is over no calamity will follow.

A very well-known superstition, which existed among many sailors up to the beginning of the 20th century, was that the possession of the caul of a new-born child was a sure prevention against death by drowning. Advertisements by sailors in newspapers for a caul were not uncommon, and the price offered was occasionally as much as £30.

On the Isle of Man, and among some other seafaring communities, possession of the feather of a wren was supposed to be a safeguard against death by *shipwreck. The origin of this belief came from the tale of a beautiful *mermaid who lured seamen to their death by singing to them in a voice so sweet that they had to follow. A knight errant, in a desire to save the seamen, discovered a means of counteracting these siren charms but was foiled by the mermaid changing herself into a wren. As a penance for thus circumventing her just deserts, she was condemned to appear as a wren on New Year's Day every year. This legend unhappily led to a brisk demand among sailors for a wren's tail or wing feather, and a considerable slaughter of these attractive small birds followed, particularly on New Year's Day, as the feather of a bird killed on that day was especially valued. The efficacy of the feather lasted for only one year, so the slaughter became annual.

Another, equally well-known, seaman's superstition is that to whistle in a calm will bring a wind, but to whistle on board when the wind is blowing is to bring a gale. Another belief is that a wind can also be brought by throwing the head of an old broom overboard in the direction from which the wind is desired. See also MOTHER CAREY'S CHICKENS; MOON-LORE.

superstructure, the constructions on board a ship that are above the level of the upper deck. It would include the whole of the *bridge structure and the deckhouse.

surface effect ship, the generic name for a ship operating on the boundary of air and water. The range includes *hovercraft and *hydrofoils as well as wave-piercing *catamarans and *SWATH ships which are designed to cut through *waves instead of riding over them. Vessels which use the lift effect of water in close proximity to the hull are known as *wing-in-surface effect ships. For illus. see CORVETTE.

surf boat, a large open craft, usually controlled by a *steering oar. Propelled by paddles, it was used in the past on beaches in Africa and India for landing passengers and goods from ships which, because there were no deep water ports and the depth of water offshore was very shallow, had to lie a long way offshore. The construction of deep water ports in even the most remote areas has long since made surf boats redundant in these places, but they are still employed in Australia for *life-saving, where they are propelled by *oars.

surge, to. **(1)** To stop the pull on a line or *hawser when it is being brought in round a *capstan or *winch. This is done by walking back on the hauling part so that the capstan or winch still revolves with the line or hawser *rendering round it without coming in, and is a means of regulating the rate of pull with a capstan or winch turning at a constant speed. **(2)** As a noun it indicates the tapered part of the *whelps of a capstan. **(3)** A *scend or exceptional run of the sea into a harbour. For a **storm surge** see WAVES.

swallow, the name given to the space between the two sides of the *shell of a *block in which the *sheave is fitted.

'swallow the anchor, to', a nautical term meaning to retire from sea life and settle down ashore.

SWATH ship (Small Waterplane Area Twin Hull), a *catamaran ship—though the technology is equally applicable to a *trimaran hull—which is shorter than a monohull or conventional catamaran of equal displacement *tonnage. The basis of the design is twin underwater torpedo-shaped hulls to which are attached two or more streamlined struts. These pierce the water surface and are connected to a platform deck designed for cargo or passengers by means of what is known as the haunch. It is usual for each submersed hull to have independent machinery. The advantage of this design is that a large proportion of the hull stays below the surface which reduces *wave drag and increases *stability, giving smaller vessels the steadiness associated with much larger ones. It is also more economical as less power is needed to climb the waves, and it can sustain higher speed in rough weather than a conventional vessel. The theory of SWATH was developed by Dr Thomas G. L. Lang in the late 1960s. and the US Navy commissioned a SWATH ship in the 1970s which has proved successful. The technology is now being employed to build *ferries and small *cruise ships. SLICE (not an acronym) technology is now being developed, using underwater propulsion pods (see PROPELLER), which allows SWATH ships higher speed through the water without sacrificing stability.

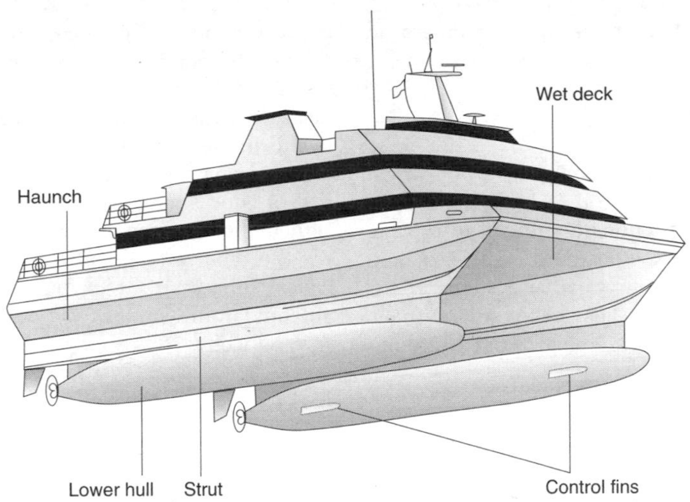

SWATH International's Super-4000 Class Ferry

sway, a term used to imply hoisting. It is particularly used where sailing ships use their own rig to hoist components such as *yards and upper masts.

sweat, to, before the days of *winches, to get the last bit of *hoist, particularly with *halyards, to avoid any slackness when setting of a sail by hand. A halyard was **sweated up** by taking a single turn round a *cleat, hauling the *standing part out from the mast horizontally while keeping tension on the end to prevent it slipping on the cleat. This raised the sail fractionally. The slack was then taken up round the cleat as the halyard was released so that the extra hoist gained was not lost.

sweep, a long, heavy *oar carried in sailing vessels, before the days of auxiliary power, for use when the wind failed. In the days of sailing navies they were carried in the smallest class of *frigates and in all vessels below that rating. Commercial craft such as *smacks and *barges, and also *yachts, would carry at least one on board.

swell, a condition of the sea resulting from *storms or high winds. It is the vertical movement of surface water in the form of *waves or undulations retaining the motion imparted to it by the wind for a period after the wind has dropped. They eventually die out as the resistance of the surrounding water takes effect and slows the motion down. The length of a swell is proportional to the *fetch.

swifter. (1) A 3.8-centimetre (1.5-in.) or 5-centimetre (2-in.) rope with a *cut splice in the centre, a *thimble at one end, and tapered at the other. Its purpose was to *lash together the ends of the *capstan bars when *weighing anchor by hand. The central cut splice was placed in the slot at the end of a capstan bar and the swifter passed from bar to bar, being secured to the end of each bar by means of two turns through the slot, the first inside and the second outside its standing part. Its purpose was to provide extra accommodation for the men weighing the anchor, as it could be manned as well as the bars. **(2)** The foremost *shrouds of each lower mast were also known as swifters.

swim, to, an old nautical verb used largely by seamen up to at least the start of the 17th century to describe the progress of a ship through the water. A ship would 'swimme well', or 'swimme ill', according to its speed under sail. Matthew Baker, who drew the designs for Queen Elizabeth I's warships, drew the underwater part of his ships in the form of a great *fish to indicate that they would swim well under sail.

swing a ship, to, to steady a ship on a succession of *magnetic compass headings to ascertain the *deviations of the compass on those headings.

swing keel, see KEEL.

synoptic chart, a weather *chart on which the isobars derived from a large number of weather station reports are drawn to provide a full picture of the position, shape, size, and depth of the various weather systems in the area covered by it. These charts are normally kept up to date in meteorological offices around the world and, by a comparison with previous ones of the same area, meteorologists can see the directions in which movements are taking place and thus predict the weather patterns in the immediate future. The distance apart of the isobars gives a basis for the prediction of wind strengths; the closer they are together, the stronger the wind is likely to be. Weather forecasts broadcast from meteorological offices are based on the information obtained from synoptic charts. See also MARINE METEOROLOGY.

T

tabernacle, a wooden or metal trunk fixed to the deck of a sailing vessel to support a mast which has its *heel at deck level and is not *stepped below decks. It is used when it is necessary occasionally to lower the mast to deck level, as in inland waters for passing under bridges etc. The mast is pivoted on a steel pin which passes through the top of the tabernacle, the forward side of the tabernacle being left open to allow the heel of the mast to swing forward as the mast is lowered *aft. A slightly different fitting, known as a *lutchet but serving the same purpose, is used in *spritsail *barges and *wherries.

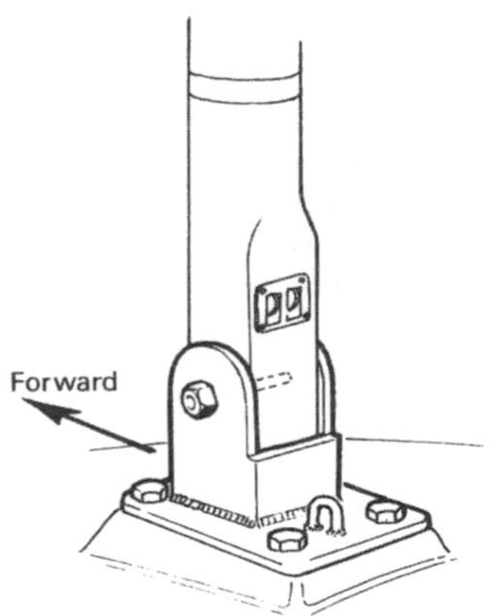

Tabernacle

table, to, a sailmaker's term meaning to sew *reef bands and *buntline bands onto sails to add extra strength to the sail where the *reef-points are fixed, and to prevent chafe in a square sail where the buntline lies along it. It is only the larger sails, particularly in *square-rigged ships, that have these bands tabled onto them.

tabling, the name given to an extra strip of sailcloth sewn around the edges of sails to reinforce them where the *bolt-rope is sewn on.

tack. (1) A *board or *reach sailed in a sailing vessel with the wind kept on one side of the vessel. See also LEG; PORT TACK; STARBOARD TACK. **(2)** The name given to the lower forward corner of a sail in a *fore-and-aft rig. **(3)** In *square-rigged sailing ships, it is the name of the rope used to hold in the *weather lower corners of *courses and *staysails when sailing *close hauled. Also, when *studding sails were set, it was the name given to the rope employed to haul out the lower outer *clew of the sail to the end of the boom. **(4)** When used as a verb, it describes the operation of bringing a sailing vessel head to wind and across it so as to bring the wind on the opposite side of the vessel.

tackle (pron. taykle), a *purchase in which two or more *blocks are used in order to multiply the power exerted on a rope. The gain in power is equivalent to the number of parts which enter and leave the moving block of the tackle, depending on whether it is rigged to *advantage or disadvantage. Before the introduction of *auxiliary power, tackles were employed for most lifting and or moving jobs in a vessel. There were many types, depending on their purpose and also on the number and nature of the blocks used.

tackline. (1) A 1.8-metre (6-ft) length of signal line with signal clips, known as inglefield clips, at each end. It is used, mainly in naval vessels, for inserting in a flag signal hoist to indicated a break in the signal, and that the flags below it form a new signal. All flags used in *signals at sea have an inglefield clip at each end of the *hoist so that they can be clipped quickly to each other to form a particular signal; those on the tackline are of the same pattern and can be clipped equally quickly to signal flags when it is required to insert a break in the hoist. See also INTERNATIONAL CODE OF SIGNALS. **(2)** A rope, or 'tack', used to control the lower corner of a *course when a *square-rigged ship is going to *windward.

tactical diameter, the distance a ship is displaced to *port or *starboard of its original line of advance after a turn of 180° under full *helm at full speed.

taffrail. **(1)** In strict definition, the *after rail at the stern of a ship, but formerly the curved wooden top of the stern of a sailing warship or *East Indiaman, usually carved or otherwise decorated. It is a contraction of taffarel, the original name for this adornment. In its modern meaning it is often used to indicate the deck area right at the stern of a vessel. **(2)** The pseudonym of a British naval captain, Henry Taprell Dorling (1883–1968), a writer of popular stories of the sea.

tail, to, to haul in on a sheet or *halyard that is wrapped around the drum of a *winch.

Talbot, Mary Anne (1778–1808), known as the 'British Amazon', the youngest of sixteen illegitimate children of Lord William Talbot, later Earl Talbot, all by the same mother. As a young girl Mary Anne was seduced by a captain in the army and, suitably disguised, she accompanied him, first as a servant and then as a member of his regiment. She was twice wounded, deserted after her lover was killed, and signed on to a French *lugger which she subsequently found to be operating as a *privateer. After four months the lugger was captured by warships of the British Navy's Channel Fleet commanded by Lord Howe, and Mary Anne was taken aboard the flagship for questioning as a renegade. She convinced Lord Howe of her bona fides and was sent by him to serve aboard one of the fleet's warships, first as a *powder monkey and later as the captain's principal cabin boy, and in 1794 took part in the battle of the Glorious First of June in which she was wounded. She then served, according to her own account, as a *midshipman in a *bomb vessel, but was captured and imprisoned at Dunkirk for sixteen months. On being released, she served as second *mate on an American merchant ship but this, too, ended in disaster when, after a voyage to New York and back, she was taken by a *press gang. Her only means of escaping their clutches was to reveal her sex, and from then on she seems to have had an even more chequered career: she worked as a goldsmith's assistant before becoming an actress, was in and out of prison for debt, and was even a prostitute on the side. She wrote an account of her adventures which was first published in the second volume of Kirby's *Wonderful Museum of Remarkable Characters*, and in 1809 was published separately as a pamphlet called *The Life and Surprising Adventures of Mary Anne Talbot*.

tall ships, non-nautical term for ships with high masts, usually *square-rigged ones. See also SAIL TRAINING.

Talurit® splicing, a trademarked method of splicing wire rope when a *thimble or *eye is required at the end. The end of the wire is threaded through a non-corrosive alloy ferrule of a size convenient for the wire and then threaded back to form a loop round the thimble. The ferrule is then gripped lightly in a hydraulic press while the wire is pulled through to make the loop the required size or to lie closely round the thimble. Further pressure is then exerted to make the metal of the ferrule flow round the strands of the wire, thus holding each firmly in position, and the splice is complete.

A Talurit® splice is as strong as a fully tucked eyesplice and is more economical in the use of the rope. When making an eyesplice by hand, 30 centimetres (1 ft) of the wire is needed for tucking for every 2.5 centimetres (1 in.) of its circumference; the Talurit® method uses only 2.5 centimetres for the whole splice.

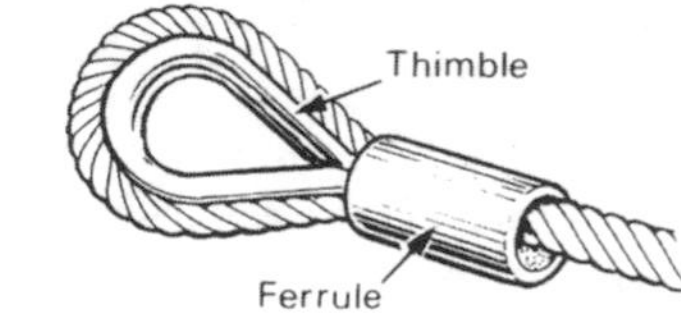

Talurit® splicing

tan, to, in the days of sail, to preserve the life of *canvas sails by dressing them with *cutch. The sails were immersed in a cutch solution for two or three hours, then hung over a *spar to dry. The resultant colour was a rich deep red. When the sail was dry the cutch was fixed in the canvas by brushing into the sail, or immersing it in a solution of 0.45 kilograms (1 lb) of bichromate to 18.2 litres (4 gals.) of fresh water, and this fixing process changed the colour of the sails to mahogany.

tanker. Since time immemorial ships have carried casks of wine, water, and other liquids. Around 1860 the carriage of cased oils across the Atlantic commenced, and by 1886 the experience gained enabled two vessels dedicated to the carriage of oil, the *Gluckauf* and the *Bakuin*, to be delivered by shipyards in north-east England. It signalled the start of a massive industry.

Tankers have always been recognizable by having their machinery and *bridges *aft and all cargo carried amidships, in the widest and most capacious part of the ship. For *stability in all conditions the cargo tanks have longitudinal *bulkheads which divide the tanks *athwartships into three or four and longitudinally into any number up to eleven or twelve, ensuring the ship has 'packets' of cargo.

The size of tankers has risen dramatically from the time of *Gluckauf*, which lifted 2,700 tons of oil. The blocking of the *Suez Canal during the 1956 Suez war prompted much larger tankers to be built to make it economical to transport oil round the Cape of Good Hope, and by the mid-1960s, tankers began to exceed 200,000 deadweight *tonnage. The deadweight is the mass of cargo carried, the two largest groups of tanker types being known as VLCC (Very Large Crude Carrier), which carry from 150,000 tonnes up to 300,000 tonnes deadweight, and ULCC (Ultra Large Crude Carrier), which carry 300,000 tonnes upwards. Today the largest tankers can take over 500,000 tonnes of cargo.

Since the Second World War (1939–45), tankers traditionally built for the oil trade,

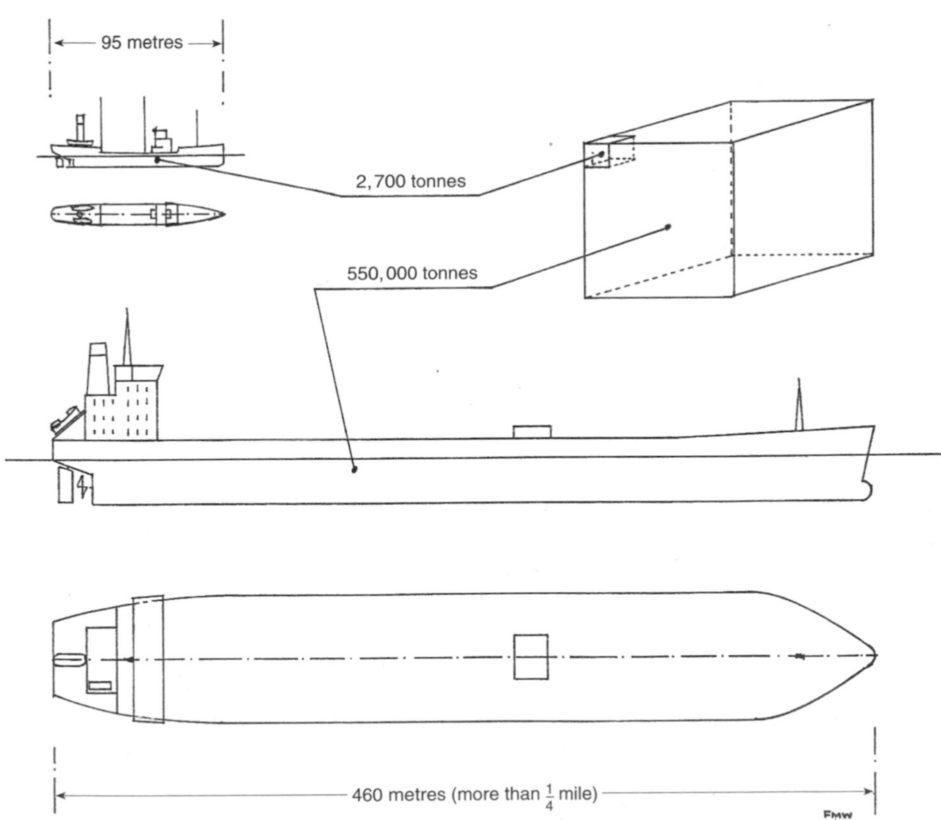

Relative size and cargo capacity of tankers c.1890 and 2001

have been delivered to carry cargoes as diverse as orange juice, vegetable oil, and even beer—the *Miranda Guinness*, completed in Bristol in 1976, could carry 2 million pints of stout across the Irish Sea! Tankers transporting bituminous materials carry this at temperatures reaching 250 °C, and must maintain these temperatures throughout the voyage. There are also what is known as Products Tankers which are designed to carry several cargoes ranging from noxious compounds through to specialist oils. Such tankers have independent piping systems, which guarantee that each cargo is free from contamination; often they have stainless steel tanks and their construction has been monitored throughout by 100% X-rays.

The most advanced Product Tankers are the LPG (Liquid Petroleum Gas) and LNG (Liquid Natural Gas) carriers. The former carries butane, propane, and similar gases which are liquefied under pressure. But the LPG has never achieved the success of its 'high-tech' sister, the LNG ship, which transports methane-type gases liquefied by temperature reduction to –163 °C or 100° Kelvin. This light gas can be compressed to less than one-six hundredth of its original volume and it then forms a liquid about half the density of water enabling efficient transportation to take place. The difficulty is that at 100° Kelvin, the steel structure of the ship becomes as brittle as sheet *ice, which means the tanks carrying the gas must be insulated from the structural hull of the ship.

Since the 1960s there have been several serious accidents to tankers, resulting in oil spillage which has raised serious *environmental issues. After consideration, the international community, through the *International Maritime Organization, has decreed that all new tankers must have *double bottoms to reduce the risk of *pollution following collision or grounding. This has brought other problems, in particular with corrosion, but has set new benchmarks for safety. See also RED TIDES.

Fred M. Walker

tar, the residue after distillation of the gum extracted from pine trees and used during the days of sail, among many other purposes, for the preservation of the standing *rigging and rope such as *hemp and *sisal. See also JACK TAR; SAILORS' DRESS.

tarpaulin, orig. **tarpawling,** originally the weatherproof *sailors' dress seamen made on board. However, from about 1750 it became the description for the painted *canvas used for covering the *hatches of cargo ships and for the protection of other gear, such as the reels on which wire rope is wound, which might suffer from sea water in rough weather.

tarpaulin captain, a captain of a British naval ship in the reigns of the Tudor and Stuart monarchs who had risen by promotion through service in the navy, as opposed to the courtiers who were appointed to posts of command simply because of their influence at court. There was always great bitterness between tarpaulin captains and what were known as *gentlemen captains, for, as Sir Henry Mainwaring wrote in his *Discourse on Pirates* (1617), the ability to command a ship with 'discretion and judgement, to manage, handle, content and command the company, both in fear and love' was beyond the capability of the gentleman captain. That crews also preferred to be commanded by a tarpaulin captain can be appreciated by the example of a dozen seamen at the funeral of a tarpaulin captain, Sir Christopher Myngs, who was killed in 1666 during the Second Anglo-Dutch War (1665–7). They begged to be given a *fireship, a notoriously dangerous form of attacking an enemy, so that they could 'do that that shall show our memory of our dead commander and our revenge'. See also WARFARE AT SEA.

tarpaulin muster, a sailor's name in the days of sail for the pooling of the financial resources of a group of seamen for a run ashore.

tarry-breeks, a north of England name for a seaman, probably from the same origin as *'Tar' or 'Jack Tar', and from the Scottish word for breeches. In a sailor's song, popular in the 18th century, a girl whose mother wanted her to marry a rich husband sings:

> I know you'd have me wed a farmer
> And not give me my heart's delight.
> Mine's the lad whose tarry trousers
> Shine to me like diamonds bright.

tartan, or **tartane,** a small coasting vessel of the Mediterranean, possibly a development of the medieval tarette, which originated with the Arabs for use as a cargo-carrying vessel. Tartans were single masted with a *lateen mainsail and a small *foresail set on a *bowsprit. They carried a crew of about 30 men. Simultaneously, there were in the Mediterranean fishing vessels known as tartanas; unlike the true tartan they had a flat bottom.

Tasman, Abel Janszoon (*c.*1603–59), Dutch *navigator. He was born at Lutjegast, Groningen, and was employed in the service of the Dutch *East India Company from the early 1630s. His first voyage of *exploration by sea was in 1834 when as captain of the *Mocha* he sailed to Ceram (now Seram). Then in 1639 he took part in an expedition to search for 'islands of gold and silver' supposed to exist to the eastward of Japan. But beyond surveying the Bonin Islands, little was found beyond the emptiness of the Pacific Ocean in these northern latitudes.

For the next two years Tasman reverted to his mercantile command, mainly in trading voyages in the Indian Ocean, but in 1642 he was selected by the governor-general of the Dutch East Indies, Antony van Diemen, to command a more ambitious expedition to discover, among other things, if Australia was part of *Terra Australis Incognita that was thought to take up much of the southern hemisphere. Already several Dutch navigators had discovered various parts of the northern and western coasts of Australia, and van Diemen wanted to know more about it.

Tasman's two ships, *Heemskerk* and *Zeehaen*, sailed from Batavia (now Jakarta) to Mauritius, and then sailed south and east, reached the *Roaring Forties. At a *latitude of 49° S., he turned north and saw land which he named Antoonij van Diemen's Landt, in honour of the governor-general, the name being later changed to Tasmania, in honour of himself. He sailed on round the south of Tasmania, not realizing that it was an island separated from Australia, and set a course for the Solomon Islands which, if he was successful, would prove that the 'Great South Land' was not, in fact, part of the great southern continent.

Eight days later he sighted high land ahead of him, which he named Staten Landt (now New Zealand). He sailed along the west coast, mistaking the strait between the two islands, now Cook Strait, for a deep bay, and after rounding the northern end of North Island, which he named Cape Maria van Diemen, he sailed north-north-east, discovering several islands in the Tonga group and the eastern part of the Fiji archipelago, and finally returned to Batavia via the New Hebrides, Solomon Islands, and New Guinea after a voyage lasting ten months. He was thus the first man to make a circumnavigation of mainland Australia, though he never saw it, and so proved it was an island and not a part of the mythical southern continent.

Despite this epic voyage, the authorities were displeased with Tasman for he had failed either to find a route to Chile, as he had been supposed to do, or to explore the new land he had found, and in 1644 he was dispatched on another expedition. This time his voyage, also planned by van Diemen, was designed to discover whether New Guinea and van Diemen's Land were part of the Australian continent. He was given command of three ships, the *Limmen*, *Zeemeeuw*, and *Brak*. After leaving Batavia, he sailed along the west coast of New Guinea, but either mistaking what is now the Torres Strait for a bay, or being unable to penetrate the mass of small islands or *reefs which guard its western entrance, he sheered south into the Gulf of Carpentaria, the southern and western coasts of which he explored and surveyed with some accuracy. He then proceeded westwards along the northern Australian coast, charting the coastline as far south as latitude 22° S., before returning to Batavia. Again, he was not well received on his return, having failed in both the main objectives of his voyage, but was reluctantly confirmed in the rank of commander, a rank which in fact he had already been using for some time.

In 1647 he was placed in command of a trading fleet to Thailand (then Siam), and the following year commanded a war fleet dispatched to operate against the Spaniards in the Philippine Islands in defence of Dutch interests in the East Indies. By now he had amassed a considerable fortune, and in 1653 retired from the Dutch East India Company to settle down and enjoy his wealth as one of the leading citizens of Batavia.

Tasman is generally considered to be the greatest of the Dutch navigators and explorers.

Details of his voyages are published in the *Hakluyt Society's volume *Early Voyages to Terra Australis* (1859).

Sharp, A., The Voyages of Abel Janszoon Tasman (1968).

tattoo. **(1)** A traditional skin decoration for seamen, initially encountered by Captain *Cook in 1769 during his first voyage of circumnavigation. In an entry of his journal he wrote: ' "Tattow" as it is called in their [the natives of Tahiti] language, this is done by inlaying the Colour of black under their skins in such a manner to be indelible. Some have ill-design'd figures of men birds or dogs, the women generally have this figure Z simply on ever(y) joint of their fingers and toes. . . . As this is a painfull operation especially the tattowing their buttocks it is perform'd but once in their life time.' The honour of inaugurating the long tradition of sailors being tattooed fell to Robert Stainsby, one of Cook's able seamen, who underwent this operation during this first voyage.

Tattooing was prevalent among tribal people, particularly in the Pacific area, and the custom certainly pre-dated Cook's account by a great many years. Its purpose was to protect the wearer from malevolent spirits as it kept sealed a person's 'tapu' or 'sacredness', and tattoos were also said to make a person attractive to the opposite sex. According to Captain *Marryat, writing in 1830, the practice of tattooing was very common among sailors in the Royal Navy; French soldiers and criminals were also said to like tattoos; and it has been estimated that by that time about 90% of seamen in the US Navy were tattooed. However, in 1909 the US government forbade the recruitment of seamen with 'indecent or obscene tattooing'. Mostly tattoos were thought of as a form of decoration, but sometimes sailors' *superstitions were attached to them. **(2)** The last call of the day aboard ship, signalling all hands to turn in. This meaning came from the Dutch 'taptoe', the signal in waterfront taverns that the taps were being closed and drinking was at an end for the day.

taunt, an old expression for a sailing ship with very high masts and narrow sails. Such a rig enabled a ship to point higher to the wind, but it was apt to wring, or twist, a ship's side because of the relatively narrow base for the *shrouds supporting the masts. North European ships—German, Dutch, and Scandinavian—were usually very taunt during the sailing era; British ships used shorter masts and broader sails, and in general enjoyed a longer life, being subject to less strain through wringing. See also ALL-A-TAUNT-O.

taut, the maritime word meaning tight, usually in relation to a sailing vessel's *rigging or the hauling of ropes. The word is also used for many similar meanings, as 'He's a taut hand', meaning 'he's a stern disciplinarian'; 'a taut ship', meaning that it is a smart ship and well disciplined.

taut wire measurement, a means developed in the British Navy during the First World War (1914–18) for providing an accurate measurement of the distance over the ground run by a ship, as opposed to through the water where the ship was affected by such factors as wind, *tide, *current, etc. As the ship moved forward a thin wire was pulled off a reel on the ship's stern. A dial on the reel then recorded the amount run out which equated with the distance the ship had travelled over the ground. It had a particular value in such naval operations as minelaying, which needed exact measurements when laying a minefield. It was also useful for hydrographic surveys.

Teach, or **Thatch, Edward** (d. 1718), English pirate, widely known as 'Blackbeard' from his odd habit of tying up the ends of his long black beard with ribbons and curling them back over his ears. He was born in Bristol and is said to have served as a *privateer in the West Indies during the War of the Spanish Succession (1702–13) and to have turned to *piracy on the declaration of peace. In 1717 he captured a large French merchant vessel, renamed her the *Queen Anne's Revenge*, fitted her out as a warship of 40 guns, and manned her with local riff-raff. His captures and robberies with this ship were, it is said, shared by him with the governor of North Carolina who certainly provided him with many facilities for refitting and victualling his ship. In 1718, however, Teach's activities so enraged the neighbouring governor of Virginia that he fitted out two *sloops, manned by men of the Royal Navy, and sent them to

Captain Edward Teach; engraving, 1734

hunt Teach down. On 22 November 1718 Lieutenant Robert Maynard, commanding one of the sloops, found and boarded Teach's ship in Beaufort Inlet, NC. A fierce fight ensued which caused high casualties on both sides before Teach was killed by one of Maynard's crew with a sword. Teach's head was cut off and suspended from the end of the *bowsprit of Maynard's ship and the surviving pirates were taken to Virginia where all but two were hanged. The remains of what is almost certainly the *Queen Anne's Revenge* were found in 1996 and exploration of the site was still ongoing in 2004.

tea clippers, see CLIPPER.

telltale. **(1)** A word which originally referred only to a *magnetic compass which the *master of a ship had in his cabin so that he always knew the direction in which his ship was heading. It was often fixed to hang face downwards from the deck *beams so that he could read the ship's course while lying in his *bunk. **(2)** The name for pieces of light material tied to the *stays of a *yacht to detect a shift in the wind, or sewn at intervals just *abaft the *luff of a sail to indicate the airflow.

tender, the name given to a *yacht's dinghy and to the larger vessels which service *navigation aids which are the responsibility of lighthouse authorities like *Trinity House. Originally, it was a small vessel attached temporarily to a larger ship for general harbour duties. A **press tender** was a small vessel under the command of a lieutenant which, in the days of *impressment in the British Navy, took on board volunteers or pressed men and delivered them to the receiving ships in home ports. Conditions aboard press tenders were notorious, and it was their filth and overcrowding that were mainly responsible for the great incidence of typhus fever which decimated British fleets during the Revolutionary (1793–1801) and Napoleonic (1803–15) Wars against France when impressment was at its height.

teredo, a bivalve *mollusc, of the family Teredinidae, also known as a shipworm because of the damage they cause to any wood in the sea. They bore long cylindrical holes in the wood, digesting the wood they carve out. They have digestive enzymes that are able to break down cellulose; most other woodborers rely on symbiotic micro-organisms to break it down. The tunnel connects to the outside water via a tiny hole through which the teredo obtains the oxygen it needs. A fully grown teredo can be nearly a metre in length, and carve a hole 2.5 cm (1 in.) in diameter. They occur at all depths in all seas, but are most common in warmer seas. During the 18th century wooden-hulled vessels were clad with *copper sheathing to prevent teredo infestations, which could cause catastrophic failure of the ship's timbers. Special paints have been developed which, when applied to the hulls of ships, deter both teredos and *fouling organisms, but these have raised serious *environmental issues and the *International Maritime Organization has begun a process which will ban them.

M. V. Angel

Terra Australis Incognita, the name given to the great and unknown southern continent required by the classical Greek geographers, who knew that the earth was spherical, to balance the land mass which was known to exist north of the equator. For a period in the Middle Ages the Church's insistence that the earth was flat led to the complete eradication of all belief in a southern continent, but the great years of *exploration by sea in the 15th and early 16th centuries confirmed the approximately spherical shape of the earth. Maps of that period showed Terra Australis as a vast continent centred on the South Pole, and extending as far north as approximately *latitude 60° S., and in the Pacific Ocean almost up to the equator. The rounding of the Cape of Good Hope by Bartholomew *Diaz in 1478 and of South America by Ferdinand *Magellan in 1520 stimulated the search for this unknown continent by many *navigators, but notably by *Tasman and then by *Cook, which gradually reduced the 'unknown land' to two smaller continents, Antarctica and Australia.

territorial waters, that area of sea adjacent to a nation's coasts which is under the full control of that nation. It was a contentious issue for centuries, and books like **Mare Clausum* were written about it. Eventually a suggestion put forward by the Dutch jurist Cornelis van Bynkershoek (1673–1743), in his book *De Dominio Maris* (*On the Dominion of the Sea*), published in 1703, was adopted. He proposed that a nation should exercise dominion over the adjacent seas only to the extent that it could defend them from the shore. This was taken as the existing range of a cannon, and agreed to be 3 miles (5 km). However, it took until 1822 for this to be formally agreed when France, Germany, the Netherlands, Denmark, and Britain signed the North Sea Fisheries Convention at The Hague. It was also agreed that waters outside this limit should be open to all ships without hindrance.

After the Second World War (1939–45) this limit was challenged by a number of maritime nations. In 1945 the US President, Harry Truman, stated that his country had the right to the *offshore oil and gas resources on its *continental shelf, an entirely new concept. A number of countries followed suit and others began to claim extended limits, too, mainly to preserve to themselves their inshore *fisheries. When Iceland extended its territorial limits to 19 kilometres (12 mls.) in 1958 it sparked with Britain the first of three confrontations, known as the 'cod wars', before most nations eventually accepted this distance as marking territorial waters. However, as *fish stocks dwindled, the pressure was on to extend the limits still further, and in February 1976, following Iceland's decision to extend its limits to 320 kilometres (200 mls.), the European Economic Community established a similar European zone, and soon afterwards most maritime nations followed suit. In 1994 the *United Nations Conference on the Law of the Sea (UNCLOS) introduced the *Exclusive Economic Zone and codified territorial waters as 12 *nautical miles, though in 1999 US agencies were ordered to enforce US law up to double that distance. UNCLOS also confirmed the right of a ship on innocent passage to pass through the territorial waters of another nation.

Tethys, the greatest of the Greek sea goddesses, was the wife of *Oceanus, and by legend the mother of the world's greatest rivers, including the Nile. She also had up to 3,000 daughters, known as the *Oceanides. By some, she has been identified with *Thetis, who in fact was her granddaughter. Her name is frequently used poetically to express the sea itself.

Thames Measurement, generally abbreviated to TM, a formula for the measurement of the *tonnage of *yachts. It was introduced in the mid-1850s by a London-based *yacht club, the Royal Thames, to produce a fairer method of handicapping yachts for racing. Until that year the tonnage of yachts had been calculated by the *Builders Old Measurement formula, but some astute *yacht designers had found a means of reducing a yacht's tonnage measurement, and thus increasing its handicap allowance, by shortening the keel as much as possible. In an attempt to prevent freak and unseaworthy yachts—such as *skimming dishes—being built to beat the racing rules, and to introduce a more equitable means of handicapping yachts of widely differing sizes, the Thames Measurement rule was introduced. The new formula, still based on the Builders Old Measurement, was

$$\frac{(L - B) \times B \times \tfrac{1}{2}B}{94}$$

where L equals the length in feet taken from the forward side of the *stem under the *bowsprit and measured at deck level to the *after side of the *sternpost, and B equals the *beam in feet measured to the outside of the hull planking. After its foundation, what is now the *Royal Yachting Association decreed that L should be measured on the waterline not the deck.

This measurement system was adopted generally by British yachtsmen and long after it had been superseded as a rating rule it was still used to describe a yacht in terms of tonnage, though the formula bore little relation to its displacement or weight. So universal did Thames Measurement become—and it is sometimes still applied to describe a classic yacht—that it was one of the details listed by a yacht's name in *Lloyd's Register of Yachts* right up until it ceased publication in the 1980s.

Johnson, P., *Yacht Rating* (1997).

thermocline, a zone of sharp temperature change in the water, across which there is a sufficient increase in the density of the water to inhibit mixing between the water mass above and below it. Seasonal thermoclines occur year-round within a 100 metres (325 ft) or so of the surface in the tropics and develop in late spring as the surface ocean warms up at temperate *latitudes (>40°) and then get eroded in autumn as the weather cools down. There is a permanent thermocline in deeper water that divides the warm upper ocean from the colder deep water. Along the polar *fronts, such as the *Antarctic Convergence, the permanent thermoclines outcrop at the surface and mark the equatorward boundary of the polar oceans. For illus. see EL NIÑO. M. V. Angel

Thermopylae, a famous British tea *clipper built in 1868 by Hood of Aberdeen. *Ship rigged, she had a gross *tonnage of 991 tons and was a long-time rival of the **Cutty Sark*. On her maiden voyage she created the first of several records, when she took just 60 days from Gravesend to Melbourne, a time that has never been beaten by a sailing ship. Though the *Cutty Sark* was the only ship seriously to contest the *Thermopylae*'s claim to be the fastest sailing clipper in the world, they only raced home in company once, and on that occasion the *Cutty Sark* lost her *rudder when in the lead. After the loss of the tea trade to *steam propulsion soon after the opening of the *Suez Canal, the *Thermopylae* continued in the Australian wool trade. After working in the North Pacific in the 1890s, where she was reputed to have kept pace with the *ocean liner *Empress of India* for several days, she was sold to the Portuguese Navy who renamed her *Pedro Nunes* and used her for *sail training. She ended her days as a coal *hulk and was *scuttled in 1907.

Thetis, one of the *Nereides in Greek legend; she married Peleus and by him became the mother of Achilles. Thetis has been frequently used in many European navies as a ship's name. It was the name of a Royal Navy *submarine which was accidentally sunk in 1938 in Liverpool Bay while on her trials, with heavy loss of life. See also TETHYS.

thimble, a circular or heart-shaped ring, usually of iron or aluminium, grooved on the outside to receive a rope which is *spliced round it to form an *eye. A thimble spliced into the *bolt-rope of a sail forms a *cringle. See also HEART.

thole pin, a wooden pin fixed in the *gunwale of a rowing boat to which, by means of a *grommet, an *oar is held when it is being pulled. A more usual method is to use two thole pins close together, with the oar between them. They are a substitute for a *crutch or a *rowlock.

Thomas W. Lawson, believed to be the largest *schooner ever built, was a ship of 5,000 gross *tonnage with a waterline length of 118 metres (385 ft). Designed by the American *yacht designer B. B. Crowninshield, she had seven masts, each nearly 60 metres (195 ft) high, and all her *halyards, *topping lifts, *sheets, etc. were led to two large steam *winches, one on the *forecastle and the other on the after *deckhouse. Built in Quincy, Mass., in the last decade of the 19th century, she had, because of her use of *auxiliary power, a crew of only sixteen hands. She was lost in heavy weather off the Scilly Isles in 1907 with the loss of all but one of her crew.

Thomson, William, first Baron Kelvin (1824–1907), Scottish physicist, who had a profound influence as a synthesizer on 19th-century physics, and helped lay the foundations for this discipline today. He also made a great impact on maritime affairs when, in 1873, he undertook to write a series of articles on the *magnetic compass for the magazine *Good*

Words. After writing the first of them he realized that there were more problems concerning a compass than he had originally thought. For the next five years he experimented and improved its capability and reliability, partly by reducing the weight of the compass card itself and increasing the time of its swing, but mainly by working out and laying down rules for compensation by which the temporary and permanent magnetism of an iron or steel ship could be easily counteracted. Through his research, the compass *binnacle was completely redesigned to house what became known as Kelvin spheres, balls of soft iron placed either side of the compass, which helped, with *Flinders bars, to compensate for a ship's *deviation. It was only after the completion of this work that he was in a position to write the second article of his series, five years after the publication of the first.

His other important contributions in the maritime field included his *sounding apparatus, but he also invented a *tide gauge, tidal harmonic analyser, and tide predictor, and worked on the advantages of the *bulbous bow.

thorough foot, to. **(1)** A method of taking out a large number of turns in a rope after it has been unduly twisted. If the turns are left handed, the rope is coiled down left handed and the end dipped through the coil. If the coil is then hauled out, the turns will be taken out. If the turns are right handed the rope is coiled down right handed, and the same process will remove the turns. **(2)** A method of joining two ropes when they have an *eye spliced into their ends.

'three sheets in the wind', a phrase, with a nautical derivation, describing someone who is intoxicated. It implies that even if a man who has had too much to drink had three sheets with which to trim his sails, he would still be too incapacitated to steer a steady *course.

'three sisters', the name given to a somewhat sinister, and wholly illegal, badge of office of a *master-at-arms or a *boatswain's mate in the British Navy, comprising three rattans bound together with waxed twine. They were used indiscriminately on the backs of seamen so as to *start them, or make them move more quickly about their work. Unlike the *cat-o'-nine-tails it was always an unofficial punishment. It was prohibited by the *Admiralty in 1809, but was not entirely eradicated for some years after that.

throat, the name given to the upper foremost corner of a four-sided sail in a *fore-and-aft rig. It was also the name sometimes given to the *jaws of a *gaff. For illus. see FORE-AND-AFT RIG.

throat halyards, those *halyards used to hoist the *throat of a sail or the *jaws of a *gaff. For illus. see GAFF RIG.

throat seizings, the name given to those *seizings, put on with twine or *spunyarn, which hold the hook and/or *thimble in the *strop which binds a wooden *block. It is also the seizing with which two parts of a rope are bound together to form an *eye in a *bight.

thrum, to, to sew short lengths of rope yarn by their *bights to a sail or piece of *canvas for use as a *collision mat. Smaller thrummed mats were sometimes used in the standing *rigging of the larger sailing vessels to prevent chafe in those places where sails or parts of the running rigging may come in contact with it. See also BAGGYWRINKLE.

thumb cleat, a *cleat with a single arm used primarily to stop *rigging slipping along a *spar. They are also *seized to standing rigging to form a hook from which a *bight of running rigging can be suspended and are often used, grouped, on *deckhouse faces for the storage of *warps.

thumb knot, another name for an overhand knot, which is no more than laying the end of a rope over its own part and bringing the end under and through the loop thus made. It is sometimes used in place of a *figure of eight knot to prevent the end of a rope or *fall unreeving through a *block, but most seamen advise against its use because it can jam.

Thurot, François (1726–60), one of the boldest and most accomplished *privateers, born at Nuits, France, the son of a small innkeeper. He was apprenticed to a druggist and then went to sea as a surgeon in a privateer in 1744, during the War of the Austrian Succession

(1739–48). He was captured by the British and imprisoned but, like another French privateer, Jean *Bart, managed to escape and returned to privateering with great success. During the Seven Years War (1756–63) he was commissioned into the French navy and commanded a *frigate. However, his reputation as a privateer was so outstanding that his ship was allowed mainly to act independently against British trade, and he captured many *prizes in the North Sea and English Channel. In 1757 he was appointed to a larger frigate and given a regular *squadron of six ships with the rank of commodore, though still operating a **guerre de course*, and was very successful in the number of merchant ships he captured. In 1760 he was despatched with a force of 1,300 troops to Ireland, for a descent on Carrickfergus and Belfast. However, little was achieved and in the ensuing battle with British men-of-war he was killed.

thwart, the transverse wooden seat in a rowing boat on which the oarsman sits. Thwarts are normally supported by grown wooden *knees (i.e. grown so that the grain of the wood follows the curve of the knee), fitted to the *ribs of the two sides. In some boats they are also supported by hanging knees. These are fixed to the ribs above the level of the thwarts so that the thwart is held securely between a knee above it and one below it.

ticket, the name that used to be given in the British merchant navy to the certificate of an officer's competency and experience. On passing the relevant exams the candidate was issued a pass slip—a 'ticket'—that was then presented to the desk or marine office for a certificate of competency to be issued. Nowadays, it is just a slang term for the certificates issued by the *Maritime and Coastguard Agency, the responsible agency for certification of British seafarers. These certificates are now based on the *International Maritime Organization's International Convention on Standards of Training, Certification and Watchkeeping for Seafarers.

tidal atlas, a collection of twelve small *charts covering the same area, each showing the direction of the tidal streams in the area for an hour while the *tide rises or falls at a standard port, in Britain usually Dover. The directions are shown by arrows, figures against the arrows indicating the speed in knots. Where only one figure is given, it indicates the rate at *springs; where two figures are given, the higher is the spring rate, the lower is the rate at *neaps. Tidal *atlases are included in some *nautical almanacs, and many are published separately.

tidal power. The twice daily *ebb and *flow of the *tides have the potential to provide considerable amounts of renewable energy. The first attempts to harness tidal energy were the tidal mills; the earliest found in Northern Ireland date from the 7th century. The principle is that water is stored behind a barrage during high tide and this drives turbines, both as it flows in during the flood and as it flows out again during the ebb. Tidal power stations are currently operating in Canada, France, Russia, and China. The largest is the one on the Rance estuary in France, which produces 320 megawatts of power. Plans to build one in the Severn Estuary in Britain were shelved because of the *environmental issues it raised and the enormous expense of building the barrage. The other difficulty is that tidal power stations generate power during the flow of the tides and not at times of peak demand, a difficulty which can only be resolved if technologies for storing huge quantities of energy can be devised. Smaller-scale technology includes tidal fences that use the tidal flows through narrow channels, and underwater turbines that resemble wind generators and may be useful in remote areas and on islands. See illustration overleaf.

www.iclei.org/EFACTS/TIDAL.HTM

M. V. Angel

'tiddley', the seaman's word for smart or neat. His shore-going uniform suit is tiddley if it is well pressed and brushed, *cheeses on deck are tiddley, *sinnet work is tiddley, and so on.

tide-race, a sharp acceleration in the speed of flow of a *tide by reason of a break or fault in the bottom formation, where the depth of water rises or falls suddenly, as over rocky ledges below water.

tide-rip, short *waves or ripples caused by *eddies made by a *tide as it rises or falls over an uneven bottom, or at sea where two *currents meet. Waves in a tide-rip do not break

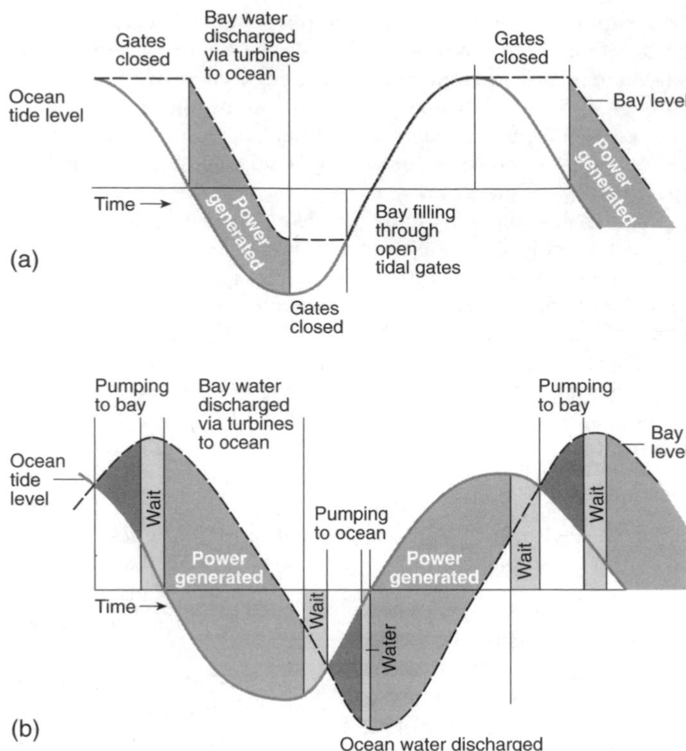

[a] A single-action tidal power system. Power is generated on the ebb tide [b] A double-action tidal power system. Power is generated on the ebb and flood tides

whereas in an *overfall they do, this being the principal difference between the two.

tide-rode, the situation of a vessel lying at anchor when it is swung to its anchor by the force of the *tide. See also WIND-RODE.

tides are shallow-water *waves generated by the gravitational forces of the moon and sun acting on the oceans. The earth's rotation results in high tides occurring both on the side nearest to the moon and on the opposite side. When the moon and sun are most closely aligned, at full and new moon, their gravitational pulls work in concert to produce *spring tides, the highest tides of the cycle. *Neap tides, the lowest-ranging tides, occur at the first and third quarters of the moon's cycle when the sun and moon are unaligned. The earth rotates every 24 hours 50 minutes relative to the moon, so the two daily tides are often of different heights. The earth spins too quickly for the tide's wave to keep up with the maximum gravitational pull of the moon, so it lags behind. This lag acts as a form of friction, which is slowing the earth's rotation.

Tidal ranges are also affected by the shapes of ocean basins. The **tidal wave** (not to be confused with *tsunamis, also colloquially known as tidal waves) circulates within a basin around an amphidromic point, which is a point at which the tidal range is zero. Islands also affect tides. In the Solent in southern Britain the tidal wave, which comes from the west, arrives earlier along the shorter route round the north of the Isle of Wight than along the longer route around the south and east of the island. The two peaks of high tide arrive separately generating high- and low-water stands; periods when the sea neither rises nor falls.

The tidal heights are also affected by weather conditions. When atmospheric pressure is low the water can rise higher than expected, and if in addition there are stronger winds blowing

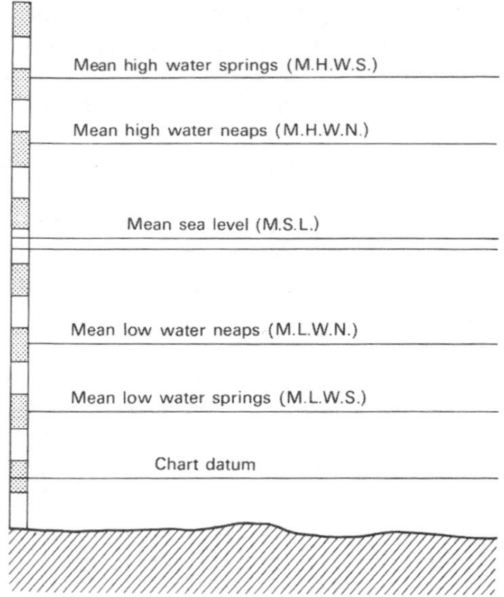

Tidal ranges

from the sea even more water can pile inshore. Such events are known as **storm surges**. During *tropical storms in coastal regions, more people are drowned by the storm surge than by the direct effects of the wind's violence. In 1953 a 3-metre (10-ft) storm surge in the southern North Sea killed 300 people in Britain and 1,800 in Holland, and resulted in the building of the Thames Barrier and the Delta project across the Eastern Scheldt. See also TIDAL POWER. M. V. Angel

tideway, a name given to a main *fairway in tidal waters, where the direction of *ebb and flow of the *tide is straight up and down the *fairway.

tiding over, an old expression to describe the method of working the *tides, in the days of *square-rigged ships. It meant making progress against a contrary wind, especially in the English Channel where the prevailing wind, being south-westerly, is *foul for sailing ships proceeding down channel. It involved anchoring during the *flood, or east-running tide, then *weighing anchor at high water and *beating to *windward, relying on the strength of the *ebb or west-running tide to carry the ship in the required direction. When the tide turned, the ship anchored again until the next high water, when the process was repeated.

tier. (1) Also spelt **tyer,** the *gasket used aboard *yachts to secure a sail to the main boom. **(2)** The name given to a row of *mooring *buoys in a port for *barges or *lighters, or a *wharf or *quay where barges can lie alongside three or four deep, with the inside barge secured to the wharf. See also TROT. **(3)** A regular row or layer of anything, such as a tier of casks in the *hold of a ship. See also CABLE-TIER; COIL; GROUND TIER.

tierce, a regular measurement of maritime victuals in the old days of salt beef and pork in casks. A tierce of salt beef was 127 kilograms (280 lb), a tierce of pork only 118 kilograms (260 lb). In the early 19th century, when casks were made larger, the beef tierce was raised to 152 kilograms (336 lb) and the pork tierce to 136 kilograms (300 lb). A tierce of port was one-third of a pipe, or 191 litres (42 gals.).

tiller, a wood or metal bar which fits into or round the head of the *rudder and by which the rudder is moved as required. Until the introduction of the steering wheel at the beginning of the 18th century, all ships, no matter how large, were steered by a tiller, the larger ones with the aid of a *whipstaff. As ships grew in length and size it needed many more men to control the tiller when sailing, especially in strong winds, hence the need for *relieving tackles. Nowadays, tillers are only used in small craft. That part of a *tiller which is furthest away from the *rudder head, is known as the **tiller head**. See also HELM; STEERING GEAR.

tiller ropes, the lines, made of rope or chain, which lead from the *rudder head, or an extension fitted to it, to the barrel of the steering wheel, whereby the rudder is moved as the wheel is put over. See also HELM; STEERING GEAR.

tilt, the name, now defunct, for a small boat's *awning which covered the *sternsheets to protect passengers from the sun.

timber heads, the prolongation of some of the *timbers in the hull of a wooden ship above the deck level so that they projected above the *gunwale to serve as *bitts.

timber hitch, a method of securing a rope round a *spar. The rope's *standing part is taken round the spar with a *half hitch round itself,

Timber hitch

and the end is then tucked three or four times round its own part. This forms a running, but self-jamming, *eye.

timbers, the *frames or *ribs of a ship, connected to the keel, which give a ship's hull both its shape and its strength. In wooden ships of any size, the timbers are made of several pieces of wood *scarfed together to the required shape. In steel ships the frames are of steel angle iron, bent to the desired shape.

timenoguy (pron. and sometimes written, timonoggy), originally a rope stretched *taut between different parts of a *square-rigger to prevent one of the *tacks or *braces from *fouling some projection. This applied especially to the *fore-sheets and tacks fouling the *stocks of the anchors when tacking. Later, it was a rope made fast in the *mizzen *rigging with a *thimble in the end through which passed the *hauling part of the main brace. The object was still to prevent fouling, particularly of the boat *davits.

timoneer, an old word occasionally used to describe the helmsman of a vessel. It is the Anglicized version of the French *timonier*, helmsman, both being derivations of the older word *tymon*, a wooden staff, and thus a *tiller or *whipstaff. As William Falconer, in his poem *The Shipwreck*, has it:

> The helm the attentive timoneer applies.

The word remained in use throughout the 19th century perhaps used rather more by writers more than by seamen. G. C. Davies, writing in the magazine *Norfolk Broads* in 1884, talks about a boat's 'timoneer sitting with the tiller in one hand and the sheet in the other'.

Titanic, the 46,328-ton *ocean liner owned by the British White Star Line which sank on her maiden voyage in April 1912 after hitting an iceberg. Built to safety flotation standards higher than required by regulations, and with sixteen watertight compartments, she was regarded as being virtually unsinkable. The largest ship in the world when she was built, she sailed from Southampton for New York on 10 April 1912. On 14 April, as she was approaching the *Grand Banks, she received four warnings of *ice ahead from other ships, but the last message, describing a field right across her track, never reached the captain.

As usual in clear weather, she was steaming at her service speed of 22 knots. There are rumours, but no evidence, that she was out to break records; in fact she had insufficient coal aboard to try. At 2340 the *crow's nest lookout reported an iceberg close ahead and the first officer immediately ordered a full turn to port. The bows missed the iceberg, but an underwater spur of ice ripped an intermittent gash down the ship's starboard side extending 91 metres (300 ft) and puncturing six forward watertight compartments. She could not survive this damage, but the passengers were not told for fear of panic. Board of Trade regulations for lifeboats had not kept pace with the increased size of ships, and while there were 1,316 passengers and 885 crew aboard, the lifeboats could only hold 1,178. However, the boats were lowered only partly filled with passengers who refused at first to believe the ship would or could sink.

*SOS wireless signals were sent, and *rockets were fired when a light appeared on the *horizon at about 0100 on 15 April. But the light moved away and the nearest ship to receive the SOS, the Cunard liner *Carpathia*, could not reach the scene before 0400. The *Titanic*, after settling slowly by the bows, sank at 0220 leaving 824 passengers and 673 crew members to die in the icy water. Only 25% of the third, or emigrant, class survived and all the engineer officers who were working below until the last moments were lost. Two inquiries into the disaster found a scapegoat in the captain of the steamer *Californian*. Both stated that the *Californian* was the source of the light seen on the horizon from the *Titanic*, though the evidence is quite clear that the light could not have come from this ship. Captain Smith of the *Titanic* was not blamed as it was not normal practice for liners to reduce speed in clear weather. There is no reason to question this finding: it is likely that the iceberg had recently overturned and was showing a dark side; there was no wind or swell to create ripples around it. The disaster led to the *International Convention for the Safety of Life at Sea and an ice patrol which continues to this day.

In 1985 the remains of the *Titanic* were found by a joint expedition from two *oceanographic institutes, Woods Hole, led by Dr Robert *Ballard, and the Institut Français de Recherches pour l'Exploitation de la Mer (IFREMER), led by Jean-Louis Michel. Later expeditions brought to the surface a large number of artefacts which are now on permanent expedition at the National Maritime Museum, Greenwich. Legal wrangles about who was allowed to *salvage what, and under what conditions, were ongoing in 2004 and there have been calls for the ship's remains to be protected.

tjalk, a Dutch *barge-type vessel for the carriage of cargo, dating from the 17th century. It originally had the normal barge rig of *jib and *spritsail, but today is built of steel and fitted with a *diesel engine. The design has been adapted to construct *yachts, and a tjalk yacht (*pavilijoen tjalk*) closely resembles an enlarged *boeier.

tjotter, the smallest of the traditional Dutch types of small craft, much like a *boeier in rig but only 4.6–6 metres (15–20 ft) in overall length. They are normally half-decked, and are popular for racing in inland waters.

toggle. **(1)** A strong wooden pin, which, in the days of sail, was usually made of **lignum vitae*. It is occasionally still used through the *bight of a rope to hold it in position and for similar purposes. When sailing warships went into battle, toggles were fixed in the running parts of the *topsail sheets and in the *jeers, so that if the rope was shot away, the *yards might still be held aloft by the toggles. **(2)** A metal link, usually in stainless steel, used in the standing *rigging of a *yacht to allow movement in two directions so as to avoid bending loads on fittings.

'Tom Bowling' or **'Tom Bowline',** the name of the most famous of Charles Dibdin's *sea songs. It began:

> Here, a sheer hulk, lies poor Tom Bowling,
> The darling of our crew . . .

The original name is that of a naval character in Tobias Smollett's *Roderick Random*, but Dibdin modelled his Tom Bowling on his brother, Captain Thomas Dibdin. One of the verses of the song is engraved on Dibdin's tombstone.

tonnage, originally the charge for the hire of a ship at so much a ton of its *burthen. It was also a tax, first levied in 1303 by Edward I of England, on all imports brought by ship into England. A second tax, known as tunnage, of three shillings on each *tun of wine imported, was levied in 1347 by Edward III.

It was from the first of these meanings, the cost of the hire of a ship, that the word tonnage came into use as an alternative to burthen. Although tonnage was still theoretically based on the number of tuns of wine that a ship could carry in its *holds, it became necessary, both for taxation purposes and for calculating the harbour dues payable by a ship, to devise a rough and ready formula by which the tonnage could be quickly calculated. It was found, in the general design of ships of those early days, that the vessel's length in feet, multiplied by its maximum *beam in feet, multiplied by the depth of its hold below the main deck in feet, with the product divided by 100, gave a reasonably accurate measurement of its tonnage, and this was the formula used for measuring warships as well as merchant vessels.

In 1694, when a law was introduced in Britain requiring the marking of a waterline on merchant ships, both when in *ballast and fully laden, this tonnage formula was officially adopted, though marginally amended to make the product of length, beam, and depth divisible by 94 instead of 100. This remained the standard of ship measurement until 1773, when more accurate limits of measurement were established by a formula known as the *Builders Old Measurement (BOM). This remained in force until the advent of iron for *shipbuilding and *steam propulsion revolutionized the design and shape of ships.

The BOM served its purpose well for the typical bluff-bowed, full-bodied ship of the timber and sail era but had no relevance to the longer, finer hulls of the iron ship in which the ratio of length to beam increased from the average three to one to four, five, and even six to one. In place of the old BOM a new calculation, known as **Moorsom's Rule**, devised by the *Admiralty at the request of the Board of Trade in the mid-19th century, was introduced. The total capacity of a ship's hull below the upper deck was calculated in cubic feet and, by dividing it by 100, the resultant figure became known as a ship's **gross tonnage**.

But this figure did not, of course, bear very much resemblance to its cargo-carrying capacity, since it was calculated on the total hull space below the ship's upper deck and made no allowance for space taken up by crew's *quarters, ship's stores, fuel, engines, etc. So a second calculation was made of the capacity in cubic feet of these spaces and, still taking 100 cubic as equivalent to one ton, was deducted from the figure of its gross tonnage to give a **net tonnage**.

Both these tonnages are known as **register tonnages** as they are entered on the ship's certificate of registration. It is on the figure of a ship's net register tonnage that such charges as port and harbour dues, dues for navigational aids, towage charges, and *salvage assessments are normally levied.

Another tonnage measurement of a merchant vessel is **deadweight tonnage**, normally shortened to dwt. This is a measurement of the weight of the cargo it carries based on the long ton of 2,240 pounds (1,017 kg). The figure is arrived at by calculating the amount of water displaced by a ship when it is unloaded, but with its fuel tanks full and stores on board, and the amount of water similarly displaced when it is fully loaded with its cargo holds full. The difference expressed in tons (35 cubic ft of seawater = one ton) gives the ship's deadweight tonnage.

Naval vessels are usually measured in terms of **displacement tonnage**. This is the weight of the water a ship displaces when it is floating with its fuel tanks or bunkers full, and with all stores on board. This, at the rate of 35 cubic feet per ton, is the actual weight of the ship, since a floating body displaces its own weight in water. During the last half of the 19th century, and for the first half of the 20th century, *yachts were measured by the *Thames Measurement rule.

The introduction of the metric system into most countries that previously used the imperial measurement has led to ships' displacement being given in metric tonnes. However, as the weight of the metric tonne (1,000 kg) and the avoirdupois, or imperial, long ton (2,240 lb) are so close—there is only 1.16% difference between the two—large-scale reregistration of vessels has not been necessary.

In 1969 the *International Maritime Organization adopted the International Convention on Tonnage Measurement of Ships which entered into force in 1982. This was the first successful attempt to introduce a universal tonnage measurement system, the new rules applying to all ships built on or after 18 July 1982. Those ships built before that date were allowed to retain their existing tonnage for twelve years before they needed to be remeasured. The Convention meant a transition from the traditional gross register tons (GRT) and net register tons (NRT) to gross tonnes (GT) and net tonnes (NT). Gross tonnage forms the basis for manning regulations, safety rules, and registration fees, while both are used to calculate port dues. The gross tonnage is a function of the moulded volume of all enclosed spaces of the ship, while the net tonnage is produced by a formula which is a function of the moulded volume of all cargo spaces of the ship.

top, originally, a platform set on the mastheads of medieval ships to carry small masts and sails to help to reduce rolling. They were also used for lookouts and as a station for archers when fighting other ships, hence the term **fighting tops**. As ships developed, tops were built at the head of the main and *topgallant masts supported by the *trestle and *crosstrees to aid access to the *yards and provide working and lookout stations aloft.

top-armours, cloths which in older days were hung around the *tops of fighting ships, partly for show, being painted red, and partly to hide the men there who acted as snipers or hurled *stinkpots onto the enemy ship's deck. See also QUARTER-CLOTHS.

top-chain, the name given to the chain *slings used for the *yards of *square-rigged warships in time of battle to prevent the yards from falling on deck if the rope slings were shot through. They were also rigged to the normal rope slings before a ship went into action.

topgallant mast, a mast raised above the *topmast in *square-rigged ships or the equivalent length of mast in a modern vessel with one-piece masts. It is raised through a *cap and supported by *trestle-trees. The origin of the name is thought to come from the use of the word gallant to indicate being grand or showing off. Topgallant *royal masts were originally a further mast raised above the topgallant, but they later became a pole extension of the topgallant mast itself. For illus. see SQUARE RIG.

topgallant sail, the sail set from the *topgallant yard of a *square-rigger. They are sometimes split into two parts, each with its own yard, and are then called the upper and lower topgallants. For illus. see SQUARE RIG.

topgallant yard, the *yard from which a *topgallant sail is set on a *square-rigger. When double topgallant sails are used the yards are named as the upper and lower topgallant yards. For illus. see SQUARE RIG.

topmark, see BUOY; IALA MARITIME BUOYAGE SYSTEM.

topmast, a mast raised above the lower mast in a sailing ship. It is usually raised through a *cap and supported by *trestle-trees.

topmen, or **yardmen,** seamen whose station in the *watch-bill, in the days of *square-riggers, was on the masts and *yards. They were the picked men of a ship's company, with the upper yardmen, those who worked on the *topsail and *topgallant sail yards, the aristocrats of the lower deck.

topping lift, a rope or flexible wire *tackle by which the end of a *spar is hoisted or lowered. In *yachts a topping lift is usually attached at or near the after end of the boom, and takes the weight of the boom while the sail is being hoisted or stowed. In the past twin topping lifts were sometimes rigged so that when the sail was being set the topping lift on the *lee side could be slacked away clear of the sail, while the *weather topping lift took the weight of the boom. See also LAZYJACKS.

topsail. In *fore-and-aft-rigged sailing vessels a topsail is a sail set above the working sails. This can be in the form of a high-setting *jib topsail or set above *gaff-rigged sails, usually from the *topmast, as a main topsail or fore topsail. In this application it can take the form of a triangular *jib-headed topsail or set with additional spars as a *jackyard topsail. In a *square-rigger it is the sail set from a topsail yard. It is sometimes split into two parts each with its own yard and those are then called upper and lower topsails. The lower topsail is often made of heavy *canvas and kept set in heavy wind.

topsail yard, the *yard from which a *topsail is set on a *square-rigger. When double topsails are used the yards are called the upper and lower topsail yards.

topsides. **(1)** That part of the side of a ship which is above the main *wales. The term referred particularly to *square-rigged sailing warships, where the main wales ran level with the bottom of the upper deck *gunports. In its modern meaning it usually refers to that portion of the ship's side which rises above the upper deck though the term is often loosely used to refer to the upper deck itself. For example 'I'm going topsides' means 'I'm going on the upper deck.' **(2)** The sides of *yachts, above the *boottop, are also known as topsides.

torsion, a form of strain on a ship's hull caused when *waves attempt to twist the forward end of the ship one way and the after end the other way. See also HOG; SAG, TO.

total loss, see CONSTRUCTIVE TOTAL LOSS.

touching, an old sailing term used in *square-rigged ships to indicate that the ship was *on the wind, with the leading *leech of the sails just beginning to shiver, or 'touching' the wind.

tow. **(1)** A name for a vessel or vessels being towed. See also TUG. **(2)** When used as a verb it means to haul another vessel through the water by means of a towing *hawser.

towage, the charge made by a *tug owner for towing another vessel. In the case of *salvage at sea, it is the amount of the bargain struck between the tug company and the representatives of the ship requiring assistance.

trabacolo, or **trabaccolo,** a 17th–19th-century coasting vessel of medium size, peculiar to the Adriatic and the waters around Italy. They were used mainly for trade but occasionally as transports for troops. Some had one mast, some two, and they were variously rigged according to the choice of the owner, but frequently with a *lateen rig.

track. **(1)** A strip of metal on the mast or boom of a *Bermudan-rigged sailing boat. It takes the slides fixed to the *luff or *foot of a Bermudan-rigged mainsail, replacing the mast hoops and *lacing for the mainsail of the old-fashioned *gaff rig. It superseded the original method, when the Bermudan rig was first introduced, of setting the luff on a *taut *stay running from masthead to deck. In modern *yachts the luff-rope feeds directly into a C-section track, or into a groove which is part of the mast itself. Tracks are also used on deck in many *yachts for the sliding sheet leads. **(2)** The path of a vessel through the water or over the ground (seabed), known as water track or ground track. Also, the path of a *storm.

trade winds are prevailing winds that blow steadily from the high-pressure zones. These occur in the *horse latitudes that lie close to the Tropics of Cancer and Capricorn, between 25° and 30° both to the north and to the south of the equator, towards the *doldrums now known as the Intertropical Convergence Zone or ITCZ. Intense solar heating at the equator causes the air to rise and this draws in the winds from the high-pressure regions. These winds are deflected by *Coriolis forces so, instead of blowing directly from north or south, they blow from the north-east in the northern hemisphere and from the south-west in the southern hemisphere. During the age of sail, ships voyaging across the North Atlantic from east to west exploited the trade winds, with the return voyage following a more northerly route where the prevailing winds are south-westerly.

www.oar.noaa.gov/spotlite/archive/spot_pacs.html M. V. Angel

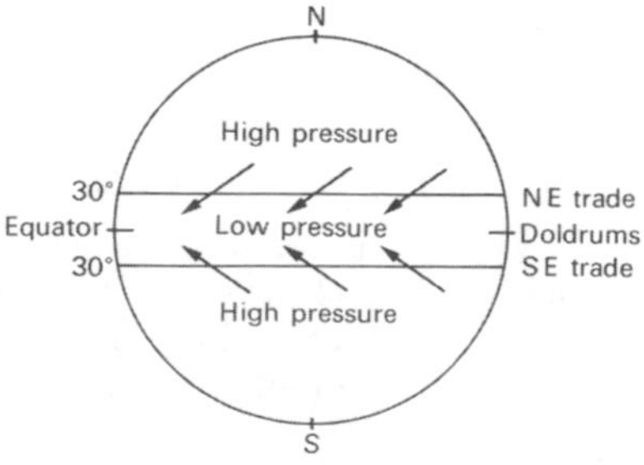

Trade winds

traffic separation schemes, areas designated by the *International Maritime Organization (IMO), and authorized by the *International Convention for the Safety of Life at Sea, or SOLAS, for separating marine traffic where it converges. Their purpose is to reduce traffic density, and usually lessen the incidence of encounters between ships on reciprocal or nearly reciprocal *courses, which are the most dangerous kind. In 1963 the Institutes of Navigation in Great Britain and France with the Deutsche Gesellschaft für Ortung und Navigation issued a report on traffic regulation in the Dover Strait which in the following year was accepted by the Inter-governmental Maritime Consultative Organization (now IMO).

The situation as it appeared to the Dover Strait Working Group at the time was that, in an area bounded by the Elbe and the English Channel where almost half the collisions in the world then took place, and through which something like 750 ships passed each day (a somewhat inflated figure as it turns out based on port returns), almost all the traffic used a passage barely 5 *nautical miles wide between the Varne Bank and the English coast, irrespective of which way it was going. The report proposed a voluntary separation of the through traffic by the Varne Bank, the observance of which would be governed by the Ordinary Practice of Seamen as envisaged in Rule 29 of the *International Regulations for Preventing Collisions at Sea, or Colregs.

A further report from the same three institutes entitled 'The Separation of Traffic at Sea' proposed measures to enable ships to navigate through heavily congested areas with more efficiency and greater safety, and in due course this was accepted by the IMO. It outlined the principles of routeing which now form the basis of traffic separation schemes throughout the world. In 1967 the first traffic separation scheme in international waters was implemented in the Dover Strait and its adjacent waters. Within the next few years some 50 other separation schemes were adopted, mainly in north-west Europe and the USA. Today some hundred separation schemes have been adopted by the IMO and over two hundred, some imposed by governments within their territorial waters, appear on official charts. In 1977 revised Collision Regulations came into force and it became mandatory to comply with the new Rule 10 which deals with the observance of traffic separation schemes.

The high incidence of collisions between vessels going in opposite directions has now been largely eliminated and there has been a substantial reduction of collisions worldwide since the introduction of traffic separation schemes.

Mike Richey

trail-board, a carved or painted board extending each side *aft from the *figurehead of a ship. Originally it extended from the head *knee to the *cheeks.

train, the name given to the after part of a wooden gun carriage as used in sailing warship. It was to an *eyebolt in the train of the carriage that the *train-tackle was hooked during battle. See also WARFARE AT SEA.

training ships, see SAIL TRAINING.

train-tackle, a *tackle used during battle in the days of the muzzle-loading broadside guns of the wooden ships of war. It was hooked to an *eyebolt in the *train of a wooden gun carriage and to a ringbolt in the deck, and used to prevent the gun from running out of the *port while it was being loaded, and for running it in after firing for reloading.

tramontana, the cold northerly wind of the Mediterranean, particularly around the western coast of Italy and northern Corsica, but also in the Balearic Islands and the Ebro Valley in Catalonia. It is the same wind that in other localities is the called the *bora, and on the Côte d'Azur and in eastern Provence it is sometimes known as the montagnère or montagneuse.

tramp ship, a cargo-carrying merchant vessel, before the days of *bulk carriers and *container ships. It did not work a regular route but carried general cargo to any destination as required, and could be diverted to any port to pick up available cargo.

trane, or **train, oil,** an old term for whale or seal oil. See also SEALING; WHALING.

transom. **(1)** The *athwartship *timbers bolted to the *sternpost of a ship to give it a flat stern. In the older *square-rigged ships, particularly men-of-war, they were usually rather heavier than other timbers in order to support the overhang of the stern and *quarter galleries. In modern vessels there is no overhang with a transom stern, and in consequence no need for the stern timbers to be heavier than any others. **(2)** A name often given to the vane of a *cross-staff, that part which slid along the staff by means of a square socket cut in the centre of the vane. **(3)** The cross-piece of timber which connected the *cheeks of a wooden gun carriage during the days of sailing navies.

transport, a ship, either naval or hired, employed in the transport of troops.

traveller. **(1)** The ring of a lower sheet *block. When *shackled to a *horse on the deck or *counter of a sailing vessel—and thus free to travel from side to side according to the direction in which the sail is *trimmed—it is usually known as a traveller. **(2)** A metal ring fitted to slide up and down a *spar, or to run in and out on a boom or *gaff to extend or draw in the *tack or *clew of a sail. Thus, a traveller was normally fitted to a long *bowsprit so that the tack of the *jib could be hauled out when being set. **(3)** A metal ring around a mast, with a hook welded onto it, which was used for hoisting a *lugsail. A *strop around the *yard, to which the lugsail was *laced, was hooked onto the traveller and the sail was then hoisted with a *halyard. **(4)** Another name for a *parrel, by which the yards in *square-rigged ships were held close to the mast. **(5)** A rope about a metre (3 ft) in length with a *thimble *spliced in one end, used to control the swing of a *topgallant yard during hoisting or lowering in a square-rigged ship. Two of these travellers were fixed on each *backstay, the thimbles travelling up and down them. The rope tails were secured to the ends of the topgallant yard to stop it swinging backwards and forwards while being *swayed up or *struck down at sea.

traverse board, an early, say late 16th-century, method of keeping track of the *boards and traverses the helmsman had made during his *watch in his attempt to make good the *course ordered. The various boards must be resolved into north–south and east–west components which add up to the course made good. The distance sailed on each *tack was recorded on the traverse board which normally hung before the helmsman. It was a circular piece of wood on which the *rhumb lines were marked by equidistant holes representing hourly and two-hourly periods during which the ship sailed a particular course. Pegs attached to the centre of the board were put into the holes to mark the number of hours. At the end of the watch the mean course made good would be calculated from the position of the pegs. The officer of the watch would have decided the measured or estimated speed, from which all directions and distances made good would be calculated.

As literacy increased among seamen the traverse board was replaced by the *log board on which the courses and distances were written up.

traverse table, a table, included in all standard books of navigational tables, which gives the measurement of the two sides of any right-angled triangle subtended by the hypotenuse. In navigational terms, it provides the *navigator with the difference of *latitude and *departure (from which he could find the change in his *longitude) for any distance along a *rhumb line *course, the course and distance forming the hypotenuse. In conventional *dead reckoning navigation this is the information the navigator needs to calculate his position. Conversely, the navigator can find from the traverse table the distance and the rhumb line course to steer between two points of known latitude and longitude. The table gives difference of latitude and departure for each degree between 0° and 90°, and for a hypotenuse length from 0 usually to 600.

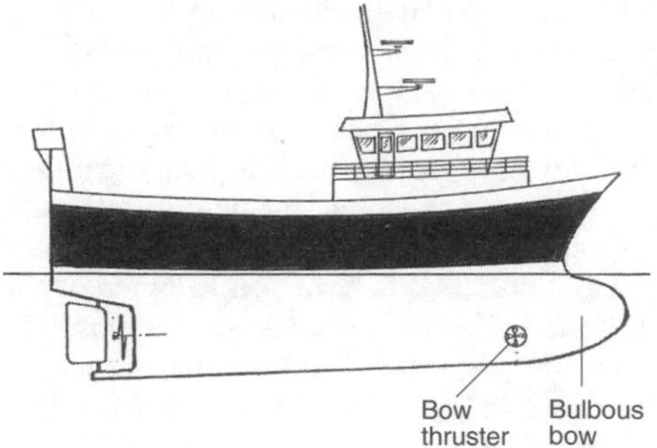

A state-of-the-art trawler with bulbous bow and bow thruster

trawler, a fishing vessel specially designed to operate a *trawl to catch bottom-lying *fish. Sailing trawlers operated a trawl to a depth of 55–73 metres (180–240 ft), but a modern one powered by *diesel engines can fish to the depth of 600 metres (almost 2,000 ft). The largest trawler afloat in 2004 was the 14,000-tonne *Irish Dawn*, part of the Irish fishing fleet. She is 144 metres (472 ft) long, with a *beam of 24.3 metres (80 ft), and in addition to her trawls, she operates a *purse seine net, which is reputed to be 1,100 metres (3,600 ft) in circumference and nearly 170 metres (550 ft) deep, to catch mackerel, sardines, and anchovies. She can freeze up to 300 tonnes of fish a day and has a storage capacity of 7,000 tonnes. With a crew of 100 she is nothing less than a floating fish factory.

trawls are large nets dragged along the bottom by commercial fishing boats. The mouth of the net is kept open by trawl doors, which not only help to weight the net down, but act like hydroplanes to keep the mouth of the net open. The bottom rope is weighted and has rollers to lift it over seabed obstructions. The head rope is lined with floats. Mesh sizes have to comply with a legal minimum so that undersized *fish are allowed to escape. The *cod-end is lined with fine mesh to reduce damage to the catch and is tied off with a throttling rope, which is released when the trawl is retrieved. Scientists in *research ships who are studying *biological oceanography also use different types of trawl, which are smaller, designed so the volumes of water filtered are accurately

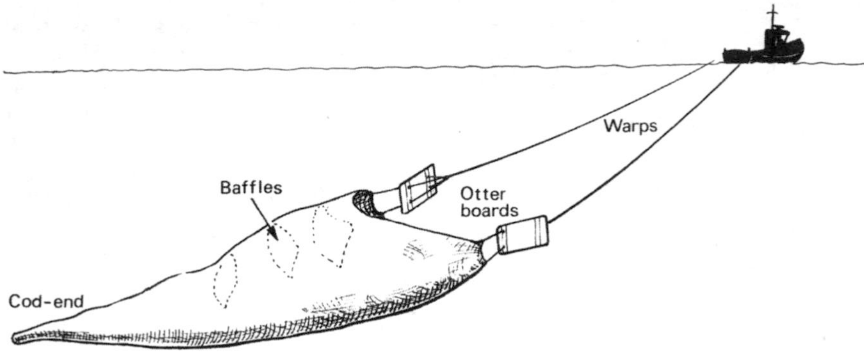

A trawl

known, and fitted with electronic sensors. See also FISHERIES. M. V. Angel

treasure ship. **(1)** A Chinese warship built during the Ming dynasty (1368–1644). Renowned for their *exploration by sea during the first half of the 15th century, they were large, *junk-rigged vessels with as many as nine masts, certainly larger than any western sailing vessel of that era. Commanded by the eunuch Cheng Ho, fleets of these ships undertook extensive voyages. The first one set sail in 1405 to find the emperor's nephew, who had fled the country, and to trade. The size and power of these treasure ships, and the riches they carried, so overawed the rulers of the places they visited that when the ships returned to China they were quickly followed by envoys eager to pay tribute to the emperor. The emperor's nephew was never found, but so much status and new knowledge had been gained that the emperor mounted six more voyages. The last sailed in 1431, but soon afterwards there was a change in policy and China lost interest in the maritime power it had built up.

Ordinary seagoing trading junks were up to 52 metres (170 ft) long, the biggest, according to the 13th-century explorer *Marco Polo, having a *draught of about 6 metres (20 ft). However, treasure ships were, according to what records remain, much larger. There has been much discussion about the size of these vessels (see, *inter alia*, A. Sleeswyk, 'The *Liao* and Displacement of Ships of the Ming Navy', *Mariner's Mirror*, 82 (1996), 1: 3) as the records are difficult to interpret. It has been thought that they almost certainly exaggerate their size as it is generally agreed that it is impossible to build a structurally safe seagoing ship of wood which exceeds 80 metres (260 ft) in length unless it is reinforced with iron or steel. However, the naval architect Colin Mudie has shown that it is quite possible that they were longer than this (see Figs. (a) and (b) overleaf).

The Chinese are intensely interested in the exploits of their treasure ships and are building a number of *replica ships to exhibit in various parts of the world, the first starting from Hong Kong in 2005. They have no engines but will be towed to 80 or so major coastal cities where they will be put on display.

(2) The Spanish *carracks, and later *galleons, known as *register ships, which brought back treasure from Spanish colonies in Central and South America during the 16th–18th centuries. The silver, and later the gold, extracted from these colonies was carried up the western coast of South America in treasure ships to the port of Panama, or to Vera Cruz on Mexico's east coast. The treasure unloaded at Panama was taken by mule trains across the Isthmus, though some, particularly during the rainy season, was shipped down the Chagres River to the Caribbean. It was stored at Nombre de Dios and then loaded onto the fleet of ships which arrived every autumn from Spain carrying supplies and merchandise for the Spanish colonists. Unlike the swift *galizabra, these ships returned to Spain in heavily escorted *flotas. Treasure ships also sailed from Mexico to Manila carrying silver which was used mainly to purchase Chinese silk.

Treasure ships were always in danger from Elizabethan seamen such as *Drake, *Grenville, and *Hawkins, and they were constantly harried by the French and the Dutch, too.

(a)

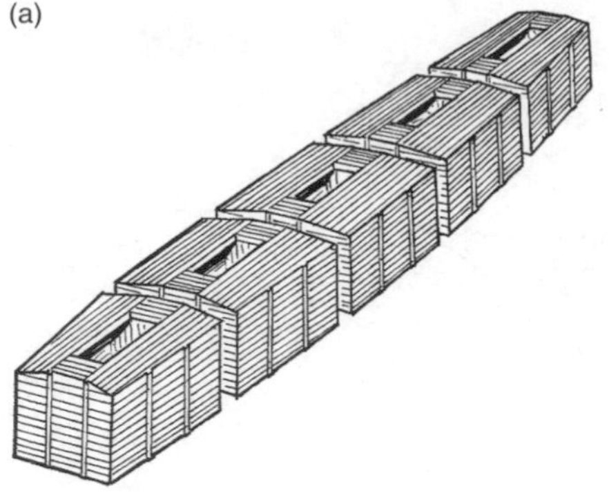

(b)

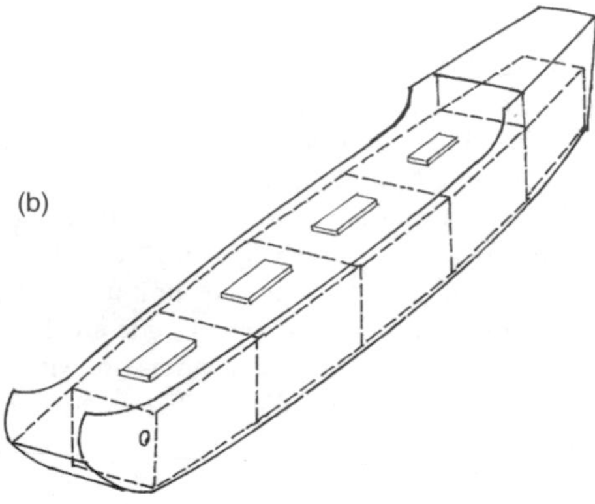

A possible form of Chinese hull construction for treasure ships with nine masts. For simplicity the principal of the construction shown here is for a smaller four-master built on five compartment boxes. Colin Mudie writes: 'if the masts were stepped at the junctions of the boxes, see (a), this infers ten boxes longitudinally and if the longest timber with which these could be built in a watertight manner was 12 metres (40 ft), it is easy to think of a vessel 122 metres (400 ft) long. The boxes could then be locked and bolted together to make the hull size and form required, as in (b), what we nowadays call volumetric construction. This would result in a suitably strong and efficient basic structure with a succession of transverse bulkheads of good watertight integrity. The resulting shell might then be clad with another skin, probably separated from the first. The planking of this skin would be subject to panel strains rather than longitudinal loads, and plank butts would not be a matter of structural concern. Such an approach might explain the watertight bulkheads and double bottoms, both of which were renowned Chinese inventions.'

They were also the targets of *piracy. One, the *Santa María de la Consolación*, was shipwrecked off Ecuador in 1681 when trying to escape from Bartholomew *Sharp, and its remains—and its treasure—were not finally located until 2003. Eleven treasure ships were sunk by a hurricane in 1715 off the eastern coast of Florida, close to Cape Canaveral, and all except one of another flota of 22 ships met the same fate on the *reefs of Florida Keys in 1733. Both sites have long been the focus of interest for treasure hunters after valuable *salvage and those working in *marine archaeology. See also SHIPWRECKS.

Broadwater, J. (ed.), *Ships and Shipwrecks in the Americas: A History Based on Underwater Archaeology* (1988).

Wagner, K., *Pieces of Eight: Recovering the Riches of a Lost Spanish Treasure Fleet* (1976).

treenails (pron. trennels or trunnels), long cylindrical pins of oak used to secure the planks of a wooden ship's sides and bottom to its *timbers. Holes were bored with an auger through the planks and into the timbers, and the treenails driven home with a mallet. Their diameter was 2.5 centimetres (1 in.) for every 30 metres (100 ft) of a ship's length; thus a ship with an overall length of 46 metres (152 ft) would use treenails 3.8 centimetres (1.5 in.) in diameter.

trench, a linear feature in the ocean where the depth exceeds 6,000 metres (19,700 ft). Trenches occur along the active margins of oceans where the oceanic crust is sliding under continental land masses or island arcs. They are highly active seismically; one of the most violent earthquakes ever recorded was associated with a trench off Chile. The active margin of the Pacific Ocean is known as the 'Ring of Fire'; ocean crust is sliding under the continents at a rate of 6 centimetres (2.4 in.) a year. Onshore a great chain of volcanoes stretches from the Philippines, along Japan, Kamchatka, the Aleutian Islands, and then down the full length of the west coast of the Americas. Offshore lies a series of trenches. The older the ocean crust, the deeper the trench, because the crust is colder and stiffer. The deepest of all is the Marianas Trench. Scientists aboard HMS *Challenger* were the first to try and plumb it, and in 1960 the *bathyscaphe *Trieste* made the deepest manned descent of it. It was

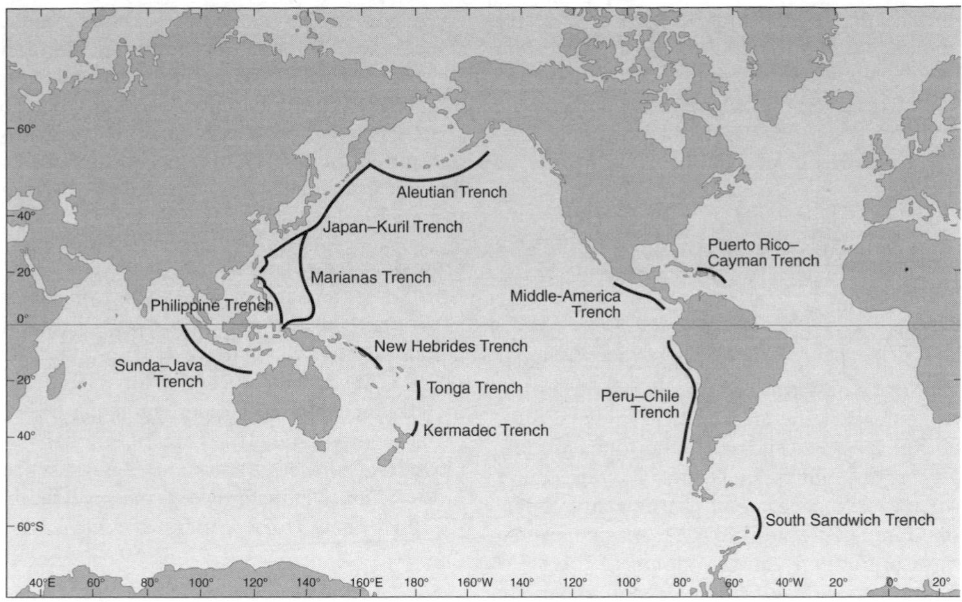

Distribution of the world's major ocean trenches

remeasured in 2001 and was found to be 10,926 metres (35,838 ft) deep. The seabed of each trench is inhabited by a unique community of animals, but their remoteness means that their faunas remain poorly known. See also GEOLOGICAL OCEANOGRAPHY.

www.geocities.com/thesciencefiles/marianas/trench.html M. V. Angel

trestle-trees, sometimes written **tressel-trees,** two short pieces of timber fixed horizontally fore and aft on each side of the lower masthead of a *square-rigged vessel and used to support the *topmast, the lower *crosstrees, and the *top. Smaller trestle-trees are similarly fitted to the topmast-head to support the topmast crosstrees and the *topgallant mast. For illus. see RIGGING: STANDING RIGGING.

triatic, a stay between the mastheads of a ship for mutual support. In powered vessels it is used to carry light *halyards along its length for the hoisting of flags.

trice up, to, in boats or ships, to haul or tie up using a small rope or line.

trick, the usual name given to the spell of duty allotted to a helmsman at the wheel.

trident, a three-pronged spear or sceptre, an attribute of the sea god *Poseidon or *Neptune. From this origin it has come to be accepted as a symbol of sovereignty over the seas. It is also the name of a nuclear *submarine missile.

trim. **(1)** The way in which a ship floats on the water, in relation to its fore-and-aft line. Most ships have trimming tanks so their trim can be adjusted by admitting or pumping out sea water acting as fore-and-aft *ballast. It is also used as a verb to describe the act of flooding or emptying trimming tanks. See also RED TIDES. **(2)** Also as a verb, it is the act of setting the sails of a sailing vessel so that they take the best advantage of the wind.

trimaran, a type of vessel with a central hull and twin floats, or hulls, on either side. See also CATAMARAN.

Trinity House was originally granted a royal charter by Henry VIII in 1514 to regulate *pilotage on the River Thames, and in 1566 Elizabeth I extended the Corporation's powers to include the erection of *sea-marks. Today, Trinity House is part of the **General Lighthouse Authority** which also comprises the **Northern Lighthouse Board** and the **Commissioner of Irish Lights**. These, respectively, provide and service the navigational lights and marks for Scotland and the Isle of Man, and for those in the waters of the Republic of Ireland and Northern Ireland. Trinity House, which is responsible for England, Wales, the Channel Islands, and Gibraltar, provides nearly 600 aids to *navigation in these areas and services them with two lighthouse *tenders, *Patricia* and *Mermaid*, and three *launches. It is therefore responsible for the aids to navigation provided by local port and harbour authorities, and it has powers to mark, remove, or destroy *shipwrecks, except Royal Naval ships, which are a danger to navigation. It is also a marine charity responsible for the education, training and welfare of mariners, and is a Deep Sea Pilotage Authority, having lost its responsibilities for District Pilotage under the 1987 Pilotage Act. The Court of Elder Brethren under the leadership of the master governs the Corporation. Administration of the lighthouse service and charities, and deep sea pilotage is delegated to the Lighthouse and Corporate Boards respectively. See also BRANCH.

trip an anchor, to, to break out the *flukes of a ship's anchor from an obstruction on the bottom. This is done by hauling up the anchor by its *buoy-rope which is always made fast to its *crown. This buoy-rope is by some erroneously called a *tripping line.

triple expansion engine, a further development of the marine *reciprocating engine. It was introduced in ships between 1870 and 1880 by adding a third cylinder to the two-cylinder *compound engine. The third cylinder was introduced between the compound engine's high- and low-pressure cylinders, and its effect was to use the available steam three times instead of twice as in the compound engine. The steam was first led to a high-pressure cylinder, the exhaust steam from that cylinder being led into an intermediate pressure cylinder, and then into a low-pressure cylinder before being converted by a *condenser back into the boiler feed water. It drove three pistons connected to the same crankshaft to add to the power transmitted to the *propeller shaft, and was made possible by improved boiler design which produced higher steam pressures. In the 1890s **quadruple expansion engines** were introduced by adding a fourth stage in the expansion of the steam, and were fitted in some ships, notably the four big German *ocean liners built between 1897 and 1902. And even after the introduction of the steam turbine some ships had engines on the quadruple expansion principle, using three cylinders for the first three stages and a low-pressure steam turbine for the fourth.

tripping line, a small rope made fast to the *yardarm of a *square-rigged ship's *topgallant *yard when the *lifts and *braces were removed before the yard was *struck down on deck. Its purpose was to hold one end of the yard so that it could be canted to the perpendicular before being lowered. Similarly, a tripping line was employed when lowering a *topmast, being used to hoist the mast sufficiently to take its weight off the *fid to allow it to be withdrawn before lowering.

trireme, a Mediterranean war *galley propelled by three banks of *oars. See also WARFARE AT SEA.

Triton, a sea deity of Greece and Rome, son of *Neptune by Amphitrite or, according to some, by Celeno Salacia. He was powerful among the sea deities and was said to be able to calm the ocean and abate *storms at pleasure. His body above the waist was that of a man, and below the waist a *dolphin, but he has also been represented with the forefeet of a horse. He is generally depicted in the act of blowing a conch or seashell. The name has also been allocated to all sea deities who are half men and half *fish.

tropical storms develop when the upper 50 metres (165 ft) or more of tropical ocean warms to over 26.5°C (80 °F) in regions that are over 500 kilometres (300 mls) from the equator, where *Coriolis forces are strong. They are intense low-pressure cyclonic systems that do not contain *fronts between warm and cold air masses. Once their wind speeds reach 17 metres per second, or m/s, (32 knots/59 kph/37 mph) they are termed tropical storms and are given names. Since the energy fuelling these damaging storms is the heat that is rapidly being transferred from the ocean to the atmosphere by convection, while they stay over the ocean they continue to grow in intensity. Once wind speed reaches 33 m/s (64 knots/

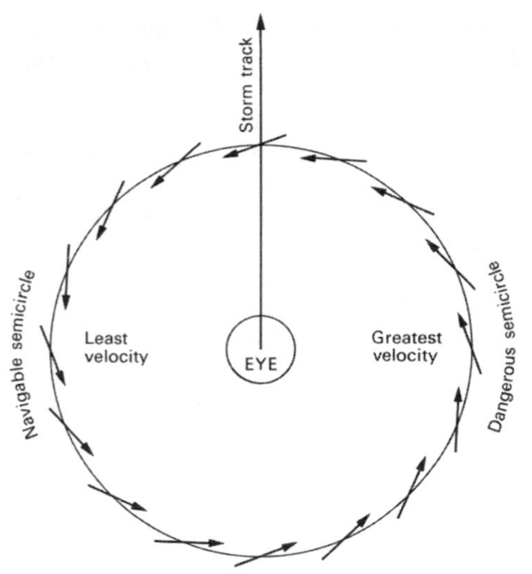

Tropical storms, northern hemisphere

118 kph/74 mph) they are designated as hurricanes (or typhoons in the North Pacific west of the dateline, or tropical cyclones in the Indian Ocean). The speed with which they can intensify is alarming. In 1988 winds in hurricane 'Gilbert' rose from 203 kph (127 mph) to 294 kph (184 mph) in 24 hours as the pressure in the *eye dropped from 960 to 888 mb. The highest winds recorded in a hurricane were 304 kph (190 mph) associated with Typhoon 'Tip' in 1979, but since such winds often destroy the recording instruments, wind speed records are seldom trustworthy.

The destructive force of tropical storms is not necessarily the result of the winds, as rainfall can cause serious flooding. In 1980 cyclone 'Hyacinth' deposited 566 centimetres (223 in.) of rain in ten days on the island of Réunion. **Storm surges** (see TIDES) generated by hurricanes cause immense death and destruction. The highest storm surge on record of 13 metres (42 ft) occurred in Australia in 1899, but it is along low-lying coastlines like that of Bangladesh that storm surges have drowned hundreds of thousands of people in a single event.

http://tropical.atmos.colostate.edu/

M. V. Angel

trot, a multiple *mooring for small boats or *yachts. The base mooring is laid in a straight line and from it individual moorings rise at intervals spaced to allow the boats room to swing with the *tide. Trots save considerable space in harbours, *marinas, and congested anchorages, and are also more economical in *ground tackle. Small vessels secured alongside each other are also said to be moored in a trot.

truck. **(1)** A circular wooden cap fitted to the tip of a vessel's wooden mast. It sometimes has one or two small *sheaves through which to *reeve signal *halyards. **(2)** The wooden wheels of the carriages on which the guns of a sailing warship were mounted were known as the trucks of the carriage. **(3)** See PARREL.

true, the direction of the North Pole from any place on the earth's surface, or of any *course or *bearing in its relation to the North Pole, as opposed to the *north magnetic pole.

trundle-head, an old term which was applied to the lower drumhead of a *capstan when it was double and worked, through a single shaft, on an upper and lower deck. Later, it was also sometimes used to describe the capstan head into the holes of which the squared ends of the capstan bars are inserted.

truss, originally the *parrel which bound a *yard to its mast in a *square-rigged ship. However, the introduction of a metal *gooseneck, which centred and secured the yard well free of the mast, made the original truss obsolete and itself took on the name of truss. It is pivoted to allow both vertical and horizontal rotation of the yard.

trysail, a small sail set for heavy weather in place of the normal sails, especially in small sailing craft. Originally a rectangular sail with its own *gaff, which was used to replace a *gaff-rigged mainsail, but currently a triangular sail usually set over the main boom when the mainsail has been *handed and stowed. In this state it is sheeted to the boom or independently.

trysail mast, in the US Navy during the days of sail, a light mast stepped aft of the *mizzen-mast. The *spanker, and sometimes the *spencer, was set on it, and it was stepped in such a way that the *stays from the *spider band of the mizzen-mast did not interfere with its *gaff or boom. It was sometimes called a snow mast, but see also SNOW.

try works, the name given to the iron pots set in brickwork and used in the days of sail for boiling the oil out of the blubber of *whales. When *whaling was widespread during the 18th–19th centuries these would normally be set up either on the deck of a whaling ship if out at sea or on shore if a suitable operating base was available. The process was called 'trying out' the oil.

tsunami, a Japanese term (*tsu*, harbour, *nami*, wave) for *waves triggered by earthquakes, landslides, volcanic eruptions, or large meteorites splashing down in the ocean. They are sometimes mistakenly called tidal waves but they are nothing to do with *tides. They are very large scale versions of the ripples that radiate out when a stone is dropped into water. They occur most frequently in the Pacific Ocean where major earthquakes are common occurrences along the ocean's active margins where the oceanic plates are slipping down below the continents. So the disaster in the Indian Ocean on Boxing Day 2004 was unexpected. Associated with the major plate boundary between the Indian and Eurasian tectonic plates, it was triggered by a major earthquake over more than 100 kilometres (63 mls.) of seabed off the north-west coast of Sumatra. Its epicentre was in deep water at 3.32° N., 95.85° E. and measured 9.0 on the Richter Scale, the fourth largest earthquake recorded for a century. The displacement of the seabed represented about 130 years of sea-floor spreading (see GEOLOGICAL OCEANOGRAPHY), hence the violence of the shock. The fault line is orientated north/south so the waves spread more east/west; fortunately for vulnerable countries like Bangladesh it did not travel far in a northerly direction, otherwise the subsequent loss of life would have been even more shocking. Another factor was the earthquake occurred only just below the seabed; if it had been deeper within the Earth's crust the shock waves would have stayed within the rocks and would not have radiated out in the ocean.

A tsunami is not one but a series of waves. Over deep water each wave is only about a metre high, and the distance between wave crests is over 100 kilometres (63 mls.). They travel at speeds of up to 700 kph (437 mph), about as fast as a passenger jet flies, but are almost impossible to detect out in the open ocean. The waves from the 2004 tsunami took just fifteen minutes to reach Sumatra, 30 minutes to reach the Andaman Islands and 90 minutes to reach Thailand, so even if a tsunami warning system had been in place, as it has been for some time in the Pacific, it is unlikely that it would have saved many lives in those countries. A warning system, which at the time of writing is due to be installed in 2005, may have helped save life in Sri Lanka, where the wave took two hours to arrive and the Maldives where it took three and a half hours. It took seven hours to reach East Africa. Television gave some warning of its approach and only one life was lost on the Kenyan coast. But there was no warning for Somalia and hundreds died.

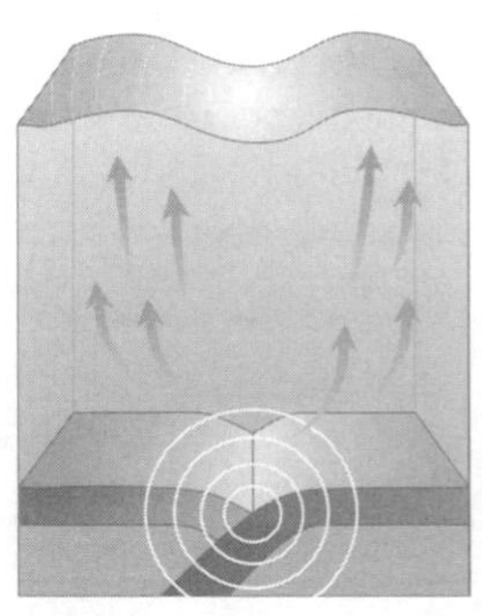

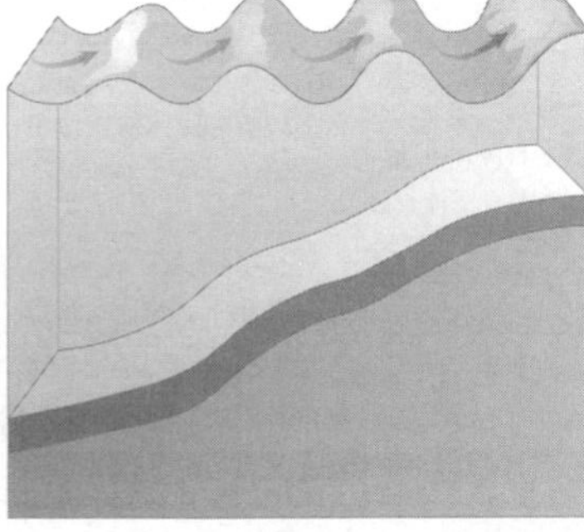

Creation of a tsunami

A tsunami can cross the Pacific in a less than a day. In 1960 a powerful underwater earthquake off Chile, measuring 8.6 on the Richter scale, generated a tsunami that killed many people locally. Fifteen hours later it came ashore at Hilo in Hawaii. Its height was 10.7 metres (35 ft) and despite warnings it killed 61 people. This was mainly because, after the first wave, people began to return to their homes only to be drowned when the second wave struck the shore. In Hilo alone this tsunami caused damage costing $US24 million.

As the tsunami waves reach shallow water, the drag of the seabed slows them so their heights build up in excess of 10 metres (33 ft), even so they can be still travelling at speeds of over 100 kph (63 mph). They come ashore as a great river of water, so their destructive power is awesome. If they are funnelled into harbours or bays they can resonate back and forth like sound in a musical instrument, which increases their destructiveness. One interesting observation of the impact of the 2004 Indian Ocean tsunami was that coastlines with intact *mangrove swamps and offshore *coral reefs were far less seriously affected than those where the mangroves had been cleared and the coral reefs degraded, so the degradation of coastal habits led to greater damage and loss of life (see also ENVIRONMENTAL ISSUES).

Tsunamis give little warning of their approach, but often the sea *ebbs away from shallow bays leaving boats high and dry before the arrival of the first destructive wave within about half an hour. This first wave is usually followed by several more, and, as was experienced in Thailand on Boxing Day 2004, it is not always the first of the waves that is the largest. This tsunami immediately killed over 200,000 people and rendered millions homeless and exposed them to serious health risks and economic ruin. Previous to that the most destructive tsunami on record resulted from the explosion of Krakatoa, a volcanic island in the Sunda Strait between the south of Sumatra and Java. A large volcano had collapsed in AD 416, forming an underwater caldera—a cauldron-like cavity—and leaving a few remnant islands, one of which was Krakatoa. On 27 September 1883, after a long series of volcanic eruptions, the island exploded. It is believed that the eruptions had cracked open the magma chamber beneath the volcano and water had flowed in. The resulting explosion had a force estimated to be 20,000 times that of the Hiroshima atom-bomb, and caused the island to collapse back into the caldera. The resulting tsunami that came ashore in Sumatra and Java reached an estimated 40 metres (130 ft) in height, and it wiped out all the coastal communities along the shoreline, killing an estimated 30,000 people.

Another destructive tsunami was the one which hit Japan in 1896. Fishermen fishing out at sea off Sanriku were unaware that it had passed beneath them, but when they returned to port they found 28,000 people had been killed by the waves. Between 1995 and 2005 about 2,000 people were killed by tsunamis around the Pacific.

Recently concern has been expressed about the lack of stability of Cumbre Vieja, a volcano on the island of La Palma in the Canaries. Some, but not all, geologists, have speculated that if this volcano erupts its flanks may collapse and triggered a major underwater landslip. This might generate a **mega-tsunami** that would have a devastating impact on the eastern seaboard of North America. No such mega-tsunami has been experienced during historical times, but about 5,000 years ago during the Bronze Age there is archaeological evidence that a giant wave over-topped a number of Scottish islands wiping out settlements at least 65 metres (200 ft) above sea-level. This was probably triggered by a massive failure of the *continental shelf off south-west Norway.

M. V. Angel

Bryant, E., *Tsunami: The Underrated Hazard* (2001).

Simon Winchester, S., *Krakatoa: The Day the World exploded, August 27 1883* (2003).

http://observe.arc.nasa.gov/nasa/exhibits/tsunami/tsun-start.html

tuck, the shape of the *afterbody of a ship under its stern or *counter, where the ends of the bottom planks or plates fit into the tuck-rail or tuck plate.

tug, a specially designed vessel which *tows other vessels, or *dumb barges, though it pushes them, too. In the West the earliest known ones were *paddle-wheel boats, and among the first to use *steam propulsion were two Royal Navy tugs, the *Comet* and *Monkey*. These

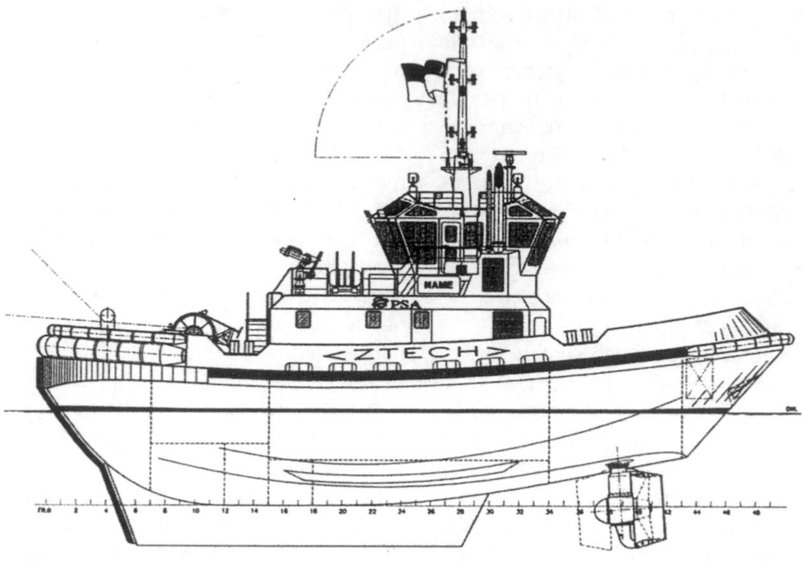

Fig.1: The Z-TECH is a tug design which aims to combine the best characteristics of the ASD and Z-drive tugs. Speed and bollard pull *astern is almost the same as when it goes *ahead, and because it works in either push or pull mode it has a very flat forward *sheer for working under the flared bows of *container ships, with a rounded, well-fendered bow. This makes it look in profile as if its bow is its stern, and vice versa, as in open water it operates stern first in tractor mode

were purchased in 1822 and were employed to tow *ships of the line out of harbour when the wind was unfavourable. The port or harbour tug aids large vessels to enter and leave their *berths; the larger ocean-going one is mainly concerned with *salvage work, though nowadays seagoing tugs also fight oil *pollution at sea, and can be used for fire-fighting as nearly all are suitably equipped for this. There are also the tugs which service the *offshore oil and gas industry. One kind positions and anchors offshore drilling rigs, another supplies them. Often these roles are combined into one powerful anchor-handling supply vessel. This can be a ship of about 2,300 tonnes and about 74 metres (240 ft) in length which is capable of carrying on its long afterdeck over 1,000 tonnes of cargo. There are also various forms of pusher tugs—known in the USA as towboats—designed for inland waterways, and the 'notch tug'. This pushes a specially designed *barge which has a notch in its stern into which the tug's bows are secured.

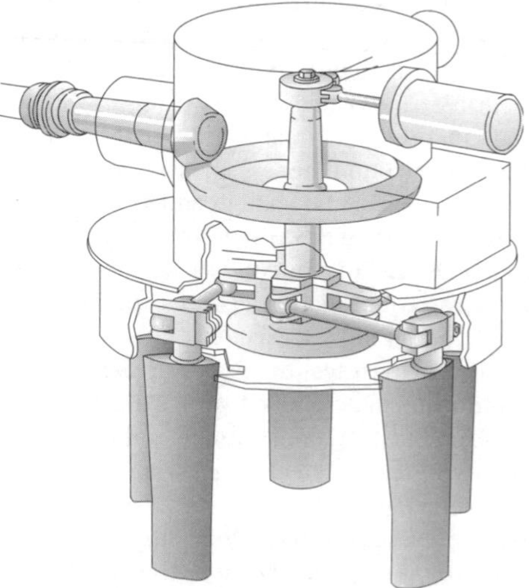

Fig. 2: A very simplified diagram of a Voith Schneider Cyloidal propulsion unit. The cutaway section shows the kinematic linkage which controls the pitch of each blade as the assembly rotates

The traditional tug had the *bridge right forward and a pronounced overhang on its *counter. Most of the length of the vessel was taken up by the after working deck which was clear of anything that might obstruct the bows of the towed vessel, and allowed the tug crew to handle the tow ropes safely. Today a tug's profile

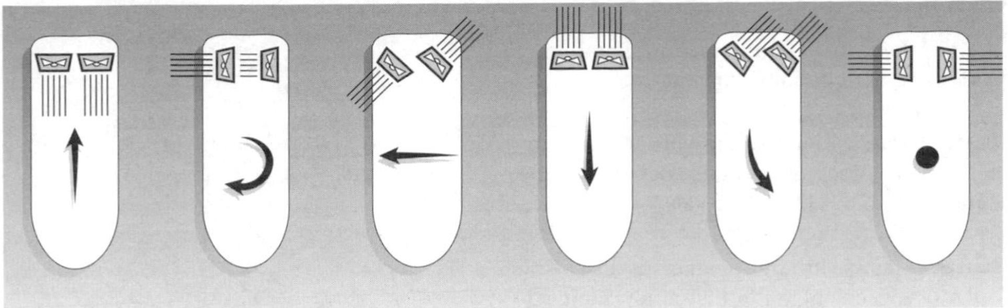

Fig. 3: The relative positions of the propulsion units of an ASD tug while performing the manoeuvres shown by the arrows. The same techniques are used by a Z-drive tractor tug with azimuthing units fitted forward

has altered (see Fig. 1), its manoeuvrability and power more so. Different kinds of propulsion systems have largely replaced the traditional single or twin screws fitted to rigid *propeller shafts at the stern, while the early *diesel engines have been replaced by ones that are often turbocharged and have six to eight cylinders. These engines have considerably increased a tug's **bollard pull**—the power, expressed in tonnes, produced by a tug when pulling against a fixed object like a *bollard. They also power the vessel's propulsion system, whether it be azimuthing—a propulsion unit with a conventional propeller which can be rotated about its vertical axis to achieve the maximum thrust—the Voith Schneider Cycloidal propeller system (see Fig. 2), or the tubular-shaped Kort nozzle which can improve a tug's bollard pull by up to 30–40%. There are two forms of Kort nozzle within which the propellers rotate: the fixed nozzle is part of the hull structure and has the ship's *rudder immediately *aft of it; the steerable one has a rudder, or rudders, incorporated into it which fits around the tug's screw(s).

With the development of these propulsion units have come different types of tug. The **combi-tug** has a conventional single propeller on a fixed shaft, but also has a small retractable azimuthing unit beneath its bows; the azimuthing **stern-drive tug** (ASD) is similar to a conventional twin-screw tug except that the propellers and fixed shafts have been replaced by azimuthing propulsion units (see Fig. 3); and the **tractor tug**, known as a Z-drive tractor tug. This has either two Voith Schneider Cycloidal propeller systems, or azimuthing propulsion units, that are fitted, not at the stern, but about a third of its length from the bow. This allows it to push as efficiently as it pulls which makes it ideal for ship-handling. The tractor tug also has a large *skeg fitted beneath its stern for directional stability and those with the Schneider Cycloidal system have a plate to protect the propellers. The plate also acts as a nozzle effect to the flow of water which improves the tug's performance.

Gaston, M., *Tugs Today* (1996).

tumble-home, or **tumbling-home,** the amount by which the two sides of a ship are brought in towards the centreline after reaching their maximum *beam. It is the opposite of *flare, in which the sides curve outwards. Wooden ships of the 15th–18th centuries, and particularly wooden warships, were built with a very pronounced tumble-home, making the width of the upper deck considerably less than that of the main and lower decks. Warships had to have the tumble-home to accommodate the main- and lower-deck guns, which were much larger than those mounted on the upper gun-

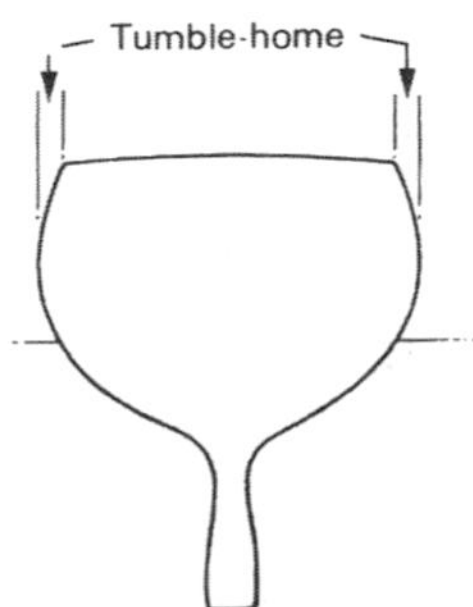

Tumble-home

deck and needed more space for the gun crews to work them. The older term, tumbling-home, had an even earlier one, housing-in.

tun, a large cask for carrying wine. It had a capacity of two pipes, usually considered to be the equivalent to 477 litres (105 gals.).

tuna are fast-swimming predacious *fish of the open ocean belonging to the family Scombridae. They are important both for commercial *fisheries and as sports fish. They are caught by *purse seine nets, *long-lining, and trolling, and like many commercial species are overfished. The thirteen species of true tunas include tunny (*Thunnus maccoyii*), albacore (*T. alalunga*), big-eye (*T. obesus*), yellow-fin (*T. alacares*), and black-fin tunas (*T. atlanticus*) and there are numerous other smaller tuna-like bonitos (*Katsuwonus* sp. and *Sarda* sp.) and Spanish mackerels (*Scoberomorus* sp.). The largest is the blue-fin (*Thunnus thynnus*), which in twenty years grows to a length of over 3 metres (10 ft) and a weight of 680 kilograms (1,500 lbs). Tracking devices have shown that a large blue-fin spends most of its time in the upper 30 metres (100 ft), but makes frequent excursions to depths of 300 metres (1,000 ft). Its average swimming speed is around 6 kph (4 mph), but it can achieve bursts of 20–30 kph (12–19 mph). The fastest recorded burst was 70 kph (43.4 mph). A tuna can achieve such fast speeds because its body is highly streamlined but also because, like *marlin, it has red muscle that keeps its body 10 °C (50 °F) warmer than the surrounding sea water. Blue-fin undertake long migrations. Fish tagged off the east coast of the USA have been recaptured off Africa and in the Mediterranean. Commercially large tunas demand high prices, because of the Japanese passion for eating the flesh raw in sushi and sashimi. However, eat them in moderation because, being top predators, they accumulate high concentrations of pollutants such as mercury and organohalogens in their bodies. See also ENVIRONMENTAL ISSUES; POLLUTION.

www.flmnh.ufl.edu/fish/Gallery/Descript/BluefinTuna/BluefinTuna.html M. V. Angel

turk's head, an ornamental knot to provide a *stopper on the end of a rope. It is a continuation of a simple manrope, or double *wall and crown, knot by tucking the strands of the rope a second time. A running turk's head is formed by making the knot around the other part of the rope.

Turk's head

turnbuckle, see BOTTLESCREW.

turret, the armoured housing for a warship's main guns of 6-in. (15-cm) *calibre, or more. It was fitted onto a bearing ring on top of an armoured *barbette. Turrets were usually used on *cruisers, or larger warships, all of which are now all but defunct.

turtle-boat, an American craft designed by the US engineer Robert *Fulton (1765–1815), one of the pioneers of the development of the *submarine, for operations against British warships during the Anglo-American War (1812–14). It was completely decked over and driven through the water by a screw *propeller worked by hand through a series of cranks inside the hull. Its weapon consisted of a number of floating charges towed *astern, with their firing mechanism operated by long trigger *lanyards. The proposed method of attack was to swing the towed charges against the side of the British warship and explode them by pulling the lanyard. With a *freeboard of a few centimetres, it was hoped the turtle-boat could be mistaken for a floating tree trunk or some other object and so be able to approach an enemy without causing suspicion. But it was driven ashore on Long Island during a *gale, where it was destroyed by the British before it could do any damage or its capabilities could be tested.

turtle deck, the upper deck of a vessel constructed with a pronounced curve from the centreline of the vessel down to the sides. Its purpose is to assist overboard the flow of any sea water shipped over the bows. See also XEBEC.

twice laid. **(1)** The name given to rope made from a selection of the best yarns from old rope which has been unlaid. **(2)** A sea dish, in the days of sailing navies, made from salt *fish left over from the previous day's rations and mashed up with potatoes or yams. It was not one of the most popular dishes.

'two blocks', a maritime term to describe a *purchase in which there is no more travel by reason of the moving *block having been hauled up to the standing block. By extension it has also come to mean a rope or wire which has been hauled as *taut as possible. A similar term with the same meaning is 'chock-a-block'.

tye, a heavy rope used to extend the pull of a *tackle through a masthead *block. It is typically used in conjunction with the *jeers to hoist the *yards of *square-riggers during the rigging of the ship.

typhoon, see TROPICAL STORMS.

U

U-boat, see SUBMARINE.

ullage. **(1)** The amount of wine or other liquor which has leaked from a cask, rendering the remainder of little worth and fit only to be thrown away. Damaged goods, particularly in relation to victuals, are commonly known on board ship as **ullaged.** **(2)** A lazy or cack-handed sailor who is of little use in a ship.

umiak, see KAYAK.

Una rig, a small sailing boat which has either a *gaff rig or a *lugsail set on a mast stepped very close to the boat's *stem, and carrying no *foresails. This rig was common enough in lightly built upriver racing boats in the 19th century, and obtained its name in Britain from the 5-metre (16-ft 6-in.) racing boat called *Una* on which it was first tried in 1852. For generations it was the regular rig of the Cape Cod *catboats in the USA.

under bare poles, see BARE POLES.

under-run, to, to haul a *hawser or *warp over a *skiff or boat in order to clear it from an underwater obstruction. To under-run a *tackle is to separate all the moving parts so that none is crossing and the tackle is clear for use.

underwater vehicles are used by those studying *oceanography and *marine archaeology, and they also have application in the *offshore oil and gas industries, and for marine *salvage and military surveillance. Free-swimming divers can only reach depths of 100 metres (300 ft) with any degree of safety, so if humans are to observe what is deeper than that they either need to descend in pressure-protected containers like a *submarine, or send down devices that can 'see' into the depths, either on an umbilical, like **remotely operated vehicles** (ROVs), or free-ranging robotic devices known as **autonomous underwater vehicles** (AUVs). Early versions had limited manoeuvrability and carried simple *sonar and cameras, but modern devices are more manoeuvrable and sophisticated, for example carrying 'Television and Search and Salvage System', or TVSS. These have made the use of manned underwater vehicles for commercial and defence applications all but redundant.

The first attempts to make first-hand observations in water as deep as 300 metres (1,000 ft) were by William Beebe who in 1934 had himself sealed in a *bathysphere. Then Auguste Piccard (1884–1962), one of the pioneers of underwater vehicles, built the *bathyscaphe *Trieste*, in which his son Jacques, together with Don Walsh, dived to the bottom of the Marianas *Trench in January 1960; an achievement repeated in 1995 by a Japanese ROV. In the early 1960s deep submersibles, often referred to as **deep submergence vessels** (DSVs), began to be developed.

The best known of these DSVs is the *Alvin*. Funded by the US Navy, it first came into operation in 1964. Among its many achievements, it found a hydrogen bomb lost in the sea off Spain and discovered the rich biological communities that live around *hydrothermal vents. *Alvin* can carry three people, a pilot and two observers, to a maximum depth of 4,500 metres (14,850 ft) from its *catamaran support vessel, *Lulu*. Other underwater vehicles have much shallower depth capabilities, but in the case of the *Johnson Sea Link*, run by the Harbor Branch *oceanographic institute, its Plexiglas compartment gives far better facilities for scientific observation and sample collection.

During the 1980s the Deep Submergence Laboratory at the Woods Hole Oceanographic Institution developed two underwater vehicles, *Argo* and *Jason*. They were designed to be used simultaneously from the same support vessel. The *Argo* was a towed survey vehicle capable of scanning large areas of the ocean bed with sonar, film, and video, but also functioned as the mother ship of the much smaller ROV *Jason*. When *Argo* detects something on the seabed that merits closer inspection *Jason* is sent to look at it. During an expedition led by Dr *Ballard, it was these two vehicles that discovered the **Titanic* in 1985. They and similar ROVs have also explored the remains of the German *battleship *Bismarck*, *ocean liners **Lusitania* and *Britannic*, and numerous other *shipwrecks of interest to those working in *marine archaeology.

Manned underwater vehicles are not only more expensive to run but also, for safety reasons, can only be operated in good sea conditions. So as technology has improved sensors design, information storage, battery power, propulsion, underwater *navigation, and the streamlining of the hulls, the ranges of AUVs have increased to hundreds of kilometres with depth capabilities of over a thousand metres. The stimulus for their development has come from the exploitation of deep-water hydrocarbons, science, and military requirements. AUVs can undertake pre-programmed tasks without the need for communication, so they are ideal instruments for seabed surveys, covert surveillance, deep-water inspections, and *cable-laying tasks, as well as making scientific observations. The cost of conducting an AUV survey may be a third less than a conventional research ship, and AUVs reach regions that are otherwise inaccessible, such as beneath *ice sheets. Robotics will probably have the same sort of impact in revolutionizing our understanding of the ocean as did the development after the Second World War (1939–45) of electronics, sonars, and computers.

www.diveweb.com/rovs/features/mayjune2000.01.htm

http://seawifs.gsfc.nasa.gov/OCEAN_PLANET/HTML/oceanography_how_deep.html

M. V. Angel

under way, the description of a ship which has movement through the water. The term is sometimes written as **under weigh.** Theoretically, a ship is considered to be under weigh only when its anchor has been broken out of the bottom while the ship itself is still stationary; it is under way as soon as it begins to move under its own power. However, the two terms have become virtually synonymous, under weigh being a modern spelling distortion of an older term. As a ship's *rudder is only effective when the ship is moving through the water, the importance of being under way is that the ship will then answer to its *helm and so becomes subject to the *International Regulations for Preventing Collisions at Sea.

underwriter, an insurer of ships and cargoes from loss and damage, the name coming from the insurer writing his name under the policy of insurance. The request for insurance is termed the offering of a 'risk', and in marine insurance the word risk is equivalent to the liability of the underwriter. Each underwriter of a marine insurance puts opposite his name the percentage of the total risk for which he accepts liability. See LLOYD'S.

United Nations Conference on the Law of the Sea (UNCLOS). In the years following the Second World War (1939–45) it became apparent that ocean resources needed to be regulated and partitioned in some way. The 17th-century doctrines, which eventually led to the three-mile limit and *territorial waters, were proving totally inadequate in the 20th century for solving international disputes over fishing rights, the regulation of *navigation, the prevention of marine *pollution and other *environmental issues, and the exploitation of *offshore oil and gas deposits. Some nations were already claiming extensions to their territorial waters and a new codification of international law was needed if international instability and conflict was to be avoided.

The first United Nations Conference on the Law of the Sea was therefore convened in 1958, and was the first conference to consider the law of the sea internationally. Eighty-six nations participated and adopted four conventions which were more or less based on existing customary law: the Territorial Sea and the Contiguous Zone; the *Continental Shelf; the High Seas; and Fishing and Conservation of the Living Resources of the High Seas. Apart from the problem of the width of the Territorial Sea, the first three became legally enforceable, but the fourth failed to attract enough support, and a second conference in 1960 failed to reach agreement on it and on fishing limits. Further conferences were held in 1973 and in 1982, and after nine years of vigorous bargaining between 160 sovereign states the convention containing the concept of an *Exclusive Economic Zone was finally adopted. Most importantly, it creates a procedure for the settlement of disputes that is binding. On 16 November 1994, a year after the convention had been ratified by the 60th state signing, it became international law. The convention has probably been one of the most important legal instruments formulated by the United Nations for sustaining international peace. For illus. see EXCLUSIVE ECONOMIC ZONE.

www.un.org/Depts/los/index.htm M. V. Angel

Universal Rule, the *rating rule developed by the great American *yacht designer Nat *Herreshoff in the early 1890s. The New York Yacht Club eventually adopted it in December 1902 instead of the Seawanhaka Rule and it was called the Universal Rule from 1904. It was used by many American *yacht clubs and many changes were made to it, but it never varied much from the original formula. Unlike the rule which governed *International Metre Class *yachts, the waterline length of a yacht built to the Universal Rule could be increased with hardly any penalty for sail area provided the *displacement was also increased. The rule's most famous products were the *J-class racing yachts built in the 1930s. It governed all *America's Cup matches between 1920 and 1937.

unstayed rig, used in small craft such as the Laser *dinghy, and in cruising boats like the Freedom and Nonsuch *yachts from the US and Canadian *yacht designers Garry Hoyt and Mark Ellis, respectively. The mast is free standing without stays and so it bends in gusts to spill wind and keep the boat from heeling excessively. Often the *luff of the mainsail (or *mizzensail and mainsail in a *ketch rig) is wrapped around the mast or masts, which are built of *carbon fibre or aluminium for high strength, to permit them to bend in a fair arc. The Freedoms, Nonsuches, and similar boats use *wishbone booms, which permit relatively easy handling of the large mainsail. Having no *rigging cuts costs and maintenance expenses, although the mast and the *partners around it must be unusually strong. In the ketch rig, when

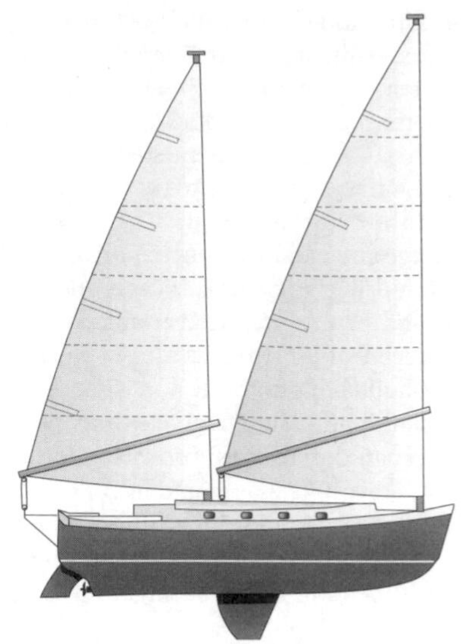

Freedom 33 designed by Garry Hoyt

*running free there are no *spreaders to interfere with the sails, and the sails can be *goose winged when the wind is dead *astern to give optimum speed and balance. Some larger boats like these do not have *jibs, but several do.

Another development of the unstayed rig is the Aerorig where the unstayed mast carries a boom which extends forward of the mast and takes a forestay for a jib. See also 'DYNASHIP'; JUNK RIG; LJUNGSTROM RIG; ROTATING RIG.

John Rousmaniere

up and down, the situation of the *cable when it has been hove in sufficiently to bring the *bows of the ship directly over its anchor.

'up funnel, down screw', the order given in British warships during the early days of *steam propulsion when it was decided to *furl the sails of a ship and proceed on the *reciprocating engine. At that time, when no ship could carry enough coal to work its engine for a complete passage, the engine was used only as an auxiliary means of propulsion when the wind failed. At the order, the boiler funnel was rigged on deck and the *propeller lowered in its *banjo until it was clear of the hull and could be coupled to the engine shaft.

uphroe, or **euphroe.** (1) From the Dutch *juffrouw*, maiden, the name given to a crow's foot *deadeye, a number of small lines spreading from a long wooden *block and used to suspend an *awning when spread over a deck. It was applicable only to vessels with two or more masts, the uphroe being secured between two masts and the lines supporting the ridge of the awning. Why the Dutch word for maiden should provide the origin of this term is obscure, except that the Dutch word for deadeye is *juffer* or *juffrouw*. **(2)** Large mast timbers from Norway for use in the largest ships. The term dates from the 17th century, when the sizes of ships built, both for trade and war purposes, increased significantly. The word was also used in Norway to describe a fir pole.

upper deck, the highest of the continuous decks which run the full length of a ship without a fall or interruption. It is the deck next above the main deck in those ships which have more than a single deck. In *ocean liners, the decks are numbered, or designated by letters, instead of having names.

upwelling describes the process in which water from deep down is brought up to the surface along divergent *fronts in the open ocean, in the *lee of headlands along coasts, and as a result of the interaction between *Coriolis force and the effects of alongshore winds. Where the upwelled water comes from below the *thermocline, the concentrations of the nutrients needed to stimulate the growth of the *marine plant phytoplankton are enhanced, so rich communities of *plankton and *fish develop. Upwelling occurs regularly along the coasts of California, Peru, north-west and south-west Africa, and in the north-west Arabian Sea, so these regions are major centres for commercial *fisheries.

M. V. Angel

urca or **uxer. (1)** A type of 16th-century ship similar to a *galleon in rig but usually smaller and more lightly armed and used to carry military stores from place to place. The name was Spanish, and it was the Spaniards who chiefly used them in the Mediterranean. **(2)** A type of Spanish *fly-boat of the 17th–18th centuries, flat bottomed with a high stern, of upto about 300 tons and armed with half a dozen or so guns according to size. Their rig varied from square to *lateen according to individual taste. Though mainly designed for, and used for, the carriage of coastal trade, some were attached to the main fighting fleets for service as dispatch boats.

US Coast Guard (USCG), created in 1915 when Congress directed the amalgamation of the Revenue Cutter Service, the Steamboat Inspection Service, the Bureau of Navigation, and the Lifesaving Service into a single agency under the Treasury Department. In the process, the new service inherited all of the responsibilities of its several parts, dating back to 1790. From the Revenue Cutter Service, the guard became responsible for enforcing all US maritime laws and suppressing *piracy, and so is authorized to make civil arrests. The Inspection Service contributed the inspection of shipping to ensure compliance with American regulations concerning construction, operation, crew skills and conditions, and ship safety. The guard acquired the Bureau of Navigation's responsibility for the identification and marking of *navigation hazards and channels, and, from the Lifesaving Service, the maintenance and operation of the many shore stations equipped with small craft for rescuing mariners in distress. *AMVER is now part of its *lifesaving organization. It was the American agency involved in supporting the International Ice Patrol established after the loss of the **Titanic*.

The principal task of the Coast Guard effort during the inter-war years was the enforcement of US Prohibition laws, 1920–33. To help it intercept major 'rum runners', it was loaned six *destroyers by the US Navy, 1930–2, to beef up offshore patrols. These were returned in mid-1934 and decommissioned.

In 1939, the Lighthouse Service was absorbed into the Coast Guard organization, thereby adding the maintenance and operation of more than 1,000 *lighthouses and *lightships to its responsibilities. Over the succeeding 60 years, some were eliminated and most of the remainder automated. At the start of the 21st century, only the Boston Light, dating from 1715, remained under human operation.

During the Second World War (1939–45), in keeping with a role inherited from the Revenue Cutter Service, the Coast Guard was transferred to the control of the Navy Department for the duration of the war. While its lesser units were involved in port security and coastal patrols, its high-endurance *cutters became *convoy escorts, as they had done in the First World War (1914–18). Coast Guardsmen were also assigned to the navy's amphibious forces to man the many landing craft coming into service.

In the succeeding half-century, the Coast Guard, in addition to its ongoing responsibilities, has been deeply involved in enforcing the 320-kilometre (200-ml.) *Exclusive Economic Zone, in the maritime aspects of environmental protection, in stemming the tide of illegal immigrants, particularly in the Caribbean area, and in the war against drugs, an effort as labour intensive as its earlier efforts during Prohibition.

The guard, too, has acquired a proportionally larger role in assisting the US Navy as a result of the great reduction in the latter service. Guardsmen were actively involved in Vietnam in the interdiction of coastal shipping, and in both Gulf wars, specializing in port security and control of shipping. Shifted from the Treasury Department to the Transportation Department, when that department was created in 1967, the Coast Guard again changed masters to the Department of Homeland Security, formed in 2002.

Johnson, R., *Guardians of the Sea* (1987).
www.uscg.mil/history Tyrone G. Martin

US Power Squadrons (USPS), the largest non-profit-making national boating organization in the USA. It has 60,000 members organized into 450 different squadrons. It gives instruction in sailing and *navigation, and related subjects and, in cooperation with the *US Coast Guard Auxiliary, it conducts safety checks of vessels at the request of their owners. It celebrates its centenary in 2014.

John Rousmaniere

USS, United States Ship, the prefix placed before the name of a warship of the US Navy.

US Sailing Association (US Sailing), the national governing body of sailing in the USA. It was first formed as the North American Yacht Racing Union (NAYRU) in 1897, its original purpose being to promote yacht racing and to unify the *racing and *rating rules in the USA and Canada, and throughout the yachting world. However, early efforts to achieve this latter aim failed and the NAYRU ceased to function until it was revived in 1925; thereafter some progress was made towards unifying the rules at an international level. However, in 1931 Canada formed its Canadian Yachting Association and by the 1970s it became evident that American sailors needed a governing body to represent them, and in 1975 the NAYRU, with the support of the US Olympic Committee, changed its name to the US Yacht Racing Union (USYRU) and was restructured to take a more active role in promoting the sport. Then in 1991 the USYRU voted to change its name to the United States Sailing Association, Inc., and to do business as US Sailing. Its current functions include certifying training instructors and race officers, and administering seventeen national championships.

Anderson, H., and MacArthur, R., *The Centennial History of the United States Sailing Association* (1998).

V

vail, to, an old seafaring word meaning to lower sails in token of submission or salute. A foreign warship meeting another in its own *territorial waters or *narrow seas would vail its *topgallant sails as a salute and acknowledgement that ownership of the waters through which it was sailing was represented by the other ship. A merchant ship would similarly vail its *topsails. See also SALUTES AT SEA.

vakka, a type of large *canoe with an *outrigger, and paddled by several men, found in the Friendly Islands.

vale, to, an old seafaring term meaning, of a ship, to drop down a river before starting on a sea voyage. Thus, a ship loaded with cargo in London would **vale down** the River Thames to the sea. The word probably derives from Latin *vale*, farewell.

van, the division of a fleet of warships which leads the *line of battle. The word comes from *vant*, a corruption of the French *avant*, in front.

Vancouver, George (1757–98), English *navigator and explorer. He began his career in the Royal Navy as a midshipman when he served under Captain James *Cook in his second and third voyages. He subsequently served in the West Indies, taking part in the victory of Lord Rodney (1719–92) over the French in the battle of the Saints in 1782.

In 1791 Vancouver was appointed to command an expedition to the north-west coast of America and on 1 April he sailed in HMS *Discovery*, a new ship of 530 tons, accompanied by the *Chatham* of 135 tons. Proceeding by way of the Cape of Good Hope and the south-west coast of Australia, where he discovered and surveyed King George Sound, he continued on to Dusky Bay, New Zealand, which he was the first to explore and survey, and arrived at Tahiti on 30 December.

After a stay of three weeks at Tahiti and a month at the Hawaiian Islands, the two ships sailed on to sight the Californian coast near Cape Mendocino on 18 April 1792 and then sailed northwards until reaching Juan de Fuca Strait. Passing through it, Vancouver entered and surveyed the island-studded water beyond, a deep inlet which he named Puget Sound after one of his officers aboard the *Discovery*. Continuing his survey, Vancouver discovered the insularity of the island that bears his name, and sailed down its western coast to Nootka Sound where, in accordance with his instructions, he accepted the cession of the territory by the Spanish who had occupied it since 1789.

After the midwinter months had been spent at Hawaii, exploration of the American coast was resumed in April 1793, the stretch between 35° N. and 56° N. being surveyed before the end of the year. During Vancouver's third stay in Hawaii, in January 1794, the Polynesian King Kamehameha formally ceded the island to the King of Great Britain; Vancouver accepted this, but the annexation appears never to have been officially ratified.

In March 1794, the expedition, having completed a survey of the other islands of the Hawaiian group, sailed north again to survey Cook's Inlet and Prince William Sound in Alaska, proving that the former was not a river estuary as had been surmised. Further surveys southwards down the coast were made to connect with the work of the preceding year, after which the two ships steered for home via Cape Horn, visiting, among other places, Valparaiso, where it was necessary to stay some weeks to make repairs. Both ships finally reached the Thames in October 1795.

Though Vancouver lacked Cook's humanity and acquired a reputation for harsh and even brutal disciplinary methods, he was otherwise a worthy disciple of the great navigator. His surveys were of a very high standard; and though there was one short outbreak of *scurvy during the voyage, the expedition lost only six men, all killed in accidents, during the four years and nine months it was away. See also EXPLORATION BY SEA.

Anderson, B., *Surveyor of the Sea* (1960).

vane. **(1)** A narrow *pennant or strip of *bunting mounted on a spindle. It was flown at the masthead of a sailing vessel to indicate the direction of the wind, though in most modern *yachts wind direction is transmitted from an electronic wind vane at the masthead to a dial in the *cockpit. In *square-riggers, where the helmsman was unable to see the mastheads because of the sails, a small vane, known as a **dog-vane**, was attached to a pike and placed on the *weather side of the *quarterdeck. The dog-vane usually consisted of thin strips of cork strung on a piece of twine and sometimes stuck round with feathers. **(2)** The sights of a variety of *quadrants, by which *altitudes were measured, were also known as vanes.

vane self-steering gear, a method by which the wind, acting on a rotatable *vane linked to a *rudder, can be set to steer a sailing *yacht on a given *course. This principle of wind-vane-operated gear was introduced in the mid-1920s to control model racing yachts while sailing downwind. Known as the Braine gear, after the name of its inventor, it proved highly effective, and in the model-yacht-racing world quickly superseded the older hit-and-miss contrivances with weights and springs then in use.

It was first applied to full-sized yachts about 1948. The gear comprised an upright metal or hardboard vane, like a small sail, mounted on a freely turning swivel plate. With the vane adjusted like a weathercock to the wind relative to the desired course, and connected by means of rods and linkage to a servo-tab on the yacht's rudder, or to a separate small rudder mounted right *aft, the yacht is made to keep her course whether *close hauled, or with the wind *abeam, or with a following wind.

These self-steering gears, which are manufactured in a variety of types and sizes, have been widely used by ocean-going yachtsmen, particularly when cruising short handed or solo. See also STEERING GEAR.

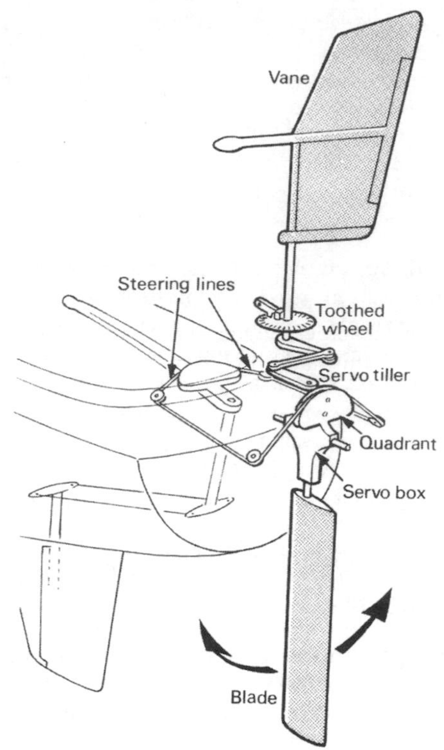

Vane self-steering gear of pendulum-servo type

vangs, the ropes leading from the outer end of a *gaff to the rail of sailing vessels, one on each side, to steady the gaff and prevent the sail from sagging away to *leeward when sailing *close hauled or *off the wind. They were used in *square-rigged ships on the gaff of the *mizzen, from which mast a gaff sail, known as a *spanker, was set. The *sprit mainsails of *barges are also fitted with vangs. The *kicking strap on the *boom of a *yacht is also often known as a vang, with a rope *purchase for the smaller sizes but hydraulically operated on the larger ones.

variation, or magnetic *declination, is the angle at any place between the magnetic *meridian and the geographical, or true, meridian. It is named east if the north end of the compass needle points to the right and west if it points to the left of the true meridian. With other corrections, notably *deviation, variation is applied to the compass course or compass *bearing. At any location, the variation may increase or decrease from year to year according to the movement of the *north magnetic pole, and such differences will be indicated on the chart. The first *chart to show lines of equal variation was that by the English astronomer Edmund Halley (1656–1742), which was published in 1701. This was also the first printed isoline map of any kind. For illus. see COMPASS ERROR.

Vasa, a 64-gun wooden warship, just over 45 metres (147 ft) in length, built at Stockholm to the order of the Swedish king Gustavus Adolphus, and the only surviving example of the complete hull of a 17th-century warship. On 10 August 1628 she sank in Stockholm harbour on her maiden voyage after a strong gust of wind heeled her over so far that she was flooded through her open *gunports. Attempts to raise her later that century failed, but she was rediscovered in 1956. In April 1961 a complicated *salvage operation brought the almost complete wooden hull to the surface from a depth of 33 metres (110 ft). Though all her iron nails and bolts had disintegrated, the hull had remained almost intact because it was held together by a large number of *treenails. About 25,000 objects, including carvings, textiles, leather, coins, equipment, and a number of skeletons were recovered, as well as parts of the ship. She was housed in a temporary museum and over a number of years her *timbers were treated with polyethylene glycol to preserve them, and she was eventually fully restored. In 1990 she was housed in a new *Vasa* museum in Stockholm where the temperature is controlled. See also MARINE AND UNDERWATER ARCHAEOLOGY; SHIPWRECKS.

veer, to. (1) To pay out a rope or *cable in a ship. The word is most usually applied to a vessel's anchor cable. There are many occasions when it is necessary to veer the cable, as for example when *mooring or unmooring, one of the two cables being veered while the other is shortened in. If a ship is lying to a single anchor and the weather deteriorates seriously, veering more cable frequently adds to its safety as, generally speaking, the greater the *scope of the cable, the greater the security. *Hawsers used in securing a ship to a *buoy or alongside a *quay are veered when they are paid out, but a sheet is never veered. **(2)** The wind when it changes direction in a clockwise direction is said to veer. A wind which veers is frequently a sign of settled weather in the northern hemisphere, of unsettled weather in the southern. See also MARINE METEOROLOGY.

veer and haul, to, to obtain an extra pull on a rope by alternately slackening it and hauling on it three or four times in preparation for a heavy haul. It gave the men hauling on the rope a sense of timing that, along with singing a *shanty, coordinated their efforts. In a *square-rigged ship, when hauling the *bowlines on the *tacks of the sail, the order was normally 'veer and haul'.

Verne, Jules (1828–1905), French author, who was born at Nantes and was an accomplished yachtsman. He originally studied for the Bar, but went to Paris where he wrote the librettos for a couple of comic operas which were reasonably successful. This encouraged him into a writing career, and with the publication in a magazine of some travel stories, he found his true *métier* in travel tales with a background of scientific knowledge and invention, which proved immensely popular all through Europe. If *Around the World in Eighty Days* (1872) is his most famous book, his *Twenty Thousand Leagues under the Sea* (1869) runs it very close. He has now given his name to a round-the-world *yacht race. See YACHTING: RACING AGAINST TIME.

Verrazzano, Giovanni da (1485–1528), Italian *navigator, born at the Castello Verrazzano in the Chianti district near Florence, a son of a noble family. At the age of 21 or 22 he moved to Dieppe to take up a maritime career, and from then on sailed in the service of France. During the next ten or twelve years he made a number of trading voyages to the Levant and appears to have met, and discussed *navigation with, Ferdinand *Magellan before the latter set off on his circumnavigation.

By 1523 Verrazzano had interested François I in a project of exploration and discovery in the New World with the idea of discovering for France a new passage into the Pacific Ocean and thus access to the wealth of the Far East. The king lent him a ship, the 100-ton *Dauphine*, and with financial backing from Florentine bankers, together with a second, smaller, ship, the *Normande,* he sailed from Dieppe to Madeira where the *Normande* left him to return to France. The *Dauphine* crossed the Atlantic alone and reached the American coast in the vicinity of the present Cape Fear in North Carolina and sailed north along the Carolina Outer Banks round Cape Hatteras and up to the present Kitty Hawk, mistaking the great extent of the Pamlico Sound, inside the Outer Banks, for the Pacific Ocean, and naming it the Sea of Verrazzano. He continued north and, encouraged by friendly Indians, entered New York Bay, probably anchoring in the narrows between Staten Island and the Long Island shore, the first European known to visit these waters. He continued northwards, visiting Narragansett Bay, the site of the present Newport in Rhode Island, rounding Cape Cod, and finally reached the Newfoundland coast. From there he returned to Dieppe, reaching there in July 1524.

Verrazzano was one of the first navigators to realize that America was a new continent, and not part of Asia, but he had difficulty in persuading either the king or the bankers to finance another voyage since he had brought back nothing of value from the new lands he had visited. But in 1527 he led a new expedition across the Atlantic, still in search of the mythical northern strait to the Pacific. Mutinous crews cut short his exploration, and all he achieved was a quick visit to Brazil, returning to France with a profitable cargo of wood from which valuable dyes could be extracted.

With the profits from the wood, and the hope of more, Verrazzano set off from Dieppe on his third voyage in the spring of 1528. He had the intention of searching for the strait into the Pacific, south of his previous exploration, and reached America at the Florida coast hoping to find signs of a strait around the Isthmus of Darien. Instead, after reaching the Bahamas, he sailed down the Lower Antilles, anchoring probably off the coast of Guadeloupe. Here he decided to go ashore, not knowing that instead of the friendly natives they had encountered during their first voyage, the Antilles were inhabited by man-eating Caribs. As soon as Verrazzano waded ashore, he was cut up and eaten on the spot.

vertex, the two points on a *great circle which have the maximum *latitude north and south, each being antipodal to the other. The only great circle without vertices is the equator.

vertical sextant angle, the angle in the vertical plane between the top of (say) a moderately close *lighthouse, or other prominent feature, and the *sea level below it read on a *sextant. If the height of the top of the observed object is known, the distance off the object can be found either by trigonometry or from a table included in most *nautical almanacs and tables. Allowance for tidal heights must be made when necessary. Vertical sextant angles are particularly useful to the *navigator who wants to keep a definite distance off a particular point, when the angle corresponding to the required distance can be pre-set on the sextant.

very lights (pron. veery), coloured pyrotechnic lights fired from a very pistol on board ship in order to communicate with another ship or with the shore. The very pistol has now been superseded by more modern means of communicating a ship's identity or as a *distress signal, etc.

Vespucci, Amerigo (1454–1512), a Florentine merchant-adventurer. His claims as an explorer and as the first European to reach mainland America, which he said he did in June 1497, have been doubted owing to the impossible distances and positions quoted in the letters in which the claims were made. Nevertheless, it is from the Latin version of his name, *Americus,* that the New World came to be called.

Vespucci's letters described four voyages to the New World, the first a private venture, the second under the Spaniard Alonzo de Ojeda, and the last two in the service of King Manoel of Portugal. In 1505 he became a naturalized Spaniard. That his accounts of his voyages had a basis of truth, and that he was by that time an experienced *navigator, is indicated by his appointment on 6 August 1508 as *piloto mayor,* or chief *pilot, of Spain, an office he held until his death.

***Victory,* HMS,** the fifth warship in the British Navy to bear this name, the first being the flagship of Sir John *Hawkins during the defeat of the *Spanish Armada in 1588. She was laid down at Chatham in 1759 as a first-*rate ship of the line of 2,162 tons, mounting 100 guns.

Her overall length was 69 metres (226 ft 6 in.) and her beam 16 metres (51 ft 10 in.). Work stopped on her when the Seven Years War (1756–63) ended, and she was not *launched until 1765. During the years of peace very little work was done on her and she was not completed until 1778, the year the French joined the Americans in their War of Independence (1775–82). Her first commission was as *flagship of Admiral August Keppel (1725–86), and during 1778 she was involved in her first action, off Ushant, and she subsequently saw action, always as a flagship, during the Revolutionary War with France (1793–1801). Between 1798 and 1800 she served as a hospital ship for the prison *hulks before undergoing an extensive refit—almost a rebuild—which lasted two years.

At the start of the Napoleonic War (1803–15) she became *Nelson's flagship in the Mediterranean, and carried him to the West Indies in his chase across the Atlantic after Admiral *Villeneuve. Then, in October 1805, he sailed in her from Portsmouth to take command of the fleet watching the combined Franco-Spanish fleet at Cadiz, and in the same month he was killed on her *quarterdeck during the battle of Trafalgar. She was badly damaged during the battle and had to be towed to Gibraltar for repairs before sailing for England with Nelson's body aboard.

After another extensive refit she was recommissioned in March 1808 and for much of the next five years served in the Baltic as the flagship of Admiral Saumarez (1757–1836). In December 1812 she was paid off and never saw action again. She remained in reserve until 1824 when she became the static flagship of the Portsmouth Command. Although she was always recognized as a historic ship, and particularly so by the closing years of the 19th century, no steps, beyond essential repairs to keep her afloat, were taken to preserve her. It was the naval historian Sir Geoffrey Callender (1875–1946), who, as honorary secretary and treasurer of the *Society for Nautical Research, instigated the drive to raise sufficient funds to restore her. She was put in *dry-dock at Portsmouth dockyard in 1921, and £120,000 was raised to return her to how she had looked at Trafalgar. When this was completed she was opened to the public in July 1928, a permanent memorial to Nelson, Trafalgar, and the British Navy as a whole.

Victory ships, a follow-on to the *Liberty ships produced during the Second World War (1939–45). They were intended for post-war use to fill the immediate gap in overall *tonnage left by the immense number of merchant ships sunk. They were built to a less spartan standard than the Liberty ships; the hull was lengthened and strengthened although remaining all-welded; a *forecastle was added; and steam turbines (see STEAM PROPULSION) replaced the *triple expansion engines of the Liberty ships. The standard gross tonnage was 7,607 and they had a top speed of 16 knots.

victualler, a merchant ship, during the days of sailing navies, taken up for naval use to carry victuals for a fleet when it was at sea for long periods. They were required because the ships had insufficient space on board to stow all the food needed. Once empty they were either sent home or broken up, in the latter case with the crews being taken on board the ships that had been replenished. Both Francis *Drake and George *Anson had victuallers with them on the first stages of their circumnavigations.

Victualling Board, an autonomous subsidiary of the British Navy Board which, until 1832, was charged with the administration of the Royal Navy. It was responsible for all naval victuals and *slops, placing on board every ship a *purser to issue these, and to keep all accounts. In the earlier years of the board's existence, this led to widespread dishonesty. However, by about the mid-18th century most of the more blatant dishonesty had been removed. In 1832 the Navy Board was amalgamated with the *Admiralty, and its subsidiary boards, including that of victualling, were abolished. All victualling for the fleet was put into the hands of the director of victualling who was a member of the Admiralty secretariat. See also PETTY WARRANT.

vigia, a term in *hydrography meaning a rock or shoal marked on a *chart, usually by report of a ship's *master, but whose actual existence has not yet been proved by a hydrographic survey.

Viking compass, a bearing-dial or sun-compass that works on the principle that the tip of the sun's shadow on a gnomon will trace curves that, within specific *latitudes and dates, can be used to maintain a *course at sea. The principle is that of the sundial.

In 1948, at a Greenland farm ruin that can be traced back to the settlement period of about AD 1000, the Danish archaeologist C. L. Vebaek excavated a half wooden dial with what are taken to be gnomon lines incised on the back and compass points cut around the outer edge. The navigational significance of the find has long been discussed and extensive sea trials have over the years been held using reproduction dials. A curve traced from the shadow of the sun over a whole day can certainly, within certain constraints, provide a means of following a particular direction. The extent to which such a device was adopted by the Norsemen is perhaps more open to question. Mike Richey

Villeneuve, Pierre Charles Jean Baptiste Silvestre, Comte de (1763–1806), French admiral, who gained rapid promotion in the navy under the Republic, reaching the rank of captain in 1793 and rear admiral in 1796. In 1798 he commanded a division of the French fleet under Admiral Brueys (1753–98) which had escorted Napoleon's army to Egypt and which was brought to action by *Nelson in the battle of the Nile, and was almost annihilated. However, Villeneuve's rear division was only lightly engaged during this action, and his *flagship and three others were the only French survivors.

Villeneuve was later promoted and in November 1804 was selected to command the French Toulon *squadron, which, in Napoleon's 'grand design', was to cross the Atlantic to combine in the West Indies with squadrons from Brest, Ferrol, and Rochefort. This whole force was then to return in overwhelming strength to dominate the English Channel while Napoleon ferried his army across it to invade Britain. The scheme broke down when Nelson pursued Villeneuve across the Atlantic, forcing him to return. Intercepted off Finisterre by a British squadron, Villeneuve fought an indecisive action, losing two ships before seeking shelter in Ferrol. According to his instructions, he should now, in company with the ships already in Ferrol, have attempted to evade the British *blockade and join the squadron in Brest, but he had little confidence in Napoleon's plan. Convinced that his main duty was to preserve his fleet and believing, incorrectly, that a superior British fleet lay between him and Brest, he took his squadron to Cadiz instead.

Once in Cadiz, Villeneuve's Franco-Spanish fleet was blockaded by an inferior British squadron which was soon reinforced by one under Nelson's command. Again Villeneuve refused to obey orders, this time to sail for the Mediterranean, and was only induced to do so on 19 October 1805 by the news that a successor had been sent to relieve him of his command. In the disastrous battle of Trafalgar two days later, Villeneuve was taken prisoner and carried to England. He was released on parole, and was found stabbed to death in a hotel at Rennes on 22 April 1806. Whether he was murdered or committed suicide has been argued by historians ever since, but as he left a farewell letter to his wife, suicide would seem to have been his most probable end.

Villiers, Alan John (1903–82), British *master mariner and maritime author, born in Melbourne, Australia. He went to sea at the age of 15 in the *barque *Rothesay Bay* and served altogether five years in *square-rigged ships. He then tried his hand as a journalist in Australia and in 1931 became part-owner of the four-masted barque *Parma* which twice won the grain race from Australia to England. In 1934 he purchased the Danish *sail training ship *George Stage*, renamed her *Joseph Conrad*, manned her with cadets, sailed round the world in her, logging 92,800 kilometres (58,000 mls.), and then wrote an account of his experiences in *The Cruise of the Conrad* (1937). Before the Second World War (1939–45) he sailed in Arab *dhows on the Persian Gulf–Zanzibar run and during it, as an officer in the *RNVR, commanded landing craft *squadrons during the invasions of Italy and Normandy, and afterwards in the Far East. After the war, he commanded the *Warspite*, the training ship of the Outward Bound Sea School, Aberdovey; sailed with the Portuguese *cod fishing fleet in the *schooner *Argus*; commanded square-rigged ships in such films as *Moby Dick* and *Billy Budd*; and commanded a *replica ship of the **Mayflower* in which he sailed to the USA in 1957 to commemorate the voyage of the Pilgrim Fathers in 1620. His other publications included: *Falmouth for Orders* (1928), *The*

Making of a Sailor (1938), *The Coral Sea* (1950), *The Quest of the Schooner Argus* (1951), *The Way of a Ship* (1954), *The New Mayflower* (1959), and *The Battle of Trafalgar* (1965).

Vinland, unknown region on the eastern coast of North America, possibly part of the Canadian maritime provinces, which is described in several Norse sagas. It was reached by the Norse explorer Leif Eriksson (*fl.* 11th century), the son of *Erik the Red, who set out from Greenland in about the year AD 1000 to search for a coastline which had been reported some years earlier. It was, apparently, thickly wooded, and the Norse settlers colonizing Greenland, made possible by *climate change, needed timber. Eriksson landed first on what could have been Baffin Island and on sailing south found a more hospitable place which he named *Markland*—a land of forests—which was possibly Labrador. He continued to sail south until he reached what seems, from the sagas, to be Nova Scotia or the northern coast of Newfoundland. However, Eriksson's description of the coastline has been the cause of much speculation, for he noted that 'wild grapes' grew there which is why he named the area Vinland. Since it was impossible for grapes to grow so far north some historians have suggested that Eriksson must have travelled further south, but it has also been suggested that what he described as grapes were in fact berries, possibly cranberries. According to the Norse sagas, further expeditions to colonize the area were undertaken but were unsuccessful.

Excavations on the northern tip of Newfoundland (L'Anse aux Meadows) in the 1960s, spurred by the fact that Vinland could also be interpreted as meaning 'grassland', conclusively proved that Norsemen had reached the island around AD 1000. Of particular interest was that butternuts, and pieces of carved butternut wood, were found on the site, and though grapes could never have grown in Newfoundland they do grow further south where butternuts can be found. As further confirmation of the presence of Norsemen in North America, a species of soft-shelled clam (*Mya arenaria*), identical to one that grows in low-*salinity waters in North American estuaries, has been found in 12th-century Viking excavations in Denmark.

What is known as the Vinland map was published in 1965. Owned by Yale University it was valued at $20 million (£13 million) and was supposed to date from about 1440. Its publication aroused tremendous controversy, and in 1973 it was declared a fake by the chemical analyst Walter McCrone. In 2002 his judgement was confirmed by chemists at University College London, who agreed with him that the map was drawn with synthetic ink that was not available until 1923. See also EXPLORATION BY SEA.

viol, violl, voyal, or **voyol,** the old name for the large *messenger used to assist in *weighing an anchor in cases where the anchor *cable was of too great a circumference conveniently to go round the barrel of a *capstan.

Voss, John Claus (*c.*1854–1922), Canadian sea captain and pioneer small-boat ocean *navigator. He spent many years at sea in *square-rigged ships before being induced in 1897 to buy a 9-metre (30-ft) *sloop, *Xora*, and sail with a companion some 9,600 kilometres (6,000 mls.) on a treasure-seeking voyage to the Cocos Islands. No treasure was found, but during this cruise Voss learned how safe even such a small vessel could be at sea. *Slocum's solo circumnavigation in his 11-metre (36-ft) *Spray* had caused widespread interest after its completion in 1895, and in 1901 a Canadian newspaper reporter suggested to Voss that a fortune could be made from stories if, between them, they sailed round the world in a boat that was smaller than the *Spray*. Voss was attracted by the idea, but instead of acquiring a smaller version of the *Spray*, he fitted out an old 11.6-metre (38-ft) Indian war *canoe, rigged her as a *schooner with three short masts, and, accompanied by the reporter, set sail from Victoria, British Columbia. A severe *gale in which the *Tilikum*, as Voss had named the canoe, rode to a *drogue which he had contrived proved enough ocean experience for the reporter, who left at the next port of call. Voss continued the voyage across the Pacific to Australia and New Zealand, across the Indian Ocean to the Cape, and thence by way of Pernambuco in Brazil to London after a combined sailing and lecture tour of some three and a quarter years. The *Tilikum* was shown at a marine exhibition at Earls Court, London, in 1905, while Voss continued to give lectures on the voyage and was elected a Fellow of the Royal Geographical Society.

After parting with his war canoe Voss next bought a tiny *yawl, 5.8 metres (19 ft) on the waterline, and called her *Sea Queen.* Sailing with a companion around the islands of Japan he rode out a *typhoon, again using the sea anchor he advocated for small craft. His voyages are described in his book *The Venturesome Voyages of Captain Voss*, which was first published in Japan in 1913. He died in reduced circumstances near San Francisco.

Vulcan, the first iron-built vessel ever constructed and as such a landmark in the history of *shipbuilding. In 1816 a committee set up by the Forth and Clyde Canal Company recommended the construction of an experimental fast passage *barge of iron, at the time a completely unknown material in shipbuilding. Her 'gestation period' of nearly three years enabled the designs to be assessed and someone sought to build her. A young shipwright, Thomas Wilson (1781–1873), was appointed and, with the aid of two blacksmiths, he started work in 1818 on the 20-metre (66-ft 6-in.) barge which was laid down near Coatbridge on the bank of the Monkland Canal. She was built throughout with plates and sections forged from puddled iron blooms, and everything was riveted, the constructional technique differing little from all later iron and steel vessels. As there were no iron rolling mills, every item had to be forged by the two blacksmiths, which made the appropriately named *Vulcan* one of the most labour-intensive ships ever built. She was *launched in May 1819 and was an outstanding success, first as a horse-drawn passenger ship between Edinburgh and Glasgow, and later as a cargo carrier. She was broken up in 1873. A *replica was constructed in 1988. See also CHARLOTTE DUNDAS.

Fred M. Walker

W

waft, to, old naval term meaning to escort a *convoy. Merchant ships in time of war were wafted from place to place by wafters, the equivalent of modern escort vessels.

waist, that part of the upper deck of a ship between the *forecastle and the *quarterdeck. In sailing ships, that part of the upper deck between the fore- and mainmasts. See also BOOMS.

waistcloth, or **wastecloath,** a decorative length of cloth which, during the 16th and 17th centuries, was hung, on occasions of state and on royal anniversaries, along the sides of a warship between the *poop and the *forecastle.

waister, the term in sailing-ship days for a seaman employed in the *waist of a ship for working ship, though there was little to do beyond hauling on ropes or swabbing the deck. Hence, the name came to be used to describe an untrained or incompetent seaman, or one who was worn out after many years of employment.

wale, an extra thickness of wood bolted to the sides of a ship in positions where protection is needed. Sailing men-of-war had a wale fixed between each row of *gunports to prevent the port-lids being damaged when going alongside an enemy in order to *board it. The wale below the lower gunports was the channel-wale, those between the upper rows of gunports were main-wales. Shorter wales, known as **chain-wales**, were bolted to the ship's sides opposite the masts to carry the ends of the *shrouds, the object being to hold the shrouds clear of the gunwale to prevent them rubbing against the ship's side. See also RUBBING STRAKE.

walking beam engine, a type of *steam propulsion engine developed in the USA from the early pumping engines installed by James Watt in many Cornish mines, in which a beam is pivoted in the centre above a vertical cylinder and transmits the motion of the piston down a crankshaft by a long connecting rod. This type of engine, used at first on land in mills and factories, was adapted in the USA for river *paddle steamers from about 1830. It was to be seen on almost all the side-wheelers on the Mississippi, Ohio, and other western rivers, as well as on New York *ferries and eastern seaboard coastal steamers.

To make local manufacture simple and to save top weight, the A-frames or entablature on which the beam was mounted in the vessel were almost entirely of wood, and the beam itself was made rigid by means of iron truss rods in the form of a flattened diamond. Owing to the height of these frames, the beam stood in full view above the upper deck of even the largest steamboats, and its movement as it rocked up and down turning the paddle wheels earned it the Native Americans' description 'mill walkee on river'.

Because of the weight of this lofty structure and its effect on the vessel's *stability, beam engines of this kind were seldom fitted to ocean-going ships. It was entirely American in conception and ideal for its purpose in smooth waters, but not to be found in quite the same form anywhere else in the world. In Europe its counterpart was the *side lever engine.

wall knot, a *stopper knot on a rope to prevent anything passing beyond it. The rope is unlayed to a distance of four or five times the circumference of the rope and the individual *strands tucked over the strand behind and under the strand in front. They are then each tucked again under the two strands in front and brought up to the centre. After each strand is hauled *taut they are *whipped together close to the knot and the ends cut off. A double wall knot is known as a **manrope knot**.

Wall knot

walt, an old term used of a ship when it was emptied of its *ballast so that it was not *stiff enough in the sea to carry a sail. Such a ship was said to be walt.

wardrobe, the name used to describe the various sails carried on board a racing or cruising *yacht.

wardroom, the name of the commissioned officers' mess in a British warship.

warfare at sea. As soon as seafaring began ships were used for warlike purposes.

Ancient Tactics and Weapons. By about the 7th century BC specialized warships were being used in the Mediterranean. These oared *galley-type vessels, with considerable operational and tactical mobility, would be the major warship type in this region for the next millennium. Galley warfare was essentially about *boarding and *entering, a land battle at sea in which enemy ships were taken in hand-to-hand combat. Other weapons could be mounted in the bows, such as projectors or *Greek fire and, later, guns. The ship itself could be used as a weapon, although *ramming was better directed at the *oars of hostile ships to deny mobility rather than sinking the enemy outright. Galley battles were fought bow to bow, in line abreast, and could be large-scale events with hundreds of ships on each side. To be powerful on land meant being powerful at sea as well.

In the Orient, too, maritime power became more important. 'China must now', wrote one commentator in 1131, 'regard the Sea and the River as her Great Wall, and substitute warships for watch-towers.' Within a century China had warships whose armament included trebuchets firing gunpowder bombs, and *paddle-wheel boats protected with iron plates.

In northern European waters a very different type of oared ship originated. These *longships and *knarrs were capable of longer voyages under sail. Their oarless merchant ship derivatives and other northern cargo vessels, such as the *cog, also began to be used for war, fitted with both after castles and forecastles to give a height advantage for weapon projection and entering. The expense of maintaining a Mediterranean-style galley navy was beyond all but the richest states, and ships that could double as warships and merchant vessels were at a premium. The *treasure ships of the Ming dynasty (1368–1644), which dominated the Indian Ocean, were both traders and warships, and with them China had, around 1420, a navy as powerful as any European nation.

During this early period naval battles took place in coastal waters and were parts of maritime campaigns in which the movement of troops and their supplies were the dominant objectives. *Piracy on seaborne commerce was always endemic in a situation where state power at sea was limited. Rulers had to work with the pirates rather than against them, encouraging them to direct their activities against the political opponents of the day.

The Ship of the Line. The 16th century saw the development of the ocean-going sailing ship armed with guns. Though guns were added to the castles of ships, and later through *gunports in the sides, naval tactics remained dominated by galley thinking. Engagements were still bow to bow with the side-mounted guns trained as far fore and aft as possible, and well-handled gun-armed galleys and larger *galleasses still had advantages. They were necessary complements to the sailing ships. Only with the development of the *galleon, combining a galley's prow with a sailing ship's range and flexibility, did the oared fighting ship face obsolescence. The gun-armed sailing ship also gave Europeans the military superiority to spread over the world. Still, however, the expense of naval operations forced states, notably England, to attempt to utilize private enterprise both as an aid in waging naval war and as a way of raising additional income. Although large fleets could be mobilized for specific operations, naval power was still episodic and uncertain; the weather played a greater part in the defeat of the repeated Spanish attempts to invade England, including the *Spanish Armada of 1588, than the English fleet.

During the 17th century recognizably modern navies came into being, permanent national maritime fighting forces maintained by funds raised by increasingly powerful states. The pressure to put more and more guns on ships—originally as much for prestige as to increase fighting capability—led to the main power of warships being in their *broadsides. The *line of battle replaced the line abreast and *fighting instructions were introduced to organize these long and unwieldy formations. Gunnery power was still limited, and taking rather than sinking the enemy remained the primary aim. It was not easy to achieve decisive results, and in the mid-17th century battles often lasted for days. Success, however, might lead to the *blockade of an enemy's coast. Maritime commerce also continued to be attacked but in a more organized manner. The system of *privateers, authorized commerce raiders who often employed the *stinkpot as a weapon, was regularized. The French **guerre de course* against commerce did much to neutralize the effects of English victories in fleet actions in the war of 1689–97.

The dynamics of war at sea created in the 17th century reached maturity in the 18th. The line of battle continued to hold sway. Only ships of 50 guns or more that could hold their own against the largest enemy warships could stand in the line of battle and these ships became known as *ships of the line, or 'line of battleships', the components of the battle fleet. Smaller vessels were used for 'cruising' duties for commerce protection and destruction, as well as scouting for the battle fleet. By the middle of the century the *frigate had emerging as the main *cruiser type and in the second half of the century the two-deck 74-gun ship became the backbone of the line of battle; 50-gun ships were no longer considered suitable.

The Anglo-French Struggle for Supremacy at Sea. Navies increased in reach and endurance as Britain and France fought globally for empires from the 1740s onwards. Long blockades could be carried out and ships attempting to escape them were intercepted in the open ocean. Major actions, which had previously been close to shore, could now be undertaken on the open seas, such as the two battles of Finisterre in which French *convoys escorted by battle squadrons were attacked by small British fleets of ships of the line. Escorted convoys continued, however, to neutralize the *guerre de course* of smaller warships and privateers.

Blockades encouraged fine *seamanship. In 1759, in stormy conditions, the British Admiral Hawke (1705–81) drove a major portion of the French fleet to disastrous and decisive defeat in Quiberon Bay during the Seven Years War (1756–63). France then improved its navy and put it to good effect in the War of American Independence (1775–82). By driving away the British fleet off the Virginia Capes in September 1781, Admiral de Grasse (1722–88) enabled the Franco-American land forces to force the surrender of the isolated British at Yorktown.

The French Revolution was a disaster for the French Navy. Its gunnery and tactical skills declined and, combined with the longer-term decline of the Spanish Navy, allowed daring commanders such as *Nelson to score stunning victories against long odds. Such battles, even Trafalgar in 1805, should not, however, be overrated. It was the blockade that prevented the invasion of Britain and exerted the economic pressure on France that eventually forced Napoleon to overreach himself, just as it was the trade convoyed in and out of Britain that allowed it to continue the conflict and support allies ashore.

The Age of Steam Arrives. The 19th century began, in naval terms, after the Napoleonic Wars ended in 1815. New technologies and techniques began to revolutionize war at sea. As early as the 1820s, commanders were beginning to consider *paddle steamers powered by *steam propulsion as key components of any fleet. They gave extra mobility to sailing ships as well as being useful warships in themselves; China, whose maritime heritage had been in decline for centuries, had nothing to match them during the Opium Wars (1839–42 and 1856–60). Paddle steamers, however, were pre-

The battle of Trafalgar (detail); oil painting by N. Pocock, 1806

vented from acquiring the fighting power of the broadside sailing ship, as the paddles took up much of the space normally allotted to guns. Paddle sloops and frigates were therefore used with sailing ships of the line in mutual support.

Naval firepower was also decisively improved in this period by more powerful guns, new forms of explosive and incendiary projectiles, and new, more accurate gunnery. Ships could more easily sink others; the days of boarding, entering, and taking were finally coming to an end. Ironically, these technical factors that allowed ships more safely to engage forts, combined with the strategic dynamics of a long peace and a stable balance of power, led to shore bombardments becoming the standard form of naval engagement. The last fleet action under sail did, however, take place in 1827 as part of some robust peace enforcement by a British-led coalition fleet during the Greek War of Independence.

The advent of the screw *propeller in the 1840s allowed steam propulsion to be applied to the battle fleet in the following decade. Although steam had great benefits in operational and tactical mobility it did diminish the strategic reach of navies, and operations close to the shore (littoral operations) remained the norm. Armour was developed in the first instance to protect ships from the fire of forts. Ship-to-ship engagement became a secondary, though important, dynamic in the development of armour-plated ships, colloquially known as *ironclads. The major battle between Austrian and Italian ironclads, off Lissa in 1866, demonstrated the difficulties of contemporary guns penetrating armour and the importance of damaging the enemy underwater by ramming. The age of the galley seemed to have returned.

Technology increased the underwater threat with the development of 'torpedoes', underwater explosive charges. At first static—what were later known as 'mines'—or carried on spars in front of small craft, known as *spar torpedoes, these were developed by Robert Whitehead (1823–1905) into self-propelled torpedoes powered by compressed air. Adopted avidly by the world's navies from the 1870s, these weapons promised more than they delivered, being slow and short ranged, and it was only

The battle of Lissa, 1866; lithograph by F. Kollarz

in 1891 that the first armoured ship succumbed to a torpedo, in an attack in harbour during the Chilean Civil War.

Despite a lack of evidence, there were those, especially in the French *Jeune École*, who argued that the torpedo boat had made the armour-plated ship obsolete. The latter was following an uncertain developmental path, evolving towards low *freeboard vessels—the smaller examples of which were sometimes known as *monitors—with a few big slow-firing guns that were only really useful for attacking enemy bases. In the 1880s, however, a combination of new, more economical engines giving longer range, lighter armour utilizing steel that allowed high freeboard and greater seaworthiness, and rapid-firing, higher-accuracy medium-calibre guns made the *battleship fully practical once more. These improvements also allowed the development of faster cruisers, the largest of which were armoured, making them usable as fast components of the battle fleet. Torpedo boat *destroyers were also developed.

The reversion to a seagoing fleet designed to operate as the earlier sailing fleets had done led to a renaissance in naval strategy. Writers like *Mahan in the USA and Colomb and Corbett in Britain drew lessons from the age of sail in developing concepts such as 'sea power' and 'command of the sea'. All emphasized the role of the battle fleet. These ideas seemed to be vindicated by events. In the Spanish–American War of 1898 a US fleet of battleships and armoured cruisers annihilated a Spanish armoured cruiser squadron off Santiago. The Russo-Japanese War of 1904–5 culminated in the battle of Tsushima, a Trafalgar-like defeat of the Russian fleet by Admiral Togo's mixed fleet of battleships and armoured cruisers.

Enter the Submarine and Air Power. The torpedo came of age at the end of the 19th century and in the early years of the 20th with the development of, first, gyroscopes to allow reliable long-distance running and then heaters to improve automotive performance. This had the effect of forcing improvements in gun accuracy to allow longer-range firing that culminated in the development of the all-big-gun, Dreadnought battleship, and *battle cruiser. The rapid deployment of these *capital ships from 1905 made existing surface fleets obsolete, especially as it went together with the development of new types of light cruisers and larger destroyers better able to accompany fleets at sea.

During the First World War (1914–18) the strategic situation discouraged major fleet action. The British *Grand Fleet, based at *Scapa Flow, commanded the world's oceans by its very existence, as it barred the path of the inferior German *High Seas Fleet to the open sea. Risking its superiority to underwater attack did not seem to offer commensurate strategic return. Equally, the weaker Germans had to avoid the annihilation that a full-scale battle would bring. In 1916, when the Germans began a systematic policy of wearing down British strength, they were lucky, in what turned into a favourable battle of attrition, to escape off Jutland. Their next attempt at attrition also almost ended in disaster and the German high command began to look for a different approach to naval victory over the British.

The combination of the *diesel engine and the gyroscope torpedo made the *submarine practical at the beginning of the 20th century. At first considered as weapons to deny the *narrow seas to warships, they began to be used by the Germans as commerce raiders. American pressure limited the activities of the 'U-boats', but in 1917 the Germans made a supreme effort. Hundreds of thousands of tons of Allied and neutral shipping were sunk. Yet attacks on, and the defence of, merchant ships had played little part in pre-war naval thinking. *Privateering had been abolished and the coming of steam and growth in merchant navies had, it was thought, created an insuperable escort problem. Only belatedly was the historic strategy of convoy adopted which neutralized the new raiders as effectively as it had the *guerre de course* of old.

Aircraft made vital contributions to the war at sea in the convoy escort role and the period 1919–39 saw *aircraft carriers develop as a vital adjunct to the surface fleet. The major maritime powers also built bigger and better fast *capital ships that combined speed and armour protection, but the Second World War (1939–45) confirmed the superiority of air power over battleships. In the Mediterranean a British carrier strike on Taranto helped neutralize the Italian fleet, a Japanese one crippled the US Pacific Fleet at Pearl Harbor, and Japanese land-based naval torpedo bombers destroyed the British battleship *Prince of Wales* and battlecruiser *Repulse*, the first capital ships sunk at sea by aircraft.

The US carriers had been at sea during the Pearl Harbor attack and, beginning with the Pacific battles of the Coral Sea and Midway in 1942, the Americans and Japanese developed a new kind of fleet warfare in which the primary striking weapons were carrier-based aircraft and long-range fleet submarines. Battleship rarely fought battleship, the last occasion being in the Surigao Strait action in the battle of Leyte Gulf in October 1944. The disproportionate manpower demands of battleships led to their almost complete demise after the war. Only the United States could afford to continue to use them, primarily for shore bombardment.

US submarines carried out one of the most successful commerce raiding campaigns in history, destroying much of Japan's mercantile marine which did not use a proper convoy system. Convoys were again successful in a renewed U-boat offensive in the Atlantic. However, they were threatened by the new 'wolf-pack' surface attack as this tactic neutralized the new *sonar systems that many in the inter-war period had thought had compromised the submarine. Nevertheless, most ships sunk were those caught sailing alone. Air cover, either land based or from small escort carriers, proved crucial to victory and new generations of escort vessels, *corvettes and frigates, were added to the escort groups that finally defeated the U-boats in 1943. New technology, fast battery-driven submarines, *schnorkels that allowed boats to use diesel power underwater, and heavier anti-aircraft armaments, could do little against the mature Allied escort system that was the foundation of victory in the West.

The Missile Age. After 1945, the western Allies prepared to fight a new battle of the Atlantic against a Soviet submarine force supported by an increasingly powerful surface fleet. The coming of nuclear-powered submarines revolutionized submarine potential and made such boats rivals to carriers for the title of capital ship. Submarine-launched ballistic missiles became the foundation of mutual nuclear deterrence, while anti-ship and anti-aircraft guided missiles also became important weapons.

By the end of the Cold War in 1989 a sophisticated forward maritime strategy had been developed in which western nuclear-powered submarines planned to attack Soviet ballistic-missile-armed submarines in their 'bastions' defended by the Soviet Navy, so holding down assets that might otherwise be used in the open ocean. At the same time, carriers would take on and defeat the Soviet land-based naval air arm.

The Cold War ended before the practicality of such concepts could be tested. It was an era that saw much sparring but relatively little actual fighting at sea. The loss of an Israeli destroyer in 1967 to Soviet-made Egyptian anti-ship missiles dramatically demonstrated the effectiveness of these weapons—though German aircraft had been the first to do so when, in 1943, a guided bomb sank the Italian battleship *Roma* on its way to surrender to the British. The Israelis developed their own missiles, which they used effectively against Arab craft in 1973. Two years earlier, Indian missile craft had attacked ships in harbour to some effect, while a Pakistani submarine torpedoed and sank an Indian frigate.

In the 1980s the Iran–Iraq War saw a *guerre de course* with missiles and small boats against merchant shipping, plus engagements in which the Americans attacked Iranian warships with bombs and missiles. In the same area in 1991, British ship-based missile-firing helicopters and US aircraft easily sank Iraqi missile craft captured from Kuwait, undermining the reputation such vessels had gained since 1967. Events in the Gulf also reinforced the lessons of the Korean War about the vital role of mines and mine countermeasures.

During the Falklands conflict of 1982 the sinking of its cruiser by a British nuclear submarine drove the Argentine Navy into port, allowing the carrier task group to concentrate its resources on defeating the Argentine air attacks. Nevertheless, Argentine aircraft sank two British frigates, a destroyer, and a landing ship with bombs, and another destroyer and a vital supply ship with Exocet missiles.

Naval strategy since the Cold War has swung even more to amphibious operations and land attack, but with sea control a necessary prerequisite. This requires a robust mix of anti-air, anti-submarine, and anti-surface capabilities. Just as in the earliest days, a desire to use the sea requires an ability to fight to ensure such use and, just as in previous centuries, the pendulum will no doubt swing back to fighting at sea as well as from it. See also ADMIRALTY; ARTICLES OF WAR; BOMB KETCH; CARCASS; CAROUS; CARTEL; CINQUE PORTS; 'CROSSING THE T'; 'DAVID'; DEPTH CHARGE; EXPLOSION VESSEL; FIRESHIP; FIREWORKS; FLOATING BATTERY; FLOTILLA; GAGE; GAS-TURBINE ENGINES; GENERAL CHASE; LINE OF BATTLE; Q-SHIP; RATE; SQUADRON; TURRET.

Harding, R., *Seapower and Naval Warfare 1650–1830* (2001).
Ireland, B., and Grove, E., *Jane's War at Sea 1897–1997* (1997).
Lambert, A., *War at Sea in the Age of Sail* (2000).
Sondhaus, L., *Naval Warfare 1815–1914* (2000).
—— *Navies in Modern World History* (2004).

Eric Grove

warm the bell, to, a phrase used in the British Navy during the days of sail meaning to do something unjustifiably, or unnecessarily, early. On board warships in the days of sail, time was measured by a half-hour *sand-glass. Each time the sand ran through, the glass was turned, usually by the midshipman of the *watch, and the appropriate number of bells struck on the *ship's bell. It was supposed, perhaps rightly, that if the glass were warmed the expansion of the neck would allow the sand to run through a little more quickly. Hence the idea that if midshipmen of night watches put the glass under their coats and grasped it tightly, eight bells, and the return to one's *hammock, would come gratifyingly earlier than it should.

warp. **(1)** A light *hawser used in the movement of a ship from one place to another by means of a *kedge anchor, a *capstan, or of men hauling on it. It is not a tow-rope, which involves the power of another ship. When used as a verb it describes the operation of moving a ship by means of warps from one position in harbour to another. **(2)** As a verb, it was also a term used in *rigging lofts in the days of sail to mean the measurement and laying out of rigging before it was cut to the proper lengths. In this case the rigging was said to be warped before it was cut out. **(3)** The ropes used for securing a ship alongside a *quay, *jetty, etc., or another ship. See also BERTHING HAWSERS. **(4)**

A packet of four *herrings is known as a warp, though the term is mainly confined to the east coasts of Britain which border the North Sea herring *fishery. **(5)** The ropes or wires attached to a *trawl by which it is *veered to the sea bottom.

Warrior, HMS, the first *ironclad ship built for the British Navy, a reply to the French armoured ship **Gloire*. Designed by Isaac Watts, the Royal Navy's chief constructor, with the assistance of the marine engineer John Scott Russell (1808–82), she was *launched at Blackwall on the River Thames in 1860. With an overall length of 127.4 metres (418 ft) and a beam of 17.6 metres (58 ft), she was originally classified as a steam *frigate of 9,210 tons, but in 1887 was reclassified as a 3rd-class armoured screw *battleship. She had a complement of 705 officers and men, was armed with 26 68-pounder muzzle loaders, and ten 110-pounder and four 40-pounder breech loaders, and was protected by 11.4 centimetres (4.5 in.) of iron armour with 45.7 centimetres (18 in.) of teak backing. Her two-cylinder Penn steam engine and single two-bladed *propeller gave her a maximum speed of 14.3 knots, but she also had a full outfit of masts and sails which totalled 4,495 square metres (48,400 sq. ft) which gave her a maximum speed of 13 knots. In 1904 she was renamed *Vernon III* and became part of the *Vernon* torpedo school at Portsmouth, continuing there until 1923 when she was removed from the Navy List. She served as an oil fuel pier at Pembroke for the next 50 years before being towed to Hartlepool to be restored to her original glory by the Warrior Preservation Trust at a cost of £7 million. She returned to Portsmouth in June 1987 as an outstanding example of *ship preservation and is now open to the public at her purpose-built jetty in the Naval *Dockyard.

washstrake, or **washboard,** a movable upper *strake which can be attached to the *gunwales of some open boats to keep out spray when under sail. The sliding boards that close off a *yacht's interior from her *cockpit are also known as washboards.

watch. **(1)** The division of the 24 hours of the seaman's day into periods of duty of four hours. Thus there should be six four-hour watches in a day, but as this would entail ships' companies, organized into two or three watches, keeping the same watches every day, the evening watch from 1600 to 2000 is divided into two two-hour watches, known as the first and last **dog watches**. Starting at midnight, the names of the watches are: Middle Morning, Morning, Forenoon, Afternoon, First Dog, Last Dog, and First. Those on duty during a watch are known as **watchkeepers**. See also SHIP'S BELL. **(2)** The basis of the internal organization of a ship's company whereby men can obtain regular periods of rest although the work of the ship must go on day and night. The crew is divided either into two watches (*port and *starboard) with each watch alternating their periods of duty, or into three watches (usually red, white, and blue), so that every man gets two periods of rest to every one period of duty. The periods of duty correspond to the watches into which the seaman's day is divided. **(3)** As a verb, a navigational *buoy is said to be watching when it is floating in the correction position as indicated on a *chart, and that its light, or other signal, if it has one, is in working order. Other buoys are watching when they are carrying out the purpose for which they are intended, e.g. an *anchor buoy.

watch-bill, a nominal list of officers and men on board a ship giving the *watches and stations to which each is quartered for all purposes on board. Thus any officer or man, on consulting the list, will know which watch he is in, to which part of the ship he is allocated, his station for *abandoning ship, for entering or leaving harbour, and for any other particular purpose on board. See also QUARTER-BILL.

watch buoy, a *buoy *moored in the vicinity of *lightships, in the days when they were manned, so that those aboard could check that the lightship was not *dragging.

water-laid rope, see CABLE-LAID ROPE.

water sail, a small sail spread in *square-rigged ships in calm weather and a following breeze to increase the area of sail spread to the wind. There were two places where such sails could be spread: below the lower *studding sail or below the boom of the *driver.

waterspout. This resembles a tornado over land and is formed by an intense vortex in the air that sucks water from the sea surface forming a dark funnel and creating high winds within and around it. They form in two ways. The majority occur in fine weather when the sea temperatures are high and the air is very humid; these form at sea level and then ascend into the sky. Less common, but more destructive, are those that form like tornadoes as vortices at the base of a thundercloud and then extend down to the sea's surface. They have been known to suck up *shoals of *fish, which then rain down from the top of the vortex.

The maxi-*yacht *Nicorette* only just survived a waterspout when one hit it during the 2001 Sydney–Hobart race (see YACHTING: SAIL). The skipper afterwards reported that the upward suction was so immense that it was like being in, and looking up at, a huge vacuum cleaner. See also MARY CELESTE. M. V. Angel

waterway, the outboard planks of a ship's deck, often hollowed to provide a shallow channel to carry off water on deck through the *scuppers.

wave line theory, one which explains the pattern of *waves caused by floating bodies when moving along the surface of the water. It was formulated by the British engineer and naval architect John Scott Russell (1808–82), who found that when a floating body, such as a ship, moves through the water it creates a wave system around itself which is the complex result of varying pressures below the surface of the water. From these observations Russell developed a theory of wave formation and pattern which, although not accepted by naval architects today, was very influential in *naval architecture and *shipbuilding in the late 19th and early 20th centuries. See also HYDRODYNAMICS.

waves transmit energy across surfaces, both at the surface and in the ocean's interior. They range from high-frequency ripples and capillary waves, to low-frequency long waves generated by *tides, and the planetary effects of the earth's orbiting and spinning that, for example, send the signal of *El Niños over the Pacific.

The most familiar waves are those that are generated by the frictional energy of winds blowing across the sea surface which have frequencies of 5 to 10 seconds. Wave heights (the height between the crests and the troughs), increase with increasing wind speeds. The longer the wave length (distance between successive crests) the faster a wave travels. Long waves generated by a *storm travel faster and appear as swell before an approaching storm. Swells often travel across the local wind-generated waves, creating the confused seas so hated by those who suffer from sea-sickness. *Tsunamis are some of the fastest travelling waves while **rogue waves** can generate a wall of water up to 30 metres (100 ft) high. They occur, though rarely, in regions where strong *currents flow against the prevailing winds, and can cause immense damage to ships. In 2000 the *cruise ship *Oriana* was struck by a 21-metre (70-ft) wave that smashed windows and sent water cascading through six of its decks.

In the open ocean waves do not result in flows of water. A cork floating in the water just bobs up and down and does not move laterally. However, as a wave approaches a shore, the frictional drag of the bottom slows its speed, so its leading face steepens and the distance between it and the wave before and after shortens. Eventually the wave crest overtakes the base of the wave and it breaks.

Waves predominantly travel in the direction of the prevailing wind. When waves approach a sandy beach at an angle they push the sand along the beach as they break, and then the swash moves the sand perpendicularly back down the beach. This results in longshore drift whereby sand moves sideways along a beach.

Waves contain considerable amounts of energy and can be very destructive. However, if we can learn to capture their energy efficiently, as

Code	*Description*	*Maximum height of waves in metres/feet*
0	glassy calm	0
1	calm (ripples)	0.3/0–1
2	smooth (wavelets)	0.3–0.6/1–2
3	slight	0.6–1.2/2–4
4	moderate	1.2–2.4/4–8
5	rough	2.4–3.9/8–13
6	very rough	3.9–6.1/13–20
7	high	6.1–9.1/20–30
8	very high	9.1–13.7/30–45
9	phenomenal	over 13.7/45

we are beginning to do with *tidal power, a vast amount of renewable energy will become available to us, and perhaps we will also be better able to protect our shore and installations from their destructive power.

A code of the sea state, in the same form as for the *Beaufort Scale for winds, is: M. V. Angel

'wavy navy', see RNVR.

way, the movement of a ship through the water by means of its own power, or the force of the wind on its sails. See also UNDER WAY.

waypoint, a destination or intermediate point in a vessel's passage. Its geographic position is stored in the memory of a *GPS or other *satellite navigation device, which automatically calculates and displays the range and *bearing (distance and *course) to the point.

ways, the parallel platforms of timber down which the cradle (in which a ship being built is held) travels when the ship is *launched. The fixed platforms are known as standing ways (or ground ways) and the sliding part as the sliding or launching ways. See also SLIPWAY.

wear, to. **(1)** The operation of bringing a sailing vessel onto the other *tack by bringing the wind around the stern, as opposed to tacking, when the wind is brought round the bow. It has been suggested that the word originated from *veer, which has a similar meaning, but the term to wear a ship is the earlier of the two. In the past tense, a ship is wore, not worn. **(2)** A term used afloat in connection with the flying of flags. In nautical parlance a ship flies its national flag or *ensign, but wears a personal flag, such as an admiral's flag. In the past tense a flag is worn, not wore. See also FLAG ETIQUETTE.

weather, in addition to its normal meteorological meaning (see MARINE METEOROLOGY), weather is also used by seamen as an adjective applied to anything which lies to *windward. Thus a ship is said to have the **weather gage** of another when it lies to windward; a ship *under way has a **weather side**, which is that side which faces the wind; a vessel under sail has **weather shrouds** on its windward side; and a coastline that lies to windward is a **weather shore**.

weather helm. A ship under sail is said to carry weather helm when, due to the balance of the hull and sails, the *tiller, or helm, is held a few degrees to the *weather side to maintain a straight *course. This is a safety factor because, if the helm is released for any reason, the vessel will turn into the wind and the sails will lose their power. A vessel with an excess of weather helm is called hard mouthed, and is also called **ardency**. See also GRIPE, TO.

weather lore, the ability of the seaman, before the days of *marine meteorology, to foretell the weather by the appearance of the sky, change of direction of the wind, cloud formations, variation of atmospheric pressure, etc. It was often expressed in jingles:

> If the wind is north-east three days without rain,
> Eight days will go by before south again.
>
> If woolly fleeces deck the heavenly way
> Be sure no rain will mar a summer's day.
>
> With the rain before the wind
> *Stays and *topsails you must mind,
> But with the wind before the rain
> Your topsails you may set again.
>
> When the sea-hog [porpoise] jumps,
> Stand by at your *pumps.
>
> First rise [of a *barometer] after low
> Foretells a stronger blow.
>
> *Seagull, seagull, sit on the sand,
> It's never good weather when you're on the land.
>
> Mackerel sky and mare's tails
> Make tall ships carry low sails.
>
> When the glass rises high,
> Your kites you may fly.
>
> When the wind shifts against the sun,
> Trust it not for back it will run.
> When the wind follows the sun,
> Fine weather will never be done.

Although often true of the northern hemisphere, the reverse holds good in the southern.

weatherly. A sailing vessel is weatherly when it can steer closer to the wind than the average.

weather ship, a vessel which occupied a station in the ocean to accumulate weather data for overflying aircraft and passing ships. After the loss of a US airliner in 1938, because of bad weather during a trans-Pacific flight, tests were carried out at sea using instrumented upper-air balloons. When these proved successful the Atlantic Weather Observation Service was inaugurated in 1940 using two *US Coast Guard *cutters and US Weather Bureau personnel. Once the USA entered the war the service, and the number of transoceanic flights, increased, and by 1945 there were 22 Atlantic and 24 Pacific stations. These were reduced to thirteen, the ships, and the costs, being shared by those nations operating transoceanic aircraft. A ship's station was a 336-kilometre (210-m.) grid of 16-kilometre (10-m.) squares, each being assigned a letter of the alphabet. A ship's position was transmitted by a *radio beacon and overflying aircraft were able to contact it to receive the data it required. The ships were also used to obtain data for *oceanography and on at least three occasions mounted *lifesaving operations to rescue passengers and crew from foundering ships and downed aircraft. Once jet aircraft and satellite weather information arrived in the 1970s, the traditional weather ship quickly became redundant, and the last one (station M) was withdrawn in 1981. See also MARINE METEOROLOGY.

http://oceanusmag.whoi.edu/v39n/dinsmore.html

wedding garland, an 18th- and 19th-century custom in British warships of hoisting a garland of evergreens in the *rigging of a warship when she entered harbour to indicate that she was out of discipline and women would be allowed on board. It was also hoisted on the day any member of the crew was married; if the captain, to the main *topgallant *stay, if a seaman, on the mast to which he was stationed in the *watch-bill. The custom exists in the British Navy to the present day, and a garland is still hoisted on the day when a member of the ship's company is being married.

weigh, to, see A-WEIGH; UNDER WAY.

well, a vertical cylindrical trunk in a ship through which the suction pipes of the *bilge *pump pass, reaching right down into the lowest part of the hull. Its object is to prevent *ballast or other objects from entering and choking the suction boxes of the pumps. In older wooden ships it was the trunk in which the ship's pump worked. It was the carpenter's duty, particularly in warships after battle, to sound the well continually to make sure that the ship was not making water through damage to its hull. As the trunk led to the lowest portion of the hull, water inside the ship would naturally flow there and thus give a maximum reading of the amount inboard.

well deck, the two spaces on the main deck of the old type of merchant ship, one between the *forecastle and the midships housing which supports the *bridge, the other between the latter and the *poop deck.

well found, the description of a vessel which is adequately and fully equipped with all gear required for its efficient operation.

West Country whipping, a method of whipping the end of a rope. The whipping twine is centred around the part of the rope to be *whipped. At every half turn it is half knotted with an overhand knot so that each consecutive knot is on the opposite side of the rope. The whipping is finished off with a *reef knot. See also COMMON WHIPPING; SAILMAKER'S WHIPPING.

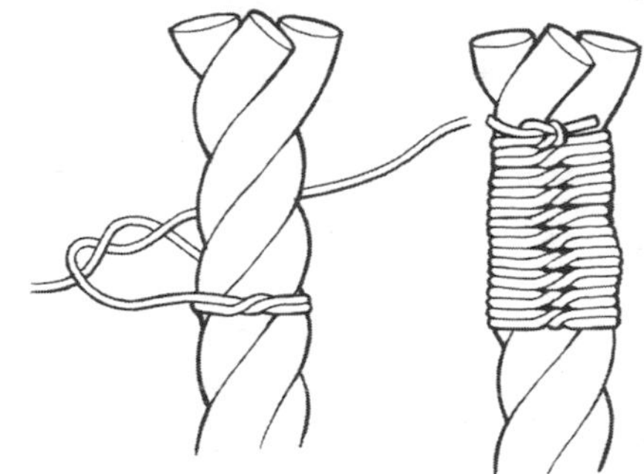

West Country whipping

'wet', a maritime term meaning stupid. 'Wet as a scrubber', extremely stupid or pathetic.

wetted surface, that part of the hull of a vessel below the water level when it is upright in the water. It varies, of course, with the loading of the vessel. The wetted surface is an element of the calculations of a vessel's speed; the greater the wetted surface, the less the speed.

whack, the old seaman's term for his daily ration of victuals—the exact amount and no more—according to the scale laid down by the various national Merchant Shipping Acts in force at the time.

whale, the most charismatic of *marine mammals. Whales are a popular tourist attraction and to see a whale *breaching is an exciting moment. They belong to the order Cetacea, which consists of about 76 species of whales, porpoises, and *dolphins. There are two main groups, baleen whales (Mysticeti) and the toothed whales (Odontoceti).

There are twelve species of baleen whales belonging to four families, and includes the largest of all animals on earth, the **blue whale**

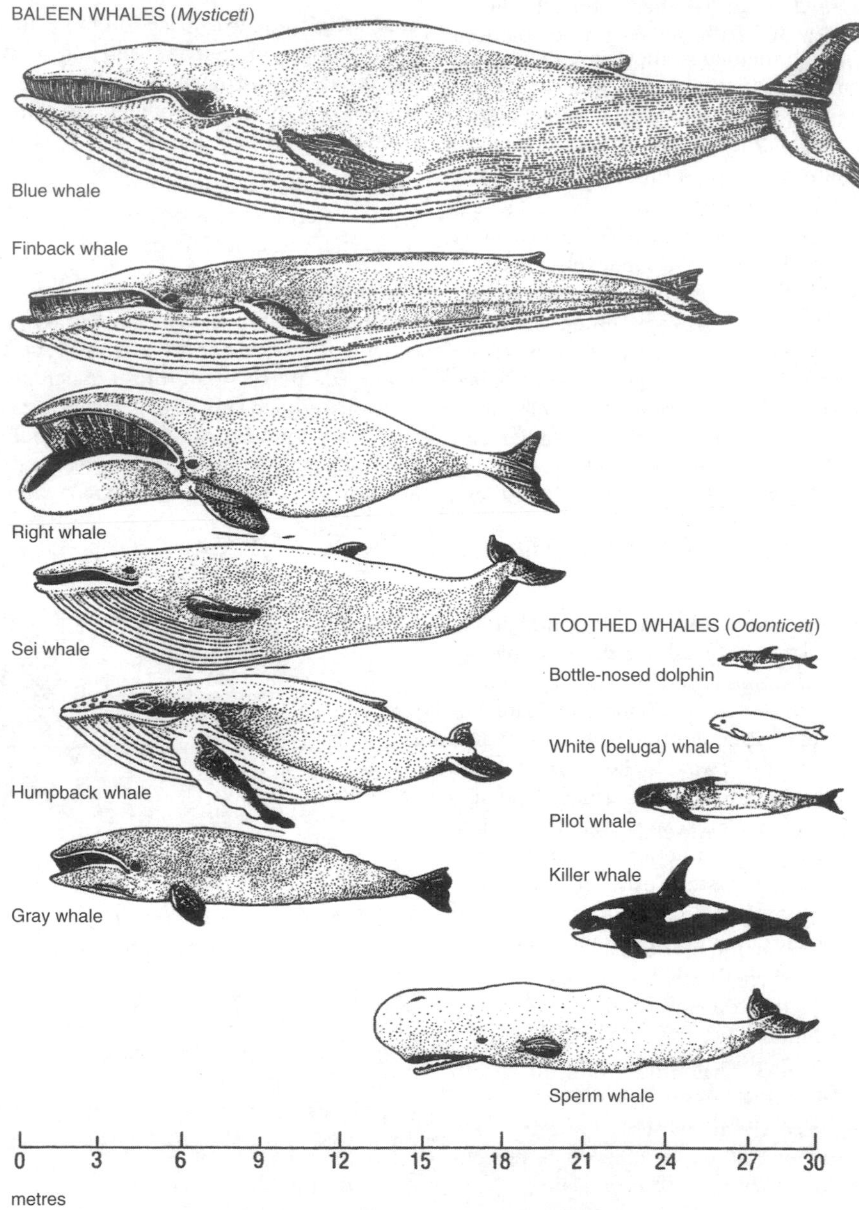

Diagram illustrating the relative sizes and shapes of baleen and toothed whales

(*Balaenoptera musculus*). A new species, a small species similar to a **fin whale** (*Balaenoptera physalus*), was recognized in 2003 by Japanese scientists using molecular techniques. **Baleen whales** are characterized by having flexible horny plates with hairy fringes hanging from their upper jaws. The plates consist of a protein called keratin, which is the structural element of human hair. The whales take huge mouthfuls of water and use their tongues to squirt the water through the plates; they sieve out *krill, *plankton, and small *fish. The whales undertake extensive migrations, moving into polar waters to exploit the rich populations of plankton that develop in the spring and summer. In winter they migrate into warm tropical seas to conserve energy and stop feeding. Calving tends to occur when they are in warm waters, so the newborn calves can use the energy from their mother's milk for growth rather than keeping warm.

The toothed whales comprise ten families and include dolphins, beaked whales, the porpoise and the narwhal (*Monodon monoceros*), and the beluga (*Delphinapterus leucas*) or white whale. The **male narwhal**, which has one of its teeth developed into a long tusk, gave rise to the medieval myth of the unicorn. **Belugas** are also known as sea canaries, because of the loud chirping noises they produce when hunting under pack ice in the Arctic. The largest toothed whale is the **sperm whale** (*Physeter macrocephalus*), which feeds mainly on *squid.

Whales are totally aquatic, although still dependent on the atmosphere for their oxygen. Their fusiform bodies are well insulated with fatty tissue known as blubber, which when rendered down was the source of the whale oil which created the *whaling industry. They have tail flukes that are horizontal and beat vertically, and on the top of the head is the blowhole through which they inhale. They exhale or 'blow' before they dive or 'sound'. Most dives last a few minutes, but the deeper-diving species, like the sperm whale and **beaked whales** (e.g. *Ziphius* spp.), can stay submerged for over an hour and can reach depths well in excess of 1,000 metres (3,000 ft). All species are highly vocal, using sound both to communicate between themselves and as *sonar to detect their prey.

Whale populations are still threatened by whaling, but the biggest current threat is the use of powerful sonars by navies which are thought to disorient the whales' own sonar system. There have been several mass strandings of whales since the 1980s, which have coincided with NATO naval exercises. In 2002 fourteen beaked whales stranded themselves just four hours after new powerful sonars were switched on by warships exercising in the vicinity. Another potential threat is increases in the occurrences of *red tides of the toxic algae (*Alexandrium fundyense*) which produces a poison, saxitoxin.

Evans, P., *The Natural History of Whales and Dolphins* (1987).

Perrin, W., Wirsig, B., and Thewissen, J., *Encyclopaedia of Marine Mammals* (2002).

www.smru.st-and.ac.uk/GeneralInterest.htm/whalesGandS.htm M. V. Angel

whaleboat, the name given to an open rowing boat, pointed at both ends so that it was convenient for beaching either bow- or stern-to. It had no *rudder and was steered by an *oar over the stern. Of robust construction, they were used for a variety of coastal work which entailed beaching frequently and were modelled on the original whaleboats carried in 19th-century *whaling ships.

whaler. **(1)** The generic, and older, name for ships of all types engaged in the *whaling industry. **(2)** A warship's boat, usually fitted with *oars and sails and taking its design from the original whaleboats used for whaling. In the British Navy a whaler *pulls five oars and is *yawl rigged with *jib and *mizzen and a *gunter mainsail. It was in a whaler that *Shackleton sailed nearly 500 kilometres (300 mls.) in 1916 to fetch help for his stranded Antarctic party.

whaling is the catching of *whales, which has been practised since the Neolithic period. The first large-scale whaling was carried out by the Basques, who were hunting the Atlantic right whale (*Balaena glacialis*) as early as the 10th century. They harpooned them from rowing boats, then towed the carcasses ashore where they were cut up and processed.

The use of hand-held harpoons thrown from small boats was the basis of most whaling until the invention of the explosive harpoon gun by a

Norwegian, Sven Foyn, in the 1850s. By the 17th century even these primitive whaling operations had pushed the whale populations in the Bay of Biscay into a terminal decline and the Basques were forced to go further afield. By then whaling in the Arctic had already begun, following the discovery of Spitsbergen by the Dutch explorer Willem *Barents in 1596.

The English and Dutch companies were set up using whaling ships of about 200 tons displacement. Small boats were *launched from the whaler, to chase and harpoon the whales. Once killed, the whales were then cut up either aboard the ship or ashore, so the blubber could be rendered with *try works to extract the oil. One of the most famous accounts of 19th-century whaling was written by William Scoresby Jr. (1789–1857). He undertook some of the first oceanographic observations in the Arctic to try and understand more about the whales' habits.

Britain's North American colonies began whaling initially hunting humpback whales (*Megaptera novaeangliae*), then sperm whales (*Physeter macrocephalus*). When the first sperm whale was caught in 1712 by a Nantucket whaler it triggered a new wave of whaling in warmer waters, for the sperm whales' waxy oil and spermaceti, used to make wax candles and other useful commodities, quickly proved more profitable than the right whale's oil.

The key characteristic of the 'right' to hunt whales was that when killed they floated, and so their carcasses could be retrieved. It was not possible to harvest several of the baleen whales including the blue whale (*Balaenoptera musculus*) until the technique of inflating the carcasses with compressed air was invented. Yankee whalers operating out of Nantucket and New Bedford roamed the oceans of the world mostly in the search for sperm whales, a way of life well described by Herman *Melville's novel *Moby-Dick*. In the Pacific, whalers operated mainly out of San Francisco hunting mostly gray (*Eschrictius robustus*) and bowhead whales (*Balaena mysticetus*). After the American Civil War (1861–5) this whaling operation flourished for several years until in 1871 almost the whole fleet was crushed in *ice.

The Norwegians had probably been taking whales for several centuries before they opened a land-based whaling station in South Georgia. The main target initially was humpback whales, whose carcasses were towed back to the onshore factory for processing. The British government raised a levy on every barrel of oil collected to finance research and instigated the **Discovery* Investigations, but in the late 1920s the introduction of factory ships to process the whales at sea enabled whaling to spread to all sectors of the Southern Ocean beyond the limits of any national jurisdiction. Whale stocks had started to show signs of decline before the Second World War (1939–45), and minimum size limits were agreed internationally. After the war the whale populations temporarily showed some signs of recovery. The International Whaling Commission was established in 1947 to provide the industry with effective scientific advice. The hunting of some species—humpback, bowhead, and some of the right whales—was banned. Even so in the 1970s the populations of Southern Ocean whales were in such sharp decline that a moratorium on whaling was agreed, although some whaling for scientific purposes was still allowed. Limited aboriginal whaling was still permitted. For example, the Inuit continued to hunt for the beluga and bowhead, and the traditional pilot-whale (*Globicephala melas*) hunt continued in the Faeroes, though the islanders have now stopped eating them because the meat is heavily contaminated with pollutants. The Japanese, Russians, Norwegians, and Icelanders, who hunt mainly for meat for human consumption, also continued to take small numbers, particularly of minke whales (*Balaenoptera acutorostrata*), whose populations were still quite large, and they still do.

In 1992 the North Atlantic Marine Mammal Commission was established by Norway, Iceland, Greenland, and the Faeroes to argue the case for the continuation of whaling particularly for minkes, stressing the importance of whale meat to some of their more remote communities, but also pointing out that the whales are competing with fishermen for *fish stocks. In the North Atlantic minke whales are estimated to take up to a million tonnes of commercial fish including *herring, *cod, and capelin, and despite the rapid growth of whale-watching as an ecotourism activity, whaling in those countries which still have a market for whale products seems likely to restart.

Philbrick, N., *In the Heart of the Sea: The Tragedy of the Whaleship Essex* (2001).
www.whaling.fo/index.htm
www.iwcoffice.org/iwc.htm#Contents

M. V. Angel

wharf. (1) A projection built of wood or stone constructed along the banks of an *anchorage or in a harbour to provide accommodation for ships to lie alongside for the loading or unloading of cargo, embarkation, and disembarkation of passengers, etc. The word is virtually synonymous with *quay, though in general the latter is thought of as being built only in stone. **(2)** A term used in *hydrography to describe an underwater scar or rocky accretion, or even a sandbank, where the *tides will throw up an *overfall or *race.

wharfage, the charge made to a shipowner for the use of a *wharf by his ship.

wharfinger, the name given to a man who owns or has charge of a *wharf.

wheelhouse, the deckhouse of a vessel within which the steering wheel is fitted. In most large ships it forms part of the *bridge. In smaller vessels without a bridge, it is a separate compartment raised above deck level to provide all-round visibility to the helmsman.

whelps, the name given to the projections which stand out from the barrel of a *capstan or *winch to provide extra bite for a rope under strain than if the barrel were smooth.

wherry. (1) A decked sailing vessel of very shallow *draught used for the transport of small quantities of freight on the Norfolk Broads in England. They have a considerable *beam in relation to their length and are fitted with a single mast carrying a large *loose-footed *gaff-rigged mainsail and no headsails. The mast is normally *stepped with its *heel on deck and supported in a *lutchet, similar to a *tabernacle, so that it can be lowered to the deck when passing under bridges, etc. **(2)** An open boat of the 17th and 18th centuries used for the carriage of passengers on the tidal reaches of the River Thames in England. They were propelled by *oars, and varied in size from about 4 metres (13 ft) with a single rower, to about 8 metres (26 ft) with four rowers.

whip. (1) The name given to a single rope *rove through a single *block and used for hoisting objects. Where greater power is required, another single block can be introduced to make a **double whip**, or another single whip can be applied to the fall of the first to form what is known as **whip-upon-whip**. **(2)** When used as a verb it is the operation of binding twine or yarn around the strands at the end of a rope or wire *rope to prevent them from unlaying or fraying. The final result is known as a **whipping**, of which the *common whipping, *sailmaker's whipping, and *West Country whipping are in the most general use at sea.

whipstaff, originally the name given to a wooden rod attached to a *yoke on the *rudder of a vessel, by which the vessel was steered. Its original purpose was to replace the *tiller, or rather to offset it, so that with a *mizzen-mast stepped right *aft the rudder could still be moved from side to side. The whipstaff proper was a vertical lever attached by an eyebolt and *gooseneck to the forward end of the tiller of a sailing vessel. In all such vessels of any size, the tiller came in along the lower deck, and as ships began to have their sterns built high, so it became necessary to place the helmsman equally high so that he could see the sails and adjust the ship's *course accordingly. The whipstaff achieved this, being led up through slots in the decks to the helmsman's position, thus giving a gain in power of about four to one. As the helmsman pushed his end of the whipstaff over to one side, it acted through its fulcrum to push the tiller over in the opposite direction and tiller movement was transmitted directly

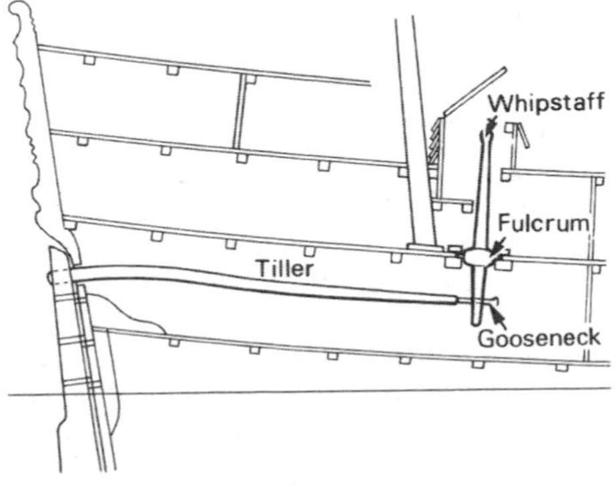

Whipstaff

to the rudder. The maximum amount of helm which could be put on with a whipstaff was about 5° either side of centre. The whipstaff was superseded early in the 18th century with the introduction of the steering wheel, having lasted about 250 years.

whisker pole, a short bearing-out *spar used in *yachts and sailing *dinghies to bear out the *clew of the *jib on the opposite side of the mainsail when running before the wind, thus obtaining some of the advantage which would be gained in a larger vessel when it sets a *spinnaker. See also GOOSE-WINGS.

whiskers, the name given to the short horizontal *spars fitted to the *bowsprit of a large sailing vessel when it is extended by a *jib-boom.

white ensign, the *ensign flown by all ships of the British Navy, and by *yachts over a certain *tonnage which belong to The Royal Yacht Squadron, Britain's senior *yacht club. When the division of the British fleet into *squadronal colours was abolished in 1864, only the white ensign was retained for all naval ships. See also BLUE ENSIGN; RED ENSIGN.

widows' men, fictitious names entered in the *muster-books of British warships during the days of sail so that their notional pay and the value of their rations could be used to swell the fund to provide pensions for the widows of men who died on board. Originally, money for such a purpose was raised by the old custom of *dead shares, but in 1733 the addition of widows' men to the muster-books was made official at the rate of two men for every 100. The practice lasted until 1829, when the payment of widows' pensions was organized on a more adequate and less haphazard basis.

Wilkes, Charles (1798–1877), American naval explorer and Antarctic explorer of English parentage. After three years in the merchant service, he joined the US Navy as a midshipman in 1818, studied under Ferdinand Hassler, founder of the US Coast and Geodetic Survey, and from 1826 to 1833 served in two surveying expeditions. He was appointed in 1834 as head of the recently established depot of *charts and navigational instruments of the Navy Department, out of which were to grow the National Observatory and the Navy Hydrographic Office.

When in 1836 Congress approved plans for a national expedition to the South Atlantic and South Pacific Oceans, to explore the islands and waters with a view to the promotion of *whaling and of commerce in general, Wilkes was sent to Europe to purchase the necessary scientific instruments. On his return he was promoted lieutenant and given the command of the expedition of six ships.

The expedition sailed in 1838, and after a season of surveying and scientific studies in the Samoa group of islands, Wilkes set out on an Antarctic cruise with the object of sailing as far south as possible between the *longitudes of 160° E. and 45° E. Antarctic land was sighted on 19 January 1840, and in spite of adverse weather and *ice conditions, and the poor state of his ship and crews, Wilkes sailed along the coast of the present Wilkes Land for a distance of 2,400 kilometres (1,500 mls.), sighting land at frequent intervals and naming the region, for the first time, the Antarctic Continent.

After returning from Antarctica Wilkes spent most of 1841 in a long survey of the coast of western North America, finally returning to New York in June 1842, having accomplished a monumental task of surveying and scientific exploration. Far from being loaded with honours, however, Wilkes was court-martialled for exceeding his authority. He was acquitted and spent the next few years writing up the official narrative of the expedition.

In 1861, at the start of the American Civil War (1861–5), he was in command of the Federal *cruiser *San Jacinto* and figured in an international incident when he stopped a British mail steamer in the Bahama Channel, north of Cuba, and removed two Confederate commissioners, James Mason and John Slidell. Although Confederate sympathizers in Britain hoped to use this incident to involve Britain against the USA, the British government contented itself with a polite protest and a successful request for the release of the two men. The incident made Wilkes something of a naval hero to the American public, and in 1862, with the rank of acting rear admiral, he was placed in command of a special *squadron to operate against the Confederate commerce raiders in the West Indies and around the Bahamas.

Although Wilkes accomplished as much as was possible considering the small number of vessels under his command, he was court-martialled again in 1864 and convicted of disobedience, disrespect, insubordination, and conduct unbecoming an officer. He was sentenced to be reprimanded and suspended from duty for three years, but the suspension was later reduced to one year, and in 1866 he was placed on the retired list with the rank of rear admiral.

Wilkins, Sir George Hubert (1888–1958), Australian polar explorer, born at Mount Bryan East, South Australia. He served as second in command and photographer to the Canadian Vilhjalmur Stefansson (1879–1962) on the latter's third expedition to the Canadian Arctic in 1913. He left it in 1917 to join the Australian Flying Corps then fighting in France during the First World War (1914–18), being seconded to the military historical section as an official photographer. In 1919 he was *navigator of a Blackburn Kangaroo aircraft on a flight from England to Australia and in 1920–1 was appointed second in command and naturalist to the British Imperial Antarctic expedition under Sir Ernest *Shackleton. Between 1926 and 1928 he commanded an Arctic expedition sponsored by the *Detroit News* during which, with a co-pilot, he flew 3,360 kilometres (2,100 mls.) across the Arctic from Point Barrow, Alaska, to Spitsbergen, a feat for which he was knighted. The following year he led the Hearst Antarctic expedition and in 1931 an expedition in the conventionally powered *submarine **Nautilus*, attempting to reach the North Pole under the ice. However, defects in the submarine obliged him to return after reaching a *latitude of 82° 15' N. An account of the voyage is given in his book *Under the North Pole*. Between 1933 and 1939 he managed the four Lincoln Ellsworth Antarctic expeditions and 1942–52 he was consultant to the US Army military planning division. After his death his ashes were scattered at the North Pole from the nuclear-powered USS *Skate* when it became, in 1959, the first submarine to surface there.

williwaw, a sudden violent gust of wind that can occur unpredictably along high-*latitude, mountainous coastlines, particularly around the Aleutian Islands and the Straits of Magellan. Cold air from over the mountains, especially where there are glaciers, becomes heavier and heavier, and suddenly descends as a fierce katabatic gust. M. V. Angel

winch, a small *capstan fitted to the decks and masts of *yachts to obtain the maximum *purchase on running *rigging. They came into general use after the First World War (1914–18) and were initially hand powered, with a winch handle being used to turn the drum. However, from the 1970s onwards they became the subject of much development and much larger winches, powered by multiple hand-cranked pedestals, known as **coffee grinders**, were introduced, which had gear boxes that allowed for reverse rotation and different gear ratios. Later, electric and hydraulic motors were fitted, often with remote control air switches. The mechanisms were then further developed with roller bearings and up to four gear ratios. For racing yachts, the weights have been reduced by the use of aluminium, titanium, and carbon composites. Many winches also have a device on top of them which automatically *tails the rope off the drum when under load, and so is called a **self-tailer**. The rope is held in the jaw so that it does not need to be *cleated.

In large ships all winches are, of course, powered by their generators. Jeremy Lines

wind is motion of the air relative to the earth's surface. At large scales, wind blows from a region of high atmospheric pressure to one of low pressure. However, once the air starts to move, it is subject to *Coriolis force and so tends to blow along isobars (lines of equal pressure) rather than across them. Locally winds are also generated by differences in heating and cooling. This give rise to phenomena like sea breezes which blow onshore during the day as the land heats up more quickly than the ocean, but offshore at night as the land cools faster. *Monsoons are large-scale versions of the same process. As winds blow across the sea surface, they exert frictional forces on the water, which generate *currents and create *waves. By convention, winds are described by the direction from which they are coming, whereas ocean currents are described by the direction in which they are flowing. Thus, a north wind blows in the opposite direction to the flow of a northerly current. In some regions the winds are reasonably predictable and are described as *trade winds. Winds are sometimes given specific names, usually because of the unpleasant conditions they generate, like the *mistral in the Mediterranean and the barat around Indonesia, but some, like zephyrs, are pleasant. See also AUSTER; BAYAMO; BEAUFORT SCALE; BLACK SQUALL; BORA; CATSPAW (2); CHOCOLATE GALE; GALE; GREGALE; KHAMSIN; LAND BREEZE; LEVANTER; MARINE METEOROLOGY; PAMPERO; PAPAGAYO; ROARING FORTIES; SHAMAL; SIROCCO; SQUALL; STORM; TRAMONTANA, TROPICAL STORMS; WEATHER LORE; WILLIWAW. M. V. Angel

windjammer, a non-nautical name by which *square-rigged sailing ships are sometimes known.

windlass, originally a small *capstan-like fitting, but on a horizontal shaft, in the fore part of a small vessel by which it rode to its anchor. It was also used sometimes for *weighing an anchor if this could be done without recourse to the capstan. Like the old-time capstan, windlasses were fitted with bars to be worked by manpower, and had a *pawl and ratchet gear to provide rotary motion to the spindle on which the windlass was mounted from an up and down motion of the bars.

A windlass still sometimes takes the place in smaller vessels of the capstan and allied *cableholders of a larger ship. Powered by electricity, the motor drives a warping drum at each end of the horizontal shaft with, inboard of the drums, a pair of *gypsies for working the chain cables of the *bower anchors.

wind-rode, a vessel is said to be wind-rode when it is riding head to wind in spite of the influence of the *tide which may be running across the wind or even in the opposite direction.

wind-rose, a circular diagram displayed on modern *charts to show the average strength and direction of winds from different directions and the frequency of other meteorological phenomena.

windrow, a line of debris lying in *slicks roughly parallel to the wind's direction. When the sea is calm, gentle winds blowing across the sea's surface generate counter-rotating vortices of water in the upper few metres of the water. These are named Langmuir circulation cells after the scientist who gave a scientific explanation for their development. The axes of the vortices lie parallel to the wind, and along the lines where they are generating weak converging *currents at the surface floating animal life and debris accumulate. In subtropical waters the stinging *Portuguese man-of-war and *sargasso weed are often lined up along windrows. The floating blue-green alga (*Trichodesmium*) that gave the Red Sea its name is often aligned in parallel lines on the surface of the Arabian Sea. M. V. Angel

windsail, a *canvas funnel, the upper end of which is guyed to face the wind. It was used to ventilate a ship by deflecting the wind below decks, the funnel being led below through a *hatch.

windseeker, US term for a small, lightweight jib used on a *yacht to catch what little wind there is in a calm. John Rousmaniere

windward, the weather side, or that from which the wind blows. It is the opposite side to *leeward. See also GAGE.

wing-in-surface effect ship (WISES), also called a **wing-in-ground effect ship**, **wingship** (USA), **Aerodynamic Ground Effect Craft** (Germany), or **ekranoplan** (Russia). This hybrid works on the same principle as the *hovercraft. Most types take off and land on water and while travelling move just above the surface, progressing on a cushion of air. This cushion is created by ground effect, the *aerodynamic interaction between the surface and the wing. WISE ships could be the next generation of cargo or passenger vessel and they also have military applications. They can be larger than conventional aircraft—the Russians have built one of 540 tonnes. So they can transport more cargo or passengers than a conventional aircraft, can do so more economically, and they travel much faster than any other surface vessel such as a *hydrofoil or *Seacat. They have been around for decades and come in all shapes and sizes, but so far none has reached commercial production. See also SURFACE EFFECT SHIP.

wire rope, see ROPE.

wishbone, a divided *spar whose two arms are pivoted together at the fore end and arched on either side in a roughly parabolic curve. The wishbone spar extends the *clew of the sail which is hoisted between the two arms, and the curves in the arms allow the sail to take up its natural flow without *girt or chafe. It was originally used as a *gaff, but was later developed as part of an *unstayed rig.

woolding, wolding, or **woulding,** binding rope around a mast or *spar to support it where has been *fished. The rope used for this purpose is also called a woolding. For illus. see FISH, TO.

worm, to, the operation of passing a small rope spirally between the lays of a *hemp *cable, or to pass *codline between the lays of a rope, as a preparation for *parcelling and *serving. In the days before synthetic *rope, rope was wormed, parcelled, and served to protect it against the wet, which was liable to rot it. See also CONTLINE.

wreck, as defined by the UK's Merchant Shipping Act 1995, includes *jetsam, *flotsam, *lagan, and *derelict. Any wreck or wreck material found in UK *territorial waters, or outside territorial waters but brought within them, has to be reported to the **Receiver of Wreck**, however unimportant it may appear to the finder. Nowadays, most material recovered comes under the heading of derelict or flotsam. The Receiver only deals with what is found in tidal waters. Material from non-tidal waters is treated as if it was on land, and comes under different legislation. Once a find has been reported the Receiver, whose job it is to protect the interests of both salvor and owner—and, if necessary, to involve other interested parties such as museums—will investigate the ownership of what has been found. Salvors of it must assume that anything recovered by them has a legitimate owner who has one year in which to prove title to it. If the owner wants it returned, they will first have to settle *salvage fees with the salvor. If it is unclaimed after a year it generally becomes the property of the crown, and the Receiver is required to dispose of it, usually by sale or auction. However, the finder is often allowed to keep items in lieu of being paid a salvage fee. The crown does not make any claims on anything recovered from outside UK territorial waters and it is returned to the finder if ownership is not established. The Receiver of Wreck used to be one of the functions of Customs & Excise officers, but is now part of the *Maritime and Coastguard Agency.

There are three other UK laws that are relevant to wrecks: the Protection of Wrecks Act 1973, the Protection of Military Remains Act, 1986, and the Merchant Shipping and Maritime Security Act 1997. The first is designed to protect *shipwrecks which are of historic, archaeological, or artistic merit. *Diving is prohibited on these sites, as it is on those of sunken vessels that contain dangerous cargoes. The second deals with the remains of military aircraft and ships, and these are designated either a Protected Place or a Controlled Site. Divers may visit the former but may not touch anything, while visiting the latter is prohibited. The third, which used to protect the remains of the **Titanic*, enshrines international agreements regarding wrecks outside UK waters. The Ancient Monuments and Archaeological Areas Act, 1979, has also been used to protect shipwrecks.

wreck buoy, a *buoy, painted green with the letter W painted prominently on it in white. It has now been replaced by the *IALA maritime buoyage system's *isolated danger mark.

wreckers. Stories about wreckers are legion, and Dame Ethel Smythe even composed an opera about them.

> Haste to the shore, the storm is nigh,
> The breakers roar, the sea-birds cry;
> Wreckers awake, for luck has come!
> What sound was that?
> Some gallant ship has come to port,
> Striking the rocks ...
> Some ship upon the rocks has struck
> With noise of thunder.
> Quick, ere she founder,
> Haul in the plunder!

Since time immemorial they have been alleged to have lured ships ashore with false lights, or by deliberately extinguishing genuine ones, and then plundering them and killing anyone from them still alive. This activity has allegedly been going on since pre-Christian times, and as late as 1905 a German pilot book of the Mediterranean warned of false lights being displayed on the North African coastline.

A favourite method of luring a vessel ashore was said to have been deployed by the inhabitants of Block Island, RI. Known as 'jibber the kibber', it entailed tying a lantern round the neck of a hobbled horse, which made the motion of the lantern very similar to the light of a ship at sea. Many other ingenious ways of luring a ship ashore have also been recounted, and laws were even passed in several countries threatening execution to any wrecker apprehended.

During the days of sail ships driven ashore were an essential part of the local economy for many British communities, if not the only one. When Sir John Killigrew built a stone *lighthouse on Cornwall's Lizard Point in 1619, the local inhabitants forced him to extinguish it. In Devon and Cornwall children in their evening prayers requested that 'a ship might be sent ashore before morning' (*Sea Breezes*, vii. 71), and Danish children made similar requests. In the middle of the 18th century the Revd Troutbeck of St Mary's in the Scilly Isles prayed: 'Oh Lord, bless the sea and the strand! Protect the poor sailors from evil and lead them to a safe harbour. But if it is Thy divine will that their ship shall be lost, then, we pray Thee, let it happen on our coast.'

That *stranded ships were plundered, and the crews sometimes killed, is well documented—the fate of Sir Clowdisley *Shovel is just one example—but those investigating the legends have found no evidence that any were ever actively caused by wreckers. (See, *inter alia*, J. de Courcy Ireland, *Mariner's Mirror*, 70 (1984), 44, H. Henningsen, *Mariner's Mirror*, 71 (1985), 215–18, and G. Place, *Mariner's Mirror*, 76 (1990), 167.)

wreck vessel, an unpowered vessel, painted green, with the word WRECK in white letters painted on each side. Like the *wreck buoy it has been replaced by the *IALA maritime buoyage system's *isolated danger mark.

xebec, or sometimes **chebeck,** a small three-masted vessel of the 16th–19th centuries which originated in the Mediterranean. It is similar in many respects to a *polacre but with a distinctive hull which had a pronounced overhanging bow and stern. They were greatly favoured by Mediterranean nations as *corsairs, and for this purpose were built with a narrow *floor to achieve a higher speed than their victims, but with a considerable *beam to allow them to carry an extensive sail plan. They had a rig which varied with the strength of the wind. In normal conditions they were *square rigged on the foremast and *lateen rigged on the main and *mizzen, but when the wind was light extremely long *yards were hoisted on the main in place of the lateen yards and immense square sails were spread on them. When sailing *close hauled, a full lateen rig was substituted, but with over-length yards which were replaced by normal ones in strong winds. When used as *corsairs, xebecs could carry a crew of 300–400 men and mounted up to 24 guns. That xebecs covered great distances for their day in search of plunder has been proved by the discovery of the remains of one close to the Cornish shoreline, and they also spread to the Baltic.

yacht, from the Dutch *jacht*, which comes from another Dutch word, *jachten*, meaning to hurry or hunt, for the Dutch were the first to use commercial vessels for pleasure. The word also applies to large powered pleasure vessels, steam or motor yachts, as well as sailing vessels deemed too big to be called a boat or a *dinghy. See also YACHTBUILDING; YACHT CLUBS; YACHT DESIGNERS; YACHTING.

yachtbuilding. Yacht design was originally carried out by the shipwright or boatbuilder commissioned to build the *yacht, and quite often to the shape agreed of a half model produced by the builder. A successful design would be copied and modified so that existing patterns could be used. In the late 19th century the advent of *rating rules influenced the previous, more traditional shapes, so that more extreme types, such as the *skimming dish, were developed to try and beat these rules.

The introduction of *steam propulsion led to many large iron auxiliary and full-powered steam yachts being built. However, it was not until about 1870 that yacht design began as a separate profession, though most *yacht designers retained strong links with building yards. Each developed his own style and yachts could be recognized as being from a particular designer.

In the 1930s the increase in ocean racing (see YACHTING: SAIL) and *dinghy racing led to an increasing number of designers producing race-winning designs so that design offices expanded. After the Second World War (1939–45) yacht design was generally low key with small simple yachts, but by the 1950s the introduction of *GRP provided a boost, and the spread of various forms of ocean racing provided battlegrounds for designers. Many of the successful ones from this period later became involved in the design of larger and larger yachts where a lot of the detail work again devolved upon the building yard.

Following modern *shipbuilding practice, the modern yacht designer will work closely with a stylist and interior designer, as yachts become ever more sophisticated. However, he will still be responsible for the yacht's fitness for its purpose, and for performance, *stability, structural integrity, and safety. To establish these he will first of all normally produce, for a sailing yacht, a preliminary general arrangement and a sail plan for the owner's approval and as a

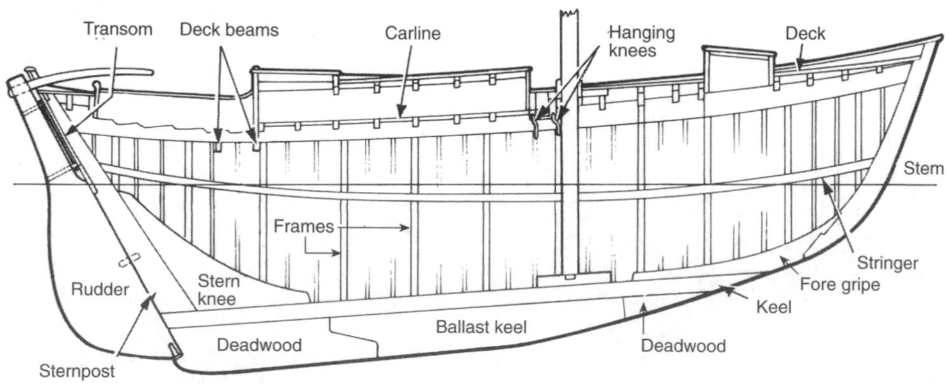

Profile construction of a typical wooden cruising yacht of the 1920s–30s

basis for a written specification with which to obtain building estimates. A *lines plan is then produced, so that stability and performance checks can be made together with detailed weight estimates, and a construction plan, including decks and the *scantling section. These, together with other structural drawings such as *bulkheads, tanks, machinery seatings, stern gear, and *rudder arrangements, may all need approval by a *classification society. At this stage it is likely that the builder and the interior designer will become involved with the development of all the systems and the detail of the interior. Other specialists may also be brought in to design the *spars, *rigging, sails, and deck gear. There may be as many as 100 drawings for a 10-metre (32-ft) yacht or 400 for a 20-metre (65-ft) yacht.

Early Yachtbuilding. From the inception of *yachting, yachtbuilding followed the traditional methods used to build small commercial wooden vessels such as *barges and *smacks, with one of the main tools being the *adze. The wood keel, of oak, elm, pitch pine, or other local timber, was laid on the *slipway or on building blocks, and the wooden *stem, *sternpost, and stern *frame bolted into place. The various frames (or ribs) were sawn to shape and erected in their respective positions along both sides of the keel from stem to stern, the lower ends of each pair being fastened to floor frames which were commonly oak crooks laid athwart the top of the keel. An inner keel, or *keelson, was sometimes bolted on to the tops of the floor frames and running from the inside of the stem to the sternpost. Beam shelves, running from bow to stern and fastened to the inside of the head of every frame, carried the outboard ends of the deck beams which in turn were fastened to the shelves, often with a half-dovetail joint. Openings in the deck for *hatches or *skylights were joined by *carlings to which the *coamings were fastened. At all junctions beneath the deck where the racking strains of hard sailing in heavy seas were greatest, oak crooks or wrought iron *knees were bolted to give more rigidity, hanging knees being vertical and lodging knees horizontal.

The planking of the hull was fastened to the frames and *floors with galvanized iron spikes, bronze bolts, or, in smaller yachts, with copper square-sectioned nails riveted over copper collars (or roves) on the inside of every frame. The work of planking the vessels was started at the *garboard strake on each side, and continued in sequence up to the turn of the *bilge. Other planks were then fastened on from the *sheer strake downwards, until the final gap between the two sets of planks could be filled in with an exactly fitting shutter *strake. Deck planks, traditionally of white pine or teak, were laid fore and *aft usually following the curve of the wide *covering board at the yacht's side. The *seams between the planks, cut in the form of a deep V, were *caulked with cotton and *payed with hot *pitch. The seams of the hull planking were likewise caulked with cotton and finished smooth and flush with a patent stopping mixture which never set hard enough to crack when the seams worked in a seaway.

Towards the end of the 19th century sawn frames were replaced in the smaller yachts by steam-bent *timbers, and this remained standard boat-building practice for wood-built yachts under about 14 metres (45 ft). In building a hull for steam-bent framing, the keel was laid first, and the stem and sternpost erected. Next, *moulds, or patterns, were cut to the shape and measurements on the designer's plan. These were fitted inside the planking and spaced at their appropriate stations through the vessel. Then, on each side wooden battens called *ribbands were temporarily screwed to the edges of the moulds, running from bow to stern and spaced roughly 15–23 centimetres (6–9 in.) apart. Each frame-timber was then made pliable by heating in a steam box, and while still boiling hot was smartly bent into shape on the inside of the ribbands, with its lower end fitting into a check slot already cut in the side of the keel. When all the timbers were in place and temporarily fastened to the ribbands, the ribbands were removed one by one as the planks of the hull were laid in place, being fastened to the timbers by copper nails and roves. Steam-bent timbering was suitable for either *carvel or *clinker planking.

Developments after the Second World War. Design and building techniques, together with the introduction of many new materials, revolutionized yachtbuilding during the 1950s. Water-resistant marine plywood, introduced during the war, opened up the possibilities for amateur builders to construct their own boats,

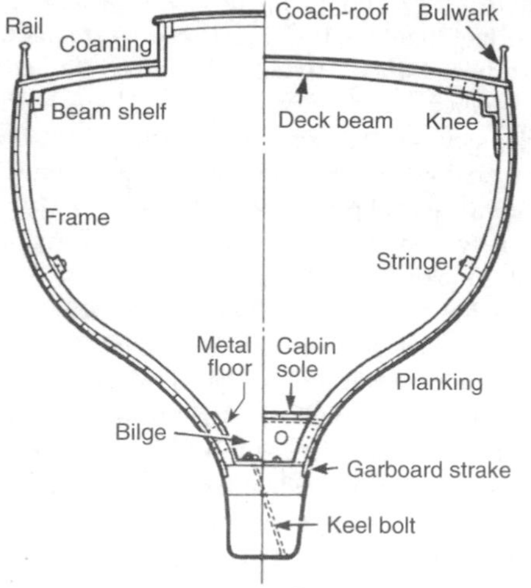

Sections through typical early 20th-century yacht of wooden construction

and numerous new designs were made available to plank in plywood from small dinghies up to cruising yachts of 12 metres (39 ft) in length.

Another popular material for the amateur boatbuilder which came into vogue at this time was ferrocement, or ferroconcrete. This method employed several layers of wire mesh, generally of the welded type, which were wired to the intersections of steel rods and tubes forming a close-knitted framework of the vessel's hull. When complete the whole fabric was rendered waterproof by an application, simultaneously from both inside the hull and outside, of a semi-liquid mortar mix, composed of cement and very fine sand. When cured and set over a period of a week or more, the resulting surface is smooth, hard, and resilient. Many *barges and *pontoons have also been made this way.

For yachts over 12 metres, the strength and durability of steel makes it favoured by those undertaking long ocean voyages and it is fairly easy to repair in any part of the world. Aluminium is also popular and, being lighter, is used to build racing yachts, but it has now been largely superseded by the composites mentioned below.

Modern Yachtbuilding by Jeremy Lines

By far the most popular material today for constructing yachts, both power and sailing, is glassfibre, or GRP, a revolution which occurred in the 1960s. After a female mould for the hull and deck has been made it is coated and polished to a high degree as this will be the finished surface of the actual yacht. This is then coated with a release agent which is followed by two gel coats before the first layer of glassfibre is laid. Resin is then rolled into this mat before the succeeding layers of reinforcement are laid and again impregnated with resin. The most usual resin is a polyester but other more expensive types such as vinylester and epoxy may be used for greater strength or less weight. A simple small hull such as a dinghy may have just a single laminate lay-up, but as size increases a cored laminate may be used to get more panel stiffness, and additional *frames, *stringers, and bulkheads may be fitted.

The unique property of a composite structure is that the designer can specify not only the thickness and size of the material but also the physical properties of the material itself by adjusting the type and orientation of the reinforcement and using different core materials and resins. Because the actual material is being made at the time of manufacture close control has to be maintained over the whole process as it cannot be remade.

Nowadays state-of-the-art racing yachts are built on the foam sandwich principle, the hull generally being formed over a male mould from two composite skins enclosing a central core of end-grain balsa wood, pvc foam, or other lightweight material. Some extremely light but stiff epoxy honeycomb materials are available today and, combined with an enormous range of reinforcement materials such as *Kevlar and *carbon fibre in woven, unidirectional, and combinations of the two, the hull structure can be built to the minimum weight in every part.

Using techniques adapted from the aerospace industry the reinforcements may be pre-impregnated with resin, thus ensuring the minimum resin weight, and then cured by controlled heating in an oven.

Resins are also used to seal and glue wood and this has helped to overcome many of the disadvantages—rot, high maintenance costs—of this type of construction and has led to a modest revival of wood in the yachtbuilding industry. Other methods such as cold-moulded wooden laminates glued with resin over a mould have produced many lightweight *dinghies and racing yachts, but, worldwide, GRP production yachts now far outnumber other types of construction.

The introduction of GRP hulls and decks, and the standardization of yachts, led to batch production where the interiors were produced on jigs and then lifted in large sections into the hulls before the decks were bonded in. To reduce the cost still further, more and more of the interior is also now moulded in GRP so that the fitting-out time can be reduced to days instead of weeks. The decks may also be fitted out separately, both above and below, before being bonded to the hull. Most boat factories have the working area arranged at deck level with everything possible being prefabricated and tested before installation. Another great advantage of this type of construction, if done properly, is the close quality control that can be achieved. It also means easier maintenance, even if it means replacement rather than repair.

Watts, C., *Practical Yacht Construction*, 3rd edn. (1970).

yacht clubs came into existence, in the UK first of all, when sailing for pleasure became an established pastime. The first *yachts had been introduced from Holland in 1660 and the oldest known club for yachtsmen, the Cork Harbour Water Club, was functioning by 1720. However, its activities thereafter were sporadic until it was rehabilitated in 1828 as the Cork Yacht Club (now the Royal Cork Yacht Club). In its early years it was probably no more than a dinner club for those interested in sailing. The Starcross Club in Devon, founded in 1772, was almost certainly started for the same reason and it organized its first race in 1775. It still exists as the Starcross Sailing Club. In the same year the Duke of Cumberland, a brother of King George III, donated a cup for a race on the River Thames which resulted in the formation of the Cumberland Sailing Society, and by 1830 this had evolved into the Royal Thames Yacht Club.

The Revolutionary and Napoleonic Wars (1793–1815) brought the new sport virtually to a halt, but in 1815 The Yacht Club was formed in London with its base at East Cowes. It, too, was primarily a dining club. However, some of its early members cruised extensively and many liked to mimic the manoeuvres and signals of the Royal Navy aboard their yachts in the sheltered waters of the Solent, coming to regard themselves as a kind of auxiliary fleet. Cruising in company was also popular, but the club did not hold its first race until 1826, though members had match-raced against one another before then. The club received royal patronage and in 1820 it became The Royal Yacht Club and, in 1833, The Royal Yacht Squadron. Today a number of British and Commonwealth yacht clubs have also been granted the right to call themselves 'Royal', as do the principal ones belonging to European maritime nations which have monarchies.

In Britain only the Royal Yacht Squadron calls itself a *squadron, but elsewhere a number of yacht clubs use the word. Some yacht clubs have the word *Corinthian in their names while others call themselves associations. Nearly all yacht clubs have clubhouses, some of them very grand indeed, but there is at least one without a location and another, formed by the head of the New Zealand syndicate which won the *America's Cup in 1995, which was no more than a rusting car on a beach.

All British subjects are entitled to fly the *red ensign, and the members of some yacht clubs have an *Admiralty warrant to fly a defaced one with the club's insignia on it. Other yacht clubs have the right to fly a defaced *blue ensign, but only members of the Royal Yacht Squadron owning yachts over a certain *tonnage are entitled to fly a *white ensign. No yacht can fly the Union flag, though it can fly one with a white border. American yachts fly a special yacht ensign.

So far as is known the first yacht club to be founded outside the British Isles was the Royal Gibraltar Yacht Club (1829) and in the following decades several were founded in Australia, Canada, and New Zealand, the Halifax Yacht Club, founded in 1837, being the earliest. The first European one, formed in 1830, was the Royal Swedish Yacht Club, followed by the Société des Régates du Havre in 1838. The Yacht Club de France, formed in 1867, is unusual in that it was state founded.

John Parkinson's official *History of the New York Yacht Club* lists the first American yacht club as the Detroit Boat Club, founded in 1839. The New York Yacht Club was founded in 1844, and in his book *Traditions and Memories of American Yachting* W. P. Stephens lists 33 yacht clubs that had become established in the United States by 1872. The *US Sailing Association records show that there are now just under 2,000 yacht clubs and class associations in the United States; its British national authority equivalent, the *Royal Yachting Association, lists about 1,200.

Johnson, P., *Yacht Clubs of the World* (1994).

yacht designers, until relatively recently, were not all qualified in *naval architecture, a lack which did not stop many from rising to the top of their profession. However, with the expansion of tertiary education and the intricacies of designing on a computer, it must be rare nowadays for a professional yacht designer not to have formal qualifications, though there are probably still plenty of talented amateurs without them who are more than capable of designing fast, seaworthy boats.

The term yacht designer—which covers designing both sailing *yachts and power yachts—seems to have been introduced by an Englishman, Dixon Kemp (1839–99). Kemp worked for many years as the yachting editor of a magazine and as secretary of the Yacht Racing Association, now the *Royal Yachting Association. He formulated the length and sail area *rating rule, adopted first in the USA (1882) and then Britain (1887), which did much to improve yacht racing and yacht design, and became an established yacht designer during the latter half of the 19th century, producing a number of seminal works on the subject.

Kemp worked during the great boom in the sport of *yachting which followed the visit to England of the *schooner **America*, in 1851, and the introduction of *steam propulsion in leisure craft which caught on at about the same time. It was this popularity that led to the work of the yacht designer diverging from that of the yachtbuilder who had traditionally designed what he was constructing.

Some of the most famous yacht designers during this period emerged from the *yacht-building firms they ran. Among the most eminent were the Scottish builders of Fairlie, William Fife II (1821–1902) and his son William III (1857–1944); Charles E. Nicholson (1868–1954) of Camper & Nicholsons, who designed everything from *skimming dishes to *J-class yachts as well as luxurious power yachts and speedboats; and Nat *Herreshoff of Bristol, RI, perhaps the greatest of all American yacht designers, who was equally versatile. All three firms built and designed many famous yachts during the decades 1850–1939, a number of which are still sailing today as classic yachts.

Archibald Cary Smith (1837–1911) was the first to specialize exclusively in yacht design in the USA, after initially earning his living by *marine painting. As a child, he played around *America* as she was being built, and was later apprenticed to a boat-builder. In 1870 he designed *Vindex*, the first iron-built yacht in America. In doing so he broke from the established concepts, employed by the boat-builders of the day, of designing by 'rule of thumb' and with carved models. Instead, every conceivable part of the vessel was calculated and then transferred to paper plans before construction started. Later, with the iron-built *Mischief*, the 1881 defender of the America's Cup, he advanced the cause of yacht designing by producing a revolutionary yacht.

In the same period a number of British yacht designers emerged from different backgrounds, some more qualified than others, but all highly skilled. Four outstanding examples are George L. Watson (1851–1904), who designed **Britannia*, perhaps the most famous racing yacht of all time; Alfred Mylne (1873–1951), the designer of some outstanding *International Metre Class yachts; and the Boston designer B. B. Crowninshield (1867–1948), a prolific designer of the smaller yacht as well as some contenders to defend the *America's Cup, and the trading schooner **Thomas W. Lawson*.

It was in Crowninshield's design office that John Alden (1884–1962), a name synonymous with a distinctive type of schooner yacht, learned his trade. Another whose name is always associated with his own designs is the Norwegian Colin Archer (1832–1921). In 1873 he designed the first Norwegian yacht, but his real interest was working boats—*pilot boats, fishing craft, and those specially built for *lifesaving—some of which were later converted into outstandingly seaworthy cruising boats. Another Norwegian, Johan Anker (1871–1940), a one-time pupil of Nat *Herreshoff, became equally well known for his Dragon-class yacht which is still popular today.

The skills of yacht designing were, and are, often passed from father to son, and sometimes to a third generation, as well. Two of Herreshoff's sons, L. Francis (1890–1972) and A. Sidney (1886–1977), were successful designers, as is Sidney's son Halsey (b. 1933). Starling Burgess (1878–1947) was, perhaps, even better known than his father Edward (1848–91), both of whom, before and after the Herreshoff era, produced designs that successfully defended the America's Cup. The Germán Frers family from Argentina, father (1898–1986), son (b. 1941), and grandson (b. 1969), have an international reputation for their yachts.

Charles E. Nicholson always described yacht design as an art, but by the time a new generation of designers began to appear during the late 1930s, when the tank testing of hulls was enormously improved, it was more a science than an art. Certainly, this is how the leader of this new wave of designers, Olin J. Stephens (b. 1908), looked upon it; and between the 1930s and the 1980s his firm of Sparkman & Stephens produced many, if not most, of the top ocean racers as well as designing the America's Cup 12-metre (39-ft) boats that successfully defended the Cup up to 1983.

Stephens, of course, had his rivals during this era. Outstanding among these were the English designers Robert Clark (1909–88) and Jack Laurent Giles (1901–69); the American Bill Lapworth (b. 1919), who in the 1960s produced some of America's most popular racing classes such as the Cal-40; the Dutchman E. G. Van de Stadt (1910–99); the New Zealanders Ron Holland (b. 1947) and Bruce Farr (b. 1949); and the Australian Ben Lexcen, formerly Bob Miller (1936–88), whose design eventually wrestled the America's Cup from the Americans in 1983. The American Ray Hunt (1908–78) was a top designer of powerboats, while Jon Bannenberg (1929–2002), Australian born, but British based, designed nearly 200 luxury state-of-the-art motor yachts for the super-rich.

For the technical aspects of yacht design see NAVAL ARCHITECTURE; YACHTBUILDING.

Del Sol Knight, L., and MacNaughton, Daniel B. (eds.), *The Encyclopedia of Yacht Designers* (2005).

Kinney, F., *You Are First: The Story of Olin and Rod Stephens of Sparkman & Stephens* (1978).

Robinson, W., *The Great American Yacht Designers* (1974).

Stephens, W., *Traditions and Memories of American Yachting*, new edn. (1989).

yachting, the sport of racing or cruising in *yachts, the term applying to both sailing and power vessels built for pleasure, or converted for it. The word has rather an old-fashioned, elitist ring to it, but Britain has not yet adapted the more democratic American word 'boating', so 'yachting' will have to suffice here as a generic term to cover the various ways of sailing for pleasure. In order to compete most types of sailing yachts are given a *rating and all are subject to international *racing rules.

In his *History of Yachting* (1974) Douglas Phillips-Birt writes that the Dutch, who gave the name 'yacht' to the world, were almost certainly the first to use their commercial boats for pleasure. This is confirmed in *The Feadship Story* (1999) by Andrew Rogers, who dates yachting in Holland to the end of the 16th century, and says the first yacht harbour was created within Amsterdam harbour in 1604. The pleasures of yachting may have been spread across the Atlantic by the Dutch to their colony of New Amsterdam—New York after 1664.

Sail

Inshore Racing. The earliest known sailing race in England was noted in John Evelyn's diary. In this he records that he was on board Charles II's yacht *Katherine* when she raced, and beat, the Duke of York's *Anne* on 1 October 1661. The *course was on the River Thames, from Greenwich to Gravesend and back, and Evelyn noted that the king sometimes steered his yacht himself.

In the 18th century yacht races were organized by the first *yacht clubs, but it was not until the 19th century that racing really began as a sport, and it was not until after the visit of the *schooner **America* (see Fig. 1) in 1851 that it became in Britain something other than an esoteric pastime for the aristocracy. The creation of what is now the *Royal Yachting Association in 1875 and the introduction of proper rating rules established the sport in Britain on proper foundations. The earliest yachts were mostly schooners, but during the latter

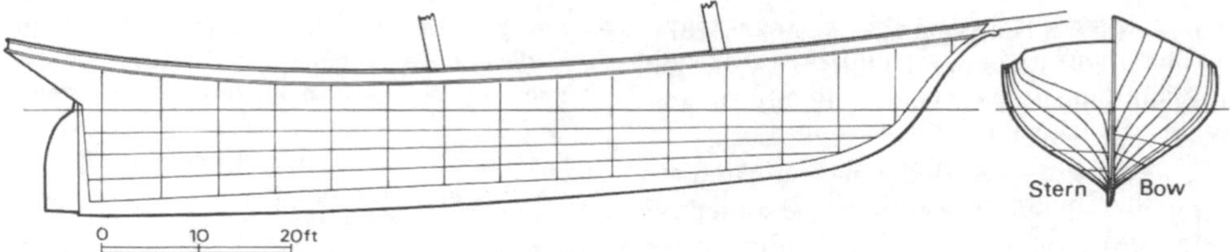

Fig. 1: *America*, 28.5 m (94 ft), 1851

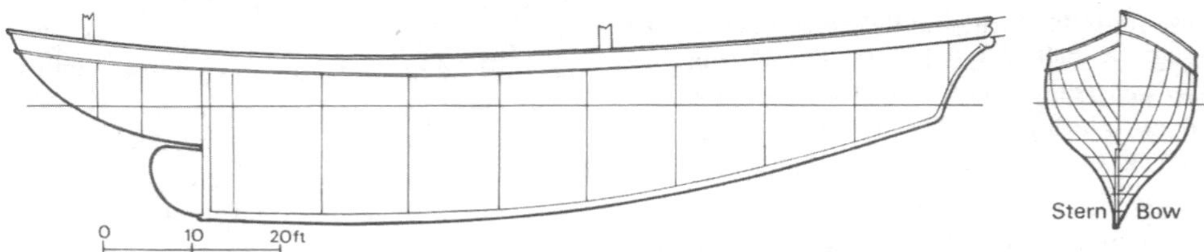

Fig. 2: *Jullanar*, 33 m (110 ft), 1875

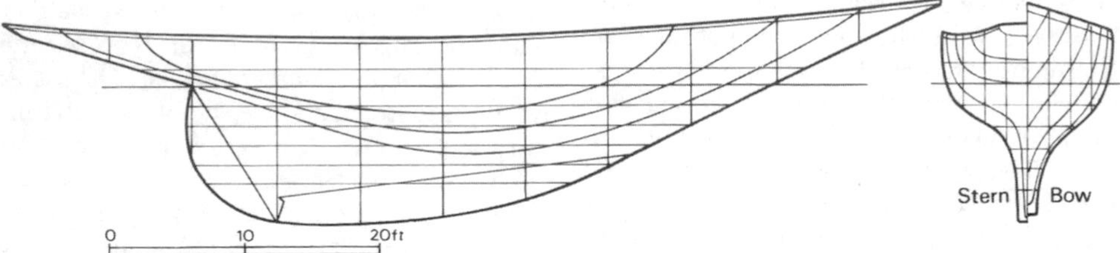

Fig. 3: *Gloriana*, 21 m (70 ft), 1891

half of the century the *cutter rig predominated, though *yawls were also built.

The latter half of the 19th century was a boom time for yachting, particularly in Britain where the Prince of Wales encouraged the new sport with his presence on the water. Many notable yachts were constructed, but perhaps the most important from the point of view of racing design was the yawl-rigged *Jullanar* (see Fig. 2). She was built and designed by an agricultural engineer, E. H. Bentall, to have, in his own words, 'the longest waterline, the smallest frictional surface, and the shortest keel'. She proved phenomenally fast and during her racing life won more races than any other yacht. Her design was the direct forerunner of such famous yachts as the Prince of Wales's **Britannia*, *launched in 1893, and Lord Dunraven's *Valkyrie II* and *Valkyrie III*, both challengers for the *America's Cup during the 1890s.

In the USA Nathanael *Herreshoff was experimenting with hull forms for racing yachts. In 1891 he produced the *sloop *Gloriana* (see Fig. 3). She was a small boat with a waterline length of 14 metres (46 ft) but was completely different in hull form from anything yet seen in American waters. Built with very long overhangs at bow and stern, her *forefoot was cut away to produce an *entry that was almost a straight line from the *stem to the bottom of the keel. It was a revolutionary design, and in every race in which she sailed that season there was nothing that could touch her.

Early English rating rules produced the 'plank-on-edge' cutter where the *beam became narrower and narrower and the *draught deeper and deeper. Those yachtsmen in the USA who adopted this type of design became known as **'cutter cranks'** and in both countries new rating rules were adopted to counter this extreme type. These formulae worked with varying degrees of success at first, but in trying to evade them designers eventually produced the *skimming dish. To counter these extreme designs the *Universal Rule was introduced in the USA and the International Rule, which produced the *International Metre Classes, was introduced in Europe.

By 1911 the *Bermudan rig was beginning to be adopted by some of the smaller racing classes. However, the first large racing yacht to adopt it, the *Nyria*, did not do so until 1920, though a halfway stage to the Bermudan from the *gaff rig, known as the *marconi rig, was introduced into the larger racing classes in 1913. While it was the big racing yachts, like the *J-class, which attracted most public attention—yacht racing was very much a spectator sport right up to the Second World War (1939–45)—yachting grew astonishingly quickly during the first three decades of the 20th century. But after the Second World War (1939–45) everything changed. By then the Universal Rule was dead and yachts built to the International Rule were falling from favour. The age of the racing *dinghy arrived, and the ocean racer became confirmed as the racing yacht of the future.

Offshore Racing. Ocean, or offshore, racing in the modern meaning of the phrase began off the east coast of the USA in 1904 when a 480-kilometre (300-m.) offshore race, from New York to Marblehead, was organized. The competitors were cruising yachts skippered by amateurs, with mostly amateur crews. There was a similar race in 1905 and then, in 1906, the first Bermuda race, a distance of 960 kilometres (600 mls.), was run. The same year, the first Transpac Race, from Los Angeles to Honolulu, also took place. Both are still held today, though both became defunct before the First World War (1914–18) and were revived after it.

The British were slower to take to this type of racing, but in 1925 seven yacht owners took up the challenge of racing round the Fastnet Rock off the coast of south-west Ireland, starting from the Isle of Wight and finishing at Plymouth, a distance of some 968 kilometres (605 mls.) The event was won by E. G. Martin in his French pilot cutter *Jolie Brise*, and at dinner afterwards the Ocean Racing Club was formed. In 1931 this became the Royal Ocean Racing Club (RORC), now the governing body of offshore racing in Britain. The early competitors in the RORC's races were all cruising boats, many of them gaff rigged and built more for comfort than speed, but in 1931 a young American yacht designer, Olin Stephens, sailed his 16-metre (52-ft) LOA yawl *Dorade* across the Atlantic to compete in that year's Fastnet race, by now a biennial event. She won easily, and did so again in 1933, and won many other races as well. Then in 1935 the Stephens-designed *Trenchemer* was launched. She was the first yacht built specifically to the RORC rating rule, though Stephens knew nothing of it at the time as his design had been stolen from a book!

At least *Trenchemer*'s owner knew a good design when he saw one, for Stephens's creations won every Fastnet race between 1931 and 1937, and many other races besides; and after the Second World War his yachts not only dominated ocean racing for many decades, but the America's Cup as well. But in 1939 the run of American wins in the Fastnet Race was broken when the English designer Charles E. Nicholson produced *Bloodhound*. Because of her royal ownership during the 1960s, she is perhaps the best-known ocean racer of all time.

In the USA the Cruising Club of America (CCA), founded in 1922, had the same role as the RORC in Britain. It, too, introduced its own rating rule and organized long-distance events. It did not organize the revival of the 1923 Bermuda race but did so after that year, and the influence of its rating rule steadily expanded along both coasts of the USA. So in 1941, when the Southern Ocean Racing Circuit (SORC) properly began, its organizers adopted the CCA rule. A series of winter events, which included the Miami–Nassau and St Pete–Havana races, the SORC quickly became popular and by the 1970s was a top event. It is still held each year, though the courses have changed.

Admiral's Cup and Ton Cups. After the Second World War, ocean racers dominated the racing scene, and new long-distance events, like the Sydney–Hobart Race (started 1945) and the Mediterranean Giraglia Race (started 1953), were inaugurated. Then in 1957 the RORC initiated the first international ocean racing event by inviting an American three-boat team to compete against a British one for a new trophy, the Admiral's Cup, so called after the RORC's admiral. The teams raced against one another in the Fastnet and Channel races, and two inshore ones, with triple points being scored in the Fastnet and double points in the shorter Channel race. In somewhat dubious circumstances—it was found afterwards that one of the British competitors had inadvertently infringed the rules and the Americans were not informed of this—the British won by 70 points to 68. Two years later the competition was thrown open to any nation and similar competitions were started in the USA (Onion Patch series) and Australia (Southern Cross Cup), each, like the Admiral's Cup, being held biennially. Another important international competition was the One Ton Cup, a challenge trophy for yachts of equal rating donated by the Cercle de la Voile de Paris in 1965. The success of this series encouraged championships for Quarter Ton, Half Ton, Three-Quarter Ton, and Mini-Ton classes.

These competitions drew yachts from every corner of the world—there were nineteen national teams in the Admiral's Cup competitions of 1975–9—but during the 1990s interest dwindled. The Admiral's Cup was cancelled in 2001, and though in 2003 it was re-established on an inter-club basis efforts to make it an international event in 2005 failed, and it was again cancelled.

Transoceanic Racing. This has a long history, for the first organized race was held in 1866. It was contested by three schooners, *Henrietta*, *Fleetwing*, and *Vesta*. The owner of each yacht put up a stake of US $30,000, with the winner—*Henrietta*—taking all. Other transatlantic races followed, most notably the one held in 1905 in which the schooner *Atlantic* won in a time not beaten until 1980, and they are still held today. However, attention is now centred on the astonishing speed achieved by racing *multihulls in transocean racing, and on those who take part in the various round-the-world races.

In the late 1950s two yachtsmen, Francis (now Sir Francis) Chichester and 'Blondie' Hasler, wagered half a crown (25p/65 cents) as to who could win a single-handed race across the Atlantic east to west. Transatlantic races in small yachts were not a new idea—a similar event to what Chichester and Hasler were proposing had taken place as early as 1891—but the race, which attracted three other starters, caught the public's imagination. It was held in 1960, was won by Chichester, and developed into a quadrennial race sponsored by a newspaper. Called the OSTAR (*Observer* Single-Handed Trans Atlantic Race), it started a trend in single-handed, and double-handed, competitions. It is still held today (2004) with multihulls and monohulls competing in different classes, but the spotlight has long since shifted to the even longer events it spawned.

Among the best known of these are the French-organized single-handed Route du Rhum (Saint-Malo–Guadeloupe) and double-handed Transat Jacques Vabre (Le Havre–Brazil). These events are dominated by multihulls, though monohulls, especially those with *swing keels, have their successes. All are high-tech 'formula one' machines which use state-of-the-art materials and the latest design expertise, and their crews are funded by sponsorship deals which run into millions.

Round-the-World Competitions. Even longer events were prompted by the first single-handed round-the-world race held in 1968–9. Sponsored by a British national newspaper, the *Sunday Times*, it was a non-stop race and was won by Robin (now Sir Robin) Knox-Johnston in his ketch *Suhaili*, in a time of 313 days. This, too, captured the imagination of the public—and the eye of the advertising industry—and has led to an ever-increasing number of round-the-world events. Regular quadrennial ones include the Volvo (previously Whitbread) Round-the-World Race, a crewed monohull race first held in 1973; the single-handed 'Around Alone' Race; and the Global Challenge in which identical yachts, with crews who pay for the privilege, race round the world against the prevailing winds. All these are held in stages, but the Everest among round-the-world races is the non-stop single-handed Vendée Globe. Yachtsmen taking part in all single-handed, or short-handed, events, including those described in the next sections, use a *vane self-steering gear.

Racing Against Time. Not exactly racing, but certainly not cruising, are the yachtsmen who race, not against anyone else, but against time.

In previous centuries the *clipper ships had raced to be first home with their cargoes and this gave Francis Chichester the idea of trying to beat the 100 days it usually took them between England and Australia, and to do it single-handed. It took him 107 days in his 16-metre (53-ft) ketch *Gipsy Moth IV*, but he then went on to circumnavigate the world, returning to a knighthood and acclaim in May 1967.

This voyage, too, set a trend and soon everyone was trying to establish new speed records. In 1970–1 Chay (now Sir Chay) Blyth made the first single-handed circumnavigation against the prevailing winds in a time of 293 days, but the current record-holder for this feat, Jean Luc van den Heede, finished the same course in 2004 in just 122 days. Women have accomplished equally astonishing voyages racing against time; in 1988 Australian Kay Cottee became the first woman to complete a solo non-stop circumnavigation, finishing in 189 days. The present holder, for both men and women, is Englishwoman Ellen (now Dame Ellen) MacArther. In February 2005 she beat the then current world record of just under 73 days, established by Frenchman François Joyon in 2004, by completing her non-stop circumnavigation in her *catamaran *B&Q* in 71 days, 14 hours, 18 minutes, and 33 seconds.

The Jules Verne Trophy, awarded to the fastest circumnavigation by a crewed yacht, was conceived by the Frenchman Yves Le Cornec, who based his idea on the Jules *Verne novel *Around the World in Eighty Days*. Frenchman Bruno Peyron was the first skipper to compete for it in 1993, and Sir Peter *Blake was among others who later held the trophy. In April 2004 Steve Fossett established the fastest crewed circumnavigation in a time of 58 days, 9 hours, 32 minutes, and 45 seconds, but he was not racing for the trophy. Its current holder is Bruno Peyron who in March 2005 completed his crewed circumnavigation in the catamaran *Orange II* in a new world record time of 50 days, 16 hours, 20 minutes, and 4 seconds.

Cruising Under Sail. What must have been one of the earliest cruises took place in 1809 when Sir William Curtis decided to sail to Spain to view the Peninsular War at first hand. He was allowed to do so provided he put his yacht under the command of a naval squadron, which he gladly agreed to. Then in 1815 he took a party of friends aboard his yacht at Ramsgate and visited St Petersburg. In those days wars attracted the attention of cruising yachtsmen. Despite a demand from some professional crews for 'no Baltic cruizing', several English yachtsman sailed there during the Crimean War (1854–6) to see if they could witness any actions against the Russian fleet, and one nearly got blown out of the water. Others sailed to the Crimea with supplies for the soldiers fighting there. The first yacht to cruise across the Atlantic was the 25-metre (83-ft) LWL American *brigantine *Cleopatra's Barge* which sailed to the Mediterranean, via the Azores and Madeira, in 1817, and then returned.

All these voyages were undertaken in large yachts crewed by professional seamen, indeed some were so large and fast that they rivalled anything the Royal Navy could build. But by the middle of the 19th century, cruising was no longer a rich man's pastime and yachtsmen were sailing their own yachts. Among the best known of these was E. F. Knight, who cruised to the Baltic in a 9-metre (29-ft) converted ship's lifeboat, and R. T. McMullen, who cruised in British waters, often alone, and their writings inspired a generation of enthusiasts to follow in their wake. Other cruising yachtsmen have also been adept at writing about their experiences and encouraging their readers to copy them. The first man to sail around the world alone, Joshua *Slocum, wrote about his adventures in a book which is still in print. In the 20th century, the books written by Susan and Eric Hiscock, Bill Tillman and others, inspired a whole generation of cruising yachtsmen.

A feature of modern cruising is the rallies and meets held by yacht clubs where owners and their families cruise, either alone or in company, to an agreed destination, or series of destinations, so as to socialize at the end of the voyage. Perhaps the best known of these is the Atlantic Rally for Cruisers (ARC), which held its first meet in 1986. The participants do compete on each of its legs, but in a low-key kind of way. There are different divisions for different types of yachts, and the prizes reflect the relaxed nature of the contest.

Power

Steam and Motor Yachts. With the introduction of *steam propulsion during the early 19th century it was only to be expected that some yachtsmen should look to this new means of propulsion. A steam yacht, as well as being more popular with ladies, was also far more suitable for the lavish entertaining of the period as well as being a status symbol. Most of the steam yachts of that century were luxuriously fitted out, with heavy carving and panelling, thick carpeting, and large *staterooms equipped with every conceivable convenience.

Like many innovations, the introduction of steam was not accepted immediately. Indeed, The Royal Yacht Club, as The Royal Yacht Squadron was then called, banned members from owning steam yachts. In 1829 one of its members, Thomas Assheton-Smith, preferred to resign rather than accept the ban, and the following year he built the 400-ton *Menai*, the first steam yacht to be built in Britain. In the USA the first steam yacht was the 1,876-ton *North Star*, for Commodore Cornelius Vanderbilt, which was *launched in 1853. Both vessels were *paddle steamers, and steam had no rival in pleasure craft until about 1885, when *launches fitted with an engine using naphtha gas in place of coal and water in the boiler appeared in both Britain and the USA. However, fires were a frequent occurrence, and when a few years later the more compact, if noisy, internal combustion engine was introduced the naphtha launch disappeared.

The first yacht to have steam turbines fitted was the *Turbinia*, which was launched in 1897 and the first large yacht to be powered by *diesel engines, the 360-ton *Pioneer*, was launched in 1913. From that time the *diesel engine quickly became accepted as the easiest, cleanest, and most economical way of powering a yacht, and without boilers and bunkers there was much more room for the passengers.

The largest privately owned motor yacht ever built was the 4,646-ton American designed *Savarona III*. Just over 125 metres (408 ft) long and with a crew of 107, she was owned by an American, Mrs E. R. Cadwalader, from 1931 to 1938, and subsequently became a school ship in the Turkish Navy. The American magnate J. P. Morgan built four yachts called *Corsair*. The last, 105 metres (343 ft) long and 2,142 tons gross, was the largest of them, and was the second largest motor yacht ever built.

Some of the motor yachts built between the wars are still afloat, and grace the harbours of Monte Carlo and the French Riviera, but many were commandeered at the start of the Second World War (1939–45), as their predecessors had been in 1914, and were sunk or had to be scrapped. Only one, T. O. M. Sopwith's 1,620-ton *Philante*, was large enough to be armed and serve in the Royal Navy during the Second World War, as a *convoy escort, and is now the Norwegian royal yacht *Norge*. In the USA the larger motor yachts were also commandeered and used as anti-submarine patrol boats in the *US Coast Guard. Today, the successors of these luxury vessels, or super-yachts as they are now called, reflect the enormous wealth of their owners as well as the talent of their designers to produce a beautiful, visually dramatic, vessel.

Offshore Powerboats. Racing powerboats offshore began as soon as the marine internal combustion engine had been introduced. By the early 20th century it had become almost as popular as racing motor cars, and it was given further impetus when the International Harmsworth Trophy was first awarded in 1903. The trophy was competed for until 1939 when it was withdrawn, and it was not resurrected until 2002, when it was awarded to powerboats up to 12.2 metres (40 ft) in length, manned by a crew of two.

Initially, powerboat racing took place in sheltered water, and the first offshore event in Britain was not held until 1905. Though the British held offshore races before the First World War (1914–18), from London to Cowes, by the 1950s the Americans had begun to dominate the sport. The first 295-kilometre (184-m.) Miami–Nassau Race was held in 1956—it later became the 580-kilometre (362-m.) Miami–Nassau–Miami event still held annually—and other long-distance events included the Around Long Island marathon and the Miami–Key West Race. Then, in 1961, the newspaper magnate Max Aitken, inspired by the Miami–Nassau event, started the 286-kilometre (179-m.) Cowes–Torquay Powerboat Race—it became the Cowes–Torquay–Cowes Race from 1968—and the following year the Italians began the 317-kilometre (198-m.) Viareggio–Bastia–Viareggio Race.

The modern powerboat is a huge advance on the 10-metre (34-ft), 21-horsepower wooden monohulls that raced in the 1950s at an average speed of 32 kph (20 mph). Today *catamaran powerboats made of advanced composites such as *Kevlar and *carbon fibre race at speeds that sometimes exceed 200 kph (125 mph). In the 1950s and 1960s the two-man crew would stand at the controls; nowadays they are enclosed in canopies made of materials borrowed from the aerospace industry, and in 2003 the Cowes–Torquay–Cowes Race was won at an average speed of 122.4 kph (76.5 mph).

As in sailing, speed for its own sake is also a great challenge to those who drive or own powerboats and in 1985 Richard (now Sir Richard) Branson's *Virgin Atlantic Challenger II* beat the transatlantic *blue riband record held since 1952 by the *ocean liner *United States*. She did so at an average speed of 67.3 kph (42.1 mph), the six-man crew covering the 4,757 kilometres (2,973 mls.) in 3 days, 8 hours, and 31 minutes. However the trustees of the blue riband prize, the Hales Trophy, later ruled that powerboats were not eligible to compete for it.

yacht routine, see FLAG ETIQUETTE.

yankee, a light-weather *foresail used in *yachts, set on the topmast *stay with its *luff extending almost the whole length of the stay. It was similar to a *genoa but cut narrower, with its *leech not overlapping the mainsail as a genoa does, and with its *clew higher than is normally the case with genoas. A yankee was used in winds of up to about force 4 on the *Beaufort Scale, but has now been superseded by new foresails like the *ghoster.

yard. (1) A large wooden or metal *spar crossing the masts of a sailing vessel horizontally or diagonally, from which a sail is set. Yards crossing the masts of a *square-rigged ship horizontally are supported from the mastheads by *slings and *lifts and are held to the mast by a *truss or *parrel. Square sails are *laced by their *heads to the yards. By means of *braces, the yards can be turned at an angle to the fore-and-aft line of the vessel in order to take the greatest advantage of the wind direction in relation to the required *course of the vessel. When a yard crosses a mast diagonally, it is

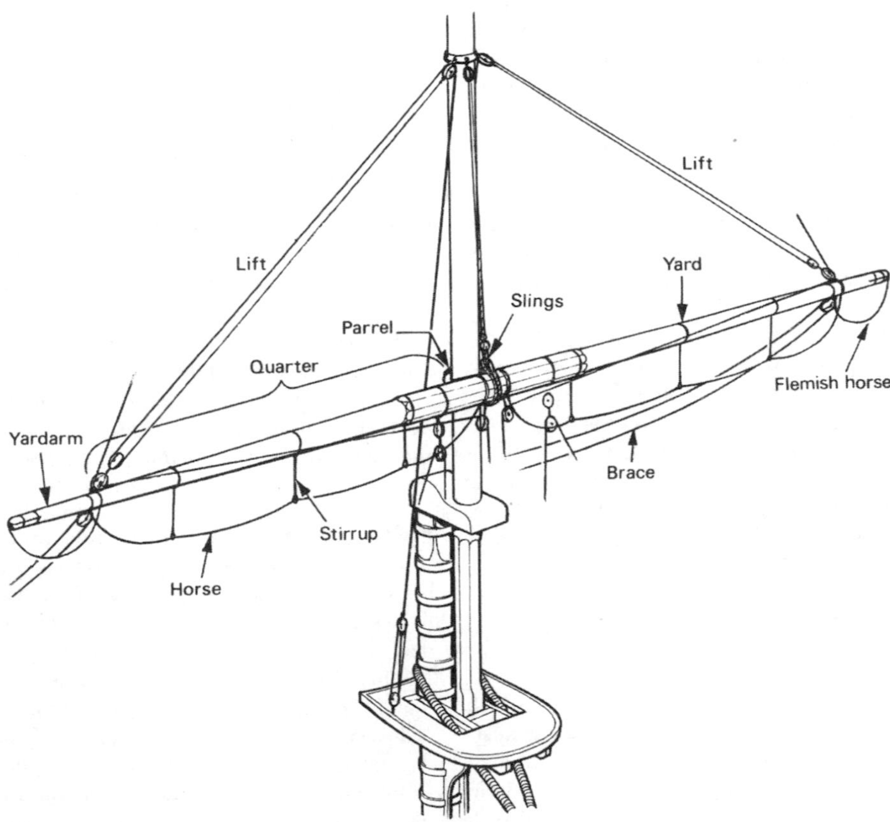

Yard

known as a *lateen yard and is not supported by braces but hoisted by a *halyard attached to a point on the yard about one-third of its length from the forward end. **(2)** A shortened form of *dockyard.

yardarm, the outer end of a *yard outboard of the *leeches of the sail and the *lifts. It is also used for the hoisting of flags for *signals at sea and it was the traditional place for hangings in the days of such punishments.

yardmen, see TOPMEN.

yaw, to. **(1)** The effect on a ship's *course produced by a following wind or sea. With the vessel travelling through the water in the same direction as that in which the sea is running or the wind blowing, the effect of the *rudder is diminished and the vessel yaws away from the desired course. A good helmsman can often anticipate the moment when a vessel is most likely to yaw, and correct the tendency to do so by applying the requisite *helm to counteract it. **(2)** When used as a noun, it denotes the involuntary movement caused by wind or sea by which a ship deviates from its chosen course. A yaw can also be caused by a careless helmsman.

yawl, a type of rig of a small sailing boat or *yacht, apparently an adaptation of the Dutch word *jol*, or *skiff. The true yawl rig consists of two masts, *cutter rigged (in the English meaning of the word) on the foremast, with a small *mizzen-mast *stepped *abaft the *rudder head carrying a sail. However, the term refers more to the position of the masts than to the particular rig they carry, and thus a sailing boat with masts stepped as above but *sloop rigged on the foremast would also be termed a yawl. The rig is very similar to a *ketch, the difference being the position in which the mizzen is stepped. Until about the mid-19th century, the term was also occasionally used for a ship's boat rowed by four or more *oars, but this use of it is now obsolete.

'yellow admiral', a term used in the British Navy during the days of sail to denote a *post-captain promoted to rear admiral on retirement without ever serving in that rank. The term dates from the days before 1864 when British admirals took their rank from their *squadronal colour. There was no yellow squadron so a 'yellow admiral' therefore had no rank at all in the flag list.

The pressure to create 'yellow admirals' arose after the Napoleonic War (1803–15) when the list of post-captains was so large that the prospect of promotion was remote. Under the system of promotion then prevailing, every officer who had reached post-captain's rank was automatically promoted when his seniority brought him to the top of the list and a vacancy in the flag list occurred. It was to keep some movement in these lists that post-captains, on reaching the top by seniority, were promoted to *flag rank and placed on the retired list on the following day, so that they did not automatically swell the rear-admirals' list.

yellow jack, the sailor's name for yellow fever, and also the slang name given to the quarantine flag in the *International Code of Signals, 'Q' flag, which is coloured yellow. It was, too, the name often given to a naval pensioner in Greenwich Hospital who was too fond of his drink. Such a man was made to wear a particular coat in which yellow was the predominant colour so that the other pensioners might be warned that he was a man who might try to wheedle their daily ration of beer out of them.

yoke, a transverse board fitted to the top of a *rudder in a small boat instead of a *tiller, the rudder being moved by yoke lines attached to the ends of the yoke and operated by the helmsman. Yokes are mainly to be found in small boats which are pulled by *oars; and very occasionally in small, open sailing craft where the position of a *mizzen or *jigger-mast makes the operation of a tiller impossible. See also STEERING GEAR.

yuloh, from a verb, *yao lu*, meaning 'to shake the oar', and of ancient origin, probably going back to the Han dynasty which was established in 206 BC. It is a form of long *oar or *sweep used over the stern by Chinese boatmen to propel *sampans and the smaller *junks. It is usually made in two parts, either *scarfed and pegged or lashed together, giving the yuloh a distinct bow which causes the blade to be very whippy or flexible and which makes the inboard end parallel with the deck. It is mounted loosely over a peg on the boat's stern, and the *loom, or inboard, end is attached to the deck by a length of line. This allows the loom to be roughly waist high, while the blade on the outboard end enters the water at an angle of about 30°. By alternately pushing and pulling the loom of the yuloh *athwartships the sampan man or girl causes the blade to flex from side to side in the water with a fish's tail motion, or *sculling action, and so drives the vessel forward.

In the 15th century the yuloh was used on much larger junks, as the description by the Arabian traveller Ibn Battutah shows: 'There are in the junk about 20 very great oars, like masts, each of which have about 30 men to work them, standing in two rows facing each other. The oar, like a club, is provided with two strong cords or cables, and one of the two rows of men pulls on the cable then lets it go, while the others pull on the second cable.'

Z

zenith, in nautical astronomy the point in the heavens immediately above an observer on the surface of the earth. A line through the centre of the earth and the observer on its surface points directly to the observer's zenith. See CELESTIAL NAVIGATION.

zenith distance, the angle between an observer's *zenith and an observed celestial body subtended at the earth's centre. It is the complement of the true *altitude of a celestial body, and forms one side of the astronomical triangle which is the basis of *celestial navigation at sea.

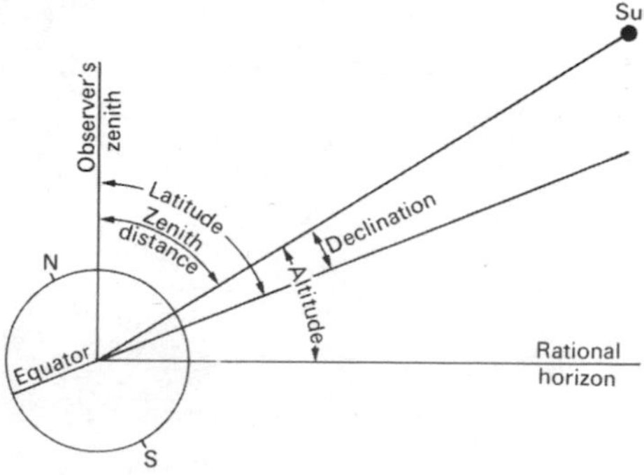

Zenith distance

zone times, the division of the globe by *meridians of *longitude into zones where the same time is kept, particularly in ships at sea. The sun crosses each meridian of longitude at its local noon and four minutes later crosses the next degree of longitude at its local noon. Without some system of time zones all *chronometers would show the times at their longitude. The world is thus divided into zones of 15° of longitude, and adjacent zones differ from each other by one hour. Zone times are measured east and west of the longitude of Greenwich (0°). Zones east of Greenwich are minus and zones to the west are plus. The longitude of 180°, where zones are +12 and –12, is known as the *International Date Line. See also GREENWICH MEAN TIME.

zulu, a type of fishing vessel, now obsolete, peculiar to the north-east coastal ports of Scotland. It had a broad-beamed *carvel-built hull with a straight *stem and a pointed *stern with a pronounced rake, at times as much as 45°. These boats were rigged with a *dipping lug foresail and a *standing lug *mizzen. They were introduced by a boat-builder named Cameron as an improvement on local types of fishing craft and were first produced during the Zulu War (1878–9), hence their name. See also FISHERIES.

SELECT INDEX

PICTURE ACKNOWLEDGEMENTS

The publishers are grateful to the following for their permission to reproduce the illustrations.
Although every effort has been made to contact copyright holders, it has not been possible to do so in every case and we apologise for any that may have been omitted.
Should the copyright holders wish to contact us after publication, we would be happy to include an acknowledgement in subsequent reprints.

Page number

14 © 1994 P .F. Collier
30 © Hulton/Getty
71 C.32.h.14. By permission of the British Library
99 © Hulton/Getty
137 *Case Studies in Oceanography and Marine Affairs*, 1991
154 Ronan Picture Library and Royal Astronomical Society
168 Ronan Picture Library
176 © National Maritime Museum, London
246 © Hulton/Getty
247 © Hulton/Getty
262 © Hulton/Getty
267 © Hulton/Getty
278 © National Maritime Museum, London
293 © Hulton/Getty
295 *Practical Junk Rig*, Hasler, H. G., & McLeod, J. K., Adlard Coles Nautical, 1988
305 © Hulton/Getty
311 Fred Walker
345 *An Introduction to the World's Oceans*, Duxbury, A., & Duxbury, A. Published by Wm. Brown, copy right Addison Wesley 1984
366 © Hulton/Getty
379 Fred Walker
429 © Hulton/Getty
435 © National Maritime Museum, London
455 Courtesy of the National Portrait Gallery, London
464 Fred Walker
500 *Avian Biology* Vol.1. Ashmole, N. P. Academic Press, 1971
507 *Biological Oceanography: an Introduction*, Lalli, C., & Parsons, T. Open University 1996
520 Fred Walker
522 Fred Walker
542 © National Maritime Museum, London
576 Fred Walker
573 Fred Walker
579 © Hulton/Getty
584 *Fundamentals of Oceanography*, Duxbury, A., & Duxbury, A. Published by Wm. Brown, copyright Wm. Brown Communications Inc. 1993
592 Fred Walker
600 Z-Tech 6000 image, courtesy of Robert Allan Ltd, and PSA Marine Ltd
601 *Tugs Today*, Gaston, M. (Patrick Stevens 1996)
620 © National Maritime Museum, London
622 © National Maritime Museum, London
629 *Biological Oceanography: an Introduction*. Lalli, C., & Parsons, T. (Open University) 1996